THE GENDER AND MEDIA READER

THE UNIVERSITY OF
WINCHESTER

The Gender and Media R▬▬▬ ̄ ̄sential text for those interested in gender and media studies, its primary topics, debates, and theoretical approaches. The primary objective of this collection is to expand readers' knowledge of how gender operates within media culture through engagement with foundational writings as well as more contemporary research in this field. Taking a multiperspectival approach that considers gender broadly and examines media texts alongside their production and consumption, *The Gender and Media Reader* enables readers' critical thinking about how gender is constructed, contested, and subverted in different sites within media culture. Along with the main introduction, individual section introductions facilitate readers' understanding of the development of gender and media studies by contextualizing the various topics, debates, and theoretical approaches that have shaped it, as well as by highlighting current trends.

Mary Celeste Kearney is Associate Professor of Radio-Television-Film and Women's and Gender Studies at the University of Texas at Austin. She is author of *Girls Make Media* (Routledge, 2006) and editor of *Mediated Girlhoods: New Explorations of Girls' Media Culture* (Peter Lang, 2011).

THE GENDER AND MEDIA READER

Edited by
MARY CELESTE KEARNEY

Routledge
Taylor & Francis Group

NEW YORK AND LONDON

First published 2012
by Routledge
711 Third Avenue, New York, NY 10017

Simultaneously published in the UK
by Routledge
2 Park Square, Milton Park, Abingdon, Oxon OX14 4RN

Routledge is an imprint of the Taylor & Francis Group, an informa business

Library of Congress Cataloging in Publication Data
The gender and media reader / editor Mary Celeste Kearney.
p. cm.
1. Mass media and se. 2. Sex role in mass media. Mass media and culture.
I. Kearney, Mary Celeste, 1962–
P96.S45G44 2011
305.3—dc22
2010044187

ISBN13: 978–0–415–99345–6 (hbk)
ISBN 13: 978–0–415–99346–3 (pbk)

Typeset in Amasis by Swales & Willis Ltd, Exeter, Devon
Printed and bound in the United States of America on acid-free paper by Sheridan Books, Inc.

CONTENTS

ACKNOWLEDGMENTS

My gratitude to Routledge editors Matthew Byrnie for his enthusiastic support of this reader's development and Erica Wetter for her graceful guidance during its production process. Thanks also to Morgan Blue for her careful work on the index.

This book is dedicated to the memory of my father, Terrence John Kearney, whose love for such disparate forms of entertainment as NASCAR, Irish ballads, and kitties taught me much about the complexities of gender.

INTRODUCTION
Mary Celeste Kearney

Commonly understood as the most influential feminist text of the early twentieth century, Simone de Beauvoir's *The Second Sex*, published in 1949, was a powerful catalyst for the women's liberation movements of the 1960s and 1970s.[1] Among her wide-ranging analyses of how woman is constructed as man's lesser "Other" in patriarchal societies, Beauvoir urged readers to think beyond conventional explanations of femininity, and instead offered a provocative alternative theory that has profoundly shaped contemporary ideas about gender:

> One is not born, but rather becomes, a woman. No biological, psychological, or economic fate determines the figure that the human female presents in society; it is civilization as a whole that produces this creature, intermediate between male and eunuch, which is described as feminine. Only the intervention of someone else can establish an individual as an *Other*.[2]

In these few sentences, Beauvoir boldly introduced a new way of understanding gender as an identity that is socially produced rather than biologically determined, thereby motivating women to imagine experiences for themselves that were not tied to the domestic sphere and the traditional roles of wife and mother. Moreover, she revealed how gender is used to regulate human behavior and social relations, and thus helped women to understand how their treatment by men, as well as their own complicity in gender norms, is connected to a much larger power structure: patriarchy.

A less-often quoted passage from *The Second Sex* has had similar significance for those interested in how gender operates in culture: "Representation of the world, like the world itself, is the work of men; they describe it from their own point of view, which they confuse with absolute truth."[3] Nevertheless, Betty Friedan's *The Feminine Mystique*, published in 1963, is more typically cited as the text responsible for inaugurating the study of gender and media, the primary topic of this collection.[4] For while Beauvoir and other feminist writers of the mid twentieth century investigated women's construction in literature and the arts, Friedan was the first to examine the portrayal of women in mass media, specifically women's magazines, the primary medium produced by, centered on, and directed to women. Surveying women's magazines from the early to mid twentieth century, Friedan demonstrated a notable change in the female roles privileged in such texts: while the "New Woman," who focused largely on her career, dominated women's magazines during the 1930s and early 1940s, by the 1950s that figure had been replaced by the "Happy Housewife," who subjugated her own desires and ambitions while finding her utmost fulfillment in her children and husband. Much as Beauvoir was instrumental in the shift to theorizing gender as socially constructed, Friedan pioneered an understanding of the significance of media texts as sites of gender (re)production.

In the forty-some years since Friedan's book was published, the study of gender and media not only has crystallized into a unique form of critical inquiry, but also has been instrumental in shaping the larger field of media scholarship while at the same time contributing to the development of gender studies in many other disciplines. The number of scholars researching gender and media has grown significantly over the last few decades. So, too, have the number of colleges and universities that offer undergraduate and graduate courses in this special area. Meanwhile, scholars who study gender and media now have several academic journals in which to publish their work, including *Camera Obscura*, *Feminist Media Studies*, *Frauen und Film* (Women and Film), and *Women's Studies in Communication*. In turn, feminist media scholars have formed the Women's Media Studies Network, and several professional organizations for media scholars, including the International Communication Association, the Media, Communication and Cultural Studies Association, and the Society for Cinema and Media Studies have divisions devoted to gender-based scholarship. Numerous conferences have been organized to support and promote this unique type of research also. Once confined largely to American and British scholars' analyses of women's representation in news coverage and Hollywood films, gender and media studies is now a global field whose practitioners commonly examine gender alongside other components of identity, such as race, class, age, ethnicity, religion, sexuality, ability, and nationality. Moreover, gender and media studies now addresses multiple forms of gendered experience (including masculinity and transgenderism), all sites within media culture (including production and reception), and numerous forms of commercial, independent, and amateur media (including popular music and video games).

The primary objective of *The Gender and Media Reader* is to expand readers' knowledge of how gender operates within media culture through engagement with both foundational studies and more contemporary research in this field. Although it takes a multi-perspectival approach that considers both gender and media broadly, this collection is meant to be neither comprehensive nor definitive. Rather, the readings included here have been selected in order to familiarize readers with a variety of approaches for analyzing gender in various sites across media culture. Thus, this collection is best approached as an introduction to the field, yet one meant to inspire further critical thinking,

research, and activism with regard to media and gender. Many of the foundational studies included here explore older media texts; however, the primary focus of the studies collected here is contemporary entertainment media, particularly fictional films, popular magazines, music videos, television programs, and video games. In turn, interpretive, qualitative methods figure dominantly in this reader, and the academic fields most commonly represented are those with roots in the humanities, especially film studies, television studies, and cultural studies.[5]

The goal of this Introduction is to facilitate readers' familiarity with gender and media studies as a particular form of critical inquiry. For those readers with less exposure to media studies, a discussion of the need for and significance of this particular form of research is offered. In turn, a historical survey of feminist and LGBTQI (lesbian, gay, bisexual, transgender, queer, intersex) activism is provided so that readers can make better sense of how those movements have impacted feminist and LGBTQI research and thus gender studies, all of which receive short overviews here also. This history is meant to familiarize readers with the particular approaches to gender used by early media scholars, including those who have written the foundational articles in this reader. Additionally, a discussion of current trends in gender and media studies provides a context for the contemporary research collected here. This Introduction also includes a short survey of the collection's five parts and an Alternate Table of Contents for those readers interested in organizing their reading in a different manner than the one used here.

Why Study Media and Gender?

Since the mid twentieth century, the media have become increasingly present in most individuals' lives. Today, many of us wake up (and go to sleep) to sounds from our radios and mp3 players. In turn, numerous people read newspapers, watch television, or surf the Web when eating meals. When we are away from home or in transit, individualized communication and information technologies, such as cell phones, mp3 players, and personal digital assistants, help to keep us entertained, informed, and connected to others. In most waiting rooms, magazines and TV monitors help to keep us distracted and occupied. For most students and middle-class adults, personal computers with Internet access have become not only essential tools for work, but also primary facilitators of our leisure activities, be they playing video games, listening to music, watching television, or reading books. Yet globally many individuals still turn to older media for information and entertainment also. Going to the movies remains a primary non-domestic pastime, as does watching television on TV sets. Meanwhile, billboards and print advertisements alert us to the latest commercial trends, and radio and television broadcasts keep us tapped into current events. Whether used autonomously or collectively, the media have permeated almost every moment of our everyday lives. Yet media technologies are no longer just mechanisms for media consumption. Much of today's media equipment now merges the practices of production and consumption, offering even those of us without training or experience the opportunity to create our own media texts and distribute them broadly to numerous individuals well beyond our home communities.

As a result of the media's extensive presence in most human lives today, many of us have considerable savvy about the narrative strategies, performance styles, editing techniques, special effects, and other practices commonly used in media production. Nevertheless, a significant amount of knowledge about media production, representation, and consumption is difficult to access not to mention comprehend merely through exposure. Fortunately, the field of media studies provides us with the tools we need to become more media literate so that we can participate fully and demonstrate good judgment as both consumers and citizens in a media-saturated society.

Today, the media are among our most powerful agents of entertainment, information, and socialization. While older social institutions, such as the family, church, state, and educational system, still play important roles in our lives, the media have increasingly become powerful regulators of individual behavior and social practices. For, as systems of communication, they are better able than other social institutions to produce and circulate images and messages that consumers use to construct knowledge and values. For example, the media regularly model particular

forms of human identity that consumers use to judge themselves and others. Gender, the primary topic of this collection, is just one of the many identities constructed in media culture (among other places). It is no surprise therefore that, as the media have become more ubiquitous in everyday life and thus play a greater role in setting social norms, they have received considerable attention from both activists and scholars interested in the social production of gender.

At the same time, media are sites of considerable ideological negotiation and contestation, that is, sites of struggle over meaning and values. While most media images and discourses are polysemous and can be interpreted in different ways (thus facilitating debate among their consumers), few of us blithely accept the messages media offer, particularly when it comes to representations of our specific social group. Indeed, as a result of decades of marginalization and stereotyping in the media, many members of disenfranchised social groups, including women, have challenged media portrayals of their communities which they find offensive and unrealistic yet are used by others to affirm stereotypes. While some consumers have demonstrated such opposition through boycotts and letter-writing, others have refused to let control remain in the hands of the media industries and have seized the tools of media production to create their own images and discourse, thus helping to expand the diversity of our cultural landscape.

Yet changes in media culture and systems of representation do not happen only at the level of consumers' involvement in media production. Research can also help to effect change in media-related policies. For example, many marginalized social groups have used the findings of media scholars to advocate for more representation by publishers, film studios, recording labels, television networks, and software companies. When it comes to gender, feminists and members of the LGBTQI community have been at the forefront of such actions and have long relied on scholarly research to support their arguments about media stereotyping and other practices of negative representation. In this regard, quantitative data have been especially useful in quickly calling attention to disparities in, for example, the percentage of male versus female characters in prime-time television programming, feature films, and video games.

Analyzing the superficial, manifest details of media phenomena is just the initial step for humanities-based scholars, however. Qualitative research, such as that found in this collection, is also crucial to effecting long-term change in media culture. Skilled in interpretive analysis and armed with critical theories of human behavior, culture, and society (e.g., semiotics, narratology, discourse theory), qualitative scholars have been central to the development of media studies and media literacy. For while quantitative data can paint a general picture of what is happening in sociohistorically specific sites of media representation, production, and reception, qualitative studies pursue the more difficult questions of "how?," "why?," and "what's at stake?" It was in the spirit of answering those questions and contributing to progressive transformations in both media culture and gender politics that the studies collected here were originally conducted, and it is in that same spirit that this collection reprints them and brings them into conversation with each other.

Gender-Based Activism

As one of the primary systems used to categorize human beings and to regulate our behavior, gender plays an important role in any society's media, and thus has been a dominant site of media studies for most of that field's history. Yet to appreciate fully the development of gender-based media scholarship, including the readings collected here, it is necessary to be familiar with the history of gender studies, whose roots are firmly grounded in both feminist and LGBTQI activism. With a goal of eliminating oppression based on gender and sexuality, feminists and members of the LGBTQI community have been required to articulate clearly their understanding of gender norms and the effect of those norms on individual identity and behavior, as well as relationships and social institutions. Yet, as a closer look at those two groups' political histories reveals, their ideas about gender are not unified, nor have they remained stable over time. Rather, considerable disagreement has occurred among such activists over how gender should be defined and how gender norms are best subverted, which in turn has profoundly shaped the development and use of gender

theory, including among scholars involved in media studies.

Feminist Activism

Although many individuals trace feminism back to only the early twentieth century and the women's suffragist movement, gender-based political philosophy is over two hundred years old. As a result of the involvement of numerous individuals and organizations motivated by such philosophy on behalf of women since that time, many different types of feminist activism and ideology have developed which, in turn, have contributed to the development of several different forms of feminist scholarship. In other words, it is more correct to use "feminisms" rather than "feminism." Nevertheless, all of these feminisms can be considered part of a larger social movement whose primary concern is women's lack of equality with men and whose primary goal is the eradication of gender oppression. No agreement exists among feminists, however, about the cause of such inequality and oppression or the most effective means for their elimination.

Many historians trace the origins of feminist activism to American, British, and French women's social reform of the mid nineteenth century, a community composed primarily of middle-class women whose goal was to improve the lives of poor women through volunteerism and charitable acts.[6] This community of activists grew out of the larger reform movement that had developed in the early 1800s in response to the social transformations caused by industrialization and urbanization. Through their involvement with widows, prostitutes, unmarried mothers, and other deprivileged women, female social reformers began to understand themselves and other women as members of a sex category, a concept that was crucial for the development of a social movement organized specifically for the betterment of women.[7]

Feminist opposition to women's inequality emerged well before the nineteenth century, however. For example, Olympe de Gouges's "Declaration of the Rights of Woman and the Female Citizen" was published in France in 1791, and Mary Wollstonecraft's *A Vindication of the Rights of Women* was published in 1792.[8] Nevertheless, feminists did not begin to organize formally until the mid-1800s, when industrialization's transformation of sex roles and women's unfair social treatment and subjugated social status became unbearable and cause for outcry. In order to improve women's everyday lives, the "woman movement" that emerged during this period advocated women's equality with men, particularly in the public sphere, and thus the elimination of legal barriers to women's civil rights.

Women's suffragism became the primary goal of feminists in the U.S., U.K., Europe, New Zealand, and Australia during the late nineteenth and early twentieth centuries. Because suffragism is typically understood as the initial period of feminist activism, the women's suffragist movement is often referred to as the "first wave" of feminism. In contrast to early reformers who sought to improve women's health and education, suffragists had a primarily liberal approach to activism that located the cause of gender inequity, as well as the elimination of it, in law. In 1880, the Isle of Man became the first country to grant women the right to vote. Some twenty-six years later, Finland became the first European country to allow women's suffrage. As a result of suffragists' global activism during the first half of the twentieth century, numerous nations followed suit, including the United States and United Kingdom.

Following the success of the suffragist movement in most Western countries, feminist sentiment declined in such areas between the 1920s and 1950s, largely as a result of common struggles experienced by men and women, boys and girls during World War II. (Meanwhile, women's suffrage became a primary political issue in Africa, East Asia, South Asia, Central America, and South America during this period.) Indeed, while many women were liberated from the domestic sphere during that war as a result of the need for more laborers, veterans eventually displaced the majority of women workers, and the traditional idea that "a woman's place was in the home" gained popular acceptance once the battles were over. Yet, despite the media's promotion of traditional femininity, as Western economies increasingly embraced consumer capitalism, more women were required to participate in the work force. In fact, the expenses associated with the consumerist lifestyle forced many middle-class married women into work outside the

home, a situation that was compounded by their desire to keep up with the "Happy Housewife" ideal prevalent in popular culture during that time. Nevertheless, women's rising discontent with the traditional roles of wife and mother, along with the publication of feminist texts, like Beauvoir's *The Second Sex*, helped to fuel the re-emergence of feminist sentiment in many Western countries during the 1950s. It was not until the early 1960s, however, that a movement for the improvement of women's rights and social status began to receive broad-based support again.

The women's liberation movement of the 1960s and 1970s is commonly referred to as the "second wave," a period when women, already granted suffrage in many countries, advocated their full social and economic equality with men.[9] Many of the feminists involved in the earliest years of the women's liberation movement had been radicalized to systems of social oppression via their involvement in other progressive movements, such as the New Left and the civil rights movement.[10] Yet these women reconfigured Karl Marx's theory of economic oppression by arguing that society is primarily divided not by class, but by sex via a patriarchal ideology that valorizes males and oppresses females.[11] In particular, these feminists emphasized the gendered division of labor in patriarchal societies, where men's work is primarily public and paid and women's work is largely private and unpaid. Because of their leftist leanings, interest in exploring the root cause of gender inequity, and their advocacy for a social revolution that would eliminate the division of society based on sex, these activists became known as radical feminists in the United States.[12]

By the early 1970s, radical feminism had declined, making way for two other feminist ideologies to achieve dominance over the next decade: liberal feminism and cultural feminism. As noted with regard to suffragists, liberal feminists advocate women's equality with men (hence its other moniker, "equality feminism") and see policy change as the key to women's betterment, particularly in the realms of work, education, and politics. By promoting women's non-domestic abilities, liberal feminists cleared a path for understanding gender as fluid and not biologically determined. Nonetheless, liberal feminists have traditionally placed less emphasis on improving women's experiences in the private sphere, which has contributed to the persistence of traditional gender roles within domestic relations. Indeed, while many men see their homes as places of leisure, most women—including those who work outside the home—continue to experience the domestic sphere as a place of labor because of their greater participation in childcare, cooking, and household maintenance. Moreover, because liberal feminists have failed to fully problematize their use of men (especially white, wealthy, heterosexual men) as role models for liberated women, they have uncritically advocated women's adoption of roles, behaviors, and even appearances historically associated with men and masculinity and thus the devaluing of those associated with women. In turn, working-class women have faulted liberal feminists for asserting an elitist perspective that addresses only middle-class concerns about women's education and non-domestic labor. (Women of lower socioeconomic status have never had a choice of whether or not to work outside the home.)

Once several important liberal feminist battles were won and feminist sentiment began to circulate more broadly in the mid-1970s, a different ideology, known in the U.S. as cultural feminism (and elsewhere as radical feminism), developed. Unlike liberal feminists who conceive of men and women as equal under the law, cultural feminists believe that women are biologically, psychologically, and spiritually different from men (a perspective that has contributed to this ideology being referred to as "difference feminism").[13] Moreover, rather than understanding men as the norm to which women should aspire, as liberal feminists do, cultural feminists purposely privilege females and femininity so as to counteract years of their marginalization and disparagement under patriarchy. Because of its women-centered approach, cultural feminism was a privileged ideology for many lesbian feminists during the 1970s and 1980s. Since lesbians were somewhat marginalized in both the women's and gay liberation movements of that period, many lesbian feminists argued that women should separate from men and patriarchal society to form a separate culture where women could feel safe, legitimate, and supported. Since deprivileged groups are already marginalized by dominant society, lesbian feminists' self-separation via this "women's culture" reconfigured that phenomenon by putting women in control of their own social location.

Cultural feminism's pro-female perspective has

been diffused broadly and has helped to bring to light women's many accomplishments as well as to legitimate character traits traditionally associated with women and femininity, like collaboration and nurturance. Nonetheless, cultural feminism is more controversial and thus less popular than liberal feminism, which requires little social change on the part of men. In particular, cultural feminism is critiqued for homogenizing women as a monolithic social group whose primary identity is feminine (much as patriarchal gender norms do), and thus failing to address the broad diversity of women's identities and experiences, which also include those conventionally labeled "masculine."

Cultural feminism has also received considerable criticism from feminists of color who find it difficult to focus solely on gender issues when their deprivileged racial and ethnic identities simultaneously constitute their subjectivities. Although long excluded from earlier histories of modern feminism, women of color have played an active role in the feminist movement since the nineteenth century. Arguing against the one-dimensional perspective on identity commonly held by white, middle-class feminists who have the privilege of being able to isolate gender from other modes of identity, feminists of color were involved in the women's liberation movement[14] yet achieved greater attention in the 1980s, helping to form a unique feminist ideology referred to today as womanism, black feminism, and women of color feminism.[15] Energized by postcolonialist politics, many non-Western feminists have similarly demanded further attention to the intersections of gender, race, and ethnicity, while adding that nationality and globalism must also be considered by the feminist movement.[16] Importantly, these feminists have helped to denaturalize the terms "woman" and "women" by foregrounding the multiplicity of identity and, in the process, have radically reconfigured feminist ideologies of gender.

Feminist ideologies and activism have shifted considerably since the early 1990s and the emergence of what is now commonly referred to as third wave feminism.[17] In continuing the project of feminists of color and non-Western feminists by bringing to light many of the problems associated with liberal and cultural feminism, third wave feminists have embraced an intersectional approach to identity that acknowledges the multiple, interdependent modes of human sub-jectivity and thus promotes diversity.[18] One of third wave feminists' primary contributions in this regard has been their attention to age and generational differences, with a specific focus on girls, girlhood, and girls' culture.[19] In turn, much like queer activists and scholars (discussed below), third wave feminists understand gender to be socially constructed. Yet, unlike liberal feminists, who valorize women's masculinity, and cultural feminists, who affirm women's femininity, third wave feminists advocate all individuals' access to the wide spectrum of gendered identities and work to validate all forms of gender expression. (Nevertheless, much third wave activism is specific to women, thus demonstrating the continuity of cultural feminism as well as the difficulty of working outside traditional social structures.)

Third wave feminists have also attempted to reclaim for women two aspects of society long ignored or disparaged by earlier feminists: sexuality and popular culture. While many feminists have developed an anti-sex perspective, primarily because sexuality is so commonly defined as patriarchal and heterosexual, third wave feminists advocate a pro-sex perspective, which has contributed to more critical thinking and activism related to women's sexual agency and sex work. In doing so, third wave feminists continue the legacy of Beauvoir, who argued for women's sexual liberation in *The Second Sex*. In turn, rather than seeing feminism as being brought to popular culture by activists and progressive industry professionals, third wave feminists understand popular culture (including media) as a dominant site where feminism is constructed and negotiated. Thus, third wave feminists have been more inclined than feminists of previous generations to use media technologies (particularly the Internet) and to create spaces for themselves and other women both within and outside the media industries. Indeed, third wave feminism has been strongly shaped by the "do-it-yourself" ethos of punk culture, which challenges individuals to express themselves and participate in the creation of popular culture.[20] Although third wave feminism has been commonly conflated with postfeminism, the latter term is now typically reserved for contemporary commercial discourse that promises women's access to historically male-dominated roles and structures of power without the loss

of traditional feminine attributes, especially heterosexual attractiveness.[21]

LGBTQI/Queer Activism

Equally important to the contestation of patriarchal and heterosexual gender norms, and thus theories of gender, is LGBTQI activism—that is, advocacy of sociopolitical change specifically in relation to homosexual, bisexual, transgender, queer, and intersex individuals.[22] Chief among the concerns for this community are legal, religious, and medical policies that oppress its members by limiting their everyday activities and curtailing their civil rights, in particular, laws against sodomy and cross-dressing.

Although France was the first nation to decriminalize homosexual activity in 1791, most other countries have been quite slow in following this lead, and some still list sodomy as a crime. The modern movement to expand the rights of homosexuals did not emerge until after World War II. Several homosexual rights organizations were formed in the United States in the 1950s, including the Mattachine Society and the Daughters of Bilitis. Nevertheless, 1969 is often cited as the birth year for modern gay politics, since that was the year that the Gay Liberation Front (GLF) emerged in response to a police raid on the Stonewall Inn in New York City.[23] The riots following that raid helped to provoke significant activism among both male and female homosexuals, as well as bisexuals, transvestites, and transgender people, who at that point in history were still prevented from meeting publicly and engaging in sexual behavior as a result of state and church laws. Like many other social movements of the mid twentieth century, the GLF had radical social transformation as part of its agenda, not just the elimination of sexual oppression. Thus, the eradication of gender- and race-based oppressions, as well as consumerism and militarism, was part of its political platform. Gay radicalism diminished over the course of the 1970s as the GLF lost support from more moderate gays and lesbians, who went on to form the Gay Activists' Alliance. Yet the GLF contributed to the rise of gay political activism in other countries during the early 1970s, including the U.K., encouraging gays and lesbians around the world to "come out" and show public pride in their sexual identity.

Much like the feminist community of the 1970s, the early gay movement included a diverse range of individuals who had different values with regard to gender. While some radical gay men took pride in their non-conformist effeminate behavior, moderate gay activists of the 1970s often responded negatively to sissies, drag queens, transvestites, and transgendered individuals, who considered themselves part of the movement yet refused to assimilate to the gender norms of heterosexual society via the gay community's norms of "passing." In turn, bisexuals were commonly ignored during this period, while lesbians and other queer women were similarly marginalized by many gay male activists. Other forms of difference, such as race, were often ignored or downplayed within the early gay movement, resulting in the common conflation of gay activists with white masculine male homosexuals.

Despite internal tensions over diversity, assimilation, and other political values and practices, organized opposition to homosexuals' social disenfranchisement continued in the 1970s. One of the first major victories for the U.S. gay movement was the removal of homosexuality from the American Psychiatric Association's *Diagnostic and Statistical Manual of Mental Disorders* in 1973. In the 1980s, the gay community was united politically as a result of the HIV/AIDS epidemic and the conservative backlash against homosexuals at that time. In response to this increased oppression, more activist groups formed within the gay and lesbian community during the early 1990s, including several which revived the radical politics of the GLF, such as ACT UP, Queer Nation, and the Lesbian Avengers. As the name Queer Nation suggests, many younger gays, lesbians, and bisexuals adopted the historically negative moniker of "queer" in the 1990s as a signifier of a new phase of anti-assimilationist activism within the gay community as well as solidarity across non-normative sexualities and gender identities.

Since the 1990s, many members of the LGBTQI community have been involved in various civil rights activities, including lobbying for gay adoption, gay marriage, outing gays in the military, and the decriminalization of sodomy. Meanwhile, other gay activists have advocated for more collaboration with activists of other marginalized communities, including people with disabilities, while also drawing more attention to issues of diversity within their own community,

including bisexuality, transgenderism, and intersexuality. While "queer" is commonly used today as an umbrella term for this diverse community, many of its members believe that specificity with regard to identity is politically important and thus insist on using "LGBTQI" (or some shorter version) instead. In the meantime, the LGBTQI community has received considerable commercial interest from mainstream manufacturers, advertisers, and retailers, thus contributing to the increased visibility of queer individuals as well as the mainstreaming of queer culture.[24] Although the relation of this community's recent commercial exploitation to its greater legitimacy and social power should not be ignored, such commercial attention to queer culture has contributed significantly to the dismantling of traditional gender norms in many countries today.

As among feminist activists, ideas about gender have not been stable in the LGBTQI community. Although many individuals assume queer individuals to be non-normative with regard to gender because of their non-normative sexuality, the range of gender identities and performances among members of this community is not limited to feminine males and masculine females. Indeed, while stereotypes of the butch lesbian and gay sissy are still dominant in many societies because they help to reaffirm heteronormative constructions of gender (i.e., masculine males and feminine females), gender in the queer community has varied widely across different places and times. For example, "butch–femme" couples were popular during the mid twentieth century among working-class lesbians, yet have been understood as politically incorrect at other times in this community based on assumptions about heterosexual mimicry.

Masculine gay men who are able to "pass" as straight males in mainstream society have commonly held the most power in the LGBTQI community, and many have contributed to what is now known as homonormativity as a result of their assimilationist values and practices which reaffirm conservative, heteronormative ideologies.[25] Meanwhile, effeminate men, queer women at large, and those individuals who mix traits and/or performances associated with masculinity and femininity—that is, cross-dressers, transgender people, and intersex individuals—have often been marginalized within this community as a result of being genderqueer and thus have had to struggle harder for legitimacy and support.[26] Indeed, some gays, lesbians, and bisexuals are uneasy with the inclusion of cross-dressers, intersex people, and transgender individuals in the queer community, since members of these latter groups do not construct their identities around sexuality in particular. Nevertheless, numerous individuals see compelling connections between those who are genderqueer and those who are sexually queer, since these groups have been similarly persecuted for their failure to adhere to heterosexual norms.

Gender Studies

While scholarly research is often considered outside the world of direct political action today, one of the most significant developments resulting from feminist and LGBTQI activism has been the formation of two academic fields related to such political work: women's studies and LGBTQI studies. An overview of the development of those fields helps in understanding how political ideologies of gender have informed academic theories of gender and what has come to be known as gender studies, a form of scholarship with strong connections to women's studies and LGBTQI studies.

The primary ideology of gender that feminist and LGBTQI scholars have challenged is what Gayle Rubin refers to as the "sex/gender system," which positions heterosexuality as the only normal form of sexual relations and thus bifurcates human beings into "males" and "females" to suppress their similarities and to organize their (hetero)sexual activity.[27] To better ensure the distinction of these two sexes, the sex/gender system demands that males always behave in ways conventionally understood as "masculine" (what R. W. Connell later labeled "hegemonic masculinity") while females must behave in a traditionally "feminine" manner (Connell's "emphasized femininity").[28] By linking these sexes to these specific genders, Rubin argues, the sex/gender system works as a powerful regulator of individual behavior and social relations, particularly with regard to the subjugation of women. With the exception of cultural feminists, who understand women's femininity to be inherent, feminist and LGBTQI activists and scholars have long opposed the sex/gender system because,

in addition to suggesting that masculinity and femininity are stable and universal categories, it relies on the faulty logic that "biology is destiny" and thus severely limits the options human beings have with regard to appearance, behavior, relationships, and even physical location. Nevertheless, as the following discussion of the development of gender studies demonstrates, the various ways feminist and LGBTQI scholars have theorized "sex" and "gender," and thus the best methods to subvert the oppressive norms associated with them, have been anything but uniform.

In an effort to raise awareness of women's contributions to society and challenge the male bias of academic inquiry and public knowledge, women's studies research was primarily a recuperative practice during its initial period in the early 1970s.[29] Influenced by liberal feminism, many early feminist scholars focused their attention on women who were influential in the formation of culture, politics, business, and the academy yet largely ignored by male historians. As with the majority of feminist activists of that era, many feminist researchers rarely questioned how their naturalized assumptions about female identity led them to recuperate primarily privileged women (i.e., those who were white, middle-class, heterosexual, able-bodied, Western) for critical inquiry under the singular frame of "women." Nevertheless, liberal approaches in women's studies have contributed greatly to the larger field of gender studies by calling attention to women's unequal treatment and representation in history, law, culture, education, business, and politics. Through critical analyses of women's social subjugation, liberal feminist scholars have been able to argue more effectively for women's increased presence and improved treatment in public arenas long dominated by men. Two of the foundational essays in gender and media studies, Laura Mulvey's "Visual Pleasure and Narrative Cinema" and Gaye Tuchman's "The Symbolic Annihilation of Women by the Mass Media" (both of which are reprinted in this collection), can be considered part of this early period of liberal feminist scholarship, for both of these projects analyzed the representation of women in relation to portrayals of men, recognizing that the latter formed the ideal subject of most media texts.[30]

Rather than trying to insert women into male-dominated realms of academic thought and society, some women's studies scholars began to explore women's uniqueness in the mid-1970s. This gynocentric approach was clearly influenced by the dominance of cultural feminism during this period, yet it has been used by numerous feminist scholars since that time to analyze those roles, behaviors, character traits, relationships, and institutions that have historically been identified with women and femininity. Such work has not only expanded knowledge about human beings and society, but has also given further legitimacy to women's experiences. For example, without the cultural, women-centered approach to feminist research, little scholarly attention would have been given to the domestic arts, motherhood, or shopping, or to the various ways in which women have challenged patriarchy by developing their own forms of culture, politics, business, education, and health care. This culturalist approach has also impacted gender and media studies, thus leading many feminist scholars to analyze media texts that specifically focus on or are consumed by women, including fashion magazines, soap operas, family melodramas, and women's music.[31] Several of the scholars whose work is included in this collection have been influenced by cultural feminism, although they may not be explicit about that in their writing.

For much of the 1970s and 1980s, liberal and cultural feminist ideologies of gender dominated women's studies. Unfortunately, despite revealing the social construction of women's inequality (and thus gender), many liberal and cultural feminist scholars of that period failed to problematize their isolation of gender as an object of critical inquiry that precluded their attention to how gender intersects with other modes of identity. In turn, many of these scholars failed to perceive how their understanding of sex and gender was essentialist, which in turn prevented them from exploring fully the different processes and effects of gender-based oppression.

Fortunately, the exclusive and universalizing perspectives on gender uncritically promoted by early women's studies scholars (most of whom were white, middle-class, heterosexual, and Western) were increasingly subverted on numerous fronts over the last decades of the twentieth century. For example, scholars supportive of socialist feminism, which had grown out of radical feminism in the 1960s, foregrounded the connection of gender, labor, and economics and thus revealed that class and socioeconomic status are significant components of gender identity.[32] Meanwhile, non-white and non-Western researchers demanded more attention to race, ethnicity, and nationality,[33] and lesbian and other queer scholars challenged the heterocentrism of feminist theories of gender while initiating more studies into gender and sexuality.[34] As a result of feminist scholars' increased attention to difference and diversity, contemporary research on gender has been profoundly affected by what Kimberlé Williams Crenshaw calls an "intersectional" approach, which insists on the multiplicity and interdependence of identities and thus precludes the isolation of gender in discussions of human behavior and social relations. (One of Crenshaw's pioneering articles on intersectionality is reprinted in this collection.)[35]

Yet new theories of gender have not been facilitated only by marginalized groups advocating for simultaneous attention to other components of identity. Poststructuralist theories, such as those put forth by Jacques Derrida, Roland Barthes, Michel Foucault, and Julia Kristeva, have also transformed gender studies, in particular by helping researchers to realize more fully the project Beauvoir started with *The Second Sex*: understanding the social construction of gender.[36] Poststructuralist theory developed in response to structuralism, a theoretical approach used to explore the larger frameworks through which human experience is constructed and understood, such as language. One of the main criticisms of the structuralist approach is that contradictions in social structures must be ignored or marginalized in order for scholars to arrive at generalizable theories. Poststructuralists challenge structuralism's generalized theories about human beings and society, which are often presented as natural and universal, by paying close attention to the specific historical and geographic context of social phenomena, for poststructuralists understand meaning to shift with changes in such contexts. This attention to the specificity of sociohistorical context has profound significance for feminist and LGBTQI scholars who attempt to demonstrate how gender is (re)produced through social interaction.

Poststructuralists have also challenged the dualist form of meaning-making that has been dominant in Western society for centuries. Westerners have long made sense of the world by categorizing concepts and social phenomena into two opposing groups, such as good and evil, self and other, man and woman. Poststructuralist theorists have noted that in Western societies binary opposites are never equally balanced: one term is always more privileged than the other. Poststructuralists argue that dualist forms of meaning-making are reductive and thus unuseful in explaining human reality, which is richly complex and thus rarely composed of such absolute opposites. The poststructuralist challenge to dualism has been important for feminists and LGBTQI scholars wanting to subvert the sex/gender system, whose regulatory power is maintained via human beings' complicity in reaffirming links between the binary opposites of male/female and masculine/feminine.

Numerous theories of gender have been written since Beauvoir delineated femininity's social construction and Rubin extended that line of thought through her theory of the sex/gender system. In particular, Judith Butler's work (some of which is reprinted here) has been overwhelmingly influential.[37] Whereas many earlier scholars had unwittingly reproduced the biological division of human beings into male and female (sex) even when asserting that women's inequality was socially produced (gender), from Butler's social constructionist perspective, neither sex nor gender are determined by biology, and, indeed, sex is "always already gender" since they are culturally produced through similar mechanisms.[38] According to Butler, gender is secured and naturalized in society through numerous repetitive performances that cohere into patterns of identity which human beings are encouraged to see as normal and thus reproduce daily via their own appearance and behavior. Only by refusing to repeat such patterns, Butler argues, can gender be "troubled" and new possibilities of identity be asserted.

In addition to its widespread impact on gender studies, Butler's work, like Rubin's, has been key to the development of queer theory, a form of poststructuralist scholarship which grew out of gay and lesbian studies, has been strongly influenced by anti-assimilationist queer politics, and questions normalizing structures associated with gender and sexuality. Like queer activists, queer theorists are typically open to non-normative sexualities and genders, such as sadomasochism and transgenderism, and thus do not restrict their work to homosexuals and homosexuality. Some queer theorists who have been influential within gender studies are Teresa de Lauretis, Eve Kosofsky Sedgwick, Michael Warner, Judith Halberstam, and José Esteban Muñoz.[39] The fact that many queer scholars focus on media culture in their work suggests the powerful connection between queer theory and media studies today.

Gender and Media Studies

Interestingly, the field of gender studies has developed somewhat in tandem with that of humanities-based media studies, which deserves a brief overview here as well. While social scientific studies of mass media emerged in the 1930s, humanities-based media studies coalesced as a unique field of critical inquiry some forty years later, largely as a result of a dramatic increase in scholarly attention to film during that period.[40] With roots in literary analysis, theatre studies, and visual arts, 1970s' film scholars had a wealth of theoretical and methodological tools at their disposal, including semiotics, historiography, narrative theory, psychoanalytic theory, and Marxist theory.[41] Television studies, by contrast, took much longer to establish, largely because of that medium's historical construction as the "low other" to film, literature, and the fine arts. Cohering as a discipline in the 1980s, television studies owes a great deal to cultural studies, a multiperspectival and antidisciplinary approach to humanities scholarship which has been shaped by poststructuralist theory.[42] Foregrounding the mechanisms of power and pleasure at work in culture, cultural studies scholars also take seriously elements of culture that have long been considered unworthy of scholarly attention, including popular media, and thus have helped to legitimate television, magazines, and other forms of popular entertainment as worthy objects of study.[43] Indeed, popular music studies, which formed in the 1980s,[44] owes its development to cultural studies, as do radio studies and game studies, which developed more recently.[45]

While film studies has long privileged textual analysis as its primary methodology, cultural studies scholars' affiliations with both sociology and anthropology have inspired numerous ethnographically informed analyses of media audiences, particularly fans of popular musicians and television programs. Analyses of media producers have traditionally been a part of media studies, as authorship has been a primary focus for film and music scholars in particular. Yet only recently have media production and media industries been afforded as much attention as media texts and consumers, in part because of the changing nature of mediamaking. Most media scholars have been interested in exploring the mainstream or commercial media texts, media reception, and media production; however, a smaller number of researchers have investigated these practices within independent, non-corporate media culture. This latter arena has been important to feminist and queer media scholars, since women and homosexual producers have long been marginalized within the media industries and thus have often worked in the realm of independent media.

Since the mid-1990s, media culture and media studies have been radically transformed by the introduction of digital technologies, especially the World Wide Web, which offers media producers the ability to construct, exhibit, distribute, and archive their works all via the same apparatus. Moreover, with the increased interactivity of the Web, users can now interact simultaneously with numerous individuals, a practice that has significantly shifted the power dynamics between producers and consumers and has challenged media scholars to rethink the ways in which they have conceived of the different roles and practices within media culture. While digital media technologies, such as computers, cell phones, video games, and the Web, are often constructed as central to contemporary and future media studies, a considerable amount of media history remains to be explored, particularly with regard to radio and television, whose earliest transmissions were not recorded. Nevertheless, digital technologies will hopefully facilitate more historical research, as archival material is increasingly digitized and made available online.

Because of the coterminous development of women's studies and film studies, scholars focused on gender have been involved in critical media studies from its inception. In fact, scholarly attention to gender in media representation, production, and reception has significantly shaped all forms of media scholarship to date. Several scholars have written historical surveys outlining the basic themes, theories, and methodologies that have been privileged in gender and media studies.[46] Liesbet van Zoonen's "Feminist Perspectives on the Media" is included in this collection in order to provide an overview of how various feminist ideologies have shaped the study of gender in media studies since the early 1970s. In turn, her essay addresses how gender and media scholarship has been transformed by cultural studies. Van Zoonen's overview is quite useful, therefore, in helping readers to understand major directions in gender-based media studies in the 1970s and 1980s. Nevertheless, because that survey ends in the early 1990s, it is necessary to comment on some of the primary ways gender and media studies has developed since that time in order to contextualize the more recent work collected in this reader.

Several trends are evident within contemporary gender and media studies.[47] The first and perhaps most noticeable trend is that men and masculinity have been receiving much more attention recently than when this form of scholarship was launched four decades ago. Such studies have contributed to the diversification of scholars doing gender-based media research and complicated what we know of as feminist media studies. In large part, this turn towards more analyses of manhood and masculinity has resulted from an increase in male scholars' interest in exploring representations of their own social group.[48] While early attempts to study men and masculinity met with some skepticism and resistance from female feminist scholars who worried that their field would become as male-dominated as older disciplines, analyses of manhood and masculinity have enriched considerably gender-based media studies as well as queer and feminist scholarship. Indeed, such studies have helped to reveal the processes through which masculinity and manhood are socially produced through media and thus have exposed some of the mechanisms of patriarchy as well as the processes through which boys are socialized. While several gay male scholars have been active within media studies focused on men and masculinity, lesbian and queer scholars have expanded such research in provocative new directions more recently by exploring female masculinity and thus subverting male entitlement to this particular gender.[49] Unfortunately, however, little attention has been paid to date to straight and bisexual women's masculine performances in media culture.

As a result of contemporary gender scholars' use of the intersectional approach to identity, a second trend evident in today's gender and media studies is the *de rigueur* exploration of sexuality, race, ethnicity, and other components of identity alongside gender. While studying these convergent identities is not a recent phenomenon within media studies, the naturalization of this approach is, which reveals the difficulty of categorizing contemporary research of this nature (not to mention titling this collection). Chief among the intersecting identities studied within gender and media studies is sexuality, particularly homosexuality and queerness.[50] Indeed, within contemporary film studies, the amount of queer research is on par with, if not exceeding, feminist scholarship. Attention to blackness dominated race-oriented studies of gender and media in the 1980s and early 1990s, particularly in the United States. Yet, with the increased diversity and internationalism of this field, media scholars have paid more attention to the intersections of gender and whiteness as well as Latino/a, East Asian, South Asian, and Middle Eastern identities since the late 1990s.[51] While class and disability remain understudied areas within gender-based media studies,[52] the recent coalescing of girls' studies as a specific form of scholarship has increased attention to how age and generation intersect with gender in media culture.[53]

A third trend in contemporary gender-based media studies is more attention to contemporary ideologies associated with feminism, particularly postfeminism and third wave feminism.[54] While some scholars have used postfeminism to describe an anti-feminist perspective in media culture, other researchers have complicated this theory by noting the simultaneous incorporation of empowerment discourse within postfeminist media texts. Nevertheless, most feminist scholars agree that postfeminism has emerged from the commercial rather than the feminist sector and therefore should not be considered a feminist ideology. As debates about the particular characteristics of postfeminist ideology continue, further attention to how this primarily commercial discourse affects males, people of color, and members of the LGBTQI community is needed.[55] Meanwhile, the term "third

wave" can be applied to feminist media studies that adhere to third wave feminist ideologies, particularly valuing diversity, understanding identities as intersectional and socially constructed, and reclaiming sexuality and popular culture as sites for feminist agency.

While representation continues to be the dominant site of analysis for gender-based media scholars, the gendering of media consumption and production is receiving much more critical attention than in the past.[56] This fourth trend—the expansion of media studies beyond textual analysis and towards reception and production studies—has been influenced by the rise of cultural studies as well as the development of digital technologies, which have altered media consumption, production, and distribution significantly. Of particular interest to scholars today are consumers-cum-producers ("prosumers") who maximize the Web's facilitation of interactive media experiences.[57] Unfortunately, far less gender-specific work has been conducted in relation to conventional forms of media production, particularly within the film, broadcasting, and recording industries; however, the studies included in Part II of this collection have helped to bring more attention to this area.

The fifth trend in contemporary gender and media studies is that this field is no longer restricted to scholars with training in media studies, as evidenced by several of the studies reprinted in this collection. Indeed, this form of analysis is now undertaken by scholars associated with a variety of disciplines, including education, sociology, legal studies, and information science. How gender and media studies will develop as a result of the participation of scholars with such diverse professional backgrounds remains unclear. At the very least, however, such interdisciplinarity demonstrates the broad concern today about gender in media culture. Moreover, it suggests that, despite four decades' worth of scholarship in this area, much research remains to be done, for in most societies the media have become dominant sites of gender performance and contestation.

Organization

The Gender and Media Reader is organized into five parts intended to facilitate readers' attention to particular sites of scholarship related to gender-based media studies. That said, many of the chapters include subject material that connects to essays located in this collection's other parts. Therefore, readers are encouraged to use the Alternate Table of Contents below in order to discern chapters that cohere around particular themes of interest. To facilitate readers' understanding of the history and development of gender and media studies, separate introductions to the book's five parts provide context for the various topics, debates, methodologies, and theoretical approaches that have shaped different areas of this unique field.

Part I of *The Gender and Media Reader* exposes readers to some of the foundational works in the study of gender and media, while also including past and present surveys of this field as well as scholarship outside media studies that has forged important new paths for those working within it. The topics, ideas, and questions in these essays are considered pivotal to scholarship on gender and media and thus are essential reading for anyone currently engaged in this work.

Part II contains both foundational and more contemporary studies of gender and media production. Problematizing the common association of media production with Hollywood, some of the readings in this section explore mediamaking among amateurs, activists, and others working independently of the commercial, industrial realm of media production. In addition to an examination of how gender functions alongside economics and business practices, other issues pertinent to mediamaking, such as authorship and technology, are explored here also.

Recent studies of gender and media representation compose Part III. One of the most fruitful areas of feminist and LGBTQI scholarship to date, the practices of media representation, is crucial to anyone interested in how the identities and bodies of socially disenfranchised individuals are performed and positioned in media texts. Yet, as noted above, recent scholarship in this area is now attending to the performance of hegemonic gender identities as well. Moving beyond the foundational studies of representation that appear in Part I, the essays here take an intersectional approach to subjectivity in order to examine how gender is constructed in media texts alongside other components of identity, such as race, class, and sexuality.

Part IV includes foundational and contemporary gender-based studies of media narratives and genres. Since critical media studies emerged in part from literary and theatre studies, questions of narrative have been privileged by media scholars as well. Building from pioneering studies of gender representation, the scholarship included here explores how gender norms are constructed, negotiated, and challenged in different genres, modes, and narrative structures.

Part V exposes readers to studies of gender and media consumption. Moving past the abstract, ahistorical spectator at the heart of much psychoanalytic film scholarship, the studies here were conducted to better understand everyday individuals' real-life experiences with and uses of media texts. Important to the field are those studies that analyze how members of socially disenfranchised groups, such as women and queer individuals, respond to media texts that exclude, marginalize, or stereotype them. Helping to complicate the traditional divide between consumption and production are several studies that focus on gaming and media fandom.

Alternate Table of Contents

The overall contents of this reader could have been organized in several different ways. To facilitate readers' focus on a particular identity or medium, the table below categorizes the collection's chapters according to subtopics within those two larger areas. The chapters are listed by author's last name.

Identity

Females (girls and/or women)

Banet-Weiser and Portwood-Stacer	Meehan
Bayton	Molina Guzmán and Valdivia
Bielby and Bielby	Mooney
Carrillo Rowe and Lindsey	Mulvey
Ciasullo	Railton
Citron	Royse et al.
Cooper	Schilt
Crenshaw	Sellen
Cumberland	Sgroi
D'Acci	Shade
De Lauretis	Shohat
Gill	Stacey
Gledhill	Tuchman
Gray	Van Doorn et al.
hooks	Van Zoonen
Kelley	Walser
Kuhn	Williams
Levine	

Males (boys and/or men)

Ashcraft and Flores	MacCallum-Stewart
Bayton	Messner et al.
Bielby and Bielby	Mooney
Brookey and Westerfelhaus	Mulvey
Cohan	Nochimson
De Lauretis	Schiavi
Douglas	Sgroi
Farmer	Straw
Fung	Tasker
Gray	Van Doorn et al.
Jenkins	Walser
Kelley	Williams

Femininity

(Most of the articles listed above under "Females" explore female displays of femininity. Those listed here emphasize femininity in their studies, and some focus on male displays of femininity.)

Banet-Weiser and Portwood-Stacer	MacCallum-Stewart
Ciasullo	Schiavi
Gill	

Masculinity

(Most of the articles listed above under "Males" explore male displays of masculinity. Those listed here emphasize masculinity in their studies, and some focus on female displays of masculinity.)

Cooper	Messner et al.
Douglas	Straw
Jenkins	Walser

Transgender

(While many of the articles collected here, particularly those noted in the "LGBTQI" section below, deal with the subversion of the sex/gender system, these articles deal explicitly with transgender identities.)

Cooper
MacCallum-Stewart
Schiavi

LGBTQI

Brookey and Westerfelhaus	D'Acci
Butler	Doty
Ciasullo	Farmer
Cohan	Fung
Cooper	Van Doorn et al.

Heterosexuality/Heteronormativity

(With the exception of studies listed under "LGBTQI," most studies in this collection focus on heterosexual gender performances. Those listed here foreground a critique of heteronormativity.)

Brookey and Westerfelhaus	Cooper
Cohan	Sgroi

Race/Ethnicity/Nationality

(With the exception of studies listed here, most studies in this collection focus on, but do not foreground a critique of, white/Anglo individuals.)

Ashcraft and Flores	Kelley
Carrillo Rowe and Lindsey	Molina Guzmán and Valdivia
Crenshaw	Sellen
Fung	Shohat
hooks	Tasker

Class

(Most of the studies contained herein focus on middle-class individuals but do not foreground a critique of class. The articles noted in this category focus specifically on class; some focus specifically on working-class individuals.)

Ashcraft and Flores	Meehan
Jenkins	Sgroi
Kelley	Walser

Age/Generation

(Most of the studies in this collection focus on adults. Those listed below focus on youth and foreground issues of age and generation.)

Kelley	Schiavi
MacCallum-Stewart	Schilt

Medium

Digital Media/Video Games

Cumberland	Shade
MacCallum-Stewart	Van Doorn et al.
Royse et al.	

Film/Video

Ashcraft and Flores	Gill
Bielby and Bielby	Gray
Brookey and Westerfelhaus	hooks
Carrillo Rowe and Lindsey	Kuhn
Citron	Mulvey
Cooper	Schiavi
De Lauretis	Shohat
Doty	Stacey
Farmer	Tasker
Fung	Williams

Magazines/Advertising

Ciasullo	Mooney
Gill	Schilt

Music/Music Video

Bayton	Railton
Crenshaw	Sellen
Farmer	Straw
Kelley	Walser

Radio

    Douglas

Television

Banet-Weiser and Portwood-Stacer	Kuhn
Cohan	Levine
D'Acci	Meehan
Gledhill	Messner et al.
Gray	Nochimson
Jenkins	Sgroi

Transmedial or multiple forms of media

Gill	Molina Guzmán and Valdivia
Gledhill	Tuchman
Levine	Van Zoonen

Notes

1. Simone de Beauvoir, *The Second Sex*, H. M. Parshley, trans. (1949; New York: Vintage, 1989).
2. Beauvoir 267.
3. Beauvoir 143.
4. Betty Friedan, *The Feminine Mystique* (New York: Norton, 1963).
5. For a collection that is specific to gender and communication studies and thus includes more quantitative, social science analyses, see Bonnie J. Dow and Julia T. Wood, eds., *The Sage Handbook of Gender and Communication* (Thousand Oaks, CA: Sage, 2006).
6. See Nancy Cott, *The Grounding of Modern Feminism* (New Haven, CT: Yale University Press, 1987).
7. See Barbara Ryan, *Feminism and the Women's Movement: Dynamics of Change in Social Movement, Ideology, and Activism* (New York: Routledge, 1992).
8. Olympe de Gouges, "Declaration of the Rights of Woman and the Female Citizen" (1791), *Women in Revolutionary Paris, 1789–1795*, eds. Darline Gay Levy, Harriet Branson Applewhite, and Mary Durham Johnson (Urbana: University of Illinois Press, 1980) 87–96; Mary Wollstonecraft, *A Vindication of the Rights of Women* (1792; Buffalo: Prometheus, 1989).
9. For a historical overview, see Kathleen C. Berkeley, *The Women's Liberation Movement in America* (Westport, CT: Greenwood Press, 1999).
10. See Sara M. Evans, *Personal Politics: The Roots of Women's Liberation in the Civil Rights Movement and the New Left* (New York: Knopf, 1979).
11. For example, see Shulamith Firestone, *The Dialectic of Sex: The Case for Feminist Revolution* (New York: Morrow, 1970). For a history of radical feminism in the U.S., see Alice Echol's *Daring to Be Bad: Radical Feminism in America, 1967–1975* (Minneapolis: University of Minnesota Press, 1989).
12. Outside the U.S., "radical feminism" is commonly used to describe what Americans refer to as "cultural feminism."
13. See Gayle Kimball, ed., *Women's Culture: The Women's Renaissance of the Seventies* (Metuchen, NJ: Scarecrow Press, 1981). See also Verta Taylor and Leila J. Rupp, "Women's Culture and Lesbian Feminist Activism: A Reconsideration of Cultural Feminism," *Signs: Journal of Women in Culture and Society* 19.1 (1993) 32–61.
14. See Kimberly Springer, *Living for the Revolution: Black Feminist Organizations, 1968–1980* (Durham, NC: Duke University Press, 2005).
15. For example, see Cherríe Moraga and Gloria Anzaldúa, eds., *This Bridge Called My Back: Writings by Radical Women of Color* (Watertown, MA: Persephone Press, 1981).
16. See Chandra Talpade Mohanty, Ann Russo, and Lourdes Torres, eds., *Third World Women and the Politics of Feminism* (Bloomington: Indiana University Press, 1991). For a discussion of the effects of women of color feminism and postcolonial theory on U.S. feminism, see Chela Sandoval, "U.S. Third World Feminism: The Theory and Method of Oppositional Consciousness in the Postmodern World," *Genders* 10 (1991) 1–24.

PART I

FOUNDATIONS: STUDYING GENDER AND MEDIA

Introduction

In order to introduce readers to gender-based media studies, Part I of the reader includes pioneering work by some of the scholars who helped to form this field, as well as several others who have significantly shaped how the intersections of gender and media are analyzed today. This part begins with a survey of feminist media studies through the early 1990s by Liesbet van Zoonen, which helps readers to contextualize the older articles included in this reader. In particular van Zoonen's survey offers a guide to understanding how specific feminist ideologies have informed different approaches to gender and media studies over the years.

The field of gender-based media studies is now almost forty years old. Emerging from feminist scholars working in cinema studies and communication studies in the 1970s, the history of this particular form of critical inquiry is complex and thus difficult to trace in any linear fashion. Early film and communication scholars came to their research with different objects of study, different questions, and different analytical toolkits. As represented by Gaye Tuchman's "The Symbolic Annihilation of Women," quantitative content analysis of commercial mass media forms, especially news media, was privileged in communication studies during the 1970s. Laura Mulvey's "Visual Pleasure and Narrative Cinema" exemplifies the dominance of semiotic and psychoanalytic analyses of Hollywood movies in film studies during that same period. Despite these divergent approaches, feminist scholars working in these two branches of media studies during the 1970s had similar concerns, particularly the representation of women, which they found in varying degrees unrealistic, stereotypical, and offensive. More disturbingly, as Tuchman argues, women were virtually absent ("symbolically annihilated") from 1970s' media culture.

Meanwhile, Mulvey's work on classical Hollywood cinema revealed the male dominance of that specific medium with regard to not only film characters, but also directors, writers, and cinematographers, a situation that, according to Mulvey, places all spectators in the position of the male viewer. Although Tuchman's and Mulvey's studies have been critiqued by numerous feminist media scholars since their publication, both are foundational in gender and media studies and thus are considered necessary reading for researchers in this field. In addition to facilitating more attention to women's representation in media (the topic in Parts 3 and 4 of this reader), given Mulvey's and Tuchman's discussions of who controls media representation and how media portrayals of women impact viewers and social norms, their work helped to inspire research on gender in both media production (Part II) and media consumption (Part V).

Since the early 1980s, several new approaches have been introduced to the study of gender and media that have impacted the manner in which scholars approach this research today. With regard to theoretical perspectives, feminist media scholars have been increasingly drawn to poststructuralist theories of language, discourse, identity, and power in order to articulate better the mechanisms by which gender is constructed, negotiated, and contested. The field of cultural studies took up many of these issues in the 1980s and, given such scholars' attention to popular culture, the media, especially televi-sion, became important objects of study. This poststructuralist, cultural studies approach is exemplified by Julie D'Acci's "Defining Women," which focuses on *Cagney & Lacey* (CBS 1982–1988), a U.S. television drama, and the multiple, conflicting perspectives on gender and power evident in the creation, promotion, and consumption of that series. By extending her methodological reach beyond textual analysis, the typical approach in media studies to that date, D'Acci's study (which was expanded to a book)[1] is understood by many scholars as a foundational and exemplary cultural studies-based media analysis, as well as a media-based cultural studies analysis.

A new direction for gender and media studies in the early 1990s was the analysis of gender along-side other components of identity, such as race, ethnicity, class, sexuality, and nationality. Such work was powerfully influenced by the development of postcolonial theory during that period. Ella Shohat's "Gender and the Culture of Empire" was one of the first feminist studies to mesh film analysis, gender analysis, and postcolonial analysis. By exploring themes of sexual difference in Western films, Shohat's work paved the way for other scholars to address the convergence of patriarchy and colonialism in representations of Third World cultures. Her secondary focus on independent films with anti-colonialist or anti-patriarchal coun-ter-narratives can be understood as part of a larger trend in the 1990s of scholars' increased attention to alternative media, a subject considered more closely by several studies included in Part II of this reader.

Kimberlé Williams Crenshaw's theorization of intersectional identities in "Beyond Racism and Misogyny" has been crucial to the development of feminist media studies. In her study, Crenshaw explores the complex intersections of gender, race, and class in media representations of women of color, and the negative effects of such stereotypes on real women of color. Her article not only has encouraged greater focus on race and class, like Shohat's, but has helped to transform the feminist study of identity by dislocating gender from the center of analysis and insisting on attention to our multiple, interdependent modes of subjectivity.

Gender studies, and thus gender-based media scholarship, was expanded considerably during the 1990s, particularly through the work of Judith Butler, who is also a pioneering figure in queer studies. In addition to offering provocative new ideas on the discursive construction of both sex and gender, Butler theorized the subversion of the sex/gender system and heteronormativity. In "Imitation and Gender Insub-ordination," Butler discusses how gender and sexuality are produced through reiterative acts, the problem the lack of originary identities poses for identity-based politics, and the possibility of troubling gender and sexual norms through acts that expose them as socially constructed. Although Butler has addressed media culture only intermittently over the course of her career, her work is now considered essential reading for scholars involved in gender-based media scholarship.

The final essay in this section, Rosalind Gill's "Postfeminist Media Culture," focuses on one of the most recent issues within contemporary gender and media studies. Postfeminism has been hotly debated by feminists since the 1991 publication of Susan Faludi's *Backlash: The Undeclared War against American Women*, which focuses on the media's construction of second wave feminism as the cause for women's difficulties in the 1980s.[2] While some feminists have critiqued postfeminism as a form of anti-feminist discourse meant to contain women and the feminist enterprise, others have explored postfeminism's con-vergence of empowerment rhetoric and heteronormative femininity. Gill takes this latter, more popular approach in her survey of various tenets of a postfeminist sensibility, thus helping to guide scholars through the complexly contradictory terrain of postfeminist media culture.

Notes

1. Julie D'Acci, *Defining Women: Television and the Case of* Cagney & Lacey (Chapel Hill: University of North Carolina Press, 1994).
2. Susan Faludi, *Backlash: The Undeclared War against American Women* (New York: Crown, 1991).

1.
FEMINIST PERSPECTIVES ON THE MEDIA
Liesbet van Zoonen

With the current proliferation and fragmentation of feminist theory and politics, reviewing feminist perspectives on the media has become a hazardous task. A general overview of the field can hardly do justice to the variety of feminist discourse while advancing one's own particular approach inevitably excludes other, often equally valid feminist discourses. In this chapter I shall use both approaches. While I cannot deny my own political and academic preferences, I do hope to provide a framework general enough to understand historical developments and recent trends in feminist media studies.

How does feminist media theory distinguish itself from other perspectives such as postmodernism, pluralism, neo-marxism, etc.? Its unconditional focus on analyzing *gender* as a mechanism that structures material and symbolic worlds and our experiences of them, is hard to find in other theories of the media. Even by mid and late seventies mainstream communication scholars did not seem to be very interested in the subject 'woman'. 'And why should they? Before the advent of the women's movement these [sex-role] stereotypes seemed natural, "given". Few questioned how they developed, how they were reinforced, or how they were maintained. Certainly the media's role in this process was not questioned' (Tuchman, 1978:5). Nor were critical communication scholars in the forefront of recognizing the importance of gender, as the account of the Women's Studies Group of the Centre for Contemporary Cultural Studies (CCCS) at Birmingham confirms: 'We found it extremely difficult to participate in the CCCS groups and felt, without

being able to articulate it, that it was a case of the masculine domination of both intellectual work and the environment in which it was being carried out' (*Women Take Issue*, 1978: 11).

The situation has improved to a certain extent. There seems to be a hesitant acknowledgement of the necessity and viability of feminist approaches to the media. Academic journals of communications have published review articles of feminist media studies and sometimes devoted whole issues to it (*Communication*, 1986; Dervin, 1987; Foss and Foss, 1983; *Journal of Communication Inquiry*, 1987; McCormack, 1980; Rakow, 1986; Smith, 1983; Steeves, 1987; Van Zoonen, 1988). However, in 'general' reviews of main trends in communication theory and research one finds few traces of this growing body of feminist scholarship. To mention some arbitrary examples: in Denis McQuail's bestselling *Introduction to Mass Communication Theory* there is no reference to 'woman', 'gender', 'sexuality', or other feminist concerns. The revised second edition has one paragraph about feminist content analysis added. In special issues about communications research in western and eastern Europe published by the *European Journal of Communication* and *Media, Culture and Society* (1990) references to gender or feminism are all but absent.

In the field of cultural studies feminist concerns have gained more ground. Many innovating studies about 'women's genres' such as soap operas, romance novels and women's magazines and their audiences, have informed and have been informed by this approach (e.g. Hobson, 1982; Modleski, 1982;

Radway, 1984; Winship, 1987). Moreover, authors such as Fiske (1987) and Morley (1986) addressing other issues in cultural studies, have incorporated gender in their research as one of the crucial mechanisms in structuring our cultural experiences and our outlook on daily life. Notwithstanding the successful and inspiring conjunction of feminist and cultural studies, not all feminist studies are cultural studies, and not all cultural studies are feminist studies. I shall elaborate the former as I review different feminist perspectives later on. The latter brings me to a second distinctive feature of feminist media studies.

The feminist academic venture is intrinsically political. In the early years of the revived movement, a concurrence of research, writing and political activism was common practice. A typical example is Betty Friedan's research about the construction of the American cultural ideal of 'the happy housewife-heroine' in women's magazines and advertisements.[1] The book *The Feminine Mystique* (1963) was an immediate best seller and gave rise to a revival of the women's movement which had been dormant since the successful struggle for women's suffrage. One of the first 'second wave' feminist groups was the *National Organisation of Women,* headed by Betty Friedan. Not surprisingly, NOW declared the media to be one of the major sites of struggle for the movement: in the spring of 1970 approximately 100 women occupied the offices of *The Ladies Home Journal* demanding among other things a female editor in chief, a child care centre for employees and the publication of a 'liberated issue' to be compiled by the protestors. At least one feminist supplement to the *Journal* appeared. A nationwide research project monitoring television networks and local stations for sexist content was conducted with the intention to challenge the licence of any station with a sexist record when it came up for renewal before the Federal Communications Commissions (Hole & Levine, 1972: 264). Although by the beginning of the eighties much feminist research came from the academy, its political nature remained, therewith fundamentally undermining the dominant academic, paradigm, of objectivity, neutrality and detachment. For example, Tuchman (1978: 38) introducing one of the first volumes about women and the media, asks herself: 'How can the media be changed? . . . How can we free

women from the tyranny of media messages limiting their lives to hearth and home?' The book concludes with a chapter discussing the policy implications of the research material presented. Numerous other academic publications conclude with recommendations for change (e.g. Creedon, 1989; Gallagher, 1980; Thoveron, 1986).

With its substantial project, it is the reciprocal relation between theory, politics and activism, the commitment of feminist academics to have their work contribute to a larger feminist goal—however defined, the blurred line between the feminist as academic and the feminist as activist, that distinguishes feminist perspectives on the media from other possible perspectives. Paradoxically, as I shall try to show in this review, the growing theoretical and empirical sophistication of feminist media studies has not only jeopardized its relevance for a critical feminist media politics but also diminished its potential as a comprehensive cultural critique. For example, as we acknowledge the pleasure women derive from watching soap operas, it becomes increasingly difficult to find moral justifications for criticizing their contribution to the hegemonic construction of gender identities. To disentangle this paradox I shall first discuss liberal, radical and socialist feminist discourses which share—in spite of their many differences—a social control model of communication, and a conceptualization of gender as a dichotomous category with a historically stable and universal meaning.

Liberal, Radical and Socialist Feminism

Classifying feminism in three neatly separated ideological currents is certainly at odds with the present fragmentation of feminist thought. It seems hard to include, for example, postmodern and psychoanalytic trends satisfactorily in this tripartition. Also, feminist theory and practice is often rather eclectic, incorporating elements from different ideologies as circumstances and issues necessitate. As a result few feminist media studies can be unequivocally classified in one of the three categories. However, taken as ideal types—which I shall do here—they are indicative of the various ways in which feminists perceive the media. Although less dominant than in the seventies and early eighties, they still underlie many feminist selfperceptions and analysis.[2]

Liberal Feminism

In liberal feminist discourse irrational prejudice and stereotypes about the supposedly natural role of women as wives and mothers account for the unequal position of women in society. General liberal principles of liberty and equality should apply to women as well. 'Equal Rights' or 'reformist' feminism are other labels for these principles which find their political translation in attempts to change legislation, in affirmative action programs, in stimulating women to take up non-traditional roles and occupations and to develop masculine qualities to acquire power. Such role reversal is much less strongly advocated for men.

Sex role stereotypes, prescriptions of sex-appropriate behaviour, appearance, interests, skills and self-perceptions are at the core of liberal feminist media analyses (Tuchman, 1978: 5). Numerous quantitative content analyses have shown that women hardly appear in the mass media, be it depicted as wife, mother, daughter, girlfriend; as working in traditionally female jobs (secretary, nurse, receptionist); or as sex object. Moreover they are usually young and beautiful, but not very well educated. Experimental research done in the tradition of cognitive psychology tends to support the hypothesis that media act as socialization agents—along with the family—teaching children in particular their appropriate sex roles and symbolically rewarding them for appropriate behaviour (cf. Busby, 1975; Gallagher, 1980). It is thought that media perpetuate sex role stereotypes because they reflect dominant social values and also because male media-producers are influenced by these stereotypes.

The solutions liberal feminism offers are twofold: women should obtain more equal positions in society, enter male dominated fields and acquire power. With a time lag mass media will reflect this change. Meanwhile, media can contribute to change by portraying more women and men in non-traditional roles and by using non sexist language. The strategies liberal feminists have developed to reach these goals are many: teaching 'non-sexist professionalism' in Schools of Journalism (Van Zoonen, 1989); creating awareness among broadcasters and journalists

about stereotypes and their effects; putting 'consumer pressure' on media institutions, especially on advertisers; demanding affirmative action policies of media institutions (cf. Thoveron, 1986). Liberal media strategies have had some unwarranted consequences. The emphasis on role reversal for women in particular has created a new stereotype of 'Superwoman', the response of commercial culture to the demands of liberal feminism. Women's magazines and advertisements portray her as an independent and assertive career woman, a successful wife and mother, who is still beautiful and has kept the body she had as a girl in perfect shape. Real women trying to live up to this image, end up suffering from serious burn out symptoms (Dowling, 1989).

Another unforeseen consequence of liberal strategies is showing painfully in developments in the media workforce. The numbers of female journalists have increased considerably in recent years with the United States in the forefront (MRTW, 1989). Sad enough however, as American researchers have observed 'a female majority in the field does not translate into superior power or influence for women: instead, it has been translated to mean a decline in salaries and status for the field' (Creedon, 1989: 3). In part these problems arise from liberal feminism's disregard for socio-economic structures, and power relations. Social conflict is presented as a difference of opinion which can be resolved through rational argumentation. This assumption is reflected in the emphasis on strategies which imply teaching and raising awareness of (male) mediaproducers, and in the rather optimistic belief that media-institutions can be changed from within by female mediaprofessionals. That men—as radical feminists would argue—or consumer capitalism—as socialist feminists would argue—have vested interests in maintaining their power over women, does not easily fit in the ideal of rational disinterested argumentation.

Radical Feminism

In radical feminist discourse 'patriarchy', a social system in which all men are assumed to dominate and oppress all women, accounts for women's position in society. Patriarchy is conceived to be the result of men's innately wicked inclination to dominate women, a genetically determined need which they can fulfil—in the last instance—by exercising their physical strength. Radical feminists have been in the forefront of exposing male abuse of women and politicizing issues formerly considered as private: sexual violence, wife battering, incest, pornography, and more recently, sex tourism and trafficking in women. It is obvious that men can have no place in radical feminist utopias. In order to free themselves completely women have to cut off all ties with men and male society, and form their own communities. Lesbianism therefore is necessarily following political choice—another example of the radical politicization of the personal.

Since mass media are in the hands of male owners and producers, they will operate to the benefit of a patriarchal society. Apparently this premise does not need further research, given the few media studies that have been conducted from a radical feminist perspective. The main focus is on pornography and rather polemical: 'Pornography exists because men despise women, and men despise women because pornography exists' (Dworkin, 1980: 289). In radical feminist media analyses the power of the media to affect men's behaviour towards women and women's perception of themselves is beyond discussion: 'Researchers may have been unable to prove a direct connection between any particular instance of media and any particular act, but *there can be no doubt* that media distortion contributes to a general climate of discrimination and abuse of women' (Davies et al., 1988: 6, author italics).

The media strategies of radical feminism are straightforward: women should create their own means of communication. Technological developments in print and audiovisual media made the proliferation of feminist writing, newsletters, magazines, radio and TV programmes, video and film groups possible. A host of feminist ideas would otherwise have not received a public forum (Kessler, 1984). Most media are produced by a collective of volunteers, who usually work without profits motives and share responsibilities. Radical feminist logic does not allow for hierarchies; they are thought to be a perversion of masculine society. Contributions are anonymous or signed with first names only since it is assumed that all women share the same kind of patriarchal oppression.

Radical media strategies have been more problematic than they seemed at first sight: the belief that women together—all innately good people—would be able to work without competition, hierarchy or specialization, and would write or film from the same source of essential femininity, proved an illusion. A constant feature of radical feminist media has been internal conflict about organization and editorial policy. Power differences, difference of opinion and interests appear to exist among women also, and are not a male preserve. Another dilemma has been posed by the inability of feminist media to attract readers and audiences beyond the feminist parish. While their self proclaimed aim often is to inform and mobilize larger audiences, movement media tend to fulfil more of a ritual function. With the waning enthusiasm for collective expressions of feminism, the circulation figures of feminist media declined rather dramatically resulting in the demise of many of them.[3]

In its pure form, radical feminist media analyses have not gained much ground. However, many elements of it are also found in other theories. Socialist feminism incorporates the concept of patriarchal ideology in its marxist analysis of women's position, without however adopting its essentialist stance. The conviction that differences between men and women are essentially biological has emerged in other feminist perspectives as well. French feminists drawing heavily from psychoanalytic theory have very sophisticatedly located the difference between men and women in the different structure of male and female genitals, considering, for example, classic linear narrative structure as an expression of masculine, goal oriented sexuality. French feminist theory has particularly influenced literary and film studies, but is rare in studies of mass media (e.g. Mattelart, 1986). The solution for women's position is not sought in withdrawing from patriarchal culture, but in creating new and legitimate spaces for the feminine voice, supposedly more process-oriented. This has been extremely successful in the area of women's writing, but the feminist avantgarde film of the seventies never acquired a large following (e.g. Pribram, 1988).

Socialist Feminism

Unlike radical and liberal feminism, socialist feminism does not focus exclusively on gender to account for women's position, but attempts to incorporate an analysis of class and economic conditions of women as well. Central concepts are 'the reproduction of labour' and 'the economic value of domestic labour'. Although not recognized as such, the nurturing, moral, educational and domestic work women do in the family is said to be indispensable for the maintenance of capitalism. Were all this labour to be paid, the profit margins of capitalism would be critically diminished (cf. Zaretsky, 1986). Socialist feminism shares with liberal feminism an emphasis on the need for women to take up paid labour. However, at the same time a fundamental restructuring of the labour market is called for, in which the average labour week is reduced to 25 hours so that women and men have time left to share nurturing and domestic responsibilities.

More recently, socialist feminism has tried to incorporate other social divisions along the lines of ethnicity, sexual preference, age, physical ability, since the experience of, for example, black, lesbian and single women did not fit nicely in the biased gender/class earlier model. This has resulted in an increasingly complicated and incoherent theoretical project, which until now has not produced a satisfactory account of the way material and cultural conditions interact. More and more, ideology in itself has become the main object of study. The work of Althusser, stating the relative autonomy of ideological *apparatuses* like the family, school, church and the media vis à vis the economic conditions, and the work of Gramsci analyzing how dominant ideology takes on the form of common sense (*hegemony*) have been particularly influential in socialist feminism. Cultural Studies approaches to gender and media that I shall discuss later, build on these concepts of ideology. Many authors (e.g. Steeves, 1987) place them in the same category. I suggest it is important to distinguish between socialist feminist discourse and cultural studies approaches due to their different conceptualizations of power. In socialist feminist discourse power remains located in socio-economic structures, be it mediated through the relatively autonomous level of ideology. Cultural studies approaches account for power as a discursive practice that can appear independent from material conditions. The distinction however is one of emphasis, both are reluctant to focus on gender exclusively and try to incorporate

material and cultural conditions in accounting for women's position in society.

In its most crude form, the socialist feminist communication model of the seventies clings to radical models in which media are perceived to be ideological instruments presenting the capitalist and patriarchal society as the natural order. However, socialist feminism is distinguished by a much greater concern for the way in which ideologies of femininity are constructed in the media, and to whose avail. Much of its research consists of ideological analysis of mediatexts, using the analytic instrumentarium offered by structuralism and semiology (e.g. Coward, 1984). The solutions socialist feminism offers are not so much different from liberal or radical media strategies. Usually a double strategy is advocated: reforming the mainstream media as well as producing separate feminist media. What distinguishes the socialist call for female media producers, is an awareness of the middle class bias of that strategy, (e.g. Baehr, 1981) and the acknowledgement that at the same time structural changes in the organization of media labour are necessary. For example, a Dutch pressuregroup of feminist journalists campaigned rather successfully for affirmative action policies in journalism, increase of part time job possibilities, parental leave and childcare facilities at the newspapers office (Diekerhof et al., 1985).

Concepts of Gender and Communication

Strategies for change follow logically from liberal, radical and socialist feminist media analyses. They aim either at reforming existing media institutions and professions, or at creating new feminist 'institutions' and developing proper feminine and feminist interpretations of professionalism. However, with the privilege of hindsight, we are now in a position to observe how useful these strategies have been. It would appear that some of them have not been very successful. Some even seem to have been counterproductive, as in the case of American journalism becoming a female dominated field reduced in status and salaries. Such political disillusions are intricately linked to theoretical flaws which all three perspectives share. These flaws concern the conceptualization of gender as a dichotomous category with a homogeneous and universal meaning, and the premise of mass media being instrumental to the control needs of respectively, society, patriarchy, and capitalism.

Gender

Radical and liberal feminism share their appreciation of gender as an inevitable consequence of sex differences, consisting of two binary and universal canons of behaviour, characteristics and values found in either women—the feminine canon—or in men—the masculine canon. Femininity is supposed to be composed of emotionality, prudence, cooperation, communal sense, compliance, etc. Masculinity supposedly is its opposite: rationality, efficiency, competition, individualism, ruthlessness, etc. Liberal feminism has it that we learn to accept these canons as normal through women's mothering role in the family and through other socialization agents like the media, while radical feminism believes in the essential nature of these differences. Transgressions of this dichotomy, manifested for example in androgynous appearances like Grace Jones and Prince; in certain types of lesbian and homosexual culture; in the phenomenon of transsexuality; and more routinely in daily lives and experiences of women and men whose behaviour and characteristics do not fit easily in the feminine or masculine canon, are considered exceptions to the thus defined universal 'sex-gender system'.

Consider the 'sameness-difference' dilemma such a universal transcendent concept of gender runs into: for liberal feminism women are *essentially the same as men but not equal*, for radical feminism women are *essentially different from men and not equal*. (It is most easy to explain this dilemma by juxtaposing liberal and radical feminism. That is not to say, however that socialist feminism is less bothered by it). Liberal feminism urges women in particular to regain that sameness becoming equal in the process. Radical feminism tells women to celebrate their being different and to struggle for a social revaluation of femininity. Both solutions are intrinsically problematic. Liberal feminism implicitly accepts the values of the protestant work ethic basic to modern capitalism by telling women to leave their domestic world, enter the (male) workforce and develop the masculine features necessary to acquire power. Masculinity is advocated as an

ideal to live up to, at the expense of human values traditionally associated with women. Role reversal might render equality to women, but in the process important 'feminine' values are dismissed and lost. This is an outcome no liberal feminist aspires to, it is thus argued that women should go public without forsaking their femininity. Moreover their supposedly moral superiority should feed and improve the degenerated public world (cf. Elshtain, 1981). In feminist media studies this liberal dogma is reflected in the call for more female journalists whose specific feminine input of concern for human relations and personal experiences would improve the current distanced and dehumanized news style (e.g. Neverla & Kanzleiter, 1984). There is a theoretical inconsistency here: whilst the essential sameness of women and men is used to legitimize demands for equality, difference enters again through the backdoor as women need their specific 'feminine' features to modify the egalizing consequences of the struggle for equality. The rather naive assumption that dominant masculine culture would easily make room for its necessary feminine complementation has more important practical consequences. As already mentioned, the recent increase of the number of female journalists in the US has not led to an increase in their influence, but instead to a devaluation of the status and the salaries of the field (Creedon, 1989: 3). The remaining option for liberal feminism then seems to be a mere adjustment strategy: equality as defined by dominant masculine culture; 'equal but the same'.

Radical feminist assumptions of essential differences between women and men, and their call for separate women's spaces and communities are equally problematic. They imply a return to an ontological explanation of human differences introducing a tyranny of biological destiny historically used to circumscribe women's place in society. As such radical feminism has the same totalitarian tendencies as its main antagonist patriarchal society. How, for instance, can radical feminism perceive women who do not conform to their supposedly innate femininity, other than as genetical deviations? (cf. Elshtain, 1981: 204–228). Radical feminist strategies inevitably condemn women to a marginal position: they will be either oppressed suffering from false consciousness within patriarchal society which is supposed to be beyond reform. Or they choose to step out of patriarchal society being free and true to their nature but remaining isolated and marginal, as for instance the lifecycle of radical feminist media illustrates. The problem is similar in psycho-analytic essentialist currents: 'For if, as some psychoanalytic theories appear to suggest, social subjects are determined, through family relations and language acquisition, *prior* to the introduction of other considerations, including race, class, personal background or historical moment, the social construct thus described is a closed system unamenable to other subject formations' (Pribram, 1987: 6). In radical feminist discourse the inevitable outcome of the sameness-difference dilemma is 'different but not equal'.

This paralyzing dilemma is a product of radical and liberal conceptualizations of gender as having universal and transcendent meaning. Feminist philosophers and historians have pointed to the historical specificity of the idea that men are political and rational, while women would be more personal, emotional and inclined to nurture. Landes (1988) locates the origins of these ideas in the work of Rousseau. Montesquieu and other philosophers of the French Revolution, who inspired republicans to banish women to the home and called men to their supposedly natural fulfilment in the world of politics. The resulting gendering of the public and the private sphere as we know it today, feeding many (feminist) discourses about the meaning of gender, can thus be considered to be a historically specific construction, by no means universal and transcendent. Thus not only has the French Revolution banished women to the family, it has also succeeded in imprisoning feminist theory and politics in its philosophical framework (cf. Van Zoonen, 1991). An acknowledgement of the historical specificity of current dominant beliefs about women and men, opens up new ways of conceptualizing gender, not as universally given, but as socially constructed. The issue then, is no longer how to promote a certain type of femininity as in radical feminism, or how to dismiss femininity and masculinity altogether as in liberal feminism, but rather to analyze how and why particular constructions of masculinity and femininity arise in historical contexts, how and why certain constructions gain dominance over others and how dominant constructions relate to the lived realities of women and men.

Communication

Liberal, radical and socialist feminist discourse share an instrumental perspective on communication. Media are perceived as the main instruments in conveying respectively stereotypical, patriarchal and hegemonic values about women and femininity. They serve as mechanisms of social control: in liberal feminist discourse media pass on society's heritage—which is deeply sexist—in order to secure continuity, integration, order and the transmission of dominant values (Tuchman, 1978); radical feminism argues that patriarchal media serve the needs of patriarchal society by suppressing and distorting women's experiences which, if expressed in their true form, would seriously disturb the patriarchal set up (Mattelart, 1986); socialist feminism assumes that media present the capitalist, patriarchal scheme of things as the most attractive system available. Direct social control becomes unnecessary since dominant ideology has been translated into 'common sense' (*Women Take Issue*, 1978). Media fulfil the structural needs of respectively democratic, patriarchal and capitalist society by transmitting its distorted dominant values about women. What feminism of each kind advocates, is the transmission of the reality of women's lives instead: media should be instrumental to creating feminist utopias. Feminist value judgements are thus completely cast in future oriented political terms, with 'political' referring to the complete social set up. As a result 'good' media—contributing to feminist goals—and 'bad' media—maintaining the status quo, are easily distinguished. Supposedly, it is only a matter of time for women's collective awareness to surface resulting in a massive exchange of 'bad' women's magazines, romance novels, etc. for 'good' feminist media.

But anno 1990, having more than 20 years of organized feminism behind us, Utopia is still far from near. A variety of new women's magazines have entered the market successfully adapting to the fragmentation of a formerly unified female readership: girls, young women, older women, career women, rich housewives, the avid cook or gardener, ordinary working women, travelling women and the traditional housewife all happily subscribe to their own kind of women's magazine; romance novels have introduced new heroines profoundly touched by feminist calls for independence, but still longing for and always attaining heterosexual everlasting romance; soap operas like *Dallas*, *Dynasty*, *Falcon Crest* and its successors—a typical 1980s television genre—attract a predominantly female audience in spite of its 'overtly' sexist, patriarchal and capitalist content; and feminist media struggle with reaching a larger audience, attracting advertisers, maintaining their old audience, or suffer from internal conflict or simply boredom.[4] Obviously the feminist transmission model of communication cannot account for these developments, other than plaintively reproaching the avid consumers of the 'bad' media with 'false consciousness'. I suggest instead to ascribe this ineptitude to the realistic bend and the passive audience conception of the model.

Realism

It is obvious that many aspects of women's lives and experiences are not very well reflected by the media. Many more women work than media-output suggests, very few women are like the 'femme fatales' of soap operas and mini series, and women's desires consist of a lot more than the hearth and home of traditional women's magazines. A call for more realistic images of women might seem self-evident, but is quite problematic. Gender stereotypes for instance do not come out of the blue, but have social counterparts which many might perceive as 'real'. Thus a common negation of the accusation that media distort reality is: 'But many women are mothers and housewives?' Who can define the objective reality media should transmit? Feminists? They are divided among themselves as the previous paragraphs have only minimally illustrated. Women? They can even much less be considered a uniform category. As Brunsdon (1988: 149) duly argues: 'Thus for feminists to call for more realistic images of women is to engage in the struggle to define what is meant by "realistic", rather than to offer easily available "alternative" images. . . . Arguing for more realistic images is always an argument for the representation of "your" version of reality.'

A related problem of the 'reality reflection thesis' is the implication that media output has unequivocal meanings: they are either real or not real. This denies the complex and multiple meanings of media texts implied by the commercial logic of mass media

needing to be popular among a variety of social groups and subcultures (cf. Fiske, 1987). In facing the dilemmas of the reflection thesis, feminist media studies have been profoundly influenced by cultural studies and by its own shift to a constructivist theory of gender. Although not a unified approach with a consistent program, cultural studies' central tenet of 'communication as a process through which a shared culture is created, modified and transformed' (Carey, 1989: 43), implies a conceptualization of media texts as sites of struggle over meaning (e.g. of gender), rather than as transparent cultural prescriptions. The reality media offer is a product of ongoing negotiation at the level of media-institutions, -texts and -audiences (Gledhill, 1988). As a result media texts are inherently 'polysemic' (Fiske, 1987) and construct diverging and sometimes conflicting articulations of femininity. Although it is often quite clear which articulations of femininity are to be preferred according to media producers (the dominant meaning of the text), the idea of a polysemic nature of media texts undermines the possibility of thinking of audiences as onesidedly and unambiguously affected by media. Which of the many meanings of the texts will they take up? This brings me to the second major problematic of the feminist transmission model of communication: its passive audience conception.

The Audience and 'US'

In feminist transmission models of communication audiences don't have much choice in interpreting media texts. Either they can accept them as true to reality, in which case they are successfully socialized (liberal feminism), brainwashed (by patriarchy) or lured to the idea that what they see and read is 'common sense' (socialist feminism). Or they see through the tricks mass media play on them and reject the sexist, patriarchal, capitalist representation of things. It seems clear that many feminists consider themselves among the latter 'enlightened' people raising themselves 'to the lofty pedestal of having seen the light' (Winship, 1987: 140). A deep gap is constructed between 'us' feminists, and 'them' the audience. Objectionable in particular are soap operas, romance novels, and women's magazines which create a 'cult of femininity and heterosexual romance that—since these media are predominantly consumed by women—set the agenda for the female world (cf. Ferguson, 1983). Such a strong conviction about the value (or rather lack of it) of these media for women's lives, is remarkably similar to the patriarchal attitudes of men knowing what is best for women. Dismissing women's genres for their supposedly questionable content, carries an implicit rejection of the women who enjoy them. That is obviously at odds with the feminist mission to acknowledge and gain respect for women's experiences and view-points. Moreover, it does not contribute to our understanding of how contending constructions of gender are articulated in such cultural phenomena. Why, then are these genres so popular among women? How do women use them to give meaning to their daily experiences? How do 'discourses of femininity' articulated in them interact with other non mediated discourses of femininity such as motherhood and sexuality (cf. Brunsdon, 1981).

The above questions have activated an unprecedented concern with the female audience, expressed in a boom of mainly ethnographic studies about female recipients of particular genres, soap operas and romance novels leading the field (see Ang and Hermes in this volume [Mass Media and Society]). However, the problem of 'us' feminists versus 'them' the audience is not solved by the ethnographic twist in feminist media studies and might in some cases even be intensified as the feminist researcher puts herself in the authoritative position of the all knowing expert of female media pleasures, while in the end still rejecting them as unproductive for 'the' feminist revolution. This is utterly problematic in Radway's by now almost classic study *Reading the Romance*. After respectfully analyzing the romance reading experiences of married working women, she claims that romance reading contains an act of protest against patriarchal culture. Briefly and bluntly summarized: by the social act of reading romance, women signal a time out for their domestic and caring labour; and by taking up romances in particular with their omnipresent androgynous hero capable of nurturing woman herself, they deny the legitimacy of patriarchal culture in which such men are quite hard to find. Radway now militantly concludes that '*we*, who are committed to social change' (my italics), should keep looking for and encouraging these traces of social protest: 'If we

do not, we have already conceded the fight and, in the case of the romance at least, admitted the impossibility of creating a world where the vicarious pleasure supplied by its reading would be unnecessary' (Radway, 1984: 222). In the end the only value of romance reading Radway acknowledges, is its potential—however far hidden—for the feminist revolution.

But what to make of those feminists who enjoy soap operas, who revel in harlequin novels and who are addicted to their weekly subscription of their favourite women's magazine, to mention just a few 'bad' genres. Winship (1987) addressing precisely this question in her analysis of women's magazines confesses that she has been a 'closet reader' of *Cosmopolitan* and *Woman's Own* for years, since a 'true' feminist is not supposed to derive pleasure from such ghastly products. Hers is one of the few examples of a study in which the personal experiences and pleasures of the researchers are an integrated element of the study, thus releasing the tension between 'us' and 'them'. As Skirrow (1986: 115) has argued: 'In investigating popular culture the only way not to feel like a snooping health investigator, sniffing out whether someone's environment is fit to live in, is to examine some aspect or form of it which evokes passionate feeling in oneself.'[5]

Feminism and Cultural Studies

From the points of criticism to feminist transmission models of communication that I laid out in the previous paragraphs, the contours of a 'cultural feminist media studies' project emerge. Though it would be hard to defend the existence of a well defined theoretical and empirical program, to which a majority of feminist communication scholars adhere, it does seem justified to say that cultural studies approaches are gaining momentum given the growing number of publications in this vein (e.g. Baehr & Dyer, 1987; Brown, 1990; Gamman & Marshment, 1988; Pribram, 1988; Shevelow, 1989).

My own formulation of its theoretical premises would start from Harding's (1986: 17) definition of gender 'as an analytic category within which humans think about and organize their social activity, rather than as a natural consequence of sex-difference, or even merely as a social variable assigned to individual people in different ways from culture to culture'. Such a conceptualization of gender implies that its meaning is never given but varies according to specific cultural and historical settings, and that its meaning is subject to ongoing discursive struggle and negotiation, the outcome having far reaching socio-cultural implications. This struggle over meaning is not a mere pluralistic 'debate' of equal but contending frames of reference. It is circumscribed by existing ethnic and economic power relations, and by the fact that 'in virtually all cultures, whatever is thought of as manly, is more highly valued than whatever is thought of as womanly' (Harding, 1986: 18).

What part do media play in the ongoing social construction of gender? Much depends on their location in economic structures (e.g. commercial vs. public media), on their specific characteristic (e.g. print vs. broadcast), on the particular genres (e.g. news vs. soap opera), on the audiences they appeal to and on the place they occupy in those audiences' daily lives. But obviously all media are among the central sites in which struggle over meaning takes place. Stuart Hall's (1980) encoding-decoding mode is a good starting point in case. According to Hall the production structure yields an 'encoded' text which does not constitute a closed ideological system but in which contradictions of the production process are discounted. The thus encoded structure of meaning is brought back into the practices of audiences by their similar but reverse 'decoding' process. Encoding and decoding need not to be symmetrical, i.e. audiences don't need to understand media texts as producers have intended them. In fact, a certain 'misunderstanding' is likely, because of 'the a-symmetry between the codes of "source" and "receiver" at the moment of transformation in and out of the discursive form. What are called 'distortions' or 'misunderstandings' arise precisely from *the lack of equivalence* between the two sides of production' (Hall, 1980: 131, original italics). Gledhill's (1988) analysis of meaning production as cultural negotiation at the level of institutions, texts and audiences builds on the encoding/decoding model.

Institutional negotiation results from conflicting frames of reference within media organizations. 'Creative' personnel is guided mainly by professional and aesthetic logic, while managing directors predominantly have economic and ideological interests

in mind. D'Acci's (1987) analysis of the American police series *Cagney and Lacey*, featuring two female detectives, illustrates the intricate interplay between institutional and textual negotiations indicative of the complexities and contradictions of the encoding process. Having a female buddy pair at the heart of the series satisfied two institutional needs at once: to revitalize the popular but somewhat stale genre of police series, and to respond to social changes caused by the women's movement. In practice these two claims were not easily realized. A continuous struggle between the writers and the network accompanied the production of the series, the conflicts all boiling down to the question how to reconcile the treatment of feminist issues with the commercial interest of the network to keep away from controversial topics. The negotiations about an episode in which unmarried career cop Cagney thinks she is pregnant shows how diverging frames of reference enter at the level of script development. The writers did not even consider to let Cagney have an abortion, anticipating that the network would never allow that solution. So a miscarriage was proposed, but the network rejected the story anyway, not wanting 'to shine the spotlight on pregnancy and the problems of an unmarried pregnant woman' (D'Acci, 1987: 219). Obviously, negotiation at this point concerns the ideological implications of the script. The networks countered the writers with a proposal of a story in which Cagney (in her late thirties) has to decide whether she will ever have children. This was unacceptable to the writers for its lack of narrative resolution, the negotiation here being about professional standards of sound scripts. Finally, the contending claims were reconciled by letting Cagney *think* she is pregnant. As becomes clear by the end of the episode, she is not. How her pregnancy could happen and what she means to do about it, is hardly discussed in the rest of the episode, since that would involve such politically and socially explosive issues as birth control and abortion. A rather dim narrative remains to which each woman can bring her own experiences with (un)wanted pregnancies and 'career/children' dilemmas. D'Acci's analysis of *Cagney and Lacey* is a rare exception to the tendency within feminist media studies to focus on gender only as explaining particularities of media content.

Negotiations at the level of texts concern the availability of meanings in a text as expressions of the encoding process, and as a result of independent and unpredictable interactions between contending elements in the text. Next to that textual interactions allow audiences to take up different 'subject positions'. To take another analysis of *Cagney and Lacey* as an example: Clark (1989) argues that the series' narrative form, representational codes and structures of looking, empowers women and encourages women-identified constructions of meaning. The series combines the linear narrative of the police series—a crime usually related to such feminist issues like sexual harassment, rape, prostitution, etc. is committed and solved—with the more circular structure of the soap opera. Integrated in the linear narrative is the personal life of the heroines which follows a more open and fragmented course. In that narrative the emphasis is on process rather than action, on dialogue rather than solution: 'We don't know from any cause effect structure what Chris [Cagney] will decide about marriage or how Mary Beth (Lacey] will cope with having breast cancer' (Clark, 1990: 119). What we do see are their considerations, their ideas and feelings which are extensively played out, while the outcome of their deliberations (not to marry, what kind of treatment to take) does not get much emphasis. According to Clark representation of the decision making *process* 'invites the participation of the spectator to complete the process of meaning construction in ways that are meaningful to her' (119).

Textual analysis such as described above, utilizing concepts from psychoanalysis, structuralism and semiotics, has been quite common in film studies (Pribram, 1988) but more and more television text are being analyzed in a similar vein. For example, Ang (1990) analyzes how the textual construction of Sue Ellen, one of the major female characters of *Dallas* provides several imaginary subject positions for women: Lewis (1989) and Kaplan (1988) discuss how music videos appeal to a gendered audience; Holland (1987) and Van Zoonen (1991) examine the significance of women newsreaders for the ongoing construction of traditional femininity. Older research about romance novels and women's magazines can also be considered part of this body of work (Modleski, 1982; McRobbie, 1982, Winship, 1987).

The concept of polysemic media texts should be embraced with caution, however. In spite of its essential ambiguity, the range of meanings and subject positions a text offers is not infinite. 'Encoding will have the effect of constructing some of the limits and parameters within which decodings will operate' (Hall, 1980: 135). So most texts do have a 'preferred reading' which, given the economic and ideological location of most media, will tend to reconstruct dominant values of a society—unless we are dealing with alternative media which should also be thought of as polysemic and encoded, within a rather different set of constraints, however. Moreover, meanings in texts need to be activated by real audiences before they can take on any social significance. The negotiation over meaning at the level of audience 'reception' has the most radical potential. 'Reception' implies two related sets of audience practices: use and interpretation.

In Hall's encoding-decoding model three hypothetical positions from which audiences may interpret television texts are identified: the viewer who takes up a *dominant-hegemonic* position reads the texts in terms of its encoding which makes the model symmetrical; the *negotiated positions* entail many more contradictions since the negotiating viewer accepts the global sense of the dominant encoding, but lets her own logic prevail at a more situated level; the most radical reading comes from an *oppositional position* in which the reader/viewer recognizes the text as inflected with dominant codes and recodes it within her own alternative frame of reference. Hall's hypothetical positions have been empirically validated by Morley's (1980) research on *Nationwide Audience*, a British current affairs program which indeed proved to be subject to a variety of interpretations of the audience. The situation in which audiences actually turn on the television set or pick up a magazine—their social use of media—circumscribe their interpretations. Some examples illustrate this: Bausinger (1984) describes a family in which the man returns home from work and immediately turns on the TV, seemingly to watch the news, but effectively expressing a desire to be left alone. Gray (1987) observes how watching rented videos and discussing soap operas form an important part of the friendship of a group of neighbours: 'These popular texts (. . .) give a focus to an almost separate female culture which they can share together within the constraints of their positions as wives and mothers' (Gray, 1987:49). Ang and Hermes (in this volume) present a detailed analysis of studies about gender and reception.

The concept of negotiated meaning and the emphasis on reception practices implies acknowledgement of gender construction as a social process in which women and men actively engage. In transmission models of communication women are perceived as victims of dominant culture as expressed in media messages. Supposedly, they are bombarded by disempowering images all but alien to their true selves. The interaction between media and female audiences thus takes on the form of a one way street. However, people do not only take media as expressions of dominant culture, they also use media to express something about themselves, as women or as men. Being a woman (or a man) implies 'work' since modern society offers so many distinct and sometimes contradicting subject positions (cf. Rakow, 1986). In each social situation an appropriate feminine identity has to be established and expressed. Women can use media to pick up and try out different feminine subject positions at the level of fantasy. But the actual use of media can also be expressive as the glossy existence of expensive 'life style' magazines, read by many not so well off readers, proves. Another illustration comes from Turkle's analysis of the reticence of women to bother about the relatively new social domain of information technologies. She argues that 'women use their rejection of computers (. . .) to assert something about themselves as women . . . It is a way to say that it is not appropriate to have a close relationship with a machine' Turkle (1988: 50). Although many men reject information technologies for exactly the same reason, the attitude of women takes on extra meaning considering the continuous social construction of gender differences.

Feminist Media Politics Reconsidered

The concepts of gender as a social construction and culture as negotiated meaning, release feminist media studies from many of the tensions of transmission models of communication. Paralyzing debates about the autonomous gendered contribution of individual female media producers become redundant by giving precedence to the institutional context of media production. The multiple realities of media

texts are acknowledged as is the relative autonomy of audiences to accommodate them to their own situation. Women are taken seriously as active creators of their own daily lives and experiences, instead of being 'medicalized' as helpless victims of dominant culture. By way of conclusion, in true feminist tradition of undermining certainties rather than advancing them, I would like to raise some new problems associated with current theoretical and empirical practices of feminist media studies. Since the field is fully in motion, I can only call attention to them and consider some possible angles from which to approach them. Offering definite and authoritative solutions is beyond my capacity and my conviction that feminism should develop in mutual deliberation, not by the prescriptions of academic 'elites'.

I'll begin with a relatively easy problem of empirical emphasis. In spite of the theoretical recognition that gender construction involves both women and men, we have focused on constructions of femininity in media and genres that are read and appreciated predominantly by women; soap operas, romance novels and women's magazines. Alongside this focus we have limited our attention to implied and actual female audiences of those genres, more often than not drawn from traditional family situations. The knowledge we have accumulated by now, concerns a very particular group of media consumed by a very particular group of women. This is a focus born out of necessity since these are precisely the genres and audiences that have been neglected by mainstream research. An academic community preoccupied with such prestigious issues as new communication technologies, the future of public broadcasting or the effects of political communication, does not come down very easily to the more profane level of media use in the daily lives of 'ordinary women'. But consider the implicit message of our research focus: do we really think *gender* is only constructed in 'women's media'? How about the constructions of masculinity found in sports programs, war movies, *Playboy* and *Penthouse*, to ventilate just a few stereotypes about men. How do men use those media to construct their gender identity, to express that they are not women? And to cut across the dichotomy of 'women's' and men's' media: how do men's 'feminine' activities such as reading a women's magazine or enjoying a soap opera relate to dominant constructions of masculinity?

With some exceptions men and masculinity have managed to remain invisible in media research: 'This has always been its ruse in order to hold on its power. Masculinity tries to stay invisible by passing itself off as normal and universal. (. . .) If masculinity can present itself as normal it automatically makes the feminine seem deviant and different' (Easthope, 1986: 1). Moreover, the focus on the reception of soaps, romances and women's magazines seriously narrows our potential for articulating a comprehensive cultural critique for we tend to ignore whole areas of social and cultural practice: at the level of institutional nego-tiation, of the production of actual texts there is little research that goes beyond the observation that women work in a male dominated field: at the level of textual negotiation there are many genres we do not know much about yet, e.g. news and current affairs, qual-ity and popular press, sports, quizzes, etc. New media developments and 'the information society' do attract considerable funding for Research and Development, but have only recently gained feminist attention (e.g. Jensen, 1989, Van Zoonen, 1990). I have called the narrow focus of current feminist media studies a relatively easy problem, since its solution involves in theory a 'mere' incorporation of new fields of atten-tion (transforming mainstream studies seems less likely). In practice however, given the minimally triple burden of feminist academics (with personal, feminist and academic responsibilities) this might not be an easy task at all.

There is a more fundamental problem to culturalist feminist media studies. As the importance of specific contextual and textual features for the construc-tion of meaning suggest, it seems unlikely that from this field a general theory of gender and media that goes beyond abstract premises, will emerge. For our understanding of contemporary cultural processes, fragmented and unpredictable as they are, I suggest this a pro rather than a contra. But the particularist shift in theory and research does raise some disturb-ing questions about the political nature of feminist media studies, precisely the feature which I suggest determines the exceptional nature of the feminist aca-demic project. If meaning is so dependent on context, can we still pass valid feminist judgements about the

political tendencies and implications of texts? For we don't know how audiences will use and interpret texts A feminist judgement of obvious textual oppression does not need to be shared by other (female) audience groups. If one interpretation is not by definition better or more valid than another, what legitimation do we have to discuss the politics of representation, to try to intervene in dominant culture?

The above problem has been recognized and responded to in several ways: Ang (1985: 135) pro-poses to consider the fantasies and pleasures involved in watching *Dallas* as independent and relatively iso-lated dimensions of subjectivity, making daily life enjoyable in expectation of feminist utopias: 'Fiction and fantasy, then function by making life at present pleasurable, or at least liveable, but this does not by any means exclude a radical political activity or con-sciousness' (Ang. 1985: 136). A radical activity that applies to the politics of representation in a very lim-ited sense. Ang's argument implies that as feminists we are allowed to produce new fantasies and fictions ourselves, but we should not interfere with the plea-sures of the audience, since 'no fixed standards exist for gauging the "progressiveness" of a fantasy' (ibid). Brown (1990) does not follow this reticence to evalu-ate soap operas and the like. She appreciates 'soap operas, like women's talk or gossip and women's bal-lads as part of women's culture that exists alongside dominant culture and that insofar as the women who use these cultural forms are conscious of the form's otherness, they are practising feminine discourse'. According to Brown 'feminine discourse' implies acknowledgement of women's subordination often expressed in parodic form by making fun of domi-nant culture. Feminine discourse thus implies an act of resistance, albeit with cultural tools provided by the dominant order. Brown's appropriation of women's pleasure is useful for it implies a conception of poli-tics that incorporates power relations in the private domestic sphere of media consumption. For example, women's televisual pleasures tend to be ridiculed by other (male) family members and often have to yield to sports and other male favourites. Brown's notion that research can contribute to the legitimation of women's fantasies can thus mean quite a relief in the here and now of daily life. However, Brown's appraisal of feminine discourse borders on simple populism, for how women's 'nomination, valuation and regulation' of their own pleasure relate to the dominant social order, remains undiscussed.

The problems of cultural relativism and populism are not privileges of feminist media studies, but haunt each contemporary attempt to formulate a progressive cultural critique. Schudson (1987: 66) discusses the new validation of popular culture in academic research and wonders how to respond to it: 'I end up caught between a belief that the university should be a moral educator, holding up for emulation some values and texts (and not others), and a reluctant admission that defining the basis of moral education is an unfinished often unrecognized task.' Schudson's doubts can be translated almost literally to the dilemmas of a contemporary feminist media critique: where can a feminist media critique derive legitimacy from and how do our academic efforts contribute to feminism's larger political project? If current research has taught us anything, it is that general judgements and strategies are not likely to gain much support or to be successful. The strategical implications of our research are much less self evident as they were in the case of liberal, radical and socialist feminism. However, I will attempt to conclude with some possibly relevant general considerations and questions.

I suggest a feminist media critique should start from the reception of specific genres in specific social context. To give an example: genre codes and conventions of news produce a relatively closed structure of meanings when compared to soap operas for instance. Considering that news claims an unambiguous relation with reality—a claim many people think justified—we need quite a different set of moral considerations from which to develop evaluations and strategies when analysing news, which may not be applicable in the case of soap operas. Acknowledging that news too is a social construction, would it still be very inappropriate to expect a decent and ethical representation, of, for example, feminist issues and the women's movement?

Another issue that might be explored is a consequence of the importance given to audience-text relations. Does it not seem logical, now that we are assuming and finding actively interpreting audiences, to develop strategies aimed at the 'semiotic empowerment' of female media recipients? Schudson (1987)

makes a similar point when he argues that a task for the universities should be to educate readers in reading critically and playfully. I do not mean anything like making female audiences aware of the 'true' sexist, patriarchal of capitalist meanings of a text. But rather I refer to the pleasures of discovering multiple and sometimes contending constructions in a text, a pleasure that I would gather is not so much different for 'academics and ordinary women'.[6] Finally, we should not define our sense of 'a larger feminist political project' too narrowly. Our own academic work is still inevitably political, for unfortunately the relation between gender and culture is, as yet, far from being a legitimate and integrated academic concern, with the exception of a few enlightened places.

Notes

1. 'Construction' is not a label that Friedan would have used, but the word summarizes her project in the vocabulary of current feminist theory.
2. The reader with a more specific interest in connecting authors and studies to perspectives is referred to Steeves (1987).
3. My discussion of the policies and problems of feminist media is based on knowledge of the Dutch situation but I would be surprised if the gist of this analysis does not apply to other western countries as well.
4. See note 3.
5. I am indebted to Joke Hermes for this passage.
6. At least from my experience in teaching extramural courses about advertisements and soap operas.

References

Ang, I., 1985: *Watching Dallas: Soap Opera and the Melodramatic Imagination*, London: Methuen.

Ang, I., 1990: 'Melodramatic Identifications: Television Fiction and Women's Fantasy', pp. 75–88 in M. E. Brown (ed.) *Television and Women's Culture: The Politics of the Popular*, London: Sage.

Baehr, H., 1981: 'Women's Employment in British Television', *Media, Culture and Society*, 3(2), 125–34.

Baehr, H. and Dyer, G., (eds) 1987: *Boxed In: Women and Television*, London: Pandora.

Brown, M. E., (ed.) 1990: *Television and Women's Culture: The Politics of the Popular*, London: Sage.

Brunsdon, C., 1981: "Crossroads": Notes on a Soap Opera', *Screen*, 22(4), 32–37.

Brunsdon, C., 1988: 'Feminism and Soap Opera', pp. 147–50 in K. Davies, J. Dickey and T. Stratford (eds) *Out of Focus:*

Writing on Women and the Media, London: The Women's Press.

Busby, L., 1975: 'Sex-role Research on the Mass Media', *Journal of Communication*, autumn, 107–131.

Carey, J., 1989: *Communication as Culture: Essays on Media and Society*, Boston: Unwin Hyman.

Clark, D., 1989: 'Cagney & Lacey: Feminist Strategies of Detection', pp. 117–133 in M. E. Brown (ed.) *Television and Women's Culture: The Politics of the Popular*, London: Sage.

Communication, 1986: 'Feminist Critiques of Popular Culture', 9(1).

Coward, R., 1984: *Female Desire: Women's Sexuality Today*, London: Paladin Books.

Creedon, P., (ed.) 1989: *Women in Mass Communication: Challenging Gender Values*, London: Sage.

D'Acci, J., 1987: 'The Case of Cagney and Lacey', pp. 203–226 in H. Baehr and G. Dyer (eds) *Boxed In: Women and Television*, London: Pandora.

Davies, K., Dickey, J., and Stratford, T., (eds) 1988: *Out of Focus: Writing in Women and the Media*, London: The Women's Press.

Dervin, B., 1987: 'The Potential Contribution of Feminist Scholarship to the Field of Communication', *Journal of Communication*, autumn, 1987, 107–120.

Diekerhof, E., Elias, M, and Sax, M., 1985: *Voor zover plaats aan de perstafel*, Groningen: Meulenhoff.

Dowling, C, 1989: *Perfect Women*, New York: Summit Books.

Dworkin, A., 1980: 'Pornography and Grief', pp. 286–291 in L. Lederer (ed.) *Take Back the Night*, New York: William Morrow.

Easthope, A., 1986: *What a Man's Gotta Do: The Masculine Myth in Popular Culture*, London: Paladin Books.

Elshtain, J., 1981: *Public Man, Private Woman*, Oxford: Martin Robinson.

European Journal of Communication, 1990: 'Communications Research in Europe: The State of the Art', 5(2–3).

Ferguson, M., 1983: *Forever Feminine: Women's Magazines and the Cult of Femininity*, London: Heinemann.

Fiske, J., 1987: *Television Culture*, London: Methuen.

Foss, K., and Foss, S., (1983): 'The Status of Research on Women and Communication', *Communication Quarterly*, 31, 195–204.

Friedan, B., 1963: *The Feminine Mystique*, London: Penguin Books.

Gallagher, M., 1980: *Unequal Opportunities: The Case of Women and the Media*, Paris: Unesco.

Gamman, L., and Marshment, M., (eds) 1988: *The Female Gaze: Women as Viewers of Popular Culture*, London: The Women's Press.

Gledhill, C., 1988: 'Pleasurable Negotiations', pp. 64–79 in E. D. Pribram (ed.) *Female Spectators: Looking at Film and Television*, London: Verso.

Gray, A., 1987: 'Behind Closed Doors: Video Recorders in the Home', pp. 38–54 in H. Baehr and G. Dyer (eds) *Boxed In: Women and Television*, London: Pandora.

Hall, S., 1980: 'Encoding/decoding', pp. 128–138 in S. Hall, D. Hobson, A. Lowe and P. Willis (eds) *Culture, Media, Language*, London: Hutchinson.

Harding, S., 1986: *The Science Question in Feminism*, London: Cornell University Press.

Hobson, D., 1982: *Crossroads: The Drama of Soap Opera*, London: Methuen.

Hole, J. and Levine, E. 1972: *Rebirth of Feminism*, New York: Quadrangle.

Holland, P., 1987: 'When a Woman Reads the News', pp. 133–150 in H. Baehr and G. Dyer (eds) *Boxed In: Women and Television*, London: Pandora.

Jansen, S., 1989: 'Gender and the Information Society: A Socially Structured Silence', *Journal of Communication*, summer, 196–215.

Journal of Communication Inquiry, 1987: 'The Feminist Issue', 11(1).

Kaplan, E., 1988: 'Whose Imaginary? The Television Apparatus, the Female Body and Textual Strategies in Select Rock Videos on MTV', pp. 132–156 in E. D. Pribram (ed.) *Female Spectators: Looking at Film and Television*, London: Verso.

Kessler, L., 1984: *The Dissident Press: Alternative Journalism in American History*, London: Sage.

Landes, J., 1988: *Women and the Public Sphere in the Age of the French Revolution*, London: Cornell University Press.

Lewis, L., 1990: 'Consumer Girl Culture: How Music Video Appeals to Girls', pp. 89–101 in M. E. Brown (ed.) *Television and Women's Culture: The Politics of the Popular*, London: Sage.

Mattelart, M., 1986: *Women, Media, Crisis: Femininity and Disorder*, London: Comedia.

McCormack, T., 1978: 'Machismo in Media Research: A Critical Review of Research on Violence and Pornography', *Social Problems*, 25(5), 544–555.

McQuail, D., 1933, 1987: *Mass Communication Theory: an Introduction*, London: Sage.

McRobbie, A., 1982: 'Jackie: An Ideology of Adolescent Femininity', pp. 263–283 in B. Waites, T. Bennett and G., Martin (eds) *Popular Culture: Past and Present*, London: Croom Helm.

Media, Culture and Society (1990) 'The Other Europe?', 12(2).

MRTW (Media Report to Women) (1989) 'Women gained editorship in 1988', pp. 3–4, March/April.

Modleski, T., 1982: *Loving with a Vengeance: Mass Produced Fantasies for Women*, London: Methuen.

Morley, D., 1980: *The Nationwide Audience: Structure and Decoding*, London: British Film Institute.

Morley, D., 1985: *Family Television: Cultural Power and Domestic Leisure*, London: Comedia.

Neverla, I. and Kanzleiter, G., 1984: *Journalistinnen*, Frankfurt: Campus Verlag.

Pribram, E. D., (ed.) 1988: *Female Spectators: Looking at Film and Television*, London: Verso.

Radway, J., 1984: *Reading the Romance: Women, Patriarchy and Popular Literature*, Chapel Hill: University of North Carolina Press.

Rakow, L., 1986: 'Rethinking Gender Research in Communication', *Journal of Communication*, winter, 11–26.

Schudson, M., 1987: 'The New Validation of Popular Culture: Sense and Sentimentality in Academia', *Critical Studies in Mass Communication*, 4, 51–68.

Shevelow, K., 1989: *Women and Print Culture: The Construction of Femininity in the Early Periodical*, London: Routledge.

Skirrow, G., 1986: 'Hellivision: An Analysis of Videograms', pp. 115–143 in C. MacCabe (ed.) *High Theory, Low Culture*, London: Methuen.

Smith, M. Y, 1983: 'Research Retrospective: Feminism and the Media', pp. 213–227 in E. Wartella and D. C. Whitney (eds.) *Mass Communication Review Yearbook*, London: Sage.

Steeves, H. L., 1987: 'Feminist Theories and Media Studies', *Critical Studies in Mass Communication*, 4, 95–135.

Thoveron, G., 1986: 'European Televised Women', *European Journal of Communication*, 1, 289–300.

Tuchman, G., 1978: *Hearth and Home: Images of Women and the Media*, New York: Oxford University Press.

Turkle, S., 1988: 'Computational Reticence: Why Women Fear the Intimate Machine', pp. 41–62 in C. Kramarae (ed.) *Technology and Women's Voices: Keeping in Touch*, London: Routledge.

Van Zoonen, L., 1988: 'Rethinking Women and the News', *European Journal of Communication*, 1, 35–52.

Van Zoonen, L., 1989: 'Professional Socialization of Feminist Journalists in the Netherlands', *Women's Studies in Communication*, 1, 1–21.

Van Zoonen, L., 1990: 'Intimate Strangers?: Toward a Cultural Approach of Women and New Media', pp. 43–53 in GRANITE (eds) *For Business Only? Gender and New Information Technologies*, Amsterdam: SISWO.

Van Zoonen, L., 1991: 'A Tyranny of Intimacy? Women, Femininity and Television News', in P. Dahlgren and C. Sparks (eds) *Communications and Citizenship*, London, Routledge.

Winship, J., 1987: *Inside Women's Magazines*. London: Pandora Press.

Women Take Issue, 1978: Women's Studies Group, Centre for Contemporary Cultural Studies, London: Hutchinson.

Zaretsky, E., 1976: *Capitalism, the Family and Personal Life*, London.

2.

THE SYMBOLIC ANNIHILATION OF WOMEN BY THE MASS MEDIA

Gaye Tuchman

Americans learn basic lessons about social life from the mass media, much as hundreds of years ago illiterate peasants studied the carvings around the apse or the stained glass windows of medieval cathedrals. As Harold Lasswell (1948) pointed out almost thirty years ago, today's mass media have replaced yesterday's cathedrals and parish churches as teachers of the young and of the masses. For our society, like any other society, must pass on its social heritage from one generation to the next. The societal need for continuity and transmission of dominant values may be particularly acute in times of rapid social change, such as our own. Then, individuals may not only need some familiarity with the past, if the society is to survive, but they must also be prepared to meet changing conditions. Nowhere is that need as readily identifiable as in the area of *sex roles*—sex roles are social guidelines for sex-appropriate appearance, interests, skills, behaviors, and self-perceptions.

It is in this area, in the past few decades, where social expectations and social conditions have been changing most rapidly. In 1920, twenty-four percent of the nation's adult women worked for pay outside the home and most of them were unmarried. Fifty years later, in 1976, over half of all American women between the ages of eighteen and sixty-four were in the labor force, most of them married and many of them with children who were of preschool age.

One-third of all women with children between the ages of three and five were employed in 1970. Such a transformation not only affects women: it affects their families as members make adjustments in their shared life; and as working men in the factory and office increasingly encounter economically productive women who insist on the abandonment of old prejudices and discriminatory behaviors. In the face of such change, the portrayal of sex roles in the mass media is a topic of great social, political, and economic importance.

This book* concerns the depiction of sex roles in the mass media and the effect of that portrayal on American girls and women. In each chapter [in *Hearth and Home*], social science researchers ask, What are the media telling us about ourselves? How do they say women and men should behave? How women should treat men? How women should view themselves? What do the media view as the best way for a woman to structure her life? What do they tell a little girl to expect or hope for when she becomes a woman?

Based on original research, each [chapter in *Hearth and Home*] helps break a new path in communications research. Not surprisingly, little research appeared on these topics until the modern women's movement gained strength in the late 1960s and early 1970s. Until then, psychology, sociology, economics, and history were mainly written by men, about men, and for

---

* Tuchman's chapter is the introduction to *Hearth and Home: Images of Women in the Mass Media*, eds. Gaye Tuchman, Arlene Kaplan Daniels, and James Benét (New York: Oxford University Press, 1978).

men. As Jessie Bernard (1973) points out, the interactions of men were viewed as the appropriate subject for social science research, and upwardly mobile male researchers were fascinated with the topics of power and social stratification. No one considered the way women experienced the world. Instead, they were seen as men's silent or unopinionated consorts. (The term "unopinionated" is used, because studies of attitudes by survey researchers frequently neglected to ask women their opinions, concentrating instead upon the attitudes of men. The most well-known exception to this role is a study of influences upon women's consumer habits, funded by a women's magazine in the 1940s [Katz and Lazarsfeld, 1955].)

These generalizations are, unfortunately, equally true of communications researchers. Generations of researchers studied the impact of the media upon political life. In the past, the main topic of concern was male voting behavior. (It was assumed women voted like their husbands; women were swayed by a husband's or father's personal influence [see McCormack, 1975].) More recently, researchers have become fascinated by agenda setting—the way the media structure citizens' priorities and definitions of political issues. Since the women's movement is not a top priority for the news media, little is known about its place in citizens' political agendas. Nobody seemed to care about the effect of the mass media upon the generation and maintenance of sex-role stereotypes. And why should they? Before the advent of the women's movement these stereotypes seemed natural, "given." Few questioned how they developed, how they were reinforced, or how they were maintained. Certainly the media's role in this process was not questioned.

But the importance of stereotyping was not lost on the women's movement; for stereotypes are confining. Sex-role stereotypes are set portrayals of sex-appropriate appearance, interests, skills, behaviors, and self-perceptions. They are more stringent than guidelines in suggesting persons *not* conforming to the specified way of appearing, feeling, and behaving are *inadequate* as males or females. A boy who cries is not masculine and a young woman who forswears makeup is not feminine. Stereotypes present individuals with a more limited range of acceptable appearance, feelings, and behaviors than guidelines do. The former may be said to limit further the human

possibilities and potentialities contained within already limited sex roles.

This volume hopes to delineate a national social problem—the mass media's treatment of women. It is a crucial problem, because as Lasswell (1948) points out, the mass media transmit the social heritage from one generation to the next. In a complex society, such as ours, the mass media pass on news from one segment of society, classes, regions, and subcultures to another. Additionally, they enable societal institutions to coordinate activities. Like the Catholic Church in the middle ages—"that great broadcasting center of medieval Europe" (Baumann, 1972, p. 65), the mass media can disseminate the same message to all classes at the same time, with authority and universality of reception, in a decidedly one-directional flow of information. But, if the stereotyped portrayal of sex roles is out-of-date, the media may be preparing youngsters—girls, in particular—for a world that no longer exists.

Suppose for a moment that children's television primarily presents adult women as housewives, non-participants in the paid labor force. Also, suppose that girls in the television audience "model" their behavior and expectations on that of "television women." Such a supposition is quite plausible for

> what psychologists call "modeling" occurs simply by watching others, without any direct reinforcement for learning and without any overt practice. The child imitates the model without being induced or compelled to do so. That learning can occur in the absence of direct reinforcement is a radical departure from earlier theories that regarded reward or punishment as indispensable to learning. There now is considerable evidence that children do learn by watching and listening to others even in the absence of reinforcement and overt practice. . . .
>
> (Lesser, quoted in Cantor, 1975, p. 5)

And psychologists note that "opportunities for modeling have been vastly increased by television" (Lesser, quoted in Cantor, 1975, p. 5). It is then equally plausible that girls exposed to "television women" may hope to be homemakers when they are adults, but not workers outside the home. Indeed, as adults these girls may resist work outside the home unless necessary for the economic well-being of their families. Encouraging such an attitude in our nation's girls can present a problem in the future: As noted, over forty percent of the labor force was female in 1970, and married women dominate the female labor force. The active participation of women in the labor force is vital to the maintenance of the American economy. In the past decade, the greatest expansion of the economy has been within the sectors that employ women. Mass-media stereotypes of women as housewives may impede the employment of women by limiting their horizons.

The possible impact of the mass media sex-role stereotypes upon national life seems momentous. As the studies collected here demonstrate, this supposition may accurately predict the future. As an illustration of that possibility, the following sections of this introduction examine the media used by an American girl as she completes school, then becomes a worker and, probably, a spouse and mother.[1] Following the format of this book, this introduction starts with an examination of the dominant medium American children and adults watch—television—and then turns to two media especially designed for women—the women's pages of newspapers and women's magazines. But because of the plethora of research about television, we concentrate upon that medium. Finally, we review studies of the impact of the media upon girls and women, again stressing studies of television.

Two related ideas are central to our discussion. These are *the reflection hypothesis* and *symbolic annihilation*. According to the reflection hypothesis, the mass media reflect dominant societal values. In the case of television (see Tuchman, 1974, 1976), the corporate character of the commercial variety causes program planners and station managers to design programs for appeal to the largest audiences. To attract these audiences (whose time and attention are sold to commercial sponsors), the television industry offers programs consonant with American values. The pursuit of this aim is solidified by the fact that so many members of the television industry take those very values for granted: Dominant American ideas and ideals serve as resources for program development, even when the planners are unaware of them, much as we all take for granted the air we breathe. These ideas and ideals are incorporated as *symbolic representations of American society, not as literal portrayals*. Take the typical television

family of the 1950s: mother, father, and two children living in an upper middle-class, single-residence suburban home. Such families and homes were not the most commonly found units in the 1950s, but they were the American ideal. Following George Gerbner (1972a, p. 44), we may say that "representation in the fictional world," such as the 1950s ideal family, symbolizes or "signifies social existence"; that is, representation in the mass media announces to audience members that this kind of family (or social characteristic) is valued and approved.

Conversely, we may say that either condemnation, trivialization, or "absence means symbolic annihilation" (Gerbner, p. 44). Consider the symbolic representation of women in the mass media. Relatively few women are portrayed there, although women are fifty-one percent of the population and are well over forty percent of the labor force. Those working women who are portrayed are condemned. Others are trivialized: they are symbolized as child-like adornments, who need to be protected or they are dismissed to the protective confines of the home. In sum, they are subject to *symbolic annihilation*.

The mass media deal in symbols and their symbolic representations may not be up-to-date. A time lag may be operating, for nonmaterial conditions, which shape symbols, change more slowly than do material conditions. This notion of a time lag (or a "culture lag," as sociologists term it) may be incorporated into the reflection hypothesis. As values change, we would expect the images of society presented by the media to change. Further, we might expect one medium to change faster than another. (Because of variations in economic organization, each medium has a slightly different relationship to changing material conditions.)

The reflection hypothesis also includes the notion that media planners try to build audiences, and the audiences desired by planners may vary from medium to medium. For instance, television programmers may seek an audience of men and women, without distinguishing between women in the labor force and housewives. But the executives at women's magazines may want to attract women in the labor force in order to garner advertisements designed for those women. (Magazine ads essentially support that medium, since each copy costs much more to produce than it does to purchase.) Accordingly, we might expect the symbolic annihilation of women by television to be more devastating than that of *some* women's magazines.

Without further ado, then, let us turn to images of women in the mass media.

Television: Symbolic Annihilation of Women

To say television is the dominant medium in American life is a vast understatement. In the average American household, television sets are turned on more than six hours each winter day. More American homes have television sets than have private bathrooms, according to the 1970 census. Ninety-six percent of all American homes are equipped with television, and most have more than one set. As Sprafkin and Liebert note in Chapter 15 [of *Hearth and Home*], by the time an American child is fifteen years old, she has watched more hours of television than she has spent in the classroom. And since she continues watching as she grows older, the amount of time spent in school can never hope to equal the time invested viewing television.

The use of television by children is encouraged because of parental use. The average adult spends five hours a day with the mass media, almost as much time as she or he spends at work. Of these five hours, four are occupied by the electronic media (radio and television). The other hour is taken up with reading newspapers, magazines, and books. Television consumes

forty percent of the leisure time of adult Americans. To be sure, despite increased economic concentration there are still 1,741 daily newspapers in this country. And studies indicate that 63,353,000 papers are sold each day. But the nation's nine hundred-odd television stations reach millions more on a daily basis. In 1976, over seventy-five million people watched one event via television, football's annual Super Bowl spectacular (Hirsch, 1978); and when "All in the Family" first appeared on Saturday night, it had a weekly audience of over 100,000,000, more than half the people in the nation. Each year, Americans spend trillions of hours watching television.

What are the portrayals of women to which Americans are exposed during these long hours? What can the preschool girl and the school girl learn about being and becoming a woman?

From children's shows to commercials to prime-time adventures and situation comedies, television proclaims that women don't count for much. They are underrepresented in television's fictional life—they are "symbolically annihilated." From 1954, the date of the earliest systematic analysis of television's content, through 1975, researchers have found that males dominated the television screen. With the exception of soap operas where men make up a "mere majority" of the fictional population, television has shown and continues to show two men for every woman. Figure 2.1

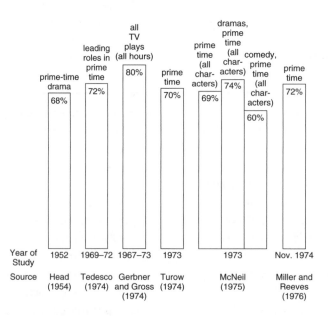

Fig 2.1 Percentage of Males in TV Programs, 1952–1974

indicates that proportion has been relatively constant. The little variation that exists, occurs between types of programs. In 1952 sixty-eight percent of the characters in prime-time drama were male. In 1973, seventy-four percent of those characters were male. Women were concentrated in comedies where men make up "only" sixty percent of the fictional world. Children's cartoons include even fewer women or female characters (such as anthropomorphized foxes or pussy-cats) than adult's prime-time programs do. The paucity of women on American television tells viewers that women don't matter much in American society.

That message is reinforced by the treatment of those women who do appear on the television screen. As seen in Figure 2.2, when television shows reveal someone's occupation, the worker is most likely to be male. Someone might object that the pattern is inevitable, because men constitute a larger share of the pool of people who can be professionals. But that objection is invalidated by the evidence presented by soap operas, where women are more numerous. But the invariant pattern holds there too, despite the fact that men have been found to be only about fifty percent of the characters on the "soaps" (see Downing, 1974; Katzman, 1972).

Additionally, those few working women included in television plots are symbolically denigrated by being portrayed as incompetent or as inferior to male workers. Pepper, the "Police-woman" on the show of the same name (Angie Dickinson) is continually rescued from dire and deadly situations by her male colleagues. Soap operas provide even more powerful evidence for the portrayal of women as incompetents and inferiors. Although Turow (1974) finds that soap operas present the most favorable image of female workers, there too they are subservient to competent men. On "The Doctors," surgical procedures are performed by male physicians, and although the female M.D.'s are said to be competent at their work, they are primarily shown pulling case histories from file cabinets or filling out forms. On other soap operas, male lawyers try cases and female lawyers research briefs for them. More generally, women do not appear in the same professions as men: men are doctors, women, nurses; men are lawyers, women, secretaries; men work in corporations, women tend boutiques.

The portrayal of incompetence extends from denigration through victimization and trivialization. When television women are involved in violence, unlike males, they are more likely to be victims than aggressors (Gerbner, 1972a). Equally important, the pattern of women's involvement with television violence reveals approval of married women and condemnation of single and working women. As Gerbner (1972a) demonstrates, single women are more likely to be victims of violence than married women, and working women are more likely to be villains than housewives. Conversely, married women who do not work for money outside the home are most likely to escape television's mayhem and to be treated sympathetically. More generally, television most approves those women who are presented in a sexual context or within a romantic or family role (Gerbner, 1972a; cf. Liebert *et al.*, 1973). Two out of three television-women are married, were married, or are engaged to be married. By way of contrast, most television men are single and have always been single. Also, men are seen outside the home and women within it, but even here, one finds trivialization of women's role within the home.

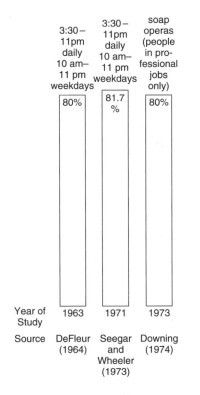

Fig 2.2 Percentage of Males Among Those Portrayed as Employed on TV, 1963–1973

According to sociological analyses of traditional sex roles (such as Parsons, 1949), men are "instrumental" leaders, active workers and decision makers outside the home; women are "affective" or emotional leaders in solving personal problems within the home. But television trivializes women in their traditional role by assigning this task to men too. The nation's soap operas deal with the personal and emotional, yet Turow (1974) finds that on the soap operas, the male sex is so dominant that men also lead the way to the solution of emotional problems. In sum, following the reasoning of the reflection hypothesis, we may tentatively conclude that for commercial reasons (building audiences to sell to advertisers) network television engages in the symbolic annihilation of women.

Two additional tests of this tentative conclusion are possible. One examines noncommercial American television; the other analyzes the portrayal of women in television commercials. If the commercial structure of television is mainly responsible for the symbolic annihilation of women, one would expect to find more women on public than on commercial television. Conversely if the structure of corporate commercial television is mainly responsible for the image of women that is telecast, one would expect to find even more male domination on commercial ads. To an even greater extent than is true of programs, advertising seeks to tap existing values in order to move people to buy a product.

Unfortunately, few systematic studies of public broadcasting are available. The best of these is Caroline Isber's and Muriel Cantor's work (1975), funded by the Corporation for Public Broadcasting, the source of core programming in the Public Broadcasting System. In this volume [*Hearth and Home*], in an adaptation of her report for the CPB, Cantor asks, "Where are the women in public television?" Her answer, based on a content analysis of programming is "in front of the television set." Although a higher proportion of adult women appear on children's programming in public television than is true of commercial television, Cantor finds "both commercial and public television disseminate the same message about women, although the two types of television differ in their structure and purpose." Her conclusion indicates that commercialism is not solely responsible for television's symbolic annihilation of women and its portrayal of stereotyped sex roles. Rather, television captures societal ideas even when programming is partially divorced from the profit motive.[2]

Male domination has not been measured as directly for television commercials, the other kind of televised image that may be used to test the reflection hypothesis. Since so many of the advertised products are directed toward women, one could not expect to find women neglected by commercials. Given the sex roles commercials play upon, it would be bad business to show two women discussing the relative merits of power lawn mowers or two men chatting about waxy buildup on a kitchen floor. However, two indirect measures of male dominance are possible: (1) the number of commercials in which only men or only women appear; and (2) the use of males and females in voice-overs. (A "voice-over" is an unseen person speaking about a product while an image is shown on the television screen; an unseen person proclaims "two out of three doctors recommend" or "on sale now at your local. . . .")

On the first indirect measure, all-male or all-female commercials, the findings are unanimous. Schuetz and Sprafkin [in *Hearth and Home*], Silverstein and Silverstein (1974) and Bardwick and Schumann (1967), find a ratio of almost three all-male ads to each all-female ad. The second indirect measure, the use of voice-overs in commercials, presents more compelling evidence for the acceptance of the reflection hypothesis. Echoing the findings of others, Dominick and Rauch (1972) report that of 946 ads with voice-overs, "only six percent used a female voice; a male voice was heard on eighty-seven percent." The remainder use one male and one female voice.

The commercials themselves strongly encourage sex-role stereotypes. Although research findings are not strictly comparable to those on television programs because of the dissimilar "plots," the portrayals of women are even more limited than those presented on television dramas and comedies. Linda Busby (1975) summarized the findings of four major studies of television ads. In one study,

- 37.5% of the ads showed women as men's domestic adjuncts
- 33.9% showed women as dependent on men
- 24.3% showed women as submissive

- 16.7% showed women as sex objects
- 17.1% showed women as unintelligent
- 42.6% showed women as household functionaries.

Busby's summary of Dominick and Rauch's work reveals a similar concentration of women as homemakers rather than as active members of the labor force:

- Women were seven times more likely to appear in ads for personal hygiene products than not to appear [in those ads]
- 75% of all ads using females were for products found in the kitchen or in the bathroom
- 38% of all females in the television ads were shown inside the home, compared to 14% of the males
- Men were significantly more likely to be shown outdoors or in business settings than were women
- Twice as many women were shown with children [than] were men
- 56% of the women in the ads were judged to be [only] housewives
- 43 different occupations were coded for men, 18 for women.

As Busby notes, reviews of the major studies of ads (such as Courtney and Whipple, 1974) emphasize their strong "face validity" (the result of real patterns rather than any bias produced by researchers' methods), although the studies use different coding categories and some of the researchers were avowed feminist activists.

In sum, then, analyses of television commercials support the reflection hypothesis. In voice-overs and one-sex (all male or all female) ads, commercials neglect or rigidly stereotype women. In their portrayal of women, the ads banish females to the role of housewife, mother, homemaker, and sex object, limiting the roles women may play in society.

What can the preschool girl, the school girl, the adolescent female and the woman learn about a woman's role by watching television? The answer is simple. Women are not important in American society, except *perhaps* within the home. And even within

the home, men know best, as the dominance of male advice on soap operas and the use of male voice-overs for female products, suggests. To be a woman is to have a limited life divorced from the economic productivity of the labor force.

Women's Magazines: Marry, Don't Work

As the American girl grows to womanhood, she, like her counterpart elsewhere in industrialized nations, has magazines available designed especially for her use. Some, like *Seventeen,* whose readers tend to be young adolescents, instruct on contemporary fashions and dating styles. Others, like *Cosmopolitan* and *Redbook,* teach about survival as a young woman— whether as a single woman hunting a mate in the city or a young married coping with hearth and home.

This section reviews portrayals of sex roles in women's magazines, seeking to learn how often they too promulgate stereotypes about the role their female readers may take—how much they too engage in the symbolic annihilation of women by limiting and trivializing them. Unfortunately, our analyses of images of women in magazines cannot be as extensive as our discussion of television. Because of researchers' past neglect of women's issues and problems, few published materials are available for review.

Like the television programs just discussed, from the earliest content analyses of magazine fiction (Johns-Heine and Gerth, 1949) to analyses of magazine fiction published in the early 1970s, researchers have found an emphasis on hearth and home and a denigration of the working woman. The ideal woman, according to these magazines, is passive and dependent. Her fate and her happiness rest with a man, not with participation in the labor force. There are two exceptions to this generalization: (1) The female characters in magazines aimed at working-class women are a bit more spirited than their middle-class sisters. (2) In the mid-1970s, middle-class magazines seemed less hostile toward working women. Using the reflection hypothesis, particularly its emphasis upon attracting readers to sell advertisements, we will seek to explain the general rule and these interesting exceptions to it.

Like other media, women's magazines are interested in building their audience or readership. For a magazine, attracting more readers is *indirectly* profitable. Each additional reader does not increase the magazine's profit margin by buying a copy or taking out a subscription, because the cost of publication and distribution per copy far exceeds the price of the individual copy—whether it is purchased on the newsstand, in a supermarket, or through subscription. Instead a magazine realizes its profit by selling advertisements and charging its advertisers a rate adjusted to its known circulation. Appealing to advertisers, the magazine specifies known demographic characteristics of its readership. For instance, a magazine may inform the manufacturer of a product intended for housewives that a vast proportion of its readership are homemakers, while another magazine may appeal to the producer of merchandise for young working women by lauding its readership as members of that target group. Women's magazines differentiate themselves from one another by specifying their intended readers, as well as the size of their mass circulation. Additionally, they all compete with other media to draw advertisers. (For example, *Life* and *Look* folded because their advertisers could reach a larger group of potential buyers at a lower price per person through television commercials.) Both daytime television and women's magazines present potential advertisers with particularly appealing audiences, because women are the primary purchasers of goods intended for the home.

Historically, middle-class women have been less likely to be members of the labor force than lower-class women. At the turn of the century, those married women who worked were invariably from working-class families that required an additional income to assure adequate food, clothing, and shelter (Oppenheimer, 1970). The importance of this economic impetus for working is indicated by the general adherence of working-class families to more traditional definitions of male and female sex roles (Rubin, 1976). Although middle-class families subscribe to a more flexible ideology of sex roles than working-class families, both groups of women tend to insist that the man should be the breadwinner. The fiction in women's magazines reflects this ideology.

Particularly in middle-class magazines, fiction depicts women "as creatures . . . defined by the men in their lives" (Franzwa, 1974a, p. 106; see also Franzwa,

1974b, 1975). Studying a random sample of issues of *Ladies' Home Journal, McCall's,* and *Good Housekeeping* between the years 1940 and 1970, Helen Franzwa found four roles for women: "single and looking for a husband, housewife-mother, spinster, and widowed or divorced—soon to remarry." All the women were defined by the men in their lives, or by their absence. Flora (1971) confirms this finding in her study of middle-class (*Redbook* and *Cosmopolitan*) and working-class (*True Story* and *Modern Romances*) fiction. Female dependence and passivity are lauded; on the rare occasions that male dependence is portrayed, it is seen as undesirable.

As might be expected of characterizations that define women in terms of men, American magazine fiction denigrates the working woman. Franzwa says that work is shown to play "a distinctly secondary part in women's lives. When work is portrayed as important to them, there is a concomitant disintegration of their lives" (1974a, p. 106). Of the 155 major female characters depicted in Franzwa's sample of magazine stories, only 65 or forty-one percent were employed outside the home. Seven of the 65 held high-status positions. Of these seven, only two were married. Three others were "spinsters" whose "failure to marry was of far greater importance to the story-line than their apparent success in their careers" (pp. 106–7). One single woman with a high status career was lauded: She gave up her career to marry.

From 1940 through 1950, Franzwa found, working mothers and working wives were condemned. Instead, the magazines emphasized that husbands should support their spouses. One story summary symbolizes the magazines' viewpoint: "In a 1940 story, a young couple realized that they couldn't live on his salary. She offered to work; he replied, 'I don't think that's so good. I know some fellows whose wives work and they might just as well not be married' " (p. 108). Magazines after 1950 are even less positive about work. In 1955, 1960, 1965, and 1970 not one married woman who worked appeared in the stories Franzwa sampled. (Franzwa selected stories from magazines using five-year intervals to enhance the possibility of finding changes.)

Since middle-class American wives are less likely to be employed than their working-class counterparts, this finding makes sociological sense. Editors

Table 2.1 Female Dependence and Ineffectuality by Class, by Percentage of Stories*

Female Dependence			*Female Ineffectuality*			
	Undesirable	*Desirable*	*Neutral*	*Undesirable*	*Desirable*	*Neutral*
Working Class	22	30	48	38	4	58
Middle Class	18	51	31	18	33	49
Total	20	41	40	28	19	53

* Adapted from Flora (1971).

and writers may believe that readers of middle-class magazines, who are less likely to be employed, are also more likely to buy magazines approving this lifestyle. More likely to work and to be in families either economically insecure or facing downward mobility, working-class women might be expected to applaud effective women. For them, female dependence might be an undesirable trait. Their magazines could be expected to cater to such preferences, especially since those preferences flow from the readers' life situations. Such, indeed, are Flora's findings, presented in Table 2.1.

However, this pattern does not mean that the literature for the working-class woman avoids defining women in terms of men. All the women in middle-class magazines dropped from the labor force when they had a man present; only six percent of the women in the working-class fiction continued to work when they had a man and children. And Flora explained that for both groups "The plot of the majority of stories centered upon the female achieving the proper dependent status, either by marrying or manipulating existing dependency relationships to reaffirm the heroine's subordinate position. The male support—monetary, social, and psychological—which the heroine gains was generally seen as well worth any independence or selfhood given up in the process" (1971, p. 441).

Such differences as do exist between working-class and middle-class magazines remain interesting, though. For they indicate how much more the women's magazines may be responsive to their audience than television can be. Because it is the dominant mass medium, television is designed to appeal to hundreds of millions of people. In 1970, the circulation of *True Story* was "only" 5,347,000, and of *Redbook*, a "mere" 8,173,000. Drawing a smaller audience and by definition, one more specialized, the women's magazines

can be more responsive to changes in the position of women in American society. If a magazine believes its audience is changing, it may alter the content to maintain its readership. The contradictions inherent in being women's magazines may free them to respond to change.

A woman's magazine is sex-typed in a way that is not true of men's magazines (Davis, 1976). *Esquire* and *Playboy* are for men, but the content of these magazines, is, broadly speaking, American culture. Both men's magazines feature stories by major American writers, directed toward all sophisticated Americans, not merely to men. Both feature articles on the state of male culture as American culture or of male politics as American politics. Women's magazines are designed in opposition to these "male magazines." For instance, "sports" are women's sports or news of women breaking into "men's sports." A clear distinction is drawn between what is "male" and what is "female."

Paradoxically, though, this very limitation can be turned to an advantage. Addressing women, women's magazines may suppose that some in their audience are concerned about changes in the status of women and the greater participation of women in the labor force. As early as 1966, before the growth of the modern women's movement, women who were graduated from high school or college assumed they would work until the birth of their first child. Clarke and Esposito (1966) found that magazines published in the 1950s and addressed to these women (*Glamour, Mademoiselle,* and *Cosmopolitan*) stressed the joys of achievement and power when describing working roles for women and identifying desirable jobs. Magazines addressed to working women were optimistic about these women's ability to combine work and home, a message that women who felt that they should or must work would be receptive to. Indeed, in 1958 Marya and David Hatch criticized *Mademoiselle, Glamour*, and *Charm* as "unduly optimistic" in their "evaluation of physical and emotional strains upon working women." Combining work and family responsibilities may be very difficult, particularly in working-class homes, since working class husbands refuse to help with housework (Rubin, 1976). But even working-class women prefer work outside the home to housework (Rubin, 1976, Vanek, forthcoming) since it broadens their horizons. Wanting to please and to attract a special audience of working women, magazine editors and writers may be freed to be somewhat responsive to new conditions, even as these same writers and editors feature stereotyped sex roles in other sections of their magazines.

Additional evidence of the albeit limited responsiveness of women's magazines to the changing status of women in the labor force is provided by their treatment of sex-role stereotypes since the advent of the women's movement. The modern women's movement is usually said to begin in the mid-1960s with the founding of the National Organization for Women. The date is of consequence for the study of sex roles in women's magazines because of Betty Friedan's involvement in the National Organization for Women. Her book, *The Feminine Mystique*, published in 1963, provided much of the ideology for the young movement. And, its analysis of sexism ("the problem with no name") was based in part on an analysis of the portrayal of sex roles in women's magazines. In an undated manuscript cited in Busby (1975), Stolz and her colleagues compared the image of women in magazines before and after the advent of the women's movement. Like others, they found no changes between 1940 and 1972. However, a time lag ("culture lag") is probably operating since nonmaterial conditions (ideas and attitudes) change more slowly than do material conditions (such as participation in the labor force).

Several very recent studies affirm that women's magazines may be introducing new conceptions of women's sex roles that are more conducive to supporting the increased participation of women in the labor force. Butler and Paisley[3] note that at the instigation of an editor of *Redbook*, twenty-eight women's magazines published articles on the arguments for and against the Equal Rights Amendment, a constitutional change prompted by the women's movement and the increased participation of women in the labor force. Franzwa's impression of the women's magazines she had analyzed earlier is that they revealed more sympathy with working women in 1975.[4] Sheila Silver (1976) indicates that a "gentle support" for the aims of the women's movement and a "quiet concern" for working women may now be found in *McCall's*. By the terms "gentle support" and "quiet concern," she means to indicate that the magazine approves equal pay for equal work and other movement aims, although it does not approve of the women's movement itself. That magazine and others, such as the *Ladies' Home Journal*, continue to concentrate upon helping women as housewives: They still provide advice on hearth and home. The women's magazines continue to assume that every woman will marry, bear children and "make a home." They do not assume that every woman will work some time in her life.

In sum, the image of women in the women's magazines is more responsive to change than is television's symbolic annihilation and rigid typecasting of women. The sex roles presented are less stereotyped, but a woman's role is still limited. A female child is always an eventual mother, not a future productive participant in the labor force.

Newspapers and Women: Food, Fashion, and Society

Following the argument developed thus far, one might expect the nation's newspapers to be even more responsive than magazines to the changing status of women in American society. With smaller circulations than the magazines and supposedly more responsive to a local population rather than a national one, newspapers might cater to their female readers in order to maintain or even increase the base of their circulation. Such an expectation seems particularly plausible because contemporary newspapers face increased costs and are suffering from the economic competition of the electronic media. But this expectation flies in the face of the actual organization of news-work, for newspapers are *not, strictly speaking, local media*. Rather, local newspapers' dependence upon national news services is sufficiently great for them to be considered *components of a national medium,* designed to appeal to as many Americans as possible. As we have just seen, such a design encourages a rigid treatment of sex roles. An historical review of newspapers' treatment of news about women makes this result clearer.

Unlike the women's magazines, newspapers seek to appeal to an entire family. Historically, they have sought to attract female readers by treating them as a specialized audience, given attention in a segregated women's page, an autonomous or semi-autonomous department whose mandate precludes coverage of the "hard news" of the day. Although women's magazines have been published in the United States since the early nineteenth century, it took the newspaper circulation wars of the 1880s to produce the notion of "women's news." At that time, it appeared that every man who would buy a newspaper was already doing so. To build circulation by robbing each other of readers and attracting new readers, newspapers hired female reporters to write about society and fashion, as well as to expand "news" to include sports and comic strips. Items of potential interest to women were placed near advertisements of goods that women might purchase for their families. The origin of women's news reveals how long newspapers have traditionally defined women's interests as different from men's and how items of concern to women have become non-news, almost oddities. That view continues today. The budget for women's pages rarely provides for updating those pages from edition to edition, as is done for the general news, sports, and financial pages, sections held to be of interest to men. Finally, as is true of other departments as well, women's page budgets are sufficiently restricted to force that department's dependence upon the wire services.

During the nineteenth century's circulation wars, newspapers banded into cooperative services intended to decrease the costs of total coverage for each participating newspaper. A reporter would cover a story for newspapers in different cities, decreasing the need for scattered newspapers to maintain extensive bureaus in a variety of cities, such as Washington and New York. Furthermore, a newspaper in a small out-of-the-way town could be requested to share its story about an important event with newspapers from distant places that would not, under normal circumstances, have a reporter on hand. Aside from

playing a limited role in the development of journalistic objectivity (Schudson, 1976), since stories were designed to meet the political-editorial requirements of diverse news organizations, the news services encouraged the expansion of definitions of news. Some provided features, such as comics and crossword puzzles. Others provided sports items, financial stories, and features of concern to women, as well as "hard news." Sometimes the women's items were scandalous revelations of the activities of "Society." More often, they were advice for the homemaker, such as recipes and articles about rearing children. In this century, syndicated and wire-service features include gossip columns about the celebrated and the notorious and advice to the lovelorn, such as that fictionalized in Nathanael West's *Miss Lonelyhearts* or that represented by "Dear Abby."

For women's pages, items like these represent more than an economic investment purchased by a newspaper on behalf of its women's department. They are also an investment of space in the paper. Expected by readers to appear on a Monday, the column inches set aside for advice or gossip cannot be withdrawn for news of the women's movement. Similarly, it may be difficult to turn aside essentially prepaid feature stories about clothing and fashions supplied by the Associated Press or some other news syndicate in order to hire additional women's page staff interested in covering the changing status of women in American society. Commitments like these "nationalize" the local media, because the news syndicate or wire service reaches virtually every daily newspaper in the United States. Because the wire services *as businesses* are necessarily committed to pleasing all (or as many as possible) of their subscribing newspapers, they must shrink from advocating vast social changes. As in the case of television, what goes in New York may not go in Peoria, Illinois or Norman, Oklahoma. National in scope, syndicated and wire-service items for the women's page must seek an American common denominator. For the sex stereotyping of the women's pages to cease, the leadership of the Associated Press and the syndicates would have to be convinced that most of their subscribing papers wanted a different kind of story for their women's pages. Only then, it seems safe to say, would the papers serviced by the syndicates run the kinds of news about changes in the status of women that may be found in the *New York Times* and the *Los Angeles Times,* whose women's pages develop their own stories through independent staffs.

For now, a characterization of women's pages provided by Lindsay Van Gelder (1974) seems apt. She speculates thus: Suppose a Martian came to earth and sought to learn about American culture by reading the women's pages. Bombarded by pictures of wedding dresses, the Martian might suppose that American women marry at least once a week. After all, a Martian might reason that newspapers and their women's pages reflect daily life. That view, we might add, would seem justified by the women's pages' intense involvement with the social life of the upper class, because upper-class power is a daily aspect of American life. Women's pages feed upon the parties, marriages, engagements, and clothing and food preferences of the wealthy and the celebrated. In this, like newspapers in general (Lazarsfeld and Merton, 1948), the women's pages encourage all citizens to emulate the upper class and to chase after positions of high status and institutionalized importance.

Newspapers' very emphasis upon established institutions and those with institutionalized power may account in part for their denigration of women and the women's movement (Morris, 1974). Most information in the general sections of newspapers concerns people in power, and newspapers justify this emphasis by stressing that such people work in or head societal institutions that regulate social intercourse. But communications researchers view the matter somewhat differently. They argue that newspapers exercise social control: By telling stories about such people, newspapers lend status to approved institutions and chastise lawbreakers. Historically, those few women mentioned in the general news pages belonged to the powerful groups in society. Gladys Engel Lang (Chapter 8 [in *Hearth and Home*]) suggests "the most admired woman" list probably reflects the publicity given to specific women. They are mainly wives of the powerful, celebrities and stars, and the few women who are heads of state. But women are mainly seen as the consorts of famous men, not as subjects of political and social concern in their own right.

This situation appears to be changing. Once ignored or ridiculed (Morris, 1974), the women's movement has received increasing coverage as it has passed through the stages characteristic of any social movement. As the women's movement became sufficiently routinized to open offices with normal business hours, some newspapers established a "women's movement beat" that required a reporter to provide at least periodic coverage of new developments (Chapter 11 [in *Hearth and Home*]). When increased legitimation brought more volunteers and more funds to wage successful law suits against major corporations and to lobby for the introduction of new laws, newspapers concerned with major institutions were forced to cover those topics (Chapter 12 [in *Hearth and Home*]). In turn, these successes increased the movement's legitimation. Legitimation also brought support of sympathizers within other organizations who were not movement members (Carden, 1973). Reporters having those other organizations as their beats are being forced to write about the ideas of the women's movement and women's changing status. For instance, the position of women and minorities in the labor force is becoming a required topic for labor reporters and those who write about changing personnel in the corporate world.

On the whole, though, despite coverage of women forcibly induced by the legitimation of the women's movement, newspapers continue to view women in the news as occasional oddities that must be tolerated. Attention to women is segregated and found on the women's page. As a recent survey of women's pages demonstrates (Guenin, 1975), most women's pages continue to cater to a traditional view of women's interests. They emphasize home and family, only occasionally introducing items about women at work. And those items are more likely to concern methods of coping with home and office tasks than they are with highlighting problems of sex discrimination and what the modern women's movement has done in combatting it. Like the television industry, appealing to a common denominator encourages newspapers to engage in the symbolic annihilation of women by ignoring women at work and trivializing women through banishment to hearth and home.

The Impact of the Media

As of this writing, women continue to enter the labor force at a faster rate than in the past—a rate that has far exceeded the predictions of demographers and specialists on the labor force. What are we to make of this discrepancy between the sex-role stereotypes reflected in the media and the employment pattern of women? Does the discrepancy mean that because of culture lag, the mass media reflect attitudes discarded by the population and that the mass media have no effect on the behavior of women? That conclusion seems quite seductive, given the patterns we have described. By entering the labor force at increasing rates, women seem to be ignoring the media's message. But that conclusion flies in the face of *every* existing theory about the mass media. Communications theorists agree that the mass media are the cement of American social life. They are a source of common interest and of conversation. Children and adults may schedule their activities around favorite television programs. And the mass media serve to coordinate the activities of diverse societal institutions. To paraphrase Gerbner and Gross (1976), the mass media in general and television in particular have replaced religion as a source of social control in American life. Like the medieval church that broadcast one message to all social classes, all the mass media disseminate the same theme about women to all social classes: They announce their symbolic annihilation and trivialization.

Equally important, all available evidence about the impact of the media upon sex-role stereotyping indicates that the media encourage their audiences to engage in such stereotyping. They lead girls, in particular, to believe that their social horizons and alternatives are more limited than is actually the case. The evidence about the impact of television is particularly compelling.

Aimee Dorr Leifer points out (1975) that television provides many of the same socialization processes as the family. Like the family, television provides examples of good and bad behavior. The family socializes children through the patterning and power of those examples, and television programming also provides variation in the frequency, consistency, and power of examples. Leifer notes some indications that variations in these factors may have an impact on the child viewer (1975, p. 5). Finally, like the family, television can provide reinforcers (rewards and punishments) for behaviors. However, although the family can tailor reinforcers to the individual child, television cannot.

Most of the documentation regarding the impact of television upon children considers the effect of televised violence, primarily because of the national push for such research after the political assassinations and riots of the 1960s. That research is particularly interesting, for our purposes, because of the unanimity of the findings and because of the diverse methods used to analyze the topic.

Social science researchers frequently squabble about which methods of research are appropriate to explore a problem. All seem ready to admit that the ideal way to explore television's impact would be to perform a controlled experiment in a natural setting. Ideally, one would isolate a group that did not watch television, matching characteristics of individuals in that group with the characteristics of others whose viewing was designed by the researchers. The groups would be studied over a period of some years to see whether the effects of television are cumulative. Unfortunately, such a research design is impossible. Virtually all American homes have at least one television set; and so, one cannot locate children for the "control group"—those not exposed to television. To get around this problem, the violence researchers used both laboratory and field experiments. In the former, children were exposed to carefully selected (and sometimes specially prepared) videotapes, lasting anywhere from ten minutes to an hour. Behavior was analyzed before viewing the tape, while viewing it, and after viewing it. By carefully controlling which children would see what tape (designing "control groups"), the experimenters could comment upon the effect of televised violence on the children. Unfortunately, laboratory studies are artificial. For one thing, both sets of children are already dosed with violence in normal viewing, and both watch television under conditions different from their homes or classrooms. Thus, researchers cannot state in any definitive way how the research findings are related to activities in the real world.

The second approach, field experiments, also has difficulties. Such studies are invariably "correlational." The studies demonstrate that two kinds of behavior are found together, but cannot state whether one behavior causes the other or whether both are caused by a third characteristic of the children studied. For instance, in the violence studies, teams of researchers asked youths and children about their viewing habits (and in one case tried to control those habits) and also measured (in a variety of ways) their antisocial behavior. Although viewing aggression and antisocial behavior were invariably found together, it remains possible that some third factor accounts for the variation.

The fact that different research teams interviewed children of different sexes, ages, social classes, and races from different parts of the country makes it fairly certain that a third factor was not responsible for the association of television viewing and antisocial behavior. And this conclusion is strengthened by the evidence provided by the laboratory studies. Furthermore, since the Surgeon General issued his report in 1973, additional field studies have found "that viewing televised or filmed violence in naturalistic settings increases the incidence of naturally-occurring aggression, that long-term exposure to television may increase one's aggressiveness, and that exposure to televised violence may increase one's tolerance for everyday aggression" (Leifer, 1975).

Although there are not as many studies, researchers have also established that television programming influences racial attitudes. Again, both laboratory and field studies were used. They demonstrate that white children may take their image of blacks from television (Greenberg, 1972), that the longer a white child watches "Sesame Street," the less likely that child will have negative attitudes toward blacks, and that positive portrayals of blacks produce more positive attitudes toward blacks, with negative portrayals producing little attitude changes (Graves, 1975). Aimee Leifer writes of these findings: "Apparently black children increase their [positive] image of their own group by seeing them portrayed on television, while white children are influenced by the portrayal, especially when it is uncomplimentary to blacks" (1975, p. 26). The evidence on the impact of the depiction of race is important in assessing television's impact on sex roles because content analyses provide strong documentation that television treats blacks and whites differently. For instance, in this volume Schuetz and Sprafkin's analysis of children's commercials and Lemon's analysis of patterns of domination document differential treatment by race as well as by sex.

Since the documentation on violence is extensive and the documentation on race is strong, it seems more than reasonable to expect that the content of television programs leads children to hold stereotyped images of sex roles. The power of the evidence on race and violence is important, because researchers have just started to ask about the impact of television on societal sex roles. What, then, do we know now?

Suppose, we asked earlier, that television primarily presents adult women as housewives. Also suppose that girls in the television audience "model" their behavior and expectations on that of television women. Such a supposition is quite plausible for psychologists note that "opportunities for modeling have been vastly increased by television" (Lesser, quoted in Cantor, 1975, p. 5). It is then equally plausible that girls exposed to television women may hope to be homemakers when they are adults, but not workers outside the home.

Do girls actually model their attitudes and behavior on the symbolically annihilated and dominated television woman?

This general question may be broken down into several component questions:

1. Do girls pay closer attention to female television characters than to male characters?
2. Do girls value the attributes of female characters or those of male characters?
3. Does television viewing have an impact on the attitudes of young children toward sex roles?
4. Do these attitudes continue as children mature?

As in the studies on violence and race, the available evidence includes laboratory and field studies.

1. *Do girls pay closer attention to female characters than to male characters?* In this volume, Joyce Sprafkin and Robert Liebert report the results of three laboratory experiments designed to see whether (a) boys and girls each prefer television programs featuring actors of their own sex; (b) whether the children pay closer attention when someone of the same sex is on the television screen; and (c) whether the children prefer to watch members of their own sex engaging in sex-typed (playing with a doll or a football) or nonsextyped (as in reading with one's parents) behavior. To gather information, they enabled the tested children to switch a dial, choosing between an episode of "Nanny

and the Professor" and one of the "Brady Bunch." (Children like to watch situation comedies [Lyle and Hoffman, 1972].) For each program, episodes featuring male or female characters were selected with different episodes showing a boy or a girl engaging in sex-typed or nonsex-typed behavior. The findings are clear: In their viewing habits, children prefer sex-typing. They prefer programs featuring actors of their own sex; they watch members of their own sex more closely; and they also pay more attention when a member of their own sex engages in sex-typed behavior. According to Sprafkin and Liebert (1976), such behavior probably involves learning, for according to psychological theories children prefer to expose themselves to same-sex models as an information-seeking strategy; children are presumed to attend to same-sex peers because they already know that much social reinforcement is sex-typed and must discover the contingencies that apply to their own gender (see also Grusec and Brinker, 1972).

2. *Do girls value the attributes of female characters or of male characters?* The evidence on evaluation is not as clear. A variety of communications researchers, particularly a group working at Michigan State University, have performed a series of laboratory experiments to determine which specific characters boys and girls prefer, and why they do so. They found that invariably boys identify with male characters. Sometimes though (about thirty percent of the time) girls also identify with or prefer male characters (Miller and Reeves, 1976). When girls choose a television character as a model, they are guided by the character's physical attractiveness; boys are guided by strength (Greenberg, Held, Wakshlag, and Reeves, 1976; Miller and Reeves, 1976). Indeed, even when girls select a male character they appear to be guided by his physical attractiveness (Greenberg *et al.,* 1976). Girls who select male characters do *not* state they are basing their choices on the wider opportunities and fun available to men, although the girls who select female characters state that the characters do the same kind of things as they themselves do (Reeves, 1976).

3. *Does television viewing have an impact on the attitudes of young children toward sex roles?* Here the evidence is clearer. Frueh and McGhee (1975) interviewed children in kindergarten through sixth grade, asking them about the amount of time they spent watching television and testing the extent and direction of their sex-typing. The children who viewed the most television (twenty-five hours or more each week) were significantly more traditional in their sex-typing than those who viewed the least (ten hours or less per week). Because this study is correlational, one cannot know whether viewing determines sex-typing or *vice versa.* But television does seem to be the culprit, according to laboratory studies on television viewing and occupational preferences.

Miller and Reeves (1976; see also Pingree, 1976) asked children to watch television characters in nontraditional roles and then asked them what kind of jobs boys and girls could do when they grew up. Children exposed to programs about female police officers, for instance, were significantly more likely to state that a woman could be a police officer than were children who watched more traditional fare.

Beuf (1974) reports similar results from sixty-three interviews with boys and girls between the ages of three and six. Some girls had even abandoned their ambitions:

> One of the most interesting aspects of the children's responses lay in their reactions to the question: "What would you want to be when you grew up, if you were a girl (boy?)" Several girls mentioned that this other-sex ambition was their true ambition, but one that could not be realized because of their sex. Doctor and milkman were both cited in this regard. . . . One blond moppet confided that what she really wanted to do when she grew up was fly like a bird. "But, I'll never do it," she sighed, "because I'm not a boy." Further questioning revealed that a TV cartoon character was the cause of this misconception. (p. 143)

A boy said, "Oh, if I were a girl, I'd have to grow up to be nothing." Beuf reports, "Children who were moderate viewers appeared to exert a wider range of choice in career selection than heavy viewers. Seventy-six percent of the heavy viewers (compared with fifty percent of the moderate viewers) selected stereotyped careers for themselves" (p. 147).

4. *Do these attitudes continue as children mature?* It is known that sex-typing increases as children mature.

Second graders are more insistent in their sex-typing than first graders are. Adolescent boys and girls insist upon discriminating between behavior by sex. But little is known about the impact of television on this process. A longitudinal study presently underway at the University of Pennsylvania's Annenberg School of Communication is the first attempt to answer this question systematically. Chapter 14 [in *Hearth and Home*], which contains a summary of that research, indicates that definitive answers are not yet available. However, analyses based on data from the second year of the study do tentatively indicate an association between television viewing and sexist attitudes. The association is weak, but it does suggest that the more a youngster watches television, the more likely the child will be to hold sexist attitudes.

What can we make of all this? The answer is: The mass media perform two tasks at once. First, with some culture lag, they reflect dominant values and attitudes in the society. Second, they act as agents of socialization, teaching youngsters in particular how to behave. Watching lots of television leads children and adolescents to believe in traditional sex roles: Boys should work; girls should not. The same sex-role stereotypes are found in the media designed especially for women. They teach that women should direct their hearts toward hearth and home.

At a time when over forty percent of the American labor force is female and when women with pre-school children are entering the labor force in increasing numbers, the mass media's message has severe national consequences. As demographers (for example, Oppenheimer, 1970) and economists (for example, Bowen and Finegan, 1969) have shown, the maintenance and expansion of the American economy depends upon increasing the rate of female employment. Discouraging women from working presents a national dilemma. Furthermore, it is quite probable that the media's message discourages women from working up to their full capacity in the labor force. And by limiting the *kinds* of jobs held by fictional women, it may encourage the underemployment of women, a severe problem for those working-class families who can barely scrape by with two incomes (Rubin, 1976). And rigid sex-role stereotypes make the burden heavier for all working women who must still shoulder the responsibilities of home and family with limited assistance from their

husbands. This problem is particularly acute in blue-collar families (Rubin, 1976). For the nation and for individuals, the message "women belong in the home" is an anachronism we can ill afford.

Throughout this book, in original essays reporting new research, social scientists delve further into the media's symbolic annihilation and trivialization of women. In introductions to each section of this volume, we relate the individual chapters to the themes we have considered here. Finally, in our last chapter we explore the policy implications of all these materials. How can the media be changed? we ask. How can we free women from the tyranny of media messages limiting their lives to hearth and home?

Notes

1. Government data indicate that at age twenty, American women are more likely to be members of the labor force than to be married. U.S. Dept. of Labor, 1976.
2. Sponsors do play a role in public broadcasting. As underwriters of programs, they may refuse to fund controversial materials. Some critics claim the Corporation for Public Broadcasting has avoided controversial topics to maintain corporate grants, and has designed dramatic series to appeal to corporations and foundations. According to informants at WNET, corporate underwriters object when the station delays airing their programs to squeeze in public appeals for contributions to the station.
3. Matilda Butler and William Paisley. Personal communication, Fall 1976.
4. 1976, personal communication.

References

Bardwick, Judith and Suzanne Schumann. 1967. "Portrait of American Men and Women in TV Commercials." *Psychology* 4(4): 18–23.

Baumann, Zygmunt. 1972. "A Note on Mass Culture: On Infrastructure." In Denis McQuail (ed.), *Sociology of Mass Communication*. Baltimore: Penguin Books, pp. 61–74.

Benét, James. 1976. "Will Media Treatment of Women Improve?" In Gaye Tuchman, Arlene Kaplan Daniels, and James Benét (eds.), *Hearth and Home: Images of Women in the Mass Media*. New York: Oxford University Press, pp. 266–271.

Bernard, Jessie. 1973. "My Four Revolutions: An Autobiographical History of the ASA." *American Journal of Sociology* 78(4): 773–91.

Beuf, Ann. 1974. "Doctor, Lawyer, Household Drudge." *Journal of Communication* 24(1): 142–45.

Bowen, William G. and T. Aldrich Finegan. 1969. *The Economics of Labor Force Participation.* Princeton: Princeton University Press.

Busby, Linda J. 1975. "Sex-role Research on the Mass Media." *Journal of Communication* 25(4): 107–31.

Cantor, Muriel G. 1975. "Children's Television: Sex-Role Portrayals and Employment Discrimination." In *The Federal Role in Funding Children's Television Programming.* Vol. 2. Ed. K. Mielke *et al.* United States Office of Education, USOE OEC-074–8674.

——. 1976. "Where are the Women in Public Broadcasting?" In Gaye Tuchman, Arlene Kaplan Daniels, and James Benét (eds.), *Hearth and Home: Images of Women in the Mass Media.* New York: Oxford University Press, pp. 78–90.

Carden, Maren Lockwood. 1973. *The New Feminist Movement.* New York: Russell Sage.

Clarke, Peter and Virginia Esposito. 1966. "A Study of Occupational Advice for Women in Magazines." *Journalism Quarterly* 43: 477–85.

Courtney, Alice E. and Thomas W. Whipple. 1974. "Women in TV Commercials." *Journal of Communication* 24(2): 110–18.

Davis, Margaret. 1976. "The *Ladies' Home Journal* and *Esquire*: A Comparison." Unpublished manuscript. Dept. of Sociology, Stanford University.

Domhoff, G. William. 1976. "The Women's Page as a Window on the Ruling Class." In Gaye Tuchman, Arlene Kaplan Daniels, and James Benét (eds.), *Hearth and Home: Images of Women in the Mass Media.* New York: Oxford University Press, pp. 161–175.

Dominick, Joseph and Gail Rauch. 1972. "The Image of Women in Network TV Commercials." *Journal of Broadcasting* 16(3): 259–65.

Downing, Mildred. 1974. "Heroine of the Daytime Serial." *Journal of Communication* 24(2): 130–37.

Epstein, Cynthia Fuchs. 1976. "The Women's Movement and the Women's Pages." In Gaye Tuchman, Arlene Kaplan Daniels, and James Benét (eds.), *Hearth and Home: Images of Women in the Mass Media.* New York: Oxford University Press, pp. 216–222.

Flora, Cornelia. 1971. "The Passive Female: Her Comparative Image by Class and Culture in Women's Magazine Fiction." *Journal of Marriage and the Family* 33(3): 435–44.

Franzwa, Helen. 1974a. "Working Women in Fact and Fiction." *Journal of Communication* 24(2): 104–9.

——. 1974b. "Pronatalism in Women's Magazine Fiction." In Ellen Peale and Judith Senderowitz (eds.), *Pronatalism: The Myth of Motherhood and Apple Pie.* New York: T. Y. Crowell, pp. 68–77.

——. 1975. "Female Roles in Women's Magazine Fiction, 1940–1970." In R. K. Unger and F. L. Denmark (eds.), *Woman: Dependent or Independent Variable.* New York: Psychological Dimensions, pp. 42–53.

Friedan, Betty. 1963. *The Feminine Mystique.* New York: Dell.

Frueh, Terry and Paul E. McGhee. 1975. "Traditional Sex Role Development and Amount of Time Spent Watching Television." *Development Psychology* 11(1): 109.

Gerbner, George. 1972. "Violence in Television Drama: Trends and Symbolic Functions." In G. A. Comstock and E. A. Rubenstein (eds.), *Media Content and Control.* Television and Social Behavior, vol. I. Washington, DC: U.S. Government Printing Office, pp. 28–187.

—— and Larry Gross. 1976. "Living with Television: The Violence Profile." *Journal of Communication* 26(2): 17–99.

Graves, S. B. 1975. "How to Encourage Positive Racial Attitudes." Paper presented at the biennial meeting of the Society for Research in Child Development. Denver, Colorado, April.

Greenberg, Bradley. 1972. "Children's Reaction to TV Blacks." *Journalism Quarterly* 49: 5–14.

——, Gary Held, Jacob Wakshlag and Byron Reeves. 1976. "TV Character Attributes, Identification and Children's Modeling Tendencies." Paper presented at International Communication Association, Portland, OR, April.

Gross, Larry and Suzanne Jeffries-Fox. 1976. "What Do You Want To Be When You Grow Up?" In Gaye Tuchman, Arlene Kaplan Daniels, and James Benét (eds.), *Hearth and Home: Images of Women in the Mass Media.* New York: Oxford University Press, pp. 240–65.

Grusec, Joan E. and Dale B. Brinker, Jr. 1972. "Reinforcement for Imitation as a Social Learning Determinant with Implications for Sex-Role Development." *Journal of Personality and Social Psychology* 21(2): 149–58.

Guenin, Zena B. 1975. "Women's Pages in Contemporary Newspapers: Missing Out on Contemporary Content." *Journalism Quarterly* 52(1): 66–69, 75.

Hatch, Marya G. and David L. Hatch. 1958. "Problems of Married and Working Women as Presented by Three Popular Working Women's Magazines." *Social Forces* 37(2): 148–53.

Hirsch, Paul. 1978. "Television as a National Medium: Its Cultural and Political Role in American Society." In David Street (ed.), *Handbook of Urban Life.* San Francisco: Jossey-Bass, pp. 389–427.

Isber, Caroline and Muriel Cantor. 1975. *Report of the Task Force on Women in Public Broadcasting.* Washington, DC: Corporation for Public Broadcasting.

Johns-Heine, Patricke and Hans H. Gerth. 1949. "Values in Mass Periodical Fiction, 1921–1940." *Public Opinion Quarterly* 13(1): 105–13.

Katz, Elihu and Paul F. Lazarsfeld. 1955. *Personal Influence.* New York: The Free Press.

Katzman, Natan. 1972. "Television Soap Operas: What's Been Going on Anyway?" *Public Opinion Quarterly* 36(2): 200–12.

Lang, Gladys Engel. 1976. "The Most Admired Woman: Image-Making in the News." In Gaye Tuchman, Arlene Kaplan Daniels, and James Benét (eds.), *Hearth and Home: Images of Women in the Mass Media*. New York: Oxford University Press, pp. 147–60.

Lasswell, Harold. 1948. "The Structure and Function of Communication in Society." In L. Bryson (ed.), *The Communication of Ideas*. New York: Harper Brothers, pp. 37–51.

Lazarsfeld, Paul F. and Robert K. Merton. 1948. "Mass Communication, Popular Taste and Organized Social Action." In L. Bryson (ed.), *The Communication of Ideas*. New York: Harper Brothers, pp. 95–118.

Leifer, Aimee Dorr. 1975. "Socialization Processes in the Family." Paper presented at Prix Jeunesse Seminar, Munich, Germany, June.

Lemon, Judith. 1976. "Dominant or Dominated? Women in Prime-Time Television." In Gaye Tuchman, Arlene Kaplan Daniels, and James Benét (eds.), *Hearth and Home: Images of Women in the Mass Media*. New York: Oxford University Press, pp. 51–68.

Liebert, R. M., J. M. Neal, and E. S. Davidson. 1973. *The Early Window: Effects of Television on Children and Youth*. New York: Pergamon.

Lyle, J. and H. R. Hoffman. 1972. "Children's Use of Television and Other Media." In E. A. Rubenstein, G. A. Comstock, and J. P. Murphy (eds.), *Television in Day to Day Life: Patterns of Use*. Television and Social Behavior, vol. 4. Washington, DC: U.S. Government Printing Office, pp. 129–256.

McCormack, Thelma. 1975. "Toward a Nonsexist Perspective on Social and Political Change." In Marcia Millman and Rosabeth Moss Kanter (eds.), *Another Voice: Feminist Perspectives on Social Life and Social Science*. New York: Doubleday/Anchor, pp. 1–33.

Miller, M. Mark and Byron Reeves. 1976. "Dramatic TV Content and Children's Sex-Role Stereotypes." *Journal of Broadcasting* 20(1): 35–50.

Morris, Monica B. 1974. "The Public Definition of a Social Movement: Women's Liberation." *Sociology and Social Research* 57(4): 526–43.

Oppenheimer, Valerie Kincaid. 1970. *The Female Labor Force in the United States: Demographic and Economic Factors Governing Its Growth and Changing Composition*. Population Monograph Series No. 5. Institute of International Studies, University of California, Berkeley.

Parsons, Talcott. 1949. "Age and Sex in the Social Structure of the United States." *Essays in Sociological Theory*. New York: The Free Press, pp. 89–103.

Pingree, Suzanne. 1976. "The Effects of Nonsexist Television Commercials and Perceptions of Reality on Children's Attitudes towards Women." Paper presented at the annual meetings of the International Communication Association, Portland, OR, April.

Reeves, Byron. 1976. "The Dimensional Structure of Children's Perception of TV Characters." Ph.D. dissertation. Michigan State University.

Rubin, Lillian. 1976. *Worlds of Pain. Life in the Working-Class Family*. New York: Basic Books.

Schudson, Michael. 1976. "Origins of the Ideal of Objectivity in the Professions: Studies in the History of American Journalism and American Law, 1830–1940." Ph.D. dissertation. Harvard University.

Schuetz, Stephen and Joyce N. Sprafkin. 1976. "Spot Messages Appearing Within Saturday Morning Television Programs." In Gaye Tuchman, Arlene Kaplan Daniels, and James Benét (eds.), *Hearth and Home: Images of Women in the Mass Media*. New York: Oxford University Press, pp. 69–77.

Silver, Sheila. 1976. "Then and Now—Content Analysis of *McCall's* Magazine." Paper presented at the annual meetings of Association for Education in Journalism. College Park, MD.

Silverstein, Arthur Jay and Rebecca Silverstein. 1974. "The Portrayal of Women in Television Advertising." *Federal Communications Bar Journal* 27(1): 71–98.

Sprafkin, Joyce N. and Robert M. Liebert. 1976. "Sex and Sex-Roles as Determinants of Children's Television Program Selections and Attention." Unpublished manuscript. State University of New York at Stony Brook.

——. 1976. "Sex-typing and Children's Television Preferences." In Gaye Tuchman, Arlene Kaplan Daniels, and James Benét (eds.), *Hearth and Home: Images of Women in the Mass Media*. New York: Oxford University Press, pp. 228–39.

Stolz, Gale K. et al. n.d. "The Occupational Roles of Women in Magazines and Books." Unpublished manuscript. Loyola University, Chicago.

Tuchman, Gaye. 1974. *The TV Establishment: Programming for Power and Profit*. Englewood Cliffs, N.J.: Prentice-Hall.

——. 1976a. "Mass Media Values." *Society* 14(1): 51–54.

——. 1976b. "The Newspaper as a Social Movement's Resource." In Gaye Tuchman, Arlene Kaplan Daniels, and James Benét (eds.), *Hearth and Home: Images of Women in the Mass Media*. New York: Oxford University Press, pp. 186–215.

Turow, Joseph. 1974. "Advising and Ordering: Daytime, Prime Time." *Journal of Communication* 24(2): 138–41.

United States Department of Labor, Women's Bureau. 1976. *Handbook on Women Workers*. Washington, DC: U.S. Government Printing Office.

Vanek, Joann. Forthcoming. *Married Women and the Work Day: Time Trends*. Baltimore, MD: Johns Hopkins University Press, chapter 4.

Van Gelder, Lindsay. 1974. "Women's Pages: You Can't Make News Out of a Silk Purse." *Ms.* (Nov.): 112–16.

3.
VISUAL PLEASURE AND NARRATIVE CINEMA
Laura Mulvey

I Introduction

A. A Political Use of Psychoanalysis

This paper intends to use psychoanalysis to discover where and how the fascination of film is reinforced by pre-existing patterns of fascination already at work within the individual subject and the social formations that have moulded him. It takes as starting point the way film reflects, reveals and even plays on the straight, socially established interpretation of sexual difference which controls images, erotic ways of looking and spectacle. It is helpful to understand what the cinema has been, how its magic has worked in the past, while attempting a theory and a practice which will challenge this cinema of the past. Psychoanalytic theory is thus appropriated here as a political weapon, demonstrating the way the unconscious of patriarchal society has structured film form.

The paradox of phallocentrism in all its manifestations is that it depends on the image of the castrated woman to give order and meaning to its world. An idea of woman stands as lynch pin to the system: it is her lack that produces the phallus as a symbolic presence, it is her desire to make good the lack that the phallus signifies. Recent writing in *Screen* about psychoanalysis and the cinema has not sufficiently brought out the importance of the representation of the female form in a symbolic order in which, in the last resort, it speaks castration and nothing else. To summarise briefly: the function of woman in forming the patriarchal unconscious is two-fold, she first symbolises the castration threat by her real absence of a penis and second thereby raises her child into the symbolic. Once this has been achieved, her meaning in the process is at an end, it does not last into the world of law and language except as a memory which oscillates between memory of maternal plenitude and memory of lack. Both are posited on nature (or on anatomy in Freud's famous phrase). Woman's desire is subjected to her image as bearer of the bleeding wound, she can exist only in relation to castration and cannot transcend it. She turns her child into the signifier of her own desire to possess a penis (the condition, she imagines, of entry into the symbolic). Either she must gracefully give way to the word, the Name of the Father and the Law, or else struggle to keep her child down with her in the half-light of the imaginary. Woman then stands in patriarchal culture as signifier for the male other, bound by a symbolic order in which man can live out his phantasies and obsessions through linguistic command by imposing them on the silent image of woman still tied to her place as bearer of meaning, not maker of meaning.

There is an obvious interest in this analysis for feminists, a beauty in its exact rendering of the frustration experienced under the phallocentric order. It gets us nearer to the roots of our oppression, it brings an articulation of the problem closer, it faces us with the ultimate challenge: how to fight the unconscious structured like a language (formed critically at the moment of arrival of language) while still caught within the language of the patriarchy. There is no way in which we can produce an alternative out of the blue, but we can begin to make a break by examining patriarchy with the tools it provides, of which psycho-analysis is not the only but an important one. We are still separated by a great gap from important issues for the female unconscious which are scarcely relevant to phallocentric theory: the sexing of the female infant and her relationship to the symbolic, the sexually mature woman as non-mother, maternity outside the signification of the phallus, the vagina. . . . But, at this point, psychoanalytic theory as it now stands can at least advance our understanding of the status quo, of the patriarchal order in which we are caught.

B. Destruction of Pleasure as a Radical Weapon

As an advanced representation system, the cinema poses questions of the ways the unconscious (formed by the dominant order) structures ways of seeing and pleasure in looking. Cinema has changed over the last few decades. It is no longer the monolithic system based on large capital investment exemplified at its best by Hollywood in the 1930's, 1940's and 1950's. Technological advances (16mm, etc) have changed the economic conditions of cinematic production, which can now be artisanal as well as capitalist. Thus it has been possible for an alternative cinema to develop. However self-conscious and ironic Hollywood managed to be, it always restricted itself to a formal mise-en-scène reflecting the dominant ideological concept of the cinema. The alternative cinema provides a space for a cinema to be born which is radical in both a political and an aesthetic sense and challenges the basic assumptions of the mainstream film. This is not to reject the latter moralistically, but to highlight the ways in which its formal preoccupations reflect the psychical obsessions of the society which produced it, and, further, to stress that the alternative cinema must start specifically by reacting against these obsessions and assumptions. A politically and aesthetically avant-garde cinema is now possible, but it can still only exist as a counterpoint.

The magic of the Hollywood style at its best (and of all the cinema which fell within its sphere of influ-ence) arose, not exclusively, but in one important aspect, from its skilled and satisfying manipulation of visual pleasure. Unchallenged, mainstream film coded the erotic into the language of the dominant

patriarchal order. In the highly developed Hollywood cinema it was only through these codes that the alien-ated subject, torn in his imaginary memory by a sense of loss, by the terror of potential lack in phantasy, came near to finding a glimpse of satisfaction: through its formal beauty and its play on his own formative obsessions. This article will discuss the interweaving of that erotic pleasure in film, its meaning, and in par-ticular the central place of the image of woman. It is said that analysing pleasure, or beauty, destroys it. That is the intention of this article. The satisfaction and reinforcement of the ego that represent the high point of film history hitherto must be attacked. Not in favour of a reconstructed new pleasure, which cannot exist in the abstract, nor of intellectualised unpleasure, but to make way for a total negation of the ease and plenitude of the narrative fiction film. The alternative is the thrill that comes from leaving the past behind without rejecting it, transcending outworn or oppres-sive forms, or daring to break with normal pleasurable expectations in order to conceive a new language of desire.

II Pleasure in Looking/Fascination with the Human Form

A. The cinema offers a number of possible pleasures. One is scopophilia. There are circumstances in which looking itself is a source of pleasure, just as, in the reverse formation, there is pleasure in being looked at. Originally, in his *Three Essays on Sexuality*, Freud iso-lated scopophilia as one of the component instincts of sexuality which exist as drives quite independently of the erotogenic zones. At this point he associated sco-pophilia with taking other people as objects, subjecting them to a controlling and curious gaze. His particular examples centre around the voyeuristic activities of children, their desire to see and make sure of the private and the forbidden (curiosity about other people's geni-tal and bodily functions, about the presence or absence of the penis and, retrospectively, about the primal scene). In this analysis scopophilia is essentially active. (Later, in *Instincts and their Vicissitudes*, Freud developed his theory of scopophilia further, attaching it initially to pre-genital auto-eroticism, after which the pleasure of the look is transferred to others by analogy. There is a close working here of the relationship between the active instinct and its further development in a narcissistic form.) Although the instinct is modified by other factors, in particular the constitution of the ego, it continues to exist as the erotic basis for pleasure in looking at another person as object. At the extreme, it can become fixated into a perversion, producing obsessive voyeurs and Peeping Toms, whose only sexual satisfaction can come from watching, in an active controlling sense, an objectified other.

At first glance, the cinema would seem to be remote from the undercover world of the surreptitious observation of an unknowing and unwilling victim. What is seen of the screen is so manifestly shown. But the mass of mainstream film, and the conventions within which it has consciously evolved, portray a hermetically sealed world which unwinds magically, indifferent to the presence of the audience, producing for them a sense of separation and playing on their voyeuristic phantasy. Moreover, the extreme contrast between the darkness in the auditorium (which also isolates the spectators from one another) and the brilliance of the shifting patterns of light and shade on the screen helps to promote the illusion of voyeuristic separation. Although the film is really being shown, is there to be seen, conditions of screening and narrative conventions give the spectator an illusion of looking in on a private world. Among other things, the position of the spectators in the cinema is blatantly one of repression of their exhibitionism and projection of the repressed desire on to the performer.

B. The cinema satisfies a primordial wish for pleasurable looking, but it also goes further, developing scopophilia in its narcissistic aspect. The conventions of mainstream film focus attention on the human form. Scale, space, stories are all anthropomorphic. Here, curiosity and the wish to look intermingle with a fascination with likeness and recognition: the human face, the human body, the relationship between the human form and its surroundings, the visible presence of the person in the world. Jacques Lacan has described how the moment when a child recognises its own image in the mirror is crucial for the constitution of the ego. Several aspects of this analysis are relevant here. The mirror phase occurs at a time when the child's physical ambitions outstrip his motor capacity, with the result that his recognition of himself is joyous in that he imagines his mirror image to be more complete, more perfect than he experiences his own body. Recognition is thus overlaid with mis-recognition: the image recognised is conceived as the reflected body of the self, but its misrecognition as superior projects this body outside itself as an ideal ego, the alienated subject, which, re-introjected as an ego ideal, gives rise to the future generation of identification with others. This mirror-moment predates language for the child.

Important for this article is the fact that it is an image that constitutes the matrix of the imaginary, of recognition/mis-recognition and identification, and hence of the first articulation of the 'I', of subjectivity. This is a moment when an older fascination with looking (at the mother's face, for an obvious example) collides with the initial inklings of self-awareness. Hence it is the birth of the long love affair/despair between image and self-image which has found such intensity of expression in film and such joyous recognition in the cinema audience. Quite apart from the extraneous similarities between screen and mirror (the framing of the human form in its surroundings, for instance), the cinema has structures of fascination strong enough to allow temporary loss of ego while simultaneously reinforcing the ego. The sense of forgetting the world as the ego has subsequently come to perceive it (I forgot who I am and where I was) is nostalgically reminiscent of that pre-subjective moment of image recognition. At the same time the cinema has distinguished itself in the production of ego ideals as expressed in particular in the star system, the stars centring both screen presence and screen story as they act out a complex process of likeness and difference (the glamorous impersonates the ordinary).

C. Sections II. A and B have set out two contradictory aspects of the pleasurable structures of looking in the conventional cinematic situation. The first, scopophilic, arises from pleasure in using another person as an object of sexual stimulation through sight. The second, developed through narcissism and the constitution of the ego, comes from identification with the image seen. Thus, in film terms, one implies a separation of the erotic identity of the subject from the object on the screen (active scopophilia), the other demands identification of the ego with the object on the screen through the spectator's fascination with and recognition of his like. The first is a function of the sexual instincts, the second of ego libido. This dichotomy was crucial for Freud. Although he saw the two as interacting and overlaying each other, the tension between instinctual drives and self-preservation continues to be a dramatic polarisation in terms of pleasure. Both are formative structures, mechanisms not meaning. In themselves they have no signification, they have to be attached to an idealisation. Both pursue aims in indifference to perceptual reality, creating the imagised, eroticised concept of the world that forms the perception of the subject and makes a mockery of empirical objectivity.

During its history, the cinema seems to have evolved a particular illusion of reality in which this contradiction between libido and ego has found a beautifully complementary phantasy world. In *reality* the phantasy world of the screen is subject to the law which produces it. Sexual instincts and identification processes have a meaning within the symbolic order which articulates desire. Desire, born with language, allows the possibility of transcending the instinctual and the imaginary, but its point of reference continually returns to the traumatic moment of its birth: the castration complex. Hence the look, pleasurable in form, can be threatening in content, and it is woman as representation/image that crystallises this paradox.

III Woman as Image, Man as Bearer of the Look

A. In a world ordered by sexual imbalance, pleasure in looking has been split between active/male and passive/female. The determining male gaze projects its phantasy on to the female figure which is styled accordingly. In their traditional exhibitionist role women are simultaneously looked at and displayed, with their appearance coded for strong visual and erotic impact so that they can be said to connote *to-be-looked-at-ness*. Woman displayed as sexual object is the leit-motif of erotic spectacle: from pin-ups to strip-tease, from Ziegfeld to Busby Berkeley, she holds the look, plays to and signifies male desire. Mainstream film neatly combined spectacle and narrative. (Note, however, how in the musical song-and-dance numbers break the flow of the diegesis.) The presence of woman is an indispensable element of spectacle in normal narrative film, yet her visual presence tends to work against the development of a story line, to freeze the flow of action in moments of erotic contemplation. This alien presence then has to be integrated into cohesion with the narrative. As Budd Boetticher has put it:

> What counts is what the heroine provokes, or rather what she represents. She is the one, or rather the love or fear she inspires in the hero, or else the concern he feels for her, who makes him act the way he does. In herself the woman has not the slightest importance.

(A recent tendency in narrative film has been to dispense with this problem altogether; hence the development of what Molly Haskell has called the 'buddy movie', in which the active homosexual eroticism of the central male figures can carry the story without distraction.) Traditionally, the woman displayed has functioned on two levels: as erotic object for the characters within the screen story, and as erotic object for the spectator within the auditorium, with a shifting tension between the looks on either side of the screen. For instance, the device of the show-girl allows the two looks to be unified technically without any apparent break in the diegesis. A woman performs within the narrative, the gaze of the spectator and that of the male characters in the film are neatly combined without breaking narrative verisimilitude. For a moment the sexual impact of the performing woman takes the film into a no-man's-land outside its own time and space. Thus Marilyn Monroe's first appearance in *The River of No Return* and Lauren Bacall's songs in *To Have or Have Not*. Similarly, conventional close-ups of legs (Dietrich, for instance) or a face (Garbo) integrate into the narrative a different mode of eroticism. One part of a fragmented body destroys the Renaissance space, the illusion of depth demanded by the narrative, it gives flatness, the quality of a cut-out or icon rather than verisimilitude to the screen.

B. An active/passive heterosexual division of labour has similarly controlled narrative structure. According to the principles of the ruling ideology and the psychical structures that back it up, the male figure cannot bear the burden of sexual objectification. Man is reluctant to gaze at his exhibitionist like. Hence the split between spectacle and narrative supports the man's role as the active one of forwarding the story, making things happen. The man controls the film phantasy and also emerges as the representative of power in a further sense: as the bearer of the look of the spectator, transferring it behind the screen to neutralise the extra-diegetic tendencies represented by woman as spectacle. This is made possible through the processes set in motion by structuring the film around a main controlling figure with whom the spectator can identify. As the spectator identifies with the main male[1] protagonist, he projects his look on to that of his like, his screen surrogate, so that the power of the male protagonist as he controls events coincides with the active power of the erotic look, both giving a satisfying sense of omnipotence. A male movie star's glamorous characteristics are thus not those of the erotic object of the gaze, but those of the more perfect, more complete, more powerful ideal ego conceived in the original moment of recognition in front of the mirror. The character in the story can make things happen and control events better than the subject/spectator, just as the image in the mirror was more in control of motor coordination. In contrast to woman as icon, the active male figure (the ego ideal of the identification process) demands a three-dimensional space corresponding to that of the mirror-recognition in which the alienated subject internalised his own representation of this imaginary existence. He is a figure in a landscape. Here the function of film is to reproduce as accurately as possible the so-called natural conditions of human perception. Camera technology (as exemplified by deep focus in particular) and camera movements (determined by the action of the protagonist), combined with invisible editing (demanded by realism) all tend to blur the limits of screen space. The male protagonist is free to command the stage, a stage of spatial illusion in which he articulates the look and creates the action.

C.1 Sections III. A and B have set out a tension between a mode of representation of woman in film and conventions surrounding the diegesis. Each is associated with a look: that of the spectator in direct scopophilic contact with the female form displayed for his enjoyment (connoting male phantasy) and that of the spectator fascinated with the image of his like set in an illusion of natural space, and through him gaining control and possession of the woman within the diegesis.

(This tension and the shift from one pole to the other can structure a single text. Thus both in *Only Angels Have Wings* and in *To Have and Have Not*, the film opens with the woman as object of the combined gaze of spectator and all the male protagonists in the film. She is isolated, glamorous, on display, sexualised. But as the narrative progresses she falls in love with the main male protagonist and becomes his property, losing her outward glamorous characteristics, her generalised sexuality, her show-girl connotations; her eroticism is subjected to the male star alone. By means of identification with him, through participation in his power, the spectator can indirectly possess her too.)

But in psychoanalytic terms, the female figure poses a deeper problem. She also connotes something that the look continually circles around but disavows: her lack of a penis, implying a threat of castration and hence unpleasure. Ultimately, the meaning of woman is sexual difference, the absence of the penis as visually ascertainable, the material evidence on which is based the castration complex essential for the organisation of entrance to the symbolic order and the law of the father. Thus the woman as icon, displayed for the gaze and enjoyment of men, the active controllers of the look, always threatens to evoke the anxiety it originally signified. The male unconscious has two avenues of escape from this castration anxiety: preoccupation with the re-enactment of the original trauma (investigating the woman, demystifying her mystery), counterbalanced by the devaluation, punishment or saving of the guilty object (an avenue typified by the concerns of the *film noir*); or else complete disavowal of castration by the substitution of a fetish object or turning the represented figure itself into a fetish so that it becomes reassuring rather than dangerous (hence over-valuation, the cult of the female star). This second avenue, fetishistic scopophilia, builds up the physical beauty of the object, transforming it into something satisfying in itself. The first avenue, voyeurism, on the contrary, has associations with sadism: pleasure lies in ascertaining guilt (immediately associated with castration), asserting control and subjecting the guilty person through punishment or forgiveness. This sadistic side fits in well with narrative. Sadism demands a story, depends on making something happen, forcing a change in another person, a battle of will and strength, victory/defeat, all occurring in a linear time with a beginning and an end. Fetishistic scopophilia, on the other hand, can exist outside linear time as the erotic instinct is focussed on the look alone. These contradictions and ambiguities can be illustrated more simply by using works by Hitchcock and Sternberg, both of whom take the look almost as the content or subject matter of many of their films. Hitchcock is the more complex, as he uses both mechanisms. Sternberg's work, on the other hand, provides many pure examples of fetishistic scopophilia.

C.2 It is well known that Sternberg once said he would welcome his films being projected upside down so that story and character involvement would not interfere with the spectator's undiluted appreciation of the screen image. This statement is revealing but ingenuous. Ingenuous in that his films do demand that the figure of the woman (Dietrich, in the cycle of films with her, as the ultimate example) should be identifiable. But revealing in that it emphasises the fact that for him the pictorial space enclosed by the frame is paramount rather than narrative or identification processes. While Hitchcock goes into the investigative side of voyeurism, Sternberg produces the ultimate fetish, taking it to the point where the powerful look of the male protagonist (characteristic of traditional narrative film) is broken in favour of the image in direct erotic rapport with the spectator. The beauty of the woman as object and the screen space coalesce; she is no longer the bearer of guilt but a perfect product, whose body, stylised and fragmented by close-ups, is the content of the film and the direct recipient of the spectator's look. Sternberg plays down the illusion of screen depth; his screen tends to be one-dimensional, as light and shade, lace, steam, foliage, net, streamers, etc, reduce the visual field. There is little or no mediation of the look through the eyes of the main male protagonist. On the contrary, shadowy presences like La Bessière in *Morocco* act as surrogates for the director, detached as they are from audience identification. Despite Sternberg's insistence that his stories are irrelevant, it is significant that they are concerned with situation, not suspense, and cyclical rather that linear time, while plot complications revolve around misunderstanding rather than conflict. The most important absence is that of the controlling male gaze within the screen scene. The high point of emotional drama in the most typical Dietrich films, her

supreme moments of erotic meaning, take place in the absence of the man she loves in the fiction. There are other witnesses, other spectators watching her on the screen, their gaze is one with, not standing in for, that of the audience. At the end of *Morocco*, Tom Brown has already disappeared into the desert when Amy Jolly kicks off her gold sandals and walks after him. At the end of *Dishonoured*, Kranau is indifferent to the fate of Magda. In both cases, the erotic impact, sanctified by death, is displayed as a spectacle for the audience. The male hero misunderstands and, above all, does not see.

In Hitchcock, by contrast, the male hero does see precisely what the audience sees. However, in the films I shall discuss here, he takes fascination with an image through scopophilic eroticism as the subject of the film. Moreover, in these cases the hero portrays the contradictions and tensions experienced by the spectator. In *Vertigo* in particular, but also in *Marnie* and *Rear Window*, the look is central to the plot, oscillating between voyeurism and fetishistic fascination. As a twist, a further manipulation of the normal viewing process which in some sense reveals it, Hitchcock uses the process of identification normally associated with ideological correctness and the recognition of established morality and shows up its perverted side. Hitchcock has never concealed his interest in voyeurism, cinematic and non-cinematic. His heroes are exemplary of the symbolic order and the law—a policeman (*Vertigo*), a dominant male possessing money and power (*Marnie*)—but their erotic drives lead them into compromised situations. The power to subject another person to the will sadistically or to the gaze voyeuristically is turned on to the woman as the object of both. Power is backed by a certainty of legal right and the established guilt of the woman (evoking castration, psychoanalytically speaking). True perversion is barely concealed under a shallow mask of ideological correctness—the man is on the right side of the law, the woman on the wrong. Hitchcock's skilful use of identification processes and liberal use of subjective camera from the point of view of the male protagonist draw the spectators deeply into his position, making them share his uneasy gaze. The audience is absorbed into a voyeuristic situation within the screen scene and diegesis which parodies his own in the cinema. In his analysis of *Rear Window*, Douchet takes the film as a metaphor for the cinema. Jeffries is the audience, the events in the apartment block opposite correspond to the screen. As he watches, an erotic dimension is added to his look, a central image to the drama. His girlfriend Lisa had been of little sexual interest to him, more or less a drag, so long as she remained on the spectator side. When she crosses the barrier between his room and the block opposite, their relationship is re-born erotically. He does not merely watch her through his lens, as a distant meaningful image, he also sees her as a guilty intruder exposed by a dangerous man threatening her with punishment, and thus finally save her. Lisa's exhibitionism has already been established by her obsessive interest in dress and style, in being a passive image of visual perfection; Jeffries' voyeurism and activity have also been established through his work as a photo-journalist, a maker of stories and captor of images. However, his enforced inactivity, binding him to his seat as a spectator, puts him squarely in the phantasy position of the cinema audience.

In *Vertigo*, subjective camera predominates. Apart from one flash-back from Judy's point of view, the narrative is woven around what Scottie sees or fails to see. The audience follows the growth of his erotic obsession and subsequent despair precisely from his point of view. Scottie's voyeurism is blatant: he falls in love with a woman he follows and spies on without speaking to. Its sadistic side is equally blatant: he has chosen (and freely chosen, for he had been a successful lawyer) to be a policeman, with all the attendant possibilities of pursuit and investigation. As a result, he follows, watches and falls in love with a perfect image of female beauty and mystery. Once he actually confronts her, his erotic drive is to break her down and force her to tell by persistent cross-questioning. Then, in the second part of the film, he re-enacts his obsessive involvement with the image he loved to watch secretly. He reconstructs Judy as Madeleine, forces her to conform in every detail to the actual physical appearance of his fetish. Her exhibitionism, her masochism, make her an ideal passive counterpart to Scottie's active sadistic voyeurism. She knows her part is to perform, and only by playing it through and then replaying it can she keep Scottie's erotic interest. But in the repetition he does break her down and succeeds in exposing her guilt. His curiosity wins

through and she is punished. In *Vertigo*, erotic involvement with the look is disorientating: the spectator's fascination is turned against him as the narrative carries him through and entwines him with the processes that he is himself exercising. The Hitchcock hero here is firmly placed within the symbolic order, in narrative terms. He has all the attributes of the patriarchal super-ego. Hence the spectator, lulled into a false sense of security by the apparent legality of his surrogate, sees through his look and finds himself exposed as complicit, caught in the moral ambiguity of looking. Far from being simply an aside on the perversion of the police, *Vertigo* focuses on the implications of the active/looking, passive/looked-at split in terms of sexual difference and the power of the male symbolic encapsulated in the hero. Marnie, too, performs for Mark Rutland's gaze and masquerades as the perfect to-be-looked-at image. He, too, is on the side of the law until, drawn in by obsession with her guilt, her secret, he longs to see her in the act of committing a crime, make her confess and thus save her. So he, too, becomes complicit as he acts out the implications of his power. He controls money and words, he can have his cake and eat it.

III Summary

The psychoanalytic background that has been discussed in this article is relevant to the pleasure and unpleasure offered by traditional narrative film. The scopophilic instinct (pleasure in looking at another person as an erotic object), and, in contradistinction, ego libido (forming identification processes) act as formations, mechanisms, which this cinema has played on. The image of woman as (passive) raw material for the (active) gaze of man takes the argument a step further into the structure of representation, adding a further layer demanded by the ideology of the patriarchal order as it is worked out in its favourite cinematic form—illusionistic narrative film. The argument returns again to the psychoanalytic background in that woman as representation signifies castration, inducing voyeuristic or fetishistic mechanisms to circumvent her threat. None of these interacting layers is intrinsic to film, but it is only in the film form that they can reach a perfect and beautiful contradiction, thanks to the possibility in the cinema of shifting the emphasis of the look. It is the place of the look that defines cinema, the possibility of varying it and exposing it. This is what makes cinema quite different in its voyeuristic potential from, say, striptease, theatre, shows, etc. Going far beyond highlighting a woman's to-be-looked-at-ness, cinema builds the way she is to be looked at into the spectacle itself. Playing on the tension between film as controlling the dimension of time (editing, narrative) and film as controlling the dimension of space (changes in distance, editing), cinematic codes create a gaze, a world, and an object, thereby producing an illusion cut to the measure of desire. It is these cinematic codes and their relationship to formative external structures that must be broken down before mainstream film and the pleasure it provides can be challenged.

To begin with (as an ending), the voyeuristic-scopophilic look that is a crucial part of traditional filmic pleasure can itself be broken down. There are three different looks associated with cinema: that of the camera as it records the pro-filmic event, that of the audience as it watches the final product, and that of the characters at each other within the screen illusion. The conventions of narrative film deny the first two and subordinate them to the third, the conscious aim being always to eliminate intrusive camera presence and prevent a distancing awareness in the audience. Without these two absences (the material existence of the recording process, the critical reading of the spectator), fictional drama cannot achieve reality, obviousness and truth. Nevertheless, as this article has argued, the structure of looking in narrative fiction film contains a contradiction in its own premises: the female image as a castration threat constantly endangers the unity of the diegesis and bursts through the world of illusion as an intrusive, static, one-dimensional fetish. Thus the two looks materially present in time and space are obsessively subordinated to the neurotic needs of the male ego. The camera becomes the mechanism for producing an illusion of

Renaissance space, flowing movements compatible with the human eye, an ideology of representation that revolves around the perception of the subject; the camera's look is disavowed in order to create a convincing world in which the spectator's surrogate can perform with verisimilitude. Simultaneously, the look of the audience is denied an intrinsic force: as soon as fetishistic representation of the female image threatens to break the spell of illusion, and the erotic image on the screen appears directly (without mediation) to the spectator, the fact of fetishisation, concealing as it does castration fear, freezes the look, fixates the spectator and prevents him from achieving any distance from the image in front of him.

This complex interaction of looks is specific to film. The first blow against the monolithic accumulation of traditional film conventions (already undertaken by radical film-makers) is to free the look of the camera into its materiality in time and space and the look of the audience into dialectics, passionate detachment. There is no doubt that this destroys the satisfaction, pleasure and privilege of the 'invisible guest', and highlights how film has depended on voyeuristic active/passive mechanisms. Women, whose image has continually been stolen and used for this end, cannot view the decline of the traditional film form with anything much more than sentimental regret.[2]

Notes

1. There are films with a woman as main protagonist, of course. To analyse this phenomenon seriously here would take me too far afield. Pam Cook and Claire Johnston's study of *The Revolt of Mamie Stover* in Phil Hardy, ed: *Raoul Walsh*, Edinburgh 1974, shows in a striking case how the strength of this female protagonist is more apparent than real.
2. This article is a reworked version of a paper given in the French Department of the University of Wisconsin, Madison, in the Spring of 1973.

4.
DEFINING WOMEN

The Case of Cagney and Lacey

Julie D'Acci

On Monday nights between 1983 and 1988, CBS attracted millions of American women to its "ladies' night line-up."[1] The last program in this line-up, a thorn in the network's side for its controversial women characters and its mediocre ratings, was also renowned for delivering a deluxe "quality audience" to CBS and its advertisers week after week.[2] According to CBS research department vice president David Poltrack, *Cagney and Lacey* attracted women viewers who, by and large, watched less television than the average audience member, were college educated, over thirty-five, and earned over $40,000 a year.[3]

Upscale female audiences were the coveted plum of the television industry in its 1980s quest for the "working-women's market," and female characters—acting out the industry's fantasies of the "new working women"—were fashioned to lure their "real-life" counterparts to prime time as never before. However, the territory of 1980s working women and the adjacent territory of feminism posed difficulties for network television. Clashes over exactly what these new women characters could or could not be, in fact, left scars in the prime-time offerings of the period that demonstrate just how well guarded particular definitions of women are by those who hold them and just how dangerous new ones are perceived to be. Many of the new working-women shows introduced during the early 1980s—*9 to 5, Remington Steele, Gloria, It Takes Two*, and *Cagney and Lacey*—underwent overhauls and modified their depictions of women in order to bring their characters back in line with conventional television notions of femininity. Because of

its six-year run, its departure from traditional norms of the "TV woman," and its embattled history, *Cagney and Lacey* provides a rich case study of the struggles over competing definitions of what it means to be a woman.

In 1981, the time of *Cagney and Lacey*'s first production as a made-for-TV movie, the cultural definitions of "woman," both in American society at large and in the representational practices of television, were multiple and open to debate. Traditional cultural meanings of femininity in a number of spheres (economy, labor, family, and sexuality, to name a few) were challenged by the women's movements. Television, in its general quest for "relevance" and its specific attempt to reach the new working-women's market, was producing representations of women that drew, in varying ways and degrees, on the new feminist consciousness—particularly that of the American liberal women's movement. Some of these representations, especially those of *Cagney and Lacey* in its initial stages, were in sharp contrast to television's conventional ways of depicting women. But these innovations would be tempered and transformed as a backlash against feminism gained force (notably evident in the defeat of the Equal Rights Amendment), and as television's tendency to filter out potentially controversial subject matter began to take hold.

A detailed study of *Cagney and Lacey* generally, then, offers to reveal the *actual terms* of cultural struggle over the meanings of femininity as this was played out on prime-time television during the period from 1981 to 1988. Since the original *Cagney and Lacey* script was written in 1974 and offered (without takers) to every major motion picture studio in Hollywood, it also offers insight into that earlier period. Furthermore, the issues contested during the late 1970s and through the 1980s continue to provoke the television industry and its audiences today.

Cagney and Lacey was the first dramatic program in television history to star two women. It appeared on CBS between 1982 and 1988 and dealt with two white middle-class and upper middle-class female detectives in the New York City Police Department. Created by Barbara Avedon and Barbara Corday, its executive producer was Barney Rosenzweig and its production company was Orion Television. The characters—Cagney (played by Meg Foster and Sharon Gless, respectively) and Lacey (played by Tyne Daly)—were represented as active heroines who solved their own cases (both mentally and physically), were rarely shown as "women in distress" and were virtually never rescued by their male colleagues.[4] In addition to their roles as active protagonists in the narrative, they were also active subjects, rarely objects, of sexual desire. Christine Cagney, a single woman, had an ongoing sexual life in which she often pursued men who interested her. Similarly, Mary Beth Lacey, a married woman, was a sexual initiator with her husband, Harvey. Lacey was also the primary breadwinner of the family, while Harvey, an often unemployed construction worker, cooked and took care of the house and their two children. Cagney and Lacey were depicted as close friends who took a lot of pleasure in one another's company and spent a lot of screen time talking to each other.

When the program first appeared, the actresses and characters were in their mid-thirties, and there was a distinct minimization of glamour in their clothing, hairstyles, and makeup. The characters were originally from working-class backgrounds and were both "working women." Much of the initial script material was modeled on the concerns of the early liberal women's movement in America, especially equal pay and sexual harassment at work. The first scripts dealt with male discrimination on the job and contained such material as a riff between Cagney and Lacey about the various ways in which Lt. Samuels, their commanding officer, was a "pig."

During its creation, and for the whole of its production, *Cagney and Lacey* became the site of intense public debates over various definitions of femininity. Many of the key players involved in the series' production and reception continuously battled over what women on television should and should not be. Among these players were those we would expect to be part of any negotiation of television content—the network, the individual production company and production team, the television audience, the press, and various interest and pressure groups.

These players, of course, were invested in definitions of women that suited their particular interests, whether those were political, economic, social, personal, or some combination thereof. The television industry, for instance, was looking for relevance and topicality while simultaneously hoping to preserve many of its conventional ways of depicting female characters. These conventions included the depiction of women as young, white, middle class, stereotypically "beautiful," and demure. They also included the presentation of female characters who were wives, mothers, heterosexual sex objects, subsidiaries to men, "vulnerable," and "sympathetic."[5] Within such conventions women were destined to be cast in situation comedies rather than in prime-time dramas. *Cagney and Lacey*'s production company, Orion Television (formerly Filmways), was at least somewhat committed to generating more innovative representations of women. Richard Rosen-bloom, Orion Television's president, was, in fact, known in Hollywood at the time for producing the highest percentage of properties written by women.[6] The individual production team was, for its part, directly influenced by the liberal women's movement, and quite explicitly fashioned *Cagney and Lacey* according to early feminist terms. A significant segment of the women's audience for *Cagney and Lacey*, and for other programs aimed at working women, was actively seeking progressive, interesting, and, in an often-cited viewer term, "real" representations of women in television fiction. As can be imagined, the mainstream press was extremely varied in its interests. One sector, very much influenced by feminism, agitated for a wider range of women characters, and specifically for roles shaped by the concerns of the women's movements. Other segments called for a return to "tried and true" femininity. Similarly, a number of interest and pressure groups had stakes in greatly divergent depictions of women. The National Gay Task Force, for example, vehemently protested the network's effort to ward off connotations of lesbianism in *Cagney and Lacey* by replacing one Cagney actress (Meg Foster) with another "more feminine" one (Sharon Gless). The National Right to Life Committee fiercely opposed Cagney and Lacey's support of a woman character who chooses to have an abortion. Planned Parenthood and the National Abortion Rights League applauded the series' embrace of reproductive rights. And spokespeople for the liberal women's movement generally and consistently championed the series for depicting "independent" working women and women's friendship.[7]

Getting New Representations of Women to the Screen

Cagney and Lacey's earliest period, from its conception in 1974 to its production as a made-for-TV movie in 1981, is rife with conflicts over different definitions of women. Generally speaking, representations of women in motion pictures and television programs were highly contradictory throughout the 1970s. Films such as *Alice Doesn't Live Here Anymore, Julia, The Turning Point*, and *An Unmarried Woman* expressed tensions between the emerging interests of the women's movements and more traditional notions of femininity. On prime-time television, social, economic, and political conditions combined to spawn a collection of amazingly paradoxical depictions. Beginning in 1970, the television industry's search for the upscale urban audience produced "socially conscious" or "socially relevant" programs that drew in large measure on the civil rights, black power, anti-war, and women's movements of the period.[8] Simply keeping its programming up to date might have led the industry to draw on the social ferment of the late 1960s and early 1970s for subject matter, but the push to attract specifically upscale urban audiences intensified the mining of thematic material that television executives thought would appeal to young, educated city-dwellers. Programs featuring working women, black women, older women, divorced women, single mothers, and working-class women suddenly filled the screen. *The Mary Tyler Moore Show, Rhoda, Alice, Good Times, The Jeffersons, Maude, One Day at a Time*, and

All in the Family are prominent examples of the new fare. However, as scholars such as Lauren Rabinovitz and Serafina Bathrick have pointed out, these programs often produced contradictory representations of women.[9]

Beginning in the mid-1970s and continuing until the end of the decade, different industry and social conditions combined once again to generate even more paradoxical female characters. This time, pressure on the industry to reduce incidents of televised violence led quite directly to the display of women's bodies as sexual attractions. "If you can't have Starsky pull a gun and fire it fifty times a day on promos," said Brandon Tartikoff (at the time vice president of NBC's programming), "sex becomes your next best handle."[10] Prior to this period, images of women on television were not charged with the sexual spectacle of motion picture imagery; instead, female television characters were domesticated. From the mid-1970s to the early 1980s, however, female sex objects populated the television landscape in what is often called the "jiggle" era, or in the industry's non-euphemistic tag, the "T&A" (for "tits and ass") period. It is, of course, no accident that these representations coincided with a time of mounting backlash over the concerns and demands of the woman's movements. One of the major paradoxes of this period, however, is that women starred in more dramatic programs than at any other time in television history. Series such as *Police Woman, Get Christie Love, Charlie's Angels, Wonder Woman, Flying High*, and *American Girls* are major legacies of the time.

Cagney and Lacey's first: script was conceived in 1974 squarely within the conceptual terms of the liberal women's movement: it featured role reversals, that is, women in a traditionally male profession, and women in a standard male public-sphere genre. Historically and industrially speaking, its creators considered it an idea whose time had come.[11] According to Barbara Avedon, Barbara Corday, and Barney Rosenzweig, *Cagney and Lacey* was specifically conceived as a response to an early and influential book from the women's movement, Molly Haskell's *From Reverence to Rape: The Treatment of Women in the Movies*. Avedon and Corday were engaged in the literature and politics of the early women's movement, and both were in women's groups. Rosenzweig was "setting out to have his consciousness raised."[12] They read Haskell's book and were intrigued by the fact that there had never been a Hollywood movie about two women "buddies" comparable to *M*A*S*H* or *Butch Cassidy and the Sundance Kid*.[13] According to Rosenzweig:

> The Hollywood establishment had totally refused women those friendships, the closest thing being perhaps Joan Crawford and Eve Arden in *Mildred Pierce*, the tough lady boss and her wise-cracking sidekick. So I went to my friend Ed Feldman, who was then head of Filmways (now Orion), and I said, "I want to do a picture where we turn around a conventional genre piece like *Freebie and The Bean* with its traditional male situations and make it into the first real hit feminist film."[14]

One of the main motivations behind *Cagney and Lacey* from its inception was the creators' notion that two women could, in fact, be represented as friends who worked and talked together, rather than as conventionally portrayed competitors. Both Avedon and Corday recall the ways in which the relationship between Cagney and Lacey was modeled (if somewhat unconsciously) on their own eight-year relationship as writing partners and friends.

Ed Feldman at Filmways was interested in the idea Rosenzweig had pitched to him, and he gave the seed money to hire Avedon and Corday as writers.[15] Barbara Avedon recalls that although Filmways was "excited" about the idea, they had difficulty understanding the view of women involved. They persisted in situating the characters in the film industry's terms of women as spectacles and sex objects. According to Avedon, "They [Filmways] told us things like, when [Cagney or Lacey] rips her shirt back and shows her badge to the guys, they can all stare [at her breasts]." "That," continued Avedon, "was the level of consciousness, even though they [Filmways] were doing a women-buddy movie."[16]

Avedon and Corday prepared for writing the script by spending ten days with New York policewomen. Avedon recalled, "The women cops we met were first and foremost cops. Unlike Angie Dickinson in *Police Woman* who'd powder her nose before she went out to make a bust, these women took themselves seriously as police officers."[17] Both Corday and Avedon were convinced that the only way for *Cagney and Lacey* to work was if they cast "strong, mature" women, with

"senses of humor." They envisioned Sally Kellerman as Cagney and Paula Prentiss as Lacey.[18] Corday, Avedon, and Rosenzweig all felt that because they were dealing with potentially controversial "feminist" material, their film would have to be first and foremost "entertaining."[19] The original script, "Freeze," was a spoof in which *Cagney and Lacey* uncover the existence of The Godmother, the female intelligence behind a brothel where men are the prostitutes and women the patrons.[20] Again, the major narrative device was the early women's movement's notion of role reversals.

After getting the script financed by Filmways, Rosenzweig needed a major motion picture studio to pick it up and do the actual production. He took the original property to every studio in Hollywood and got predictably "Hollywood" responses, such as "these women aren't soft enough, aren't feminine enough."[21] At MGM, Sherry Lansing (who was later to become the first woman head of a major motion picture studio, Twentieth Century Fox) persuaded her boss, Dan Melnik, to make the movie. MGM said it would but only if well-known "sex symbols" Raquel Welch and Ann-Margret starred. (Welch and Ann-Margret had not yet demonstrated their true versatility as actresses at this point in Hollywood history.) The other stipulation was a 1.6-million-dollar budget which, in a kind of Catch-22 fashion, prohibited the hiring of such high-priced actresses.[22] The property, therefore, lay dormant for the next five years.

In 1980, Rosenzweig decided to have another go at it. This time, he took it to the television networks as a pilot for a weekly series. Corday and Avedon reconceived the script to update it and make it less of a spoof and more of a "realistic" crime drama.[23] Although CBS would not pick up *Cagney and Lacey* as a series, it decided it would take it as a less costly, less risky, made-for-TV movie, and it also suggested that Rosenzweig cast "two sexy young actresses."[24] According to Rosenzweig, he told CBS:

> You don't understand, these policewomen must be mature women. One has a family and kids, the other is a committed career officer. What separates this project from *Charlie's Angels* is that Cagney and Lacey are women; they're not girls and they're certainly not objects.[25]

During this impasse, CBS, which had an outstanding

"pay-or-play" commitment to Loretta Swit of *M*A*S*H*, asked Rosenzweig to cast her as Cagney.[26] Avedon and Corday, who had recently worked with Sharon Gless on the TV series *Turnabout*, wanted her for the part.[27] Avedon said she had actually considered Gless the model for Cagney while writing the new script.[28] Because Gless could not be released from her contract to Universal, Rosenzweig cast Swit as Cagney, even though her contract with *M*A*S*H* would preclude her availability should an opportunity to turn *Cagney and Lacey* into a series arise. He cast Tyne Daly as Lacey. The movie was scheduled for broadcast on October 8, 1981, and was publicized in various ways by the women's movement, the television industry, and the mainstream press.

The pre-production publicity represented Cagney and Lacey as important for the causes of the women's movement. Gloria Steinem at *Ms.* magazine had been sent a script by the creators and was so enthusiastic that she appeared with Loretta Swit on the *Phil Donahue Show* to plug the movie. According to one media critic, they were so "reverential" it "sounded as though they were promoting the first woman president."[29] Steinem also featured Loretta Swit and Tyne Daly, in police uniforms as Cagney and Lacey, on the cover of the October issue of *Ms.*[30] The issue contained a feature article on *Cagney and Lacey* written by Marjorie Rosen, a well-known feminist film critic and author of *Popcorn Venus: Women, Movies and the American Dream*. The article told the troubled history of the property, emphasized its importance for feminism, underscored specific feminist characteristics it saw Cagney and Lacey as bringing into "distinctive focus," and ended with a pitch for a weekly series. The feminist characteristics especially applauded by *Ms.* included women as the subjects of narrative action and adventure, as active in traditionally male-dominated genres and jobs, and as friends. Also emphasized were the notions of women as autonomous, individualistic, and independent.[31]

CBS's promotion department, with its own motivations and vested interests, publicized the movie according to a standard television industry advertising practice called "exploitation advertising." This is a practice, with precedents in the Hollywood film industry, in which a sensational (usually sexual or violent) aspect of a program is highlighted for the purposes of attracting audiences. In the *Cagney and Lacey* movie

advertisement in *TV Guide*, a large close-up of Loretta Swit with long blonde hair dominates the left side of the composition, while her clasped, outstretched hands contain a pointed revolver, which dominates the right. A significantly smaller medium shot of the lesser-known (at the time) Tyne Daly in police coat, shirt, and tie is under the Swit close-up. On the far left of the page, under and smaller than the Daly image, is a shot of Swit lying on her back (presumably naked) with a sheet draped over her. One bare shoulder and arm, and one bare leg bent at the knee, are exposed. A man, depicted only from his waist up (also naked) is leaning over and on top of her, his arm across her body. The copy reads, "It's their first week as undercover cops! Cagney likes the excitement. Lacey cares about the people she protects. They're going to make it as detectives—or die trying."[32]

Various conceptions of women are set into play here, and it seems evident that the television industry, in dealing with a movie about women in non-traditional roles, is careful to invoke not only connotations regarding the "new woman" but also more traditional notions of femininity. Swit is shown as a cop with an aimed revolver but also as a conventionally beautiful woman with eye makeup, lipstick, and long blonde hair. She is also shown as a conventional object rather than subject of sexual desire. Lacey is shown in traditionally male clothing but is described in the conventionally feminine way of "caring about the people she protects." And although they are both trying to "make it" as detectives, they are also stereotypical "women in distress" who may "die trying." The emphasis on stereotyped feminine behaviors and predicaments in an ad for a movie about women in new roles fulfills the formula for exploitation advertising by suggesting sexual and dangerous content to the audience, while also reassuring the audience about women's traditional role and position in relation to social power.

The movie aired at 8:00 P.M. on Thursday, October 8, 1981, and captured an astonishing 42 share of the television audience (CBS had been getting a 28 or 29 share in this time period).[33] Within 36 hours, CBS was on the telephone to Barney Rosenzweig asking him to get a weekly program together.[34] Gloria Steinem and *Ms.* magazine staff members had already lobbied members of the CBS board, urging them to make a series out of the movie.[35]

Controversial Representations of Women

The second phase of *Cagney and Lacey's* history, the television series starring Tyne Daly and Meg Foster (as Swit's replacement for Cagney), was aired from March 25, 1982, to August 1982 (including summer reruns). This period coincides with that during which the network was most ardently courting an audience of working women. The massive entry of women into the labor force in the 1970s and 1980s produced what advertisers in the mid-1970s began to call the "new working women's market," a demographic group made up of American women in control of and spending their own disposable income. Other culture industries including magazines, movies, radio, and cable TV channels had pursued such women well before prime-time network television did, but in the late 1970s the three major networks began casting about for programs to attract them. The prime-time soaps (beginning with *Dallas* in 1978) and a series of made-for-TV movie melodramas were the first forms successful at capturing this new target audience. By the early 1980s, the television industry, having cloned and spun off a crop of prime-time soaps, was looking for other vehicles with which to do the same. The huge ratings success of the *Cagney and Lacey* made-for-TV movie seemed to indicate that women-oriented programming that drew on feminist discourses and subject matter was a good bet. Such a hunch, in the midst of the Reagan years' backlash against the women's movements, only intensified the contestatory nature of the negotiations surrounding the production and reception of female television characters at the time.

The first *Cagney and Lacey* series script was written by Barbara Avedon, Barbara Corday, and Barney Rosenzweig. Gloria Steinem and *Ms.* magazine, keeping alive the link between the women's movement and the program, organized a reception for the stars and creators in early March.[36] The series was publicized by Filmways in press releases as "two top-notch female cops who fight crime while proving themselves to male colleagues."[37] The angle of women working in non-traditional jobs, in roles that called for rough physical action, and as fighting sexism was emphasized both in the industry's publicity for the series and the scripts.

The very night and hour *Cagney and Lacey* premiered, the series 9 *to* 5, based on the hit movie of the same name (and dealing with secretaries agitating for better working conditions), premiered on the competing ABC network.[38] The fact that *Cagney and Lacey* and 9 *to* 5 were scheduled opposite one another would prove costly for both series in terms of ratings. Gloria Steinem, speaking at a Hollywood Radio and Television Society luncheon a month before the premieres, had protested this scheduling, saying it might "split the audience and hurt each other's [the two series'] chances."[39]

Of the thirty-five press reviews I read on the series' premiere, most were lukewarm or favorable. Most mentioned the feminist elements in the script: the exposure of "chauvinism" among the male detectives, Mary Beth and Harvey's role reversals, and the "juggling" of women's personal lives and careers.[40] Several articles said such things as "the show's message of female discrimination is too obvious and heavy-handed," and "the not-too-subtle message here is that women have to be twice as good to look equal with a man—a topic which could be the Achilles' heel of the series if pounded home too strongly."[41] Many also pointed out the difference between Cagney and Lacey and other female television characters. Such phrases as "no racy 'Charlie's Angels'-style glamour here," "mature women, not girls or sex objects," "not clothes horses à la Angie Dickinson," and "realistic crimebusting from the female perspective minus the giggle and jiggle," were common.[42] Other articles commented with impunity on the women's bodies, appraising them with regard to conventional television notions of glamour. "Ms. Daly," one of the articles reads, "has a plain face, a schlumpy figure, a thick Eastern accent. She's not sexy on the outside . . . . Meg Foster is the better looking but far more of a tomboy than a sex symbol."[43] Another reads, "While Foster and Daly are attractive, they look and act ordinary enough to be believable. . . . They are even occasionally permitted to look rumpled, discouraged, crabby."[44] And again:

> Past shows have had one token woman—with the exception of "Charlie's Angels," which featured a team of Wonder Women dressed and coifed from Rodeo Drive rather than DC Comics. Cagney and Lacey, on the other hand, are cops. They look like real people. They are cute rather than beautiful.[45]

For the next full year, such running commentary on the bodies of the two characters was standard in many articles on the series. The practice demonstrates several things. First, the critics perceived a difference between Cagney and Lacey and other television representations of women on the level of the body. This difference, of course, is produced through the televisual technique of *mise en scène* and relates to the characters' hairstyle, makeup, clothing, gestures, and mannerisms.[46] However, the critical commentary evidences a tendency to halt the play of difference with regard to representations of women. By focusing on the bodies of the women represented, the critics reproduced a traditional way of assessing the value of women and thus worked (at least in part and in many instances despite themselves) to *contain* the difference set into play by *Cagney and Lacey.* Women in this commentary become identified with, and to some degree limited to, their bodies. The phenomenon demonstrates how difficult it is for women to escape being "pinned to" their biological difference, or to exceed the conventional equation of women with sex or sex object. It also demonstrates the presumed access to women's bodies and the license to discuss and evaluate them that television, film, and photographic representations have helped to routinize.

Despite the favorable press, and without much consideration for the fact that it was scheduled in competition with *9 to 5*, the network wanted to cancel *Cagney and Lacey* after two episodes.[47] In fact, CBS did not allocate advertising money to promote the series' third episode in *TV Guide* (*9 to 5* had a half-page ad).[48] There is no doubt that the first episodes of *Cagney and Lacey* were a ratings disappointment to the network and were responsible for losing the large lead-in audience attracted by *Magnum P.I.,* the program that immediately preceded it.[49]

The show would have been canceled abruptly had not Rosenzweig persuaded Harvey Shephard, vice president in charge of programming for CBS, to give *Cagney and Lacey* a *Trapper John* rerun spot on Sunday, April 25, at 10:00 PM. Rosenzweig argued that *Cagney and Lacey* was an adult program that required a time slot later than 9:00 PM.[50] Shephard reluctantly agreed, but once again voiced CBS's ambivalence by telling Rosenzweig to "save his money" when Rosenzweig told him that Filmways planned to spend $25,000 on

new publicity.[51] However, Filmways did take the financial risk, sending Foster and Daly on a cross-country tour. In a one-week campaign, organized by the Brocato and Kelman public relations company, Daly and Foster traveled to major urban areas and gave approximately fifty radio, television, and print interviews, including a Washington, D.C., television talk show interview with Tyne Daly and Betty Friedan "on the topic of women's rights."[52]

The Sunday, April 25, episode of *Cagney and Lacey* pulled in an impressive 34 share and ranked 7 in the overall ratings. Despite the success, Harvey Shephard told Rosenzweig that many members of the CBS board (responsible for the final renewal decisions) would consider the 34 share "a fluke."[53] He said he would fight for the series' renewal only if Rosenzweig made a significant change in the program. The change was to replace Meg Foster.[54]

At this point in the history of *Cagney and Lacey,* a number of factors influencing CBS's ambivalence about the program began to emerge. These factors are directly related to notions of femininity generated by the series and seem to be the most salient in CBS's hesitation. In a *Daily Variety* article on May 25, 1982, and a *Hollywood Reporter* article on May 28, Harvey Shephard spoke publicly about Foster's replacement. Shephard was quoted in both articles as saying that "several mistakes were made with the show in that the stories were too gritty, the characterizations of both Cagney and Lacey were too tough and there was not enough contrast between these two partners."[55] Several weeks after the statements appeared, an article in *TV Guide* revealed yet other factors behind CBS's ambivalence and its decision to replace Foster. According to critic Frank Swertlow, *Cagney and Lacey* was to be "softened" because CBS believed the main characters were "too tough, too hard and not feminine." The article quoted an unnamed CBS programmer who said the show was being revised to make the characters "less aggressive." "They were too harshly women's lib," he continued. "These women on 'Cagney and Lacey' seemed more intent on fighting the system than doing police work. We perceived them as dykes."[56]

It would appear that the association of *Cagney and Lacey* with the "masculine woman" and with lesbianism gave CBS a way in which to think about and cast its objections to the unconventional and apparently threatening representations of women on the series. This would explain why CBS rushed to cancel the program and remove Foster. It would also explain why the network gave such importance to the comments it may have picked up in the audience research rather than, for instance, to the positive comments in the press reviews cited earlier.

New and expanded representations of women could not, apparently, include even a hint of lesbianism. This, of course, must be situated within the history of lesbianism's representation on prime time, but space permits only a few comments. During the 1970s quest for "relevance" and socially "hip" subject matter, several programs featured episodes about lesbians, including *All in the Family.* Likewise, into the 1980s, prime-time programs such as *Kate and Allie, Hotel, Hill Street Blues, St. Elsewhere,* and *The Golden Girls* included lesbianism as a single-episode storyline, and the daytime serial *All My Children* had an ongoing lesbian character for several weeks in 1983. By the late 1980s, *Heartbeat* featured an ongoing lesbian character whose inclusion was instrumental in the show's cancellation by ABC after protests from religious groups. The main point to be made here is that each of these "liberal" representations of lesbianism, in one way or other and to varying degrees (*Heartbeat* and *All My Children* trying to downplay this facet), underscore the "social problem" aspect of lesbianism and play off the notion that lesbianism is an "aberration."[57] That viewers would interpret the relationship between Cagney and Lacey as having lesbian overtones, or that two strong women characters would be perceived as "dykey" without the accompanying suggestion that "dykeyness" was considered a deviation from the norm, was something the television industry simply could not permit. Indeed, this stretched the limits of difference regarding the representation of women well beyond the boundaries of television's permissible zone.

CBS's official explanation of Meg Foster's removal from the show was that audience research had discovered objections to the characters. According to Arnold Becker, chief of research for CBS, audience research drawn from a sample of 160 persons had picked up such comments on *Cagney and Lacey* as "inordinately abrasive, loud and lacking warmth" and

"they should be given a measure of traditional female appeal, especially Chris."[58] However, Becker also gave his own (not based on audience research) opinion about the characters: "Even in the first show," he said, "when they [Cagney and Lacey] dressed like hookers, they weren't sexy looking—they were sort of like burlesque." And, "There's a certain amount of resistance to women being in male-oriented jobs. I think it's fair to say, in light of what has happened to ERA, that most people favor equal pay for equal work, but not women as truck drivers or ditch diggers or that sort of male work." He added that the allusion "to homosexuality" in *TV Guide* was "quite unfair." "Those tested," he said, "thought of Cagney and Lacey as masculine, not that they were lovers."[59]

The differential treatment given to the characters and the actresses during this incident demonstrates some of the specific dimensions of the network's anxiety. The *TV Guide* article says the *married* character played by Tyne Daly was being kept because CBS considered her "less threatening." Conversely, CBS thought that the original Chris Cagney's nonglamorous, feminist, sexually active image and her working-class and single status manifested too many "non-feminine" traits. She also had no acceptable class, family, or marriage context that could contain, domesticate, or "make safe" those threatening differences.

The press and viewer response to the changes in the series and the firing of Meg Foster generated significant public discussion and debate over the meanings of "femininity" (and "masculinity"). These definitions touched on many dimensions of *mise en scène:* the characters' clothing, hairstyles, facial mannerisms, and the use of props such as cigarettes. The debates consistently referred to femininity and women's bodies in the social world beyond the domain of the television characters.

Howard Rosenberg of the *Los Angeles Times* began a satiric column on many of the issues raised by the incident, with the questions "What is feminine? What is masculine? What is CBS doing?" He then asked, "Are the old Cagney and Lacey too strident? Even too masculine?" He continued, "For the definitive answer, I contacted Detective Helen Kidder and Detective Peggy York, partners in the Los Angeles Police Department." He quoted Kidder as saying:

I watched the show once and I was so turned off. They looked rough and tough, and they weren't terribly feminine, just in the way they dressed and acted. They were so, you know, New York. ... Peggy and I wear good suits, nylons and pretty shoes, silk blouses, the hair, everything. Not that that keeps you from being a dyke.

Rosenberg concluded with his own analysis of the characters:

Although Cagney is the character to be softened, Lacey seemed to be far the toughest of the two. ... Many of the symbols were conflicting, however. Cagney frequently spoke admiringly of men, which was good, but wore slacks more than Lacey did, which was suspicious. Yet, Cagney had pink bed sheets and longer and curlier hair than Lacey. ... In Lacey's favor, there was a scene in which she sank amorously into bed with Hawvey [sic] and another in which she cooked breakfast for the family. Good signs. Yet she also dangled a cigarette from her mouth like Bogie. Cagney always drove, and Lacey didn't, which could mean something. But Lacey talked without moving her mouth. Lacey convinced me, however, when she took off her skirt in one sequence, she was wearing a slip, not boxer shorts.[60]

Rosenberg's column was one among many that appeared after the removal of Meg Foster, and numerous women reporters vented their outrage. Sharon Rosenthal of the *New York Daily News* wrote, "Not feminine enough? By whose standards? I wondered. Wasn't the whole point of the show to portray women on television in a new, more enlightened manner?"[61] And Barbara Holsopple of the *Pittsburgh Press*, in writing about what the network wanted for *Cagney and Lacey*, said, "Not tough cops, mind you. Nice feminine, good ones. Those yo-yos at the network were second-guessing us again."[62]

As Howard Rosenberg's interview with the Los Angeles policewomen indicates, it is plausible and even predictable that a portion of viewers would find Cagney and Lacey problematic, and some for the specific reasons mentioned by CBS. The viewer reaction in the letters I have seen, however, was critical of

CBS.[63] A sample of *Cagney and Lacey* audience letters in Rosenzweig's files contains such remarks as, "The program *Cagney and Lacey* is being ruined. I have thoroughly enjoyed it: the actresses had good chemistry and I enjoyed seeing a tough female." Another viewer commented:

I read in last week's *TV Guide* something about replacing Meg Foster for such reasons as she is too threatening? I don't understand where TV executives come up with such craziness. I get the feeling there's a card game at the Hillcrest Country Club called "Let's go with the path of least resistance when it comes to women on TV." There seems to be a NEED for all women TV stars to be a carbon copy of Cheryl Ladd. Where's the female Al Pacino? Where's the female Bobby de Niro?

Still another viewer stated, "Foster and Daly did a marvelous job of portraying strong, confident women living through some trying and testing circumstances. Too strong? Too aggressive? Come on! They are cops in the city. They aren't supposed to be fragile, delicate wimps." And a final one from England: "The excuse that Cagney and Lacey are too butch is pathetic. A policewoman in America let alone Britain not butch enough wouldn't last in the public streets."[64]

Two months after the removal of Meg Foster, CBS may have, in the words of one reviewer, "shuddered a little" when a previously unaired Meg Foster/Tyne Daly episode, which was broadcast on June 21, scored a 38 share and ranked number 2 in the overall ratings.[65] However, the network continued to manifest its caution and discomfort regarding potentially controversial representations of women when it pulled the other new Foster/Daly episode scheduled for June 28 from the lineup a few hours before air time. The network said it had received phone calls and letters protesting the episode, which was about a Phyllis Schlafly-type anti-ERA spokesperson whom Cagney and Lacey were assigned to protect.[66] Even though the attempt to move the Equal Rights Amendment into the constitution had already failed, CBS decided to avoid controversy, pull the episode and air it later in August. The network, furthermore, had asked Rosenzweig not to invite Gloria Steinem to appear on the episode as he had originally intended.[67] In the two

TV Guide advertisements for these June episodes, a considerable "feminization" of the images of Daly and Foster is evident—especially when compared to the previous *TV Guide* advertisements for the series.

Bringing Women Back in Line

CBS's ultimate decision on Cagney and Lacey was that the series should be revised to "combine competency with an element of sensuality."[68] Its solution was twofold: to replace Meg Foster with someone more "feminine" (Sharon Gless) and to change Chris Cagney's socio-economic background.[69] The Gay Media Task Force, in light of the allegations that the original characters were "too masculine," protested the replacement, saying that Gless's acting was "very kittenish and feminine."[70]

Instead of being from the working class, Cagney would now have been raised by a wealthy Westchester mother and grandmother. Her father, a retired New York policeman who had already been featured in the series, would be the divorced husband of that mother, and the marriage a cross-class mistake. A new CBS press kit was issued to publicize the series in a different way. "Cagney and Lacey," it read, "are two cops who have earned the respect of their male counterparts and at no expense to their femininity."[71]

Furthermore, after the Meg Foster episodes, Cagney underwent a radical fashion change to accompany her class transformation. A network memo stated that "the new budget will include an additional $15,000 for wardrobe costs, the revised concept for character calls for Cagney to wear less middle-class, classier clothes so that her upward mobility is evidenced."[72] This revision must also be seen in relation to the history of television's skewed representations of class and to the advertising industry's decision, at this time, to target the upscale professional segment of the working women's market.[73]

The new Chris Cagney was more of a rugged individualist than a feminist and was actually conservative on many social issues. Lacey espoused most of the feminism and liberal politics. A CBS promo for the 1982–1983 season made these new differences between the characters explicit and also foregrounded Cagney's heterosexuality. The promo ran like this:

MARY BETH: Ya know Chris, there've been some great women in the 20th century.

CHRIS: Yeah! And some great men (dreamily).

MARY BETH: Susan B. Anthony!

CHRIS: Jim Palmer!

MARY BETH: Madame Curie. . .

CHRIS: Joe Montana . . . ooo can he make a pass!

MARY BETH: (lightly annoyed with Chris) Amelia Airhart! [*sic*]

CHRIS: The New York Yankees!

MARY BETH: Chris, can't you think about anything else than men?[74]

Struggling over Femininity: The Press and the Viewers

The new and revised *Cagney and Lacey* with Sharon Gless and Tyne Daly began in the fall of 1982 and generated a good deal of attention and enthusiasm in the press. This revised program makes the most sense when seen in the context of the overall changes in the new television programs directed toward working women and drawing on feminism, and in the context of a backlash against the women's movements. During this same period, the program *9 to 5*, with Jane Fonda as executive co-producer, endured revisions that led to an episode in which the once-politicized secretaries spent much of the program dressed in negligées. *Remington Steele*, about a woman running her own detective agency, underwent changes in which the lead female character became considerably less aggressive and much more traditionally feminine in her relationship with the male character.[75]

The mainstream, press, in commenting on the first season of the Gless/Daly *Cagney and Lacey*, focused on the "changes" from the previous run. Many wrote of the general "softening" and "feminization" of the program. For example, one critic noticed that "the entire show this season appears less gritty than last year's style," while another remarked, "some of the rougher, tougher edges are gone."[76]

A large number of articles appeared in response to Gless's replacement of Foster and the feminization of the program. They read like a semiotic register of the word "feminine," and function (not always intentionally) to problematize its various meanings. Many singled out specific elements such as clothing, hairstyles, makeup, voice qualities, body movements, personality traits, and behaviors as evidence for the presence or absence of "femininity," while some also wrote of the unconventional, potentially problematic character of Gless's and Cagney's "femininity." Carol Wyman of the *New Haven Register* said of Gless/Cagney, "She's one of those people who is very pretty, and at the same time a jock, the kind of person who ruins her good stockings to chase a crook, talks loud when she gets drunk and gets impatient with a woman witness who cries too much."[77]

Some articles that commented on the "feminization" also wrote of the changes in the relationship between the characters and the innuendos of lesbianism:

> Miss Daly's tomboy quality was balanced by the introduction of a partner with more feminine characteristics than her original co-star. . . . This second-season rematch [is] perhaps more compatible with the network's definition of a conventional female relationship. . . [but] who cares if a cop is gay or not as long as he or she shoots straight.[78]

Judging from audience letters, viewers were at first reluctant to accept Gless, but within two months a large and avid following began to develop. An exemplary letter from a woman who had been angered by Meg Foster's removal reads:

> I thought Meg Foster and Tyne Daly were a great combination, but apparently some "genius" of the male persuasion, obviously, decided that Meg Foster wasn't "feminine" enough. My Gawd, should cops wear aprons and be pregnant? Gimme a break! However, *Lady* Luck was with you when you found Sharon Gless. I must admit that you did something right by putting her in the Cagney role. . . . She's extremely feminine with just the right amount of "butch" to strike a very appealing balance.[79]

An irony in the history of the series, and a strong testament to the operation of multiple and contradictory viewer interpretations, is that Sharon Gless (according to published articles and viewer letters) had a large lesbian following at the time of the series' first run and now in reruns.[80] And this audience interpreted the Cagney character according to a variety of unpredictable and unconventional viewing strategies. When seen in relation to the viewer response letters surrounding the removal of Meg Foster and the press comments on the appeal of the friendship between Cagney and Lacey, this development demonstrates the ways in which the television industry's investments in particular notions of "femininity" and at least certain viewer investments can be at odds. The potential homoerotic overtones in the representation of the two women that formed the basis for the network's discomfort were, in fact, the bases of certain viewers' pleasure. There was, of course, a continuum of response ranging from viewers who responded pleasurably to the fictional representation of a close friendship between Cagney and Lacey to those whose viewing strategies purposely highlighted the homoerotic overtones in the relationship.

After the initial run of articles on the "feminization" of the characters and the series, a wide array of feminist-oriented pieces highlighting the importance of *Cagney and Lacey* to women appeared in mainstream newspapers. The series was hailed as "pioneering the serious role of women on TV" and "helping to break new TV ground."[81] Many of these articles emphasized the notion that Cagney and Lacey, unlike previous television characters, portrayed "real women." Despite this critical acclaim the first season of the Gless/Daly *Cagney and Lacey* did not do well in the overall ratings and did only marginally well with a women-only target audience. Its competition during much of the season was female-oriented prime-time movies. Consequently, CBS put *Cagney and Lacey* on its cancellation list. In an effort to save the series, Barney Rosenzweig coordinated a large letter-writing campaign in which CBS and major newspapers throughout the country were deluged with thousands of viewer letters protesting the impending cancellation.[82] The Los Angeles chapter of the National Organization for Women and National NOW publicized the campaign and urged their members to write. According to state delegate Jerilyn Stapleton, the Los Angeles chapter had only two goals for the period: to get Ronald Reagan out of office and to keep *Cagney and Lacey* on the prime-time schedule.[83]

Virtually all the letters mentioned the uniqueness of *Cagney and Lacey*'s representation of women and the relationship between the two characters. The writers repeatedly suggested that Cagney and Lacey were good "role models" for women and girls; that they were unique because they were "real" and "different from all previous TV portrayals of women"; and that they were extremely important to the culture, to the individual writers, and to the writers' friends and families. Almost all related *Cagney and Lacey's* depictions of women to their own everyday lives, the writers often placing themselves in a particular social situation and at a specific point on the "feminism spectrum." Phrases such as, "I'm a thirty-three year old nursing administrator," a "single working mother," a "married woman and mother who works inside the home," "a feminist" or "not a women's libber—just a concerned woman" appeared often. Many of the letters reverberated with discourses stemming from the liberal women's movement and demonstrated the workings of an "interpretive community" or a "community of heightened consciousness" described in the work of such feminist scholars as Elizabeth Ellsworth and Jacqueline Bobo.[84] They also displayed many specific ways in which the women letter writers were reconfiguring and redefining their notions of what it means to be a woman.

Repeatedly, writers said such things as "It's good to see smart, functioning, strong women"; "It's a pleasure to see women in such active roles"; "It's one of the few programs that neither glamorizes nor degrades women"; and "At last women are being portrayed as three-dimensional human beings." There were numerous long letters describing the particular significance of the series to the writer. One viewer wrote:

My office alone contains six technical editors, RABID fans of "Cagney and Lacey." We're all highly paid, well-educated women in our forties with very different life-styles. Since we are "specialists" and work very closely with each other, each of us regards the others as "extended family," and we nurture and support each other in the best ways possible. We enjoy "Cagney and Lacey" because it contains so many moments that ring familiar in a woman's daily life. We see ourselves in it so often, even though OUR jobs are unbelievably unexciting. It's gotten so that Tuesday mornings are spent hashing over Monday night's episode. We're really addicted.

Another said:

It's such an exciting show from a woman's point of view. Watching those two women makes one realize how much more attractive we are as women when we dare to be all our possible dimensions rather than the stereotypical images we have been taught to be and continually see on the screen. You have affected some of us profoundly.

The relationship between the two actresses and characters and its effect on the viewers were written about with equal enthusiasm. The actresses, Tyne Daly and Sharon Gless, were described as a "superb combination," a "winning team," who "together have great charisma" and "natural and genuine chemistry." "The vivid interaction of Chris and Mary Beth," wrote one viewer, "has actually made honest female relationships into major dramatic entertainment." Another claimed, "In the final analysis, it was the friendship between the two lead characters wherein lay the show's strongest appeal for me."

Despite the volume of viewer mail, and despite the fact that it primarily came from the desired target audience (upscale working women between the ages of 18 and 54), the series was canceled in the spring of 1983. However, several factors combined to cause CBS to reverse its decision and bring it back on the air. First, people continued to send letters. Second, after cancellation, *Cagney and Lacey* received four Emmy nominations, and Tyne Daly won an Emmy for best dramatic actress. Third, *Cagney and Lacey* scored number one in the ratings for the first week of summer reruns and remained in the top ten throughout the period. Nonetheless, CBS hedged its bets by reinstating the series with a very limited seven-episode trial run.

The Struggle Continues: The Production Team, the Network, and Interest Groups

The period of *Cagney and Lacey's* history that begins with the reinstated Gless/Daly series in the spring of 1984 reveals several industry trends occurring at the time. With regard to television's portrayal of feminism, the period was characterized by "mainstreaming." Hence, the radical edge of feminist issues was tempered and channeled into character traits and behaviors. In addition, the meaning of feminism itself was becoming increasingly ambiguous so that programs offered "something for everyone" to fulfill many different viewers' political positions and interpretations. Terry Louise Fisher, a producer/writer for *Cagney and Lacey*, described this as a move from political issues to "entertainment value."[85] During this period, some of the key players on *Cagney and Lacey*'s production team, particularly Barney Rosenzweig, began to think more in industry terms and less in women's movement terms when it came to portraying the characters. This resulted in disputes among the production team members over the representations of Cagney's and Lacey's hairstyles, makeup, and clothing. Determined to get the series renewed beyond the limited seven episodes, Rosenzweig called for a general upgrading of the style and "looks" of the two characters.[86] He wanted a renovation of the Cagney "look" to include more "stylish," "glamorous" outfits, and a new hairstyle that would "move" and "bounce."

For several months, Rosenzweig had wanted to change Lacey's wardrobe and hairstyle. Tyne Daly, who had designed the Mary Beth Lacey "look" by shopping with wardrobe designer Judy Sabel in the sale and basement sections of New York department stores, continually refused to change the character's plain, eccentric style.[87] Battles over Lacey's hair were also frequent occurrences on the set. Rosenzweig would ask Daly's hairdresser to get to her between takes and tease and spray her hair.[88] During one such incident, Daly shouted to the crew and staff, "Can anyone tell me why my producer wants me to look like Pat Nixon?"[89]

During this period, there were also negotiations and struggles over the representation of female characters at the level of script development. An episode involving Cagney's pregnancy scare (the last of the seven trial episodes in May 1984) is a powerful example. The negotiations revolved around how to represent a single woman, an unmarried woman's pregnancy, the topic of working women and childbearing, and the issues of contraception and abortion. A synopsis from my personal observation and notes gathered during producer-writer meetings in February and March of 1984 reveals some of the actual processes involved.

Conceived by Terry Louise Fisher, the story originally dealt with Cagney's discovery that she was pregnant. Fisher had struggled with how to resolve the pregnancy. Knowing that the network would never allow abortion as a possibility for Cagney, Fisher self-censored the consideration and was less than satisfied in resorting to the hackneyed miscarriage route. After working on the script, however, she felt it opened up interesting possibilities. Tony Barr, an executive at CBS, rejected the script, saying that the network did not "want to shine the spotlight on pregnancy" and the problems of a pregnant unmarried woman. Barney Rosenzweig, Barbara Corday (creative consultant for the series), Terry Louise Fisher (writer-producer), P. K. Knelman (co-producer), and Peter Lefcourt (writer-producer) discussed various options at a meeting. CBS had suggested that they turn the episode into a "biological clock" story in which Cagney is faced with the decision of whether or not she will ever have children. Fisher felt that the biological clock angle was not dramatically sound because it would offer no "resolution" or "closure." She asked Rosenzweig if he would fight for the original story with the network. But Corday wondered if they wanted to fight for it at this point, thinking it would be better to hold off and do it next season (if CBS were to renew the series) in, for instance, the fifth show so they could build up to Cagney being seriously involved with one person. Since the subplot of the script involved the officers at the precinct preparing for the sergeant's exam, and since attaining the rank of sergeant was one of Cagney's immediate ambitions, Lefcourt suggested that the issue revolve around a "my job or having a baby kind of choice." Fisher said she refused to do that to working women: "It sounds too much like waiting for Prince Charming" to come. Lefcourt agreed, "You're right, the Cinderella story."

Finally, Rosenzweig suggested they leave the first act exactly as it was—Cagney *thinks* she's pregnant. In actuality, however, she is not. Since the network had seemed so adamant about not focusing at all on pregnancy, Rosenzweig immediately called Tony Barr with his compromise option. Barr agreed that Cagney could *think* she was pregnant, but only on the condition that Lacey accuse her of being totally irresponsible. A long discussion on how they would cast Cagney's irresponsibility then followed. Someone wondered,

"Should we say it was a night of passion?" Another suggested, "Cagney could say something like, 'I know it was my fault, I was acting like a teenager;' or 'Well, it happens, I mean the diaphragm is not foolproof.' " Rosenzweig objected that "as the father of four daughters, I don't want to put down the diaphragm." The other four agreed that it was the only "safe method for women's bodies," and they did not want to represent Cagney as "being on the pill."

In the final episode entitled "Biological Clock," Cagney thinks she is pregnant but is not, and Lacey is only mildly accusatory. There is no mention of specific birth control technologies or how the "mistake" might have happened. There is no mention of what Cagney would do if she were pregnant, although Lacey strongly pushes marriage. Cagney seems to be developing a relationship with the alleged baby, and abortion is never mentioned.

During this period, the producers and writers also talked about where, in general, to go with the Cagney character.[90] The discussions revolved around making Cagney a more "sympathetic" character. They decided they would do this by making her more "committed" as a character, and this would be done by having her become seriously involved with one man. According to Terry Louise Fisher and Barbara Avedon the word "sympathetic" is industry jargon directed almost exclusively toward female characters and used to describe female roles that evoke "feminine" behavior and situations.[91] But the decision to make Cagney sympathetic by having her in a committed relationship with her boyfriend, Dory, was unpopular with viewers. One of the reporters on *60 Minutes* during the "letters-from-viewers" segment read a viewer letter that called for the removal of Dory from the *Cagney and Lacey* series.

During the 1984–1985 season, the Cagney character was once again associated with some conventionally feminist actions. In the episode in which she brings an end to her relationship with Dory, she overtly rejects (in a long conversation with Lacey) the institution of marriage. In other episodes, she files sexual harassment charges against a captain in the police department, urges Lacey to get a second opinion on a mastectomy, and consequently introduces the option of a lumpectomy. The season concludes with Cagney being the only one in her precinct to make the rank

of sergeant, thereby emphasizing the importance of her career and her goal to become the first woman chief of detectives. With critical and industry acclaim, a more secure place in the ratings (at least with the target female audience) and the requisite changes in class and glamour, the network, it appears, became less skittish about the less conventional representations of women.

A number of episodes between 1984 and 1988, particularly those dealing with wife-beating, abortion, breast cancer, sexual harassment, date rape, and alcoholism, treated issues of enormous social importance to women and raised questions about the use of "exploitation topics" in programs for and about women.[92] These episodes both "cashed in on" and became part of intense public debates involving the institutional and social control over women's bodies and what women generally should and should not be. They also brought several social interest groups and institutions into the overall discursive struggle over defining what it meant to be a woman.

An episode about abortion, for example, broadcast November 11, 1985, became a central part of the ongoing public battles over the issue. Anti-abortion groups, led by the National Right to Life Committee (a group heavily invested in traditional definitions of women and their bodies), appealed to CBS to pull the episode, which centered on the bombing of an abortion clinic and the support by Cagney and Lacey (after considerable debate) of a woman's choice to have an abortion. The NRLC called the program a "piece of pure political propaganda."[93] After CBS said that they found the program to be "a fair and well-balanced view" and refused to pull it from the schedule, the NRLC asked CBS affiliates to black it out. If the affiliate did not want to black it out, NRLC asked it to offer to show a half-hour film of NRLC's choice (such as the anti-abortion film *Matter of Choice*) or to make available to NRLC a half-hour to "put some of our folks on to rebut this." If none of this worked, NRLC's next plan was to "call for a nationwide blackout of CBS during the balance of the month of November which is their rating month."[94]

Tyne Daly and Barney Rosenzweig flew to Washington, D.C., for a luncheon co-sponsored by the National Abortion Rights Action League and Orion Television to "counter [the] opposition" to the episode.[95] Daly said, "We feel we've done something very balanced. . . . I don't think I know a woman who hasn't struggled or knows someone who hasn't struggled with this issue."[96] Planned Parenthood also organized a press conference in New York on the episode, and NRLC President John Wilke and Barney Rosenzweig debated the issue on the *MacNeil/Lehrer News Hour.* To Wilke's charges that "this program is the most unbalanced, most unfair program we've seen in a number of years. . . . We did not hear a single right-to-life answer properly given," Rosenzweig replied:

> A year ago we had an episode in which Christine Cagney believed she was pregnant, and never once considered abortion as an alternative. I didn't hear from the National Organization for Women or the Voters for Choice then about banning the show or boycotting us. I just got some rather nice letters from the pro-life people.[97]

One CBS affiliate "pulled the show," while WOWT-TV in Omaha, Nebraska, agreed to offer equal time to NRLC.[98] After the broadcast, the political struggle continued: an anti-abortion spokesperson suggested that "any further violence at abortion clinics would be on CBS's conscience."[99] In an article in the *Washington Post*, Judy Mann praised the actions of CBS and the episode, and she said of television that "no other medium is as capable of dramatizing and educating the public about some of life's most difficult experiences."[100]

Closing Thoughts

Many more things, of course, can be said about women, television, and *Cagney and Lacey.* But the case I have outlined does raise some general points. First, as is obvious by now, television is a social institution and discursive practice which must be studied in all its complexity. On the one hand, it is, as Teresa de Lauretis (following Foucault) might say, a "technology of gender"—an apparatus that contributes to the social and cultural construction of femininity and masculinity that defines the possibilities of what it means to be a woman or a man.[101] On the other hand, as with any mass medium, it attracts diverse audiences who can interpret its texts in many different ways. As we

have seen in *Cagney and Lacey*, different players in the overall television enterprise generate, and compete for, their own definitions of femininity according to their own investments and imaginations.

One of the most vexing issues for popular culture scholars at the present time involves the relationship of polysemy (or the multiplicity of meaning) to the limitations on meaning in texts produced by mainstream culture industries. From my point of view, television should be seen as a negotiation among the industry, the texts, and audience members.[102] But it is similarly apparent to me that we must acknowledge and analyze more thoroughly the many ways the television industry works to pin down meaning in particular and often predictable ways. This involves, among other things, attending to the ways in which the industry continues to depict women on the basis of its own institutional and advertising-based exigencies. Just as the 1970s quest for young, urban audiences led to a spate of "socially relevant" television programs and to the increased representation of black women, working-class women, and single mothers, the quest for the working women's market in the late 1970s and 1980s led to women-oriented programs and feminist subject matter in prime time. But as we have seen, when these representations deviated too much from the acceptable conventions of the industry, they were quickly brought back in line. Given the outpouring of letters about *Cagney and Lacey* from women viewers who were desperate for new representations, and the fact that *Cagney and Lacey* attracted so many working women to the prime-time screen, we might have expected the networks to be more adventurous in future programs, more eager to please female audiences. Although they have featured some female leads in dramatic programs since the mid-1980s (*Kay O'Brien, The Days and Nights of Molly Dodd, China Beach, Heartbeat, Nightingales*, and *The Trials of Rosie O'Neill*), many of which met with cancellation or controversy, the networks continued to channel women, and especially "transgressive" women (such as Roseanne and Murphy Brown) into situation comedies.

The case of *Cagney and Lacey* ultimately illuminates, I think, two major facets of a complex phenomenon: the specific ways television texts tend to "shut down" and limit the meanings of "woman," and the ways in which large numbers of viewers, voracious for innovative representations, continued throughout the history of the series and its changes to read the text for meanings that echoed and shored up their conceptions of themselves as "non-traditional" women. The fact, moreover, that many lesbian viewers continued to find homoerotic overtones in the program and continued to generate pleasure from active "misreadings" confirms that textual limits do not shut down audience interpretations. But, from my point of view, the production of oppositional or alternative readings is not, finally, enough. I am confident that those of us who spend time in front of television sets will always interpret programming in creative ways, always produce meanings that escape the confines of the text. I hope, however, we will also continue to analyze television texts and industry practices for the ways they contribute to constraining the representations of gender, sexuality, race, class, and ethnicity. And finally, I hope we continue to agitate for a greater representation of *difference* in all the mass media.

This seems particularly necessary in the current cultural retrenchment from feminism now manifest on our television screens. ABC, for example, canceled *Heartbeat* after religious watchdog groups protested its lesbian characters; and NBC, besieged by the same groups in early 1991, assured advertisers and the public that it had no intention of continuing a storyline on *L.A. Law* involving a possible love relationship between two women characters. Later in 1991, however, CBS (fearing it was losing viewers to less conservative cable channels) announced it would continue stories about its bisexual female character; and for the same reason, the Network Television Association (a trade group representing ABC, CBS, and NBC) urged marketers not to be "intimidated" by boycott organizations.[103] Faced with these developments, I see it as strategic to generate ways of intervening in the popular struggle over meanings. Although agitating for changes in television does not necessarily change the world, the alternative course of resignation leaves the outlook even more bleak. At the very least, it is important not to concede television and its representations to the discourses and energies of the New Right.

Notes

1. For articles on the "ladies' night line-up" see Ella Taylor, "Ladies' Night: CBS's Monday Night Mystique," *Village Voice* (December 3, 1985), pp. 55–56; and Pat Dowell, "Ladies' Night," *American Film* (January–February 1985), pp. 44–49.

2. A quality audience is an audience made up of the exact demographic characteristics desired by the network for the particular time slot the program occupies. Upscale, working women between the ages of 23 and 54 were the desired demographics for Monday night prime time on CBS. For a discussion of quality audiences and "quality" programs see Jane Feuer, Paul Kerr, and Tise Vahimagi, eds., *MTM: "Quality Television"* (London: BFI, 1984).

3. Quoted in Karen Stabiner, "The Pregnant Detective," *New York Times Magazine* (September 22, 1985), p. 103. *Cagney and Lacey*, as audience letters and rating information demonstrate, also drew in many working women from a lower range on the economic spectrum.

4. At the conclusion of the *Cagney and Lacey* made-for-TV movie, Swit's Cagney appears as a "woman in distress" and is rescued by the squad (most of whom, with the exception of Lacey, are men). The representation of the protagonists as classic "women in distress," however, is absent from the Foster/Daly series. The Gless/Daly series does have a few sequences that feature "women in distress" figures. Lacey, for instance, is rescued from a high beam by Harvey, and Lacey is taken hostage. Mimi White, "Ideological Analysis and Television," *Channels of Discourse*, ed. Robert Allen (Chapel Hill: University of North Carolina Press·, 1987), pp. 154–158 cites two instances in which Cagney is shown as "trapped" or "caged" by the framing and the *mise en scène*. White finds this problematic for the series' representation of women. By and large, however, the characters are not, I would maintain, regularly produced as the classic "women in distress" or in need of help from male colleagues.

5. These are the two terms used most often by the television networks to describe what they want in women characters. From Terry Louise Fisher and Barbara Avedon, personal interviews, February 1984, Los Angeles.

6. Michael Leahy and Wallis Annenberg, "Discrimination in Hollywood: How Bad Is It?" *TV Guide* (October 13–19, 1984), p. 14. According to Leahy and Annenberg, Orion TV hired women to write 37% of its projects.

7. The liberal women's movement had such an enormous effect on *Cagney and Lacey*'s production and reception that I want to clarify my conception of it here. In America, the movement is generally associated with *Ms.* magazine, with Gloria Steinem and with the National Organization for Women. Its primary emphasis, especially in the 1970s and early 1980s,

was on equality in the labor force, with a focus on white middle-class women, and its programs for social change were oriented toward reform rather than radical structural reorganization of American social and cultural life. Nonetheless, the movement was vigilant in keeping public attention on the material conditions of women's everyday lives, on women's solidarity, and on the importance of mass media to social change.

8. Jane Feuer, in "MTM Enterprises: An Overview," Feuer et al., pp. 1–28. Todd Gitlin, *Inside Prime Time* (New York: Pantheon, 1983), p. 266.

9. Serafina Bathrick, "*The Mary Tyler Moore Show*: Women at Home and at Work," in Feuer et al., pp. 99–131. Lauren Rabinovitz, "Sitcoms and Single Moms: Representations of Feminism on American TV," *Cinema Journal* 29:1 (Fall 1989), pp. 3–19.

10. Cited in Todd Gitlin, p. 72.

11. Barbara Corday, personal interview, February 1984, Los Angeles; Barney Rosenzweig, personal interview, October 1983, Los Angeles.

12. Barney Rosenzweig, personal interview.

13. Barbara Corday, personal interview; Barney Rosenzweig, personal interview.

14. Marjorie Rosen, "Cagney and Lacey," *Ms.* 4 (October 1981), pp. 47–50, 109.

15. Rosen, p. 49; Barbara Corday, "Dialogue on Film," *American Film* 9 (July–August 1985), p. 12.

16. Barbara Avedon, personal interview.

17. Avedon quoted in Rosen, p. 49.

18. Barbara Corday, personal interview; Barbara Avedon, personal interview.

19. Barney Rosenzweig, personal interview; Rosen, p. 49.

20. Rosen, p. 49.

21. Rosen, p. 49.

22. Rosen, p. 49.

23. Rosen, p. 50.

24. Barney Rosenzweig, personal interview.

25. Rosen, p. 50.

26. Barney Rosenzweig, personal interview, October 1983.

27. Barbara Avedon, personal interview; Barbara Corday, personal interview.

28. Barbara Avedon, personal interview.

29. Sharon Rosenthal, "Cancellation of 'Cagney and Lacey' to Mean Loss of 'Rare' TV Series," *New York Daily News* (June 3, 1983), pp. 31, 35.

30. Barney Rosenzweig, personal interview; *Ms.* 4 (October 1981), cover.

31. Some of these characteristics demonstrate the ways in which advertising definitions of women and the liberal women's movement definitions (particularly at this point in the history of the American women's movement) may be brought together without much trouble. Later in the 1980s, the liberal women's movement was more attentive to issues involving women of color, poor and working-class women, and lesbians, and it also recognized structural reasons for women's oppression which require more than personal solutions. In the early 1980s, however, the emphasis of the movement was most squarely on equality in the labor force, primarily for white, middle-class women.

32. *TV Guide* (October 3–10, 1981), p. A-137.

33. Richard Turner, "The Curious Case of the Lady Cops and the Shots That Blew Them Away," *TV Guide* 41 (October 8–14, 1983), p. 52.

34. Turner, p. 52.

35. *Soho News* (March 9, 1982), page unknown, from clipping file of Barney Rosenzweig, Los Angeles.

36. *Soho News* (March 9, 1982), page unknown, from clipping file of Barney Rosenzweig, Los Angeles.

37. Filmways News Release, "Meg Foster to Join Tyne Daly as CBS 'Cagney and Lacey' Duo," (1982), Barney Rosenzweig files.

38. Six months later, in the fall of 1982, three other working-women-oriented and women's movement-influenced programs, *Gloria, Remington Steele*, and *It Takes Two*, also joined the schedule.

39. Tom Bierbaum, "Steinem Takes Right Turn on TV Violence," *Daily Variety* (February 2, 1982), p. 25.

40. See, for example, Bowden's Information Service, "Tyne Daly Returns to Detective Role," *The Leader Post* (March 12, 1982), page unknown, from clipping file of Barney Rosenzweig.

41. Barbara Holsopple, "Two New Series on Women: All Work, No Play," *Pittsburgh Press* (March 25, 1982), page unknown, from clipping file of Barney Rosenzweig, Los Angeles.

42. Beverly Stephen, "Policewomen: TV Show on the Case," *Los Angeles Times* (April 11, 1982), page unknown, from clipping file of Barney Rosenzweig, Los Angeles; Bonnie Malleck, "Real Women at Last: Pinch-Hitter 'Cagney and Lacey' Is a Mid-Season Bonus," *Kitchner-Waterloo Record* (April 1982), page unknown, from clipping file of Barney Rosenzweig.

43. Ed Bark, "Ratings May Kill Quality Cop Show," *Dallas Texas Morning News* (April 1, 1982), page unknown, from clipping file of Barney Rosenzweig, Los Angeles.

44. Malleck, page unknown.

45. Bill Musselwhite, "No There's No Farm Raising Tiny Animals for Airlines," *Calgary Herald* (April 3, 1982), page unknown, from clipping file of Barney Rosenzweig, Los Angeles.

46. The technique of *mise en scène* includes, among other things, characters' body size, makeup, hairstyle, clothing or costume; character movement, gestures, mannerisms, and use of props. See David Bordwell

and Kristin Thompson, *Film Art* (New York: Alfred A. Knopf, 1985), pp. 119–150.

47. Turner, p. 53; Barney Rosenzweig, personal interview.

48. *TV Guide* (April 3–10, 1982), pp. A-116–117.

49. *Magnum PI* was getting an average share of 38. When *Cagney and Lacey* aired it pulled in a 25 share the first week and 24 the second week. According to Rosenzweig, "At 9 o'clock all over America, 12 million people were getting up out of their seats *en masse* and walking away, or leaving the network." Cited in Turner, p. 53.

50. Turner, p. 53.

51. Turner, p. 53.

52. Brocato and Kelman, Inc., Public Relations, "Itinerary for Tyne Daly and Meg Foster" (April 27, 1982), Barney Rosenzweig files.

53. Turner, p. 54.

54. Turner, p. 54; Barney Rosenzweig, personal interview. After Meg Foster was released from her contract she had initial difficulty getting other work. According to a United Feature syndicate article (Dick Kleiner, "TV Scout Sketch 1: Cagney and Lacey Situation, The Story Behind Meg's Ouster," week of August 23, 1982), prior to that she "was an in-demand actress. But there was no official announcement of why she was fired, so people jumped to some pretty wild conclusions. . . . They want no part of a troublemaker." The article continues, "Later an official story came out and from then on Meg's offers picked up again." Rosenzweig says he tried to save Foster's job by suggesting to CBS that they dye her hair blonde (as a way of achieving character contrast with the brunette Daly). He admits, however, to giving in to the network rather quickly and making Foster the "scapegoat" in order to save the series. Barney Rosenzweig, personal interview, 1983, Los Angeles. As of this writing, Foster appears as a district attorney on *The Trials of Rosie O'Neil*, starring Sharon Gless and produced by Barney Rosenzweig.

55. Richard Hack, "TeleVisions," *The Hollywood Reporter* (May 28, 1982), p. 6; Dave Kaufman, "CBS Ent Prez Grant Asks Crix for Fair Chance," *Daily Variety* (May 25, 1982), p. 19.

56. Frank Swertlow, "CBS Alters 'Cagney' Calling it 'Too Women's Lib,'" *TV Guide* (June 12–18, 1982), p. A-l.

57. My point here is that even though the programs were presenting "positive" representations of lesbians, they highlighted the fact that lesbianism is considered socially "deviant" as the organizing principle of the story–the point of the humor or drama.

58. Howard Rosenberg, "'Cagney and (Uh) Lacey,' a Question of a Pink Slip," *Los Angeles Times* (June 23, 1982), Calendar Section, p. 7.

59. Rosenberg, p. 7. It is possible, of course, that the research survey also inadvertently elicited particular responses from the viewers tested.

60. Rosenberg, pp. 1, 7.

61. Rosenthal, pp. 31, 35.

62. Barbara Holsopple, "'Cagney and Lacey' Hanging by (Blond) Thread," *Pittsburgh Press* (November 19, 1982), p. B-38.

63. *TV Guide* printed a series of angry responses in its subsequent issue. *TV Guide* (June 10–16, 1982), p. A-4.

64. Viewer letters, 1982, Rosenzweig files.

65. Frank Torrez, "TV Ratings," *Los Angeles Herald Examiner* (July 2, 1983).

66. Sal Manna, "Sorry This Show Wasn't Seen," *Los Angeles Herald Examiner*, 1982, pp. B-l and B-7, exact date unknown, from clipping file of Barney Rosenzweig, Los Angeles.

67. Manna, pp. B-l and B-7. Steinem, due to an overcrowded schedule, had actually already declined.

68. Arnold Becker quoted in Rosenberg, p. 7.

69. John J. O'Connor, in speaking of the "new" Cagney, described Gless as "blond, single, [and] gorgeous in the imposing manner of Linda Evans on *Dynasty*." See his "'Cagney and Lacey'—Indisputably a Class Act," *The New York Times* New Service to *The Patriot Ledger* (July 5, 1984), p. 42.

70. Tim Brooks and Earle Marsh, *The Complete Directory to Prime Time Network TV Shows: 1946–The Present* (New York: Ballantine Books, 1985), p. 136.

71. Rick Du Brow, "Cagney and Lacey Hang Tough," *Los Angeles Herald Examiner* (January 25, 1983), pp. C-l, C-4.

72. *Cagney and Lacey* offices, "Analysis of Costs for CBS for 'Cagney and Lacey,'" 1982, Rosenzweig files.

73. Since the mid-1950s advertisers made it clear that they did not want their products associated with lower-class characters and settings. See Eric Barnouw, *The Image Empire* (New York: Oxford University Press, 1970), pp. 5–8.

74. CBS Entertainment, Advertising and Promotion, "Program Promotion," 1982, Rosenzweig files.

75. Elaine Warren, "Where Are the Real Women on TV?" *Los Angeles Herald Examiner* (October 31, 1983), Section E, pp. 1, 10.

76. "Review," *Daily Variety* (October 28, 1982), p. 9.

77. Carol Wyman, "'Cagney and Lacey' Has Grown," *New Haven Register* (February 24, 1983), page unknown, from clipping file of Barney Rosenzweig, Los Angeles.

78. Terrence O'Flaherty, "Women in the Line of Fire," *San Francisco Chronicle* (October 11, 1983), p. B-9.

79. Viewer letters from Barney Rosenzweig files, Los Angeles.

80. Barbara Grizzuti Harrison, "I Didn't Think I Was Pretty:

An Interview with Sharon Gless," *Parade Magazine* (February 23, 1986), pp. 4–5.

81. Caption for cover photo of Tyne Daly and Sharon Gless, *Los Angeles Herald Examiner* (January 25, 1983).

82. I am quoting from a sample of 500 letters from this period which I arbitrarily pulled and duplicated from Barney Rosenzweig's files. The letters are written to Bud Grant (president of CBS entertainment), Barney Rosenzweig, Tyne Daly, Sharon Gless, and Orion Television. Since each letter was written to save the series from the network's ax, the sample is thoroughly biased in favor of the series and its representations. No critical letters or letters of complaint are present.

83. Jerilyn Stapleton, personal interview, February 1984, Los Angeles.

84. Elizabeth Ellsworth, "Illicit Pleasures: Feminist Spectators and *Personal Best*," in *Becoming Feminine*, ed. Leslie G. Roman, Linda K. Christian-Smith, and Elizabeth Ellsworth (Philadelphia: The Farmer Press, 1988), pp. 102–119. Jacqueline Bobo, "*The Color Purple*: Black Women as Cultural Readers," in *Female Spectators*, ed. E. Deidre Pribram (London and New York: Verso, 1988), pp. 90–108. This work draws on that of Stanley Fish, David Morley, and Charlotte Brunsdon.

85. Terry Louise Fisher, personal interview, February 1984, Los Angeles.

86. Barney Rosenzweig, personal interview, January 1984, Los Angeles.

87. Judy Sabel, personal interview, February 1984, Los Angeles.

88. Personal observation on the set of *Cagney and Lacey* and conversation with Eddie Barron, hairdresser for Tyne Daly, February 1984, Los Angeles.

89. Personal observation on the set of *Cagney and Lacey*, February 1984.

90. Personal notes, writer-producer meetings, January–March, 1984, Los Angeles.

91. Terry Louise Fisher, personal interview, January 1984, Los Angeles. Barbara Avedon, personal interview.

92. Exploitation topics use sensational, usually sexual or violent subject material in order to attract an audience.

93. "An Episode of 'Cagney' Under Fire on Abortion," *The New York Times* (November 11, 1985), page unknown, from files of Barney Rosenzweig, Los Angeles.

94. CBS vice president George Schweitzer, cited in Nancy Hellmich, "Daly Defends 'Cagney' Show on Abortion," *USA Today* (November 6, 1985), Section D, p. 1; John Wilke cited on *MacNeil/Lehrer News Hour*, PBS (November 8, 1985).

95. Hellmich, p. 1.

96. Hellmich, p. 1.

97. *MacNeil/Lehrer News Hour* (November 8, 1985).

98. Judy Mann, "Cagney and Lacey, and Abortion," *Washington Post* (November 15, 1985), page unknown, from files of Barney Rosenzweig, Los Angeles; Hellmich, p. 1.

99. Mann.

100. Mann.

101. Teresa de Lauretis, *Technologies of Gender* (Bloomington: Indiana University Press, 1987), pp. 1–30.

102. For more on industry (institution), text, and reception, see Christine Gledhill, "Pleasurable Negotiations," *Female Spectators: Looking at Film and Television* (London and New York: Verso, 1988), pp. 64–77.

103. See Kate Oberlander, "Network Group Hits Boycotts," *Electronic Media*, August 5, 1991, p. 4; and "TV News: New Emphasis on Gay Themes," *TV Guide* (August 17–23, 1991), pp. 25–26. In December 1991, *L.A. Law* featured its bisexual female character in an episode about her lesbian relationship.

5.
GENDER AND THE CULTURE OF EMPIRE
Toward a Feminist Ethnography of the Cinema
Ella Shohat

Although recent feminist film theory has acknowledged the issue of differences among women, there has been little attempt to explore and problematize the implications of these differences for the representation of gender relations within racially and culturally non-homogeneous textual environments.[1] While implicitly universalizing "womanhood," and without questioning the undergirding racial and national boundaries of its discourse, feminist film theory, for the most part, has not articulated its generally insightful analyses vis-a-vis the contradictions and asymmetries provoked by (post)colonial arrangements of power. This elision is especially striking since the beginnings of cinema coincided with the height of imperialism between the late 19th century and World War I. Western cinema not only inherited and disseminated colonial discourse, but also created a system of domination through monopolistic control of film distribution and exhibition in much of Asia, Africa, and Latin America. The critique of colonialism within cinema studies, meanwhile, has tended to downplay the significance of gender issues, thus eliding the fact that (post)colonial discourse has impinged differently on the representation of men and women. It is between these two major theoretical frameworks that my essay is situated, attempting to synthesize feminist and postcolonial cultural critiques.

In this essay I explore Western cinema's geographical and historical constructs as symptomatic of the colonialist imaginary generally but also more specifically as a product of a gendered Western gaze, an imbrication reflective of the symbiotic relations between patriarchal and colonial articulations of difference. I emphasize the role of sexual difference in the construction of a number of superimposed oppositions—West/East, North/South—not only on a narratological level but also on the level of the implicit structuring metaphors undergirding colonial discourse. While referring to some resistant counternarratives, I also examine the structural analogies in the colonialist positioning of different regions, particularly in sexual terms, showing the extent to which Western representation of otherized territories serves diacritically to define the "West" itself.

(A) Gendered Metaphors

Virgins, Adams, and the Prospero Complex

An examination of colonial discourse reveals the crucial role of gendered metaphors in constructing the colonial "subaltern." Europe's "civilizing mission" in the Third World is projected as interweaving opposing yet linked narratives of Western penetration into inviting virginal landscape[2] *and* resisting libidinal nature. The early exaltation of the New World paradise, suggested for example by Sir Walter Raleigh's report—". . . a country that hath yet her mayden head, never sakt, turned, nor wrought"[3]—and by Crévecoeur's letters—"Here nature opens her broad lap to receive the perpetual accession of new comers, and to supply them with food"[4]—gradually centered around the idealized figure of the pioneer. Linked to nineteenth century westward expansionism, the garden symbol embraced metaphors related to growth, increase, cultivation, and blissful agricultural labor.[5] At the same time, the discourse of Empire suggests that "primitive" landscapes (deserts, jungles) are tamed; "shrew" peoples (Native Americans, Africans, Arabs) are domesticated; and the desert is made to bloom, all thanks to the infusion of Western dynamism and enlightenment. Within this Promethean master-narrative, subliminally gendered tropes such as "conquering the desolation," and "fecundating the wilderness," acquire heroic resonances of Western fertilization of barren lands. The metaphoric portrayal of the (non-European) land as a "virgin" coyly awaiting the touch of the colonizer implied that whole continents—Africa, America, Asia, and Australia—could only benefit from the emanation of colonial praxis. The revivification of a wasted soil evokes a quasi-divine process of endowing life and meaning ex nihilo, of bringing order from chaos, plenitude from lack. Indeed, the West's *Prospero complex* is premised on an East/South portrayed as a Prospero's isle, seen as the site of superimposed lacks calling for Western transformation of primeval matter. The engendering of "civilization," then, is clearly phallocentric, not unlike the mythical woman's birth from Adam's Rib.[6]

The American hero, as R. W. B. Lewis points out, has been celebrated as prelapsarian Adam, as a New Man emancipated from history (i.e., European history) before whom all the world and time lay available.[7] The American Adam archetype implied not only his status as a kind of creator, blessed with the divine prerogative of naming the elements of the scene about him, but also his fundamental innocence. Here colonial and patriarchal discourses are clearly interwoven. The Biblical narration of Genesis recounts the creation of the World; the creation of Adam from earth (*adama* in Hebrew) in order for man to rule over nature. The power of creation is inextricably linked to the power of naming—God lends his naming authority to Adam as mark of his rule, and the woman is "called Woman because she was taken out of man." The question of naming played an important role not only in gender mythology but also in colonial narratives in which the "discoverer" gave names as a mark of possession ("America" as celebrating Amerigo Vespucci) or as bearers of a European global perspective ("Middle East," "Far East"). "Peripheral" places and their inhab-

itants were often stripped of their "unpronounceable" indigenous names and outfitted with names marking them as the property of the colonizer. The colonial explorer as depicted in *Robinson Crusoe* creates, demi-urge-like, a whole civilization and has the power of naming "his" Islander "Friday," for he "saves" his life on that day; and Friday, we recall, is the day God created Adam, thus further strengthening the analogy between the "self-sufficient" Crusoe and God.

The notion of an American Adam elided a number of crucial facts, notably that there were other civilizations in the New World; that the settlers were not creating "being from nothingness"; and that the settlers had scarcely jettisoned all their Old World cultural baggage, their deeply ingrained attitudes and discourses. Here the notion of "virginity," present for example in the etymology of Virginia, must be seen in diacritical relation to the metaphor of the (European) "motherland." A "virgin" land is implicitly available for defloration and fecundation. Implied to lack owners, it therefore becomes the property of its "discoverers" and cultivators. The "purity" of the terminology masks the dispossession of the land and its resources. A land already fecund, already producing for the indigenous peoples, and thus a "mother," is metaphorically projected as virgin, "untouched nature," and therefore as available and awaiting a master. Colonial gendered metaphors are visibly rendered in Jan Van der Straet's pictorial representation of the discovery of America, focussing on the mythical figure of Amerigo Vespucci, shown as bearing Europe's emblems of meaning (cross, armor, compass).[8] Behind him we see the vessels which will bring back to the Occident the treasures of the New World Paradise. In front of him we see a welcoming naked woman, the Indian American. If she is an harmonious extension of nature, he represents its scientific mastery.[9] Here the conqueror, as Michel de Certeau puts it, "will write the body of the other and inscribe upon it his own history."[10]

In Nelson Pereira dos Santos' *How Tasty Was My Frenchman* (*Como Era Gostoso Meu Françes*, 1970), the patriarchal discourse on the encounter between Europeans and Native Americans is subverted.[11] Partly based on a diary written by the German adventurer, Hans Staden, the film concerns a Frenchman who is captured by the Tupinamba tribe and sentenced to death in response to previous massacres inflicted by Europeans upon them. Before his ritualized execution and cannibalization, however, he is given a wife, Sebiopepe (a widow of one of the Tupinamba massacred by the Europeans) and he is allowed to participate in the tribe's daily activities.[12] In the last shot, the camera zooms into Sebiopepe's face as she is emotionlessly devouring her Frenchman, despite the fact that she has developed a close relationship with him. This final image is followed by a citation from a report on Native American genocide by Europeans, which undermines the possibly disturbing nature of the last shot.[13] If pictorial representations of the "discovery" tend to center on a nude Native American woman as metaphorizing the welcoming "new-found-land," in *How Tasty Was My Frenchman* the Native American woman is far from being an object of European discourse. Presented as linked to her communal culture and history, she herself becomes part of history. Her nudity is not contrasted with the discoverer's heavy clothing; rather, she is part of an environment where nudity is not a category. The fact that the film employs largely longshots in which characters appear nude in the performance of their banal daily activities undermines voyeurism and stands in contrast to the fetishistic Hollywood mode that tends to fragment the (female) body in close shots.[14] In her interaction with the Frenchman, Sebiopepe represents, above all, the voice of the Native American counter narrative.[15] In one scene, for example, a myth of origins prefigures the symbolic revolt of the Tupinamba. Sebiopepe begins to narrate in Tupi a Tupinamba Promethean myth concerning the God, Mair, who brought them knowledge. The Frenchman, at one point, takes over the narration and, in French, further recounts the deeds of the God, while we see him performing the divine deeds. The Whitening of the Tupinamba God on the image track evokes the Promethean colonial discourse concerning the redemption of the Natives, but here that discourse is relativized, especially since the Native American woman ends the myth in Tupi, recounting the rebellion of the people against the God, while the image track shows the destruction of the Frenchman's work. Her voice, then, recounts the tale of the people who revolted, undercutting the masculinist myth of availability, submissiveness, and redemption.

Graphological Tropes

The inclination to project the non-Occident as feminine is seen even in the nineteenth century Romantic depiction of the ancient Orient of Babylonia and Egypt, reproduced in films such as D. W. Griffith's *Intolerance* (1916) and Cecil B. DeMille's *Cleopatra* (1934). In *Intolerance* Babylon signifies sexual excess, building on the Book of Revelation as "Babylon, the Great, the Mother of Harlots and of the Abominations of the Earth." DeMille's *Cleopatra* explicitly expresses this view by having the sexually manipulative Cleopatra addressed as Egypt[16] and by presenting the Orient as exclusively the scene of carnal delights. The ultimate subordination of the woman Cleopatra and her country Egypt is not without contemporary colonial overtones, suggested for example in the Anglo-aristocratic "Roman" court where sarcastic jokes are made at the expense of a presumably Black Cleopatra, asserting that Rome could never be turned into the Orient, or ruled by an Egyptian. (The historically dark Cleopatra is turned by Hollywood conventions of Beauty into a European looking White woman, just as the iconography of Christ has gradually de-Semitized him.)[17] The visual infatuation with Babylon and Egypt's material abundance emphasized through a mise-en-scene of monumental architecture, domestic detail, and quasi-pornographic feasts, cannot be divorced from the inter-text of colonial travel literature whose reports also obsessively recounted the details of Oriental sensual excesses.

Cinema, in this sense, enacted a historiographical and anthropological role, writing (in-light) the cultures of others. The early films' penchant for graphological signifiers such as hieroglyphs (in the different versions of *Cleopatra*), Hebrew script (*Intolerance*), or the image of an open book as in "The Book of Intolerance" and the marginal "notes" accompanying the intertitles (which pedagogically supply the spectator with additional information) imply Hollywood as a kind of a Western popular griot. By associating itself with writing, and particularly with "original" writing, early cinema lent a pedagogical, historical, and artistic aura to a medium still associated with circus-like entertainments. (It is not a coincidence, perhaps, that Siegfried Kracauer, for example, referred to films as "visible hieroglyphs.") And by linking a new apprentice art to ancient times and "exotic" places cinema celebrated its ethnographic and quasi-archaeological powers to resuscitate forgotten and distant civilizations, a celebration implicit in the construction of pseudo-Egyptian movie palaces. The "birth" of cinema itself coincided with the imperialist moment, when diverse colonized civilizations were already shaping their conflicting identities vis-a-vis their colonizers. These films about the ancient world suggest, perhaps, a Romantic nostalgia for a "pure" civilization prior to Western "contamination." They also represent a Romantic search for the lost Eastern origins of Western civilizations, analogous to Schlieman's excavations in Troy. It is within this context that we can understand the "structuring absence"—in the representation of Egypt, Babylonia, and the (Biblical) Holy Land—of the contemporary colonized Arab Orient and its nationalist struggles.[18] Through a historiographical gesture, the films define the Orient as ancient and mysterious, participating in what Jacques Derrida in another context calls the "hieroglyphist prejudice." The cinematic Orient, then, is best epitomized by an iconography of Papyruses, Sphinxes, and Mummies, whose existence and revival depend on the "look" and "reading" of the Westerner. This rescue of the past, in other words, suppresses the voice of the present and thus legitimates by default the availability of the space of the Orient for the geopolitical maneuvers of the Western powers.

The filmic mummified zone of ancient civilizations, then, is dialectically linked to the representation of the historical role of the West in the imperial age. Reproducing Western historiography, First World cinema narrates European penetration into the Third World through the figure of the "discoverer."[19] In most Western films about the colonies (such as *Bird of Paradise* (1932), *Wee Willie Winkie* (1937), *Black Narcissus* (1947), *The King and I* (1956), *Lawrence of Arabia* (1962), and even Buñuel's *Adventures of Robinson Crusoe* (1954) we accompany, quite literally, the explorer's perspective. A simple shift in focalization to that of the "natives," as occurs in the Australian-Aboriginal *Nice Coloured Girls* (1987)[20] or in the Brazilian *How Tasty Was My Frenchman* where the camera is placed on land with the "natives" rather than on ship with the Europeans, reveals the illusory and intrusive nature of the "discovery." More usually, however, heroic status is attributed to the voyager (often a male scientist) come to master a new land and its treasures, the value of which the "primitive" residents had been unaware.[21] It is this construction of consciousness of "value" as a pretext for (capitalist) ownership which legitimizes the colonizer's act of appropriation. The "discovery," furthermore, has gender overtones.[22] In this exploratory adventure, seen in such films as *Lawrence of Arabia* and the *Indiana Jones* series, the camera relays the hero's dynamic movement across a passive, static space, gradually stripping the land of its "enigma," as the spectator wins visual access to Oriental treasures through the eyes of the explorer-protagonist. *Lawrence of Arabia* provides an example of Western historical representation whereby the individual Romantic "genius" leads the Arab national revolt, presumed to be a passive entity awaiting T. E. Lawrence's inspiration. (Arab sources obviously have challenged this historical account.)[23] The unveiling of the mysteries of an unknown space becomes a *rite de passage* allegorizing the Western achievement of virile heroic stature.

Mapping Terra Incognita

The masculinist desire of mastering a new land is deeply linked to colonial history and even to its contemporary companion, philosophy, in which epistemology partially modeled itself on geography. The traditional discourse on nature as feminine—for example Francis Bacon's idea that insofar as we learn the laws of nature through science, we become her master, as we are now, in ignorance, "her thralls"[24]—gains, within the colonial context, clear geopolitical implications. Bacon's search for expanding scientific knowledge is inseparable from the contemporaneous European geographical expansion, clearly suggested by his language of analogies and metaphors: "[A]s the immense regions of the West Indies had never been discovered, if the use of the compass had not first been known, it is no wonder that the discovery and advancement of arts hath made no greater progress, when the art of inventing and discovering of the sciences remains hitherto unknown."[25] And Bacon finds it "disgraceful," that "while the regions of the material globe . . . have been in our times laid widely open and revealed, the intellectual globe should remain shut up within the narrow limits of old discoveries."[26]

Travelling into the indefiniteness of the ocean, the Faustian overreacher's voyage beyond the Pillars of Hercules aims at the possibility of a *terra incognita* on the other side of the ocean. Studying topography, systematizing the paths, as Hans Blumenberg points out, guarantees that the accidents of things coming to light ultimately lead to a universal acquaintance with the world. "So much had remained concealed from the human spirit throughout many centuries and was discovered neither by philosophy nor by the faculty of reason but rather by accident and favorable opportunity, because it was; all too different and distant from what was familiar, so that no preconception (*praenotio aliqua*) could lead one to it."[27] The logic of explorers from Robinson Crusoe to Indiana Jones is, in this sense, based on the hope that "nature" conceals in its "womb" still more, outside the familiar paths of the power of imagination (*extra vias phantasiae*). It is within this broader historical and intellectual context that we may understand the symptomatic image of penetration into a cave placed in a non-European land to discover that "Unknown," seen for example in the Rudyard Kipling-based *The Jungle Book* (1942), *Raiders of the Lost Ark* (1981), *Indiana Jones and the Temple of Doom* (1984), and the E. M. Forster-based *A Passage to India* (1984).

Colonial narratives legitimized the embarking upon treasure hunts by lending a scientific aura, encapsulated especially by images of maps and globes. Detailed descriptions of maps were probably inspired by the growing science of geography which determined the significance of places through its power of inscription on the map, with the compass on top as the signature of scientific authority. Geography, then, was microcosmically reflected in the map-based adventures which involved the drawing or deciphering of a map, and its authentication through the physical contact with the "new" land. Western cinema, from the earliest anthropological films through *Morocco* (1930) to the *Indiana Jones* series, has relied on map imagery for plotting the Empire, while simultaneously celebrating its own technological power—implicitly vis-a-vis the novel's reliance upon words or static drawings, and later still photographs—to illustrate vividly the topography. For example, venture-narrative films mark maps with moving arrows to signify the progress of the Westerner in his world-navigation,

a practice characterizing even the recent *Raiders of the Lost Ark* and *Indiana Jones and the Temple of Doom*. By associating itself with the visual medium of maps, cinema represents itself scientifically, as being a twentieth-century continuation of Geography.

Films often superimposed illustrative maps on shots of landscapes, subliminally imposing the map's "claim" over the land, functioning as a legal document. *King Solomon's Mines* (1937, 1950, 1985), as Anne McClintock suggests in her discussion of Rider Haggard work, explicitly genderizes the relation between the explorer and the topography.[28] Menahem Golan's version, for example, reveals in the second shot of the film a small nude female sculpture engraved with Canaanite signs, explained by the archeologist to be a map leading to the twin mountains, the Breasts of Sheba, below which, in a cave, are hidden King Solomon's diamond mines. The camera voyeuristically tilts down on the female body/map, scrutinizing it from the excited perspective of the archeologist and the antique dealer. The road to Utopia involves the deciphering of the map, of comprehending the female body; the legendary twin mountains and the cave metaphorize the desired telos of the hero's mission of plunder. The geology and topography of the land, then, is explicitly sexualized to resemble the physiology of a woman.

The recurrent image of the spinning globe, similarly, entitles the scientist to possess the world, since the globe, as the world's representation, allegorizes the relationship between creator and creation. Cinema's penchant for spinning globe logos serves to celebrate the medium's kinetic possibilities as well as its global ubiquity, allowing spectators a cheap voyage while remaining in the metropolitan "centers"—Lumières' location shootings of diverse Third World sites, such as India, Mexico, and Palestine being symptomatic of this visual national-geographics-mania. The spinning globe virtually became the trade-mark of the British Korda brothers' productions, many of whose films, such as *Sanders of the River* (1935), *The Drum* (1938), *The Four Feathers* (1939), and *The Jungle Book*, concerned colonial themes.[29] The overarching global point-of-view sutures the spectator into a Godlike cosmic perspective. Incorporating images of maps and globes, the Jules Verne-based film *Around the World in 80 Days* (1956), for example, begins by its omniscient narrator hailing the "shrinking of the world" as Verne was writing the book.[30] The "shrinking" relates the perspective of upper-class British men whose scientific confidence about circling the world in eighty days is materialized, thus linking the development of science to imperialist control: "Nothing is impossible. When science finally conquers the air it may be feasible to circle the globe in eighty hours," says the David Niven character.

Science, knowledge, and technology can also be read allegorically as linked to imperial expansionism in the film's citation of Georges Méliès' film *A Trip to the Moon* (*Le Voyage dans la Lune*, 1902) (based on Verne's *From the Earth to the Moon*, 1865) in which the "last frontier" explored is seen first in the imagistic phallic penetration of the rounded moon.[31] This imagination of the "last frontier," in a period when most of the world was dominated by Europe, reproduces the historical discourse of the "first frontier." The narrative is structured similarly to the colonial captivity narrative where the skeleton creatures carrying spears burst from the moon's simulacrum of a jungle but are defeated by the male explorers' umbrella-like guns which magically eliminate the savage creatures. Such a film, not in any obvious sense "about" colonialism, but one produced in a period when most of the world was dominated by Europe, can thus be read as an analogue of imperial expansion.[32] Similarly in recent films such as *Return of the Jedi* (1983) the conquest of outer space exists on a continuum with an imperial narrative in which the visualization of the planet provides the paradigm for the representation of Third World "underdevelopment" (deserts, jungles, and mountains). The Manichean relationship between the American hero and the new land and its natives involves exotic creatures, teddy-bear-like Ewoks whose language remains a mystery throughout the film, who worship the technologically well-equipped hero and who defend him against evil ugly creatures who have unclear motives. The American hero's physical and moral triumph legitimizes the destruction of the enemy, as does the paternal transformation of the friendly "elements" into servile objects, along with his assumed right to establish new outposts (and implicitly to hold on to old outposts, whether in Africa, Asia, or America).

The Dark Continent

The colonial films claim to initiate the Western spectator into an unknown culture. This is valid even for films set in "exotic" lands and ancient times which do *not* employ Western characters (for example, *Intolerance*,[33] *The Ten Commandments* (1923, 1956), *The Thief of Baghdad* (1924), and *Kismet* (1944), yet whose Oriental heroes/heroines are played by Western stars. The spectator is subliminally invited on an ethnographic tour of a celluloid-"preserved" culture, which implicitly celebrates the chronotopic magical aptitude of cinema for panoramic spectacle and temporal voyeurism, evoking Andre Bazin's formulation of cinema as possessing a "mummy complex."[34] Often the spectator, identified with the gaze of the West (whether embodied by a Western male/female character or by a Western actor/actress masquerading as an Oriental), comes to master, in a remarkably telescoped period of time, the codes of a foreign culture shown, as Edward Said suggests, as simple, unselfconscious, and susceptible to facile apprehension. Any possibility of dialogic interaction and of a dialectical representation of the East/West relation is excluded from the outset. The films thus reproduce the colonialist mechanism by which the Orient, rendered as devoid of any active historical or narrative role, becomes the object of study and spectacle.[35]

The portrayal of a Third World region as undeveloped, in this same vein, is reinforced by a topographical reductionism, for example the topographical reductionism of the Orient to desert, and metaphorically, to dreariness. The desert, a frequent reference in the dialogues and a visual motif throughout the Orientalist films, is presented as the essential unchanging decor of the history of the Orient. While the Arabs in such films as *Lawrence of Arabia, Exodus* (1960), and the *Raiders of the Lost Ark* are associated with images of underdevelopment, the Westerner, as the antithesis of the Oriental desert, is associated with productive, creative pioneering, a masculine redeemer of the wilderness. The films reflect a culturally over-determined geographical-symbolic polarity; an East/West axis informs many films on the Oriental theme. As if in a reversion to deterministic climate theories such as those of Madame de Stael or Hippolyte Taine, the films present the East as the locus of irrational primitivism and uncontrollable instincts. The exposed, barren land and the blazing sands, furthermore, metaphorize the exposed, unrepressed "hot" passion and uncensored emotions of the Orient, in short, as the world of the out-of-control Id.

The Orient as a metaphor for sexuality is encapsulated by the recurrent figure of the veiled woman. The inaccessibility of the veiled woman, mirroring the mystery of the Orient itself, requires a process of Western unveiling for comprehension. Veiled women in Orientalist paintings, photographs, and films expose flesh, ironically, more than they conceal it.[36] It is this process of exposing the female Other, of literally denuding her, which comes to allegorize the Western masculinist power of possession, that she, as a metaphor for her land, becomes available for Western penetration and knowledge. This intersection of the epistemological and the sexual in colonial discourse echoes Freud's metaphor of the "dark continent." Freud speaks of female sexuality in metaphors of darkness and obscurity often drawn from the realms of archeology and exploration—the metaphor of the "dark continent," for example, deriving from a book by the Victorian explorer Stanley.[37] Seeing himself as explorer and discoverer of new worlds, Freud in *Studies on Hysteria* compared the role of the psychoanalyst to that of the archeologist "clearing away the pathogenic psychical material layer by layer" which is analogous "with the technique of excavating a buried city."[38] The analogy, made in the context of examining a woman patient, Fräulein Elisabeth Von R., calls attention to the role of the therapist in locating obscure trains of thought followed by penetration, as Freud puts it in the first person: "I would penetrate into deeper layers of her memories at these points carrying out an investigation under hypnosis or by the use of some similar technique."[39]

Speaking generally of "penetrating deeply" into the "neurosis of women" thanks to a science which can give a "deeper and more coherent" insight into femininity,[40] Freud is perhaps unaware of the political overtones of his optical metaphor. Penetration, as Toril Moi suggests, is very much on Freud's mind as he approaches femininity,[41] including, one might add, the "dark continent of female sexuality." The· notion of the necessary unveiling of the unconscious requires an obscure object in order to sustain the very desire

to explore, penetrate, and master. David Macey's suggestion that psychoanalysis posits femininity as being in excess of its rationalist discourse, and then complains that it cannot explain it,[42] is equally applicable to the positing of the Other in colonial discourse. Furthermore, Freud uses the language of force; for example, "we force our way into the internal strata, overcoming resistances at all times."[43] Looking at the Eastern roots of civilizations, Freud employs ancient myths and figures such as the Sphinx and Oedipus to draw parallels between the development of the civilization and that of the psyche. (Although Freud did not speculate at any great length on Egyptian mythology, over half of his private collection of antiquities reportedly consisted of ancient Egyptian sculptures and artifacts.)[44] The psychoanalyst who heals from the suppressed past (most of Freud's studies of hysteria were conducted in relation to women) resembles the archeologist who recovers the hidden past of civilization (most of which was "found" in Third world lands). As in archeology, Freud's epistemology assumes the (white) male as the bearer of knowledge, who can penetrate woman and text, while she, as a remote region, will let herself be explored till truth is uncovered.

The interweaving of archeology and psychoanalysis touches on a nineteenth-century motif in which the voyage into the origins of the Orient becomes a voyage into the interior colonies of the "self." ("Un voyage en Orient [était] comme un grand acte de ma vie intérieure," Lamartine wrote.)[45] The origins of archeology, the search for the "roots of civilization" as a discipline are, we know, inextricably linked to imperial expansionism. In the cinema, the *Indiana Jones* series reproduces exactly this colonial vision in which Western "knowledge" of ancient civilizations "rescues" the past from oblivion. It is this masculinist rescue in *Raiders of the Lost Ark* that legitimizes denuding the Egyptians of their heritage, confining it within Western metropolitan museums—an ideology implicit as well in the Orientalist *Intolerance*, *Cleopatra*, and the *Mummy* series. (These films, not surprisingly, tend to be programmed in museums featuring Egyptological exhibitions.) *Raiders of the Lost Ark*, symptomatically, assumes a disjuncture between contemporary and ancient Egypt, since the space between the present and the past can "only" be bridged by the scientist. The full significance of the ancient archeological objects within the Eurocentric vision of the Spielberg film is presumed to be understood only by the Western scientists, relegating the Egyptian people to the role of ignorant Arabs who happen to be sitting on a land full of historical treasures—much as they happen to "sit" on oil. Set in the mid-thirties when most of the world was still under colonial rule, the film regards the colonial presence in Egypt, furthermore, as completely natural, eliding a history of Arab nationalist revolts against foreign domination.

The American hero—often cinematically portrayed as a Cowboy—is an archeologist implicitly searching for the Eastern roots of Western civilization. He liberates the ancient Hebrew ark from illegal Egyptian possession, while also rescuing it from immoral Nazi control, subliminally reinforcing American and Jewish solidarity vis-a-vis the Nazis and their Arab assistants.[46] The geopolitical alignments here are as clear as in the inadvertent allegory of *The Ten Commandments*, where a WASPish Charlton Heston is made to incarnate Hebrew Moses struggling against the Egyptians, thus allegorizing in the context of the fifties the contemporary struggle of the West (Israel and the U.S.) against Egyptians/Arabs.[47] That at the end of *Raiders of the Lost Ark* it is the American Army which guards the "top secret" ark—with the active complicity of the ark itself—strengthens this evocation of geopolitical alliances.[48] *Raiders of the Lost Ark* significantly develops parallel linked plots in which the female protagonist, Marion, and the ark become the twin objects of the hero's search for harmony. The necklace which leads to the ark is first associated with Marion who becomes herself the object of competing nationalist male desires. She is abducted by the Nazis and their Arab assistants much as the ark is hijacked by them, followed by Dr. Jones's rescue of Marion and the ark from the Nazis. The telos of the voyage into unknown regions—whether mental or geographical—then, is that the Westerner both knows the Orient (in the epistemological and Biblical senses) and at the same time brings it knowledge, rescuing it from its own obscurantism.

Egyptology and The Mummy

A different perspective on these issues is suggested in the Egyptian film *The Mummy/The Night of Counting the Years* (Al Mumia, 1969).[49] Based on the actual case of the discovery of Pharaonic tombs in the Valley of the Kings in 1881, a year before the full British colonization of Egypt, the film opens with the French Egyptologist, Gaston Maspero, informing his colleagues about the black market trade in antiquities coming from the reigns of Pharaohs such as Ahmose,[50] Thutmose III,[51] and Rameses II.[52] The government's archeological commission, under Maspero, delegates an expedition, headed by a young Egyptian archeologist, to investigate the location of the tombs in Thebes in order to end the thefts. In Thebes, meanwhile, the headman of the Upper Egyptian Horobbat tribe, which had been living off extracting artifacts from the pharaonic tombs, has just died, and his brother must initiate his two nephews into the secret of the mountain. Still in grief over their father's death, the sons are repelled by the dissection of the mummy merely to get at a gold necklace depicting the sacred "Eye of Horus." The protesting brothers must choose between two betrayals, both of them grave: the vulture-like lootings of ancient kingdoms and the desecration of their mummies, or the betrayal of their father's secret with the consequence of cutting off their source of income and therefore their ability to feed hungry Horobbat mouths. Any revelation of the secret would mean ultimately destroying their family and tribe in the name of respect for "the dead" now viewed by the elders as nothing more than leathery mummies. The older brother is assassinated by the village elders when he refuses to sell the artifact on the black market, while the younger brother, Wannis, is torn between his guilt over owing his life to ancient Egyptian corpses ("How many bodies did my father violate in order to feed us?" he asks his mother) and the condemnation of his people. Wandering through the ruins of Thebes and Karnak—for him not simply a memento of an older civilization, but the very living reminder of his childhood playground—the long-take swirling camera movements reflect his ethical and even epistemological vertigo, his conflicting internalized responsibility for his Egyptian heritage vis-a-vis his immediate responsibility for present-day lives. After being reassured that the "effendi archeologists" are trying to understand Egypt's past and not plunder it, he reveals the secret knowledge to Maspero's assistant. The expedition, before the village can prevent it, empties the graves, and carries out the mummy- coffins, destined for the museum.

The Mummy/The Night of Counting the Years is set in the late nineteenth-century, at the height of imperial Egyptology. By the time Britain occupied Egypt in 1882, the country was bankrupt of its archeological treasures which were exhibited in London and Paris as testimony of Western scientific progress. In the heroic, almost sanctimonious, language of the Egyptological mission, archeological reports on the 1881 discovery describe their rescue of the ancient East's powerful kings from Arab clans in a way which associates the Westerner with emperors and royal dynasties. The simplistic positing of a rupture between present and past Egypt conveniently empowers the Western claim over Egypt's past,[53] thus naturalizing the presence of the Rosetta Stone, for example, in the British Museum. Shadi Abdel Salam's film implicitly challenges the archeological master-narrative by foregrounding the voices of those on the margins of Egyptological texts. If the film opens with an archeological project and ends with its successful accomplishment, it also undermines that mission by focussing on the concrete dilemmas of living Egyptians. The non-diegetic musical motif based on Upper Egypt popular music ("Al Arian"), and the slow rhythm evocative of the regional atmosphere, furthermore, cinematically convey the cultural force of their environment.[54] The film does not end, significantly, with the narrative closure of safe placement of the artifacts in a museum, but rather with the slow vanishing of the boat carrying the Egyptologists and the mummies, all from the perspective of the devastated tribe. If *How Tasty Was My Frenchman* opens with the penetration of the Europeans seen from the perspective of the Native Americans, *The Mummy/The Night of Counting the Years* ends with the emptiness left behind by the intrusion of Europe. Reportedly, the Egyptian women of the tribe mourned when the mummies were taken, yet Shadi Adbel Salam presents, in longshot and through depsychologized editing, a unified communal silent gaze where the whistling wind becomes a voice of protest. Their gaze, far from conveying the triumphant conclusion of the archeological narrative, unveils the disastrous rupture in their very lives, thus subverting the self-celebratory Egyptological definitions of dispossession and theft.[55]

Archeological reports often inadvertently display metaphors which suggest capitalist values attached to their own profession. In his account of the 1881 discovery, the archeologist Howard Carter who worked on the discovery of Tut-ankh-Amen's tomb, writes: "Incredible as it may seem the secret was kept for six years, and the family, with a banking account of forty or more dead pharaohs to draw upon, grew rich."[56] Abdel Salam's *The Mummy/The Night of Counting the Years*, in contrast, emphasizes the ambivalent relationships between the tribe and the treasures, between the Egyptian people and their ancient heritage. The tribe lives on theft, yet its circumstances of hunger imply a critique of the imperial class system. The archeological redemption, in other words, must be seen in its historical and cultural context, i.e., taking the only power the tribe possessed without bringing anything in return. It would be simplistic, however, to view *The Mummy/The Night of Counting the Years* as a mere condemnation of Egyptology. The film illuminates class relations within a colonial dynamics in which the tribe, in order to survive, is obliged to deal with the "small" black market dealers, for the "effendies" from Cairo will not even pay them and arrest them. Class formations of Egyptian society, particularly within imperial context, force the small village to regard the ancient artifacts as a means of survival, a system in which the only power of the tribe is their secret. The effendies are viewed from the perspective of the tribe as strangers, cut off, in other words, from the national reality. *The Mummy/The Night of Counting the Years* in contrast with Western representations of Egypt, does not stress the grandeur of ancient Egypt at the expense of contemporary Arab lives; rather, it exposes the complex, multi-layered dimensions of Egyptian identity.

An allegory on Egyptian identity, the film offers a meditation on the destiny of a national culture. To cite Shadi Abdel Salam: "We have a national culture but it lies buried at the bottom of the memory of the people who are not always aware of its great values."[57] Speaking in an improbably literary Arabic (rather than an existing dialect), the villagers represent the Arab cultural heritage, while they are simultaneously presented as continuous with the ancient past, emphasized, for example, through the ancient Egyptian eye make-up worn by the actress Nadia Lutfi. In a symbolic syncretic continuity of Pharaonic and

Arab Egypt, the film associates the ancient "Eye of Horus," first shown in a close shot looking presumably at the brothers (directly at the spectator), with the Arab sign of "hamsa," against casting evil eye, seen on the boat on which the older brother is murdered. Similarly images of a closed gigantic hand of a monument is accompanied by a dialogue between Wannis and a stranger about "a hand holding a fate no one can read," or "what fate can you read in a stone hand?," stating that it is impossible to read fate at the hands of the monuments, i.e., a contemporary popular Middle Eastern culture of reading fate in the hand is implicitly contrasted with the immortal greatness but also the lifelessness of monuments.[58] A kind of visual dialogue of Arab Egypt with its past, furthermore, is rendered through montage, for example, when the image of the agonizing Wannis, looking up at the gigantic monument, is juxtaposed with a high-angle shot of Wannis, this time presumably from the monument's point-of-view. The presentation of Egypt's national identity as an amalgam of histories and cultures evokes the formulations, for example by the writers Taha Hussain and Tawfiq al-Hakim, of Egyptian identity as a synthesis of Pharaonic past, Arabic language, and Islamic religion. The film's opening intertitle, drawn from *The Book of the Dead*, promising that the one who shall go shall also return, and the final intertitle calling for the dead to "wake up," must also be seen within the context in which *The Mummy/The Night of Counting the Years* was produced.[59] During the post-1967 war period, after the defeat to Israel, the Gamal Abdel Nasser regime lost much of its allure, and the general mood of despair went hand in hand with a felt need for critical reassessments. In this sense, the ancient inscription of resurrection is also allegorically a call to Egypt of the late sixties for national rebirth.

(B) Textual/Sexual Strategies

The Colonial Gaze

Still playing a significant role in postcolonial geopolitics, the predominant trope of "rescue" in colonial discourse forms the crucial site of the battle over representation. Not only has the Western imaginary metaphorically rendered the colonized land as a female to be saved from her environ/mental disorder, it has also projected rather more literal narratives of rescue, specifically of Western and non-Western women—from African, Asian, Arab, or Native American men. The figure of the Arab assassin/rapist, like that of the African cannibal, helps produce the narrative and ideological role of the Western liberator as integral to the colonial rescue phantasy. This, projection, whose imagistic avatars include the polygamous Arab, the libidinous Black buck, and the macho Latino, provides an indirect apologia for domination. In the case of the Orient, it carries with it religious/theological overtones of the inferiority of the polygamous Islamic world to the Christian world as encapsulated by the monogamous couple. The justification of Western expansion, then, becomes linked to issues of sexuality.

The intersection of colonial and gender discourses involves a shifting, contradictory subject positioning, whereby Western woman can simultaneously constitute "center" and "periphery," identity and alterity. A Western woman, in these narratives, exists in a relation of subordination to Western man and in a relation of domination toward "non-Western" men and women. This textual relationality homologizes the historical positioning of colonial women who have played, albeit with a difference, an oppressive role toward colonized people (both men and women), at times actively perpetuating the legacy of Empire.[60] This problematic role is anatomized in Ousmane Sembène's *Black Girl* (*La Noire de . . .*, 1966) in the relationship between the Senegalese maid and her French employer, and to some extent by Mira Hamermesh's documentary on South Africa *Maids and Madams* (1985), in contrast to the White-woman's-burden ideology in films such as *The King and I* (1956), *Out of Africa* (1985), and *Gorillas in the Mist* (1989). In many films, colonial women become the instrument of the White male vision, and are thus granted a gaze more powerful than that not only of non-Western women but also of non-Western men.

In the colonial context, given the shifting relational nature of power situations and representations, women can be granted an ephemeral "positional superiority" (Edward Said), a possibility exemplified in *The Sheik* (1921). Based on Edith Hull's novel, George Melford's *The Sheik* first introduces the spectator to the Arab world in the form of the "barbarous ritual" of the marriage market, depicted as a casino lottery ritual from which Arab men select women to "serve as chattel slaves." At the same time, the Western woman character, usually the object of the male gaze in Hollywood films, tends to be granted in the East an active (colonial) gaze, insofar as she now, temporarily within the narrative, becomes the sole delegate, as it were, of Western civilization. The "norms of the text" (Boris Uspensky) are represented by the Western male but in the moments of His absence, the white woman becomes the civilizing center of the film.[61] These racial and sexual hierarchies in the text are also clearly exemplified in Michael Powell and Emeric Pressburger (*Black Narcissus*), where most of the narrative is focalized through the British nuns and their "civilizing mission" in India. But ultimately the "norms of the text" are embodied by the British man, whose initial "prophecy" that the wild mountains of India are not suitable for and are beyond the control of the Christian missionaries is confirmed by the end of the narrative, with the virtual punishment of the nuns as catastrophes and mental chaos penetrate their order. Yet in relation to the "Natives" (both Indian men and women) the British women are privileged and form the "filter" and "center of consciousness" (Gerard Genette) of the film.

The discourse on gender within a colonial context, in sum, suggests that Western women can occupy a relatively powerful position on the surface of the htext [sic], as the vehicles less for a sexual gaze than a colonial gaze. In these friction-producing moments between sexual and national hierarchies, particularly as encapsulated through the relationship between Third World men and First World women, national identity (associated with the white female character) is relatively privileged over sexual identity (associated with the dark male character). At the same time, the same ambivalence operates in relation to Third World men, whose punishment for inter-racial desire is simultaneously accompanied by spectatorial gratification for a male sexual gaze as ephemerally relayed by a darker man. These contradictions of national and sexual hierarchies, present in embryo in early cinema, are accentuated in the recent nostalgia-for-empire (liberal) films which foreground a female protagonist, presumably appealing to feminist codes, while reproducing colonialist narrative and cinematic power arrangements. The desexualization of the "good"

African or Indian (servant) man in *Gorillas in the Mist*, *A Passage to India*, and *Out of Africa*, not unlike the desexualization of the female domestic servant as in *The Birth of a Nation* (1915) and *Gone with the Wind* (1939), is dialectically linked to the placement of the Western woman in the (White) "Pater" paradigm vis-a-vis the "natives."

Rape and the Rescue Phantasy

The chromatic sexual hierarchy in colonialist narratives, typical of Western racial conventions, has White women/men occupy the center of the narrative, with the White woman as the desired object of the male protagonists and antagonists. Marginalized within the narrative. Third World women—when not inscribed as metaphors for their virgin land as in *Bird of Paradise*—appear largely as sexually hungry subalterns.[62] In one scene in *The Sheik*, Arab women—some of them Black—fight quite literally over their Arab man. While the White woman has to be lured, made captive, and virtually raped to awaken her repressed desire, the Arab/Black/Latin women are driven by a raging libido. Here one encounters some of the complementary contradictions in colonial discourse whereby a Third World land and its inhabitants are the object of the desire for chastity articulated in the virgin metaphors, while also manifesting Victorian repression of sexuality, particularly female sexuality, through unleashing its pornographic impulse.[63]

The positing of female sexual enslavement by polygamous Third World men becomes especially ironic when we recall the subjection of African-American women slaves on Southern plantations with the daily lived polygamy of White men slaveowners.[64] Images of Black/Arab woman in "heat" versus "frigid" White woman also indirectly highlight the menacing figure of the Black/Arab rapist and therefore mythically elide the history of subordination of Third World women by First World men. The hot/frigid dichotomy, then, implies three interdependent axioms within the sexual politics of colonialist discourse: 1) the sexual interaction of Black/Arab men and White women can *only* involve rape (since White women, within this perspective, cannot possibly desire Black men); 2) the sexual interaction of White men and Black/Arab women cannot involve rape (since Black/Arab women are in perpetual heat and desire their White master); and 3) the interaction of Black/Arab men and Black/Arab women also cannot involve rape, since both are in perpetual heat. It was this racist combinatoire that generated the (largely unspoken) rationale for the castration and lynching of African-American men and the non-punishment of White men for the rape of African-American women.

It is within this logic that *The Birth of a Nation* obsessively links sexual and racial phobias. The animalistic "Black," Gus, attempts to rape the virginal Flora, much as the "mulatto" Lynch tries to force Elsie into marriage, and the "mulatta" Lydia blames an innocent White man of sexual abuse, while simultaneously manipulating the unaware politician Stoneman through sexuality. The threat of African-American political assertion is subliminally linked to Black sexual potency. It is not surprising, therefore, that the only non-threatening Black figure, the "loyal" mammy, is portrayed as completely de-sexualized. The thematization of Blacks' hyper-sexuality diacritically foils (White) masculinist acts of patriotism. It is the attempted rape of Flora that catalyzes the grand act of White "liberation." The opening intertitle, which states that the very presence of the African in America "planted the first seed of disunion," and the portrayal of idealized harmony between North and South (and Masters and Slaves) before the abolition suggest that libidinal Blacks destroyed the nation. The rescue of Flora, of Elsie, and of the besieged Northerners and Southerners (who are now once again united "in common defence of their Aryan Birthright"), operates as a didactic allegory whose telos is the Klansmen's vision of the "order of things." The closure of "mixed"-marriage between North and South confirms national unity and establishes a certain sexual order in which the virginal desired White woman is available only to White man. The superimposition of the Christ figure over the celebrating family/nation provides a religious benediction on the "birth." This abstract, metaphysical Birth of the Nation masks a more concrete notion of birth—no less relevant to the conception of the American nation—that of children from raped Black women, just as the naming of the mulatto as "Lynch" crudely blames the victims. Furthermore, the White man, who historically raped Third World women, manifests latent rapist desires toward innocent White

women via a projected Black man, here literally masked in black-face.

Even when not involving rape, the possibilities of erotic interaction in films prior to the sixties were severely limited by apartheid-style ethnic/racial codes. The same Hollywood that at times could project mixed love stories between Anglo-Americans and Latins and Arabs (especially if incarnated by White American actors and actresses such as Valentino in *The Sheik*, Dorothy Lamour in *The Road to Morocco* (1942), or Maureen O'Hara in *They Met in Argentina* (1941) was completely inhibited in relation to African, Asian, or Native American sexuality. This latent fear of blood-tainting in such melodramas as *Call Her Savage* (1932) and *Pinky* (1949) necessitates narratives where the "half breed" ("Native American" in *Call Her Savage* and "Black" in *Pinky*) female protagonists are prevented at the closure of the films from participating in mixed-marriage, ironically despite the roles being played by "pure White" actresses. It is therefore the generic space of melodrama that preoccupies itself with "inter-racial" romantic interaction. The trajectory of constituting the couple in the musical comedy, for example, could not allow for a racially "subaltern" protagonist.

The Production Code of the Motion Picture Producers and Directors of America, Inc.: 1930–1934, an even stricter version of the Hays Office codes of the 20s, explicitly states: "Miscegenation (sex relation between the white and black races) is forbidden."[65] The delegitimizing of the romantic union between "white" and "black" "races" is linked to a broader exclusion of Africans, Asians, and Native Americans from participation in social institutions. Translating the obsession with "pure blood" into legal language. Southern miscegenation laws, as pointed out by African-American feminists as early as the end of the last century,[66] were designed to maintain White (male) supremacy and to prevent a possible transfer of property to Blacks in the post-abolition era. "Race" as a biological category, as Hazel Carby formulates it, was subordinated to race as a political category.[67] It is within this context of an exclusionary ideology that we can understand the Production Code's universal censorship of sexual violence and brutality where the assumption is one of purely individual victimization, thus undermining a possible portrayal of the racially-sexually-based violence toward African-Americans, and implicitly wiping out the memory of the rape, castration, and lynching from the American record.[68] The Production Code, in other words, eliminates a possible counter-narrative by Third World people for whom sexual-violence has often been at the kernel of their historical experience and identity.[69]

The Spectacle of Difference

An analysis of the history of First World cinema in racial and colonial terms uncovers a tendency toward national "allegory," in Jameson's sense, of texts which, even when narrating apparently private stories, manage to metaphorize the public sphere, where the micro-individual is doubled, as it were, by the macro-nation and the personal and the political, the private and the historical, are inextricably linked.[70] The national and racial hierarchies of the cinema allegorize, in other words, extra-discursive social intercourse. In the period of the Good Neighbor Policy, Hollywood attempted to enlist Latin America for hemispheric unity against the Axis. As European film markets were reducing their film consumption due to the beginning of the war, Hollywood, in hopes for South American markets and pan-American political unity, flooded the screens with films featuring "Latin American" themes. Interestingly the trope of "good neighbor" very rarely extended to winning family status through inter-racial or inter-national marriage. Marginalized within the narrative, and often limited to roles as entertainers, the Latin American characters in *The Gang's All Here* (1943), *Too Many Girls* (1940), and *Weekend in Havana* (1941) at the finale tend to be at the exact point from which they began, in contrast with the teleologically evolving status of the North American protagonists. Displaying "exoticism," the musical numbers in these films provide the spectacle of difference, functioning narratively by uniting the North American couple vis-a-vis the South Americans.

Films such as *The Gang's All Here* demonstrate a generic division of labor, whereby the solid, "serious" or romantic numbers such as "A Journey to a Star" tend to be performed by the North American protagonists Alice Faye and James Ellison, while the Latin American characters perform "unserious," "excessive" numbers involving swaying hips, exagger-ated facial expressions, caricaturally sexy costumes, and "think-big" style props embodied by Carmen Miranda. Her figure in the number "The Lady with the Tutti-Frutti Hat" is dwarfed by gigantesque vegetative imagery in which the final image of her as a virtual fertility goddess links this idealized quality with the beginning of the number where goods are unloaded from the South; the North here celebrates the South as the feminine principle capable of giving birth to goods consumed by the North. The bananas in Miranda's number, furthermore, not only enact the agricultural reductionism of Latin America but also form phallic symbols, here raised by "voluptuous" Latinas over circular quasi-vaginal forms. (But the Latina, as the lyrics suggest, will take her hat off "only for Johnny Smith," much as the "Oriental" woman in films such as *The Road to Morocco* would only remove her veil for the Anglo-American.) This construction of Latinness (or Orientalness) as the locus of exoticism is not subsumable by hegemonic North American cultural codes. The South American characters therefore do not form part of any narrative development and their presence is "tolerable" only on the folkloric level. Character interaction, in this sense, allegorizes the larger relation between the North and South (or West and East) and reflects an ambivalence of attraction/repulsion towards those on the "margins" of the Western Empire.

The gender and colonial discursive intersection is revealed in the ways that Hollywood exploited the Orient, Africa, and Latin America as a pretext for eroticized images, especially from 1934 through the mid-fifties when the restrictive production code forbade depicting "scenes of passion" in all but the most puerile terms, and required that the sanctity of the institution of marriage be upheld at all times. Miscegenation, nudity, sexually suggestive dances or costumes, "excessive and lustful kissing" were prohibited, while adultery, illicit sex, seduction, or rape could never be more than suggested, and then only if absolutely essential to the plot and severely punished at the end. The Western obsession with the Harem, for example, was not simply crucial for Hollywood's visualization of the Orient but also authorized the proliferation of sexual images projected onto an otherized elsewhere, much as the Orient, Africa, and Latin America played a similar role for Victorian culture.

Exoticizing and eroticizing the Third World allowed the imperial imaginary to play out its own fantasies of sexual domination. Already in the silent era, films often included eroticized dances, featuring a rather improbable melange of Spanish and Indian dances, plus a touch of belly-dancing (*The Dance of Fatima, The Sheik*, and *Son of the Sheik* (1926)). This filmic practice of melange recalls the frequent superimposition in Orientalist paintings of the visual traces of civilizations as diverse as Arab, Persian, Chinese, and Indian into a single feature of the exotic Orient[71]—a colonialist process that Albert Memmi terms the "mark of the plural." An Oriental setting (most of the films on the Orient, Africa, and Latin America were studio-shot) thus provided Hollywood filmmakers with a narrative license for exposing flesh without risking censorship; they could display the bare-skin of Valentino, Douglas Fairbanks, and Johnny Weissmuller as well as that of scores of women, from Myrna Loy, Maureen O'Sullivan, and Marlene Dietrich dancing with her legs painted gold to Dolores Grey moving her hips with the "realistic" excuse of other, less civilized cultures. (The code which turned Jane's two piece outfit into one piece in later films, did not affect, for the most part, the nude breasts of African women at the background of the *Tarzan* series,[72] evoking *National Geographic*'s predilection for "Native" nudity.) In the desert and the jungle, the traditional slow-paced process of courtship leading to marriage could be replaced with uninhibited fantasies of sexual domination and "freedom," and specifically with fantasies of polygamy and even rape of presumably repressed White women. The display of rape in a "natural" despotic context continues to the present, for example, in the several attempted rapes of Brooke Shields in *Sahara* (1983). The Orient, like Latin America and Africa, thus is posited as the locus of eroticism by a puritanical society, and a film industry, hemmed in by a moralistic code.

The Imaginary of the Harem

As with voyeuristic anthropological studies and moralistic travel-literature concerning non-normative conceptions of sexuality, Western cinema diffused the anachronistic but still Victorian obsession with sexuality through the cinematic apparatus. The outlet for Western male heroic desire is clearly seen in *Harum*

Scarum (1965), a reflexive film featuring a carnival-like Orient reminiscent of Las Vegas, itself placed in the burning sands of the American desert of Nevada, and offering harem-like nightclubs. The film opens with Elvis Presley—attired in an "Oriental" head wrap and vest—arriving on horseback in the desert. Upon arrival Presley leaps off his horse to free a woman from two evil Arabs who have tied her to a stake. The triumphant rescuer later sings:

> I'm gonna go where desert sun is; where the fun is; go where the harem girls dance; go where there's love and romance—out on the burning sands, in some caravan. I'll find adventure where I can. To say the least, go East, young man.

You'll feel like the Sheik, so rich and grand, with dancing girls at your command. When paradise starts calling, into some tent I'm crawling. I'll make love the way I plan. Go East—and drink and feast—go East, young man.

Material abundance in Orientalist discourse, tied to a history of imperial enterprises, here functions as part of the generic utopia of the musical, constituting itself, in Jamesonian terms, as a projected fulfillment of what is desired and absent within the socio-political status quo. Yet the "absence" is explicitly within the masculinist imaginative terrain. The images of harems offer an "open sesame" to an unknown, alluring, and tantalizingly forbidden world, posited as desirable to the instinctual primitive presumably inhabiting all men. In *Kismet* (1955), for example, the harem master entertains himself with a panopticon-like device which allows him to watch his many women without their knowledge. Authorizing a voyeuristic entrance into an inaccessible private space, the Harem dream reflects a masculinist utopia of sexual omnipotence.[73]

The topos of the harem in contemporary popular culture draws, of course, on a long history of Orientalist phantasies. Western voyagers had no conceivable means of access to harems—indeed, the Arabic etymology of the word "harem," Kharim, refers to something "forbidden." Yet Western texts delineate life in the harems with great assurance and apparent exactitude, rather like European Orientalist studio paintings, for example the famous *Turkish Bath* (1862) which was painted without Ingres ever visiting the Orient. The excursions to the Orient, and on-location paintings by painters such as Ferdinand-Victor-Eugene Delacroix, similarly, served largely to authenticate an a priori vision. Inspired by the Arab popular tradition of fantastic tales, the travellers recounted the Orient to fellow-Westerners according the paradigms furnished by European translations of *A Thousand and One Nights* (*Alf Laila wa Laila*), tales which were often translated quite loosely in order to satisfy the European taste for a passionately, violent Orient.[74] This Orient was perhaps best encapsulated in the figure of Salomé, whose Semitic origins were highlighted by the nineteenth- century Orientalist ethnographic vogue (e.g., Hugo von Habermann, Otto Friedrich).

The historical harem—which was largely an upper class phenomenon—was in fact most striking in its domesticity. Memoirs written by Egyptian and Turkish women[75] depict the complex familial life and a strong network of female communality horizontally and vertically across class lines. The isolated but relatively powerful harem women depended on working class women who were freer to move, and therefore became an important connection to the outside world.[76] Despite their subordination, harem women, as Leila Ahmed points out, often owned and ran their property, and could at times display crucial political power, thus revealing the harem as a site of contradictions.[77] Whereas Western discourse on the harem defined it simply as a male-dominated space, the accounts of the harem by Middle Eastern women testify to a system whereby a man's female relatives also shared the living space, allowing women access to other women, providing a protected space for the exchange of information and ideas safe from the eyes and the ears of men. (Contemporary Middle Eastern vestiges of this tradition are found in regular all-female gatherings, whereby women, as in the harems, carnivalize male power through jokes, stories, singing, and dancing.) In other words, the "harem," though patriarchal in nature, has been subjected to an ahistorical discourse whose Eurocentric assumptions[77] left unquestioned the sexual oppression of the West. The Middle Eastern system of communal seclusion, then, must also be compared to the Western system of domestic "solitary confinement" for upper-middle class women.[78]

European women constituted an enthusiastic audience for much of the nineteenth-century Orientalist poetry written by Beckford, Byron, and Moore, anticipating the spectatorial enthusiasm for exoticist films. As travellers, however, their discourse on the harems oscillates between Orientalist narratives and more dialogical testimonies. Western women participated in the Western colonial gaze; their writings often voyeuristically dwell on Oriental clothes, postures, and gestures, exoticizing the female "other."[79] If male narrators were intrigued by the harem as the locus of lesbian sexuality, female travellers, who as women had more access to female spaces, undermined the pornographic imagination of the harem. Interestingly, the detailed description of Turkish female bodies in Lady Mary Wortley Montagu's letters, particularly those drawn from her visit to the *hammam* (baths), points to a subliminal erotic fascination with the female "other," a fascination masquerading, at times, as a male gaze:

> I perceiv'd that the Ladys with the finest skins and most delicate shapes had the greatest share of my admiration, th'o their faces were sometimes less beautiful than those of their companions. To tell you the truth, I had the wickedness enough to wish secretly that Mr. Gervase had been there invisible. I fancy it would have very much improv'd his art to see so many fine Women naked in different postures . . .[80]

Female travellers, furthermore, were compelled to situate their own oppression vis-a-vis that of Oriental women. Lady Mary Wortley Montagu often measures the freedom endowed to English vis-a-vis Turkish women, suggesting the paradoxes of harems and veils:

> 'Tis very easy to see that they have more liberty than we have, no woman of what rank soever being permitted to go in the streets without two muslins, one that covers her face all but her eyes and another that hides the whole dress . . . You may guess how effectually this disguises them, that there is no distinguishing the great lady from her slave, and 'tis impossible for the most jealous husband to know his wife when he meets her, and no man dare either touch or follow a woman in the streets . . . The perpetual masquerade gives

them entire liberty of following their inclinations without danger of discovery.[81]

In fact, Lady Mary Wortley Montagu implicitly suggests an awareness, on the part of Turkish women, not simply of their oppression but also of that of European women. Recounting the day she was undressed in the *hamman* by the lady of the house, who was struck at the sight of the stays, she quoted the lady's remark that "the Husbands in England were much worse than in the East; for they ty'd up their wives in boxes, of the shape of their bodies."[82]

The popular image-making of the Orient internalized, in other words, the codes of male oriented travel-narratives. The continuities between the representation of the native body and the female body, are obvious when we compare Hollywood's ethnography with Hollywood's pornography. Ironically, we find a latent inscription of harems and despots even in texts not set in the Orient. *Harem structures*, in fact, permeate Western mass-mediated culture. Busby Berkeley's musical numbers, for example, project a harem-like structure reminiscent of Hollywood's mythical Orient. Like the harem, his musical numbers involve a multitude of women who, as Lucy Fischer suggests, serve as signifiers of male power over infinitely substitutable females.[83] The mise-en-scene of both harem scenes and musical numbers is structured around the scopic privilege of the master and his limitless pleasure in an exclusive place inaccessible to other men. Berkeley's panopticon-like camera links visual pleasure with a kind of surveillance of manipulated female movement. The camera's omnipresent and mobile gaze, its magic-carpet-like air-borne prowling along confined females embodies the over-arching look of the absent/present master—i.e., of both the director/producer, and vicariously of the spectator. The production numbers tend to exclude the male presence, but allow for the fantasies of the spectator, positioning his/her gaze as that of a despot entertained by a plurality of females. Rendered virtually identical, the women in Berkeley's numbers evoke the analogy between the musical show and the harem not only as a textual construct but also as a studio practice whose patriarchal structure of casting is conceived as a kind of beauty contest (a "judgment of Paris"). Speaking of his casting methods, Berkeley himself recounted

a day in which he interviewed 723 women in order to select only three: "My sixteen regular girls were sitting on the side waiting; so after I picked the three girls I put them next to my special sixteen and they matched just like pearls."[84]

The Desert Odyssey

The exoticist films allow for subliminally transexual tropes. The phantasm of the Orient gives an outlet for a carnivalesque play with national and at times gender identities. Isabelle Adaani in *Ishtar* is disguised as an Arab male-rebel and Brooke Shields as an American male racer in the Sahara desert, while Rudolph Valentino (*The Sheik* and *Son of the Sheik*), Douglas Fairbanks (*The Thief of Bagdad*), Elvis Presley (*Harum Scarum*), Peter O'Toole (*Lawrence of Arabia*), Warren Beatty and Dustin Hoffman (*Ishtar*) wear Arab disguise. Masquerading manifests a latent desire to transgress fixed national and gender identities. In *The Sheik*, the Agnes Ayres character, assisted by Arab women, wears an Arab female dress in order to penetrate the Oriental "marriage market," assuming the "inferior" position of the Arab woman in order, paradoxically, to empower herself with a gaze on Oriental despotism. The change of gender identities of female characters in more recent films such as *Sahara* and *Ishtar* allows as well for harmless transgressions of the coded "feminine" body-language. In counter narratives such as *The Battle of Algiers* (*La Battaglia di Algeri*, 1966), however, gender and national disguises take on different signification.[85] FLN Algerian women wear Western "modern" dress, dye their hair blond, and even act coquettishly with French soldiers.[86] Here it is the Third World which masquerades as the West, not as an act of self-effacing mimicry but as a way of sabotaging the colonial regime of assimilation.

Since clothing over the last few centuries, as a result of what J. C. Flugel calls "the Great Masculine Renunciation,"[87] has been limited to austere, uncolorful, and unplayful costumes, the projection to the phantastic locus of the Orient allows the imagination to go exuberantly "native." Historically, the widely-disseminated popular image in newspapers and newsreels of T. E. Lawrence in flowing Arab costume have partially inspired films such as *The Sheik* and *Son of the Sheik*, whose bi-sexual appeal can be located in the closet construction of Western man as "feminine."[88] The coded "feminine" look, therefore, is played out within the safe space of the Orient, through the "realistic" embodiment of the "Other." David Lean's Lawrence, despite his classical association with norms of heroic manliness, is also portrayed in a homoerotic light. When he is accepted by the Arab tribe he is dressed all in white, and at one point set on a horse, moving delicately, virtually captured like a bride. Drawing a sword from his sheath, the Peter O'Toole character shifts the gendered signification of the phallic symbol by using it as a mirror to look at his own newly acquired "feminine" Oriental image. More generally, the relationship between Lawrence and the Omar Sharif character gradually changes from initial male rivalry to an implied erotic attraction in which Sharif is associated with female imagery, best encapsulated in the scene where Sharif is seen in close-up with wet eyes, identifying with the tormented Lawrence. The inter-racial homo erotic subtext in *Lawrence of Arabia* forms part of a long tradition of colonial narratives from novels such as *Robinson Crusoe* (Crusoe and Friday), and *Huckleberry Finn* (Huck and Jim) to filmic adaptations such as *Around the World in 80 Days* (Phileas Fogg and his dark servant Passepartout).[89] Most texts about the "Empire," from the Western genre to recent nostalgia-for-Empire films such as *Mountains of the Moon* (1989), however, are pervaded by White homoeroticism in which male explorers, deprived of women, are "forced" into physical closeness, weaving bonds of affection and desire, in the course of their plights in an unknown, hostile land.

Homoeroticism, then, can simultaneously permeate homophobic colonialist texts. Within this symptomatic dialectic we may also understand the textual (dis)placement of the heterosexual African/Arab/Latino man, as playing the Id to the Western masculinist Superego. In *The Sheik*, for example, Valentino, as long as he is known to the spectator only as Arab, acts as the Id, but when he is revealed to be the son of Europeans, he is transformed into a superego figure who nobly risks his life to rescue the English woman from "real" Arab rapists.[90] And the English woman overcomes her sexual repression only in the desert, after being sexually provoked repeatedly by the Sheik. Valentino, the "Latin lover," is here projected into another "exotic" space where he can act out sexual

phantasies that would have been unthinkable in a contemporaneous American or European setting. The desert, in this sense, functions narratively as an isolating element, as sexually and morally separate imaginary territory. The Orientalist films tend to begin in the city—where European civilization has already tamed the East—but the real dramatic conflicts take place in the desert where women are defenseless, and White woman could easily become the captive of a romantic sheik or evil Arab. The positioning of rapeable White woman by a lustful male in an isolated desert locale gives voice to a masculinist fantasy of complete control over the Western woman, the woman "close to home," without any intervening protective code of morality. Puritanical Hollywood thus claims to censure female adventurousness, and the male tyranny of harems and rapes—but only, paradoxically, as a way of gratifying Western inter-racial sexual desires.

In the more recent reworking of *The Sheik* and *Son of the Sheik*, in Menahem Golan's *Sahara*, the male rescue phantasy and the punishment of female rebellion undergird the film. In *Sahara* the central figure, Dale (Brooke Shields), feisty race car driving and only-daughter of a 20s care manufacturer, is presented as reckless, daring, and assertive for entering the male domain of the Oriental desert and for entering the "men only" race. She also literally disguises herself as a man, and adopts His profession and His mastery of the desert land through technology. Captured by desert tribesmen, she becomes a commodity fought over within the tribe and between tribes; the camera's fetishization of her body, however, is the ironic reminder of the Western projection of stars' bodies as commodity. Scenes of Brooke Shields wrestling with her captors not only suture the Western spectator to a national rescue operation but also invite the implied spectator into an orgiastic voyeurism. The desire for the Western woman and the fear of losing control over her is manifested in her punishment through several attempted rapes by Arabs. But at the end the courageous winner of the race decides "on her own" to return to the noble light-skinned sheik who had rescued her from cruel Arabs at the risk of his own life. The woman, who could have won independence, still "voluntarily" prefers the ancient ways of gender hierarchies.

At times, it is implied that women, while offended by Arab and Muslim rapists, actually *prefer* masterful men like Valentino.[91] Following the screening of *The Sheik*, newspaper columnists were asking "Do women like masterful men?" To which Valentino replied: "Yes." "All women like a little cave-man stuff. No matter whether they are feminists, suffragettes or so-called new women, they like to have a masterful man who makes them do things he asserts."[92] Edith Hull expressed similar opinions. "There can be only one head in a house. Despite modem desire for equality of sexes I still believe that physically and morally it is better that the head should be the man."[93] Edith Hull's novel and Monic Katterjohn's adaptation, gratify, to some extent, a projected Western female desire for an "exotic" lover, for a Romantic, sensual, passionate, but non-lethal, play with the *Liebestod*, a release of the Id for the (segregated) upper-middle-class occidental woman.[94] (The author of the source novel claimed to have written the book for relaxation when her husband was in the war and she was alone in India. She decided to visit in Algeria, where she was impressed with the fine work the French government was doing.) In this sense the phantasm of the Orient can be incorporated by Western women, forming part of the broader colonial discourse on the "exotic," while simultaneously constituting an imaginary locus for suppressed sexual desires.

The rescue phantasy, when literalized through the rescue of a woman from a lascivious Arab, has to be seen not only as an allegory of saving the Orient from its libidinal, instinctual destructiveness but also as a didactic *Bildungsroman* addressed to women at home, perpetuating by contrast the myth of the sexual egalitarianism of the West. The exoticist films delegitimize Third World national identities and give voice to anti-feminist backlash, responding to the threat to institutionalized patriarchal power presented by the woman's Suffrage movements and the nascent feminist struggle. In this sense the narrative of Western women in the Third World can be read as a projected didactic allegory insinuating the dangerous nature of the "uncivilized man" and by implication lauding the freedom presumably enjoyed by Western women. In *The Sheik* and *Sahara* the Western woman directly rebels against the "civilized tradition" of marriage at the beginning of the film, calling it "captivity," only to later become literally captive of lusting Dark men. Transgressing male space (penetrating the marriage market by masquerading as an Arab woman in *The Sheik*, and participating in a male race by masquerading as a young man in *Sahara*), the female protagonist begins with a hubris vis-a-vis her Western male protectors (against the Arabians from the desert), and then goes through the "pedagogical" experience of attempted rapes. The telos, or quite literally, "homecoming" of this desert Odyssey is the disciplinary punishment of female desire for liberation and renewed spectatorial appreciation for the existing sexual, racial, and national order.

* * *

My discussion of colonial constructions of gender has aimed at analyzing the crucial role of sexual difference for the culture of Empire. Western popular culture, in this sense, has operated on the same Eurocentric discursive continuum as such disciplines as Philosophy, Egyptology, Anthropology, Historiography, and Geography. From the erotic projections of *The Sheik* to the spectacular historiography of *Lawrence of Arabia*, or from the fantastic tale of *The Mummy* (1932) to the Egyptological mission of *Raiders of the Lost Ark*, my reading has tried to suggest that despite some differences, having to do with the periods in which the films were produced, hegemonic Western representation has been locked into a series of Eurocentric articulations of power. Although a feminist reading of (post)colonial discourse must take into account the national and historical specificities of that discourse, it is equally important also to chart the broader structural analogies in the representation of diverse Third World cultures. (Post)Colonial narratives, as we have seen, serves to define the "West" through metaphors of rape, phantasies of rescue, and eroticized geographies. The popular culture of Empire has tended to rely on a structurally similar genderized discourse within different national and historical moments, a discourse challenged by resistant counter-narratives such as *How Tasty Was My Frenchman, Nice Coloured Girls*, and *The Mummy/The Night of Counting the Years*.

Notes

1. Different sections of this essay were presented at several conferences: Third World Film Institute, New York University (1984); The Middle East Studies Association,

University of California, Los Angeles (1988); Humanities Council Faculty Seminar on Race and Gender, New York University (1988); The Society for Cinema Studies, Iowa University (1989); The Conference on "Gender and Colonialism," University of California, Berkeley (1989); The Conference on "Rewriting the (Post)Modern: (Post)Colonialism/Feminism/Late Capitalism," The University of Utah, Humanities Center (1990).

2. Here some of my discussion is indebted to Edward Said's notion of the "feminization" of the Orient, *Orientalism* (New York: Vintage, 1978). See also Francis Barker, Peter Hulme, Margaret Iversen, Diana Loxley, eds. *Europe and Its Others* Vols. 1 and 2. Colchester: University of Essex, 1985, especially Peter Hulme, "Polytropic Man: Tropes of Sexuality and Mobility in Early Colonial Discourse" (Vol. 2); Jose Rabasa, "Allegories of the Atlas" (Vol. 2). Some of my discussion here on gendered metaphors appears in Ella Shohat, "Imagining Terra Incognita: The Disciplinary Gaze of Empire," *Public Culture*, Vol. 3, No. 2.

3. Sir Walter Raleigh, "Discovery of Guiana." Cited in Susan Griffin, *Woman and Nature: The Roaring Inside Her* (New York: Harper & Row, 1978), p. 47.

4. St. John de Crèvecoeur, *Letters from an American Farmer*, 1782. Cited in Henry Nash Smith, *Virgin Land: The American West as Symbol and Myth* (Cambridge, Massachusetts: Harvard University Press, 1950), p. 121.

5. See Henry Nash Smith, *Virgin Land: The American West as Symbol and Myth*. For 19th century North American expansionist ideology, see Richard Slotkin, *The Fatal Environment: The Myth of the Frontier in the Age of Industrialization, 1800–1890* (Middletown, Connecticut: Wesleyan University Press, 1985).

6. For an examination of the representation of the American frontiers and gender issues see Annette Kolodny, *The Lay of the Land: Metaphors as Experience and History in American Life and Letters* (Chapel Hill: The University of North Carolina Press, 1975); and *The Land Before Her: Fantasy and Experience of the American Frontiers, 1630–1860* (Chapel Hill: The University of North Carolina Press, 1984).

7. R. W. B. Lewis, *The American Adam: Innocence, Tragedy, and Tradition in the Nineteenth Century* (Chicago: The University of Chicago Press, 1959). Hans Blumenberg, interestingly, points out in relation to Francis Bacon that the resituation of Paradise, as the goal of history, was supposed to promise magical facility. The knowledge of nature for him is connected to his definition of the Paradisiac condition as mastery by means of the word. (*The Legitimacy of the Modern Age*. Translated by Robert Wallace. Cambridge, Massachusetts: MIT Press, 1983).

8. Jan Van der Straet's representation of America has been cited by several scholars: Michel de Certeau,

'Avant propos' in *L'Ecriture de l'histoire* (Paris: Gallimard, 1975); Olivier Richon, "Representation, the Despot and the Harem: Some Questions Around an Academic Orientalist Painting by Lecomte-du-Nouy" (1885) in *Europe and Its Others* (Vol. 1).

9. The gendering of colonial encounters between a "feminine" nature and "masculine" scientist draws on a pre-existing discourse which has genderized the encounter between "Man and Nature" in the West itself. For a full discussion see, for example, Susan Griffin, *Woman and Nature: The Roaring Inside Her*.

10. Michael de Certeau, 'Avant propos' in *L'Ecriture de l'histoire*.

11. The film was distributed in the U. S. as *How Tasty Was My Little Frenchman*.

12. For a close analysis of *How Tasty Was My Frenchman* see Richard Peña, "How Tasty Was My Little Frenchman," in Randal Johnson and Robert Stam, *Brazilian Cinema* (East Brunswick, New Jersey: Associated University Presses, 1982) (re-printed by University of Texas Press, 1985).

13. The report concerns another tribe, the Tupiniquim who were massacred by their "allies," the Portuguese, confirming the Native American stance, mediated in the film through the Tupinamba tribe, that despite tactical alliances, the Europeans, whether French or Portuguese, have similar desires in relation to the Native American Land.

14. The film which was shot in Parati (Brazil) has the actors and actresses mimic Native American attitudes towards nudity by living rude throughout the duration of the shooting. This production method is, of course, different from the industrial approach to shooting scenes of nudity. *How Tasty Was My Frenchman* can also be seen as part of a counterculture of the late sixties, and its general interest in non-Western societies as alternative possibilities.

15. *How Tasty Was My Frenchman* does not criticize patriarchal structures within Native American societies.

16. Although Cleopatra was addressed as Egypt in the *Antony and Cleopatra* play, Shakespeare here and in *The Tempest* offers a complex dialectics between the West and "its Others."

17. Colonialist representations have their roots in what Martin Bernal calls the "Aryan model," a model which projects a presumably clear and monolithic historical trajectory leading from classical Greece (constructed as "pure," "western," and "democratic") to Imperial Rome and then to the metropolitan capitals of Europe and the United States. (See *Black Athena: The Afroasiatic Roots of Classical Civilization. Volume I, The Fabrication of Ancient Greece 1785–1985*. New Brunswick: Rutgers University Press, 1987.) "History" is made to seem

synonymous with a linear notion of European "progress." This Eurocentric view is premised on crucial exclusions of internal and external "others": the African and Semitic cultures that strongly inflicted the culture of classical Greece; the Islamic and Arabic-Sephardi culture which played an invaluable cultural role during the so-called "dark" and "middle" ages; and the diverse indigenous peoples, whose land and natural resources were violently appropriated and whose cultures were constructed as "savage" and "irrational."

18. Egyptology's mania for a mere ancient Egypt, for example, is ironic in an Arab context where Egypt is often perceived as *the* model of an Arab country.

19. This is true even for those films produced after the great wave of national liberation movements in the Third World.

20. Tracey Moffatt's *Nice Coloured Girls* explores the relocations established between White settlers and Aboriginal women over the last two hundred years, juxtaposing the "first encounter" with present-day urban encounters. Conveying the perspective of Aboriginal women, the film situates their oppression within a historical context in which voices and images from the past play a crucial role.

21. Female voyagers occupy very rarely the center of the narrative (*The King and I, Black Narcissus*). In contrast to scientist heroes, they tend to occupy the "feminine" actantial slot: educators and nurses.

22. The passive/active division is, of course, based on stereotypically sexist imagery.

23. See for example Suleiman Mousa, *T. E. Lawrence: An Arab View.* Translated by Albert Burros (New York: Oxford University Press, 1966).

24. See Francis Bacon, *Advancement of Learning* and *Novum Organum* (New York: The Colonial Press, 1899).

25. Francis Bacon, *Advancement of Learning* and *Novum Organum*. In *Advancement of Learning*, p. 135.

26. Francis Bacon, *Novum Organum* in *The Works of Francis Bacon*. James Spedding, Robert Ellis and Douglas Heath, eds. (London: Longmans & Co., 1870), p. 82.

27. Hans Blumenberg, *The Legitimacy of the Modern Age*, p. 389.

28. For an illuminating reading of Haggard's *King Solomon's Mines* see Anne McClintock, "Maidens, Maps, and Mines: The Reinvention of Patriarchy in Colonial South Africa," *The South Atlantic Quarterly*, Vol. 87, No. 1 (Winter 1988).

29. Television has incorporated this penchant for spinning globe logos especially in News programs, displaying its authority over the world.

30. *Around the World in 80 Days* feminizes national maps by placing images of "native" women on the backs of maps of specific countries. The balloon used by the protagonist is referred to as "she" and called "La Coquette."

31. The feminine designation of "the moon" in French, "La Lune," is reproduced by the "feminine" iconography of the moon.

32. Georges Méliès' filmography includes a relatively great number of films related to colonial explorations and Orientalist phantasies such as *Le Fakir-Mystère Indien* (1896), *Vente d'Esclaves au Harem* (1897), *Cleopatre* (1899), *La Vengeance de Bouddah* (1901), *Les Aventures de Robinson Crusoe* (1902), *Le Palais des Milles et Une Nuits* (1905). Interestingly, Méliès' early fascination with spectacles dates back to his visits to the Egyptian Hall shows, directed by Maskelyne and Cooke and devoted to fantastic spectacles.

33. I am here referring especially to the Babylon section.

34. Bazin's Malraux-inspired statement in the opening of "The Ontology of the Photographic Image" suggests that "at the origin of painting and sculpture there lies a mummy complex." (*What Is Cinema*, translated by Hugh Gray, Berkeley: University of California Press, 1967, p. 9.) The ritual of cinema, in this sense, is not unlike the Egyptian religious rituals which provided "a defence [sic] against the passage of time," thus satisfying "a basic psychological need in man, for death is but the victory of time." In this interesting analogy Bazin, it seems to me, offers an existentialist interpretation of the mummy, which, at the same time, undermines Egyptian religion itself; since the ancient Egyptians above all axiomatically assumed the reality of life after death—toward which the mummy was no more than a means.

35. In this essay, I refer to some of the various subgenres of the Hollywood Orientalist film of which I have identified seven: 1) Stories concerning contemporary Westerners in the Orient (*The Sheik* [1921], *The Road to Morocco* [1942], *Casablanca* [1942], *The Man Who Knew Too Much* [1956], *Raiders of the Lost Ark* [1981], *Sahara* [1983], *Ishtar* [1987]); 2) Films concerning "Orientals" in the first world (*Black Sunday* [1977], *Back to the Future* [1985]); 3) Films based on ancient history such as the diverse versions of *Cleopatra*; 4) Films based on contemporary history (*Exodus* [1960], *Lawrence of Arabia* [1962]); 5) Films based on the Bible (*Judith of Bethulia* [1913], *Samson and Delilah* [1949], *The Ten Commandments* [1956]); 6) Films based on *The Arabian Nights* (*The Thief of Baghdad* [1924], *Oriental Dream* [1944], *Kismet* [1955]); 7) Films in which ancient Egypt and its mythologized enigmas serve as pretext for contemporary horror-mystery and romance (the *Mummy* series). I view these films partially in the light of Edward Said's indispensable contribution to anti-colonial discourse, i.e., his genealogical critique of Orientalism as the discursive formation by which European culture was able to manage—and even produce—the Orient during the post-Enlightenment period.

36. Mallek Alloula examines this issue in French postcards of Algeria. See *The Colonial Harem*. Translated by Myrna Godzich and Wlad Godzich. (Minneapolis: University of Minnesota Press, 1986).

37. Freud associates Africa and femininity in *The Interpretation of Dreams* when he speaks of Haggard's *She* as "a strange book, but full of hidden meaning . . . the eternal feminine . . . *She* describes an adventurous road that had scarcely even been trodden before, leading into an undiscovered region. . . ." *The Standard Edition of the Complete Psychological Works of Sigmund Freud*, ed. James Strachey. (London: The Hogarth Press, 1953–74), SE IV-V, pp. 453–4.

38. Joseph Breuer and Sigmund Freud, *Studies on Hysteria*. Translated by James Strachey in collaboration with Anna Freud. (New York: Basic Books, 1957), p. 139.

39. Breuer and Freud, *Studies on Hysteria*, p. 193.

40. Sigmund Freud, "On Transformations of Instinct as Exemplified in Anal Erotism," in *The Standard Edition of the Complete Psychological Works of Sigmund Freud*, SE XVII, pp. 129, 135.

41. Toril Moi, "Representation of Patriarchy: Sexuality and Epistemology in Freud's Dora," in Charles Brenheimer and Claire Kahane, eds. *In Dora's Case: Freud, Hysteria, Feminism*. (London: Virago, 1985), p. 198.

42. David Macey, *Lacan in Contexts*. (London, New York: Verso, 1988), pp. 178–180.

43. Breuer and Freud, *Studies on Hysteria*, p. 292.

44. Stephan Salisbury, "In Dr. Freud's Collection, Objects of Desire," *The New York Times*, September 3, 1989.

45. "My voyage to the Orient was like a grand act of my interior life."

46. Linking Jews to the history, politics and culture of the West must be seen as continuous with Zionist discourse which has elided the largely Third World Arab history and culture of Middle Eastern Sephardic Jews. For a full discussion of the problematics generated by Zionist discourse, see Ella Shohat, "Sephardim in Israel: Zionism from the Standpoint of Its Jewish Victims," *Social Text* 19/20 (Fall 1988). This debate was partially continued in *Critical Inquiry* Vol. 15, No. 3 (Spring 1989) in the section "An Exchange on Edward Said and Difference." See especially, Edward Said, "Response," pp. 634–646.

47. *The Ten Commandments*, partially shot on location in Egypt, was banned by the Egyptian government.

48. On another level we might discern a hidden Jewish substratum undergirding the film. In the ancient past Egypt dispossessed the Hebrews of their ark and in the present (the thirties) it is the Nazis; but in a time tunnel Harrison Ford is sent to fight the Nazis in the name of a Jewish shrine (the word "Jewish" is of course never mentioned in the film) and in the course of events the rescuer is rescued by the rescues. A phantasy of liberation from a history of victimization is played out by Steven Spielberg, using Biblical myths of wonders worked against ancient Egyptians this time redeployed against the Nazis—miracles absent during the Holocaust. The Hebrew ark itself performs miracles and dissolves the Nazis, saving Dr. Jones and his girlfriend Marion from the Germans who, unlike the Americans, do not respect the divine law of never looking at the Holy of Holies. The Jewish religious prohibition of looking at God's image and the prohibition of graven images (with the consequent cultural de-emphasis on visual arts) is triumphant over the Christian predilection for religious visualization. The film, in the typical paradox of cinematic voyeurism, punishes the hubris of the "Christian" who looks at divine beauty while at the same time nourishing the spectator's visual pleasure.

49. *Al Mumia* (*The Mummy*) was exhibited in the U. S. under the title *The Night of Counting the Years*.

50. Ahmose freed Egypt from the Hyksos invaders and ushered in the "New Empire" period of ancient Egyptian history.

51. Thutmose III was Egypt's greatest warrior pharaoh who conquered Palestine and Syria.

52. Rameses II is the reputed Pharaoh of the Exodus.

53. Howard Carter and A. C. Mace's narrative of their predecessor's 1881 discovery, for example, links the Egyptologists' rescue of mummies to the ancient Egyptian priests' protection of their Kings: "There, huddled together in a shallow, ill-cut grave, lay the most powerful monarchs of the ancient East, kings whose names were familiar to the whole world, whom no one in his wildest moments had ever dreamed of seeing. There they had remained, where the priests in secrecy had hurriedly brought them that dark night three thousand years ago; and on their coffins and mummies, neatly docketed, were the records of their journeyings from one hiding place to another. Some had been wrapped, and two or three in the course of their many wanderings had been moved to other coffins. In forty-eight hours—we don't do things quite so hastily nowadays—the tomb was cleared; the kings were embarked upon the museum barge." (Shirley Glubok, ed., *Discovering Tut-ankh-Amen's Tomb*. [Abridged and adapted from Howard Carter and A. C. Mace, *The Tomb of Tut-ankh-Amen*] New York: Macmillan Publishing, 1968, p. 15.)

54. In a relatively recent interview following the screening of *The Mummy* on Egyptian television, Shadi Abdel Salam was slightly criticized for relying on a Western musician when Egypt has its own musicians. Abdel Salam insisted that the Italian musician was chosen for his technical knowledge, and that his role was basically to arrange a pre-existing popular Egyptian music. Khassan Aawara, "*Al Mumia*," *Al Anba*, October 30, 1983 (Arabic).

55. In addition to Edward Said's pioneering critical writings on Orientalist discourse and specifically on Egypt, see also Timothy Mitchel, *Colonising Egypt* (Cambridge: Cambridge University Press, 1988).

56. Shirley Glubok, p. 15.

57. Guy Hennebelle, "Chadi Abdel Salam Prix Georges Sadoul 1970: 'La momie' est une reflexion sur le destin d'une culture nationale," *Les Lettres Francaises*, No. 1366, December 30, 1977, p. 17.

58. "They were the mightiest Pharaohs. What became of them?"—a meditation in the film reminiscent in some ways of Shelly's "Ozymandias."

59. See *The Book of the Dead*, ed. E. A. Wallis Budge (London: Arkana, 1989).

60. See for example Cynthia Enloe, *Bananas, Beaches and Bases: Making Feminist Sense of International Politics* (Berkeley: University of California Press, 1989), pp. 19–41.

61. See Boris Uspensky, *A Poetics of Composition* (Berkeley: University of California Press, 1973).

62. For a critical discussion of the representation of Black female sexuality in the cinema see Jane Gaines, "White Privilege and Looking Relations—Race and Gender in Feminist Film Theory," *Screen* Vol. 29, No. 4 (Autumn 1988). On Black spectatorship and reception of dominant films see for example Jacqueline Bobo, "*The Color Purple*: Black Women as Cultural Readers" in Diedre Pribram, ed. *Female Spectators: Looking at Films and Television* (New York: Verso, 1988); Manthia Diawara, "Black Spectator-ship: Problems of Identification and Resistance" in *Screen* Vol. 29, No. 4 (Autumn 1988).

63. The mystery in the *Mummy* films which often involves a kind of Liebestod or haunting heterosexual attraction—for example *The Mummy* (1932), *The Mummy's Curse* (1944), *The Mummy's Hand* (1940)—can be seen in this sense as allegorizing the mysteries of sexuality itself.

64. In her striking autobiography, Harriet Jacobs, for example, recounts the history of her family, focussing especially on the degradation of slavery and the sexual oppression she suffered as a slave woman. Her daily struggle against racial/sexual abuse is well illustrated in the cases of her master, who was determined to rum her into his concubine, his jealous wife, who added her own versions of harassments, and the future congressman, who, after fathering her children, did not keep his promise to set them free. *Incidents in the Life of a Slave Girl Written by Herself*, Fagan Yellin, ed. (Cambridge, Massachusetts: Harvard University Press, 1987).

65. Citations from The Production Code of the Motion Picture Producers and Directors of America, Inc.—1930–1934 are taken from Garth Jowett, *Film: The Democratic Art* (Boston: Little, Brown and Company, 1976).

66. Here I am especially thinking of Anna Julia Cooper and Ida B. Wells.

67. Hazel V. Carby, "Lynching, Empire, and Sexuality" *Critical Inquiry* Vol. 12, No. 1 (Autumn 1985).

68. For discussion of rape and racial violence see for example Jacquelyn Dowd Hall, "'The Mind that Burns in Each Body': Women, Rape, and Racial Violence" in Ann Snitow, Christine Stansell and Sharon Thompson, eds. *Powers of Desire* (New York: Monthly Review Press, 1983).

69. Haile Gerima's *Bush Mama* anatomizes contemporary American power structure in which rape performed by a white policeman is subjectivized through the helpless young Black woman.

70. Fredric Jameson, "Third World Literature in the Era of Multinational Capitalism" *Social Text* 15 (Fall 1986). Although Jameson speaks of allegory in a Third World context, I found the category germane for the First World, increasingly characterized by "othernesses" and "differences" within itself.

71. For example, Ferdinand-Victor-Eugene Delacroix, as Lawrence Michalak points out, borrowed Indian clothing from a set designer for his models, threw in some "Assyrian" motifs from travel books and Persian miniatures, and invented the rest of the Maghreb from his imagination. ("Popular French Perspectives on the Maghreb: Orientalist Painting of the Late 19th and Early 20th Centuries," in *Connaissances du Maghreb: Sciences Sociales et Colonisation*, Jean-Claude Vatin, ed. Paris: Editions du Centre National de la Recherche Scientifique, 1984.)

72. Images of nude breasts of African women in the *Tarzan* series relied on travelogues. Trinh T. Minh-ha in *Reassemblage* (1982) attempts to question the focus on breasts in ethnological cinema. For her broader critique of anthropology see *Woman, Native, Other* (Bloomington: Indiana University Press, 1989), pp. 47–76.

73. Fellini's *8½*, meanwhile, self-mockingly exposes this pornographic imagination of the King Solomon-style harem as merely amplifying the protagonist's actual lived polygamy.

74. For the Orientalist ideology undergirding the translations of *A Thousand and One Nights* to European languages see Rana Kabbani, *Europe's Myths of Orient* (Bloomington: Indiana University Press, 1986).

75. See for example Huda Shaarawi, *Harem Years: The Memoirs of an Egyptian Feminist (1879–1924)*. Translated by Margot Badran (New York: The Feminist Press at The City University of New York, 1987).

76. See Lois Beck and Nikki Keddie, eds. *Women in the Muslim World*. (Cambridge, Massachusetts: Harvard University Press, 1978); Mervat Hatem, "The Politics of Sexuality and Gender in Segregated Patriarchal Systems: The

Case of Eighteenth- and Nineteenth-Century Egypt," *Feminist Studies* 12, No. 2 (Summer 1986).

77. For a critique of Eurocentric representation of the Harem see Leila Ahmed, "Western Ethnocentrism and Perceptions of the Harem," *Feminist Studies* 8, No. 3 (Fall 1982).

78. The artistic representation of the solitary confinement of upper-middle class Western women within the household is fascinatingly researched and analyzed by Bram Dijkstra, *Idols of Perversity* (New York: Oxford University Press, 1986).

79. Protofeminist Western women such as Hubertine Auclert, Françoise Correze, Mathea Gaudry, and Germaine Tillion, as Marnia Lazreg suggests, reproduced Orientalist discourse in their writings. For a critique of Western feminism and colonial discourse see for example Marnia Lazreg, "Feminism and Difference: The Perils of Writing as a Woman on Women in Algeria," *Feminist Studies* 14:3 (Fall 1988); Chandra Talpade Mohanty, "Under Western Eyes: Feminist Scholarship and Colonial Discourses," *Boundary* 2:12 (Spring/Fall 1984); Gayatri Chakravorty Spivak, "French Feminism in an International Frame," *Yale French Studies* 62 (1981); *In Other Worlds: Essays in Cultural Politics*, Chapter 3 "Entering the Third World" (New York and London: Methuen, 1987).

80. Robert Halsband, ed., *The Complete Letters of Lady Mary Wortley Montagu*, Vol. I (London: Oxford University Press, 1965), p. 314.

81. Robert Halsband, ed., *The Selected Letters of Lady Mary Wortley Montagu*, (New York: St. Martin's Press, 1970), pp. 96–97.

82. Robert Halsband, ed., *The Complete Letters of Lady Mary Wortley Montagu*, Vol. I, pp. 314–315.

83. For an analysis of the "mechanical reproduction" of women in Busby Berkeley's films, see Lucy Fischer, "The Image of Woman As Image: The Optical Politics of *Dames*," in Patricia Erens, ed. *Sexual Stratagems: The World of Women in Film* (New York: Horizon Press, 1979).

84. Quoted in Lucy Fischer, "The Image of Woman As Image: The Optical Politics of *Dames*," p. 44.

85. For a detailed analysis of *The Battle of Algiers*, see Robert Stam, "Three Women, Three Bombs: *The Battle of Algiers* Notes and Analysis" *Film Study Extract* (Macmillan Press, 1975). See also Barbara Harlow's introduction to Malek Alloula, *The Colonial Harem*, pp. ix–xxii.

86. In *Battle of Algiers* FLN Algerian men at one point wear Arab female dress—a disguise whose ultimate goal is to assert Algerian national identity. This ephemeral change of gender identities within anti-colonial texts requires a more elaborate analysis of the Third World masculine rescue operation of Third World women from the violation of First World men. Such feminist criticism directed at the works of Frantz Fanon and Malek Alloula within the Algerian/French context has been addressed, in the Black/White North American context, at Malcolm X and the Black Panthers.

87. See J. C. Flugel, *The Psychology of Clothes* (London: Hogarth Press, 1930). For an extended discussion of Flugel writing on fashion see Kaja Silverman "The Fragments of a Fashionable Discourse," in *Studies in Entertainment: Critical Approaches to Mass Culture*, ed. Tania Modleski (Bloomington: India University Press, 1986); also Silverman, *The Acoustic Mirror: The Female Voice in Psychoanalysis and Cinema* (Bloomington: Indiana University Press, 1988), pp. 24–27.

88. The American journalist Lowell Thomas was instrumental in the popularization of T. E. Lawrence in the West; his show, which consisted of lecture and footage he shot from the Middle East front, was, after a short time, moved to Madison Square Garden. See John E. Mack, *A Prince of Our Disorder: The Life of T. E. Lawrence* (Boston: Little Brown and Company, 1976).

89. Leslie Fiedler argues that homoerotic friendship between White men and Black or indigenous men is at the core of the classical American novel. See *Love and Death in the American Novel* (New York: Criterion Books, 1960).

90. Interestingly Leslie Fiedler's *The Inadvertent Epic* comments on another white woman novelist, Margaret Mitchell, whose *Gone With the Wind* is structured according to scenarios of inter-ethnic rapes.

91. For an analysis of Valentino and female spectatorship, see Miriam Hansen, "Pleasure, Ambivalence, Identification: Valentino and Female Spectatorship," *Cinema Journal* 25, No. 4 (Summer, 1986).

92. *Movie Weekly*, November 19, 1921.

93. *Movie Weekly*, November 19, 1921.

94. Denis de Rougemont partially traces the liebestod motif to Arabic poetry. See *Love in the Western World*, Translated by Montagnery Belgion (New York: Harper & Row Publishers, 1974).

6.
BEYOND RACISM AND MISOGYNY

Black Feminism and 2 Live Crew

Kimberlé Williams Crenshaw

Violence against women is a central issue in the feminist movement. As part of an overall strategy to change patterns of individual and institutional behavior to better women's lives, academics and activists have challenged the ways violence against women—primarily battering and rape—is perpetuated and condoned within our culture.

Much of this challenge has occurred within legal discourse because it is within the law that cultural attitudes are legitimized through organized state power. Feminists have struggled with some success to end the representation of battering and rape as a "private family matter" or as "errant sexuality" and make clear these are specific sites of gender subordination. These battles have taken place over issues such as mandatory arrest for batterers, the admissibility of a victim's sexual history in sexual assault cases, and the admissibility of psychological evidence, such as the battered women's syndrome in cases involving women who kill their batterers and rape trauma syndrome in sexual assault cases.

If recent events are indicative, the process may continue to bear some political fruit. The governors of Ohio and Maryland have commuted sentences of women convicted of murdering abusive husbands, and other states are considering similar actions. Moreover, legislation is pending before Congress that would make violence "motivated by gender" a civil rights violation.[1]

The emphasis on gender, however, tends to downplay the interaction of gender subordination with race and class. The attitude is largely consistent with doctrinal and political practices that construct racism and sexism as mutually exclusive. Given the assumption that all women stand to benefit from efforts to politicize violence against women, concerns about race may initially seem unnecessarily divisive. Indeed, it seems that what women have in common—the fact that they are primary targets of rape and battering—not only outweighs the differences among them but may render bizarre the argument that race should play a significant role in the analysis of these issues.

Although racial issues are not explicitly a part of the politicization of gender, public controversies show that racial politics are often linked to gender violence in the way that the violence is experienced, how the interventions are shaped, or the manner in which the consequences are politicized and represented. The controversies over the Central Park jogger case, the 2 Live Crew case, the St. John's rape trial, and the perhaps lesser known issue of Shahrazad Ali's *The Blackman's Guide to the Blackwoman*,[2] all present issues of gender violence in which racial politics are deeply implicated but in ways that seem impossible to capture fully within existing frameworks that separate racial politics from gender politics. These separations are linked to the overall problem of the way racism and sexism are understood and how these understandings inform organizing around antiracism and feminism.

Reformist efforts to politicize these issues exclusively around gender are thus problematic both for women of color and for those engaged in feminist and antiracist politics generally. Discursive and political practices that separate race from gender and gender from race create complex problems of exclusion and distortion for women of color. Because monocausal frameworks are unlikely to provide a ready means for addressing the interplay of gender and race in cultural and political discourse on violence, it is necessary to recenter inquiries relating to violence against women from the vantage point of women of color. On the simplest level, an intersectional framework uncovers how the dual positioning of women of color as women and as members of a subordinated racial group bears upon violence committed against us. This dual positioning, or as some scholars have labeled it, double jeopardy, renders women of color vulnerable to the structural, political, and representational dynamics of both race and gender subordination. A framework attuned to the various ways that these dynamics intersect is a necessary prerequisite to exploring how this double vulnerability influences the way that violence against women of color is experienced and best addressed.

Second, an intersectional framework suggests ways in which political and representational practices relating to race and gender interrelate. This is relevant because the separate rhetorical strategies that characterize antiracist and feminist politics frequently intersect in ways that create new dilemmas for women of color. For example, political imperatives are frequently constructed from the perspectives of those who are dominant within either the race or gender categories in which women of color are situated, namely, white women or men of color. These priorities are grounded in efforts to address only racism or sexism—as those issues are understood by the dominant voices within these communities. Political strategies that challenge only certain subordinating practices while maintaining existing hierarchies not only marginalize those who are subject to multiple systems of subordination but also often result in oppositionalizing race and gender discourses. An intersectional critique is thus important in uncovering the ways in which the reformist politics of one discourse enforce subordinating aspects of another.

The observations that follow are meant to explore the ways in which intersections of race and gender bear upon depictions of violence against women, particularly women of color. My observations are also meant to explore the bearing of these intersections

on the broader efforts to politicize violence against all women. I explicitly adopt a Black feminist stance in my attempt to survey violence against women of color. I do this with cognizance of several tensions that this perspective entails. The most significant one relates to the way in which feminism has been subject to the dual criticism of speaking *for* women of color through its invocation of the term "woman" even as it fails to examine differences and the problem of *excluding* women of color through grounding feminism on the experiences and interests of white women. I think it is important to name the perspective from which my own analysis is constructed, and that is as a Black feminist. I also think it is important to acknowledge that the materials upon which my analysis are based relate primarily to Black women. At the same time, I see my own work as part of a broader effort among feminist women of color to broaden feminism to include, among other factors, an analysis of race. Thus, I attempt to reach across racial differences to share my thinking and tentatively suggest ways in which the theory may apply to other women of color.

This chapter focuses on the problem of representational intersectionality. After a brief introduction to the theory of intersectionality, I will consider the ways in which media representations of women of color reinforce race and gender stereotypes. These stereotyped representations encourage and incite violence against us. But they do much more than that: They create a dominant narrative that forces actual women of color to the margins of the discourse and renders our own accounts of such victimization less credible. These media images define the spaces that women of color may occupy in dominant consciousness and problematize our efforts to construct a political practice and cultural critique that address the physical and material violence we experience.

This project is not oppositional to the overall effort to recode violence against women, rather, it is an attempt to broaden and strengthen the strategies available by exploring sites where race and gender converge to create the cultural and political grounding for gender violence. It is important also to ensure that these reform efforts do not reinforce racist sensibilities within the larger culture or ignore the need to challenge patriarchy within subcultures.

An Examination of Intersectionality

Intersectionality is a core concept both provisional and illustrative. Although the primary intersections that I explore here are between race and gender, the concept can and should be expanded by factoring in issues such as class, sexual orientation, age, and color. I conceive of intersectionality as a provisional concept that links contemporary politics with postmodern theory. In examining the intersections of race and gender, I engage the dominant assumptions that these are essentially separate; by tracing the categories to their intersections, I hope to suggest a methodology that will ultimately disrupt the tendencies to see race and gender as exclusive or separable categories. Intersectionality is thus in my view a transitional concept that links current concepts with their political consequences, and real world politics with postmodern insights. It can be replaced as our understanding of each category becomes more multidimensional. The basic function of intersectionality is to frame the following inquiry: How does the fact that women of color are simultaneously situated within at least two groups that are subjected to broad societal subordination bear upon problems traditionally viewed as monocausal—that is, gender discrimination or race discrimination. I believe three aspects of subordination are important: the structural dimensions of domination (structural intersectionality), the politics engendered by a particular system of domination (political intersectionality), and the representations of the dominated (representational intersectionality). These intersectionalities serve as metaphors for different ways in which women of color are situated between categories of race and gender when the two are regarded as mutually exclusive. I hope that a framework of intersection will facilitate a merging of race and gender discourses to uncover what lies hidden between them and to construct a better means of conceptualizing and politicizing violence against women of color. It is important to note that although I use these concepts in fairly specific ways, as metaphors their boundaries are neither finite nor rigid. Indeed, representational intersectionality is not only implicated in the political interactions of race and gender discourses, it can also be inclusive of these intersections. Moreover, political and representational intersectionality can also be included as aspects of structural intersectionality.

Structural Intersectionality

I use the term *structural intersectionality* to refer to the way in which women of color are situated within overlapping structures of subordination. Any particular disadvantage or disability is sometimes compounded by yet another disadvantage emanating from or reflecting the dynamics of a separate system of subordination. An analysis sensitive to structural intersections explores the lives of those at the bottom of multiple hierarchies to determine how the dynamics of each hierarchy exacerbates and compounds the consequences of another. The material consequences of the interaction of these multiple hierarchies in the lives of women of color is what I call structural intersectionality. Illustrations of structural intersectionality suggest that violence toward women usually occurs within a specific context that may vary considerably depending on the woman's race, class, and other social characteristics. These constraints can be better understood and addressed through a framework that links them to broader structures of subordination that intersect in fairly predictable ways.

One illustration of structural intersectionality is the way in which the burdens of illiteracy, responsibility for child care, poverty, lack of job skills, and pervasive discrimination weigh down many battered women of color who are trying to escape the cycle of abuse. That is, gender subordination—manifested in this case by battering—intersects with race and class disadvantage to shape and limit the opportunities for effective intervention.

Another illustration of structural intersectionality is the way in which battered immigrant women's vulnerabilities were particularly exploited by the Immigration Marriage Fraud Amendments of 1986,[3] which imposed a two-year wait for permanent-resident status on women who moved to this country to marry U.S. citizens or permanent residents, and which required that both spouses file the application for the wife's permanent-resident status. When faced with what they saw as a choice between securing protection from their batterers and securing protection from deportation, many women, not surprisingly, chose the latter. Even now that these provisions have been amended—primarily at the urging of immigration activists, not feminists, which is perhaps another testament to immigrant women's isolation under intersecting structures of subordination—immigrant women are still at risk. The amendment waives the two-year wait only for battered women who produce evidence of battering from authorities (such as police officers, psychologists, and school officials) to which immigrant women may have little access, and immigrant women may still lack the English-language skills, the privacy on the telephone, and the courage to transgress cultural barriers to ask for help. Further, women married to undocumented workers may suffer in silence for fear that the security of their entire family will be jeopardized should they seek help.

A final illustration of structural intersectionality is the way in which rape crisis centers in poor minority or immigrant communities must address rape survivors' homelessness, unemployment, poverty, hunger, distrust of law-enforcement officers, and perhaps their lack of English-language skills as well, often hindered by funding agency policies premised on the needs of middle-class white rape survivors.

Political Intersectionality

I use the term *political intersectionality* to refer to the different ways in which political and discursive practices relating to race and gender interrelate, often erasing women of color. On some issues, the frameworks highlighting *race* and those highlighting *gender* are oppositional and potentially contradictory. These discourses are sometimes presented as either/or propositions, with the validity of each necessarily precluding the validity of the other. Manifestations of this oppositionality are found in antiracist and feminist rhetorical postures that implicitly or explicitly legitimize the dynamics of either racial or gender subordination. An extreme example is Shahrazad Ali's controversial book, *The Blackman's Guide to the Blackwoman* (1989), which blames the deteriorating conditions within the Black community on the failure of Black men to control their women. Ali recommends, among other practices, that Black men "discipline" disrespectful Black women by slapping them in the mouth—the mouth "because it is from that hole, in the lower part of her face, that all her rebellion culminates into words. Her unbridled tongue is a main reason she cannot get along with the Blackman."[4] More commonly, the

need to protect the political or cultural integrity of the community is interpreted as precluding any public discussion of domestic violence. But suppressing information about domestic violence in the name of antiracism leaves unrevealed, and thus unaddressed in public discourse within our communities, the real terror in which many women of color live.

In other instances, women of color are erased when race and gender politics proceed on grounds that exclude or overlook the existence of women of color. Such an erasure took place in the rhetorical appeals made by sponsors of the Violence Against Women Act (1991).[5] White male senators eloquently urged passage of the bill because violence against women occurs everywhere, not just in the inner cities. That is, the senators attempted to persuade other whites that domestic violence is a problem because "these are *our* women being victimized." White women thus came into focus, and any authentic, sensitive attention to our images and our experience, which would probably have jeopardized the bill, faded into darkness.

But an erasure need not take place for us to be silenced. Tokenistic, objectifying, voyeuristic inclusion is at least as damaging as exclusion. We are as silenced when we appear in the margins as we are when we fail to appear at all.

Political intersectionality as it relates to violence against women of color reveals the ways in which politics centered around mutually exclusive notions of race and gender leave women of color without a political framework that will adequately contextualize the violence that occurs in our lives.

Representational Intersectionality

A final variant on the intersectional theme is *representational intersectionality*, referring to the way that race and gender images, readily available in our culture, converge to create unique and specific narratives deemed appropriate for women of color. Not surprisingly, the clearest convergences are those involving sexuality, perhaps because it is through sexuality that images of minorities and women are most sharply focused. Representational intersectionality is significant in exploring violence against women of color because it provides cues to the ways in which our experiences are weighed against counternarratives that cast doubt upon the validity and harm of such violence. I will analyze examples of representational intersectionality in images of violence against women—images that wound—in the next section.

Representational Intersectionality and Images that Wound

Representational intersectionality is manifest in the familiar images of women of color within popular culture. Here I examine the cultural images widely disseminated in the mainstream movies *Angel Heart, Colors, Year of the Dragon*, and *Tales from the Darkside: The Movie*. Next, I will discuss a video game called *General Custer's Revenge*. Finally, I will consider in more detail the debate surrounding the obscenity prosecution of 2 Live Crew's album *Nasty As They Wanna Be*.

Media images provide cues to understanding the ways in which women of color are imagined in our society. The images of Latina, African-American, Asian-American, and Native American women are constructed through combinations of readily available race and gender stereotypes. Because the stereotypes depicted in these presentations are quite familiar, collectively they form images of women of color that are specific and categorically unique.

Consider first the film *Colors. Colors* was a controversial film, but unfortunately none of the criticism addressed its portrayal of women. Yet the film was rife with familiar stereotypes. The obligatory sexual relationship in that movie occurred between a hot-headed white cop played by Sean Penn and a young Latina played by Maria Conchita Alonso, whom he encountered working at a fast-food stand. Their relationship and her characterization progressed as follows: In Scene 1, he flirts, she blushes. In Scene 2, she accompanies him to a family outing at his partner's home. In Scene 3, the crucial scene, he drops her off at her home. She almost maintains the "good girl" image that had been carefully constructed from the onset, but when she reaches her door, she reconsiders and turns back to invite him in for a night of sex. In subsequent scenes this nice, hardworking ethnic girl increasingly turns into a promiscuous schizophrenic Latina. In her final appearance, the transformation is complete. The scene begins with the young cop arriving to investigate a noisy house party. She is seen putting on her

clothes in a bedroom from which a black man has departed. She wears a low-cut, loud dress and six-inch heels. She is very loud and brash now, laughingly tormenting the distraught and disappointed Sean Penn who upon seeing her, attempts to escape. She follows him and with her hands on her hips, demanding now in a very heavy and exaggerated accent: "Look at me. This is part of me too!"

This image of the good ethnic fiery Latina is contrasted with an image of Black sexuality also constructed in *Colors*. In another scene, the police converge on a house to serve a warrant on a suspect named Rock-it. As they approach the house, the viewer hears a rhythmic squeaking and loud screams. The camera takes several seconds to track through the ramshackle house. There is little in the house except a stereo apparently playing and loud, pulsating music accenting the sound track. The camera turns a corner and finds a Black man and a Black woman on a bed, atop a single white sheet, so earnestly and frantically copulating that they are wholly oblivious to the several police officers surrounding them with guns drawn. When they finally became aware of the officers' presence, the man makes a sudden move and is shot several times in the back. As his lover screams hysterically, he gasps that he was simply reaching for his clothes.

In *Angel Heart*, the descent of an African-American woman into her own uncontrolled sexuality ends in tragic horror. Epiphany Proudfoot, played by Cosby-kid Lisa Bonet, is introduced washing her hair at a well. She appears at first the model of youth, reticent and exotic. Yet she's slightly fallen: She has a child whose father is unknown. Later we see her as a voodoo priestess dancing a blood-curdling ritual and collapsing in an uncontrolled sexual frenzy. The movie culminates in a vicious pornographic scene between Epiphany and Harry Angel (played by Mickey Rourke) that gives new meaning to the phrase "sex and violence." Sex—initiated by Epiphany— soon becomes gruesome as dripping water turns into blood, intercut with rivers of blood, deep thrusting, and screams of agony and horror. The visual narrative splits after this scene: Epiphany appears normal, singing a lovely lullaby and wistfully twisting her hair as she bathes, but later we discover that Epiphany is in fact dead. Her body sprawls across the bed, her legs spread open. A deep pool of blood surrounds her pelvic area. The movie's final scene plays out across her dead body. We discover the cause of her death when the Southern sheriff questioning Angel drawls, "Is that your gun up her snatch?" The horror is not yet complete, for we have still to discover that not only has Harry Angel killed his lover, but that this lover is actually his daughter. So this Cosby kid hits big time, being multiply victimized by incest, rape, and murder.

Perhaps it is happenstance that Lisa Bonet played Epiphany and that the imagery in this big-budget Hollywood film is so violent. Yet I wonder whether a Michelle Pfeiffer, a Kim Basinger, or even a Madonna would be asked to play such a role? I don't think so. The film, by relying on race-sex exoticism, works differently from the way it would with a white female. In fact, the presence of a woman of color often "makes" the story, as is still more clearly shown in an episode from *Tales from the Dark Side: The Movie.* The life of a young white artist is spared by a sixteen-foot talking gargoyle upon the artist's promise that he will never tell anyone that he has ever seen this gargoyle. Later that night he meets a Black woman, played here by Rae Dawn Chong, whom he later marries and with whom he has two lovely children. With the support of his wife he becomes enormously successful, and they live a happy, fulfilled life. On their tenth anniversary, he decides to tell his wife this secret as a part of his expression of affection to her. Presenting her with a full-sized sculpture of the monster he tells her how his life was spared upon making a vow never to reveal that the monster exists. After he tells her the story, she becomes hysterical and, as "fate" would have it, begins to turn into the sixteen-foot gargoyle. Their two children emerge from the adjoining room as baby gargoyles. The wife disregards the artist's frantic efforts to profess his love for her, stating that she "loved him too but when the vow was broken their fate was sealed." She monstrously tears out his throat, gathers up the "children," and swoops through the ceiling. Here the drop-of-blood rule really works: The children, although half human, are little monsters, too. Can anyone doubt the message—white male miscegenators, beware! Exotica and danger go hand in hand.

Mickey Rourke, apparently bidding to be everybody's favorite racist/sadomasochist/rapist/ murderer, turns up again in *Year of the Dragon.* There he plays Captain Stanley White, a New York cop, who pursues a brash and independent Asian-American TV newscaster. He encounters her on the street, addresses her as a prostitute, taunts her with racist epithets (apparently learned from his days in Vietnam). After she invites him up to her apartment, he continues to assault her verbally, before physically doing so. He tells her that he hates everything about her, and then taking down his pants, he queries, "So why do I want to fuck you so badly?" The worst is yet to come: As our heroine rallies enough outrage to ask him to leave, he calls her a slant-eyed cunt. She slaps him once, pauses, and slaps again. He then grabs her, throws her down, rips off her clothes, and has forcible sex with her.

The next image comes not from a movie but from a video game, *General Custer's Revenge.* A Native American woman is tied to a pole. The player, General Custer, must traverse an obstacle course to get to the woman before getting shot. His saberlike penis leads him forward. The player wins when General Custer reaches the Native American woman and pounces on her. She "kicks up her legs in dubious delight" as he commits "what opponents call a rape and the manufacturer claims is a willing sex act." (A spokesman for the manufacturer commented, "There is a facsimile of intercourse. The woman is smiling.") Every stroke is a point. The motto: "When you score, you score."[6]

These four representations confirm both the feminist claim that women are legitimate targets for violence and the more specific observation that these targets are often represented with distinct racialized images. The Latina is two sided: She is both a sweet, hardworking ethnic and a loud, unscrupulous, racialized "other." The Black woman is wild and animal-like. In *Tales from the Darkside: The Movie*, she *is* an animal or, worse yet, a monster. The Asian-American woman is passive. She can be verbally abused and physically assaulted, yet she still stands ready to please. The Native American woman is a savage. She has no honor and no integrity. She doesn't fight rape; in fact, being tied up and ravished makes her smile. She enjoys it.

In each of these cases the specific image is created within the intersection of race and gender. Although some claim that these images reflect certain attitudes that make women of color targets of sexual violence, the actual effect of images on behavior is still hotly contested. Whatever the relationship between imagery and actions is, it seems clear that these images do function to create counternarratives to the experiences of women of color that discredit our claims and render the violence that we experience unimportant. These images not only represent the devaluation of women of color, they may also reproduce it by providing viewers with both conscious and unconscious cues for interpreting the experiences of "others." Because both the actual experience of violence and the representations of those experiences constitute the "problem" of gender violence, feminists of color must address how race and gender intersect in popular discourse as well as in feminist and antiracist politics.

Addressing the Intersectionalities in the 2 Live Crew Controversy

The different intersectionalities discussed above converge in my thinking on the controversy surrounding the obscenity prosecution of 2 Live Crew. The entire problem spurred by the prosecution of 2 Live Crew—the question of how to construct a Black feminist approach to the virulent misogyny in some rap music—has vexed me for some time, and as I suggested at the outset, prompted my attempt to construct a Black feminist understanding of gender violence.

The prosecution of 2 Live Crew began several months after the release of their *As Nasty As They Wanna Be* album. In the midst of the Mapplethorpe controversy and Tipper Gore's campaign to label offensive rock music, the Broward County sheriff, Nick Navarro, began investigating 2 Live Crew's *Nasty* recording at the behest of Jack Thompson, a fundamentalist attorney in Miami, Florida. The sheriff obtained an ex parte order declaring the recording obscene and presented copies of the order to local store owners, threatening them with arrest if they continued to sell the recording. 2 Live Crew filed a civil rights suit, and Sheriff Navarro sought a judicial determination labeling 2 Live Crew's *Nasty* recording obscene.[7] A federal court ruled that *Nasty* was obscene but granted 2 Live Crew permanent injunctive relief because the sheriff's action had subjected the recording to unconstitutional prior restraint. Two

days after the judge declared the recording obscene, 2 Live Crew members were charged with giving an obscene performance at a club in Hollywood, Florida. Additionally, deputy sheriffs arrested a merchant who was selling copies of the *Nasty* recording. These events received national attention and the controversy quickly polarized into two camps. Writing in *Newsweek*, political columnist George Will staked out a case for the prosecution. He argued that *Nasty* was misogynistic filth. Will characterized the performance as a profoundly repugnant "combination of extreme infantilism and menace" that objectified Black women and represented them as suitable targets for sexual violence.[8]

The most prominent defense of 2 Live Crew was advanced by Professor Henry Louis Gates, Jr., an expert on African-American literature. In a *New York Times* op-ed piece and in testimony at the criminal trial, Gates contended that 2 Live Crew were literary geniuses operating within and inadvertently elaborating distinctively African-American forms of cultural expression.[9] Furthermore, the characteristic exaggeration featured in their lyrics served a political end: to explode popular racist stereotypes in a comically extreme form. Where Will saw a misogynistic assault on Black women by social degenerates, Gates found a form of "sexual carnivalesque" with the promise to free us from the pathologies of racism.

As a Black feminist, I felt the pull of each of these poles but not the compelling attractions of either. My immediate response to the criminal charges against 2 Live Crew was a feeling of being torn between standing with the brothers against a racist attack and standing against a frightening explosion of violent imagery directed to women like me. This reaction, I have come to believe, is a consequence of the location of Black women at the intersection of racial and sexual subordination. My experience of sharp internal division—if dissatisfaction with the idea that the "real issue" is race or gender is inertly juxtaposed—is characteristic of that location. Black feminism offers an intellectual and political response to that experience. Bringing together the different aspects of an otherwise divided sensibility, Black feminism argues that racial and sexual subordination are mutually reinforcing, that Black women are marginalized by a politics of race and of gender, and that a political response to each form of subordination must at the same time be a political response to both. When the controversy over 2 Live Crew is approached in light of such Black feminist sensibilities, an alternative to the dominant poles of the public debate emerges.

At the legal bottom line I agree with the supporters of 2 Live Crew that the obscenity prosecution was wrongheaded. But the reasons for my conclusion are not the same as the reasons generally offered in support of 2 Live Crew. I will come to those reasons shortly, but first I must emphasize that after listening to 2 Live Crew's lyrics along with those of other rap artists, my defense of 2 Live Crew, however careful, did not come easily.

On first hearing 2 Live Crew I was shocked; unlike Gates I did not "bust out laughing." One trivializes the issue by describing the images of women in *As Nasty As They Wanna Be* as simply "sexually explicit." We hear about cunts being fucked until backbones are cracked, asses being busted, dicks rammed down throats, and semen splattered across faces. Black women are cunts, bitches, and all-purpose "hos." Images of women in some of the other rap acts are even more horrifying: battering, rape, and rape-murder are often graphically detailed. Occasionally, we do hear Black women's voices, and those voices are sometimes oppositional. But the response to opposition typically returns to the central refrain: "Shut up, bitch. Suck my dick."

This is no mere braggadocio. Those of us who are concerned about the high rates of gender violence in our communities must be troubled by the possible connections between such images and violence against women. Children and teenagers are listening to this music, and I am concerned that the range of acceptable behavior is being broadened by the constant propagation of antiwomen imagery. I'm concerned, too, about young Black women who together with men are learning that their value lies between their legs. Unlike that of men, however, women's sexual value is portrayed as a depletable commodity: By expending it, boys become men and girls become whores.

Nasty is misogynist, and a Black feminist response to the case against 2 Live Crew should not depart from a full acknowledgement of that misogyny. But such a response must also consider whether an exclusive focus on issues of gender risks overlooking aspects of the prosecution of 2 Live Crew that raise serious questions of racism. And here is where the roots of my opposition to the obscenity prosecution lie.

An initial problem concerning the prosecution was its apparent selectivity. Even the most superficial comparison between 2 Live Crew and other mass-marketed sexual representations suggest the likelihood that race played some role in distinguishing 2 Live Crew as the first group to ever be prosecuted for obscenity in connection with a musical recording, and one of only a handful of recording groups or artists to be prosecuted for a live performance. Recent controversies about sexism, racism, and violence in popular culture point to a vast range of expression that might have provided targets for censorship, but that were left untouched. Madonna has acted out masturbation, portrayed the seduction of a priest, and insinuated group sex on stage. But she has never been prosecuted for obscenity. Whereas 2 Live Crew was performing in an adult's-only club in Hollywood, Florida, Andrew Dice Clay was performing nationwide on HBO. Well known for his racist "humor," Clay is also comparable to 2 Live Crew in sexual explicitness and misogyny. In his show, for example, Clay offers: "Eeny, meeny, miney, mo, suck my [expletive] and swallow slow," or "Lose the bra bitch." Moreover, graphic sexual images—many of them violent—were widely available in Broward County where 2 Live Crew's performance and trial took place. According to the trial testimony of a vice detective named McCloud, "Nude dance shows and adult bookstores are scattered throughout the county where 2 Live Crew performed."[10] But again, no obscenity charges were leveled against the performers or producers of these representations.

In response to this charge of selectivity, it might be argued that the successful prosecution of 2 Live Crew demonstrates that its lyrics were uniquely obscene. In a sense, this argument runs, the proof is in the prosecution—if they were not uniquely obscene, they would have been acquitted. However, the elements of 2 Live Crew's performance that contributed initially to their selective arrest continued to play out as the court applied the obscenity standard to the recording. To clarify this argument, we need to consider the technical use of "obscenity" as a legal term of art. For the purposes of legal argument, the Supreme Court in the 1973 case of *Miller v. California* held that a work is obscene if and only if it meets each of three conditions: (1) "the average person, applying community standards, would find that the work, taken as a whole, appeals to the prurient interest"; (2) "the work depicts or describes, in a patently offensive way, sexual conduct specifically defined by the applicable state law"; and (3) "the work, take as a whole, lacks serious literary, artistic, political, or scientific value."[11] The Court held that it is consistent with first amendment guarantees of freedom of expression for states to subject work that meets each of the three prongs of the *Miller* test to very restrictive regulations.

Focusing first on the prurient interest prong of the *Miller* test, we might wonder how 2 Live Crew could have been seen as uniquely obscene by the lights of the "community standards" of Broward County. After all, as Detective McCloud put it, "Patrons [of clubs in Broward] can see women dancing with at least their breasts exposed" and bookstore patrons can "view and purchase films and magazines that depict vaginal, oral and anal sex, homosexual sex and group sex."[12] In arriving at its finding of obscenity, the court placed little weight on the available range of films, magazines, and live shows as evidence of the community's sensibilities. Instead, the court apparently accepted the sheriff's testimony that the decision to single out *Nasty* was based on the number of complaints against 2 Live Crew, "communicated by telephone calls, anonymous messages, or letters to the police."[13]

Evidence of this popular outcry was never substantiated. But even if it were, the case for selectivity would remain. The history of social repression of Black male sexuality is long, often violent, and all too familiar. Negative reactions against the sexual conduct of Black males have traditionally had racist overtones, especially where that conduct threatens to "cross over" into the mainstream community. So even if the decision to prosecute did reflect a widespread community perception of the purely prurient character of 2 Live Crew's music, that perception itself might reflect an established pattern of vigilante attitudes directed toward the sexual expression of Black males. In short, the appeal to community standards does not undercut a concern about racism; rather, it underscores that concern.

A second troubling dimension of the case against 2 Live Crew was the court's apparent disregard for the culturally rooted aspects of 2 Live Crew's music. Such disregard was essential to a finding of obscenity given the third prong of the *Miller* test, requiring that obscene material lack any literary, artistic, or political value. 2 Live Crew argued that this test was not met because the recording exemplified such African-American cultural modes as "playing the dozens," "call and response," and "signifying." As a storehouse of such cultural modes, it could not be said that *Nasty* could be described as completely devoid of literary or artistic value. In each case the court denied the group's claim of cultural specificity by recharacterizing those modes claimed to be African American in more generic terms. For example, the court reasoned that playing the dozens is "commonly seen in adolescents, especially boys, of all ages." "Boasting," the court observed, appears to be "part of the universal human condition." And the court noted that the cultural origins of one song featuring call and response—a song about fellatio in which competing groups chanted "less filling" and "tastes great"—were to be found in a Miller beer commercial, not in African-American cultural tradition. The possibility that the Miller beer commercial may have itself evolved from an African-American cultural tradition was lost on the court.

In disregarding this testimony the court denied the artistic value in the form and style of *Nasty* and, by implication, rap music more generally. This disturbing dismissal of the cultural attributes of rap and the effort to universalize African-American modes of expression flattens cultural differences. The court's analysis here manifests in the law a frequently encountered strategy of cultural appropriation. African-American contributions accepted by be mainstream culture are considered simply "American" or found to be "universal." Other modes associated with African-American culture that resist absorption and remain distinctive are neglected or dismissed as "deviant."

An additional concern has as much to do with the obscenity doctrine itself as with the court's application of it in this case. The case illustrates the ways in which obscenity doctrine asks the wrong questions with respect to sexual violence and facilitates the wrong conclusions with respect to racially selective enforcement. As I mentioned earlier, obscenity requires a determination that the material be intended to appeal to the prurient interest. In making this deter-mination, the court rejected the relevance of 2 Live Crew's admitted motives—both their larger motive of making money and their secondary motive of doing so through the marketing of outrageous sexual humor. Although the prurient interest requirement eludes pre-cise definition—recall Potter Stewart's infamous dec-laration that "I know it when I see it"—it seems clear that it must appeal in some immediate way to sexual desire. It would be difficult to say definitively what does or does not constitute an appeal to this prurient interest, but one can surmise that the twenty-five-cent peep shows that are standard fare in Broward County rank considerably higher on this scale than the sexual tall tales told by 2 Live Crew.

2 Live Crew is thus one of the lesser candidates in the prurient interest sweepstakes mandated by the obscenity standard, and it is also a lesser contender by another measure that lies explicitly outside the obscenity doctrine: violence. Compared to groups such as N.W.A., Too Short, Ice Cube, and the Geto Boys, 2 Live Crew's misogynistic hyperbole sounds minor league. Sometimes called gangsta' rap, the lyr-ics offered by these other groups celebrate violent assault, rape, rape-murder, and mutilation. Had these other groups been targeted rather than the compara-tively less offensive 2 Live Crew, they may have been more successful in defeating the prosecution. The graphic violence in their representations militates against a finding of obscenity by suggesting an intent to appeal not to prurient interests but instead to the fantasy of the social outlaw. Indeed, these appeals might even be read as political. Against the histori-cal backdrop in which the image of the Black male as social outlaw is a prominent theme, gangsta' rap might be read as a rejection of a conciliatory stance aimed at undermining fear through reassurance in favor of a more subversive form of opposition that attempts to challenge the rules precisely by becom-ing the very social outlaw that society has proscribed. Thus, so long as obscenity remains preoccupied with finding prurient interests and violent imagery is seen as distinct from sexuality, obscenity doctrine is inef-fectual against more violent rappers.

Yet even this somewhat formal dichotomy between sex, which obscenity is concerned about, and vio-lence, which lies beyond its purview, may provide little

solace to the entire spectrum of rappers ranging from the Geto Boys to 2 Live Crew. Given the historical link-ages between Black male sexuality and violence, the two are likely to be directly linked in the prurient inter-est inquiry, even if subconsciously. In fact, it may have been the background images of Black male sexual violence that rendered 2 Live Crew an acceptable tar-get for obscenity in a lineup that included many stron-ger contenders.

My point here is not to suggest that the distinc-tion between sex and violence should be maintained in obscenity, nor more specifically, that the more vio-lent rappers ought to be protected. To the contrary, these groups trouble me much more than 2 Live Crew. My point instead is to suggest that obscenity doctrine does nothing to protect the interests of those who are most directly implicated in such rap—Black women. On a formal level, obscenity separates out sexual-ity and violence, thus shielding the more violently misogynist groups from prosecution. Yet the histori-cal linkages between images of Black male sexuality and violence simultaneously single out lightweight rappers for prosecution among all other purveyors of explicit sexual imagery. Neither course furthers Black women's simultaneous interests in opposing racism and misogyny.

Although Black women's interests were quite obvi-ously irrelevant in this obscenity judgment, their bod-ies figured prominently in the public case supporting the prosecution. George Will's *Newsweek* essay pro-vides a striking example of how Black women's bodies were appropriated and deployed in the broader attack against 2 Live Crew. In "America's Slide into the Sew-ers," Will told us, "America today is capable of terrific intolerance about smoking, or toxic waste that threat-ens trout. But only a deeply confused society is more concerned about protecting lungs than minds, trout than black women. We legislate against smoking in restaurants; singing 'Me So Horny' is a constitutional right. Secondary smoke is carcinogenic; celebration of torn vaginas is 'mere words.'"[14]

Notwithstanding these expressions of concern about Black women, Will's real worry is suggested by his repeated references to the Central Park jogger. He writes, "Her face was so disfigured a friend took 15 minutes to identify her. 'I recognized her ring.' Do you recognize the relevance of 2 Live Crew?" Although the connection between the threat of 2 Live Crew and the image of the Black male rapist was suggested subtly in the public debate, it is manifest throughout Will's discussion and in fact bids to be its central theme. "Fact: Some members of a particular age and societal cohort—the one making 2 Live Crew rich—stomped and raped the jogger to the razor edge of death, for the fun of it." Will directly indicts 2 Live Crew in the Central Park jogger rape through a fictional dialogue between himself and the defendants. Responding to one defendant's alleged confession that the rape was fun, Will asks: "Where can you get the idea that sexual violence against women is fun? From a music store, through Walkman earphones, from boom boxes blaring forth the rap lyrics of 2 Live Crew"; because the rapists were young Black males and *Nasty* presents Black men celebrating sexual violence, surely 2 Live Crew was responsible. Apparently, the vast American industry that markets misogynistic representation in every conceivable way is irrelevant to understanding this particular incident of sexual violence.

Will invokes Black women—twice—as victims of this music. But if he were really concerned with the threat to Black women, why does the Central Park jogger figure so prominently in his argument? Why not the Black woman from Brooklyn who, within weeks of the Central Park assault, was gang-raped and then thrown down an air shaft? What about the twenty-eight other women—mostly women of color—who were raped in New York City the same week the Central Park jogger was raped? Rather than being centered in Will's display of concern, Black women appear to function as stand-ins for white women. The focus on sexual violence played out on Black women's bodies seems to reflect concerns about the threat to Black male violence against the strategy of the prosecutor in Richard Wright's novel *Native Son*.[15] Bigger Thomas, the Black male protagonist, is on trial for killing Mary Dalton, a white woman. Because Bigger burned her body, however, it cannot be established whether Mary was raped. So the prosecutor brings in the body of Bessie, a Black woman raped by Bigger and left to die, to establish that Bigger had raped Mary.

Further evidence that Will's concern about sexual imagery and rape is grounded in familiar narratives of Black sexual violence and white victimhood is suggested by his nearly apoplectic reaction to similar attempts to regulate racist speech. In his assault on 2 Live Crew, Will decries liberal tolerance for lyrics that "desensitize" our society and that will certainly have "behavioral consequences." Proponents of campus speech regulations have made arguments that racist speech facilitates racist violence in much the same way that Will links rap to sexual violence. Yet Will has excoriated such proponents.

Despite his anguish that sexual lyrics "coarsen" our society and facilitate a "slide into the sewer," in Will's view,[16] racist speech is situated on a much higher plane. Apparently, the "social cohort" that is most likely to engage in racial violence—young white men—has sense enough to distinguish ideas from action whereas the "social cohort" that identifies with 2 Live Crew is made up of mindless brutes who will take rap as literal encouragement to rape. Will's position on racist speech not only indicates how readily manipulable the link between expression and action is, but suggests further reasons why his invocation of Black women seems so disingenuous. One can't help but wonder why Will is so outraged about attacks on Black women's vaginal walls and not concerned about attacks on our skin.

These concerns about selectivity in prosecution, about the denial of cultural specificity, and about the manipulation of Black women's bodies convince me that race played a significant if not determining role in the shaping of the case against 2 Live Crew. While using antisexist rhetoric to suggest a concern for women, the attack simultaneously endorsed traditional readings of Black male sexuality. The fact that most sexual violence involves intraracial assault fades to the background as the Black male is represented as the agent of sexual violence and the white community is represented as his victim. The subtext of the 2 Live Crew prosecution thus becomes a re-reading of the sexualized racial politics of the past.

Although concerns about racism fuel my opposition to the obscenity prosecution, I am also troubled by the uncritical support for and indeed celebration of 2 Live Crew by other opponents of that prosecution. If the rhetoric of antisexism provided an occasion for racism, so too, the rhetoric of antiracism provided an occasion for defending the misogyny of Black male rappers.

The defense of 2 Live Crew took two forms, one political and one cultural, both of which were advanced most prominently by Henry Louis Gates, Jr. The political argument was that 2 Live Crew represents an attack against Black sexual stereotypes. The strategy of the attack is, in Gates's words, to "exaggerate [the] stereotypes" and thereby "to show how ridiculous the portrayals are."[17] For the strategy to succeed, it must of course highlight the sexism, misogyny, and violence stereotypically associated with Black male sexuality. But far from embracing that popular mythology, the idea is to fight the racism of those who accept it. Thus, the argument goes, 2 Live Crew and other rap groups are simply pushing white society's buttons to ridicule its dominant sexual images.

I agree with Gates that the reactions by Will and others to 2 Live Crew confirm that the stereotypes still exist and still evoke basic fears. But even if I were to agree that 2 Live Crew intended to explode these mythic fears, I still would argue that its strategy was wholly misguided. These fears are too active and African Americans are too closely associated with them not to be burned when the myths are exploded. More fundamentally, however, I am deeply skeptical about the claim that the Crew was engaged—either in intent or effects—in a postmodern guerrilla war against racist stereotypes.

Gates argues that when one listens to 2 Live Crew, the ridiculous stories and the hyperbole make the listener "bust out laughing." Apparently, the fact that Gates and many other people react with laughter confirms and satisfies the Crew's objective of ridiculing the stereotypes. The fact that the Crew is often successful in achieving laughter neither substantiates Gates's reading, nor forecloses serious critique of its subordinating dimensions.

In disagreeing with Gates, I do not mean to suggest that 2 Live Crew's lyrics are to be taken literally. But rather than exploding stereotypes as Gates suggests, I believe that the group simply uses readily available sexual images in trying to be funny. Trading in racial stereotypes and sexual hyperbole are well-rehearsed strategies for achieving laughter; the most extreme representations often do more to reinforce and entrench the image than to explode it. 2 Live Crew departs from this tradition only in its attempt to up the ante through more outrageous boasts and more explicit manifestations of misogyny.

The acknowledgement, however, that the Crew was simply trying to be funny should not be interpreted as constituting a defense against its misogyny. Neither the intent to be funny nor Gates's loftier explanations negate the subordinating qualities of such humor. An examination of the parallel arguments in the context of racist humor suggests why neither claim functions as a persuasive defense for 2 Live Crew.

Gates's use of laughter as a defensive maneuver in the attack on 2 Live Crew recalls similar strategies in defense of racist humor. Racist humor has sometimes been defended as antiracist—an effort to poke fun at or to show the ridiculousness of racism. More simply, racist humor has often been excused as just joking; even racially motivated assaults are often defended as simple pranks. Thus, the racism and sexism of Andrew Dice Clay could be defended either as an attempt to explode the stereotypes of white racists or more simply as simple humor not meant to be taken seriously. Implicit in these defenses is the assumption that racist representations are injurious only if they are devoid of any other objective or are meant to be taken literally. Although these arguments are familiar within the Black community, I think it is highly unlikely that they would be viewed as a persuasive defense of Andrew Dice Clay. Indeed, the historical and ongoing criticism of such humor suggests widespread rejection of such disclaimers. Operating instead under a premise that humor can be nonliteral, perhaps even well intended, but racist nonetheless, African Americans have protested such humor. This practice of opposition suggests a general recognition within the Black community that "mere humor" is not inconsistent with subordination. The question of what people find humorous is of course a complicated one that includes considerations of aggression, reinforcement of group boundaries, projection, and other issues. The claim of intending only a joke may be true, but representations function as humor within a specific social context and frequently reinforce patterns of social power. Even though racial humor may sometimes be intended to ridicule racism, the close relationship between the stereotypes and the prevailing images of marginalized people as well as a presumed connection between the humorist and the dominant audience complicates this strategy. Clearly, racial humor does not always undermine the racism of the character speaking nor indict the wider society in which the jokes have meaning. The endearment of Archie Bunker seems to suggest at least this much.

Thus, in the context of racist humor, neither the fact that people actually laughed at racist humor nor the usual disclaimer of intent have functioned to preclude incisive and often quite angry criticism of such humor within the African-American community. Although a similar set of arguments could be offered in the context of sexist humor, images marketed by 2 Live Crew were not condemned, but as Gates illustrates, defended, often with great commitment and skill. Clearly, the fact that the Crew is Black, as are the women it objectifies, shaped this response. There is of course an ongoing issue of how one's positioning vis-à-vis a targeted group colors the way the group interprets a potentially derisive stereotype or gesture. Had 2 Live Crew been whites in blackface, for example, all of the readings would have been different. Although the question of whether one can defend the broader license given to Black comedians to market stereotypical images is an interesting one, it is not the issue here. 2 Live Crew cannot claim an in-group privilege to perpetuate misogynistic humor against Black women. Its members are not Black women, and more important, they enjoy a power relationship over them.

Sexual humor in which women are objectified as packages of bodily parts to serve whatever male-bonding/male-competition the speakers please subordinates women in much the same way that racist humor subordinates African Americans. That these are "just jokes" and are not taken as literal claims does little to blunt their demeaning quality—nor, for that matter, does it help that the jokes are told within a tradition of intragroup humor.

Gates offered a second, cultural defense of 2 Live Crew: the idea that *Nasty* is in line with distinctively African-American traditions of culture. It is true that the dozens and other forms of verbal boasting have been practiced within the Black community for some time. It is true as well that raunchy jokes, insinuations, and boasts of sexual prowess were not meant to be taken literally. Nor, however, were they meant to disrupt conventional myths about Black sexuality. They

were meant simply to be laughed at and perhaps to gain respect for the speaker's word wizardry.

Ultimately, however, little turns on whether the "wordplay" performed by 2 Live Crew is a postmodern challenge to racist sexual mythology or simply an internal group practice that has crossed over into mainstream U.S. society. Both versions of the defense arc problematic because both call on Black women to accept misogyny and its attendant disrespect in the service of some broader group objective. Whereas one version argues that accepting misogyny is necessary to antiracist politics, the other argues that it is necessary to maintain the cultural integrity of the community. Neither presents sufficient justification for requiring Black women to tolerate such misogyny. The message that these arguments embrace—that patriarchy can be made to serve antiracist ends—is a familiar one, with proponents ranging from Eldridge Cleaver in the 1960s to Shahrazad Ali in the 1990s. In Gates's variant, the position of Black women is determined by the need to wield gargantuan penises in efforts to ridicule racist images of Black male sexuality. Even though Black women may not be the intended targets, they are necessarily called to serve these gargantuan penises and are thus in the position of absorbing the impact. The common message of all such strategies is that Black women are expected to be vehicles for notions of "liberation" that function to preserve Black female subordination.

To be sure, Gates's claim about the cultural aspects of 2 Live Crew's lyrics do address the legal issue about the applicability of the obscenity standard. As I indicated earlier, the group's music does have artistic and potentially political value; I believe the court decided this issue incorrectly and Will was all too glib in his critique. But these criticisms do not settle the issue within the community. Dozens and other wordplays have long been within the Black oral tradition, but acknowledging this fact does not eliminate the need to interrogate either the sexism within that tradition or the objectives to which that tradition has been pressed. To say that playing the dozens, for example, is rooted in a Black cultural tradition or that themes represented by mythic folk heroes such as Stagolee are Black does not settle the question of whether such practices are oppressive to women and others within the community. The same point can be made about the relentless homophobia in the work of

Eddie Murphy and many other comedians and rappers. Whether or not the Black community has a pronounced tradition of homophobic humor is beside the point; the question instead is how these subordinating aspects of tradition play out in the lives of people in the community, people who are otherwise called upon to share the benefits and the burdens of a common history, culture, and political agenda. Although it may be true that the Black community is more familiar with the cultural forms that have evolved into rap, that familiarity should not end the discussion of whether the misogyny within rap is acceptable.

Moreover, we need to consider the possible relationships between sexism in our cultural practices and violence against women. Violence against women of color is not centered as a critical issue in either the antiracist or antiviolence discourses. The "different culture" defense may contribute to a disregard for women of color victimized by rape and violence that reinforces the tendency within the broader community not to take intraracial violence seriously. Numerous studies have suggested that Black victims of crime can count on less protection from the criminal justice system than whites receive. This is true for Black rape victims as well—their rapists are less likely to be convicted and on average serve less time when they are convicted. Could it be that perpetuating the belief that Blacks are different with respect to sexuality and violence contributes to the disregard of Black female rape victims like Bessie in *Native Son* or the woman thrown down an air shaft in Brooklyn?

Although there are times when Black feminists should fight for the integrity of Black culture, this does not mean that criticism must end when a practice or form of expression is traced to an aspect of culture. We must also determine whether the practices and forms of expression are consistent with other interests that we must define. The legal question of obscenity may be settled by finding roots in the culture. But traditional obscenity is not our central issue. Performances and representations that do not appeal principally to "prurient interests" or that may reflect expressive patterns that are culturally specific may still encourage self-hatred, disrespect, subordination, and various other manifestations of intragroup pathology. These problems require an internal group dialogue. Although we have no plenary authority to

grapple with these issues, we do need to find ways of using group formation mechanisms and other social spaces to reflect upon and reformulate our cultural and political practices.

I said earlier that the political goals of Black feminism are to construct and empower a political sensibility that opposes misogyny and racism simultaneously. Merging this double vision in an analysis of the 2 Live Crew controversy makes clear that despite the superficial defense of the prosecution as being in the interests of women, nothing about the anti-2 Live Crew movement is about Black women's lives. The political process involved in legal prosecution of 2 Live Crew's representational subordination of Black women does not seek to empower Black women; indeed, the racism of that process is injurious to us.

The implication of this conclusion is not that Black feminists should stand in solidarity with the supporters of 2 Live Crew. The spirited defense of 2 Live Crew was no more about defending the Black community than the prosecution was about defending women. After all, Black women—whose assault is the very subject of the representation—are part of that community. Black women can hardly regard the right to be represented as rape-deserving bitches and whores as essential to their interests. Instead the defense primarily functions to protect the cultural and political prerogative of male rappers to be as misogynistic as they want to be.

The debate over 2 Live Crew illustrates how the discursive structures of race and gender politics continue to marginalize Black women, rendering us virtually voiceless. Fitted with a Black feminist sensibility, one uncovers other issues in which the unique situation of Black women renders a different formulation of the problem than the version that dominates in current debate. Ready examples include rape, domestic violence, and welfare dependency. A Black feminist sensibility might also provide a more direct link between the women's movement and traditional civil rights movements, helping them both to shed conceptual blinders that limit the efficacy of their efforts. In the recent controversy over the nomination of Clarence Thomas to the U.S. Supreme Court, for example, organized groups in both camps—in particular women's groups—initially struggled to produce evidence showing Thomas's negative disposition toward their respective constituencies. Thomas's repeated derogatory references to his sister as the quintessential example of welfare dependency might have been profitably viewed from a Black feminist framework as the embodiment of his views on race, gender, and class, permitting an earlier formulation of a more effective coalition.

The development of a Black feminist sensibility is no guarantee that Black women's interests will be taken seriously. For that sensibility to develop into empowerment, Black women will have to make it clear that patriarchy is a critical issue that negatively impacts the lives of not only African-American women, but men as well. Within the African-American political community, this recognition might reshape traditional practices so that evidence of racism would not constitute sufficient justification for uncritical rallying around misogynistic politics and patriarchal values. Although collective opposition to racist practice has been and continues to be crucially important in protecting Black interests, an empowered Black feminist sensibility would require that the terms of unity no longer reflect priorities premised upon the continued marginalization of Black women.

Notes

1. 137 Cong. Rec. S597, S610 (1991) (S. 15, H.R. 1502).
2. S. Ali, The Blackman's Guide to Understanding the Blackwoman (Philadelphia: Civilized Publications, 1989).
3. Pub. L. 99–639 (Nov. 10, 1986), Pub. L. 100–525, § 7(a)–(c) (Oct. 24, 1988).
4. S. Ali, *supra* note 2, at 169.
5. H.R. 1502, S. 15 (102d Cong.).
6. Coraham, *Custer May Be Shot Down Again in Battle of Sexes over X-Rated Video Game*, People Magazine, Nov. 15, 1982.
7. Santoro, *How 2B Nasty: Rap Musicians 2 Live Crew Arrested*, The Nation, July 2, 1990, at 4.
8. Will, *America's Slide into the Sewer*, Newsweek, July 30, 1990, at 64.
9. Gates, *2 Live Crew Decoded*, N.Y. Times, June 19, 1990, at A23.
10. *2 Live Crew*, UPI (Oct. 19, 1990).
11. 413 U.S. 15, 24 (1973).
12. *2 Live Crew*, UPI (Oct. 19, 1990).
13. 739 F. Supp. 578, 589 (S.D. Fla. 1990).
14. Will, *supra* note 8.
15. R. Wright, Native Son (1940; New York: Harper & Collins, 1966).
16. Will, *supra* note 8.
17. *An Album Is Judged Obscene; Rap: Slick, Violent, Nasty and, Maybe Helpful*, N.Y. Times, June 17, 1990, at 1.

7.
IMITATION AND GENDER INSUBORDINATION[1]

Judith Butler

So what is this divided being introduced into language through gender? It is an impossible being, it is a being that does not exist, an ontological joke.

(Monique Wittig)[2]

Beyond physical repetition and the psychical or metaphysical repetition, is there an *ontological* repetition? . . . This ultimate repetition, this ultimate theatre, gathers everything in a certain way; and in another way, it destroys everything; and in yet another way, it selects from everything.

(Gilles Deleuze)[3]

To Theorize as a Lesbian?

At first I considered writing a different sort of essay, one with a philosophical tone: the "being" of being homosexual. The prospect of *being* anything, even for pay, has always produced in me a certain anxiety, for "to be" gay, "to be" lesbian seems to be more than a simple injunction to become who or what I already am. And in no way does it settle the anxiety for me to say that this is "part" of what I am. To write or speak *as a lesbian* appears a paradoxical appearance of this "I," one which feels neither true nor false. For it is a production, usually in response to a request, to come out or write in the name of an identity which, once produced, sometimes functions as a politically efficacious phantasm. I'm not at ease with "lesbian theories, gay theories," for as I've argued elsewhere,[4] identity categories tend to be instruments of regulatory regimes, whether as the normalizing categories of oppressive structures or as the rallying points for a liberatory contestation of that very oppression. This is not to say that I will not appear at political occasions under the sign of lesbian, but that I would like to have it permanently unclear what precisely that sign signifies. So it is unclear how it is that I can contribute to this book [*Inside/Out: Lesbian Theories, Gay Theories*] and appear under its title, for it announces a set of terms that I propose to contest. One risk I take is to be recolonized by the sign under which I write, and so it is this risk that I seek to thematize. To propose that the invocation of identity is always a risk does not imply that resistance to it is always or only symptomatic of a self-inflicted homophobia. Indeed, a Foucaultian perspective might argue that the affirmation of "homosexuality" is itself an extension of a homophobic discourse. And yet "discourse," he writes on the same page, "can be both an instrument and an effect of power, but also a hindrance, a stumbling-block, a point of resistance and a starting point for an opposing strategy."[5]

So I am skeptical about how the "I" is determined as it operates under the title of the lesbian sign, and I am no more comfortable with its homophobic determination than with those normative definitions offered by other members of the "gay or lesbian community." I'm permanently troubled by identity categories, consider them to be invariable stumbling-blocks, and understand them, even promote them, as sites of necessary trouble. In fact, if the category were to offer no trouble, it would cease to be interesting to me: it is precisely the *pleasure* produced by the instability of those categories which sustains the various erotic practices that make me a candidate for the category to begin with. To install myself within the terms of an identity category would be to turn against the sexuality that the category purports to describe; and this might be true for any identity category which seeks to control the very eroticism that it claims to describe and authorize, much less "liberate."

And what's worse, I do not understand the notion of "theory," and am hardly interested in being cast as its defender, much less in being signified as part of an elite gay/lesbian theory crowd that seeks to establish the legitimacy and domestication of gay/lesbian studies within the academy. Is there a pregiven distinction between theory, politics, culture, media? How do those divisions operate to quell a certain intertextual writing that might well generate wholly different epistemic maps? But I am writing here now: is it too late? Can this writing, can any writing, refuse the terms by which it is appropriated even as, to some extent, that very colonizing discourse enables or produces this stumbling block, this resistance? How do I relate the paradoxical situation of this dependency and refusal?

If the political task is to show that theory is never merely *theoria*, in the sense of disengaged contemplation, and to insist that it is fully political (*phronesis* or even *praxis*), then why not simply call this operation *politics*, or some necessary permutation of it?

I have begun with confessions of trepidation and a series of disclaimers, but perhaps it will become clear that *disclaiming*, which is no simple activity, will be what I have to offer as a form of affirmative resistance to a certain regulatory operation of homophobia. The discourse of "coming out" has clearly served its purposes, but what are its risks? And here I am not speaking of unemployment or public attack or violence, which are quite clearly and widely on the increase against those who are perceived as "out" whether or not of their own design. Is the "subject" who is "out" free of its subjection and finally in the clear? Or could it be that the subjection that subjectivates the gay or lesbian subject in some ways continues to oppress, or oppresses most insidiously, once "outness" is claimed? What or who is it that is "out," made manifest and fully disclosed, when and if I reveal myself as lesbian? What is it that is now known, anything? What remains permanently concealed by the very linguistic act that offers up the promise of a transparent revelation of sexuality? Can sexuality even remain sexual-

ity once it submits to a criterion of transparency and disclosure, or does it perhaps cease to be sexuality precisely when the semblance of full explicitness is achieved?[6] Is sexuality of any kind even possible without that opacity designated by the unconscious, which means simply that the conscious "I" who would reveal its sexuality is perhaps the last to know the meaning of what it says?

To claim that this is what I *am* is to suggest a provisional totalization of this "I." But if the I can so determine itself, then that which it excludes in order to make that determination remains constitutive of the determination itself. In other words, such a statement presupposes that the "I" exceeds its determination, and even produces that very excess in and by the act which seeks to exhaust the semantic field of that "I." In the act which would disclose the true and full content of that "I," a certain radical *concealment* is thereby produced. For it is always finally unclear what is meant by invoking the lesbian-signifier, since its signification is always to some degree out of one's control, but also because its *specificity* can only be demarcated by exclusions that return to disrupt its claim to coherence. What, if anything, can lesbians be said to share? And who will decide this question, and in the name of whom? If I claim to be a lesbian, I "come out" only to produce a new and different "closet." The "you" to whom I come out now has access to a different region of opacity. Indeed, the locus of opacity has simply shifted: before, you did not know whether I "am," but now you do not know what that means, which is to say that the copula is empty, that it cannot be substituted for with a set of descriptions.[7] And perhaps that is a situation to be valued. Conventionally, one comes out *of* the closet (and yet, how often is it the case that we are "outed" when we are young and without resources?); so we are out of the closet, but into what? what new unbounded spatiality? the room, the den, the attic, the basement, the house, the bar, the university, some new enclosure whose door, like Kafka's door, produces the expectation of a fresh air and a light of illumination that never arrives? Curiously, it is the figure of the closet that produces this expectation, and which guarantees its dissatisfaction. For being "out" always depends to some extent on being "in"; it gains its meaning only within that polarity. Hence, being "out" must produce the closet again and again in order to maintain itself as "out." In this sense, *outness* can only produce a new opacity; and *the closet* produces the promise of a disclosure that can, by definition, never come. Is this infinite postponement of the disclosure of "gayness," produced by the very act of "coming out," to be lamented? Or is this very deferral of the signified *to be valued*, a site for the production of values, precisely because the term now takes on a life that cannot be, can never be, permanently controlled?

It is possible to argue that whereas no transparent or full revelation is afforded by "lesbian" and "gay," there remains a political imperative to use these necessary errors or category mistakes, as it were (what Gayatri Spivak might call "catachrestic" operations: to use a proper name improperly[8]), to rally and represent an oppressed political constituency. Clearly, I am not legislating against the use of the term. My question is simply: which use will be legislated, and what play will there be between legislation and use such that the instrumental uses of "identity" do not become regulatory imperatives? If it is already true that "lesbians" and "gay men" have been traditionally designated as impossible identities, errors of classification, unnatural disasters within juridico-medical discourses, or, what perhaps amounts to the same, the very paradigm of what calls to be classified, regulated, and controlled, then perhaps these sites of disruption, error, confusion, and trouble can be the very rallying points for a certain resistance to classification and to identity as such.

The question is not one of *avowing* or *disavowing* the category of lesbian or gay, but, rather, why it is that the category becomes the site of this "ethical" choice? What does it mean to *avow* a category that can only maintain its specificity and coherence by performing a prior set of *disavowals?* Does this make "coming out" into the avowal of disavowal, that is, a return to the closet under the guise of an escape? And it is not something like heterosexuality or bisexuality that is disavowed by the category, but a set of identificatory and practical crossings between these categories that renders the discreteness of each equally suspect. Is it not possible to maintain and pursue heterosexual identifications and aims within homosexual practice, and homosexual identifications and aims within heterosexual practices? If a sexuality is to be disclosed,

what will be taken as the true determinant of its meaning: the phantasy structure, the act, the orifice, the gender, the anatomy? And if the practice engages a complex interplay of all of those, which one of this erotic dimensions will come to stand for the sexuality that requires them all? Is it the *specificity* of a lesbian experience or lesbian desire or lesbian sexuality that lesbian theory needs to elucidate? Those efforts have only and always produced a set of contests and refusals which should by now make it clear that there is no necessarily common element among lesbians, except perhaps that we all know something about how homophobia works against women—although, even then, the language and the analysis we use will differ.

To argue that there might be a *specificity* to lesbian sexuality has seemed a necessary counterpoint to the claim that lesbian sexuality is just heterosexuality once removed, or that it is derived, or that it does not exist. But perhaps the claim of specificity, on the one hand, and the claim of derivativeness or non-existence, on the other, are not as contradictory as they seem. Is it not possible that lesbian sexuality is a process that reinscribes the power domains that it resists, that it is constituted in part from the very heterosexual matrix that it seeks to displace, and that its specificity is to be established, not *outside* or *beyond* that reinscription or reiteration, but in the very modality and effects of that reinscription. In other words, the negative constructions of lesbianism as a fake or a bad copy can be occupied and reworked to call into question the claims of heterosexual priority. In a sense I hope to make clear in what follows, lesbian sexuality can be understood to redeploy its 'derivativeness' in the service of displacing hegemonic heterosexual norms. Understood in this way, the political problem is not to establish the specificity of lesbian sexuality over and against its derivativeness, but to turn the homophobic construction of the bad copy against the framework that privileges heterosexuality as origin, and so 'derive' the former from the latter. This description requires a reconsideration of imitation, drag, and other forms of sexual crossing that affirm the internal complexity of a lesbian sexuality constituted in part within the very matrix of power that it is compelled both to reiterate and to oppose.

On the Being of Gayness as Necessary Drag

The professionalization of gayness requires a certain performance and production of a "self" which is the *constituted effect* of a discourse that nevertheless claims to "represent" that self as a prior truth. When I spoke at the conference on homosexuality in 1989,[9] I found myself telling my friends beforehand that I was off to Yale to be a lesbian, which of course didn't mean that I wasn't one before, but that somehow then, as I spoke in that context, I *was* one in some more thorough and totalizing way, at least for the time being. So I *am* one, and my qualifications are even fairly unambiguous. Since I was sixteen, being a lesbian is what I've been. So what's the anxiety, the discomfort? Well, it has something to do with that redoubling, the way I can say, I'm going to Yale to be a lesbian; a lesbian is what I've been being for so long. How is it that I can both "be" one, and yet endeavor to be one at the same time? When and where does my being a lesbian come into play, when and where does this playing a lesbian constitute something like what I am? To say that I "play" at being one is not to say that I am not one "really"; rather, how and where I play at being one is the way in which that "being" gets established, instituted, circulated, and confirmed. This is not a performance from which I can take radical distance, for this is deep-seated play, psychically entrenched play, *and this "I" does not play its lesbianism as a role.* Rather, it is through the repeated play of this sexuality that the "I" is insistently reconstituted as a lesbian "I"; paradoxically, it is precisely the *repetition* of that play that establishes as well the *instability* of the very category that it constitutes. For if the "I" is a site of repetition, that is, if the "I" only achieves the semblance of identity through a certain repetition of itself, then the I is always displaced by the very repetition that sustains it. In other words, does or can the "I" ever repeat itself, cite itself, faithfully, or is there always a displacement from its former moment that establishes the permanently non-self-identical status of that "I" or its "being lesbian"? What "performs" does not exhaust the "I"; it does not lay out in visible terms the comprehensive content of that "I," for if the performance is "repeated," there is always the question of what differentiates from each other the moments of identity that are repeated. And if the "I" is the effect of a certain repetition, one which

produces the semblance of a continuity or coherence, then there is no "I" that precedes the gender that it is said to perform; the repetition, and the failure to repeat, produce a string of performances that constitute and contest the coherence of that "I."

But *politically*, we might argue, isn't it quite crucial to insist on lesbian and gay identities precisely because they are being threatened with erasure and obliteration from homophobic quarters? Isn't the above theory *complicitous* with those political forces that would obliterate the possibility of gay and lesbian identity? Isn't it "no accident" that such theoretical contestations of identity emerge within a political climate that is performing a set of similar obliterations of homosexual identities through legal and political means?

The question I want to raise in return is this: ought such threats of obliteration dictate the terms of the political resistance to them, and if they do, do such homophobic efforts to that extent win the battle from the start? There is no question that gays and lesbians are threatened by the violence of public erasure, but the decision to counter that violence must be careful not to reinstall another in its place. Which version of lesbian or gay ought to be rendered visible, and which internal exclusions will that rendering visible institute? Can the visibility of identity *suffice* as a political strategy, or can it only be the starting point for a strategic intervention which calls for a transformation of policy? Is it not a sign of despair over public politics when identity becomes its own policy, bringing with it those who would 'police' it from various sides? And this is not a call to return to silence or invisibility, but, rather, to make use of a category that can be called into question, made to account for what it excludes. That any consolidation of identity requires some set of differentiations and exclusions seems clear. But which ones ought to be valorized? That the identity-sign I use now has its purposes seems right, but there is no way to predict or control the political uses to which that sign will be put in the future. And perhaps this is a kind of openness, regardless of its risks, that ought to be safeguarded for political reasons. If the rendering visible of lesbian/gay identity now presupposes a set of exclusions, then perhaps part of what is necessarily excluded is *the future uses of the sign*. There is a political necessity to use some sign now, and we do, but how to use it in such a way that its futural signi- fications are not *foreclosed?* How to use the sign and avow its temporal contingency at once?

In avowing the sign's strategic provisionality (rather than its strategic essentialism), that identity can become a site of contest and revision, indeed, take on a future set of significations that those of us who use it now may not be able to foresee. It is in the safeguard- ing of the future of the political signifiers—preserving the signifier as a site of rearticulation—that Laclau and Mouffe discern its democratic promise.

Within contemporary U.S. politics, there are a vast number of ways in which lesbianism in particular is understood as precisely that which cannot or dare not *be*. In a sense, Jesse Helms's attack on the NEA for sanctioning representations of "homoeroticism" focuses various homophobic fantasies of what gay men are and do on the work of Robert Mappletho- rpe.[10] In a sense, for Helms, gay men exist as objects of prohibition; they are, in his twisted fantasy, sado- masochistic exploiters of children, the paradigmatic exemplars of "obscenity"; in a sense, the lesbian is not even produced within this discourse as a prohibited object. Here it becomes important to recognize that oppression works not merely through acts of overt prohibition, but covertly, through the constitution of viable subjects and through the corollary constitution of a domain of unviable (un)subjects—*abjects*, we might call them—who are neither named nor prohib- ited within the economy of the law. Here oppression works through the production of a domain of unthink- ability and unnameability. Lesbianism is not explicitly prohibited in part because it has not even made its way into the thinkable, the imaginable, that grid of cultural intelligibility that regulates the real and the nameable. How, then, to "be" a lesbian in a political context in which the lesbian does not exist? That is, in a political discourse that wages its violence against lesbianism in part by excluding lesbianism from discourse itself? To be prohibited explicitly is to occupy a discursive site from which something like a reverse-discourse can be articulated; to be implicitly proscribed is not even to qualify as an object of prohibition."[11] And though homosexualities of all kinds in this present climate are being erased, reduced, and (then) reconstituted as sites of radical homophobic fantasy, it is important to retrace the different routes by which the unthink-

ability of homosexuality is being constituted time and again.

It is one thing to be erased from discourse, and yet another to be present within discourse as an abid- ing falsehood. Hence, there is a political imperative to render lesbianism visible, but how is that to be done outside or through existing regulatory regimes? Can the exclusion from ontology itself become a rallying point for resistance?

Here is something like a confession which is meant merely to thematize the impossibility of confession: As a young person, I suffered for a long time, and I suspect many people have, from being told, explicitly or implicitly, that what I "am" is a copy, an imitation, a derivative example, a shadow of the real. Compulsory heterosexuality sets itself up as the original, the true, the authentic; the norm that determines the real implies that "being" lesbian is always a kind of miming, a vain effort to participate in the phantasmatic plenitude of naturalized heterosexuality which will always and only fail.[12] And yet, I remember quite distinctly when I first read in Esther Newton's *Mother Camp: Female Imper- sonators in America*[13] that drag is not an imitation or a copy of some prior and true gender; according to Newton, drag enacts the very structure of imperson- ation by which *any gender* is assumed. Drag is not the putting on of a gender that belongs properly to some other group, i.e. an act of *ex*propriation or *ap*propria- tion that assumes that gender is the rightful property of sex, that "masculine" belongs to "male" and "feminine" belongs to "female." There is no "proper" gender, a gender proper to one sex rather than another, which is in some sense that sex's cultural property. Where that notion of the "proper" operates, it is always and only *improperly* installed as the effect of a compulsory sys- tem. Drag constitutes the mundane way in which gen- ders are appropriated, theatricalized, worn, and done; it implies that gendering is a kind of impersonation and approximation. If this is true, it seems, there is no origi- nal or primary gender that drag imitates, but *gender is a kind of imitation for which there is no original;* in fact, it is a kind of imitation that produces the very notion of the original as an *effect* and consequence of the imita- tion itself. In other words, the naturalistic effects of het- erosexualized genders are produced through imitative strategies; what they imitate is a phantasmatic ideal of heterosexual identity, one that is produced by the imitation as its effect. In this sense, the "reality" of heterosexual identities is performatively constituted through an imitation that sets itself up as the origin and the ground of all imitations. In other words, heterosexuality is always in the process of imitating and approximating its own phantasmatic idealization of itself—*and failing*. Precisely because it is bound to fail, and yet endeavors to succeed, the project of heterosexual identity is propelled into an endless repetition of itself. Indeed, in its efforts to naturalize itself as the original, heterosexuality must be understood as a compulsive and compulsory repetition that can only produce the *effect* of its own originality; in other words, compulsory heterosexual identities, those ontologically consolidated phantasms of "man" and "woman," are theatrically produced effects that posture as grounds, origins, the normative measure of the real.[14]

Reconsider then the homophobic charge that queens and butches and femmes are imitations of the heterosexual real. Here "imitation" carries the meaning of "derivative" or "secondary," a copy of an origin which is itself the ground of all copies, but which is itself a copy of nothing. Logically, this notion of an "origin" is suspect, for how can something operate as an origin if there are no secondary consequences which retrospectively confirm the originality of that origin? The origin requires its derivations in order to affirm itself as an origin, for origins only make sense to the extent that they are differentiated from that which they produce as derivatives. Hence, if it were not for the notion of the homosexual *as* copy, there would be no construct of heterosexuality *as* origin. Heterosexuality here presupposes homosexuality. And if the homosexual *as* copy *precedes* the heterosexual as *origin*, then it seems only fair to concede that the copy comes before the origin, and that homosexuality is thus the origin, and heterosexuality the copy.

But simple inversions are not really possible. For it is only *as* a copy that homosexuality can be argued to *precede* heterosexuality as the origin. In other words, the entire framework of copy and origin proves radically unstable as each position inverts into the other and confounds the possibility of any stable way to locate the temporal or logical priority of either term.

But let us then consider this problematic inversion from a psychic/political perspective. If the structure of gender imitation is such that the imitat*ed* is to some degree produced—or, rather, *re*produced—by imitation (see again Derrida's inversion and displacement of mimesis in "The Double Session"), then to claim that gay and lesbian identities are implicated in heterosexual norms or in hegemonic culture generally is not to *derive* gayness from straightness. On the contrary, *imitation* does not copy that which is prior, but produces and *invents* the very terms of priority and derivativeness. Hence, if gay identities are implicated in heterosexuality, that is not the same as claiming that they are determined or derived from heterosexuality, and it is not the same as claiming that heterosexuality is the only cultural network in which they are implicated. These are, quite literally, *inverted* imitations, ones which invert the order of imitated and imitation, and which, in the process, expose the fundamental dependency of "the origin" on that which it claims to produce as its secondary effect.

What follows if we concede from the start that gay identities as derivative inversions are in part defined in terms of the very heterosexual identities from which they are differentiated? If heterosexuality is an impossible imitation of itself, an imitation that performatively constitutes itself as the original, then the imitative parody of "heterosexuality"—when and where it exists in gay cultures—is always and only an imitation of an imitation, a copy of a copy, for which there is no original. Put in yet a different way, the parodic or imitative effect of gay identities works neither to copy nor to emulate heterosexuality, but rather, to expose heterosexuality as an incessant and *panicked* imitation of its own naturalized idealization. That heterosexuality is always in the act of elaborating itself is evidence that it is perpetually at risk, that is, that it "knows" its own possibility of becoming undone: hence, its compulsion to repeat which is at once a foreclosure of that which threatens its coherence. That it can never eradicate that risk attests to its profound dependency upon the homosexuality that it seeks fully to eradicate and never can or that it seeks to make second, but which is always already there as a prior possibility.[15] Although this failure of naturalized heterosexuality might constitute a source of pathos for heterosexuality itself—what its theorists often refer to as its constitutive malaise—it can become an occasion for a subversive and proliferating parody of gender norms in which the very claim to originality and to the real is shown to be the effect of a certain kind of naturalized gender mime.

It is important to recognize the ways in which heterosexual norms reappear within gay identities, to affirm that gay and lesbian identities are not only structured in part by dominant heterosexual frames, but that they are *not* for that reason *determined* by them. They are running commentaries on those naturalized positions as well, parodic replays and resignifications of precisely those heterosexual structures that would consign gay life to discursive domains of unreality and unthinkability. But to be constituted or structured in part by the very heterosexual norms by which gay people are oppressed is not, I repeat, to be claimed or determined by those structures. And it is not necessary to think of such heterosexual constructs as the pernicious intrusion of "the straight mind," one that must be rooted out in its entirety. In a way, the presence of heterosexual constructs and positionalities in whatever form in gay and lesbian identities presupposes that there is a gay and lesbian repetition of straightness, a recapitulation of straightness—which is itself a repetition and recapitulation of its own ideality—within its own terms, a site in which all sorts of resignifying and parodic repetitions become possible. The parodic replication and resignification of heterosexual constructs within non-heterosexual frames brings into relief the utterly constructed status of the so-called original, but it shows that heterosexuality only constitutes itself as the original through a convincing act of repetition. The more that "act" is expropriated, the more the heterosexual claim to originality is exposed as illusory.

Although I have concentrated in the above on the reality-effects of gender practices, performances, repetitions, and mimes, I do not mean to suggest that drag is a "role" that can be taken on or taken off at will. There is no volitional subject behind the mime who decides, as it were, which gender it will be today. On the contrary, the very possibility of becoming a viable subject requires that a certain gender mime be already underway. The "being" of the subject is no more self-identical than the "being" of any gender; in fact, coherent gender, achieved through an apparent repetition of the same, produces as its *effect* the illusion of a prior and volitional subject. In this sense,

gender is not a performance that a prior subject elects to do, but gender is *performative* in the sense that it constitutes as an effect the very subject it appears to express. It is a *compulsory* performance in the sense that acting out of line with heterosexual norms brings with it ostracism, punishment, and violence, not to mention the transgressive pleasures produced by those very prohibitions.

To claim that there is no performer prior to the performed, that the performance is performative, that the performance constitutes the appearance of a "subject" as its effect is difficult to accept. This difficulty is the result of a predisposition to think of sexuality and gender as "expressing" in some indirect or direct way a psychic reality that precedes it. The denial of the *priority* of the subject, however, is not the denial of the subject; in fact, the refusal to conflate the subject with the psyche marks the psychic as that which exceeds the domain of the conscious subject. This psychic excess is precisely what is being systematically denied by the notion of a volitional "subject" who elects at will which gender and/or sexuality to be at any given time and place. It is this excess which erupts within the intervals of those repeated gestures and acts that construct the apparent uniformity of heterosexual positionalities, indeed which compels the repetition itself, and which guarantees its perpetual failure. In this sense, it is this excess which, within the heterosexual economy, implicitly includes homosexuality, that perpetual threat of a disruption which is quelled through a reenforced repetition of the same. And yet, if repetition is the way in which power works to construct the illusion of a seamless heterosexual identity, if heterosexuality is compelled to *repeat itself* in order to establish the illusion of its own uniformity and identity, then this is an identity permanently at risk, for what if it fails to repeat, or if the very exercise of repetition is redeployed for a very different performative purpose? If there is, as it were, always a compulsion to repeat, repetition never fully accomplishes identity. That there is a need for a repetition at all is a sign that identity is not self-identical. It requires to be instituted again and again, which is to say that it runs the risk of becoming *de*-instituted at every interval.

So what is this psychic excess, and what will constitute a subversive or *de*-instituting repetition? First, it is necessary to consider that sexuality always exceeds any given performance, presentation, or narrative which is why it is not possible to derive or read off a sexuality from any given gender presentation. And sexuality may be said to exceed any definitive narrativization. Sexuality is never fully "expressed" in a performance or practice; there will be passive and butchy femmes, femmy and aggressive butches, and both of those, and more, will turn out to describe more or less anatomically stable "males" and "females." There are no direct expressive or causal lines between sex, gender, gender presentation, sexual practice, fantasy and sexuality. None of those terms captures or determines the rest. Part of what constitutes sexuality is precisely that which does not appear and that which, to some degree, can never appear. This is perhaps the most fundamental reason why sexuality is to some degree always closeted, especially to the one who would express it through acts of self-disclosure. That which is excluded for a given gender presentation to "succeed" may be precisely what is played out sexually, that is, an "inverted" relation, as it were, between gender and gender presentation, and gender presentation and sexuality. On the other hand, both gender presentation and sexual practices may corollate such that it appears that the former "expresses" the latter, and yet both are jointly constituted by the very sexual possibilities that they exclude.

This logic of inversion gets played out interestingly in versions of lesbian butch and femme gender stylization. For a butch can present herself as capable, forceful, and all-providing, and a stone butch may well seek to constitute her lover as the exclusive site of erotic attention and pleasure. And yet, this "providing" butch who seems *at first* to replicate a certain husband-like role, can find herself caught in a logic of inversion whereby that "providingness" turns to a self-sacrifice, which implicates her in the most ancient trap of feminine self-abnegation. She may well find herself in a situation of radical need, which is precisely what she sought to locate, find, and fulfill in her femme lover. In effect, the butch inverts into the femme or remains caught up in the specter of that inversion, or takes pleasure in it. On the other hand, the femme who, as Amber Hollibaugh has argued, "orchestrates" sexual exchange,[16] may well eroticize a certain dependency only to learn that the very power to orchestrate that dependency exposes her own incontrovertible power,

at which point she inverts into a butch or becomes caught up in the specter of that inversion, or perhaps delights in it.

Psychic Mimesis

What stylizes or forms an erotic style and/or a gender presentation—and that which makes such categories inherently unstable—is a set of *psychic identifications* that are not simple to describe. Some psychoanalytic theories tend to construe identification and desire as two mutually exclusive relations to love objects that have been lost through prohibition and/or separation. Any intense emotional attachment thus divides into either wanting to have someone or wanting to be that someone, but never both at once. It is important to consider that identification and desire can coexist, and that their formulation in terms of mutually exclusive oppositions serves a heterosexual matrix. But I would like to focus attention on yet a different construal of that scenario, namely, that "wanting to be" and "wanting to have" can operate to differentiate mutually exclusive positionalities internal to lesbian erotic exchange. Consider that identifications are always made in response to loss of some kind, and that they involve a certain *mimetic practice* that seeks to incorporate the lost love within the very "identity" of the one who remains. This was Freud's thesis in "Mourning and Melancholia" in 1917 and continues to inform contemporary psychoanalytic discussions of identification.[17]

For psychoanalytic theorists Mikkel Borch-Jacobsen and Ruth Leys, however, identification and, in particular, identificatory mimetism, *precedes* "identity" and constitutes identity as that which is fundamentally "other to itself." The notion of this Other *in* the self, as it were, implies that the self/Other distinction is *not* primarily external (a powerful critique of ego psychology follows from this); the self is from the start radically implicated in the "Other." This theory of primary mimetism differs from Freud's account of melancholic incorporation. In Freud's view, which I continue to find useful, incorporation—a kind of psychic miming—is a response to, and refusal of, *loss*. Gender as the site of such psychic mimes is thus constituted by the variously gendered Others who have been loved and lost, where the loss is suspended through a melancholic and imaginary incorporation (and preservation) of those Others into the psyche. Over and against this account of psychic mimesis by way of incorporation and melancholy, the theory of primary mimetism argues an even stronger position in favor of the non-self-identity of the psychic subject. Mimetism is not motivated by a drama of loss and wishful recovery, but appears to precede and constitute desire (and motivation) itself; in this sense, mimetism would be prior to the possibility of loss and the disappointments of love.

Whether loss or mimetism is primary (perhaps an undecidable problem), the psychic subject is nevertheless constituted internally by differentially gendered Others and is, therefore, never, as a gender, self-identical.

In my view, the self only becomes a self on the condition that it has suffered a separation (grammar fails us here, for the "it" only becomes differentiated through that separation), a loss which is suspended and provisionally resolved through a melancholic incorporation of some "Other." That "Other" installed in the self thus establishes the permanent incapacity of that "self" to achieve self-identity; it is as it were always already disrupted by that Other; the disruption of the Other at the heart of the self is the very condition of that self's possibility.[18]

Such a consideration of psychic identification would vitiate the possibility of any stable set of typologies that explain or describe something like gay or lesbian identities. And any effort to supply one—as evidenced in Kaja Silverman's recent inquiries into male homosexuality—suffer from simplification, and conform, with alarming ease, to the regulatory requirements of diagnostic epistemic regimes. If incorporation in Freud's sense in 1914 is an effort to *preserve* a lost and loved object and to refuse or postpone the recognition of loss and, hence, of grief, then to become *like* one's mother or father or sibling or other early "lovers" may be an act of love and/or a hateful effort to replace or displace. How would we "typologize" the ambivalence at the heart of mimetic incorporations such as these?[19]

How does this consideration of psychic identification return us to the question, what constitutes a subversive repetition? How are troublesome identifications apparent in cultural practices? Well, consider the

way in which heterosexuality naturalizes itself through setting up certain illusions of continuity between sex, gender, and desire. When Aretha Franklin sings, "you make me feel like a natural woman," she seems at first to suggest that some natural potential of her biological sex is actualized by her participation in the cultural position of "woman" as object of heterosexual recognition. Something in her "sex" is thus expressed by her "gender" which is then fully known and consecrated within the heterosexual scene. There is no breakage, no discontinuity between "sex" as biological facticity and essence, or between gender and sexuality. Although Aretha appears to be all too glad to have her naturalness confirmed, she also seems fully and paradoxically mindful that that confirmation is never guaranteed, that the effect of naturalness is only achieved as a consequence of that moment of heterosexual recognition. After all, Aretha sings, you make me feel *like* a natural woman, suggesting that this is a kind of metaphorical substitution, an act of imposture, a kind of sublime and momentary participation in an ontological illusion produced by the mundane operation of heterosexual drag.

But what if Aretha were singing to me? Or what if she were singing to a drag queen whose performance somehow confirmed her own?

How do we take account of these kinds of identifications? It's not that there is some kind of *sex* that exists in hazy biological form that is somehow *expressed* in the gait, the posture, the gesture; and that some sexuality then expresses both that apparent gender or that more or less magical sex. If gender is drag, and if it is an imitation that regularly produces the ideal it attempts to approximate, then gender is a performance that *produces* the illusion of an inner sex or essence or psychic gender core; it *produces* on the skin, through the gesture, the move, the gait (that array of corporeal theatrics understood as gender presentation), the illusion of an inner depth. In effect, one way that genders gets naturalized is through being constructed as an inner psychic or physical *necessity*. And yet, it is always a surface sign, a signification on and with the public body that produces this illusion of an inner depth, necessity or essence that is somehow magically, causally expressed.

To dispute the psyche as *inner depth*, however, is not to refuse the psyche altogether. On the contrary, the psyche calls to be rethought precisely as a compulsive repetition, as that which conditions and disables the repetitive performance of identity. If every performance repeats itself to institute the effect of identity, then every repetition requires an interval between the acts, as it were, in which risk and excess threaten to disrupt the identity being constituted. The unconscious is this excess that enables and contests every performance, and which never fully appears within the performance itself. The psyche is not "in" the body, but in the very signifying process through which that body comes to appear; it is the lapse in repetition as well as its compulsion, precisely what the performance seeks to deny, and that which compels it from the start.

To locate the psyche within this signifying chain as the instability of all iterability is not the same as claiming that it is inner core that is awaiting its full and liberatory expression. On the contrary, the psyche is the permanent failure of expression, a failure that has its values, for it impels repetition and so reinstates the possibility of disruption. What then does it mean to pursue disruptive repetition within compulsory heterosexuality?

Although compulsory heterosexuality often presumes that there is first a sex that is expressed through a gender and then through a sexuality, it may now be necessary fully to invert and displace that operation of thought. If a regime of sexuality mandates a compulsory performance of sex, then it may be only through that performance that the binary system of gender and the binary system of sex come to have intelligibility at all. It may be that the very categories of sex, of sexual identity, of gender are produced or maintained in the *effects* of this compulsory performance, effects which are disingenuously renamed as causes, origins, disingenuously lined up within a causal or expressive sequence that the heterosexual norm produces to legitimate itself as the origin of all sex. How then to expose the causal lines as retrospectively and performatively produced fabrications, and to engage gender itself as an inevitable fabrication, to fabricate gender in terms which reveal every claim to the origin, the inner, the true, and the real as nothing other than the effects of *drag*, whose subversive possibilities ought to be played and replayed to make the "sex" of gender into a site of insistent political play? Perhaps this

will be a matter of working sexuality *against* identity, even against gender, and of letting that which cannot fully appear in any performance persist in its disruptive promise.

Notes

1. Parts of this essay were given as a presentation at the Conference on Homosexuality at Yale University in October, 1989.
2. "The Mark of Gender," *Feminist Issues 5* no. 2 (1985): 6.
3. *Différence et répétition* (Paris: PUF, 1968), 374; my translation.
4. *Gender Trouble: Feminism and the Subversion of Identity* (New York and London: Routledge, 1990).
5. Michel Foucault, *The History of Sexuality, Vol. I,* trans. John Hurley (New York: Random House, 1980), 101.
6. Here I would doubtless differ from the very fine analysis of Hitchcock's *Rope* offered by D. A. Miller in this volume [*Inside/Out: Lesbian Theories, Gay Theories*].
7. For an example of "coming out" that is strictly unconfessional and which, finally, offers no content for the category of lesbian, see Barbara Johnson's deftly constructed "Sula Passing: No Passing" presentation at UCLA, May 1990.
8. Gayatri Chakravorty Spivak, "Displacement and the Discourse of Woman." In *Displacement: Derrida and After,* ed. Mark Krupnick (Bloomington: Indiana University Press, 1983).
9. Let me take this occasion to apologize to the social worker at that conference who asked a question about how to deal with those clients with AIDS who turned to Bernie Segal and others for the purposes of psychic healing. At the time, I understood this questioner to be suggesting that such clients were full of self-hatred because they were trying to find the causes of AIDS in their own selves. The questioner and I appear to agree that any effort to locate the responsibility for AIDS in those who suffer from it is politically and ethically wrong. I thought the questioner, however, was prepared to tell his clients that they were self-hating, and I reacted strongly (too strongly) to the paternalistic prospect that this person was going to pass judgment on someone who was clearly not only suffering, but already passing judgment on him or herself. To call another person self-hating is itself an act of power that calls for some kind of scrutiny, and I think in response to someone who is already dealing with AIDS, that is perhaps the last thing one needs to hear. I also happened to have a friend who sought out advice from Bernie Segal, not with the belief that there is an exclusive or even primary psychic cause or solution for AIDS, but that there might be a psychic

contribution to be made to surviving with AIDS. Unfortunately, I reacted quickly to this questioner, and with some anger. And I regret now that I didn't have my wits about me to discuss the distinctions with him that I have just laid out.

Curiously, this incident was invoked at a CLAGS (Center for Lesbian and Gay Studies) meeting at CUNY sometime in December of 1989 and, according to those who told me about it, my angry denunciation of the social worker was taken to be symptomatic of the political insensitivity of a "theorist" in dealing with someone who is actively engaged in AIDS work. That attribution implies that I do not do AIDS work, that I am not politically engaged, and that the social worker in question does not read theory. Needless to say, I was reacting angrily on behalf of an absent friend with AIDS who sought out Bernie Segal and company. So as I offer this apology to the social worker, I wait expectantly that the CLAGS member who misunderstood me will offer me one in turn.

10. See my "The Force of Fantasy: Feminism, Mapplethorpe, and Discursive Excess," *differences* 2, no. 2 (Summer 1990). Since the writing of this essay, lesbian artists and representations have also come under attack.

11. It is this particular ruse of erasure which Foucault for the most part fails to take account of in his analysis of power. He almost always presumes that power takes place through discourse as its instrument, and that oppression is linked with subjection and subjectivization, that is, that it is installed as the formative principle of the identity of subjects.

12. Although miming suggests that there is a prior model which is being copied, it can have the effect of exposing that prior model as purely phantasmatic. In Jacques Derrida's "The Double Session" in *Dissemination*, trans. Barbara Johnson (Chicago: University of Chicago Press, 1981), he considers the textual effect of the mime in Mallarmé's "Mimique." There Derrida argues that the mime does not imitate or copy some prior phenomenon, idea, or figure, but constitutes—some might say *performatively*—the phantasm of the original in and through the mime:

He represents nothing, imitates nothing, does not have to conform to any prior referent with the aim of achieving adequation or verisimilitude. One can here foresee an objection: since the mime imitates nothing, reproduces nothing, opens up in its origin the very thing he is tracing out, presenting, or producing, he must be the very movement of truth. Not, of course, truth in the form of adequation between the representation and the present of the thing itself, or between the imitator and the imitated, but truth as the present unveiling of the present.... But this is not the case.... We are faced then

with mimicry imitating nothing: faced, so to speak, with a double that couples no simple, a double that nothing anticipates, nothing at least that is not itself already double. There is no simple reference.... This speculum reflects no reality: it produces mere "reality-effects". ... In this speculum with no reality, in this mirror of a mirror, a difference or dyad does exist, since there are mimes and phantoms. But it is a difference without reference, or rather reference without a referent, without any first or last unit, a ghost that is the phantom of no flesh ... (206)

13. Esther Newton, *Mother Camp: Female Impersonators in America* (Chicago: University of Chicago Press, 1972).

14. In a sense, one might offer a redescription of the above in Lacanian terms. The sexual "positions" of heterosexually differentiated "man" and "woman" are part of the *Symbolic*, that is, an ideal embodiment of the Law of sexual difference which constitutes the object of imaginary pursuits, but which is always thwarted by the "real." These symbolic positions for Lacan are by definition impossible to occupy even as they are impossible to resist as the structuring telos of desire. I accept the former point, and reject the latter one. The imputation of universal necessity to such positions simply encodes compulsory heterosexuality at the level of the Symbolic, and the "failure" to achieve it is implicitly lamented as a source of heterosexual pathos.

15. Of course, it is Eve Kosofsky Sedgwick's *Epistemology of the Closet* (Berkeley: University of California Press, 1990) which traces the subtleties of this kind of panic in Western heterosexual epistemes.

16. Amber Hollibaugh and Cherríe Moraga, "What We're Rollin Around in Bed With: Sexual Silences in Feminism," in *Powers of Desire: The Politics of Sexuality*, ed. Ann Snitow, Christine Stansell, and Sharon Thompson (New York: Monthly Review Press, 1983), 394–405.

17. Mikkel Borch-Jacobsen, *The Freudian Subject* (Stanford: Stanford University Press, 1988); for citations of Ruth Leys's work, see the following two endnotes.

18. For a very fine analysis of primary mimetism with direct implications for gender formation, see Ruth Leys, "The Real Miss Beauchamp: The History and Sexual Politics of the Multiple Personality Concept," in *Feminists Theorize the Political*, eds. Judith Butler and Joan W. Scott (New York and London: Routledge, 1992). For Leys, a primary mimetism or suggestibility requires that the "self" from the start is constituted by its incorporations; the effort to differentiate oneself from that by which one is constituted is, of course, impossible, but it does entail a certain "incorporative violence," to use her term. The violence of identification is in this way in the service of an effort at differentiation, to take the place of the Other who is, as it were, installed at the

foundation of the self. That this replacement, which seeks to be a displacement, fails, and must repeat itself endlessly, becomes the trajectory of one's psychic career.

19. Here again, I think it is the work of Ruth Leys which will clarify some of the complex questions of gender constitution that emerge from a close psychoanalytic consideration of imitation and identification. Her forthcoming book manuscript will doubtless galvanize this field: *The Subject of Imitation.*

8.
POSTFEMINIST MEDIA CULTURE
Elements of a Sensibility
Rosalind Gill

Introduction

The notion of postfeminism has become one of the most important and contested terms in the lexicon of feminist, cultural analysis. In recent years, debates about everything from the history and exclusions of feminism to the gender consciousness (or otherwise) of young women and the ideological nature of contemporary media, have crystallized in disagreements about postfeminism. As with 'postmodernism' before it, the term has become overloaded with different meanings. As Dick Hebdige (1988) noted in relation to postmodernism, this is an indication that there is something over which it is worth struggling. Arguments about postfeminism are debates about nothing less than the transformations in feminisms and transformations in media culture—and their mutual relationship.

However, after nearly two decades of argument about postfeminism, there is still no agreement as to what it is and the term is used variously and contradictorily to signal a theoretical position, a type of feminism after the Second Wave, or a regressive political stance. Such disagreement would not necessarily be cause for alarm (but might merely be a sign of vibrant debate) were it not for two additional problems: first, the difficulty of specifying with any rigour the features of postfeminism; second, the problem of applying current notions to any particular cultural or media analysis. What makes a text postfeminist? What features need to be present in order for any media scholar to label something as postfeminist? In order to use the term 'postfeminism' for analytical purposes, at minimum we need to be able to specify the criteria used to identify something as postfeminist.

To this end, this article aims to propose a new understanding of post-feminism which can be used to analyse contemporary cultural products. It seeks to argue that postfeminism is best thought of as a sensibility that characterizes increasing numbers of films, television shows, advertisements and other media products. Elsewhere (Gill and Herdieckerhoff, 2006) I have discussed the theoretical basis for this conceptualization, highlighting the problems of three dominant accounts of postfeminism which regard it as an epistemological or political position in the wake of feminism's encounter with 'difference' (Alice, 1995; Brooks, 1997; Lotz, 2001; Yeatman, 1994), an historical shift within feminism (Dow, 1996; Hollows, 2000, 2003; Moseley and Read, 2002; Rabinovitz, 1999) or as a backlash against feminism (Faludi, 1992; Whelehan, 2000; Williamson, 2003). Rather than defending the argument for considering postfeminism as a sensibility, this article begins the process of exploring and tentatively explicating the themes or features that characterize this sensibility. To do so, rather than staying close to the (relatively few) texts that have dominated discussions of postfeminism, such as *Sex and the City, Ally McBeal and Desperate Housewives*, it will engage with examples from a range of different media—from talk shows to lad magazines, and from 'chick lit' to advertising. It hopes to demonstrate the utility of the notion of postfeminism as a sensibility, and to contribute to the task of unpacking postfeminist media culture.

Unpacking Postfeminist Media Culture

This article will argue that postfeminism is understood best neither as an epistemological perspective nor as an historical shift, nor (simply) as a backlash in which its meanings are pre- specified. Rather, postfeminism should be conceived of as a sensibility. From this perspective postfeminist media culture should be our critical object—a phenomenon into which scholars of culture should inquire—rather than an analytic perspective. This approach does not require a static notion of one single authentic feminism as a comparison point, but instead is informed by postmodernist and constructionist perspectives and seeks to examine what is distinctive about contemporary articulations of gender in the media.

This new notion emphasizes the contradictory nature of postfeminist discourses and the entanglement of both feminist and anti-feminist themes within them. It also points to a number of other relatively stable features that comprise or constitute a postfeminist discourse. These include the notion that femininity is a bodily property; the shift from objectification to subjectification; the emphasis upon self-surveillance, monitoring and discipline; a focus upon individualism, choice and empowerment; the dominance of a makeover paradigm; a resurgence in ideas of natural sexual difference; a marked sexualization of culture; and an emphasis upon consumerism and the commodification of difference. These themes coexist with, and are structured by, stark and continuing inequalities and exclusions that relate to 'race' and ethnicity, class, age, sexuality and disability as well as gender.

Femininity as a Bodily Property

One of the most striking aspects of postfeminist media culture is its obsessive preoccupation with the body. In a shift from earlier representational practices, it appears that femininity is defined as a bodily property rather than a social, structural or psychological one. Instead of regarding caring, nurturing or motherhood as central to femininity (all of course highly problematic and exclusionary), in today's media, possession of a 'sexy body' is presented as women's key (if not sole) source of identity. The body is presented simultaneously as women's source of power and as always unruly, requiring constant monitoring, surveillance, discipline and remodelling (and consumer spending) in order to conform to ever-narrower judgements of female attractiveness.

Indeed, surveillance of women's bodies constitutes perhaps the largest type of media content across all genres and media forms. Women's bodies are evaluated, scrutinized and dissected by women as well as men, and are always at risk of 'failing'. This is most clear in the cultural obsession with celebrity, which plays out almost exclusively over women's bodies. Magazines such as *Heat* offer page after page of big colour photographs of female celebrities' bodies, with scathing comments about anything from armpit hair to visible panty lines, but focusing in particular upon 'fat' and, more recently, censuring women deemed to be too thin. So excessive and punitive is the regulation of women's bodies through this medium that conventionally attractive women can be indicted, for having 'fat ankles' or 'laughter lines'. No transgression is too small to be picked over and picked apart by paparazzi photographers and writers. The tone of comments is frequently excoriating: 'Yes, that really is Melanie Griffith's wrinkly skin, not fabric' and 'There's so much fabric in Angelica Huston's dress it looks like it could be used to house small animals on cold nights. Despite that, it's straining over Anje's stomach and fits like a skintight bodysuit' (*Heat*, 19 March 2005).

Ordinary (non-celebrity) women are not exempt. TV programmes such as *What Not To Wear* and *10 Years Younger* subject women to hostile scrutiny for their bodies, postures and wardrobes, and evaluations including the like of 'very saggy boobs' and 'what a minger'. Angela McRobbie notes the following from her viewing of *What Not To Wear*.

> 'What a dreary voice', 'look at how she walks', 'she shouldn't put that ketchup on her chips', 'she looks like a mousy librarian', 'her trousers are far too long', 'that jumper looks like something her granny crocheted, it would be better on the table', 'she hasn't washed her clothes', 'your hair looks like an overgrown poodle', 'your teeth are yellow, have you been eating grass?' And 'Oh my God she looks like a German lesbian'.
>
> (McRobbie, 2004a: 118)

McRobbie comments that this last insult was considered so hilarious that it was trailed as a promotion for the programme across the junctions of BBC TV for almost two weeks before it was broadcast. Importantly, the female body in postfeminist media culture is constructed as a window to the individual's interior life. For example, in *Bridget Jones's Diary* (Fielding, 1997) when Bridget Jones smokes 40 cigarettes a day or consumes 'excessive' calories, we are invited to read this in psychological terms as indicative of her emotional breakdown. Today, a sleek, toned, controlled figure is normatively essential for portraying success. Yet there is also—contradictorily—an acknowledgement that the body is a canvas affording an image which may have little to do with how one feels inside. For example, after their break-ups with Brad Pitt and Tom Cruise respectively, Nicole Kidman and Jennifer Aniston were heralded across the media as 'triumphant' when they each first appeared in public—meaning that they successfully performed gleaming, commodified beauty and dazzling self-confidence, however hurt or vulnerable they actually may have felt. There was no comparable focus on the men.

The Sexualization of Culture

The intense focus on women's bodies as the site of femininity is closely related to the pervasive sexualization of contemporary culture. Sexualization here refers both to the extraordinary proliferation of discourses about sex and sexuality across all media forms, referred to by Brian McNair (2002) as part of the 'striptease culture', as well as to the increasingly frequent erotic presentation of girls', women's and (to a lesser extent) men's bodies in public spaces. Newspapers' use of rape stories as part of a package of titillating material is well documented, and in the news media all women's bodies are available to be coded sexually, whether they are politicians, foreign correspondents or serious news anchors.

Different forms of sexualization are evident also in popular magazines. In the 'lad mags', sex is discussed through a vocabulary of youthful, unselfconscious pleasure-seeking, while in magazines targeted at teenage girls and young women it is constructed as something requiring constant attention, discipline, self-surveillance and emotional labour. Girls and women are interpellated as the monitors of all sexual and emotional relationships, responsible for producing themselves as desirable heterosexual subjects as well as pleasing men sexually, protecting against pregnancy and sexually-transmitted infections, defending their own sexual reputations and taking care of men's self-esteem. Men, by contrast, are hailed as hedonists just wanting 'a shag'. The uneven distribution of these discourses of sex, even in a resolutely heterosexual context, is crucial to understanding sexualization (Gill, 2006; Tincknell et al., 2003). Put simply, in magazines aimed at straight women, men are presented as complex, vulnerable human beings. But in magazines targeted at those same men, women only ever discuss their underwear, sexual fantasies, 'filthiest moments' or body parts (Turner, 2005).

The lad magazines are emblematic of the blurring of the boundaries between pornography and other genres which has occurred in the last decade. 'Porno chic' has become a dominant representational practice in advertising, magazines, internet sites and cable television. Even children's television has adopted a sexualized address to its audience and between its presenters. The commercially-driven nature of this sexualization can be seen in the way that clothing companies target girls as young as five with thongs (G-strings), belly tops and T-shirts bearing sexually provocative slogans, such as 'When I'm bad I'm very, very bad, but when I'm in bed I'm better'. The use of the Playboy bunny icon on clothing, stationery and pencils aimed at the pre-teen market is but one example of the deliberate sexualization of children (girls). The 'girlification' of adult women such as Kylie Minogue and Kate Moss is the flipside of a media culture that promotes female children as its most desirable sexual icons.[1]

From Sex Object to Desiring Sexual Subject

Where once sexualized representations of women in the media presented them as passive, mute objects of an assumed male gaze, today sexualization works somewhat differently in many domains. Women are not straightforwardly objectified but are portrayed as active, desiring sexual subjects who choose to present themselves in a seemingly objectified manner because it suits their liberated interests to do so (Goldman, 1992). Nowhere is this clearer than in advertising which has responded to feminist critiques by constructing a new figure to sell to young women: the sexually autonomous heterosexual young woman who plays with her sexual power and is forever 'up for it'.

This shift is crucial to understanding the postfeminist sensibility. It represents a modernization of femininity to include what Hilary Radner has called a new 'technology of sexiness' (Radner, 1999) in which sexual knowledge and practice are central. Furthermore, it represents a shift in the way that power operates: from an external, male judging gaze to a self-policing, narcissistic gaze. It can be argued that this represents a higher or deeper form of exploitation than objectification—one in which the objectifying male gaze is internalized to form a new disciplinary regime. In this regime, power is not imposed from above or the outside, but constructs our very subjectivity. Girls and women are invited to become a particular kind of self, and are endowed with agency on condition that it is used to construct oneself as a subject closely resembling the heterosexual male fantasy found in pornography. As Janice Turner has argued:

> Once porn and real human sexuality were distinguishable. Not even porn's biggest advocates would suggest a porn flick depicted reality, that women were gagging for sex 24/7 and would drop their clothes and submit to rough, anonymous sex at the slightest invitation. But as porn has seeped into mainstream culture, the line has blurred. To speak to men's magazine editors, it is clear they believe that somehow in recent years, porn has come true. The sexually liberated modern woman turns out to resemble—what do you know!—the pneumatic, take-me- now-big-boy fuck-puppet of male fantasy after all.
>
> (Turner, 2005: 2)

The humorous tone that characterized early examples of this shift—the amusing bra adverts in which billboard models confidently and playfully highlighted their sexual power or traffic-stopping sexiness—should not imply that this shift is not, in fact, profoundly serious and problematic. In the last decade it has gone from being a new and deliberate repre-

sentational strategy used on women (i.e. for depicting young women) to being widely and popularly taken up by women as a way of constructing the self. For example, TV presenter Denise van Outen 'confides' in a TV interview, 'I do have a lovely pair. I hope they'll still be photographing my tits when I'm 60'; 'readers' wives' write in to lad magazines with their favourite sexual experiences: 'he turned me around, bent me over the railings and took me from behind, hard'; and girls and women in the West queue up to buy T-shirts with slogans such as 'Porn Star', 'Fcuk Me' and 'Fit Chick, Unbelievable Knockers'.

To be critical of the shift is not to be somehow 'anti-sex'—although in postfeminist media culture this position (the prude) is the only alternative discursively allowed (itself part of the problem, eradicating a space for critique).[2] Rather it is to point to the dangers of such representations of women in a culture in which sexual violence is endemic, and to highlight the exclusions of this representational practice—only *some* women are constructed as active, desiring sexual subjects: women who desire sex with men (except when lesbian women 'perform' for men) and only young, slim and beautiful women. As Myra MacDonald (1995) has pointed out, older women, bigger women, women with wrinkles, etc. are never accorded sexual subjecthood and are still subject to offensive and sometimes vicious representations. Indeed, the figure of the unattractive woman who wants a sexual partner remains one of the most vilified in a range of popular cultural forms. Above all, to critique this is to highlight the pernicious connection of this representational shift to neoliberal subjectivities in which sexual objectification can be (re-)presented not as something done to women by some men, but as the freely chosen wish of active, confident, assertive female subjects.

Individualism, Choice and Empowerment

Notions of choice, of 'being oneself' and 'pleasing oneself', are central to the postfeminist sensibility that suffuses contemporary western media culture. They resonate powerfully with the emphasis upon empowerment and taking control that can be seen in talk shows, advertising and makeover shows. A grammar of individualism underpins all these notions—such that even experiences of racism, homophobia or domestic violence are framed in exclusively personal terms in a way that turns the idea of the personal-as-political on its head. Lois McNay (1992) has called this the deliberate 'reprivatization' of issues which have become politicized only relatively recently.

One aspect of this postfeminist sensibility in media culture is the almost total evacuation of notions of politics or cultural influence. This is seen not only in the relentless personalizing tendencies of news, talk shows and reality TV, but also in the ways in which every aspect of life is refracted through the idea of personal choice and self-determination. For example, phenomena such as the dramatic increase in the number of women having Brazilian waxes (to remove pubic hair entirely and reinstate a prepubes-cent version of their genitalia) or the uptake of breast augmentation surgery by teenage girls, are depicted widely as indicators of women 'pleasing themselves' and 'using beauty' to make themselves feel good. Scant attention is paid to the pressures that might lead a teenager to decide that major surgery will solve her problems, and even less to the commercial interests that are underpinning this staggering trend, such as targeted advertising by cosmetic surgery clinics and promotional packages which include mother and daughter special deals and discounts for two friends to have their 'boobs' done at the same time.

The notion that all our practices are freely chosen is central to postfeminist discourses, which present women as autonomous agents no longer constrained by any inequalities or power imbalances whatsoever. As Kate Taylor puts it, twentysomething women

> already see themselves as equal to men: they can work, they can vote, they can bonk on the first date . . . if a thong makes you feel fabulous, wear it. For one thing, men in the office waste whole afternoons staring at your bottom, placing bets on whether you're wearing underwear. Let them. Use that time to take over the company. But even if you wear lin-gerie for you, for no other reason than it makes you feel good, that is reason enough to keep it on.
> (Taylor, 2006)

In this account, two versions of the empowered female subject are presented. In one, women deliber-ately use their sexual power to distract men so as to take over the business while the guys are salivating. In the other, women are depicted as simply following their own desires to 'feel good'. This latter theme of pleas-ing oneself is by far the more common and is captured in this decade-old comment from Fay Weldon:

> Young girls seem to be getting prettier all the time. There is a return to femininity, but it seems to me that most girls don't give two hoots about men. It is about being fit and healthy for *themselves* not for men.
> (Narayan, 1996: 13; emphasis in original)

Of course the idea that in the past women dressed in a particular way purely to please men is ridiculous: it suggests a view of power as something both over-bearing and obvious, which acted upon entirely doc-ile subjects—as well as implying that all women are heterosexual and preoccupied with male approval. But this pendulum shift to the notion that women just 'please themselves' will not do as a substitute. It pres-ents women as entirely free agents and cannot explain why—if women are just pleasing themselves and fol-lowing their own autonomously generated desires—the resulting valued 'look' is so similar—hairless body, slim waist, firm buttocks, etc. Moreover, it simply avoids all the interesting and important questions about the relationship between representations and subjectivity, the difficult but crucial questions about how socially-constructed, mass-mediated ideals of beauty are internalized and made our own.

What is striking is the degree of fit between the autonomous postfeminist subject and the psychologi-cal subject demanded by neoliberalism. At the heart of both is the notion of the 'choice biography' and the contemporary injunction to render one's life knowable and meaningful through a narrative of free choice and autonomy, however constrained one actually might be (Rose, 1996; "Walkerdine et al., 2001). Take this typical example from *Glamour*'s 'Relationtips' column, October 2005:

> It is possible to make the euphoria of the first date last. In the early weeks, says Balfour, it's best to be the first to end the date. 'It leaves him wanting more.' Then remember the golden rules: don't talk endlessly about your ex, be bitter about men or

moan about your awful job/family/life. Most men agree a confident, secure, optimistic and happy woman is easier to fall in love with than a needy, neurotic one. 'It's not about "I need to be more sexy for him and he'll love me more", it's about being confident in yourself.'

Here—as in *Bridget Jones's Diary* and in 'chick lit' more generally—achieving desirability in a heterosexual context is explicitly (re-)presented as something done for yourself, not in order to please a man. In this modernized, neoliberal version of femininity, it is absolutely imperative that one's sexual and dating practices be presented as freely chosen (however traditional, old-fashioned or inegalitarian they may be—involving strict adherence to rules, rationing oneself and not displaying any needs). In this example, some of the strain of this position—the messy suturing of traditional and neoliberal discourses—can be seen very clearly in both the need to disavow explicitly a potential reading that 'you' would be doing this to please a man, and the attempt to gloss 'leaving him wanting more' somehow as a modern and powerful position.

Self-Surveillance and Discipline

Intimately related to the stress upon personal choice is the new emphasis on self-surveillance, self-monitoring and self-discipline in postfeminist media culture. Arguably, monitoring and surveying the self have long been requirements of the performance of successful femininity—with instruction in grooming, attire, posture, elocution and 'manners' being 'offered' to women to allow them to emulate more closely the upper-class white ideal. In women's magazines femininity has been portrayed always as contingent—requiring constant anxious attention, work and vigilance, from touching up your make-up to packing the perfect capsule wardrobe, from hiding 'unsightly' pimples, wrinkles, age spots or stains to hosting a successful dinner party. However, what marks out the present moment as distinctive are three features. First, the dramatically increased intensity of self-surveillance, indicating the intensity of the regulation of women (alongside the disavowal of such regulation). Second, the extensiveness of surveillance over entirely new spheres of life

and intimate conduct. Third, the focus upon the psychological—the requirement to transform oneself and remodel one's interior life.

Something of the intensity and extensiveness of the self-surveillance and discipline now normatively required of women can be seen in women's magazines in which bodily shape, size, muscle tone, attire, sexual practice, career, home, finances, etc. are rendered into 'problems' that necessitate ongoing and constant monitoring and labour. Yet, in an extraordinary ideological sleight of hand, this labour must be understood nevertheless as 'fun', 'pampering' or 'self-indulgence' and must *never* be disclosed. Magazines offer tips to girls and young women to enable them to continue the work of femininity but still appear as entirely confident, carefree and unconcerned about their self-presentation (as this is now an important aspect of femininity in its own right); for example, the solution to continuing a diet while at an important business lunch where everyone else is drinking is to order a spritzer (and surreptitiously ask the waiter to make it largely mineral water), *J17* includes the following advice to girls texting a 'lad love':

> Do: be flirtatious—no lad can resist an ego massage; text him before he goes to bed—you'll be the last thing on his mind; put in a deliberate mistake to give it that "I'm not so bothered aboutcha" air; wait a minimum of 10 minutes before you reply—yes, 10 minutes!
>
> (*J17*, March 2001)

From sending a brief text message to ordering a drink, no area of a woman's life is immune from the requirement to self-survey and work on the self. More and more aspects of the body come under surveillance: you thought you were comfortable with your body? Well think again! When was the last time you checked your 'upper arm definition'? Have you been neglecting your armpits or the soles of your feet? Do you sometimes have (ahem) unpleasant odours?

But it is not only the surface of the body that needs ongoing vigilance—there is also the self: what kind of friend, lover, daughter or colleague are you? Do you laugh enough? How well do you communicate? Have you got emotional intelligence? In a culture saturated by individualistic self-help discourses, the self has become a project to be evaluated, advised, disciplined and improved or brought 'into recovery'. However, what is so striking is how unevenly distributed these quasi-therapeutic discourses are. In magazines, contemporary fiction and television talk shows, it is women, not men, who are addressed and required to work on and transform the self. Significantly, it appears that the ideal disciplinary subject of neoliberalism is feminine.

The Makeover Paradigm

More broadly, it might be argued that a makeover paradigm constitutes postfeminist media culture. This requires people (predominantly women) to believe, first, that they or their life is lacking or flawed in some way; second, that it is amenable to reinvention or transformation by following the advice of relationship, design or lifestyle experts and practising appropriately modified consumption habits. Not only is this the implicit message of many magazines, talk shows and other media content, but it is the explicit focus of the 'makeover takeover' (Hollows, 2000) that dominates contemporary television. It began with food, homes and gardens, but has now extended to clothing, cleanliness, work, dating, sex, cosmetic surgery and raising children.

Such shows begin with the production of 'toxic shame' (Peck, 1995) in their participants through humiliation—inadequacies in the wardrobe, cleanliness, dating or childrearing department, alongside the gleeful and voyeuristic display of their failings to the audience ("Oh my GOD—what is THAT? No, NO! What's she DOING?!"). Participants are then variously advised, cajoled, bullied or 'educated' into changing their ways and becoming more 'successful' versions of themselves (looking younger, getting past the first date, having a better relationship with their children, etc.). A frequent 'third chapter' of the show's format allows the hapless victim to be set free to 'go it alone' (on a date or buying clothes) while, behind the watchful eye of the hidden camera, the 'experts' offer their judgements.

As Helen Wood and Beverly Skeggs (2004) have argued, the ubiquity of such shows produce 'new ethical selves' in which particular forms of modernized and upgraded selfhood are presented as solutions to the dilemmas of contemporary life. The scenarios are profoundly classed and gendered and, as Angela McRobbie (2004a) points out, racialized too (if largely through exclusion), since the kind of hostile judgements routinely made of white working-class women would risk being heard as racist if made by white experts about black bodies, practices and lives. The shows reinvigorate class antagonisms which, in this moment of compulsory individuality, no longer work on such 'crude' categories as occupation or social location, but play out on the women's bodies, homes, cooking skills and ability as mothers, through notions of good taste and cultural capital:

> Choice mediates taste, displaying the success and the failure of the self to make itself, for instance in lifestyle programmes such as *Changing Rooms* (BBC), *House Doctor* (Channel 4) and *Better Homes* (ITV) where the domestic and thus the everyday is transformed through appropriating 'better' taste.
>
> (Wood and Skeggs, 2004: 206)

McRobbie points to the appalling nastiness and viciousness of the gendered and class animosities enacted, as the audience is encouraged to laugh at those less fortunate. However, in a programme such as *Wife Swap*, in which two married women (usually from dramatically different class backgrounds) swap lives, the orchestrated morality is sometimes more complicated, with middle-class 'career women' the target of attack for devoting too little time or attention to their children (alongside the attacks on working-class women's poor food preparation or incompetence at helping with homework, which McRobbie describes). What is clear from even a cursory viewing of such shows is that women simply cannot win; inevitably, they will always 'fail'. But rather than interrogating femininity or social relations, or what we as a society expect of women, the shows offer no way of understanding this other than through the dramatized spectacle of conflict between two women.

As has been noted previously, most of the participants and a large part of the assumed audience for makeover shows are women. One exception is *Queer Eye for the Straight Guy*, in which 'five gay professionals in fashion, grooming, interior design, culture, food and wine come together as a team to help straight men of the world find the job, get the look and get the girl' (executive producer, quoted in Allatson, 2004: 209). Here, gay men occupy an explicitly feminized position, offering advice based on their cultural capital as wealthy, successful, middle-class and, above all, stylish. There is no space here to reflect on the debates about the show, such as its elision or equation of gayness with stylishness, its eradication of any female 'queer' perspectives, and its role in bolstering and maintaining a heterosexist economy. But it is worth pointing to the difference in tone between this show and similar formats aimed at transforming women—in particular, the ironic distance and lack of a sense of punitive regulation that marks out *Queer Eye*. This is also notable in other shows featuring male participants: they are marked in subtle ways as 'less serious' and as offering a kind of symbolic revenge against men. This can be seen most clearly in the now iconic moment in each show (such as *10 Years Younger*) in which male 'victims' are told that they must have their back (or sometimes chest) hair removed. This procedure is lingered over by the camera in a way that seems designed to appeal to female viewers, for whom waxing or electrolysis is assumed to be routine. The 2005 box-office hit *Hitch*, in which Will Smith plays a life and relationship coach to the sweet but inept Kevin James, features a similar scene, while also being wrapped in a narrative that reassures male viewers that such self-transformations are not really necessary: being oneself (unmade-over) is all that is required to win the woman's heart, and 'authentic masculinity' wins the day.

The Reassertion of Sexual Difference

For a short time in the 1970s and 1980s, notions of male and female equality and the basic similarity of men and women took hold in popular culture, before this was resolutely dispensed with in the 1990s. A key feature of the postfeminist sensibility has been the resurgence of ideas of natural sexual difference across all media from newspapers to advertising, talk shows and popular fiction. One arena in which this played out was the media debate about masculinity, in which the figure of the 'New Man' was attacked by both women and men as asexual and not manly enough. New man was condemned as inauthentic and

fake, and understood by many as an act or pose that had arisen through what was presented as the hegemonic dominance of feminism, but had little to do with what men were actually like. Against this, the rise of the 'New Lad' in the 1990s was widely reported as an assertion of freedom against the stranglehold of feminism and—crucially—as an unashamed celebration of true or authentic masculinity, liberated from the shackles of 'political correctness'. New lad championed and reasserted a version of masculinity as libidinous, powerful and, crucially, different from femininity.

Importantly, these discourses of sexual difference were nourished both by the growing interest in evolutionary psychology, and developments in genetic science which held out the promise of locating a genetic basis for all human characteristics. Such developments, from concern about the existence of a 'gay gene' to attempts to identify the parts of the brain responsible for risk-taking (and to demonstrate that they were larger in men than in women), were accorded a huge amount of coverage in the press and on television, and it is significant that this interest coincided with a moment in which the lifestyle sections of newspapers were expanding and proliferating, filled in large part by articles focusing on the nature of gender and gender relations (see Gill, 2006).

In addition, notions of sexual difference were fed by the explosion of self-help literature which addressed—at least as its subtext—the question of why the 'battle of the sexes' continued despite (or, in some iterations, because of) feminism. One answer rang out loud and clearly from many texts: because men and women are fundamentally different. Feminism was deemed to have lost its way when it tried to impose its ideological prescriptions on a nature that did not fit; what was needed, such literature argued, was a frank acknowledgement of difference rather than its denial. Spearheading the movement (or at least the publishing phenomenon) was John Gray, whose 'Mars and Venus' text (2002) soon became a whole industry. Gray's genius was in locating sexual difference as a psychological rather than essentially biological matter, and transposing old and cliched notions through the new and fresh metaphor of interplanetary difference, while (superficially at least) avoiding blame and criticism (a closer reading tells a different story).

Gray's work has become an important part of postfeminist media culture in its own right, as well as in its citations in other popular cultural texts from magazines to 'chick lit', and its inauguration of the notion of (interplanetary) translation. The idea (also found in more expressly feminist texts such as Deborah Tannen's (1992) work on language), is that men and women just do not understand each other. A large role for the popular media, then, is translating or mediating men's and women's communication, customs and 'funny ways' to each other (in a manner, one could argue, that still systematically privileges male power).

Discourses of sexual difference also serve to (re-) eroticize power relations between men and women. On one level this simply means that difference is constructed as sexy. On another, discourses of natural gender difference can be used to freeze in place existing inequalities by representing them as inevitable and—if read correctly—as pleasurable.

Irony and Knowingness

No discussion of the postfeminist sensibility in the media would be complete without considering irony and knowingness. Irony can serve many functions. It is used in advertising to address what Goldman (1992) calls 'sign fatigue', by hailing audiences as knowing and sophisticated consumers, flattering them with their awareness of intertextual references and the notion that they can 'see through' attempts to manipulate them. Irony is used also as a way of establishing a safe distance between oneself and particular sentiments or beliefs, at a time when being passionate about anything or appearing to care too much seems to be 'uncool'. As Ian Parker has noted in relation to declarations of love, the postmodern and ironic version of 'I love you' might be, 'as Barbara Cartland would say, "I love you madly"' (Parker, 1989: 157). Here the quotation or reference sets up a protective distance between the speaker and the expression of love. Jackson et al. (2001) have argued that irony may offer an internal defence against ambivalent feelings, as well as outwardly rebutting charges of taking something (or worse still, oneself) too seriously.

Most significantly, however, in postfeminist media culture irony has become a way of 'having it both ways', of expressing sexist, homophobic or otherwise unpalatable sentiments in an ironized form, while claiming this was not actually 'meant'. It works in various ways. As Whelehan (2000) and Williamson (2003) have argued, the use of retro imagery and nostalgia is a key device in the construction of contemporary sexism. Referencing a previous era becomes an important way of suggesting that the sexism is safely sealed in the past while constructing scenarios that would garner criticism if they were represented as contemporary. In the recent '*Happy Days*' advert for Citroen C3 cars, for example, the first frame shows a young woman having her dress entirely ripped off her body to reveal her bright red underwear (which matches the car). She screams, but the action soon moves on as the interest is in her body, not her distress. The 1950s iconography and soundtrack from the *Happy Days* show protects the advert from potential criticism: it is as if the whole thing is in ironic and humorous quotation marks.

The return and rehabilitation of the word 'totty' in popular culture marks another example of this, allowing middle-class television presenters to refer to women in an entirely dehumanizing and objectifying manner, while suggesting that the sexism is not meant seriously. The word has a nostalgic quality, redolent of 'naughty' seaside postcards.

Irony can operate through 'silly' neologisms. This happens routinely in the lads' magazines. For example, in evaluating photographs of readers' girlfriends' breasts, *FHM* makes such comments as 'if we're being fussy, right chesticle is a tad larger than the left'—the sheer silliness of the term 'chesticle' raises a smile so that one might almost overlook the fact that this is a competition ('breast quest') to find the 'best pair of tits' in Britain (in 2005).

Irony also functions through the very extremeness of the sexism expressed: as though the mere fact that women are compared to 'rusty old bangers' or posed against each other in the 'dumbest girlfriend' competition is (perversely) evidence that there is no sexism (the extremeness of the sexism is evidence that there is no sexism). Magazine editors routinely trot out the line that it is all 'harmless fun' (when did 'harmless' and 'fun' become yoked together so powerfully?). And some academic commentators agree. David Gauntlett argues that the sexism in such magazines is 'knowingly ridiculous, based on the assumption that it's silly to be sexist (and therefore is funny in a silly way)' (2002: 168).

Yet if we suspend our disbelief in the notion that it is 'just a laugh', we are left with a fast- growing area of media content (which profoundly influences other media) that is chillingly misogynist, inviting men to evaluate women only as sexual objects. A recent issue of *FHM* asks men: 'How much are you paying for sex?' Readers are invited to calculate their 'out-goings' on items such as drinks, cinema tickets and bunches of flowers, and then to divide the total by the number of 'shags' they've had that month in order to calculate their 'pay per lay'. Under a fiver per shag is 'too cheap—she is about the same price as the Cam-bodian whore'; around £11 to £20 is 'about the going rate for a Cypriot tart', and each shag should be com-pared with the value and pleasure to be obtained from purchasing a new CD. Any more expensive than this and the lad should expect a performance worthy of a highly-trained, sexy showgirl (Turner, 2005).

It is hard to imagine any other group in society being so systematically objectified, attacked and vili-fied with so little opposition—which tells us something about the power of irony. Any attempt to offer a cri-tique of such articles is dismissed by references to the critic's presumed ugliness, stupidity or membership of the 'feminist thought police'. Frequently, criticisms are pre-empted by comments which suggest that the article's writer is expecting 'blundering rants' from the 'council of women'. In this context, critique becomes much more difficult—and this, it would seem, is pre-cisely what is intended.

Feminism and Anti-feminism

Finally, this article will turn to constructions of femi-nism, which are an integral feature of the postfemi-nist sensibility considered here. One of the things that makes the media today very different from the television, magazines, radio or press of the 1960s, 1970s and early 1980s, is that feminism is now part of the cultural field. That is, feminist discourses are expressed within the media rather than simply being external, independent, critical voices. Feminist-inspired ideas burst forth from our radios, television screens and print media in TV discussions about date rape and sexualized imagery, in newspaper articles about women's experiences of war or the increasing beauty pressures on young girls, in talk shows about domestic violence or anorexia. Indeed, it might be argued that much of what counts as feminist debate in western countries today takes place in the media rather than outside it.

However, it would be entirely false to suggest that the media has somehow become feminist and has adopted unproblematically a feminist perspec-tive. Instead it seems more accurate to argue that the media offers contradictory, but nevertheless patterned, constructions. In this postfeminist moment, as Judith Stacey (1987) has put it, feminist ideas are simulta-neously 'incorporated, revised and depoliticised', and—let us add here—attacked. Angela McRobbie (2004b) has referred to this as the contemporary 'dou-ble entanglement' of neoliberal values in relation to gender, sexuality and family life, and a feminism that is part of common sense yet also feared, hated and fiercely repudiated.

What makes contemporary media culture distinc-tively postfeminist, rather than pre-feminist or anti-feminist, is precisely this entanglement of feminist and anti-feminist ideas. This can be seen clearly in the multimillion dollar publishing phenomenon of 'chick lit' in the wake of the success of *Bridget Jones's Diary*. In contemporary screen and paperback romances, feminism is not ignored or even attacked (as some backlash theorists might have it), but is simultane-ously taken for granted and repudiated. A certain kind of liberal feminist perspective is treated as common-sense, while at the same time feminism and feminists are constructed as harsh, punitive and inauthentic, not articulating women's true desires (Tasker and Negra, 2005). In some instances feminism is set up as police-man, disallowing women the pleasures of traditional femininity. In a recent interview, Marian Keyes, author of a series of successful 'chick lit' novels, refers to her-self as part of a 'postfeminist generation' that grew up in fear of being 'told off' by feminists and 'having everything pink taken out of my house' (*Start the Week*, BBC Radio 4, 7 June 2004). This caricature captures well what Esther Sonnet has called the 'naughty but nice' effect, where 'disapproval from Big Sister inten-sifies the secret/guilty pleasures offered to the "post-feminist" consumer of the forbidden pleasures of the unreconstructed "feminine"' (Sonnet, 2002: 193).

Perhaps this also relates to the pleasures of the sexism in lad magazines, targeted as they are at men 'who should know better' (to use *Loaded*'s strapline). It is precisely the knowingness of the 'transgression', alongside the deliberate articulation of feminist and anti-feminist ideas, that signifies a postfeminist sensibility.

In such romances, postfeminist heroines are often much more active protagonists than their counterparts in popular culture from the 1970s and 1980s. They value autonomy, bodily integrity and the freedom to make individual choices. However, what is interesting is the way in which they seem compelled to use their empowered postfeminist position to make choices that would be regarded by many feminists as problematic, located as they are in normative notions of femininity. They choose, for example, white weddings, downsizing, giving up work or taking their husband's name on marriage (McRobbie, 2004b). One reading of this may highlight the exclusions of Second Wave feminism, suggesting that it represents the 'return of the repressed'; the pleasures of domesticity or traditional femininity (Hollows, 2003). Another (not necessarily contradictory) reading might want to stress the ways in which pre-feminist ideals are being (seductively) repackaged as postfeminist freedoms (Probyn, 1997) in ways that do nothing to question normative heterosexual femininity. Two things are clear, however: postfeminism constructs an articulation or suture between feminist and anti-feminist ideas, and this is effected entirely through a grammar of individualism that fits perfectly with neoliberalism.

Conclusion

This article has attempted to outline the elements of a postfeminist sensibility, against a backdrop in which 'postfeminism' is routinely invoked but rarely explored or specified. Of necessity, this outline has been brief and schematic, highlighting a variety of themes that, taken together, constitute a distinctively postfeminist sensibility. I am conscious of having paid insufficient attention to differences of various kinds, and would be interested in exploring the extent to which a postfeminist sensibility re-centres both heterosexuality and whiteness, as well as fetishizing a young,

able-bodied, 'fit' (understood as both healthy, and in its more contemporary sense as 'attractive') female body. The ways in which postfeminism marks a racialized and heterosexualized modernization of femininity require much more analysis than was possible here. In conclusion, however, this article highlights two key points about the sensibility sketched here: its intimate relation to feminism and to neoliberalism.

What makes a postfeminist sensibility quite different from both pre-feminist constructions of gender and feminist ones, is that it is clearly a response to feminism. In this sense, postfeminism articulates a distinctively new sensibility. Some writers have understood this as a backlash (Faludi, 1992; Whelehan, 2000; Williamson, 2003) but one could argue that it is more complex than this, precisely because of its tendency to entangle feminist and anti-feminist discourses. Feminist ideas are at the same time articulated and repudiated, expressed and disavowed. Its constructions of contemporary gender relations are profoundly contradictory. On the one hand, young women are hailed through a discourse of 'can-do girl power', yet on the other hand, their bodies are powerfully reinscribed as sexual objects; women are presented as active, desiring social subjects, but they are subject to a level of scrutiny and hostile surveillance which has no historical precedent.

Yet these contradictions are not random, but contain the sediments of other discourses in a way that is patterned and amenable to elaboration—much as this article has tried to do. It is precisely in the apparent contradictions of the postfeminist sensibility that the entanglement of feminist and anti-feminist discourses can be seen. The patterned nature of the contradictions is what constitutes the sensibility, one in which notions of autonomy, choice and self-improvement sit side-by-side with surveillance, discipline and the vilification of those who make the 'wrong' 'choices' (become too fat, too thin or have the audacity or bad judgement to grow older).

These notions are also central to neoliberalism and suggest a profound relation between neoliberal ideologies and postfeminism. In recent years a number of writers have explored neoliberalism in order to highlight the ways in which it has shifted from being a political or economic rationality to a mode of governmentality that operates across a range of social spheres (Brown, 2003; Rose, 1996). Neoliberalism is understood increasingly as constructing individuals as entrepreneurial actors who are rational, calculating and self-regulating. The individual must bear full responsibility for their life biography, no matter how severe the constraints upon their action.

However, what has not yet been examined is the relationship of neoliberalism to gender relations. But it appears from this attempt to map the elements of a postfeminist sensibility that there is a powerful resonance between postfeminism and neoliberalism. This operates on at least three levels. First, and most broadly, both appear to be structured by a current of individualism that has replaced almost entirely notions of the social or political, or any idea of the individual as subject to pressures, constraints or influence from outside themselves. Second, it is clear that the autonomous, calculating, self-regulating subject of neoliberalism bears a strong resemblance to the active, freely choosing, self-reinventing subject of postfeminism. These two parallels suggest, then, that postfeminism is not simply a response to feminism but also a sensibility at least partly constituted through the pervasiveness of neoliberal ideas. Third, however, is a connection which might imply that the synergy is even more significant: in the popular cultural discourses examined here, *women* are called on to self-manage and self-discipline. To a much greater extent than men, women are required to work on and transform the self, regulate every aspect of their conduct, and present their actions as freely chosen. Could it be that neoliberalism is always already gendered, and that women are constructed as its ideal subjects? Further exploration of this intimate relationship is needed urgently to illuminate both postfeminist media culture and contemporary neoliberal social relations.

Notes

1. See Tincknell (2005) for a nuanced discussion of this phenomenon.
2. The language of feminism's sex wars is also unhelpful in this respect, counterposing the 'anti-pornography' feminists with the 'sex positive' feminists, with the implication that those who are against pornography are somehow less than positive about sex.

References

Alice, L. (1995) 'What Is Postfeminism? Or, Having it Both Ways', in L. Alice and L. Star (eds) *Feminism/Postmodernism/Postfeminism: Conference Proceedings*, pp. 5–17. Auckland: Massey University Press.

Allatson, P. (2004) '*Queer Eye*'s Primping and Pimping for Empire et al', *Feminist Media Studies* 4(2): 208–11.

Brooks, A. (1997) *Postfeminisms: Feminism, Cultural Theory and Cultural Forms*. London: Routledge.

Brown, W. (2003) 'Neo-Liberalism and the End of Liberal Democracy', *Theory and Event* 7(1). [Accessed 4 December 2006: http://muse.jhu.edu/ journals/tae/]

Dow, B. J. (1996) *Prime-Time Feminism: Television, Media Culture, and the Women's Movement Since 1970*. Philadelphia: University of Pennsylvania Press.

Faludi, S. (1992) *Backlash: The Undeclared War Against Women*. London: Chatto & Windus.

Fielding, H. (1997) *Bridget Jones's Diary*. London: Picador.

Gauntlett, D. (2002) *Media, Gender and Identity: An Introduction*. London: Routledge.

Gill, R. (2006) *Gender and the Media*. Cambridge: Polity Press.

Gill, R. and E. Herdieckerhoff (2006) 'Rewriting the Romance: New Femininities in Chick Lit', *Feminist Media Studies* 6(4), 487–504.

Goldman, R. (1992) *Reading Ads Socially*. London: Routledge.

Gray. J. (2002) *Men Are from Mars, Women are from Venus*. London: HarperCollins.

Hebdige, D. (1988) *Hiding in the Light*. London: Routledge.

Hollows, J. (2000) *Feminism, Femininity, and Popular Culture*. Manchester: Manchester University Press.

Hollows, J. (2003) 'Feeling Like a Domestic Goddess: Postfeminism and Cooking', *European Journal of Cultural Studies* 6(2): 179–202.

Jackson, P., N. Stevenson and K. Brooks (2001) *Making Sense of Men's Magazines*. Cambridge: Polity Press.

Lotz, A. (2001) 'Postfeminist Television Criticism: Rehabilitating Critical Terms and Identifying Postfeminist Attributes', *Feminist Media Studies* 1(1): 105–21.

MacDonald, M. (1995) *Representing Women: Myths of Femininity in the Popular Media*. London: Hodder.

McNair, B. (2002) *Striptease Culture: Sex Media and the Democratisation of Desire*. London: Routledge.

McNay, L. (1992) *Foucault and Feminism: Power, Gender and the Self*. Cambridge: Polity Press.

McRobbie, A. (2004a) 'Notes on "*What Not To Wear*" and Post-Feminist Symbolic Violence', in L. Adkins and B. Skeggs (eds) *Feminism after Bourdieu*, pp. 99–109. Oxford: Blackwell.

McRobbie, A. (2004b) 'Post Feminism and Popular Culture', *Feminist Media Studies* 4(3): 255–64.

Moseley, R. and J. Read (2002) '"Having it *Ally*": Popular

Television and Postfeminism', *Feminist Media Studies* 2(2): 231–50.

Narayan, N. (1996) 'Cleavage Divides Postfeminists', *Observer* (25 Aug.): 13.

Parker, I. (1989) *The Crisis in Modern Social Psychology and How to End It.* London: Routledge.

Peck, J. (1995) 'TV Talk Shows as Therapeutic Discourse: The Ideological Labour of the Televised Talk Cure', *Communication Theory* 5(1): 58–81.

Probyn, E. (1997) 'New Traditionalism and Post-Feminism: TV Does the Home', in C. Brunsdon, J. D'Acci and L. Spigel (eds) *Feminist Television Criticism: A Reader*, pp. 126–37. Oxford: Blackwell.

Rabinovitz, L. (1999) 'Ms-Representation: The Politics of Feminist Sitcoms', in M.B. Haralovich and L. Rabinovitz (eds) *Television, History and American Culture*, pp. 144–167. Durham, NC: Duke University Press.

Radner, H. (1999) 'Queering the Girl', in H. Radner and M. Luckett (eds) *Swinging Single*, pp. 1–38. Minneapolis, MN: University of Minnesota Press.

Rose, N. (1996) *Inventing Ourselves: Psychology, Power and Personhood.* New York: Cambridge University Press.

Sonnet, E. (2002) 'Erotic Fiction by Women for Women: The Pleasures of Post-Feminist Heterosexuality', *Sexualities* 2(2): 167–87.

Stacey, J. (1987) 'Sexism by a Subtler Name? Postindustrial Conditions and Post-Feminist Consciousness in the Silicon Valley', *Socialist Review* 17(6): 7–28.

Tannen, D. (1992) *You Just Don't Understand: Women and Men in Conversation.* London: Virago.

Tasker, Y. and D. Negra (2005) '"In Focus" Postfeminism and Contemporary Media Studies', *The Cinema Journal* 44(2): 107–10.

Taylor, K. (2006) 'Today's Ultimate Feminists are the Chicks in Crop Tops', *Guardian* (23 March). [Available at: http://www.guardianunlimited.co.uk]

Tincknell, E. (2005) *Mediating the Family: Gender, Culture and Representation.* London: Hodder Arnold.

Tincknell, E., C. Chambers, J. Van Loon and N. Hudson (2003) 'Begging for It: "New Femininities", Social Agency and Moral Discourse in Contemporary Teenage and Men's Magazines', *Feminist Media Studies* 3(1): 47–63.

Turner, J. (2005) 'Dirty Young Men', *Guardian Weekend* (22 Oct.) [Accessed 4 December 2006: http://www.guardian.co.uk/weekend/story/0,,1596384,00.html]

Walkerdine, V., H. Lucey and J. Melody (2001) *Growing Up Girl: Psychosocial Explorations of Gender and Class.* Basingstoke: Palgrave.

Whelehan, I. (2000) *Overloaded: Popular Culture and the Future of Feminism.* London: Women's Press.

Williamson, J. (2003) 'Sexism with an Alibi', *Guardian* (31 May). [Accessed 4 December 2006: http://www.guardian.co.uk/comment/story/0,3604,967618,00.html]

Wood, H. and B. Skeggs (2004) 'Notes on Ethical Scenarios of Self on British Reality TV', *Feminist Media Studies* 4(2): 205–8.

Yeatman, A. (1994) *Postmodern Revisionings of the Political.* New York: Routledge.

PART II

PRODUCTION: LABOR, CREATIVITY, MARKETING, AND TECHNOLOGY

Introduction

Part II of the reader focuses on studies of gender and media production. Once confined primarily to questions of authorship, industry, and political economy, the field of media production studies has developed at a rapid pace since the expansion of cultural studies in the late twentieth century, moving beyond both traditional literary and political economy approaches.[1] Researchers interested in the gender dynamics of media production now commonly use a combination of ethnographic practices, discourse analysis, and critical theory to understand how and why this cultural realm continues to operate via a patriarchal logic that limits female involvement and constrains women's advancement, as well as how women media producers and consumers negotiate this difficult terrain. Albeit to a lesser extent, the gender politics of independent and amateur media have received critical attention from media scholars of late also.

Although their concerns were primarily with women's representation, several of the scholars who founded the field of gender-based media studies drew attention to how the media industries' gender politics shape the portrayals of women, thereby suggesting new paths for future research in production studies. For instance, in her early work on the symbolic annihilation of women in mass media, Gaye Tuchman discusses how male media professionals draw from and reproduce dominant social norms in their texts as a result of their goal of attracting the largest number of consumers possible for the commercial sponsors who fund their work.[2] Meanwhile, Laura Mulvey's early work suggests that the male gaze of Hollywood cinema is produced through male dominance of three primary roles within film production: the screenwriter, who creates protagonists with whom viewers are encouraged to identify; the director, who works with actors and crew members to adapt the screenwriter's ideas for the screen; and the cinematographer, who controls what the camera and thus viewers see.[3] Because of these traditional gender politics, Mulvey advocated the development of women's counter-cinema.

Although many feminist scholars conducting media research after Mulvey and Tuchman have operated under the assumption of the media industries' patriarchal legacy, Denise and William Bielby's "Women and Men in Film" was one of the first studies to specifically examine the gender dynamics of employment and career development in such industries.[4] Focusing on the realm of feature film writing in the early 1990s, the Bielbys' study reveals considerable barriers to female advancement and equal pay in this male-dominated trade, thus pointing to specific areas requiring attention from scholars and activists alike. The sociological approach the Bielbys modeled in their research on the media industry labor practices is similar to a more contemporary, cultural studies-inflected approach referred to as "culture of production" scholarship.[5]

Michelle Citron's "Women's Film Production" concerns a different arena of filmmaking, specifically that independent of the commercial film industry. As one of the filmmakers who took up Mulvey's challenge to create an alternative cinema for women, Citron explores various transformations in feminist independent film during the late twentieth century, while also providing a contextual analysis for such changes. Although most feminist filmmakers of the 1970s were opposed to producing narrative films and to working in the media industries, Citron exposes how a lack of funding, criticisms of elitism, and the diminishment of feminist film distribution and exhibition have resulted more recently in feminist filmmakers working within narrative cinema and the Hollywood industry. (While not addressed specifically by Citron, queer filmmaking has taken a similar path since the 1970s, although the entrance of queer themes and producers into the media industries has been much slower than it has for those associated with feminism.)

Scholarship focusing on gender and media production does not preclude questions about texts and reception. Indeed, Tuchman's and Mulvey's early studies revealed the intersections linking all of these sites of media culture. Moving from assumptions to theories about patriarchy and heterocentrism in the media industries, more research has been conducted recently in order to understand the effects of the media industries' gender politics on media texts, marketing, and consumers. For instance, Eileen Meehan's political economy analysis, "Gendering the Commodity Audience," examines the interdependence of capitalism and patriarchy in the broadcast and advertising industries' ratings practices, revealing such industries' overvaluing of wealthy men as consumers at the expense of women—even female professionals with as much buying power as their male peers.

Shifting this discussion of audience commodification in a new direction, Robert Alan Brookey and Robert Westerfelhaus's "Hiding Homoeroticism in Plain View" problematizes the notion of inherently gendered and sexualized audiences by exploring the practices used within the media industries to develop particular audiences. Using the film *Fight Club* (2000) as their test case, Brookey and Westerfelhaus demonstrate how the construction of DVD supplemental features for films imbued with homoeroticism works to "closet" queer readings and thus to (re)produce a normative straight male viewership.

As much as white, heterosexual, upper-middle-class men continue to be constructed by advertisers and the media industries as the most lucrative market, media professionals have never ignored female consumers entirely. In fact, during certain historical periods when female employment and buying power has been greater than that of males, such as the World War II era, the media industries have catered directly to women. Partially owing to the influence of cultural feminism, numerous feminist studies have explored the media industries' development of content for females via such texts as soap operas, family melodramas, and fashion magazines. Contributing to such scholarship through a focus on contemporary media culture, Elana Levine's "Fractured Fairy Tales and Fragmented Markets" considers the synergistic practices involved in the production and promotion of *Weddings of a Lifetime* (Lifetime 1995). Levine's study reveals the complicated effects of media conglomeration on women-targeted texts as well as the Disney studio's image, which has long privileged discourses of heterosexual romance and family values in its appeal to girls and women.

Leslie Regan Shade's "Gender and the Commodification of Community" brings feminist concerns about gender and production to our youngest mediascape, the Internet. In this chapter, Shade charts the transformation of online discourse by exploring the corporate history of websites originally designed with feminist objectives and content, such as gURL.com and women.com. As she argues, such feminist sites were transformed into commercial entities that construct their users not as agential members of a community but as individual consumers who can be further commodified by the e-marketplace.

One of the areas more recently examined by scholars interested in gender and media production is amateur, particularly youth, media. Kristen Schilt's "'I'll Resist With Every Inch and Every Breath'" examines girl-made zines (small, independent magazines) in the context of 1990s' rhetoric about female youths' loss of voice during adolescence and the rise of riot grrrl, a feminist punk youth culture. Schilt's study explores girls' authorship and creation of these texts to form supportive communities as well as safe spaces from which they can resist dominant gender norms.

Robin D. G. Kelley's chapter, "Looking to Get Paid," discusses youth media also, specifically music. With U.S. racial and class relations as his backdrop, Kelley explores how poor African American youths' cultural production is sometimes successfully commodified and turned into a livelihood, thus refashioning play as work. Nevertheless, Kelley is keen to address imbalances of power in this cultural realm, especially in his examination of the gender norms that restrict female involvement and advancement in hip-hop production.

This theme of constraining female creativity is addressed also by Mavis Bayton, whose "Women and the Electric Guitar" concerns the historical construction of the electric guitar as masculine. Providing insight into how this gendering of technology impacts the different roles and practices open to males and females in popular music culture, Bayton's work reveals the numerous hurdles girl and women musicians face and thus more sites requiring intervention by those who value gender parity in the roles and practices of media production.

Notes

1. For an overview of different types of media authorship studies, see Janet Staiger, "Authorship Approaches," *Authorship and Film* (New York: Routledge, 2003) 27–57. For an overview of the development of media production studies beyond political economy analyses and toward cultural studies, see Timothy Havens, Amanda D. Lotz, and Serra Tinic, "Critical Media Industry Studies: A Research Approach," *Communication, Culture & Critique* 2.2 (2009) 234–253.
2. Gaye Tuchman's essay is reprinted in Part I of this reader.
3. Laura Mulvey's article is reprinted in Part I of this reader.
4. See the "Celluloid Ceiling" reports on gender employment in the U.S. media industries conducted by Martha Lauzen at the Center for the Study of Women in Television and Film: http://womenintvfilm.sdsu.edu.
5. See Paul du Gay, ed., *Production of Culture/Cultures of Production* (Thousand Oaks, CA: Sage, 1997).

9.
WOMEN AND MEN IN FILM

Gender Inequality among Writers in a Culture Industry

Denise D. Bielby and William T. Bielby

In previous research, we (Bielby and Bielby 1992) documented how unstructured labor market arrangements in the television industry generate a process of "continuous disadvantage," whereby women television writers are disadvantaged relative to men throughout their careers, regardless of their previous accomplishments in the industry. This model proved to be a better representation of the data than the model of "cumulative disadvantage," whereby men and women begin their careers with more or less similar opportunities, but women encounter a "glass ceiling," falling further and further behind their male counterparts over time. That research also rejected the hypothesis that the level of gender inequality among writers in the television industry had declined throughout the 1980s.

In our 1992 article, we argued that five distinctive features of the organization of production sustained this pattern of gender inequality among television writers: (1) the employment relation is based on short-term contracting for the duration of a specific project; (2) the quality and commercial viability of the completed work cannot be unambiguously evaluated based on technical and measurable features of the finished product, but it can only be evaluated post hoc; (3) career success is largely dependent on a writer's current reputation among a small group of "brokers" who match creative talent with commercial projects; (4) reputations are based on perceptions of an artist's success in currently fashionable styles or genres; and (5) the overwhelming majority of those who make decisions about matching creative talent to commercial projects are men. Given the skewed sex-ratio,

women's marginal location within networks of decision makers, and the high levels of ambiguity, risk, and uncertainty surrounding employment decisions, social similarity and gender stereotypes are likely to have a strong impact on employment decisions. Indeed, empirical results of that study show that compared to male television writers of similar age, experience, and track record, women earn 11 to 25 percent less throughout their careers (Bielby and Bielby 1992).

This research examines whether a similar pattern of gender inequality exists among writers for feature film. There are good reasons to expect that the findings for television will apply to the feature film industry as well. The overall structure of the two industries is quite similar—what DiMaggio (1977) calls "centralized brokerage administration" and Faulkner and Anderson (1987) describe as "recurrent short-term contracting." Each of the five distinctive characteristics of television production apply to feature film as well.

However, there are differences between film and television production in their organization and business contexts, and some of these differences may be of consequence for labor market dynamics of writers and other "culture workers." First, the levels of ambiguity, risk, and uncertainty facing producers in feature film are substantially greater in the film industry than in television. Production costs are many times higher than in television, and predicting which film projects will become hits is much more difficult than in television. In their study of the film industry, Baker and Faulkner (1991, 286) observe, "Filmmaking is a tenuous enterprise. It occurs in a business and technical environment characterized by high stakes, risk, and uncertainty. It requires substantial investments of financial capital for properties, artists, and support personnel. And it entails high personal and career risks."

Compared to television network programmers, risk-adverse production executives in feature film might be more likely to imitate prior successful projects and to rely on rules of thumb that tend to typecast women writers. For example, no one wants to be the first to develop a script from a woman writer for a big-budget action-adventure film. In a recent interview, Callie Khouri, who won an Academy Award for her script for *Thelma & Louise*, put it this way:

> There is a certain stigma, I think that there is a set of expectations that women write a certain type of picture, so you don't look for an action movie that's written by a woman. You don't look for a thriller. There are certain types of movies that you don't expect to be written by a woman. People still call things "women's pictures." If it has a female audience then there is always a somewhat derogatory connotation to a so-called woman's picture.
>
> (Danquah 1994)

Carolyn Shelby who wrote *Class Action* has expressed similar sentiments:

> You come in with an action project, and they see you're a woman, and you can see it's not something they're comfortable with. They're thinking "small picture" rather than *Terminator 2* when you're sitting there talking to them.
>
> (Voland 1992)

Second, the level of uncertainty facing the writers themselves is greater in feature film than in television. Several thousand episodes of network, cable, and syndicated television series are produced in the United States each year, and the writers on the staff of a successful series can generally count on being employed for an entire season if not the series' entire run. In contrast, a film project is a one-shot deal, and only about 300 feature films are released domestically in the United States each year. At the same time, tens of thousands of individuals aspire to careers as screenwriters, and they register about 36,000 scripts or script treatments with the Writers Guild of America

each year. In short, the labor market for film appears much more competitive than that for television writers, and as a result the barriers faced by women might be more formidable as well.

Third, in television, successful writer-producers (also known as "hyphenates") can become powerful brokers in the industry, gaining autonomy in running their own shows and negotiating long-term development deals. Women hyphenates such as Diane English, Linda Bloodworth-Thomason, Beth Sullivan, and Marcy Carsey have joined the ranks of male writer-producers such as Steven Bochco, Aaron Spelling, and Stephen J. Cannell in the industry elite. As research for the Writers Guild of America, West, shows, when women become writer-producers of ongoing series, the number of women writers employed increases substantially (Bielby and Bielby 1987, 1989, 1993). In feature film, in contrast, very few women have joined the ranks of top writers during the same period. Moreover, elite film writers might be very well paid, but unless they also direct, they have virtually no say in the production process. In the absence of arranging a writer-director hyphenate combination for film projects, writers find themselves pitted against directors over creative control of a film's final form (Baker and Faulkner 1991; Cox 1995; Robb 1994).

Although the factors noted above are likely to generate greater gender inequality in feature film than in television, other differences between the two industries suggest a lesser degree of typecasting by gender of screenwriters compared to television writers. First, genre categories are much more highly institutionalized in television than in feature film. Although film genres such as "action-adventure," "romantic comedy," and "adult drama" are widely recognized, television genres are much more highly institutionalized in the organizational structures of the studios and networks. For example, each of the broadcast networks has separate development divisions for drama, comedy, daytime, and so on, whereas genre distinctions are not built into the film divisions of the major studios (Bielby and Bielby 1994). In television, female executives are likely to be segregated into divisions dealing with female-typed genres (e.g., television movies and miniseries, children's programming, daytime programming), whereas—at least officially—a woman vice president of production at a film studio is not charged with working within a specific film genre. And by 1990, women accounted for nearly one third of the executives in the ranks of vice president or higher in the production divisions of the major film studios (Bernstein 1990).

Second, in television, advertising revenues are sold on the basis of the demographic composition of the audience. In television, *who* is watching can be as important as *how many* people are watching. For example, an action-adventure series in development at a network might be targeted to an 18- to 35-year-old male audience, and advertising rates might be set based on a network guarantee regarding the size of the audience within that age/gender group. In contrast, a film's profitability depends on the number of people who pay to view it. Although the film might be developed to appeal to a younger male audience, a ticket purchased by a 45-year-old woman earns the studio the same amount as one bought by a 19-year-old man. Thus, the less intense age/gender targeting of film audiences may reduce the incentive to typecast writers by gender. On the other hand, there is a tremendous amount of typecasting of "on screen" talent in feature film, where there is a widely held belief that a female star cannot successfully carry a big budget film. In the words of one studio head:

> It's almost impossible for a female to "open" a movie now. It just doesn't work. People don't come. A movie like *Ghost* succeeded conceptually, on its own terms, not because of Demi Moore.
> (Dutka 1990, 8)

Thus, it is reasonable to assume that the often explicit devaluation of female talent on screen carries over to a devaluation of women's contributions to film off screen.

Overall, the similarities between television and feature film are probably more consequential than the differences. Although distribution channels differ, the same large corporations—the major studios—dominate production in both TV and film, and with the advent of new technologies of production and distribution, the distinctions between the two sectors of the entertainment industry are increasingly blurred. To a significant extent, the two sectors draw on the same pool of writers; in any given year, about one third of those writing for feature film are also employed in television. Thus,

we expect the structure and dynamics of labor markets in the two sectors to be largely similar, although on balance, if there is a detectable difference in the levels of gender inequality, we expect it to be somewhat larger in film than in television.

Below, we first present an overview of women writers' participation in feature film from the silent era to the present, relying on both historical scholarship and quantitative data from the membership files of the Writers Guild of America, West. Then we describe the data, measures, models, and hypotheses used to assess alternative models of gender inequality in labor market dynamics among film writers. Following the presentation of our results, we discuss the implications of our findings for gender inequality in the mass media and in culture industries more generally.

Women Writers' Participation in Feature Film from the Silent Era to the Age of the Blockbuster

Film writing is one of the few professional occupations in which a labor force with a substantial female presence has been displaced by men. Many of the most successful early scenarists, as screenwriters of the silent film era were called, were women (Francke 1994; McCreadie 1994). The highest-paid writer of the 1920s was Frances Marion, whose silent credits include *Humoresque, Stella Dallas,* and *Love,* and who went on to write the sound films *The Champ* and *Dinner at Eight* (Schwartz 1982). Although definitive statistics are not available, estimates of the gender composition of screenwriters during the silent era (from the early 1900s to 1927) range from 50 percent (Martin and Clark 1987) to 90 percent (McCreadie 1994), and it is generally agreed that women screenwriters played a major role in establishing the narrative form and conventions of the film scenario (Francke 1994).

The process whereby screenwriting was transformed from a profession with substantial opportunities for women to one that became male dominated appears similar to that described by Tuchman (1989) in her account of the masculinization of authorship of the Victorian novel. Tuchman's evidence indicates that before 1840 at least half of all novelists were women. She argues that the occupation of novelist was a relatively lucrative "empty field" for woman of the educated classes at this time, albeit one with relatively low prestige.

Over the next half century, men "invaded" the empty field, drawn to the profession as demand increased and the field became more lucrative. Moreover, the centralization and rationalization that accompanied the industrialization of the publishing industry placed men in control of production and distribution. The transformation of authorship into "men's work" was legitimated ideologically in the late nineteenth and early twentieth century, as the narrative form of the novel was redefined as a valued cultural object, and a critical double standard was applied that valued the contributions of male novelists over women.

Tuchman suggests that the same process of invasion, redefinition, and institutionalization should be apparent in other professions that experience masculinization, even when the transformation occurs rapidly. The transformation of screen-writing in the late 1920s and early 1930s appears to fit this pattern. With the advent of sound movies in 1927, those with a talent for storytelling—playwrights, novelists, journalists—were recruited to Hollywood in large numbers (Beranger 1950; Schwartz 1982). The Depression accelerated the trend toward consolidation of production that began in the 1920s, so that by the early 1930s the financing, production, distribution, and exhibition of feature films was dominated by eight vertically integrated corporations: Warner Brothers, RKO, Twentieth Century Fox, Paramount, MGM, Universal, Columbia, and United Artists (Stanley 1978). This consolidation was accompanied by a rationalization of production, including writing. Under the studio system, the role of the scenarist had become elaborated, subdivided, and formalized (Staiger 1983). Within the story department of each studio, a story editor had responsibility for identifying viable literary properties for producers and would supervise a dozen or so script readers who would evaluate books, plays, stories, or treatments for their cinematic potential. Studios generally relied on their own staff of screenwriters to write the actual scripts, with others such as continuity clerks and script clerks doing much of the routine work in processing the filming of a script (Work Projects Administration, American Guide Series 1941).

Some of the more established women writers of the silent era continued to thrive under the studio system (Francke 1994; McCreadie 1994; Schwartz 1982). Among them were Frances Marion, who was a founding member and first vice president of the Screen Writers Guild (the predecessor of the Writers Guild of America), and Anita Loos, whose credits range from *Intolerance* (1916) to *Gentlemen Prefer Blondes* (1953). However, the male "invasion" of the profession was an accomplished fact by the mid-1930s. Membership statistics from the Writers Guild of America, West, show that women accounted for less than 15 percent of those working as screenwriters in the late 1930s (see Figures 9.1 and 9.2). In sharp contrast to the early years of the industry—when the lines dividing production roles were fluid and women moved with relative ease across the tasks of scenarist, editor, director, and producer—under the studio system, women writers were likely to be assigned to administrative or support roles such as reader or script supervisor (Francke 1994) or as "corpse rougers" who "brightened the dialogue of other people's scripts" (Mary McCall, Jr., quoted in McCreadie 1994, 111).

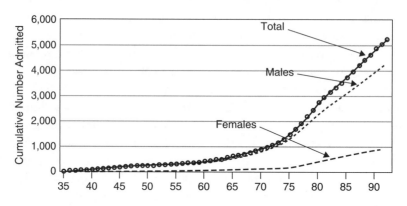

Fig 9.1 Cumulative Number of Screenwriters Admitted to WGA, West, by Gender, 1935–1992

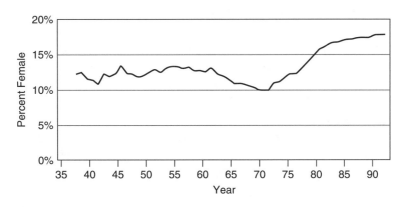

Fig 9.2 Gender Composition of the Cumulative Membership, Screenwriter Members of the WGA, West, 1936–1992

The institutionalization of the male invasion of the screenwriting profession was legitimated by the typecasting of women writers. Women's work on story adjustments, scene polishes, and dialogue rewrites was regarded as the "tyranny of the woman writer" by male writers of the time (Frances Marion, cited by McCreadie 1994, 28). Studio chiefs believed women were especially well suited for writing for "women's films," for writing dialogue for female stars, and for infusing the "women's angle" into films more generally (Francke 1994). Of course, the reality is quite different; women screenwriters have been associated with successful scripts in every film genre, and many "women's films" have been scripted by men.[1] But the ideology that women's talents are best suited for women's themes or female stars (an ideology shared by many women writers themselves) legitimates the notion that outside of narrow genres and specialties, screenwriting is men's work.

With men's dominance of screenwriting fully institutionalized, the decline of the studio system and the trend toward independent production during the 1950s had little impact on women's representation among screenwriters. From the 1950s through the early 1960s, women continued to constitute about 12 to 13 percent of those entering the screenwriting profession. Perhaps not coincidentally, the decline in women's representation among new screenwriters from 1962 through 1971 to its lowest level in the history of the industry (see Figure 9.3) corresponds exactly with the era feminist film critic Molly Haskell (1987, 323) calls "the most disheartening in screen history" regarding the portrayals and prominence of women.

Not until the early 1970s is there a noticeable increase in women's representation among those entering the profession: from 1972 to the present, women have accounted for about one in five screenwriters qualifying for membership in the Writers Guild (Figure 9.3). It is not clear what accounted for the modest upturn in women's representation in the early 1970s. On the one hand, feminist themes were beginning to appear in commercially successful films of the 1970s

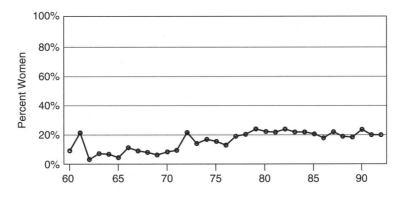

Fig 9.3 Women as a Percentage of Screenwriters Admitted to WGA, West, Annually, 1960–1992

such as *Klute* (1971), *Alice Doesn't Live Here* (1974), *A Woman Under the Influence* (1974), and *An Unmarried Woman* (1977),[2] and women in the industry began organizing to advance their interests through groups such as Women in Film and the Women's Committee of the Writers Guild of America. These developments may have both encouraged talented women to pursue careers in the industry and persuaded producers to be more open toward material from women screenwriters. On the other hand, the early 1970s also marked the beginning of the "blockbuster" era, which greatly increased the financial risk involved in pursuing projects with potential box office sales in excess of $100 million (Baker and Faulkner 1991). Increasingly, the "blockbuster" mentality encouraged producers to seek out established directors, writers, and actors who have track records of consistent success and forgo serious consideration of writers who seek to transcend proven formulae and established genres. As a result, the salaries of a small group of elite screenwriters have been bid up to levels in excess of $750,000 per film, while the gap in career trajectories between this group and other screenwriters widens. *Daily Variety* analyst Paul F. Young observes:

> Why the red carpet? Studio executives and agents unanimously agree that a writer can't "open" a film like a star. But veteran agents and producers alike say the trend to shop at Tiffany reflects the paranoia felt by studio executives who don't read much themselves, or who fear rocking the corporate boat. Says one high-profile producer, "I can't get the studio to pay a writer *less* than $750,000. It makes them nervous. Another producer with a studio deal explains, "They think an expensive writer will get it right the first time. And if he doesn't, the executive has protected himself by using a pre-approved writer."
>
> (Young 1995, 5, 18)

Our quantitative data on film writers' employment and earnings cover the years 1982 to 1992. This period is of interest because of potentially countervailing forces affecting the careers of women writers. On the one hand, by the mid-1980s the talent guilds for writers, directors, and actors were issuing statistical studies documenting women's underrepresentation in

the industry, and the industry press began giving widespread coverage to the issue of gender discrimination. And as noted above, during the same period, women were finally moving into the top executive ranks of the motion picture studios, paralleling women's gains in management in other sectors of the economy. On the other hand, men's dominance of screenwriting (and all other aspects of the industry) had been fully institutionalized for half a century, and the business environment of the period appears not to be conducive to innovative ways of reaching out to groups previously excluded by the industry. Given these countervailing if not contradictory trends, it is not surprising that many feminist film analysts look on the past decade as "the age of ambivalence" (Haskell 1987; also see Francke 1994). Our data allow us to bring systematic quantitative evidence to bear on the question of whether efforts to challenge men's institutionalized dominance are beginning to create new opportunities for women writers.

An overview of trends in employment and earnings of screenwriters suggests that women writers are encountering an impenetrable glass ceiling in the era of the blockbuster. From 1982 through 1992 there was no perceptible change in the gender composition of those employed in screen writing; women accounted for about 18 percent of employed screenwriters throughout this period. (In comparison, according to 1990 census statistics, women account for 49.5 percent of all authors in the United States.) Figure 9.4 shows gender differences in earnings trends over the same period. While the gender gap in median earnings closed modestly from the mid-1980s to the early 1990s, in both absolute and relative terms the gap at the 90th percentile is significantly greater in the early 1990s than it was in 1982. In other words, among the industry's most successful screenwriters, women are falling further behind their male counterparts.

These descriptive statistics tell just part of the story. For example, one cannot tell from these statistics whether the closing of the gender gap in median earnings is simply attributable to the increasing levels of experience of women screenwriters. Nor can one compare the career trajectories of men and women screenwriters who enter the industry at the same time. With multivariate analyses we can explore the dynamics of disadvantage faced by women film

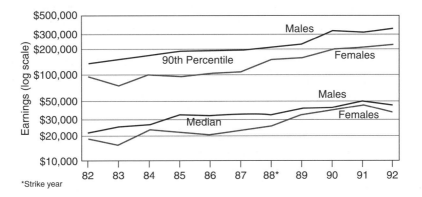

Fig 9.4 Gender Differences in Earnings among Employed Screenwriters at Median and at 90th Percentile, 1982–1992

writers that generate the overall trends. How great is the disadvantage faced by women writers—in terms of employment and earnings—compared to men with similar qualifications and track records? Do labor market dynamics generate a pattern of "cumulative disadvantage" whereby men and women begin their careers with more or less similar opportunities, but with women subsequently encountering a "glass ceiling" as the careers of their male counterparts take off? And finally, is the magnitude of women's disadvantage declining over time as more women move into positions of power and authority in the industry?

Data, Measures, and Models

The data for our study describe the employment and earnings trajectories of 4,093 screenwriters who were employed at least once during the period from 1982 through 1992. These data are from the employment and membership records of the Writers Guild of America, West (WGAW). Each quarter, guild members report earnings from all employment covered by the "MBA," the WGAW's major collective bargaining agreement with producers. Because virtually all active producers are signatory to the MBA, these earnings declarations cover nearly all writing for feature films produced in Hollywood.

In their earnings declarations, members report total earnings; employing organization; type of employment; whether the writing is for screen, television, radio, or pay-TV; the title of the film, series, or program; and its length. In most cases, writers also report whether they worked on a first draft, polish, final draft, revision, and so forth.

Our model is a pooled cross-section time series specification of the form:

$$Y_{ict} = a + b_1 X_i + b_2 W_{it} + Z_c + d_t + e_{ict} \qquad (1)$$

where Y_{ict} is log earnings for the ith individual in cohort c in year t, and cohort is defined as year admitted to membership in the Writers Guild of America. Attributes of individuals that do not vary over time (e.g., minority status) are included in X_j and individual traits that vary over time (e.g., years of experience) are included in W_{it}. The term Z_c captures effects on earnings that are unique to a specific cohort over time, while d_t captures year-specific effects on earnings. The disturbance, e_{ict} is assumed to have a mean of zero and constant variance and to be uncorrected with the other independent variables.

Minority status is represented by a binary variable coded 1 for minority writers and 0 otherwise. Gender is coded 1 for females, 0 for males. Work experience is measured in two ways. The first is years of membership in the WGAW. Because less than half of all writers are employed in any given year, years of membership does not equal years of employment experience. Consequently, in some models we also include binary variables for lagged employment status one, two, and three years prior to year t.

Age is measured as year t minus year of birth. Year effects are captured by 10 binary variables, with 1982 as the reference category. Cohort effects are captured by two binary variables, the first coded 1 for those admitted to the WGAW prior to 1971 and the second coded 1 for those admitted between 1971 and 1975. Finally, because many writers work in both television and film, our models include a binary variable coded 1 if the writer received earnings from work in television during year t.

Descriptive statistics reporting gender differences in age, experience, and employment appear in Table 9.1. On average, women screenwriters employed at least once between 1982 and 1992 are younger and have fewer years of experience than their male counterparts. Just more than one third of the men and women screenwriters were employed in feature film in 1992, and about 30 percent were employed in television. Finally, Table 9.1 shows that writers of color are virtually absent in the industry, accounting for just more than 3 percent of the screenwriters employed from 1982 through 1992. Indeed, because so few women of color are employed to write for feature film (only 26 over the 11-year period), our statistical models are not able to provide reliable estimates of the interaction of race and gender as they influence the earnings of screenwriters.

Table 9.1 Means by Gender on Age, Experience, Employment, and Minority Status, WGA West Members Employed at Least Once in Film, 1982–1992

Variable	Metric	Female Means (N = 752)	Male Means (N = 3,341)
Cohort (year admitted to WGA)			
Pre-1971	0–1	0.064	0.155
1971–75	0–1	0.094	0.110
1976–80	0–1	0.243	0.226
1981–85	0–1	0.258	0.196
1986–90	0–1	0.270	0.251
1991–92	0–1	0.070	0.062
Years experience in 1992		10.5	12.8
Age in 1992			
<30	0–1	0.025	0.032
30–39	0–1	0.262	0.257
40–49	0–1	0.460	0.369
50–59	0–1	0.141	0.160
60–64	0–1	0.020	0.051
65+	0–1	0.040	0.080
Age NA	0–1	0.052	0.052
Employed in film, 1992	0–1	0.359	0.379
Employed in TV, 1992	0–1	0.309	0.290
Employed (TV or film):			
1982	0–1	0.360	0.392
1983	0–1	0.390	0.412
1984	0–1	0.408	0.433
1985	0–1	0.457	0.479
1986	0–1	0.489	0.509
1987	0–1	0.517	0.534
1988 (strike year)	0–1	0.495	0.508
1989	0–1	0.539	0.552
1990	0–1	0.553	0.594
1991	0–1	0.555	0.571
1992	0–1	0.552	0.559
Minority status	0–1	0.035	0.030

Cumulative Versus Continuous Disadvantage: Hypotheses

Table 9.2 summarizes our hypotheses regarding the determinants of earnings under alternative conceptualizations of labor market dynamics. The main effects of gender, experience, and control variables are assumed to be the same across models. Each assumes a net negative effect of being female, effects of years of experience that increase at a decreasing rate, and positive effects of prior employment and earnings.

The three models of labor market dynamics, "cumulative disadvantage," "continuous disadvantage," and "declining disadvantage," are differentiated by their implications for interaction effects by gender. We choose between the cumulative disadvantage and continuous disadvantage models based on interaction effects between gender and experience, between gender and prior employment, and between gender and prior earnings.

The cumulative disadvantage model assumes that access to opportunity early in the career pays off more for men than for women. As a result, the gender gap in wages is expected to increase with experience. In other words, according to the cumulative disadvantage model, the net returns to experience are expected to be lower for women than for men (i.e., a negative interaction between gender [coded 1 for female] and the experience variables). Similarly, if women have more volatile

careers and find it difficult to sustain career success from year to year, then the impact of prior earnings and employment should be lower for women than for men. Accordingly, the cumulative disadvantage model also predicts a negative interaction between gender and the lagged employment and earnings variables.

In contrast to the cumulative disadvantage model, the continuous disadvantage model implies a pervasive bias against women that affects them equally through all stages in their careers. Under the continuous disadvantage model, the earnings disparity between men and women at entry is neither greater nor worse than at later stages in the career. According to this model, the shape of the earnings trajectory over the course of a career is the same for men and women, but women start their careers with a substantial earnings "penalty" and never catch up. Thus, the continuous disadvantage model implies *no* interaction between gender and measures of experience, prior employment, and prior earnings; but it implies a strong "main effect" of gender, with women earning significantly less than men with similar levels of experience.

Neither the cumulative disadvantage nor the continuous disadvantage model provides an explicit prediction about trends over time in the aggregate gender gap in earnings. Over time and net of all other factors in these two models, the earnings gap between men and women might be increasing, decreasing, or not changing at all. In contrast, according to the model

Table 9.2 Hypothesized Effects of Independent Variables on Earnings for Different Models of Labor Market Dynamics

Variable	Cumulative Disadvantage	Continuous Disadvantage	Declining Disadvantage
Female	−	−	−
Experience (years in industry)	∩	∩	∩
Lagged employment	+	+	+
Lagged earnings	+	+	+
Gender interactions			
Female by			
Experience	−	0	?
Lagged employment	−	0	?
Lagged earnings	−	0	?
Year	?	?	−

Note: Hypothesized relationships: + = hypothesized positive relationship, − = hypothesized negative relationship, ∩ = hypothesized curvilinear relationship (increasing at a decreasing rate), ? = no relationship hypothesized.

of declining disadvantage, there is a trend toward an erosion of gender barriers and a resulting decline in the gender gap in earnings over time. According to this model, whether the underlying dynamic is one of cumulative or continuous disadvantage, forces are at work that are slowly but surely dismantling the sources of that disadvantage. Thus, the declining disadvantage model predicts that the impact of gender declines over time (a negative interaction between gender [coded 1 for female] and year).

In sum, if we find strong evidence of lower returns among women than among men in the effects of experience, prior employment, and prior earnings (i.e., negative interactions between gender and each of these traits), then the cumulative disadvantage model will be favored over the continuous disadvantage model. In contrast, if there is a large net effect of gender but no interaction of gender with measures of experience, prior employment, or prior earnings, then the continuous disadvantage model will be favored. Regardless of the outcome of this comparison, a large negative interaction of female-by-year will provide evidence of declining disadvantage, that is, an erosion of gender barriers over time.[3] Absence of such an interaction will suggest that the barriers faced by women writers have persisted throughout the 1980s and into the early 1990s, despite women's increasing representation in positions of power and responsibility, and despite increased attention to the problem of gender bias in the industry.

Findings from Multivariate Models

We choose between the cumulative and continuous disadvantage models of gender inequality in labor market dynamics based on whether there are interactions between gender and measures of experience, prior employment, and prior earnings, and we evaluate the declining disadvantage model based on whether there is a negative interaction between gender and year. Accordingly, our analytic strategy is to estimate and contrast models with and without gender interactions and to assess whether statistically significant gender interactions correspond to the patterns hypothesized by the cumulative and declining disadvantage models as summarized in Table 9.2. To fully exploit the longitudinal data, we estimate and test models under three alternative specifications. The first specification (Models 1 and 2) includes our measure of experience, but not lagged employment and lagged earnings. This specification has the advantage of exploiting all 11 years of data from 1982 through 1992, reflecting the earnings trajectories of the 4,093 writers who worked at least once during that period. The second specification (Models 3 and 4) adds binary variables for whether a writer was employed in years t–1, t–2, and t–3. Because data on employment are not available for years prior to 1982, estimates for this specification are based on a shorter time span, from 1985 through 1992, and pertain to the 3,645 writers who worked at least once during this period. The final specification (Models 5 and 6) includes effects of earnings in years t–1 and t–2 and is limited to writers with at least one employment spell of three consecutive years between 1983 and 1992 (i.e., nonzero earnings in years t, t–1, and t–2). Accordingly, the results of this specification apply to a select subgroup of 1,606 more successful writers with relatively continuous employment histories in the industry.

Results for the first two specifications (Models 1 through 4) appear in Table 9.3 and for the third specification (Models 5 and 6) in Table 9.4. The results for the models with no gender interactions (Models 1 and 3 in Table 9.3) show a substantial net disadvantage faced by women writers compared to men of similar age, experience, minority status, and recent employment history. Evaluated at the mean, the effect of being female of −.282 in Model 1 corresponds to a net gender gap in earnings of 25 percent, and the effect of −.234 in Model 3 corresponds to a net gender gap of 21 percent. Thus, if there were no gender interactions, we would conclude that women writers face an earnings penalty of 21 to 25 percent throughout their careers. However, because results reported below reveal significant gender interactions, the 21 to 25 percent estimate of the earnings penalty represents an average across a gender gap in earnings that is in fact contingent on the amount of experience screenwriters have in the industry.

Overall, the results support the model of cumulative disadvantage. First, in each instance, a global test of the gender interactions rejects the null hypothesis of no interaction (see row labeled "all interactions" at the bottom of Tables 9.3 and 9.4). Models 2, 4, and

Table 9.3 Determinants of Earnings among All Employed Film Writers 1982–1992[a]

Variable	Model 1	Model 2	Model 3	Model 4
Cohort				
Pre-1971	0.163**	0.140*	0.532**	0.506**
1971–75	−0.057	−0.062	0.246**	0.240**
Year				
1983	0.046	0.066	—	
1984	0.205**	0.214	—	
1985	0.330**	0.368**	—	
1986	0.372**	0.420**	0.047	0.061
1987	0.471**	0.515**	0.150**	0.167**
1988 (strike year)	0.485**	0.494**	0.103*	0.081
1989	0.596**	0.596**	0.283**	0.258**
1990	0.702**	0.706**	0.413**	0.387**
1991	0.776**	0.792**	0.450**	0.426**
1992	0.777**	0.782**	0.436**	0.403**
Age 30–39	−0.063	−0.067	−0.159**	−0.164**
Age 40–49	−0.186**	−0.192**	−0.236**	−0.242**
Age 50–59	−0.548**	−0.554**	−0.448**	−0.455**
Age 60–64	−0.864**	−0.881**	−0.725**	−0.741**
Age 65+	−1.074**	−1.088**	−0.928**	−0.945**
Age NA	−0.329**	−0.337**	−0.272**	−0.281**
Experience	0.0795**	0.0854**	0.0017	0.0073
Experience squared	−0.0016**	−0.0018**	−0.0003*	0.0004**
Female	−0.282**	−0.045	−0.234**	−0.203*
Minority	−0.243**	−0.207*	0.010	0.018
TV employment	−0.274**	−0.301**	−0.171**	−0.215**
Lag TV employment			−0.024	−0.019
Employed—lag 1	—	—	0.495**	0.515**
Employed—lag 2	—	−0.435**	0.424**	
Employed—lag 3	—	—	0.479**	0.474**
Interactions, Female by				
Experience	—	−0.0374**	—	0.0389**
Experience^2	—	0.0010**	—	0.0010**
1983	—	−0.118	—	—
1984	—	−0.066	—	—
1985	—	−0.240	—	—
1986	—	−0.293	—	−0.067
1987	—	−0.290	—	−0.114
1988	—	−0.072	—	0.123
1989	—	−0.021	—	0.148
1990	—	−0.046	—	0.150
1991		−0.116		0.137
1992		−0.053		0.191
TV employment	—	0.173*	—	0.256**
Minority		−0.250		−0.069

cont.

Table 9.3 Continued

Variable	Model 1	Model 2	Model 3	Model 4
Employed—lag 1			—	−0.097
Employed—lag 2			—	0.057
Employed—lag 3			—	0.048
Constant	9.823	9.788	9.789	9.786
Root mean squared error	1.393	1.392	1.300	1.299
R^2	0.081	0.084	0.186	0.188
N (person-years)	14,439	14,439	11,296	11,296
Tests	df	F ratio	df	F ratio
All interactions	14	2.009*	14	2.271**
Experience interactions	2	6.793**	2	5.741**
Lag employment interactions	—	—	3	0.727
Year interactions	10	1.042	7	1.497

a. Pooled cross-sectional time-series regression models, ordinary least squares estimates. Dependent variable is log earnings.
* $p < .05$; ** $p < .01$.

Table 9.4 Determinants of Earnings among Film Writers Employed in Three Consecutive Years, 1985–1992[a]

Variable	Model 5	Model 6
Cohort		
Pre-1971	0.074	0.049
1971–75	0.078	0.071
Year		
1986	−0.142*	−0.141*
1987	−0.060	−0.068
1988 (strike year)	−0.130*	−0.136*
1989	0.030	0.002
1990	0.117*	0.127*
1991	−0.085	−0.122*
1992	−0.069	−0.117
Age 30–39	−0.023	−0.023
Age 40–49	−0.119	−0.120
Age 50–59	−0.220**	−0.221**
Age 60–64	−0.393**	−0.397**
Age 65+	−0.274**	−0.280**
Age NA	−0.068	−0.068
Experience	0.0050	0.0096
Experience^2	−0.0001	−0.0002
Female	−0.039	−0.060
Minority	0.009	0.010
TV employment	−0.244**	−0.279**
Lag TV employment	0.122**	0.129**
Employed—lag 3	0.062*	0.062*
Log earnings—lag 1	0.518**	0.519**
Log earnings—lag 2	0.267**	0.263**

Table 9.4 Continued

Variable	Model 5	Model 6
Interactions, female by		
Experience	—	−0.0405*
Experience squared	—	0.0011*
1986	—	0.021
1987	—	0.084
1988	—	0.071
1989	—	0.198
1990	—	−0.058
1991		0.302*
1992		0.347*
Minority	—	−0.039
TV employment		0.248**
Employed—lag 3	—	0.0472
Log earnings—lag 1	—	−0.0189
Log earnings—lag 2	—	0.019
Constant	2.526	2.556
Root mean squared error	0.968	0.967
R^2	0.500	0.502
N (person-years)	5,049	5,049
Tests	df	F *ratio*
All interactions	14	1.708*
Experience interactions	2	3.072*
Lag earnings interactions	2	0.134
Year interactions	7	1.84

a. Pooled cross-sectional time-series regression models, ordinary least squares estimates. Dependent variable is log earnings.
* $p < .05$;** $p < .01$.

6 (with interactions) provide significant improvement in fit over Models 1, 3, and 5 (without interactions), respectively. Second, specific tests of the gender-by-experience interactions reject the null hypothesis of no interaction in all three comparisons (see row labeled "experience interactions" at the bottom of Tables 9.3 and 9.4). In each instance, the estimated parameters for the linear and quadratic experience effects imply that earnings increase with experience at a decreasing rate for men, and the gender-by-experience interaction implies that the rate of earnings growth is slower for women than for men (or even negative for women). In other words, the gender gap in earnings grows as screenwriters move through their careers, even after controlling for gender differences in prior career success. The pattern of cumulative disadvantage with years of experience is portrayed in

Table 9.5, based on the main and interaction effects of gender and experience estimated in Models 2, 4, and 6. Although the precise pattern depends on whether prior employment and earnings are controlled, Table 9.5 shows that for each model the net gender gap in (log) earnings increases dramatically with years in the industry. At career entry, the gender gap in earnings is as low as 4 to 6 percent (and not statistically significant according to the estimates of the main effects of gender in Models 2 and 6). But the results in Table 9.5 show that within five years of career entry, the gender gap in earnings grows to 20 percent or more, and by the fifteenth year the gap is on the order of 40 percent or more.

Although the gender gap in earnings increases with years in the industry, we find no evidence that the effects of prior employment on earnings are

Table 9.5 Estimates of Cumulative Disadvantage: Net Effect of Gender on Log Earnings at Different Levels of Industry Experience

Years of Experience	Model 2 No Lags	Model 4 Net of Lag Employment	Model 6 Net of Lag Employment, Earnings
0 Years	−0.045	−0.203	−0.060
1 Year	−0.081	−0.241	−0.099
5 Years	−0.207	−0.373	−0.235
10 Years	−0.321	−0.492	−0.356
15 Years	−0.386	−0.561	−0.422
20 Years	−0.402	−0.581	−0.433

greater for men than for women (see row labeled "lag employment interactions" at the bottom of Table 9.3 and "lag earnings interactions" in Table 9.4). Nor do the results in Tables 9.3 and 9.4 show any evidence of declining disadvantage, because the gender-by-year interaction is not statistically significant. That is, there is no statistical evidence that the disadvantages faced by female screenwriters are declining over time. In each instance, we fail to reject the null hypothesis of no gender-by-year interactions (row labeled "year interactions" at the bottom of Tables 9.3 and 9.4).[4] In short, with respect to the impact of gender on earnings, consistent with research on television writers (Bielby and Bielby 1992), the structure of disadvantage was essentially static during the 1980s and early 1990s. The apparent decline in the gender gap in median earnings shown in Figure 9.4 is actually a spurious trend generated by shifts over time in the number of years of experience women screenwriters have relative to men.[5]

In sum, our findings support a model of cumulative disadvantage whereby the gender gap in earnings grows with years of experience in the industry. Women writers in the industry face gender barriers that reduce their earnings substantially compared to men of similar age and experience, and these barriers increase the longer they work as screenwriters. We also found no evidence that the barriers faced by women screenwriters are eroding over time. Our confidence in these results is reinforced by two features of our analysis. First, by using a pooled cross-section design, we are exploiting both intra- and interindividual variation, and with such large sample sizes we certainly would

have detected substantively significant interactions by year had they existed.[6] Second, the pattern of coefficients for the control variables is consistent with what we know about the structure of the labor market for screenwriters. Year effects increase monotonically. Older writers face a net disadvantage, consistent with descriptive statistics for the industry (W. Bielby and D. Bielby 1993) and with findings for television writers (D. Bielby and W. Bielby 1993). Minority writers are disadvantaged according to models 1 and 2, although the other models show this to be largely mediated by differences between minority and nonminority writers in prior employment and earnings.[7] Finally, the effect of work in television is negative in all our models, consistent with the notion that writers achieving success in television are less likely to be pursuing film work, where the odds of success are much lower.

Conclusion

Women compose about half of those who are classified as authors by the U.S. Census, but the screenwriting profession is more than 80 percent male. Those women who are able to break into the profession experience a process of cumulative disadvantage: the longer they work in the industry, the more their earnings lag behind their male counterparts. It has not always been this way. In the early years of the industry, women participated fully in the writing of film narratives and were among the highest-paid scenarists in the industry. However, in the late 1920s and 1930s, the profession went through a transition that Tuchman (1989) has described as the "empty field" phenomenon. As filmmaking became industrialized and rationalized, men dominated key roles in corporate channels of production, distribution, and exhibition. As screenwriting became more lucrative, men entered the profession in large numbers, and their dominance was legitimated by an ideology that valued men's contributions across the board but considered women's talent as appropriate only for a narrow range of genres. By the end of the 1930s, male dominance of the profession was fully institutionalized, and with the exception of a slight upturn in the early 1970s, women's representation among screenwriters has changed little over the last half century.

The typecasting of women writers seems as prevalent today as it was when "women's pictures" were at the height of their popularity in the 1930s and 1940s. Bettye McCartt, a prominent Hollywood talent agent, describes her encounters with typecasting as follows:

> When we get a call for a writer, they'll say, "Who do you have who can write an action-adventure piece?" If I suggest a woman, well they laugh at me. There are certain genres where a woman won't even be considered. By the same token, they'll call and say, "What woman writers do you have for a piece on so-and-so."
>
> (Writers Guild of America, West 1990, 12)

Although we have no quantitative data on the extent of typecasting of women writers, it is easy to imagine how it generates a pattern of cumulative disadvantage. The typical woman writer is likely to break into the industry writing material that is either currently fashionable or viewed by producers as appropriate for a woman writer, and she is paid at a rate comparable to that for a new male writer (Guild minimums under the collective bargaining agreement place a floor on compensation of novice writers). But as her career progresses, the woman writer's opportunities are limited to a narrow range of genres, whereas her male counterpart faces no such limitations. Even if she achieves a modest degree of success as a screenwriter, her long-term marketability is vulnerable to the inevitable cycles in the popularity of specific genres in the way that a male writer's is not. Such a dynamic is consistent with anecdotal accounts from women writers and their agents, and it is with our empirical

findings of cumulative gender disadvantage in earnings, even when women writers are compared to men who have similar patterns of employment and earnings over a three-year period.

Among feature film writers, a gender gap in earnings emerges and widens over the course of writers' careers. Our earlier research (Bielby and Bielby 1992) detected a different dynamic in the labor market for television writers. For them, there is a substantial earnings gap at career entry that persists throughout the career. The two patterns probably reflect different routes to career entry in film and television. In film, there are more ways for both male and female aspiring writers to participate at the periphery of the labor market (e.g., by selling an option on a story or treatment, by doing a rewrite or "polish" on a screenplay). Typically, both male and female film writers start at the margins of the industry, and although few succeed beyond that level, men have better prospects for breaking into the ranks of successful writers of feature film, and success breeds success once they do. In contrast, the market for television writers is more highly structured. An aspiring writer either participates by gaining access to the interconnected social network of writer-producers, studio development executives, and network programmers or does not participate at all. In that kind of market, women writers are likely to face a substantial disadvantage from the very beginning.

Despite the somewhat differing dynamics of cumulative versus continuous disadvantage, it is important to recognize that there is substantial gender stratification in both segments of the industry, and in neither film nor television have we found any evidence of a decline since the early 1980s in the barriers faced by women writers. The similarities in the organizational, business, and labor market arrangements in television and film are no doubt more important than the differences in understanding the nature of those barriers. Short-term contracting in a context of ambiguity, risk, and uncertainty encourages the reliance on closed social networks of interpersonal ties and the use of informal, subjective criteria for the hiring and evaluation of writers and other creative workers. A large body of social research demonstrates that these are precisely the conditions under which gender stereotypes reinforce structural barriers to women's career advancement (Bielby 1992; Deaux 1984; Eagly and Wood 1982; Williams and Best 1986), especially when there is no system for holding those responsible for decisions about hiring and compensation accountable for doing so in a way that is free from bias (Salancik and Pfeffer 1978; Tetlock 1985). So in one sense, our findings are exactly what one would expect from established theories of gender inequality in the workplace. At the same time, prevailing theories of gender-segregated job ladders and a bureaucratically legitimated gendered division of labor (Acker 1990) are less relevant to television, film, and related media industries than they are to the corporate, government, blue-collar, and pink-collar settings that have been the focus of most research on gender inequality in the workplace. Although there is some research and theory on how gender is created and reinforced symbolically in the workplace (Cockburn 1985; Hearn and Parkin 1983; Hochschild 1983), none of it addresses how it occurs in mass culture industries that deliberately and self-consciously attempt to reflect and trade on cultural idioms about gender. The women and men who finance, write, produce, market, and distribute feature films and television programming are "doing gender" in a way that simultaneously shapes the work experiences and opportunities of those who participate in the industry and determines the images of gender consumed by a global audience. Mass culture industries are sites where symbolic representations of gender are literally produced, and they provide new challenges to the way we understand gender inequality in organizations. Our research highlights the importance of attending to the industrial context, social networks, organizational arrangements, and the symbolic content of the commodities produced to fully understand the barriers to women's full participation in the production of media narratives.

Notes

This research was completed with support from the National Science Foundation (SES 89–10039) and the Academic Senate of the University of California, Santa Barbara.

1. Even feminist film critics are vulnerable to these stereotypes. McCreadie (1994) suggests that the rise of "women's films" in the 1940s opened new opportunities for women writers, which then declined with the demise of that genre in the postwar period. But Writers Guild of America, West membership statistics suggest that women's representation among screenwriters remained steady at about 13 percent from the mid-1930s to the early 1960s (Figure 9.2). Thus, although it is widely believed that women are best suited for writing almost exclusively for women's films, for approximately three decades, women's representation among screenwriters remained constant regardless of the dominant genre of the day.

2. None of these films was written by a woman.

3. Strictly speaking, if the cumulative disadvantage model is favored over the model of continuous disadvantage, then a process of declining disadvantage would imply a three-way interaction between time, gender, and the effects of experience, prior employment, and prior earnings.

4. Although the hypothesis that the year-by-gender interaction coefficients are jointly zero cannot be rejected, the point estimates seem to suggest a pattern of declining gender effects over time. To examine this possibility, we replaced the 10 binary interaction terms, female × (year—1982). This provides a more powerful 1 degree of freedom test of the hypothesis that the gender gap in earnings declined linearly from 1982 to 1992. However, even with this more powerful test, the null hypothesis of no interaction could not be rejected.

5. From the early 1980s to the early 1990s, there was a substantial shift in employment favoring younger writers. So by the end of the period covered by our study, the industry was relying more heavily on writers who were just launching their careers. Because the gender gap in earnings is smaller among writers who are early in their careers, this trend has the effect of attenuating the bivariate association of gender and earnings, even though the net gender gap, controlling for experience, is not shrinking.

6. Moreover, inspection of collinearity diagnostics indicated that our failure to detect interaction is not due to inflated levels of sampling variation and covariation.

7. As noted above, because so few minority women are employed as screenwriters, we are unable to obtain reliable estimates of the interaction of minority status and gender. In each of our models, the interaction of female by minority status is negative (substantially so in model 1), suggesting that minority women face additional barriers. However, due to the small number of cases, the test of the interaction has very little power, and even a substantial gender-by-minority status interaction would fail to be detected as statistically significant in our models.

References

Acker, Joan. 1990. Hierarchies, jobs, bodies: A theory of gendered organizations. *Gender & Society* 4:139–58.

Baker, Wayne E., and Robert R. Faulkner. 1991. Role as resource in the Hollywood film industry. *American Journal of Sociology* 97:279–309.

Beranger, Clara. 1950. *Writing for the screen.* Dubuque, IA: W.C. Brown.

Bernstein, Sharon. 1990. But is there hope for the future? *Los Angeles Times,* 11 November, 9, 82–3.

Bielby, Denise D., and William T. Bielby. 1993. The Hollywood "graylist"? Audience demographics and age stratification among television writers. In *Current research on occupations and professions (Creators of Culture),* vol. 8, edited by Muriel G. Cantor and Cheryl Zollars. Greenwich, CT: JAI.

Bielby, William T. 1992. The structure and process of sex segregation. In *New approaches to economic and social analyses of discrimination,* edited by Richard Cornwall and Phanindra Wunnava. New York: Praeger.

Bielby, William T., and Denise D. Bielby. 1987. *The 1987 Hollywood writers' report: A survey of ethnic, gender and age employment factors.* West Hollywood, CA: Writers Guild of America, West.

——. 1989. *The 1989 Hollywood writers' report: Unequal access, unequal pay.* West Hollywood, CA: Writers Guild of America, West.

——. 1992. Cumulative versus continuous disadvantage in an unstructured labor market. *Work and Occupations* 19:366–489.

——. 1993. *The 1993 Hollywood writers' report: A survey of the employment of writers in the film, broadcast, and cable industries for the period 1987–1991.* West Hollywood, CA: Writers Guild of America, West.

——. 1994. "All hits are flukes:" Institutionalized decision-making and the rhetoric of network prime-time program development. *American Journal of Sociology* 99:1287–1313.

Cockburn, Cynthia. 1985. *Machinery of dominance.* London: Pluto Press.

Cox, Dan. 1995. WGA cuts into DGA territory. *Daily Variety* 246:1, 26.

DiMaggio, Paul. 1977. Market structure, the creative process, and popular culture: Toward an organizational reinterpretation of mass culture theory. *Journal of Popular Culture* 11:433–51.

Dutka, Elaine. 1990. Women and Hollywood: It's still a lousy relationship. *Los Angeles Times,* 11 November, 8, 85–8.

Danquah, Mari. 1994. Crashing the glass ceiling: Women writers in Hollywood. *The Journal of the Writers Guild of America* 7:12–7.

Deaux, Kay. 1984. From individual differences to social categories: Analysis of a decade's research on gender. *American Psychologist* 39:105–15.

Eagly, Alice H., and W. Wood. 1982. Inferred sex differences in status as a determinant of gender stereotypes about social influence. *Journal of Personality and Social Psychology* 43:915–28.

Faulkner, Robert R., and Andy B. Anderson. 1987. Short-term projects and emergent careers: Evidence from Hollywood. *American Journal of Sociology* 92:879–909.

Francke, Lizzie. 1994. *Script girls: Women screenwriters in Hollywood.* Bloomington: Indiana University Press.

Haskell, Molly. 1987. *From reverence to rape: The treatment of women in the movies,* 2d ed. Chicago: University of Chicago Press.

Hearn, Jeff, and P. Wendy Parkin. 1983. Gender and organizations: A selective review and critique of a neglected area. *Organization Studies* 4:219–42.

Hochschild, Arlie R. 1983. *The managed heart: Commercialization of human feeling.* Berkeley: University of California Press.

McCreadie, Marsha. 1994. *Women who write the movies.* New York: Birch Lane Press.

Martin, Ann, and Virginia Clark. 1987. *What women wrote: Scenarios, 1912–1929.* Cinema History Microfilm series. Frederick, MD: University Publications of America.

Robb, David, 1994. Writers Guild, DGA in clash over credits. *The Hollywood Reporter* 334: 1, 94.

Schwartz, Nancy Lynn. 1982. *The Hollywood writers' wars.* New York: Knopf.

Salancik, Gerald R., and Jeffrey Pfeffer. 1978. Uncertainty, secrecy, and the choice of similar others. *Social Psychology* 41:264–6.

Staiger, Janet. 1983. "Tame" authors and the corporate laboratory: Stories, writers, and scenarios in Hollywood. *Quarterly Review of Film Studies* 8 (Fall):33–45.

Stanley, Robert. 1978. *The celluloid empire: A history of the American motion picture industry.* New York: Hastings.

Tetlock, P. E. 1985. Accountability: The neglected social context of judgment and choice. In *Research in organizational behavior,* vol. 7, edited by L. L. Cummings and B. M. Staw. Greenwich, CT: JAI.

Tuchman, Gaye. 1989. *Edging women out: Victorian novelists, publishers, and social change.* New Haven, CT: Yale University Press.

Voland, John. 1992. The sun also rises: Confronting discrimination in the entertainment industry. *The Journal of the Writers Guild of America* 5:9–12.

Williams, John E., and Deborah L. Best. 1986. Sex stereotypes and intergroup relations. In *Psychology of intergroup relations,* edited by S. Worchel and W. G. Austin. Chicago: Nelson-Hall.

Work Projects Administration, American Guide Series. 1941. *Los Angeles: A guide to the city.* New York: Hastings.

Writers Guild of America, West. 1990. Women in Hollywood. *The Journal of the Writers Guild of America* 3:10–15.

Young, Paul F. 1995. Scripters caught in studio squeeze. *Daily Variety* 247:5, 18.

10.
WOMEN'S FILM PRODUCTION

Going Mainstream

Michelle Citron

A recent issue of *Time* magazine contains an article about women directors in Hollywood: Martha Coolidge, Susan Seidelman, Amy Heckerling, Barbra Streisand, Elaine May, Penelope Spheeris, Lee Grant, Donna Deitch, Joyce Chopra, Joan Micklin Silver, and others.[1] The article has a self-congratulatory tone; there are plenty of anecdotes to prove that things are still tough for women directors, yet the conditions are getting measurably better. The women mentioned in the article arrived at their current positions from a variety of places. Some started in the women's political-documentary independent film movement of the 1960s and 1970s (Coolidge, Deitch, Chopra). A few came from within the ranks of Hollywood itself (Grant, Streisand and May are actresses, Silver is married to a producer). The remainder are the first post-feminist generation of women to come out of film schools (Heckerling, Seidelman). The journalistic approach taken by *Time* is entertaining—in our still disenfranchised state there is a certain pleasure derived from a good horror story with a clear villain, in this case the male power structure in Hollywood—but not very insightful. The real question that must be asked is: What does it mean for women to decide to enter into the production of mainstream popular culture?[2]

I want to try and answer this question with the interweaving of two different perspectives. One is the macro-view: to look historically and politically at women in film-making in the United States, particularly as it relates to the broader movements of feminism and feminist film theory. The second is the micro-view: to analyse my own development as

an American feminist film-maker and to look at this development both at a personal level and as a member of this larger group. I use myself not to suggest that my development was either particularly unique or common, but rather as an entry into certain ideas about the relationship of the personal and psychological to the social and political.

What Does It Mean?

The question, 'What does it mean for a significant number of women to be making narrative films?', immediately presents a problem. The question is abstract and implies some kind of homogeneity, while the motivations, decisions and experiences of each woman entering into narrative film-making are concrete and diverse. This question implies one thing if asked by an intellectual/theorist and something quite different if asked by a film-maker making a decision about her next project. Even among film-makers the question is slippery. As asked by a woman who has worked her way up through the Hollywood hierarchy it has a different implication than as asked by me, a film-maker who comes out of the political film-making movement of the 1960s and 1970s, has a university teaching job, and is well aware of semiotics, psychoanalysis and feminist aesthetic issues. I am now in the process of making a narrative film more mainstream than my previous work. I have yet to find funding and thus it is not yet produced. My perspective on the issues is obviously influenced by where I am in this process. I find I move easily between cynicism and optimism. And I am aware that if I had already completed and exhibited a mainstream narrative film, my analysis might be quite different.

The first problem is terminology. Director, producer/director, film-maker . . . each word implies not only a particular relationship to the product and defines a different degree of control and power, but an ideology as well. When I made avant-garde films in the early 1970s, I called myself a film-maker, a designation that implied I was the sole controlling force behind the work. When my work evolved into films that were more conventionally (though not entirely) narrative in form, I was still a film-maker, still solely responsible for the work. I conceptualized and wrote the film, raised the money, directed the actors, and shot and edited it. I needed people to assist me, to load the magazines, help hang lights and record sound, but it was truly my film, and I took pride in understanding all aspects of the film-making process. In this sense the term 'film-maker' implies artisan: it is associated with the long history of independent film-making and with a deliberate dissociation from what Hollywood, with its job specification and hierarchy, produced. When I made *Daughter Rite* in 1978 I was a film-maker. When I made *What You Take For Granted . . .* in 1983 I went into the project as a film-maker but came out of it thinking of myself as a producer/director. I conceptualized and wrote it, raised the money and directed the actors. But the film was much larger in scope, too big for me to do everything. I needed others to light it, do the cinematography, record the sound, even assistant-direct. This film, more complex to produce, necessitated job specificity and some structure whereby all the different people could work efficiently with each other. Yet there is another level at work here, because when people now, ten years later, ask me what my role was on *Daughter Rite* I answer, 'producer/director'.

In the United States at least, the term 'film-maker' has lost some of its currency and, with the exception perhaps of small avant-garde films, is now rarely used. Its replacement with 'director' implies a shift towards a desire to associate oneself with Hollywood, or at least with the power that implies. In addition, the term 'director' has gained popular recognition and mythical status in our culture. This has been aided by the prevalence of the *auteur* theory regarding Hollywood directors, as indicated by mass media promotion of

directors as superstars: feature articles in *People* magazine, entire television programmes devoted to various directors on *At the Movies* and *Sneak Previews*. My use of the term 'film-maker' as opposed to 'director' in this essay is of necessity inconsistent: but hopefully the context will supply the appropriate meaning and resonance.

Mainstream narrative film is also a slippery term. Should it be defined by the text itself, by its mode of production, or by the nature of its distribution and exhibition? Both Hollywood-produced and independently produced films are theatrically distributed. For example, Donna Deitch's *Desert Hearts* (1985) was produced independently and distributed by Samuel Goldwyn, Jr, mainly to theatrical venues in large cities. Independent films can also be lower budget/alternative works, such as Bette Gordon's *Variety* (1983) or Lizzie Borden's *Born In Flames* (1983). Such films will never be shown in mass-audience theatrical distribution, but will be exhibited internationally on the art house circuit, or on the festival and museum circuit, and on foreign television. What I mean here by a mainstream narrative film is one that is aesthetically accessible to a broad audience and relies to a large extent on classical narrative conventions (whether of plot, of characterization, or of cinematic techniques). I also mean a film which is theatrically distributed: that is, seen in venues other than museums, film festivals and the like. A mainstream narrative is defined by the text itself and by its distribution and exhibition pattern and not necessarily by its production history. The simplest test is to ask, 'Is it likely to be reviewed in the mainstream press and on television?' If the answer is yes, for my purposes it is a mainstream narrative film.

Except for the earliest years of film-making, before film became a large-scale business, there have been only two women 'directors' (and here I mean directors of classic Hollywood mainstream narratives): Dorothy Arzner in the 1930s and 1940s, and Ida Lupino in the 1950s. The remaining smattering of women film-makers worked within the avant-garde (for example, Maya Deren), in documentary (for example, Shirley Clarke), or in small entrepreneurial operations (such as educational films, industrial films and commercials). All of these practices were more marginal and thus, in differing degrees, more accessible to women. There were relatively few women film-makers until the

1960s, when increasing numbers of us stepped behind the camera.

I was one of those women in the early 1970s who could suddenly conceive of herself as a film-maker. This was made possible by the general climate of feminism which was challenging the limited options we had previously seen for ourselves. In the film department at the university I was attending, there was also a shift in attitude in response to demands from women for more access to this traditionally male programme. Even so, in the two production classes I took as a student—both classes of twenty-five students—there was only one other woman besides myself.

I was immediately attracted to the avant-garde. I analysed my attraction with the simplistic phrase: new forms for new feminist contents. I wanted to make films that articulated women's experiences and saw the need for a new film language with which to do so. In retrospect, I realize there was another, deeper reason—my attraction to the avant-garde was one manifestation of an almost relentless intellectual upward mobility.

I was determined to rise above my working-class family by proving I was an intellectual. I would make ART, not movies. Movies I associated with all the other cultural products that abounded in my childhood home—*Reader's Digest Condensed Books, Popular Mechanics, Queen for a Day, The Price is Right* and *Mantovani's 101 Strings*. The making of ART was the clearest way for me to put distance between my parents (who embarrassed me) and myself. It was my tool of self-definition and it allowed me to create a world they could not enter. In a house where too many people lived in too few rooms, where I always shared a bedroom with my sister, where most of the rooms didn't have doors that could be closed, ART was a world that separated me from them. I vividly remember bringing my early films home to show my parents, who were very confused by what they saw. And even after viewing them, they insisted to all their friends that their daughter made educational films. It was the label that in their limited experience was the most accurate; although, with my film experience, I knew it wasn't accurate at all. I was secretly pleased by the misunderstanding. My choice of avant-garde was not psychologically self-indulgent. It was tied to an analysis of the regressive ideology of traditional narrative (that is, Hollywood) forms. But my choice of avant-garde over the more popular choice of documentary was also shaped by my personal history.

I was very much influenced by the 'expanded cinema'[3] movement of the 1960s and tried, in isolation, to synthesize it with feminist politics of the early 1970s and my own notions of a feminist aesthetic. At the time I was unaware of the feminist film conference being held in Edinburgh in 1972 and did not read the articles generated by that meeting until 1974 or 1975. I was working, then, in isolation from the film theorists who were using semiotics and psychoanalysis to develop a feminist film theory and feminist aesthetic. In this I was no different from other women film-makers in the United States. Even my position within a major university did not give me an advantage over my community-based contemporaries in terms of access to theoretical work; an indication, perhaps, of the slow filter-down process that usually occurs with intellectual thought.

I made *Self-Defense* in 1972–3. This is a film that presents, through the metaphor of self-defence, women's anger, their coming to consciousness and their ultimate bonding in sisterhood. These ideas are expressed with images of women that have been manipulated through various techniques of optical printing, layering, filtering, and so on. The images in the first half of the film consist of shapes or moving colours that slowly transform into a woman practising T'ai Chi. The later images of the film are silhouettes of women, first one then two, then three, performing karate forms. The silhouettes are played against highly saturated images of women's 'finery'—jewellery, make-up, fabric—which at first exist within the figures, then outside of the figures, and ultimately disappear altogether. I was surprised by the audience's reaction to my film. It was not, I discovered, just my parents who were confused. On the one hand, the women for whom the film was intended were befuddled and alienated by *Self-Defense*. They had no experience with avant-garde film language and therefore no entry into the film. On the other hand, my fellow film-makers, all men, had no inkling that there was a deeper metaphorical level at work in the film. All they saw were the optically printed images and the technical expertise they implied.

In reaction to this response I separated out the two audiences by making two distinct films—*Integration* (completed in 1974) for the male film-makers, *Parthenogenesis* (completed in 1975) for the women. *Integration* is a structuralist film, once again using techniques of the optical printer. It is an avant-garde film exploring the manipulation of form, detached from feminist concerns at the levels of both medium and content (it is not an example of an attempt at a political 'alternative film practice').

Parthenogenesis, my only documentary, was a conscious attempt to place myself in the context of the feminist film movement of the early 1970s. In the United States, documentaries were seen by feminists as the politically appropriate film form. There were many reasons for this. Documentary, particularly in the 1950s and 1960s, allowed 'outsiders' some access into the relatively closed world of film production. These two decades saw a broadening of the documentary form (influenced by the Free Cinema movement, *cinéma vérité*, television and new technologies), in terms of production techniques, subjects and aesthetics. This atmosphere of experimentation and openness permitted the entry of some women, particularly at the lower levels of the hierarchy, as editors and associate producers. Ironically, the editor turned out to have a position of creative control, and thus of power, since many of these films were, in effect, shaped in a fundamental way during the editing process. By the time the feminist movement of the 1960s emerged with its changing notions of what women could achieve, a group of trained and experienced women documentary film-makers already existed.[4] In addition, documentary's changing and broadening of aesthetic standards and production values had very practical implications. Provided the topic was of compelling interest, a film could be made for less money than, and could look different from, a mainstream narrative yet still be accessible to audiences and critics. This made the documentary form seem even more desirable to film-makers, especially to women with no previous film-making experience.

But there were also clear political reasons why women chose to make documentary films. Documentary, with its long political history and didactic potential, was—given the political situation that motivated most women film-makers at the time—an appropriate form. Documentary film was also seen, particularly in the United States, as a healthy and necessary reaction to the 'unreality' of mainstream narrative film. Women, finally becoming politically aware and self-aware, desired to present 'real' women on the screen, something that Hollywood not only failed to do, but actively worked against. Film theory of the 1970s, with its analysis of realism and ideology, put to rest the naive notion that film is a transparent reflection of reality. And yet documentary film seemed able to be a viable, accessible and powerful means of capturing, or representing, a certain 'lived experience'.

In making *Parthenogenesis*, I saw myself as part of the feminist film movement in the United States. The film follows a week of daily violin lessons between a female teacher and her young female student as they learn the Bach Double Violin Concerto in D minor. It explores the teacher/student interaction, the importance of women as artistic role models, and seeks to demystify the 'creative' process. This last was represented by the one avant-garde technique of the film. The film starts with an abstract image that recurs at various points during the learning of the piece. With each of its appearances, this image becomes more concrete so that by the end of the film it is clearly identifiable as the student and teacher performing the piece they have been practising. This final image of the film represents, simultaneously, the demystified abstracted image and the end result of the learning process documented in the film. With this final image, documentary and avant-garde become one. Although flawed as a film, *Parthenogenesis* was very satisfying in terms of audience response. Not only was it highly accessible, but the device and meaning of the abstracted image were always a focus of viewer response so that awareness of form, as well as of content, was an important aspect of audience discussion.

The political climate of the 1970s also created an environment that encouraged the production of avant-garde films. The use of semiotics and psychoanalysts in analysing classical Hollywood film led to a desire to develop a film practice—defined as avant-garde—that transcended the traditional regressive nature of the medium. I found this investigation of form inspired by feminist film theory very exciting. Examples include the films of Laura Mulvey and Peter Wollen—*Penthesilia* (1974) and *Riddles of the Sphinx* (1976), although many other films and film-makers could be cited as well. Their theoretical investigation offered a more thorough analysis and understanding of the importance of avant-garde film than did the 'expanded cinema' context in which I had been working; and, in making theory concrete, they were very important for what they taught about that theory. I found these films intellectually stimulating and visually beautiful. And yet I also found them lacking; they suppressed the affective, that is the emotional, sphere. But this is precisely the point of these films—which were, as a result, theoretically interesting and politically sound, but flat. They offer intellectual pleasure but rarely emotional pleasure, the consequences of which are both theoretical and practical.

I hadn't always wanted to be a film-maker. In 1970, after completing an undergraduate degree in psychology, I had started graduate work in cognitive psychology at the University of Wisconsin in Madison. Academic psychology was in the grip of behaviourism and I was directed to design empirical experiments—the only methodology recognized by the institution—to research the subtle phenomenon of cognition. My master's thesis was intended to investigate the way in which we synthesize complex concepts from multiple channels of information. I created a multi-media presentation about water that included the simultaneous projection of five slides and three channels of sound. Experimental method required that I project the stimuli in different arrangements (for instance, simultaneous versus linear) to unsuspecting eight-year-olds. I then performed sophisticated multi-variance statistical analysis on the data. I received my degree for the work, but the numbers that emerged from the computer told me nothing about how we make sense out of our experiences: the behaviourist approach, in other words, seemed futile and wrong to me. I concluded that empiricism might be helpful in understanding the brain, but was useless for understanding the mind. My discontent inspired many confrontations with the faculty in my department. Finally, I turned in frustration to a study of the underlying assumptions of empiricism—a study of the history and philosophy of science. In 1974, I was awarded my PhD and immediately became a film-maker, leaving behind for ever the intellectual mire created by committing oneself to an empirical methodology—or so I thought.

Years later, while watching feminist avant-garde films grounded in contemporary film theory, I was struck by their similarity to empiricism. Positivism—as manifested in empiricism, which had had its genesis in philosophy and the hard sciences and had subsequently moved into the social sciences in the late 1940s and early 1950s—had finally, so it seemed to me, reached the humanities. These avant-garde films perpetuated one of the dichotomies that underlies positivism: the higher world of the mind (the intellect) over the baser world of the body (the emotions). They represented a kind of artistic empiricism.[5] Useful and intellectually pleasurable as these films and the theory informing them are, both are limited because their underlying meaning is one of separation, not integration. This separation of the intellectual from the emotional and the implied subordination of the latter to the former in some ways paralleled my own attraction, as a beginning film-maker, to ART and not to movies.

Daughter Rite (1978) should be seen in this context. The film is the story of two pairs of sisters and their relationship to their respective mothers. The themes of betrayal, anger, love and manipulation between mothers and daughters and between sisters are presented through an interweaving of cinematic techniques: scripted and acted scenes shot in the visual language of *cinéma vérité* and optically printed home movie images accompanied as voice-over by a narrator reading entries from her journal.

My experiences with audience reactions to my earlier work, as well as my intellectual development in graduate school, led me to want to make accessible avant-garde films. For *Daughter Rite* I tried to solve the problem of accessibility through the device of mixing modes (documentary, narrative and avant-garde) and genres (*cinéma vérité* and melodrama), in order both to critique film language itself and also to open it up to non-avant-garde audiences. A play on genres, with its mass culture familiarity and appeal, seemed to offer a way of entry into what would otherwise be an avant-garde film. It would allow me to use conventions (of visual style, acting technique, narrative scene pacing and development, characterization) familiar enough to audiences to provide a 'hook'. And by juxtaposing different generic conventions, I hoped to critique and illuminate, as well as to entertain (or perhaps give pleasure). My understanding of accessibility involved embryonic ideas about the validity of the emotional sphere and its importance in film. When I chose to use melodramatic conventions, my choice was dictated by the fact that melodrama is a genre historically associated with women, and was among the earliest issues addressed by feminist film theory and criticism. It is also a genre infused with a highly charged emotional layer. My use of it reflected my desire to integrate the intellectual and affective realms.

Many feminist avant-garde films are inaccessible in that they strain the tenuous relationship of communication which binds the film-maker, through the film, to the audience. Through its use of popular genres, this relationship is stronger in narrative film than in other forms. Feminist avant-garde films reject generic convention, relying on the subject-matter of the film to provide entry into an otherwise inaccessible work. But the language and style of the avant-garde, being unfamiliar, create a gap that many viewers cannot bridge. *Daughter Rite* is usually programmed with a second more purely avant-garde feminist film, often Sally Potter's *Thriller* (1979) or Su Friedrich's *The Ties That Bind* (1985), two very important works. Though both are avant-garde, these two films come from different traditions. *Thriller*, a feminist reworking of the story of Puccini's opera *La Bohème*, makes its consciousness of contemporary feminist film theory evident in both sound and image, and uses an avant-garde film language to suppress a potential emotional response from the viewer despite its wonderful use of humour. *The Ties That Bind* is more in keeping with the American avant-garde tradition; it is consciously aware of its use of an unconscious or intuitive language as opposed to a theoretical language in expressing and encouraging an emotional response from the viewer. Both these avant-garde approaches—whether the separation of the emotional from the intellectual or the use of a personal language to explore the emotional—create a distance from the film for the viewer. If the audience is an art museum or cinema audience having previous experience with avant-garde film language, there is usually little problem with either film. But if the viewers are a general non-film gathering (for instance a women's centre), or a community based group), I often find myself having to explain and defend these films to a confused and sometimes hos-

tile group, angry at being shut out. There is no question that these audiences learn a lot from the experience of viewing and then discussing these avant-garde films. But the experience is dependent upon teaching; the film cannot stand alone. This in itself is not bad, and does in fact expand the audience for future films. I in no way think that all films should reach all audiences and I love and staunchly defend avant-garde work; but from my own political perspective, this kind of avant-garde film practice, although important and necessary, is inevitably circumscribed.

I don't mean to imply that *Daughter Rite* never suffers misunderstanding on the part of 'general' audiences. This is not in fact true, although misunderstanding seems to happen in a somewhat limited way. Of particular difficulty are the home movies/narration sequences in the film. Individual viewers seem to attend *either* to the visual channel *or* to the auditory channel. This does not seem to close the viewer off entirely from the film's meaning and experience, rather it creates a 'hole' for them in an otherwise accessible film.

The film *What You Take for Granted . . .* (1983) was my attempt to resolve further this issue of accessibility. It concerns the contradictions of women working in non-traditional blue-collar and professional jobs. Structurally, the film consists of the interweaving of three cinematic components: first, six women who talk directly to camera about their lives and jobs; secondly, two of the six women—a truck-driver and a doctor—engaged in a narrative; and thirdly, documentary footage of women doing various types of work. Thus, cinematic tension is set up which parallels the tension between the public and private spheres of the characters' lives. But while *What You Take For Granted . . .* merges cinematic styles, it is nevertheless the most conventionally narrative of my work.

Women's independent/political films in the 1970s, whether documentary or avant-garde, existed in a larger social/political context. This broad context included such varied elements as grassroots political movements (civil rights, anti-war, feminist, gay rights, labour, and so on) with their numerous centres and identifiable members; a more liberal and responsive government agenda than at present regarding social and art programmes; and a lively intellectual environment fuelled by a new political awareness. This made possible independent/political film funding (from government as well as from alternative sources, such as progressive private foundations like the Film Fund), distribution and exhibition.

The context has changed since the 1970s, so those of us working within it must also change. On the simplest level, we have lost our audiences as previously defined (for example, the large network of broad-based women's centres has greatly diminished). Serious Business Company and Iris Films, two important distributors of women's films throughout the 1970s, have ceased to exist (Serious Business ceased trading in 1983, Iris in 1985).[6] Only two distributors of women's films remain in the United States: New Day Films (which has expanded to include labour movement and health films) and Women Make Movies. Other films are occasionally picked up by broader-based independent distributors; this in itself is a kind of mainstreaming. In such a context, films are seen not as women's films but as independent films. In some cases, this can have the advantage of broadening a film's audience; in others, it can bury them out of sight.

But no matter who distributes 'alternative' films, there are fewer companies handling fewer films and exhibiting to smaller audiences. This is in response to a changing market. Women Make Movies can serve as an example. Although their revenues have increased, it is due to an expanded list (they took over a number of Serious Business and Iris films) and a few films that subsidize the rest of the collection by frequent university film department rentals. Demand by women's groups, centres, and so on, has declined as these groups have decreased in number in the United States. Those audiences we reached in the 1970s are no longer out there in the same simply defined way. In this changed context, one could say that women entering into the production of mainstream narrative films are film-makers following their audience. This may be questionable as a political strategy—certainly as judged by the criteria of the 1970s—but it is at least pragmatic. If a film-maker wants her films to be seen by women, she must reach out to them in a different way in the 1980s. She can do this by exploring different distribution strategies—exploiting the half-inch home video market for instance—or more easily by making films that fit into current distribution and exhibition markets, usually meaning mainstream narrative.

For fifteen years feminists have made films which allowed for a privileged communication between film-maker and audience. The film-maker might have travelled with the film and engaged with the audience, answering questions after the screening. Sometimes such a dialogue took place in the classroom between teacher (the film-maker's surrogate) and students. This kind of film-maker/film/audience relationship is difficult to maintain with changing distribution patterns and the decrease in exhibition venues. There are now fewer women's or feminist exhibition situations and less money at universities for film rental or women's studies programmes. My own experience is that over the past ten years or so invitations to screen my films have clearly shifted from women's organizations and women's studies departments to university film and English departments.

Mainstream narrative film, a popular form relying on accepted conventions, has always allowed for an immediate relationship between audience and film. Traditionally, the only mediating devices have been those of the popular film critic and audience word of mouth, which are useful but not necessary for an individual viewer's understanding of a particular film. Given the decrease in political and educational outlets in the United States, narrative film's traditionally unmediated relationship to an audience is increasingly appealing.

One further point may be made about the changed context: the political atmosphere of the 1970s and early 1980s fostered dialogue between film-makers and film-makers, film-makers and audiences, film-makers and film theorists. This dialogue took place at film festivals (Edinburgh Festival in 1972 and 1979), at conferences (the Alternative Cinema Conference at Bard in 1979, the Milwaukee conferences in the late 1970s and early 1980s, the International Conference of Feminist Film and Video Makers in Amsterdam in 1981, to name just a few), in university classes and grassroots community meetings everywhere. This activity was linked to a focused and broad-based feminist political movement. What I see as the mainstreaming of film, whether in terms of film theory or in terms of production, is part of a larger mainstreaming of feminism.

Mainstreaming

Independent production can mean many things, but particularly important is independence of the need for large sums of money. I think the magic number is probably around $200,000 for production costs alone. Less than that a film-maker can probably raise and thus maintain personal control of a project and remain a 'film-maker', in the sense discussed above. More than that necessitates different sources of, and strategies for, obtaining money and consequently a loss of total control over the production. The exception to this would be the director who has a lot of power in the industry, which few women in Hollywood have.[7] In the past I did not need to be concerned with my films selling advertising on television or returning an investment. At my level of financing the profit margin was quickly reached and, once there, I defined the meaning of profit. This gave me the freedom to make what I wanted when I wanted. I still needed resources, but these were attainable. I could get a grant for $6,000 or $20,000. I could use the equipment at the institution where I taught, or borrow a camera for a week from a friend who was not working. Of course this was not easy. A film took four years to make instead of one. I paid heavily with free labour, my own and that of my friends. I was marginal (which had its own special status) but I also took full responsibility for what I produced.

I was a 'film-maker', not a 'director'. I controlled the entire process of making a product that was small enough for control to be maintained. Every film I started I knew I would finish, and I did finish because completion depended solely on my own tenacity. For a director, the situation is different. Within the institution of mainstream theatrical narrative production (whether one works under a studio or independently, in Hollywood, New York or elsewhere) the script can be great, but still unmarketable. A script can be sold, but not produced. A film can be shot but not finished. And a film can be completed yet not distributed or adequately marketed. These become financial, not aesthetic decisions, decisions made by people who probably do not share my priorities regarding film.

The shift from film-maker to director can be seen as trading control for power. The director has the power fed by large sums of money, experienced crew and actors, good equipment, and so on. The director works in a form and with production values that can reach large audiences because the product is familiar to audiences and thus is what theatrical distributors want. In this context, power means a number of things: the opportunity to reach a larger audience, the potential of using mainstream culture to critique or subvert it, the freedom to define and test one's own personal boundaries as film-maker. This is all very seductive. But in the hierarchy of mainstream narrative film the director, in gaining this power, relinquishes control to the producer, to the distributor. Will the film get made and distributed? Who will make the really pivotal decisions? What kinds of compromises to the market-place will have to be made?

A lot of women now desire the kind of power available through mainstream narrative film-making. This change of priorities is one manifestation of our changing social/political context. If women are no longer a clearly definable political movement, then the focus shifts from the group to the individual. This is one understanding of the phenomenon of mainstreaming. When a defined political group is dispersed and submerged within a dominant culture, it can then only be defined by its individual members; power can be exercised only in an individualistic manner. Ironically such personal power is now possible because women collectively have obtained film-making experience and a new level of self-confidence: this is one consequence of the women's movement. It is easier to contemplate making a mainstream narrative film when you've shot a $250,000 documentary or have been to film school and learned to direct a large crew.

But power is double-edged. A desire to make mainstream narrative films can also indicate an acceptance of our culture's definition of progress and success. The myth is that bigger is better: more money for production, higher production values, stars, wider distribution and larger audiences means a BIGGER film which means progress and thus a better product.

The politics of the 1970s provided us with alternative myths to those of the dominant culture: politically correct is better; the artisan grounded in the community, however small, is better. Feminist film-makers had little desire to enter into the mainstream film world; our goal was to make films in direct opposition to that world. We wanted to make films that challenged the status quo. Whether documentary or avant-garde, these were films for a purpose, for political organizing and consciousness-raising in the broadest sense. This film practice challenged ideas about film language, the relationship between viewer and film, and the function of cinema in our society. But in a changing political context, the dominant film world has become more enticing. This is not to argue that the desire to make mainstream narrative features has no legitimacy. But it does reflect part of the paradox and contradiction of wanting to do so.

One interpretation of women's move into the production of narrative film is that women now feel a willingness to take different kinds of risks: to perhaps be the woman who, while accepting the parameters of mainstream narrative film as dictated by both the market-place and the strong psychological pull of narrative, can subvert it. In one way, this acceptance of power can be seen as a desire, reinforced by self-confidence, to 'win on our own terms'. This might be easier for younger women who are entering into narrative production today, the field changed by the women who came before them; they enter film-making with a kind of self-confidence bred of their age and environment. These women can build on a now visible history of women film-makers and directors, including directors of feature films, both narrative and documentary. In entering film-making through main-stream narrative production, they do not have to first reassess, and in a sense reject, their own prior non-narrative work. These women can define compromise differently because, both personally and culturally, they have come out of a different historical moment.

The situation is different for women who have already worked in film and are moving into narrative production from other forms. Any kind of film production is a compromise forged on a constantly shifting matrix of content, aesthetics, accessibility, access to financial and production resources, distribution and exhibition potential, and so on: As political film-makers of independent avant-garde and documentary films, our choices were based on our priorities at the time. What we sacrificed in a particular compromise was not in that context as important as what we gained. A film-maker might make a seventeen-minute film that would be seen by no more than 10,000 women. But the film had a clarity of political and aesthetic vision

completely in the film-maker's control. Audience size was augmented if the film could be used as an edu-cational or organizing tool. But the shifting historical moment creates both a willingness and a need to make different compromises. Today, a woman direc-tor can make a low-budget feature which gets theatri-cally distributed and seen by hundreds of thousands of women. But in this case, the demands of the market as 'safeguarded' by the producer circumscribe risks at the level of either form or content. The contradictions here are unlimited. Martha Coolidge tells of a conver-sation she had with the producer of *City Girl*, a film she directed in 1981 but which has never been completed. 'The first thing the producer said to me was, "Are you a feminist?" Well, of course I'm a feminist. But I knew that if I said yes, I'd lose the job. So I said no.'[8]

How do the compromises made by women work-ing within Hollywood with limitations imposed from above differ from those faced by women working inde-pendently? At what point does a practical compro-mise become a betrayal of past goals, experience and work? When is a compromise valuable? The answers to these questions are difficult, as they are shaped by continually shifting cultural contexts and the changing experiences of women film-makers. Nevertheless, it is important that women are entering into narrative film production; though I make this statement with full awareness of its contradictions and ambiguities.

What Is the Meaning of Narrative?

Narrative film's enduring quality as popular art implies some deep psychological attraction which the form holds for us: attempts to understand this phenomenon have provided a central focus for contemporary film theory. This has often meant a study of genre. With women's entry into the production of mainstream narrative films, understanding genre becomes doubly important, since to make a mainstream narrative film today is to work within a genre. The questions raised by women's move into mainstream narrative film pro-duction are therefore not only about accepting power and losing or relinquishing control, but about the power of genre itself. What is our attraction to genre? Can women create new genres? Can we work within the context of old genres, while creating a different point of view or subverting it in some other way? I would like to look at Martha Coolidge's film *Valley Girl* (1983) as an example.

Valley Girl is a romantic comedy about Los Angeles Valley high schooler Julie, who is bored with her Valley steady Tommy, a conservative egocentric stud. Julie becomes attracted to Randy, a working-class punk from the inner city (Hollywood). Her romance with Randy is played out in the context of the values of her own upper-middle-class culture, as represented by her friends who greatly discourage her new romance because Randy comes from the 'wrong side' of the Hollywood Hills.

Early in the film there is a party scene. Tommy, recently rejected by Julie, responds by cornering Loryn, one of Julie's close friends. He coaxes her away from the party into an upstairs bedroom where he comes on to her sexually. At first Loryn resists, insisting it would be wrong for them to make out because of her loyalty to Julie. Tommy tells her he is emotionally devastated, that it is Julie's fault, and that he needs the solace that only Loryn, with her sexual favours, can provide. His flattery gradually breaks down Loryn's initial protests, and he succeeds in getting her to undress. At the point when Loryn is most vulnerable, lying on the bed with her breasts exposed, she asks, 'Tommy, does this mean we're going together?' Tommy, who by now has got what he wants from Loryn replies, 'No. I think it means you're a pretty lousy friend . . . messing around with your girlfriend's boyfriend while he's in a bad way. But I'll tell you what. I won't tell anybody if you won't.' Loryn is stunned by the betrayal but before she can respond, Tommy bolts, leaving her alone on the bed crying.

This bedroom scene, composed of only one shot—camera angled slightly above Loryn and Tommy as they lie on the bed—is presented exclusively from the emotional point of view of Loryn. The characters are positioned in the frame with Loryn beneath Tommy so that we clearly see Loryn's full face and body. Tommy, looming over her, is little more than a barely identified male back. This shot set-up privileges Loryn's emotional point of view by enabling us to see her changing body language and facial expressions as the scene unfolds. We see her vulnerability, humiliation and doubt of her own perception as she trusts Tommy, yielding to his need to be nurtured and succumbing to his flattery, only to be

used by him. In this context, Loryn's nudity becomes an indictment of Tommy's sexist manipulations, and not the presentation of a women's body for male visual pleasure. The female nudity in this film was a demand made by the producer, a demand to which Coolidge knew she would have to acquiesce. In this particular instance Coolidge's only choice was how to film the nudity. Coolidge took the producer's demand for female nudity and used it towards her own feminist ends.

This scene, moreover, is intercut with the party going on downstairs and the first verbal interaction between Julie and Randy, her new romantic interest. This meeting is initiated by Julie's aggressive gaze at Randy across the crowded room. The scene between Loryn and Tommy in the bedroom makes public a common exchange experienced privately by women in the male/female sexual game. The scene between Julie and Randy at the party presents an alternative scenario for female/male interaction. The intercutting of the meeting downstairs with the scene of sexual humiliation upstairs presents a sequence in which a young woman's relationship to sex and power is explored in a strong and unusual manner.

However, this scene occurs in a film which is, for the most part, fairly conventional. *Valley Girl* falls into the genre of romantic comedy in its presentation of a female protagonist who must make a decision about her life, a decision defined by conventionality versus individuality. But the choice is only between two boys: should she date the young, upper-class stud Tommy, who comes from and represents the conservative values of her own class, or should she date the young, working-class punk Randy and so choose the 'other'? Despite peer group pressure she chooses the punk, thus affirming her strength of character and imagination. Yet ultimately, the choice can be framed only in the context of a conventional male/female relationship. The film is not particularly progressive on a narrative level, but rather is similar to others in the romantic comedy genre, from *The Philadelphia Story* (1940) to *Kiss Me Goodbye* (1982) to *Desperately Seeking Susan* (1985).

The nudity in *Valley Girl*, as well as the genre itself, were demands made by the producer, not choices made by the director. But Coolidge is able to work within the constraints of a popular genre and subvert it in small but significant ways by offering a point of view informed by a feminist awareness. She is able to work within an established genre and deliberately play on audience expectations. I am not suggesting that all women directors wish, or have the ability, insight or position, to twist formulas, just as subversion cannot be assured simply because a woman director works independently. But the potential for subversion in a mainstream context nevertheless does exist.

Most women directors working in Hollywood have been confined to traditional women's genres such as melodrama—Lee Grant's *Tell Me a Riddle* (1980), Amy Jones's *Love Letters* (1983); or comedy—Amy Heckerling's *National Lampoon's European Vacation* (1983), Lisa Gottlieb's *One of the Boys* (1985), Susan Seidelman's *Desperately Seeking Susan* (1985). Few have been allowed to direct detective films, thrillers, or science fiction, genres which are 'male' as well as more expensive to produce. The exceptions have been light comic science fiction such as Seidelman's *Making Mr Right* (1987) and Coolidge's *Real Genius* (1985), and Penelope Spheeris's two low-budget exploitation films *Hollywood Vice Squad* (1985) and *The Boys Next Door* (1984). But even women working independently outside Hollywood have chosen for the most part to work within traditional women's genres. For example, both Donna Deitch's *Desert Hearts* and Joyce Chopra's *Smooth Talk* (1985) are melodramas.

What does this mean? Is it some recognition of the psychological validity of these genres that have historically been regarded as women's domain? Or is it a result of what will 'sell' and therefore be safe? What is the relationship between the psychological, the social, the political and the historical? What is so compelling about specific genres? What is so compelling about narratives? Can stories and myths be created that are different from the ones currently popular? What is the relationship between the meaning of the form and the meaning of the myth? How can point of view function? Contemporary film theory has attempted to answer some of these questions. But we need to broaden our theoretical approach to include along with work on film texts, analyses of their social, economic, political and historical dimensions. The consequences of this broadening will become clear only when we are in a position to examine a large body of narrative films directed by women. Only then can we ask different questions, or ask the same questions in a different way.

The social and political thought and activity of the 1960s and 1970s provided a focus for what we, as film-makers, wanted to say. Documentary, the form of the didactic, flourished. The theoretical analysis of film in the 1970s provided a focus for the experimentation of the avant-garde. These two approaches and the resultant film practices had an underlying assumption of 'political correctness'. Narrative film, however, is more ambiguous. It allows for contradictions, paradoxes, uncertainties. My own desire to explore narrative is an acknowledgement and acceptance that all is not clearly understood. It is an attempt consciously to explore the meaning of myth and ambiguity, and it is only at the present historical and personal moment that I can do so. This is not to imply that all women going 'Hollywood' share my motives, nor that all women film-makers should be making narrative films. Women should not focus exclusively on narrative films: documentary and avant-garde films still need to be made. I only suggest that the entry of women into mainstream narrative film-making will broaden the work we do and expand our understanding of visual culture and of ourselves. Ultimately, my argument is for heterogeneity; to add to the production of documentary and avant-garde, not to replace it.

To make narrative films is to take risks. However, these are risks we need now to take. We will lose a certain amount of control of our films, despite our best intentions and preparedness. We will make bad judgements. We will even make bad films. But we need new 'data' in order to refine our understanding of film and our relationship to it. By making narrative films, we can accumulate such material. What we need now are narrative films made by as many women as possible in as many ways as possible about as many things as possible.

Notes

I would like to thank Fina Bathrick and Chuck Kleinhans for their valuable feedback on earlier drafts of this essay.

1. *Time*, 24 March 1986, pp. 82–3.
2. For two other approaches, written by film-makers concerned with experimental narrative, see Jill Godmillow, 'A Little Something on Narrativity', the *Independent*, vol. 9,

no. 3 (April 1986). And Yvonne Rainer, 'Some Ruminations around Cinematic Antidotes to the Oedipal Net(tles) while Playing with De Lauraedipus Mulvey, or, He May Be Off Screen, But . . .', the *Independent*, vol. 9, no. 3 (April 1986).

3. 'Expanded Cinema' was a label coined by Gene Young-blood in the early 1970s to describe a varied body of avant-garde film work being produced in the United States. The work, which included the films of Stan Brakhage, Scot Bartlett, Bruce Baillie, and Will Hindle, among others, was noted for its use of varied formal experimentation which reflected the 'expanded consciousness' of the film-maker in the 1960s.

4. It is not surprising that New Day Films, the first feminist film distributor in the United States, had its inception at a Flaherty Seminar; its creation was motivated by the sense of disenfranchisement felt by a number of women documentary film-makers at the time.

5. Terry Lovell has a much more refined discussion of the similarities between empiricism and contemporary film theory in her book *Pictures of Reality: Aesthetics, Politics and Pleasure*, London: British Film Institute, 1980. What I call empiricism, Lovell more accurately defines as three different intellectual approaches (empiricism, conven-tionalism and realism). In addition, my analysis comes from a viewing of contemporary avant-garde feminist films, products of the theory, while Lovell's analysis is based on an analysis of the theory itself. Empiricism is even more transparent in mainstream communication studies as practised by the majority of radio–television–film departments in universities in the United States. This is analogous to my experiences of psychology in the late 1960s and early 1970s; the embracing of a methodology that represents a simplistic understanding of the powers of empiricism and a misplaced attempt to make the intellectual work of cultural studies 'scientific'.

6. Two good articles on the reality of independent film funding, production, distribution and exhibition are Freude Bartlett's, 'Distributing Independent Films', *Jump Cut*, no. 31, and 'Freude Bartlett Interviewed: Doing Serious Business', *Jump Cut*, no. 31 (1986).

7. The May 1986 issue of *Life* magazine is devoted entirely to Hollywood. The cover shows a group photo captioned 'Hollywood's most powerful women'. Pictured are five actresses: Sally Field, Jane Fonda, Goldie Hawn, Jessica Lange and Barbra Streisand.

8. *Time*, p. 83.

11.
GENDERING THE COMMODITY AUDIENCE
Critical Media Research, Feminism, and Political Economy
Eileen R. Meehan

Throughout the 1970s and 1980s, media scholars sorted the field into the categories of "mainstream" versus "critical" research. These adjectives instantly communicated where one stood in terms of the root assumptions and valuations undergirding one's work—as well as which side you rooted for at the staged debates where administrative researchers like Elihu Katz or Wilbur Schramm debated some representative of the opposition—perhaps James Carey, or Herbert Schiller, or Stuart Hall (Meehan 1999; see Poole and Schiller 1981). At the time, the administrative paradigm so dominated the field that its practitioners often assumed it was the only way to do research, rejecting other approaches as subjective, unsystematic, and impractical—as "armchair theorizing" little better than wishful thinking. Thus George Gerbner underplayed the intellectual hostility associated with the paradigmatic debates when he titled his special 1983 issue of the *Journal of Communication* "Ferment in the Field." Glancing back, I am struck by the "mainstream" paradigm's ability to unify its opposition—to place Carey, Schiller, and Hall on the same side. But I am also struck by the absence of feminist work in that benchmark publication, despite the *Journal's* openness to feminist work under Gerbner's editorship (e.g., Busby 1975; Cantor 1977, 1979; Lemon 1977; Poe 1976; Streicher 1974) as well as the tremendous outpouring of feminist research across media studies in the 1970s generally (e.g., Arnold 1976; Brabant 1976; Holly 1979; Janus 1977; Marzoff, Rush, and Stern 1974–1975; Morris 1973; Ogan and Weaver 1978–1979; St. John 1978; Tuchman et al. 1978).

One decade later, in two issues of the same journal, Michael Gurevitch and Mark Levy published essays addressing "the future of the field," which were republished under the title *Defining Media Studies: Reflections on the Future of the Field* (1994). The book organized its forty-eight contributions into seven categories (disciplinarity, new directions, influencing public policy, audiences and institutions, critical research, history of the field, and academic curriculum and legitimacy). Administrative research dominated the volume and critical scholarship was sprinkled across four of the categories. In the critical category, two essays focused on political economy. (Meehan, Mosco, and Wasko 1994; Schiller 1994); the other two on cultural studies (Grossberg 1994; McChesney 1994). Overall, only one essay offered a feminist perspective: H. Leslie Steeves's "Creating Imagined Communities: Development Communication and the Challenge of Feminism" (1993) in the public policy category. Yet, in describing the collection, Gurevitch and Levy state:

> The paradigmatic debate (or "dialogue") that dominated communication scholarship in the '70s and early '80s has been replaced by new and different intellectual nudgings, by the injection into communication scholarship of *recently emergent perspectives such as feminism*, post-modernism, and neofunctionalism.
>
> (1994, 7, emphasis mine)

As a political economist, trained during the period leading up to "Ferment," and as a coauthor of an essay in *Defining*, I find this all rather disturbing, yet oddly unsurprising.

That contradictory reaction motivates this essay. As a political economist, I have focused my research mainly on the internal structures of media-based corporations—which shape the form and content of cultural commodities (e.g., Meehan 1991)—and the external relationships between such corporations—which also shape cultural commodities and which construct media markets (e.g., Meehan 1990). Working at this level of abstraction generally has meant treating large-scale, impersonal institutions as agents with little reference to the actions, struggles, or alliances of human beings. Much of the feminist scholarship in communications takes a less abstracted point of entry: women working in the industries (Martin 1991); women's use of mediated artifacts (Radway 1984; Steeves et al. 1988); the fictional men and women offered as role models by the media (Byars 1991; Byars and Dell 1992); or some combination of these concerns (Andersen 1995; Stabile 1995).

Connections between feminist lines of research and institutional lines of research may not be readily apparent. The conditions of people's work and leisure, and the artifacts that they employ in each sphere, may seem fairly remote from the impact of transindustrial conglomeration on blockbuster films or the structure of markets in the broadcasting industry. Yet political economists and feminist scholars understand that patriarchy and capitalism have been historically intertwined in the United States from the nation's founding. This suggests that important connections between patriarchy and capitalism can be discovered by scholars who synthesize feminist and political-economic approaches to media research. It also suggests that our research heritages can be taken as one starting point from which to articulate that synthesis.

To test this, I return to a defining moment in political economy—the Blindspot Debate over the commodity audience, which raged in print in the *Canadian Journal of Political and Social Theory* (Smythe 1977, 1978; Murdock 1978; Livant 1979) and in person (Smythe, Murdock, Garnham) at the 1978 conference of the International Association for Mass Communication Research in Poland. After summarizing the Blindspot Debate, I then return to my own analysis of the commodity audience in national television. I

review that work to tease out the dynamics of patriarchy and capitalism that undergird the markets for commodity ratings and commodity audiences. This particular intersection of feminism and political economy suggests that much can be gained by such revisionist exercises, which, in concert with new syntheses and new approaches to research, may generate an intellectual rapprochement between feminism and political economy in media studies.

What Do the Media Make?

This seemingly innocent question drove the Blindspot Debate. Having posed the question, Smythe (1977) suggested that most critical researchers of the period would respond thus: the media were consciousness industries that made texts (films, television shows, etc.) embodying the dominant ideology, which was absorbed by the average audience member as naturalized, common sense. Hence, media were best studied by decoding texts to uncover the ideology that produced consciousness. Smythe dismissed this as a blindspot of Western Marxism, caused by academic Marxists' overriding concern with ideology and their rejection of both political economy and political action. Smythe next posed his own, then-startling, answer: the media manufactured only one commodity—audiences. By this, Smythe meant that all media assembled, packaged, and sold audiences to advertisers. Content was secondary—a free lunch at best. Media industries were neither dream factories nor consciousness industries: they were hunter-gatherers of the audience.

These bold claims generated considerable debate, with Murdock (1978) taking the lead. Murdock offered a series of differentiations to scale back Smythe's claims. For Murdock, media earning revenues from advertisers were clearly different from media earning revenues directly from audience members. This separated movie studios, book publishers, and recording labels from television networks, newspapers, and magazines. Only advertiser-supported media produced commodity audiences but, for Murdock, even those media could not be reduced to transactions between corporations. He argued that any media artifact operated at two levels: economic and cultural. While the economic level was of greatest interest to media companies, it was less relevant to audiences being processed for sale. The images, ideas, visions, narratives, characters, and performances embodied in the media artifact, and the people comprising the audiences for such artifacts, also needed study. Murdock called for research recognizing the economic and cultural dimensions of commercial media.

Smythe responded by critiquing Murdock and reasserting his central claims. Over the years, other scholars engaged these issues, shifting the focus and testing the claims of the original debate (D'Acci 1994; Jhally 1982; Livant 1982; McCormack 1983; Meehan 1984; Wasko et al. 1993). The phrases "audience commodity" and "commodity audience" entered the critical lexicon. That such a commodity existed and played a crucial role in advertiser-supported media generally became axiomatic in political-economic research on media. Further, as advertising ("product placement") increasingly shaped content in movies and books, the demarcation between advertiser-supported and audience-supported media artifacts thinned. However, for scholars working on reception or representation, the significance of the audience commodity in their decoding of texts or reconstruction of readers' reactions was little appreciated, as pointed out by such critical cultural scholars as Stabile (1995) or Budd, Entman, and Steinem (1990).

Case Study: Broadcasting and Ratings

As Smythe's notion of the audience commodity became established, it also became a focus for research. In my case, that meant exploring the audience commodity in the U.S. system of national broadcasting. My research focused on the corporations that oligopolized network broadcasting (RCA's NBC and CBS in radio; RCA's NBC, CBS, and ABC in television) and in the market where those networks sold, and advertisers bought, the audience commodity. These transactions were highly routinized. The employees who made the deals relied entirely on the ratings book, which specified the number of people in the audience and described them in rough demographic categories. These employees were not executives; they were relatively low-paid and generally female. Yet their labor put together the basic transactions from which networks earned revenues.

These crucial transactions were routinized through dependence on the ratings. This suggested a structural dependence between the market for the audience commodity and the market for ratings. From 1929 to the present, advertisers and networks had typically purchased ratings from a single provider. The buyers' apparent willingness to allow a monopoly suggested that the dynamics in this market deserved closer inspection. Rather than rehearse my research into the history of the ratings industry and the rating market's structuration, I will focus on the results of that research. Four elements that emerged from it are relevant for this discussion.

The first element was shared demand: advertisers and networks demanded measurements of bona fide consumers. Bona fide consumers had the disposable income, access, and desire to loyally purchase brand names and to habitually make impulse purchases. This consumerist caste expanded and contracted in response to capitalism's boom-and-bust cycle. To accommodate the shared demand for consumers, the ratings monopolist selected methods that discriminated against mere listeners or viewers. For example, during the Great Depression, the C. E. Hooper Company used telephone interviews to measure the commodity audience; in the 1975–80 recession, the A. C. Nielsen Company (ACN) based its sample on cable households. In both cases, the measurement method ensured that the sampled households had the funds, desire, and location that allowed them to subscribe to nonessential services. This clearly differentiated the methods and reports of such ratings "research" from social-scientific studies of audience behavior. In ratings, unified demand for the consumerist caste shaped measurement practices.

The second element was the connection between demand and price, which revealed a discontinuity between advertisers' and networks' interests in the size of the commodity audience. The larger the number of bona fide consumers viewing, the higher the price charged by networks. Conversely, the smaller the number, the lower the price. This discontinuity allowed the ratings monopolist to play networks against advertisers, and corporations to form alliances across industries. During the early 1960s, NBC tried to restructure the market by persuading advertisers to shift demand from "how many viewers overall" to "how many viewers between 18 and 34." ABC joined in the campaign and the two networks persuaded advertisers that 18-

to-34-year-olds were better consumers. By 1963, ACN was shifting its sample to emphasize the new demographic; the networks followed by replacing "old favorites" like *The Beverly Hillbillies* and *Petticoat Junction* with "youth-oriented" and "socially relevant" programs like *Mod Squad* and *Storefront Lawyers*. Similarly, in the early 1970s, cable channels used this discontinuity to insert themselves into the relationships among advertisers and networks, and to persuade ACN to measure cable audiences. Discontinuity in demand, then, was used by "players" to renegotiate relationships and restructure the market, thereby changing how the commodity audience was defined and measured.

The third element to emerge was the cybernetic nature of the commodity audience (Mosco 1996). The commodity audience was knowable only through the ratings that measured it and those ratings were the outcome of corporate rivalries, alliances, and manipulations.

This led to the fourth and last element; television's commodity audience had nothing to do with the people who watched television.[1]

These four claims emerged from my institutional analysis of the long-term, impersonal relationships between corporations constituting the markets for commodity ratings and commodity audiences. Building on these claims, I then organized "television" into three markets. The market for commodity ratings served as the fundamental market that set the parameters within which the market for the commodity audience and the market for programming worked.

Three of the Markets Constituting Broadcast Television

The ratings monopolist balanced continuities and discontinuities in demand through its selection of measurement practices. The monopolist responded to continuities in demand by targeting the bona fide consumers demanded by advertisers and broadcasters; unless demanded, the rest of the viewership was unimportant. Discontinuities meant that either the ratings monopolist or blocs of buyers could attempt restructuration of the market for commodity ratings; the monopolist's methods and its definition of the commodity audience responded to shifts in market structuration and participants' power.[2] Given its monopoly position and the pricing conflict that

separated advertisers and networks, the ratings monopolist exercised some agency in selecting its methods, thereby controlling costs of production. All of these economic concerns shaped the ratings reports and ensured that they were commodities—not research.

Based on the ratings commodity, advertisers and networks set to work low-paid, female employees relying on ratings to conduct the transactions in which networks sell their portions of the commodity audience to advertisers. This market and the routinization of its transactions depended entirely on the power relations embodied in the market for commodity ratings. Ratings became the proverbial floor upon which this market rested. And, although ratings were widely dismissed as misleading or inadequate in the trade press, they were treated as absolute truths in this market.

Upon that market was erected yet another structure: the market for programs in which networks, their internal production units, and independent producers negotiated over programs. Decisions here relied on track record, that is, on previous success in the ratings. A proven track record meant either that the production unit's previous series had earned high ratings or that elements of the proposed show had been featured in last year's top-rated programs. Elements included the proposed stars, type of cast, typical plot, genre, and "twist" in the genre's formula.[3] Networks assumed that past success was a predictor of future success—always defining success in terms of the ratings. The ratings, then, shaped decisions about contracts for new series and employment, about casting and plots, about routine and innovative representations.

With track record as the main prognosticator of success, no network would accept—and no producer would propose—a series without a track record.[4] But even the best prognostications go wrong. Historically, most new series are canceled due to poor ratings. Indeed, a tenth of a rating point can mean the difference between retention and cancellation. Thus, commodity ratings set the limits of broadcast programming in the present and the future.

Engendering Markets

For broadcasting, then, Smythe was both correct and incorrect. His analysts revealed that the main product manufactured by networks and sold to advertisers was the commodity audience. But his belief that the ratings monopolist exercised no agency misled him. The political economy of ratings, as summarized above, demonstrated the key role played by the market for commodity ratings and traced the structural forces that constructed ratings as truly *manufactured* commodities whose content depended on changing power relations within that market.

Returning to the main concern of this essay, I now ask: what does a feminist perspective illuminate about these ungendered markets and the ungendered corporations operating within them? My answer is twofold: taking a feminist perspective reveals that societal divisions of labor based on gender, plus prejudicial assumptions about gender, played a significant role in defining and differentiating the commodity audience. To see this, let us return to industrial concerns about the demographics of the commodity audience.

Although age grade became a central concern in the 1960s, the demographic category of gender was an industrial concern for the rating monopolist, advertisers, and broadcasters from at least 1929. Indeed, the female commodity audience had a special place in network schedules: in the daytime, doing housework, listening to talk shows and episodic serials. Both forms of programming were geared toward advertising, whether indirectly using product placements in the script or directly as commercial interruptions. Episodic serials were called soap operas as much for their content as their ownership: soap manufacturers produced the shows and contracted for broadcast time on NBC or CBS to run them. The ratings monopolist[5] treated female audiences as the normal, naturally occurring listenership for daytime programming. During the Great Depression, there was no interest in households without telephones, women who worked outside the home, or men who did not. This carried over into the 1960s and was reflected in Nielsen reports on daytime viewership by women, which carried such titles as *Where the Girls Are.*

Opposite daytime and its female commodity audience was "prime time" and its highly prized male commodity audience. However, prime time was not "where the boys were" but rather where *the* audience was. Networks that couldn't draw *the* audience counterprogrammed for niche audiences, meaning women, or women and children, or African Americans, or Hispanic Americans, or some combination thereof.[6] This subtle shift in language gendered the commodity audience as male and assumed its descent line to be European. Thus the commodity audience was differentiated into the valuable and desired audience of white men produced by the network that won the ratings contest versus the niche audiences begrudgingly produced by networks that lost the ratings contest. As *the* audience, the white male commodity audience had a "higher quality" for which advertisers willingly paid.

The industrial definition of "higher quality" shifted when NBC and ABC succeeded in joining age to gender as the crucial markers of *the* audience. That commodity audience narrowed to the white men aged 18 to 34 within the ACN sample. As cable channels squirmed their way into the mix, cable subscription was added to the industrial definition of *the* audience, yet again narrowing the commodity audience, this time to white male cable subscribers 18 to 34.

With two further modifications in this industrial definition, ACN adjusted its ratings to take into account social status and women's employment outside the home. The long recessionary cycle that spanned 1975–1989 coincided with second-wave feminism. Through the same period, the Reagan and Bush administrations' monetarist policies effectively transferred wealth from the general population to the elite, promoted the exportation of heavy industrial operations, discouraged wage increases for workers of middle or lower social status, and encouraged companies to replace employees with temporary contractees (Bluestone and Harrison 1982). Among other things, these synergistic policies brought more women generally, and more college-educated women specifically, into the documented workforce. In such two-income households may be seen one effect of second-wave feminism: these women generally retained some control over their earnings.

In any case, ACN expanded its demographic categories to include "working women" as well as the terms "upscale" and "downscale" to identify the social status attached to occupation and income. For advertisers, upscale white male cable subscribers aged 18 to 34 watching television during prime time became the most valued and demanded commodity audience. Daytime remained women's time, although upscale women 18 to 34 and upscale working women 18 to 34 using video-cassette recorders to tape programs were more highly valued than mere housewives. Among the new niche audiences for prime time, the category of upscale white working women aged 18 to 34 and subscribing to cable had sufficient attraction for advertisers that networks designed programs blending elements of soap operas into action-adventure programs.[7]

This periodic narrowing of *the* audience demonstrates the difference between the commodity audience and the people who actually watch television. It also suggests that noneconomic assumptions undergird beliefs about what sorts of people *ought* to be *the* audience and that those assumptions follow familiar patterns of discrimination on the grounds of gender, race, social status, sexual orientation, and age. Given limitations of space, I will discuss only the assumptions about gender.

Such institutionalized sexism might be dismissed as pragmatic given certain assumptions about gender and money: most of the workforce was male; men earned more than women; thus more men had more to spend than women regardless of women's occupations. Advertisers wanted spenders, so networks and cable channels had to target men to meet advertisers' demand for spenders.

According to these assumptions, the three markets operated rationally by discriminating against women. The market for commodity ratings necessarily placed greater value on measurements of males than on measurements of females. The market for the commodity audience rationally preferred buying the male commodity audience in prime time and treated the female commodity audience as a special niche with limited and time-specific appeal. When some of that latter commodity audience gained and controlled income, they become a very special niche—one that could be attracted through the manipulation of subtexts in male-oriented programming. That left the market for prime-time programming gearing production for the male commodity audience, but with female-friendly elements to attract the subniche of upscale women. Television was largely in the business of men—counting them, characterizing them, selling them, and programming for them. As long as "society" defined men as the proverbial breadwinners, that social reality

governed the decisions of advertisers, networks, and the ratings monopolist.

Of course, that argument could be countered on its own stereotypical grounds: a sexist society may have defined men as breadwinners, but it also defined women as spenders. In the patriarchal division of domestic labor, woman's work included shopping for the household's general needs, for her own needs, and for the man's needs. The idealized version of that division of labor sent men outside the home to work for wages and women to spend those wages by shopping. Through their shopping, women assembled the materials necessary for men to rest and recuperate. If advertisers wanted to reach spenders, then they needed to target that category of people socially designated as spenders: women. Could advertisers have been blinded by sexism?

That question, posed ironically, has played out concretely in the history of two cable channels: ESPN and Lifetime. ESPN was launched in 1979 as a twenty-four-hour sports channel. It quickly gained acceptance from advertisers and cable operators. Now 80 percent owned by the Walt Disney Company, ESPN has added three more sports channels (ESPN-2, ESPN Classic, and ESPN News) and a chain of restaurant/entertainment complexes called ESPNZone. While ESPN attracts mostly male viewers, it has not been categorized as a narrowcaster—that is, a channel serving a niche audience with highly defined and delimited tastes (Walt Disney 1998).

In contrast, since its launch in 1984, Lifetime has consistently been treated as a narrowcaster reaching a small niche audience—women. As part of ABC's and Hearst's joint ventures in cable (A&E, Lifetime), the channel enjoyed success in terms of inclusion on cable systems but struggled to attract advertisers (Byars and Meehan 1994). Eventually, Lifetime reorganized its prime time schedule in an attempt to attract upscale heterosexual couples.[8] That seemed to turn the trick for Lifetime, which now carries extensive advertising for everything from aspirin to cars.

With Disney's acquisition of ABC, Lifetime seemed poised to launch a second channel targeting women in their teens and twenties, but nothing came of it.[9] Although Disney's 1998 annual report extolled the transformation of ESPN from cable channel into franchise, no similar plans seem to be on the horizon for Lifetime (Walt Disney 1998). While audience gender is not the only variable differentiating the corporate histories of these two channels, this sketch suggests that being a "channel for men who love sports" places a company in a position significantly different from being "television for women."

Feminism and Political Economy

When reanalyzed from a feminist perspective, my case study of broadcast ratings yielded an unexpected finding: a structural contradiction between patriarchy and capitalism embodied in a fundamental market in the television industry, and effecting the structure of two derivative markets. The structure of the market for commodity ratings assumed that men controlled both wages and spending, making them *the* audience. But the market structure ignored similarly patriarchal assumptions about the domestic division of labor that assigned the household's shopping to women. While men as breadwinners and women as shoppers fits into the patriarchal division of labor that was idealized in the 1950s, the fact remains that women have always worked in this country. Not only have women been allotted a considerable share of the caretaking and household purchasing, but women have sought and secured paid work.

Paralleling the social status of men's blue-collar occupations have been women's pink-collar jobs: grocery clerk, secretary, domestic worker, telephone operator, nurse, farm worker, court reporter, teacher, etc. These occupations typically offered lower wages than those paid for blue-collar jobs, regardless of the levels of skill—suggesting that the patriarchal devaluation of women was echoed in capitalism's wage structure. For the market in commodity audiences, that would make male earners a better buy, but only if they adhered to a nonpatriarchal division of domestic labor. With a patriarchal division, an audience of female shoppers was the better buy. Because this contradiction was not articulated in the demand for commodity ratings, the ratings monopolist had no reason to investigate or to resolve it.

One might expect that contradiction to emerge and be resolved in the 1980s as political-economic changes forced more women into the workplace and into white-collar occupations. As women achieved

greater—though not perfect—economic equality, they would seem likely candidates for inclusion in *the* audience. Yet, despite the ratings monopolist's adoption of categories to sort viewers by occupational status, women remained marginalized as niches. Males remained the object of the rating firm's art, with upscale males the most prized trophies.

This makes little economic sense. In capitalism, money is supposed to be the great leveler. Arbitrary social distinctions that unfairly oppress individuals are supposed to evaporate when people enter the market for goods and services as consumers, or when they offer themselves as labor. The logic of profit should drive advertisers to demand shoppers regardless of the gender, social status, race, age, ethnicity, sexual orientation, etc., of the particular people buying the bars of soap, rolls of toilet paper, or cans of beans. Why, then, do such distinctions persist in the markets for commodity ratings and commodity audiences—in markets where companies essentially trade in people?

A feminist political economy allows us to answer that question in terms of both gender and social status. The overvaluing of a male audience reflects the sexism of patriarchy as surely as the overvaluing of an upscale audience reflects the classism of capitalism. Each practice is rooted in the illogic of prejudice, that is, in the ideologies naturalizing the oppression of women and of working people.[10] Those ideologies shape corporate decisions such that corporations structure markets as instruments of oppression and not as liberatory spaces. Indeed, restructuring markets to foster the liberation of women and working people would actually undermine the interests of individual capitalists and of capitalism, which profit from disparities in income and oppressive social relations. From this perspective, television is structured to discriminate against anyone outside the commodity audience of white, 18-to-34-year-old, heterosexual, English-speaking, upscale men. This recognition is crucial to scholarly work on television. Whatever amenities or pleasures television offers to viewers outside *the* commodity audience, television is an instrument of oppression.

Notes

1. Because Smythe assumed that the audience commodity and the viewership were identical, I use commodity

audience to differentiate the manufactured audience from the viewership.

2. Other possibilities may exist; these are the two that I have identified.

3. "Twists" are minor innovations in plot, character, props, setting, etc., that are used to differentiate among series building on similar track records. Twists and track record are typically balanced. For example, the more recent series *Nash Bridges* was derived from *Miami Vice*. Both starred Don Johnson; both were crime dramas about an ensemble of undercover police officers who wore stylish outfits, talked tough, raced about in luxury cars, and were frequently lectured by a senior officer. In *Miami Vice*, the authority figure was the unit's enigmatic captain; in *Nash Bridges*, an internal affairs officer investigating the unit. Here the twist is gender: the investigator was cast as a stylishly dressed woman who also served as Bridges's love interest. Where officers in *Miami Vice* experienced considerable moral ambiguity, *Nash Bridges* maintained a clear division between cops and robbers. Where *Miami Vice* specialized in a brooding, enigmatic atmosphere, *Nash Bridges* struck an upbeat note through the use of bright lighting for indoor scenes. Where Johnson's character and his partner drove through Miami at night, Nash and his partner raced around an eternally sunny San Francisco. On *Miami Vice*, Johnson's character lacked stable and fulfilling relationships outside his work. On *Nash Bridges*, Johnson's character had good relationships at work and at home: he easily led his unit, had established a personal friendship with his investigator, acted as a loving and protective father to his daughter, and seemed to be a dutiful, if skeptical, son to his father.

4. This has encouraged producers "pitching" innovative shows in terms of old shows; the best-known example, perhaps, being Gene Roddenberry's attempt to persuade network executives that a science fiction drama targeting adults should be thought of as a Western: *Star Trek* was really *Wagon Train* set in outer space.

5. The American Association of Advertising Agencies and the Association of National Advertisers owned the Cooperative Analysis of Broadcasting, which provided ratings only to those AAAA and ANA members that subscribed to the service. CAB conducted telephone surveys with a long list of questions asking respondents to recount every fifteen minutes of radio listening done the day prior to contact. Unsurprisingly, CAB reported low ratings. The C. E. Hooper Company capitalized on the networks' discontent while offering advertisers and agencies results from telephone surveys that asked for a report of current listening and of listening during the previous fifteen minutes. Greater accuracy combined with a lower cost from expanding the buyer base worked: CEH

monopolized broadcast ratings throughout the "golden age" of radio. ACN achieved monopolistic control over network radio and television in the 1950s. It maintains its monopoly over television ratings to the present day and has extended operations into web site ratings.

6. Little if any interest has been expressed in Native Americans or viewers descended from immigrants from Asia or the Pacific Rim.

7. For example, in *Miami Vice*, the melodrama centered on whether Johnson's character would recover from the death of his previous partner, form a bond with his current partner, and sort out his love life. In *Nash Bridges*, the melodrama focuses on the continuing story of one man's family. Johnson's character must deal with the romance between his daughter and one of his subordinates, maintain his relationship with his father, and transform the woman investigating his operations from antagonist to friend and, perhaps, lover.

8. Personal interview with Judy Girard, head of programming, Lifetime, New York, 1995.

9. Personal interview with Douglas McCormack, Chief Executive Officer, Lifetime, New York, 1995.

10. Although the particular dynamics shift as demographic categories shift, I believe that the basic analysis holds for people of color, speakers of languages other than English, people younger or older than the valued age grade, gay men, lesbians, etc. One would look for dynamics rooted in colonialism, ageism, heterosexism, etc., and trace the connections to patriarchy and/or capitalism.

References

Andersen, Robin. 1995. *Consumer Culture and TV Programming.* Boulder: Westview Press.

Arnold, June. 1976. "Feminist Presses and Feminist Politics." *Quest: A Feminist Quarterly* 3(1): 18–26.

Bluestone, Barry and Bennett Harrison. 1982. *The Deindustrialization of America: Plant Closings, Community Abandonment, and the Dismantling of Basic Industries.* New York: Basic Books.

Brabant, Sarah. 1976. "Sex Role Stereotyping in the Sunday Comics." *Sex Roles* 2(4): 331–37.

Budd, Mike, Robert M. Entman, and Clay Steinman. 1990. "The Affirmative Character of U.S. Cultural Studies." *Critical Studies in Mass Communication* 7(2): 169–84.

Busby, Linda J. 1975. "Sex-Role Research on the Mass Media." *Journal of Communication* 25(4): 107–31.

Byars, Jackie. 1991. *All That Hollywood Allows: Re-Reading Gender in 1950s Melodrama.* Chapel Hill: University of North Carolina Press.

—— and Chad Dell. 1992. "Big Differences on the Small Screen: Race, Class, Gender, Feminine Beauty, and the Characters in *Frank's Place*." In *Women Making Meaning:*

New Feminist Directions in Communication, ed. L. Rakow. New York: Routledge. 191–208.

——— and Eileen R. Meehan. 1994. "Once in a Lifetime: Constructing 'The Working Woman' through Cable Narrowcasting." *Camera Obscura* 33–34: 13–41.

Cantor, Muriel G. 1977a. "Women and Public Broadcasting." *Journal of Communication* 27(1): 14–19.

———. 1977b. "Our Days and Our Nights on TV." *Journal of Communication* 29(4): 66–73.

Carey, James. 1995. "Abolishing the Old Spirit World." *Critical Studies in Mass Communication* 12(1): 82–89.

D'Acci, Julie. 1994. *Defining Women: Television and the Case of "Cagney and Lacey."* Chapel Hill: University of North Carolina Press.

Gerbner, George, ed. 1983. "Ferment in the Field," *Journal of Communication* 33(3).

Grossberg, Lawrence. 1994. "Can Cultural Studies Find True Happiness in Communication?" In *Defining Media Studies: Reflections on the Future of the Field*, eds. M. Gurevitch and M. Levy. New York: Oxford University Press. 331–39.

Gurevitch, Michael and Marc Levy, eds.1994. *Defining Media Studies: Reflections on the Future of the Field*. New York: Oxford University Press.

Holly, Susan. 1979. "Women in Management of Weeklies." *Journalism Quarterly* 56(4): 810–15.

Janus, Noreene Z. 1977. "Research on Sex-Roles in the Mass Media: Toward a Critical Approach." *Insurgent Sociologist* 7(3): 19–32.

Jhally, Sut. 1982. "Probing the Blindspot: The Audience Commodity." *Canadian Journal of Political and Social Theory* 6(1–2): 204–10.

Lemon, Judith L. 1977. "Women and Blacks on Primetime Television." *Journal of Communication* 27(4): 70–79.

Livant, Bill. 1979. "The Audience Commodity: On the 'Blindspot' Debate." *Canadian Journal of Political and Social Theory* 3(1): 91–106.

———. 1982. "Working at Watching: A Reply to Sut Jhally." *Canadian Journal of Political and Social Theory* 6(1–2): 211–15.

Martin, Michele. 1991. *Hello, Central? Gender, Technology, and Culture in the Formation of Telephone Systems*. Montreal: McGill-Queen's University Press.

Marzolf, Marion, Ramona R. Rush, and Darlene Stern. 1974–1975. "The Literature of Women in Journalism History." *Journalism History* 1(4): 117–28.

McChesney, Robert W. 1994. "Critical Communications Research at the Crossroads." In *Defining Media Studies: Reflections on the Future of the Field*, eds. M. Gurevitch and M. Levy. New York: Oxford University Press. 340–46.

McCormack, Thelma. 1983. "The Political Content and the Press of Canada." *Canadian Journal of Political Science* 16(3): 451–72.

Meehan, Eileen R. 1984. "Ratings and the Institutional Approach." *Critical Studies in Mass Communication* 1: 216–25.

———. 1990. "Why We Don't Count." In *Logics of Television*, ed. P. Mellencamp. Bloomington: Indiana University Press. 117–37.

———. 1991. "Holy Commodity Fetish, Batman!: The Political Economy of a Commercial Intertext." In *The Many Lives of Batman: Critical Approaches to a Superhero and His Media*, eds. W. Uricchio and R. Pearson. New York: Routledge. 47–65.

———. 1999. "Commodity, Culture, Common Sense: Media Research and Paradigm Dialogue." *Journal of Media Economics* 12(2): 149–63.

Meehan, Eileen R., Vincent Mosco, and Janet Wasko. 1994. "Rethinking Political Economy: Change and Continuity." In *Defining Media Studies: Reflections on the Future of the Field*, eds. M. Gurevitch and M. Levy. New York: Oxford University Press. 347–58.

Morris, Monica B. 1973. "Newspapers and the New Feminists: Blackout as Social Control?" *Journalism Quarterly* 50: 37–42.

Mosco, Vincent. 1996. *The Political Economy of Communication*. London: Sage.

Murdock, Graham. 1978. "Blindspots about Western Marxism: A Reply to Dallas Smythe." *Canadian Journal of Political and Social Theory* 2(2): 109–19.

Ogan, Christine L., and David H. Weaver. 1978–79. "Job Satisfaction in Selected U.S. Daily Newspapers: A Study of Male and Female Top Managers." *Mass Communications Review* 6: 20–26.

Poe, Alison. 1976. "Active Women in Ads." *Journal of Communication* 26(4): 185–92.

Poole, Ithiel de Sola, and Herbert L. Schiller. 1981. "Perspectives on Communications Research: An Exchange." *Journal of Communication* 31(3): 15–23.

Radway, Janice. 1984. *Reading the Romance: Women, Patriarchy, and Popular Culture*. Chapel Hill: University of North Carolina Press.

Schiller, Dan. 1994. "Back to the Future: Prospects for Study of Communication as a Social Force." In *Defining Media Studies: Reflections on the Future of the Field*, eds. M. Gurevitch and M. Levy. New York: Oxford University Press. 359–66.

Smythe, Dallas W. 1977. "Communications: Blindspot of Western Marxism." *Canadian Journal of Political and Social Theory* 1(3): 1–27.

———. 1978. "Rejoinder to Graham Murdock." *Canadian Journal of Political and Social Theory* 2: 120–29.

St. John, Jacqueline D. 1978. "Sex Role Stereotyping in Early Broadcast History: The Career of Mary Margaret McBride." *Frontiers: Journal of Women's Studies* 3(3): 31–38.

Stabile, Carole A. 1995. "Resistance, Recuperation, and Reflexivity: The Limits of a Paradigm." *Critical Studies in Mass Communication* 12(4): 403–22.

Steeves, H. Leslie. 1993. "Creating Imagined Communities: Development Communication and the Challenge of Feminism." *Journal of Communication* 43(3): 218–29.

Steeves, H. Leslie, Sam Becker, and Hyeon Choi. 1988. "The Context of Employed Women's Media Use." *Women's Studies in Communication* 11(2): 21–43.

Streicher, Helen White. 1974. "The Girls in the Cartoons." *Journal of Communication* 24(2): 125–29.

Tuchman, Gaye, Arlene Kaplan Daniels, and James Benet, eds. 1978. *Hearth and Home: Images of Women in the Mass Media.* New York: Oxford University Press.

Walt Disney Corporation. 1998. *1998 Annual Report.* http://corporate.disney.go.com/investors/annual_reports/1998/index.html

Wasko, Janet, Vincent Mosco, and Manjunath Pendakur, eds. 1993. *Illuminating the Blindspots: Essays Honoring Dallas W. Smythe.* Norwood: Ablex.

12.
HIDING HOMOEROTICISM IN PLAIN VIEW
The Fight Club *DVD as Digital Closet*
Robert Alan Brookey and Robert Westerfelhaus

During an interview at Yale University, Edward Norton had this to say about his recent film, *Fight Club:*

> I hope it rattles people. I hope it dunks it very squarely in your lap because I think one of the things we strove very specifically to do with this was on some levels retain a kind of a moral ambivalence or a moral ambiguity–not to deliver a neatly wrapped package of meaning into your lap. Or in any way that let you walk away from the film like this, comfortable in having been told what you should make of it. (Norton, 2000)

As explained by Norton, *Fight Club* was deliberately designed to activate the audience, to force them to draw their own moral conclusions, to antagonize them. The film's goal, according to Norton, is summed up in words he attributes to its director, David Fincher: "If it doesn't piss off a healthy number of people then we've done something wrong."

Norton's comments were available to a much larger audience than the one he addressed at Yale when his interview was included on the *Fight Club* DVD. The DVD format has gained popularity in part because it can offer this type of supplemental material to the consumer. In the first half of 2000, approximately 2.7 million DVD players were shipped (DVD video, 2000). For the year 2001, it is projected that 28 million players will be shipped worldwide, making the DVD "the fastest-growing consumer electronics product in history" (Abraham, 2001, p. 12). A casual glance around the local video store reveals that more and more shelf space has been given over to DVD products. In short,

the DVD has emerged as an increasingly popular method for delivering cinematic products, one that may soon replace VHS videotape as the preferred medium for viewing at-home movies.

The rising popularity of DVDs is understandable, given the advantages the format has over standard VHS videotape. The overall quality of the digital image and sound is superior to that of analog videotape. The DVD format holds substantially more information than the VHS format, and is thus able to offer consumers features previously unavailable. Many DVDs include interviews, like the interview with Norton on the *Fight Club* DVD. These interviews are often with those involved in making the film: actors, directors, screenwriters, and so on. Some DVDs include running commentaries, in which such people discuss the film while it is playing. Additionally, DVDs often include "behind the scenes" clips, production notes, and storyboards. DVD technology makes all this material available interactively, allowing viewers to decide what they want to view, when, and in what order. Thus, the DVD offers more material for the viewer to consume than either the theatrical release of a film or the standard VHS version, and it does so in a way that affords the viewer greater control over the viewing experience.

To illustrate our point, we offer a critical analysis of the DVD for the film *Fight Club*. We argue that the supplemental material included on the DVD is used to make the product more marketable to mainstream audiences by framing the homoerotic elements of the film as homosocial behavior. In the following section, we explain our theory of the DVD. We then go on to identify and discuss issues relevant to our analysis of the *Fight Club* DVD, and then we offer the analysis itself. Although Norton suggests that *Fight Club* is a film open to interpretation, we conclude that the DVD version may actually limit interpretation.

Extra Text and Auteuristic Residue

As we have noted, the DVD version of a film typically offers consumers additional material not included in the film's theatrical release or video version. The *Fight Club* DVD is no exception. These materials are similar to the "secondary texts" that John Fiske (1987) describes in his book *Television Culture*. In addition to "primary texts" (actual television programs), Fiske argues that there exist "secondary texts" (criticism, interviews, promotional articles, and other materials) that function intertextually to favor selected readings of primary texts. Fiske notes that while his use of these concepts is specific to television, they are informed by theories of intertextuality that have been applied to film. For example, such inter-textual relationships have helped the producers of the James Bond films change preferred readings to accommodate cultural and political shifts and thus maintain the economic viability of the franchise (Bennett & Woollacott, 1987).

Like traditional secondary texts, the additional material included on DVDs also can be used to increase a film's profitability. We suggest, however, that they do so in a way that blurs the distinction between primary and secondary texts as they have been conceived and made use of in the past. For example, many DVDs offer running commentaries that provide the viewer with the option of listening to the film's director, actors, and even screenwriters voice opinions about the film as it is playing. Given this blurred distinction, we have decided to call the additional material available on the DVD-"extra text." We use the word "extra" because the material resides outside of, and in addition to, the cinematic text as traditionally defined by film criticism–i.e., the parameters of the theatrical release. Although extra-text materials function in a way similar to secondary texts, we do not believe the term "secondary" fully conveys the signifying relationship they have with the primary-cinematic text. Primary and secondary texts are usually physically distinct from one another and are often read at

different times, creating an intertextual relationship that is marked by both temporal and spatial distance. However, by including such distinct but interrelated texts in a self-contained package, the DVD turns this intertextual relationship into an intratextual relationship. Thus, the DVD is perhaps the ultimate example of media-industry synergy, in which the promotion of a media product is collapsed into the product itself. Judicious use of DVD-extra text can exploit this intratextual advantage as a means of promoting the film.

Although citing negative reviews is not a traditional method of promoting a film, the packaging of the *Fight Club* DVD prominently displays excerpts from negative reviews and does so in a way that simultaneously celebrates the reviews and mocks the reviewers. Included with the DVD is a pamphlet entitled "How to Start a Fight," which contains several negative quotes from reviews of the film interspersed with positive quotes from people involved in the film's production that serve as rebuttals. This juxtaposition works to undermine the credibility of the negative reviews. For example, Alexander Walker of the *London Evening Standard* is quoted as attacking *Fight Club* as: "an inadmissible assault on personal decency. And on society itself" (How to Start a Fight, 2000, p. 14). This quote is juxtaposed with one from Kevin McCormick, identified as "Former Executive Vice President of Production, Fox 2000 Pictures," the studio that produced the film:

> I was really surprised by the intensity of the reaction, but for me it only made it more clear what an extraordinary movie it was, and made me certain that it will be well remembered. Remember that the witch in *Snow White* was controversial in its day. Anything new is going to be controversial.
>
> (How to Start a Fight, 2000, p. 14)

In contrasting the two quotes thus, McCormick's observation provides a rebuttal that suggests Walker's negative comments are, at best, shortsighted.

This is but one example that illustrates how DVD-extra text can function rhetorically in attempting to shape viewer interpretation. Individuals involved in the film's production are presented in the extra text as having privileged insights regarding a film's meaning and purpose and, as such, they are used to articulate a "proper" (i.e., sanctioned) interpretation. This privileged positioning may be best understood as a return to "auteurism." As Lapsley and Westlake (1988) explain, auteurism was an approach to film criticism that "grounded itself in the commonplaces of the romantic notion of the artist, thereby gaining film entry to the hallowed canon of Art" (p. 105). According to "auteurism" theory, a film is an expression of a unique artistic vision, usually that of its director. In the past, this notion was rendered problematic by the structure of the traditional studio industry that valued profit before art. This problem has been further exacerbated in recent years by the emergence of media conglomerates that produce films which reflect a variety of commercial as well as aesthetic decisions reached by corporate committees (Bart, 2000). Therefore, it is difficult to view such films as expressions of some auteur's unique artistic vision. Lapsley and Westlake (1988) note that the auteur was pretty much abandoned as a theoretical construct for scholarly film criticism back in the late sixties. They go on to point out, however, that auteurism remains in the mainstream discussion of film like an ideological residue. In contemporary popular discourse on film, the concept of the auteur has expanded to include actors and screenwriters in addition to directors who, because of their involvement in the making of a film, are also thought to possess privileged knowledge about it.

Media conglomerates have a vested interest in maintaining the ideology of the auteur because it facilitates the promotion of their products. For example, when Warner Brothers releases a film, it has those involved in the making of the film appear in magazines and on television programs owned by AOL/Time Warner; the director might be interviewed in *Time* and the actors in *Entertainment Weekly* (a publication owned by AOL/Time Warner). In this way, media conglomerates exercise partial control over the publicity for their products. However, they can never be sure that those who view the film are the same people who read the magazine articles or see the television shows.

In contrast, DVD-extra text offers those marketing a film an intratextual advantage that significantly increases the chances that promotional tactics will reach their target audience. By collapsing promotion into the product, DVD-extra text can more effectively

exploit the ideology of the auteur than is possible through the use of traditional secondary texts. The extra text offers consumers access to commentary by those involved with making the film, and it positions this commentary as authoritative. Such extra-text features can direct the viewer toward preferred interpretations of the primary text while undermining unfavorable interpretations, especially those that might hurt the product's commercial success. The DVD format increases the likelihood that viewers will be exposed to these promotional tactics, thereby lending such tactics greater rhetorical force. In the past, the comments of a screenwriter–for example, in the context of a magazine or newspaper interview–enjoyed very little rhetorical force because they were far removed from the cinematic experience of viewing the film in a theater. The DVD format, however, collapses exposure to promotional material into the experience of viewing the film by bringing the film and its makers' commentary about it into close proximity, temporally and spatially; hence, DVD-extra text's intratextual advantage over traditional forms of secondary texts.

Another rhetorical advantage of DVD intertextuality is the fact that it is experienced interactively, investing the viewer with a greater (perceived) sense of agency. The extra text of the *Fight Club* DVD, and the preferred interpretation that it seeks to promote, are not forced upon the viewer.[1] Instead, the viewer must actively explore the DVD in order to discern how the film's makers believe it should be interpreted. In this way, the viewers are positioned as active agents who do not passively subject themselves to the privileged opinions of the film's auteurs, but instead uncover them through acts of digital discovery–or so it would seem. In theorizing about the "interactivity" of digital media, Greg Smith (1999) argues that a "fantasy" is perpetuated in which such interactivity is perceived as providing the viewer choice about and control over media consumption. Smith notes that this fantasy of interactivity presupposes that other older forms of media (TV and film) are consumed passively, though it has been established that people actively engage these. Smith argues critics should expose the "hype" of digital interactivity, and the contradiction of the DVD reveals the hype surrounding its own interactivity. DVD technology seems to empower the consumer by making available a wider range of viewing choices than were previously available on other formats. These choices, however, have been carefully selected by those involved in making and marketing the product, and may include material that points to a preferred interpretation of the film. These limited "choices," and the way they are strategically arranged for access, can serve to circumvent alternative interpretations.

The participation of the DVD viewer, however, does not begin and end with the interactivity that we have described. The terrain of media technology is littered with embarrassing failures: the eight-track tape player, quadraphonic sound, Beta-Max, and even earlier versions of videodisk technology. Therefore, the consumers of a new and emerging media technology have a financial and personal investment in the technology they purchase: no one wants to believe they have just bought the next eight-track. Not only does purchasing a DVD player involve a financial investment, but the rental and purchase cost of DVDs can also be higher than that of the VHS format. DVD consumers have an economic incentive to access and view DVD-extra text (it justifies the additional expenditure) and to regard it as a valuable addition to their viewing experience. Indeed, if they felt that the extra text added nothing to their viewing experience, they might well conclude that they are not realizing the full value of their investment. We suggest, then, that DVD viewers are "invested viewers," who have an incentive to allow their viewing experience to be directed–at least in part–by the DVD-extra text, and to believe that the interpretation that text offers is worth their time and money.

In summary, we contend that DVD-extra text operates as a complex rhetorical object. It collapses the functions of the secondary texts into the product of the primary text, and gives the signifying force of intertextual relationships an intratextual advantage. It can evoke the ideological residue of the "auteur," and do so in a way that directs the viewers' experiences of the film. Finally, because it is a new, interactive, technology, the DVD may actually invest the viewers in the interpretation that it offers. Simply put, the DVD is not just a new way of repackaging a film for distribution; it is a synergistic package comprised of product and promotion. Perhaps the best evidence of this rhetorical use of extra text can be found in reviews of the *Fight Club* DVD.

When it was first released in theaters, *Fight Club* received mixed reviews and earned box office receipts that dropped precipitously after the first weekend. This drop might have been due to scathing reviews given the film by several high profile critics. For example, Kenneth Turan (1999) of the *Los Angeles Times* wrote, "What's most troubling about this witless mishmash of whiny, infantile philosophizing and bone-crunching violence is the increasing realization that it actually thinks it's saying something of significance. That is a scary notion indeed" (p. 1). David Thomson (1999), writing for *The New York Times*, had such a low opinion of *Fight Club* that he spent most of his review discussing Fincher's other films. The extent of Thomson's contempt is brought home when, in the conclusion of his review, he gives away the film's ending. Finally, Roger Ebert of the *Chicago Sun-Times* (1999) joined his fellow critics in denouncing the film's violence: "*Fight Club* is the most frankly and cheerfully fascist big-star movie since *Death Wish*, a celebration of violence in which the heroes write themselves a license to drink, smoke, screw and beat one another up" (p. 1).

When *Fight Club* was released on DVD, however, some critics suggested that the extra text it included offered fresh and valuable insights about the film. Some of these critics used Ebert's review as a point of contrast. For example, in a review for *DailyRadar. com*, Tom Chick (2000) mentions how Norton, in the running commentary, explains the Buddhist principle "[t]hat is the arc of the movie" (p. 5). Accordingly, Chick suggests the film is not a celebration, but a rejection of fascism. As he notes, "The fact that this last step is lost on Ebert is a fine example of not only how lazy a critic he is but also how widely the movie was misinterpreted" (Chick, 2000, p. 5). In a review for the *WCBE Public Arts* web page, Mikel Ellis (2001) also cites Ebert's negative review, but argues that the *Fight Club* DVD provides an understanding of the film's violence:

> Perhaps *Fight Club*'s paradox is that it consciously provokes response and is still able to sidestep the pedantic overkill that usually accompanies mainstream filmmaking. Your appreciation of *Fight Club* becomes a Rorschach for your willingness to tolerate the existential stick in the eye. The DVD doesn't ameliorate the stick, but it does a brilliant job of showing you who is holding the other end.
>
> (p. 2)

The reviews by Ellis and Chick illustrate the point we have made about the rhetorical force of the DVD.

The popular press treated the DVD as a new and different product, and many publications devoted separate sections to DVD criticism. Critical reviews of the *Fight Club* DVD provide an interesting comparison and contrast to the reviews of the film. As a point of comparison, both the film and DVD critics operate under the ideology of the auteur, and make frequent references to Fincher and other people involved in the film. As a point of contrast, reviewers of the DVD suggest that the extra material it includes provided them with deeper and better insights than they otherwise would have had. For example, in *American Cinematographer*, Chris Pizzello (2000) offers this observation about the running commentaries on the *Fight Club* DVD: "[a]ll of the commentaries are worthy and interesting, but the writers deliver the most illuminating observations. *Fight Club* is a movie of provocative ideas, and who better to explain them than [Chuck] Palahniuk" (p. 23). Gary Crowdus (2000), in his review for *Cineaste*, is even more direct in his assessment of the value of the *Fight Club* DVD. After noting that many of the film's "critics became morally exercised over the film's mano-a-mano violence," and were "apoplectic about what they perceived to be its 'fascist' politics" (p. 47), he goes on to argue that those critics "seemed almost willfully oblivious to the fact that the filmmakers provided a comic or dramatic context for every fight" (p. 47). Crowdus argues that the DVD version goes "a long way toward clarifying the filmmaker's intentions," and he expresses the hope that "at least one of the major critics who trashed the film on its theatrical release will screen the DVD, reconsider their critical stance, and . . . publicly and remorsefully confess the obtuseness of their initial pronunciamento in a *Variety* cover story" (pp. 46 & 48).

That the critics claim to have divined the proper interpretation of *Fight Club* from the DVD illustrates that text's rhetorical function. This text challenges the film critic because it can be used to delegitimate unfavorable critiques–both by addressing those that have already been voiced and by attempting to preempt those that might be expressed. In order to meet this challenge, the critics of the DVD must not only critique the text of the film, but also analyze how their interpretation is addressed by the extra text. Our analysis of the *Fight Club* DVD illustrates how this type

of critical approach might proceed. We do not offer this analysis as the definitive critical approach to this emerging technology, but as a starting point for future theorizing and criticism. Before proceeding with our analysis, we point out why we believe our interpretation is one that the producers and promoters of *Fight Club* might want to dismiss.

The Queer Take

Fight Club's violence was not the only aspect of the film to attract attention. Some critics found the film implicitly homoerotic. Andrew O'Hehir (1999) of *Salon.com* writes: "You certainly can't say that Fincher or screenwriter Jim Uhls . . . hold back on the film's psychological subtext–*Fight Club* opens with our nameless narrator [Norton] tied to a chair with Tyler's, uh, gun in his mouth" (1999, p. 1).[2] In an interview in the *Village Voice*, director Fincher discounts the homoerotic subtext. After the interviewer, Amy Taubin (1999) mentions what she describes as the "strong homoerotic undercurrent," Fincher remarks, "I think it's beyond sexuality. The way the narrator looks up to Tyler and wants to please him and get all of his attention doesn't seem to me to have anything to do with sex" (p. 2). Although we do not offer Fincher's denial of homoerotic subtext in the film as evidence of collusion with the producers of *Fight Club*, his comments were economically judicious considering that *Fight Club* was marketed to a young male audience, the type of audience to which overt male homosexual representation seldom appeals (Nilles, 2001).

Although the representation of queer experience has increased dramatically over the last few years, this increase has not necessarily coincided with mainstream commercial success. As R. Ruby Rich (2000) notes, in spite of the crossover success of such films as *Boys Don't Cry* and *Gods and Monsters*, Queer cinema has remained, for the most part, a niche market targeted to a specific and limited audience. In addition, mainstream media depicting queer experience have been very careful to avoid sexual representation (Brookey, 1996; Brookey & Westerfelhaus, 2001; Dow, 2001). In spite of the qualified successes of Queer cinema, homoerotic representation in general, and male homosexual representation in particular, do not deliver big box office receipts.

In a more general sense, the mass media are driven by a meta-ideology that Sender (1999) calls the ethic of consumption. Success is measured in profits, and the greatest profits are earned by appealing to the largest possible demographic market, the so-called mainstream, which as a group has proven to be heterosexist and homophobic in its consuming habits. The exclusion of gay characters–and consequently gay culture, relationships, and sexuality–has been one simple and effective method used to appeal to this profitable market (Kielwasser & Wolf, 1992; Russo, 1987).[3] There are, however, compelling commercial reasons for including depictions of gays in the mass media. A segment of the gay community–affluent, urban, well educated, and predominantly white males–now comprise a very appealing and profitable niche market (Fejes & Petrich, 1993). In addition, inclusion of certain sanctioned types of gay characters–though not overt gay sexuality–has proven capable of attracting mainstream audiences and thus generating large profits.

Advertisers, filmmakers, television programmers, and others employ several rhetorical strategies to market media offerings that include gay themes and gay characters to mainstream audiences. One strategy that comforts mainstream audiences depicts gays in ways that support rather than threaten the heterosexist order. This taming is done by having gay characters serve as comedic foils to heterosexual leads, by portraying them as asexual and apolitical, and by depicting them as self-policing and impossibly perfect protectors of the heterosexist socio-sexual order (Brookey & Westerfelhaus, 2001; Dow, 2001; Fejes, 2000; Russo, 1987). A second strategy portrays gays in negative terms–as depressed and disturbed, as pathetic victims, or as dangerous predators–and thus reaffirms homophobic biases held by many mainstream audience members (Fejes & Petrich, 1993; Russo, 1987). A third strategy hides the presence of gays–and any gay sexuality–through the inclusion of subtextual cues that are easily read by gay audiences but are virtually invisible to unsympathetic and unknowledgeable mainstream audiences (Bronski, 1984; Russo, 1987; Sender, 1999).[4] Such hiding rarely is complete, however, nor is it intended to be. According to Bronski (1984), though "blatant homosexuality does not have mass appeal . . . the exotic implications

of hidden homosexuality have huge sales potential" (p. 186; see also Clover, 1992).

Sedgwick's (1985) concept of the "homosocial desire" continuum provides a useful way to theorize the practice of revealing and hiding homosexuality. She defines the homosocial as "social bonds between people of the same sex" (p. 1) and suggests that homosocial practices such as male bonding can be mapped onto the same continuum of desire as homosexuality, even when those practices are homophobic or aggressively heterosexual. She argues that cultural representation, however, often tries to rupture this continuum in order to establish the homosocial as distinct from, and dichotomous to, homosexuality. In this way, homosocial practices, especially those that can signify homoeroticism, are prevented from sliding onto the homosexual side of the continuum. A common form of cultural representation that achieves this purpose is the use of violence as a socially sanctioned means of relieving homoerotic tension that results in "re-confirming heterosexual masculinity" (Nakayama, 1994, p. 171). In this way, homoeroticism in a homosocial context can be evoked and then beaten back, quite literally in the case of *Fight Club*, before it slides into homosexuality.

The homoeroticism that permeates *Fight Club* is complex and multilayered. At one level, the film includes numerous subtextual signifiers that appeal to, and are thus suggestive of, gay erotic sensibility. An example of such is the fuss that Jack and Tyler make about a Gucci ad, which depicts a male model, whose build and pose echo those found in gay pornography. The inclusion of such subtextual signifiers iconically ties *Fight Club* to other media expressions of contemporary American homoeroticism. At another level, homoeroticism is evident in the fighting from which the film derives its name. *Fight Club*'s ritualistic fights foster male bonding and render acceptable intimate and prolonged physical contact between the contestants. In this way, when *Fight Club* signifies homo-eroticism–as for example when the camera lingers over bare-chested, sweaty men with their muscles flexed and bodies pressed together–it does so in a way that passes it off as homosocial. The DVD, however, provides another line of defense against an interpretation that attempts to render this homoeroticism as homosexual experience.

Earlier we argued that DVD-extra text could be used to direct the viewer's interpretation of a film. In the next section, we argue that *Fight Club*'s extra text is employed to discourage the viewer from interpreting the homosocial practices represented as signifying homosexual experience. More specifically, we contend that the extra text is used to deny the presence of homoeroticism, to dismiss homoerotic elements, and to divert attention away from these elements. In our analysis of *Fight Club* and the DVD-extra text that accompanies it, we point out how these tactics of denial, dismissal, and diversion are used by the product's makers and marketers to maintain at least a veneer of heterosexuality, and thus uphold the socio-sexual status quo. This is yet another example of what Gross (1991) notes is the media's tendency to preserve the mainstream's false façade of heteronormity.[5]

The *Fight Club* DVD consists of two disks. The first contains the theatrical release, foreign language versions, and running commentaries by the director (David Fincher), the actors, (Brad Pitt, Edward Norton, and Helena Bonham Carter), the author of the original book and the screenwriter (Chuck Palahniuk and Jim Uhls), and others involved in the production. The second disk contains scenes deleted from the theatrical release, promotional materials, storyboards, location scouting, and principle photography. All inclusive, the *Fight Club* DVD contains over eight hours of viewable material, not counting material repeated in different versions (Spanish subtitles, Dolby surround sound). As noted earlier, even the physical packaging of the DVD contains a pamphlet that could be counted as extra text.

Examples of homoeroticism can be found in many elements of the DVD, including the pamphlet entitled "How to Start a Fight," which features a picture of Brad Pitt on the cover, flexing his muscles in a way reminiscent of gay erotica/porn. The press kit featured on disk two takes the form of a mail-order catalogue, offering a "Hard Core Tank" shirt depicting porn stars, and available in a "Boys at the Backdoor" style. In one of the location shots included in disk two, a crewmember refers to a substance made to resemble liposuctioned fat as his "jizz." Clearly these are signifiers of the male sexual body, male-on-male sex, and the sexual "product" of the male. It could be argued that these extra-text elements reveal seep-

age of homosexual experience, but it is a seepage that is easily contained. If the authority of the auteurs is established by the extra text, and this authority in turn asserts an interpretative grammar that views the homoerotic elements of the film as homosocial and not homosexual, then these extra-text elements could also be viewed as homosocial.

Indeed, different materials included in the *Fight Club* DVD-extra text work to establish the authority of the auteurs and assert their opinions. For example, the extra text includes features about location scouting, principle photography, and special effects elements that reinforce, and are anchored in, the auteur ideology. In the location scouting shoots, Fincher is the center of attention as other crewmembers listen to him articulate his vision of the scenes. In the principal photography, the focus is on the actors as they interact with the crew, rehearse their blocking, and give their input as to how a scene should play. The special effects scenes include commentary by the crewmembers that often refer to Fincher as the final judge of how a scene should look, or discuss how an actor influenced decisions about an effect. For a specific special effect included in a sex scene, the final determination for a computer-generated image was that it had to make Helene Bonham Carter look pretty. Although these aspects of the DVD show how the film crew contributed to the film, they also clearly indicate that Fincher or the actors held the opinions that mattered most. If theirs are the opinions that matter, then their running commentaries are the most important elements of the extra text in that they provide an ongoing forum for these opinions. We should note that the DVD reviewers discussed previously also point out the importance of the director's, actors', and writers' running commentaries in influencing their response to, and interpretation of, *Fight Club*. Therefore, we focus our critical attention on these specific running commentaries in our analysis of the extra text.[6]

We will begin our analysis with a description of the film in order to illustrate how the narrative supports a homoerotic interpretation. We then isolate four segments where we believe homoeroticism is most pronounced, and where the erasure of homosexual experience as an assurance of mainstream acceptance is most necessary. We interpret the homoerotic elements in these segments, and then show how the running commentaries offered by the director, actors, and writers use denial, dismissal, and distraction to undermine the validity of a homosexual interpretation. In this way the ideology of the homosexual erasure dovetails with the ideology of the auteur.

Narrative

Fight Club opens with the image of a man's brain and closes with the image of a penis. In between, the film explores the psychic and sexual crisis of contemporary white, middle-class American masculinity—or one version of it—through the experiences and observations of "Jack," *Fight Club*'s protagonist, who is played by Norton. When we first meet Jack, he is a slave to materialism who attempts to find emotional connections in the support groups he compulsively cruises. It is at one of these, a group for men with testicular cancer, that Jack meets Marla Singer, the film's main female character. When Jack challenges Marla's right to be there, she states that she has a greater right to attend the group than does Jack (the implied argument: like many of the men attending, she has no testicles, while Jack's are intact and cancer free). This conflict illustrates that Jack's relationship with Marla, initially, is hardly romantic. In fact, he goes so far as to blame her for his problems.

Jack is much more interested, however, in a man that he meets on one of the countless business flights he takes, Tyler Durden, a charismatic soap salesmen whose passion for life is a sharp contrast to Jack's general ennui. The two strike up a conversation, during which Tyler makes seductive reference to pursuing the kind of active, exciting, subversive life of which Jack has only dreamed. After the flight, Jack arrives at his condo to find it has been blown-up in a mysterious explosion. Jack then contacts Tyler and the two men agree to meet at a bar. After a night of drinking, Jack mentions the need to find himself a hotel. Jack agrees to go home with Tyler, but before they leave Tyler requests an unusual favor: "Hit me as hard as you can." They begin a sparring match during which they bond.

So much so, in fact, that the two men set up house in a manner Jack describes as "Ozzie-and-Harriet." During one scene that highlights their domestic familiarity, Tyler bathes while he and Jack discuss whom they would most like to fight. Tyler mentions he would fight his dad, who he says was indifferent. Jack claims he does not know his dad because "he left when I about six years old." Tyler observes, "We're a generation of men raised by women. I'm wondering if another woman is really the answer we need." This sense of abandonment by and anger toward male-father figures, and their suspicion directed toward maternal substitutes, are important shaping influences in the relationship of Tyler and Jack and the unfolding of the film's plot.

The routine of their domestic arrangement is punctuated by periodic fights in the bar's parking lot, which attract a growing crowd of men who function first as voyeurs and then as enthusiastic participants in the ritualistic pugilism. Tyler and Jack find themselves at the center of a growing phenomenon. The fights are more than mere physical recreation: they are a means for men to explore themselves and their masculinity while connecting with other men. As the fights absorb more of Jack's time and energy, he no longer regularly attends support groups. Instead, he and Tyler fashion a support group of their own in the bar's basement, where the fighting has now moved. The club's members form a clandestine bond that extends beyond the confines of the club. They exchange secret, knowing glances at work, while dining, and in other public places. Through what they come to call Fight Club, they are able to distinguish themselves in ways denied them by the demeaning and emasculating jobs of the contemporary service economy.

Not surprisingly, Jack's absence from the support groups is noticed by Marla, who calls and asks where he has been. In a desperate bid for attention, she claims she has swallowed a whole bottle of tranquilizers. Jack sets down the receiver and walks away as the film fades to a sex scene that morphs several images of Marla. The next morning, as Jack eats breakfast he hears someone enter the room, and imagining that he is speaking to Tyler, he says, "You won't believe this dream I had last night." To his surprise, Marla enters. Marla then begins an ongoing sexual relationship with Tyler, who it seems had picked up the receiver Jack had dropped and had come to her rescue. Jack is annoyed and threatened by Marla's presence because she seems to compete with Jack for Tyler's attention.

In other words, Jack sees Marla as a threat to his relationship with Tyler.

Marla, however, is not Jack's only threat. Tyler begins a new form of Fight Club called Project Mayhem, in which members engage in petty acts of vandalism. Over time, the number and severity of these acts increase as does the number of club members. Jack and Tyler's home becomes filled with young men who make claims upon Tyler's attention and strain his relationship with Jack. In one scene, Jack takes out his growing frustration upon a club member, whom Tyler had affectionately embraced, by brutally pummeling him during a fight. Jack finally confronts Tyler, and Tyler states that Jack does not understand the full implications of their relationship.

At this point in the film, Tyler disappears. Jack searches for him in the Fight Club underground that has emerged in major cities throughout the United States. He always arrives in Tyler's wake, and to his puzzlement is recognized and referred to as "Mr. Durden." Seeking to address newly aroused suspicions, Jack calls Marla to ask if they have had sex. Marla replies, "You fuck me, then snub me. You love me, and then hate me. You show me your sensitive side, and then you turn into a total asshole. Is that a pretty accurate description of our relationship, Tyler?" Jack asks, "What did you call me? Say my name." Marla replies, "Tyler Durden."

Jack now realizes that he and Tyler are the same person and that he is the author of Project Mayhem's increasingly violent agenda. To protect Marla, who has been targeted as a threat to the project, Jack sends her away on a bus. In an attempt to stop the project's next act of terrorism, Jack tries to disconnect one of the bombs Project Mayhem has set to explode in an office-building parking garage. Tyler stops him and the two men engage in a fight that is filmed by security cameras, which capture images of Jack throwing himself around the garage. This fight is continued from the garage to an office at the top of the building, and the film returns to the opening scene: Tyler holding a gun in Jack's mouth. From his vantage point, Jack looks down to see Fight Club members carry Marla off a bus. Jack reasons that he can resolve the situation: if Tyler is not real but the gun is, then the gun is not in Tyler's hand but in his own. Jack puts the gun to his head and pulls the trigger. It is Tyler, however, who

dies. When the Fight Club arrives with Marla, Jack takes Marla's hand and says, "You met me at a very strange time in my life."

This narrative depicts a homosocial relationship in a homoerotic manner that easily could be interpreted as representing homosexual experience. We have a man undergoing a masculinity crisis attributed to an unresolved relationship with his father. He responds to this crisis by forming a relationship with another man that proves to be both narcissistic and self-destructive. Once the relationship is dissolved (literally destroyed) the man can then pursue a relationship with a woman. In fact, the narrative seems to have taken a page from Freud (1949) in its depiction of the conflict and resolution of a proper sexual object choice. The narrative includes violence as a means of simultaneously relieving the homo-erotic tension in a way deemed acceptable to mainstream sensibilities (Nakayama, 1994). We believe that the film's homoeroticism is made even more acceptable by its erasure in the extra text. Now that the larger narrative of the film has been considered, we turn our attention to specific segments in which we feel the homoerotic elements of the film are the most pronounced. We will provide a close analysis of these segments and their treatment in the running commentaries.

Segment One

After discovering his condo has been destroyed, Jack contacts Tyler and the two agree to meet at a bar. Over beer Tyler tells Jack that he is lucky, that things could be worse: "A woman could cut off your penis while you're sleeping and toss it out the window of a speeding car." That is, Tyler suggests, Jack could have lost his manhood—literally as well as symbolically. Though seemingly out-of-place, Tyler's sexual non sequitur makes sense within the larger context of the film's narrative, which compares the enervating effect of material possessions with emasculation. Tyler's comment, however, is more than a metaphoric indictment of contemporary consumerism, as becomes clear as the scene unfolds. Outside the bar, the now homeless Jack mentions the need to find himself a hotel. Tyler responds, "Just ask." Jack: "What are you talking about?" Tyler: "After three pitchers of beer, you still can't ask. . . . Cut the foreplay and just ask." Jack then asks if he can come home with Tyler, and Tyler agrees. The scene plays out as a coy, homoerotic flirtation. After a night of drinking, one man wants to ask if he can go home with another, but he cannot bring himself to raise the question directly. Perhaps Jack is reluctant because he senses the sexual significance of two men going home together after last call. Tyler too seems to understand the sexual significance of Jack's unstated request when he tells Jack to "cut the foreplay." Before they leave Tyler asks Jack to "hit me as hard as you can."

At this point, the film makes one of its many scenic shifts that disrupt the chronological progression of the narrative. The camera focuses upon a slide of a penis, while in a voice-over Jack says, "Let me tell you something about Tyler Durden." Jack informs the audience that, in addition to selling soap, Tyler has several other low-paying, service-oriented jobs. We are told that Tyler works as a projectionist who splices single frames of pornographic images (e.g., "A nice, big cock") into family films. Jack also tells us that Tyler is also a banquet waiter who functions as a food-industry guerilla terrorist. Indeed, in another act of penile subversion we see Tyler insert his own where its presence is neither expected nor welcome: he is shown peeing into a soup tureen. Tyler's sexual subversion, however, is also sexual aggression. His phallic insertions position him as the film's dominant—and dominating—sexual force, as well as the object of Jack's sexual desire. After this digression, the film returns to the bar's parking lot where tentatively at first, and then with great enthusiasm, Jack and Tyler slug it out. Afterwards, they share a beer as Tyler smokes in a way suggestive of post-coital relaxation. Jack casually proposes, "We should do this again sometime."

In this segment the film begins to conflate homoeroticism with sadomasochism, a point addressed by Fincher in his commentary. Although Fincher begins his comments immediately following Tyler's severed penis comparison, his remarks are not about this sexual reference. Instead, he talks about the difficulty in conceptualizing this "thesis" scene, and his final decision to shoot it with two cameras. It is certainly proper for a director to discuss camera work, but given that the movie is about the crisis of contemporary masculinity, the dryly technical focus of his comments seem a bit odd directly following a reference to castration.

These comments, however, can be understood as a means of distracting the viewer from the sexual implications of the reference.

This distraction is quickly followed by a denial when Fincher describes the fight between Jack and Tyler. He avers that the scene may have "undercurrents of sadomasochism," but claims that Jack and Tyler's interactions come from an "innocent place," implying that the scene is not about sex per se. The use of the word "innocent" is also important because sex serves as a signifier for the loss of innocence; therefore, innocence signifies the absence of sex. Immediately after Fincher refers to the scene as innocent, the slide of the "nice big dick" appears on the screen. Fincher explains that Tyler's phallic insertions were inspired by a man he once knew who clipped scenes from films Fincher claims were not really "pornographic," and although the clips that Fincher describes are sexually suggestive (female breasts, a woman's panties), he describes the man's actions as "innocent." Through this comparison, Fincher's comments invite the viewer to see that Tyler's insertions are equally "innocent" and void of any serious sexual import.

In another running commentary track with Fincher and the actors, the "innocence" of these scenes is supplemented by joking banter between Fincher and Pitt. During the bar scene, Fincher compliments Pitt on the reference to "Viagra," and Pitt compliments Fincher on the reference to "Olestra," which Fincher then describes as a reference to "anal leakage." The obvious and unseemly connection between a sexual stimulate and the act of sodomy is humorously dismissed, as is the sexual subtext of the scene after Jack and Tyler's fight. In the running commentary with Palahniuk and Uhls, Palahniuk–author of the book on which the film is based–comments that he thought the scene was "weird" because it was "shorthand" for a love relationship. Screenwriter Uhls, however, seems to chuckle knowingly at Palahniuk's confusion. Fincher jokingly remarks that he loves the "post-coital smoking scene," and Pitt says that he finds it "touching." The two seem to suggest that the scene operates as a joke, and the homoerotic subtext should not be taken seriously. Perhaps that is why Uhls chuckles at Palahniuk's confusion; because he actually worked with Fincher, Uhls understands the joke. Earlier comments by Norton suggest that the viewer will get the joke, too. He claims that those who watch the film and the DVD are probably fans, or as he puts it, "anyone listening in here is cool." In other words, Norton positions the viewer in the role of an accomplice who is privy to Fincher and Pitt's jokes and understands that what might appear to be overtly homosexual is really only an expression of "innocence." As for the slide of the "nice big dick," Norton jokingly observes that Fincher appears in all of his movies. This joking serves to parody critical practices of homoerotic interpretation, thereby dismissing such practices as comical.

Segment Two

As more men flock to the fights, they move from the bar's parking lot to its basement. It is into this basement that Tyler descends and lays out the rules of what comes to be called "Fight Club." As Tyler promulgates the rules, men remove their belts, shoes, and shirts. Soon, two shirtless men fight as others cheer. Jack comments in voice over: "This kid from work, Ricky, he couldn't remember if he orders pens with blue ink or black. But Ricky was a god for ten minutes when he trounced the maître d' at a local food court." In close-up, Jack observes the fight with a hint of lust on his face. The fight concludes with the loser lying on the floor in a passive sexual position, a look of ecstasy on his face. It would seem that these fights carry a sexual tension that makes them more than mere brawls; they signify a relationship that dares not speak its name: "The first rule of Fight Club is: you do not talk about Fight Club."

Jack later encounters "Ricky" while at work and the maître d'—whose face is bruised and bandaged—at the food court. They exchange knowing glances that resemble the type of homoerotic cruising gay activist Harry Hay once described as "the eye lock" (Timmons, 1990). Jack describes the men's connection in transformative terms: "A guy came to Fight Club for the first time, his ass was a wad of cookie dough; after a few weeks, he was carved out of wood." Jack's description links participation in Fight Club with sexual empowerment: When a member first begins Fight Club, his "ass" is weak, malleable, and easily penetrated; but through the act of fighting, he quickly becomes "wood," a common metaphor for an erection ("a woody") and thus a sign of sexual potency.

The sexual nature of these encounters is given more texture in an exchange between Jack and Tyler. As the two walk down the street they pass a bus stop with a Gucci ad that depicts a young man's rather doughy "ass." After they board the bus, Jack motions to another Gucci ad depicting a well-defined, muscular male body. He asks, "Is that what a man looks like?" Tyler responds, "Self-improvement is masturbation, now self-destruction. . . ." A quick cut to the Fight Club shows two men fighting as others watch and cheer. When finished, the men fall apart as though sexually spent. The juxtaposition of Tyler's comments with this image connects the inward focus of most self-improvement schemes to the self-absorbed isolation of solo sex, while implying that the necessarily social act of fighting is linked to real sex. To bring Tyler's response to its logical conclusion, if self-improvement is masturbation, then self-destruction is real sex (with real men). This view, of course, reaffirms the mainstream conception of gay sex as dangerous and destructive, and thus helps the film build to its heteronormative conclusion.

In the DVD-extra text, Fincher does not address these scenes except to comment upon how funny Jack looks in his sunglasses in the food court scene. Bonham Carter is a bit more engaged. Her comments, however, ignore the film's sexual elements and focus instead upon the violence and how its depiction offered her insight into why men fight: it gives them the sensation of being alive. Norton suggests the film is the contemporary equivalent of *The Graduate*, because it deals with "youthful dislocation" and how it feels to be out-of-sync with society's accepted values. Palahniuk comes closest to addressing the sexual aspects of these scenes. He does so indirectly, however, in suggesting that the use of alcohol in some scenes was important because, just as some people have to consume alcohol to have sex, it "seemed natural that people would have to have alcohol to fight for the first time." With this possible exception, these running commentaries illustrate how the extra text distracts the viewer from the presence of homoerotic elements. Within this segment a man's "ass" is mentioned and two men's naked bodies are visually represented with a reference to masturbation. However, Norton's statement that *Fight Club* is an ambiguous film along the lines of *The Graduate* directs viewer attention away from the film's homoerotic elements by comparing it to a film known for its heterosexual elements.

Segment Three

As the personal violence of Fight Club evolves into the public violence of Project Mayhem, Tyler inducts new recruits and turns the house into a crowded barracks. The presence of so many men packed into the house heightens the club's homoerotic tension. This tension is visually expressed in a scene in which Jack gazes upon a shirtless young recruit while he shaves; the recruit's body is framed in the doorway of the bathroom, and Tyler stands by the doorway as though he were presenting the young man for Jack's erotic enjoyment. An implication of this heightened homoeroticism is depicted later when Tyler affectionately embraces a young, blond recruit after a successful Project Mayhem adventure. Jack gazes enviously upon the recruit and expresses his sense of rejection as Tyler's attention turns to another. Later in the Fight Club basement, Jack takes on the recruit, knocks him to the floor, and pummels his face into a bloody pulp. When Tyler asks, "Why did you go psycho, boy?" Jack replies, "I wanted to destroy something beautiful." More to the point, Jack wanted to destroy a masculine object of beauty that was occupying Tyler's attention.

This heightened homoerotic tension has caused a rift in Jack and Tyler's relationship. While driving, Tyler raises this issue: "Is something on your mind, dear?" Jack wonders why he was not told about Project Mayhem, especially given that he and Tyler started Fight Club together. Tyler replies that Project Mayhem goes beyond the two of them, and that Jack should forget what he thinks he knows "about life, about friendship, and especially about you and me." Project Mayhem thus signals the beginning of the end of Jack and Tyler's relationship.

In commenting on this segment, Fincher notes he is often asked in interviews about the homoerotic elements of *Fight Club*. He suggests that if the story line of the film is followed, it is clear that *Fight Club* is more of a "self-love story" than a homosexual love story. Apart from its direct denial of homosexual love, Fincher's distinction ignores how homosexuality has frequently been associated with narcissism. In the running commentary with the actors, Fincher also disparages critic Amy Taubin, who raised the issue of homoeroticism in an interview she conducted. Fincher mentions that Taubin may have accused him of violating the "cardinal rule" against having a character played by two different actors. The actors laugh at the absurdity of the rule, and offer examples of films that defy its application. The fact that Fincher's comments deny the issue of homosexuality in one running commentary, and then dismiss a critic that has raised the issue in another, may be coincidental. Nevertheless, the two running commentaries suggest to the viewer that *Fight Club* is not to be interpreted as representing homosexual experience.

It is also interesting to note how Jack's jealousy is treated. Norton ignores the emotion entirely and focuses instead upon the technical aspects of the scene: how the shot of his jealous gaze was "undercranked" (filmed at 40 frames, according to Fincher). Pitt, on the other hand, suggests that the scene depicts a "brotherly" jealousy, motivated by fraternal rather than sexual interests. Screenwriter Uhls suggests that Jack's jealousy can be understood from a "hetero point of view," as a person resenting their best friend paying attention to another. He then goes on to observe that the scene "obviously has homosexual connotations." Palahniuk, however, laughs at this suggestion. The extra text comments make it clear that, from the perspective of those involved in making the film, a heteronormative reading of the scene has greater legitimacy than does a homo-erotic one. In turns, Norton's comments distract the viewer from the homoeroticism, Pitt's and Uhls' comments deny it, and Palahniuk's comments dismiss it.

Segment Four

After Jack discovers that Tyler is a projection of his own psyche, he no longer sees Marla as a threat but rather as threatened. Before he can pursue a relationship with Marla, however, Jack must first finish off Tyler. Jack confronts Tyler in the parking garage of one of the buildings targeted to be blown-up as part of Project Mayhem. The two struggle, Tyler subdues Jack, and the film returns to the same scene with which it began: Tyler holding a gun in Jack's mouth.

When Jack wonders why he cannot rid himself of Tyler, Tyler claims he was created from Jack by Jack to satisfy Jack's unmet needs. Jack then realizes what he must do: he puts the gun to his head and pulls the trigger. With smoke coming out of his mouth, Tyler turns and falls to the ground with the back of his head blown out. In this way, Jack both consummates and ends his relationship with Tyler, and thus rids himself of his homoerotic projection. As noted earlier, other critics have also recognized the homoerotic significance of this scene. We should add, however, that the discovery that Tyler is Jack's narcissistic projection also serves to code their relationship as homosexual.

Now that Jack has killed off Tyler, he turns to Marla. Fight Club members then arrive with Marla in custody (Tyler had instructed them to "take care of her" because she "knows too much"). Jack directs them to leave him and Marla alone. Marla asks Jack what "sick game" he is playing, but stops mid-sentence when she sees his face. He informs her he shot himself, but that he is now okay. He adds that she can trust him that "everything is going to be fine." At that very moment, in a strange mockery of clichéd sexual fireworks, the buildings targeted by Project Mayhem implode in the distance as Jack takes Marla's hand and says, "You met me at a very strange time in my life." Indeed, but now that he is with Marla, it seems that Jack's masculinity crisis may finally have a heterosexual resolution. Or, maybe not: the film concludes with the image of a penis (the same one inserted in a previous scene) flashing briefly on the screen. The visual reappearance of an object of homoerotic desire seems to raise the question: "The End?"

Norton and Fincher's comments provide perhaps the best example of dismissal. He claims Jack resists the escalation of Fight Club's violence only when Marla's safety is overtly threatened, and argues that this threat is the film's pivotal point because it precipitates Jack's break from his alter ego (Tyler). Norton also observes that, though Jack was looking to Tyler for "some kind of intimacy," in the end Jack transfers his "desire for connection to Marla, where it should have been in the first place, maybe." Allowing for the equivocal "maybe," Norton provides the definitive heteronormative reading to this segment, and to the film's conclusion. This reading, however, infers that Jack's desire for "intimacy" with Tyler was homosexual and thus inappropriate;

otherwise it makes little sense to suggest that Jack's "desire for connection" should have been directed to Marla "in the first place." This inference, however, is easily dismissed when Fincher jokes as the film flickers to a close: "Did you know there is a six-frame splice of a penis at the end?" Norton: "You're kidding." At a point when homosexuality is almost acknowledged, albeit inferentially, it is ultimately laughed off and dismissed.

Conclusion

We have argued that Fight Club's narrative, coupled with the interpretation of it offered in the running commentaries, protects the film's commercial appeal through dual forms of homosexual erasure. The narrative, while depicting a relationship that can easily be interpreted as homosexual, incorporates violence and a heteronormative ending to render the homoeroticism merely homosocial. The running commentaries provide a second line of defense, with the film's auteurs providing an interpretation that either denies that the homoeroticism represents homosexuality, or dismisses the possibility of homosexuality, or distracts the viewer from the issue. In this way, the Fight Club DVD constructs a digital closet that provides pleasures associated with such eroticism while at the same time assuaging any guilt that might potentially accompany such pleasure on the part of homophobic and/or heterosexist consumers. Although Fight Club was not a blockbuster by any definition, it has attracted a large and loyal–and predominantly young male–cult following inspiring websites, conferences, and even actual fight clubs where young men meet and beat one another (Nilles, 2001). While this cult following among young, presumably heterosexual males may merely be an effect of the erasure included in the film's narrative, the DVD-extra text adds an additional layer of plausible deniability for those who need it. Norton may be correct when he quotes Fincher; perhaps Fight Club was designed to "piss off a healthy number of people"; but if the DVD is any indication, Fight Club does not achieve this by forcibly challenging the male heterosexual viewer's sexual identity.

We have also argued that the DVD, with its interactive mix of media product and promotion, not only offers consumers a new way to view films, but also presents critics with new challenges in analyzing and critiquing them. In particular, we have pointed out through our analysis of the *Fight Club* DVD how the extra text can be employed to discourage and discount some interpretations while encouraging others. In the case of the *Fight Club* DVD, the running commentaries included in the extra text serve to delegitimate a homoerotic interpretation of the film. We suggest that the effectiveness of this privileging of the director's, actors', and writers' commentary–what we have referred to as a return to the ideology of the auteur–is made possible by the blurring of the traditional distinction between primary and secondary texts. As an integral part of the DVD, and not something apart from it, these opinions are now included in the viewing experience of many consumers as well as critics. This provides the DVD with an intratextual advantage not enjoyed by other means of packaging and distributing films. Furthermore, we suggest that this new technology may have created an invested consumer who, by buying the DVD, is also predisposed to buy the interpretation that the DVD offers.

The DVD is an important media product that is gaining in popularity, and likely is to claim a prominent place in the digital-media marketplace. Given the DVD's potential as a media product, it deserves theoretical consideration, and this is what we have attempted to provide. The concepts that we have included in our analysis do not exhaust the critical potential of DVD analysis, but we hope that we have established some groundwork from which additional theorizing might proceed. DVD-extra text is very fertile terrain. Although we believe it is used to evoke the auteur in the case of *Fight Club*, we can see other ways that extra text can be used to promote a film. In the case of *Austin Powers: International Man of Mystery*, the DVD-extra text includes several humorous devices that draw on the persona of Austin Powers, but do not actually introduce Mike Myers as an auteur. In the case of a classical film, the cast and crew may no longer be around to offer interviews and running commentaries to accompany the DVD release. For example, the DVD for *All About Eve* is very thin on extra text, including only promotional photos of the cast in character, and a promotional trailer. It may well be that older films may carry enough of a reputation that people will purchase the DVD without the addition of extra text as an enticement. Simply put, differ-

ent films, and different genres of film, require different promotional strategies; extra text can be employed in ways that accommodate these differences. Additional critical work is needed to chronicle these various accommodations.

We believe that the concept of intratextuality, on the other hand, may find applications outside the DVD. Although the Internet has usually been regarded as the embodiment of intertextuality, as media become more web-based, media conglomerates have a vested interested in reining in the web surfer. Robert McChesney (1999) has argued that the media have become more centralized and more concerned about cross-promotion and product re-packaging, and that these practices are designed to keep the consumer focused on product options offered by a single corporate interest. If the intratextuality of the DVD signifies intertextual relations with predetermined restraints and boundaries, then these same restraints can be put in place as more media access is introduced on the Internet. In other words, web pages for a media conglomerate may offer links that only connect to other products and companies related to the conglomerate. The Fox Network web page may some day allow viewers to watch reruns of *Ally McBeal*, and also to buy a CD of music from the show, but it will not link them to another network. The intratextual advantages of convenience and proximity enjoyed on the DVD can also be enjoyed on the web; and similar to the DVD, intertextuality on the web may become intratextuality that is carefully crafted to serve corporate interests.

The invested viewer, however, may be a concept with a short shelf life for the DVD. After all, as we have argued, the viewer is invested because DVD technology is so new; it will not be as new next year. As the DVD player becomes more common, those purchasing the technology will no longer be ahead of the curve. These consumers will be purchasing a tested technology, and may be less likely to worry about the value of their purchase. Will these consumers believe the extra text to be an important part of their investment? That may depend on how the early consumers set the trend for the technology's use. If the DVD reviews we noted earlier are any indication, DVD-extra text is considered a highly desirable attribute of this new technology. Perhaps the trend is already set and future consumers of DVDs will be as interested in the extra text as contemporary consumers, and will come to expect it. Furthermore, although the viewer's investment in the DVD may dissipate, the concept of the invested viewer may be useful in explaining how other emerging media technologies are received. In other words, those pioneers who first purchase a technology may be motivated to believe the technology has value, even when that value primarily serves corporate interests.

Finally, we wonder about the politics of representation in light of our analysis of the *Fight Club* DVD. Queer experience is not the only type of experience that has been erased in mainstream media. In fact, an important critical project in the field of media studies has advocated readings that challenge the representation, or lack thereof, of numerous marginalized groups. The *Fight Club* DVD illustrates how digital technology can be used to delegitimate resistant and politically activated readings. We do not believe that digital technology can be used to eradicate politically activated readings, but it does present new challenges to media critics who believe that the practices of media representation are often classist, racist, sexist, and homophobic. Perhaps the important questions are not about the existence of a digital closet, but how many and what kinds of people can it hold?

Notes

1. Our use of the term "viewer" is informed by John Fiske's (1987) definition. He claims the term is specifically applicable to television, and that it suggests an active agent who contributes meaning to the media text. Although we are dealing with a film text, DVDs are mainly consumed at home via television sets. We also feel that it is important to imagine the viewer of the DVD as active though the extra text appears to be designed to constrain the active viewer.
2. The theatrical release only referred to this character as "the narrator." In the DVD, however, the character is referred to as "Jack."
3. Borrowing from Gerbner and Gross (1976), Kielwasser and Wolf (1992) argue that the invisibility engendered by such absence with respect to gays (and gay youth in particular) results in a form of symbolic annihilation.
4. From a queer perspective, this strategy poses two problems: first, it helps render gays invisible to much of the mainstream, contributing to their symbolic annihilation; and second, it privileges the gay experience of affluent,

urban, white gays and lesbians to the exclusion of other gays and their experiences (Gluckman & Reed, 1993).
5. Our use of the term "homoeroticism" refers to erotic experience between two people of the same biological sex. We do not suggest that the characters in *Fight Club* actually participate in sexual acts, a distinction clarified by Bataille, who views eroticism as a uniquely human attribute. Bataille (1989) argues: "Eroticism, unlike simple sexual activity, is a psychological quest independent of the natural goal: reproduction" (p. 11). Moreover, he states that pain, whether seen or experienced, is a primary means of undertaking this quest because it mediates between life and death. The fact that the homoeroticism in *Fight Club* is often framed by physical pain illustrates Bataille's point.
6. A fourth running commentary includes the opinions of the director of photography, costume designer, and special effects artists. As expected, these technicians talk mostly about aspects of their craft as represented in scenes, but seldom comment on the narrative or visual elements as these relate to homoeroticism. We could have argued that their comments distract from the homoeroticism, because they do. However, we felt that such an argument would be too easy and a little disingenuous. Furthermore, the residue of the auteur does not seem to encompass these individuals, as evidenced in the reviews of the DVD, and the materials included on the DVD. In fact, these individuals in their commentaries often refer and defer to Fincher and the actors. Therefore, we have decided not to include this running commentary in our analysis.

References

Abraham, M. (2001, January 29). DVD will continue as fastest-growing consumer product. *ENEWS*, sec. In-Stat, p. 12.

Bart, P. (2000). *The gross.* New York: St. Martin's Griffin.

Bataille, G. (1989). *Tears of Eros.* San Francisco: City Lights.

Bennett, T., & Woollacott, J. (1987). *Bond and beyond: The political career of a popular hero.* London: Macmillan Education.

Bronski, M. (1984). *Culture clash: The making of gay sensibility.* Boston: South End Press.

Brookey, R. A. (1996). A community like Philadelphia. *Western Journal of Communication, 60*(1), 40–56.

Brookey, R. A., & Westerfelhaus, R. (2001). Pistols and petticoats, piety and purity: *To Wong Foo*, the queering of the American monomyth, and the marginalizing discourse of deification. *Critical Studies in Media Communication, 18*(2), 141–156.

Chick, T. (2000). *There: Tom Chick breaks the first (and*

second) rule of Fight Club. [On-line]. DailyRadar.com, 1–3. Retrieved February 11, 2001. Available http://www.dailyradar.com/ columns/showbiz_column_283.html.

Clover, C. J. (1992). *Men, women, and chain saws: Gender in the modern horror film.* Princeton, NJ: Princeton University Press.

Crowdus, G. (2000). *Fight Club. Cineaste, 25* (4), 46–47.

Dow, B. J. (2001). Ellen, television and the politics of gay and lesbian visibility. *Critical Studies in Media Communication, 18* (2), 123–140.

DVD video to beat industry sales projections. (2000, September). *Emedia, 13* (9), 12.

Ebert, R. (1999, October 15). *Fight* stresses frightful ideas; Fascism wins by knockout. *Chicago Sun-Times*, sec. Weekend Plus; Movies, p. 31. [On-line]. Retrieved February 11, 2001. Available http://www.suntimes.com/ebert/ebert_reviews/1999/10/101502.html.

Ellis, M. (2001). *Fight Club*, and then some. [On-line]. *WCBE Public Arts*, 1–2. Retrieved February 11, 2001. Available http://www.publicbroadcasting.net/wcbe/arts/movies/article/157.html.

Fejes, F. (2000). Making a gay masculinity. *Critical Studies in Media Communication, 17* (1), 113–116.

Fejes, F., & Petrich, K. (1993). Invisibility, homophobia, and heterosexism: Lesbians, gays, and the media. *Critical Studies in Mass Communication, 10* (3), 396–422.

Fiske, J. (1987). *Television culture.* New York: Routledge.

Freud, S. (1949). *Three essays on the theory of sexuality.* London: Imago.

Gerbner, G., & Gross, L. (1976). Living with television: The violence profile. *Journal of Communication, 26* (2), 172–199.

Gluckman, A., & Reed, B. (1993, November 1). The gay marketing movement: Leaving diversity in the dust. *Dollars and Sense*, 190, 16–19 and 34–35.

Gross, L. (1991). The contested closet: The ethic and politics of outing. *Critical Studies in Mass Communication, 8* (3), 352–388.

How to Start a Fight. (2000). *Fight Club DVD* [Brochure]. Beverly Hills, CA: Twentieth Century Fox Home Entertainment, Inc. [On-line]. Available http://www.foxhome.com/cgi-bin/adtrack/ fightclub_dvd1/getform.pl?PAGE=booklet.html&MANUF=FOXHOME_SW&AD=DOMAIN& CAMPGN=FCDVD1.

Kielwasser, A. P., & Wolf, M. A. (1992). Mainstream television, adolescent homosexuality, and significant silence. *Critical Studies in Mass Communication, 9* (4), 350–373.

Lapsley, R., & Westlake, M. (1988). *Film theory: An introduction.* Manchester, UK: Manchester University Press.

McChesney, R. (1999). *Rich media, poor democracy.* Urbana: University of Illinois Press.

Nakayama, T. K. (1994). Show/down time: "Race," gender, sexuality, and popular culture. *Critical Studies in Mass Communication, 11* (2), 162–179.

Nilles, K. (2001, January 22). *Fight Club* packs a wallop with young fans. *Milwaukee Journal Sentinel*, p. 1E. [On-line]. Available http://www.jsonline.com/Enter/movies/jan01/fclub22011901.asp.

Norton, E. (2000). *Fight Club DVD* [Disk Two]. Interview. Beverly Hills, CA: Twentieth Century Fox Home Entertainment, Inc.

O'Hehir, A. (1999, October 15). *Fight Club.* [On-line]. *Salon.com*, 1–3. Retrieved December 30, 2000. Available http://www.salon.com/ent/movies/review/1999/10/15/fight_club/print.html.

Pizzello, C. (2000, September). DVD playback. *American Cinematographer, 81* (9), 22–24.

Rich, B. R. (2000, March). Queer and present danger. *Sight and Sound, 10* (3), 22–25.

Russo, V. (1987). *The celluloid closet: Homosexuality in the movies* (rev. ed.). New York: Harper & Row.

Sedgwick, E. (1985). *Between men: English literature and male homosocial desire.* New York: Columbia University Press.

Sender, K. (1999). Selling sexual subjectivities: Audiences respond to gay window advertising. *Critical Studies in Media Communication, 16* (2), 172–196.

Smith, G. M. (1999). Introduction: A few words about interactivity. In G. M. Smith (Ed.), *On a silver platter: CD-ROMs and the promises of a new technology* (pp. 1–34). New York: New York University Press.

Taubin, A. (1999, October 13–19). 21st century boys. [On-line]. *The Village Voice*, 1–3. Retrieved September 20, 2000. Available http://www.villagevoice.com/issues/9941/taubin.php.

Thomson, D. (1999, October 17). Brilliance and promise will only go so far. *The New York Times*, Sec. 2, p. 15.

Timmons, S. (1990). *The trouble with Harry Hay: Founder of the modern gay movement.* Boston: Alyson.

Turan, K. (1999, October 15). Movie review: *Fight Club. Los Angeles Times*, F1. [On-line]. Retrieved February 11, 2001. Available http://www.calendarlive.com/top/1,1419,L-LATimes-Search-X!ArticleDetail-5276,00.html?search_area=Articles&channel=Search&search_text=Movie+review%3A+Fight+Club.

13.
FRACTURED FAIRY TALES AND FRAGMENTED MARKETS

Disney's Weddings of a Lifetime *and the Cultural Politics of Media Conglomeration*

Elana Levine

The summer of 1995 proved a particularly prolific season for new unions. As couples worldwide exchanged conjugal vows, the Walt Disney Company trumpeted its purchase of broadcasting giant Capital Cities/ABC, a merger the entertainment industry pronounced "a marriage made in heaven" (Gibbs 1995, 24). Meanwhile, weddings both romantic and remunerative unfolded at the Disney World theme park in Orlando, Florida, where David Cobb and Suzanne Mackie became the first couple to be married at Disney's Fairy Tale Wedding Pavilion. Cobb and Mackie's nuptials were soon featured in the first episode of *Weddings of a Lifetime*, an ongoing series of specials airing on Lifetime, the women-targeted cable television network. Co-owned by ABC and the Hearst Corporation, Lifetime Television joined the Disney family with the Disney/ABC merger.

Each of the early episodes of *Weddings of a Lifetime* traced the history of a "real-life" heterosexual couple's romance, including the planning of their Lifetime-sponsored fantasy wedding, before presenting the wedding ceremony itself. The program has aired quarterly since 1995, although beginning in 2000, the series turned away from showcasing the Lifetime-sponsored weddings of average Americans and turned instead to celebrity wedding coverage and more narrowly focused wedding specials (e.g., *Dream Weddings on a Budget*). This article focuses on the earliest episodes in the series, for they best exemplify the program's synergistic potential. The first two install-

ments, in the mid-1990s, were set at the Walt Disney World theme park in Orlando, Florida, and succeeding episodes continued to promote Disney properties. For example, a February 1997 edition celebrated the theme park's twenty-fifth anniversary in conjunction with a young couple's wedding and the bride's parents' renewal of vows in honor of *their* twenty-fifth anniversary. A March 1999 episode featured the first couple to wed during a Disney Cruise Line Vacation. The intervening episodes were staged in alternately glamorous or quirky locales, among them the Sandals Caribbean Resorts, the Windows on the World restaurant in New York City, and the U.S. Naval Academy in Annapolis, Maryland. To host the program, Lifetime hired a succession of celebrity couples, all of whom had ties to the cable network's part owner, the U.S. broadcast network, ABC. Married in real life, on one of ABC's daytime soap operas, or both, hosts such as Jack and Kristina Wagner, Michael E. Knight and Catherine Hickland, and John and Eva LaRue Callahan guided viewers through the fairy-tale weddings of the featured couples. The series thus teemed with layered images of weddings and romance—the real-life couples getting married, Disney fairy tales like *Cinderella*, the celebrity couples' real-life relationships, and the fictional romantic histories of their soap opera characters.

In this article, I argue that the synergistic melding of Disney, ABC, and Lifetime in *Weddings of a Lifetime* not only typifies media industry strategies in an age of conglomeration but also evidences the complex textual meanings produced through such institutional practices. In the case of *Weddings*, Disney's cross-promotional efforts at once bolster and challenge the company's vested interests in the ideologies of heterosexual romance and marriage. While the linkages between Disney properties maximize the program's selling power, those same linkages, along with the series' blurred generic boundaries and pretensions to "reality," fracture the idealized fairy tale that its stories of romance and marriage ostensibly relate. This article attempts to move beyond large-scale denunciations of media conglomeration that, while compelling, do not always grapple with the cultural politics of the media conglomerates' products.[1] Following Janet Wasko's (1996) call for studies that combine "political economic analysis with insights drawn from cultural analysis . . . emphasizing the economic as well as the ideological" (p. 349), this article investigates the institutional and textual implications of Disney's *Weddings of a Lifetime*.[2] In so doing, I hope to extend the discussion of media conglomeration into specific case studies that examine the effects of this pervasive institutional development on the media products we consume.

It's a Small World After All: Disney and the Institutions of Media Conglomeration

By the time of *Weddings of a Lifetime*'s debut in the mid-1990s, Disney's status as a global media conglomerate was emblematic of the economic trends that have increasingly come to rule most industries, perhaps none more so than the culture industries. Selling to global markets, trafficking in ephemeral images instead of material goods, depending on cross-promotional synergies to support its horizontally integrated subsidiaries, Disney and its fellow media superpowers have both created and been created by our global economy. One result has been what Michael Curtin (1997) has termed a "globalization/fragmentation dialectic" (p. 187), a tension between global and local profit bases, mass and niche markets. Each side of the dialectic enables the existence of the other: niche markets are profitable because they buy a specialized alternative to mass-targeted products; global operations are feasible because local resources provide

reliable income. Almost as often, however, the two sides can conflict. In Disney's case, expanded holdings and cross-promotion have given the company a globalizing boost, but the conglomerate's attempts at fragmentation, at niche marketing their products, have created some serious problems. Protests against films such as *Priest* (1994) and *Kids* (1995), both distributed by the Disney subsidiary Miramax, indicate the difficult balancing act Disney has faced in diversifying its customer markets. The trickiness of the act is particularly intense for Disney because its image as creator of family entertainment has been as central to its success as (and perhaps the most impressive of) its corporate machinations. In this way, the company's image is deeply wedded to its economic status as a successful media conglomerate as well as to its cultural status as a bastion of family values.

Today's global media conglomerates, Disney among them, realize the globalization/fragmentation dialectic that defines their existence through the mixed strategies of mass expansion and niche marketing. To manage these two potentially contradictory goals, the conglomerates often rely on synergies between their various operations. In the early 1990s, for example, the Time Warner empire marketed the rap music created by its Death Row Records to a narrow audience of "urban" youth. Such niche marketing could be profitable for Time Warner because it was neatly balanced by the media giant's more global, or mass, market stakes in subsidiaries like Warner Television productions. This variety of product allows Time Warner and the other companies in similar circumstances to circulate creative content between their various operations while also allowing more profitable outlets to distribute or promote products from the more limited arms of the company (Curtin 1997, 191).

Disney's participation in the mergers and synergies that earmarked the late-twentieth-century media industries was significantly maximized with its purchase of Capital Cities/ABC and attendant half-ownership of Lifetime. Such ownership structures have helped Disney and others to create a commercial intertextuality, a textually evidenced synergy, which gets played out in the conglomerate's products (Kinder 1991, 172). For example, Disney's Touchstone Television productions, *Home Improvement* and *Ellen*, both aired on ABC in the mid-1990s while the stars of each series made the Disney-produced films *The Santa Clause* (1994) and *Mr. Wrong* (1996). Meanwhile, Disney's television syndication distributor, Buena Vista, originated the popular daytime talk show *Live with Regis and Kathie Lee* from ABC's owned and operated WABC-TV in New York.[3] ABC sitcoms such as *Roseanne, Family Matters, Step by Step,* and *Boy Meets World* sent their characters to Disney World for special "vacation" episodes in the early days of the merger (Nashawaty 1996, 8). And the Disney-MGM Studios theme park began an annual ABC Super Soap Weekend in 1996, featuring ABC soap stars and attractions such as "gift shops . . . a suds-themed restaurant and re-creations of such daytime trademarks as the *General Hospital* nurses' station" (It's a Soap World 1996, 54). Disney's cable properties also proved to be potent realms for synergy, with the kids-targeted Disney Channel, the male-targeted ESPN, and the female-targeted Lifetime reinforcing the Disney image as a family company that could also meet the individual needs of different family members.

ABC's half-ownership of Lifetime has provided multiple opportunities for commercial intertextuality throughout the relationship's synergistic history. As co-owners, the Hearst Corporation and ABC created series such as *Lifetime Magazine* (coproduced by ABC News) and *Our Home* (which drew on Hearst properties like *Good Housekeeping* magazine) (Bronstein 1994). *Weddings of a Lifetime,* in employing the celebrity couples as hosts, capitalizes on ABC's in-house production of the network's daytime soap operas *All My Children, One Life to Live,* and *General Hospital.* Real-life married couple John and Eva LaRue Callahan, for example, played married couple Edmund and Maria on the network's *All My Children* until LaRue's departure from the show in 1997. When Jack and Kristina Wagner hosted the first three *Weddings* episodes in 1995 and 1996, Jack had already left his *General Hospital* role as Frisco Jones, but Kristina remained on contract to the soap as Felicia Jones, Frisco's then ex-wife.[4] In addition, regular mention of Jack's character and his occasional guest appearances since his departure kept the actor very much identified with the ABC soap. Viewer crossover between the ABC soaps and *Weddings* was undoubtedly strong, given soap viewers' high level of knowledge of the actors' personal lives (the real-life marriages of the host couples) and professional work outside the soaps.

In addition to these media industry synergies, Disney spent the mid-1990s expanding its business in other areas of the marketplace. For example, a 5 million person drop in attendance at Disney World between 1990 and 1994 spurred the company to extend the theme park's appeal beyond families with young children to include teens and childless adults. To these ends, Disney added new resort hotels, cruise ships, and a sports-training complex (DeGeorge and Grover 1994). The new Disney town of Celebration, located "just 15 miles south of Cinderella's Castle and the Pirates of the Caribbean," has attempted to extend the Disney experience through all ages and spheres of life, creating a utopian middle-class community where all public space is owned and controlled by Disney (Rothchild 1995).[5] The new Wedding Pavilion, home of the Disney Fairy Tale Wedding, was another step in this direction, redrawing young adults into the Disney experience midway between their childhood visits and their trips as the parents of young children and potential Celebration homeowners.

The creation of the Disney World Wedding Pavilion allowed Disney to capitalize on those aspects of its business that best exemplified late-twentieth-century economic trends. Among these trends was a shift in consumption patterns from goods to services, a shift that has encouraged faster consumer turnover and repeat consumption and that, as a result, has helped to circumvent the more limited sales potential of durable material goods.[6] Disney has long been as famous for selling experiences of intangible spectacle as it has been for selling goods, and the Disney World Fairy Tale Wedding Department opened in 1991 as yet another Disney service that trafficked in transient spectacle. Since couples regularly traveled to Disney World to get married anyway, the company found a way to profit even further from those couples' patronage. When the Fairy Tale Wedding Department opened the Disney Wedding Pavilion in the Florida theme park in the summer of 1995, they were taking the next logical step of providing a setting specifically designated for an already thriving part of their business.

At the time of *Weddings of a Lifetime*'s debut, Disney marketed its fairytale weddings in an elegantly designed promotional package sent to interested parties on request. An ivory-colored folder, embossed with tiny flowers and held together by a delicate piece of gold lame ribbon, opened to feature a personalized letter from the Fairy Tale Weddings senior sales manager on *Cinderella* stationary. A glossy brochure fit into a precut pocket and featured a couple in wedding attire gazing lovingly at each other as Cinderella's castle glowed in the background and the long white train of the bride's gown framed the bottom of the photo. Similarly romantic photos filled the brochure's pages, along with text such as, "Where could you find a more memorable place to turn your wedding dreams into reality? [Disney's Fairy Tale Weddings will] create for you the memories of a lifetime!" The individual sheets with pricing information and other un-fairytale-like details were placed behind the brochure and contained such warnings as, "It is necessary that all of your guests stay in a Walt Disney World owned and operated resort during your wedding. This way each guest is able to participate in the ultimate Disney experience." Seemingly, the $7,500 minimum wedding expenditure and the rental of Cinderella's Glass Coach (including six white ponies and three costumed footmen) for $2,200 would not generate enough of the Disney experience—or enough Disney income—in and of themselves. In true Disney style, the entire family had to be immersed in the world of Disney, expanding the consumer base surrounding the wedding in the name of the "Disney experience" and the normalizing power of the heterosexual nuclear family.

Although the spectacular dimensions of the Disney Fairy Tale Wedding experience logically assisted Disney's attempts to expand its market to include more and more consumers, the focus on weddings instead of the company's previous target of the family with children also functioned as a fragmentation or narrowing of the Disney market. As a promotion for the Fairy Tale Wedding Department, *Weddings of a Lifetime* contributed to this more fragmented marketing effort. When the series began in 1995, Lifetime held the enviable position of being the only cable network exclusively targeted to women. Lifetime's positioning as *the* women's network was particularly attractive to commercial sponsors because of its ability to offer the most sought-after audience demographic, women aged 18 to 49 with an average household income exceeding $40,000. In addition, the network had built up an aura of social responsibility due

to well-received dramatic and nonfiction programming on women's health concerns and social issues such as sexual harassment, which allowed advertisers to adopt the network's "pro-woman" stance through association (Bronstein 1994). The network further emphasized its target audience to advertisers and viewers with its "Television for Women" promotional campaign, a campaign that led the network to an initial increase in prime-time ratings of 25 percent in the summer of 1995 (over the previous year) and 46 percent by November of that year (McConville 1995). *Weddings* contributed to the network's positive numbers upon its debut—the June 1995 episode was the network's "best performing special" (Haugsted 1995, 34). Each of the first two episodes drew more than 4.5 million viewers, and the series has remained the network's highest-rated nonmovie special (Jim Hjelm Dresses 1996; Vejnoska 1999).

In targeting the upscale, young to middle-aged segment of the women's market, Lifetime provides Disney with a safe and successful niche to go along with the conglomerate's more mass-targeted holdings. This is precisely the safe kind of niche market that Disney, or any media conglomerate, hopes to develop, as whenever the company has attempted to fragment its product to less mainstream markets, it has come under attack. For example, the Disney-produced and ABC-distributed sitcom *Ellen* came under the media spotlight as early as 1996 when rumors began circulating that the series' lead character would come out as a lesbian. Disney was widely criticized for the impropriety of this move, particularly because of *Ellen*'s 8:00 p.m., "family hour" time slot. *TV Guide* chastised the company for airing a suggestive promotional spot for the series during ABC's broadcast of Disney's child-friendly feature, *The Lion King* (Cheers & Jeers 1996). Christian conservative Pat Robertson, one of the many voices soon to criticize the conglomerate, protested Ellen's potential declaration by arguing, "Disney is trying to position itself as a family company. You can't be a family company if that's the kind of posture you have" (Battaglio 1996). Pressures such as these, along with disappointing ratings, uneven scripting, and half-hearted promotion, resulted in *Ellen*'s cancellation soon after the show's eponymous main character did indeed come out (Becker 1998).

Another mid-1990s' Disney controversy centered on the company's decision to offer health benefits to domestic partners of employees. As the last major Hollywood studio to provide these benefits, Disney had been under significant pressure to accommodate its gay and lesbian workers. According to one industry analyst, "There are a lot of talented people in Hollywood who happen to be gay, so Disney faces a lot of competition to get employees if they don't offer benefits for partners" (Muller 1996, E1). In the face of these intraindustrial pressures, Disney's new policy was attacked by groups such as the Southern Baptists, which called for a Disney boycott because "the Disney Company has given the appearance that the promotion of homosexuality is more important than its historic commitment to traditional family values" (SBC to Boycott Disney 1996, 81).

Not only do such attacks on Disney suggest the problems the company has faced as it has expanded its operations and targeted new niche markets, but they also illustrate Disney's heightened vulnerability when it comes to questions of sexuality and its relationship to family values. As gays and lesbians have gained greater voice in a culture that is increasingly tolerant of diversity, mainstream powers within the same culture have sought to sustain the hegemonic hold of heterosexual privilege. When Disney, longstanding advocate of the heterosexual nuclear family, institutes products and policies that question this cultural mainstay, anxieties about sexuality and the family intensify. Disney's economic position, one that has used fragmented marketing as a profit-inflating corrective to its ever-expanding global reach, requires the kinds of products that might appeal to niche markets, such as a sitcom with a lesbian lead. But products like these represent cultural and economic threats to Disney's mass-marketed profit base of "wholesome" family entertainment. For Disney, a profitable globalization/fragmentation dialectic employing synergistic connections and targeting niche markets potentially endangers the ideological stronghold of its past success—the normalized sovereignty of the heterosexual nuclear family.

How to Live Happily Ever After: Disney and the Synergistic Media Text

Given the industrial dialectic within which Disney is embroiled, and given the pertinence of issues of

sexuality and family to the company's cultural posture, a media text like *Weddings of a Lifetime* seems the ideal outlet for the conglomerate's needs. Yet, because the program appears within a social climate brimming with such disruptive forces as divorce, domestic violence, gay and lesbian life-partnerships, and feminism, a context within which the idealized heterosexual nuclear family could seem more a fiction than a reality, *Weddings of a Lifetime* is also a text whose ideological foundation is under duress. Thus, in an intensified effort to assert believably the family ideal upon which the Disney empire (and much of Western culture, for that matter) depends, *Weddings of a Lifetime* has called upon real-life stories of "true love" and employed real-life married couples whose fame rests on the fairy-tale romances of their television characters to attest to the viability of the Disney image and of traditional heterosexual romance.

In this section, I explore the features of the *Weddings of a Lifetime* text and focus on the series' first three episodes. Two of these episodes were set at Disney World, and these opening installments established a pattern that the beginning years of the series followed. In addition, these initial episodes were hosted by married soap actors Jack and Kristina Wagner, a factor that allows for an in-depth analysis of the intertextual associations the celebrity hosts bring to the text. Through these intertextual associations, the program's blurred generic boundaries, and its pretensions to reality, *Weddings of a Lifetime* asserts prescriptions for normative sexuality and its attendant gender and racial roles. At the same time, these textual features introduce a degree of ambiguity that has the potential to undermine the program's prescriptive tendencies.[7]

Weddings of a Lifetime participates in the ongoing circulation of a Disney specialty, the traditional romance narrative. In the construction of the gendered, sexual, and racial identities of the series' first three couples in particular, Disney-friendly romance and family values reign.[8] The rigid inscription of gender roles within the couples' relationships is one locus of these values. Although the program targets a women's audience, the gender roles most explicitly identified are the men's. All three grooms in the first episodes perfect the art of the romantic gesture, as David illustrates when he fashions a *Cinderella*-inspired proposal for Suzanne. The young men are constructed as creative, charming, romantic, and head over heels in love.

The young women have less distinctive identities. Unlike their male partners, Suzanne, Anne, and Stacy become most active when selecting their wedding dresses and the other accouterments (e.g., invitations, flowers, bridesmaid dresses) associated with the wedding. The dress selection process features prominently in each episode, with the bride's final choice revealed only as she walks down the aisle. The centrality of consumable goods to the wedding fantasy not only encourages the consumptive desires vital to Disney's success but also locates those desires in the hearts of women. Constructed primarily as consumers, the *Weddings of a Lifetime* brides receive their bridegrooms' romantic attentions much as they receive the trappings of their Disney-sponsored weddings. Disney is thus able to promote consumption alongside heterosexual romance, as if the two were naturally suited partners. In this portrayal, marriage and consumption are constructed as privileges rather than duties, the embrace of each allowing the women to enjoy more of the other. Such a fantasy sanctions Disney's role as wedding provider both literally and figuratively (as the progenitor of fairy-tale romance). It also suggests a situation beneficial to women, freeing them from oppressive relationships to men and the market, offering the Lifetime target audience happiness in exchange for prescriptive gender roles and uninhibited spending.

Another major function of gender roles within *Weddings of a Lifetime* is to assist the continuation of heterosexual hegemony through the creation of a new family unit. Although heterosexuality is such a deeply naturalized ideological construct that it is most strongly enforced by the program's efforts to take it completely for granted, it is foregrounded at certain moments. In the first two episodes, at the Disney World weddings, heterosexuality is subsumed under ethereal romance; sex itself remains unspoken. However, in the third episode, set at Sandals Resort in Ocho Rios, Jamaica, the "sex" in heterosexuality becomes central to Jon and Stacy's romance fantasy. Jon gleefully relates, "We're saving ourselves for each other—waiting until our wedding night," and describes the heart necklace Stacy wears to help them "stay strong" in this resolve. The episode heightens the sexual tension Jon and

Stacy ostensibly experience as their wedding draws closer by featuring their scantily clad bodies reveling in the beaches of the Sandals resort, including a sexually suggestive kiss under a waterfall. In addition, the couple learns about the Jamaican custom of the groom drinking from a coconut to build strength for his wedding night. When Jon heartily imbibes, the episode reinforces myths of heterosexual male potency, even as it sustains those of premarital celibacy. This contradictory mix of myths remains Disney-appropriate because the episode is not set in Disney World but in Jamaica, an "exotic" foreign locale that allows for a franker discussion of sexuality. Because Jon and Stacy's virginal pact preserves Disney identities even in Jamaica, the episode ultimately separates sexuality from romance, displacing the boldly sexual onto a foreign, and racialized, other.

The Jamaican episode makes most evident the necessary whiteness of Disney's fairy-tale couples, although their racial identities are significant in each of the first three episodes. Each wedding features an African American guest singer (Peabo Bryson, Patty Austin, and Bryan McKnight) who is briefly introduced early in the program, sings over a montage of photos of the couple, and then reappears in the middle of the wedding ceremony to perform a love song. With the song as a backdrop, the couples bring flowers to their mothers and hug and kiss their families before pausing to watch the singer. Juxtaposed with the visibly nonwhite singer and referencing the musical montages that have encapsulated many a white, on-screen romance, the moment affirms white familial solidarity in the presence of the hired entertainment. The Jamaican episode takes the affirmation of the white family even further, with its black hired help frequently hovering in the background as resort employees, wedding coordinator, and wedding officiator. These blacks, with the added weight of their national difference to their racial difference, distinctly mark Jon and Stacy's American whiteness. The couple's pronounced southern accents also set them apart from the Jamaicans who serve them. Racial identity, along with gender and sexual identity, works to instill Disney-appropriate images of romance and marriage in *Weddings of a Lifetime*, images that Disney needs to sustain its reputation as reliable provider of family entertainment and reliable supporter of family values.

As I have suggested, however, Disney's preferred meanings are far from assured in the *Weddings of a Lifetime* texts. The program's attempts to mix reality with fantasy raise doubts about the believability of each and thus about the idealized family values the company represents.

One aspect of *Weddings of a Lifetime* that at times fractures the narratives of the real-life couples and their fairy-tale romances is the intertextual associations evoked through the programs' hosts, Jack and Kristina Wagner. The hosts' real-life relationship and their behavior during the programs simultaneously work to reinscribe the unified identities represented by the real-life couples and to upset the authority of the romance fantasy. For example, the dialogue between the Wagners and the lines they address directly to the audience comment on the gender roles taken up by the featured couples. Kristina Wagner matches the brides' roles in her enthusiasm for the wedding dresses and the romantic details of the weddings. She embodies the connection between the brides and the target audience of women by directly addressing that audience. For example, in the second episode, when Jack does not seem to understand the significance of the top designer who created the wedding party's dresses, Kristina turns to the camera, winking in gender solidarity, "But *we* do, don't we, ladies?"

At the same time as Kristina's role reinforces the prescriptive gender identities represented by the brides, her interactions with Jack suggest a different sort of romantic relationship than that experienced by the featured couples, one that might be read as a counterpoint to the fantasy romances. For instance, when she interviews the bridesmaids in the third episode, she tells them, "My husband and I, we have two little boys," then calls to Jack, "Jack, can we have a baby girl?" His response, cutesy and dismissive, is, "No, honey. No. Sorry, Bryan," as he returns to his interview with singer Bryan McKnight. While Kristina's behavior here is appropriately feminine and maternal, her cajoling, even slightly nagging, tone suggests that fairytale romance has a limited shelf life; less romantic concerns will likely overtake the new marriages. Jack's response to her behavior is an even more significant contributor to this fracturing of the romance fantasy. Instead of serving as the enthusiastic initiator of romance, as do the grooms he interviews, Jack

takes on the more passive role of the wearily tolerant, detached husband. The Wagners' interactions thus contribute to the program's narrative of heterosexual family life in ways that both support the romance fantasy and begin to suggest its vulnerability. As attractive an example of heterosexual marital bliss as they are, the Wagners also embody the less glamorous role of the old married couple. For the Wagners, the fairy tale is seemingly over; reality has set in. This representation of married life offers no more fluidity in gender roles than does the fairy-tale romance narrative, but it does allow for a reading of fairy-tale romance as a fleeting fantasy, one far removed from reality, despite the evidence of the program's "real-life" couples.

Another aspect of the Wagners' role that suggests the vulnerability of the romance fantasy is the complex intertextuality of the Wagners' real-life relationship and their soap characters' on-screen relationship. In real life, the Wagners had a child out of wedlock and lived together for several years before getting married in 1993.[9] Such a nontraditional pattern of heterosexual romance presents a potential disruption of the fantasy wedding stories told in the Lifetime series. The Wagners' relationship is inextricably bound up with their soap characters' lives as well. Like many a soap opera couple, the characters of Frisco and Felicia Jones originally had a fairy-tale romance, complete with a fantasy wedding. Felicia even has royal blood; she is an Aztec princess. But Jack Wagner's departure from the soap and subsequent short visits to revive his character have substantially changed the relationship between Frisco and Felicia. The couple divorced when Frisco chose his work as a secret agent over his family, and his periodic reappearances have emphasized Frisco's need to continue his work and Felicia's need to care for their daughters. Although this disruption to the fairy tale seemingly leaves intact traditional gender roles, Felicia's long period as a single mother has led her to criticize these roles and their implications for her life. A December 1995 *General Hospital* scene, set in the middle of the night, featured Felicia pacing the floor with her screaming baby as she sarcastically muttered:

> It's Mommy's responsibility to deal with things like this, even if Daddy was here. . . . But he's off, he's off saving the free world from the threat of

the month, which is what he does. . . . And this is what I do. Would I want to be off saving the free world from the threat of the month? No, I certainly wouldn't.

Regular viewers well knew that the adventuresome Felicia *would* like to be off saving the world, as much as she loved her daughters, and that she deeply resented Frisco's abdication of his responsibilities to his family. Thus, while certain moments in Frisco and Felicia's on-screen relationship lived up to the fairy-tale romance ideal, the ongoing nature of soap storytelling had led to developments that questioned the desirability of that fairy tale and its gender-specific roles. When Jack and Kristina exchange gender-prescriptive dialogue during *Weddings of a Lifetime*, the intertextual associations between *Weddings*, the actors' personal relationship, and their soap opera characters suggest not only the permeability of boundaries between fact and fiction but also the disputability of ideals like fairy-tale romance and marriage. In one sense, the Wagners and their soap character counterparts represent ideals of heterosexual romance and marriage, perfect, synergistic reflections of the fairy-tale romances featured on the show. In another sense, the Wagners' unorthodox romance (an on-and-off relationship, a baby out of wedlock) and the disruption of Frisco and Felicia's love story might suggest that heterosexual partnering is rarely as ideal as Disney makes it seem, that Disney's fairy tales—even the real-life ones featured on *Weddings*—only exist in fantasy.

An additional feature of the *Weddings of a Lifetime* texts that hints at the vulnerability of the Disney wedding fantasy is their use of genre. *Weddings* features a blend of genres, most prominently combining the two broad categories of fantasy (e.g., the Disney fairy tales) and reality (e.g., the real-world couples). Recent genre theorists have argued that generic combination is a regular feature of Hollywood film and television texts and a primary source of their polysemy.[10] *Weddings of a Lifetime* supports such an understanding of genre mixing, for its combination of generic elements allows for a range of potential readings. More so than the average instance of genre blending in mainstream texts, however, *Weddings'* amalgamation of genres multiplies even the typical range of readings available. In bringing together the fairy tale and nonfictional

genres such as the live event, the tabloidized reality show (e.g., *Cops*), and the infomercial, *Weddings* fuses genres that are rarely fused. In crossing and recrossing the line between fantasy and reality, the series cross-promotes multiple Disney products, including the ideals of heterosexual family life on which the empire's fortunes rest. At the same time, this generic mixing can be seen to challenge the believability of the fairy-tale fantasy and its Lifetime-documented reality.

The program's fairy-tale elements are the most predictable and the most Disney influenced of its generic parts and, as such, they rely most heavily on other Disney texts, particularly *Cinderella*. Heterosexuality pervades the 1950 Disney cartoon, from the birds that awaken Cinderella to the king's obsessive desire for grandchildren. The king's need for children produced within the heterosexual nuclear family matches Disney's need for such families to sustain its empire, while Cinderella's focus on goods such as her ball gown and her coach romanticizes the consumptive desires Disney hopes to instill in its young audiences. The Disney Fairy Tale Wedding department offers the lived experience of Cinderella's trip to the ball for a substantial fee, and *Weddings of a Lifetime* featured real-life couples getting to play *Cinderella*. In the first episode, David proposes to Suzanne in an evening-long *Cinderella* fantasy, complete with a new dress, glass slipper, and bended-knee proposal in front of that Disney World trademark, Cinderella's Castle. In the second episode, the "fairy godmother" who saw Michael propose to Anne on Sally Jesse Raphael's talk show describes how she was moved to write to Disney to request a fairy-tale wedding for the couple. These intertextual references fulfill Disney's synergistic promotional aims as well as assist its efforts in reifying heterosexual romance. The presence of the fairy tale within *Weddings'* generic mix is perhaps Disney's strongest push for its version of heterosexual romance.

However, the intersection of these fairy-tale elements with elements of nonfictional programming, particularly the live event, the reality program, and the infomercial, complicate the program's assertion of heterosexual marital bliss. In the first two episodes, *Weddings of a Lifetime* makes pretensions of "liveness" a central feature, one designed to authenticate the fairy tales as real. Jack and Kristina Wagner carry handheld microphones, using them to directly address the audience and to interview the wedding party and the guest singer. Other markers of the program's liveness include flubbed lines, awkward performances by the couples and wedding parties during the ceremonies, and even a "Live" graphic in the corner of the screen. Such features of the live television event succeed in reinforcing the reality of the on-screen tale, analogizing it to breaking news and to sports programming, a likeness also assisted by the Wagners' "play-by-play" analysis of the prewedding and postwedding rituals. However, because such genres are usually so unrelated to stories of fantasy romance, their invocation might also disrupt the seamlessness of the Disney fairy tale. The inclusion of live television as a generic element thus helps perpetuate the polysemy of the *Weddings* text.

Like the elements of the live event, those of the tabloidized reality program also attempt to inject a sense of truth into the fairy-tale-like stories. Faithful to the reality genre, *Weddings of a Lifetime* features interviews with the couples and their families and reenactments of significant moments in the pairs' romances. In the second episode, for example, Anne and Michael narrate the story of their initial meeting at (where else?) Disney World. A reenactment of their first encounter on the Disney monorail, followed by recreations of their day together throughout the theme park (including stops at Space Mountain, Pirates of the Caribbean, and the Electric Light Parade), ends on a cable car, the young lovers kissing as fireworks light up the night sky. Like much of the program, this segment invokes the infomercial as much as any other genre, but its use of the reenactment is specific to the reality program. Although the genre's title suggests an adherence to truth, the tabloidized reputation of reality television makes its brand of truth immediately suspect. Much as reality programs like *Cops* and *Rescue 911* rely on past television images of police and emergency work to construct their images of real cops and paramedics, so, too, does *Weddings of a Lifetime* rely on past images of fairy-tale romance and marriage (like *Cinderella*) to construct its images of heterosexual happiness. In addition, the reality replayed on *Weddings of a Lifetime* is specifically created for the television event. Not only the reenactments, but also the wedding preparations and ceremonies themselves

are Disney's and Lifetime's constructions, staged for the cameras even though they result in legally binding marriage contracts between the couples. The "reality" of the reality program, suspect in any case, works in particularly convoluted ways in *Weddings of a Lifetime*, attempting to authenticate the fairy-tale romances, but inevitably pointing to their constructedness.

The other nonfiction genre that fractures the fairy-tale world of the Disney romances is the infomercial genre, present throughout the program. While the first two episodes openly hawk Disney and the Fairy Tale Wedding Pavilion, the third episode features Jon and Stacy frolicking around the Sandals Resort, another purveyor of fantasy "destination" weddings. Each of the first three episodes also includes plugs for the dress designers and tuxedo manufacturers. Yet the program's infomercial tendencies are so overt as to be ironic at points. As Jack Wagner narrates over visuals of the reception room in the first episode:

> Guests will be taken through an enchanted forest to a replica of Cinderella's castle by crossing a drawbridge over a moat past the armed guards into the courtyard with fountains, flowers, and endless greenery for a feast fit for kings and queens.

Reading like a game show announcer's description of the sponsor's prize, Wagner's breathless delivery mocks the excessiveness of the arrangements while fulfilling a promotional role. Because the infomercial has become such a well-known television genre, and because it clashes so harshly with the idealized world of the fairy tale, *Weddings of a Lifetime*'s infomercial elements not only undercut its fairy-tale elements but undercut themselves too. Neither the reality nor the fantasy of the program are undisputed; its generic mix fractures the text's meaning such that Disney's reaffirmation of heterosexual romance and marriage is left in tenuous standing.

After "The End": The Cultural Politics of Media Conglomeration

Weddings of a Lifetime is a product low on the Walt Disney Company's chain of significance and profitability. As a quarterly series of specials on a cable network the conglomerate half-owns, its fortunes rank nowhere close to those of feature film and merchandising bonanzas like *Beauty and the Beast* or *Aladdin*. Yet the very smallness of this product, its specificity as a niche-marketed offering from a media giant, allows it to represent the micro-instances of Disney's hold on our wallets and our imaginations. In addition, *Weddings*' organizing ideologies of heterosexual romance and family values foreground the significance of these issues for Disney's image, an image that has been constitutive of its economic success. The deeply wedded connections between Disney's industrial standing as a global conglomerate seeking to balance mass and niche markets while maximizing synergistic ties and its cultural standing as a bastion of family values and heterosexual hegemony come to the fore in *Weddings of a Lifetime* in ways that make this small-scale program a highly representative case study of late-twentieth-century media.

At the center of *Weddings*' significance, and of the late-twentieth-century media's significance, are the blurred boundaries between reality and fantasy, fact and fiction, truth and falsity, which many claim earmark the cultural period of postmodernity.[11] When these boundaries are blurred in *Weddings of a Lifetime*, it is possible to see the progressive potential of such cultural confusion, although this potential could be even more clearly delineated with evidence of actual audience readings of the program. Without such evidence, we can speculate that the influence of the tabloidized reality genre throws into doubt the authenticity of the featured couples' fairy-tale romances and consequently throws into doubt the truth of sexual hierarchies that privilege the heterosexual nuclear family to the detriment of other human relationships of love and support. This is not to say that those hierarchies do not continue to hold great sway. Much of the success of *Weddings of a Lifetime* is due to the persistent appeal of fantasy images of heterosexual romance to many viewers. Just as appealing are the program's pretensions to reality; the fantasy images are so compelling because they are supposed to be real. Perhaps what *Weddings of a Lifetime* most assuredly says about the cultural politics of media conglomeration is that, as powerful as synergistic ties can be, the multiplicity of meanings they contribute to a single text can keep that text from fully endorsing any one ideological stance, even one as deeply ingrained as that of heterosexual romance and marriage.

Notes

1. See McChesney (2000), Turow (1992), and Barber (1995) for examples of scholarship that justifiably denounces media conglomeration and its consequences for a media-saturated public sphere.

2. Wasko (1996) notes that the Disney empire is an ideal case for this sort of integrated analysis.

3. For details on these synergies and those throughout all arms of the Disney conglomerate, see Gloede et al. (1995).

4. When the episodes hosted by the Wagners aired, Jack Wagner was starring in the FOX series *Melrose Place* as the lying and womanizing Dr. Peter Burns. Thus, the intertextual associations generated through this role might be seen as disruptive to the fairy-tale romance represented in *Weddings*.

5. See Andrew Ross (1999) for an in-depth discussion of Celebration.

6. David Harvey's (1989) *The Condition of Postmodernity* elaborates on these industrial shifts of the late twentieth century.

7. In what follows, I offer my own analysis of the polysemic potential of *Weddings of a Lifetime*. A study of actual audience responses to the show would tell us whether this resistant potential is realized by the program's everyday viewers.

8. The gendered, racial, and sexual identities of the couples remained relatively consistent in all of the episodes aired before the series' format change in 2000. The occasional aberrations, such as one episode that featured an Asian American couple, did not substantially change the formula or disrupt the Disney-friendly messages about traditional romance.

9. Although irrelevant at the time of the initial *Weddings* airings, the Wagners have since divorced, as have David and Suzanne Cobb, the couple married in the first *Weddings* episode.

10. On film genres, see Rick Altman (1999). On television genres, see Jason Mittell (2001).

11. For the purposes of this analysis, the characterization of postmodernity by theorist Jean Baudrillard may be most appropriate. Baudrillard (1983) points to Disney as the disturbing epitome of the hyperreal and often as an emblem of postmodern America itself. His argument that Disneyland—and, I would add, the entire Disney empire—is "a deterrence machine set up in order to rejuvenate in reverse the fiction of the real" understands the Disney theme park as the fulfillment of an

imaginary world apart from the "real" world that thus helps to sustain a distinction between real and imaginary, truth and falsity that does not exist (p. 25). In Baudrillard's thinking, Disney deters us from recognizing that reality and fiction have become one and, thus, that the truths we believe in are mere constructs.

References

Altman, Rick. 1999. *Film/Genre*. London: British Film Institute.

Barber, Benjamin R. 1995. *Jihad vs. McWorld*. New York: Ballantine Books.

Battaglio, Stephen. 1996. Ellen's Sex Life Scrutinized. BPI Entertainment News Wire, September 16.

Baudrillard, Jean. 1983. *Simulations*. Translated by Paul Foss, Paul Patton, and Philip Beitchman. New York: Semiotext(e).

Becker, Ron. 1998. Prime-Time Television in the Gay Nineties: Network Television, Quality Audiences, and Gay Politics. *The Velvet Light Trap* 42 (Fall): 36–47.

Bronstein, Carolyn. 1994. Mission Accomplished? Profits and Programming at the Network for Women. *Camera Obscura* 33–34: 213–42.

Cheers & Jeers. 1996. *TV Guide*, November 23, 14.

Curtin, Michael. 1997. On Edge: Culture Industries in the Neo-Network Era. In *Making and Selling Culture*, edited by Richard Ohmann. Hanover, NH: University Press of New England.

DeGeorge, Gail, and Ronald Grover. 1994. Reanimating Disney World. *Business Week*, December 5, 41.

Gibbs, Nancy. 1995. Easy as ABC. *Time*, August 14, 24.

Gloede, W. F., B. Sharkey, R. Brunelli, M. Freeman, L. Miles, M. Murgi, M. Adams, M. Krantz, A. Sacharaow, A. Mundy, and C. Hurton. 1995. The Company Eisner Keeps. *Mediaweek*, August 7, 14–24.

Harvey, David. 1989. *The Condition of Postmodernity*. Oxford, UK: Basil Blackwell.

Haugsted, Linda. 1995. Critics Still Skeptical of Cable's On-Air Offerings. *Multichannel News*, July 17, 34.

It's a Soap World After All. 1996. *TV Guide*, March 16, 54.

Jim Hjelm Dresses Featured on Lifetime Television. 1996. *Business Wire*, February 9.

Kinder, Marsha. 1991. *Playing with Power in Movies, Television, and Video Games*. Berkeley: University of California.

McChesney, Robert W. 2000. *Rich Media, Poor Democracy: Communication Politics in Dubious Times*. New York: New Press.

McConville, Jim. 1995. Lifetime Adds Threesome for Fall. *Broadcasting & Cable*, August 7, 22.

Mittell, Jason. 2001. A Cultural Approach to Television Genre Theory. *Cinema Journal* 40 (3): 3–24.

Muller, Joann. 1996. Foes to Mickey: You Dirty Rat; Boycott Bandwagon Rolls on as Churches Say Firm Forsakes Morals for Money. *Boston Globe*, September 1, E1.

Nashawaty, Chris. 1996. A Shot in the Park. *Entertainment Weekly*, March 8, 8.

Ross, Andrew. 1999. *The Celebration Chronicles: Life, Liberty, and the Pursuit of Property in Disney's New Town*. New York: Ballantine Books.

Rothchild, John. 1995. A Mouse in the House. *Time*, December 4, 62–63.

SBC to Boycott Disney, Evangelize Jews. 1996. *The Christian Century*, July 3, 81.

Turow, Joseph. 1992. The Organization Underpinnings of Contemporary Media Conglomerates. *Communication Research* 19 (6): 682–704.

Vejnoska, Jill. 1999. Lights . . . camera . . . I do. *The Atlanta Journal and Constitution*, June 21, 1B.

Wasko, Janet. 1996. Understanding the Disney Universe. In *Mass Media and Society*, edited by James Curran and Michael Gurevitch. London: Arnold.

14.
GENDER AND THE COMMODIFICATION OF COMMUNITY

Women.com and gURL.com

Leslie Regan Shade

This chapter will chronicle the transformation of two online communities designed specifically for women (Women.com) and young girls (gURL.com), whose origin stories in the early to mid-1990s began as earnest attempts to produce feminist-oriented content for a demographic that was not then adequately represented on the Internet. Feminist pioneers created their communities in the heady days of Internet utopianism, when the North American female population of the Internet was paltry, in comparison to its current gender parity. Women.com and gURL.com are interesting case studies because, as we shall see, both communities became part of the wave of dot.com euphoria, merging with other companies and creating commercial ventures, capitalizing on Internet stock speculation, and, in the process, diluting the nature of its feminist content to appeal to a mainstream female audience, thus targeting and commodifying a particular female demographic.

Women.com and gURL.com are cautious tales of how cutting-edge online feminist communities became part of the feminization of the Internet, by which I refer to the process whereby the creation of popular content privileges women's consumption, rather than encouraging their production or critical analysis. The corporate history of Women.com and gURL.com will be detailed, and the elements that shape their notion of community (such as discussion boards, content forums, user agreements and privacy policies) will be analyzed. As will be shown, the case studies of Women.com and gURL.com illustrate how

community has been transformed by the process of commodification, and how users are conceived not as active agents or citizens, but as consumers. What were once burgeoning feminist communities have since been transmogrified into female-oriented spaces where empowerment is often equated with consumer sovereignty.

Women.com

> Did you expect a feminist revolution online, empowering women to toss aside those astrology readings and turn off Ally McBeal, to run for president on a platform of halting genital mutilation in Africa? Those who thought the Web would be more like *Ms.* than *Mademoiselle*—believing that all women were itching for more intellectualism—were deluded.[1]

Women.com emerged in 1993 as Women's WIRE (Worldwide Information Resource & Exchange). As this was before graphical interfaces and even the earliest incarnation of the World Wide Web, Mosaic, was popularized, Women's WIRE was launched as a dial-up service, and then moved on to the commercial bulletin board service CompuServe, before establishing in 1995 a presence on the World Wide Web. It used First Class software, which bundled together chat, message boards, libraries, and upload and download areas. Subscription costs were $15/month for two hours, with additional hours billed at $2.50/hour.

Women's WIRE was founded by Ellen Pack, former chief operating officer at Torque Systems Inc., a software company, and Nancy Rhine, who worked in customer support at the Well, a famous online network, known for its communitarian zeal, emanating from the Bay Area.[2]

In the early 1990s, estimates of women's online participation were approximately 15% of all Internet participants, with most women accessing the Internet through universities and in high-tech workplaces. Access to the Internet for women was an emerging social and political issue. Exemplary in this regard was a loose coalition of women called BAWIT (Bay Area Women in Telecommunications) who presented one of the earliest 'manifestos' on gender issues in online communication at the Computers, Freedom, and Privacy Conference in 1993. Issues BAWIT identified included the need for women to become more active users and designers of computer networking, identification of online harassment and sexist forms of online interaction, the prevalence of pornography, and the paucity of women in computer science programs.[3] Early Internet content for women included a variety of feminist-oriented listservs and Usenet newsgroups, emphasizing academic and technical interests.[4]

In 1994, subscription information for Women's WIRE read:

> WOMEN'S WIRE draws its content from the media, newswires, women's organizations, government sources and, most importantly, from its subscribers—offering a central source for the latest women's news and information. Topic areas include news & politics, the environment, parenting, education, health & fitness, technology, arts & leisure, careers & finance, and more. Subscribers can access the latest legislative updates, reports, health abstracts, event calendars, and other information resources on issues impacting women. In addition, there are cultural resources like book, music and movie reviews, and conversations on a multitude of topics. Not only that, but WOMEN'S WIRE offers Internet email, mailing lists, AP and Reuters newswires, and Usenet newsgroups, too![5]

Content on Women's WIRE emphasized current news and affairs, and encouraged political activism.

Subscribers were expected to participate and interact on diverse conferences, and take a role in building community content. According to Ellen Pack, Women's WIRE started off with 500 'founding subscribers' enlisted to develop an online community that would "foster diversity . . . people with something to contribute, personally, intellectually or through their involvements. While many subscribers will already be familiar with computer conferencing, our goal is to make it so easy to get around online that it's completely unnecessary to be technologically sophisticated."[6] The emphasis on creating community content was a natural for co-founder Nancy Rhine, who got her start in community development when she was a member of The Farm, an intentional community in Tennessee formed in 1971, famous for their role in promoting home births and midwifery.[7] When Rhine relocated to California, she joined other ex-Farm members who were at the Well, where she realized that "women, especially, would adopt the Internet on a global scale for exchanging ideas and information on everything from politics and discrimination issues to day-to-day child-rearing, career, and health information."[8]

According to Rhine, Women's WIRE became very popular as "Word spread like wildfire as activist-minded women joined to converse with a global, online population that was 90 percent female. The support and excitement was palpable among the first thousand paying customers, as women realized what this tool could do to help them make a living, raise their kids, and find support and information of all kinds."[9]

In 1995 Women's WIRE established a presence on the World Wide Web, and in 1996 it received more than 7.5 million hits a month, which represented 300,000 individual visitors. Original content was repackaged with wire stories from Reuters, and distribution relationships, corporate partnerships, and advertisers, including Levi's, signed on.[10] In 1997 Women's WIRE changed its name to Women.com, which reflected their domain name. Marlene McDaniel became CEO and Chairman. She had previously spent 30 years in the technology field (her senior executive marketing positions included stints at Sun Microsystems, 3Com, and publisher Ziff-Davis). At that time Women.com consisted of three separate entities: its popular Women's Wire online site, Beatrice's Web Guide (a guide to women's activities and Web sites), and Prevention's Healthy Ideas (health tips from Rodale's health and fitness magazine).[11] Later distribution agreements were struck with AOL, Microsoft's WomenCentral and Yahoo!, a partnership with Bloomberg News, and agreements with foreign media companies in Japan, Korea, Malaysia, and Latin America.

Under McDaniel, Women.com merged with Hearst New Media & Technology Home Arts.com in 1999. Each company held an equal 50% stake in the venture. The terms of agreement with Hearst obliged Women.com to access content from Hearst, which included their cable, television and magazine content, including their HomeArts.com site, their popular Astrology.com site, and distribution of online magazine sites including *Country Living Gardener, Country Living's Healthy Living, Good Housekeeping, Redbook,* and *Town & Country.*[12] Promotion of Women.com was via Hearst's television cable properties Lifetime, A&E, and the History Channel. Although Hearst's audience was more traditional and mainstream than Women.com's users, the business rationale was that an amalgamation of a wider female audience would create more advertising and e-commerce business ventures. Said McDaniel about the revamped Women.com: "It's a place to go where women can find a whole variety of things that appeal their interests. And it will give us the opportunity to serve our advertisers and our audience with better programming."[13]

By then, women's presence on the Internet had increased substantially, and corporations realized that one of the ways to attract more lucrative e-commerce traffic would be to target the 'elusive' female market, purportedly responsible for over half of household purchases. Marketers dissected the female online population to ascertain what strategies to employ in their bid to capture their spending dollars. Advertisers eagerly signed on for partnerships and joint ventures, and several 'one-stop shopping' women's portals were created, including competitors Oxygen Media and iVillage.com.[14] At that time, the climate for women's commercial online climate was heating up. The media paid much attention to the $87.6 million IPO in March 1999 of iVillage.[15] The stakes were up for "supremacy in the online battle to attract women Web users, prized as a growing and highly coveted (read: they spend a lot)."[16] Women.com executives recognized

this, and participated in a joint study with Proctor & Gamble, the consumer-products company, and Harris Interactive, a market research firm, to uncloak the psychographics of women's online behavior. Because men design most websites, McDaniel contended, "We want to understand how women use the Web to better design products and services for them."[17]

In the late 1990s, like so many Internet based ventures, Women.com decided to jump on the IPO bandwagon. Their 1999 IPO was launched at 3.75 million shares at $10 each. Early trading saw the stock price rise to almost $24. One month later the stock price was at 80% above initial offering price, but later plummeted to half of the IPO.

With the downturn in the Internet economy in 2000 and the intense competition for advertising monies, many women's Internet portals sunk, and their stock valuation plummeted.[18] In 2001 Women.com and iVillage announced a $36M merger.[19] As reported in *The Wall Street Journal,* "the deal supports the notion that the Internet cannot sustain several major ad-dependent sites catering to the niche market of women's interest."[20]

iVillage was co-founded by Nancy Evans and Candice Carpenter in 1995. Carpenter had previously worked with Time-Life and cable home shopping channels QVC. Evans was a well-known publishing executive, having been a columnist for *Glamour* magazine, the editor-in-chief of the Book-of-the-Month Club, and a president and publisher of Doubleday. In 1995 Carpenter and Evans, noting the paucity of online content for women, created Parent Soup, dedicated to parenting resources for women, which later changed into iVillage.

When iVillage began selling common stock in 1999 as part of their initial public offering (IPO), the opening bid was $95.88, and by the end of the first day Carpenter's stake—690,001 shares of stock—was worth over $80M.[21] Media attention was both adulatory and hostile because co-founders Candice Carpenter and Nancy Evans "were neither 'Webheads' nor computer geeks, but two women in their forties with controversial reputations rooted in the realm of books, magazines, and television."[22] The media paid particular attention to Carpenter, who also parlayed the media into a process she dubbed 'self-branding.'[23] Although Carpenter was frequently profiled in the media as one of the quintessential female Internet entrepreneurs, in November 2000 she left the company after receiving a one-time payment of $1.3-million.[24] Carpenter married, took the last name of her husband (Olson), and wrote a book published by McGraw-Hill, *Chapters: Create a Life of Exhilaration and Accomplishment in the Face of Change.*[25]

The iVillage Community

iVillage pioneered 'integrated sponsorships', wherein advertisers participate in the creation of online content and services; examples of early sponsorships included iVillage's Pet Channel, sponsored by pet food manufacturer Ralston Purina, and a 'behavior modification program' sponsored with the milk industry, consisting of e-mail reminders and message boards to drink three glasses of milk per day. Described as a "ganglion of corporate alliances and digital pathways that together form a network of seventeen Web sites, or 'channels,' through which the company seeks to build a community of women on the Internet."[26]

iVillage also had aspirations to 'monetize' its community by selling enough products and advertising to create profits. It purchased Lamaze Publishing (publisher of information for new and impending parents), and The Newborn Channel, broadcaster of instructional information to new mothers distributed in hospitals across the U.S. Like many emergent e-commerce ventures, iVillage attempted to exploit the 'stickiness' factor—the attributes that draw users into the websites and keep them online for long sessions. Quantifying the number of 'unique visitors' (also called 'eyeballs') and page tracks is the Web equivalent to Nielson Media television ratings and in its early days, iVillage reported more than 100-million page views per month.[27]

According to Cliff Figallo (an early member of the Well and known for his work on building online communities), since it's founding in 1995 iVillage has adopted several different business models. These include its origins as an advertiser-sponsored community site, to e-commerce ventures targeting women as the main household purchasers, to its acquisition

Table 14.1 Commodifying Community: The View from iVillage

Magazine sites include *Cosmopolitan, Country Living, Good Housekeeping, House Beautiful, Marie Claire, Redbook, Town & Country,* and *Victoria.*

iVillage advertising partners include: Clairol (hair coloring products), Country Crock (cooking and home decorating resources), Dewey Color System (psychological color profiling), eDiets (fitness and meal plans), Kraft (food processor and recipes), Match.com (dating service), Olay (facial and skin products), SmartSource (household consumer coupons), and WestPoint Stevens (home bed and bath linens).

Online integrated sponsorships and advertising include "deep integration of brand messages including sponsored content, customized bridge sites, special promotion, market intelligence, and problem-solving interactive tools". Marketing partners include Ford Motor Company; financial service companies PNC Bank, Visa, and Charles Schwab; consumer products companies Kimberly-Clark, Proctor & Gamble, Johnson & Johnson, and Unilever; pharmaceutical companies Pfizer and Glaxo-Wellcome; dog food company Ralston Purina; and online drugstore Planet RX.

Nineteen iVillage channels are loosely organized around subject matter, including family, health, work, money, food, relationships, beauty, shopping, diet and fitness, travels, pets, astrology. Channel features include interactive tools, access to experts, special features, and resources.

Member services include e-mail, games, coupons, newsletters, quizzes, and personals.

Community Challenges is a trademarked "behavior-changing program" featuring a "combination of defined steps and group collaboration" providing women "with a structured and supportive program through which to tackle—and conquer—common and pressing problems. Led by top experts, Community Challenges generally last six weeks and include weekly 'assignments' as well as special message boards and chats so that participants can interact with other women pursuing the same goals". Topics have included organizational skills, walking for fitness, and "thinking for thinness".

of Women.com when it moved to a paid subscription model, "leveraging on the needs and wants of the community."[28]

iVillage has several different types of community-related content, according to Kellie Gould, iVillage's senior vice president for programming: ". . . about 3,000 message boards about 900 weekly hosted chats, and we have roughly 2,500 'community leaders'". These leaders and community managers are volunteers who lead and guide the weekly-hosted chats, message boards, and interactive forums.[29] Gould refers to iVillage's content as 'evergreen issues': "They're about parenting and dieting and financial management–these kinds of things are so important to women for so many years–and their needs change. What we're really excited about is offering that information throughout their lives."[30]

iVillage's strategy is what Figallo refers to as "a lifecycle approach to community", wherein women return to the community as they go through different stages of their lives, from marriage to pregnancy to child rearing to careers to divorce (see Table 14.1 for details of iVillage community content).

Although iVillage boasts reaching 12.6% of the Internet population, claims that it ranks 13th among all digital media properties for women aged 18 and older, and "is the leading destination and brand and touches 31 million unique people", it is not without its critics. Commented Janelle Brown: "Other than a certain emphasis on resourcefulness, do-it-yourself-ism and pro-female positivity, there isn't much difference between the front page of iVillage and the cover of *Family Circle*, that of Women.com and *Cosmopolitan* (whoops, *Cosmopolitan* is now part of Women.com)."[31] Indeed, a recent look at iVillage featured a Women.com link to a spread on "Rock Star Workouts! How to get: Gwen's Abs, Britney's Bust, Madonna's arms, and Shakira's butt". Another feature, "Spring Cleaning for Real Women" linked to columnist "Clean-It Queen" Mary Ellen Pinkham, with sidebars to a feng shui quiz and links to storage products ("Organizing your CD or video collection has never been easier!!") to purchase.

Under the ownership of iVillage, Women.com has certainly shifted gears, going from intelligent women's commentary and oftentimes feminist content to a content slate concentrating on "gossip, sex & style". At Women.com ". . . you can leave life's pressures behind,

kick back and laugh at hilarious dating stories, get the hottest celebrity scoop, check out styles for your home and your closet, talk about sex, take revealing quizzes and amuse yourself with games that women love."[32] At *Girl Talk*, Sexual Bloopers are revealed (featuring bodily functions gone awry); *Date This Dude* allows one to vote for their favorite hottie; while Cosmo Sex reveals the secrets in Sex University (Oral Studies and Kinky Curriculum!). The site is littered with flash java-scripted pop-up and banner ads.

How is community conceptualized at Women.com and iVillage? Gustafson[33] has analyzed three popular women's sites—iVillage.com. Women.com, and Oxygen.com—to ascertain their rhetoric of community through design and its implication in the creation of the feminization of community online. She concludes that these sites, through their rules and coding practices, reinforce women's traditional roles as consumers. Integrated sponsorships and commercial partnerships are just one part of this package. Membership benefits include access to message boards, discounts, coupons, 'freebies', interactive quizzes, newsletters, and the ability to create ones own webpage. Becoming a member of iVillage (membership in Women.com is linked to iVillage) involves registering identification (name, e-mail address, gender, birth date, country and zip code are required fields) and agreeing to the Terms of Service. 'The Women's Network' (TWN) Terms of Service cover a range of issues; for instance, members who provide iVillage with false or misleading information may have their iVillage e-mail account and webpage terminated. Spam is not allowed, nor is anonymity or impersonating another member. Content is strictly enforced, as the following excerpt from the Terms of Service reads:

> . . . unlawful, harassing, libelous, defamatory, abusive, threatening, harmful, vulgar, obscene, profane, sexually oriented (unless within the scope of the topic area of a message board as determined by iVillage in its sole discretion), racially offensive, inaccurate, or otherwise objectionable material of any kind or nature or that encourages conduct that could constitute a criminal offense, give rise to civil liability or otherwise violate any applicable local, state, national or international law or regulation, or encourage the use of controlled substances.

For purposes of the immediately preceding sentence, "masked" vulgarity, obscenity or profanity (e.g. "f*ck") is deemed to be equivalent to including the actual objectionable word, phrase or symbol in your post, message or otherwise on TWN. iVillage reserves the right to delete any such material from TWN. [34]

Messages posted on iVillage in public areas are the property of iVillage. Members thus waive their intellectual property rights and grant to iVillage the use of any of their content:

> . . . royalty-free, perpetual, irrevocable, non-exclusive right (including any moral rights) and license to use, reproduce, modify, adapt, publish, translate, create derivative works from, distribute, communicate to the public, perform and display the content (in whole or in part) worldwide and/or to incorporate it in other works in any form, media, or technology now known or later developed, for the full term of any Rights that may exist in such content.[35]

In their Privacy Policy, iVillage assures its members that information they collect is to provide a better community for their members:

> iVillage uses the information it gathers for several purposes, such as to understand more about our audiences interests, to communicate with you and to give you a better experience when visiting the iVillage Network by personalizing tools, content, services and email messages. iVillage also uses this information to build new services and develop offers that iVillage believes are more relevant and valuable to you.[36]

However, at one time, a serious glitch at the iVillage Website allowed women to view other users' personal messages.[37] This infraction was quickly resolved.

Members are told that information collected about them from either iVillage or third parties is collected from server logs and cookies. Information is aggregated to create anonymous statistical demographic profiles of the iVillage members, which is used to determine trends and market research for potential advertisers and partners. As Gustafson writes: "iVillage is perhaps the most overt in its intention to promote tailored marketing and encourage organized, traditionally feminine modes of consumption. Surveys and discussion groups may bond community members to one another, while serving the broader purpose of providing detailed marketing information."[38]

iVillage is heavily dependent on sponsorships and advertising, which represent 78% and 81% of their revenues. Advertising revenues derive from short and long-term contracts, typically featuring banner advertisements on each page view, from which viewers may hyperlink to each advertiser's homepage. In their 2002 10K report to the Securities and Exchange Commission, it was stressed that iVillage's business depends on the market acceptance of the Internet as a medium for advertising. For year-end 2002 and 2001, revenues from the five largest iVillage customers accounted for approximately 38% and 37% of total revenues, respectively. The three largest advertisers (Proctor & Gamble, Hearst Communications, and Unilever) accounted for approximately 11%, 11% and 10% of total revenues. According to the 10K filing, "iVillage has not achieved profitability and iVillage expects to continue to incur operating losses for the foreseeable future. iVillage incurred net losses of approximately $33.9 million for the year ended December 31, 2002, $48.5 million for the year ended December 31, 2001, and $191.4 million for the year ended December 31, 2000. As of December 31, 2002, iVillage's accumulated deficit was approximately $466.7 million."[39]

gURL.com

The Internet simultaneously expands on and explodes the image of the teenybopper with a phone welded to her ear, giving teenage girls an open forum to talk to anyone about anything. With her personally crafted identity, a Web-wise girl can be free from the judgment she feels in real life and find out what she needs to know without worrying about whispers of her dilemma leaking out in gym class the next day. Girls no longer have to wait until they are 27 (and drunk) to admit to a girlfriend that they masturbate. Now they can go online and get advice on how to get the most out of the showerhead technique.[40]

gURL.com began as a project initiated in 1996 by students Rebecca Odes, Esther Drill, and Heather McDonald at New York University's Interactive Telecommunications Program. According to Odes, "The lack of interesting media was the subject of a lot of high school late-night discussions . . . after we started studying at NYU, we thought maybe the Web would be the place to do something different."[41]

gURL.com differed from other websites set up for teen girls because it presented a frank and feisty attitude towards dating, sex, and beauty. According to its creators, it was "committed to discussing issues that affect the lives of girls age 13 and up in a non-judgmental, personal way. Through honest writing, visuals and liberal use of humour, we try to give girls a new way of looking at subjects that are crucial to their lives. Our content deals frankly with sexuality, emotions, body image, etc."[42] Popular content included "Paper Doll Psychology" which allowed one to dress a figure and receive a pseudo-psychological assessment of what the chosen outfit says about the outfitter. "The Boob Files" included first person essays on breasts, and "Deal With It" tackled issues regarding sexuality, parents, growing up, and body issues.

The gURL.com founders were often featured as part of New York's Silicon Alley 'digerati', multimedia artists who pioneered a hip new style on the burgeoning Web.[43] Drill, McDonald, and Odes parlayed their gURL.com content into a best-selling book, *Deal With It!*, published by Pocket Books.[44] For 'mature teens', the book covered a gamut of issues, from sex and sexuality, to the body (functions and image), to careers. Described by *New York Magazine* as "Our Bodies Ourselves for teenagers—minus the 100% cotton", it received critical acclaim for its honesty and spunkiness. A few years later they created *The Looks Book*[45], an eclectic examination of beauty throughout the ages, the body (images, parts, modification), and the creation of style (including Bombshell, Baby Doll, African Queen, California Girl, Chick Geek, and Modern Primitive). The books reinforced Odes' intention that "Our job is not to give girls a reason to be online, but to have them realize that this message can exist offline."[46]

In December 1997, gURL.com was acquired by dELiA*s Corporation, a direct-market fashion retailer to teenage girls and young women. They folded gURL.com into their network of teen-centered Internet properties, the iTurf Network.[47] Two years later iTurf issued an IPO for $92.4M, and stock sold for $66/share the first day. One of their initiatives was with Upoc, a wireless media company targeting youth, with the goal "to send updates on news, shopping and local events from the gURL.com Web site to pagers and mobile phones."[48]

With the downtown in Internet stocks a year later, dELiA*s shut down or sold off all their Internet properties except for gURL.com. Then, in 2001 Primedia, a large special-interest magazine publisher, acquired gURL.com from dELiA*s for an undisclosed price. The purchase of gURL.com was meant to augment their existing teen properties, which they had started to build up in October 2000 when they brought in former MTV Networks Online President Fred Seibert to head their Teen Internet Initiative, designed to leverage the Web assets of their offline publications, including *Seventeen, Teen Beat,* and *Tiger Beat* magazines.

Primedia's magazine holdings include over 150 general interest publications covering an array of topics: entertainment, automobiles, sports, crafts and jewelry, equine, gardening, high technology, hunting and fishing, marine sports, motorcycles, quilting and sewing, shooting sports, action sports, and sports news. Primedia's Youth Entertainment Group includes several magazines focusing on music (*Bop, Teen Beat, Tiger Beat*) and teen celebrities (*Teen Stars, Teen, BB*) but also Channel One Network, a commercial newscast seen in many U.S. high schools, which has not been without its critics as a blatant example of the commercialization of public space.[49]

Cross-promotion of Primedia's holdings is evident with gURL.com and *Seventeen* magazine, with the ability for gURL.com members to contribute content to *Seventeen,* and with *Seventeen* ads appearing on the site. However, in April 2003 Primedia announced the sale of *Seventeen* and other branded properties to Hearst Publishing for $182.4M.[50] It is not yet known how this will affect gURL.com.

The demographic of tweens (pre-teens aged 8–12) and teens in North America is huge. Generation Y, as it is often referred to, consists of 71M teens and young adults in the U.S. alone. Between 1990–2000, the number of teens aged 12–19 increased to 32M, and it is expected to increase to 34.6 million by 2006. It is also a very multi- and intra-cultural demographic.[51] Concomitant with this increase in youth is an exponential growth in tween targeting and marketing. YTV (Youth Television Network) in Toronto estimates that in Canada, tweens "control about $1.9 billion in spending every year", with $15 billion in the U.S., from "gifts (particularly from doting grandparents who live longer and have fewer grandkids than their counterparts of a generation ago), allowances, [and] money from jobs such as babysitting and other spending money."[52] Globally, the youth market is growing dramatically, and represents "a ripe and growing consumer base for U.S. marketers, with $100 billion in spending power, even if they live in developing countries, among chaotic economic circumstances (in Argentina, for example), or in countries not considered the States' political allies."[53]

Targeting teenagers for their spending prowess in the marketplace is nothing new. Record has chronicled the post-World War II courting of the teen consumer, when advertisers seized teens as a viable consumer demographic. Particularly attractive were teenage women, who were wooed by a bevy of products that were the precursor for their future role in the domestic sphere. The emergence of *Seventeen* magazine in 1944 exemplified how advertisers and publishers saw opportunities to enlist young women in "embracing white middle-class heteronormativity . . . [focusing] primarily on the young women's domestic role and her need to spend money in order to achieve domestic bliss."[54]

The gURL.com Community

Unlike other web-based communities for young women, gURL.com has an edgier–and even feminist–attitude. Content is organized around the topics of everyday management ("Deal With It"), fashion and beauty ("Looks Aren't Everything"), Shopping ("Stop, Look, and Listen"), careers ("Where Do I Go From Here?"), celebrities ("Movers, Shakers, and Media Makers") and Sports. Interactive features include advice columns, polls, "shout outs", comics, games, e-cards, and contests.

Drill, Odes, and McDonald were prescient in realizing that girls wanted to be not mere consumers of content, but creators. As Kearney[55] has observed, young women have created a vibrant zine and ezine culture, often parodying mainstream commercial culture and dominant discourses on femininity. Early content on gURL.com was hailed for its irreverent nature and interactive features. Current games include "Make Your Own Rock Band", "Make Your Own Reality TV Show" and "Try the Prom Dress Selector." The Deal With It! section includes "Sucky Emotion Comics" and "Mizbehavior." Members may contribute comics and poems, and are invited to give their opinions on various topics of current news interest; recent headlines have included "Georgians plan whites-only program", "War on the Environment", "Madonna Slams American Values", and "Senate Passes Bill Limiting Abortion".

Despite gURL.com's alliance with *Seventeen* magazine (banner ads entreating members to subscribe to the magazine appear throughout a gURL.com session), content encourages young women to think in careerist modes, and the "Movers and Shakers" section features interviews with women working in diverse fields: included have been a civil rights lawyer, a Congresswomen, a gURL.com web designer, a journalist, archeologist, writer, neuroscientist, and astronaut.

Membership in gURL.com is free and includes participation in chatrooms, access to free webpages, ability to participate in surveys, and publishing opportunities. To sign up for membership, users are asked for a nickname, password, first name, birth date, zip/postal code, state/province, and country, plus a current e-mail address. Users may opt out of receiving e-mail updates from gURL.com partners, and as well can opt out of participating in the gURL.com survey. Upon registering, members receive the following notice:

> I agree to treat other gURL members with respect in all interactions: on the chat, in the shoutouts, in emails, etc. I am aware that attacking another gURL member is not allowed and that all comments of this nature will be removed, as will the people who say them.

A lengthy legal notice agreement is also appended, which tells the member that 1) they use gURL.com at their own risk and that "we cannot guarantee the accountability or reliability of any information obtained through gURL.com"; 2) intellectual property rights adhere to any text, images, or sounds transmitted through gURL.com, and that any content submitted through gURL.com remains the property of gURL.com—"a royalty-free, perpetual, irrevocable, worldwide, non-exclusive right and license to use, reproduce, modify, adapt, publish, translate, create derivative works from, distribute, perform, transmit and display such Content (in whole or part) and/or to incorporate it in other works in any form, media or technology now known or later developed for the full term of any Rights that may exist in such Content"; 3) gURL.com is not liable for any damages resulting from the use of gURL.com, such as downloading inappropriate or buggy content; 4) modifications to the agreement can be made at any time.

After agreeing to these legal notices (it is doubtful that most young girls actually wade through the convoluted legalese), members are brought to their personal survey profile, where they are asked to give their opinion on what they like to do in their spare time (a wide range of choices are given, from reading, mak-

ing crafts, cooking, e-mailing, to participating in an organized religion), what sorts of electronic devices they intend to purchase in the next six months, survey topics interested in (cars, foods, jobs/money, politics, shopping), whether or not one intends to go to college, modem speed, access to credit card, how much money is spent in an average week, how much time spent online per week, how often one visits gURL.com, and whether one is a reader of *Seventeen* magazine.

Members can then create a gURL.com profile. They are asked to provide information on their age (junior high, high-school, college, or older), provide personal comments without providing full name or real addresses, click on interests, sports, music, and arts genres preferred, academic interests, and choose an icon to represent themselves (includes cartoons of a sun, red lips, daisy, basketball, star, fox, television set, soccer ball, hamburger). Member services are plentiful, and members are encouraged to provide input on the types of features they want (see Table 14.2: Commodifying Community: The View from gURL.com).

Table 14.2 Commodifying Community: The View from gURL.com

gURL Chat:	Includes chatrooms and live chats. Chats are "a place where members of the gURL connection can chat with and meet each other. If that is not what you have in mind, i.e. you hope to meet boys or to cyber, please go elsewhere!", and "Live chats with celebrities, health experts, and goofballs".
gURL Grams:	Allows members to send messages to each other
gURL Profiles:	When users are signing up for membership, they create a profile which "lists your likes, interests, and a personal message to the gURL community. Other members of the gURL community can view your profile and, from there, send you a gURLgram or add you to their friends list".
gURL Pages:	Free webpage sites for members.
Shout-Outs:	These are bulletin boards where members can read, post, and respond to various topics. These include Shout Out to gURL—for advice on gURL.com; Shout Out for Advice—subtopics include dating, friends, school, family, bodies, emotions; Poetry Shout Out—subtopics include emotion, hate, love poems, my self, nature, relationships, the state of the world; Shout Out a Story—fiction, horror, mystery, romance, sci-fi and fantasy; HTML Shout Out—learn and practice hypertext markup language; College Shout Outs—academics, getting in, freshman year, living situations, social stuff, vacation, working; Spirituality Shout Out—beliefs, religions, faith, God, the Bible, the occult, spiritual practices; Media Shout Out; Sports Shout Out.
gURL Mall:	An online store, where one can buy books (*Deal With It!*), subscribe to *Seventeen* magazine, order CDs from Sony Music, purchase *Seventeen* home bedding fashions (hyperlinked to retailer JC Penney), and other items. The *Classifieds* section also provides links to shopping and events sites.
gURL Contests:	Includes links to various retail contests (CoverGirl Summer Stylin' Sweepstakes, Rockstar Sweepstakes, Clearasil's 'Celebrate Your Prom in Style')

A "Note to Parents" tells them that the operating ethos behind gURL.com is that "information is a positive thing":

> We created gURL to be an alternative to prescriptive traditional girls' magazines, and our site strives to present a variety of experiences that are relevant to teen girls. Because of this, gURL sometimes contains mature content dealing with sexuality, body image, emotions, self-destructive behavior, etc. Our honesty is part of what makes our site resonate with our audience . . . We recognize that not every girl is ready to deal with these issues at the same age. If your daughter is younger than our recommended age or you think she is not ready to deal with mature content at whatever age, we suggest you direct her to another site.[56]

gURL.com adheres to the Children's Online Privacy Protection Act (COPPA), a FTC regulation that restricts the personal information children's websites can collect from individuals under the age of 13. Their Privacy Statement says that "they sometimes collect personal information from our users", but that information collected during membership will not be sold to third parties outside Primedia "although you may occasionally receive mailings from advertisers". Members are cautioned to be aware of the privacy policies for sites outside of gURL.com.

Although gURL.com contends that its editorial content and expressed views are "independent of any influence by advertisers or marketing partners", one has to wonder if this is always the case. gURL. com persuades its members, through its various discursive strategies (particularly its hip language and humour and its recognition of the importance of popular culture in the everyday lives of girls) that they are part of a community whose viability and energy depends upon their contributions. But this captive community is also a temptation for online marketers, who see a sizable demographic of affluent and active consumers.

gURL.com illustrates the increasing debate surrounding the ethics of online marketing targeted to children and young people. The blurring lines between content and advertising, particularly with media convergence, has created for many marketers a new and exciting challenge. But for others—academics and children's media advocates—the brave new world of digital media for children portends a perilous decline in non-commercial media spaces.[57]

Conclusion

Tracing the corporate history and examining their discourses of community reveal howWomen.com and gURL.com exemplify both the feminization of the Internet and the commodification of community. The creation of consumer-oriented content targeting women and young girls by media behemoths and a new breed of competitive entrepreneurs is one facet of the feminization of the Internet. The other is the erasure of race and class. As Nakamura contends, "Gender and race can just as easily be co-opted by the e-marketplace. Commercial sites such as these tend to view women and minorities primarily as potential markets for advertisers and merchants rather than as 'coalitions' ".[58]

The commandeering of the semblance and sensibility of community has been an objective of many commercial sites on the Internet. This contrasts with utopian sentiments of virtual communities, wherein a gift economy flourishes regardless of geographic locale. The tension between the Internet as a marketplace of ideas constituted by citizens, versus the Internet as a mere market controlled by corporations, is expressed well by Fernback who writes

> When community becomes as purchasable as any other commodity, it loses its meaning as a fundamental social institution . . . people are empowered as consumers rather than as citizens when they participate in communities that are designed to be advertising billboards. If we are empowered as consumers, we make democratic decisions based on our roles as consumers rather than as citizens. The audience becomes a market rather than a public.[59]

The late 1990s were heady days for the Internet. Fueled by media adulation, Wall Street hi-jinks, and a faith in market incentives, digital capitalism, or as pundits dubbed it, the "new economy", became a short-lived bust. Described as a "technicist neo-liberal mythology"[60], many of the products of the Internet, which burst onto the scene with much hype and hurrah, quickly went the way of vapor ware—here today, gone tomorrow. The original feminist qualities inherent in Women.com—and to a certain extent gURL.com—have been, similar to our current cultural backlash—diluted and packaged for a homogeneously idyllic audience commodity. The question is: will these 'communities' be sustainable, given the vicissitudes of convergence, or will they be merely passing fads?

Notes

1. Janelle Brown, "From Feminism to Fluff: Economics forces top sites to push content into line with print media," *The Vancouver Sun* (September 7, 2000): F14.
2. Howard Rheingold, *The Virtual Community: Homesteading on the Electronic Frontier*, revised edition. (Cambridge, MA: MIT Press, 2000).
3. Hoai-An Truong, "Gender Issues in Online Communications," version 4.3, 1993. URL: http://www.cpsr.org/cpsr/gender/bawit.cfp93 (May 1, 2003)
4. In August 1993, I delivered a talk on gender issues in networking at the first international conference on community networking (the International Free-Net Conference), at Carleton University in Ottawa, Canada. My paper detailed activity over the last few months on gender issues in computer networking, and discussed issues such as the participation of women in computer science and networking, social interactions, ethical issues including pornography, use of networks by women, and included a variety of references and online resources. The ascii text of the talk circulated widely on the Internet for years, and appeared on newsgroups, through private e-mails, on computer conferences, and later, on many sites on the World Wide Web. What was fascinating was the viral fashion in which the text circulated online, and the incredible interest and passion the topic—that of feminism and the Internet—generated. See *Gender Issues in Computer Networking* at URL: http://www.cpsr.org/cpsr/gender/leslie_regan_shade.txt
5. See http://www.cs.berkeley.edu/~jmankoff/women.wire.txt.
6. "Women's Wire Gets Serious About Business," *The Tampa Tribune* (August 19, 1995).
7. See http://www.thefarmcommunity.com/.
8. Nancy Rhine, "Populist Activism—Online Facilitation," *TechTV* (2001). URL: http://www.techtv.com/screensavers/print/0,23102,3335135,00.html (accessed May 1, 2003).
9. Nancy Rhine, "Populist Activism."
10. "Women's Wire Gets Serious."
11. Gary M. Sterne, "Women's Wire," *Link-Up* 15, no. 2 (March–April 1998): 20.
12. Jennifer Oldham, "Women.com, Hearst to Build Site for Women," *Los Angeles Times* (January 29, 1999); Greta Mittner, "Hearst.com Gives Muscle to Women.com," *Red Herring* (January 29, 1999). URL: http://www.redherring.com/insider/1999/0129/vc-women.html (accessed May 1, 2003).
13. "Women.com Gets Makeover," *Wired News* (January 28, 1999). URL: http://www.wired.com/news/culture/0,1284,17606,00.html (accessed May 1, 2003).
14. Leslie Regan Shade, *Gender and Community in the Social Construction of the Internet.* (New York: Peter Lang, 2002).
15. Erik Larson, "Free Money," *The New Yorker* (October 11, 1999): 76–85.
16. Chris Nerney, "Women.com IPO Turns Heads on Wall Street," *The Internet Stock Report* (October 15, 1999).
17. Lindsey Arendt, "How Women Buy, and Why," *Wired News* (November 17, 1999). URL: http://www.wired.com/news/business/0,1367,32483,00.html (accessed May 1, 2003).
18. Shelley Emling, "Web sites battle to lure women: Many full-service portals are struggling," *Edmonton Journal* (March 15, 2001): F2.
19. Jennifer Rewick, "iVillage.com to Buy Rival Women.com For $30 Million," *Wall Street Journal* (February 6, 2001): B8.
20. Ibid.
21. Larson, 85.
22. Larson, 76.
23. Ibid
24. Brad Reagan, "Openers—Where are they now? (Candice Olson)," *Wall Street Journal* (February 11, 2002): R4.
25. Ibid.
26. Larson, 78.
27. Ibid.
28. Cliff Figallo, "iVillage: Investing in community and banking on trust," *Econtent* 25, no. 6 (June 2002): 52–53.
29. Ibid.
30. Cited in Figallo, 2002.
31. Brown, "From Feminism to Fluff."
32. From "Women.com—About Us" at www.women.com.
33. Karen E. Gustafson, "Join Now, Membership is Free: Women's Web Sites and the Coding of Community", 168–188 in *Women & Everyday Uses of the Internet: Agency & Identity*, ed. Mia Consalvo and Susanna Paasonen. (New York: Peter Lang, 2002).
34. iVillage Terms of Service, June 22, 2001.
35. iVillage Terms of Service, June 22, 2001.
36. iVillage Privacy Policy, June 22, 2001.
37. Eugene Schultz, "More privacy breaches occur," *Computers & Security* 21, no. 7, 2002: 583–584.
38. Gustafson, 183.

39. iVillage Form10-K for Annual And Transition Reports Pursuant To Sections 13 or 15(d) of the Securities Exchange Act of 1934, For the fiscal year ended December 31, 2002. URL: http://www.edgar-online.com/bin/edgardoc/finSys_main.asp?dcn=0001125282-03-002637&nad= (accessed May 1, 2003).

40. Rebecca Odes, co-founder of gURL.com, quoted in Amanda Griscom, "Vital Signs: New Media Savants Check the Pulse of Silicon Alley." *The Village Voice,* January 19–25, 2000). URL: http://www.villagevoice.com/issues/0003/griscom.php (accessed May 1, 2003).

41. Michael J. Martinez, "gURLs Online and Out Loud." *ABC News* (April 10, 1998). URL: http://more.abcnews.go.com/sections/tech/dailynews/gurl980410.html (accessed May 1, 2003).

42. From www.gurl.com

43. Vanessa Grigoriadia, "Generation 1.0: Oldest Silicon Alley Veterans Tell All," *New York* (March 6, 2000).

44. See http://www.dealwithit.com.

45. See http://www.thelooksbook.com/.

46. Quoted in Martinez.

47. Brian Morrissey, "Primedia Scoops Up gURL.com from Delia's," *Silicon Valley Reporter* (May 29, 2001). URL: http://siliconalley.venturereporter.net/issues/sar05292001.html#Headline8615 (accessed May 1, 2003).

48. Deborah Mendez-Wilson, "Targeting gen 'Y': You go gURL!, *Wireless Week* 6, no. 28 (July 10, 2000):26.

49. See Ronald V. Bettig and Jeanne Lynn Hall, *Big Media, Big Money: Cultural Texts and Political Economics* (Lanham, MD: Rowman & Littlefield, 2003) and Henry A. Giroux, *Impure Acts: The Practical Politics of Cultural Studies.* (New York: Routledge, 2000).

50. Press release archive of April 24, 2003 at www.primedia.com.

51. Alison Stein Wellner. "The Teen Scene," *Forecast* 22, no. 9 (September 2002):1.

52. Elizabeth Payne, "Tweens: The latest sale bait: Too young to woo?," *Edmonton Journal* (April 28, 2002): D3.

53. Arundhati Parmar, "Global youth united," *Marketing News* v.36(22) (October 28, 2002): 1, 49.

54. Angela R. Record, "Born to Shop: Teenage Women and the Marketplace in the Postwar United States," 181–195 in *Sex & Money: Feminism and Political Economy in the Media,* ed. Eileen R. Meehan and Ellen Riordan. (Minneapolis: University of Minnesota Press, 2002), 188.

55. Mary Celeste Kearney, "Producing Girls: Rethinking the Study of Female Youth Culture," 285–310 in *Delinquents & Debutantes: Twentieth Century Girls' Cultures,* ed. Sherrie A. Inness. (New York: NYU Press, 1998).

56. Note to Parents, undated, at http://www.gurl.com/connect/bbs/bb.epl/gurlV3/default.

57. Kathryn C. Montgomery, "Digital Kids: The New On-line Children's Consumer Culture," 635–650 in *Handbook of Children and the Media,* ed. Dorothy and Jerome Singer. (Thousand Oaks, CA: Sage, 2000).

58. Lisa Nakamura, "After/Images of identity: Gender, technology, and identity politics," 321–331 in Mary Flanagan & Austin Booth, eds., *Reload: Rethinking Women + Cyberculture.* Cambridge, MA: MIT Press, 2002, 328.

59. Jan Fernback, "Community as Commodity: Empowerment and Consumerism on the Web," 224–230 *Internet Research Annual Volume 1: Selected Papers from the Association of Internet Researchers Conferences 2000–2002,* ed. Mia Consalvo. (New York: Peter Lang, 2004, 228).

60. Gadrey, Jean. *New Economy, New Myth.* (London: Routledge, 2003), 111.

References

Arent, Lindsey. "How Women Buy, and Why." *Wired News,* November 17, 1999. URL: http://www.wired.com/news/business/0,1367,32483,00.html (May 1, 2003).

Bettig, Ronald V. and Jeanne Lynn Hall. *Big Media, Big Money: Cultural Texts and Political Economics.* Lanham, MD: Rowman & Littlefield, 2003.

Brown, Janelle. "From Feminism to Fluff: Economics forces top sites to push content into line with print media." *The Vancouver Sun,* September 7, 2000: F14.

"WIRE: Women's Information Resource & Exchange Opens Doors." *EFFector Online* v6(2), October 1, 1993. URL: http://www.eff.org/effector/HTML/effect06.02.html#wire (May 1, 2003).

Emling, Shelley. "Web Sites Battle to Lure Women: Many Full-service Portals are Struggling." *Edmonton Journal,* March 15, 2001: F2.

Fernback, Jan. "Community as Commodity: Empowerment and Consumerism on the Web." *Internet Research Annual Volume 1: Selected Papers* From the Association of Internet Researchers Conferences 2000–2002, ed. Mia Consalvo. New York: Peter Lang, 2003.

Figallo, Cliff. "iVillage: Investing in Community and Banking on Trust." *Econtent* v.25(6), June 2002: 52–53.

Gadrey, Jean. *New Economy, New Myth.* London: Routledge, 2003.

Giroux, Henry A. *Inpure Acts: The Practical Politics of Cultural Studies.* New York: Routledge, 2000.

Gordon, Joanne. "MeVillage." *Forbes* v.168(11), October 29, 2001: 54.

Grigoriadia, Vanessa "Generation 1.0: Oldest Silicon Alley Veterans Tell All." *New York,* March 6, 2000

Griscom, Amanda. "Vital Signs: New Media Savants Check

the Pulse of Silicon Alley." *The Village Voice*, January 19–25, 2000). URL: http://www.villagevoice.com/issues/0003/griscom.php (May 1, 2003).

Gustafson, Karen E. "Join Now, Membership is Free: Women's Web Sites and the Coding of Community," pp. 168–188 in *Women & Everyday Uses of the Internet: Agency & Identity*, ed. by Mia Consalvo and Susanna Paasonen. New York: Peter Lang, 2002.

iVillage ownership. See Edgar Online: http://www.edgar-online.com/lycos/quotecom/search/default.asp?sym=IVIL (May 1, 2003).

iVillage Form 10-K for Annual And Transition Reports Pursuant To Sections 13 or 15(d) of the Securities Exchange Act of 1934, For the fiscal year ended December 31, 2002. URL: http://www.edgar-online.com/bin/edgardoc/finSys_main.asp?dcn=0001125282-03-002637&nad=(May 1, 2003).

Kearney, Mary Celeste. "Producing Girls: Rethinking the Study of Female Youth Culture," pp. 285–310 in *Delinquents & Debutantes: Twentieth Century Girls' Cultures*, ed. Sherrie A. Inness. New York: NYU Press, 1998.

Larson, Erik. "Free Money." *The New Yorker*, October 11, 1999): 76–85.

Martinez, Michael J. "gURLs Online and Out Loud." *ABC News*, April 10, 1998. URL: http://more.abcnews.go.com/sections/tech/dailynews/gurl980410.html (May 1, 2003).

Mendez-Wilson, Deborah. "Targeting Gen 'Y': You Go gURL! *Wireless Week* v.6(28), July 10, 2000):26.

Mittner, Greta. "Hearst.com Gives Muscle to Women.com." *Red Herring*, January 29, 1999). URL: http://www.red-herring.com/insider/1999/0129/vc-women.html (May 1, 2003).

Montgomery, Kathryn C. Digital Kids: "The New On-line Children's Consumer Culture," pp. 635–650 in *Handbook of Children and the Media*, ed. Dorothy and Jerome Singer. Thousand Oaks, CA: Sage, 2000.

Morrissey, Brian. "Primedia Scoops Up gURL.com from Delia's." *Silicon Valley Reporter*, May 29, 2001. URL: http://siliconalley.venturereporter.net/issues/sar05292001.html#Headline8615 (May 1, 2003).

Nakamura, Lisa. "After/Images of identity: Gender, Technology, and Identity Politics" pp. 321–331 in Mary Flanagan

& Austin Booth, eds., *Reload: Rethinking Women + Cyberculture*. Cambridge, MA: MIT Press, 2002.

Nerney, Chris. "Women.com IPO Turns Heads on Wall Street." *The Internet Stock Report*, October 15,1999). http://stocks.internetnews.com/tracker/article/0,1785,219591,00.html (May 1, 2003).

Oldham, Jennifer. "Women.com, Hearst to Build Site for Women." *Los Angeles Times*, January 29, 1999.

Parmar, Arundhati. "Global Youth United." *Marketing News* v.36(22), October 28, 2002: 1, 49.

Payne, Elizabeth. "Tweens: The Latest Sale Bait: Too Young to Woo?" *Edmonton Journal*, April 28, 2002: D3.

Reagan, Brad. "Openers—Where Are They Now? (Candice Olson)." *Wall Street Journal*, February 11, 2002: R4.

Record, Angela R. "Born to Shop: Teenage Women and the Marketplace in the Postwar United States," pp. 181–195 in *Sex & Money: Feminism and Political Economy in the Media*, ed. Eileen R. Meehan and Ellen Riordan. Minneapolis: University of Minnesota Press, 2002.

Rewick, Jennifer. "iVillage.com to Buy Rival Women.com for $30 Million." *Wall Street Journal*, February 6, 2001: B8.

Rheingold, Howard. *The Virtual Community: Homesteading on the Electronic Frontier* (revised edition). Cambridge, MA: MIT Press, 2000.

Rhine, Nancy. "Populist Activism—Online Facilitation." *TechTV*, 2001. URL: http://www.techtv.com/screensavers/print/0,23102,3335135,00.html (May 1, 2003).

Schultz, Eugene. "More Privacy Breaches Occur." *Computers & Security* v.21(7), 2002: 583–584.

Shade, Leslie Regan. *Gender and Community in the Social Construction of the Internet*. New York: Peter Lang, 2002.

Stern, Gary M. "Women's Wire." *Link-Up* v. 15(2), March-April 1998: 20.

Truong, Hoai-An. "Gender Issues in Online Communications," version 4.3, 1993. URL: http://www.cpsr.org/cpsr/gender/bawit.cfp93 (May 1, 2003).

Wellner, Alison Stein. "The Teen Scene." *Forecast* v22(9), September 2002: 1.

"Women.com Gets Makeover." *Wired News*, January 28, 1999. URL: http://www.wired.com/news/culture/0,1284,17606,00.html (May 1, 2003).

"Women's Wire Gets Serious About Business." *The Tampa Tribune*, August 19, 1995.

15.
"I'LL RESIST WITH EVERY INCH AND EVERY BREATH"

Girls and Zine Making as a Form of Resistance

Kristen Schilt

If popular culture can be read as reflecting popular attitudes and opinions, girls appear to be living in a society that is beginning to validate their experience and encourages them to develop into strong, productive women. Teen apparel catalogues (such as *Delia's* and *Brat*) offer a myriad of girl-positive clothing. Girls can choose to wear "girls kick ass," "happy to be a girl," or "I will not lose to boys" on T-shirts as their personal empowerment slogan. Television shows such as *Xena* and *Buffy the Vampire Slayer* offer girls new images of strong, female heroines who use wits and martial arts to defeat male attackers. In addition, girls are also now viewed as a viable target market for items beyond apparel and makeup. Companies ranging from software producers to snowboard makers are now marketing their products—with a feminine spin—to girls. Lionel trains and Legos, as in the 1950s, now come in bold colors for boys and pastel colors for female consumers. Even Nintendo, a notorious marketer to boys, made their new GameBoy in hot pink in an attempt to attract female players. With this new marketing trend of providing girls with empowering consumer choices, American culture appears to be encouraging girls to grow into strong women who can negotiate work, home, and romance, while still retaining their femininity.

This new focus on girl power products stems from the growth of sociological and psychological research on the need for empowering adolescent girls that emerged in the mid-1990s. Although psychologists like Carol Gilligan (1982) have long advocated that

adolescence is a difficult time for girls, the publication of the American Association of University Women's (AAUW) report, *Shortchanging Girls, Shortchanging America,* brought attention to what has come to be known as "the confidence gap" (Orenstein, 1994). The AAUW found that although both sexes experience a drop in self-esteem in adolescence, girls suffer more from lack of belief in their intelligence and self-worth. Following the AAUW report came a plethora of research that focused on the adolescent female experience as one of immense turmoil (Lees, 1995; Orenstein, 1994; Pipher, 1994; Sadker & Sadker, 1994). In addition to supporting the AAUW's (1991) finding that girls lose their belief in themselves as creative and talented beings as they approach adolescence, these works tended to paint a bleak picture of adolescent girls as "saplings in a hurricane" (Pipher, 1994, p. 22) who were "in danger of drowning in the Bermuda Triangle of adolescence" (Pipher, 1994, p. 73).

Is the situation really this desperate for adolescent girls, however? Certainly adolescence is a time fraught with trauma for girls, and providing information about the problems girls experience is an important research goal. For example, information from psychological clinical studies and sociological ethnographic work with girls allows parents and teachers to identify problems girls are experiencing and helps to outline plans to overcome these obstacles to girls' success. However, although these techniques elicit important data, they place the researchers in the position of talking to girls who either are placed in psychological care, volunteer to be in research projects, or seek out researchers in schools. I argue that these research methods may miss girls who do not seek out researchers but still may be offering resistance to the crisis of adolescence. Thus, to gain a wider perspective on girls' experiences in adolescence, I argue that it is necessary to focus attention on how girls describe their own lives outside of the gaze of the researcher. To this end, I juxtapose academic research on adolescent girls with writing by girls gathered from zines.[1] Analyzing girls' writing in zines illustrates how some girls are able to resist losing their voice in adolescence by receiving validation for their experiences and being encouraged to speak up from their zine support networks. I argue that examining these zine support networks reveals not only how beneficial peer support networks can be in adolescence in terms of giving girls a safe space to articulate their thoughts and feelings but also the difference between girl-based and consumer-market-driven strategies of girl empowerment.

Methodology

This research was conducted through a combination of written interviews with female zine makers and textual analysis of girl-produced zines. I chose to do my primary analysis on girl-made zines for several reasons. First, "girl-zines" (which Green and Taormino [1997] defined as "do-it-yourself publications made primarily by and for girls and women" [p. xi]) deal with many of the same topics as academic research on girls. Therefore, I found them to be an excellent resource for analyzing the differences between how adults construct the problems of adolescence and how girls actually experience their lives. Second, most research that attempts to access girls' thoughts and feelings relies on participant observation, focus groups, or interviews. Using zines as a research tool provides a unique opportunity to hear girls speaking about their experiences outside of a clinical or research setting, because zines are examples of girls writing about their lives without an adult audience in mind. Thus, examining girls' writings in zines is an unobtrusive method that captures how girls choose to represent their lives in writing rather than how they describe their lives to researchers.

To begin my analysis, I did a content analysis of girl-zines in my own personal collection. Having been a zine maker for several years, I had amassed an archive of over 100 girl-produced zines that I used in my analysis. Most of the zines I traded for with my zine or ordered from *Factsheet Five* (a now-defunct resource guide that contained contract addresses and ordering information for zines). As I was interested in girl-zines, I eliminated zines that dealt mainly with music, fiction, or poetry. In addition, as I was focusing on teenagers, I eliminated zines that were produced by girls older than the age of 18. After this selection process, I had 33 issues of zines that I viewed as representative of the girl-zine genre as they contained articles about a range of topics about the female experience, such as feminism, rape and sexual abuse, and sexual relationships. I devised codes for a variety of subjects, ranging from sexual abuse to discussions of feminism. For a final analysis, I narrowed my focus down to five topics: sexuality, sexual abuse, sexual harassment, self-destructive behaviors (such as self-mutilation), and puberty (especially menarche). I selected these topics because they occurred frequently in the zines and were areas that researchers who focus on adolescent girls frequently discuss (Martin, 1996; Orenstein, 1994; Pipher, 1994). As I was juxtaposing girls' personal writing with the academic literature about them, I wanted to examine comparable subject matter. Twenty-seven of the zines contained writings on these topics (see the appendix for a list of zines used in the final analysis).

After conducting the content analysis, I focused on what the zines said about these topics, performing a textual analysis of the articles. When I had finished this analysis, I conducted written interviews with a sample of girl-zine editors whose zines I had analyzed to examine what function zine making served in their lives and to see what they were doing currently. Zine makers leave very little contact information, as they are often anonymous, have an address that is no longer correct, or simply lack contact information at all. For these reasons, I had only mail contacts for 20 of the girl-zine makers. I was able to reach 18 by mail, and all agreed to participate. I opted to do the interviews via mail for two reasons. First, the respondents were geographically widespread, so face-to-face interviews would have been financially prohibitive. Second, because I was interviewing zine editors, I surmised they would be most comfortable in a situation in which they were able to write their responses. Many of them mentioned in their zines that they felt uncomfortable talking to others in person or on the phone. Thus, written interviews seem to be the best option for making the respondents comfortable. I mailed 18 interviews, and I received 17 back. On the form, I provided blank space for racial and ethnic identity and age. The respondents ranged between the ages of 14 and 20. Fifteen labeled themselves as Caucasian or White, whereas two identified their ethnic backgrounds as Italian American and Polish American.

Obviously, the written interviews were not a random or representative sample, as I was using zine editors whose zines I had in my collection. However, as zines are not formally published and there is no central location (such as a zine library) to access all zines produced, collecting a random sample of girl-zines would have been impossible. The zines in my collection did come from diverse regional locations, and the demographics of the zine makers I interviewed did reflect the demographics of most girl-zine makers (Carlip, 1995; Leonard, 1997). Zine making is mainly a middle-class phenomenon, as it requires access to time and resources. Most of the printing costs are absorbed by the editor, as are the costs of paper, layout, and distribution. Zines are also largely produced by White people, as they emerged from the predominantly White punk subculture. In addition, it is mainly an adolescent format, as teenagers, in general, have more leisure time than adults. For these reasons, girl-zine editors are usually reported to be White, young, and middle-class (Kearney, 1998; Leonard, 1997). As my sample reflected these same demographics, I argue that this research contains fairly representative examples of zines made by adolescent girl-zine makers in the United States in the mid-1990s.

On a final note, although zines are public and available as research tools, it is important to remember that girls did not expect them to be used in research. For this reason, I exclude the real names of my respondents, opting to identify them through their zine identity. I did this to help maintain the anonymity that many zine makers desire, especially around extremely personal subjects.

Problematizing Adolescence for Girls

As adolescence marks the difficult transition between childhood and adulthood, boys and girls have been found to experience a myriad of problems as they chart the unfamiliar territory of puberty and increasing responsibility. However, psychological studies that examine adolescent development have found that girls consistently suffer a wider variety of negative consequences as they begin to mature (Freud, 1905; Gilligan, 1982; Horney, 1926; Peterson, 1988). The 1991 AAUW report found that compared to boys, girls emerged from adolescence with lower self-esteem, a higher vulnerability to depression and eating disorders, and less belief in their intellectual abilities, especially in the areas of math and science.[2] The report found that boys' confidence, on the other hand, did not drop as severely as girls.[3] This differential between boys and girls' self-esteem, labeled the "confidence gap" (Orenstein, 1994), became the focus for a body of research on adolescent girls in the 1990s. In this section, I provide a brief overview of research on the confidence gap specifically for White, middle-class girls, as this is the demographic of my research.

The adolescent stage of development is viewed as a time for boys and girls to begin developing independence and autonomy from the adults in their lives. Yet, early studies on boys and girls' developmental differences suggested that this development of autonomy was particularly difficult for adolescent girls. Examining the experiences of White, middle-class girls in the 1980s, for example, Carol Gilligan (1982) argued that girls have a different relational style than boys. This female style privileges sharing, communicating, and cooperating. As girls enter adolescence, however, Gilligan argued that they begin to realize that this relational style is not valued in society, a realization that causes them to go underground with their thoughts and feelings. For Gilligan, this emotional closing off results in girls becoming silent and passive, in effect losing their voice.

Since the publication of *In A Different Voice* (Gilligan, 1982), a steady stream of work on girls, adolescence, and self-esteem has emerged. These studies suggest that White, middle-class, adolescent girls have difficulty maintaining confidence in their appearance, their intellectual abilities, and their own emotions and feelings (Gilligan & Brown, 1992; Lees, 1995; Martin, 1996; Orenstein, 1994; Pipher, 1994). One salient theme that emerges from this body of work is girls' lack of authentic relationships. Gilligan and Brown (1992) and Pipher (1994) located girls' drop in self-esteem within the context of the societal negation of girls' relational style, a negation that forces girls to begin to form false friendships with little true emotional context. In addition to sacrificing authentic relationships, adolescent girls are socialized to believe that "good girls" are quiet, passive, and willing to sacrifice their needs for the needs of others. With anger and depression outlined as unacceptable emotions for girls who want to be feminine, girls often feel scared or trapped by their "bad" emotions. As a result, girls' depression and anger is often internalized and surfaces in self-destructive behaviors, which may explain the higher rates of eating disorders and depression found in adolescent girls (Pipher, 1994).

Moving beyond girls' psychological development, research has also focused on the role of the education system in socializing girls into gender-appropriate behavior (Lees, 1995; Orenstein, 1994; Sadker & Sadker, 1994). In ethnographic studies of classroom behavior, researchers have documented the myriad of ways in which girls are rewarded for silence and passivity (Orenstein, 1994; Sadker & Sadker, 1994) whereas boys receive positive reinforcement for aggressive behavior and are given more freedom to express negative emotions such as anger.[4] This treatment in the education system serves to reinforce societal messages about gender appropriate behavior and encourages girls to place a higher value on being nice than on being smart, which often leads girls to lower their career expectations from "mean," competitive professions (such as lawyers and doctors) to more caring (and lower-paying) professions (such as nursing and teaching) (Orenstein, 1994).

Research that examines the loss of voice also looks at the confidence gap in relation to sexuality and sexual agency. Puberty—the most visible marker of the transition from childhood to adulthood—raises complex issues for girls. Although menarche is considered to be a rite of passage into womanhood, it is frequently denigrated in society and has come to have a negative, dirty image (Lees, 1995). In addition, girls' bodily development, such as breast growth (which is

occurring at increasingly early ages), attracts male sexual attention that often is confusing or unwanted. With little sexual or emotional education in schools, girls begin to think of themselves as the sum of their physical attributes, which leaves them vulnerable to male sexual advances. These negative images of female puberty result in many girls leaving adolescence with no voice with which to articulate their thoughts and beliefs, especially in regard to sexual desire (Martin, 1996; Tolman & Debold, 1994).

In summation, although a definitive answer to the question of what causes girls' adolescent loss of voice remains to be found, the majority of the research on girls suggests that, whether it is psychological or structural, girls largely are unable to retain their pre-adolescent strength, determination, and voice in their teenage years. Yet a great deal of the most publicized research on girls comes from clinical studies (Gilligan, 1982; Gilligan et al., 1995; Pipher, 1994), focus groups (Lees, 1995; Martin, 1996), or participant observation in schools (Orenstein, 1994). I argue that these research methods may leave out girls who do not seek out researchers but still may be offering resistance to the crisis of adolescence. My analysis of girl-produced zines reveals that the form of resistance that girls present may often fail to register with those seeking examples of outright rebellion or concise verbal descriptions of how girls are resisting. In the next section, I outline how and why zines are an important research tool for examining girls' apparent loss of voice from their own perspective.

Using Zines to Examine Girls' Experiences

In her essay, "Telling a Girl's Life," Lyn Mikel Brown (1991) posed the question, "What would it mean for a girl at the edge of adolescence to tell the truth about her life, to speak honestly and openly about her experience?" (p. 71). Although her comment is an attempt to solve the problem of girls' losing their voice in adolescence, it has a resonance for examining research on adolescent girls. As I argued earlier, because clinical studies place girls as the research participant, responses to questions about girls' experiences are always filtered through the research process. With ethnographic research questions of how much adult authority the researcher should exercise frequently arise. As most researchers do not want to be too intrusive, they often opt to remain outside of girls' real or nonschool lives, which excludes them from an important sector of activity (Kenny, 2000). Those who do participate in leisure activities with girls, however, acknowledge that the research they gather is always mediated through their position as adults in an adolescent world and, therefore, cannot be seen as a true reflection of what girls do when not under the adult gaze (Griffiths, 1995). Obviously, I am not advocating for the removal of the researcher from the research process; however, I am arguing that using girls' personal writing—whether it is notes to adolescent friends (Hey, 1996) or zines—as a research tool offers a new way to look at adolescent girls' lived experiences because these writings are composed for peer groups and personal use, not for adult audiences.

Not being written for an adult audience is the main lure of zine writing, which has the ability to be simultaneously public and private. As Green and Taormino (1997) noted, many girls do zines to share their experiences with their readers. For girls, the experience of having a space to talk about their lives can be very important, as there are few chances for girls to express their thoughts and feelings without fear of ridicule or censure. As one zine maker said, "Sometimes paper is the only thing that will listen to you" (Green & Taormino, 1997, p. xi). Yet, although girls can be open about their lives, they also are able to control the audience of their zines and how much personal identification they provide for the reader. Girls often use only first names, employ pseudonyms, or give no names at all. Zine makers leave zines anonymously at book and record stores, or trade them with people who express interest in reviews they have read. Controlling the audience allows girls to feel they are still anonymous while revealing their inner-most thoughts on paper.

Zines are also unique in that they exemplify a girl-driven strategy for empowerment. Although a girl-power movement has sprung up in response to widely read works on adolescent girls, such as *Reviving Ophelia* (Pipher, 1994), much of these empowerment strategies have been consumer based. Thus, girls are supposed to be empowered through buying girl-power products, such as T-shirts with girl-positive slogans. Although these consumer slogans may be empowering for some, they do not encourage girls' own creativity or input into empowerment strategies. Zines, on the other hand, are a do-it-yourself project that teaches girls how to be cultural producers (Kearney, 1998), rather than consumers of empty girl-power products. By making a zine, girls learn that if they do not like the cultural products offered to them, they can produce their own. Learning this do-it-yourself ethos can encourage girls to be more critical consumers of cultural products and lead them to feel more empowered to express their own ideas and opinions. In addition, as argued earlier, trading zines can lead to the creation of a supportive, zine network with whom to share new ideas and opinions. Thus, zines allow girls to take part in and actively direct girl-based empowerment strategies for negotiating their specific problems in adolescence, rather than market-driven strategies created by adults that often fall short of offering girls the tools to effect change in their own lives.

Finally, girls can use zines to form friendships that provide them with emotional validation. Although zine makers do not use Gilligan et al.'s (1995) term "false" friendships, they often do express a sense of suffering from a lack of real friendships in their everyday life. For example, the author of *Pussycat* #2 wrote:

> It seems that I have friends but . . . we talk about T.V., movies, or some dumb thing that's funny. No one wants my real [sic]. "Oh, you are so funny!" So I make you laugh, then I laugh. But I really want to cry.

However, girl-zine makers are often able to bypass this isolation by forming zine peer support groups that allow for the formation of close, emotional candid relationships with other girl-zine makers. In my written interviews, all of the girls discussed the importance of their zine friends and provided me with examples of personal support they received from these relationships. One girl remarked about her zine friends, "There are people who understand completely. That's amazing. It makes you feel like you can do anything when you connect." Another girl notes the importance of zine making to her:

> It is my therapy and the way I reach out to others. Recently a lot of people have told me reading me stuff helps them—and "I'm not the only one who

feels this way" sort of reaction. I HAVE to zine to pour out the pain from my self and knowing it helps others is further impetus.

Finally, one girl wrote, "I don't have a social life, I have a zine," illustrating the centrality of zine making to her life. Zines offer girls a way of making connections with other girls who share and sympathize with their experiences and become a unique communication tool that allows them to express their thoughts and feelings in a safe community of other zine-makers. Moreover, as Gilligan et al. (1995) have argued, "Girls' active attempts to maintain connection with others and with their own thoughts and feelings, are acts of resistance and courage" (p. 27). Using this definition, zines can be seen as a form of resistance, a concept I expand in the next section.

Reframing Resistance

In terms of defining resistance, I find it useful to employ a psychological definition as my research takes on the predominantly psychological debate about girls losing their voice in adolescence. Carol Gilligan et al. (1995) discussed two different types of what they term "political resistance" (p. 26). The first type is covert resistance, a situation in which girls go underground with their feelings and knowledge. In this situation, they realize that they are in a culture that does not value their experience and retreat from it. The downside to covert resistance is these girls lack a confiding relationship and may ultimately end up feeling alienated. A second strategy is overt resistance, in which girls manage to speak out and reject stereotypes about the proper roles for women and femininity.

Although researchers who focus on girls would welcome overt resistance if they could find it, it rarely occurs as many overt resisters are censured. Girls know what consequences await those who speak out, as parents and teachers are the absolute authority in most disputes with teenage girls (Brown, 1998; Orenstein, 1994). Even if teachers are displaying openly sexist behavior, they still have the ability to punish girls who challenge them. In addition, girls have little ability to express their anger and frustration because, as Pipher (1994) pointed out, our language does not allow girls to fully articulate their experiences. If they protest sexist or racist treatment, they may be labeled delinquents or troublemakers (Gilligan et al., 1995; Orenstein, 1994). Many girls, therefore, reject overt forms of resistance because there is too much punishment involved. Not employing overt resistance, however, is not necessarily bad, as LeBlanc (1999) argued, "No form of resistance can be pure, untainted by strains of accommodation" (p. 133). To resist, girls need to find a balance between secret and open resistance. Therefore, in my work on zines, I looked for a combination of the two, a sort of c/overt resistance that allows girls to overtly express their anger, confusion, and frustration publicly to like-minded peers but still remain covert and anonymous to authority figures.

An example of how this c/overt resistance operates is through using zines to write about humiliating or unfair experiences that girls may not have discussed with other people. For example, one zine editor wrote in *Good Faerie #12* about the sexist treatment she received at the hands of her math teacher. He called her a "reverse sexist" in front of the class for wearing a feminist T-shirt. She wrote:

> I'm not going to defend myself of anything. It doesn't work usually. It wouldn't have helped me either really. Perhaps the point is this: the "down-look" that was cast on me for wearing a shirt with a feminist statement, which I would say that I support by means of my feminist ideals. Which, yes, are really not often "voiced." It did rather throw me off guard, and I didn't really know what I'd say about it. I thought he twisted the words and meanings a bit. I saw it more optimistically and toward high achievement as opposed to supremacy. I resent that this made me doubt and left me unprepared. I still don't know the proper response.

The example in this zine is interesting, as from the teachers' perspective, it would appear that the author was not defending herself. Moreover, had this interaction been observed by a researcher, it could be read as exemplifying adolescent girls' loss of voice.[5] Reading this passage, however, reveals that girls are not passive in these situations as much as they are unable or unwilling to speak freely and risk being ridiculed or censured. This discussion exemplifies c/overt resistance, as the zine author worked out her feelings in the safety of her zine where she can speak about her experience yet still remain anonymous.

Although the c/overt resistance of zines could be easily dismissed as little more than ideological resistance, it can lead to more overt political action for some girls. As cultural producers, girls are able to make cultural products that encourage participation in girl-driven empowerment. As one zine maker wrote about zine making and politics in *Out of the Vortex #6:*

> Zines are many people's first contact with the idea of the do-it-yourself ethic. I know this was true for me. It's quite staggering, the first time you truly digest the revolutionary concept that you don't have to depend on other people to do the things you want to do. You can have full power over that. For me, this zine was my first time being the final critic of my work before it was seen by the public. Always in my life I had handed in my writing to teachers, parents, older writer friends, to give me their opinions about what I'd done. Suddenly, all this seemed unnecessary. The confidence people gain from this tremendous self-sufficiency can carry over into all aspects of their lives. This is particularly important to kids, girls, minorities, anyone who is discouraged from taking charge in their lives.

In addition to passing on the sense of the importance of the do-it-yourself kind of empowerment, girl-zines also pass on a great deal of information about how to become involved in feminist, political, and antiracist action. Speaking to the importance of this spread of information, many of the zine makers I interviewed noted that they learned about feminism from zines, which led many of them to become involved in feminist groups, such as NOW or Riot Grrrl, and to study women's studies or feminist theory in college. This reveals how zine making can move beyond the c/overt resistance of giving girls a safe space to practice articulating their thoughts and feelings about feminism to the more overt space of feminist activism. In addition, it illustrates that c/overt resistance should not be discounted as it is a much more feasible form of resistance for adolescent girls—particularly younger girls—who are more regulated by structures of authority.

In summation, zines can operate as a safe format for girls to explore their thoughts and feelings without fear of censure. As evidenced through my written interviews, having this safe space for c/overt resistance can lead girls to adopt more overt forms of resistance as they mature. For researchers, zines can also be a useful tool for examining how girls speak about their lives outside of the gaze of researchers. In the next section, I compare academic writing on adolescent girls with girls' own writing, focusing on five topics: sex, self-mutilation, sexual abuse, menstruation, and sexual harassment. Through this analysis, I explore how girls' discussions can be read as c/overt resistance to the loss of voice, and, finally, how girls' perspectives on these issues may differ from academic assessments.

"Sex. It's So Fucked." Sexual Agency and Zines

Karen Martin (1996) argued that one reason for the drop in girls' self-esteem in adolescence is lack of sexual agency. In her analysis, she pointed out that the female body and femininity are degraded in American culture. Thus, girls enter adolescence with a fear of the changes that are occurring in their bodies and the sexual treatment they receive. Girls feel removed from their sexuality—which they view negatively. She noted that girls often describe their first sexual encounters with bewilderment, describing them as "just happening." These comments reveal a feeling that sexual encounters are beyond girls' control. Moreover, girls are unable to discuss sex with their partners and have trouble resisting unwanted sexual intimacy (Martin, 1996; Orenstein, 1994). Tolman and Debold (1994) pointed out that there is very little language for girls to voice their sexual desire, which often leads them to disconnect from their bodily feelings. Gilligan et al. (1995) argued that "this disconnection . . . puts girls in serious danger, as they can be mistreated and abused without acknowledging to themselves the extent of their hurt and loss" (p. 101).

Although these same feelings of disconnection from sexuality often appear in zines, the zine format is often used as a location for discussing this sense of alienation from sexuality, as well as sexual relationships, sexual desire, and general information about sex, such as birth control options. Fourteen of the zines I analyzed discussed sex in one of these formats. The most common was discussions of sexual relationships and birth control issues. For example, in *Out of the Vortex #6*, one of the zine makers recounts her sexual history, going into great detail about whether the man or the woman should be responsible for introducing the subject of condoms. Another zine discussed the author's AIDS test and how frightening waiting for the results was for her. These articles work to normalize the sexual experience of girls and take away the idea that sexually active females are "sluts." Other zines encouraged sexual desire. *Riotemptresses #1* gives a description of how female masturbation works and encourages readers to try it themselves. These zines provide examples of girls who take control of their sexual lives and have a safe space to talk about their own desire.

Other zines become a format to discuss sexual problems and agency. For example, in *Yawp #12*, the editor wrote about having sex with her boyfriend:

> Sex. It's so fucked. I know that Peter would not do anything against my wishes. So why did I have such a hard time telling him when I don't want to do some/anything? Good girl. Always the good girl, always got to please. I was 17 and he was 22 and I didn't want to take any chances of him losing interest. And I knew that he would understand if I said no. Later on he said quite sincerely, "I hope I didn't make you do anything you didn't want to do." I said no. Liar that I am.

Although she is expressing her lack of agency in her inability to be honest about her sexual desires, she is using her zine to work through the thought process of why she feels unable to be candid. She adds that she wrote this article after receiving a letter from a zine friend dealing with similar topics, revealing that she was able to think more about her lack of sexual agency because of support she was receiving from her zine network. In our written interview, she remarked that her boyfriend did eventually break up with her but added, "After getting my zine [which

discussed the break up], my friend Caroline ransacked her house looking for my phone number, couldn't find it, and instead wrote me a long e-mail assuring me that I didn't need my ex-boyfriend, she understood what I was going through, I was beautiful and she loved me." This type of support can enable girls to reject the feeling that they need to comply with a boy's sexual desire. It also allows them to feel supported in the decision not to have sex, either for the first time or when they simply do not want to. Although they are not overtly resisting unwanted sexual advances, they are using c/overt resistance to develop more autonomy in their sexual relationships. Developing this sense of autonomy is an important step in recognizing one's sexual agency and feeling secure in expressing it, which Martin (1996) maintained will aid girls in developing a more positive sense of self. Thus, through zine discussions, some girls do appear able to begin the process of developing a positive sense of sexual agency in adolescence and manage to gain some voice for expressing their sexuality.

"No One but the Razor": Talking about Self-Mutilation and Sexual Abuse

In addition to discussing sexual experiences, zines are also arenas for writing about painful experiences that are not normally discussed, such as sexual abuse and self-mutilation. Pipher (1994) and Orenstein (1994) found examples of girls who reported cutting themselves with razors and knives as an attempt to "feel better." Pipher (1994) noted that self-mutilation illustrates how anger that cannot be expressed in an overt way can act as a destructive force for girls who often think they are the only ones engaging in such hurtful behavior. Four of the girl-zines I analyzed contained reports of cutting in an attempt to deal with feelings of depression, anger, and hopelessness. *Scratch N Sniff* and *Look Behind the Scenes* wrote about telling a close friend about the mutilation and being rejected for their "abnormal" behavior. The other two zines discussed the why of self-mutilation. The editor of *Yawp #12* wrote about her response to feeling depressed over a breakup: "I cut myself last week, which I haven't done in a long time. But I was alone and abysmally depressed so out came the scissors slash slash on my rib cage." Another wrote in *Good Faerie #10* about her frustration with her life, adding that sometimes there is "no one but the razor." In these examples, girls have developed survival strategies (Gilligan et al., 1995) that allow them to deal with bottled-up emotions. Although these strategies aid girls in resisting giving up their anger, they are ultimately negative, as they are causing the girls to put themselves in bodily harm.

In our written interview, the editors of *Yawp* and *Good Faerie* reported that they received many letters of support from other girl-zine makers who had similar stories of self-mutilation. The editor of *Good Faerie* recounts her happiness at receiving these letters because "everybody is afraid to talk about their own fucked-up-ness and they are not building connections like they should." Receiving this support helped her to stop using cutting as a form of anger release. Thus, much like feminist consciousness-raising sessions in the 1960s, talking about cutting among female zinc-makers takes it out of a hidden space, which is an important precursor to political action. As Alice Echols (1989) noted, talking about personal experiences in consciousness-raising groups allows women to recognize what they had previously thought of as personal problems are actually social problems shared by other women. Zines provide girls with a similar experience, as hearing from girls who have the same self-destructive behavior can lead girls to question why their valid anger is being turned on themselves. This questioning can, in turn, lead girls to see their problems as part of a larger political situation and not unique to themselves. Zines, therefore, give girls the power to realize they are not alone in their struggles to navigate the contradictions of adolescence and allow them to turn negative resistance like cutting into the c/overt resistance of sharing experiences in zines.

Zines also provide a realm in which to share experience for sexual abuse survivors. Lees (1995), Kaplan (1997), and Pipher (1994) all encountered examples of girls discussing sexual abuse and incest. However, these topics receive little attention in most academic work, as they are difficult to broach with teenage respondents because researchers are not encouraged to ask directly about sexual activity without parental consent. In the case of incest, asking for parental permission is impossible, as the girls fear retaliation for speaking out. Again, zines provide a safe space to talk about abuse with others. Twelve of the zines I

analyzed talked about sexual abuse and rape. The discussions came in many different forms. Several were written as stories or in a poem format. For example, the editor of *Pussycat #2* wrote, "Father your hands are holding my life/Sometimes when you don't look/I go to the kitchen and get a knife/Someone needs to remind you/I'm not your fucking wife." *Riotempresses #1* contains several poems and essays about rape and sexual abuse. Finally, *Sewer* is almost one long continuous sentence about incest. With this story format, it is difficult to decide whether girls are reporting their own experience or dramatizing an issue that is particularly resonant for them. However, that this topic is mentioned reveals that it is something girls are thinking about and, as Hilary Carlip (1995) argued, many girls actually are experiencing this abuse. Therefore, I included the stories about incest and sexual abuse in my analysis because they still reflected girls' perceptions of sexuality and the dangers of adolescence.

Other zines provide the reader with detailed accounts of personal abuse, particularly incest. *Fantastic Fanzine #3.5* describes the sexual abuse the editor suffered at the hands of her father and outlines how she is beginning her healing process. I found this same focus on the healing process in other zines that dealt with sexual abuse. For example, the editor of *Unite Grrrls Love Yourselves* wrote:

You have to talk to someone. You really do have to tell . . . someone. Anyone. Once I began to accept it and deal with it, once I told one person, I just kept telling people. Once you tell one person, it is not enough. I feel I've got to tell the whole world cause I kept such a secret locked up inside of me for so long that I start to feel free telling more and more people. And see, right now there is an 11-year-old girl (on the *Sally Jesse Raphael* show) she is telling her story. She too was sexually molested. She is crying. I am crying too. I just want to hold her and tell her I am proud of her. And that she is brave. And I wanna tell her that maybe everything isn't alright right now, but we can make it alright. I wish for every one of us to come out, that could change things. We can come out, come on strong. Yell and kick until the world finally listens and takes action.

(Carlip, 1995, p. 25)

She urges girls to make a connection, to share their story, noting that she has been empowered to talk about her experience by being able to discuss it in her zine. This illustrates how girls can deal with their painful experiences and start a healing process instead of turning their anger and hurt inwards. Zines provide girls with a safe space in which to share experiences and to begin to recognize them as part of a bigger political problem. Also, using zines provides researchers a way to examine what girls are writing about a topic that is especially hard to discuss in research settings but may have a great deal more salience to White, middle-class girls than previously addressed by academic research.

"I Knew All about Periods, Technically": Puberty

In *Puberty, Sexuality, and the Self*, Karin Martin (1996) argued that the biggest flaw in research about the loss of self-esteem in adolescent girls is that researchers do not look at puberty and the effects it has on girls. Sue Lees (1995) found that boys frequently denigrate puberty for girls (especially menstruation). In his study of working-class boys, for example, Paul Willis (1977) found that boys called each other "jam rags," referring to used sanitary napkins as an insult. There is no comparable language for girls to ridicule boys' puberty changes. Ridiculing menstruation can also be a tactic used to belittle or trivialize girls' valid anger. Mary Pipher (1994) noted that if girls show unacceptable emotions, such as anger or depression, it is frequently written off as PMS or "being on the rag." Moreover, Lees (1995) noted, "A girl is constantly warned that her body may let her down, by emitting odors or by leaking" (p. 107). Such a negative view of puberty, especially menarche, makes it hard for girls to feel comfortable about their changing bodies, which Martin (1996) argued adds to decreased sexual agency.

In zine writing, puberty is a frequently discussed topic, particularly feelings about menarche and menstruation. Of the seven zines I found that discussed menstruation, the majority focused on menarche. Frequently, there are articles in which the zine maker gets several of her friends to write about their first periods. Many of the stories mention not knowing what

was going on or being scared at the arrival of their first period. One girl wrote in *Pink Noise* of puberty: "When I found out what being a girl actually meant, I was scared! I found out from a neighbor who said I'd grow tits that hurt when they bounced and I'm gonna [sic] get a cut that won't stop bleeding." Although most girls wrote that they knew what menstruation was due to watching films about it in classes, they seemed unprepared for it to happen to them. In *Pussycat #2*, the editor wrote that when she got her first period, she cried and felt dirty. She added, "My father tried to make me stop crying by telling me in some countries they celebrate menstruation. I wished we did in the U.S." Her example shows how negatively many girls perceive puberty, especially menarche. A guest author wrote in *Pussycat* of carrying around a pack of Kotex for a year after seeing the menstruation film in the 5th grade. She was worried that she might be unprepared when it started and then ridiculed. Menarche discussions in zines are another example of sharing negative experiences. Although girls are not openly contesting society's denigration of menstruation, they have a safe space to c/overtly discuss their experiences and get support from other girls who feel the same way. Writing about periods—and the shame and confusion attached to them—helps girls to realize they are not alone in their experience; other girls have similar feelings of being dirty or ashamed.

Not all stories about menstruation and menarche are negative, however. Another guest editor of *Pussycat* wrote:

> I was a freshman and while having a conversation with my best friend, the subject of Midol came up. She asked if I had my period yet, I said no. About two weeks later, I started. I immediately called my best friend. The next day at school she brought me 2 dozen red cupcakes with pink and red frosting. When girls asked me what they were for, I gave them this look. Only two of them figured it out.

In this example, menstruation is a positive experience for the girl because her best friend supports her. Other zincs move to a more challenging stance in regard to the denigration of menstruation in American culture. In *Scratch N Sniff*, the editor wrote:

Ya [sic] see the other day my mom and I went to the grocery store. I needed to buy some tampons. I looked by the make-up, by the shampoo, and such, even by the Depends—still no sign of my trusty Tampax biodegradable tampons. By this time I was getting very irritated aimlessly strolling by the fruit, spices, and various canned goods. Eventually I came to the baby isle [sic] and right there between the Gerber strained peas and the pull up Pampers were the tampons and pads. What is the fucking symbolism in that? To think that some dumb ass male grocery store organizer decided that tampons and baby shit go hand and hand really annoyed me. Just because I bleed once a month does not mean I need a pacifier.

She challenged what she saw as a patriarchal culture (in the form of a male grocery store executive) denigrating what to her is a natural experience. In discussing why menstruation is considered "dirty," girls can begin to investigate where those feelings of shame come from and begin to eradicate them. For many girls, menstruation is the first step toward the realization that they were now sexual beings. Sharing stories about menarche, menstruation, and the stigma attached to it can help girls start to gain more sexual agency as they realize that other girls share their feelings of confusion about puberty and its changes. Feeling positively about menstruation is part of achieving sexual subjectivity and agency.

"It's Not Fair that You, Me, or Any Woman Should Have to Put Up with that Shit": Sexual Harassment

Sexual harassment of adolescent girls in schools is a heated topic of debate. One side argues that sexual harassment is often boys simply expressing their natural sexual curiosity (Gurian, 1998; Pollack, 1999). The other side views any form of harassment of girls as wrong and in need of regulation. In *Reviving Ophelia*, Mary Pipher (1994) discussed the AAUW report, "Hostile Hallways" (AAUW, 1993), that examined sexual harassment in schools in the early 1990s. The report states that 70% of girls experience harassment, and 50% experience unwanted sexual touching at their schools. Peggy Orenstein

(1994) also focused on sexual harassment in schools, following a case in the middle-class junior high she studied. Ultimately, she found that—despite the new rules against harassment—the principal is unable to punish the boys who did the harassing because of fear of lawsuits from parents. Sue Lees (1995) examined how boys' violent sexual behavior is actually condoned by teachers. After interviewing boys and girls, she concluded her book by arguing that sexual harassment will continue until boys are made to be accountable for their behavior.

Of the eight zines that discussed sexual harassment, most focused on the question of why sexual harassment occurs. For example, in *Boredom Sucks #8* the editor questioned why men felt the need to yell at women on the streets and argued that it was not fair that women were forced to put up with such negative treatment. Other zines such as *Pussycat #2, Riotempresses #1*, and *Slambook #2* dissect the assumption that women bring on sexual harassment themselves through what they are wearing. In addition, zines are used as a way to encourage sharing harassment stories and supporting girls who have been harassed. The author of *Pussycat #2* wrote:

I know most people know but it is hard to get anything done about sexual harassment. Even though I fancy myself a strong feminist, it happened to me and I found there was no one to back me up. All the other girls the same asshole did the same thing to thought nothing of it or didn't want to speak up. I know what it's like to stand up for myself and have everyone laugh and then have no one behind you. So if you have been harassed, even if I don't know you, I'll be behind you.

Knowing that someone is there to support you if you have been harassed can be important for creating an environment in which girls feel safe to speak out. Zines are limited by the fact that zine friends are often geographically separated and thus not able to give local support. However, as my research on zine makers revealed, when you do not have anyone around you who is supportive, zine friends can make an important difference. The most useful function of zines in regard to sexual harassment is sharing experiences that are not usually voiced. It appears to be the support that matters, whether it is physical or written. As one of the editors of *Out of the Vortex #7* wrote about sharing experiences with zine friends: "Every time I talk with girls about sexual harassment and assault, my own memories get a little less painful." Knowing that a safe space for this kind of discourse exists can encourage girls to be more vocal about their experiences and, hopefully, become more comfortable speaking out against them.

Conclusion

Academic research on teenage girls has been an integral force in awakening society to the problems girls experience in adolescence, such as sexual harassment and gender-bias teaching (Lees, 1995; Orenstein, 1994; Sadker & Sadker, 1994). It is the conclusion of this article, however, that in addition to focusing on these problem areas, greater academic attention needs to be paid to how girls also develop their own strategies to navigate adolescence. Zine making is one example of a strategy that provides girls with a safe space to talk about their lives to the audience of their choice. Zines offer girls a way to practice their voices and opinions and work as a sounding board for speaking about experiences and emotions. Because zines remain outside of the adult world and often are written anonymously, they offer girls a c/overt forum for discussing topics that are normally not spoken about openly, such as sexual abuse and self-mutilation. This safe space for writing about their lives is important, for, as Mary Pipher (1994) pointed out, "Our daughters need time and protected places in which to grow and develop socially, emotionally, intellectually, and physically. They need safe spaces where they can go to learn about themselves and others" (p. 230). As girls are able to trade zines with other girls, this safe space can translate into a support network that operates as a girl- produced strategy for staying connected with others and navigating the "Bermuda Triangle" (Pipher, 1994, p. 73) of adolescence.

Although zine making is a c/overt form of resistance, the importance of it as a safe space and support network system for teenage girls should not be underestimated. As James C. Scott (1990) pointed out, overt resistance is rare, as it takes time and support to build up to political action. This is especially true in the case of teenage girls who are constrained by teachers, parents, and student peer cultures. Expressing opinions in zines in a c/overt manner allows girls to begin to build confidence in their thoughts and feelings. Much like the feminist consciousness-raising groups of the 1960s, sharing experiences through zines can lead girls to begin to realize that much of what they had previously thought of as personal problems are actually social problems shared by many other girls. Having this supportive community, even if they are not local friendships, can allow girls to feel more comfortable speaking out against sexist treatment or sexual abuse. Moreover, the confidence gained from having this safe, supportive space to express c/overt resistance can lead to further, more overt involvement in political movements, such as feminism. This is why zine making is so important as a form of c/overt resistance, as it gives girls a safe space to practice articulating their thoughts and feelings and aids in the creation of political action.

In addition, analyzing zines provides researchers with a method for examining girls' lives on their own terms. Although psychological studies and school ethnographies offer important insights into girls' adolescent problems and the structural and cultural constraints on their lives, zines are an example of girls writing without an adult audience in mind. Reading and analyzing zines aids in understanding how girls grapple with the negative messages they receive in society and reveals how they often resist or alter these messages. Zine articles also give insight into what issues girls see as critical to their lives, rather than what issues adult researchers view as central. For example, from the analysis of girl-zines—in my work and in other work such as Carlip (1995)—sexual abuse and the negativity focused around menarche appear to deserve much more focus than they have been given in academic research. Thus, zines and other girl-produced writing offers an important addition to research on adolescent girls as this body of work reveals girls' active role in creating strategies to make their way through the difficult period of adolescence.

Finally, as argued by Kearney (1998), zine making allows girls to move away from being passive consumers and encourages them to be cultural producers who make cultural products relevant to their own lives. This aspect of cultural production has

particular salience in light of the girl-power market that has emerged with the popularity of books
such as *Reviving Ophelia* (Pipher, 1994). Although
these more consumer-based strategies indeed may
be empowering to some adolescent girls, they offer
little practical guidance for girls interested in challenging their treatment in society. Having the power
to produce a cultural artifact that speaks about your
own life and over which you exercise complete creative control gives a new dimension to the empowerment of adolescent girls as it teaches them the
tools for seeking their own strategies for navigating
adolescence. Even though these strategies may not
always be successful or positive and are constrained
by girls' race and class positions, it is important to
look at girls' active involvement in creating new strategies, rather than casting them as passive Ophelias.
In conclusion, I argue that if educators, mentors, and
researchers want to create strategies to empower
girls, there needs to be more academic work that
focuses on how girls represent, create, and produce
their own lives within the social and cultural constraints of adolescence.

Appendix

List of Zines Included in Analysis

All zines in this list were produced between
    1992–1996.
Billy's Mitten, Vol. 5.
Boredom Sucks, Vol. 3.
Dux Femina Facti, Vol 3.
Fantastic Fanzine, Vol. 3.5.
Good Faerie, Vol. 10.
Good Faerie, Vol. 12.
Kusp, Vol. 1.
Look Behind the Scenes.
Out of the Vortex, Vol. 6.
Out of the Vortex, Vol. 7.
Patti Smith, Vol. 3.
Pink Noise.
Pussycat, Vol. 2.
Pussycat, Vol. 3.
Riotempresses, Vol. 1.
Scratch N Sniff.
Sewer.

Slambook, Vol. 2.
Smart Like Eve, Vol. 3.
Smile for Me, Vol. 2.
Soeur, Vol. 1.
Sometimes I'm a Pretty Girl, Vol. 2.
Sourpuss, Vol. 3.
Sourpuss, Vol. 8.
Teenagewhorebook, Vol. 11.
Unite Girls and Love Yourselves.
Yawp!, Vol. 12.

Notes

1. Zines, short for "fanzines," are small, independently
   published magazines. The authors, called editors, write
   the content or solicit articles from others. They are
   usually made on computers or handwritten and then
   photocopied and stapled. They tend to have limited
   distributions, ranging from 20 to 100 and are usually
   handed out for free, traded for other zines, or sold for
   a small fee.
2. In the AAUW report, self-esteem was estimated by asking participants to self-report how content they were with
   their bodies, intellectual abilities, and personalities. Boys
   reported liking themselves more, had more confidence in
   their intelligence, listed a wider range of talents, and were
   more content with their bodies than girls.
3. The concept of the confidence gap between boys and
   girls has come under fire recently. Researchers who work
   with adolescent male populations now argue that boys
   have lower confidence, lower test scores, and higher rates
   of depression than girls. As I only address the literature
   on adolescent girls for this article, I am not engaging
   these debates. For an overview of this position, however,
   see Gurian, 1998; Kindlon & Thompson, 1999; Pollack,
   1999; and Sommers, 2000.
4. These gender differences are complicated also by class
   and race. For example, compared with girls from other
   race/ethnic backgrounds, African American girls exhibit
   the highest confidence in their nonacademic abilities and
   the most satisfaction with their bodies. However, although
   African American girls in some studies were able to speak
   up in classroom settings, they were labeled as troublemakers by teachers (Orenstein, 1994). For more discussion on racial and class differences, see Ferguson, 2000;
   Gilligan, Sullivan, and Taylor, 1995; and Orenstein, 1994.
5. Arguably, some researchers may read this silence as
   resistance (see for instance, Lewis, 1993). However, I am
   arguing that this example is not simply silence but more
   c/overt resistance, as the author rehashes the incident
   openly in her zine.

References

American Association of University Women. (1991). *Shortchanging girls, shortchanging America* [videocassette] (available from the AAUW). Washington, DC: The Foundation.

American Association of University Women. (1993). *Hostile hallways: The AAUW survey on sexual harassment in America's schools.* Commissioned by the American Association of University Women Educational Foundation. Researched by Harris/Scholastic Research. Washington DC: The Foundation.

Brown, L. M. (1991). Telling a girl's life. In C. Gilligan, A. Rogers, & D. Tolman (Eds.), *Women, girls, and psychotherapy: Reframing resistance* (pp. 71–86). New York: Haworth.

Brown, L. M. (1998). *Raising their voices: The politics of girls' anger.* Cambridge, MA: Harvard University Press.

Carlip, H. (1995). *Girlpower: Young women speak out.* New York: Warner Books.

Echols, A. (1989). *Daring to be bad: Radical feminism in America 1967–1975.* Minneapolis: University of Minnesota Press.

Ferguson, A. (2000). *Bad boys: Public schools in the making of Black masculinity.* Ann Arbor: University of Michigan Press.

Freud, S. (1905). *The standard education of the complete psychological works of Sigmund Freud* (Vol. XXII). London: Hogarth Press.

Gilligan, C. (1982). *In a different voice: Psychological theory and women's development.* Cambridge, MA: Harvard University Press.

Gilligan, C., & Brown, L. M. (1992). *Meeting at the crossroads.* New York: Ballantine.

Gilligan, C., Sullivan, A., & Taylor, J. (1995). *Beyond voice and silence: Women and girls, race and relationships.* Cambridge, MA: Harvard University Press.

Green, K., & Taormino, T. (1997). *A girl's guide to taking over the world: Writings from the girl 'zine revolution.* New York: St Martin's Griffin.

Griffiths, V. (1995). *Adolescent girls and their friends: A feminist ethnography.* Aldershot: Avebury Press.

Gurian, M. (1998). *A fine young man: What parents, mentors, and educators can do to shape adolescent boys into exceptional men.* New York: Jeremy P. Tarcher/Putnam.

Hey, V. (1996). *The company she keeps: An ethnography of girls' friendships.* Buckingham, UK: Open University Press.

Horney, K. (1926). The flight from womanhood. *International Journal of Psychoanalysis, 7,* 324–339.

Kaplan, E. B. (1997). *Not our kind of girl: Unraveling the myths of Black teenage motherhood.* Berkeley: University of California Press.

Kearney, M. (1998). Producing girls: Rethinking the study of female youth culture. In S. Inness (Ed.), *Delinquents and debutants: Twentieth century American girls' cultures* (pp. 285–310). New York: New York University Press.

Kenny, L. D. (2000). *Daughters of suburbia: Growing up White, middle class and female.* New Brunswick. NJ: Rutgers University Press.

Kindlon, D., & Thompson, M. (1999). *Raising Cain: Protecting the emotional life of boys.* New York: Ballantine.

LeBlanc, L. (1999). *Pretty in punk: Girls' gender resistance in a boy's subculture.* New Brunswick, NJ: Rutgers University Press.

Lees, S. (1995). *Sugar and spice: Sexuality and adolescent girls.* London: Penguin Books.

Lewis, M. (1993). *Without a word: Teaching beyond women's silence.* New York: Routledge.

Leonard, M. (1997). Rebel girl you are the queen of my world: Feminism, subculture and grrrl power. In S. Whiteley (Ed.), *Sexing the groove: Popular music and gender* (pp. 230–256). New York: Routledge.

Martin, K. (1996). *Puberty, sexuality, and the self: Girls and boys at adolescence.* New York: Routledge.

Orenstein, P. (1994). *Schoolgirls: Young women, self-esteem and the confidence gap.* New York: Anchor.

Peterson, A. (1988). Adolescent development. *Annual Review of Psychology, 39,* 583–607.

Pipher, M. (1994). *Reviving Ophelia: Saving the selves of adolescent girls.* New York: Ballantine.

Pollack, W. (1999). *Real boys: Rescuing our sons from the myths of boyhood.* New York: Henry Holt.

Sadker, D., & Sadker, M. (1994). *Failing at fairness: How America's schools cheat girls.* New York: Scribner.

Scott, J. (1990). *Domination and the arts of resistance.* New Haven, CT: Yale University Press.

Sommers, C. H. (2000). *The war against boys: How misguided feminism is harming our young men.* New York: Simon & Schuster.

Tolman, D., & Debold, E (1994). Conflicts of body image: Female adolescents, desire, and the no-body body. In M. Katzman, P. Fallon, & S. Wolley (Eds.), *Feminist perspectives on eating disorders* (pp. 301–317). New York: Guilford.

Willis, P. (1977). *Learning to labor: How working class kids get working class jobs.* New York: Columbia University Press.

16.
LOOKING TO GET PAID

How Some Black Youth Put Culture to Work

Robin D. G. Kelley

I don't like to dream about gettin paid, so I
Dig into the books of the rhymes that I made. . . .
> —Eric B and Rakim, "Paid in Full"

If you can run ball for 6–7 hours, you have already
established your ability to work.
> —James Spady, "Running Ball"

Graffiti writing for the unemployed black ghetto
kid may have developed because there is little else
to do but street wisdom tells you to turn it to your
advantage. The rap insists on self-realisation but
on your own terms, to be unafraid of established
channels, but to use them on your own terms, i.e.,
rip them off.
> —Atlanta and Alexander,
> "Wild Style: Graffiti Painting"

Nike, Reebok, L.A. Gear, and other athletic shoe conglomerates have profited enormously from postindustrial decline. TV commercials and print ads romanticize
the crumbling urban spaces in which African American
youth must play, and in so doing they have created a
vast market for overpriced sneakers. These televisual
representations of "street ball" are quite remarkable;
marked by chain-link fences, concrete playgrounds,
bent and rusted netless hoops, graffiti-scrawled walls,
and empty buildings, they have created a world where
young black males do nothing *but* play.

And yet, representations of the ghetto as a space
of play and pleasure amid violence and deterioration
are more than simply products of the corporate imagi-

nation. Inner city public parks and school facilities *are*
falling apart or disappearing at an alarming rate. The
writings of "aerosol artists" *have* altered concrete walls,
abandoned buildings, and public transportation; some
have created masterpieces amidst urban rubble, and
most have highlighted the rubble by "tagging" public
structures with signs and signatures. Play areas—like
much of the inner city—have become increasingly fortified, caged in by steel fences, wrought iron gates, pad-
locks, and razor ribbon wire. The most striking element
in this postindustrial urban spectacle are the people
who occupy these urban spaces. Parks and schoolyards
are full of brown bodies of various hues whose lack of
employment has left them with plenty of time to "play."
In other words, while obscuring poverty, unemployment,
racism, and rising police repression, commercial representations of the contemporary "concrete jungles"
powerfully underscore the link between urban decline,
joblessness, and the erosion of recreational spaces in
the inner city. At the same time, they highlight the historic development of "leisure" time for the urban working class and, therefore, offer commodities to help fill
that time. The difference between the creation and commodification of urban leisure at the turn of the century
and now, however, is that opportunities for wage labor
have virtually disappeared and the bodies of the displaced workers are overwhelmingly black and brown.

In this chapter I hope to offer some suggestive
observations about the relationship between the rise
of permanent unemployment, the transformation of
public space, and the changing meanings and practices of play for African American urban youth. The

approach I take challenges the way in which work and leisure have been dichotomized in studies of the U.S. working class. In much of this literature, play is seen as an escape from work, something that takes place on the weekends or evenings in distinctive spaces set aside for leisure. Indeed, these leisure spaces constitute the flip side of work for, as Paul Gilroy puts it, the body "is here celebrated as an instrument of pleasure rather than an instrument of labor."[1] What I am suggesting, however, is that the pursuit of leisure, pleasure, and creative expression is *labor*, and that some African American urban youth have tried to turn that labor into cold hard cash. Thus, play has increasingly become, for some, more than an expression of stylistic innovation, gender identities, and/or racial and class anger—increasingly it is viewed as a way to survive economic crisis or a means to upward mobility. Having stated the essential outlines of my argument, however, let me add a few clarifications and caveats. First, I am in no way suggesting that this kind of self-commodification of play is emancipatory, revolutionary, or even resistive. Rather, it comprises a range of strategies within capitalism—some quite entrepreneurial, in fact—intended to enable working-class urban youth to avoid dead-end, low-wage labor while devoting their energies to creative and pleasurable pursuits. These strategies do not undermine capitalism; profits generated by the most successful ventures simply buttress capital and illustrate, once again, its amazing resilience and elasticity, even when the commodities themselves offer ideological challenges to its basic premise. Furthermore, these strategies do not necessarily improve the position of the entire black community, nor are they intended to. On the contrary, in some instances they might have negative consequences for African Americans—that is, through the circulation of representations that ultimately undergird racist ideologies, or "success" narratives that let racism off the hook by demonstrating that "hard work" in the realm of sports or entertainment is all one needs to escape the ghetto. Second, I am not suggesting that all or even most youth engaged in these forms of play are trying to turn their efforts and skills into a commodity. Nor am I suggesting that the self-commodification of "play-labor" is unique to the black community—though the structural position of working-class African Americans in the political

and cultural economy of the U.S. terrain lends itself to these kinds of opportunities. In a nation with few employment opportunities for African Americans and a white consumer market eager to be entertained by the Other, blacks have historically occupied a central place in the popular culture industry. Thus, while the postindustrial city has created a different set of opportunities and limitations on black youths' efforts to turn play into a means to escape wage labor, what I discuss below has a much older trajectory.

Economic restructuring leading to permanent unemployment; the shrinking of city services; the rising number of abandoned buildings; the militarization of inner city streets; and the decline of parks, youth programs, and public schools altered the terrain of play and creative expression for black youth. The loss of manufacturing jobs was accompanied by expansion of low-wage "service" jobs—retail clerks, janitors, maids, data processors, security guards, waitresses, and cooks, which tend to be part-time and offer limited health or retirement benefits. By Reagan's second term, over one-third of black families earned incomes below the poverty line. For black teenagers, the unemployment rate increased from 38.9 to 43.6 percent under Reagan. And in Midwestern cities—once the industrial heartland—black teenage unemployment rates ranged from 50 to 70 percent in 1985.[2] Federal and state job programs for inner city youth were also wiped out at an alarming rate. In California, both the Neighborhood Youth Corps and the Comprehensive Employment and Training Act (CETA) were dismantled, and the Jobs Corps and Los Angeles Summer Job Program have been cut back substantially.[3]

Massive joblessness contributed to the expansion of the underground economy, and young people, not surprisingly, are among its biggest employees. The invention and marketing of new, cheaper drugs (PCP, crack, and synthetic drugs) combined with a growing fear of crime and violence, the transformation of policing through the use of new technologies, and the erosion of youth programs and recreational facilities have had a profound impact on public life. When the crack economy made its presence felt in poor black communities in Los Angeles, for instance, street violence intensified as various gangs and groups of peddlers battled for control over markets. Because of its unusually high crime rate, Los Angeles gained the dubious distinction of having the largest urban prison population in the country. Yet, in spite of the violence and financial vulnerability that went along with peddling crack, for many black youngsters it was the most viable economic option.[4]

While the rise in crime and the ascendance of the crack economy, however, might have put money into some people's pockets, for the majority it meant greater police repression. Black working-class communities in Los Angeles were turned into war zones during the mid- to late 1980s. Police helicopters, complex electronic surveillance, even small tanks armed with battering rams became part of this increasingly militarized urban landscape. Housing projects, such as Imperial Courts, were renovated along the lines of minimum security prisons and equipped with fortified fencing and a Los Angeles Police Department substation. Imperial Courts residents were suddenly required to carry identity cards and visitors were routinely searched. As popular media coverage of the inner city linked drugs and violence to black youth, young African Americans in Los Angeles and elsewhere were subject to increasing police harassment and, in some cases, feared by older residents.[5]

In trying to make sense of the intensification of violence and crime in the inner city during the past two decades, we must resist the tendency to romanticize the past, to recall a golden age of urban public life free of violence and conflict. At the turn of the century, for example, bloody turf wars were common among European immigrant youth. Recalling his youth on the Lower East Side of Manhattan, Communist writer and activist Mike Gold wrote:

> The East Side, for children, was a world plunged in eternal war. It was suicide to walk into the next block. Each block was a separate nation, and when a strange boy appeared, the patriots swarmed. . . . The beating was as cruel and bloody as that of grown-ups; no mercy was shown. I have had three holes in my head, and many black eyes and puffed lips from our street wars. We did it to others, they did it to us. It was patriotism, though what difference there was between one East Side block and another is now hard to see.[6]

In addition to Jewish and Italian gang violence, historian Cary Goodman points out that some of the most vicious fights that erupted in the Lower East Side during this era took place between socialists and anarchists. Likewise, in Philadelphia during the 1950s, gangs fought with zip guns and switchblades, which resulted in even more deaths and serious injuries than the turn-of-the-century street wars.[7]

The difference between then and now is not the levels of violence or crime (indeed, few criminologists are willing to admit that the crime rate in predominantly white turn-of-the-century cities was often higher than it is now). Rather, it is a combination of the growing importance of street gangs in the urban political economy and the dramatic improvement in technology that is different. Taking advantage of the gaping hole left by the disappearance of a viable local economy, some gangs have become businesses, distributors of illegal and *legal* goods and services, and they generally define their markets by territory. The very technological revolutions that enable them to connect up with international cartels, expand their ventures, or maintain contact with one another (through reasonably priced pagers, laptop computers, and hand-held fax machines) have also increased the stakes by facilitating greater investment diversity and territorial reach.[8]

More importantly, the proliferation of inexpensive and powerful semi-automatic weapons is what distinguishes the 1990s from the 1950s, or for that matter, from the 1890s. The National Rifle Association (NRA), the nation's largest lobby against gun control, played a major role in ensuring the availability of firearms. Backed by huge weapons manufacturers and armed with one of the wealthiest political action committees in the country (its annual budget is close to $30 million and in the 1992 elections it contributed $1.7 million to House and Senate candidates), the NRA has fought tenaciously against bans on the kinds of automatic assault weapons that are appearing more frequently in inner city communities. Under Reagan, whose presidential campaign received strong backing from the NRA, the regulatory power of the Bureau of Alcohol, Tobacco, and Firearms (ATF) was weakened considerably. By the mid-1980s, obtaining a license to sell guns became so easy that potential dealers needed only to pay a mere thirty-dollar fee and undergo an unusually casual background check. According to one report, "the ATF's background checks were once so lax that the agency even issued licenses to dogs." Ironically, the *fear* of crime partly explains the success of the NRA lobby and their closest allies, gun manufacturers and distributors. During the past decade, the gun industry has banked on crime fears to sell its products, focusing attention less on the hunting market and more on citizens' desire to protect themselves and their property. After a sales slump in the early 1980s, gun sellers not only expanded their marketing strategy to women and teens but brought back cheap semi-automatic pistols, which are frequently used in street crimes. In the end, however, middle-class families concerned about crime, not criminals, are the primary consumers of handguns. In 1992 alone, estimated sales of firearms totaled more than $774 million.[9]

The fear of crime has also spawned new developments in late-twentieth-century urban architecture. The design of the built environment has had a profound impact on how public space is defended and protected, which in turn shapes the way people interact with one another. The work of Camilo José Vergara and Mike Davis powerfully illustrates the degree to which cities are built and conceived as fortifications against the presumed criminality and chaos of the streets. Vergara writes:

> Buildings grow claws and spikes, their entrances acquire metal plates, their roofs get fenced in. . . . Even in areas where statistics show a decrease in major crime, fortification continues to escalate, and as it does, ghettos lose their coherence. Neighborhoods are replaced by a random assortment of isolated bunkers, structures that increasingly resemble jails or power stations, their interiors effectively separated from the outside. . . . In brick and cinderblock and sharpened metal, inequality takes material form.[10]

Recession and Reagan-era budget cuts, combined with the militarization of urban life, have devastated inner city public recreational facilities and altered the landscape of play significantly. Beginning in the 1970s, a wave of public recreational service employees were either furloughed, discharged, or allowed to retire without replacement; the service and maintenance of parks and playgrounds was cut back substantially; many facilities were eliminated or simply

deteriorated; and the hours of operation were drastically reduced. During the mid-1970s, for instance, Cleveland's recreation department had to close down almost $50 million dollars worth of facilities. In New York City, municipal appropriations for parks dropped by more than $40 million between 1974 and 1980—a sixty-percent cut in real dollars. Staff cutbacks were even more drastic: between the late 1960s and 1979, the number of park employees dropped from almost 6,100 to 2,600. To make matters worse, a growing number of public schoolyards in inner city communities have become inaccessible during after-school hours.[11]

More recently, we have witnessed a growing number of semipublic/private play spaces like "people's parks" which require a key (such as the playground in Greenwich Village that services residents of New York University-owned apartments) and highly sophisticated indoor play areas that charge admission. The growth of these privatized spaces has reinforced a class-segregated play world and created yet another opportunity for investors to profit from the general fear of crime and violence. Thus, in the shadows of Central Park, Frederick Law Olmsted's great urban vision of class integration and public sociability, high-tech indoor playgrounds such as WonderCamp, Discovery Zone, and PlaySpace charge admission to eager middle- and upper-class children whose parents want a safe play environment. Protection from the outside is emphasized; at PlaySpace, for example, young workers are expected to size up potential customers before "buzzing" them in. While these play areas are occasionally patronized by poor and working-class black children, the fact that most of these indoor camps/playgrounds are built in well-to-do neighborhoods and charge an admission fee ranging between five and nine dollars prohibits poor families from making frequent visits.[12]

Privatization has also adversely affected public parks. Parks directors in several big cities, notably New York, have turned to "public-private partnerships" and begun to charge "user fees" in order to make ends meet. New York City's Department of Parks and Recreation has already transferred zoos, skating rinks, and parking lots to private operators, and there has been discussion of contracting out recreational and maintenance services to private companies. Moreover, during the 1980s, the city and state used tax abatements as a way of encouraging private developers to build parks and plazas, which usually manifest themselves as highly surveilled "arcades, interior atriums, and festival marketplaces attached to office and condominium towers." The move toward private ownership of public space is powerfully captured in a plaque located on a plaza in midtown Manhattan: "PUBLIC SPACE, Owned and Maintained by AT&T."[13]

Of course, I do not want to exaggerate the impact of the disappearance of public play areas on urban youth. In New York, for example, the sidewalks and streets have long been a desirable place to play, not just for children but for adults as well. In the immigrant working-class neighborhoods of the Lower East Side during the early twentieth century, parents preferred to be within hearing distance of their children, and the streets were often crowded with kids. Scenes of dozens of Jewish and Italian kids surrounding an open fire hydrant on a hot summer day in the 1920s are not much different from scenes in Harlem in the early 1970s. Young and old kids have constantly carved out space on the sidewalk for jacks, craps, double dutch, hopscotch, and handball, and the streets have been used as stickball diamonds that incorporate existing landmarks (such as cars and fire hydrants) as bases. Moreover, since 1909, the New York Police Athletic League has run an annual program whereby it blocks off traffic through selected streets during the summer in order to create more safe places to play.[14]

But as the streets become increasingly dangerous, or are perceived to be so, more and more young children are confined indoors, limited to backyards, or (for those who can afford it) shuttled to the city's proliferating "discovery zones." For inner city families, the threat of drive-bys has turned porches and front doors, which once spilled out onto sidewalks and streets as extensions of play areas, into fortified entrances with iron "screen" doors that lock from the inside. Sadly, the increasingly common practice of placing iron gates over windows and doors is partly responsible for a rise in fire-related deaths in urban black communities.

The simultaneous decline in employment opportunities; public leisure spaces for young people; and overly crowded, poorly funded public schools and youth programs simply expanded an urban landscape in which black teenagers—the throwaways of a new, mobile capitalism—became an even larger, more permanent (and in the minds of many, more menacing) presence in parks and on street corners. The growing numbers of young brown bodies engaged in "play" rather than work (from street-corner bantering, to "malling" [hanging out at shopping malls], to basketball) have contributed to popular constructions of the "underclass" as a threat and shaped urban police practices. The invention of terms such as *wilding*, as Houston Baker points out, reveal a discourse of black male youth out of control, rampaging teenagers free of the disciplinary strictures of school, work, and prison.[15]

I want to argue that many of these young bodies are not merely idle bystanders. They are not uniformly devoid of ambition or a work ethic. Increasingly, young people have tried to turn play into an alternative to unfulfilling wage labor. Basketball, for black males at least, not only embodies dreams of success and possible escape from the ghetto. In a growing number of communities pickup games are played for money much like cards or pool. While it is true that some boys and young men see basketball as a quick (though *never* easy) means to success and riches, it is ludicrous to believe that everyone on the court shares the same aspirations.[16] In the context of a game with competition, it becomes clear very quickly who can play and who cannot. Most participants are not deluding themselves into believing that it is an escape from the ghetto; rather, they derive some kind of pleasure from it. But for that small minority who hold onto the dream and are encouraged, the work ethic begins quite early and they usually work harder than most turn-of-the-century child wage workers. As cultural critic James Spady observes in the epigraph to this chapter, running ball all day long is evidence of a work ethic. Besides, black working-class men and their families see themselves as having fewer career options than whites, so sports have been more of an imagined possibility than becoming a highly educated professional—"it was *the* career option rather than *a* career option," writes Michael Messner.[17] Nowhere is this better illustrated than in the highly acclaimed documentary film *Hoop Dreams*. Charting the tragic lives of Arthur Agee and William Gates, two young talents from the South Side of Chicago who were recruited by a white suburban Catholic high school to play ball, the filmmakers capture the degree to which many black working-class families have invested their hopes and aspirations in the game of basketball.[18]

Not surprisingly, the vast majority are disappointed. Of the half-million high school basketball players in the United States, only 14,000 (2.8 percent) play college ball, and only twenty-five of those (.005 percent) make it to the National Basketball Association. More generally, only 6 or 7 percent of high school athletes ever play college sports; roughly 8 percent of draft-eligible college football and basketball players are drafted by the pros, and only 2 percent ever sign a contract. The chances of attaining professional status in sports are approximately 4 in 100,000 for white men, 2 in 100,000 for black men, and 3 in 1,000,000 for U.S.-born Latinos.[19]

Practically all scholars agree that young women and girls have had even fewer opportunities to engage in either work or play. They have less access to public spaces, are often responsible for attending to household duties, and are policed by family members, authorities, and boys themselves from the "dangers" of the streets. Aside from the gender division of labor that frees many boys and men from child care responsibilities and housecleaning, the fear of violence and teen pregnancy has led parents to cloister girls even more. Thus, when they do spend much of their play time in the public spaces of the city, parent-imposed curfews and other pressures limit their time outside the household.

Controlling women's access to public space is just part of the story. Because sports, street gambling, hanging out in parks and street corners, and other forms of play are central to the construction of masculinity, boys, young men, and authority figures erect strict gender boundaries to keep women out. In fact, one might argue that play is at least as, if not more, important than work in shaping gender identities. After all, our sense of maleness and femaleness is made in childhood, and the limits, boundaries, and contestations in the world of play constitute key moments in the creation and shaping of gender identity.[20] And given the transformation of the labor market in the age of multinational capital, the gendering and gender policing of play has enormous implications. With the extension of a service-based economy (often

gendered as feminized or servile labor) and the rise of permanent unemployment, work no longer seems to be a primary factor in the construction of masculinity—if it ever was.

The policing of these boundaries has a material element as well; it ultimately helps reproduce gender inequalities by denying or limiting women's access to the most potentially profitable forms of creative leisure. Of course, girls and young women do participate in mixed-gender play, and some even earn the right to participate in the men's world of play. For instance, women do play basketball, occasionally with the fellas, but they have fewer opportunities for pickup games, to participate in organized street leagues, or to dream that honing one's skills could land a college scholarship or trip to the pros. Yet, despite the policing of gender boundaries, which tends to become more rigid when children reach preadolescence, girls find forms of homosocial play and pleasure which they defend and protect. And like boys' games and mixed-gender play in declining urban centers, modern social reformers have occasionally tried to turn these forms into "supervised play" as a way to build self-esteem, discipline, and the work ethic (though these virtues were allegedly instilled in young girls through "domestic science" programs). The most fascinating example is the Double Dutch League of New York, originally founded in 1973 by the Police Athletic League (PAL) and later sponsored by McDonald's restaurant. Girls were organized into teams that competed at Lincoln Center for scholarship money and other prizes. Some of the crews, like the Jazzy Jumpers and the Ebonnettes, became fairly big in New York and nationally.[21]

Double dutch is a very old jump-rope game in which participants skip over two ropes spinning in opposite directions. Although it is not exclusive to African American youth, it has been a cultural mainstay among black urban girls for decades. Double dutch is not a competitive sport; rather, it is a highly stylized performance accompanied by (frequently profane) songs and rhymes and can involve three or more girls. Two girls turn the rope (though boys occasionally participate as turners, especially if they are under big sister's supervision) while one or sometimes two participants "jump in."[22] The good jumpers perform improvised acrobatic feats or complicated body movements as a way of stylizing and individualizing the performance. What is particularly interesting about the Double Dutch League is the degree to which its male founders, like its president David Walker, saw the game in terms of the peculiar needs and interests of girls. Walker explained that he had been thinking about activities for girls, especially after failing to attract many girls to his bicycling program. Walker explained, "When I heard the expression double dutch about a thousand bulbs lit in my mind. I started realizing it was an activity that girls really related to. . . . Mothers did it when they were kids. . . . see the relationship—mother—clothesline—daughter." Moreover, he believed it was an important activity for controlling inner city girls and teaching them the benefits of competition. Once PAL and other groups began institutionalizing double dutch, the jumpers who participated in these formal contests found the improvisational character of the game sharply circumscribed. Within the PAL-sponsored contests and demonstrations, moves became highly formalized and choreographed, despite the fact that League organizers encouraged innovation. Contestants were judged on speed and accuracy—criteria that simply were less important on the streets. The organizers even tried to sever its inner city linkages by referring to double dutch as "street ballet" and by practically eliminating the verbal component so essential to double dutch. Few girls participated in these tournaments, in part because there was little incentive. The financial promise of basketball (which could still be played without supervision) was missing in double dutch.[23]

Even more than sports and various schoolyard games, forms of "play" that fall outside the pale of recreation—visual art, dance, and music—offered black urban youth more immediate opportunities for entrepreneurship and greater freedom from unfulfilling wage labor. Performance and visual arts, in particular, powerfully dramatize how young people have turned the labor of play into a commodity, not only to escape wage work but to invest their time and energy in creative expression, or what ethnographer and cultural theorist Paul Willis calls "symbolic creativity." As Willis argues, constructing an identity, communicating with others, and achieving pleasure constitute the labor of creating art in everyday life. Hence, it is in the realm of symbolic creativity that the boundaries between work and play are perhaps most blurred, especially as these forms become commodified.[24]

The struggle to carve out a kind of liminal space between work and play, labor and performance, is hardly new. Today in the streets of New Orleans, children as young as five years old maintain a tradition of street performance, playing "second line" jazz in makeshift marching bands through the French Quarter. And the subway stops and downtown sidewalks of New York; Washington, D.C.; Atlanta; Oakland; and elsewhere are filled with young black musicians of mixed talent trying to make a living through their craft. Perhaps the most famous young black "street musician" is Larry Wright, a talented percussionist who milked a plastic bucket and a pair of drumsticks for every timbre and tonality imaginable. He began performing on street corners in New York City as an adolescent, earning change from passersby who found his complex polyrhythms appealing. His mother encouraged Larry to pursue his art, which ultimately earned him acceptance into New York's highly competitive High School for the Performing Arts. When he was still only fifteen, two filmmakers "discovered" him and made a half-hour video about his life and music that put his name in circulation—and the rest, as they say, is history. After an appearance in the film *Green Card*, a Levi's commercial shot by Spike Lee, and a Mariah Carey video, his example spawned a number of imitators throughout the country. I have seen kids in front of the Pavilion (an eatery and shopping center on Pennsylvania Avenue in Washington, D.C.) with white buckets and sticks trying to reproduce his sound.[25]

While street performance is as old as cities themselves, new technologies and the peculiar circumstances of postindustrial decline have given rise to new cultural forms that are even more directly a product of grassroots entrepreneurship and urban youth's struggle over public space. These forms demanded specific skills, technical knowledge, and often complicated support systems that provided employment and investment opportunities for nonperformers. The most obvious example is Hip Hop culture, a broad cultural movement that emerged in the South Bronx during the 1970s. But even before the Hip Hop scene blew up in New York City as an alternative vocation for black and Latino kids, the slums of Washington, D.C., became a source of both musical inspiration and entrepreneurial imagination. Out of D.C.'s black ghettos emerged a highly percussive music called Go-Go, which indirectly influenced the direction of East Coast Hip Hop. Originating in the late 1960s, when Go-Go guru Charles Brown formed a dynamic band called the Soul Stirrers, Go-Go had always been a distinctive Washington, D.C., style. The bands tended to be large—sometimes a dozen pieces—and were characterized by heavy funk bass, horns, rhythm guitar, and various percussion instruments—from snares, congas, and cow bells to found objects. Like Hip Hop and other black Atlantic musical traditions, Go-Go music places a premium on sustaining the rhythm and getting the dancers involved in the performance through call and response. Just as Hip Hop deejays keep the dancers on the floor by playing a seamless array of break beats, Go-Go bands play continuously, linking different songs by using a relentless back beat and bass guitar to string the music together into an intense performance that could last an hour or more.[26]

Go-Go groups like Trouble Funk, E.U. (Experience Unlimited), Redds and the Boys, Go-Go Allstarz, Mass Extension, and the appropriately named Junkyard Band were products of high school and junior high inner city music programs. Some band members met at high school marching band competitions or were involved in summer youth projects intended to get kids off the streets. As black D.C. artist and activist Malik Edwards remembers, "It was just kids trying to play their music, bands trying to outjam each other. E.U. came out of the Valley Green Courtesy Patrol summer project, which got them some instruments through the community center and a place to practice." Performing on cheap, often battered instruments, young Go-Go musicians created a distinctive "pot-and-pan" sound. "The sound was created out of inefficient instruments, just anything they could do to make an instrument," recalls Go-Go promoter Maxx Kidd.[27] Yet, these artists still made the most popular music in the District, sometimes performing to capacity dance crowds in school gyms, parks, recreation centers, empty warehouses, rented hotel ballrooms, and a vast array of "Go-Go's" (clubs) in the neighborhood.

With few exceptions, no one really got rich off of Go-Go. Throughout the 1970s, neither radio stations nor the record industry took an interest in this new urban music. Despite the initial lack of commercial interest, Go-Go gave up-and-coming musicians a space to learn their craft, perform for audiences, make a little money on the side, and an opportunity for creative expression. Ironically, it is precisely because the early Go-Go scene remained free of major corporate investment that it spawned a fairly lucrative underground economy for inner city youth who sold bootleg tapes, made posters, organized dances, made and repaired musical instruments, and indirectly benefited from the fact that black working-class consumers spent their money on local entertainment.[28] Unfortunately, just as Go-Go began building an international following and the record industry took a greater interest in the mid-1980s, its popularity in D.C. began to decline. Moreover, it never achieved the kind of following Hip Hop enjoyed; after hit songs by E.U., Trouble Funk, and Charles Brown, the big studios lost interest in Go-Go soon thereafter. There is still a vibrant Go-Go scene in Washington, but it is only a fraction of what it was a decade ago.

Hip Hop, on the other hand, was more than music; it embraced an array of cultural forms that included graffiti art and break dancing as well as rap music. Because each of these forms generated different kinds of opportunities and imposed different sorts of limitations, we must examine them separately. We might begin with the oldest—and perhaps least lucrative—component of Hip Hop culture; graffiti. Of course, various forms of wall writing go back centuries, from political slogans and gang markings to romantic declarations. But the aerosol art movement is substantially different. Calling themselves writers, graffiti artists, aerosol artists, and subterranean guerrilla artists, many of the young pioneers of this art form treated their work as a skilled craft and believed they were engaged in worthwhile labor. During the 1970s, some graffiti artists sold their services to local merchants and community organizations, and a handful enjoyed fleeting success in the Soho art scene.

Subway trains provided the most popular canvases. They enabled the artist to literally circulate his or her work through the city. Moreover, many young people thought of themselves as waging war against the Metropolitan Transit Authority (MTA). They felt the transit police were repressive, the fares were too high, and trains assigned to poor communities like Harlem and the South Bronx were inferior. Writers often "bombed" the interiors of trains with "tags"—quickly executed and highly stylized signatures, often made with fat markers rather than spray cans. Outside the trains they created "masterpieces," elaborate works carefully conceived and designed ahead of time. Good writers not only had to be skilled artists but because they were breaking the law by defacing property, they had to work quickly and quietly. They often executed their work in complete darkness, sometimes beginning around 2:00 or 3:00 A.M. The threat of arrest was constant, as was the potential of being seriously injured by a moving train or the electrified third rail. Most artists protected themselves by working in crews rather than as lone individuals. From the outset women writers like Lady Pink, Charmin, and Lady Heart were part of these crews and most worked alongside male artists, though female writers had to battle male sexism and protect themselves from possible sexual assault while executing their work.[29]

By the early 1970s, graffiti writing became a widely debated and discussed phenomenon, becoming the subject of several dramatic and documentary films. Although this partly explains the mainstream art world's fleeting interest in aerosol art, the fact is that graffiti writers themselves took the first initiative. Through organizations such as United Graffiti Artists (UGA) and the Nation of Graffiti Artists (NOGA), some of the leading artists attempted to collectively market their work and establish ties to art dealers and downtown galleries. Launched in 1972, UGA's initial mission was to redirect graffiti into socially acceptable avenues and to get black and Puerto Rican kids off the street. Very quickly, however, it became a primary vehicle for exposing a fairly exclusive group of aerosol artists to galleries and dealers. A year after its founding, the UGA exhibited graffiti on canvases at the Razor Gallery in SoHo (downtown Manhattan). The paintings were priced between $200 and $3,000, and several of the pieces sold.[30] NOGA artists also enjoyed a few fleeting successes in the mid-1970s. Unlike UGA, which had a small membership of selected artists, NOGA was founded as a community youth artists' collective open to just about everyone. With the assistance of former dancer and entrepreneur Jack Pelsinger and graphic artist and gallery manager Livi French, two veterans of the New York

arts scene, NOGA arranged several exhibits in public venues throughout the city. They could not command as much as the UGA artists for their work; NOGA writers rarely sold canvases for more than $300 and 25 percent of their proceeds went back to the organization to pay for supplies. Because they were not regarded as legitimate artists, institutions that hired them to paint large-scale murals frequently saw no need to pay them. Author Craig Castleman relates one such incident in which Prospect Hospital in the Bronx commissioned NOGA artists to produce a mural:

> When the mural was complete, Jacob Freedman, director and owner of the hospital, thanked the artists and had the mural rolled and taken into the hospital. He then started back to his office. At that point, Jack [Pelsinger] related, "I asked him for the money. 'What money?' he said. 'The money for the artists!' He acted like he didn't understand. It was like he was saying 'What! Pay kids for painting a mural for my hospital!' Well, I kept after him and finally he coughed up a hundred dollars. A hundred dollars for a mural that had taken all day to complete."[31]

While UGA members demanded higher prices, in some ways they did not fare much better in terms of earning respect as legitimate artists. Those who tried to branch out beyond graffiti were often discouraged, and gallery and museum directors who invited them to show their work tended to treat them in an incredibly disrespectful manner. After arranging a show at the Chicago Museum of Science and industry in 1974, museum staff not only refused to help them hang their own show but put the artists up at the YMCA rather than a nearby hotel.[32]

In any event, the American and European art world's fascination with aerosol artists did not last long, and it was largely limited to male writers since "high art" critics viewed graffiti as the embodiment of an aggressive masculine street culture. (Many of the artists also promoted this image; the UGA, for example, systematically denied women membership.) The only writers who made it big were Jean Michel Basquiat and a white artist named Keith Haring, both of whom have since died. To most veteran writers, Basquiat and Haring were peripheral to the graffiti scene since neither had done a train piece.[33] Nevertheless, the overnight success of these major artists, especially Basquiat, gave hope to some writers that the visual arts might offer a lucrative alternative to low-wage labor and an opportunity to live off of their own creativity. And for some writers, hard work and talent paid off. St Maurice, a veteran writer from Staten Island whose parents were artists, pursued his art professionally and eventually opened a framing shop. All twelve original members of UGA went on to either college or art school. Most of them became professional artists.[34]

Writers most committed to the genre, however, wanted to get paid but were unwilling to "sell out." Despite a strong desire to make money from their work and to become full-time artists, few writers wholeheartedly embraced the downtown art scene. As Lady Pink explained it: "Painting on canvas or a gallery's walls removes the element of risk, of getting one's name around, of interaction with one's peers and one's potential younger rivals. The pieces in galleries cease to be graffiti because they have been removed from the cultural context that gives graffiti the reason for being, a voice of the ghetto."[35]

And as the risks increased, the number of masterpieces in the public sphere slowly dwindled, and with them went the excitement of the downtown art world. By the late 1970s; the city launched a fairly successful (and very expensive) war against subway graffiti. In 1977, the MTA began spending $400,000 per year cleaning the trains with petroleum hydroxide and huge buffing machines. They also protected the train yards with attack dogs and 24 million dollars' worth of new fencing topped with ribbon wire, a razor-sharp, form of barbed wire that ensnares and shreds the body or object attempting to cross it. Ironically, while the MTA largely succeeded in keeping the trains graffiti free, aerosol art exploded throughout other city spaces and has spread throughout the world during the 1980s and 1990s. Tagging can be found in virtually every urban landscape, and masterpieces continue to pop up on the sides of housing projects, schoolyards, abandoned buildings and plants, under bridges, and inside tunnels that service commuter trains. Furthermore, writers have developed vehicles in which to circulate their work—mainly 'zines devoted exclusively to graffiti and independently produced videos.[36]

Why does aerosol art lose its value as soon as it is removed from its site of origin—the urban jungle? On the surface, the answer seems obvious: it is regarded by artists and critics as more authentic when it is produced illegally and can simultaneously deface property while conveying a message. Yet, when we compare graffiti with basketball, it is interesting to note that the latter does not lose its street credentials once individuals take their skills into more bourgeois, institutionalized contexts. Indeed, stories of black college players who were "discovered" on the playgrounds of some horrific metropolitan ghetto have become stock narratives among sports-casters and columnists. By contrast, once a piece of aerosol art enters the hallowed space of a museum or gallery, it is instantly dismissed as inauthentic or constructed for viewers as an extreme example of "outsider art." The different responses to sports and graffiti, I believe, are linked to the very nature of sports as a spectacle of performing bodies. The physicality of certain sports (like basketball); the eroticizing and racializing of the bodies participating in these spectacles; and the tendency to invest those bodies with the hopes, dreams, and aspirations of a mythic, heroic working class keep most popular, commercialized team sports at a safe distance from the world of high culture. Visual arts are a different story; it is precisely the similarities in form and technique (not to mention aesthetics) that push graffiti uncomfortably close to the official realm of modern art. And as residents of newly gentrified communities know, policing becomes more intense when the threat is in close proximity. Moreover, when the creative product is the body itself rather than a painting, a sculpture, a book, or even a musical score, it is rendered as less cerebral or cognitive and thus, inadvertently, devalued. It is not ironic, for example, that the media paid as much attention to Jean Michel Basquiat's physical appearance as to his paintings.[37]

As aerosol art was pushed further underground, rap music emerged from the underground with a vengeance. Young West Indian, African American, and Puerto Rican deejays and emcees in the South Bronx plugged their sound systems into public outlets and organized dance parties in schoolyards and parks, partly as a means to make money. A whole underground economy emerged, which ranged from printing and selling T-shirts advertising crews (Hip Hop groups), to building speakers, reconfiguring turntables, buying and selling records and bootleg tapes, even to selling food and drink at these outdoor events.[38] The real money, however, was in promoting, deejaying, and rapping. In fact, production and performance of Hip Hop music not only required musical knowledge but skills in electronics and audio technology. It is not an accident, for instance, that most pioneering Hip Hop deejays and graffiti artists had attended trade and vocational schools. Others got their start deejaying for house parties, a practice particularly common in Los Angeles. Los Angeles Hip Hop deejay G-Bone recalls, "I got out of high school, working at Fox Hills [mall I] must have been making minimum wage, about three dollars then, we came up with the DJ idea . . . we started buyin' records from Music Plus with our whole paycheques. . . . All we had was two speakers, Acculab speakers and a home amp with tubes and a Radio Shack mixer that didn't have crossfaders. They made it with buttons."[39] Calling themselves Ultrawave Productions, they started out making $60 a gig before muscling out another neighborhood deejay company (Baldwin Hills Productions) for clients. Then their fee shot up to $150. Young rappers and deejays also made money by selling homemade tapes on the streets or through local record shops willing to carry them. Toddy Tee's hit song "Batteram" started out as a street tape, and Oakland rapper Too Short sold homemade tapes for several years before getting a record contract.

Serious deejays invested the money they made doing dances and house parties in better equipment. Dr. Dre, formerly of the now defunct tap group Niggas With Attitude (NWA), used the money he made deejaying in high school to set up a four-track recording studio above his mother's garage in Compton, California. "That's how I learned how to use the board and everything. From the four track I advanced to the eight track and then fucking around in a little demo studio we had, using the money we had from DJing we bought a few things for a little twelve track studio." After selling street tapes for a while, he finally put his music on vinyl—before he got a record contract. Dre remembers, "We was just sellin' 'em out the trunk, trying to make money, we sold close to ten thousand records right out the car before we got signed."[40]

Break dancing, like rap music, apparently emerged in the South Bronx during the 1970s. The word *break* refers to "break beats"—fragments of a song that dancers enjoyed most and that the deejay would isolate and play over and over by using two turntables. The breakers were sometimes called "B-boys" or "B-girls" for short. Thanks to popular films such as *Flashdance*, most people have some familiarity with break dancing—the head and backspins, the jerky body movements of the "Electric Boogie" and the "Egyptian,"[41] Performed by men and women, sometimes in "crews" that did choreographed and "freestyle" moves before audiences and often in competition with other crews, breaking involved incredible body contortions and acrobatic feats. What many outsiders take for granted, however, is the extent to which moves like spinning on one's hand or head requires an enormous amount of practice and body conditioning. Besides rigorous physical preparation, break-dancers constantly risked injury, particularly since they generally performed on the streets and sidewalks. Some placed a flattened cardboard box between themselves and the hard concrete, but it was not enough to protect them from serious injuries ranging from stress fractures and scrotal contusions to brain hemorrhaging. Training and discipline were of utmost importance if dancers wanted to avoid injury. One particularly dangerous move was the "suicide," where the dancer does a front flip and lands on his/her back. As Dee-rock of The Furious Rockers put it, "It can be dangerous. . . . If you don't learn right, you'll kill yourself,"[42]

Perhaps more than most dance crazes, breaking ultimately became a contest over public space. It was a style performed in malls, hallways, and especially city streets. Historian and cultural critic Tricia Rose explains:

Streets were preferred practice spaces for a couple of reasons. Indoor community spaces in economically oppressed areas are rare, and those that are available are not usually big enough to accommodate large groups performing acrobatic dances. In addition, some indoor spaces had other drawbacks. One of the breakers with whom I spoke pointed out that the Police Athletic League [of New York], which did have gymnasium-size space, was avoided because it was used as a means of community surveillance for the police. Whenever local police were looking for a suspect, kids hanging out in the PAL were questioned.

But, despite the fantasy scenes of dancers taking to the streets in films like *Fame* and *Flashdance*, breakers did not go unmolested. There were several cases in which break-dancers were arrested for disturbing the peace or "attracting undesirable crowds" in public spaces such as shopping malls.[43]

One of the main reasons break-dancers performed in public was simply to make money. Like practitioners of sports, graffiti, and rap music, break-dancers were not only willing to work within the marketplace, but actively promoted the commodification of the form as an alternative to dead-end wage labor. The Furious Rockers, a predominantly Puerto Rican group from Brooklyn, were typical of most crews—at first. They began performing at Coney island amusement park for nickels and dimes, carrying only a boom box and a flattened cardboard box, and within months graduated to local gigs in New York public schools. Then they got a real break: choreographer Rosanne Hoare "discovered" them and arranged appearances on NBC's *Today* show and in Gene Kelly's film *That's Dancing*.[44]

While most break-dancers continued to hustle coins and dollar bills for their street-corner performances, the overnight success of the style itself and its rapid appropriation by advertising firms, professional dance schools, and the entertainment industry raised the stakes considerably. It suggested to young practitioners that break dancing was worth pursuing professionally. Some, like Rock Steady Crew, appeared in several movies that focus on Hip Hop culture, including *Beat Street*, *Breaking*, and *Wild Style*. Burger King, Panasonic, Pepsi, and Coca Cola have all used break-dancers in their commercials. All of these "breaks" left a deep imprint on young up-and-coming breakers that their craft might lead them out of the ghetto and into a worthwhile career and financial security.[45] But as one of the pioneers of break dancing, Rock Steady Crew's Crazy Legs, put it, "We got ripped off by so many people." As inner city-black and Puerto Rican youth who lacked professional status within the entertainment industry, they were frequently hired by downtown clubs to perform for their elite clientele and paid virtually nothing. Indeed, the very fact that The

Furious Rockers even had an agent was rare. The film industry did not do much better, either paying break-dancers less than union scale or hiring professional dancers to learn the moves so as to bypass the problem of hiring nonunion labor. Besides, like most dance trends, breaking declined almost as rapidly as it came into style.[46]

Perhaps because break dancing was both a skill that could be learned by professional dancers and a component of Hip Hop that was ultimately subordinated to rap music—serving more or less as a colorful backdrop to the emcee and deejay—breakers had far fewer opportunities to market their skills. Besides, breaking was introduced to the wider consumer audience without the overwhelming emphasis on the ghetto origins of the performers that one finds in rap and graffiti. Television shows like *Star Search* promoted suburban white preteens performing the most clichéd routines that combined breaking and gymnastics. I might add that Hip Hop culture in particular and dance and visual arts in general simply lack the institutional reward structures one finds in college and professional sports. The chances of landing a college scholarship or getting commercial endorsements (unless one is marketing malt liquor to underage drinkers) on the basis of one's skills as an emcee, break-dancer, or aerosol artist are slim indeed. Rap music is the only potential moneymaker, and the most successful artists usually earn a fraction of what star athletes make. Given the wider range of financial opportunities available in sports, is it any wonder that athletics (including basketball) continue to be the most multiracial realm of "play-labor" and the most intensely defended as a "color-blind" site of cultural practice?

None of these realms of play-labor, however, claim to be "gender-blind." Participants in and advocates for sports, Hip Hop, and Go-Go erect gender boundaries to maintain male hegemony in the areas of production, promotion, and performance. Of course, music and the arts offered women more opportunities for entry than the highly masculinized and sex-segregated world of sports. Women not only persevered to become respected graffiti artists in spite of the pressures against them; they had also been part of the rap scene since its inception. At the same time, gender boundaries within Hip Hop were vigilantly policed at all levels of production. Young men often discouraged or ridiculed women emcees; such women were often denied access to technology, ignored, or pressured by gender conventions to stay out of a cultural form identified as rough, profane, and male. Indeed, one might argue that rap music's misogyny is partly a function of efforts of male Hip Hop artists to keep it a masculine space. On the other hand, because the record industry markets rap as a profane, masculine street music, selling the bodies of the performers is as important as producing the music. Perhaps this explains why, during the formative years of rap music, it was easier for women to get on the mic at a local place like the Hevalo Club in the Bronx than to secure a record contract. Hip Hop, like other contemporary popular music, has become a highly visual genre that depends on video representations to authenticate the performer's ghetto roots and rough exterior. In a world of larger-than-life B-boys surrounded by a chaotic urban backdrop, there are few spaces for women outside the realm of hypermasculinity. Sometimes women rappers might challenge hypermasculine constructions of Hip Hop, but rarely do they step outside of those constructions. While there is something strangely empowering about women being able to occupy that profane, phallocentric space through which to express their own voices, it nonetheless sets limits on women's participation and ensures male dominance in the Hip Hop industry.[47]

On the other hand, women have been essential to the Hip Hop and Go-Go scene as consumers and participants. The pioneering deejays made their money by throwing parties, either in small underground clubs or at outdoor events. In order to ensure women's presence at these heterosocial affairs, gender differences shaped admissions policies substantially. Because women do not have the same access to cash wages, or unfettered movement through public space, they were often subsidized at these gatherings (ladies' night was almost every night; many house parties in California charged men and admitted women free). This should not be surprising since men depend on the presence of women for their own pleasure in the context of heterosexual exchange.

Indeed, it is in the world of sexuality that young men, more than young women, become consumers in the urban marketplace. In this complicated arena of public play, sex is one of the few realms of pleasure in which young women could make money. By exploring how young women have tried to turn the commodification of their own bodies and sexuality into "pleasure and profit" for themselves, however, I am not arguing that heterosexual relations are merely extensions of the marketplace. I am not suggesting that black working-class urban youth have no genuine loving relationships, even when economic transactions are involved. Rather, I am merely suggesting that because black women have less access than black men to public space, employment opportunities, entrepreneurial opportunities, and the most lucrative cultural opportunities, it has a profound impact on their daily social relations. For poor young black women, sex is one of the few "hustles" they have since virtually every other avenue is closed to them.

Sex, whether it is sexual intercourse or public expressions of sexuality, is a very complicated issue to think about in terms of the kinds of entrepreneurial activities I have outlined thus far. It is equally complicated when we consider the fact that sex is almost never performed or experienced in a context of pure pleasure. It carries with it the potential for deep emotional ties, scars, and/or obligations (such as fidelity, devotion, possession, agreed-upon codes of public behavior) between partners. Sex, therefore, is not simply another game or performance. Although all forms of play operate within discrete relations of power (indeed, the very notion of "leveling the playing field" acknowledges deep power relations in sports itself), the ideological and emotional currents that shape sexual encounters foreground the issue of power. Sex, after all, is neither competition nor an expression of aesthetic value, though in practice it might contain elements of both. For example, heterosexual courtship for men is often highly competitive, analogous to hunters competing for game which they display as a way of demonstrating their prowess. The physical attractiveness of the prey also enhances the hunter's claims of prowess. Although consensual sexual intercourse itself may contain elements of competition and value an aesthetic of form, *ideally* it is people enjoying and partaking in the erotic, sensual pleasures of the body—someone else's and/or their own. *Realistically*, I think it is safe to say, sex involves control and manipulation, not just physically and emotionally but discursively.

When we examine the commodification of sex in relation to our argument about how displaced urban youth turn forms of "play" into paid labor, discursive constructions of sex as a source of power become extremely important. These discourses powerfully reproduce a gender hierarchy in which professionalization ultimately increases the value of men's sexuality while devaluing women's sexuality. The pimp, whose very survival depends on the commodification of sex and the private ownership of women's bodies, is considered a heroic figure rich in sexual prowess. On the other hand, when women presumably use sex as a lever to obtain nice things or even decent treatment they are labelled "hos," "gold diggers," and "skeezers." It is a discourse that absolves men of responsibility, erasing their own participation in the sexual transaction. While women are constructed as possessing extraordinary sexual powers, when they do employ their sexuality as an exchange value, their prowess and worth are sharply downgraded. The contrast with other forms of play-labor I have discussed is striking. Unlike sports and most aspects of Hip Hop culture (with the possible exception of aerosol art), when a woman's sexual exercises remain just "play" and are not widely circulated, they are more highly valued. If she turns "professional" and earns money and becomes more highly circulated, she loses "value."[48]

The most unambiguous example of the professionalization of sex is obviously prostitution. The word *prostitution*, however, carries enormous moral connotations and focuses attention solely on the woman rather than the men who are equally involved in the transaction, both as consumers and employers. Few female prostitutes describe their work as creative or fulfilling in the same way that graffiti artists, athletes, or musicians do. And, in most cases, it is not autonomous work but an exploitive wage relationship—piece work is perhaps a better description. Because streets are dominated and controlled by men, prostitutes often require protection; even if they are not assaulted, the fear of assault is constantly circulated. Most importantly, women turn to prostitution for the money.[49]

On the other hand, when discussing prostitution in a heterosexual context, we run the risk of stripping women of any agency or removing from the transaction the issue of female desire. For instance, while prostitution offers women a means of income, we

must consider the extent to which anonymous sex is a source of pleasure. Furthermore, in light of the ways in which black women's sexual expression or participation in popular amusements (especially in heterosocial public places) has been constrained historically, black women's involvement in the pleasure industry might be seen as both typical and transgressive. Typical in that black women's bodies have historically been exploited as sites of male pleasure and embodiments of lasciviousness; transgressive in that women were able to break the straitjacket of what historian Evelyn Brooks Higginbotham calls the "politics of respectability" in exchange for the possibility of female pleasure. It is also potentially empowering since it turns labor not associated with wage work—sexual play and intercourse—into income.[50]

One young Harlem woman, simply identified as "Margo," who turned to prostitution as early as fifteen, took pleasure in the fact that she could earn an average of $200 per customer for doing something she enjoyed—having sex. As the product of an abusive home and grinding poverty, Margo sold her body as a means of survival. At the same time, by describing prostitution as her "pastime" rather than her job, she indirectly illustrated the pleasure she sometimes derived from the transaction: "If a guy approached me and said I was beautiful and asked how much would it cost him to have me, I would tell him whatever came to my mind. If he looked well dressed and clean I would say $200, $300, $400. It depended on my mood. If I was real horny, I would react quicker but that didn't mean the price went down. I would just choose someone who I thought was good looking. Someone who I thought would be pleasant to fuck."[51]

Sex, in Margo's view, was undoubtedly labor, but it was unlike the wage relationships that dominate the labor market. Besides, she found a way to bypass a pimp and work for herself, which meant that she kept all of her earnings. "It was sort of like getting your cake and eating it too," she pointed out. "You wake up, eat, sleep, you don't punch no clocks, you don't conform to no rules and regulations or courtesy to co-workers, customers, bosses, clients, patients, staff, etc. Best of all, you don't pay taxes either."[52]

Margo's world is hardly ideal and it certainly does not challenge the structures of capitalism. On the contrary, her decisions are driven somewhat by capitalist principles: namely, reducing labor expenditures and maximizing profit. However, she is resisting what would otherwise be her fate in an increasingly service-oriented, low-wage economy with shrinking opportunities for working-class ghetto residents. She exercises some control over her labor time, retains the full fee for her services, and often enjoys the work she performs. For her, sex is both work she can earn money from and play she can enjoy.

All of these examples, in their own unique way, reveal the dialectical links between work and play within the context of capitalism. Although the concept of play in the modern era is inextricably tied to the creation of leisure time as a form of consumption and recuperation for wage workers in capitalist political economy, play is a form of agency that is generally regarded as pleasurable activities that take place in "free" time. Play undeniably requires labor, but it is usually thought to be creative and fulfilling to those involved; it is autonomous from the world of work. In a postindustrial economy with fewer opportunities for wage work that might be financially or even psychologically fulfilling, art and performance—forms of labor not always seen as labor—become increasingly visible as options to joblessness and low-wage service work. Of course, the opportunities that music, sports, visual arts, and sex offer as alternative roads to upward mobility are actually quite limited. Nevertheless, these arenas have provided young people with a wider range of options for survival, space for creative expression, and at least a modicum of control over their own labor. In other words, neither an entrepreneurial spirit nor a work ethic is lacking in many of these inner city youths. Indeed, the terms *work* and *play* themselves presume a binarism that simply does not do justice to the meaning of labor, for they obscure the degree to which young people attempt to turn a realm of consumption (leisure time/play time) into a site of production. Their efforts are clearly within the spirit of laissez faire, but the definition of *profit* is not limited to monetary gain; equally important are the visceral pleasures of the form, the aesthetic quality of the product, the victory, the praise.

Of course, turning the labor of play into a commodity is hardly new. What is new, however, are the particular cultural forms that have emerged in this era and the structural context of the postindustrial urban

political economy. As I have argued, the decline of recreational facilities and accessible play spaces for inner city youths has coincided with the transformation of a criminal justice system in which reform is clearly no longer on the agenda. Today, policing the inner city is geared toward the corralling and managing of a young, displaced, and by most estimates permanently unemployed, black working-class population. Ironically, while city and state expenditures on parks and recreation dwindle and the corporate sector invests in more class-segregated, forbidding "public" play spaces, a growing number of voices have called for a return to supervised play in order to get kids "off the streets" and instill them with discipline and a strong work ethic. The movement sounds strikingly similar to Progressive Era efforts to replace what appeared to be disorganized street life with middle-class norms and behavior.[53] Not surprisingly, the introduction of an old idea to solve relatively new problems is in keeping with the new conservative agenda of the current Republican-dominated Congress under the leadership of Newt Gingrich. (Ironically, whereas the Republicans' "Contract with America"—a highly publicized commitment to sharply limit government and pass a broad plank of extremely conservative legislation—emphasizes "family values," crime, and personal safety, they have deeply cut expenditures on recreation and urban development. Instead of supervised play, Gingrich and his followers have favored forms of incarceration, from longer prison sentences to orphanages for children whose parents are deemed incompetent. Suddenly, supervised play seems like the liberal answer to "juvenile delinquency.")

While the movement for organized play has plenty of virtues, I hope we do not make the same mistakes of a century ago; more social control will do little to unleash and develop the creative capacities of black urban youth. Rather than try to change the person through rigid regimentation and supervised play, we need to change the streets themselves, the built environment, the economy, and the racist discourse that dominates popular perceptions of black youth. The presence of large numbers of African American and Latino youth together in parks, schoolyards, subway stations, or on street corners does not necessarily mean they are conspiring to rob somebody. Nor does it mean they are leading a life of idleness.

Finally, in the struggles of urban youths for survival and pleasure inside capitalism, capitalism has become both their greatest friend and greatest foe. It has the capacity to create spaces for their entrepreneurial imaginations and their "symbolic work," to allow them to turn something of a profit, and to permit them to hone their skills and imagine getting paid. At the same time, it is also responsible for a shrinking labor market, the militarization of urban space, and the circulation of the very representations of race that generate terror in all of us at the sight of young black men and yet compels most of America to want to wear their shoes.

Notes

1. Paul Gilroy, "One Nation under a Groove: The Culture Politics of 'Race' and Racism in Britain," in *Anatomy of Racism*, ed. David Theo Goldberg (Minneapolis: University of Minnesota Press, 1990), 274.

2. Nearly half of the unemployed in the 1980s were teenagers, and blacks and Latinos had the highest percentage. Terry Williams and William Kornblum, *Growing Up Poor* (Lexington, Mass.: D.C. Heath, 1985), 5–6.

3. Mike Davis, *City of Quartz: Excavating the Future of Los Angeles* (London: Verso, 1990), 304–7; Edward Soja, *Postmodern Geographies: The Reassertion of Space in Critical Social Theory* (London: Verso, 1989), 197, 201.

4. The idea that unemployed black youth turn to crime because it is more rewarding than minimum-wage, service-oriented work has been explored by a number of social scientists. See, for example, Richard B. Freeman, "The Relation of Criminal Activity to Black Youth Employment," in *The Economics of Race and Crime*, eds. Margaret C. Simms and Samuel L. Myers, Jr. (New Brunswick, N.J.: Transaction Books, 1988), 99–107; Llad Phillips and Harold Votey, Jr., "Rational Choice Models of Crimes by Youth," Ibid., pp. 129–87; Llad Phillips, H. L. Votey, Jr., and D. Maxwell, "Crime, Youth, and the Labor Market," *Journal of Political Economy* 80 (1972): 491–504; and Philip Moss and Chris Tilly, *Why Black Men Are Doing Worse in the Labor Market: A Review of Supply-Side and Demand-Side Explanations* (New York: Social Science Research Council Committee for Research on the Underclass, Working Paper, 1991), 90–93. For a discussion of the role of gangs in the illicit economy, see Martin Sanchez Jankowski, *Islands in the Street: Gangs and American Urban Society* (Berkeley, Calif.: University of California Press, 1991), 119–31. Despite the general perception that dealers make an enormous amount of money, at least one study suggests that the average crack peddler only makes about $700 per month. See Peter Reuter, Robert MacCoun, and Patrick Murphy, *Money for Crime: A Study of the Economics of Drug Dealing in Washington, D.C.* (Santa Monica, Calif.: Rand Drug Policy Research Center, 1990); and Davis, *City of Quartz*, 322.

5. Davis, *City of Quartz*, 244–51. For discussions of the ways in which the mass media depicts black youth gangs, violence, and the crack economy in inner city neighborhoods, see Jankowski, *Islands in the Street*, 284–302; Jimmie L. Reeves and Richard Campbell, *Cracked Coverage: Television News, the Anti-Cocaine Crusade, and the Reagan Legacy* (Durham, N.C.: Duke University Press, 1994); Herman Gray, "Race Relations As News: Content Analysis," *American Behavioral Scientist* 30, no. 4 (March–April, 1987): 381–96; Craig Reinarman and Harry G. Levine, "The Crack Attack: Politics and Media in America's Latest Drug Scare," in *Images of Issues: Typifying Contemporary Social Problems*, ed. Joel Best (New York: Aldine de Gruyter, 1989), 115–35; and Clarence Lusane, *Pipe Dream Blues: Racism and the War on Drugs* (Boston: South End Press, 1991).

6. Michael Gold, *Jews without Money* (New York: International, 1930), 42.

7. Cary Goodman, *Choosing, Sides: Playground and Street Life on the Lower East Side* (New York: Schocken Books, 1979), 9; and Nightingale, *On the Edge*, 15.

8. Jankowski, *Islands in the Street*, 119–31; Terry Williams, *Cocaine Kids: The Inside Story of a Teenage Drug Ring* (Reading, Mass.: Addison-Wesley, 1989); Jonathan Rieder, "Adventure Capitalism," *New Republic* 19 (November 1990): 36–40; and Philippe Bourgeois, "In Search of Horatio Alger: Culture and Ideology in the Crack Economy," *Contemporary Drug Problems* 16 (Winter 1989): 619–49.

9. Josh Sugarmann and Kristen Rand, "Cease Fire," *Rolling Stone Magazine* 677 (March 10, 1994): 31–42, quote on page 38. This is an excerpt from a report issued by the Violence Policy Center titled *Cease Fire: A Comprehensive Strategy to Reduce Firearms Violence* (Washington, D.C.: Violence Policy Center, 1994). See also Bruce C. Johnson, "Taking Care of Labor: The Police in American Politics," *Theory and Society* 3, no. 1 (1976): 106; Craig Wolff, "Guns Offer New York Teenagers a Commonplace Deadly Allure," *New York Times*, November 5, 1990; "Guns Take Ever Higher Toll among Young Blacks," *New York Times*, March 17, 1991; and Davis, *City of Quartz*, 240–48.

10. Davis, *City of Quartz*, chapter 4; Camilo José Vergara, "Our Fortified Ghettos," *The Nation* (January 31, 1994), 121, 122.

11. Jay S. Shivers and Joseph W. Halper, *The Crisis in Urban Recreational Services* (Rutherford, N.J.: Fairleigh

Dickinson University Press, 1981), 77–79; Roy Rosenzweig and Elizabeth Blackmar, *The Park and the People: A History of Central Park* (New York: Henry Holt, 1994), 502. The increasing cost of policing public recreational facilities also contributed to the budget crisis (Shivers and Halper, *The Crisis*, 106, 248–61).

12. Much of this I learned by taking my four year old, Elleza, to these high-tech playgrounds. When we visited Play-Space in December 1994, the employees refused to "buzz" me in at first, partly because they could not see Elleza through the window. When I picked her up and literally pointed to her, they allowed us to enter. For an interesting article about these pay-for-play spaces and the impact they are making on children's play in New York City, see Barbara Ensor, "Fun City," *New York Magazine* (October 24, 1994), 54–57. I should add that given the increasing workload of urban professionals, these "pay-for-play" spaces also offer inexpensive baby-sitting for older children.

13. Rosenzweig and Blackmar, *The Park and the People*, 508–9.

14. Goodman, *Choosing Sides*; David Nasaw, *Children of the City: At Work and at Play* (Garden City, N.Y.: Anchor Press, 1985); Amanda Dargan and Steve Zeitlin, *City Play* (New Brunswick, N.J.: Rutgers University Press, 1990), 136.

15. Houston Baker, *Black Studies, Rap, and the Academy* (Chicago: University of Chicago Press, 1993), 46–50; Robin D. G. Kelley, "Straight from Underground," *The Nation* 254, no. 22 (June 8, 1992): 793–96; Davis, *City of Quartz*, chapters 4 and 5; Rose, *Black Noise*, 106–14.

16. Nelson George, *Elevating the Game: Black Men and Basketball* (New York: HarperCollins, 1992), 200.

17. Spady and Eure, *Nation Conscious Rap*, 262; Michael A. Messner, *Power at Play: Sport and the Problem of Masculinity* (Boston: Beacon Press, 1992), 52; see also Henry Louis Gates, Jr., "Delusions of Grandeur," *Sports Illustrated* (August 9, 1991): 78.

18. Steve James, Fred Marx, and Peter Gilbert, *Hoop Dreams* (New York: Kartem-quit Films, 1994).

19. J. Hoberman, "Making It," *Village Voice* (October 18, 1994): 49; Messner, *Power at Play*, 45. Hoberman's essay is a review of *Hoop Dreams*.

20. Heidi Hartmann, "The Family as the Locus of Gender, Class, and Political Struggle: The Example of Housework," *Signs* 6 (Spring 1981): 366–94; Carolyn Steedman, *Landscape for a Good Woman: A Story of Two Lives* (New Brunswick, N.J.: Rutgers University Press, 1986), 13; Elizabeth Faue, "Reproducing the Class Struggle: Perspectives on the Writing of Working-Class History," paper presented at Social Science History Association Meeting, Minneapolis, October 19, 1990 (paper in author's possession), 8.

21. Dargan and Zeitlin, *City Play*, 157–61; Williams and Kornblum, *Growing Up Poor*, 77; June Goodwin, "Double Dutch, Double Dutch: All You Need is a Clothesline and Jet-Propelled Feet," *Christian Science Monitor*, October 7, 1980. See also Kyra Gaunt's brilliant dissertation, "The Games Black Girls Play: Music, Body, and 'Soul,'" (Ph.D. diss., University of Michigan, 1996).

22. As a boy "turner" in New York during the late 1960s and early 1970s, I remember vividly some of the accompanying songs and rhymes. My favorite was "Ain't your mama pretty/She got meatballs on her titties/She got scrambled eggs between her legs/Ain't your mama pretty." The most popular rhyme at that time went something like this: "—— and —— sitting in a tree [any name will do] / K-I-S-S-I-N-G / First comes love / Then comes marriage / Here comes —— with a baby carriage / How many babies did she have?" At that point the tempo would pick up and the other participants would count the number of times the jumper could skip without messing up. The final count, of course, equals the number of babies she and her boyfriend will have. For other examples, see Roger D. Abrahams, ed., *Jump-Rope Rhymes: A Dictionary* (Austin, Tex.: University of Texas Press, 1969); Gaunt, "The Games Black Girls Play"; Goodwin, *He-Said-She-Said*; and Bessie Lomax Hawes and Bessie Jones, ed., *Step It Down: Games, Plays, Songs, and Stories from Afro-American Heritage* (New York: Harper & Row, 1972).

23. Dargan and Zeitlin, *City Play*, 157, 160–61.

24. Willis, *Common Culture*, 1–5, 65.

25. On Larry Wright, see the film by Ari Marcopoulos and Maja Zrnic, *Larry Wright* (distributed by First Run Icarus Films, New York, 1990). I am basing some of my arguments here on my own observations in several U.S. cities. For a sensitive portrait of a young black homeless man in Washington, D.C, trying to make a living playing flute on the street, see Courtland Milloy, "Bittersweet Notes from the Street," *Washington Post*, October 3, 1985.

26. Unfortunately, there is very little written on Go-Go, so some of what I describe comes from my own observations and discussions with friends who grew up in Washington, D.C.—most notably, Marya McQuirter, a history graduate student at the University of Michigan. (I am grateful to Marya for correcting a couple of errors in an earlier draft of this book [*Yo' Mama's Disfunktional*].) Nevertheless, there are a few useful articles from the *Washington Post* which I consulted for this essay. See especially Richard Harrington, "Go-Go: A Musical Phenomenon, Bonding a Community," *Washington Post*, May 19, 1985; Michael Marriott, "Funky Sounds 'Bustin' Loose' in the District," *Washington Post*, October 5, 1984; and Courtland Milloy, "Go-Go Goes Across Town," *Washington Post*, July 15, 1985.

27. Harrington, "Go-Go."

28. Ibid.

29. Some important works on graffiti include Joe Austin, "Taking the Train: Youth Culture, Urban Crisis, and the 'Graffiti Problem' in New York City" (Ph.D. diss., University of Minnesota, 1996); Craig Castleman, *Getting Up: Subway Graffiti in New York* (Cambridge: MIT Press, 1982); Atlanta and Alexander, "Wild Style: Graffiti Painting," in *Zoot Suits and Second Hand Dresses: An Archaeology of Fashion and Music*, ed. Angela McRobbie (Boston: Unwin Hyman, 1988), 156–68; Martha Cooper and Henry Chalfant, *Subway Art* (New York: Holt, Rinehart, and Winston, 1984); Hager, *Hip Hop*; Ivor I. Miller, "Aerosol Kingdom: the Indigenous Culture of New York Subway Painters" (Ph.D. diss., Yale University, 1990); Rose, *Black Noise*, 41–47; and Jack Stewart, "Subway Graffiti: An Aesthetic Study of Graffiti on the Subway System of New York City, 1970–1978" (Ph.D. diss., New York University, 1989). On women aerosol artists, see especially Nancy Guevara, "Women Writin' Rappin' Breakin' " in *The Year Left 2*, ed., Mike Davis et al. (Verso Press: London, 1987), 160–75; and Rose, *Black Noise*, 43–44.

30. Austin, "Taking the Train," 118–75; Castleman, *Getting Up*, 117–25; Hugo Martinez, "A Brief Background of Graffiti," in *United Graffiti Artists Catalog* (n.p., 1975).

31. Quoted in Castleman, *Getting Up*, 131–32.

32. Ibid., 122–25; author conversation with St. Maurice, Staten Island, New York, January 1990.

33. Ivor Miller, "Guerrilla Artists of New York City," *Race & Class* 35, no. 1 (July–September 1993): 39; David Brendan Strasser, " 'It's the End of the World As We Know it (and I Feel Fine)': Keith Haring, Postmodern Hieroglyphics, Panic Hyperreality," (Ph.D., diss., Bowling Green State University, 1992); on the European art scene's fascination with graffiti, see Atlanta and Alexander, "Wild Style," 156–57; Kirk Varnedoe and Adam Gopnik, *High & Low: Modern Art, Popular Culture* (New York: Museum of Modern Art, New York, 1990), 337–82.

34. Austin, "Taking the Train," 186–327; Castleman, *Getting Up*, 126; author conversation with St. Maurice, Staten Island, New York, January 1990. I might add that because graffiti was one aspect of the larger Hip Hop culture, some writers, notably Freddy Brathwaite and Rammelzee, also produced and performed rap music. Brathwaite, known to the world as "Fab Five Freddy," did attend art school but went on to produce music videos, rap songs, and host the ever popular *Yo! MTV Raps*. Rammelzee rapped for a while (appearing in Charlie Ahearn's 1982 film *Wildstyle*) and eventually became a noted performance artist. See Atlanta and Alexander, "Wild Style," 158–62; and Rose, *Black Noise*, 194. The most extreme discussion of the transformation and commodification of graffiti can be found in Austin, "Taking the Train," chapter 6.

35. Quoted in Miller, "Guerrilla Artists," 39.

36. Joe Austin, "A Symbol that We Have Lost Control: Authority, Public Identity, and Graffiti Writing," (unpublished paper in author's possession).

37. On this last point, one need only look at the *New York Times Magazine*'s cover article on Basquiat in February 1985. As the physical embodiment of "primitivism" meets modernism, he appeared shoeless but with a shirt and tie. For other examples of Basquiat's body and lifestyle as spectacle, see Lorraine O'Grady, "A Day at the Races: On Basquiat and the Black Art World," *Artforum* 31 (April 1993): 10–12; "Jean-Michel Basquiat: Pop Life," *The Economist* 325 (November 21, 1992): 104–5; Martine Arnault, "Basquiat, from Brooklyn," *Cimaise* (November–December, 1989): 41–44; and Andrew Decker, "The Price of Fame," *Art News* 88 (January 1989): 96–101. On the problem of outsider/insider art and the question of boundaries, see the wonderful catalogue edited by Maurice Tuchman and Carol S. Eliel, *Parallel Visions: Modern Artists and Outsider Art* (Princeton, N.J.: Princeton University Press, 1992); and Michael D. Hall and Eugene W. Metcalf, Jr., *The Artist Outsider: Creativity and the Boundaries of Culture* (Washington, D.C.: The Smithsonian Institution Press, 1994).

38. On the early history of rap music, see Hager, *Hip Hop*; Rose, *Black Noise*; Bill Adler, *Rap: Portraits and Lyrics of a Generation of Black Rockers* (New York: St. Martin's Press, 1991); Nelson George et al., eds., *Fresh: Hip Hop Don't Stop* (New York: Random House, 1985); Spady and Eure, *Nation Conscious Rap, I* xi–xxxi; Toop, *Rap Attack 2*; and Brian Cross, *It's Not about a Salary: Rap, Race, and Resistance in Los Angeles* (London; Verso, 1993). For more on the financial side of Hip Hop, see Clarence Lusane, "Rap, Race, and Politics," *Race & Class* 35, no. 1 (1993), 42–47; and Alan Light, "About a Salary or Reality?" *South Atlantic Quarterly* 90 (Fall 1991): 855–70.

39. Cross, *It's Not about a Salary*, 162–63, 145.

40. Ibid., 196–97. It is particularly interesting to contrast Dr. Dre's story with that of his former partner, Eazy E (aka Eric Wright). Easy's more publicized version of NWA's origins suggests that drug money was used to capitalize NWA's initial productions—a narrative that reinforces the idea that "authentic" gangsta rappers have criminal backgrounds. See David Mills, "The Gangsta Rapper: Violent Hero or Negative Role Model?" *The Source* (December 1990): 32; Dan Charnas, "A Gangsta's World View," *The Source* (Summer 1990): 21–22; "Niggers with Attitude," *Melody Maker* 65, no. 44 (November 4, 1989): 33; Frank Owen, "Hanging Tough," *Spin* 6, no. 1 (April 1990): 34.

41. Rose, *Black Noise*; Guevara, "Women Writin' Rappin' Breakin' "; Dan Cox, "Brooklyn's Furious Rockers: Break Dance Roots in a Breakneck Neighborhood," *Dance*

Magazine 58 (April 1984): 79–82; Hager, *Hip Hop*; Peter J. Rosenwald, "Breaking Away '80s Style," *Dance Magazine* 58, no. 4 (April 1984): 70.

42. Quoted in Cox, "Brooklyn's Furious Rockers," 81. Much has been written on injuries caused by break dancing. For a sample, see Ronald Wheeler and Rodney Appell, "Differential Diagnosis of Scrotal Pain After Break Dancing," *The Journal of the American Medical Association* 252 (December 28, 1984): 3336; Philip J. Goscienski and Louis Luevanos, "Injury Caused by Break Dancing," *The Journal of the American Medical Association* 252 (December 28, 1984): 3367; Robert A. Norman and Michael Grodin, "Injuries from Break Dancing," *American Family Physician* 30 (October 1984): 109–112; and Kui Chung Lee, "Intracerebral Hemorrhage after Break Dancing," *The New England Journal of Medicine* 323 (August 30, 1990): 615–16.

43. Rose, *Black Noise*, 48, 50; Sally Banes, "Breaking Is Hard to Do," *Village Voice*, April 22–28, 1981: 31–33.

44. Dan Cox, "Brooklyn's Furious Rockers," 79.

45. Rosenwald, "Breaking Away '80s Style," 73–74.

46. Rose, *Black Noise*, 50; and on the training of professional dancers in break-dance techniques, see Joyce Mollov, "Getting the Breaks," *Ballet News* 6 (August 1984): 14–19; Margaret Pierpont, "Breaking in the Studio," *Dance Magazine* 58 (April 1984): 82.

47. The best discussion of women's involvement as Hip Hop artists can be found in Rose, *Black Noise*, especially chapter 5. See also Toop, *Rap Attack 2*, 93–95; and Guevara, "Women Writin' Rappin' Breakin,' " 160–75. Most of the work on women and rap focuses on representations of women or female rappers' representations of sexuality rather than their actual participation as artists or producers.

48. I am especially grateful to Wahneema Lubiano for helping me think through the valuing or devaluing of women's sexuality in relationship to the market. For examples of the celebration of the pimp in literature and popular culture, see Iceberg Slim [Robert Beck], *Pimp: The Story of My Life* (Los Angeles; Holloway House, 1969); Christina Milner and Richard Milner, *Black Players; The Secret World of Black Pimps* (New York: Little, Brown and Co., 1972). On the pimp in popular film, see Donald Bogle, *Toms, Coons, Mulattoes, Mammies and Bucks: An Interpretive History of Blacks in American Films*, new ed. (New York; Continuum, 1989), 234–42; Daniel Leab, *From Sambo to Super-spade: The Black Experience in Motion Pictures* (Boston: Houghton Mifflin, 1975); David E. James, "Chained to Devilpictures: Cinema and Black Liberation in the Sixties," in Davis et al., *The Year Left 2*, 125–38; Brown, *Die, Nigger, Die*; Bobby Seale, *Seize the Time* (New York: Random House, 1970) and *Lonely Rage* (New York: Times Books, 1978) in which Seale himself takes on the characteristics of a pimp; and Eldridge Cleaver, *Soul on Ice* (New York: McGraw-Hill, 1968).

49. For a vivid and detailed description of black teenage prostitutes and pimps during the 1970s and 1980s, see Williams and Kornblum, *Growing Up Poor*, 62–63.

50. My thinking here owes a great deal to Tera Hunter's *To 'Joy My Freedom: Southern Black Women's Lives and Labors After the Civil War* (Cambridge: Harvard University Press, 1997). esp. chapters 7 and 8; Kathy Peiss, *Cheap Amusements: Working Women and Leisure in Turn-of-the-Century New* (Philadelphia: Temple University Press, 1986); Hazel Carby, "Policing the Black Woman's Body in an Urban Context," *Critical Inquiry* 18 (Summer 1992): 738–55; Victoria Wollcort, "Remaking Respectability: African American Women and the Politics of Identity in Interwar Detroit" (Ph.D. diss., University of Michigan, 1995).

51. Williams and Kornblum, *Growing Up Poor*, 65–66.

52. Ibid., 66, 69.

53. Goodman, *Choosing Sides*, 28.

17.
WOMEN AND THE ELECTRIC GUITAR

Mavis Bayton

Where are all the great female electric guitarists? Why haven't we had an Erica Clapton, Pat Townsend or Jenny Hendrix? Ask the average person to think of some famous women guitarists and they will be hard pushed to come up with a single name. In June 1996 *Mojo* Magazine (Issue 31) celebrated 'The 100 Greatest Guitarists of All Time'. Only three of them were women: Sister Rosetta Tharpe, Joni Mitchell and Bonnie Raitt. The lack of women guitarists in rock's hall of fame is partly a result of the way in which women get written out of history and their contribution undervalued, but mainly a reflection of the fact that so very few women get a foot on even the bottom rung of the rock career ladder. So the key question is: why do so few women set out on the career of electric guitarist?

Looking at popular music as a whole, women have been music consumers rather than music producers: the main role for women is that of fan. Women performers have been more prominent in commercial 'pop' and 'folk' than in 'rock', but their place in all these worlds has been predominantly that of vocalist rather than instrumentalist. Where women have been instrumentalists they have tended to be keyboard-players. Whilst women folk singer-songwriters have played the acoustic guitar, the electric guitar (surely the instrument which most epitomises 'rock') has been left in the hands of the boys.

There have always been women vocalists. So, for example, in the early 1960s there were, in America, a large number of all-female singing groups. The 'British Invasion' of beat music, however, signalled the

end for these vocal groups. It is hard to think of any women's beat groups. This female absence is all the more surprising in that many of these beat groups, and most notably the Beatles themselves, performed quite a lot of covers of American all-girl singing groups. Why were young women not themselves performing this eminently suitable material in the new beat group format? The answer, I believe, is simple: all-girl vocal groups suddenly looked passé. The Beatles had changed the mould: it was no longer enough just to sing, you had to play your own instruments too and, above all, that meant the electric guitar. At that time, although many girls took up the acoustic guitar (in the footsteps of Joan Baez and Joni Mitchell), the idea of playing the electric guitar was alien to them. The arrival of the electric guitar, then, led to the exclusion of women from groups for some considerable time.

In the decades since, there have been more women playing electric instruments and, indeed, all-women rock bands, but it is still the case that men are the norm and women the exception. A head-count of UK musicians in local and national bands will highlight the continuing gender imbalance. In a typical small city or large town in the UK, there will be hundreds of men playing electric guitars in local bands and hundreds more playing by themselves at home. In contrast, you will find around a dozen women playing electric guitars in bands. I have recently carried out a head-count in Oxford and I estimate the proportion of women instrumentalists in local bands to be somewhere between 2 and 4 per cent. The trade magazines reflect this relative absence. They also reinforce it, for any novice or would-be female guitarist is still confronted with a solidly masculinist world.

In 1988, 1992 and 1996, as part of my ongoing research into women's popular music-making, I analysed the trade magazines for guitarists. In each year, the overwhelming majority of the photos, features and news were of male guitarists: women's presence has been absolutely minimal. Here I shall just discuss the summer of 1996. Taking the August issue of *Guitar*, there were eighty pictures of male guitarists. In contrast, there were only two of women playing guitars and one of these seemed to be stereotyping female insecurity, by showing a scantily-clad and worried looking female under the sentence 'Don't Drop That Guitar' (an advert for guitar security straps)! The back cover of the August issue of *Guitar School* magazine shows musical equipment and a sexy woman clearly positioned for the male guitarist to have sex with. In *Total Guitar* there was a handful of pictures of women but they were without exception holding acoustic instruments. The only sizeable picture of a woman was located over the advertising line 'The best players play the best pickups': the scantily dressed woman is not positioned as musician but as groupie. On the other hand, compared to 1988, I did notice that there is an absence of blatantly phallic and naively macho 'cock rock' advertisements, such as 'Make it Big with an Aphex Aural Exciter' or 'Mega-Muscle', although there were still plenty of naked hairy chests and medallions in evidence!

In terms of text, all but one magazine in the batch I purchased had no main feature articles on female musicians. The exception was *Guitar School* magazine, which had one feature article on Sinéad Lohan, whilst the other six articles were on men. This article was, however, somewhat questioning her playing abilities. The title was 'I Can Play, Really' and asks, 'Who says a woman's place is in the kitchen?' The (male) author later comments, 'As a "girl with a guitar", one might expect Sinéad to opt for a dainty acoustic, but no, her current instrument is a black Godin Acousticaster.' Has he not heard of Chrissie Hynde, Bonnie Raitt or L7?

Last, these magazines typically contained transcriptions of pieces for purchasers to learn to play. These were all written by men. Likewise, all the technical advice pages and playing advice were by men. All the covers depicted male guitarists. Two magazines came with free CDs, predictably, of male players.

How can one explain the lack of female electric guitarists? At the turn of the 1980s, when I was playing guitar in an all-women band, the question intrigued me to the extent that I embarked on a sociological research project. This research involved participant and non-participant observation and in-depth interviewing of a cross-section of female rock musicians in the mid-1980s. In 1995–6 I updated my research. In total, I have interviewed around a hundred women musicians. The points I make here are based on that research.[1]

I start from the supposition that there are no physical reasons for the lack of female guitarists. Women are just as musical as men, and at any age they can acquire the strength and skills required to play any instrument in any style of popular music. Women are just as capable of becoming rock musicians as men are. Lead guitarists are made, not born. The reasons for women's absence are entirely social.

As girls grow up, they learn (from family, school, books, magazines and, above all, their friends) how to be 'feminine' and not to engage in 'masculine' activities. Playing the flute, violin and piano is traditionally 'feminine', playing electric guitar is 'masculine'.[2] On TV and in magazines, young women are presented with repeated images of men playing electric guitar; there are few female role models to inspire them. Thus most young women do not wish to become rock guitarists, and, even if they did, would not believe it to be possible. The very first steps in learning the electric guitar force a young woman to break with one of the norms of traditional 'femininity'; long, manicured, polished fingernails must be cut down.

Yolande (bassist with Marcella Detroit): I have taught a little bit in youth clubs. . . . I have had girls saying 'I don't want to cut my nails'. I've had other women saying they don't like the idea of getting muscles.

It is difficult to stay 'feminine' in a rock band precisely because 'femininity' is an artifice: it is assumed that women do not sweat, that their noses do not go red and shiny, and that their hair stays in place. Or, in the words of Judith Butler (1990): 'gender is an identity tenuously constituted in time, instituted in an exterior space through a stylised repetition of acts'. Those 'acts' involve 'work' which is antithetical to the 'work' involved in playing electric guitar in a band. Moreover, if gender is 'tenuously constituted', then playing electric guitar jeopardises its maintenance.

> *Terri* (guitarist in 1980s jazz rock band: You find you have to keep up your feminine 'girly' thing and that doesn't particularly go with being in a hard, sloggy job, which is what music's all about.

In contrast, for young men playing guitar in a band directly enhances their masculinity. (I have known more than one male guitarist who proudly preserved the bloodstains on his fretboard.)

That minority of girls who are not discouraged from playing the electric guitar by its traditionally masculine connotations face a series of further obstacles. Compared to boys, teenage women lack money, time, space, transport and access to equipment. They are pressurised (by commercial teen culture and their schoolfriends) to get a boyfriend. The search for romance can devour their time, better preparing them for the role of fan than for that of musician and, even in this role, young women behave differently from young men. Male fans identify with their guitar-heroes and seek to emulate them by learning to play themselves. In contrast, female fans fantasise about sex, love, marriage and babies with their idols (Vermorel and Vermorel, 1985). Male fans buy a guitar; female fans buy a poster.

If, against the odds, the desire to play electric guitar persists, a girl has to contend with another major obstacle: boys. Unlike classical guitar, there are few formal settings in which to learn to play rock. Thus the informal friendship groups within which rock music-making occurs are of crucial importance as learning environments. However, teenage women are not often welcomed in male music-making cliques and thus do not generally get the insider information and tips which are routinely traded within them. Male musicians tend to be possessive about such technical information.

The vast majority of bands are male and many actively exclude women. A major preoccupation of young men is establishing their 'masculinity'. Thus, so-called masculine traits are exaggerated. It is in their younger teens that most male rock guitarists start playing in bands. To have, say, a girl on lead guitar would undermine rock's latent function of conferring 'masculine' identity on its male participants. Its 'masculinity' is only preserved by the exclusion of girls. I think that if it were traditional for girls to play electric guitar, then boys would avoid it just as much as they currently avoid embroidery. Girls fulfil the role of 'outsiders'/'negative reference group'/'the Other'. So, from the boys' point of view, girls must be kept out of rock bands just as they are kept out of cricket and football. A number of the women I interviewed told me of their early experiences. Enid, for instance, who was a heavy metal guitarist during the early 1980s:

> *Enid:* At that time, the guys we knew who could play didn't want to know at all about us. Females playing in a band, at that time, was totally unheard of. They thought, 'Oh, girls! They won't be serious and they won't carry on. And they wouldn't be any good anyway.'

Guitar shops are also 'male' terrain: they rarely employ women as assistants, and the customers are overwhelmingly male. Thus boys tend to feel at home there. In any of these shops you can observe the assertive way in which young men try out the equipment, playing the beginning of a few well-know songs time and again, loudly and confidently, even though those few bars may encompass the sum total of their musical knowledge. In contrast, nearly every one of my interviewees said that guitar shops felt like alien territory. For instance:

> *Amy* (16-year-old guitarist in 1990s Oxfordshire band, Frances Belle): At Russell Acott I feel very intimidated. Especially going to ask—they're all stood behind the counter, these massive metal blokes. Well, that's what they look like, judging by their image. I go up and go, 'Can I have a top E string?' because I don't know the proper names or anything, so it's even worse. And they go, 'What gauge? What sort?' And I'm like, 'I don't know'. So I don't like going in and looking at guitars or anything in music shops. . . . When you're trying, they're just staring at you. If you don't know much as well—and then they pick it up and go (imitates complicated guitar playing) and you're going, 'Oh no, I'll just take that!'

Novice guitarists, like Amy, reported that trying out the equipment was akin to being on trial; they were scared of showing themselves up and being 'put down' by the assistants or laughed at, whilst experienced players relayed tales of condescension or of simply being ignored. If a woman guitarist goes into a shop with a man, the assistants tend to talk to the man not the woman, even if the man is not actually a guitarist.

Fran (bass guitarist in various 1990s Nottingham bands including Sub Rosa, Mothers of the Future and The Very Good Rock and Roll Band): You go in and all the blokes are sitting in one corner talking about some riff that they came up with last night, totally ignoring you. They are very patronising. They see that you're a woman and they think, 'How did you dare come in our music shop?'

Rock is associated with technology, which is itself strongly categorised as 'masculine'. 'Femininity' involves a socially manufactured physical, mechanical and technical helplessness, whilst 'masculinity' involves a display of technical competence. In marked contrast to girls, boys get given technical toys and become confident about technical things. Women are often alienated from the essential technical aspects of rock. If they become singers, or play the sax, they may manage to avoid full immersion in this sea of technicality, but not if they play the guitar. Thus young women may be drawn towards the electric guitar but are put off by the multitude of electronic and electrical components, which are a basic requirement for a rock performance: leads, plugs, amplifiers, plug-boards, etc. They lack confidence. Some women who had been playing in rock bands for years said that they still had not completely overcome this problem of 'techno-phobia'. For instance:

Vi Subversa (guitarist in 1980s punk band, Poison Girls): I think there is a tendency for us still to be scared of equipment: the 'black-box-with-chrome-knobs' syndrome. . . . I've obviously become very familiar with what I do but I still don't feel physically as at one with my equipment as I think most men do. . . . It took me a year before I turned my volume up. Roger would see that my amp was turned up even if I turned it down, because I was still scared of it . . . of making a noise to that extent. I turned

the knobs down on my guitar for a whole year. And then, suddenly, I thought, 'Fuck it! I'm not going to do that anymore'.

Moreover, technical language is often used as a power strategy in a mystifying way in order to exclude women. This can happen informally amongst groups of male musicians, by sound crews at gigs, by technicians in recording studios and so on. So it is not only that women lack confidence, they are also deliberately excluded from this technical world.

There are, then, a number of factors which can help to explain why so few women play the electric guitar, but I believe the major reason is that the electric guitar, unlike the acoustic guitar, is seen as 'male'. The skills involved in playing the instrument are perceived as 'male' skills, inappropriate for women. A woman playing a rock instrument is breaking the gender code.[3] She faces a set of low expectations concerning her competence (woman with guitar = fish with bicycle). For a man, a good performance on the electric guitar is simultaneously a good 'performance' of 'masculinity'. The 'heavier' the rock the more true that is. When you go to a metal concert, it's the men in the audience who play 'air guitar', not the women. In doing so, they are affirming the male bond between themselves and the musicians up on the stage. The electric guitar, as situated within the masculinist discourse of rock, is virtually seen as an extension of the male body. This is always implicit and sometimes explicit, as when men mime masturbating their 'axes'. Heavy metal guitarists unashamedly hold their guitars like a penis. Prince even has a substance being 'ejaculated' from his guitar! (Male) musical skills become synonymous with (male) sexual skills. With legs firmly planted akimbo, the guitarist is able to lean back in a parody of sexual ecstasy. Metal fans may argue that this whole bodily stance is knowing, ironic and fun. That may be so. The fact remains, however, that it is an exclusively 'masculine' idiom.

It is not only the shape which is symbolic, but also the sheer volume and attack of the instrument which connotes phallic power. 'Power, the essential inherent and delineated meaning of heavy metal, is culturally coded as a masculine trait' (Weinstein, 1991). Advertisers in guitar magazines choose words with care to endow their gadgets with masculinity: 'strong', 'overpowering', 'punch', 'tough', 'cut-throat' and so on. And in both language and image, sexual innuendo abounds.

All of this causes problems for the woman guitarist, in terms of how she holds and plays her instrument. Rock guitarists (unlike classical and jazz players) typically hold their instrument low down in front of their genitals, radically adapting their fingering style to suit. Yet most players actually find it easier to hold their guitar on their chest or at their waist. The main reason given, by men and women, for playing the guitar at pelvic level (or lower) is that it 'just looks right'. I would argue that the only reason for this is the silent encoded phallocentric message. If you play it higher up it is seen as less 'masculine'. A woman with an electric guitar looks 'wrong' anyway and if she then plays it at chest height she looks even more 'wrong'. Thus, if a woman wants to look 'good' she has to play in a 'masculine' way. For instance:

Sara (guitarist in 1990s Sheffield rock band Treacle): When I record I have it really short, up here. Because it's easier to play. But when I'm on stage, obviously, I have it—not really low down like a big heavy rocker—but in the middle, so it doesn't look stupid up round my boobs.

Feminists have had particular objections to the traditional mode of playing. For example,

Alison (bass guitarist in 1980s jazz rock band): Women don't often seem to play guitars and basses so low down. . . . I don't think it's true that women can't do it. I think there are very few women who would choose to do it, feminist or not, actually. . . . I think a lot of women find using your guitar like that very obnoxious or objectionable, and if you're feminist it's that much worse, because you can see that much more in it.

Heavenly is a band not noted for its worries about being 'girly' and so it was particularly ironic that Amelia told me she was worried about playing the guitar too high:

Amelia (guitarist in 1990s indie band Heavenly): I would say that if I had been a better feminist I would have been more determined to hold it correctly. I don't hold it well . . . I used to play quite high

and it was considered very sissy. So I now wear it probably lower than I should do! It is an issue, definitely! Pete's always trying to get me to wear it higher, because he says I play it better when it's higher. But I refuse to do it 'cause I look too silly!

Most female guitarists I spoke to (whether in the 1980s or the 1990s) had considered these problems if not actually agonised over them.

Claire (guitarist in 1990s indie band Sidi Bou Said): if you wear your guitar too low you are incapable of moving anywhere and because I play lots of bar chord and stuff up the neck it's easier to have the guitar higher. But I feel a bit 'poncey' with the guitar too high. . . . I do like the idea of women playing guitars slung like men. . . . I've always thought guitars are really sexy and really strong things and I like the fact they're slung where they are. I couldn't play it up here; it wouldn't feel right. It's all about sex, really.

Debbie even risked her health by playing her guitar very low:

Debbie [from 1990s pop band Echobelly]: I started getting RSI [repetitive strain injury]. It's really bad. So my guitar started getting higher and higher. But it's really bad. I get a huge swelling up here from fretting.

The problem is partly one of a lack of female role models. Although a musician might not be consciously copying anyone, there is no doubt that she is unconsciously influenced by other (male) guitarists and absorbs masculinist performance norms. The middle-aged punk performer Vi Subversa developed an ironic solution to this problem, subverting the meaning of stereotypical macho guitar hero movements:

Vi Subversa: I know when I go in for some big chords that this is what men do. And my feeling when I do it is irony, because I know that you don't have to strut around to make a good sound. I know that you can do it anyway. For boys to see a woman doing it is feeding them an image they haven't had before.

And in Vi Subversa's case not only are the boys seeing a woman playing 'power-chords' but an older woman at that.

If playing styles raise issues concerning the female body, so does the instrument itself. Technical objects are political in their design. The electric guitar was designed for men, by men, and it has thereby functioned to exclude women. These days, guitars can be made in various shapes. Why, then, does the standard rock guitar remain decidedly phallic? I believe that if it was mainly women who played electric guitar the shape of the instrument would have changed by now; not only for symbolic reasons but also because of the female body. Perhaps guitars would typically be held above the waist and their design make allowances for the fact that women have breasts. If you hold your guitar at chest level you risk crushing them and this is particularly painful if you are pre-menstrual. Both Juliet and Kate from Oxford's 1990s band, Twist, for instance, mentioned this problem. Kate used to play a Gibson 5S, which is a big-bodied guitar, and her breasts hung over the top in a manner which sometimes embarrassed her. I used to play a Gibson Les Paul and, whilst my left breast used to get squashed, my right breast used to fit snugly into the top curve in the guitar's waisted middle. I was not the only one to attempt this partial solution. For instance,

> *Anna* (guitarist in Sub Rosa): They've got that kind of slot at the top which you can hook your tit over the top of. You can either squash it against your stomach, which is going to hurt, or you can hook it over the appropriate bit. . . . I'm going to work on a funk rhythm guitar with a concave back that you fit your tits into!

Despite all the physical and symbolic obstacles strewn in the path of would-be female electric guitarists, a small minority do set out on a musical career.[4] My research shows that they then face further problems which men do not; the entrenched sexism of the rock world. They encounter hostile male musicians, prejudiced promoters, patronising disc jockeys, obstructive technicians who sneer and make sexist jokes at their expense, inhospitable masculinist working conditions, unimaginative marketing by record companies, and sexploitative media coverage. They also face harassment and put-downs because they are women.

The most common form of harassment is verbal abuse of the 'show us yer tits' variety. This sort of abuse reflects the fact that women's place on stage is only legitimate if they take their clothes off. At gigs in the 1970s you could sense some men's incredulity: if you were not going to expose your breasts, then what were you doing up on stage? A woman is as likely to be evaluated on the size of her breasts as on her guitar playing. Moreover, such comments are meant to be heard by the performers. It can be startling and off-putting for the novice guitarist to have to deal with demands that she strip.

This kind of harassment is still as common in the 1990s as it was in the 1970s. To many of my interviewees, such abuse was so routine and taken for granted that it barely required a comment. Practically every woman musician that I interviewed had experienced it.

> *Terri* (of 1980s jazz rock band): There's always either a comment or some uneasy atmosphere or something. Every gig there'll be some little something that has to be dealt with. [But] a lot of women just have that experience happen to them so much of the time that they block it out. And it's the victim syndrome. It's like almost that you draw that kind of attention to yourself, that somehow women are responsible for those things. Or, 'Oh, it's not serious, dear. It doesn't matter.' We're so used to being harassed.

But younger women today have been strongly retaliating. Actively drawing the audience's attention to the perpetrator and confronting him usually works. My interviewees supplied me with a number of amusing and effective one-line retorts which they had used. Male hostility also often makes women musicians determined to show how good they are, although there is usually an accompanying resentment.

Sometimes harassment goes further than verbal insults, to become physically threatening. My interviewees recounted particularly scary stories of gigs abroad. For instance:

> *Shareen* (guitarist in Ms45): I remember once when I was 18. I was doing a gig in Colorado. Some guy actually came up to the stage and picked me up

and started to carry me off . . . it was scary! I hit him on the head with my guitar and a big fight started.

Emma (of Lush): We just did a tour of America and we walked off the stage at one gig. Because there are these weird radio festivals and people are just moshing and punching each other senseless. And people were just throwing things at us. Not like 'Get off the stage'; it was just a sport for them at these festivals. . . . It was a really violent atmosphere. . . . I was afraid when this massive shoe came hurtling towards my head. That's when I walked off.

So sexist prejudice and active harassment act as a handicap for the female guitarist. But the most general problem is simply not being taken seriously. The status 'woman' seems to obscure that of 'musician'. Female guitarists are expected to be sexy and incompetent and these expectations form a hurdle which must be coped with or combated in some way. Guitarists told me about men at gigs who, after admiring their instrument, played very fast up and down the neck to show how good they were and to put the woman down. Even when a woman's performance is appreciated it is not always her instrumental skills that she is complimented on:

Sara (of Treacle): After the gig, people come up to you and, instead of saying, 'I really liked what you did', they'll say, 'I like your hair.' Like, when has a male musician ever got 'You've got nice eyes' instead of . . . . They'd never say that to a male person!

Furthermore, even when the comments seem to be about a woman's musicianship they may mean something different:

Anna (of Sub Rosa): The times I've gone on stage and been wearing miniskirts or looking fairly girly, I've got more compliments on my playing than if I had been wearing jeans and a T-shirt. I've got a friend who says, 'Them right dead-legs who come up to you after gigs and go, "I thought your playing was really good", what they actually mean is, "I fancy you in a skirt".'

Finally, there is another very basic reason why female guitarists do not reach the celestial heights. Unlike men, women have to carefully juggle the demands of family and career, personal and public life. Women are typically unable to commit themselves to rock careers in the wholehearted way in which men do precisely because of these commitments elsewhere. The centrality of family and love relationships make it difficult for girls to make long-term plans. In a sense, all career plans are provisional. In contrast, for a boy having a girlfriend is not the be-all-and-end-all of his life and marriage does not interrupt his career. For a man, paid work is the central plank of his life. Apart from the minority of highly successful musicians, most women still have to choose between a rock career and motherhood. Male guitarists typically have their career serviced by the hidden labour of girlfriends and wives. Female guitarists are far less likely to get such support. Where were Erica Clapton and Pat Townsend? Washing the dishes and feeding the baby, probably.

I look forward to the day when there will be as many women playing electric guitar in bands as men. I look forward to this not merely because I want to see an end to sexist constraints on women, but also because of the effects this would have on musical performance itself. In playing styles, men would no longer be the yardstick against which women are measured. If as many women played guitar as men, particularly lead guitar, then the instrument would no longer be seen as a phallic symbol and this would also be reflected in its design. Playing rock would no longer denote masculinity. In a non-sexist world half of all electric guitarists would be women and gender would be no more relevant to playing than eye colour or height is today. I choose to end with a quote from the inveterate middle-aged guitarist Vi Subversa:

All of technology is dominated by men . . . but I'm fucked if I'm going to say it belongs to them. It's ours! Right? Every single wire that's been put together was made by a man who was fed, nurtured, supported by women somewhere. I think we've got to reclaim the lot.

Notes

1. The 1980s research led to an unpublished doctoral thesis: Mavis Bayton (1989) 'How Women Become Rock Musicians', Warwick University. The updated research has been for a book being published in the near future by Oxford University Press.

2. In many parts of the world musical instruments are sexually classified and in some tribal societies the consequences of breaking a musical taboo can be serious. But exactly which instrument each sex is allowed to play varies cross-culturally.

3. I do not have space in this article to discuss clothes, but women in feminine 'drag' (satin slips, nighties, wedding dresses) 'kicking shit' out of their guitars, women like Courtney Love and Babes in Toyland, and indie women with the ironic and contradictory ballgowns-plus-Doc Martens approach, are creating exactly the sort of 'gender trouble' which Judith Butler (1990) proposes as subversive political action, upsetting the notion of a fixed, true or real gender and revealing gender to be, in itself, a fabricated performance.

4. The women who do play electric guitar are exceptional in that they have overcome the obstacles which I have been discussing. Two main routes into playing have been feminism and punk. Both of these opened up a playing space for women. It is no accident that there was an increase in women musicians in the late 1970s and early 1980s.

References

Butler, J. (1990) *Gender Trouble: Feminism and the Subversion of Identity*, London: Routledge.

Vermorel, F. and Vermorel, J. (1985) *Stardust: The Secret life of Fans*, London: Comet.

Weinstein, D. (1991) *Heavy Metal*, New York: Lexington.

PART III

TEXTS: BODIES, IDENTITIES, AND REPRESENTATION

Introduction

Part III of this reader is devoted to studies of gender in media representation, one of the oldest and, to date, most fruitful areas of feminist and queer media scholarship. Given the media industries' persistently narrow construction of women, homosexuals, and other individuals socially disenfranchised as a result of their gender, understanding the intricacies of such industries' gendered representational strategies has been crucial to advocacy for progressive change. This objective is clear in Gaye Tuchman's early work on women's symbolic annihilation in mass media, as well as in Laura Mulvey's theorization of women's sexual objectification in Hollywood cinema.[1] Although both scholars were concerned with the stereotypical and, at times, offensive portrayal of women in media, their studies are indicative of the different paths media scholars took in the early 1970s with regard to issues of representation. Tuchman's research was conducted primarily via quantitative methods that found the number of images of women in media sorely lacking, while Mulvey used semiotics and psychoanalytic theory to understand how cinematic representations of women are impacted by the fears and fantasies of those who produce them. As Suzanna Danuta Walters explains, these differing approaches are perhaps best understood as, on the one hand, the study of images of women and, on the other, the study of woman as image.[2]

Building from yet expanding beyond these foundational feminist studies of media representation, both of which focused somewhat narrowly on white, heterosexual, middle-class women in mass media, the chapters included in this section cover a much broader spectrum of gendered media representations as a result of changes in feminist and queer epistemologies since Mulvey and Tuchman published their early work in the 1970s. For example, most scholars working in this area today have been trained in queer, Marxist, critical race, and/or postcolonial theory, and thus take an intersectional approach to subjectivity in order to examine how gender is constructed alongside other components of identity, such as age, race, class, and sexuality. Additionally, studies of gendered media representation now also include explorations of representations that trouble stereotypical patriarchal, heteronormative imagery and thus can be labeled "feminist" or "queer." (This research often entails questions of authorship and production also.) In turn, manhood, masculinity, and postfeminism have received greater attention from media scholars since the early 1990s, thereby further diversifying and complicating what we know about gender and representation.

Just as the objects of study in gender and media studies have changed, so have the methods used to analyze gendered media representations, as demonstrated by the chapters included here. Moving beyond the quantitative "images of women" studies pioneered by Tuchman, most contemporary feminist and queer media studies scholars follow the more theoretical "woman as image" route paved by Mulvey in order to explore gender's construction in media texts. Nevertheless, semiotics and psychoanalytic theory are used to a much lesser extent today by media scholars interested in gender than is discourse analysis, which requires researchers to consider the specific sociohistorical context of gendered representations, their production, and targeted audiences. At the same time, contemporary media scholars commonly examine the narrative and formal strategies used to construct such representations, just as Mulvey did.

The first chapter in this part, Annabelle Mooney's "Boys Will Be Boys," considers the representation of women in contemporary British men's magazines, such as *FHM* and *Loaded*. Continuing one of the most dominant threads in feminist media studies to date, women's sexual objectification, Mooney's project reframes this discussion via her attention to "lad" magazines' use of irony, naturalization of pornography, and opposition to feminism, strategies other scholars associate with a postfeminist sensibility.[3]

Noting an increase in scholarly attention to the crisis of white masculinity in media culture, Aimee Carrillo Rowe and Samantha Lindsey, in "Reckoning Loyalties," redirect their concerns about the intersections of race and gender to focus on representations of white women. Through their analyses of *Lost Highway* (1997) and *Alien Resurrection* (1997), Carrillo Rowe and Lindsey take up the issue of women's sexual objectification, yet reframe that traditional feminist theme in relation to the representation of women's agency and aggression in such films. Ultimately determining that female power is circumscribed in order to restabilize white male authority in these texts, Carrillo Rowe and Lindsey nonetheless explore the radical possibilities of white women's refusals of loyalty to white patriarchy.

Isabel Molina Guzmán and Angharad Valdivia's "Brain, Brow, and Booty" utilizes theories of hybridity and transnational identities to study the media representation of Latinas. Focusing on the iconicity of Latina actors Salma Hayek and Jennifer Lopez as well as artist Frida Kahlo, Molina Guzmán and Valdivia aim to better understand the intersecting scripts of gender and ethnicity circulating in the Latinidad of contemporary U.S. media culture. Noting the liminal cultural position of these three figures, they argue that media Latinas are betwixt and between the processes traditionally used to contain female Others and more recent practices that allow for their agency and possible unsettling of hegemonic discourses of gender and ethnicity.

Eliza Sellen's "Missy 'Misdemeanor' Elliott" explores some of the themes broached by Molina Guzmán and Valdivia yet directs her attention to black womanhood in popular music culture. Focusing on two of Missy Elliott's music videos, Sellen explores how the performer's representations in these texts subvert both patriarchal and feminist frameworks of identity. Attending to such issues as female embodiment, sexuality, race, and science fiction, Sellen argues that Elliott creatively reconstructs a fluid, uncontained identity that reveals and ensures her political agency.

Ann Ciasullo's chapter, "Making Her (In)visible," offers a critical survey of lesbian representation in contemporary media. With particular concern about the exclusion of butch lesbians in popular culture, Ciasullo demonstrates the constraint of lesbian representation by heteronormative ideas of gender. Moreover, she exposes the convergence of heterocentrism and capitalism in her argument that the glamorous femme operates multidirectionally in popular culture, attracting not only lesbian consumers, but also straight men who desire her alleged allegiance to hegemonic femininity, and straight women who identify with her as an ideal female consumer. Attending to the intersections of gender and sexuality by race and class, Ciasullo also reveals the relative invisibility of poor lesbians and queer women of color in media culture.

"*Joe Millionaire* and Women's Positions," by Renee Sgroi, is one of the rare contemporary studies of women's media representation that has socioeconomic status as one of its dominant analytical frameworks.[4] Taking a reality dating show as her object of study, Sgroi argues that *Joe Millionaire* (FOX 2003) offers particular classed versions of gender that help to reaffirm heterosexual coupling and the nuclear family on behalf of American nationalism. In particular, Sgroi attends to the two male leads' differing class positions and their relation to how the show's female contestants are framed.

Brenda Cooper's "*Boys Don't Cry* and Female Masculinity" reveals yet another new path in feminist and queer media studies. Focusing on the representation of female masculinity in this dramatization of transsexual Brandon Teena's life and death, Cooper argues that *Boys Don't Cry* (1999) offers a liberatory narrative that challenges both heteronormativity and hegemonic (male) masculinity. Moreover, through attention to the horrific constraint of Brandon's gender fluidity, Cooper avers that the film provocatively exposes the detrimental effects of gender and sexual bigotry and thus plays a role in progressively expanding public understanding and appreciation of transgender individuals and sexual minorities.

Now a classic in gender-oriented sports studies, Michael Messner, Michele Dunbar, and Darnell Hunt's "The Televised Sports Manhood Formula" explores ten prominent themes in male-oriented televised sports, such as professional wrestling, football, and basketball. Such themes, they argue, foreground aggression, militarism, and commercialism, thus providing males with a master discourse that encourages their performance and affirmation of a particular form of masculinity conducive to the sports/media/commercial complex. Nevertheless, this study's analysis of the commercials that accompany such televised sports reveals other performances of less-than-ideal masculinities that both support the dominant manhood formula (through opposition) and offer consumers opportunities to question gender norms.

Helping to push pornography studies in new directions, Richard Fung's "Looking for My Penis" was one of the first analyses of the representation of Asian men in erotic texts. Exploring the processes of exoticization and fetishization associated with orientalist discourse, Fung examines the narrow representation of Asian males in gay pornography while also arguing that this particular cultural realm remains dominated by texts produced by and for white males with little effort to affirm racial difference and diversity.

Steven Cohan's "Queer Eye for the Straight Guise" focuses on the popular U.S. reality show *Queer Eye for the Straight Guy* (Bravo 2003–2007). Via the multiple lenses of camp, gender, sexuality, and postfeminism, Cohan explores criticism from the queer community that the series provides a comfortable representation of homosexuality for hip straight consumers through its normalizing makeovers of gender-sloppy heterosexual men by stereotypically effeminate gay males. While Cohan connects that project with the postfeminist media trend of the gay man as the fashionable straight woman's best accessory, he is also concerned with how the "Fab Five" deploy queer camp to poke fun at straight masculinity, a project that ultimately makes queerness more visible within commercial TV culture while also differentiating camp from a postfeminist sensibility.

Karen Lee Ashcraft and Lisa Flores's "'Slaves with White Collars'" analyzes two Hollywood films, *Fight Club* (1999) and *In the Company of Men* (1997), in order to explore the emerging discourse of professional masculinity in crisis as a result of shifts in labor, commerce, and women's power. Noting that both films valorize a "civilized/primitive" masculinity via narratives of tough yet weary "white-collar" males who find transcendence via bodily harm, Ashcraft and Flores argue that such conflicted representations of masculinity both demonstrate fissures in male commitment to corporatism and reveal the resilience of hegemonic masculinity as an elastic social construct.

The chapter that closes Part III of the reader, "A Body of Text," is co-authored by Niels van Doorn, Sally Wyatt, and Liesbet van Zoonen and explores the relations of gender and embodiment in text-based online communication, a practice commonly thought to allow for gender fluidity owing to the absence of imagery and thus both real and fictional bodies. Analyzing two sites of Internet relay chat, #Cyberbar, a channel mostly occupied by straight men and women, and #Queer, a channel dominated by gay males, van Doorn, Wyatt, and van Zoonen found that, although the discursive performances of embodiment in each site tended to reaffirm a connection between sex and gender, some participants in #Queer articulated alternate masculinities that challenged heteronormativity. Nevertheless, these gender performances were part of a larger project that constructed a gay male norm by prohibiting certain gender transgressions, thus demonstrating the difficulty, if not impossibility, of transcending the body and real-life experiences in cyberspace.

Notes

1. See Gaye Tuchman's and Laura Mulvey's chapters in Part I of this reader.
2. Suzanna Danuta Walters, *Material Girls: Making Sense of Feminist Cultural Theory* (Berkeley: University of California Press, 1995).
3. See Rosalind Gill's chapter in Part I, for example.
4. See Liesbet van Zoonen's chapter in Part I for a discussion of class-based feminist media studies.

18.
BOYS WILL BE BOYS

Men's Magazines and the Normalisation of Pornography

Annabelle Mooney

Introduction

The emergence of men's magazines in the UK over the last 20 years has attracted attention in the fields of marketing, publishing, and the media generally (Goff 2004; Grimshaw 2004; O'Hagan 2004). Starting with the UK launch of *Loaded* in 1994 (Crew 2003, p. 1), other publications such as *FHM* (1994; a re-branding of *For Him*, dating from 1985), *Zoo* and *Nuts* (both 2004) have appeared. It is arguable that their presence is connected to increasing markets in the area of fashion, technology, and grooming. Certainly many magazines are aimed at increasing consumerism, whether for men or women or specialised interest group markets. Publications for young men and women (adults and adolescents) have more than this in common. The contribution towards the sexualised construction of women in the West is something they also share (Tincknell, Chambers, van Loon & Hudson 2003). It is impossible to claim that men's magazines are an isolated instance of this phenomenon. Indeed, defenders of lad's magazines often refer to the availability of pornographic material on the internet and satellite television channels as evidence of their own benign and women-friendly status. Ross Brown, editor of *FHM* remarks, "Men can get sexy images from the web, cable TV, DVDs. They want something extra. Sex has been completely watered down. Sex is everywhere" (quoted in Turner 2005). The implicit claim in Brown's remarks is that it is acceptable and somehow inevitable that sex is everywhere. Such availability also means that to be competitive and to be finan-

cially viable, lad's magazines need to offer something else. What precisely these distinctive elements might be will not be directly explored here. However, the personal and "matey" mode in which readers are addressed and the use of humour are good candidates (see Benwell 2004).

Following an account of men's magazines in the UK, this paper argues that the pornography contained in lad's magazines is made to seem unremarkable and usual. This is done through an invocation of the "real woman," encouragement of various kinds of reader activity, and alignment with other magazine genres, particularly those aimed at women. I then explore, and attempt to refute, the claim that the representation of women in such publications is "ironic." The claim to irony is indefensible textually and politically. In fact, what "irony" means in this context is problematic; it seems that "irony" is used as a virtual synonym for "humour." Finally, I argue that this portrayal of women is the culmination of hegemonic gender norms which are both reactionary and essentialising and which further seek to appropriate neo-liberal values of social autonomy and financial success into a repressive construction of women as, at best, passive subjects. Indeed, the normalisation of pornographic content in lad's magazines calls for repetition of MacKinnon's question: are women human (2006)? At least in the context of these men's magazines, it would seem that "[b]eing a woman is 'not yet a name for a way of being human'" (Rorty 1991, p. 234 quoted in MacKinnon 2006, p. 43). Women are still objects.

Men's Magazines in the UK

In a necessarily short survey of the history of men's magazines in the UK, Jackson, Stevenson, and Brooks write that "the new generation of men's general interest of lifestyle magazines was launched into a relative vacuum in the early 1980s" (2001, p. 27). While publications described as "lad's magazines" have only emerged in the last 15 years, their key ingredients were already well established. Fascination with sports, extreme or otherwise, outlandish stories, and naked women were already present in daily newspapers such as the *Daily Star, Sunday Sport* and *The Sun.* While O'Hagan finds the "popularity of *Nuts*" as "hard to understand" as the success of *The Sun* (2004, p. 36), given the success of this formula in newspapers, it is perhaps surprising that such content was not translated into magazine format at an earlier date.

The current content of lad's magazines has evolved even since the launch of *Loaded*.[1] The original mock-ups of *Loaded* contained no naked women at all (Crewe 2003, p. 47). Crewe argues that *Loaded* "was distinctively British, and rooted in more recent, populist subculture" as well as speaking to their readership in a "markedly less earnest and more celebratory" manner about masculinity (2003, p. 50) than anything previously available, such as *GQ* and *Esquire. FHM*, on the other hand, was modelled on women's magazines in that it was "crammed with practical advice for readers on a range of issues" (Crewe 2003, p. 52) from relationship and sexual health advice to reviews of gadgets, computer games, and films. *Maxim* has been compared even more directly to the glossy women's magazines. Editor Gill Hudson says, "It's like the male equivalent to Cosmopolitan" (Crewe 2003, p. 54). *Zoo* and *Nuts* appear to be comparable to women's weeklies such as *Heat, Closer,* and *Grazia* with a corresponding decrease in production values and a turn to more local and less globally famous women. For the weekly lad's magazines especially, this means that rather than using Hollywood stars (as the monthlies do), the women featured tend to be (1) British soap opera actors, (2) women who are "famous" only because of frequent exposure in the magazine or (3) real (i.e. non-celebrity) women. The way the genre has evolved was apparently unintended. James Brown (a founding editor of *Loaded*) remarked, "If I'd known when I started

Loaded that the men's sector would descend into a conveyor belt of old soap stars in bikinis, I assure you I would not have done it" (Crewe 2003, p. 148). This comment was made even before the "lower end" *Nuts* and *Zoo* were launched. Indeed, the "accessibility" of women is not unrelated to the accessibility of fame. Appearing on a reality show, or within the pages of a lad's magazine, is sufficient for some degree of celebrity status. The disdain that Brown arguably shows for "old soap stars" and indeed the female viewing population may at first appear to be at odds with his claim to a "populist subculture." Nevertheless, Brown's reluctance to be directly associated with some men's magazines signals the diversity of the market.

FHM and *Loaded*, with their glossy covers, heavy paper stock, high production values and routine use of A-list celebrities are, on the face of it, more sophisticated than the thinner, cheaper weeklies (*Zoo* and *Nuts*). It is possible to argue that the latter better encapsulate the "*Loaded* culture." However, this "culture" appears to have developed out of a complex interplay between readers, the media more generally, and shifts in masculinity, rather than simply being the outcome of the *Loaded* writers' own intentions. Crewe points out that the original editors of *Loaded* (James Brown and Tim Southwell) "assumed that their audience shared their own post-political masculinities" (2003, p. 131). Meanwhile, the "*Loaded* culture" appears to celebrate essentialist forms of masculinity.

Much of the academic work dealing with men's magazines necessarily and insightfully takes account of these "post-political masculinities," how these are constructed and explored and how they often use ironic modes as a strategy (e.g. Benwell 2001, 2004, 2005; Jackson, Stevenson & Brooks 2001; Tincknell, et al. 2003). The use of "irony" in this scholarly work is entirely different from the way "irony" is used by editors and others to defend the representation of women as discussed below. I do not want to suggest that these publications cannot be variously interpreted. Certainly there are resistant (and perhaps even ironic) readers. Nevertheless, lad's magazines can be understood as complementing and continuing the reproduction of an ideology of gender which treats masculinity and femininity in polarised ways (for a recent popular science book, see Brizendine 2006) which is already well established in women's titles (e.g. *Cosmopolitan*; see

Machin & Thornborrow 2006) and the public arena more generally. I suggest that these lad's magazines can be read as holding (or rather reinstating) the view that gender is binary and essential (rather than socially constructed). They articulate such attitudes towards and ideal models of women more fully and perhaps even more "honestly" than other forms of contemporary culture, especially those designed for a female readership. In lad's magazines it is possible to see hegemonic gender norms laid bare (albeit with a veneer of "irony"). As Chris Weedon argues,

> To maintain current levels of patriarchal power it is necessary to discredit or marginalize ways of giving meaning to experience which redefine hegemonic gender norms. These norms must be constantly reaffirmed as part of the large body of common-sense knowledge upon which individuals draw for their understanding of everyday life.
>
> (1997, p. 76)

While these norms are articulated, they are not always articulate. Gauntlett, in his discussion of men's magazines, writes that he "would not want to defend the dumb excesses of some of [them]" (2002, p. 152). The choice of "dumb" here as opposed to, for example, "sexist" or "demeaning," serves to evade any feminist concerns. Nevertheless, the use of "dumb" is appropriate in the sense that these magazines arguably silence the voices of some women (Langton 1993) and portray a particularly unintelligent and unreconstructed male. In keeping with the former, I want to start with a silence, signalled formally, to gesture towards the general absence of scholarly attention to the particular question of whether the depiction of women in these publications is pornographic (Attwood 2005, p. 84; see, however, Mind the Gap (n.d.); Object (n.d.)) and the silencing of women which may be the result of these publications and the attitudes they can be read as endorsing.

Normalisation of Pornography

The lad's magazines examined in this paper are not placed on the "top shelf" with other pornographic material (*Playboy*, *Mayfair*, and so on) in retail outlets. They are issued weekly (*Nuts* and *Zoo*) or monthly (*FHM* and *Loaded*) and are available in newsagents and supermarkets, often near cash registers. Though there have been some recent moves for "modesty covers" (*Guardian* 2006) this is still voluntary, even though some businesses (notably Walmart in the U.S.) have removed the magazines altogether because of customer pressure (Younge 2003).

The location of sale of lad's magazines facilitates the claim that they are not "proper" pornography. Thus one reader claims "You obviously wouldn't classify it as pornography or they wouldn't be selling it at Safeways [supermarket]" (quoted in Jackson, Stevenson & Brooks 2001, p. 122). Some of Jackson, Stevenson, and Brooks' informants are less sure about lad's magazines status as pornography. One comments, "it obviously isn't hard core porn yet it's blurring the boundaries," another says "it's a kind of softened pornography" (Jackson, Stevenson & Brooks 2001, p. 122) suggesting a category of "soft-soft porn." Readers, however, especially when distancing themselves from the magazines, will describe them as pornographic (Benwell 2005, p. 167).

The content of the magazines extends beyond naked women. They print stories on sport, technology (gadgets, computer games, and the like), drinking, and entertaining. However, the way in which women are represented, both textually and visually, borrows from the pornographic genre. I would not want to suggest that these magazines are *simply* pornographic; indeed, I do not want to suggest that pornography itself is a homogenous genre. In this discussion, I take pornography as referring to a state of undress as well as to a mode of representation that invites the sexualised gaze of the viewer. This paper examines four magazines from the same period (March–April 2006)[2] that have been used in order to provide examples of the normalisation of pornography and, in the second part, the alleged irony of these publications. For the purposes of this paper I am considering only the content related to representations of women.

The similarities of lad's magazines to pornography are clear when one considers the poses in which women are depicted.[3] While genitalia are obscured by lingerie, people (women rather than men), products or poses, breasts are routinely exposed (though nipples are not visible on covers). The poses, props, and clothing all borrow from the pornographic repertoire. For example, a recurring feature in one of the magazines (*Loaded*) is the "flip to strip" feature in which women appear clothed on one page and naked on the next. While cruder, explicitly signalled and with fewer steps than a traditional striptease, it clearly alludes to the practice in pornographic magazines of showing women in increasing states of undress. The invocation of the pornographic genre is explicitly invoked again by *Loaded*. Stills from pornographic films are presented showing male and female porn actors who resemble "mainstream" celebrities. Any elements of the stills which are not allowable because of publishing guidelines are covered with a small cartoon beaver (which recurs in other risqué sections of the magazine as a signifier of sexual "naughtiness" because of its reference to female genitalia).

This borrowing from the pornographic repertoire is also present in the weeklies. On the double contents page of *Zoo*, a naked woman is shown lying on a sheep skin rug. She is looking at the viewer, though her face is at the extreme left of the page. Her eyes are focussed on the camera which is slightly above and to her left. She wears nothing but a small smile. Her buttocks are slightly raised and one of her breasts is exposed. On the front cover of the magazine, she is presented sitting on a piece of soft furnishing (it is impossible to tell if this is a bed or a sofa), her legs slightly apart, and again looking at the viewer, but this time the camera is placed lower than her face. This pair of pictures functions in a similar way to the explicitly signalled "flip to strip" in *Loaded*, the woman's poses obviously keying pornography in positioning of the body (with respect to the page and the viewer) and the vector of her gaze.

At the same time, there are a number of features in terms of genre, content, and participant roles which work to normalise these pornographic elements. By "normalise," I mean that the pornographic is presented as of the everyday. Thus while Hardy's (1998) work clearly shows that men's consumption of top shelf pornography takes place with a consciousness of its fantasy elements, the lad's magazines under consideration here work to frame what is presented as "real." This normalisation appears to contribute to the general display and purchase of what would otherwise be considered top shelf "reading" material. Moreover, while much of the content suggests an audience of

young adult males, it is worth bearing in mind that lad's magazines are targeted to an audience as young as 12 years old (Hatoum & Belle 2004, p. 406).

Features of normalisation have not gone unnoticed. Benwell (2004) notes in relation to *Loaded*, for example, that it includes letters pages, advice, handy hints, features, interviews, and advertising. While such inclusions can be read as creating a space for identity construction and negotiation which moves beyond the sexual, I contend that they work also to frame the display of naked women in the magazines as acceptable. In the following, I outline three features which work to normalise the pornographic elements of the magazines. The first is the explicit use of the "real." Instead of women occupying fantasy roles (with requisite fantasy names), "real women" (with ordinary names) are used. Contributions are also made by readers, in the form of "real" stories or photographs. The second strategy of normalisation is that of reader participation more broadly, as action is encouraged in the form of letters, competitions, and websites. Finally, these magazines are also positioned as more or less equivalent to weekly and monthly magazines aimed at women. Some of the lad's magazines refer explicitly to their "female equivalent" publications. This alignment is also accomplished through the inclusion of handy hints and tips (often contributed by readers) and regular advice columns covering areas of sex and relationships. I will argue that they work to frame the pornographic as a sexual norm.

Real Women and Real Life Stories

The women photographed and interviewed in lad's magazines are framed by a discourse of the real which is linked to how "accessible" they are. Accessibility can be defined in terms of whether readers would consider it possible to meet and date, if not the particular women represented, at least women who are very similar. The representation of celebrities needs also to be considered in this frame. Different "kinds" of women can be read, as Attwood points out, as a "hierarchy of female body representation" from the high ranking "fashion body," the "porn body" and, at the bottom, "ordinary women" (2005, p. 90). Nevertheless, Attwood notes a "tendency towards the flattening out of distinctions between ordinary and celebrity babes" (2005, p. 91) arguably best exemplified by the poses struck by "ordinary" and celebrity woman alike. The reader is given details about celebrity and ordinary women, but in relation to the latter, the reader is encouraged to discover, and often do, more. In the monthly *Loaded* "Casting Couch" feature, readers are urged to vote for their favourite: "Vote for your fave and next month she'll strip in her bedroom" (2006, p. 12). This incursion into the private space of the

presented.

Real women are also presented in the more *ad hoc* sections of magazines. In the edition of *Loaded* examined, there is a "Gotcha! Quiz Special" with such tasks as "Name that Nip" in which celebrities' (presumably unintentionally) exposed nipples are presented and the reader challenged to identify the women to which they belong. It is not necessary to be a celebrity, however, nor to be included in a regular section. One reader of *Loaded*, submits a photo of his topless wife with a plea for the magazine to print it to "give her a nice little confidence boost" (2006, p. 47).

It is clear from this that women are valued entirely for their constituent body parts and their sexual attractiveness and that women are encouraged to value themselves for these same attributes. *Nuts* runs

a "Boobs of Britain" competition, in which readers vote for their favourites as well as a "Boobs of the Week" feature sidebar with four pairs of breasts cropped from women's bodies. One woman is chosen to be "The Girl Behind the Boobs" and has her breasts represented in the cropped manner, in addition to a photograph which includes her face. That the woman is "behind" her "boobs" signals textually the visual foregrounding of her breasts and their salience in her overall identification. In a similar mode, *FHM* runs an annual "High Street Honeys" and ask readers to send in photographs of their wives, girlfriends, and sisters as "nothing will make her year like the sight of her own heavenly-chiselled chesticles (covered in a tiny bikini) on the cover of Britain's biggest men's mag" (2006, p. 52).

The "real" in this context and in the following discussion is, of course, a "construction" of the real. The representations are real only in the sense of being "staged authenticity" (MacCannell 1999). At the very least, the "reality" promoted is already a mediated one by virtue of the two-dimensional magazine format. Further, there is a long tradition in the UK of such "real" women in the form of, for example, reader's wives in soft pornography magazines (such as *Razzle* and *Fiesta*). The claim that lad's magazines are making nevertheless is that women really are as they are portrayed, despite indications to the contrary experienced in the real three dimensional world.[4] Indeed, read alongside women's magazines, men's publications can be understood as claiming that women's magazines represent a fantasy realm with display of prestige commodities foregrounded, whereas the bodily display (Desmond 1999) in men's magazines is authentic as the women are naked.

The terms "bodily display" and "staged authenticity" have their origins in tourism research. Used to describe the way host cultures construct and display themselves to the tourist, they are appropriate terms to deploy in the context of lad's magazines. The celebration of traditional masculine activities and values appears to be a return of essentialist arguments. As Crewe puts it, "[m]asculinity [is] conceived as something ultimately innate and unchanging" (2003, p. 130). Given that such an ontological perspective ultimately leads to a difference in approach to gender relations, lad's magazines may well be read as travel brochures for the foreign land of women (cf. Taylor 2005, p. 162). This may go some way in explaining the transfer of lexemes for male body parts into new words for women's breasts ("chesticles") which are fabricated ("chiselled") for male sexual pleasure ("fun bags" and "boy pleasers"). The transfer is at once a claim to difference and to similarity; but always in male terms.

Thus while there is similarity in some sense between men and women (see Attwood, 2005, p. 87), man is still the measure. L. D. Taylor concludes a quantitative analysis of lad's magazines with respect to women and sex:

> The message of such articles is that women want to engage in unusual sexual behaviors as much as men do, that women are driven by sexual variety just as men are. This is exemplified by articles in which women are quoted as they enthuse over bondage, sex in public, group sex, and the use and imitation of pornography during sex. The implicit message is that women's and men's sexual desires are essentially similar.
>
> (2005, p. 162)

Clearly, women do have sexual desires, drives, and selves. However, the way in which women are represented visually and textually offers only object positions *vis-à-vis* the male subject. This is not a sexual scene of reality or equality. Indeed, this may be impossible within the pornographic genre as such equality "is not simply unerotic but actually antithetical to eroticism" (Hardy 2000, p. 88; however, see Attwood 2005; Smith 2002). The logic of the "mainstream" pornographic scene is one of submission, even if this is consensual. Indeed, whether equality can be erotic is not at issue in these magazines as women are represented as objects and thus never equal to the male viewer.

Contribution and (Inter)action

The potential for reader action and interaction through contribution to these magazines has already been partly covered in the previous section. While related websites offer a chance for readers to interact with each other and develop topics of conversation over a period of time, nevertheless, readers' contributions to the magazines can be read as interactive in the form

of an adjacency pair given that such contributions are printed and commented upon by editorial staff. Even though such exchanges (limited as they are) are common in magazines, the most salient topic for this discourse community appears again to be the "opposite sex," as contributions directly related to women appear to be the most significant mode in terms of number of opportunities across the magazines examined. However, there are other opportunities for reader participation beyond voting for their favourite breasts or submitting photographs of their partners. The remaining forms of participation are more action than interaction but emphasise the "real," offer material inducements, and include the submission of true stories and (real) photographs by readers.

The importance of the real is again a claim to authenticity. This may be achieved in a number of ways. In *FHM*, a page of "True Stories" involving the "ludicrous/hilarious/bizarre" are invited from readers who are not "lying" (2006, p. 226). The best story wins a video mobile or football strip. It is possible to read these prizes as inducements to exaggerate, even (and perhaps especially) given the explicit instruction not to do thus ("Sure you're not lying?"). Readers are invited to engage in a textual game which involves balancing the credible and the incredible. This mirrors the game of "authenticity" in the balancing of the real and fantasy in respect of women represented.

Loaded also offers inducements in the form of technology and sports wear to contribute to its "Rogues Gallery" (a page of pictures on the last page; 2006, p. 194). The three categories each have a winner. "GR8 Nokias" (presumably a play on mobile phone cameras and "knockers") includes four photographs of naked or near naked women; "Stupid Stuff" speaks for itself and "Now You're Stalking" requires photographs of readers with famous people. In the issue examined here, a woman with head completely covered by a pink plastic rounded cone but breasts exposed wins the "Stupid Stuff" category, while a reader photographed with a girl band (the only women in this section) also wins "Now You're Stalking". Thus even when interaction does not necessarily involve women, sexual attractiveness is still of primary concern.

Alignment with Women's Magazines

Perhaps the most significant way these magazines have been normalised is through their cultural alignment with women's glossies in terms of their emphasis on consumerism. At the same time, there is also alignment with women's magazines and those not overtly gendered. This is done explicitly, by naming other publications, as well as by borrowing staple modes from the "house and home" genre and from light entertainment weeklies.

In *Zoo*, a "weekly look at the fluffy world of women's mags" occupies the bottom of the "News" section (2006, 20–21). This consists of a précis of and some commentary on stories from three weekly magazines (*Real People, Pick Me Up*, and *Take a Break*) which are arguably aimed at *Zoo* readers' mothers.[5] Commenting on a story in *Take a Break* about a man who has sex with one of the escorts he was responsible for chauffeuring, *Zoo* writes, "he then rather spoils things by adding, 'I'm hoping [my wife] will take me back again'." This commentary on an item aimed at women confirms the lad's magazine's opposing and masculine view of the world. The opposition is thus one of gender and age, firmly placing these women's magazines as "other" and thus a prime target for humour.

At the same time, it might be argued that the inclusion of these stories provides a common ground with which *Zoo* readers can relate to women. It seems to me, however, that it is rather a means of situating *Zoo* in relation to these publications, especially the values invoked by their titles. By doing this, *Zoo* is normalised and capitalises on the real (*Real People*) as well as laying claim to positive forms of recreation and relaxation (*Pick Me Up* and *Take a Break*).

The perennial advice column of women's magazines (especially glossies, e.g. *Cosmopolitan*) is also borrowed by men's magazines. However, the emphasis here is not on health or personal problems of the kind usually encountered in the former. Rather, the columns are framed as educational tools to make men more attractive to women or, indeed, to provide advice for conducting relationships. The latter, however, includes answering a reader's question about how to get his girlfriend to try ATM (ass-to-mouth). The columnist, Tera Patrick, is an "adult actress" willing to answer "sex queries." The other questions in Patrick's column

deal with anxieties about and techniques for satisfying girlfriends sexually. Abi Titmuss' "Bachelor School" in *Nuts* (2006, p. 38), deals with more urbane social problems such as how to tell a girlfriend she has put on weight or has halitosis. The advice Titmuss gives is as cursory as it is questionable ("it's also *proven* that a nice aftershave can be a turn on" (*Nuts* 2006, p. 38; my emphasis). Readers, thus, claim that only "sad losers" consult these sections of the magazines (Jackson, Stevenson & Brooks 2001, p. 121). Presumably one is not a "sad loser" if "consulting" the pages for amusement rather than advice.

Readers are not only given advice on how to maintain their sexual relationships, but also their possessions. In content borrowed from weeklies such as *Take a Break* and glossies in the house and home genre, handy hints and tips submitted by readers deal with how to protect leather shoes in winter and suits before storing them (*Nuts* 2006, p. 114). The best "Fact, Tip & Trick" wins five cases of beer. *FHM* also provides tips in the form of food and beer reviews giving supermarket ready meals taste tests and star ratings. This kind of utilitarian content is continued with the inclusion of television guides (in weeklies) and reviews of recent film and video game releases (monthlies).

Such content links to readers' everyday lives and thus promotes identification with the magazine, as well as providing advertisers and prize sponsors with potential customers. However, it seems to me that in terms of the normalised pornographic content, such regular features work to position the magazines firmly in at least two normalised frames. First, inclusion of product reviews and fashion items positions the magazines firmly within a frame of consumption. Indeed, subjecting women to a desiring male gaze is also to subject them to the consumerist gaze. In this way, the magazines provide a tangible, albeit two dimensional, way of purchasing, consuming, and desiring women. Second, while sexual content is certainly oriented to the "real," the inclusion of the minutiae of life anchors the publications in the everyday in more tangible ways. The framing of pornographic content with the banality of television guides and clothing maintenance tips works to normalise the content and situate it in routine schemas. Given the sustained invocation of the "real" and the celebration of "authenticity" and "honesty," claims by editors and publishers that the magazines are ironic warrant attention.

Isn't It Ironic?

In response to claims that the magazines objectify or damage women, editors and publishers claim that the material is ironic (see, e.g., Crewe 2003, p. 142; Turner 2005). However, the editors of the magazines do not make this claim to irony as often as external commentators, who describe them as "richly ironic [and] postmodern" (Walker 1999) or, as O'Hagan in the *London Review of Books* puts it "soft-core irony and hard-core sentiment" (2004).[6] Gill Hudson, editor of *Maxim*, puts irony centre stage:

> I don't want to produce a magazine that is sheerly pornographic because porn is not ironic or funny [but] if we ignore the fact that sex sells . . . we're just stupid . . . I think the humour is very important and it's also a way of making men feel comfortable with something that men are going to do anyway and not beat yourself up about it.
> (Hudson quoted in Peter Jackson, Nick Stevenson & Kate Brooks 2001, p. 69)

This looks not so much like an ideological claim about the nature of content material, but a claim about the commercial reality of publishing and the "essential" nature of men. It is also not a claim that Hudson finds problematic. Peter Howarth, when editor of *Esquire*, was more troubled, explaining: "we've got to do Caprice [on the cover] because it will sell" (Howarth, quote from 2000 cited in Crewe 2003, p. 170).

The assertion that "sex sells" is apparently enough to condone its use and obscures the gendered nature of sex in these magazines, that is, the vast majority of sexual display is done by women. Note that Hudson's use of "*sheerly* pornographic" suggests an implicit realisation that there is at least some pornographic content (or that it is pornographic to some extent). Brown, on the other hand, admits to "a huge sliver of sexism in FHM"; however, "We do it because our readers laugh at it" (quoted in Turner 2005). But this is even less than a claim to irony. It is a claim to amusement. According to Merrill, naked women are "simply a means of attracting men to the magazine's broader

content—football, facts and statistics, gadgets, and the gags" (quoted in Turner 2005). The implied desires of readers also need to be balanced with advertisers' concerns (Crewe 2003, p. 105).

While Hudson appeals to a "real world" with the claim that "men will be men," the belief that men will not, indeed cannot, change is worth exploring. This is consonant with readers' assessments of the magazines as "honest," "natural" and "unhypocritical" (Jackson, Stevenson & Brooks 2001, 116–117) as well as with reactions that see the magazines as condoning lad culture. Jackson, Stevenson, and Brooks note that "media constructions of laddishness have come to seem so "natural" that for many respondents there was no need to defend them or to consider alternative forms of masculinity" (2001, p. 119). This essentialist position was evidently held by readers to be unproblematic.

For the purposes of this paper, I take the claim of irony seriously if only because it appears to be a persistent discourse in relation to lad's magazines. In practice, however, the claims to irony appear to be no more than a claim to humour, commercial reality or innate male behaviour. Even in 2003 the claim to irony was an ambivalent claim to humour. "Lad culture worked for a while because we all thought it was ironic, funny, and typically British. And for a while," says Dylan Jones, editor of *GQ*, "it was. Now, however, lad culture is an embarrassment" (quoted in Lyle 2003).

There are three central problems with the claim that these men's magazines are ironic which will be discussed presently. The first is the mistake of treating the ironic disclaimer as authentic, especially when publication content and style are considered. This mirrors the invocation of the real which is nevertheless "constructed." The second is that the claim to irony assumes readers' recognition of it. Finally, it fails to take into account the world in which people (and especially women) live. Such a move to the political is, however, at odds with readers' understanding of their own consumption of the magazines. One of Jackson, Stevenson, and Brooks' postgraduate informants says, "I mean, buying *Loaded*'s not a political act in any shape or form" (2001, p. 115, see also p. 121). The political and the real world (at least in so far as women are concerned) are segmented off from a different but apparently "real", "honest" world that these texts invoke.

Is the Disclaimer Authentic?

The question of whether we can treat the claim that these publications are ironic rests on whether irony is retrievable or indeed identifiable. This is difficult for a number of reasons. First, even if the avowed and actual intention is to be ironic, this is no guarantee that the reader will see it as such. Benwell, following Hutcheon (1994) points out that irony depends on the interpreter (2004, p. 11). Given the way readers tend to distance themselves from these publications (Benwell 2005, p. 167), the detail of such interpretation is difficult to establish.

More problematically, whether irony is inherently innocent is far from clear. Hutcheon notes, "Irony has often been used to reinforce rather than question established attitudes" (1994, p. 10). Indeed, irony is a resource which can be used to escape censure while communicating what might otherwise be frowned upon. Van Dijk has argued that such expressions can function simply as disclaimers, "a semantic move that aims at avoiding a bad impression when saying negative things about Others" (1997, p. 32). The negative thing about the other is still said. The disclaimer seeks to remove liability even while committing an offence. Indeed, irony, like any other rhetorical strategy, has no self-evident meaning or effect in and of itself.

Admittedly, any claims or counter claims about the use of irony are difficult to establish especially when it becomes no more than a claim to humour. In linking the two, the idea that irony is always amusing is erroneously invoked. Irony is often scathing, insulting, and produced with intent to wound (Hutcheon 1994). Further, the "irony" in these magazines is directed at women. The "humour" which editors claim makes their publications innocent is potentially more degrading than "real" irony. The proliferation of lexemes for women's breasts is a case in point. While Adam Porter, editor of the *Loaded* website, claims that nothing derogatory is said about women (in Jackson, Stevenson & Brooks 2001, p. 69), describing breasts as "chest lumps," "funbags," "boy-pleasers," and "chesticles" is not, on the face of it, respectful.

It becomes even more difficult to ascertain the worthiness of the claims to irony as no argument is given. The irony is simply asserted. Indeed, to return to Hudson's comments cited above, it is difficult to reconcile the claim that "sex sells" with the assertion that the sexual representation of women is ironic. In the absence of an argument for why these texts are ironic, it seems that the use of "irony" originates in postmodernist usage. The postmodern use of "irony," the use to which these texts appear to be appealing, is more often than not a claim for a "knowing" irony or, more generally, "knowingness." Indeed, Benwell writes, "the unrelenting omnipresence of a certain knowingness, self-referentiality, and humor, [are] all commonly glossed as irony" (2004, 3–4). In this sense, modes of representation are invoked (somewhat according to the echoic theory of irony; Wilson & Sperber 1992) with full knowledge that these modes are inappropriate if used without "knowingness." However, such knowingness and self-referentiality need to be retrievable too. Simply, there are no spaces in these texts where this is clearly signalled.

Perhaps it is the case that the "knowingness" that "irony" stands for is related to the knowledge of women disrobing for the magazines. In this case, knowingness seems only to mean something like consent (rather than any self-awareness of irony). If knowingness does mean consent, the argument would run, the women who participate in these magazines are happy to take their clothes off for the male viewer. This may well be true, but it is not necessarily for the purpose of being ironic. I will return to this important issue presently.

The obvious reading of these texts is that it is permissible to look at naked women and to enjoy doing so. An ironic reading would be the exact opposite. While readers may make a claim to irony in distancing themselves from the magazines, there is for readers a "common kind of slippage between the explicitly attributed identity of detached, uninvested and even disapproving reader and the kinds of revealed values that emerge discursively in the more detailed engagement with texts" (Benwell 2005, p. 161). As noted above, consumers of these magazines read them as licensing "laddishness" at least within the confines of the reading experience. Further, the actions invited in terms of reader participation involve assessing women in terms of physical attractiveness (by voting for their favourite casting couch candidate or by sending in photographs of their own "honeys"). Such voting and participation is encouraged and materially rewarded, further ratifying women in these positions.

It seems to me that the claim to irony can only be a claim to an "irony of last resort." By this I mean, that without claiming irony, the representations of women would be indefensible. At a time in which equality between the sexes is at least theoretically and legislatively well established, in the Western world it is simply not permissible to hold the view that women are only sex objects. Such a "politically incorrect" objectification of women needs to be carefully managed. Thus, if one wants to treat women as sex objects (and not be classed in a special publishing category, that is, not be placed on the top shelf with "proper" pornography) a disclaimer has to be attempted. If sex is to sell, if consumers are to be reached in their normal day to day consuming habits, then the sex has to be normalised and/or ironicised. The claim to irony is indefensible exactly because it is itself only a defence. Perhaps, then, it is not surprising that there are no arguments for the claim to irony.

The alleged irony in these lad's magazines is clearly irony with a victim; the victim is usually a particular woman. Because the "ironic" attacks on individuals are routine and repeated, the assaults on particular women can be read as an assault on women generally. In order to demonstrate how the "ironic" attack occurs, two illustrations from *Zoo* magazine should suffice. The first, "The Zoo Thing-ometer," is a scale which rates what "we like" and what "we no like" on page 5 of the magazine (*Zoo* 2006). At the extreme bottom (i.e. things "we no like") is news that Jade Goody (a former *Big Brother* contestant) is launching a perfume. The comment provided is as follows, "Smelling of what? Kebabs and thick pigshit?" This is not ironic; it is degrading in both intention and effect. It is entirely possible that readers may find it amusing, but that does not make it ironic.

The second example comes from the same magazine. Another sidebar feature which speculates about the identity of the "crack smoking pop tart who supposedly inspired the new [The Streets] single *When*

You Wasn't Famous" (*Zoo* 2006, p. 15). Here, celebrity women are described as "dirty" and "dirty crack whores" who have "filthy bedroom tricks." It seems that such descriptions are positive in the sense of referring to desirable characteristics for a woman to have. Again, these epithets appear to be intended to be read literally (in the sense that "dirty" is good), as they are apparently compliments (of a kind). If this is the case, they are not ironic either.

Given that the magazines are pornography normalised, it is not clear that irony is even an option. Sontag points out, "pornography isn't a form that can parody itself . . . A parody of pornography, so far as it has any real competence, always remains pornography" (2001, p. 98). The magazines must deny pornographic content if they are to remain off the top shelf. At the same time some "competence" in the genre must be present if the magazines are to invite any action at all, that is, for sex to sell. The result is that the denial—like the claim to irony—cannot be authentic.

David Bennett writes,

> It has been said that postmodernism recycles modernity in "scare quotes," and what these recent rereadings of popular pornographic texts are doing, in effect, is discovering the scare quotes within the commodity, thereby making them admissible to the house of postmodern Art—if not quite to the Republic of Good Taste. Importantly, the pornography in question here isn't of a subcultural kind that affirms marginal or minority sexualities against a hegemonic mainstream; it is the pornographic mainstream itself ("primitive, male-manufactured, genitally focused raunch") recast as variously ironic, self-parodic, critical, oppositional and subversive—the familiar terms by which the post-1970s progressive humanities academy legitimates both its choices of objects to study and its own reading-practices. But when the mainstream is re-cast as oppositional, to what is it opposed?
>
> (2005, p. 5)

I suggest that the normalising of pornography in lads' magazines leaves pornography (un-normalised, as it were) as Bennett's oppositional object. The question of what is opposed by the readership of these magazines has been explored, as have reasons for the resultant constructed certitude which can be read as a return to essentialism (Benwell 2004; developed from Beck 1997). Benwell suggests that the language of men's magazines, particularly the ritual insults in letters pages, can be seen as an anti-language, "extreme versions of social dialect" (Montgomery 1986, p. 93; drawing on Halliday 1978). "Montgomery describes the users of anti-language as 'a group occupying a marginal or precarious position in society' (1986, p. 93)" (Benwell 2001, p. 29). While Bethan Benwell notes that such men

> could hardly be described as such a group, elements of anti-language in the magazine seem to function both to strengthen a sense of group membership, and also to contribute to a stance which is set in rebellious opposition to a hegemonic norm.
>
> (2001, p. 29)

But what is this group? What is the hegemonic norm that they are opposing? From Benwell's reading, they are "united by . . . their opposition to feminism" (2001, p. 31; see also Mullany 2004). It should be said that the *idea* of feminism may be hegemonic, but that does not mean that hegemony is feminist. As Benwell notes, however, "[t]o a certain degree, a collective identity is encouraged and constructed by consumer forces, the advertisers who financially underpin the magazines" (2001, p. 31).[7] This brings us back to Hudson's assertion that sex sells, as the opposition to feminism is integral to the construction of men as consumers. Bethan Benwell explains that

> men needed to be cajoled into the explicit adoption of the feminized role of the consumer. To create distance between men's titles and their equivalent publications, a very different tone was adopted, one that combined strident aspiration, unassailable confidence, a lack of intimacy, and an objectification of women.
>
> (2004, p. 4)

Thus women, often unpaid, are deployed as instruments of a consumerist agenda.[8] This is as ironic as it is obscene.

Women's Own?

Clearly the ideological processes to which women (and men) are subjected are both patriarchal and heteronormative. Though this reads like a truism, hegemonic gender norms are central in explaining the consent of women in appearing in lad's magazines. The power of hegemony, especially in relation to gender, should not be underestimated. While it may be unfashionable to talk about false consciousness and oppression in a neo-liberal, globalised world, it does not make it irrelevant. Given the essentialist views on gender retrievable from lad's magazines, the question of hegemonic gender norms is arguably becoming even more salient. The naturalisation of pornography discussed above is no more than a logical working out of these attitudes, which sees pornography inserted into the cultural landscape while shedding its loaded lexical tag. It is no longer pornography when normalised, it is, simply, normal.

While there has been important work in relation to fine grained and socially situated analysis of male magazines, there is a broader social situation in which the claims to irony specifically need to be placed. The excellent work about the complimentary role of women's magazines deserves revisiting. Indeed, one might argue that women's glossies and weeklies prepare audiences, male and female, to accept the values of lad's magazines.

In a multimodal analysis of various local editions of women's magazines, *Cosmopolitan* (India), *Glamour* (UK) and *Gioi Phu Nu* (Vietnam), Machin and Thornborrow highlight the way the real is represented, staged, and mediated (2006). Women's agency "becomes a process of signification through codes of dress and lifestyle that are drawn from consumer culture" (Machin & Thornborrow 2006, p. 187). While this is consonant with the lifestyle choices of post-traditional societies (Giddens 1991), it is not necessarily related to social empowerment. Indeed, David Machin and Joanna Thornborrow conclude,

> The discourses of sex we have described here do not serve women well. By *duping them* into thinking that they can become powerful through taking on a theatrically signified sexuality, they will

be less able to address the things that leave them powerless in their real lives.

(2006, p. 187; my emphasis)

Women's magazines appear to shift between texts which are often progressive and challenging of social structures (Budgeon & Currie 1995; Eggins & Iedema 1997), to texts which encourage superficial, consumerist behaviour in the name of "girl power" or something similar (Caldas-Coulthard 1996; Talbot 1995).[9] The subject position of women in magazines, particularly in the vein of the latter, has been further elaborated. Tincknell et al. (2003) compare men's magazines with those targeted at teenage girls, noting the stark differences in discourses of sex and sexuality. While magazines for teenage girls now present "knowing desire as the legitimate sexual discourse for young women," as well as a "'right' to sexual pleasure" and a "'right' to sexual knowledge" (Tincknell et al. 2003, p. 54), women remain objects rather than agents, even though "their objectification is re-presented as a form of self-empowerment" (Tincknell et al. 2003, p. 57). While women are presented in men's magazines "as image," men in magazines for young women are positioned as "central to the discursive production of normalised femininity" (Tincknell et al. 2003, p. 59). The achievement of lifestyle through consumer goods adds another dimension to existing hegemonic gender norms and in effect fuses late-capitalist values of product accumulation for the purposes of identity construction and performance with existing gender scripts and tropes. This is hardly novel.

The representation of women in lad's magazines can thus be understood as a logical working out of the "normalised femininity" that women are encouraged to adopt. While not my purpose here, it is well to remember the power of women's magazines to silence women by convincing them that maintaining traditional gender roles yet wearing designer shoes represents a positive revolution. The indefensible claims that lad's magazines are ironic is yet another way of silencing women. Should women object to sexualised representations of other women in these magazines, they are likely to be thought of as humourless, attacking free speech, and failing to defend the choice of other women to appear in these magazines. While anecdotal, one of my student's words on the

status of women exemplifies the last of these characteristics and lays bare the central problem. In debating the current relevance of the concept of patriarchy, a female student responded that if she wished to be photographed in lingerie for a campaign of billboards, this was her choice. There is no question that such a choice should be available to her. That this was provided as an example of the irrelevance of feminism is troubling. I suggest such an attitude demonstrates the internalisation of an ideology that values women (and asks them to value themselves) exactly and primarily as physical objects. It is a simulacrum of empowerment.

This internalisation of values is directly analogous to the Dish of the Day in Adams' restaurant at the end of the universe. "I am the main Dish of the Day" the creature tells the diners, "May I interest you in parts of my body?" (Adams 2002, p. 284). As this fictional quadruped has been bred to have the desire to be eaten, many women have internalised these hegemonic gender norms such that they desire only to be desired. This is hardly surprising. Indeed, if this were not the case, "hegemony" as a term would lose its power. *FHM* editor Ross Brown comments that "When you become a celebrity . . . you automatically tick the box saying 'Are you prepared to be photographed in your knickers and pants?'" (quoted in Turner 2005). It is possible that this order is reanalysed by young women, such that being prepared to be photographed in underwear is a *causal* factor in becoming a celebrity. Other comments are equally difficult to challenge in their own terms. Phil Hilton, then editor of *Nuts* magazine, comments that the women who pose for their magazine "hope to turn modelling into a source of income . . . [some] simply want to supplement their earnings, and some just want to get rich by being sexy. They should be free to make these choices" (*Telegraph* 2006). Arguments phrased in terms of personal autonomy and freedom can hardly be countered. The point is, however, that these choices are presented to and accepted by women as leading to appealing subject positions. Their "enthusiastic participation" (*Telegraph* 2006) is paradoxical, as women in their capacity as agents vie to become objects. But it is not a paradox which condones participation; it is a paradox which should challenge any argument for participation, enthusiastic or otherwise.

Conclusion

Men and women, in practice and often in theory, do not have equal rights. For women to get these rights, however, others, men, would have to surrender theirs. Bruce Arrigo and Christopher R. Williams write,

> The "gift" of equality, procured through state legislative enactments as an emblem of democratic justice, embodies true (legitimated) power that remains nervously secure in the hands of the majority. The ostensible empowerment of minority groups is a façade; it is the ruse of the majority gift. What exists, in fact, is a simulacrum (Baudrillard 1981, 1983) of equality (and by extension, democratic justice); a pseudo-sign image (a hypertext or simulation) of real sociopolitical progress.
>
> (2000, p. 322)

The question is, then, is a real surrender, something more than a simulacrum, likely to occur? It does not seem likely as it is not a simple turning over of power; a reconfiguration of gender positions and discourses would be required. Further, as Tincknell et al. note, the "plenitude of images of women also confirms a containment to 'woman *as* image,' so that only men can be represented as fully social subjects" (2003, p. 59). Women are not represented as "fully social subjects" because they are not considered to be fully social subjects, even by publications produced for them. Women are not yet human and this is the central problem. The "solution" to the problem is no less than a transformation of the hegemonic order with respect to gender. This calls for a war of position (Gramsci 1971). At the very least, empty claims about normalised pornography being "ironic" need to be spoken against. There is nothing new in arguing that women are not full human citizens (MacKinnon, 2006). But that there is nothing new does not mean nothing should be done; rather, the fact that the social order remains untransformed means the opposite. There has been a very real silence in the academy about lad's magazines in relation to women and the real world. This silence suggests that women are willing to tolerate representations of themselves as objects. Objects cannot logically be asked (or understood) to tolerate anything. Thus while there is no retrievable irony in men's magazines, there is a glaring irony in this apparent acceptance.

Acknowledgements

I would like to thank Dr. Betsy Evans and Dr. Christopher Marlow for very useful criticism and comments. I would also like to thank the two anonymous reviewers for their patience, hard work and extremely valuable comments and insights. Naturally, all errors remain mine. A different version of this paper was presented at the International Roundtable for the Semiotics of Law, Boulougne-sur-Mer 2006. Funding from Roehampton University made that trip possible.

Notes

1. For a longer history of men's magazines, see Crewe (2003) and Jackson, Stevenson, and Brooks (2001).
2. The weekly *Nuts* and *Zoo* are dated 3–9 March; the monthly *FHM* and *Loaded* are dated April 2006. They were all purchased the same day. *Maxim* was not examined as it was not sold with the other magazines in any nearby areas.
3. When presenting a paper on this material at a conference, I was asked by an American academic whether showing pictures from the magazine was necessary. I explained that it was important to demonstrate the similarity to pornographic poses. She was surprised to hear that the material was not generally considered pornographic.
4. Indeed, if reality really was as represented in the magazines, there would be little need for such publications.
5. While impossible to explore in this paper, it is worth noting that these magazines also valorise sexually attractive women.
6. The former is presumably a reference to ironic soft-core pornography.
7. Crewe's work (2003) suggests how complicated this may be.
8. *Nuts*, for example, does not pay the girls who pose (Turner 2005).
9. I do not want to suggest that there was a "golden age" of feminist glossies. However, there appear to have been some more (rather than less) empowering mainstream publications at certain points in time demonstrating that it is possible to be commercially viable as well as progressive.

References

Adams, Douglas (2002) *Hitchhiker's Guide to the Galaxy: The Trilogy of Four, the Restaurant at the End of the Universe*, Pan Macmillan, London.

Arrigo, Bruce A. & Williams, Christopher R. (2000) 'The (im)possibility of democratic justice and the "gift" of the majority', *Journal of Contemporary Criminal Justice*, vol. 16, no. 3, pp. 321–343.

Attwood, Feona (2005) 'Tits and ass and porn and fighting: male heterosexuality in magazines for men', *International Journal of Cultural Studies*, vol. 8, pp. 83–100.

Beck, Ulrich (1997) *The Reinvention of Politics: Rethinking Modernity in the Global Social Order*, Polity, Cambridge.

Bennett, David (2005) 'Postmodernising pornography for the 21st-century academy', Inter-Disciplinary net, Sex and Sexuality, conference paper, [Online] Available at: http://www.inter-disciplinary.net/ci/sexuality/s2/Bennett%20paper.pdf (accessed 1 July 2006).

Benwell, Bethan (2001) 'Male gossip and language play in the letters pages of men's lifestyle magazines', *Journal of Popular Culture*, vol. 34, no. 4, pp. 19–33.

Benwell, Bethan (2004) 'Ironic discourse: evasive masculinity in men's lifestyle magazines', *Men and Masculinities*, vol. 7, no. 1, pp. 3–21.

Benwell, Bethan (2005) '"Lucky this is anonymous" ethnographies of reception in men's magazines: a "textual culture" approach', *Discourse and Society*, vol. 16, no. 2, pp. 147–172.

Brizendine, Louann (2006) *The Female Brain*, Morgan Road Books, New York.

Budgeon, Shelley & Currie, Dawn H. (1995) 'From feminism to post-feminism: women's liberation in fashion magazines', *Women's Studies International Forum*, vol. 18, no. 2, pp. 173–186.

Caldas-Coulthard, Carmen Rosa (1996) '"Women who pay for sex. and enjoy it": transgression versus morality in women's magazines', in *Texts and Practices: Readings in Critical Discourse Analysis*, eds Carmen Rosa Caldas-Coulthard & Malcolm Coulthard, Routledge, London, pp. 250–270.

Crewe, Ben (2003) *Representing Men: Cultural Production and Producers in the Men's Magazine Market*, Berg, Oxford.

Desmond, Jane (1999) *Staging Tourism: Bodies on Display from Waikiki to Sea World*, University of Chicago Press, Chicago.

Eggins, Suzanne & Iedema, Rick (1997) 'Difference without diversity: semantic orientation and ideology in competing women's magazines', in *Gender and Discourse*, ed. Ruth Wodak, Sage, London, pp. 165–196.

FHM (1994–) UK.

Gauntlett, David (2002) *Media, Gender and Identity: An Introduction*, Routledge, London.

Giddens, Anthony (1991) *Modernity and Self-Identity: Self and Society in the Late Modern Age*, Polity, Cambridge.

Goff, Clare (2004) 'How often do lads want it?', *Financial Times*, 6 July, p. 10.

Gramsci, Antonio (1971) *Selections from the Prison Notebooks*, Publishers, New York.

Grimshaw, Colin (2004) 'Can you spot the difference? Two titles in search of lads', *Financial Times*, 30 March, pp. 2–3.

Guardian. (2006) 'Sainsbury's plans a cover-up for lad mags', 13 April, [Online] Available at: www.guardian.co.uk (1 July 2006).

Halliday, M. A. K. (1978) *Language as Social Semiotic: The Social Interpretation of Language and Meaning*, Edward Arnold, London.

Hardy, Simon (1998) *The Reader, the Author, his Woman and her Lover: Soft-core Pornography and Heterosexual Men*, Cassell, London.

Hardy, Simon (2000) 'Feminist iconoclasm and the problem of eroticism', *Sexualities*, vol. 3, no. 1, pp. 77–196.

Hatoum, IDA Jodette & Belle, Deborah (2004) 'Mags and abs: media consumption and bodily concerns in men', *Sex Roles*, vol. 51, no. 7/8, pp. 397–407.

Hutcheon, Linda (1994) *Irony's Edge: The Theory and Politics of Irony*, Routledge, London.

Jackson, Peter, Stevenson, Nick & Brooks, Kate (2001) *Making Sense of Men's Magazines*, Polity, Cambridge.

Langton, Rae (1993) 'Speech acts and unspeakable acts', *Philosophy and Public Affairs*, vol. 22, no. 4, pp. 293–330.

Loaded (1994–) UK.

Lyle, Peter (2003) 'Get your obits out for the lads!', *The Independent on Sunday*, 6 July, pp. 1, 2, [Online] Available at: www.lexisnexis.com (20 Aug. 2007).

MacCannell, Dean (1999) *The Tourist. A New Theory of the Leisure Class*, University of California Press, Berkeley.

Machin, David & Thornborrow, Joanna (2006) 'Lifestyle and the depoliticisation of agency: sex as power in women's magazines', *Social Semiotics*, vol. 16, no. 1, pp. 173–188.

MacKinnon, Catharine A. (2006) *Are Women Human? And Other International Dialogues*, Belknap Press of Harvard University Press, Cambridge, MA.

Mind The Gap (n.d.) [Online] Available at: http://mindthegapcardiff.blogspot.com/ (1 July 2006).

Montgomery, Martin (1986) *An Introduction to Language and Society*, Routledge, London.

Mullany, Louise (2004) '"Become the man that women desire": gender identities and dominant discourses in email advertising language', *Language and Literature*, vol. 13, no. 4, pp. 291–305.

Nuts (2004–) UK.

O'Hagan, Andrew (2004) 'Disgrace under pressure', *London Review of Books*, vol. 26, no. 11, pp. 36–38, [Online] Available at: http://www.lrb.co.uk/v26/n11/ohag01_.html (28 February 2007).

Object (n.d.) [Online] Available at: www.object.org.uk (1 July 2006).

Rorty, R. (1991) 'Feminism and pragmatism', *Michigan Quarterly Review*, vol. 30, pp. 231–258.

Smith, Clarissa (2002) '"They're ordinary people, not aliens from the Planet Sex!": the mundane excitements of pornography for women', *Journal of Mundane Behavior*, vol. 3, no. 1, Feb., [Online] Available at: http://www.mundanebehavior.org/index2.htm (30 April 2007).

Smith, Merryn (2004) 'Fertility related discourses and family subjectivity: narratives of professional women', paper presented at "To think is to experiment", Centre for Narrative Research in the Social Sciences, University of East London, London, 28 April.

Sontag, Susan [1996] (2001) 'The Pornographic Imagination' in *Styles of Radical Will*, Vintage, London, pp. 35–73.

Talbot, Mary (1995) 'A synthetic sisterhood: false friends in a teenage magazine', in *Gender Articulated: Language and the Socially Constructed Self*, eds Kira Hall & Mary Bucholtz, Routledge, London, pp. 143–165.

Taylor, L. D. (2005) 'All for him: articles about sex in American lad magazines', *Sex Roles*, vol. 52, no. 3/4, pp. 153–163.

Telegraph (2006) 'Lads mags: porn or good fun? Debate', [Online] Available at: www.telegraph. co.uk (30 April 2007).

Tincknell, Estella, Chambers, Deborah, Van Loon, Joost & Hudson, Nicola (2003) 'Begging for it: "new femininities," social agency, and moral discourse in contemporary teenage and men's magazines', *Feminist Media Studies*, vol. 3, no. 1, pp. 47–63.

Turner, Janice (2005) 'Dirty young men', *Guardian Weekend Magazine*, 22 Oct., [Online] Available at: www.guardian. co.uk (5 Nov. 2005).

Van Duk, Teun A. (1997) 'What is political discourse analysis?', *Belgian Journal of Linguistics*, vol. 11, pp. 11–52.

Walker, Gail (1999) 'Hot property', *Belfast Telegraph*, 2 Feb., [Online] Available at: http://www.lexisnexis.com (28 February 2007).

Weedon, Chris (1997) *Feminist Practice and Poststructuralist Theory*, Blackwell, Oxford.

Wilson, Deidre & Sperber, Dan (1992) 'On verbal irony', *Lingua*, vol. 87, pp. 53–76.

Younge, Gary (2003) 'When Wal-Mart comes to town', *Guardian*, 18 Aug., [Online] Available at: www.guardian. co.uk (5 July 2006).

Zoo (2004–) UK.

19.
RECKONING LOYALTIES
White Femininity as "Crisis"
Aimee Carrillo Rowe and Samantha Lindsey

The white male is the most persecuted in America.

> (Rush Limbaugh fan cited in David Gates 1993: 51)

Feminism has emasculated the American male, and that emasculation has led to physical problems. [Viagra] will take the pressure off men. It will lead to new relationships between men and women and undercut the feminist agenda. It will free the American male libido much the same way that the Pill did.

> (Bob Guccione, editor of *Penthouse*, cited in Bruce Handy 1998: 56)

The "crisis of white masculinity" is by now well documented by cultural workers who seek to call attention to its historical production and the politics at stake in such regressive articulations. The above excerpts, from *Newsweek* and *Time*, respectively, are productive of such discourses, which have emerged in the (post-) civil rights era in the U.S., at a time when political gains secured through the struggles of 1960s' social movements began to take effect (Marshall Cohen 1977; Alan H. Goldman 1979; Kent Greenwalt 1979; Barry R. Gross 1977; Kenneth Kipnis 1977). The explosion of contested public meanings surrounding the Vietnam War, the (re)emergence of the feminist, queer, and anti-racist movements within the civil rights struggles, and the end of the post-World War II economic boom are some of a whole host of socio-political forces that ushered in this crisis as early as the 1970s (Susan Jeffords 1994; David Savran 1996). Its targets are framed as the sources of white male angst, including social forces such as immigration, affirmative action, transnationalism, and feminism.

These discourses are (re)written in contemporary popular culture through a variety of cultural forms which (re)center white men through the appropriation of leftist terminologies of "victimization" that seek to redress marginalizing forces by marking modes of oppression (Liam Kennedy 1996). They circulate through a range of mainstream media sources, including such texts as: Frederick R. Lynch's *Invisible Victims: White Males and the Crisis of Affirmative Action*, in which the author describes the "New McCarthyism" as a system of "taboos" that prevent white men from describing "reality" because they get attacked from all sides (1989: xiii); Peter Brimelow's *Alien Nation: Common Sense About America's Immigration Disaster*, which describes the risks of "mass immigration" as turning America into an "alien nation" (1995: xxi); and a now well-known *Newsweek* article entitled "White Male Paranoia" (Gates 1993), a response to the film *Falling Down* (1992).[1] The naturalization of this particular logic of white male victimization is also articulated in popular films such as the aforementioned *Falling Down* (1992), as well as *Fight Club* (1999, see Henry Giroux 2001), *Grand Canyon* (1991), *Unforgiven* (1992), *Demolition Man* (1993), *Forrest Gump* (1994; see Kennedy 1996), *Lost Highway* (1997), *Saving Private Ryan* (1998; see Hilary Harris 2000), *The Ice Storm* (1997), *Kurt and Courtney* (1998), *Men in Black* (1997), *Primary Colors* (1998), *Bulworth* (1998), and Academy

Award-winning *Good Will Hunting* (1997). While these films explore different subject matters and plot lines, each portrays white men as victims to a host of political circumstances and social groups. The perpetrators range from white women (*Lost Highway*, *The Ice Storm*, *Kurt and Courtney*, *Primary Colors*), to people of color and immigration (*Men in Black*, *Bulworth*), to war and class (*Good Will Hunting*, *Saving Private Ryan*). Through a reversal of the subject and object of "persecution" within these discourses, such texts undermine the legitimacy of interrogations of white male privilege (framing them as "attacks"), thus positioning marginalized groups as social agents of domination. Thus the articulation between (white male) "subject" and "oppressor" used to challenge white male authority now becomes displaced onto "other" bodies. The criticisms of white male privilege and the advances made by marginalized groups are rewritten as evidence of the "besieged" white male.

While the contested meanings attached to white masculinity have been interrogated within cultural and feminist studies, little attention has been paid to the ways in which these discourses position white femininity. Recent studies on white women (Ruth Frankenberg 1993; Hilary Harris 2000; Jane Lazarre 1996; Dreama Moon 1999; Vron Ware 1992) reveal how whiteness functions as an unnamed and "unmarked" force in the lives of white women. In the broadest sense, these studies establish the argument that "race shapes white women's lives" in ways that may be invisible to them since "white people have too often viewed themselves as nonracial or racially neutral" (Frankenberg 1993: 1). These texts are invaluable in rendering visible the complexities of whiteness and they go a long way to address challenges by Third World women to the exclusionary practices and political erasures of white feminism (M. Jacqui Alexander and Chandra Mohanty 1997; Himani Bannerji 1993; bell hooks 1992; Aida Hurtado 1996; Chandra Talpade Mohanty 1991; Cherríe Moraga and Gloria Anzaldúa 1981) by self-consciously and self-reflexively interrogating the privileging forces that constitute white female positionalities. Ruth Frankenberg notes the "ambivalent" status of white femininity as simultaneously privileged and confined *vis-à-vis* white masculinity due to the "contract" that defines this "tropological family" as "strictly heterosexual and monoracial in its coupling"

(cited in Harris 2000: 185–6). Missing from this body of work is a close examination of such "couplings" within the current historical context, which is particularly important in order to intervene in the conservative swing enabled by the white male figures that "relentlessly take up a series of opposed positionalities" (Savran 1996: 131). Especially given the articulation of "feminism" as an emasculating force, it is vital that feminists pay close attention not only to how white masculinity gets configured, but also how such meanings inflect, constrain, and potentially radicalize the possible meanings of white femininity. Further, it is important that we interrogate the whiteness of the femininity that gets deployed within these discourses in order to avoid universalizing the racial particularity of this formation under normative or un-raced terms such as "woman" and "femininity."

This essay examines two contemporary films, *Lost Highway* and *Alien Resurrection* (1997), which centrally figure white femininity as a site of white male anxiety. The uncertainty around the (re)distribution of sexual power and what constitutes that power serves as the basis for the contentious positioning of the white female figures in these films. As they become "empowered" as sexual agents, they challenge traditional gendered equations of domination: man = subject and woman = object. Instead, white female positionalities oscillate between sexual subject and sexual object in relation to various forms of white male authority. We argue that *Lost Highway* draws upon film noir themes of an emasculating *femme fatale* who achieves agency at the very moment in which she embraces her role as sexual object—her sexual objectification becomes the precondition for her subjectivity. As sexual subject she emasculates white men in neo-noir style through her refusal to prove her loyalty or subservience to them. In *Alien Resurrection* the positioning of the white female figure of Ripley as "hybrid" alien/woman produces uncertainty as to where her loyalties lie—with the "alien" or with "humanity." Refusing sexual objectification, the alien force within Ripley evokes sexual aggression and queer desire, thus the emasculating threat she poses is to replace and displace the white male figure. Ultimately, however, this anxiety is resolved when she suppresses her queer/ "alien" desires and affiliations and proves her loyalty to white male authority by saving "humanity." If the production of white femininity revolves around the question of loyalty, Ripley's move to "stand by her men" serves a disciplinary function: the primary allegiance of "white woman" must remain directed in the service of white male authority. As such, the film circumscribes more subversive, "alien" formations of white femininity, whose affinities lie with "others."

"Gateway to the Underworld": White Male Angst and the Splitting of White Femininity

> White Woman literally embodies both a meditation on and a mediation between the white patriarch and his life's meanings, as those meanings are stored in the family he was apparently saved to reproduce.
>
> (Harris 2000: 194)

In her essay, "Flexible Sexism," Doreen Massey (1994) discusses the "splitting" of (white)[2] female subjectivity into two feminine faces, represented by "bourgeois" and "underworld" characterizations. Analyzing David Lynch's noir-style film *Blue Velvet* (1996), Massey argues that the suburban veneer of "health and order" associated with (white) femininity relies upon the "underworld" femininity of "wild sexuality and violence." This contradictory positioning of (white) woman is depicted through the visible subjectivity of the white bourgeois woman, a face of white femininity that is simultaneously belied and sustained by its counterpart, the hidden "underworld" of out-of-control sexuality. Massey argues that bourgeois (white) masculine identity is produced in relation to this paradoxical construction of (white) femininity: it draws upon the "suburban veneer" to maintain an outward appearance of legitimacy, while desiring the mastery over the sexual challenge represented by the underworld (1994: 227).

White male struggles to master "overly-empowered" white femininity, a trope of film noir, emerges here as white men both fear and desire white women. The nature of this struggle assumes and reifies a proximal[3] relationship between white men and women, producing white femininity as a preferred site through which white male anxiety gets played out. Massey argues that because "some kinds of 'otherness' remain just too threatening to be colonized in

this manner," (white) women become the "gateway to the other world" through which white men may get a "taste of the other" (Moore cited in Massey 1994: 228). Similarly, Hilary Harris notes in her analysis of *Saving Private Ryan* the "mediating" role that "White Woman" plays between her white male counterpart and his life through absolving him from "any specific historical debt, or burden, or guilt that he might reasonably be expected to feel" (2000: 195). White femininity, then, is inextricably linked to white masculinity through a host of discursive practices associated with normalizing hegemonic gender, race, and heterosexual relations. This proximity positions white femininity not only as a primary site in which the crisis of white masculinity gets played out (as "gateway to the underworld"), but also makes certain affective demands of white women (that they serve a "mediating" and moralizing function to white men).

Film critics have long called attention to the contradictory role of (white) women, both subject and object of gendered relations, and a potentially emasculating trope of film noir. As Dale E. Ewing, Jr. writes in his review of *Women in Film Noir*,

> The male gaze denotes a specific style of visual presentation in which the male is the subject and the woman is the object . . . Women in film noir are viewed through the eyes of men who measure their worth according to sexist and oppressive standards. The contradiction rests in threatening women's roles that victimize the male heroes and undermine the patriarchal order.
>
> (1999: 78)

The fluctuating role of white woman as sexual object (of the white male gaze) and sexual subject (victimizing white male heroes) is a constitutive narrative dilemma of film noir. If this plot line is consistent across historical moments, however, this is not to suggest that its contours and the gendered anxieties that it evokes are ahistorical. The role of the *femme fatale* in film noir was a figure that emerged in the wake of World War II when gender roles were disrupted as soldiers returned from the war to discover that their women had replaced them in the workplace. Stephen Farber explains,

During the war years and immediately afterward, strong women flourished in American films and were often presented as monsters and harpies, hardened by greed and lust, completely without feeling for the suffering they caused. These films undoubtedly reflected the fantasies and fears of a wartime society, in which women had taken control of many of the positions customarily held by men.

(1999: 49)

The reemergence of film noir in the 1990s may well signify a reinscription of such fears of postwar white male displacement at the hands of white women—both eras are marked by "realignments in gender relations" (Foster Hirsch 1999: 7).

If the anxieties around displaced gender roles are to be understood as both a trope of film noir and an historically contingent discursive formation, then the deployment of such dynamics within specific historical contexts becomes critical. In order to address this task, we trace some of the movements of the configuration of white femininity as "subject" and "object" of heterosexual positionalities through an analysis of *Lost Highway*. The film self-consciously reveals the terror evoked by white female power, "real" or "imagined," over white male figures. The basic storyline goes: white man becomes "obsessed" with white woman; white woman exploits his desire for her to control him.

Lost Highway follows in the wake of *Blue Velvet* and plays out similar themes of white masculinities and femininities. Yahoo!Movies (1997) provides the following synopsis of the film:

Fred Madison (Bill Pullman) is a jazz saxophonist who is married to the beautiful Renee (a brown-haired Patricia Arquette). After receiving menacing videotapes taken from inside their home, the couple begins to worry. Fred's fear is compounded when he meets a mysterious man (Robert Blake) at a flamboyant party. Fred wakes up to discover that Renee has been murdered, and Fred is convicted of the crime [as depicted in the video footage]. Trouble is, he doesn't remember anything from that night. Sitting in a jail cell, he undergoes a miraculous transformation, waking up as Pete

Dayton (Balthazar Getty), a young mechanic. When Pete meets a dangerous client's sexy girlfriend, Alice Wakefield (a blonde Arquette), a passionate affair blossoms that threatens to expose Pete.

The film may be read as a postmodern and neo-noir film for its fluid character constructions, nonlinear plot, themes, chiaroscuro lighting, and gender, race, and heterosexual dynamics. Foster Hirsch argues that the film is and is not film noir: "These routine noir stories of mischance, seduction, and entrapment are connected by an event that takes the film out of noir: in prison Fred disappears mysteriously replaced by Pete" (1999: 313). We will return to Hirsch's reading of this scene shortly.

Lost Highway depicts a suburban white woman and her "underworld" counterpart, but leaves unresolved the relationship between the two, suggesting that they are the same woman: both are played by the same actress, they appear in a sisterly pose in a photograph and then later one disappears, and each evokes the other throughout the plot. As Erik Bryant Rhodes writes in his film review, "they are the same in that each evokes a luxurious sense of carnal potency—one withheld, the other flaunted" (1998: 60). Director David Lynch scripts this form of "split" femininity to play upon the anxiety posed by a white woman who is not as she seems. By drawing attention to this dynamic, *Lost Highway* exposes the relationship between the "suburban veneer" that maintains a sense of legitimacy and the desire for mastery over the sexual challenge represented by the underworld. That Renee and Alice are "the same" simultaneously blurs and marks the distinction between the underworld and the outer world, thus providing a visual spectacle of white male angst at the hands of the split white woman.

The film depicts this splitting through the primary female character(s), Renee and Alice (both played by Patricia Arquette). Renee—with her fiery red hair, black silk robe, and high heels—approximates bourgeois white femininity. She spends most of her time in the home; she defers to Fred's wishes, judgments, and commands; she continuously tries to reassure him that she is his loyal companion. While she is depicted as playing a submissive role to Fred in their elite home, it is never entirely clear (particularly to him) whether her subordination and devotion to him are "sincere." For instance, one reviewer writes that Fred is a "jazz saxophonist at the Luna Lounge and he seems to want [Renee] to come along to watch him blow and she seems not to want to come" (Donald Lyons 1997: 4). What is interesting about this excerpt is it reveals the reviewer's own uncertainty about Renee's complicity with Fred's desires. While she generally yields to his wishes and commands, she is mildly disinterested in "watching him blow" and she "seems not to want to come." Her ambivalence, his inability to "arouse in her any enthusiastic sexual response," drives Fred to "suspicion, paranoia, and nightmares" (Lyons 1997: 4). The (in)authenticity of Renee's performance of white femininity becomes the site through which Fred's white male anxieties get played out. He becomes victimized by his own uncertainty and incapacity to remain a central figure, a privileged sexual subject, in relation to his wife. In this sense, Renee's figure departs from bourgeois femininity—she herself is a "split" figure, straddling the outer- and the under-worlds.

If Renee's ambivalence toward Fred is unsettling, Renee's "underworld" face, Alice, is outright terrifying, becoming a repository site of white male anxiety. Renee's blonde counterpart, Alice, represents the "untamable" side of white femininity that both undergirds and belies Renee's suburban and subordinated existence. If Renee's loyalty is under scrutiny, Alice explicitly betrays Pete, using his "obsession" with her as a mechanism to exploit him. The narrative of overly-sexualized Alice is situated within the broader cultural context of circulating discourses of white female "pathological" sexuality in the popular media, such as Mary Kay Letourneau's "rape," Karla Faye Tucker's orgasmic killing pleasure, and Monica Lewinsky as "predator" of the president. Each of these narratives depicts white women's out-of-control sexuality as the source of white male sexual anxiety. This discourse also couples with discourses of "the end of feminism" in which (white) women's empowerment is rewritten as "vain" forms of "self-obsession," and of the "Viagra craze" as a remedy to the "physical problems" caused by feminism's emasculation.

In Alice this form of white female empowerment, articulated through the fantasy of white male emasculation, achieves orgasmic and horrific excess. "Desire is red and desire is death and desire is woman," critic Donald Lyons writes of the film, drawing attention to "the women's shiny red lips," which "are rapturously given the whole screen as they utter urgent words into black phones" (1997: 2–3). Interestingly, Alice and Renee emerge as one character for Lyons. It is actually Alice's red lips that speak into the black phone and her red lips could be read as "desire and death," in the sense that it is she who betrays the white male figure. Renee is actually the victim of (Fred's?) murder and neither woman is herself a killer. The erasure, and indeed reversal, of Renee's death in Lyons' reading ("desire is death and desire is woman") marks the compelling way in which this film achieves its task. It simultaneously blurs the distinction between the underworld and the outer world, even as it marks it. Thus Lynch exposes that the line between the two is not so clear and that the latter emerges through the condition of possibility created by the former.

Alice remains bound within the underworld of Mafia violence and pornography. Her excessive sexuality marks her body as the ultimate site of white male heterosexual desire and conquest. Lynch depicts the compelling force of her hetero/sexuality as occupying the liminal space between image and "reality," thus raising, but never answering, the question: Is Alice merely a projection of white male desire? If so, then why is he unable to "control" the effects of his own production? Or, if Alice represents the object of white male desire, how does she return as the subject of his victimization?

While Alice eludes white male conquest (no man can ever "have" her), she secures her power through her appropriate performance of a role assigned to her within the logic of phallocentrism that drives the "underworld." The modes of empowerment available to her are circumscribed within the heteropatriarchal exploitation of her body. This theme is captured in one compelling scene, in which Renee's character seems to transform into Alice. When Renee first "arrives" in the "underworld," her innocence is depicted through her fearful composure. The camera, tight on her face, reveals her eyes darting and worried brow. She seems to be aware of the role she is to play as "woman" in this space, but she hesitates to take it, for doing so marks the moment in which her idealized femininity becomes compromised and she leaves the conventional shores of the outer world. She is ushered downstairs into a living room with very little light, where the Mafia leader ("Mr. Eddie") is seated before a fireplace. In this shadowy space, he sits like a king (or a devil) before the burning flames, the only source of light and heat in the room. As she stands before him, bodyguards surround her with guns drawn, aimed at her head. Mr. Eddie raises his hands as if to elicit an unspoken command. He does not need to *speak* his command because her purpose within this sphere is implicitly understood by all present. She takes her unspoken cue, drops her clothes, and stands naked before him.

At this moment of vulnerability, terror passes and her face is overcome with pleasure and relief as she seizes her circumscribed power within this sphere of male pleasure. Renee becomes Alice. Under Mr. Eddie's direction, her bourgeois femininity is transformed into "underworld" sexuality. This transformation is both terrifying—because it reveals that Fred was right to fear Renee, to question her sincerity, and ultimately to kill her—and affirming, because white female sexuality is positioned in the service of white male pleasure. On one hand, white woman knows her role within this dangerous and male-dominated sphere. This recognition marks the limited range in which she can function as a woman of the underworld: she is first and foremost a hetero/sexual object. To the extent that her power is defined by her capacity to take up and play this role well, she becomes an active agent, or subject, through her appropriation and abuse of her object status. In this and other scenes Lynch reveals white woman's role in the underworld as a male fantasy with a twist: Alice is the ultimate sex object, yet she locates her own agency by using her hetero/sexual power to control the men that would control her. Although the white male figure has created the female subject represented by Alice as the embodiment of sexual pleasure within *Lost Highway*, he is terrorized by his own creation. Alice is "empowered" at the moment in which she strips for the underworld king/devil.

While her power is *contingent* upon white male approval, the power Alice wields is the source of terror for the white male figure of the outer world who seeks to possess her. For instance, at a climactic point in the film, Pete commits murder for Alice. She promises that this act will free them from the dangerous underworld, exploiting his dream that the two of them can run away together. She would belong exclusively to him if they were to leave. As their escape unfolds, however, she suddenly turns on him. In one climactic scene she mocks his male authority by pointing a gun at his face. Tension mounts as the audience is asked to identify with his anxiety when it is not clear whether or not she intends to kill him. In this moment of escape from the underworld, Alice gains control of the gun-as-phallus and turns it against him. At last she hands the gun to him, saying, "Put this in your pants." His masculinity literally rests in her hands, and as gender subordination is inverted, she must empower him to "put it in his pants." Thus, the phallus does not *belong* to *him*, but rather, is *secured* only through *her* benevolence.

During this scene, a porno plays on the wall behind them showing a close-up of her face, twisted with hetero/sexual pleasure, while a faceless white male figure takes her from behind. Pete, faced with her image on the screen as both degraded sexual object and powerful sexual subject, grabs his head in anguish. Sweating and seeing double, he runs upstairs and opens a door to find Alice, on all fours, in the same position as the porno depicts. On seeing him, she speaks to him from the big screen with cold mockery: "Did you want to talk to me? Did you want to ask me why?" He quickly closes the door because he already knows the answer to her rhetorical questions. His own desire to possess Alice implicates Pete in the system of power that has produced her as a terrifying figure. He is, ironically, victimized by his ultimately failed efforts to exclusively control her. In spite of, and indeed, because of the fact that Alice is confined to operate within the "underworld" parameters of the role of sexual object "created" by white men, the uncertainty that arises out of Alice's hetero/sexual agency threatens the viability of white masculinity. This underworld theme mirrors Pete's anxiety around his inability to *know* to whom Alice is in service.

If the discourse of white masculinity gets played out within this text through the splitting of white female subjectivity, both "the underworld" and the act of splitting are actively erased within the collective, or officially intelligible, memory. Lynch depicts this "forgetting" through the trope of the video camera, which plays on themes of truth and memory. At one point in the film the police come to question Fred about Renee's murder, which was captured on video. They ask him a series of questions about video cameras, and he responds: "I hate video cameras because I like to remember things my own way, how I remembered them, not necessarily the way they happened." In marking the slippage between how Fred "*likes* to remember things" and "the way they happened," Lynch calls attention not only to the slippage between "truth" and memory, but also to the "truth" that Fred does not want to see: his need to control Renee; his anxiety around her loyalty; and ultimately, his role in the production of his own victimization.

The video camera serves the unpleasant function of capturing, legitimizing, and historicizing that which would be edited out of hegemonic cultural memory. Throughout the film a ghostly character terrorizes the white male characters in the film by continually "shooting" them with his video camera and playing their own actions back to them, thus forcing them to confront the "truth" of their own creations. When faced with the "actual" memory of the violence and insecurity in which their white masculinity is based, they are victimized by the spectacle of their lives reflected back to them. At these moments their heads literally spin out of control, shaking violently from side to side. This exposure to the underworld that is concealed from the outer world is terrifying for these men, not only because it marks the violence through which the white female "other" is produced, but also because it evidences the very process through which white masculinity itself becomes signified.

The two white male figures are also interchangeable, in a sense, as each replaces the other in mysterious ways throughout the film. When Fred is incarcerated on death row for Renee's murder, he begins to have horrible headaches. One evening, his head spins out of control, violently shaking from side to side. The next morning, the guards find that a young white male, Pete, has mysteriously replaced the "wife killer." Pete is released and returns to work as a mechanic, where he soon meets Alice when Mr. Eddie brings in his Caddy for a tune-up. Fred reemerges as Pete's replacement at the end of the film when Alice taunts, "You can never have me!" in response to Pete's desire, "I want

you, I want you." Rhodes explains these transposable figures as "representing two sides of the same self." The overriding quality that defines this "self" is "a man obsessed with possessing the wrong woman" (1998: 59). Fred and Pete mirror each other in their desire for, and thus victimization by, the white female characters they seek to control. In this way the film captures a dynamic of white male angst as it gets played out on the text of the white female body. Both the male and the female characters are "split," interchangeable, and replace each other in ways that provide compelling points of entry into analyzing the production of racialized gender relations within this text. Film noir critic Foster Hirsch (1999) calls attention to this replacement as the distinguishing feature that moves *Lost Highway* from neo-noir to horror. But Hirsch fails to grapple with the significance of Lynch's move from an individualized narration of white male angst at the hands of the *femme fatale* and the more collective sense of this experience evoked by this interchangeability. Indeed, *Lost Highway* may not narrow the boundaries of film noir, as Hirsch suggests, but rather open up a space to imagine beyond the suffering individual white male to recognize the social, political, and cultural forces that constitute a broader white male sense of self.

Lost Highway is an interesting text to analyze for the purpose of marking the relationship between the production of white femininity and white masculinity since it reveals both the slippage between the subject and object positions that each figure occupies and moves this narration from individual to collective social experience.[4] White man is no longer the unquestioned sexual subject within this narration, but rather his efforts to achieve this status, through the objectification and subordination of his white female counterparts, are turned against him. Thus he becomes the object of their sexual desires, which are ultimately not directed in his service, but rather in more selfish, or "self-obsessed" modes. While *Alien Resurrection* also draws upon this theme of white male anxiety in relation to white female loyalty, it departs from the neo-noir trope of the emasculating *femme fatale*, an anxiety that remains unresolved in *Lost Highway*. Instead, *Alien Resurrection* locates structures of white female desire through which such anxiety may be resolved. We now turn our attention to *Alien Resurrection*.

In Defense of Whiteness: Aliens, Cyborgs, and the Containment of White Femininity

The *Alien* series (*Alien* 1979; *Aliens* 1986; *Alien3* 1992; *Alien Resurrection* 1997) has received a good deal of attention by feminist and cultural critics. Some argue that the films constitute a feminist text, based on their readings of Ripley's strong femininity (Peter Lev 1998), the film's exposure of the "phallic ideal" in the second film (Robert Torry 1994), or the reversal of gender roles (Thomas Vaughn 1995). Others suggest that the series is regressive on a number of fronts: for its "humanism" (J. H. Kavanaugh 1980), its "corporate masculinism" (Susan Jeffords 1987), its individualistic corporatism, represented by Ripley's complicity in the corporate hierarchy and her failure to forge alliances among different marginalized groups (Judith Newton 1980), or its repression of an archetypal femininity (Janice Rushing 1995). Our position navigates among several of these arguments and diverges most specifically in its attempt to situate its critique within this particular historical moment. While we concur with the arguments that point to Ripley's strong femininity and the films' gender role reversal as potentially liberating impulses, we diverge in our reading of the implications of such articulations of "feminism." In this sense our analysis seeks to extend the insights provided by Jeffords (1987) and Newton (1980) by examining how the liberal, white, and/or heterosexual feminisms articulated become appropriated not only for corporate purposes, but also for those of white supremacy, heteronormativity, and U.S. global dominance.

This film succeeds as a mainstream text because it resolves white male anxiety by disciplining Ripley's white femininity—she abandons and aborts her "alien" familial ties in favor of her ties to white male authority. At the end of *Alien3* (1992) Ripley is "pregnant" with an alien and dramatically takes her own life so that she may take the life of her alien fetus in a "suicidal swan dive into boiling lead" (Leah Rozen 1997: 29). In *Alien Resurrection*, Ripley is brought back to life through cloning by "scientists working for the evil Company," who seek to extract the alien from her belly for "their own nefarious" and colonial purposes (Rozen 1997: 29). In the process of cloning her genes are fused with those of the alien so that Ripley is "half alien." While she is visibly human, she demonstrates the primal intuition and physical prowess of the alien species. As one *Newsweek* review of the film explains, "Ripley seems to have acquired superhuman powers and a new, bitterly sardonic lease on life" (David Ansen 1997: 90).

What is unsettling about Ripley's new powers is that they defy traditional and even "progressive" articulations of white femininity with which her character has historically been endowed. For instance, Thomas Vaughn (1995) reads Ripley's shaved head in *Alien3* as an erasure of her identity as "an attractive woman." He writes, "This is certainly a far cry from the objectified item of desire she becomes at the end of *Alien*, reducing the stature of her sexuality by homogenizing her with the male prison population" (1995: 432). And yet, as Vaughn points out, her de(hetero)sexualization in this film is accompanied by her "sexual emergence," signified by her first sex act in the *Alien* series. While we concur with Vaughn's interpretation of the paradoxical nature of this "annihilation of the subject" as telos, we seek to draw closer attention to the constitution of the subject who is being annihilated and/or recuperated here. The most compelling reading of this "paradox" of Ripley's simultaneous de(hetero)sexualization and sexualization is that it reveals the tension that surrounds the contemporary production of the white female subject. As Vaughn notes, this paradox emerges most clearly in *Alien3* in which there seems to be a masculinizing shift in Ripley's character, a shift that accompanies a new moment in the cultural production of white femininity within the emerging context of white male victimage. We read this paradox, then, as part of a broader, ongoing negotiation of white male angst as it gets played out on the increasingly masculinized and simultaneously increasingly heterosexualized body of the white female figure. While her new masculinized identity increasingly threatens to displace him, she must simultaneously demonstrate that she is willing to remain in service to his hegemonic status by complying with his heterosexual desire to occupy her body.

The paradox that Vaughn (1995) outlines takes on a new form in such a reading of *Alien Resurrection*. Ripley's hybridity as human/alien becomes the site of anxiety through which the white female figure's loyalty to white masculinity gets played out. Sigourney Weaver names this tension in a behind-the-scenes interview shown prior to the video in which she describes the "film's appeal" as follows: "Something has gone wrong in the cloning so that [Ripley has] had a genetic mix with the alien and there's this unease about how much she is of which and where her loyalties lie" (*Alien Resurrection* 1997). Here Weaver evokes the "unease" of the film as an effect of Ripley's new hybridity ("how much she is of which") that gets played out, ultimately, through the test of the white female character's "loyalties."

If white femininity's contemporary cultural production revolves around the central question of her "loyalties," to what, or whom, is she being asked to remain loyal? And what, or whom, is competing for her loyalties? In order to address these questions we first trace the shifting manifestations of white femininity within the *Alien* series in an effort to map this production to the emerging discourse of white male victimage. Then we more closely analyze some of the "competing" forces that hail the white female subject's loyalties. *National Review* critic James Bowman tracks the progression of white femininities in the *Alien* series when he writes:

> It is hard to remember now that in the original *Alien* (1979) Sigourney Weaver's archetypal character, Lt. Ripley, was wreathed in feminine curls, or that in the sequel, *Aliens* (1986), her chief concern was to mother a little girl . . . By the time of *Alien3* (1992), Lt. Ripley had become completely defeminized . . . At this point Lt. Ripley . . . is allowed one or two expressions of her residual femininity . . . Otherwise [she plays] the take-charge guy, the cool one in a crisis, as most of her male comrades are gibbering in terror.
>
> (1998: 35)

If the Ripley of the late 1970s and 1980s is more traditionally "feminine" (signified by her "feminine curls" and "motherly" impulse), the 1990's marks her "de-feminization." This shift threatens to displace white masculinity's hegemonic status because Ripley's character moves from feminized sexual object to masculinized sexual subject. As such her gender-bending form blurs the distinction between object and subject, producing uncertainty and anxiety through which contemporary questions of white femininity and its

relation to white masculinity are played out. If in *Alien3* this tension begins to emerge through the re-imagination of white femininity's traditional "place," *Alien Resurrection* marks a new phase of this anxiety. White female loyalty is more forcefully at stake, not only to the white male (in the gender reversal that plays through the trope of the *femme fatale*, as *Lost Highway* reveals), but also more broadly to the interests of the postcolonial U.S. nation-state. Throughout the film the viewer is continually asked to speculate where her loyalties lie: with the "alien" (read feminine, castrating, racialized "other" that lies beyond the "frontier") or with "humanity" (read "civilization," "progress," and ultimately, whiteness). Each is positioned in opposition to the other in this configuration, so that her loyalty to the alien within her functions as a betrayal to "humanity." The tension around her loyalty to humanity gets played out through her heroic efforts to save the space ship, all the white men on board, and the earth to which the ship is returning. Ultimately, then, "loyalty to humanity" is signified as loyalty to white male structures of power. It also entails the betrayal, erasure, or in this case, "abortion" of her own internal alien, a theme to which we return below.

What is so terrifying about this configuration of white femininity is that Ripley's body, her outward appearance, is still "human," yet something unseen, that which resides on her interior, is dangerous and deadly. One of the forms in which this tension plays out is Ripley's catachrestic and indeed masculinized performance of white femininity. As Bowman's review notes, the sexuality deployed in the character of the genetically cloned Ripley of *Alien Resurrection* is different from her "human" portrayals in the previous *Alien* films. She queers the category "white woman" on several fronts: in the challenge she represents to white male authority; in her masculine portrayal of white femininity; and her (homo)sexualization of the beautiful cyborg, Call. Reviewers comment that the "new Ripley" is "alluringly pansexual in brown leather" (Joe Morgenstern 1997: A8) and she is "buffer and tougher than ever" (Rozen 1997: 29). Several call attention to a scene in which Ripley dominates her male counterparts in a game of basketball. One reviewer describes this scene as "eerie" because "Ripley the super-woman, facing down the pirate thugs, plays basketball and stops the ball cold with outstretched palm as if her hand were lined with crazy glue" (David Denby 1997: 20).

While there is nothing inherently "eerie" about a woman playing basketball, the scene only achieves its "eerie-ness" in the gender reversal (she replaces the male) and the racial morphing (she dominates a white and black male in a discursively "black" sport) that the scene represents. Reviewer James Bowman reveals the threat that such a gender inversion represents when he writes, "she shows two male swaggerers who have made the mistake of regarding her as sexual prey that she is not only stronger than they . . . but also a better basketball player. Ouch! That's hitting them in a sensitive place" (1998: 36). By marking Ripley's anxiety-producing performance of white femininity, Bowman's comments draw attention to two disciplining aspects of a dynamic of subordination constitutive of its cultural production. First, she fails to respond to their efforts to (hetero)sexualize her when she refuses the role of "sexual prey." In this sense, she refuses to be the object of their sexual desire/aggression, and thus rewrites white femininity as a castrating subject. Second, and, perhaps more importantly, she responds in a competitive/masculine fashion to their advances and proceeds to dominate her male counterparts on their own terms. If part of the work of white femininity is to mirror back to white masculinity its centrality in the social order of things, then her prowess—especially in a masculine realm such as competitive sports—becomes an affront on his character as it is positioned within the broader social order. Bowman's exclamation, "Ouch! That's hitting them in a sensitive place," articulates Ripley's "strength" to their castration. His spontaneous outcry ("Ouch!") signifies his unmediated reflex to being "hit in a sensitive place."

Perhaps the most compelling evidence of the anxiety that surrounds Ripley's queer white femininity is the simultaneous evocation and erasure of the desire between the two female characters. Ripley's white female counterpart, Call (Winona Ryder) plays a beautiful and innocent—or "whey-faced," as one critic writes (Anthony Lane 1997: 102)—cyborg, who is programmed by the state to conform to its demands and serve its interests. She "reveals herself to be a runaway robot, programmed for compassion" (Kim New-

man 1997: 37). Call represents an idealized version of the former Ripley, and yet the relationship between the women evokes an unnamable uneasiness in the actors and critics alike. Weaver refers to the film as "a kinky picture!" in an interview. She grins as she explains that she "was lucky having a particularly kinky director who was interested in pushing the sensual side of the story" (cited in Matthew Hastings 1997: 39). The only explanation the interview provides for Weaver's comments is that the film's director, Jean-Pierre Jeunet, is French. Weaver's description of the film as "kinky" frames, but does not attempt to name or explain, the lesbian overtones of the film. Thus lesbianism is simultaneously evoked and erased as unnamably "other," a theme to which we return below. The sexual tension between Call and Ripley would go without comment if Ripley were a white man. The dis-ease of her role in this film is that it too closely approximates that of a white man. The threat here, that is both named and displaced by her deployment of the term "kinky," is that for white woman to do so is to doubly displace white man—not only by defeating him at his own game—but through desiring and producing desire in "his" ideal (white) woman. Thus Ripley's subjectivity in this *Alien* is figured through the displacement and replacement of white masculinity with an "unnatural," thus objectified, form of white femininity. Like the *femme fatale* of Alice/Renee in *Lost Highway*, Ripley's character displaces the subject/object sexual relations between white masculinity and white femininity. Yet this displacement turns on the logic of white male replacement, as opposed to entrapment, by (overly) empowered white female subjects.

This theme of lesbianism as evoked, but not named, recurs in almost every review we read. While the same homoerotic image of Call and Ripley in a near-kiss pose appears more frequently than any other shot in these reviews, its meaning is either ignored or contained within the text of the review itself. The photo is a profile shot of Ripley standing over Call—their faces almost touching—looking down into her face and holding it up to her own. It references a scene in which Call sneaks into Ripley's sleeping quarters with the intention of killing her, thinking the alien is inside of her. Call finds Ripley, apparently asleep, and uses her knife to expose a scar between Ripley's breasts. Ripley "awakens" to Call's queer affront—coming to her knees she is much taller than Call—then fondles her face, and finally lifts her by her throat with "alien" strength. The recursive trope of "sisterhood" in the text that accompanies the widely distributed picture contains the queer desire and violent overtones evoked by the scene and the photo by desexualizing, or heterosexualizing, the image. One critic describes the two women pictured in this image as "the pixyish Ryder, who, alongside the strapping Weaver, comes across like a futuristic Skipper doll trying to keep up with big-sister Barbie" (Rozen 1997: 29). The disjuncture between the text and the queer desire evoked by the visual image contain the latter on a number of fronts. For one, the textual depiction contradicts the image by placing Ryder in a sort of fruitless pursuit of (or "trying to keep up with") Weaver. Further, it frames the relationship as one between a youthful and older pair of sisters, thus simultaneously evoking an innocent, even child-like affection between them as well as foregrounding their difference in age. Finally, his depiction of Ryder as a "pixyish Skipper doll," following in the trail of her "strapping big-sister Barbie," desexualizes the scene by objectifying the actors as dolls. Another critic writes, "[screenwriter Joss Whedon] has even given Ripley a soul sister . . . to bond with. O.K., she's a robot, but she's got a heart of gold as well as buns of steel" (Richard Schickel 1997: 84). Again the relationship is framed in terms of sisterhood, but here the heterosexualization of the image is the containment strategy: Call is "given" to Ripley by the male screenwriter; her sensuality is offset by her robot status and her "heart of gold"; and, perhaps most strikingly, the (male) critic objectifies and heterosexualizes her body by drawing attention to her "buns of steel." Thus the threatening desire between the women is erased, the desiring women as subjects are reduced to objects, and the image is (re)framed for the heteronormative male gaze. The text belies the force of image, reassuring the reader that the homoerotic images he is consuming are produced for him (Laura Mulvey 1989). The queer pleasure that resonates between Ripley and Call is rearticulated as heterosexual pleasure through this textual framing of the image for the male gaze.

If the anxiety around Ripley's white femininity takes place on the terrain of her hybrid, human/alien body, then how does the film ultimately contain and resolve this tension? If the alien is (inside of) her, how can her white femininity be recuperated? We now turn our attention to the final scene of the film in which Ripley "aborts" her alien child in a gesture which purges the alien force from her body. In this climactic scene, the surviving crewmembers make their escape from the alien-infested "father" ship onto a smaller vessel as they try to escape from the alien. Ripley is confronted with the ultimate "choice" through which the uncertainty about her loyalties will finally be determined: she must either kill her own offspring, or let her offspring kill the surviving crewmembers and then the humans awaiting at "home." After a dramatic display of affection between Ripley and her alien child, Ripley flicks her acidic blood onto a window, creating a small hole through which the alien baby is sucked. "She at first nuzzles the horrible thing with an apparently maternal show of feeling, but then flings a drop of her blood at the window of the spaceship, creating a small hole through which the creature is sucked in disgusting ribbons of flesh and blood" (Bowman 1998: 35). Ripley cries as she watches her alien child being sucked through the hole in an eerie display that mimics an abortion procedure. Bowman continues, "It's about as close to a depiction of abortion you're ever likely to see on the Silver Screen. The ending of this inconvenient life is said to have 'saved the earth'" (1998: 35). Within the broader historical context of anti-immigration and rightist discourses surrounding the perceived crisis in Third World over-reproduction in the US, Ripley's abortion is acceptable because the alien is not viably "human" in the first place. Rather, the alien form with which Ripley was impregnated originates from beyond the frontier, in the wild zones of restless natives. This "inconvenient" and racialized "life," then, must be ended in order to "save the earth." In this "abortion" of her alien child, Ripley's otherness—as metonymic of several forms of otherness (feminism, lesbianism, immigration, miscegenation)—is contained through its violent expulsion. Within this cultural narrative, then, Ripley's white female body provides an effective site through which white male anxiety around various forms of otherness may be purged. Now divided from her alien child, the film concludes with a sense of hope that Ripley's underworld femininity is excised, restoring her viable status as white woman.

Alien Loyalties: Radicalizing White Femininity

Our readings of *Lost Highway* and *Alien Resurrection* point to two themes that constitute the cultural production of white femininity in a broader "crisis of white masculinity" relevant to feminist (re)articulations of white femininity. First, we note the displacement of traditional gender roles between white femininity and white masculinity as the roles of sexual subject and object become destabilized in both films. In *Lost Highway* Alice/Renee becomes an emasculating sexual subject and Pete/Fred becomes her sexual prey, while in *Alien Resurrection* Ripley's masculinized figure refuses sexual objectification and threatens to replace the white male subject.

In both cases, the modes of white female subjectivity are circumscribed through the centrality of the destabilized white male figure. In *Lost Highway*, for instance, sexual objectification becomes the precondition for the white female agency; Alice becomes a subject by submitting to the right man positioning her as his sexual object. The film reveals the ways in which white female power is defined in limited and hegemonic terms: white woman must conform to the disciplinary regimes of whiteness, heterosexuality, and gender in order to gain social power. In this sense, the power she secures through such routes is contingent upon her subordination and her formation as a hegemonic subject. Audre Lorde (1984: 118) writes of the "patriarchal invitation to power" wherein "white women face the pitfall of being seduced into joining the oppressor under the pretense of sharing power." The "pitfall" of this logic, Lorde continues, is that "it is easier . . . for white women to believe the dangerous fantasy that if you are good enough, pretty enough, sweet enough, quiet enough, teach the children to behave, hate the right people, and marry the right men, then you will be allowed to co-exist with patriarchy in relative peace" (1984: 119). The task, then, is not only to name and render visible the disciplinary structures through which white female power gets defined on such circumscribed terms, but also to imagine alternative modes of identity formation for white femininity.

The theme of loyalty to white male power runs through both films as the crisis of white masculinity gets played out on the bodies of white female figures.

In *Lost Highway*, we note the positioning of the white female figure as the "gateway to the underworld" through her "*femme fatale*" deployment as an emasculating force in relation to white male sexual power: her failure to prove her loyalty becomes the site of his victimization. In *Alien Resurrection* Ripley's hybridity calls into question her loyalty to "humanity," a logic which relies upon both an un-raced/white and imperialistic notion of "humanity" as well as stereotypical notions of the racialized and dangerous "frontier," miscegenation, and queer desire. White femininity is disciplined within this narrative to prove her allegiance to the former and negate her alliance with the latter.

Yet the turn of this anxiety around white female loyalties points to modes of radical rearticulations for this figure. If loyalty is a formation that operates through affinities and alliances, "choice" with regard to whom or what to direct those loyalties may be contested and rewritten. Hegemonic logic mandates loyalty to dominant structures of power, such as white masculinity, and indeed becomes destabilized by white female figures who refuse this role. If, as Harris notes, "White Woman" serves a legitimizing role *vis-à-vis* "White Man," absolving him from "any specific historical debt, or burden, or guilt that he might reasonably be expected to feel" (2000: 195), then her refusal to do so holds radical potential. As white female loyalties are rewritten in counterhegemonic terms of multiracial and transnational feminist alliances, new modes of power emerge. The proximity between white femininity and white masculinity is contingent upon white female investments in such relations of rule. "Alien" alliances—queer and multiracial—undermine this bond, forging new modes of connection that disrupt and potentially rewrite the social order.

Acknowledgements

Professor Carrillo Rowe would like to thank Daniel Gross, Susan Jeffords, Matt Sparke, Lisa McLaughlin, and the *FMS* reviewers for their important commentary on earlier versions of this manuscript, and Diane Crosby for her invaluable research assistance.

Notes

1. To take one example, the *Newsweek* article (Gates 1993: 49) sets this reversal into motion by referring

to "white male bashing" as a double standard. The author asks, "What if they talked like that about blacks? About women?" His questions suggest that any criticism of white male authority is "unfair" because "minority" and "female" authority is not also being challenged. Through the erasure of history, this logic becomes the grounds for the argument that white men are the "new minority." He is unfairly singled out and "discriminated" against for a set of qualities over which he has no control.

2. We use parentheses to signify that some authors cited here are designating a particular form of femininity: white femininity.

3. By "proximal," we mean to evoke various forms of closeness that constitute the relationship between white femininity and white masculinity: spatial (these identity groups most frequently are depicted as sharing social localities, such as home and workplace); emotional (white women and men are figured through binds of family, friendship, and profession), and sexual (white women are produced as the primary and legitimate sexual partners of white men) (see Richard Dyer 1997; Hurtado 1996).

4. Lynch's most recent film, *Mulholland Drive*, is both a thematic reiteration of *Lost Highway*, as well as a departure. In the former, Lynch draws upon themes of truth and memory, as well as the critical theme of "crisis" that makes *Lost Highway* turn. The shift between the films involves the shifting subject and object of victimization. In *Mulholland Drive* white femininity occupies the subject position of crisis, as the white female character falls victim to her (apparently) Latina lover. Just as white woman must die in *Lost Highway* for victimizing white men, brown woman must die in *Mulholland Drive* for victimizing white woman. Lynch's critique reveals the power dynamics of victimization that take place between white women and women of color as the latter have increasingly been vocal critics of the former, especially in feminist contexts. This shift in the subject of crisis also reveals the broader implications of white masculinity in crisis: that white women must ally themselves with white men, and the white male establishment, if they are to benefit from the broader racial gains secured by white victimage (i.e. claims by white women that they, like white men, are victims of "racial preferencing" in admissions and hiring practices).

References

Alexander, M. Jacqui and Chandra Mohanty. 1997. *Feminist Genealogies, Colonial Legacies, Democratic Futures*. New York: Routledge.

Alien (video recording). 1979. Ridley Scott (dir.). Gordon Carroll, David Giler, and Walter Hill (prod.).

Alien Resurrection (video recording). 1997. Jean-Pierre Jeunet (dir.). Bill Badalato, Gordon Carroll, David Giler, and Walter Hill (prod.).

Alien3 (video recording). 1992. David Fincher (dir.). Gordon Carroll, David Giler, and Walter Hill (prod.).

Aliens (video recording). 1986. James Cameron (dir.). Gordon Carroll, David Giler, and Walter Hill (prod.).

Ansen, David. 1997. "Film Clips: *Alien Resurrection*." *Newsweek*, December 1: 90.

Bannerji, Himani. 1993. *Returning the Gaze: Essays on Racism, Feminism, and Politics*. Toronto: Sister Vision.

Blue Velvet (video recording). 1986. David Lynch (dir.). Fred Caruso and Richard Roth (prod.).

Bowman, James. 1998. "*Alien* Menace." *National Review*, January 26: 35–6.

Brimelow, Peter. 1995. *Alien Nation: Common Sense About America's Immigration Disaster*. New York: HarperCollins.

Bulworth (video recording). 1998. Warren Beatty (dir.). Warren Beatty, Pieter Jan Brugge, and Lauren Shuler-Donner (prod.).

Cohen, Marshall. 1977. *Equality and Preferential Treatment*. Princeton, NJ: Princeton University.

Demolition Man (video recording). 1993. Marco Brambilla (dir.). Howard Kazanijan, Michael Levy, and Joel Silver (prod.).

Denby, David. 1997. "Movies: Garden Variety." *New York*, December 1: 120–1.

Dyer, Richard. 1997. *White*. London and New York: Routledge.

Ewing, Dale E., Jr. 1999. "Film Noir: Style and Content," in Alain Silver and James Ursini (eds.) *Film Noir: Reader*, pp. 73–84. New York: Limelight Edition.

Falling Down (video recording). 1992. Joel Schumacher (dir.). Arnon Milchan (prod.).

Farber, Stephen. 1999. "Violence and the Bitch Goddess," in Alain Silver and James Ursini (eds.) *Film Noir: Reader 2*, pp. 45–56. New York: Limelight Edition.

Fight Club (video recording). 1999. David Fincher (dir.). Arnon Milchan (prod.).

Forrest Gump (video recording). 1994. Robert Zemeckis (dir.). Wendy Finerman, Steve Starkey, and Steve Tisch (prod.).

Frankenberg, Ruth. 1993. *White Women, Race Matters: The Social Construction of Whiteness*. Minneapolis: University of Minnesota.

Gates, David. 1993. "White Male Paranoia." *Newsweek*, March 29: 48–54.

Giroux, Henry. 2001. "Private Satisfactions and Public Disorders: Fight Club, Patriarchy, and the Politics of Masculine Violence." *jac* 21 (1): 1–32.

Goldman, Alan H. 1979. *Justice and Reverse Discrimination*. Princeton, NJ: Princeton University Press.

Good Will Hunting (video recording). 1997. Gus Van Sant (dir.). Lawrence Bender (prod.).

Grand Canyon (video recording). 1991. Lawrence Kasdan (dir.). Michael Grillo, Lawrence Kasdan, and Charles Okun (prod.).

Greenwalt, Kent. 1979. *Discrimination and Reverse Discrimination: Essay and Materials in Law and Philosophy*. Chicago: Commission on Undergraduate Education in Law and the Humanities of the American Bar Association.

Gross, Barry R. 1977. *Reverse Discrimination*. Buffalo, NY: Prometheus Books.

Handy, Bruce. 1998. "The Viagra Craze." *Time*, May 4: 50–7.

Harris, Hilary. 2000. "Failing 'White Woman': Interrogating the Performance of Respectability." *Theatre Journal* 52 (2): 183–209.

Hastings, Matthew. 1997. "Back to Life." *Film Review*, December: 32–9.

Hirsch, Foster. 1999. *Detours and Lost Highways: A Map of Neo-noir*. New York: Limelight.

hooks, bell. 1992. *Eating the Other: Desire and Resistance, Black Looks*. Boston: South End.

Hurtado, Aida. 1996. *The Color of Privilege: Three Blasphemies on Race and Feminism*. Ann Arbor: University of Michigan.

Ice Storm, The (video recording). 1997. Ang Lee (dir.). Ted Hope, Ang Lee, and James Schamus (prod.).

Jeffords, Susan. 1987. "Battle of the Big Mommas: Feminism and Alienation." *Journal of American Culture* 10 (3): 73–84.

Jeffords, Susan. 1994. *Hard Bodies: Hollywood Masculinity in the Reagan Era*. New Brunswick, NJ: Rutgers University.

Kavanaugh, J. H. 1980. "Son of a Bitch: Feminism, Humanism, and Science in *Alien*." *October* 13 (Summer): 90–100.

Kennedy, Liam. 1996. "Alien Nation: White Male Paranoia and Imperial Culture in the United States." *Journal of American Studies* 30 (1): 87–100.

Kipnis, Kenneth. 1977. *Philosophical Issues in Law: Cases and Materials*. Englewood Cliffs, NJ: Prentice-Hall.

Kurt and Courtney (video recording). 1998. Nick Broomfield (dir.). Michael D'Acosta and Tine Van Den Brande (prod.).

Lane, Anthony. 1997. "Current Cinema: Under Siege." *New Yorker*, December 1: 101–2.

Lazarre, Jane. 1996. *Beyond the Whiteness of Whiteness: Memoir of a White Mother of Black Sons*. Durham, NC: Duke University Press.

Lev, Peter. 1998. "Whose Future? Star Wars, Alien and Blade Runner." *Film Literature Quarterly* 26 (1): 30–9.

Lorde, Audre. 1984. *Sister Outsider: Essays and Speeches by Audre Lorde*. Freedom, CA: The Crossing Press.

Lost Highway (video recording). 1997. David Lynch (dir.).

Deepak Nayar, Tom Sternberg, and Mary Sweeney (prod.).

Lynch, Frederick. R. 1989. *Invisible Victims: White Males and the Crisis of Affirmative Action*. New York: Greenwood.

Lyons, Donald. 1997. "La-La Limbo." *Film Commentary* 33 (1): 2–4.

Massey, Doreen. 1994. *Space, Place, and Gender*. Minneapolis: University of Minnesota.

Men in Black (video recording). 1997. Barry Sonnefeld (dir.). Laurie MacDonald and Walter Parkes (prod.).

Mohanty, Chandra Talpade. 1991. "Under Western Eyes: Feminist Scholarship and Colonial Discourses," in Chandra Talpade Mohanty, Ann Russo, and Lourdes Torres (eds.) *Third World Women and the Politics of Feminism*, pp. 51–80. Bloomington and Indianapolis: Indiana University.

Moon, Dreama. 1999. "White Enculturation and Bourgeois Ideology: The Discursive Production of 'Good White Girls,' " in Thomas K. Nakayama and Judith N. Martin (eds.) *Whiteness: The Communication of Social Identity*, pp. 177–97. Thousand Oaks, CA: Sage.

Moraga, Cherríe and Gloria Anzaldúa. 1981. *This Bridge Called My Back: Writings by Radical Women of Color*. New York: Kitchen Table.

Morgenstern, Joe. 1997. "Film: From Weird Science to Real Life." *Wall Street Journal*, November 28: A8.

Mulholland Drive (video recording). 2001. David Lynch (dir.). Pierre Edleman (II) and Neal Edlestein (prod.).

Mulvey, Laura. 1989. *Visual and Other Pleasures*. Bloomington: Indiana University Press.

Newman, Kim. 1997. "Reviews." *Sight and Sound* 7 (December): 36–7.

Newton, Judith. 1980. "Feminism and Anxiety in *Alien* in Symposium on *Alien*." *Science Fiction Studies* 7 (3): 293–7.

Primary Colors (video recording). 1998. Mike Nichols (dir.). Mike Nichols (prod.).

Rhodes, Erik Bryant. 1998. *"Lost Highway." Film Quarterly* 15 (3): 57–61.

Rozen, Leah. 1997. "Screen." *People Weekly*, December 1: 29.

Rushing, Janice. 1995. "Evolution of 'The New Frontier' in *Alien* and *Aliens*: Patriarchal Co-optation of the Feminine Archetype," in Carl. R. Burgchardt (ed.) *Readings in Rhetorical Criticism*, pp. 489–511. State College, PA: Strata Publishing Company.

Saving Private Ryan (video recording). 1998. Steven Spielberg (dir.). Ian Bryce, Mark Gordon, Gary Levinson, and Steven Spielberg (prod.).

Savran, David. 1996. "The Sadomasochist in the Closet: White Masculinity and the Culture of Victimization." *Differences: A Journal of Feminist Cultural Studies* 8 (2): 127–52.

Schickel, Richard. 1997. *"Alien Resurrection*: Less Frightening, but as Much Fun as Ever." *Time*, December 1: 84.

Torry, Robert. 1994. "Awakening to the Other: Feminism and the Ego-Ideal in *Alien." Women's Studies* 23: 343–63.

Unforgiven (video recording). 1992. Clint Eastwood (dir.). Clint Eastwood (prod.).

Vaughn, Thomas. 1995. "Voices of Sexual Distortion: Rape, Birth, and Self-annihilation Metaphors in the *Alien Trilogy." The Quarterly Journal of Speech* 81 (4): 423–35.

Ware, Vron. 1992. *Beyond the Pale: White Women, Racism, and History.* New York: Verso. Yahoo!Movies. "Lost High-way—Reviews." On-line. Available:http://movies.yahoo.com/shop?d = hv&cf = info&id = 1800023131&intl-us (April 2, 1997).

20.
BRAIN, BROW, AND BOOTY
Latina Iconicity in U.S. Popular Culture
Isabel Molina Guzmán and Angharad N. Valdivia

We were shooting on the steps of the Metropolitan Museum one night. It was lit romantically, and Jennifer was wearing an evening gown, looking incredibly stunning. Suddenly there must have been a thousand people screaming her name. *It was like witnessing this icon.* (Ralph Fiennes in the *New York Times*, 2002, p. 16, emphasis added)

This stamp, honoring a Mexican artist who has transcended "la frontera" and *has become an icon to Hispanics, feminists, and art lovers, will* be a further reminder of the continuous cultural contributions of Latinos to the United States. (Cecilia Alvear, President of National Association of Hispanic Journalists (NAHJ) on the occasion of the introduction of the Frida Kahlo U.S. postage stamp; 2001; emphasis added)

"Nothing Like the Icon on the Fridge." (column about Salma Hayek's *Frida* by Stephanie Zacharek in the *New York Times*, 2002)

The iconic location of Latinas and their articulation into commodity culture is an inescapable affirmation of the increasing centrality of Latinidad and Latinas to U.S. popular culture. We live in an age when Latinidad, the state and process of being, becoming, and/or appearing Latina/o, is the "It" ethnicity and style in contemporary U.S. mainstream culture. This construction of Latinidad is transmitted primarily, though not exclusively, through the mainstream media and popular culture. We also continue to live in an age

when women function as a sign, a stand-in for objects and concepts ranging from nation to beauty to sexuality (Rakow & Kranich, 1991). This article examines the representational politics surrounding three hypercommodified Latinas in contemporary U.S. culture, Salma Hayek, Frida Kahlo, and Jennifer Lopez. We recognize there is growing cadre of women currently circulating through U.S. popular culture, such as Cameron Diaz and Penélope Cruz, who are sometimes identified by media producers as Latinas despite their problematic location within that social identity.[1] Nevertheless, the three women central to this analysis are foreground in relation to their Latinidad and respective identities as Puerto Ricans and Mexicans. Furthermore, these three women, more so than Cruz and Diaz, are most often inscribed by journalists and other media professionals within the visual and narrative tropes associated with female Latinidad. Thus, in this project, we focus on the contemporary representations of Hayek, Kahlo, and Lopez in order to explore the gendered and racialized signifiers surrounding Latinidad and Latina iconicity; and investigate the related processes of producing and policing Latina bodies and identities in mainstream texts such as films and magazines.

Decades of research on ethnic, racial, and feminist media studies demonstrate that there exists the tendency to racialize and genderize media representations (Aparicio and Chavez-Silverman, 1997; Fregoso, 1993; Lopez, 1991; Perez-Firmat, 1994; C. E. Rodriguez, 1997; Ramirez-Berg, 2002; Shohat and Stam, 1994). The concurrent processes of racialization and gendering render feminized images less powerful and valuable than masculine images, often resulting in a double-edged construction of femininity and otherness. As a result, the female ethnic subject is othered through its categorization and marginalization in relation to dominant constructions of Whiteness and femininity, and the male ethnic subject is othered through its categorization and marginalization in relation to dominant constructions of Whiteness and masculinity. In other words, Latinos are generally devalued and feminized, and Latinas fall beyond the margins of socially acceptable femininity and beauty. By examining popular representations of Latina identity and physicality, we explore the representational dialectic created through the linked processes of racialization and gendering.

Specifically, this article bridges the theoretical approaches of Feminist Media Studies and Latina/o Studies with recent scholarship on hybridity and transnational identities (Bhabha, 1994; Brah & Coomber, 2000; García Canclini, 1995; Valdivia, 2003; Werbner & Modood, 1997). We begin by contextualizing the contemporary situation of Latina/os and Latinidad within U.S. media and popular culture, and continue by locating Hayek, Kahlo, and Lopez within the terrain of Latina iconicity. Next we examine popular representations of Hayek, Kahlo, and Lopez in order to study dominant signifiers of Latinidad and Western discourses of femininity and sexuality as well as the resulting racialized prescriptions of Latina bodies and sexuality in contemporary popular culture. Following an analysis of the representational tension between the use of Latina bodies for the commodification of ethnic authenticity and the symbolic resistance embodied in hybridized Latina bodies, identities, and cultures, we conclude by theorizing how contemporary Latina iconicity connects to broader transformative notions of transnational identities in order to problematize Western gendered and racialized narratives of ethnicity and to theorize beyond them.

Contextualizing Latina/os and Latinidad in the United States

While it is important to remember that the United States historically has been a multiracial and multiethnic society, according to the 2000 U.S. Census those identifying as Hispanic increased by 38.8% from the 1990 U.S. Census creating major demographic shifts

throughout the United States. The proportion of the population that identifies as Hispanic or Latina/o is increasing by a rate five times faster than the rest of the population. By contrast 1971 was the last year Anglo Americans reproduced at a rate that maintained their proportion of the total population (Hacker, 2000). In California, the most populated state in the United States, "non-Hispanic Whites" are no longer the majority racial group, and Latina/os have surpassed African Americans as the second largest ethnic-racial group in the United States (U.S. Census Reports, 2003). From politicians to media marketing specialists, mainstream U.S. institutions are slowly recognizing the social, economic and political presence and power of one of the fastest growing ethnic groups. (Russell Sage Foundation, 2002).

Nevertheless, U.S. Latina/o identity is a complex and contradictory post-colonial panethnic construction. Although the social formation of Latina/os as a panethnic group is recent and the label itself remains problematic and contested, the use of the terms Latina/o and Latinidad are gaining scholarly and political exigency (Darder & Torres, 1998; Flores, 2000; Oboler, 1995). As a demographic category, Latinidad describes any person currently living in the United States of Spanish-speaking heritage from more than 30 Caribbean and Latin America countries. It is an imagined community of recent, established and multi-generational immigrants from diverse cultural, linguistic, racial, and economic backgrounds. Within Latina/o studies scholarship there is much tension surrounding the use of this emerging ethnic identity category. Whereas Juan Flores (2000) asserts that Latina/o is nearly always an identity, a subjectivity, that is partially complete, so that one identifies as a Mexican-American Latina or a Chilean Latina or a Puerto Rican/Dominican Latina, Achy Obejas (2001) counters that we now have a growing community of Latina/os who identify themselves specifically as Latina/os. Long-standing roots in the United States as well as a diverse mixture of backgrounds and affiliations make such an identity possible.

As such, Latinidad epitomizes the contemporary situation of globalization and hybridity that partially defines the lived and symbolic experiences of transnational communities (Shome & Hedge, 2002a, 2002b). This dynamic, celebratory, and contested concept of Latinidad allows us to explore a broad range of popular signifiers associated with representations of Latina/o identity in the United States. We frame Latinidad as a social construct informed by the mediated circulation of ethnic-specific community discourses and practices as well as mainstream economic and political imperatives through the cultural mainstream. Thus Latinidad is a category constructed from the outside with marketing and political homogenizing implications as well as from within with assertions to difference and specificity.

Latina Iconicity in U.S. Popular Culture

The contemporary demographic shift in the United States, popularly dubbed the "browning of America," is causing the U.S. government and corporations to rethink hegemonic constructions of U.S. citizenship, marketing, and consumption (Dávila, 2000; Halter, 2000). For the past 20 years Latina/o marketing and advertising agencies have worked diligently to reframe dominant discourses about the U.S. Latino audience as ethnically homogenous, racially non-White, Spanish-dominant, socioeconomically poor and most often of Mexican origin (Astroff, 1997; Dávila, 2000; A. Rodriguez, 1999). Slowly Latina/o marketing professionals are redefining mainstream industry perceptions about the U.S. Latina/o audience by highlighting actual and projected increases in the U.S. Latina/o population; the commercial profits from dual language marketing; and, the existence of more than one million Latino/a households with incomes of more than $50,000 living in the United States (Sinclair, 1999).[2]

In the overall climate of "shopping for ethnicities" corporations are moderately increasing spending levels on "Hispanic" marketing (Goodson & Shaver, 1994; Halter, 2000). Additionally, strong demand from Latin American audiences for U.S. programming and from U.S. Latino/a audiences for more inclusive programming are increasing the production of film and television shows that appeal to audiences across a matrix of race, ethnicity, gender, and class. Beginning with Warner Brother's 1997 release of *Selena*, starring Jennifer Lopez, Hollywood has realized the potential of movies that target Latin American and U.S. Latino/a audiences, as well as a spectrum of ethnic and racial categories. Throughout the past few years Latina/o faces also have appeared in increasing numbers on television programming. ABC's *George Lopez Show* (2002) featuring a multiethnic Cuban and Mexican-American family is one of the network's more popular prime time situation comedies. Gregory Nava's dramatic PBS series *American Family* (2001) featuring a Los Angeles Chicana family continues to receive wide critical acclaim. Nick Jr.'s *Dora the Explorer* has been a resounding success in the preschool television market with a broad spectrum of synergistically successful products ranging from books and toys to clothing and food. In 2001 Jay Leno hosted Los Aterciopelados, a Colombian rock band who sing and speak only in Spanish; and in 2000, CBS and its Spanish-language network affiliates aired the first live Spanish-language program on U.S. prime-time television, the National Academy of Recording Arts and Sciences Latin Grammies. Celia Cruz's death in the summer of 2003 was covered by all mainstream news and entertainment outlets. The success of films, television shows, and popular music featuring Latina/os demonstrate the viability of Latina/o programming with both Latina/o and general audiences.

Given the media industry's growing interest in Latina/o artists, culture, consumers, and audiences, the iconic position of Latinas within U.S. popular culture presents a critical space from which to study the racialized and gendered construction of meaning surrounding transnational identities and hybrid bodies. Iconicity, as a form of representation, involves the transformation of meaning that arises through the interactive relationship between an image, the practices surrounding the production of that image, and the social context within which the image is produced and received by audiences. As Giles and Middleton (2000) propose it is not so much that iconic images communicate a specific meaning or message, but that they "resignify" the meanings surrounding a particular image, event or issue through their circulation in popular culture. Within contemporary U.S. popular culture, three women—Salma Hayek, Frida Kahlo, and Jennifer Lopez—have gained iconic status as representatives of feminine Latinidad. In other words, popular representations of each woman communicate more than the visuals, instead the images are invited to sign-in for mainstream narratives about Latina identity and sexuality. The rest of this article analyzes the representational politics surrounding these three Latinas in order to examine the ways that they signify Latinidad and Latinas as a whole. Simultaneously, we problematize the homogenizing narratives of Latina iconicity circulated through U.S. popular culture by highlighting the lived and symbolic differences between Hayek, Kahlo, and Lopez.

Jennifer Lopez

At $13 million dollars per movie, Lopez is the highest paid Latina identified actress in Hollywood history. The industry's recognition of her box-office draw places her in a unique category in relation to other actresses like Michelle Rodriguez, Salma Hayek, and Penélope Cruz, and African American actresses like Halle Berry, Vanessa Williams, and Angela Bassett. Unlike Cameron Diaz whose Latinidad remains relatively invisible by virtue of her proximity to and performance of Whiteness, Lopez has explicitly highlighted and in some instances subverted her malleable ethnic and racial identity. In unprecedented fashion Lopez has catapulted her on-screen image to multiple domains most notably the music, clothing, lingerie, perfume, and television industries. Like other actors seeking greater control through interventions behind the camera, Lopez has started her own production company Nuyorican Films. With three hit albums and a string of successful Hollywood films and spectacular romances, as well as the requisite bomb *Gigli* (2003), Lopez (a.k.a. La Lopez, J-Lo or Jenny from the Block) remains a rare film/music/dance sensation. Cosmetic and fashion line deals pushed Lopez's projected $35 million per year income into the number 12 spot on *Forbes'* (2002) top 25 list of U.S. entertainers. New perfume and fashion lines as well as forthcoming films and albums are part of a carefully orchestrated effort to remain at the forefront of the mainstream. It is impossible to predict whether these efforts will prove successful in terms of an enduring career, but contemporarily J-Lo continues to grace more magazine covers than most any other star.

Salma Hayek

The fall 2002 release of *Frida* by Miramax catapulted its producer and star Salma Hayek onto the cover of U.S. magazines, ranging from *Parade* to *Elle*. Her success in Mexican soap operas inspired Hayek to cross the entertainment border, where her first Hollywood role was a 30-second stint as a sultry and angry Chicana ex-girlfriend in Alison Ender's 1993 film *Mi Vida Loca*. As Hayek's hair has gotten progressively straighter and thus more "Anglo"-looking, her on-screen image also has become less stereotypically ethnic, consequently yielding more complex supporting and leading roles. While not achieving the multimedia profile of Lopez, Hayek is one of the most prolific contemporary Latinas in Hollywood, recently earning an Oscar nomination for her role in *Frida*, a rare achievement perceived as recognition of an actress's skill and talent. Like Rosie Perez, Hayek's inability to subvert the linguistic accent that clearly marks her as ethnically different limits the roles available to her. Despite the problematic nature of ethnically pure notions of identity, Hayek is using her accent and Spanish fluency to promote herself as "the authentic" Hollywood Latina thereby privileging her ethnicity in relation to other Latina performers, like Diaz and Lopez (Molina Guzmán, 2007). Because of Hayek's growing discomfort with the roles available to her, she founded her own production company, which among other projects produced *In the Time of the Butterflies* (2001) and directed *El Maldonado Miracle* (2003) for Showtime Television.

Frida Kahlo

Although we recognize that Kahlo differs from Hayek and Lopez along several dimensions, she occupies the representational foreground in contemporary mainstream popular culture in a very complex manner. One of the ironic ways through which Latina and Latin American women reach fame in U.S. mainstream culture, despite reaching fame while alive elsewhere, is through death—Evita, Selena, Frida, and Celia Cruz being prominent examples (Fusco, 1995). Decades after her death, Kahlo is one of the most popular and commodified mainstream images of Latinidad globally, and in the United States particularly. One can find Frida Kahlo stationery, posters, jewelry, hair clips, autobiographies, cookbooks, biographical books, chronological art books, refrigerator magnets, painting kits, wall hangings, and wrapping paper, to mention a few of the items in bookstores and novelty stores throughout the U.S., Mexico, Puerto Rico, and Spain. Kahlo exhibits, such as "Diego y Frida: Amores y Desamores," held at the Centro Cultural de Madrid; La Casa Azul in Coyoacan, Mexico (Kahlo's blue home); and assorted other collections, draw on a growing transnational fan base. Images of Kahlo circulate from the popular, in the form of U.S. Postal Service reproduction of her artwork, to the elite in the form of museum exhibits and special collections. Her paintings received the highest ever bid for a Latin American artwork auctioned at the prestigious House of Sotheby. Highlighting Kahlo's representational significance Hayek and Lopez raced to release biopics of the artists.[3] Thus, it is not so much the art works themselves, including her own self-representational images, in which we are interested, but rather how Kahlo the symbol transcends the high and low culture divide by signing in for Latina identity and authenticity.

Racializing Latina Bodies and Sexuality in U.S. Popular Culture

One of the most enduring tropes surrounding the signification of Latinas in U.S. popular culture is that of tropicalism (Aparicio & Chavez-Silverman, 1997; Perez-Firmat, 1994). Tropicalism erases specificity and homogenizes all that is identified as Latin and Latina/o. Under the trope of tropicalism, attributes such as bright colors, rhythmic music, and brown or olive skin comprise some of the most enduring stereotypes about Latina/os, a stereotype best embodied by the excesses of Carmen Miranda and the hypersexualization of Ricky Martin. Gendered aspects of the trope of tropicalism include the male Latin lover, macho, dark-haired, mustachioed, and the spitfire female Latina characterized by red-colored lips, bright seductive clothing, curvaceous hips and breasts, long brunette hair, and extravagant jewelry. The tropes of tropicalism extend beyond those people with Caribbean roots to people from Latin American, and recently to those in the United States with Caribbean and/or Latin American roots.

Sexuality plays a central role in the tropicalization of Latinas through the widely circulated narratives of sexual availability, proficiency, and desirability (Valdivia, 2000). For centuries the bodies of women of color, specifically their genitals and buttocks, have been excessively sexualized and exoticized by U.S. and European cultures (Gilman, 1985). Not surprisingly popular images of Latinas and the Latina body focus primarily on the area below the navel, an urbane corporeal site with sexualized overdetermination (Desmond, 1997). Within the Eurocentric mind/body binary, culture is signified by the higher intellectual functions of the mind/brain while nature is signified by the lower biological functions of the body. That is, Whiteness is associated with a disembodied intellectual tradition free from the everyday desires of the body, and non-Whiteness is associated with nature and the everyday needs of the body to consume food, excrete waste, and reproduce sexually. Dominant representations of Latinas and African American women are predominately characterized by an emphasis on the breasts, hips, and buttocks. These body parts function as mixed signifiers of sexual desire and fertility as well as bodily waste and racial contamination.

Contemporary Latina iconicity inherits traces of this dichotomous representational terrain. Despite Jennifer Lopez's multimedia successes, it is her buttocks insured by Lopez for $1 billion that most journalists and Lopez herself foregrounds. Like other popular Latinas, Lopez is simultaneously celebrated and denigrated for her physical, bodily, and financial excess. Whenever she appears in the popular press, whether it is a newspaper, a news magazine, or *People*, Lopez's gorgeous stereotypical Latina butt is glamorized and sexually fetishized. Indeed, she is often photographed in profile or from the back looking over her shoulders—her buttocks becoming the focus of the image, the part of her body that marks Lopez as sexy but different from Anglo female bodies. Lopez's bootie is marked as unusually large, abnormal, irregular, and by implication not Anglo-Saxon (Barrera, 2000; Beltrán, 2002; Negrón-Mutaner, 2000). Despite the successful marketing of her curves, Lopez recognizes the discourse of exotic otherness that surrounds her body. While Lopez continues to use her increasingly thinning body to commodify herself, she is also becoming frustrated with the U.S. media's obsession with the state, weight, and firmness of her butt (Beltrán, 2002).

Likewise, while news media images of Lopez foreground her buttocks, photographs of Hayek emphasize her bountiful breasts, small waist, and round hips. Hayek's petite yet hyper-curvaceous frame embodies the romanticized stereotypical Latina hourglass shape, a petite ethnic shape that stands in opposition to the resonances of blackness surrounding Lopez's hyper-buttocks and music video representations. Profile shots of Hayek in movies and magazine covers show both her breasts and her perfectly shaped booty. Frontal shots of Hayek's body highlight her deep cleavage as well as her long dark hair, worn straightened when performing a more glamorous image, and by implication Anglo identity, or curly when performing a more exotic ethnic identity.

Accompanying images of her body are journalistic texts that ultimately frame Hayek's body and identity within narratives of Latinidad, in particular references to her personality, voracious appetite, and loud, talkative nature. Thus, unlike Lopez whose sexualized image primarily foregrounds her racialized booty, sexualized representations of Hayek center on her body as the stereotyped performance of Latina femininity. However, regardless of the dichotomy in news media representations between the sexual excessiveness of Lopez and the sexual femininity of Hayek, with the exception of Lopez's roles in *Blood and Wine* (1996) and *U-Turn* (1997), cinematically it is Lopez who most often is allowed to perform "Whiteness." Although Lopez is the professional singer and dancer, it is Hayek who is depicted sexually gyrating to music in *54* (1998), *Dogma* (1999), *Dusk Till Dawn* (1996), and *Wild Wild West* (1999). Dance, especially the type involving movement below the waist, is often racialized and sexualized within mainstream U.S. culture and not surprisingly linked with the dynamic construction of Latinidad (Aparicio, 1998; Desmond, 1997; Valdivia, 2001).

The marginalization of Latina bodies is defined by an ideological contradiction—that is, Latina beauty and sexuality is marked as other, yet it is that otherness that also marks Latinas as desirable. In other words, Latina desirability is determined by their signification as a racialized, exotic Others. For example, in the movies *Blood and Wine* and *U-Turn* Lopez's body is framed as animalistic, primitive, and irresistibly dangerous to the Anglo American male characters. In both movies, Lopez's body is fetishized through extreme close-ups of her eyes, lips, breasts, legs and buttocks, visuals

that often link her highly sexualized body to the physical environment around her. Similarly, Hayek's characters in *From Dusk Till Dawn* (1996), *54*, and *Timecode* (2000) construct the ethnic feminine other as a temptress, a source of sexual and racial contamination, whose sexuality ultimately destroys her.

Consequently, representations of Hayek's body provide a symbolic bridge between the racialized and sexualized narrative of Lopez's buttocks and the ethnic and desexualized narrative of Kahlo's self-representations of her physically injured body. Whereas Lopez's body, especially her butt, signifies a racialized exotic sexuality, Kahlo's body asserts her ethnicity and foregrounds her identity beyond or outside of her sexuality. Portraits and images of Kahlo emphasize her face, in particular her hyper-eyebrow as a signifier of ethnic-difference, feminine-strength, and intellectual rather than bodily work. Nevertheless, intellectual efforts by Kahlo to complicate both her identity and Latina body do not necessarily transfer into twenty-first century commodifying practices. Instead we get the reification of difference through the everyday commodification of her face in the form of earrings, shirts, and other mainstream products, and her intellectual labor is resignified as aberrant and exotic. Within these popular products, the emphasis on her colorful-ethnic dress and facial hair, both physical markers of ethnic bodies, work to mediate her ethnic identity for capitalist consumption. In the end, the physical representations of all three women are informed by the racializing discourses of ethnic female bodies as simultaneously physically aberrant, sexually desirable, and consumable by the mainstream. These discourses cannot be examined outside of a framework of analysis that allows for fluidity and mixture.

Hybridity, Authenticity, and the Latina Body

Hybridity as a theoretical concept is particularly significant for analyzing popular representations of ethnic populations whose histories of colonialism and imperialism have resulted in the continuing construction of what Homi Bhabha defined as the "third space," Gloria Anzaldúa has called *nepantla*, and Mary Louise Pratt has termed "the contact zone" or that space where bodies and identity resist stable categories, and meaning is ambivalent, contradictory, and historically shifting. Critical hybridity theory explores the cultural arrangements and expressions arising from transcultural and intercultural exchanges between members of different social, political, and economic powers within and between particular communities (Kraidy, 2002). The contemporary experience of Latinas, which also holds true of other populations shaped by colonialism, globalization, and transnationalism, is informed by the complex dynamics of hybridity as a cultural practice and expression (García Canclini, 1995). Latinidad gains its postcolonial exigency, not from the ideological stability of dominant social classifications, but through the cultural, ethnic, and racial fluidity of Latina/o identity. Thus, Latina/o identity, as a hybrid form within U.S. culture, remaps dominant hierarchies of identity and challenges popular notions of place and nation.

Due to their mixed cultural and ethnic heritage, Hayek, Kahlo, and Lopez as hybrid women often problematize and work against the discursive field of popular ethnic and racial categories. While remaining at the margins of representations of whiteness, they also exist outside the marginalizing borders of blackness. Instead, they occupy a racialized space in between the dominant U.S. binary of Black or White identities. Given their dark, full-bodied hair, brown eyes, somatically olive skin, and a range of more or less European facial features, they are physically "any-woman"—with the perception of their identity determined both by the context of reception and the relationally encoded setting of production. Moreover, this undetermined space extends to the categorization of their ethnic backgrounds. Because of their hybrid cultural and personal histories none of the women can lay claim to an authentically pure ethnic identity, rather they may claim or reject a multiplicity of ethnic identities—Mexicana, Chicana, Latina, Nuyorican, Puerto Rican, "American." The ability to occupy and shift between racial and ethnic categories ruptures dominant identity discourses while the commodification of ethnicity within mainstream U.S. popular culture reifies difference.

Not coincidentally, within the realm of cinematic discourse Hayek and Lopez have portrayed characters whose ethnic identity is ambiguous and peripheral to the role, text and narrative action of particular movies. In at least five movies, *Dogma, Enough* (2002),

Out of Sight (1998), *Timecode* (2000), and *Gigli* (2003) Hayek and Lopez perform characters whose ethnic and/or racial identity are "absent" from the text. This narrative absence has proven historically difficult if not impossible for actresses who explicitly identify as African American and are always already marked by the relatively fixed discourse of Blackness in the United States. This is not to say that Lopez's and Hayek's race or ethnicity are not read by audiences, but rather that the dominant discourse of racial otherness is displaced within the narrative and replaced with a more complicated signification of ethnic-otherness. For instance, in at least seven films, Hayek's *54* and *From Dusk Till Dawn* and Lopez's *Anaconda* (1997), *The Cell* (2000), *Angel Eyes* (2001), and *Maid in Manhattan* (2003) the ethnicity of the characters is only subtly referenced through contextual signifiers like the character's name, splices of Spanish dialog, or passing references between characters. Lopez fought for her character in *Anaconda*, initially cast as an Anglo woman, to have a Spanish surname—Terry Flores a "home girl from the Southside of L.A." In addition to *Selena* (1997), Lopez also portrays the Mexican immigrant Maria Sanchez in *Mi Familia* (1995); in *U-Turn* she portrays a part Native-American woman; and in *The Wedding Planner* she plays a second-generation Italian American. In perhaps her most ethnically stereotypical role, the working class, single mom, hotel maid in *Maid in Manhattan*, the character's Latinidad is communicated only through splice of Spanish language, such as the use of phrases like *mi hija* or *papi*, her ethnically marked mother, and her ethnically ambiguous surname, Ventura. Likewise, although her character's ethnic identity is never mentioned, Hayek's character in *54* is identified as Latina only through her Spanish given-name, Anita. Together Hayek and Lopez are provided an unprecedented space for signification not overtly determined by racial or other physical markers of difference.

However the ability of Hayek, Lopez, and other Latina actresses to shift across racial and ethnic representations is limited by language as an additional signifier of difference, especially for Latinas whose skin tone may not be "colored" enough to create ethnic or racial ambiguity. Like the ethnically ambiguous star of James Cameron's hit sci-fi series *Dark Angel* (2000), Jennifer Lopez's English-language fluency and the lack of an accent that can be clearly coded as Spanish, and therefore coded as racial-other in the United States, allows her access to a range of cinematic texts that would normally be slated for Anglo actresses. For example, Lopez's agent convinced the producer of *The Wedding Planner* (2001), who did not want to recast it as a Latina role, that she could play the non-Latina character originally scripted as Eastern European. More so than Hayek, Lopez has tapped into the ability to perform a panethnic other in order to meet Hollywood's desire for the commodified exotic other. On the other hand, Salma Hayek directed actors to perform accents in the *Frida* (2002) movie in order to signify Latinidad in an effort to assert authenticity even though the movie was filmed in English. Thus, the accent that often serves as a professional barrier for Hayek is reframed to provide her with the role of a lifetime. Like the everyday practices of some Latina/os, language can be and is often used in a multiplicity of ways depending on the specific situation.

Despite the emancipatory potential of hybrid bodies within U.S. popular culture, Hayek and Lopez are often caught within intra-Latina conflicts over ethnic specificity and authenticity. Because of the homogenizing constructions of Latina ethnicity circulated in U.S. mainstream popular culture, the actresses themselves have sometimes engaged in a battle over who is the true or authentic Latina in order to win coveted roles. For instance, the selection of Lopez to play the role of Selena was highly criticized by Mexican American activists who wanted a Mexican American actress. Although Lopez was born in the United States, her parents are of Puerto Rican origin. By alternating between identifying herself as Puerto Rican, Nuyorican, and "American," Lopez exemplifies the transnational identity of most U.S. Latina/os. Both women, one Nuyorican and the other Tejana, embody the emerging politics of Latina/o identity (Aparicio, 2003) by problematizing mainstream tendencies toward homogenization and the erasure of difference. More recently the conflict over the *Frida* biopic foregrounds the tension between Latina panethnicity and ethnic authenticity lived through Lopez as an U.S. Nuyorican and Hayek as a Mexican woman. Whereas Lopez refused to engage in the public discussion over Latina and Mexican authenticity by privileging her identity as a Latina and the shared experiences of Latinas, Hayek waged a publicity campaign explicitly arguing that she as the "true" Mexican should be the one to portray Kahlo's life. In an interview foregrounding the debate over authenticity, Hayek stated:

> I don't believe in the so-called Latino explosion when it comes to movies. Jennifer Lopez doesn't have an accent. She grew up in New York speaking English and not Spanish. Her success is very important because she represents a different culture, but it doesn't help me. I grew up in Mexico, not the U.S., and the fact is that there just aren't any parts for Latin actresses. I have to persuade people that my accent won't be a problem.
>
> (http://www.imbd.com, 2001)

Ironically, Hayek did not engage in similar arguments when she auditioned for the role of Selena, a Tejana who did not speak Spanish, or the lead role as an Indian woman in the cinematic adaptation of Salman Rushdie's *The Ground Beneath Her Feet*. Like Kahlo and Lopez, Hayek's identity is itself complicated. Her father is a Lebanese businessman and her mother is Spanish, making her barely a first-generation Mexican. Frida herself was half Mexican and half German-Hungarian and prominently identified herself as Jewish like her father, especially in anti-Semitic circles. Indeed, she actually adopted the clothing and hairstyle most associated with her performance of Mexican ethnicity from indigenous Mexican cultures, which remain economically and politically marginalized.

Moreover, Frida Kahlo's iconicity is itself grounded within narratives of ethnic authenticity that harken back to Latin America as the mother continent. Within this narrative U.S. Latina/os are never authentic, as the boundaries of identity are policed by both the U.S. and specific Latin American national-ethnic cultures. Kahlo is such a powerful signifier of identity because she signs in for the motherland of Latin America in general and Mexico in particular. Central to narratives of the motherland are Eurocentric narratives of authenticity that erase the precolonial experiences of indigenous, African, Asian, and other populations by looking back to Europe, in this particular instance Spain. This Spanish "fantasy heritage," so prevalent in Southwest mid-twentieth century historiography (Garcia, 2001) constructs Spain as the privileged site of whiteness, regardless of the fact that the Spanish empire was fueled by the occupation of the North African Moors and remains a multicultural society (Menocal, 2002). Additionally, this fantasy heritage erases diasporic and hybrid population and cultural traces thus accomplishing the purifying function of myth (Barthes, 1973). Given that Spain is often privileged as the motherland by many Latina/os, it is unsurprising that Penélope Cruz, who does not identify as Latina and foregrounds her Spanish citizenship consistently is treated within the mainstream as a Latina. Moreover, in relation to Jennifer Lopez' embodied butt, Cruz signs in for culture and class rather that exotic nature (Valdivia, 2007). These narratives of authenticity and origin mythologize a pure White Spain as motherland—and that, like all other discourses of purity, proves to be untenable.

Contemporary Latina/o studies interrogates this vexed notion of authenticity. The fact is not all nor most U.S. Latina/os necessarily speak Spanish. For example, pop music sensation Christina Aguilera toyed with the idea of taking the "h" out of her name to more explicitly assert her Latinidad through a traditional Spanish spelling. Musical diva Mariah Carey recently considered recording in Spanish although it would mean learning a new language for her. Jennifer Lopez' much awaited concert broadcast on U.S. television in December 2001 highlighted her less than facile use of the Spanish language. The experiences of Lopez, Carey, and Aguilera as U.S. Latinas are typical in that none of them speak Spanish flawlessly or fluently. The very controversy and tensions in the Latin Grammys over the use of Spanish and the representation of specific Latina/o nationalities underscore and foreground the complex contemporary situation of hybrid communities vis-a-vis discourses of authenticity. Indeed, it is difficult to find a person of pure racial or ethnic identity, and if it were possible Latino communities would not be the place to look for racial or ethnic purity. Although Moraga and Anzaldúa (1981) may not exactly have had this in mind when they edited *This Bridge Called My Back*, Latin American women historically have been forced or have chosen to engage in mixed racial and ethnic relationships. The growing literature on La Malinche,

especially Chicana and Latina feminist scholarship, attests to this history of hybridity by refraining the masculinist framework of sexual and cultural prostitution, of selling out one's body and culture in favor of the progressive and redeeming feminine narrative of inter-cultural translator and creator of a new hybrid, cosmic race (Alarcón, 1994).

Conclusion

Whether we examine women's magazines, television programs, cinematic texts, girl's toys, clothing, pulp fiction, road signs, medical videos, or popular music and dance, it is difficult to avoid the unmistakable presence of Latinidad and its gendered components in mainstream U.S. culture. While these contemporary representations may provide the opportunity for individual Latinas to open spaces for vocality and action, they nevertheless build on a tradition of exoticization, racialization and sexualization, a tradition that serves to position Latinas as continual foreigners and a cultural threat. As such Latinas occupy a liminal space in U.S. popular culture, that is, we can be both marginal and desired. Recently popular representations of Latina booties as large, aberrant yet sexy, desirable, and consumable contribute to the reification of racial dichotomies where Latinas occupy that in between space between the White booty (or the pre-adolescent invisible androgynous White booty) and the Black booty whose excess falls beyond the boundary of acceptability and desirability within U.S. popular culture. For this booty economy to retain its value, popular culture representations of Latinidad must continue to construct that mythical brown race that falls somewhere between Whiteness and Blackness and elides the dynamic hybridity of Latinidad that spans across the entire racial spectrum.

Nevertheless, the representational tensions surrounding the three iconic Latinas highlighted in this article present a potentially emancipatory challenge or at least an unsettling intervention to Eurocentric discourses of racial and ethnic purity. Kahlo, Lopez, and Hayek are an iconic presence that engage the stereotyped representation of Latinas to sell products and open a space from which Latina bodies can vex notions of racial and national purity and therefore authentic ethnicity. Although historically Latina actresses have been relegated to exist within the racialized binary narrative of virgin and whore, popular discourses surrounding Salma Hayek, Frida Kahlo, and Jennifer Lopez disrupt some of Hollywood's symbolic boundaries surrounding ethnicity, race, gender, and sexuality. The commodification of Latinidad has signaled a homogenization of Latinidad and simultaneously provided access to roles previously unavailable to Latinas. Despite the exoticized nature of the representations surrounding the bodies of Lopez and Hayek, they successfully have marketed themselves in order to sell mainstream movie tickets, music, clothing, and perfume.

Furthermore, as transnational figures these three icons exist within the representational conflict between the hybrid and the authentic that many diasporic cultures occupy. Kahlo, a German-Hungarian-Jewish-Mexican, recuperates female sexuality and indigenous Mexican culture as a way of challenging the imperialistic Western gaze. Mainstream circulation of her image reinscribes difference, especially in terms of the ubiquitous unibrow, but also inescapably represents her head, her face, and, through her intellectual efforts, her brain. As such, given binary tendencies in our culture, one would expect Kahlo to exist outside the realm of the sensual. However Hayek's further rerepresentation of Kahlo takes Kahlo into the sensual and sexual thus fully completing her signification as a contemporary iconic Latina. Lopez, a U.S. born Puerto Rican, a Nuyorican, privileges both her U.S. Americanness and her Puerto Ricanness as way of challenging dichotomous discourses and the erasure of Latina bodies in Hollywood films. Repeated affirmations of love and marriage also firmly place her within that Roman Catholic component so predominant in popular constructions of Latinidad. Finally, Hayek, a Lebanese-Mexican, foregrounds the bodies of Latinas themselves as a way of challenging mainstream narratives about women and Latinidad and uses Eurocentric discourses of authenticity to position her self in relation to other iconic Latinas.

Hayek, Kahlo, and Lopez are not simply passive subjects manipulated by the media and popular culture, but transnational women caught in the dialectic between agency and the objectification of identity that operates within many mediated products.

Although the stereotypic representation of Latina sexuality continues, the popular representations of Hayek, Kahlo, and Lopez also problematize emerging constructions of Latinas within dominant discourses about gender, ethnicity, and race. As independent, racially and ethnically undetermined, and transnational women, Latina iconicity ruptures and affirms the borders that surround contemporary popular significations of Latinas they create territorial and deterritorialized images of Latinas that serve as both norm and periphery, of subordination and domination. Latinidad and iconic Latinas render Eurocentric discourses of racial and national purity untenable, and challenge us to acknowledge the uneasy harnessing of transnational, hybrid, and gendered bodies towards a reductionist commodification that exists in tension with a media industry acknowledgments that hybrid bodies are the contemporary site for the production and consumption of identity.

Notes

The authors would like to thank Cameron McCarthy, Lori Reed, and Kumarini Silva for their comments and suggestions to drafts of this article.

1. We recognize that the category "Latina" is fluid and porous. As such, Penélope Cruz, who is Spanish, is often categorized by both the popular press and websites as "Latina." As well, although Cameron Diaz is currently (February 2004) Hollywood's highest paid actress, only *Latina* magazine claims her as Latina. Neither she nor most coverage of her ever mentions her Latinidad.
2. Sinclair (1999) notes that many of these industry officials come from the Latin American media and middle class and reinscribe the outsider status of U.S. Latina/os and U.S. Latina/o popular culture.
3. Madonna also tried to produce a biopic of Kahlo. A Mexican-produced biopic predates all three U.S. attempts.

References

Alarcón, N. (1994). Traddutora, traditora: A paradigmatic figure in Chicana feminism in Grewal. In I. Grewal & C. Kaplan (Eds.), *Scattered hegemonies: Postmodernity and transnational feminist practices* (110–133). Minneapolis, MN: University of Minnesota. Aparicio, F. (1998). *Listening to salsa: Gender, Latino popular music and Puerto Rican culture.* Hanover, NH: Wesleyan Press.

Aparicio, F. (2003). Jennifer as Selena: Rethinking Latinidad in media and popular culture. *Latino Studies*, 190–105. Volume 1, issue 1

Aparicio, F. R., & Chavez-Silverman, S. (Eds.). (1997). *Tropicalizations: Transcultural representations of Latinidad.* Hanover, CT: University Press of New England.

Barrera, M. (2000). Hottentot 2000: Jennifer Lopez and her butt. In K. Phillips & B. Reay (Eds.), *Sexualities in history: A reader* (110–133). New York: Routledge.

Barthes, R. (1973). *Mythologies.* London: Granada.

Beltrán, M. (2002). Jennifer Lopez as Latina star body: The construction of an ambivalent crossover. *Quarterly Review of Film and Video, 19*, 1.

Bhabha, H. (1994). *The Location of Culture.* New York: Routledge.

Brah, A., & Coomber, A. (2000). *Hybridity and its discontents: Politics, science and culture.* New York: Routledge.

Darder, A., & R. Torres. (1998). *The Latino studies reader: Culture, economy and society.* New York: Blackwell.

Dávila, A. (2001). *Latinos, Inc.: The marketing and making of a people.* Berkeley: University of California Press.

Desmond, J. C. (1997). *Meaning in motion: New cultural studies of dance.* Durham, NC: Duke University Press.

Flores, J. (2000). *From bomba to hip hop: Puerto Rican culture and Latino identity.* New York: Columbia University Press.

Fregoso, R. L. (1993). *The bronze screen: Chicana and Chicano film culture.* Minneapolis, MN: University of Minnesota Press.

Fusco, C. (1995). *English is broken here: Notes on cultural fusion in the Americas.* New York: The New Press.

Garcia, M. (2001). *A world of its own: Race, labor, and citrus in the making of greater Los Angeles, 1900–1970.* Chapel Hill, NC: University of North Carolina Press.

García Canclini, N. (1995). *Hybrid cultures: Strategies for entering and leaving modernity.* Minneapolis, MN: University of Minnesota Press.

Giles, J., & Middleton, T. (2000). *Studying culture: A practical introduction.* London: Blackwell.

Gilman, S. (1985). *Difference and pathology: Stereotypes of sexuality, race, and madness.* Ithaca, NY: Cornell University Press.

Goodson, S., & Shaver, M. A. (1994). Hispanic Marketing: national advertiser spending patterns and media choices. *Journalism Quarterly, 71*, 191–198.

Hacker, A. (2000). The case against kids. *The New York Review of Books.* November 30, pp. 12–17.

Halter, M. (2000). *Shopping for identity: The marketing of ethnicity.* New York: Shocken Books.

Hayek, S. (2001). Personal quotes. [Online]. Internet Movie Database. Available: http://___www.us.imdb.com/?Hgyek,+Salma

Hindes, A. (1997). WB betting on appeal of Selena. [Online]. Available: http://www.varieiy.com

Johnson, M. (2000). How ethnic are U.S. ethnic media: The case of *Latina* magazine. *Mass Communication and Society, 3*, 229–248.

Joseph, M., & Fink, J. (1999). *Performing hybridity.* Minneapolis, MN: University of Minnesota Press.

Kennedy, D. (2002). "Holiday Movies; Homegirl, Working Woman, Empire Builder". *The New York Times*, Nov. 3. Section, 2A, p. 16.

Kraidy, M. (2002). Hybridity in cultural globalization. *Communication Theory, 12*(3), 316–339.

López, A. M. (1991). Are all Latins from Manhattan?: Hollywood, ethnography, and cultural colonialism. In L. D. Friedman (Ed.), *Unspeakable images: Ethnicity and the American cinema* (404–424). Urbana, IL: University of Illinois Press.

Menocal, M. R. (2002). *The ornament of the world: How Muslims, Jews, and Christians created a culture of tolerance in medieval Spain.* Boston: Little Brown.

Molina Guzmán, I. (2007). Salma Hayek's *Frida*: Transnational Latina bodies in popular culture. In M. Mendible (Ed.), *From bananas to buttocks: The Latina in popular film and culture* (117–128). Austin, TX: University of Texas Press.

Moraga, C. and G. Anzaldúa. (1981). *This bridge called my back: Writings by radical women of color.* Berkeley, CA. Third Women Press.

Negrón-Mutaner, F. (2000). Jennifer's butt. *Aztlán, 22*(2), 182–195.

Obejas, A. (2001). Carving out a new American identity: Nationalism is an obsolete idea as Latinos outgrow labels. *Chicago Tribune*, September 21, Section 2, pp. 1, 6.

Oboler, S. (1995). *Ethnic labels, Latino lives: Identity and the politics of (re)presentation in the United States.* Minneapolis, MN: University of Minnesota Press.

Perez-Firmat, G. (1994). *Life on the hyphen: The Cuban American way.* Austin, TX: University of Texas Press.

Rakow, L., & Kranich, K. (1991). Woman as sign in television news. *Journal of Communication, 41*, 8–23.

Ramírez Berg, C. (2002). *Latino images in film: Stereotypes, subversion, resistance.* Austin, TX: University of Texas Press.

Rodriguez, A. (1999). *Making Latino news: Race, language, class.* Thousand Oaks, CA: Sage.

Rodriguez, C. E. (1997). *Latin looks: Images of Latinas and Latinos in the U.S. media.* Denver, CO: Westview Press.

Russell Sage Foundation. (2002). Call for Papers. [Online]. Available: http://www.russellsage.org/programs/~roi reviews/immigprop.htmimmigration.htm

Shohat, E. (1998). *Talking visions: Multicultural feminism in a transnational age.* New York: New Museum of Contemporary Art and MIT Press.

Shohat, E., & Stam, R. (1994). *Unthinking Eurocentrism: Multiculturalism and the media.* New York: Routledge.

Shome, R., & Hedge, R. (2002a). Postcolonial approaches to communication: Charting terrain, engaging the intersections. *Communication Theory, 12*(3), 249–286,

Shome, R., & Hedge, R. (2002b). Critical communication and the challenge of globalization. *Critical Studies in Mass Communication, 19*(2), 172–189.

Sinclair, J. (1999). *Latin American television: A global view.* New York: Oxford University Press.

U.S. Census (2003). "Population Estimates Reports." U.S. Census Bureau. http://factfinder. census.gov

Valdivia, A. (2000). *A Latina in the land of hollywood.* Tucson, AZ: University of Arizona Press.

Valdivia, A. (2003). Latina/os as the paradigmatic transnational post-subculture. In D. Muggleton and R. Weinzierl (Eds.), *The post-subcultures reader* (151–167). London: Berg Publishers.

Valdivia, A. (2007). Is Penélope to J-Lo as culture is to nature? Eurocentric approaches to "Latin" beauties. In M. Mendible (Ed.), *Bananas to buttocks: The Latina body in popular culture* (129–148). Austin, TX: University of Texas Press.

Wernber, P., & Modood, T. (1997). *Debating cultural hybridity multi-cultural identities and the politics of anti-racism.* London: Zed Books.

Zacharek, S. (2002). "The new season/movies; Nothing like the Icon on the Fridge." The *New York Times*, Sep. 8. Section ZA, p. 41.

21.
MISSY "MISDEMEANOR" ELLIOTT

Rapping on the Frontiers of Female Identity

Eliza Sellen

Introduction

Missy 'Misdemeanor' Elliott exploded onto the rap music scene in 1997: now, five albums later, she stands as a formidable figure within the rap industry. Described on her website (Elektra, 2002) as a 'multi-media superstar, an artist, producer, writer and business woman', Elliott appears to be the woman who pulls all the strings. Her longstanding musical partnership with producer Tim 'Timberland' Mosely, and her collaboration with video directors such as Hype William and Dave Meyers, has undoubtedly changed both the visual and musical landscape of rap music.

Through this paper I will use two of Elliott's music videos, *One Minute Man* (2001) and *She's a Bitch* (1999), alongside lyrics from two of her albums, as texts that can be critiqued through feminist ideas of identity. The validity of analysing media texts in relation to identity is articulated by Stuart Hall, when he asserts that identity is constituted, 'not outside but within representation' using media texts, 'not as a second-order mirror held up to reflect what already exists, but as a form of representation which is able to constitute us as new kinds of subjects and thereby enables us to discover who we are' (Hall, cited in hooks, 1992, p. 131).

In the first three sections I will establish how Elliott disrupts and appropriates signs of race and sexuality. I will then go on to look at boundaries, both in terms of body boundaries and the boundaries of meaning associated with sign systems. The link between Elliott and boundaries will be concluded through Christine Battersby's work on female patterns of identity. Battersby develops a feminist meta-physics that is able to hold onto identity *and* fluidity, and through this paper I will argue that Elliott gives sustenance and vision to Battersby's notion of a *reconstructed* female identity.

Embodiment and the Gaze

Embodiment and the gaze are central tools of cinematic analysis, bringing with them the arguably gendered acts of looking and pleasure. bell hooks uses Laura Mulvey's (1988) reading of the cinema to highlight the 'absence' of the black female body. For Mulvey, women in film are constructed within a framework that situates men as 'the bearer of the look' (p. 63), the purpose of film being to facilitate masculine pleasure. The classic film techniques discussed by Mulvey involve the compartmentalising effect of the camera on female bodies, focusing on abstract breasts or hips. Yet, as hooks asserts, Mulvey's reading assumes white women as the norm, and as such black female bodies become absent, used by the mainstream film industry as a signifier of the exotic, and as a prop through which normalised white female sexuality is established. However, understanding the media industry as a monolithic force is questioned by Lisa Lewis (1995) in her article *Form and Female Authorship in Music Videos*, where she suggests that there are areas *within* the media that can be manipulated to the advantage of women. Lewis claims that, 'female musicians are actively participating in making the music video form work in their interest, to assert their authority as producers of culture and to air their views on female genderhood' (p. 500).

Given this, Elliott, as a black female rap artist, can be seen as inhabiting a progressive space, and resisting the absence articulated by hooks.

The body and the gaze are central to the analysis of the music video form. Female bodily comportment is heavily proscribed in the media, narrowly defining the acceptable depiction of women. This is illuminated by Iris Marion Young's (1990) essay *Throwing Like a Girl*. Young surmises that, 'the modalities of feminine bodily existence have their root in the fact that feminine existence experiences the body as a mere thing—a fragile thing, which must be picked up and coaxed into movement, a thing that exists as looked at and acted upon' (p. 150). Within the media text, and its mass audience, this objectification becomes heightened. Yet, this idea of the female body is rejected by Elliott who, in *One Minute Man* (OMM), 'acts on' her environment and *demands* to be 'looked at' on her own terms, and in doing so disrupts the masculine gaze and controls the camera.

In OMM Elliott takes her head off and holds it towards the camera. The power of the image initially lies in the super-human ability of Elliott to decapitate herself, whilst continuing to sing, breathe, and dance. The fact that the bodily manipulation is, from the audience's perspective, self-actuated, is a powerful image for women. The objectively compartmentalised female body used to reduce the presence of whole woman, is exploded by Elliott who, in a double act of agency, compartmentalises *her own* body for *her own* pleasure.

Elliott further addresses Young's idea of body comportment as she resists the idea of '*inhibited intentionality*' (p. 147 italics in original), which claims that women shrink from using their bodies in a forceful and outwardly directed manner. In contrast Elliott, in a different section of OMM, flies through the air making martial arts movements as she sings, taking up space around and above her. Elliott's active body refuses traditional codes of female comportment in film. Yet Elliott cannot be read as simply engaging in an oppositional dialogue with traditional forms of female representation. Elliott moves beyond this dichotomy by engorging and extending the boundaries of her identity through the use of multifarious cultural symbols, including symbols of female sexuality.

Jamaican Vulgarity and Blues Sexuality

Elliott blends together techniques from Jamaican dancehall music, Blues music, and male rap music in order to create a distinct and empowered sense of black female sexuality. Elliott borrows from the raw stylistics of Jamaican dancehall culture; her rap lyrics revolve primarily around the experiences of lower-class urban African-American women, and, as Carolyn Cooper (1993) articulates with reference to Jamaican dancehall culture, can be seen as articulating the voice of 'the *vulgus*, the common people' (p. 8). According to Cooper, the oral and the vulgar are linked to illiteracy, and lack formal status; yet this style, defined against the refined English text, allows Elliott to speak to the lived experience of urban African-American women in a language that refuses the dominant and normalised discourse. Elliott can be seen as importing the vulgar into her raps, mimicking Jamaican DJ's who, according to Gilroy, 'steered the dance-hall side of roots culture away from political and historical themes and towards "slackness": crude and often insulting wordplay pronouncing on sexuality and sexual antagonism' (Gilroy cited in Cooper, 1993, p. 141). This 'slackness' can be seen in Elliott's track *You Don't Know* (1999) when she raps about aggression between women when men cheat on their partners, rapping 'you been suckin' his dick, tastin' my clit/just a side chick/I'm the prize bitch/keep it silent/don't make me violent'. The language is undoubtedly vulgar, complicated by the un-feminine and un-feminist allusion to violence between women.

The role of the female in dancehall culture is ambiguous. As Cooper states, 'women who enjoy the humour and innocuous slackness of songs such as these are subject to censure', with the implication being that such, 'undomesticated female sexuality . . . has the smell of prostitution' (pp. 120–1). Elliott, whilst borrowing the vulgarity of dancehall culture, has no regard for these boundaries. She is clear that many of her records are for women, speaking to, and validating the experiences of, urban African-American women, as she asserts,

'people always say, "why your mouth so vulgar? Why you got to sing all these nasty records?" but I be representing for my ladies and we've got something to say. We've been quiet too long, lady like, very patient, . . . we always had to deal with the guys talking about how they gonna wear us out on records, and so I had to do records that were strictly representing for my ladies'.

(Elliott, 2002)

Elliott's desire to 'represent her ladies', will always, for Hortense Spillers (1984), fall outside of the empowered text. Spillers in *Interstices: A Small Drama of Words*, claims that although, 'black women have learned as much that is positive about their sexuality through the practising activity of the singer as they have from the polemicist' (p. 87), 'the non-fictional text [remains] the empowered text—not fiction' (p. 74).

Hazel Carby (1991) in, *It jus be's dat way sometime: the sexual politics of women's blues*, is clear about the value of music in establishing sexual subjectivity: 'by analysing the sexual and cultural politics of black women who constructed themselves as sexual subjects through song, in particular the blues, I want to assert an empowered presence' (p. 747). In OMM, guest-rapper, Trina (2001), illustrates how female rappers have continued to use sexual subjectivity as a way to claim an empowered presence. Trina explicitly articulates her sexual desires rapping, 'one minute, two minute, three minute, hell nah, to please me you gotta sleep in it'. Visually Trina embodies a corporeal, hyper-sexuality. Wearing a revealing outfit, she dances in the style of dancehall, lifting up her own dress to reveal her gyrating 'booty', her movements on the bed mimicking pornography. However, this sexuality remains within a female space: the camera is non-intrusive, remaining at a distance to Trina, and she never inhabits a vulnerable or passive position. Trina illustrates the difficulties at play when black women assert an aggressively sexual persona. Within a dominant discourse that already defines black women as the locus for an exotic, raw sexuality, the value in *self-consciously* inhabiting this persona is ambiguous. Yet, as Roach and Felix's (1988) discussion of black women in Britain concludes, black women should be able to express all aspects and experiences of black women's lives, 'whatever the risks of white appropriation for stereotyping' (p. 141).

Carby asserts a more diffuse and dynamic approach to black female sexuality, claiming that, 'the women blues singers occupied a privileged space and were able to, '*play out and explore the various possibilities of a sexual existence*; they are representatives of women who attempt to *manipulate and control their construction as sexual subjects*' (p. 749 italics added). Elliott, within a contemporary environment, is doing exactly this, exploring the 'various possibilities of a sexual existence'. In OMM, Trina, wholly endorsed by Elliott's own style of rapping, represents *one possibility* of sexual existence. Yet it remains that Trina and Elliott can be read as illustrating Spillers' discussion of 'the unsexed black female and the supersexed black female', who both, 'embody the very same vice, cast the very same shadow, inasmuch as both are an exaggeration' (1984, p. 85). As such, Elliott, although rapping explicitly about sex, remains sex-less, with Trina, (or in other videos, female dancers) standing in for the sexuality that remains absent.

Elliott's ambiguous sexual subjectivity is further compounded by the extent to which she appropriates the sexual language of black male rappers. The validity of accessing these masculine tools is again questionable, arguably restricting female rap music to a larger heterosexual framework, and risking female authenticity. Yet, as Irigaray (1985) claims with regard to mimicry, 'to play with mimesis is . . . for women, to try to recover the place of her exploitation by discourse, without allowing herself to be simply reduced to it' (p. 76). Elliott's mimesis of traditional male sexuality serves to combine and complicate both male and female sexual signifiers. As Perry (1995) claims, 'women rappers not only claim *their* sexual selves, but also enter the male body, generally as a metaphor for their strength and power, but also to expand self-definition' (p. 526). Elliott (1999) locates herself as the phallic symbol in her song *Dangerous Mouths* from her album *Da Real World*, when she raps, 'Let me intervene/come between/like dick through your jeans/hang down to your knees', and again in an interlude on Elliott uses the phallic gun as a metaphor for her genitalia, whilst simultaneously invoking the more traditional imagery of the warm and welcoming vagina when she sings, 'I keep my piece so sweet, yeah nice and warm'.

Elliott's sexuality appropriates many disparate sources, and remains empowered precisely because of this complexity. By pointing to sites of empowerment, stereotype and masculinity, Elliott simultaneously celebrates, challenges, and makes visible contentious ideas of female sexuality.

Blackness and Power

Elliott's refusal to be defined through the masculine gaze and her self-aware female sexuality establish a persona that is further developed by her relation to race. In *She's a Bitch* (SAB), Elliott plays with the tradition of blackface. The effect of making up white faces with black paint dates from America in the 1850s, and has traditionally been used to caricature blackness. In SAB, Elliott employs blackface and by doing so brings direct attention to the issue of race. Frantz Fanon (1993) discusses this visibility when he writes,

> '"Look a Negro!" It was an external stimulus that flickered over me as I passed by . . . assailed at various points, the corporeal schema crumbled, its place taken by a racial epidermal schema . . . I was over-determined from without . . . I am the slave . . . of my own appearance'.
>
> (pp. 111–2, 116)

One of Elliott's central techniques is her *demand* for the gaze on her own terms. This aggressive resistance to a constraining gaze is apparent in Elliott's use of blackface. In SAB Elliott takes the 'racial epidermal schema' inflates it, making it *more* visible, and throws it back out to stand as an 'external stimulus'; a revised cultural signifier. Elliott, by taking the idea of blackness visually as far as it can go, recast blackness as a locus of power, as well as questioning static ideas of race.

Elliott's self-aware manipulation of blackface involves the complex appropriation of historical black imagery in order to disrupt and question dominant cultural readings. Through SAB, Elliott recasts blackface by combining it with a digital landscape, infusing it with ideas of a black-hi-tech-female. Her appropriation of masculine rap techniques, and refusal to adhere to generic female conventions, underscores Elliott's potent sense of agency; this is further illuminated by looking specifically at power and the sublime in SAB.

SAB, the debut track from her second album *Da Real World*, is preoccupied with power, locating Elliott

outside of the tradition of female ethics that promotes caring and sisterhood as *natural* female characteristics, and instead constituting an unforgiving female appropriation of power, hierarchy and narcissism. SAB is a song about the right of women to call themselves bitches. Elliott addresses the idea that language can, like cultural symbols, be re-defined and become empowering when she states,

> 'basically a bitch to me is a power word. It's basically a female knowing what she wants and going after what she wants. If you're calling me "bitch"' cos I'm going after what I want and I'm confident about myself then that's what you're gonna have to call me'.
>
> (Elliott cited in Dreher, 2002)

Elliott claims 'bitch' as part of her own vernacular, and in doing so disrupts and loosens the masculine grasp on language, as well as injecting the notion of power into what it means to be female. SAB establishes an exclusively female space, and begins with Elliott occupying the full screen, walking towards the camera, dressed in black leather, with a metal breastplate and gloves. The video involves a large amount of footage that is solely of Elliott. Throughout SAB, Elliott demands to be looked at, as she raps, walks, and dances with *un*-inhibited intentionality; the shots offer no distraction from her female power as she exists alone and takes up her own exclusive space. The breastplate, metal gloves and bullet shape shells running down her chest signify combat; accompanied by her female foot soldiers, Elliott is ready for the fight. These signifiers of masculine power are compounded by the use of hierarchy within SAB. Elliott inhabits a world where an unequal power nexus is accepted, along with the struggle and determination that it takes to make it within such a system. Elliott celebrates her hard won position of power, holding onto the masculine hierarchical system instead of sharing or expending her power, as would be assumed under traditional feminine ethics.

Patricia Yaeger (1989) legitimises Elliott's coveting of masculine power, and the hierarchy and inequality that is implicit to it, in her essay *Toward a Female Sublime*. Yaeger claims that the sublime is heavily gendered, and given this, articulates the female sublime as distinct from the traditional masculine sublime. The masculine sublime is defined by Battersby (1994) as when one 'marvels at that which stands at the boundaries of human identity and threatens to overcome it. The ego confronts its own incapacity and its own possible annihilation, and it recuperates itself in the face of this threatened loss' (pp. 27–28). This movement between the I and the other, that ultimately rests in the reassertion of the I, is the motif of the masculine sublime, and, as Yaeger recounts, the masculine sublime inherently 'insists on aggrandising the masculine self over others' (p. 191). As such, the sublime can be seen as perpetuating the notion of hierarchy and power *over* others. Yaeger discusses the difficulties for women in appropriating the sublime as a usable genre, stating that,

'The problem with entering the realm of the sublime is that we contract to participate in a power struggle that, even when it is resisted, involved grim forces of possession and domination . . . Nevertheless, I do not want to reject this martial vocabulary out of hand because women, as writers and heroines, are clearly in need of feisty, voracious, volatile vocabularies of empowerment . . . as a moment concerned with empowerment, transport, and the self's strong sense of authority, the sublime is a genre woman writer needs'.

(pp. 198–192)

Elliott, through SAB provides an active and contemporary example of women playing with the 'forces of possession and domination', creating a martial, volatile and heroic landscape, occupied by the 'self's strong sense of authority'. The vocabulary of power, culturally revised and disrupted symbols of blackness, and the gender issues that operate within SAB, constitute a sophisticated amalgamation, imbuing Elliott with an excessive and uncompromising potency.

Science Fiction and Sign Systems

The imagery of SAB fits closely within high technology, science fiction (SF) and action-movie stylistics. De Lauretis in 'Signs of Wo/ander' (1980) claims that SF takes signs further than simply playing with signifiers, and corrupting dominant denotations. De

Lauretis discusses 'sign-vehicles', meaning a sign that has no referent within our present social reality, such as a 'female man'. These sign-vehicles 'construct a new semantic universe, or re-organise the semantic space by reapportioning meaning in different ways and changing the value of words and actions' (p. 165) By employing sign-vehicles a sense of wander is created:

'Displaced from the central position of the knowledgeable observer, the reader stands on constantly shifting ground, on the margins of understanding, at the periphery of vision: hence the sense of wander, of being dislocated to another spacetime continuum where human possibilities are discovered in the intersection of other signs with other meanings'.

(p. 166)

This sense of 'wAnder' also functions in SAB. Elliott re-organises signs of blackness, the primitive, and power, within a technological landscape, and by doing so constructs a new semantic universe.

SAB's links to the SF genre are further underscored by the use of technology in both SAB and in SF. As De Lauretis writes, 'technology shapes the very content and form of the imagination in our time' (De Lauretis, Huyssen and Woodward, 1980, p. xiii). In the video *Super Human* (2002), cultural commentator Kodwo Eshun discusses Elliott's musical and visual stylistics and their reliance on technology, asserting that,

'Tim "timberland" Mosley and Missy Elliott think in a totally digital way, in other words rhythm is information to be recombined, manipulated, rearranged in which ever way you like', and then, with the introduction of Hype Williams as video director, 'you see a vision that can capture the rhythm that's going on, he finds a way to give vision a syncopation, he finds a way to give the image a percussive rhythmic quality'.

The intimacy between culture and technology is undoubtedly central to the creation of Elliott's identity. The use of *digital* technology privileges the idea of the soft-image, whereby an image becomes endlessly malleable once it has been downloaded into a computer. As Eshun comments, 'the soft image often has a fantasy aspect to it. It is filled with super-human energies, super-human powers, it is essentially a dream landscape, a landscape filled with special effects'. Eshun, although crucial in understanding Elliott's music videos within the SF technological framework, ultimately defines the use of the soft image in Elliott's music videos as belonging to the genre of spectacle:

> '[these] music videos refer to the origins of the cinema, in which the cinema is spectacle, pleasure and surprise. In this sense the music video is the placing of giant technological skills, and giant budgets at the service of very primitive pleasure'.

Elliott's expansive and vibrant play with signs, and her continually changing imaginary can be understood as spectacle, rightly emptied of any definitive truth. Through this reading Elliott becomes 'the poet' in Richard Rorty's (1989) 'poeticized culture', refusing to 'find the real wall behind the painted ones', taking her role as poet to mean the creation of 'ever more multi-coloured artefacts' (pp. 53–54). The allusion to truth and unity has become unpopular; as Weiskel, with reference to the genre of the sublime, forthrightly states, 'the sublime must now be abridged, reduced, and parodied as the grotesque, somehow hedged with irony to assure us that we are not imaginative adolescents' (Weiskel cited in Yaeger, 1989). It is possible to locate Elliott's use of power in SAB as a parody of masculine power, a sending up of the Kantian sublime, mocking its preoccupation with nature and transcendence. In its place a black woman, digitally creating an ironic landscape that remains an artefact, resisting *any* definitive meaning, and directed by the meaningless dynamic of postmodernism.

Yet, as Eshun articulates, 'special effects [can] start to become *social* fantasies' (italics added). De Lauretis echoes this infusion of special effects and social fantasy when she claims that,

> 'The science fictional construction of a possible world . . . entails a conceptual reorganization of semantic space and therefore of material and social relations, and makes for an expanded cog-

nitive horizon, an epic vision of our present social reality'.

(p. 170)

This 'reorganisation' denies the postmodern break-up of a unified space and instead holds onto the importance and effect of 'material and social relations' on, 'our [expanded] present social reality'. The technological imagination enables Elliott to create both a re-constructed and politically charged landscape, manipulating and extending sign-systems to both get outside of naturalised hegemony, and to give vision to other possible social realities. However, the traditional relationship between the female and technology is one couched in the language of excess and otherness; the technosexual woman stands as a fearful force within masculine imagery.

The Technosexual Woman

Janet Lungstrum (1997) in *'Metropolis' and the Technosexual Woman of German Modernity*, discusses the relationship between female identity and technology, asserting that 'the effect of technology has been to cast woman in a provocative pose, a position not unlike that of woman in the male imagination: she is the sex-machine locus of her creators' fear and fascination' (p. 128). The 'fear and fascination' of woman and machine refers to the potential excess and out-of-control-ness that is implicit in the understanding of woman defined as 'technosexual Other' (p. 129)—an excess that shores up masculine identity at the same time as it feeds into masculine anxieties over the need to contain technology.

Woman, especially the embodied voice of the female singer, has, as Sarah Webster Goodwin (1994) writes, 'a particular kind of power: that of nature, the material world—and more, that of the mother, whose body and voice assimilate to the undisclosed meanings of the pre-symbolic' (p. 67). This pre-symbolic definition of woman is echoed directly by Yaeger when she assesses the sublime 'struggle between self and other', suggesting that it 'is really a subterfuge, an oedipal confrontation that masks the oral, primordial desire to merge with (rather than possess) the mother' (p. 204).

The link between a Dionysian, pre-symbolic space that is defined through ecstasy and drugs, and a technology that is equally potent and potentially uncontrollable, is expressed by Elliott in her song *Mr. DJ* (1999) which features Lady Saw, a Jamaican singer. Elliott sings, 'as I hear the record spin it seems to take over me, so I move side to side, and its something inside that controls me'. The idea of being *taken over* is echoed by Lady Saw when she chants, 'tell the guys don't come waste me time, 'cos we under with ganja and de red wine'. According to Lungstrum, this Dionysian scene becomes intensified by Elliott's simultaneous use of technology. In the middle of the song a computerised voice says, M.I.S.S.Y.Y.S.S.I.M.M. I.S.S.Y. The reversal of Elliott's name both asserts and denies a fixed identity—the sound of the string of letters is indecipherable. Elliott combines the technological and the Dionysian idea of female excess and the pre-symbolic, with a high level of sophistication and subtlety; the sounds of the computerised voice and Lady Saw's Jamaican voice form a vivid manifestation of a Dionysian, primitive, and technological female sound.

SAB also visually captures this sense of female excess and technology. Lungstrum illustrates the perceived tension and destructiveness of the relationship between woman and technology in her discussion of the scene in *Metropolis*, where Robot-Maria instigates the workers to 'destroy the machinery and flood their own homes[:] the unleashed power of female orgasm literally floods her own mechanism and short-circuits' (p. 133). The self-desiring excess of both woman and technology erupts in a moment of self-annihilation, with dire social consequences. Yet this link between female self-desiring and self-annihilation can arguably be read as part of the masculine cautionary tale, speaking more to masculine fears than to potential female realities. This tension is absent in Elliott's combination of female excess and technology. Towards the end of SAB, Elliott and her foot soldiers emerge as the song breaks down into a war-call on a giant M that rises up from the ocean. The final landscape is digitally apocalyptic; atomic clouds roll above Elliott, whilst a dark sea crashes around the giant M. It is in this scene that the ocean, representing the 'flood of the female orgasm', becomes united with the hi-tech hyper-black warrior. Elliott simultaneously inhabits the excess of the female and the power of technology, becoming a self-constructed technosexual woman, refusing to be

defined through a relation to either masculine fears or pleasures.

Lungstrum, having located the technosexual woman in *Metropolis* as powerful yet bound up with masculine fears and fantasies, refuses to dismiss her as a category, claiming that it remains a valid form for women through, 'the reappropriation, or recreation, by woman of her technosexuality . . . one adopts, adapts, and empowers a phallocentric discourse into hybrid feminist re-production' (p. 134). This reappropriation not only echoes De Lauretis' desire to 're-organise the semantic space by reapportioning meaning in different ways and changing the value of words and actions' (p. 165), but also hints at Donna Haraway's idea of the cyborg, which is present throughout Elliott's videos.

In SAB, Elliott explicitly becomes a cyborg, defined by Haraway (1991) as, 'hybrid of machine and organism' (p. 149). In one scene Elliott wears a white suit that is covered in light strips whilst rapping in the centre of an enclosed set, made up of the same light strips. Elliott becomes a part of the light technology, and looks as if she is within a computer *mother*board, pulsating and dancing within the light circuit. Haraway locates science fiction as a site (amongst others) for cyborg incarnations, 'contemporary science fiction is full of cyborgs—creatures simultaneously animal and machine, who populate worlds ambiguously natural and crafted' (p. 149). Haraway asserts that the rethinking of physical boundaries that is demanded by the cyborg (for example, where does Elliott begin and the set end?) not only destabilises the idea of bounded bodies, but also demands that we stop demonising technology and take 'responsibility for the social relations of science and technology' (p. 181). For Haraway, 'cyborg imagery can suggest a way out of the maze of dualism . . . it means both building and destroying machines, identities, categories, [and] relationships' (p. 181).

Through Haraway's notion of the cyborg, Elliott's expression of technosexuality is situated within a framework that rejects dualism, allowing for unbounded bodies, whilst holding on to the idea of responsibility. Within this framework Elliott can be seen as fearlessly revelling in, as Haraway articulates, the act of 'building and destroying machines and identities' (p. 181).

Female Identity: Unbounded *and* Re-constructed

In this final section I will look at a small selection of ideas from Christine Battersby's book *The Phenomenal Woman* (1998). Battersby builds a feminist metaphysics which is located within the broader theoretical discourse of corporeal feminism. Corporeal feminism bridges the chasm between biology and discourse: exposing discourse as normalising the male body whilst pathologizing the female, *at the same time as* privileging the corporeal leaky body as a more accurate account of both male and female bodies. The idea of the impenetrable body that both contains 'the self' and protects against external forces provides the foundation to traditional and masculine philosophical ideas of the self. As Grosz (1994) highlights, within this discourse, bodily fluids,

> 'affront the subject's aspiration toward autonomy and self-identity . . . body fluids flow, they seep, they infiltrate; their control is a matter of vigilance, never guaranteed. In this sense, they betray a certain irreducible materiality'.
>
> (p. 195)

The corporeal body is a leaky body; its parameters are unclear, seeping beyond the normalised masculine boundaries, refusing the autonomy that comes from the illusion of masculine containment.

Elliott, even as she visually thwarts the authority of the bounded biological body, endowing it with superhuman capacities, arguably skips over female corporeality, placing herself within a physically post-biological space. As Eshun comments with reference to Elliott's debut video *The Rain*, 'You don't know what she is, she's kind of a new creature, a strange new mutant'. Yet, the corporeality of Elliott's lyrics shore up her female corporeal identity.

In *The Phenomenal Woman* Battersby constructs, 'a new subject-position that makes *women* typical' (p. 2). Battersby claims that, 'for the (normalised) "female" there is no sharp division between "self" and "other"' (p. 8). Ideas of power, hierarchy, the sublime, and masculine anxieties over female excess and technology, all rely on a distinction between the 'self' and 'other', with the sub-text marking the 'other' as threatening. Battersby, by privileging the blurring of self and other

that is experienced by women through natality, offers a different foundation from which to develop identity. As Battersby writes,

> 'The boundary of my body can also be thought of as an event-horizon, in which one form (myself) meets its potentiality for transforming itself into another form or forms (the not-self). Such a body-boundary entails neither containment of internal forces nor repulsion of/protection against external forces'.
>
> (p. 52)

Battersby re-constructs body-boundaries in a way that privileges interpenetration, flow and potentiality whilst holding on to the idea of boundaries, re-constructed as an event-horizon. Elliott's engagement with the unbounded body also holds on to a boundary: her name, used as a promotional tool. As German music journalist, Mercedes Bunz (2002), comments, 'throughout her career "Missy", the "M", the dotted "Missy" appear in her videos on various occasions, while at the same time she keeps changing her character instead of clinging to an identifiable persona'. As Battersby asserts, her notion of female identity

> '*retains a notion of the self*, but construe[s] identity in terms of living forces and birth, not as a "state" of matter that is dead or characteristic of a "soul" or a "mind" that remains fixed and constant, no matter which of its qualities or attributes might change'.
>
> (p. 8 italics added)

Elliott's identity has changed throughout her career, yet, as Battersby writes, it is the, 'rhythmic repetitions' of the Missy trademark that, 'provides the "labour" that allows identity to emerge from conflictual multiplicities' (p. 9).

Battersby endorses flow and fluidity against a static state of matter, whilst simultaneously rejecting the deconstruction of identity. This re-construction resists the postmodern desire for the abandonment of all boundaries, keeping hold of the idea of responsibility. As Battersby writes, 'without talk of identity (and hence also boundaries), I do not see that there can be a basis for responsibility and action, including political action' (p. 57).

Battersby's use of chaos theory is perhaps the most direct way to connect the identity created in Elliott's music videos with the female identity established by Battersby:

'forms are not fixed things, but *temporary arrestations in continuous metastable flows*, potentialities or evolutionary events'.

(p. 52 italics added)

Given this, Elliott's shifting personas in her videos are not moments of 'acting' that exist above the fixed identity of Melissa Elliott, but rather forms of potentiality that are lived by Elliott as she continually moves into different force-fields offering other potentialities for being. Elliott's music video forms and their heightened sense of (dis)embodiment and their play of cultural sign-systems constitutes a vivid illustration of Battersby's notion of female identity.

Conclusion

Under Construction (2002), Elliott's current album, continues to provide fresh constructions of Elliott's identity. Her weight-loss has been accompanied by a shift to softer colours and texture in her outfits, her videos are more realistic, her message more political. In an interview that accompanied the launch of the album, Elliott says, 'I enjoyed that period of freaky dressing, it made me different from a lot of other artists, but now I've changed and I want to be a little more accessible. I'm going back to dope rope chains, fingers rings, and pink gold' (Elliott cited in Emery, 2002). In *Under Construction*, Elliott evokes signs of the hip hop family and hip hop history as vehicles around which the rap community can unify. Addressing the violence that exists between rap artists, Elliott cites herself as someone who is working on herself, and, by example, hopes to encourage a self-conscious, peaceful and joyful rap environment. In Battersby's language, this current 'arrestation of flow' may be maintained through the 'rhythmic repetitions' of this form of identity, or, maybe Elliott will move into a new force-field which will re-score her identity in to a different 'arrestation'—who knows? Elliott, in her entirety, remains

an enigma, and if, as Carolyn Cooper states, 'subjection to analysis is yet another form of containment' (p. 171), I would rather leave Elliott uncontained.

The focus of this paper has been two-fold; firstly to explore the ways in which Elliott exercises agency with regard to the cultural symbols that she employs and the visual imagery that she creates, and secondly the assertion that this fluid approach to identity can work alongside a re-constructed identity that is able to hold on to political agency. Elliott can be seen to illustrate Hortense Spillers' claim that, 'the singer . . . is a precise demonstration of the subject turning in fully conscious knowledge of her own resources toward her object [the song]. In this instance of being-for-self . . . the woman, in her particular and vivid thereness, is an unalterable and discrete *moment* of self-knowledge' (p. 86 italics added). Yet, through Battersby's work, the vitality of self-knowledge articulated through this quote reveals itself as *a moment*—one possible arrestation of identity amongst limitless others possibilities. As Hélène Cixous writes (1991), 'Women's imaginary is inexhaustible, like music, painting, writing: their stream of phantasms is incredible' (p. 22). It is from this incredible stream of phantasms that moments of identity endlessly configure and reconfigure.

Bibliography

Battersby, C. (1998) *The Phenomenal Woman*. Cornwall: Polity Press.

Bunz, M. contributions to the video documentary made by, Dreher, C. (2002) *Super Human*. [Video]. USA: IMC Vision.

Carby, H. (1991) 'It jus be's dat way sometime: the sexual politics of women's blues' in R. Warhol and D. Price Herndl (eds) *Feminisms: an Anthology of Literary Theory and Criticism*. USA: Rutgers.

Cixous, H. (1991) 'The laugh of the Medusa' in S. Gunew (ed.) *A Reader in Feminist Knowledge*. London: Routledge.

Cooper, C. (1993) *Noises in the Blood: Orality, Gender and the Vulgar Body of Jamaican Popular Culture*. Malaysia: Macmillan Caribbean.

De Lauretis, Teresa. (1980) 'Signs of Wo/ander' in T. De Lauretis, A. Huyssen and K. Woodward (eds) *The Technological Imagination: Theories and Fictions*. Madison/Wisconsin: Coda Press Inc.

De Lauretis, T., Huyssen, A. and Woodward, K. (eds) (1980) *The Technological Imagination: Theories and Fictions*. Madison/Wisconsin: Coda Press Inc.

Elliott, M. (1999) *Da Real World*. [CD]. Elektra.

Elliott, M. (2002) *Under Construction*. [CD]. Elektra.

Emery, A. (2002) 'Supa Fly Girl'. *Muzik*, December 2002, pp. 46–49.

Eshun, K. contributions to the video documentary made by, Dreher, C. (2002) *Super Human*. [Video]. USA: IMC Vision.

Fanon, F. (1993) *Black Skins, White Mask*. London: Pluto Press.

Felix, P. and Roach, J. (1988) 'Black looks' in L. Gammon, and M. Marshment (eds) *The Female Gaze*. London: The Women's Press

Grosz, E. (1994) *Volatile Bodies: Towards a Corporeal Feminism*. Bloomington: Indiana University Press.

Haraway, D. (1991) *Simians, Cyborgs, and Women*. London: Free Association Books.

Hills Collins, P. (2000) *Black Feminist Thought*. New York: Routledge.

hooks, b. (1992) *Black Looks: Race and Representation*. Boston, MA: South End Press.

Irigaray, L. (1985) *The Sex Which Is Not One*. New York: Cornell University Press (Trans. C. Porter with C. Burke).

Lewis, L.A. (1995) 'Form and female authorship in music video' in G. Dines, and J. M. Humez, (eds) *Gender, Race and Class in Media*. London: Sage.

Lungstrum, J. (1997) 'Metropolis and the technosexual woman of German modernity' in K. von Ankum (ed.) *Women in the Metropolis: Gender and Modernity in Weimar Culture*. Berkley, LA: University of California Press.

Meyers, D. (2001) *One Minute Man*. [Music video] Downloaded from the internet, July 2003.

Mulvey, L. (1988) Visual pleasures and narrative cinema' in C. Penley (ed.) *Feminism and Film Theory*. London: BFI Publishing.

Perry, I. (1995) 'It's my thang and I'll swing it the way I feel! Sexuality and black women rappers' in G. Dines, and J. M. Humez, (eds) *Gender, Race and Class in Media*. London: Sage.

Rorty, R. (1989) *Contingency, Irony and Solidarity*. Cambridge: Cambridge University Press.

Spillers, H. J. (1984) 'Interstices: a small drama of words' in C. S. Vance (ed.) *Pleasure and Danger: Exploring Female Sexuality*. New York: Routledge and Kegan Paul.

Webster Goodwin, S. (1994) 'Wordsworth and Romantic voice: the poet's song and the prostitute's cry' in L. Dunn and N. Jones (eds) *Embodied Voices: Representing Female Vocality in Western Culture*. Cambridge: Cambridge University Press.

Williams, H. (2001) 'She's a bitch' in *Hits of Miss E . . . The Videos. Vol. 1*. Elektra Entertainment Group. www.elektra.com/elektra/missyelliott/index.jhtml (accessed 10/11/02.)

Yaeger, P. (1989) 'Toward a female sublime' in L. Kauffman (ed.) *Gender and Theory: Dialogues on Feminist Theory*. Oxford: Basil Blackwell.

Young, I. M. (1990) *Throwing Like a Girl and Other Essays in Feminist Philosophy and Social Theory*. Bloomington: Indiana University Press.

22.
MAKING HER (IN)VISIBLE

Cultural Representations of Lesbianism and the Lesbian Body in the 1990s
Ann M. Ciasullo

We regularly punish those who fail to do their gender right.

(Judith Butler, *Gender Trouble*, 140)

In September 1999, *The Jerry Springer Show* ran an episode entitled "I'm Having an Affair—With Another Woman!" After a series of confessions between the featured wife and husband (the main revelation: they were sharing the same mistress), the "other woman" appeared on stage. In her tight black dress, she strutted over to the wife, straddled her, and started making out with her. The audience members roared with approval. Bypassing both the tradition to which these "luscious lesbians" belong[1] and the question of whether these women actually *were* lesbians, I want to ask some questions about this incident: Should we be hopeful because the audience didn't yell "dyke!" or scream words of damnation at the women? Does the audience's response suggest that lesbianism is becoming more acceptable in mainstream society? Surveying the many other cultural venues in which lesbianism has made its presence felt, it would appear that lesbianism *is* becoming more acceptable. Indeed, lesbians seem to be everywhere—in mainstream magazines ranging from *People* to *Cosmopolitan*, in movies like *Chasing Amy* and *Set It Off*, on television shows like *Friends, Mad about You*, and, of course, *Ellen*—saturating the cultural imagination. In the words of Ann Northrop, a leader of the Lesbian Avengers, "Lesbians are the Hula-Hoop of the nineties."[2]

Northrop's metaphor points to the way that lesbians are, in many ways, the 1990s' version of a novelty, a fad, something to be consumed and played with. But of course, the "novelty" status accorded to lesbians belies their long and difficult struggle for positive representation by the mainstream media; thus the present signification attached to their trendiness—popularly known as "lesbian chic"—is much more complex than the cultural experience of most fads. We must consider how the emergence of "the lesbian" is constructed, characterized, and framed by the media that are presenting it to middle America. What kind of lesbian has "come out" in the past decade? More precisely, what kind of lesbian has been *allowed* to appear on mainstream cultural landscapes? How is she (re)presented, or more specifically, how is she embodied—how is her body portrayed, described, contained or not? Drawing from a range of sources—television and film, popular magazines such as *Time* and *Newsweek*, women's magazines such as *Glamour* and *Vogue*, and current lesbian theory—I wish to analyze the phenomenon of this emerging lesbian (body). I will show how mainstream media produce and reproduce particular lesbian bodies while effacing other, equally legitimate—and perhaps even more conventionally "lesbian"—bodies. The body or image that is made invisible is the "butch," a figure that I consider better able than a "femme" body to challenge mainstream cultural fantasies about lesbianism.[3]

My argument is twofold: first, most recent mainstream representations of lesbianism are normalized—heterosexualized or "straightened out"—via the femme body. The mainstream lesbian body is at once sexualized and desexualized: on the one hand, she is made into an object of desire for straight audiences through her heterosexualization, a process achieved by representing the lesbian as embodying a hegemonic femininity and thus, for mainstream audiences, as looking "just like" conventionally attractive straight women; on the other hand, because the representation of desire between two women is usually suppressed in these images, she is de-homosexualized. Furthermore, this heterosexualization is enabled by the alignment of her femininity with specific racial and socioeconomic attributes: on mainstream cultural landscapes, the femme body is nearly always a white, upper-middle class body. Second, and equally important, those lesbians who are not femme (and, by extension, who are not white and middle or upper class) are—with perhaps one notable exception which I will discuss below—virtually invisible in media representations, and when they do appear, they are often pathologized. This might seem an odd argument; after all, as Arlene Stein, author of *Sisters, Sexperts, Queers: Beyond the Lesbian Nation*, points out, "It's the butch lesbian who's been synonymous with lesbianism in the public imagination."[4] Here it is important to underscore the distinction between the butch's presence in the cultural *imagination* and her lack of presence on cultural *landscapes*. As I will argue later in this article, this same butch who is so closely aligned with the *idea* of lesbianism is curiously absent from cultural *representation*; in mainstream images and discourses of lesbianism in the 1990s, there are few butches to be found. By surveying the various and proliferating discourses about lesbianism in popular culture, I will consider the ways in which the lesbian body is marked and made "tasteful" for the viewing public—made, in essence, palatable for mainstream consumers to consume.

"Butch," "Femme," and the Substance of Style, or Why the Categories Still Matter

Before turning directly to my discussion, I want to address some objections that might arise over my choice of terms. Aren't "butch" and "femme," and the binary to which they are usually assigned, too simplistic and too overdetermined? Hasn't postmodernism had a profound effect on style, and isn't it reductive to think about lesbian representation only in terms of "butch" and "femme"? Certainly it could be argued

that a clear-cut distinction between the "two types" of lesbians is no longer cogent. There is no doubt that lesbian communities have expanded notions of butch and femme and that the butch-femme rigidity that was so common in the 1950s and 1960s has, to a large extent, disappeared.[5] As Michele Fisher, in an humorous article entitled "Butch Nouveau," notes: "In the old days you were either butch or femme or you got made fun of. Not so in today's version of the culture: Now the butch-femme spectrum is very crowded. You've still got your stone butches and ultra or old-school femmes, but then you've also got your soft butches, tomboy femmes, stone femmes, butches of center, femmes of center, and many more."[6] Fisher's assessment of the ways that lesbian culture has changed is, for the most part, accurate; one need only attend any Gay Pride Parade or visit any lesbian bar to see the ways that styles have proliferated. Butch and femme, in their conventional sense, exist alongside dozens of other styles. As Jeanie Kasindorf proclaims of lesbian culture, "In the nineties, it seems, there is room for every style."[7]

Or so the story goes. But I would argue that the idea that we can "be whatever we want to be," the postmodern sensibility that imbues many discussions of lesbian style, is misleading, for it does not give attention to the way that cultural forces play upon the self in the self's experience of coming out, of identity formation, and of choosing "style." When I was first coming out over seven years ago, I saw anything but "room for every style." At the time I was twenty-four, and until that point I had always loved wearing dresses and skirts and makeup. Then I started dating a woman, and something odd happened: I believed that my skirt-loving tendencies and my desire to wear eyeliner had to stop. Until then, I had considered myself a relatively open-minded and intelligent person who didn't let culture dictate her beliefs. Yet when I entered into this relationship, my biggest anxiety was not whether my friends and family could accept my lesbianism, but whether I could ever "look the part." For a month I didn't wear a skirt or dress, and I spent many a night wondering if my desire to pluck my eyebrows meant I was really straight. In other words, culture *did* impinge on me: I spent a long time trying to reconcile my feminine qualities with my "new" lesbian self, a self that I believed had to eschew all things feminine.

But mainstream cultural fantasies alone did not provoke my confusion over wanting to wear dresses on occasion. Those anxieties were fueled just as much by lesbian culture as by straight culture. I spent months, if not years, feeling out of place. I remember going to gay bars with my girlfriend and fearing that I would be exposed at any minute. I honestly believed someone would come up to me and say, "Wait a minute . . . you're not *really* a lesbian; you're not butch enough! Now get out!" As a feminine woman, then, the coming-out process for me was as much about acceptance by the lesbian community as by my straight loved ones, and in my mind, both forms of acceptance hinged (in part) on how well I met the "criteria" of lesbianism that pointed back to *visibility*, or *butchness*. I felt as though my *lack* of visibility—visible only when paired with my girlfriend, who is by most standards an "obvious" lesbian, a butch—made me "unreal," inauthentic.

I relate this story because it underscores the way such categories *do* still shape and influence our experiences; we live in, by, and with these categories, whether we wish to or not. And femmes are not the only ones whose subjectivity is marked and formed by such experiences. As Lisa Walker points out in her insightful essay, "How to Recognize a Lesbian: The Cultural Politics of Looking Like What You Are," "some members of the lesbian and gay community (and the heterosexual one, for that matter) will suffer for their nonconformity to the normative visible codes for gender identity no matter how they 'choose' to identify. Some men are perceived as femme and some women are perceived as butch no matter how hard they try to conform."[8] Having spent seven years with my partner, Melanie, and hearing her called "sir" more often than "ma'am," makes me believe, like Walker, that there is something we can call "butchness." Certainly Melanie is not totally butch by many standards; if anything, she is somewhat androgynous. Yet her body, unmarked as "conventionally" female, passes as male, resulting in such situations as being kicked out of a dressing room with me because, as the clerk told us, "men have to wait outside." There is a component of *un*femininity, *non*-femaleness that characterizes the butch. To claim, then, that lesbian style has expanded to the extent that we are all "free" to choose how we look—and, by extension, how we

are received in the world—is, in my opinion, reductive. As Susan Bordo asserts, the postmodern notion of "abstract, unsituated, disembodied freedom . . . glorifies itself only through the effacement of the material praxis of people's lives."[9] I, too, would argue that the putative "liberation" associated with the proliferation of categories doesn't wholly ring true.

Thus I use the terms 'butch" and "femme" in my discussion of mainstream culture because I believe the categories obtain in ways that we are often reluctant or even loathe to acknowledge. And they obtain *especially* in mainstream culture, where ideas about "lesbian style" have not diversified or proliferated at the rate that they have in lesbian culture, and where women's appearances in general are measured against a narrow arid demanding standard of beauty. I am not saying that there is an essential butch or femme to be found, but I am saying that some women, whether by willful self-presentation and stylization or by simply "wearing what's comfortable" or what makes them feel good, will appear more butch than others, and some women will appear more femme than others. Thus we should ask, Where exactly is the butch in mainstream culture, where is the femme, and what is the significance of their relative absence or presence?

"Lesbian Chic": The Inauguration of Lesbian Visibility

The above question cannot be answered simply or easily, and in many ways, it cannot be answered at all until we begin at the beginning: 1993, the year of "lesbian chic." *New York* magazine kicked off the craze in May of 1993, featuring chanteuse k.d. lang on its cover with the caption: "Lesbian Chic: The Bold, Brave New World of Gay Women." *Newsweek* followed suit in June, offering on its cover the image of two attractive lesbians, hugging one another and smiling broadly at the camera. Finally, in August, *Vanity Fair* presented the now-famous cover of a scantily-clad Cindy Crawford shaving a pleased k.d. lang. And inside magazines as well—women's magazines in particular—lesbians were suddenly getting space. *Ladies' Home Journal*, an unlikely venue for lesbian concerns, printed a short interview with, of all people, Martina Navratilova.[10] More in step with "lesbian chic," *Mademoiselle* featured a long article entitled "Women in

Love," announcing that "lesbians are becoming more visible as a new generation of gay women are coming out and coming of age in ways that are distinctly their own."[11] (It also featured a "glossary" of lesbian terms, just in case readers couldn't follow the article.) And *Vogue* said "Goodbye to the Last Taboo," pointing out: "Not long ago, you couldn't say the word *lesbian* on television. Now everybody's gay-girl crazy. Alexis Jetter charts the trend and asks, Is this the new visibility, or the old voyeurism?"[12]

Certainly there is something to be said for the fact that mainstream culture was representing lesbianism in a relatively positive light. Yet such representation was not met without skepticism; the question posed by *Vogue* tapped into an anxiety that many lesbians felt in response to this sudden boom in "positive" images. For years, lesbian feminist critics have been concerned with the relative invisibility of the lesbian within both academic circles and in the culture at large. Summarizing these concerns, Terry Castle, in her book, *The Apparitional Lesbian: Female Homosexuality in Modern Culture*, poses the question: "Why is it so difficult to see the lesbian—even when she is there, quite plainly, in front of us? In part because she has been 'ghosted'—or made to seem invisible—by culture itself."[13] In the Second Wave of the feminist movement, lesbians—like women of color—were effaced by the white, middle-class, heterosexual image that many feminists sought to protect and promote. In the 1970s and 1980s, as the push for gay rights picked up momentum, lesbians were similarly eclipsed by gay men at the forefront of the movement. Furthermore, the images of lesbianism that have emerged throughout the twentieth century have not always been benign; one need only peruse Vito Russo's *The Celluloid Closet*, a survey of representations of homosexuality in film, to be reminded of exactly how pernicious such representations have been.[14] To be sure, representation promises visibility, but visibility means not only that one is *present* but that one is *being watched*. It also means that certain images get singled out as *watchable*. In the proliferation of lesbian images that we have witnessed since that watershed year, what images have been singled out? On mainstream cultural landscapes, what does the lesbian body of the 1990s look like?

The Consumable Lesbian

In April of 1997, amidst the increasingly loud media buzz surrounding her sexuality, Ellen DeGeneres appeared on the cover of *Time* magazine proclaiming, "Yep, I'm Gay." On this cover, Ellen is dressed in black (save the shiny white loafers she sports). Her pants look comfortable and not too tight; her shirt, long-sleeved and low-cut. Around her neck she wears what appears to be a small string of diamonds, and on her fingers are several rings. Her face, made up a little more than usual, smiles broadly for the camera, which looks down at her as she crouches on the floor. Jeanie Kasindorf points out that "the short-haired 'bulldyke' is still many Americans' idea of what a gay woman looks like,"[15] but *this* lesbian body—comfortable and comforting—doesn't look anything like the stereotypical lesbian body, the "mannish," makeup-less butch in boots and flannel so often associated with lesbianism. Here, Ellen is attractive (nice smile, light but appealing makeup), feminine (low-cut shirt—unusual for DeGeneres—and *diamonds*?), and inviting.

I think this cover photo illustrates a particular trend in representations not only of Ellen but also of lesbianism in general: the sanitizing of the lesbian through her feminizing (or, conversely, the use of the feminine to sanitize the popular conception of the lesbian). Certainly it could be argued that these carefully coded bodies offer a corrective to the relatively rigid image of the lesbian that has dominated for decades (the same one that dominated my mind when I came out): the angry, militant, lesbian feminist, the butch, the woman who deep down wants to be a man and thus eschews all accoutrements of femininity. And certainly there is something to be said for disrupting the narrative associating lesbianism with masculinity (David Greenberg, for example, reminds us that "stereotypes linking lesbianism with masculinity date back to the Romans").[16] At the same time, however, the femme or feminine images presented to mainstream audiences have the potential to be interpreted in a variety of ways, many of them not subversive at all. The result, in fact, could well be a reinscription of mainstream norms and ideals. Let me turn to some other images to illustrate how this reinscription might take place.

Ellen's predecessors were the two lesbians on the cover of *Newsweek* from 1993 heralding "LESBIANS."

The women pictured are young, white, and conventionally attractive. Presumably they are partners, as one sits behind the other, hugging her girlfriend around the waist. Both women have dark, styled hair, dark eyes, and attractive faces. The "hugger" has soft, curly hair and a slightly smiling, slightly made-up (and thus feminine) face. We see her from the waist up only; she wears a long-sleeved denim shirt—not particularly feminine attire, but it is balanced by some standard markers of both femininity and affluence: pearl earrings, pearl necklace, and a shiny ring on her finger. The other woman, leaning back in her girlfriend's arms, also is conventionally attractive, although her short, pageboy haircut isn't quite as feminine as her girlfriend's hairdo. What she does have going for her, however, is her body: lean and tanned, she wears a brown, long-sleeved button-up top with a deep scoop neck. Her neck and collarbone are thus accentuated and "marked" clearly as petite, feminine, and pretty. This photo, coupled with the Ellen cover, seems to assure mainstream audiences that there is nothing "different" about lesbians, except that they might hug one another more than straight women might. Indeed, these images—images of clean-cut, well-dressed, economically secure, feminine lesbians—promise readers that Ellen and the *Newsweek* women are, simply put, all-American girls.

A clearer case in point of this packaging of the lesbian body is the representation and transformation of Melissa Etheridge. Etheridge broke into the rock and roll scene in 1988 with the release of her self-titled debut album. The image on the cover of this album is striking: decked out in leather, hair spiked up tall and rebellious, Etheridge clenches her fists and her jaw; she looks ready to explode. Although the space she occupies is small, it is clear in this image that she is all energy and that once unleashed, she will take up as much space as she likes.

This image certainly contrasts with one from a 1994 *People* magazine: accompanying an article entitled "A House in Harmony" is a photo of Etheridge and her (now ex-)partner, Julie Cypher. Pictured in their (very nice) kitchen, Melissa sits on the counter laughing while Julie stands next to her, lifting up some wine glasses with very feminine hands—fingernails nicely polished, rings on her fingers, bracelet on one wrist. Then, in 1996, the two appear on the cover of *Newsweek*, huddled close together, looking serious and announcing, "We're Having a Baby." Inside is an interview with the two women, and the photo accompanying the article is a pleasing one: the women pose by a poolside (presumably theirs), Melissa holding Julie's wrists as the two of them laugh and play. What changes are being registered in these representations? The most obvious difference is the way Etheridge's image has shifted—from a very eighties' butch in leather to a softer, more conventionally attractive nineties' lesbian. But there are other markers to note as well. Like the other lesbians on the cover of *Newsweek*, Melissa and Julie (when they were still a couple) were typically pictured close together, hugging or playing; they usually occupied a small amount of space and, unlike the first image of Etheridge, their bodies gave no indication of breaking out of that space. Although their image on the cover of *Newsweek* might be characterized as defiant—they look the viewer in the eye and hold each other without shame—the fact remains that Etheridge and Cypher are presented as conventionally attractive women, and their attractiveness has the potential to "soften" that defiance for mainstream audiences. Finally, the positions of the women's bodies in all these photos indicate some intimacy, but they do not indicate *sexuality*. Mainstream magazines like *Newsweek* might not have a problem putting Etheridge and Cypher on the cover, but they—like other media—are careful to present bodies that are sanitized yet attractive clean of any (homo)sexual residue.

Possibly the singular exception to this image is provided by another lesbian in the music industry, the highly visible—and highly unfemme—k.d. lang. If my argument is that only femme or feminine lesbians are allowed to appear on our cultural landscapes, how might we account for someone like lang, of whom Madonna was rumored to have said, "Elvis is alive—and she is beautiful!"? I can only speculate, but I think her representation depends on both her self-presentation and the way mainstream audiences interpret her presence on cultural landscapes. For example, lang insists that she is neither butch nor femme but androgynous. As she explains, "I don't feel like a woman, and I don't feel like a man; I feel like both, simultaneously."[17] And certainly lang is one of the most *playful* lesbians around, if not one of the most playful *women* in the public eye. She's not afraid to try on different styles, as a layout in the July 1997 issue of *Vogue*—in which lang sports designer dresses—indicates. So perhaps lang can pull off the butch aspects of her self-presentation precisely because she so obviously points to the game that gender is for her. Or, finally, perhaps lang's visibility is allowed because she *is* the exception to the rule—like RuPaul, the representative "other." For however butch k.d. lang may appear to be, her popularity has certainly not produced a mainstream cultural landscape crowded with imitators.

Aside from lang, then, there is a certain homogeneity to the lesbian bodies we see in mainstream media. Take the much talked-about 1995 lesbian wedding on *Friends*, for example. The sophisticated brides "had their hair in ringlets and wore dresses out of a Merchant Ivory film"[18]; in other words, they looked *nothing* like the stereotypical lesbian. On the one hand, this representation might have been effective at dispelling some preconceptions that the public holds regarding lesbians, convincing audiences that even "straight-looking" women could be gay and that even lesbians could have such impeccable taste in clothing. Such disruption is important. At the same time, doesn't this "corrective" seem *too* correct? As an article in *Entertainment Weekly* suggests, "[television] writers may have gotten a bit too conscientious in avoiding stereotypes. Out comic Lea DeLaria, who had a cameo in the lesbian wedding on *Friends*, complains, 'They needed at least 30 or 40 more fat dykes in tuxedos. All those thin, perfectly coiffed girls in Laura Ashley prints—what kind of a lesbian wedding is that? And no one played softball afterwards?'"[19] Although DeLaria is being humorous about this instance of lesbian representation, she nonetheless raises an important point: the "thin, perfectly coiffed girls" might well be lesbians, but where were the other ones, the "dykes," to use her words? In representing lesbianism and lesbian bodies, then, television, like print media, relies upon images that seem to erase the butch lesbian.

From the *Friends* brides—who did, indeed, look more like fashion models than anything else—to the lesbian couple on *Mad about You*, to the earlier femme duo of Sandra Bernhard and Morgan Fairchild on *Roseanne*, these lesbian bodies are consumable, just like the presumably straight female bodies in women's fashion magazines. They join images from recent movies as well. One of the better-received lesbian

"crossover" films (an independent film that is relatively successful with mainstream audiences) is the 1996 *Bound*. The movie poster itself offers a tantalizing image of lesbianism—Jennifer Tilly as Violet, the film's femme in her seductive dress, tellingly glances toward Gina Gershon, who is looking tough with her muscle T-shirt and her tattooed arm. Gershon plays the butch, Corky, and she does an impressive (and undeniably sexy) job of it. But this image, and those in the movie itself, frame Gershon's butchness: she is marked as butch (and, by extension, working class—a connection that I explore later in the article) through her black shirt and tattoo, and through her proclivity for painting and plumbing, but she is simultaneously marked as feminine with her pouty, Julia Roberts lips, wispy hair hanging in her eyes, and her reputation as an actress—this is, after all, one of the women who bared it all in *Showgirls* (although in that film, too, there was a lesbian subplot in which Gershon's polymorphously perverse character was rejected by Elizabeth Berkley's straight-only femme.)[20] And notably, it is Gershon's conventionally attractive, feminine body that we see fully nude in *Bound*, not Tilly's. As a recent issue of *Girlfriends* magazine asks, "Is this the butchest woman in Hollywood?"

Similarly, we might question why one of the other recent "lesbian" films—independent filmmaker Kevin Smith's *Chasing Amy* (1997)—was such a crossover success. The plot is as follows: boy meets girl, boy discovers girl is a lesbian but pursues her anyway, boy convinces girl to give it a try with him, boy and girl find true love with one another, experience conflict, and ultimately break up. This movie was critically acclaimed for its honest portrayal of how love surpasses all boundaries, and perhaps mainstream audiences were moved by the film's message: "It's not who you love. It's how" (or so the movie poster tells us). Or perhaps it was the "lure" of the lesbian, a lure that straight audiences might experience vicariously through the main character of the film, Holden (played by Ben Affleck). Whatever the draw, certainly it didn't hurt that the film's feature lesbian, Alyssa (or, as David Ansen, movie critic for *Newsweek*, puts it, "the bright, wild, sexy Alyssa"),[21] was played by Joey Lauren Adams, a petite, traditionally attractive blond with a childlike voice. It's easy to see why Holden falls for Alyssa: he initially thinks she's straight, and even when he discovers that she's not, he nurses this belief. That is, Alyssa fulfills an *I know, but* function in the film: *I know she's a lesbian, but she can't be a lesbian,* says Holden. So, too, it is altogether possible that femme Alyssa prompted mainstream audiences to employ the *I know, but* equation: I know this character's a lesbian, but—but she's so attractive, she can't be a lesbian. But she decides to be with Holden, so maybe she's not a lesbian. But she's not a lesbian in real life, she used to date the director, Kevin Smith, who thanks his "poopie" in the closing credits. And therein lies the rub: in mainstream cultural representations of lesbianism, there is always a *but,* always the possibility—or is it the promise?—that she who is lesbian (e.g., Anne Heche) can "unbecome" lesbian (e.g., Anne Heche).

Discursive Bodies

In the May 1993 issue of *New York,* Jeanie Kasindorf's article on "lesbian chic" describes life at an upscale lesbian bar called Henrietta Hudson in New York City:

> Outside the front stands the bouncer, a short young woman with a shaved head and a broad, square body. She's covered in loose black cotton pants, and looks like an out-of-shape kung fu instructor. . . . [Inside] sits a young woman straight from a Brooks Brothers catalogue—wearing a conservative plaid jacket and matching knee-length pleated skirt, a white blouse with a Peter Pan collar, and a strand of pearls. She chats with her lover while they sip white wine and rub each other's backs. Across from them, at the bar, sits a group of young women in jeans and black leather, all with cropped hair. . . . The Brooks Brothers woman and her lover leave, and are replaced by two 26-year-old women with the same scrubbed, girl-next-door good looks. The two are celebrating their engagement and show off matching diamond rings. . . . In the other alcove is a sexy young tawny-skinned woman in her early twenties. She has thick, dark, curly hair flowing into her eyes and down her back; she wears a skintight top over tight jeans. She is talking to her pretty blond lover, also in tight jeans, with a black leather jacket. . . . These are

the faces of a new generation of women—women who have transformed the lesbian image.[22]

I quote this long passage because I want to draw attention to the way that lesbians—and lesbian bodies—are normalized, made consumable, even in print. Lesbians here fall into one of two main categories: incredibly (and conventionally) attractive, and thus described quite thoroughly (and voyeuristically), or not conventionally attractive, and thus briefly mentioned and dismissed. Take, for example, the bouncer "with a shaved head and a broad, square body" who "looks like an out-of-shape kung fu instructor." This initial figure is one of the few images of the butch body described in this excerpt, and it is presented as unappealing, if not humorous. However, following her is a luscious array of lesbians: a woman wearing pearls, the two young "scrubbed, girl-next-door good looks" women, and the "sexy young tawny-skinned" woman who, with her luxurious hair and tight, revealing clothing, is described almost excessively. The juxtaposition of the bouncer and the rest of the women both draws attention to the ways in which the bouncer is *not* attractive and, by the end of the passage, effectively erases her; she is all but forgotten in this sea of gorgeous women. Aside from the bouncer, the only other women who interrupt what seems to be a narrative tailored to evoke straight (male) desire as well as lesbian desire are the young women with cropped hair, dressed in jeans and leather. They are not dwelled upon obsessively; nor are there any adjectives assessing their beauty. In *this* landscape of lesbianism, then, the images of femme lesbians may challenge the traditional reader's sense of what a lesbian looks like; but these same images are potentially desirable to straight audiences. Such language evokes the discourse of *Sports Illustrated*'s swimsuit issue more than anything else. As Sherrie Inness notes: "By emphasizing that lesbians are beautiful, well dressed, and born to shop, . . . writers build up an image of lesbians as being 'just like us'—or, in other words, 'homosexual = heterosexual.'"[23]

Scanning a variety of magazines, it seems that the "homosexual = heterosexual" equation is now a common one. An article in *Seventeen* on lesbian teens describes one young woman, Amy, as a girl who's "gone out with guys before—she's even lost her virginity"—and another, Tonya, as a young woman "who looks a little bit like Kelly Taylor on *90210.*"[24] A *Maclean's* article on lesbian film-maker Patricia Rozema proclaims that she "looks more like a movie star than a moviemaker."[25] *Premiere* magazine characterizes Rozema's movie, *When Night Is Falling*, as "an unabashed lipstick-lesbian fest, with women who look like goddesses rolling around in crushed velvet."[26] *People* magazine, describing Melissa Etheridge and Julie Cypher, notes that while "Etheridge dresses down, eschewing even lipstick," Cypher sports "a nouveau-shag hairdo and dangling silver necklaces, embod[ying] California chic."[27]

Even *Redbook* has discovered the appeal of the femme lesbian, as evidenced in a recently published article entitled, "Why She *Had* to Leave the Husband She Adored." It tells the story of Lisa Anderson, a thirty-two-year-old white woman who, after five years of marriage, realized she was gay. Lisa now frequents what the magazine calls a "women's bar," where one can see "women of every physical description—from stunning cover-girl look-alikes wearing red lipstick and stiletto heels to plain-faced flannel-shirted types who could almost pass for men." Notably, the author assures us that Lisa is *not* one of those women who "could almost pass for men." In fact, according to the article, Lisa's "style" of lesbianism is representative of *most* lesbians: "[L]ike Anderson, who's wearing a sexy sweater and black pants, the majority [of lesbians] look like any ordinary woman you'd see at the mall on Saturday." To further assure the readers that Anderson is not one of "those" lesbians, the author relates a story about a hostile exchange between Anderson and a butch lesbian: "[Anderson] was amused when a very butch-looking lesbian accused her of not being 'gay enough' because she eschews a masculine, spiked-hair-and-leather look." This anecdote might ostensibly function as an illustration of how lesbian communities can be just as oppressive as straight communities when it comes to style, but in another way—to the mostly straight, middle-class readers of *Redbook*—it vilifies the butch lesbian as "oppressor," as the "bad" lesbian. Nevertheless, the story concludes with two hopeful messages for the readers: first, the author tells us, Anderson may be a lesbian *now*, but in the future—who knows: "Not that Anderson is ruling out the possibility of ever again being with a

man physically." Second, Anderson promises that she won't procreate: "What won't be an option, she says, is having children. She knows there are plenty of same-sex couples raising kids, but she doesn't want to be among them. 'Kids are cruel, and I'd be afraid of the abuse my kid would take in a 'two moms' scenario."[28] This article might mark a step forward for *Redbook*, but just how big a step is it?

We might ask the same question about the visibility of Guinevere Turner, an actress best known in lesbian and independent film circles as the coproducer and one of the stars of the hit *Go Fish*, who is in many ways a lesbian media darling.[29] An article in *Premiere* magazine on lesbian filmmakers features an entire-page photograph of Turner (the other filmmakers only got about a quarter of the page each) and describes her as "the glamorous writer-star of 1994's lesbian-themed succès d'estime *Go Fish*" and a "bombshell in grunge." "With her Pre-Raphaelite beauty and the saucy look in her eye," the article gushes, "Turner was the *Go Fish* girl who really whetted Hollywood's appetite."[30] A 1997 *Newsweek* article entitled "Hollywood Lesbians: It's a 'Girl World'" calls Turner "gorgeous,"[31] while another in *Entertainment Weekly* introduces her as "beautiful cowriter-star Guinevere Turner."[32] And a recent issue of *Glamour* even gave Turner a guest column (in which she discusses lesbian commitment ceremonies). The essay is decently written, but it is accompanied—of course!—by a picture of Turner, dressed stylishly and smiling prettily for the camera. Above all, however, it is noted that Turner is adamant about admitting her lesbianism up front; in fact, she "feels honesty [about her lesbianism] hasn't hurt her mainstream chances. . . . It helps, says Turner, if a gay actress is good-looking in a traditional way. 'The world isn't ready for lesbian androgyny.'"[33] But the world is ready, it appears, for Turner's lesbianism. The discursive production of *this* lesbian body—as well as the others above-functions in the same way as the pictorial production does: it presents a lesbian body that is conventionally desirable, a body marked by glamour, beauty, and above all, *sameness* to mainstream images of heterosexual bodies.

Whiteness, Femininity, and the Lesbian Body

Alexis Jetter astutely observes that lesbians represented in the mainstream media "have a few key things in common: They're white. They're middle class. And they seem more interested in makeup and clothes than in feminism. In short, they're femmes, or what the straight world prefers to call lipstick lesbians."[34] Indeed, one cannot help but notice that the images populating the cultural landscape are images of a *white* femme body. There are, in fact, only two recent mainstream representations of women of color: Whoopi Goldberg's lesbian nurturer, Jane, in *Boys on the Side* (1994), and Queen Latifah's butch lesbian, Geo, in *Set It Off* (1996). What is most striking about these representations is that they *don't* seem to conform to the mainstream narrative of lesbianism to which I have been pointing. After all, here are two nonwhite lesbian characters, neither of which could be called a femme. In this sense, it could be argued that Jane and Cleo stand as counterexamples, offering disruption to what I have been depicting as a homogeneous narrative of the feminine lesbian. But again, I think it is necessary to ask just how much of a disruption Jane and Cleo (and Goldberg and Latifah) really pose. The fact that they don't fit into the overall picture of the "lipstick lesbian" demands further consideration.

Whoopi Goldberg's *Boys on the Side* character, Jane, is an R&B singer who decides to leave her home in New York City and head out west. On her travels she is accompanied by two other women, the "whiter-than-white bread upper-middle-class straight woman"[35] Robin, played by Mary Louise Parker, and the fun-loving, straight, "white-trash" Holly, played by Drew Barrymore. Jane predictably falls for Robin, and although the love is unrequited, Jane nurses Robin through her illness and untimely death from AIDS. An inoffensive, if not innocuous, plot, and Goldberg's Jane seems to be a positive representation of lesbianism: she is tough, funny, and caring.

But still, there is something suspect about the character of Jane, something that highlights the conflation of femme-ness and whiteness in the images examined earlier. For example, although it is significant that Goldberg's character, unlike the many lesbians populating mainstream landscapes, is not conventionally feminine, it is also evident that Jane is set up as a contrast to the other two women in the film: the uptight, prissy Robin and the free-spirited, cute Holly (both of whom hook up with men over the course of the film). Goldberg's Jane is presumably neither the object

of (straight) sexual desire for mainstream audiences (that's Drew Barrymore's role) nor a *satisfied* desiring subject within the film; as Raymond Murray puts it, "Whoopi Goldberg stars as a lesbian who just can't seem to get laid (or even receive a passionate kiss). . . . [P]oor Whoopi goes loveless and untouched."[36] Compared with the earlier (white) femme images of the *Newsweek* lesbians or the *Friends* brides, images that appear clean of homosexual residue but that still function within a heterosexual economy of desire, Jane simply doesn't fit. And isn't it noteworthy that one of the few exceptions to the "lipstick lesbian" rule is a Black woman?[37]

But what about Cleo, the butch lesbian played by Queen Latifah in the film *Set It Off*? After all, if Goldberg's Jane is troubling because she is an asexual mammy figure (playing nurse to an upper-class white woman), surely Latifah's Cleo, a lesbian who is both sexual *and* butch, can be read as a positive addition to the imagery that surrounds us. But here, too, I would question the meaning of this image in relation to the dozens of white femme bodies that populate the mainstream landscape. Considering the overwhelming homogeneity of these images, it seems apparent that mainstream representations of the lesbian body are "made" femme not simply by embodying femininity but also by embodying *white* femininity. Given this configuration of lesbianism, then, it comes as no surprise that one of the few butch lesbians to appear on this landscape is *Black*. And unlike Gina Gershon's Corky, the butch masculinity of Queen Latifah's Cleo is not tempered with any markers of femininity. Furthermore, although Cleo is a sexual lesbian, her sexuality differs from that of the white lesbian images I have examined thus far: presumably, the object of sexual desire for mainstream audiences is not Latifah's Cleo but instead is Jada Pinkett's Stony, Vivica Fox's Frankie, or, most obviously, Cleo's sexy femme lover.[38] Rather than standing out as an exception to the mainstream image of the white (hetero) sexualized femme lesbian, then, Cleo stands as her *foil*: the Black (homo)sexualized butch lesbian. (And, predictably, Cleo lives in the L.A. projects and leads a working-class existence cleaning offices—hence her desire to rob several banks.) The characters of Jane and Cleo, then, are born from the same mainstream edict: the femme body is necessarily a white body, so a Black lesbian cannot be a femme. What she can be, however, is an amalgam of mythologies about Black women.

Finally, it is crucial to consider these images of Black lesbianism in relation to the larger context to which they belong—that is, to remember once again that in a world of images, the boundaries between the "reel" and the "real" are not stable; that, as in the case of Gina Gershon, there is a slippage between the characters that the actresses play and the actresses themselves, between their on-screen and off-screen lives. Mainstream audiences might not have a problem seeing Whoopi Goldberg as lesbian Jane not only because Jane plays into the mythology of the Black woman as the sexless mammy but also because Goldberg's "real-life" persona is a heterosexual woman. In other words, even though Goldberg plays lesbian Celie in *The Color Purple* or lesbian Jane on screen, audiences know that the "real" Whoopi Goldberg is definitely not a lesbian—from Ted Danson to Frank Langella, she is a woman who loves men.

Is Queen Latifah, too, a woman who loves men? Despite ongoing rumors that she is a lesbian, Latifah's not telling, one way or the other. Or *is* she, albeit indirectly? Take, for example, a recent issue of *Essence*, where Latifah appears both on the cover and inside the magazine dressed in sexy, feminine lingerie. Can these images be read as the emergence of a Black femme lesbian among the many white femmes inhabiting cultural landscapes? According to the article, no. The opening paragraph notifies the readers: "Those of you ready to skim ahead looking for answers to the sexuality question need not bother."[39] Similarly, in a 1998 interview in *The Source: The Magazine of Hip-Hop Music, Culture and Politics* (advertised on the cover as "QUEEN LATIFAH EXHALES: THE TRUTH ABOUT HER HOLLYWOOD LIFE . . . AND THOSE DAMN GAY RUMORS"), Latifah insists: "I don't have any problems with my sexuality, whatever you wanna think I am. I'll never answer the question. I'd rather have you die wanting to know." Although this statement and the statement introducing the *Essence* article might seem like admirable attempts to throw into question society's tendency to label according to sexual preferences, her later comments about the infamous "kiss" in *Set It Off* indicate an increasing anxiety on her part, a desire to align herself with the heterosexual: "That scene in *Set It Off* where I kissed that

girl? I've never watched it. I mean Dana [Latifah's real name] is not comfortable watching Dana doing stuff like that. What I do from my point of view is one thing, but seeing it is another thing. So I've never actually watched that scene, every time it comes I know it and I turn my head . . . . I tried to get out of it . . . . I didn't think it was that necessary, my mother didn't think it was that necessary, but this guy's directing the movie and he's got the last call."[40] Latifah may have "kissed that girl" *on* screen, but *off* screen, she makes it clear that someone else dictated the expression of lesbian desire.

Why the Femme?

I have spent some time now pointing to the various ways that lesbian bodies are coded in mainstream culture—coded materially, spatially, discursively, and racially. What I hope to have pointed to is the *excess* of such coding. What, then, are these representations effecting in culture at large? The answer to this question is by no means simple; certainly any image can have different and varying effects on different people. By way of response, however, I want to point out some other cultural ideas that belong to the mainstream imagination, using them to suggest why the femme is so overrepresented. Our starting point is with the obvious: within mainstream culture, the femme is not really considered a lesbian. A hundred years ago, Havelock Ellis declared that "the principle character of sexually inverted woman is a certain degree of masculinity"; femme or feminine lesbians he deemed "pseudohomosexuals."[41] Diane Hamer elaborates on this preconception: "Always, it has been the butch woman who is constructed as the authentic lesbian; rarely is the femme seen as such. Traditionally, the femme has been constructed as essentially feminine and heterosexual; her lesbianism at most a passing phase, resulting from seduction by a predatory butch or a temporary retreat from men after some damaging experience."[42] The femme, in other words, is representable not only because she is desirable but also because she is perceived as "inauthentic."

We might also note that the feminine (or feminized) lesbian bodies we see are usually shown alone (e.g., Ellen's *Time* cover), coupled with another conventionally feminine lesbian (e.g., Melissa and Julie, the *Friends* brides), or—tellingly, perhaps?—with a man (e.g., *Chasing Amy*). Virtually none of the mainstream representations pairs a femme or feminine lesbian with a butch or masculine lesbian. Perhaps the configurations of single and coupled femmes work to undo the "lesbian" signifier and to de-lesbianize the subject for mainstream audiences. Biddy Martin, explicating Teresa de Lauretis's arguments about lesbian desire, points out this quandary for the femme, writing that "as a femme alone, her lesbianism would be invisible."[43] Without the signifier of the butch, the femme's lesbianism disappears, or, more accurately, never appears in the first place. Is this, perhaps, another more important reason why "femme-looking" lesbians are the most represented in mainstream culture? Mainstream culture is thus giving with one hand and taking back with another: it makes room for positive representations of lesbianism, but the lesbian it chooses as "representative," decoupled from the butch that would more clearly signify lesbianism for mainstream audiences, in effect becomes a nonlesbian, or, as Rosanne Kennedy puts it, an "absent presence."[44] Thus, in the same moment that mainstream culture (re)presents the lesbian, challenging her longstanding invisibility, it reinscribes that very invisibility.

The Invisible Butch, or the Unrepresentable Body

I go back, now, to the question that's been a silent but present one throughout most of this article. On the cultural landscape of lesbianism, in the realm of representation, where is the butch? Given the above evidence, it's clear that she remains on the margins, rarely seen. Why? Perhaps most obviously because the butch, unlike the femme, is *not* consumable; her relative invisibility on the cultural landscape has to do with her perceived (un)attractiveness. Sue O'Sullivan points out that butch is "the caricature lesbian whipping girl, the one who serves as the repository of mainstream hatred and fear of feminism's 'excesses'. . . . She is 'mannish' but not at all stylish and at the same time she is definitely a woman. Therefore she has to be ugly—in other words, butch."[45] Or, as Sherrie Inness, nicely encapsulating this point, maintains: "Butches fail to fulfill heterosexual ideas about what is attractive and sexually appealing in women."[46] In

other words, the butch, a woman marked more by conventional masculine characteristics than feminine ones, is considered "ugly." And given the configurations of our mainstream cultural landscape, there is little room for those judged unattractive. In fact, such supposed unattractiveness is an affront to an image-based culture; as O'Sullivan contends, "the so-called loony, ugly (read not stereotypically feminine) lesbian, increasingly designated as an arbiter of political correctness, remains a figure for derision and hatred."[47]

But perhaps such "derision and hatred" toward the butch, and her invisibility on the mainstream cultural landscape, is not so simply explained. Another characteristic attributed to the butch that conceivably marks her as unrepresentable is her socioeconomic status. In *Odd Girls and Twilight Lovers: A History of Lesbian Life in Twentieth-Century America*, Lillian Faderman points out that from the 1920s through 1960s, the butch-femme pair was usually associated with the working class.[48] Indeed, one need only read Leslie Feinberg's *Stone Butch Blues* to get an idea of the type of blue-collar jobs the "stone butches" of the 1950s and 1960s held, working primarily on docks and in factories.[49] I would assert that this connection between the butch and her working-class status further contributes to her mainstream undesirability. Look for a moment at the following description of butch-femme relations, as described in a 1993 article in *New York* magazine:

> "It was very different when I came out in Texas," says Jean Sidebottom, the editor and publisher of *Sappho's Isle*, the tri-state lesbian newspaper. "That bull-dyke world was very much the scene I came out into. The first lesbian bar I ever walked into, in Houston, was owned by a woman called Papa Bear. She was mildly obese, with short-cropped, masculine, stone-butch hair. She smoked cigars and wore T-shirts and blue-jeans—she had a key chain on her belt loop and a knife in her boot. Her girlfriend was a stripper. There was a certain sleaziness associated with it that I somehow could never accept. *It gave you a feeling of being less than a real person*."[50]
>
> (Emphasis mine.)

The lesbian Sidebottom describes is a butch, coded so with her "short-cropped, masculine, stone-butch hair" and her clothes—jeans, boots, T-shirt. There are no markers of "normality" on Papa Bear; she is not only masculine, she is also masculine and *undesirable* ("mildly obese"). On James Dean, T-shirts, blue jeans, and the accessories might be sexy. On Papa Bear, these attributes contribute to a caricature of the bull dyke and her hypermasculinity, a caricature that seems to be presented as simultaneously humorous and loathsome. Couple this with the fact that the butch's girlfriend is a stripper, and the entire image—and, by extension, the entire *body* of the butch—is deemed sleazy. Finally, the last line of the quote—"it gave you a feeling of being less than a real person"—leaves me wondering: what is "it?" What *specifically* leaves Sidebottom feeling so unlike a "real person"? One reading, of course, might be that she felt uncomfortable trying to fit into butch-femme codes of the 1950s and 1960s. However, given the description that precedes this statement, I want to point to another reading: the connection between "being less than a real person" and being a butch (or, more specifically here, a bull dyke). For even if it was the whole scene that made Sidebottom feel uncomfortable, in this passage it is Papa Bear who represents the source of not only discomfort but also "sleaziness." The butch here is presented as working class, masculine, and, above all, distasteful. Given these characteristics, *this* lesbian, clearly, is *not* palatable in any way. And the ways in which class marks the butch—considerably different from the ways class marks the upwardly mobile femmes or feminine lesbians discussed earlier—only contributes to her unrepresentability.

A more recent example of this unrepresentability occurs in the *Newsweek* article by Corie Brown, "Hollywood Lesbians: It's a 'Girl World,'" in which the author details how "Gay women in showbiz are coming out and succeeding as never before." To support the claim that Hollywood is now a "Girl World," Brown cites the testimony of numerous Hollywood players—independent producers, agents, activists, actresses—all of whom attest to the changing attitudes and mores in Tinseltown. Yet, as Brown notes, the members of the "Girl World" do not all run in the same circles: "There are really two thriving but separate lesbian worlds in Hollywood: the lipstick lesbians in the executive offices and the tool-belt crowd that competes in the macho world of gaffers, grips, and carpenters on movie and television sets." Brown then gives a voice to one of the members of the "macho world": "'I'm in a field that is the last stand of the macho man,' says Amazon, as this 27-year-old grip calls herself. 'I'm a lesbian woman. I'm intimidating.'"[51] Given the media's trend for ignoring the butch, it is notable that the working-class lesbians—the "tool-belt crowd," as Brown calls them—are mentioned at all. So is one other thing: the fact that accompanying this article are four large pictures of Hollywood lesbians: Guin Turner, Chastity Bono, Amanda Bearse, and Nina Jacobson, a production executive. To which world do they belong?

In considering this question of where the butch resides on mainstream cultural landscapes, I want to begin by teasing out some of the implications of the first argument I presented above: that the butch's perceived unattractiveness renders her invisible in an image-based culture. We should note that there is a converse of this equation: at the same time that culture might render the butch invisible because she is supposedly unpleasing to the eye, this very same quality makes her highly *visible*, or noticeable, in the real world. Mainstream media employ the femme body, I have argued, because the femme can be "de-lesbianized"; she is at once marked a lesbian and not a lesbian. The butch body, on the other hand, cannot be "de-lesbianized"; because her body is already and always marked as lesbian, she is *more* visible than the femme—and thus, if represented, more "lesbian" than the femme.

There is one other point that I think important to note: in the terms of mainstream, phallocentric culture, the butch body is not a "useful" body. At the core of her unrepresentability is her masculinity, "the chief identifying trait of the butch." And, as Sherrie Inness explains: "by claiming masculine identifiers for her own use, the butch sets herself apart from the 'average' heterosexual woman by failing to present herself as traditionally feminine in order to appeal to the male gaze."[52] This point is best made by turning to the concepts of desire and identification in order to examine the ways in which the butch body accommodates neither desire nor identification for mainstream audiences. As I have pointed out earlier, the body of a femme lesbian—say, the lesbians on the cover of *Newsweek*—is one that is consumable: straight women can look for the markers on these women's bodies that "match" their own, thus identifying with the women's *bodies*, their *images*. Straight men can "imagine" away the couple's lesbianism and thus desire them. But the butch body is incapable of meeting these criteria: more likely than not, straight women will not *identify* with the butch—she looks too much like a man and thus they might *desire* her (a different story altogether). By contrast, more likely than not, straight men will not *desire* the butch, for, as Inness points out, the butch does not present herself as the object of the male gaze—and in defying such representation, she is both a challenge and a threat to straight men. But there is one other possibility: these men might *identify* with the butch lesbian in her masculinity—and what does it mean for a straight man to identify with a butch lesbian?

The butch is unrepresentable, then, because of her masculinity; as Judith Roof asserts, "Admitting the possibility that a woman can be a man, that the traits attributed to masculinity are not exclusively masculine, and perceiving lesbians as masculine reveals the threat to masculine supremacy and to a heterosexual system lesbians potentially pose."[53] The butch has the capacity to disrupt the notion that masculinity is an inherently male attribute: the butch can be as good a man as any man is. But herein lies the quandary for her: she is at once present in mainstream imagination, the lesbian who appears in the straight mind's eye when lesbianism is mentioned, and the lesbian who is so reviled that she is unrepresentable. As the unrepresented signifier of lesbianism, the butch, even in her relative invisibility, inhabits an increasingly precarious place in mainstream culture: for if the femme body is now the *de facto* lesbian body in mainstream representation, at what point will this representation replace the signifier? In other words, at what point will the "real"—that is, the represented (femme) image—replace the "imaginary" (butch) one? And if such a displacement does occur—if the femme, by virtue of her widespread presence on cultural landscapes, becomes the "new" imaginary signifier of lesbianism—where does that leave the butch? Inness thus rightly compares the butch with Ellison's Invisible Man, contending that "the butch is simultaneously the most visible and least visible member of society. She is visible because she stands out as an 'abnormal' woman who does not adhere to society's dictates

about 'correct' femininity. She is invisible for exactly the same reason. Twisted by attempts to fit her into sanctioned conceptual categories, she becomes a distorted figure, the Other, the nonperson."[54] In the cultural landscape of lesbianism, then, the body of the butch remains outside the frame—present, to be sure, but not in the picture.

Conclusion

In its initial stages, this project began as an exploration of cultural representations of the butch body in the mainstream media. It ended, as you can see, as something quite different, because in my search for mainstream representations of the butch, I found almost none. This proves my point all the more: the butch is too dangerous, too loaded a figure to be represented. What I did discover is what I have presented here: the fact that there is, indeed, an increased amount of lesbian representation but a representation marked by a striking homogeneity, a certain safeness. What we are left with, then, is a landscape of lesbianism that is at once incredibly full and altogether empty. Although the 1990s may be perceived as a decade in love with lesbianism, we would do well to consider the ways that this love, channeled through commodification and consumerism, through identification and desire, helps to determine not only who gets seen but what it means to be seen after all.

Notes

I would like to express my gratitude to Virginia Blum for her help and encouragement in writing this article, as well as for her invaluable suggestions for revision. I would also like to thank Susan Bordo, Julie Cary, David Magill, Mary Hall, Valerie Johnson, and especially Melanie Anderson for reading subsequent drafts of this article. Finally, I am grateful to the reviewers of *Feminist Studies* for raising important questions about my article and thus for helping me to develop and refine my work.

1. I use the term "luscious lesbians" to refer to a kind of lesbian representation that is directed at and meant primarily for a straight male audience—one that typically appears in straight porn films. As Michael Segell, in "Two Girls for Every Boy," explains: "All men—straight ones, anyway—are aroused by the idea of two women having sex with one another. . . . Male fascination with female

coupling is so universal, in fact, that some researchers consider the erotic response to it a reliable indicator of heterosexuality." See Michael Segell, "Two Girls for Every Boy," *Esquire*, January 1997, 31.

2. Ann Northrop, quoted in Alexis Jetter, "Goodbye to the Last Taboo," *Vogue*, July 1993, 86.

3. I want to clarify my point here: I do not believe that the femme is completely incapable of challenging hegemonic discourses about lesbianism; in many ways, she can shatter stereotypes and pose a threat to heterosexual mainstream audiences. For discussions of the subversive potential of the femme, see Judith Roof, *A Lure of Knowledge: Lesbian Sexuality and Theory* (New York: Columbia University Press, 1991), 244–54; Judith Butler, *Gender Trouble* (New York: Routledge, 1990), 122–24; Joan Nestle, "Flamboyance and Fortitude: An Introduction," in *The Persistent Desire: A Femme-Butch Reader*, ed. Joan Nestle (Boston: Alyson Publications, 1992), 13–20; and Biddy Martin, "Sexualities without Genders and Other Queer Utopias," in *Femininity Played Straight: The Significance of Being Lesbian* (New York: Routledge, 1996), 71–94. Although I find these arguments quite compelling (particularly as they take issue with the invisibility of the femme within lesbian feminist theoretical circles), at the same time I question whether the femme in *popular culture*—in movies, on television, in magazines—loses her potential for disruption and subversion.

4. Arlene Stein, quoted in Jetter, 92.

5. For further discussion of butch-femme relationships in the 1950s and 1960s, see Lillian Faderman, *Odd Girls and Twilight Lovers: A History of Lesbian Life in Twentieth-Century America* (New York: Penguin Books, 1991), 159–87.

6. Michelle Fisher, "Butch Nouveau," *Utne Reader*, July/August 1996, 27.

7. Jeanie Kasindorf, "Lesbian Chic: The Bold, Brave New World of Gay Women," *New York*, 10 May 1993, 34.

8. Lisa Walker, "How to Recognize a Lesbian: The Cultural Politics of Looking Like What You Are," *Signs* 18 (summer 1993): 878–79.

9. Susan Bordo, "'Material Girl': The Effacements of Postmodern Culture," in *Unbearable Weight: Feminism, Western Culture, and the Body* (Berkeley: University of California Press, 1993), 275.

10. The image accompanying this interview is of a rather feminine-looking Martina: she is wearing what appears to be a bejeweled gown (the photo shows her from the waist up only) and gold hoop earrings, and her shoulder-length hair is attractively styled. Given the readership of the magazine, the reasons for this feminization of Martina are obvious. I am not suggesting, however, that this photo negates the role that Martina plays as an out

lesbian. As Diane Hamer points out in her essay, "Netting the Press: Playing with Martina" (in *The Good, the Bad, and the Gorgeous: Popular Culture's Romance with Lesbianism*, ed. Diane Hamer and Belinda Budge [London: Pandora, 1994], 57–77), Navratilova was *the* representative lesbian of the 1980s, an unfriendly and judgmental decade. And although Navratilova continues to be quite visible as a political activist, I would assert that her presence on the landscapes of popular culture is rather limited.

11. Elise Harris, "Women in Love," *Mademoiselle*, March 1993, 180.

12. Jetter, 86.

13. Terry Castle, *The Apparitional Lesbian: Female Homosexuality and Modern Culture* (New York: Columbia University Press, 1993), 4.

14. Vito Russo, *The Celluloid Closet: Homosexuality in the Movies*, rev. ed. (New York: Harper & Row, 1987).

15. Kasindorf, 33–34.

16. David Greenberg, *The Construction of Homosexuality* (Chicago: University of Chicago Press, 1988), 373.

17. Charles Gandee, "Cross-Dressing for Success," *Vogue*, July 1997, 148.

18. Guinevere Turner, "'I, Melanie, Take You, Mary . . .,'" *Glamour*, February 1997, 90.

19. A. J. Jacobs, "Out?" *Entertainment Weekly*, 4 Oct. 1996, 22.

20. As Richard Dyer, in his book, *Heavenly Bodies: Film Stars and Society* (London: British Film Institute, 1986), points out, "Star images are always extensive, multimedia, intertextual" (3).

21. David Ansen, "Boy Meets Lesbian," *Newsweek*, 7 Apr. 1997, 73.

22. Kasindorf, 33.

23. Sherrie Inness, *The Lesbian Menace: Ideology, Identity, and the Representation of Lesbian Life* (Amherst; University of Massachusetts Press, 1997), 67.

24. Sadie Van Gelder, "It's Who I Am," *Seventeen*, November 1996, 142.

25. Brian D. Johnson, "Sex and the Sacred Girl," *Maclean's*, 5 May 1995, 93.

26. Rachel Abramowitz, "Girl Gets Girl," *Premiere*, February 1996, 84.

27. Peter Castro and John Griffiths, "A House in Harmony," *People*, 5 Sept. 1994, 58.

28. Ronnie Polaneczky, "Why She *Had* to Leave the Husband She Adored," *Redbook*, July 1997, 86, 106.

29. Even though *Go Fish* is one of the better-known lesbian movies of the 1990s, I do not think that it could be called either a mainstream film or a mainstream representation of lesbianism, and thus I do not offer a reading of the movie itself. Although the film does present several characters who could be considered butch (Ely and

Daria, for example), it is marketed through the advertisement of the film's femme starlet, Guin Turner. The appeal for those people browsing at the video store, I would argue, is the picture on the box, one that seems to promise yet another story of "luscious lesbians."

30. Abramowitz, 81, 95.

31. Corie Brown, "Hollywood Lesbians: It's a 'Girl World,'" *Newsweek*, 14 Apr. 1997, 69.

32. Allison Gaines, "'Chasing' Down the Rumors," *Entertainment Weekly*, 28 Nov. 1997, 87.

33. Brown, 69.

34. Jetter, 88. I want to pause here to concur with Jetter's third point, that mainstream lesbians "seem more interested in makeup and clothes than in feminism." To be sure, the visible lesbian is typically a depoliticized lesbian, divorced from her feminist roots. If current representations of the lesbian are trying to shatter the image of the 1970s' "ugly militant lesbian" by replacing her with the 1990s' "lipstick lesbian," there's no better way to achieve this goal than to sever the ties between the lesbian and her politics. The question of "style" or "fashion" and its effects on the political efficacy of lesbian feminism is one of ongoing concern. Although it is beyond the scope of my article to enter this debate, there are several excellent essays which address this issue; see, for example, Inge Blackman and Kathryn Perry, "Skirting the Issue: Lesbian Fashion for the 1990s," *Feminist Review* 34 (spring 1990): 67–78; Sue O'Sullivan, "Girls Who Kiss Girls and Who Cares?" in *The Good, the Bad, and the Gorgeous*, 78–94; Danae Clark, "Commodity Lesbianism," in *The Lesbian and Gay Studies Reader*, ed. Henry Abelove, Michèle Aina Barale and David M. Halperin (New York: Routledge, 1993), 186–201; and especially Arlene Stein, "All Dressed Up but No Place to Go? Style Wars and the New Lesbianism," in *Out in Culture: Gay, Lesbian, and Queer Essays on Popular Culture*, ed. Corey K. Creekmur and Alexander Doty (Durham: Duke University Press, 1995), 476–83.

35. Raymond Murray, *Images in the Dark: An Encyclopedia of Gay and Lesbian Film and Video* (New York: Plume, 1996), 337.

36. Ibid.

37. In *Segregated Sisterhood: Racism and the Politics of American Feminism* (Knoxville: University of Tennessee Press, 1991), Nancie Caraway points out: "Black women historically have been powerless to displace the patriarchy's monopolization of the negative imagery which has cast them variously as depraved sexual temptresses, castrating matriarchs, breeders, or sexless, deferential mammies" (78)—in other words, as excluded from the realm of "true" womanhood, of *femininity*. For further reading on the mythologies of Black womanhood, see bell hooks, *Ain't I a Woman? Black Women and Feminism* (Boston: South End Press, 1981), and *Black Looks: Race and Representation* (Boston: South End Press, 1992); and Patricia Hill Collins, *Black Feminist Thought: Knowledge, Consciousness, and the Politics of Empowerment* (New York: Routledge, 1990).

38. It is significant that Cleo's femme lover is a Black woman with blonde hair—blondeness that may well function to "whiten" her. For an incisive reading of the connection between "blonde ambition" and whiteness, see bell hooks's "Madonna: Plantation Mistress or Soul Sister?" in *Black Looks*, 157–64.

39. Joan Morgan, "The Queen of Screen: Latifah Goes to the Movies," *Essence*, January 1998, 70.

40. Amy Linden, "From Here to Royalty," *The Source: The Magazine of Hip-Hop Music, Culture, and Politics*, August 1998, 157, 158.

41. Havelock Ellis, quoted in Greenberg, 382.

42. Hamer, 70–71.

43. Martin, 86.

44. Rosanne Kennedy, "The Gorgeous Lesbian in LA Law: The Present Absence?" in *The Good, the Bad, and the Gorgeous*, 141.

45. O'Sullivan, 85.

46. Inness, 200.

47. O'Sullivan, 79.

48. Faderman, 179–81.

49. Leslie Feinberg, *Stone Butch Blues* (Ithaca, N.Y.: Firebrand Books, 1993).

50. Kasindorf, 34.

51. Brown, 68, 69.

52. Inness, 203, 188.

53. Roof, 248.

54. Inness, 204.

23.
JOE MILLIONAIRE AND WOMEN'S POSITIONS
A Question of Class
Renee M. Sgroi

Introduction

Imagine the following scene: a viewer turns on the television, and there is a man onscreen, his face in shadow. The sun is a hazy brightness that burgeons over the back of this man's shoulders. The sunlight bathes him in a white-gold aura as he bends in slow motion over his digging. The opening, tentative strains of Strauss's *Blue Danube* are heard, imbuing the man's movements with grace and beauty. This is followed by a British-sounding voiceover, almost as if in time to the music, and the slowly shifting shots of the man digging, and driving construction machinery:

> Once, there was an average Joe, ((sounds of construction trucks)) who made a humble living by < S simply, moving, dirt S >. Meet Evan Marriott. Annual income, nineteen thousand dollars. What will happen when this average Joe is transformed, into a multimillionaire?
>
> (*Joe Millionaire*, episode one)[1]

The music swells and the scene quickly moves to a French chateau. The construction worker shaves, has his hair trimmed, dresses, and emerges from a white Rolls Royce as a dashing, elegant looking man with a winning smile. The opening sequence of *Joe Millionaire* begins by transforming this "average Joe" into a fairy prince fit to meet the twenty single, attractive young women who think he is a multi-millionaire. As the voiceover explains:

> He will lavish them with riches, in order to find the woman who will love him for who he is. . . . But once this average Joe has made his choice, he will have to confess the truth. . . . Will love or money prevail? This is the story of *Joe Millionaire*.
>
> (*Joe Millionaire*, episode one)

The gist of the show is that Evan must convince the women that he is a multi-millionaire, but the test is to discover who among the women will fall for him, and who will fall for the money.

Right from the opening credits, *Joe Millionaire* foregrounds questions of class. On the one hand, there is the test of Evan's ability to "pass" as a multi-millionaire. Will the women love him for "who he truly is" or for the money? This puzzle is in itself more complex than it might seem since, as John Kirk argues, "attempting to pass as middle class involves more than masquerade, a change of outfit . . . [because] . . . Class is deeply ingrained in lived experience" (2002, p. 6). On the other hand, the women are also being tested. "True love" on this show is premised upon accepting a person's "real" self, regardless of occupation or class status. And yet, as we discover later on in the series, true love is somehow problematic or heretofore inaccessible for working-class Evan. What kinds of questions and notions does *Joe Millionaire* put forth then around issues of class and gender?

Class is receiving renewed attention in cultural studies work. Several theorists argue that class has all but disappeared from cultural studies analyses, even though, ironically, cultural studies work is valued *because* of its strong emphasis on class (Cevasco 2000; Day 2001; Kirk 2002; Munt 2000). Sally Munt (2000, pp. 7–8) argues that questions of class have slipped under the radar in part because of the failures of Marxism and the rise of neo-liberal policies and governments in the US and UK. Day (2001, p. 179) points to the shift from heavy manufacturing industries to light industries as having had an impact on "traditional work cultures" in which employees engaged in talk and gossip that was later outlawed in the necessary industrial shift towards increased speed and efficiency in the post-World War II period. As a result, notions of the working class move from local, community-based associations to cultural ones (Day 2001, p. 188). What has resulted from these economic and cultural shifts is the notion that we have apparently moved to a "classless" society (Day 2001, p. 188; Munt 2000). Similarly, John Kirk (2002, pp. 3–4) asserts that "A postmodern pluralism reigns" in which identities are formed through discourse, and as a result, there is silence around the question of class. Combined with many academics' own difficulties around having grown up working class but now living a middle-class life (and getting paid a middle-class salary), class has become extremely problematic within cultural studies research (Day 2001; Kirk 2002; Munt 2000). As Munt argues, questions of class appear to be "not sexy enough for the intelligentsia" (2000, p. 7).

And yet, it is exactly at this intersection of sexiness, class, and especially gender that I situate my paper. Alison Graham-Bertolini's (2004) recent piece on *Joe Millionaire* in *Feminist Media Studies* argues that women on this show are identified in relation to men. She demonstrates that women's positions vis-à-vis the men on the show are produced primarily through their reliance on Paul Hogan, the butler, and their dependence on Evan's gaze (Graham-Bertolini 2004, p. 342). Certainly, there are moments on the show when Evan's attention to some women over others suggests that they rank higher in his estimation, and presumably this confers a certain degree of identification, both for Evan and the viewers. But as Kirk (2002) points out, as a structuring category class is intricately linked to identification. Building on the questions Graham-Bertolini raises then, it is necessary to reconsider Evan's gaze within the context of his classed position on the show.

Class and Taste

Life is saturated with class relations as Munt (2000) asserts, and everyday life consists of the kinds of distinctions we make. As Pierre Bourdieu (1984) made clear, taste is a means for classifying a class condition because:

> It transforms objectively classified practices, in which a class condition signifies itself (through taste), into classifying practices . . . Taste is thus the source of the system of distinctive features which cannot fail to be perceived as a systematic expression of a particular class of conditions of existence.
>
> (Bourdieu 1984, p. 175)

In other words, taste provides the signs or markers with which people try to distinguish themselves as belonging (or aspiring) to a particular class. One could argue that taste is subjective, yet as Celia Lury points out distinctions of taste are always accomplished through social practices, so that taste "is always a variant of class practice" (1996, p. 86). Classed distinctions can never be fully abstracted from the workings of everyday life. Taking these assertions into account, this paper investigates how the women's classed positions[2] affect their chances to "win" Evan. As I hope to demonstrate, it is not Evan's gaze that confers identity on *Joe Millionaire*, but Paul Hogan, the butler's, classed gaze.

Paul's position as bearer of official and class knowledge begins with the opening credits of episode one where his voiceover invites viewers[3] into the fairytale. As we saw above, Paul's Australian accent[4] (which could be mistaken for British) and the Strauss music metonymically represent the marks of class, sophistication, and wealth, in contrast to Evan's "humble" origins. Each episode begins and ends with Paul sitting in his wing chair, brandy snifter in hand, reminding us about last week's episode and asking leading questions about next week's. Like Alistair Cook and *Masterpiece Theatre*, Paul presides over *Joe Millionaire* with sophistication and class.

Paul's role as host also functions as an embodiment of the implied author. Like any good host, Paul tells us what the show is about and he provides clues as to what will happen next week, thereby giving us the necessary information to make sense of the show (Norman Fairclough 1995, p. 92). The host functions as bearer of "official discourse" in a clearly gendered relation (John Fiske 1987). He[5] assumes this position through his embodiment of the show's implied author, which is the reader's concept of the person(s) who have authored a text. In contrast, the narrator is the speaker whose voice tells the story (Sarah Kozloff 1992, pp. 77–78). In a television text then, the implied author can be the amalgam of writers, producers, and television executives who make the TV program a reality in viewers' minds. By embodying the voice of the implied author, the host puts a personal face on this amorphous figure (Kozloff 1992, p. 79). Paul's position on *Joe Millionaire* is much the same: he introduces the story and embodies the organizing force (and I would also suggest power) of the implied author(s).

At the same time, Paul participates (to an extent) in the activities at the chateau. As a result, he also occupies the space of a narrator. As a heterodiegetic narrator, Paul exists outside the events of the story. He is not one of the contestants, he is not the object of the women's affections, and he occupies an ancillary, working-class position as butler. Yet he also is a homodiegetic narrator because he is embedded within the events (Kozloff 1992, p. 82). He assists Evan and takes long walks with him as Evan tries to sort out his feelings about the women. Like the other participants, Paul lives at the chateau. He is present at the key "Dress Selection" scene where the women choose their gowns for the ball, and so he possesses intimate knowledge of this critical event. Paul's ability to draw conclusions is predicated on his proximity to and knowledge of the women. Ultimately, though, I want to argue that Paul's narrative role extends beyond that of the person telling (and not necessarily authoring) the tale. Paul's gaze and his expert knowledge works to anchor the women's subject positions so that what is offered to potential viewers bears the authoritative stamp of Paul's classed distinctions.

Paul's position as bearer of "true," official, authentic, and authoritative knowledge, what Bourdieu (1984) might call "legitimate knowledge," is further established in the "Dress Selection" scene in episode one. Here, the women are ushered into a room where they are given thirty minutes to select a gown for that evening's ball. The ball, of course, is an iconic event in romantic fairytales. It is where Cinderella's "true" beauty is revealed, and this trope gets played out in the final episode where Zora accepts Evan. The ball is also where the women are formally introduced to Evan. Chaos seemingly ensues as the women appear to scurry about trying to seize a good dress, and Paul's comment here highlights an implied animal metaphor: "Naturally they all wanted to look good for their millionaire, and they were determined to get the gown which they wanted, was a bit like a, pack of angry (hungry??) wolves." The comparison of women to wolves subordinates them in terms of their supposed inability to control their sexual and animalistic urges in contrast to masculine reason. Following Paul's statement, there is an aerial shot of the women choosing their dresses. The shot appears to provide concrete evidence of the animalistic women, but importantly, the shot's angle positions viewers so that specific power relations are created. As Gunther Kress and Theo van Leeuwen argue: "The top-down angle . . . is the angle of maximum power. It is orientated towards 'theoretical,' objective knowledge. It contemplates the world from a god-like point of view" (1996, p. 149). The aerial shot here invites the viewer to see the scene from this position of maximum power and thus to judge the women's actions.

If viewers are already offered a god-like position over the women in this scene, the expert knowledge Paul extends to us strengthens the possibilities for judging the women based on their supposed irrationality. Paul stands on the sidelines, to the right of the screen. He is in the hallway looking left into the room where the women "madly" choose their dresses. Because of the camera angle, we can see that Paul watches the women. He stands and looks from a distance as an apparent objective observer. Because he is in the foreground of the shot, he appears to be closer to us than the women. As a result, we are invited to personally identify with him because of his proximity, and to distance ourselves literally and figuratively from the women. The perceived spatial closeness may also be achieved through an awareness that, as Kress and van Leeuwen suggest, the women are "not part of 'our' world" (1996, p. 143). Rather, the shot "'offers' the represented participants to the viewer as items of information, objects of contemplation, impersonally, as though they were specimens in a display case" (Kress & Van Leeuwen 1996, p. 124). If the women are "objects," they can only be so because they are "objectified" through the invitation to share in Paul's gaze.

The very next shot shows Paul's reaction to the scene: he is shaking his head, as if in utter disbelief. Paul here performs a kind of morally superior masculinity, as a rational man who is distanced from "animalistic" women, both spatially and metaphorically. It is especially significant that, because Paul does not look directly at the camera and because he stands essentially in profile, this shot creates the sense that the camera has caught him "in the act." That is to say, it looks as if he is simply reacting "naturally" to the scene and that this is not something scripted by the producers. This effect is important, because it signals a call to authenticity, authority, and "the truth." Importantly, this "truth" is premised upon Paul's closeness but also distance (metaphoric and literal) from the women and on his "superior" position. This dual position of closeness and distance produces his authority and permits him to judge the women. The effects of Paul's commentary and the use of specific camera angles in "Dress Selection" invite viewers to occupy the space of the male gaze, but importantly, Paul does not gaze at the women in a sexualized way.[6] Rather, Paul's gaze is premised upon his authoritative ability to make classed distinctions.

Viewers are therefore offered "evidence" to side with Paul's perspective and expert opinion so that his assessments of individual women work to position these participants in classed ways. Heidi, for instance, is a participant who appears to be on the show solely to steal Evan and his supposed millions. The revelation that she has left a boyfriend at home is referred to as "Heidigate," and in this same episode, goodness wins out as Heidi is eliminated. Following the elimination, we see her sitting in a hallway while Paul looks for a missing piece of her luggage. She is trying to get her belongings packed, and she attempts to speak French. The hallway shots are accompanied by accordion music playing what sounds to be a cross between a tango and a tarantella. This particular music is only used in scenes that seem to suggest comic relief, and I propose that the accordion music marks instances of the joke. According to Kathleen Rowe (1995,

p. 68), Freud's triadic model of the joke occurs when two men subvert their originally aggressive sexual impulses towards a woman through a joke—the woman thus becomes the conduit for male bonding. In this instance, however, the viewers are positioned to take up the space of the second man, if we laugh at Heidi it is because of her lack of class.

The translation of Heidi's French comments works to position us in this space. In this hallway shot, Paul, of course, has the definitive final word. He states: "Too bad Heidi can't stay in France a bit longer, perhaps her French could improve." This is followed by a shot of Heidi saying: "Je n'ai pas heureux, ((inaudible)) pain, le baggage." Heidi's comments are transcribed and translated, and appear across the bottom of the screen as: "I have no happy . . . You no find bread baggage." For viewers not familiar with the language, the translated comments are framed as ridiculous and indicative of Heidi's pompous attempts to speak French, rather than as a good try for a beginner. Her attempt to speak French is framed as her desire to aspire to social sophistication. Her ultimate inability to achieve success signals her classlessness. As Gareth Palmer (2004, p. 188) argues with reference to lifestyle and home decorating reality TV shows, participants are taught "to create a self by learning middle-classness, but it is a task that will always feel doomed to failure." While lifestyle show participants can never quite manage the "fragility of this new identity and the uncertain ways in which it is worn" (Palmer 2004, p. 188), Heidi's effort to acquire linguistic cultural capital is not only a failure, but it is a joke. Paul mocks Heidi's linguistic inability and this signals his own superior class position because he possesses this cultural capital. Yet viewers are also invited to laugh at Heidi because we have been given the information (via the translation) and the cultural capital so as to be "in the know." Paul then offers his judgement of her: "I was pleased by Evan's decision to eliminate Heidi, as I'm quite certain her motivations were suspect, couldn't find that bag fast enough."

Class Style

Style, fashion, and clothing are also markers of class on *Joe Millionaire*, and they function to determine the regulated body. The regulated body of the good, "authentic" girl is neat and tidy. She does not wear "tasteless" clothes because, as Lury argues:

> Individuals struggle to improve their social position by manipulating the cultural representation of their situation in the social field. They accomplish this, in part, by affirming the superiority of their taste and lifestyle with a view to legitimizing their own identity as best representing what it means to be "what it is right to be."
>
> (Lury 1996, p. 83)

Unfortunately for Mojo (who was eliminated in episode four) she is unsuccessful at this task. In episode three, in which she prepares for her Paris date with Evan, Evan and Paul discuss her lack of style:

Paul: I told Mojo to dress chic and with high heels.
Evan: Oh really?
Paul: It'll be interesting.
Evan: Yeah. Especially with her it'll be really interesting.

Here, Paul enacts his position of expertise in advising Mojo to wear something "chic" and with high heels. His advice and/or direction may also indicate the possibility that Mojo may lack experience with going out for dinner to a fancy restaurant (again, an indication of her class status) and especially one in Paris. Both Paul and Evan identify Mojo's lack of cultural capital, and this identification appears to be based on shared assumptions about her lack of style.

It is perhaps not surprising then that Mojo also becomes the butt of a joke in episode four. Here, Evan and Mojo have a date at the chateau in which they learn how to fence. Following the date, they sit in a room looking at Mojo's photo album. She also gives Evan a poem she wrote and a puzzle. She states: "he wasn't going to get it unless I liked him." She reads the poem to him, and then gives him the puzzle, which is a black and white photograph of her. A line across the puzzle reads: "I choose you." Mojo's stance and gaze in the photo is directed towards the viewer. Evan remarks that: "The puzzle was kind of un^usual, ((pause, starts nodding, swallows)) actually, it was a picture of her." His hesitation, and his emphasis on the fact that the puzzle was a picture of Mojo suggests

his discomfort or unease about receiving this unusual gift.[7] Following this is a shot of Evan struggling to put the puzzle together while accordion music plays in the background again, I would argue, as an indication of the carnivalesque quality of this scene. Evan indicates his surprise: "And so it's you?" and "I choose you?" The use of the accordion music and the shots of Evan's surprise reinforce the notion that the gift is odd and possibly ridiculous. Yet, Evan appears to put a positive spin on it as he observes: "No girl had ever given me anything like that before. Um, but I guess it was pretty sweet." However, if this is an attempt to temper the strangeness of the gift, it is lost at the end of the episode following Mojo's elimination. Instead, the gift becomes yet another example of her absurdity and her lack of taste.

In his fireside conclusion, Paul remarks: "Once again I didn't get a necklace, but I did swipe the puzzle. I might be the real winner here." (Here, he refers to the show's practice of giving contestants a necklace as a sign to continue to the next round.) Paul holds up the puzzle to viewers, and the look on his face suggests that he mocks the gift. Given his position as arbiter of good taste on the show, Paul's enactment of the implied author here suggests that Mojo's puzzle is tasteless. What is significant, however, is that this enactment is directed at the audience. We are invited to view Mojo's puzzle as classless, and therefore to form the triadic model with Paul so that we might laugh at Mojo. Moreover, as if to reiterate the triadic bond of the joke, Paul goes on to observe: "Anyway, don't miss our show next week, when Evan whisks our girls away to the French Riviera in a private jet. Oh, I bet Heidi would have loved that. Ah well. As always, I shall be right here, awaiting your return." Although Heidi was eliminated two episodes previously, it seems a bit unusual to be reminded of her here. Yet, the reference to Heidi is not jarring if understood within the context of the running joke; rather, it links Heidi and Mojo as subjects of the joke within a shared relationship between Paul and the audience. Thus, Paul's "objective" gaze at the women positions them as animalistic, trashy, and greedy wolves that viewers are invited to laugh at. Importantly, however, the subjects of Paul's authorial perspectives and jokes are these "classless" women.

Of course, as Graham-Bertolini (2004) points out, Evan, too, gazes at the women, but how he does so is in marked contrast to Paul's classed looks. In episode three, for instance, Evan lustfully gazes at Mojo, as she tries on dresses for their date to the Moulin Rouge. In episode four, there are numerous shots of Evan's gawkish stares at the women, as Sarah, Melissa, and Mojo join him and Zora in a hot tub at the chateau. The music in this scene is sexually suggestive. There are shots of the steam rising from the hot tub as the women appear to lick their lips, and Evan states that he "was like a deer caught in the headlights." An obligatory shot of Sarah's breasts in her bikini is sutured to this comment. Headlights? Breasts? Yes, the point is quite clear. While a shot-by-shot analysis of this scene would illustrate how Sarah, Melissa, and Mojo are positioned as aggressive, sexual, and promiscuous women, and how Zora is positioned as somewhat of a prude, without going to such lengths I think the point can be made that Evan's looking does work to position some of these women as sex objects. Yet I do not believe that Evan's gaze here is the sum total of how the women are positioned on the show. Rather, it is important to see how Evan himself is positioned in order to understand how class comes to function as an important marker of authenticity and of "true value."

Working-Class Masculinity

From the start of *Joe Millionaire*, Evan appears to be a "real man," "authentic," working in the "real world." By the time the women arrive in episode one, they are already located within a patriarchal structure in which women occupy subordinate (and perhaps in this context "inauthentic") positions. Evan's version of masculinity on the show is produced in relation to his job as a construction worker, an association that is based on his "superior" physical strength, and therefore his status as a working-class man. For instance, the show's opening sequence reveals a number of shots of Evan at a construction site, in contrast to Paul's upper-class voiceover, as we saw above. Defining Evan's masculinity in relation to construction machinery associates him with particular images of white, working-class masculinity and the notion of "separate spheres," in which men worked outside the home, and women worked within it (Robert Connell 1995; Imelda Whelehan 1995).[8] White working-class masculinity, as a

category or set of ideas or images, was established in relation to perceived notions of white men's superior physical strength (John Beynon 2002, p. 50ff; Joane Nagel 1998).[9] Yet it was also established in relation to raced bodies. As Marlon Riggs (1986) outlines in *Ethnic Notions*, the flight of southern African–Americans to the northern states following emancipation created fears and anxieties that white men's jobs would be "stolen." "Good" working-class masculinity then is valenced as white. Of course, this category of masculinity was threatened by the changing patterns of work and the shift away from the declining manufacturing industries to service industries (Jonathan Rutherford 1988, p. 23) in the twentieth century, producing a so-called "crisis" of masculinity (Rowena Chapman & Jonathan Rutherford 1988, pp. 11–12). I want to come back to this point, and turn to examine how testimonials work to produce Evan's authenticity.

In their testimonials, Evan's friends support an image of him as an "average Joe" and a romantic hero. His friend and co-worker, Jeremy, tells us about the "real" Evan.[10] Describing his first day at work, when Evan came up to help him out and show him the ropes, Jeremy states: "[it] let me know that he was willing to help somebody out if they needed something, Evan would give you the shirt off his back" (episode one). Jeremy positions Evan as an honest, generous fellow, willing to help others. Yet, like any good romantic hero, Evan has trouble finding a "real," "true" woman (Janice Radway [1985] 1991). Part of Evan's difficulty, or so it appears, is that he is working class. His transformation to multi-millionaire then suggests that the show plays on an unwritten assumption that women are incapable or unwilling to love a "true" but poor man (read: we are all gold-diggers!). As Evan states: "In dating I've noticed if you're not a doctor or lawyer, well it's you know oh he's not as successful enough for me." A "good" man/match must apparently be middle class. Yet, lest viewers presume that Evan is really a self-pitying sop, Thomas, another friend and co-worker confirms Evan's assertion that construction workers have a hard time dating:

> Not long ago, I was in a bar with Evan, and we were talking to couple of beautiful women, and one in particular took a liking to him, and you could tell he really liked her. She asked for what he did for

a living, and he said construction, and you could tell that she was really uncomfortable, so I pulled beside and I said, maybe Evan we could just leave out the part about driving a bulldozer, and he said, < Q Tom the one thing I refuse to do is to lie to a woman in order to get her to like me. You know, if she's not going to like me for who I am, then she's not a person I want in my life. Q >

(*Joe Millionaire*, episode seven)

What is interesting in Thomas's comments is how he positions Evan as someone who is loyal to his "true identity" and his job, that he shares the collegiality and affinity with his working-class brethren that is often understood to be an integral part of white working-class masculinity (Connell 1995). As a true, honest man, Evan's apparent authenticity enacts a male version of the "princess and the pea" fairytale in that his millionaire masquerade enables the women to see his "true" qualities and therefore discover the "real" prince.

Evan's "authentic" male self is carefully constructed to provide a litmus test against which the female contestants are measured. In episode two, the women go on group dates with him, and during these dates, they are tested to see how well they can perform in his "real" masculine world. The first of these dates takes place at a vineyard, where the women are expected to pick grapes in the rain. These tests are premised upon the class issues the show throws into relief. The question is: can the women accept a working-class lifestyle, or are they solely interested in the trappings of an upper-class life? Are the women "too feminine" to co-exist in Evan's working-class world? They can only be so if "creature comforts" are implicitly feminized as signs of softness associated with the domestic sphere (Connell 1995). If a woman is too feminine, she will not be able to cope with the "ruggedness" of Evan's "true" life. Thus, it becomes important to the show's plot to test the women "when they go on *outside*, when things aren't so comfortable" (emphasis mine). Evan positions the women's "natural" location within the private realm of the home, the domestic sphere, and/or the luxury of the interior of the chateau and its trappings. The purpose of the vineyard date is to take the women out of their "natural element." Indeed, Melissa takes up this process of

locating women within domestic spheres when she states: "I was so out of my element, it was cold, it was raining, and, I did not want to be picking grapes." She performs herself as a feminine woman whose "natural" space or element is not in a vineyard doing manual labor.

It is no accident, then, that *all* of the tests take place outside, beyond traditional realms of white women's working spaces. Nor is it accidental that the women are positioned as "real" women through these tests. The second group date takes place on a steam train, fuelled by coal. The women must shovel coal into the train's furnace before the group can go on a ride through the French countryside. Evan states: "I just wanted to cut through the first date chit-chat, this date was a great way for me to start gauging, which one of these girls is not afraid to get her hands dirty" (episode two). He implies that the women are not accustomed to "dirty" or "real" work, but it is important to see that this implication is based on gender divisions. For instance, he positions first date discussions as "chit-chat," and therefore frivolous, idle, and worthless. The association to women's gossip as a function of women's (subordinate) culture (Mary Ellen Brown 1994) is implicit. Evan wants to move beyond this feminine idleness and get to something "real" like men's work.

Yet how do the women react to these tests? How do they perform their femininities within these masculine terms? Several of the women indicate their surprise and displeasure with the tasks, either verbally or non-verbally through looks, gestures, and so on. For instance, reflecting on the vineyard date, Melissa states: "I'm not outdoorsy, and uh it was my turn to go out on a date, and I thought (Hx) you know, please let it be inside, it was outside!" She rolls her eyes and makes a look of disgust when she says "please let it be inside," but her look turns to what appears to be dismay as she reveals the date was outside. Sarah also expresses the contradiction of meeting a millionaire and then toiling on a vineyard. She states: "We were of course all thinking, < Q ok, here's how you pick the grapes Q > , and then we would go inside, but they hand us the buckets and shears, we were literally shin-deep in mud" (episode two). To the women's surprise, the trip to the vineyard is not about witnessing how grapes are picked, processed, and transformed into wine,[11] but it is about actually picking grapes. Sarah's comment then illustrates the women's contradictory expectations for the date. She elaborates on the contradiction when she states:

> After we picked some token grapes, we were like < Q okay ((laugh)), here you go, get a shot of us with the grapes Q > , and then we were all kind of hanging out, and Philippe ((the wine-maker)) was like, < Q no, there's ten more rows Q > like, < MRC pick the grapes MRC > .
>
> (*Joe Millionaire*, episode two)

Here, Sarah indicates the techniques of production, referring to the grapes as "token" grapes, and recognizing the use of establishing shots or filler. She also implies that all of the women on the date appeared to think along the same lines, as they were all "hanging out," not expecting to do any kind of work. Melissa's account perhaps captures the women's reactions best. She states: "I was like, Oh ha ha ha Philippe, pretty funny right, he's like < Q ((with French accent)) no, really we must cut the grapes Q > . And I'm like, you've gotta be kidding."

What is interesting about these sequences is that it is primarily Sarah and Melissa's reactions that are shown. Sarah and Melissa are positioned as gold-diggers, as Graham-Bertolini (2004, p. 342) also indicates. Sarah, for instance, appears to be too feminine to participate in Evan's world because, as he suggests, she "seems very Martha Stewart-like." He states further: "I get the impression she's pretty uptight, um, not the kind of girl I would usually go out with, uh certainly not the type of girl who would go out with me." Having positioned Sarah as a fussy, particular, and, for some, impossible version of femininity, Evan suggests here that Sarah belongs to the legions of women who would not normally date a construction worker because of her cultural capital.

Although Melissa clearly indicates her displeasure about picking grapes, she appears to throw herself into the task, suggesting that she, on the other hand, does "measure" up. Yet, her comment reveals how she uses the task for her own ends. She states: "When you date somebody, sometimes you do things, to get that person to fall for you" and "I can fake picking grapes and having fun, like that's not hard to do."

Here, Melissa admits that she works hard picking the grapes in order to make Evan fall for her. She uses the task to make it to the next round and acknowledges her own power by stating that she can fake it. Because she's playing the game, Melissa subverts the test by performing the version of femininity that the test requires and recognizing that it is a performance. She exercises a certain amount of power and moves on to the next round. That she has exercised power is confirmed with a cut to Evan's naïve comments, in which he states: "I think she had a really good time, I don't think it's something ((i.e. the grape-picking)) she gets to do very often." Of course, the irony is that this is something Melissa never "gets to do" because she chooses not to. Thus it appears that Melissa has duped Evan but her manipulation is framed as an indication of her duplicity. Because she is measured against Evan's "true" self, Melissa's supposed "realness" is shown to be lacking.

In contrast, Zora rises to the challenge of shoveling horse shit on the third group date horseback riding. Her willingness to take up the task of shoveling shit demonstrates her non-complaining "nature" as a selfless, romantic heroine (Radway [1984] 1991) and melodramatic heroine (Peter Brooks [1976] 1995; Christine Gledhill 1987). Yet when we consider this performance less as an instantiation of the romantic and melodramatic heroine, and more within the context of the construction of class distinctions on the show, we begin to see that Zora's performance serves to demonstrate her capacity to willingly participate in Evan's masculine, white, class-based, "authentic" world. She possesses the "right" cultural capital to do so. This is because Zora indicates that she is used to living in the real world. As she states in episode four when her horse spits on her: "So working with the elderly has prepared me for people spitting up on me." Evidently, then, Zora is verified through her ability to participate (although, not dominate) in a particular version of a man's "real" world.

Authenticity on *Joe Millionaire* is made possible only in relation to white, class-based forms of masculinity or domains of masculine knowledge and power. As a result, the women on the show can only acquire authenticity through their proximity to or relationship with white working-class masculinity or men.

The particular heterosexual couple that is formed on *Joe Millionaire* is thus not only classed, but also raced.

Conclusion

What I am suggesting then is that Evan's "authentic" working-class status functions ideologically and that the ideology that is "sung" to viewers (John Fiske & John Hartley 1978; McCarthy 1998) offers a particular version of masculine and feminine classed positions that are integral to the heterosexual couple and the nuclear family. Nagel (1998, p. 249) argues that current, western understandings of nationalism arose in the nineteenth century and that these are closely linked to the production of certain kinds of masculinities and femininities. In particular, women "occupy an important symbolic place as the mothers of the nation" (Nagel 1998, p. 254). Women's roles are defined in relation to a pure and chaste sexuality so that women are encoded as the embodiment of national honor (or shame) (Nagel 1998, p. 254). Without the space here to interrogate the possible links this version of sexuality may have to race, suffice to say that on *Joe Millionaire*, Zora gets situated within a traditional, "all-American" hometown and community as the proverbial girl next door, while her rival, Sarah, is shown zooming about in her car, not rooted to any one place or group of people.

While the women of *Joe Millionaire* are positioned as sexual objects through Evan's sexualized glances, the more important gaze on the show is Paul's, as we have seen. Paul's authoritative looking provides us with the class knowledge upon which to judge the women, and his knowledge is representative of the implied author. Class, and women's proximity to an "authentic" white, masculine working class, thus appears to be a determining factor in the regulation of female (and male) subject positions and in the formation of the heterosexual couple. Yet the ultimate question is why the issue of class and cultural distinctions matter at all in this arena? The answer, of course, lies in the grounds upon which the heterosexual couple is reinscribed on this show. By becoming a couple, and by extension providing the possibility for the formation of the nuclear family, I propose that Zora and Evan's coupledom works to situate, and secure, a particular

raced and classed configuration of the nuclear family within the nation.

In her analysis of *TLC* staples *A Wedding Story* and *A Baby Story*, Rebecca Stephens (2004, pp. 199–200) argues that reality TV shows that focus on heterosexual romance must be contextualized within a social and political environment in which the US government has recently passed legislation that rewards teen mothers to marry. She points out that "these legislative attempts can be seen as evidence of forced emulation of middle-class values as a panacea for poverty" (Stephens 2004, p. 200). Although she rightly indicates that a single TV show cannot be held responsible for social practices or social trends (ibid., p. 201), the ideological work accomplished on shows such as *Joe Millionaire* serves to reinforce the sets of values and forms of regulation already circulating within the culture. Like Graham-Bertolini (2004) then, what I think happens on *Joe Millionaire* is that women perform their subject positions in relation to men and to a heterosexual, patriarchal order that attempts to locate women in specific spaces within the heterosexual couple. Yet how this works is determined by women's performances as certain kinds of classed people.

Notes

1. I have transcribed the show's dialogue and disclosures using standard transcription methods (see Table 1, Appendix) because I do not believe that language is a bearer of transparent meanings that exists outside of power relations (Fairclough 1992). In so doing, my analysis attempts to recognize and capture the talk's complexities and power relations, and how the talk is sutured to particular kinds of music, camera angles, and so on.

2. Subject positions on the show are fluid. Individuals may be spoken or speak themselves into discourse at an intersection of *several* discourses, so there is always the possibility for movement, mixing, and so on. By seeing participants on the show as subjects, we can view them in terms of how they are positioned by the editing, or how they position themselves, and not in terms of their intentions (because I think we would be hard-pressed to ever fully get at anyone's intentions).

3. Although viewers are invited to see the show in particular ways, I recognize that the show nevertheless leaves itself open to resistant, oppositional, and negotiated readings. My view of audiences does not see viewers as cultural dupes; rather, like Justin DeRose, Elfriede Fürsich, and Ekaterina Haskins (2003), I propose that

there may be limits to the textual polysemy available in a reality TV show. Following the work of Henry Giroux (1999), my reading of *Joe Millionaire* similarly proposes that Paul's authorial knowledge limits the range of possible meanings available.

4. It is worth clarifying that this Australian Paul Hogan is not the same as the Paul Hogan of the *Crocodile Dundee* movies.

5. Almost every prime time reality TV show I have watched has a male host, for instance Jeff Probst on *Survivor*, Chris Harrison on *The Bachelor* and *Bachelorette* series, and so on. The exceptions are *Mr. Personality*, with host Monica Lewinsky, and Tyra Banks, on *America's Next Top Model*. Yet even on *America's Next Top Model*, Jay Manuel, the show's photo shoot stylist, make-up artist, and sometimes judge, tends to be with the models more, directing them through their photo shoots, so that he at least shares some of the limelight with Banks. In contrast, Alex McLeod is actually given the title "host" on *Joe Millionaire*, but her role and her visibility are completely overshadowed by Paul Hogan.

6. In an interview in *reality check* magazine, *The Bachelor* host Chris Harrison suggests that he was hired as host in part because he is a "family man," and would not be romantically or sexually interested in the participants on the show (J Di Lauro 2004, p. 45). In the same way, Paul's gaze is not sexualized because this would overstep an emphasis on the formation of a single heterosexual couple, a point which I argue is critical to many romance reality TV shows.

7. Mojo's gift may be unusual because the words, "I choose you" invert the rules of the game, so that Mojo appropriates the position of choosing reserved for Evan.

8. And yet the notion of separate spheres was not a reality for all, and it was not as clear-cut as it may appear. For large numbers of working-class families, women worked both in the home, and outside of the home for wages.

9. Both John Beynon (2002) and Joane Nagel (1998, pp. 244–245) point to the rise of boys training for physical strength through programs like the Boy Scouts and Boy Scouts of America, respectively, and how these societies are linked to nation-building.

10. Evan's authenticity is further supported by his friend, Stephan's testimonial in episode seven. Stephan says: "When I see Evan on the show, he's not being fake, Evan is being Evan, alright, that's him" and "You can take him to a five star restaurant, and that knife and fork doosh doosh ((sounds of throwing cutlery away)) he's going to pick up that burger and just drive it down."

11. Dates in which participants observe production or manufacturing processes and then get to nominally participate are often incorporated into shows like *The Bachelor* and *The Bachelorette*. In contrast, *The Simple Life* explores the contradictions that arise when heiress Paris Hilton and celebrity daughter Nicole Richie are put to work, often in manual workplaces.

References

America's Next Top Model (2005) (television series) United Paramount Network.

The Bachelor (2003) (television series) FOX Broadcasting Company.

The Bachelorette (2003) (television series) FOX Broadcasting Company.

Beynon, John (2002) *Masculinities and Culture*, Studies in Cultural and Media Studies Series, Open University Press, Buckingham.

Bourdieu, Pierre (1984) *Distinction: A Social Critique of the Judgement of Taste*, trans. Richard Nice, Harvard University Press, Cambridge, MA.

Brooks, Peter [1976] (1995) *The Melodramatic Imagination: Balzac, Henry James, Melodrama, and the Mode of Excess*, Yale University Press, New Haven, CT.

Brown, Mary Ellen (1994) *Soap Opera and Women's Talk: The Pleasure of Resistance*, Sage Publications, Thousand Oaks, CA.

Cevasco, Maria Elisa (2000) 'Whatever happened to cultural studies: notes from the periphery.' *Textual Practice*, vol. 14, no. 3, pp. 433–438.

Chapman, Rowena & Rutherford, Jonathan (1988) 'The forward march of men halted', in *Male Order: Unwrapping Masculinity*, eds R. Chapman & J. Rutherford, Lawrence & Wishart, London.

Connell, Robert William (1995) *Masculinities*, Polity Press, Cambridge.

Day, Gary (2001) *Class*, Routledge, London and New York.

Derose, Justin, Fürsich, Elfriede & Haskins, Ekaterina v. (2003) 'Pop (up) goes the *Blind Date*: supertextual constraints on "reality" television', *Journal of Communication Inquiry*, vol. 27, no. 2, pp. 171–189.

Di Lauro, Janet (2004) 'Reality check crashes ABC's bachelor/ette pad', *Reality Check*, winter, pp. 43–45.

Fairclough, Norman (1992) *Discourse and Social Change*, Polity Press, Cambridge.

Fairclough, Norman (1995) *Media Discourse*, Edward Arnold, London.

Fiske, John (1987) *Television Culture: Popular Pleasures and Politics*, Routledge, London.

Fiske, John & Hartley, John (1978) *Reading Television*, New Accents Series, Methuen, London.

Giroux, Henry A. (1999) *The Mouse that Roared: Disney and the End of Innocence*, Rowman & Littlefield, Lanham, CO.

Gledhill, Christine (1987) 'The melodramatic field: an investigation', in *Home Is Where the Heart Is: Studies in*

Melodrama and the Woman's Film, ed. C. Gledhill, British Film Institute, London.

Graham-Bertolini, Alison (2004) '*Joe Millionaire* as fairy tale: a feminist critique', *Feminist Media Studies*, vol. 4, no. 3, pp. 341–344.

Joe Millionaire (2003) (television series) FOX Broadcasting Company.

Kirk, John (2002) 'Changing the subject: cultural studies and the demise of class', *Cultural Logic*, [Online]. Available at: http://cologic.eserver.org/2002/kirk.html, accessed 17 December, 2005.

Kozloff, Sarah (1992) 'Narrative theory and television', in *Channels of Discourse, Reassembled*, ed. R. C. Allen, University of North Carolina Press, Chapel Hill, NC.

Kress, Gunther & Van Leeuwen, Theo (1996) *Reading Images: The Grammar of Visual Design*, Routledge, London and New York.

Lury, Celia (1996) *Consumer Culture*, Polity Press, Cambridge.

McCarthy, Cameron (1998) *The Uses of Culture: Education and the Limits of Ethnic Affiliation*. Routledge, New York and London.

Mr. Personality (2003) (television series) FOX Broadcasting Company.

Munt, Sally R. (ed.) (2000) *Cultural Studies and the Working Class: Subject to Change*, Cassell, London and New York.

Nagel, Joane (1998) 'Masculinity and nationalism: gender and sexuality in the making of nations', *Ethnic and Racial Studies*, vol. 21, pp. 242–269.

Palmer, Gareth (2004) ' "The new you": class and transformation in lifestyle television', in *Understanding Reality Television*, eds S. Holmes & D. Jermyn, Routledge, London and New York.

Radway, Janice [1984] (1991) *Reading the Romance: Women, Patriarchy, and Popular Literature*, University of North Carolina Press, Chapel Hill, NC.

Riggs, Marlon (1986) *Ethnic Notions* (videorecording), USA.

Rowe, Kathleen (1995) *The Unruly Woman*, University of Texas Press, Austin.

Rutherford, Jonathan (1988) 'Who's that man?', in *Male Order: Unwrapping Masculinity*, eds R. Chapman & J. Rutherford, Lawrence & Wishart, London.

The Simple Life (television series) (2005) FOX Broadcasting Company.

Stephens, Rebecca L. (2004) 'Socially soothing stories? Gender, race, and class in TLC's *A Wedding Story* and *A Baby Story*', in *Understanding Reality Television*, eds S. Holmes & D. Jermyn, Routledge, London and New York.

Whelehan, Imelda (1995) *Modern Feminist Thought: From Second Wave to Post-Feminism*, Lawrence & Wishart, London.

Appendix

Table 23.1 Transcription symbols

Speech Division	Symbol
Units	
Word	Space
Speaker identity/turn start	:
Transitional Continuity	
Final	.
Continuing	,
Appeal	?
Accent and Lengthening	
Primary accent	^
Pause	'
Vocal Noises	
Exhalation	(Hx)
Quality	
Singsong	<S . . . S>
Quotation	<Q . . . Q>
Marcato	<MRC . . . MRC>
Other	
Researcher's comment	((. . .))

24.
BOYS DON'T CRY AND FEMALE MASCULINITY
Reclaiming a Life and Dismantling the Politics of Normative Heterosexuality
Brenda Cooper

I just keep on laughing
Hiding the tears in my eyes
Because boys don't cry.
Boys don't cry.

(Smith, Tolhurst, & Dempsey, 1988)

The 1993 murders of three young people in Falls City, Nebraska, (population 5,200) began as just one more crime statistic when Lisa Lambert, Philip DeVine, and Brandon Teena were found shot to death in Lambert's farmhouse. But national news media picked up the story when Brandon Teena was identified as Teena Brandon, a female-to-male transsexual[1] from Lincoln, Nebraska, who had been "passing" in Falls City and dating a local teenager, Lana Tisdel. As details unfolded, the public learned that two local ex-convicts who had befriended Brandon, John Lotter and Tom Nissen, were so outraged to learn that Brandon was a biological female, they beat him up and repeatedly raped him. When Brandon filed rape charges against them, they hunted him down and shot him to death as he tried to hide under a blanket, then stabbed his body. After allowing Lisa Lambert to place her infant son in his crib, Lotter and Nissen gunned her down and shot the other witness, Philip DeVine (Gabriel, 1996; Messina, 2000).

Lotter and Nissen were convicted of first-degree murder, and the story faded from media attention until 1999, when filmmaker Kimberly Peirce brought it back in *Boys Don't Cry* (Sharp, Hart, Kolodner, Vachon & Peirce, 1999), starring Hilary Swank in her Oscar-winning role as Brandon Teena. Peirce's "long-standing interest in transvestism and transsexuality" (Leigh, 2000, p. 18) drew her to Brandon's compelling story when she read the news accounts of his murder. But Peirce wanted more than simply to make what could easily have been a lurid movie about a murdered transsexual in Nebraska: she wanted to reclaim Brandon's story from the sensationalized media accounts that followed the crime. "The coverage was focused almost exclusively on the spectacle of a girl passing as a boy, without any understanding of why a girl would want to pass," Peirce explained. "And I thought that was dangerous" (p. 18).

Given the questions about Brandon's "true" gender, it's not surprising that media reports about Brandon Teena reflected the most leering kind of tabloid coverage, as journalists sensationalized the story of Brandon's sexuality and how he had deceived the residents of Falls City (Leigh, 2000; Ricks, 1994; Sloop, 2000). Observed *New York Times* film critic Janet Maslin (1999), this "tabloid-ready tale attracted the kind of omnivorous media attention that distorts the truth beyond recognition and milks reality dry" (p. E10). Moreover, John Sloop has argued that the news media accounts not only perpetuated "caricatures of trans-gendered people" (p. 169) but also functioned to reaffirm traditional ideals of gender and heterosexuality and to discipline transgressors like Brandon Teena who challenged hegemonic sexual norms.

There's no question that the varied forms of female masculinity, including transsexuality, have been framed in the mainstream media as a spectacle —denigrating transsexuality as an aberration at best, or as stereotypical caricatures of deviant and perverted behavior at worst (Nangeroni, 1999; Sloop, 2000). Although male masculinity has been the subject of myriad research studies, Judith Halberstam (1998) asserts that scholars have shown "absolutely no interest in masculinity without men" (p. 13), and she warns that the "suppression of female masculinities allows for male masculinity to stand unchallenged as the bearer of gender stability and gender deviance" (p. 41). In light of filmmaker Peirce's goal to reclaim Brandon Teena's story from news accounts that had sensationalized it as aberrant (Leigh, 2000),[2] I explore the strategies used in the narratives of *Boys Don't Cry* to represent one form of female masculinity and examine the film's potential to "destabilize binary gender systems" (Halberstam, p. 29). My study argues that Peirce's film can function to reclaim Brandon's lifestory from the "spectacle of a girl passing as a boy" (Leigh, p. 18), presenting instead a sympathetic individual and offering film viewers narratives that challenge and confront societal boundaries related to gender and sexuality.[3]

Media Narratives, Heteronormativity, and Queerness

The most basic assumption of heteronormativity is that gender is natally ascribed, natural, and immutable. Thus, envisioning a "world of only heterosexuals" (Scheman, 1997, p. 128), heteronormativity insists "on the inbornness of gender identity, even when it is discordant with biological sex" (p. 138). Heterosexuality is thus deemed an essential aspect of human nature and intelligibility, and "homosexuality counts as the willful denial of one's true self" (p. 128). Significantly, heteronormativity is a powerful principle of social and cultural order that absorbs and disciplines all forms of gender transgressiveness into its female–male binary gender system (Shapiro, 1991).

One partner in the power of heteronormativity to order society is the media and their long history of depicting characters who transgress gender boundaries as comic, weak, or as evil (Dow, 2001; Dyer, 1999; Fejes & Petrich, 1993; Gross, 1996; Russo, 1986). These narrative strategies often establish an "additional level of deviance for such characters," by linking "homosexuality with criminality" (Dow, p. 129). As

Dyer explains, the "amount of hatred, fear, ridicule and disgust packed into those images is unmistakable" (p. 297), and, says Russo, result in "politically indefensible and aesthetically revolting" portrayals (p. 32). Even after the media began to respond to demands from the gay rights movement for equality, portrayals were still framed in terms of the problems sexual minorities posed for heterosexual society (Gross, 1996).

As evidence of societal progress, however, some popular media critics have pointed out that more positive images of sexual minorities have appeared over the past decade (e.g., Svetkey, 2000). But scholars such as Dow (2001) argue that even these recent depictions "can serve a masking function as representation is mistaken for social and political change" (p. 136). For instance, Dow critiques the coming-out discourses surrounding Ellen DeGeneres and her television sitcom character, Ellen Morgan. Ellen's coming-out—both on- and off-screen—was framed in popular media as an "escape from repression" (p. 123) for homosexuals, according to Dow. However, she cautions that "the liberation narrative in and around *Ellen* allows mainstream media to proclaim increased *visibility* for gays and lesbians as increased *legitimacy* for gays and lesbians, in presumably social and political ways" (p. 136), in much the same way as *The Cosby Show* was used in the 1980s as an example of how racism had been eliminated in American society (p. 137). Dow concludes that the "romantic narrative of autonomy and liberation" underlying *Ellen* ultimately functioned to obscure issues of homophobia and heterosexism, even among heterosexuals who are sympathetic to and supportive of gay rights (p. 135). Robert Brookey and Robert Westerfelhaus (2001) reach similar conclusions in their examination of the depictions of gay male drag queens in the film *To Wong Foo, Thanks for Everything! Julie Newmar.* Although these researchers conclude that the film's unapologetic gay characters were clearly more positive and a greater challenge to heterosexual norms than is typical in mainstream media, *To Wong Foo* nonetheless remarginalized the film's drag queens. The movie's narratives, they argue, functioned to tame and contain "gays and gay experience" (p. 142), while simultaneously reaffirming the "heterosexual order" (p. 153). Both studies demonstrate how mainstream media's depictions of queer experience "can appear to embrace them while at the same time defining queers in terms that dehumanize, marginalize, and attempt to tame" (Brookey and Westerfelhaus, p. 153). Ultimately, the vast majority of media representations of individuals who transgress gender continue to "reinforce rather than challenge" heteronormativity (Gross, 1996, p. 153): "[T]hey are still odd men and women out in a straight world. . . . confined to stereotypical characterizations" (Gross, 2001, p. 117).

In her overview and synthesis of the contributions to film theory made by gay, lesbian and queer theorists, Julia Erhart (1999) explains how previous researchers (e.g., Dyer, 1992; De Lauretis, 1984) articulated the idea that mainstream narratives are inevitably "*hetero*sexed" (p. 171). Judith Roof (1996) refers to this as "narrative's heteroideology" (p. xxvii)—the ways narrative and sexuality work together to create and perpetuate a heterosexual ideology in culture and media (p. xiv). Similarly, Teresa de Lauretis (1987) has asserted that "most of the available theories of reading, writing, sexuality, ideology, or any other cultural production are built on male narratives of gender . . . bound by the heterosexual contract" (p. 25). The argument that narratives were inevitably "*hetero*sexed" recognizes the limitations of Laura Mulvey's (1975) concept of the "sexedness" of narrative, as well as the "heterocentric and exceedingly rigid structure" of her articulation of the gaze, which many argue wrote "homosexuality out of existence" (Hanson, 1999, p. 13). One goal of gay, lesbian and queer media researchers, therefore, has been to celebrate and to foreground rather than to minimize the differences of sexual minorities from the norms of heterosexuality (Erhart, p. 173). Thus, a queer approach in media studies encourages researchers to identify and to explicate narratives that make heterosexuality rather than sexual transgression appear strange, or narratives that include "qualities of being non-, contra-, or anti-straight" (Erhart, p. 174).[4] A queer approach also provides the necessary conceptual framework for scholars to explicate queer readings within media texts that appeal not only to sexual minorities, but to heterosexual spectators as well. Ultimately, queer theory "seeks not only to analyze but also to resist, dismantle, or circumnavigate hegemonic systems of sexual oppression and normalization" (Hanson. p. 4).

According to Erhart (1999), a key component of contemporary queer media research is the "mutability of identity" (p. 175), which views sexuality as performative rather than as adhering to specific, permeable categories of gayness or straightness. Within this conceptual framework, gender is positioned as a social construction and thus the way gender functions in individuals' lives is also viewed as socially constructed (Scheman, 1997, p. 145).[5] Such an approach works to undermine the "binarily opposed and mutually exclusive" labels of woman and man, of femininity and masculinity (Erhart, p. 175), in favor of what Chris Straayer refers to as an "embraced incongruity" of femaleness and maleness (as cited in Erhart, p. 175). From this perspective, a woman character dressed in male attire may appropriate male privilege within media narratives because such performances privilege sexuality's instability and contradictoriness; thus, characters exhibiting both female and male traits work to culturally empower such performers by disrupting normative assumptions of two-sexedness (Straayer, as cited in Erhart, p. 176).

Straayer's approach suggests that the "queerness" of media narratives resides more in the potential of media texts to destabilize heteronormativity than with any "against-the-grain response" from spectators (as cited in Erhart, 1999, p. 176). Alexander Doty (1993) agrees that texts offer a flexible space for queer readings, but sees queerness as having much broader implications: "[C]ultural 'queer space' recognizes the possibility that various and fluctuating queer positions might be occupied whenever *anyone* produces or responds to culture. . . . the queer often operates within the nonqueer, as the nonqueer does within the queer (whether in reception, texts, or producers)" (p. 3). Ultimately, Doty explains that queerness—in any form—should work to complicate the ways gender and sexual categories are understood and how they function in culture and society (p. xvii). Thus, David Halperin (as cited in Scheman, 1997, p. 148) has suggested that the term "queer" is best articulated not as a particular identity, but as a flexible strategy of positioning to resist heteronormative practices.

Similar to the goals of queer media research, one goal of contemporary liberatory activism is to disrupt the perspectives and ideals of society's privileged selfhood that serve to marginalize and oppress individuals whose lives fall outside the realm of privi-lege (Scheman, 1997). Scheman says that privileged sexual subjectivity is maintained through the domi-nant narratives of a culture—the media for instance—which "facilitate the smooth telling of some lives and straitjacket, distort, or fracture others" (p. 126). As a strategy regarding media content, research, and social commentary, liberatory resistance seeks to "destabi-lize the center" of heteronormativity and its privileged subjectivity by challenging its claims to "naturalness" (p. 132). Mass media content and criticism can, there-fore, work to problematize heteroideology by expand-ing and relocating its normative gaze, providing new perspectives of sexual minorities who find themselves marginalized, stigmatized and ultimately excluded from most media content. Hence, Scheman suggests, scholars who "queer the centers" of the discursive practices of heteronormativity (p. 152) serve an activ-ist liberatory function that can challenge and expand our view of what is "normal" and free from the mar-gins those whose lives may not conform.

Thus, media narratives that challenge hegemonic masculinity have the potential to destabilize the het-eronormative gaze. Masculinity, Halberstam (1998) argues, is "what we make it" (p. 144). More provocative is Halberstam's assertion that a core principal of het-eronormativity—that the "penis alone signifies male-ness"—corresponds specifically to a tendency among gender scholars to limit their discussions of mascu-linity solely to men (1994, p. 214). Thus, Halberstam (1998) urges researchers to consider transgenderism and transsexuality as forms of a transgressive mas-culinity that disrupt the hegemonic norm. As many scholars have observed, film is one site where defini-tions of sexual difference are vehemently contested (Hanson, 1999). Hence, the story of Brandon Teena in *Boys Don't Cry* offers media critics the opportunity to explore such struggles by considering how film depictions of female masculinity may work to subvert heteromasculinity's privileged position. Further, *Boys Don't Cry* is perhaps the only film addressing the issue of female masculinity by a self-described queer film-maker[6] to reach mainstream audiences and to receive critical acclaim and prestigious awards. As such, it has significant potential to challenge the socially con-structed and circulated meanings of gender. Through an investigation of the narrative strategies employed

to dislocate and to dismantle heteronormativity and its presumptions of biological gender identity, I argue that Kimberly Peirce's film can be read as a liberatory narrative that effectively "queers the center" of het-eroideology by centering female masculinity in oppo-sition to what society and its mass media typically depict as "normal."

My reading of *Boys Don't Cry* in terms of its poten-tial to function as a form of liberatory activism may not reflect the interpretations of average spectators nor of other media scholars and critics. But this is how media criticism should be approached. Media criti-cism is not intended to be a quest for "truth," as Dow (1996) points out; nor is the goal to argue that there is only one correct way to read a text. Rather, Dow argues, criticism should be a process of argumenta-tion whereby the goal is to convince readers that their own insights into a text may be enhanced by reading the text similarly. Thus, my critical analysis of *Boys Don't Cry* is meant to present meaning possibilities, not meaning certainties (p. 4).

Framing the "Strangeness" and Paradoxes of Heteronormativity in *Boys Don't Cry*

In this essay, I argue that the narratives of *Boys Don't Cry* challenge heteronormativity and *hetero*sexed nar-ratives in four strategic ways: 1) by dismantling the myth of "American's heartland"; 2) by problematizing heteromasculinity; 3) by centering female masculinity; and, 4) by blurring the boundaries of female mascu-linity. My articulation of these subversive strategies within the film's narratives supports my contention that the film can serve a liberatory function whereby the privileged subjectivities of heterosexuality and hegemonic masculinity are dismantled, while female masculinity and gender fluidity are privileged and nor-malized.[7]

Dismantling the Myth of the Idyllic Heartland

At the center of heteronormativity is the traditional nuclear family. Perhaps no idealization of the tradi-tional American family and its inherent values is stron-ger than the mythic notion of family associated with heartland America-Mom, apple pie, baseball, and

Chevrolets. The sense of morality and virtue, individuality and freedom, and the strong "family values" of hard-working heartland Americans carry potent connotations of the heterosexual ideal at its best. This romanticism was evident in the news coverage of Brandon Teena's life and murder, which represented Brandon as a deceitful "predator" with a "sinister" intention to prey on the wholesome residents of a small, all-American town in the rural heartland (Sloop, 2000, p. 170). Indeed, a billboard at the city limits declares Falls City the "All-American Community. A Great Place to Live, Great People, Churches, Schools" (Muska & Oláfsdóttir, 1998). Invoking the mythic American heartland in news accounts of Brandon Teena's slaying encouraged people to think that Brandon's masculine performance corrupted the "innocence and normality" of America's heartland and, especially, corrupted and violated the Midwestern women who inhabited it (Sloop, p. 172). Such a news frame, Sloop asserts, reaffirmed and protected "normative heterosexist ways of making sense of gender and of disciplining gender trouble" (p. 171).

The narratives of *Boys Don't Cry* can be read as aggressively challenging this perspective and as presenting a very different and much darker vision of small-town America and its residents. The news media's idealistic images of rolling farmland and hardworking, law-abiding folks who were victimized by an outsider (Sloop, 2000) are countered in the film by lecherous, gun-toting ex-cons, bigoted police officers, seedy trailer parks and run-down farmhouses, a barren land populated by dysfunctional, fragmented families, and desperate people working dead-end jobs, whose primary forms of recreation are alcohol and drugs. In Peirce's view, Falls City is not a place where good-hearted people are content to live their lives; it's a place where most are desperate to leave but fear they never will. In offering this dark view of the place where Brandon was murdered, Kimberly Peirce's film works simultaneously to debunk the myth of the all-American heartland and to dispute the validity of its core value—the wholesome nuclear family unit and the heteronormative assumptions that underlie it.

One strategy to problematize a "primary site of heteronormativity" is to depict the traditional family unit in "counter-normative ways" (Scheman, 1997, p. 148). Clearly, the lives of all of the film's players

are far removed from the cultural ideals of America's heartland. John Lotter (Peter Saragaard) and Tom Nissen (Brendan Sexton III) are boozing, violent ex-convicts in their early 20s, trying to avoid getting busted and sent back to prison. The women who befriend Brandon are hardly innocent or wholesome. Candace[8] is a neglectful single mother who parties too much and tends bar at the town's seedy club. Lana's mother (Jeanetta Arnette) is an unemployed, divorced alcoholic who tries to reaffirm her sexual appeal through pathetic flirtations with John and Tom, and later, with Brandon. In Lana's (Chloé Sevigny) first appearance on screen, spectators see a prematurely world-weary young woman, drunk and mumbling karaoke in the bar where Candace works. Lana spends her free time abusing drugs and alcohol, and fantasizes about quitting her night shift job at the local spinach packing plant to escape Falls City for a career as a karaoke star. In one scene, Brandon encounters a staggeringly drunken Lana at the all-night Quik Stop, where she complains that she's "stuck in a town where there's nothing to do but go bumper skiing and chase bats every night of your evil, fucking life." When they return to Lana's home and find her mother passed out on the sofa, Lana tells Brandon, "God, I hate my life."

The film's perspective is both bleaker and more realistic than the idealist notions of the American heartland and its people found in popular media depictions. Falls City, like many rural communities, is populated primarily with decent, law-abiding citizens and hardworking people, but is also plagued by bigotry, unemployment, alcohol and drug abuse, dysfunctional families and a high incidence of violence that often takes the form of domestic violence (Holden, 1998; Jones, 1996; Muska & Oláfsdóttir, 1998). The film's depiction of the people who befriended Brandon thus represents an important liberatory and subversive strategy in exposing the hypocrisy and contradictions of normality inherent within both the Norman Rockwell American hometown myth and in hegemonic heterosexuality. Rather than romanticizing heartland America and its people, *Boys Don't Cry* functions to contradict the rosy stereotypes by destabilizing the center of heteroideology and relocating its gaze to the contradictions of hetero-sexuality's claims of natural and virtuous normativity (Scheman, 1997). Hence, the narratives of *Boys Don't Cry* disrupt and problematize the inherent heteroideology that structures cultural myths surrounding rural America and its All-American communities populated by "Great People." As the next section argues, Peirce's vision also reveals the intolerance of Falls City's residents in ways that work to construct normative masculinity as "strange."

Problematizing Heteromasculinity

Just as *Boys Don't Cry* relocates the mythic heartland to a "place of normative incoherence" (Scheman, 1997, p. 132), it also raises serious questions regarding the assumptions of naturalness and virtue inherent in traditional definitions of heterosexual manhood and its privileges. Ex-cons John Lotter and Tom Nissen are unemployed and regularly abuse alcohol and drugs. Tom is revealed to be an arsonist who set his family's home on fire and, as he explains to Brandon, both men have a history of using self-mutilation as a means to control their violent tempers. Heteromasculinity as exhibited through the characters of John and Tom, therefore, seems not only unnatural, strange and lacking in virtue, but also a serious threat to society.

Enter Brandon Teena. Halberstam (1998) explained that a FTM transsexual "ventures into male territory with the potential threat of violence hanging over his head" (p. 25) because he is in physical danger if discovered by a male. And this is precisely what happens to Brandon after Tom and John become suspicious about his sexuality. In fact, two of the most graphic representations of heterosexual masculinity as problematic and, in this case, pathological, occur after the two men violently turn on Brandon, ripping off his clothes in order to "prove" Brandon is a female, and, later, when they repeatedly assault and rape him. John and Tom are outraged to learn that they have been hanging around with a "dyke." The fact that "this dyke" also has been making time with Lana, toward whom John is obsessively proprietary, further inflames John's anger. After John and Tom ransack Brandon's duffel bag and find a dildo, stuffed socks, and a pamphlet on sexual identity crisis, they violently confront him. As Brandon struggles and pleads with them to let him go, they drag him into the bathroom to strip him so they can learn the "truth." Seeing no evidence of a penis,

Tom yells at John to "Touch it." He won't. Repulsed to realize that his "little buddy" is not a "real man," John yells: "What the fuck *are* you?!" While John holds him, Tom then pulls down Brandon's underwear, spreads his legs and fingers his crotch, and then says disgustedly, "Don't look like no sexual identity crisis to me." As Tom restrains a trembling and humiliated Brandon, John yanks open the bathroom door and yells at Lana, "Look at your little boyfriend!" When Lana refuses, John shoves her face next to Brandon's exposed genitals and forces her to look. Despite the "evidence" that Brandon is not biologically a man, Lana pleads with the two men to, "Leave him alone," which infuriates John further. "Him? Him?!" he screams.

John's and Tom's rage toward Brandon and his successful masculine performance is not satisfied with this humiliation. They have been cuckolded and they will make Brandon pay. The men ambush Brandon outside Lana's home and drag him into their car. They drive him to a deserted lot, haul him out of the car, and order him to strip. John ignores Brandon's pleas to stop, slugging him in the face instead and shoving him into the back seat. While they cheer each other on, John and Tom take turns raping and beating Brandon, proving to themselves that *they* are the *real* men. It is a quintessential moment of heteromasculine privilege. After Brandon reports his rape to the local authorities, however, John and Tom enact their ultimate privilege and revenge upon Brandon for having trespassed into their masculine domain, and having made them look like fools. Despite John's warnings to Brandon to "keep our little secret" or "I'll have to silence you permanently," Brandon files assault and rape complaints against them. Clearly, the men are in danger of being sent back to prison. In the brutal murder scene that follows, John and Tom find Brandon at Candace's farmhouse, where he has been hiding since the rape. As John points a gun at Brandon's head, Lana pleads with him, and looks at Brandon asking tearfully, "Teena, why didn't you leave? We can still do it." The implication that Lana is willing to leave Falls City with Brandon is the final blow to John's already threatened sense of privileged masculine ego. He shoots Brandon in the head, and after Brandon's body lies on the floor, Tom violently stabs him and John fires another shot into his body. Tom then turns his gun on Candace, killing her in front of her crying toddler.[9]

The assault and murder scenes function to expose the "rabid pathology present in John and Tom's conception of masculinity, one which assumes that committing acts of violence is their natural birth-right" (Anderson, 2000, p. 56). This perception of the acceptability of violence as a male "privilege," partic-ularly against women, is underlined immediately after Brandon is raped when John reminds him that, "You know you brought this on yourself." Brandon replies, "I know. This whole thing is my fault."[10] Violence and aggressive behavior have long been part of the codes of masculinity in American culture and, in particular, a part of the image associated with the macho-cow-boy masculinity of America's heartland. Furthermore, media rape narratives generally reinforce a hegemonic masculine ideology in which masculinity emerges as the "solution rather than the cause of the victimization of women through rape" (Cuklanz, 1998, p. 444). But in contrast, the narratives of *Boys Don't Cry* suggest to spectators that Brandon is not the one who is "sick": "[I]t is male heterosexuality–culturally assumed to be a firmly entrenched, inalienable identity–that shows the greatest signs of sickness and is in dire need of reconfiguration" (Anderson, p. 55).[11] The film's depic-tion of John and Tom's heteromasculinity as patho-logically violent and brutally enacted has the effect of making it more difficult to see their response to Brandon's "deception" as some kind of "panic" and thus somehow "defensible," or to condemn Brandon's masculine performance as "sick," which has typically been the case when individuals refuse to occupy their biologically assigned gender (Anderson).[12]

Indeed, the media have long perpetuated the per-spective that individuals who do not conform to their assigned gender are abnormal and their transgressive performance of gender is unnatural (Bennett, 1998; Fejes & Petrich, 1993). But the narrative structure of *Boys Don't Cry* suggests that the problem resides not in Brandon but, rather, within the strict construction of normative masculinity and its inherent misogynist attitudes and sexual bigotry that often lead to con-tempt for and violence against those who challenge the heterosexual norms. As a U.S. Marshal said regarding the residents of Falls City during the murder trials of Lotter and Nissen: "They don't view homosexuals—don't view people that are different from them—they don't view them as being equal.

They think it's OK. . . . Well yeah, I can shoot her—you know, she's a lesbian, she's a cross-dresser, she's a dyke. She's less than human. And they rationalize their actions by that" (Muska & Oláfsdóttir, 1998).[13] Thus, the narratives of *Boys Don't Cry* expose the bigoted mechanisms that perpetuate and maintain dominant heteromasculinity, effectively dismantling the ideals of normative masculinity and making heterosexu-ality—instead of transgressive sexuality—appear strange. The next section discusses how, in contrast, the juxtaposition of a normalizing female masculin-ity with the "strangeness" of hegemonic masculinity works to center the queer by queering the center of heteronormativity (Scheman, 1997) in the film's nar-rative structure.

Centering Female Masculinity

The film's Brandon Teena performs stereotypical macho masculinity very well, using the behavior of John and Tom as role models. Brandon's performance of masculinity, however, can be interpreted as oper-ating on two levels in the narratives: When Brandon tries to establish his male identity with his new bud-dies, he imitates the kind of overly aggressive macho machismo that John and Tom represent. But Lana falls for Brandon because of his version of mascu-linity, which contradicts and challenges traditional assumptions about what it takes to be a man and to please a woman. Brandon's articulation of manhood effectively mocks sexist masculine ideals and appro-priates the codes of normative masculinity.

Shapiro (1991) reminds us that "transsexuals must work hard at passing in their new gender status" (p. 256) in order to "live successfully in the gender of choice, to be accepted as a 'natural' member of that gender" (Stone, 1991, p. 296), and this is precisely what Brandon does. He meets his male role models during a bar brawl when Brandon tells a man to stop harassing Candace. Having survived this masculine "rite of passage" (Anderson, 2000, p. 55), a bruised but proud Brandon is befriended by John and Tom, who advise him that "if you're gonna get into fights over girls like Candace, you gotta learn a few moves." Brandon's initiation into John and Tom's articulation of masculinity continues when he accompanies them to Falls City, and decides to stay and party with them.

"One more night, Tyson. Come on, buddy," John says. Delighted by John's acceptance and the reference to his bar fight, Brandon soon finds himself in the midst of drunken rowdies, taking turns at "bumper ski-ing"—a macho contest where the goal is to hold onto a rope and stand on the rear bumper of a pickup truck as it roars around a dirt track. John taunts Brandon into trying it: "Come on, stud. Let's go cowboy. . . . Go ahead. Be a man." Eager for acceptance and to prove his masculinity, Brandon mounts the pickup and flies around the field, falling off three times before he quits. He is flattered when John calls him a "crazy little fucker." When Lana later asks Brandon why he "let John tie you to the back of a truck and drag you around like a dog?" Brandon replies, "I just thought that's what guys do around here."

But Brandon's happiness over being accepted as one of the boys is not as great as his desire to win Lana, for whom he developed an instant infatuation. For this goal, Brandon seems to know that he needs to be his own kind of man, not the kind he sees in John and Tom. Thus, when Brandon is interacting with women, it is with a shy sensitivity and tender-ness that helps redefine what is means to be a man. As Brandon pursues a relationship with Lana, he exhibits a new form of masculinity—he's the boyfriend young women dream about. He's sensitive, he buys them gifts (although with stolen credit cards and checks), and he's a tender lover who is more concerned with his partner's sexual gratification than his own. When John asks her what she sees in that "wuss," Lana retorts, "I know he's no big he-man like you, but there's something about him."[14] Soon John and Tom "find themselves decisively 'out-boyed' by the handsome, sexually adept newcomer" (Brooks, 2000, p. 44). As Halberstam (1994) said of the FTM transsexual in the film *Vera*, who is "more adept at masculinity than most men could hope to be" (p. 221), Brandon's form of masculinity is far more appealing to Lana, and seems more "normal" than the violent, abusive masculinity exhibited by either John or Tom.

Peirce's film, I argue, does far more than sim-ply celebrate Brandon's ability to "outboy" the local males. The prevailing image in the film's narratives is Brandon's self-actualization as a male. With rare exceptions, masculine pronouns are used to refer to Brandon throughout the movie, and in the few instances in which "she" is used, those referring to Brandon as a female are typically the men whose manhood has been threatened by his appropriation of masculinity. Every time Brandon looks himself in the mirror and admires the man he sees reflected, we are encouraged to share that image, to see him as a male and to share the "exhilaration he feels as a sexual being" (Anderson, 2000, p. 54). From the film's opening scenes—Brandon dressed in men's Western-style clothes, admiring his new haircut, and meeting his date at a roller rink while the lyrics of "You're Just What I Needed" play (Ocasek, 1987)—the underly-ing message is that Brandon truly sees himself as a man; therefore, living his life as a man is not an abnor-mal or deceptive act. As Shapiro (1991) explains, "[T]ranssexuals commonly believe that it is when they are trying to play the role of their anatomical sex, as opposed to their subjectively experienced gender, that they are trying to pass as someone they are not" (p. 256).[15] In *Boys Don't Cry*, the narratives privilege Brandon's self-identity over his biological body— Brandon Teena *is* a man.[16]

There's little history of a previous life as a girl—in *Boys Don't Cry*, Brandon's real life begins as a young man. Yet Peirce does not try to rationalize Brandon's transsexuality out of existence. His cousin Lonny ridicules him for stuffing such a large sock in his pants that it looks like a "deformity," and taunts Brandon to admit that he's just a "dyke." A gang of men, furious that he has been sleeping with one of their sisters, chases Brandon, calling him a "Fucking dyke! Freak! Fucking Faggot!" In another scene, Brandon's frus-tration is obvious when his menstrual period begins and he is forced to scavenge for tampons (which he shoplifts from a convenience store). Spectators see the measures he must take in order to enact his masculine identity: binding his breasts and using a dildo or stuffed socks to mimic a penis in his jeans. Each of these scenes, however, works to privilege Brandon's self-definition as a man. As Erhart (1999) has explained, the "co-presence of seemingly mutu-ally exclusive body parts and accouterment . . . under-mines normative understandings of two-sexed-ness *and* renders powerful the respective performers" (p. 176). As a result, the narratives of *Boys Don't Cry* work to demonstrate that the "way in which transsexuals go about establishing their gender in social interactions reminds us that the basis on which we are assigned a gender in the first place (that is, anatomical sex) is not what creates the reality of gender in ongoing social life" (Shapiro, 1991, p. 257).

Although Brandon finds himself in the position of having to say, "I can explain" to people, these scenes are also framed to focus attention toward Brandon's confusion and frustration over why any explanation is necessary, why others can't accept him for who he believes he is. In this way, the narratives encourage the recognition of Brandon's own experiences of sexual identity and validate what he believes to be his true nature. The underlying message in all of the scenes in which Brandon must offer some explanation for his masculine identity is that the confusion surrounding his sexual identity does not reside in him, but in others—in the intolerance they feel toward those who violate normative heterosexuality.

As the previous section argues, the narratives of *Boys Don't Cry* privilege an alternative perspective of masculinity—female masculinity—blurring the conventional boundaries of sexual identity and opening a space to experience gender and sexuality as performative rather than as biologically assigned. Brandon's masculine performance confirms the constructive nature of gender and, in turn, disrupts heteronormativity's "antiquated categories" of sexuality: by challenging the "naturalness of gender . . . penises as well as masculinity become artificial and constructible" (Halberstam, 1994, pp. 214–215).

Blurring the Boundaries of Female Masculinity

The narrative structure of *Boys Don't Cry* further confounds issues of gender fluidity through the depiction of Lana as she ignores her suspicions about Brandon's sexuality and, ultimately, chooses to overlook contradictions between his gender identity and his biologically assigned sex. For example, she sees Brandon's cleavage above his bound breasts when they make love, and Brandon pushes her hand away when she reaches for his penis. Still, she continues to date him and make plans for their future together. In another scene, Lana ignores the implications when Brandon is confined to the women's section of the jail. As he tries to explain that, "Brandon's not quite a.'he,'" Brandon's

more like a 'she,'" Lana cuts him off: "Shut up. That's your business. I don't care if you're half monkey or half ape." Later when Lana's mother and John and Tom demand proof of Brandon's gender, Lana assures him, "I'm going to tell them what we know is true. . . . I know you're a guy." She tells them, "Mom, I seen him in the full flesh. I seen it. I know he's a man." Lana even refuses to deny Brandon's masculine identity after John and Tom violently force her to look at his genitals. And when Brandon stumbles to Lana's home after being raped and beaten, her mother says, "I don't want *it* in my house." But Lana still calls him "he": "Mom stop it. He's hurt. Call an ambulance! Now!"[17]

Near the end of the movie, Lana does acknowledge Brandon's birth identity as a female, a narrative strategy that refuses to "allow gender to remain unproblematized" (Scheman, 1997, p, 127). Lana finds Brandon in a run-down shed, where Candace has allowed him to stay. Any doubt that Lana knows he is not biologically male is gone when she asks: "What were you like? Before all this? Were you like me? Like a girl-girl?" Brandon answers, "Yeah, like a long time ago. Then I guess I was just like a boy-girl, then I was just a jerk. It's weird, finally everything felt right." Further, it is Lana who initiates their love-making. She takes off Brandon's shirt and sees him naked for the first time. "I don't know if I'm gonna know how to do it," she confesses. After making love, the two make plans to return to Lincoln together. Although Lana later changes her mind about leaving town with Brandon, the implication in this scene is that like the character of Annie in *Linda/Les & Annie*, Lana "embraces the ambiguity and constructiveness" (Halberstam, 1994, p. 224) of Brandon's masculine identity.[18] Rather than conform to what Halberstam (1998) referred to as heterosexuality's "jarring need to identify the feminine partner of the transsexual man with normal sexual aims and desires" (p. 156), the film's narratives make it possible to read Lana's behavior as more ambiguous and, ultimately, as far more liberatory. By refusing to label Brandon as exclusively male or transsexual, *Boys Don't Cry* represents Brandon in terms of what Kate Bornstein refers to as a "gender outlaw" (as cited in Halberstam, 1994, p. 218), a representation that negates the "reductive rhetoric of inversion that suggests that one true identity hides within an other waiting for an opportunity to emerge" (p. 219).

Although it could be argued that by depicting Lana as acknowledging Brandon's birth sex Peirce has betrayed Brandon's self-definition as a male, I would argue that this scene is liberatory precisely because it refuses to conform to heteronormativity's categorization of gender as exclusively male *or* female. The ambiguity of Lana's attraction to Brandon as a man on one hand, and her acknowledgment and acceptance of his biological sex on the other hand, subvert heteroideology and its inherent oppression of sexual difference. As Scheman (1997) has suggested, the "more important it is for transsexuals to claim a stable and unproblematic gender" and to maintain an "illusion of the normality of 'natural' gendering . . . , the more conceptually dependent they are on their own marginality, as rare exceptions to a fundamentally natural dichotomy" (p. 146). Thus, depicting Lana and Brandon engaging in sexual relations even when she has acknowledged Brandon's biological sex can be read as a liberatory strategy that works to blur the dichotomous distinctions between female and male. Rather than denying Brandon's sense of his sexual identity, the final love-making scene between Brandon and Lana has the effect of directing the gaze *away* from Brandon's transsexuality, allowing the scene to be read as *affirming* multiple sexual identities, which was one of Peirce's stated goals for the film. "Society kept forcing them [Brandon and Lana] into these categories that I don't think they really needed. And that was so destructive," Peirce said (Allen, 1999, p. 5). By suggesting that Lana can love and defend Brandon as a male, even though she has acknowledged he is biologically a female, the film opens a space for sexuality to escape being an either-or proposition.

Thus, the seemingly conflicting depictions of sexuality in *Boys Don't Cry* work to validate and to celebrate multiple expressions of gender and sexuality. Further, by framing Brandon's gender performance as an example of legitimate female expressions of masculinity, the narratives of *Boys Don't Cry* throw into question the privileged sexual definitions of what constitutes "normal" masculinity and sexuality. In so doing, the film "queers the center" of normative heterosexuality by "centering the queer" in the narratives (Scheman, 1997, p. 124). This celebration of female masculinity in *Boys Don't Cry* and the film's departure from the norms of hegemonic heterosexuality render the unspeakability of sexual transgression speakable, expanding the heteronormative feminine–masculine dichotomy and encouraging us as spectators to reexamine our own definitions of sexual identity and personal freedom.

"Gender Outlaws" and Implications for Media Analysis

> It is perhaps preferable therefore to acknowledge that gender is defined by its transitivity, that sexuality manifests as multiple sexualities, and that therefore we are all transsexuals.
> There are no transsexuals.
>
> (Halberstam, 1994, p. 226)

Among those who have chastised the film industry for catering to the majority, heterosexual audience is Vito Russo (1986), who has said: "Mainstream cinema is plainly chickenshit when it comes to gay life and lives, and it's time we said so" (p. 34). Indeed, mainstream media have a history of allowing spectators to experience vicariously the possibilities of transgressing gender boundaries, but usually only within the safety of comedic contexts that assure audiences that heterosexuality is never jeopardized (Williams, 1996, p. 273), and where gender is categorized as if "genitals always, inevitably outweigh agency" (Hale, 1998, p. 316). Thus, says Richard Dyer (1999), "What we should be attacking in stereotypes is the attempt of heterosexual society to define us for ourselves, in terms that inevitably fall short of the 'ideal' of heterosexuality" (p. 300). This is precisely what I argue is accomplished in *Boys Don't Cry*. Rather than reassuring spectators that heterosexuality is stable and secure, Kimberly Peirce's representation of Brandon Teena and his female masculinity is read here as a liberatory discourse, exposing the arbitrary artificiality of assuming a natural and immutable gender and drawing attention to the damage inflicted both by and upon a society that requires individuals to deny their varied and multiple experiences of gender.

Peirce's film has far broader liberatory and societal implications than just contradicting media's traditionally negative stereotypes of sexual minorities. Unlike narratives such as those surrounding *Ellen*'s coming-out that facilitate "blindness toward" both "heterosexism and homophobia" (Dow, 2001, p. 135), *Boys Don't Cry* defies and denies such blindness, graphically depicting the consequences of heteronormativity's bigotry toward gender transgression and condemning the lack of social or political change that could help eradicate such prejudice. Filmmaker Peirce has explained that she needed to make audiences understand Brandon's "journey and the violence that was exacted upon him, because that's how you fight hate crimes" (O'Sullivan, 1999, p. N49). For Peirce, the most gratifying aspect of the acclaim her film received has been to bring Brandon "into the mainstream, and the audience is falling in love with Brandon, which was the main point" ("Kimberly Peirce," 2000, p. 2).

Larry Gross (1996) reminds us that, more than just entertainment, the mass media are perhaps the most dominant and pervasive storytellers in American society (p. 159). We learn how to think about the world—including about sexual minorities—from mass media. As Nangeroni (1999) observes, the "stigma against transgender people is maintained by the media's denigration and disrespect. Crossdressers and transsexuals have long been the butt of jokes, regularly depicted as something other than 'normal,' not worthy of respect or even protection under the law" (p. 17). For these reasons, films like *Boys Don't Cry* that privilege tolerance and acceptance of gender fluidity have the potential to help reduce the kind of societal bigotry and intolerance that result in hate crimes like Brandon Teena's murder. The harsh consequences of such bigotry is underlined by the film's concluding soundtrack, when we're reminded that Brandon's dream of masculine self-actualization, like his life, "ended way too soon" (Stephenson, Robbins, & Dubois, 1998). As Gross suggests, honest media portrayals of sexual minorities "have the potential to reach the hearts and minds of many Americans. This is reason enough to continue the struggle to transform the media" (p. 159). Close critiques of media performance and content is a vital part of that struggle. While there are multiple ways to interpret *Boys Don't Cry* and other media representations of sexuality, critical readings such as this one, which privilege gender fluidity and liberation from heteronormative straightjackets, also have the potential to contribute to broadening our understandings of gender and sexuality, in both mass media and in society.

Notes

1. For the purposes of my study, I'll refer to Brandon Teena as a transsexual, following the clarifications provided by Sandy Stone (1991), Nancy Nangeroni (1999) and Judith Halberstam (1998). Transsexuals are individuals who identify "his or her gender identity with that of the 'opposite' gender" (Stone, p. 281). Thus, Halberstam cautioned that misusing pronouns—using the pronoun "he" to refer to a MTF transsexual or "she" to refer to a FTM—is an insidious practice that either attempts to rationalize transsexuals "out of existence," (p. 150), or as Nangeroni explained, "disregards and disrespects our most fundamental sense of ourselves. It's about our choice to *define ourselves* differently than our birth doctors, families, and society would define us" (p. 17). It is for these reasons that many transgender activists insist that using "Brandon Teena" and "masculine pronouns as markers of transsexual or transgender configurations of this young person's identity are the only correct modes of representation" (Hale, 1998, p. 313). Hence, I use "Brandon" rather than "Teena" and masculine pronouns throughout this essay, unless citing a direct quotation from another source that uses "Teena" or "she."

2. Most critics agreed that Peirce followed the events of Brandon's life and death closely, and that her objectivity in the film's narratives resulted in well-rounded depictions of all the film's characters, including Brandon's murderers (e.g., Bloom, 1999; Strickler, 1999; Wu, 1999). My study, however, is concerned less with the artistic license of Peirce's film than with how the narratives in *Boys Don't Cry* construct a particular view of both Brandon Teena and issues of gender and sexual fluidity.

3. The purpose of my study is to articulate the potential of the film's narratives to destabilize the privileged position of heteronormativity, particularly as relates to female masculinity. This parallels some of Peirce's own stated goals for *Boys Don't Cry.* Therefore, although I make references to instances in which my reading intersects with Peirce's agency, my critique is not an examination of Peirce's intended meaning for the film.

4. See for example: Doty (1993); Burston & Richardson (1995); Evans & Gamman (1995); Hanson (1999); Mayne (2000); Nataf (1995); and Robertson (1996).

5. For additional discussions of gender as performance, see for example: Butler (1987; 1990; 1993); Condit (1997); Doane (1982); and Moi (1985).

6. Peirce explained to an interviewer that, "I identify as a queer rather than as straight, lesbian, or gay. I like the term 'queer' because it gives me the freedom to express more aspects of my personality—the boy side and the girl side" (Miller, 2000, p. 39).

7. Before beginning the discussion, it is important to clarify that I come to this study from the privileged position of a heterosexual. I have attempted to be aware of and sensitive to the rules for writing about transsexuals suggested by Jacob Hale (1997). Two rules are particularly relevant to my investigation of *Boys Don't Cry*. First, Hale advises that non-transsexed individuals must interrogate the motives for their interests in researching issues of transsexuality and sexual difference. This is simple for me: my interests in gender transgression and challenges to heteronormativity are deeply-rooted in the close relationship I shared with my gay brother, and my interests have increased in the years since he lost his battle with AIDS. Hale's next rule, however, is more challenging. Hale suggests that the most appropriate way for nontranssexed individuals to examine transsexual issues is to focus on what dominant cultural narratives tell us about heteroideology and its consequences for *everyone*, rather than attempt to write and make conclusions about transsexual subjectivity. Thus, as Hale and Scheman (1997) suggest, I've attempted to complicate my privileged location as well as make a contribution to scholarship by examining how female masculinity may transcend the "frame of anomaly" of heteroideology (Henderson, 2001, p. 22) in mediated popular culture.

8. For legal reasons, Lisa Lambert, one of Lotter and Nissen's murder victims, is portrayed as Candace (Alicia Goranson) in the movie (O'Sullivan, 1999).

9. For narrative coherence and simplicity, Peirce omitted the third murder victim, Philip DeVine, from her script (O'Sullivan, 1999).

10. That many men in this country consider committing acts of violence against women a part of their natural birthright is difficult to dispute: "Male-perpetuated violence is a major cause of fear, distress, injury, and even death for women in this country" (Koss, Goodman, Browne, Fitzgerald, Keita, & Russo, 1994, p. ix). Further, the number one cause of injury to women ages 15–54 in the United States is domestic violence ("Violence against," 2001); and the United States has one of the highest rates of reported rape among industrialized nations worldwide (Salholz, 1990).

11. Peirce told interviewers that one reason Brandon's rape and murder deeply resonated with her was because the "violence [he experienced] with men was a violence I knew" (Che, 2000, p. 50).

12. In her review of *The Brandon Teena Story*, Melissa Anderson (2000) says the documentary also relates the rage exhibited by John and Tom to their sense of powerlessness, to living lives in which "hope has been extinguished" (p. 55). The narratives of *Boys Don't Cry*, I would argue, also suggest that the men's powerlessness had the effect of emasculating John's and Tom's sense of their privileged masculinity: they had been trying to lash back at society, friends, and family long before Brandon arrived in Falls City. Consequently, Brandon and his successful performance of transgressive masculinity worked to exacerbate their already threatened heteromasculinity, and gave them a target on which to vent their long-extant rage and to reassert their damaged masculinity.

13. Such bigoted attitudes are not limited to the residents of heartland towns such as Falls City. For example, between the year when Matthew Shepard was murdered and the trial of Aaron McKinney, one of the men convicted for his murder, 35 people who had transgressed their biologically assigned gender are known to have been killed in America (Montgomery, 2000). Among openly gay and lesbian individuals, over half report they have been victims of homophobic violence (Singer & Deschamps, as cited in Dow, 2001, p. 136). Jeffrey Montgomery, executive director of The Triangle Foundation, graphically summarized the problems facing individuals who do not conform to normative heterosexuality in America: "[G]ay, lesbian, bisexual and transgender people are at risk every day of their lives. Not only are we the group most at risk of violence, we are most at risk of job discrimination, losing our families; homophobia retains its title as the last socially acceptable form of bigotry" (p. 443). Further, as Montgomery reports, post-verdict interviews with jury members in trials for some of these crimes indicate that many jurors believed that if the murdered person had "made a homosexual advance," then that person "deserved to die" and the killer should "be let off easy" (p. 443).

14. In explaining her attraction to Brandon, Lana Tisdel told documentary filmmakers Susan Muska and Greta Oláfsdóttir (*The Brandon Teena Story*, 1998) that, "It was really nice being treated like a lady instead of just like nothing, like dirt."

15. The term "passing" is associated with the idea of people trying to be accepted as someone they are not, and the connotations are generally negative. For instance, passing was frequently used as a negative reference to light-skinned African Americans who tried to live as White, a practice America's racist society viewed as deceitful and immoral. In contrast, sexual minorities often are expected to pass as heterosexuals in order to conform to the "don't ask, don't tell" mentality underlying society's heterosexism. Thus, many sexual minorities continue to pass as heterosexuals in the workplace, the military, and with their families to avoid discrimination and bigotry. In Brandon's case, Sloop (2000) reports that the news media framed Brandon's passing as a man as a dishonest and vile affront against the citizens of Falls City, Nebraska. Yet, as Shapiro (1991) points out,

passing is an essential part of performing gender for transsexuals; the most critical aspect of a transsexual's success is to be accepted as a "natural" member of their chosen gender (p. 296). And as Halberstam (1998) reminds us, transsexuals' lives are often in physical danger when their biological sex is discovered. Given such danger and prejudice as well as Brandon's need to enact his gender identity, Brandon's decision to pass seems a valid and honest response, not only for him, but also for others who must live their lives in a society that rejects and threatens them.

16. JoAnn Brandon was angered when Hilary Swank referred to her daughter as a man, thanking Brandon Teena rather than "Teena Brandon" when she accepted her Best Actress Oscar award ("Swank speech," 2000). Ms. Brandon insisted that the only reason her daughter passed as a man was to keep men from touching her, because she had been sexually molested years earlier. Considering the homophobic attitudes prevalent in Falls City (Jones, as cited in Barr, 2000, p. 48; Muska & Oláfsdóttir, 1998), it is perhaps understandable that Ms. Brandon wanted to defend her daughter as a "normal" heterosexual. Filmmaker Peirce has explained, however, that she never intended to "tell the audience what is and isn't true" (Leigh, 2000, p. 20), nor is that my intention in this essay. The goal of my research was not to determine the "facts" of Brandon's sexuality, but to examine critically the film strategies used to depict issues of gender fluidity and female masculinity in ways that can be read as working to subvert heteronormativity. Thus, I don't address Ms. Brandon's charges in my critique.

17. Lana explained her continued denials despite her growing suspicions in *The Brandon Teena Story* (Muska & Oláfsdóttir, 1998), and the film's dialogue adheres closely to her explanations.

18. Although Aphrodite Jones (as cited in Barr, 2000) states that Lana stopped dating Brandon after she learned his biological sex, Lana seemed to contradict such claims when she was interviewed and filmed for *The Brandon Teena Story* (Muska & Oláfsdóttir, 1998). For instance, Muska and Oláfsdóttir assert that Brandon's sexuality did not become a problem for Lana or his other girlfriends until it became public knowledge, when homophobia became an issue because Brandon's girlfriends were labeled as lesbians (Yabroff, 1999). Since Falls City has a reputation as a "very conservative, racist, and homophobic place" Jones, as cited in Barr, p. 48), it is perhaps not surprising that Lana Tisdel filed a defamation of character lawsuit against Peirce claiming that the depiction of her relationship with Brandon in *Boys Don't Cry* has made her the object of "contempt and ridicule" in Falls City, and as a result, she had been

"scorned and/or abandoned by her friends and family" (Barr, p. 48).

References

Allen, J. (1999, October 22). 'Boys Don't Cry' filmmaker saw past violence to love. *CNN.com entertainment.* [Online]. Available: http://www8.cnn.com/SHOWBIZ/Movies/9910/22/boys. dont.cry/index.html.

Anderson, M. (2000, February). *The Brandon Teena Story–Boys Don't Cry* [Review of the films *The Brandon Teena Story* and *Boys Don't Cry*]. *Cineaste, 25*(2), 54–56.

Barr, L. (2000, May). The other woman. *Brill's Content, 3*, 48.

Bennett, L. (1998). The perpetuation of prejudice in reporting on gays and lesbians: *Time* and *Newsweek:* The first fifty years. (Research paper R-21). The Joan Shorenstein Center. Cambridge, MA: President and Fellows of Harvard University.

Bloom, B. (1999). Boys Don't Cry. [Review of the film *Boys Don't Cry*]. [On-line]. Available: http://us.imdb.com/Reviews/223/22390.

Brookey, R. A., & Westerfelhaus, R. (2001). Pistols and petticoats, piety and purity: *To Wong Foo*, the queering of the American monomyth, and the marginalizing discourse of deification. *Critical Studies in Media Communication, 18*, 141–156.

Brooks, X. (2000, April). Boys Don't Cry. [Review of the film *Boys Don't Cry*]. *Sight and Sound, 10*(4), 43–44.

Burston, P. & Richardson, C. (Eds.). (1995). *A queer romance: Lesbians, gay men and popular culture.* London: Routledge.

Butler, J. (1987). Variations on sex and gender: Beauvoir, Wittig and Foucault. In S. Benhabib and D. Cornell (Eds.), *Feminism as critique* (pp. 128–142). Minneapolis: University of Minnesota Press.

Butler, J. (1990). *Gender trouble: Feminism and the subversion of identity.* New York: Routledge.

Butler, J. (1993). *Bodies that matter: On the discursive limits of 'sex'.* New York: Routledge.

Che, C. (2000, January). Kimberly Peirce. *Out, 74,* 50.

Condit, C. M. (1997). In praise of eloquent diversity: Gender and rhetoric as public persuasion. *Women's Studies in Communication, 20,* 91–116.

Cuklanz, L. M. (1998). The masculine ideal: Rape in prime-time television, 1976–1978. *Critical Studies in Mass Communication, 15,* 423–448.

De Lauretis, T. (1984). *Alice doesn't: Feminism, semiotics, cinema.* Bloomington, IN: Indiana University Press.

De Lauretis, T. (1987). *Technologies of gender: Essays on theory, film and fiction.* Bloomington, IN: Indiana University Press.

Doane, M. A. (1982). Film and the masquerade: Theorising the female spectator. *Screen, 23*(3/4), 74–87.

Doty, A. (1993). *Making things perfectly queer.* Minneapolis: University of Minnesota Press.

Dow, B. J. (1996). *Prime-time feminism: Television, media culture, and the women's movement since 1970.* Philadelphia: University of Pennsylvania Press.

Dow, B. J. (2001). *Ellen*, television, and the politics of gay and lesbian visibility. *Critical Studies in Media Communication, 18*, 123–140.

Dyer, R. (1992). Don't look now: The instabilities of the male pin-up. In R. Dyer, *Only entertainment* (pp. 103–119). London & New York: Routledge.

Dyer, R. (1999). Stereotyping. In L. Gross & J. D. Woods (Eds.), *The Columbia Reader: On lesbians and gay men in media, society, & politics* (pp. 297–301). New York: Columbia University Press.

Erhart, J. (1999). Laura Mulvey meets Catherine Trammell meets the She-Man: Counter-history, reclamation, and incongruity in lesbian, gay, and queer film and media criticism. In T. Miller & R. Stam (Eds.), *A companion to film theory* (pp. 165–181). Malden, MA: Blackwell.

Evans, C, & Gamman, L. (1995). The gaze revisited, or reviewing queer viewing. In P. Burston & C. Richardson (Eds.), *A queer romance: Lesbians, gay men and popular culture* (pp. 13–56). London: Routledge.

Fejes, F., & Petrich, K. (1993). Invisibility, homophobia and heterosexism: Lesbians, gays and the media. *Critical Studies in Mass Communication, 10*, 396–422.

Gabriel, D. A. (1996, February 21). Brandon Teena Murderer sentenced. *Janeway.* [On-line]. Available: http://songweaver.com/gender/teena-sentencing.html.

Gross, L. (1996). Don't ask, don't tell: Lesbian and gay people in the media. In P. M. Lester (Ed.), *Images that injure: Pictorial stereotypes in the media* (pp. 149–159). Westport, CT: Praeger.

Gross, L. (2001). The paradoxical politics of media representation. *Critical Studies in Media Communication, 18*, 114–119.

Halberstam, J. (1994). F2M: The making of female masculinity. In L. Doan (Ed.), *The lesbian postmodern* (pp. 210–228). New York: Columbia University Press.

Halberstam, J. (1998). *Female masculinity.* Durham, NC & London: Duke University Press.

Hale, J. (1997). Suggested rules for non-transsexuals writing about transsexuals, transsexuality, transsexualism, or trans_. [On-line]. Available: http://sandystone.com/hale.rules.html.

Hale, C. J. (1998). Consuming the living, dis(re)membering the dead in the butch/ftm borderlands. *GLQ 4*(2), 311–348.

Hanson, E. (1999). *Out takes.* Durham, NC & London: Duke University Press.

Henderson, L. (2001). Sexuality, feminism, media studies. *Feminist Media Studies, 1*(1), 17–24.

Holden, S. (1998, September 23). A rape and beating, later 3 murders and then the twist. [Review of the documentary *The Brandon Teena Story*]. *The New York Times*, p. E5.

Jones, A. (1996). *All she wanted: A true story of sexual deception and murder in America's heartland.* New York: Pocket Books.

Kimberly Peirce–*Boys Don't Cry.* (2000, March 21). [On-line]. gurl.com chat transcript. Available: http://nj123abcus.tripod.com/kimberlypeirceboysdontcry/id7.html.

Koss, M. P., Goodman, L. A., Browne, A., Fitzgerald, L. F., Keita, G. P., & Russo, N. F. (1994). *No safe haven: Male violence against women at home, at work, and in the community.* Washington, D.C.: American Psychological Association.

Leigh, D. (2000, March). Boy wonder. [Interview with Kimberly Peirce]. *Sight and Sound, 10*(3), 18–20.

Maslin, J. (1999, October 1). Film Festival reviews: Sometimes accepting an identity means accepting a fate, too. [Review of the film *Boys Don't Cry*]. *The New York Times*, p. E10.

Mayne, J. (2000). *Framed: Lesbians, feminists, and media culture.* Minneapolis: University of Minnesota Press.

Messina, G. (Producer). (2000, August 24). Her secret life. *20/20.* New York: ABC News.

Miller, F. (2000). Putting Teena Brandon's story on film. *Gay & Lesbian Review, VII*(4), 39 +.

Moi, T. (1985). *Sexual/textual politics.* New York: Routledge.

Montgomery, J. (2000, May 1). America . . . You kill me: "Gay panic defense." *Vital Speeches of the Day, 66*(14), pp. 443–446.

Mulvey, L. (1975). Visual pleasure and narrative cinema. *Screen, 16*(3), 6–18.

Muska, S., & Oláfsdóttir, G. (Producers & Directors). (1998). *The Brandon Teena Story.* [Documentary]. (Videotape available from New Video, 126 Fifth Avenue, New York, NY).

Nangeroni, N. (1999, February). Rita Hester's murder and the language of respect. *Sojourner, 24*(6), 16–17.

Nataf, Z. I. (1995). Black lesbian spectatorship and pleasure in popular cinema. In P. Burston & C. Richardson (Eds.), *A queer romance: Lesbians, gay men and popular culture* (pp. 57–80). London: Routledge.

Ocasek, R. (1987). You're just what I needed. *The Cars* [compact disk]. WEA/Electra Entertainment.

O'Sullivan, M. (1999, October 22). Why 'Boys Don't Cry.' *Washington Post*, p. N49.

Ricks, I. (1994, March 8). Heartland homicide. *The Advocate, 650*, 28–30.

Robertson, P. (1996). *Guilty pleasures: Feminist camp from Mae West to Madonna.* Durham, NC: Duke University Press.

Roof, J. (1996). *Come as you are: Sexuality & narrative.* New York: Columbia University Press.

Russo, V. (1986, March/April). When the gaze is gay: A state of being. *Film Comment, 22* (2), 32–34.

Salholz, E. (with Clift, E., Springen, K., & Johnson, P.). (1990, July 16). Women under assault. *Newsweek, 116,* 23–24.

Scheman, N. (1997). Queering the center by centering the queer. In D. T. Meyers (Ed.), *Feminists rethink the self* (pp. 124–162). Boulder, CO: Westview.

Shapiro, J. (1991). Transsexualism: Reflections on the persistence of gender and the mutability of sex. In J. Epstein & K. Straub (Eds.), *Body guards: The cultural politics of gender ambiguity* (pp. 248–279). New York & London: Routledge.

Sharp, J., Hart, J., Kolodner, C, Vachon, C. (Producers) & Peirce, K. (Director). (1999). *Boys Don't Cry* [Film]. (Videotape available from CBS/Fox Home Video).

Sloop, J. M. (2000). Disciplining the transgendered: Brandon Teena, public representations, and normativity. *Western Journal of Communication, 64,* 165–189.

Smith, R., Tolhurst, L., & Dempsey, M. (1988). Boys Don't Cry. *Boys Don't Cry* [compact disk]. Wea/Bektra Entertainment.

Stephenson, V., Robbins, D., & Dubois, T. (1998). Bluest eyes in Texas. *Restless Hearts Greatest Hits* [compact disk]. BMG/RCA.

Stone, S. (1991). The Empire strikes back: A posttranssexual manifesto. In J. Epstein & K. Straub (Eds.), *Body guards: The cultural politics of gender ambiguity* (pp. 280–304). New York & London: Routledge.

Svetkey, B. (2000, October 6). Is your TV set gay? *Entertainment Weekly,* 24–26, 27–28.

Swank speech upsets Brandon mother. (2000, March 28). [On-line]. Available: http://www.canoe. com/ JamOscar2000/mar28 swank.html.

Violence against women (2001). National Women's Health Information Center. [On-line]. Available: http:// www.4woman.gov/violence/.

Williams, J. P. (1996). Biology and destiny: The dynamics of gender crossing in *Quantum Leap. Women's Studies in Communication, 19,* 273–290.

Wu, G. (1999). Boys Don't Cry. [Review of the film *Boys Don't Cry*]. [On-line]. Available: http://us.imdb.com/ Reviews/211/21137.

Yabroff, J. (1999). Documentary filmmakers Susan Muska and Greta Oláfsdóttir talk about the story behind "The Brandon Teena Story." Salon.com entertainment. [On-line]: Available: http://www.salon.com/ent/movies/ int/1999/02/25int.html.

25.
THE TELEVISED SPORTS MANHOOD FORMULA

Michael A. Messner, Michele Dunbar, and Darnell Hunt

A recent national survey found 8- to 17-year-old children to be avid consumers of sports media, with television most often named as the preferred medium (Amateur Athletic Foundation of Los Angeles, 1999). Although girls watch sports in great numbers, boys are markedly more likely to report that they are regular consumers of televised sports. The most popular televised sports with boys, in order, are pro football, men's pro basketball, pro baseball, pro wrestling, men's college basketball, college football, and Extreme sports.[1] Although counted separately in the Amateur Athletic Foundation (AAF) study, televised sports highlights shows also were revealed to be tremendously popular with boys.

What are boys seeing and hearing when they watch these programs? What kinds of values concerning gender, race, aggression, violence, and consumerism are boys exposed to when they watch their favorite televised sports programs, with their accompanying commercials? This article, based on a textual analysis, presents the argument that televised sports, and their accompanying commercials, consistently present boys with a narrow portrait of masculinity, which we call the Televised Sports Manhood Formula.

Sample and Method

We analyzed a range of televised sports that were identified by the AAF study as those programs most often watched by boys. Most of the programs in our sample aired during a single week, May 23–29, 1999, with one exception. Because pro football is not in

season in May, we acquired tapes of two randomly chosen National Football League (NFL) *Monday Night Football* games from the previous season to include in our sample. We analyzed televised coverage, including commercials and pregame, halftime, and postgame shows (when appropriate), for the following programs:

1. two broadcasts of *SportsCenter* on ESPN (2 hours of programming);
2. two broadcasts of Extreme sports, one on ESPN and one on Fox Sports West (approximately 90 minutes of programming);
3. two broadcasts of professional wrestling, including *Monday Night Nitro* on TNT and *WWF Superstars* on USA (approximately 2 hours of programming);
4. two broadcasts of National Basketball Association (NBA) play-off games, one on TNT and the other on NBC (approximately 7 hours of programming);
5. two broadcasts of NFL *Monday Night Football* on ABC (approximately 7 hours of programming); and
6. one broadcast of Major League Baseball (MLB) on TBS (approximately 3 hours of programming).

We conducted a textual analysis of the sports programming and the commercials. In all, we examined about 23 hours of sports programming, nearly one quarter of which was time taken up by commercials. We examined a total of 722 commercials, which spanned a large range of products and services. We collected both quantitative and qualitative data. Although we began with some sensitizing concepts that we knew we wanted to explore (e.g., themes of violence, images of gender and race, etc.), rather than starting with preset categories we used an inductive method that allowed the dominant themes to emerge from our reading of the tapes.

Each taped show was given a first reading by one of the investigators, who then constructed a preliminary analysis of the data. The tape was then given a second reading by another of the investigators. This second independent reading was then used to modify and sharpen the first reading. Data analysis proceeded along the lines of the categories that emerged in the data collection. The analyses of each separate sport were then put into play with each other and common themes and patterns were identified. In one case, the dramatic pseudosport of professional wrestling, we determined that much of the programming was different enough that it made little sense to directly compare it with the other sports shows; therefore, we only included data on wrestling in our comparisons when it seemed to make sense to do so.

Dominant Themes in Televised Sports

Our analysis revealed that sports programming presents boys with narrow and stereotypical messages about race, gender, and violence. We identified 10 distinct themes that, together, make up the Televised Sports Manhood Formula.

White Males are the Voices of Authority

Although one of the two *SportsCenter* segments in the sample did feature a White woman coanchor, the play-by-play and ongoing color commentary in NFL, wrestling, NBA, Extreme sports, and MLB broadcasts

Table 25.1 Race and Sex of Announcers

White Men	White Women	Black Men	Black Women
24	3	3	1

were conducted exclusively by White, male play-by-play commentators.

With the exception of *SportsCenter*, women and Blacks never appeared as the main voices of authority in the booth conducting play-by-play or ongoing color commentary. The NFL broadcasts occasionally cut to field-level color commentary by a White woman but her commentary was very brief (about 3½ minutes of the nearly 3 hours of actual game and pregame commentary). Similarly, one of the NBA broadcasts used a Black man for occasional on-court analysis and a Black man for pregame and halftime analysis, whereas the other NBA game used a White woman as host in the pregame show and a Black woman for occasional on-court analysis. Although viewers commonly see Black male athletes—especially on televised NBA games—they rarely hear or see Black men or women as voices of authority in the broadcast booth (Sabo & Jansen, 1994). In fact, the only Black commentators that appeared on the NBA shows that we examined were former star basketball players (Cheryl Miller, Doc Rivers, and Isaiah Thomas). A Black male briefly appeared to welcome the audience to open one of the Extreme sports shows but he did not do any play-by-play; in fact, he was used only to open the show with a stylish, street, hip-hop style for what turned out to be an almost totally White show.

Sports is a Man's World

Images or discussion of women athletes is almost entirely absent in the sports programs that boys watch most. *SportsCenter*'s mere 2.9% of news time devoted to women's sports is slightly lower than the 5% to 6% of women's sports coverage commonly found in other sports news studies (Duncan & Messner, 1998). In addition, *SportsCenter*'s rare discussion of a women's sport seemed to follow men's in newsworthiness (e.g., a report on a Professional Golfers' Association [PGA] tournament was followed by a more brief report on a Ladies Professional Golf Association [LPGA] tournament). The baseball, basketball, wrestling, and football programs we watched were men's contests so could not perhaps have been expected to cover or mention women athletes. However, Extreme sports are commonly viewed as "alternative" or "emerging" sports in which women are challenging masculine hegemony (Wheaton & Tomlinson, 1998). Despite this, the Extreme sports shows we watched devoted only a single 50-second interview segment to a woman athlete. This segment constituted about 1% of the total Extreme sports programming and, significantly, did not show this woman athlete in action. Perhaps this limited coverage of women athletes on the Extreme sports shows we examined is evidence of what Rinehart (1998) calls a "pecking order" in alternative sports, which develops when new sports are appropriated and commodified by the media.

Men are Foregrounded in Commercials

The idea that sports is a man's world is reinforced by the gender composition and imagery in commercials. Women almost never appear in commercials unless they are in the company of men, as Table 25.2 shows.

That 38.6% of all commercials portray only men actually understates the extent to which men dominate these commercials for two reasons. First, nearly every one of the 91 commercials that portrayed no visual portrayals of people included a male voice-over. When we include this number, we see that more than 50% of commercials provide men-only images and/or voice-overs, whereas only 3.9% portray only women. Moreover, when we combine men-only and women and men categories, we see that men are visible in 83.5% of all commercials and men are present (when we add in the commercials with male voice-overs) in 96.1% of all commercials. Second, in the commercials that portray both women and men, women are often (although not exclusively) portrayed in stereotypical, and often very minor, background roles.

Women are Sexy Props or Prizes for Men's Successful Sport Performances or Consumption Choices

Although women were mostly absent from sports commentary, when they did appear it was most often in stereotypical roles as sexy, masculinity-validating props, often cheering the men on. For instance, "X-sports" on Fox Sports West used a bikini-clad blonde woman as a hostess to welcome viewers back after each commercial break as the camera moved provocatively over her body. Although she mentioned the show's sponsors, she did not narrate the actual sporting event. The wrestling shows generously used scantily clad women (e.g., in pink miniskirts or tight Spandex and high heels) who overtly displayed the dominant cultural signs of heterosexy attractiveness[2] to escort the male wrestlers to the ring, often with announcers discussing the women's provocative physical appearances. Women also appeared in the wrestling shows as sexually provocative dancers (e.g., the "Gorgeous Nitro Girls" on TNT).

In commercials, women are numerically more evident, and generally depicted in more varied roles, than in the sports programming. Still, women are underrepresented and rarely appear in commercials unless they are in the company of men. Moreover, as Table 25.3 illustrates, the commercials' common depiction of women as sexual objects and as "prizes" for men's successful consumption choices articulates with the sports programs' presentation of women primarily as sexualized, supportive props for men's athletic performances. For instance, a commercial for Keystone Light Beer that ran on *SportsCenter* depicted two White men at a baseball game. When one of the men appeared on the stadium big screen and made an ugly face after drinking an apparently bitter beer, women appeared to be grossed out by him. But then he drank a Keystone Light and reappeared on the big screen looking good with two young, conventionally beautiful (fashion-model-like) women adoring him. He says, "I hope my wife's not watching!" as the two women flirt with the camera.

As Table 25.3 shows, in 23 hours of sports programming, viewers were exposed to 58 incidents of women being portrayed as sexy props and/or sexual prizes for men's successful athletic performances or

Table 25.2 Sex Composition of 722 Commercials

Men Only	Women Only	Women and Men	No People
279 (38.6%)	28 (3.9%)	324 (44.9%)	91 (12.6%)

Table 25.3 Instances of Women Being Depicted as Sexy Props or Prizes for Men

	SportsCenter	Extreme	Wrestling	NBA	MLB	NFL
Commercials	5	5	3	10	4	6
Sport programs	0	5	13	3	0	4
Total	5	10	16	13	4	10

Note: NBA = National Basketball Association, MLB = Major League Baseball, and NFL = National Football League.

correct consumption choices. Put another way, a televised sports viewer is exposed to this message, either in commercials or in the sports program itself, on an average of twice an hour. The significance of this narrow image of women as heterosexualized commodities should be considered especially in light of the overall absence of a wider range of images of women, especially as athletes (Duncan & Messner, 1998; Kane & Lenskyj, 1998).

Whites are Foregrounded in Commercials

The racial composition of the commercials is, if anything, more narrow and limited than the gender composition. As Table 25.4 shows, Black, Latino, or Asian American people almost never appear in commercials unless the commercial also has White people in it (the multiracial category below).

To say that 52.2% of the commercials portrayed only Whites actually understates the extent to which images of White people dominated the commercials for two reasons. First, if we subtract the 91 commercials that showed no actual people, then we see that the proportion of commercials that actually showed people was 59.7% White only. Second, when we examine the quality of the portrayals of Blacks, Latinos, and Asian Americans in the multiracial commercials, we see that people of color are far more often than not relegated to minor roles, literally in the background of scenes that feature Whites, and/or they are relegated to stereotypical or negative roles. For instance, a Wendy's commercial that appeared on

several of the sports programs in our sample showed White customers enjoying a sandwich with the White owner while a barely perceptible Black male walked by in the background.

Aggressive Players Get the Prize; Nice Guys Finish Last

As Table 25.5 illustrates, viewers are continually immersed in images and commentary about the positive rewards that come to the most aggressive competitors and of the negative consequences of playing "soft" and lacking aggression.

Table 25.5 Statements Lauding Aggression or Criticizing Lack of Aggression

SportsCenter	Extreme	NBA	MLB	NFL
3	4	40	4	15

Note: NBA = National Basketball Association, MLB = Major League Baseball, and NFL = National Football League.

Commentators consistently lauded athletes who most successfully employed physical and aggressive play and toughness. For instance, after having his toughness called into question, NBA player Brian Grant was awarded redemption by *SportsCenter* because he showed that he is "not afraid to take it to Karl Malone." *SportsCenter* also informed viewers that "the aggressor usually gets the calls [from the officials] and the Spurs were the ones getting them." In

Table 25.4 Racial Composition of 722 Commercials

White Only	Black Only	Latino/a Only	Asian Only	Multiracial	Undetermined	No People
377 (52.2%)	28 (3.9%)	3 (0.4%)	2 (0.3%)	203 (28.1%)	18 (2.5%)	91 (12.6%)

pro wrestling commentary, this is a constant theme (and was therefore not included in our tallies for Table 25.5 because the theme permeated the commentary, overtly and covertly). The World Wrestling Federation (WWF) announcers praised the "raw power" of wrestler "Shamrock" and approvingly dubbed "Hardcore Holly" as "the world's most dangerous man." NBA commentators suggested that it is okay to be a good guy off the court but one must be tough and aggressive on the court: Brian Grant and Jeff Hornacek are "true gentlemen of the NBA . . . as long as you don't have to play against them. You know they're great off the court; on the court, every single guy out there *should* be a killer."

When players were not doing well, they were often described as "hesitant" and lacking aggression, emotion, and desire (e.g., for a loose ball or rebound). For instance, commentators lamented that "the Jazz aren't going to the hoop, they're being pushed and shoved around," that Utah was responding to the Blazers' aggression "passively, in a reactive mode," and that "Utah's got to get Karl Malone toughened up." *SportsCenter* echoed this theme, opening one show with a depiction of Horace Grant elbowing Karl Malone and asking of Malone, "Is he feeble?" Similarly, NFL broadcasters waxed on about the virtues of aggression and domination. Big "hits"; ball carriers who got "buried," "stuffed," or "walloped" by the defense; and players who get "cleaned out" or "wiped out" by a blocker were often shown on replays, with announcers enthusiastically describing the plays. By contrast, they clearly declared that it is a very bad thing to be passive and to let yourself get pushed around and dominated at the line of scrimmage. Announcers also approvingly noted that going after an opposing player's injured body part is just smart strategy: In one NFL game, the Miami strategy to blitz the opposing quarterback was lauded as "brilliant"—"When you know your opposing quarterback is a bit nicked and something is wrong, Boomer, you got to come after him."

Previous research has pointed to this heroic framing of the male body-as-weapon as a key element in sports' role in the social construction of narrow conceptions of masculinity (Messner, 1992; Trujillo, 1995).

This injunction for boys and men to be aggressive, not passive, is reinforced in commercials, where

Table 25.6 Humorous or Sarcastic Discussion of Fights or Near-Fights

SportsCenter	Extreme	NBA	MLB	NFL
10	1	2	2	7

Note: NBA = National Basketball Association, MLB = Major League Baseball, and NFL = National Football League.

a common formula is to play on the insecurities of young males (e.g., that they are not strong enough, tough enough, smart enough, rich enough, attractive enough, decisive enough, etc.) and then attempt to convince them to avoid, overcome, or mask their fears, embarrassments, and apparent shortcomings by buying a particular product. These commercials often portray men as potential or actual geeks, nerds, or passive schmucks who can overcome their geekiness (or avoid being a geek like the guy in the commercial) by becoming decisive and purchasing a particular product.

Boys Will Be (Violent) Boys

Announcers often took a humorous "boys will be boys" attitude in discussing fights or near-fights during contests, and they also commonly used a recent fight, altercation, or disagreement between two players as a "teaser" to build audience excitement.

Fights, near-fights, threats of fights, or other violent actions were overemphasized in sports coverage and often verbally framed in sarcastic language that suggested that this kind of action, although reprehensible, is to be expected. For instance, as *SportsCenter* showed NBA centers Robinson and O'Neill exchanging forearm shoves, the commentators said, simply, "much love." Similarly, in an NFL game, a brief scuffle between players is met with a sarcastic comment by the broadcaster that the players are simply "making their acquaintance." This is, of course, a constant theme in pro wrestling (which, again, we found impossible and less than meaningful to count because this theme permeates the show). We found it noteworthy that the supposedly spontaneous fights outside the wrestling ring (what we call unofficial fights) were given more coverage time and focus than the supposedly official fights inside the ring. We speculate that wrestling producers know that viewers already watch fights inside the ring with some skepticism as to their authenticity so they stage the unofficial fights outside the ring to bring a feeling of spontaneity and authenticity to the show and to build excitement and a sense of anticipation for the fight that will later occur inside the ring.

Give up Your Body for the Team

Athletes who are "playing with pain," "giving up their body for the team," or engaging in obviously highly dangerous plays or maneuvers were consistently framed as heroes; conversely, those who removed themselves from games due to injuries had questions raised about their character, their manhood.

This theme cut across all sports programming. For instance, *SportsCenter* asked, "Could the dominator be soft?" when a National Hockey League (NHL) star goalie decided to sit out a game due to a groin injury. Heroically taking risks while already hurt was a constant theme in Extreme sports commentary. For instance, one bike competitor was lauded for "overcoming his fear" and competing "with a busted up ankle" and another was applauded when he "popped his collarbone out in the street finals in Louisville but he's back on his bike here in Richmond, just 2 weeks later!" Athletes appear especially heroic when they go against doctors' wishes not to compete. For instance, an X Games interviewer adoringly told a competitor, "Doctors said don't ride but you went ahead and did it anyway and escaped serious injury." Similarly, NBA player Isaiah Rider was lauded for having "heart" for "playing with that knee injury." Injury discussions in NFL games often include speculation about whether the player will be able to return to this or future games. A focus on a star player in a pregame or halftime show, such as the feature on 49ers' Garrison Hearst, often contain commentary about heroic overcoming of serious injuries (in this case, a knee blowout, reconstructive surgery, and rehabilitation). As one game began, commentators noted that 37-year-old "Steve Young has remained a rock . . . not bad for a guy who a lotta people figured was, what, one big hit from ending his career." It's especially impressive when an injured player is able and willing to continue to play with aggressiveness and reckless abandon: "Kurt Scrafford at right guard—bad neck and all—is just out there wiping out guys." And announcers love the team leader who plays hurt:

> Drew Bledso gamely tried to play in loss to Rams yesterday; really admirable to try to play with that pin that was surgically implanted in his finger during the week; I don't know how a Q.B. could do that. You know, he broke his finger the time we had him on Monday night and he led his team to two come-from-behind victories, really gutted it out and I think he took that team on his shoulders and showed he could play and really elevated himself in my eyes, he really did.

Sports Is War

Commentators consistently (an average of nearly five times during each hour of sports commentary) used martial metaphors and language of war and weaponry to describe sports action (e.g., battle, kill, ammunition, weapons, professional sniper, depth charges, taking

Table 25.8 Martial Metaphors and Language of War and Weaponry

SportsCenter	Extreme	Wrestling	NBA	MLB	NFL
9	3	15	27	6	23

Note: NBA = National Basketball Association, MLB = Major League Baseball, and NFL = National Football League.

Table 25.7 Comments on the Heroic Nature of Playing Hurt

SportsCenter	Extreme	NBA	MLB	NFL
9	12	6	4	15

Note: NBA = National Basketball Association, MLB = Major League Baseball, and NFL = National Football League.

Table 25.9 Depictions of Guts in Face of Danger, Speed, Hits, Crashes

SportsCenter	Extreme	NBA	MLB	NFL
4	21	5	2	8

Note: NBA = National Basketball Association, MLB = Major League Baseball, and NFL = National Football League.

aim, fighting, shot in his arsenal, reloading, detonate, squeezes the trigger, attack mode, firing blanks, blast, explosion, blitz, point of attack, a lance through the heart, etc.).

Some shows went beyond commentators' use of war terminology and actually framed the contests as wars. For instance, one of the wrestling shows offered a continual flow of images and commentary that reminded the viewers that "RAW is WAR!" Similarly, both NFL *Monday Night Football* broadcasts were introduced with explosive graphics and an opening song that included lyrics "Like a rocket burning through time and space, the NFL's best will rock this place . . . the battle lines are drawn." This sort of use of sport/war metaphors has been a common practice in televised sports commentary for many years, serving to fuse (and confuse) the distinctions between values of nationalism with team identity and athletic aggression with military destruction (Jansen & Sabo, 1994). In the shows examined for this study, war themes also were reinforced in many commercials, including commercials for movies, other sports programs, and in the occasional commercial for the U.S. military.

Show Some Guts!

Commentators continually depicted and replayed exciting incidents of athletes engaging in reckless acts of speed, showing guts in the face of danger, big hits, and violent crashes.

This theme was evident across all of the sports programs but was especially predominant in Extreme sports that continually depicted crashing vehicles or bikers in an exciting manner. For instance, when one race ended with a crash, it was showed again in slow-motion replay, with commentators approvingly dubbing it "unbelievable" and "original." Extreme sports commentators commonly raised excitement levels by saying "he's on fire" or "he's going huge!" when a competitor was obviously taking greater risks. An athlete's ability to deal with the fear of a possible crash, in fact, is the mark of an "outstanding run": "Watch out, Richmond," an X-games announcer shouted to the crowd, "He's gonna wreck this place!" A winning competitor laughingly said, "I do what I can to smash into [my opponents] as much as I can." Another com-

petitor said, "If I crash, no big deal; I'm just gonna go for it." NFL commentators introduced the games with images of reckless collisions and during the game a "fearless" player was likely to be applauded: "There's no chance that Barry Sanders won't take when he's running the football." In another game, the announcer noted that receiver "Tony Simmons plays big. And for those of you not in the NFL, playing big means you're not afraid to go across the middle and catch the ball and make a play out of it after you catch the ball." Men showing guts in the face of speed and danger was also a major theme in 40 of the commercials that we analyzed.

The Televised Sports Manhood Formula

Tens of millions of U.S. boys watch televised sports programs, with their accompanying commercial advertisements. This study sheds light on what these boys are seeing when they watch their favorite sports programs. What values and ideas about gender, race, aggression, and violence are being promoted? Although there are certainly differences across different kinds of sports, as well as across different commercials, when we looked at all of the programming together, we identified 10 recurrent themes, which we have outlined above. Taken together, these themes codify a consistent and (mostly) coherent message about what it means to be a man. We call this message the Televised Sports Manhood Formula:

> What is a Real Man? A Real Man is strong, tough, aggressive, and above all, a winner in what is still a Man's World. To be a winner he has to do what needs to be done. He must be willing to compromise his own long-term health by showing guts in the face of danger, by fighting other men when necessary, and by "playing hurt" when he's injured. He must avoid being soft; he must be the aggressor, both on the "battle fields" of sports and in his consumption choices. Whether he is playing sports or making choices about which snack food or auto products to purchase, his aggressiveness will net him the ultimate prize: the adoring attention of conventionally beautiful women. He will know if and when he has arrived as a Real Man when the

Voices of Authority—White Males—*say* he is a Real Man. But even when he has finally managed to win the big one, has the good car, the right beer, and is surrounded by beautiful women, he will be reminded by these very same Voices of Authority just how fragile this Real Manhood really is: After all, he has to come out and prove himself all over again tomorrow. You're only as good as your last game (or your last purchase).

The major elements of the Televised Sports Manhood Formula are evident, in varying degrees, in the football, basketball, baseball, Extreme sports, and *SportsCenter* programs and in their accompanying commercials. But it is in the dramatic spectacle of professional wrestling that the Televised Sports Manhood Formula is most clearly codified and presented to audiences as an almost seamless package. Boys and young men are drawn to televised professional wrestling in great numbers. Consistently each week, from four to six pro wrestling shows rank among the top 10 rated shows on cable television. Professional wrestling is not a real sport in the way that baseball, basketball, football, or even Extreme sports are. In fact, it is a highly stylized and choreographed "sport as theatre" form of entertainment. Its producers have condensed—and then amplified—all of the themes that make up the Televised Sports Manhood Formula. For instance, where violence represents a thread in the football or basketball commentary, violence makes up the entire fabric of the theatrical narrative of televised pro wrestling. In short, professional wrestling presents viewers with a steady stream of images and commentary that represents a constant fusion of all of the themes that make up the Televised Sports Manhood Formula: This is a choreographed sport where all men (except losers) are Real Men, where women are present as sexy support objects for the men's violent, monumental "wars" against each other. Winners bravely display muscular strength, speed, power, and guts. Bodily harm is (supposedly) intentionally inflicted on opponents. The most ruthlessly aggressive men win, whereas the passive or weaker men lose, often shamefully. Heroically wrestling while injured, rehabilitating oneself from former injuries, and inflicting pain and injury on one's opponent are constant and central themes in the narrative.

Gender and the Sports/Media/Commercial Complex

In 1984, media scholar Sut Jhally pointed to the commercial and ideological symbiosis between the institutions of sport and the mass media and called it the sports/media complex. Our examination of the ways that the Televised Sports Manhood Formula reflects and promotes hegemonic ideologies concerning race, gender, sexuality, aggression, violence, and consumerism suggests adding a third dimension to Jhally's analysis: the huge network of multi-billion-dollar automobile, snack food, alcohol, entertainment, and other corporate entities that sponsor sports events and broadcasts. In fact, examining the ways that the Televised Sports Manhood Formula cuts across sports programming and its accompanying commercials may provide important clues as to the ways that ideologies of hegemonic masculinity are both promoted by—and in turn serve to support and stabilize—this collection of interrelated institutions that make up the sports/media/commercial complex. The Televised Sports Manhood Formula is a master discourse that is produced at the nexus of the institutions of sport, mass media, and corporations who produce and hope to sell products and services to boys and men. As such, the Televised Sports Manhood Formula appears well suited to discipline boys' bodies, minds, and consumption choices within an ideological field that is conducive to the reproduction of the entrenched interests that profit from the sports/media/commercial complex. The perpetuation of the entrenched commercial interests of the sports/media/commercial complex appears to be predicated on boys accepting—indeed glorifying and celebrating—a set of bodily and relational practices that resist and oppose a view of women as fully human and place boys' and men's long-term health prospects in jeopardy.

At a historical moment when hegemonic masculinity has been destabilized by socioeconomic change, and by women's and gay liberation movements, the Televised Sports Manhood Formula provides a remarkably stable and concrete view of masculinity as grounded in bravery, risk taking, violence, bodily strength, and heterosexuality. And this view of masculinity is given coherence against views of women as sexual support objects or as invisible and thus irrelevant to men's public struggles for glory. Yet, perhaps to be successful in selling products, the commercials sometimes provide a less than seamless view of masculinity. The insecurities of masculinity in crisis are often tweaked in the commercials, as we see weak men, dumb men, and indecisive men being eclipsed by strong, smart, and decisive men and sometimes being humiliated by smarter and more decisive women. In short, this commercialized version of hegemonic masculinity is constructed partly in relation to images of men who don't measure up.

This analysis gives us hints at an answer to the commonly asked question of why so many boys and men continue to take seemingly irrational risks, submit to pain and injury, and risk long-term debility or even death by playing hurt. A critical examination of the Televised Sports Manhood Formula tells us why: The costs of masculinity (especially pain and injury), according to this formula, appear to be well worth the price; the boys and men who are willing to pay the price always seem to get the glory, the championships, the best consumer products, and the beautiful women. Those who don't—or can't—pay the price are humiliated or ignored by women and left in the dust by other men. In short, the Televised Sports Manhood Formula is a pedagogy through which boys are taught that paying the price, be it one's bodily health or one's money, gives one access to the privileges that have been historically linked to hegemonic masculinity—money, power, glory, and women. And the barrage of images of femininity as model-like beauty displayed for and in the service of successful men suggest that heterosexuality is a major lynchpin of the Televised Sports Manhood Formula, and on a larger scale serves as one of the major linking factors in the conservative gender regime of the sports/media/commercial complex.

On the other hand, we must be cautious in coming to definitive conclusions as to how the promotion of the values embedded in the Televised Sports Manhood Formula might fit into the worlds of young men. It is not possible, based merely on our textual analysis of sports programs, to explicate precisely what kind of impact these shows, and the Televised Sports Manhood Formula, have on their young male audiences. That sort of question is best approached

through direct research with audiences. Most such research finds that audiences interpret, use, and draw meanings from media variously, based on factors such as social class, race/ethnicity, and gender (Hunt, 1999; Whannel, 1998). Research with various subgroups of boys that explores their interpretations of the sports programs that they watch would enhance and broaden this study.

Moreover, it is important to go beyond the preferred reading presented here that emphasizes the persistent themes in televised sports that appear to reinforce the hegemony of current race, gender, and commercial relations (Sabo & Jansen, 1992). In addition to these continuities, there are some identifiable discontinuities within and between the various sports programs and within and among the accompanying commercials. For instance, commercials are far more varied in the ways they present gender imagery than are sports programs themselves. Although the dominant tendency in commercials is either to erase women or to present them as stereotypical support or sex objects, a significant minority of commercials present themes that set up boys and men as insecure and/or obnoxious schmucks and women as secure, knowledgeable, and authoritative. Audience research with boys who watch sports would shed fascinating light on how they decode and interpret these more complex, mixed, and paradoxical gender images against the dominant, hegemonic image of the Televised Sports Manhood Formula.

Notes

1. There are some differences, and some similarities, in what boys and girls prefer to watch. The top seven televised sports reported by girls are, in order, gymnastics, men's pro basketball, pro football, pro baseball, swimming/diving, men's college basketball, and women's pro or college basketball.

2. Although images of feminine beauty shift, change, and are contested throughout history, female beauty is presented in sports programming and commercials in narrow ways. Attractive women look like fashion models (Banet-Weiser, 1999): They are tall, thin, young, usually (although not always) White, with signs of heterosexual femininity encoded and overtly displayed through hair, makeup, sexually provocative facial and bodily gestures, large (often partially exposed) breasts, long (often exposed) legs, and so forth.

Acknowledgments

Research for this study was funded by Children Now. The authors thank Patti Miller of Children Now and Wayne Wilson of the Amateur Athletic Foundation of Los Angeles. We also thank Cheryl Cole and the anonymous reviewers of the *Journal of Sport & Social Issues.*

References

Amateur Athletic Foundation of Los Angeles. (1999). *Children and sports media.* Los Angeles: Author.

Banet-Weiser, S. (1999). *The most beautiful girl in the world: Beauty pageants and national identity.* Berkeley: University of California Press.

Duncan, M. C., & Messner, M. A. (1998). The media image of sport and gender. In L. A. Wenner (Ed.), *MediaSport* (pp. 170–195). New York: Routledge.

Hunt, D. (1999). *O.J. Simpson facts and fictions.* New York: Cambridge University Press.

Jansen, S. C., & Sabo, D. (1994). The sport/war metaphor: Hegemonic masculinity, the Persian Gulf war, and the new world order. *Sociology of Sport Journal, 11,* 1–17.

Jhally, S. (1984). The spectacle of accumulation: Material and cultural factors in the evolution of the sports/media complex. *Insurgent Sociologist, 12*(3), 41–52.

Kane, M. J., & Lenskyj, H. J. (1998). Media treatment of female athletes: Issues of gender and sexualities. In L. A. Wenner (Ed.), *MediaSport* (pp. 186–201). New York: Routledge.

Messner, M. A. (1992). *Power at play: Sports and the problem of masculinity.* Boston: Beacon.

Rinehart, R. (1998). Inside of the outside: Pecking orders within alternative sport at ESPN's 1995 "The eXtreme Games." *Journal of Sport and Social Issues, 22,* 398–415.

Sabo, D., & Jansen, S. C. (1992). Images of men in sport media: The social reproduction of masculinity. In S. Craig (Ed.), *Men, masculinity, and the media* (pp. 169–184). Newbury Park, CA: Sage.

Sabo, D., & Jansen, S. C. (1994). Seen but not heard: Images of Black men in sports media. In M. A. Messner & D. F. Sabo (Eds.), *Sex, violence and power in sports: Rethinking masculinity* (pp. 150–160). Freedom, CA: Crossing Press.

Trujillo, N. (1995). Machines, missiles, and men: Images of the male body on ABC's *Monday Night Football. Sociology of Sport Journal, 12,* 403–423.

Whannel, G. (1998). Reading the sports media audience. In L. A. Wenner (Ed.), *MediaSport* (pp. 221–232). New York: Routledge.

Wheaton, B., & Tomlinson, A. (1998). The changing gender order in sport? The case of windsurfing subcultures. *Journal of Sport and Social Issues, 22,* 252–274.

26.
LOOKING FOR MY PENIS

The Eroticized Asian in Gay Video Porn

Richard Fung

Several scientists have begun to examine the relation between personality and human reproductive behaviour from a gene-based evolutionary perspective. . . . In this vein we reported a study of racial difference in sexual restraint such that Orientals > whites > blacks. Restraint was indexed in numerous ways, having in common a lowered allocation of bodily energy to sexual functioning. We found the same racial pattern occurred on gamete production (dizygotic birthing frequency per 100: Mongoloids, 4; Caucasoids, 8; Negroids, 16), intercourse frequencies (premarital, marital, extramarital), developmental precocity (age at first intercourse, age at first pregnancy, number of pregnancies), primary sexual characteristics (size of penis, vagina, testis, ovaries), secondary sexual characteristics (salient voice, muscularity, buttocks, breasts), and biologic control of behaviour (periodicity of sexual response, predictability of life history from onset of puberty), as well as in androgen levels and sexual attitudes.[1]

This passage from the *Journal of Research in Personality* was written by University of Western Ontario psychologist Philippe Rushton, who enjoys considerable controversy in Canadian academic circles and in the popular media. His thesis, articulated throughout his work, appropriates biological studies of the continuum of reproductive strategies of oysters through to chimpanzees and posits that degree of "sexuality"— interpreted as penis and vagina size, frequency of intercourse, buttock and lip size—correlates positively with criminality and sociopathic behavior inversely with intelligence, health, and longevity. Rushton sees race as *the* determining factor and places East Asians (Rushton uses the word *Orientals*) on one end of the spectrum and blacks on the other. Since whites fall squarely in the middle, the position of perfect balance, there is no need for analysis, and they remain free of scrutiny.

Notwithstanding its profound scientific shortcomings, Rushton's work serves as an excellent articulation of a dominant discourse on race and sexuality in Western society—a system of ideas and reciprocal practices that originated in Europe simultaneously with (some argue as a conscious justification for[2]) colonial expansion and slavery. In the nineteenth century these ideas took on a scientific gloss with social Darwinism and eugenics. Now they reappear, somewhat altered, in psychology journals from the likes of Rushton. It is important to add that these ideas have also permeated the global popular consciousness. Anyone who has been exposed to Western television or advertising images, which is much of the world, will have absorbed this particular constellation of stereotyping and racial hierarchy. In Trinidad in the 1960s, on the outer reaches of the empire, everyone in my schoolyard was thoroughly versed in these "truths" about the races.

Historically, most organizing against racism has concentrated on fighting discrimination that stems from the intelligence–social behavior variable assumed by Rushton's scale. Discrimination based on perceived intellectual ability does, after all, have direct ramifications in terms of education and employment, and therefore for survival. Until recently, issues of gender and sexuality remained a low priority for those who claimed to speak for the communities.[3] But antiracist strategies that fail to subvert the race–gender status quo are of seriously limited value. Racism cannot be narrowly defined in terms of race hatred. Race is a factor in even our most intimate relationships.

The contemporary construction of race and sex as exemplified by Rushton has endowed black people, both men and women, with a threatening hypersexuality. Asians, on the other hand, are collectively seen as undersexed.[4] But here I want to make some crucial distinctions. First, in North America, stereotyping has focused almost exclusively on what recent colonial language designates as "Orientals"—that is East and Southeast Asian peoples—as opposed to the "Orientalism" discussed by Edward Said, which concerns the Middle East. This current, popular usage is based more on a perception of similar physical features—black hair, "slanted" eyes, high cheek bones, and so on—than through a reference to common cultural traits. South Asians, people whose backgrounds are in the Indian subcontinent and Sri Lanka, hardly figure at all in North American popular representations, and those few images are ostensibly devoid of sexual connotation.[5]

Second, within the totalizing stereotype of the "Oriental," there are competing and sometimes contradictory sexual associations based on nationality. So, for example, a person could be seen as Japanese and somewhat kinky, or Filipino and "available." The very same person could also be seen as "Oriental" and therefore sexless. In addition, the racial hierarchy revamped by Rushton is itself in tension with an earlier and only partially eclipsed depiction of *all* Asians as having an undisciplined and dangerous libido. I am referring to the writings of the early European explorers and missionaries, but also to antimiscegenation laws and such specific legislation as the 1912 Saskatchewan law that barred white women from employment in Chinese-owned businesses.

Finally, East Asian women figure differently from men both in reality and in representation. In "Lotus Blossoms Don't Bleed," Renee Tajima points out that in Hollywood films:

There are two basic types: the Lotus Blossom Baby (a.k.a. China Doll, Geisha Girl, shy Polynesian beauty, et al.) and the Dragon Lady (Fu Manchu's various female relations, prostitutes, devious madames). . . . . Asian women in film are, for the most part, passive figures who exist to serve men—as love interests for white men (re: Lotus Blossoms) or as partners in crime for men of their own kind (re: Dragon Ladies).[6]

Further:

Dutiful creatures that they are, Asian women are often assigned the task of expendability in a situation of illicit love. . . . Noticeably lacking is the portrayal of love relationships between Asian women and Asian men, particularly as lead characters.[7]

Because of their supposed passivity and sexual compliance, Asian women have been fetishized in dominant representation, and there is a large and growing body of literature by Asian women on the oppressiveness of these images. Asian men, however—at least since Sessue Hayakawa, who made a Hollywood career in the 1920s of representing the Asian man as sexual threat[8]—have been consigned to one of two categories: the egghead/wimp, or—in what may be analogous to the lotus blossom-dragon lady dichotomy—the kung fu master/ninja/samurai. He is sometimes dangerous, sometimes friendly, but almost always characterized by a desexualized Zen asceticism. So whereas, as Fanon tells us, "the Negro is eclipsed. He is turned into a penis. He is a penis,"[9] the Asian man is defined by a striking absence down there. And if Asian men have no sexuality, how can we have homosexuality?

Even as recently as the early 1980s, I remember having to prove my queer credentials before being admitted with other Asian men into a Toronto gay club. I do not believe it was a question of a color barrier. Rather, my friends and I felt that the doorman was genuinely unsure about our sexual orientation. We also felt that had we been white and dressed similarly, our entrance would have been automatic.[10]

Although a motto for the lesbian and gay movements has been "we are everywhere," Asians are largely absent from the images produced by both the political and the commercial sectors of the mainstream gay and lesbian communities. From the earliest articulation of the Asian gay and lesbian movements, a principal concern has therefore been visibility. In political organizing, the demand for a voice, or rather the demand to be heard, has largely been responded to by the problematic practice of "minority" representation on panels and boards.[11] But since racism is a question of power and not of numbers, this strategy has often led to a dead-end tokenistic integration, failing to address the real imbalances.

Creating a space for Asian gay and lesbian representation has meant, among other things, deepening an understanding of what is at stake for Asians in coming out publicly.[12] As is the case for many other people of color and especially immigrants, our families and our ethnic communities are a rare source of affirmation in a racist society. In coming out, we risk (or feel that we risk) losing this support, though the ever-growing organizations of lesbian and gay Asians have worked against this process of cultural exile. In my own experience, the existence of a gay Asian community broke down the cultural schizophrenia in which I related on the one hand to a heterosexual family that affirmed my ethnic culture and, on the other, to a gay community that was predominantly white. Knowing that there was support also helped me come out to my family and further bridge the gap.

If we look at commercial gay sexual representation, it appears that the antiracist movements have had little impact: the images of men and male beauty are still of *white* men and *white* male beauty. These are the standards against which we compare both ourselves and often our brothers—Asian, black, native, and Latino.[13] Although other people's rejection (or fetishization) of us according to the established racial hierarchies may be experienced as oppressive, we are not necessarily moved to scrutinize our own desire and its relationship to the hegemonic image of the white man.[14]

In my lifelong vocation of looking for my penis, trying to fill in the visual void, I have come across only a handful of primary and secondary references to Asian male sexuality in North American representation. Even in my own video work, the stress has been on deconstructing sexual representation and only marginally on creating erotica. So I was very excited

at the discovery of a Vietnamese American working in gay porn.

Having acted in six videotapes, Sum Yung Mahn is perhaps the only Asian to qualify as a gay porn "star." Variously known as Brad Troung or Sam or Sum Yung Mahn, he has worked for a number of different production studios. All of the tapes in which he appears are distributed through International Wavelength, a San Francisco-based mail order company whose catalog entries feature Asians in American, Thai, and Japanese productions. According to the owner of International Wavelength, about 90 percent of the Asian tapes are bought by white men, and the remaining 10 percent are purchased by Asians. But the number of Asian buyers is growing.

In examining Sum Yung Mahn's work, it is important to recognize the different strategies used for fitting an Asian actor into the traditionally white world of gay porn and how the terms of entry are determined by the perceived demands of an intended audience. Three tapes, each geared toward a specific erotic interest, illustrate these strategies.

Below the Belt (1985, directed by Philip St. John, California Dream Machine Productions), like most porn tapes, has an episodic structure. All the sequences involve the students and *sensei* of an all-male karate *dojo*. The authenticity of the setting is proclaimed with the opening shots of a gym full of *gi*-clad, serious-faced young men going through their weapons exercises. Each of the main actors is introduced in turn; with the exception of the teacher, who has dark hair, all fit into the current porn conventions of Aryan, blond, shaved, good looks.[15] Moreover, since Sum Yung Mahn is not even listed in the opening credits, we can surmise that this tape is not targeted to an audience with any particular erotic interest in Asian men. Most gay video porn exclusively uses white actors; those tapes having the least bit of racial integration are pitched to the speciality market through outlets such as International Wavelength.[16] This visual apartheid stems, I assume, from an erroneous perception that the sexual appetites of gay men are exclusive and unchangeable.

A Karate dojo offers a rich opportunity to introduce Asian actors. One might imagine it as the gay Orientalist's dream project. But given the intended audience for this video, the erotic appeal of the dojo, except for the costumes and a few misplaced props (Taiwanese and Korean flags for a Japanese art form?) are completely appropriated into a white world.

The tape's action occurs in a gym, in the students' apartments, and in a garden. The one scene with Sum Yung Mahn is a dream sequence. Two students, Robbie and Stevie, are sitting in a locker room. Robbie confesses that he has been having strange dreams about Greg, their teacher. Cut to the dream sequence, which is coded by clouds of green smoke. Robbie is wearing a red headband with black markings suggesting script (if indeed they belong to an Asian language, they are not the Japanese or Chinese characters that one would expect). He is trapped in an elaborate snare. Enter a character in a black *ninja* mask, wielding a *nanchaku*. Robbie narrates: "I knew this evil samurai would kill me." The masked figure is menacingly running the nanchaku chain under Robbie's genitals when Greg, the teacher, appears and disposes of him. Robbie explains to Stevie in the locker room: "I knew that I owed him my life, and I knew 1 had to please him [long pause] in any way that he wanted." During that pause we cut back to the dream. Amid more puffs of smoke, Greg, carrying a man in his arms, approaches a low platform. Although Greg's back is toward the camera, we can see that the man is wearing the red headband that identifies him as Robbie. As Greg lays him down, we see that Robbie has "turned Japanese"! It's Sum Yung Mahn.

Greg fucks Sum Yung Mahn, who is always face down. The scene constructs anal intercourse for the Asian Robbie as an act of submission, not of pleasure: unlike other scenes of anal intercourse in the tape, for example, there is no dubbed dialogue on the order of "Oh yeah . . . fuck me harder!" but merely ambiguous groans. Without coming, Greg leaves. A group of (white) men wearing Japanese outfits encircle the platform, and Asian Robbie, or "the Oriental boy," as he is listed in the final credits, turns to lie on his back. He sucks a cock, licks someone's balls. The other men come all over his body; he comes. The final shot of the sequence zooms in to a close-up of Sum Yung Mahn's headband, which dissolves to a similar close-up of Robbie wearing the same headband, emphasizing that the two actors represent one character.

We now cut back to the locker room. Robbie's story has made Stevie horny. He reaches into Robbie's

pants, pulls out his penis, and sex follows. In his Asian manifestation, Robbie is fucked and sucks others off (Greek passive/French active/bottom). His passivity is pronounced, and he is never shown other than prone. As a white man, his role is completely reversed: he is at first sucked off by Stevie, and then he fucks him (Greek active/French passive/top). Neither of Robbie's manifestations veers from his prescribed role.

To a greater extent than most other gay porn tapes, *Below the Belt* is directly about power. The hierarchical dojo setting is milked for its evocation of dominance and submission. With the exception of one very romantic sequence midway through the tape, most of the actors stick to their defined roles of top or bottom. Sex, especially anal sex, as punishment is a recurrent image. In this genre of gay pornography, the role-playing in the dream sequence is perfectly apt. What is significant, however, is how race figures into the equation. In a tape that appropriates emblems of Asian power (karate), the only place for a real Asian actor is as a caricature of passivity. Sum Yung Mahn does not portray an Asian, but rather the literalization of a metaphor, so that by being passive, Robbie actually becomes "Oriental." At a more practical level, the device of the dream also allows the producers to introduce an element of the mysterious, the exotic, without disrupting the racial status quo of the rest of the tape. Even in the dream sequence, Sum Yung Mahn is at the center of the frame as spectacle, having minimal physical involvement with the men around him. Although the sequence ends with his climax, he exists for the pleasure of others.

Richard Dyer, writing about gay porn, states that

> although the pleasure of anal sex (that is, of being anally fucked) is represented, the narrative is never organized around the desire to be fucked, but around the desire to ejaculate (whether or not following from anal intercourse). Thus, although at a level of public representation gay men may be thought of as deviant and disruptive of masculine norms because we assert the pleasure of being fucked and the eroticism of the anus, in our pornography this takes a back seat.[17]

Although Tom Waugh's amendment to this argument—that anal pleasure is represented in individual sequences[18]—also holds true for *Below the Belt*, as a whole the power of the penis and the pleasure of ejaculation are clearly the narrative's organizing principles. As with the vast majority of North American tapes featuring Asians, the problem is not the representation of anal pleasure per se, but rather that the narratives privilege the penis while always assigning the Asian the role of bottom; Asian and anus are conflated. In the case of Sum Yung Mahn, being fucked may well be his personal sexual preference. But the fact remains that there are very few occasions in North American video porn in which an Asian fucks a white man, so few, in fact, that International Wavelength promotes the tape *Studio X* (1986) with the blurb "Sum Yung Mahn makes history as the first Asian who fucks a non-Asian."[19]

Although I agree with Waugh that in gay as opposed to straight porn "the spectator's positions in relation to the representations are open and in flux,"[20] this observation applies only when all the participants are white. Race introduces another dimension that may serve to close down some of this mobility. This is not to suggest that the experience of gay men of color with this kind of sexual representation is the same as that of heterosexual women with regard to the gendered gaze of straight porn. For one thing, Asian gay men are men. We can therefore physically experience the pleasures depicted on the screen, since we too have erections and ejaculations and can experience anal penetration. A shifting identification may occur despite the racially defined roles, and most gay Asian men in North America are used to obtaining pleasure from all-white pornography. This, of course, goes hand in hand with many problems of self-image and sexual identity. Still, I have been struck by the unanimity with which gay Asian men I have met, from all over this continent as well as from Asia, immediately identify and resist these representations. Whenever I mention the topic of Asian actors in American porn, the first question I am asked is whether the Asian is simply shown getting fucked.

Asian Knights (1985, directed by Ed Sung, William Richhe Productions), the second tape I want to consider, has an Asian producer-director and a predominantly Asian cast. In its first scenario, two Asian men, Brad and Rick, are seeing a white psychiatrist because they are unable to have sex with each other:

RICK: We never have sex with other Asians. We usually have sex with Caucasian guys.

COUNSELOR: Have you had the opportunity to have sex together?

RICK: Yes, a coupla times, but we never get going.

Homophobia, like other forms of oppression, is seldom dealt with in gay video porn. With the exception of safe sex tapes that attempt a rare blend of the pedagogical with the pornographic, social or political issues are not generally associated with the erotic. It is therefore unusual to see one of the favored discussion topics for gay Asian consciousness-raising groups employed as a sex fantasy in *Asian Knights*. The desexualized image of Asian men that I have described has seriously affected our relationships with one another, and often gay Asian men find it difficult to see each other beyond the terms of platonic friendship or competition, to consider other Asian men as lovers.

True to the conventions of porn, minimal counseling from the psychiatrist convinces Rick and Brad to shed their clothes. Immediately sprouting erections, they proceed to have sex. But what appears to be an assertion of gay Asian desire is quickly derailed. As Brad and Rick make love on the couch, the camera cross-cuts to the psychiatrist looking on from an armchair. The rhetoric of the editing suggests that we are observing the two Asian men from his point of view. Soon the white man takes off his clothes and joins in. He immediately takes up a position at the center of the action—and at the center of the frame. What appeared to be a "conversion fantasy" for gay Asian desire was merely a ruse. Brad and Rick's temporary mutual absorption really occurs to establish the superior sexual draw of the white psychiatrist, a stand-in for the white male viewer, who is the real sexual subject of the tape. And the question of Asian–Asian desire, though presented as the main narrative force of the sequence, is deflected, or rather refrained from a white perspective.

Sex between the two Asian men in this sequence can be related somewhat to heterosexual sex in some gay porn films, such as those produced by the Gage brothers. In *Heatstroke* (1982), for example, sex with a woman is used to establish the authenticity of the straight man who is about to be seduced into gay sex. It dramatizes the significance of the conversion from the sanctioned object of desire, underscoring the power of the gay man to incite desire in his socially defined superior. It is also tied up with the fantasies of (female) virginity and conquest in Judeo-Christian and other patriarchal societies. The therapy-session sequence of *Asian Knights* also suggests parallels to representations of lesbians in straight porn, representations that are not meant to eroticize women loving women, but rather to titillate and empower the sexual ego of the heterosexual male viewer.

Asian Knights is organized to sell representations of Asians to white men. Unlike Sum Yung Mahn in *Below the Belt*, the actors are therefore more expressive and sexually assertive, as often the seducers as the seduced. But though the roles shift during the predominantly oral sex, the Asians remain passive in anal intercourse, except that they are now shown to want it! How much this assertion of agency represents a step forward remains a question.

Even in the one sequence of *Asian Knights* in which the Asian actor fucks the white man, the scenario privileges the pleasure of the white man over that of the Asian. The sequence begins with the Asian reading a magazine. When the white man (played by porn star Eric Stryker) returns home from a hard day at the office, the waiting Asian asks how his day went, undresses him (even taking off his socks), and proceeds to massage his back.[21] The Asian man acts the role of the mythologized geisha or "the good wife" as fantasized in the mail-order bride business. And, in fact, the "house boy" is one of the most persistent white fantasies about Asian men. The fantasy is also a reality in many Asian countries where economic imperialism gives foreigners, whatever their race, the pick of handsome men in financial need. The accompanying cultural imperialism grants status to those Asians with white lovers. White men who for various reasons, especially age, are deemed unattractive in their own countries, suddenly find themselves elevated and desired.

From the opening shot of painted lotus blossoms on a screen to the shot of a Japanese garden that separates the episodes, from the Chinese pop music to the chinoiserie in the apartment, there is a conscious attempt in *Asian Knights* to evoke a particular atmosphere.[22] Self-conscious "Oriental" signifiers are part and parcel of a colonial fantasy—and reality—that

empowers one kind of gay man over another. Though I have known Asian men in dependent relations with older, wealthier white men, as an erotic fantasy the house boy scenario tends to work one way. I know of no scenarios of Asian men and white house boys. It is not the representation of the fantasy that offends, or even the fantasy itself, rather the uniformity with which these narratives reappear and the uncomfortable relationship they have to real social conditions.

International Skin (1985, directed by William Richhe, N'wayvo Richhe Productions), as its name suggests, features a Latino, a black man, Sum Yung Mahn, and a number of white actors. Unlike the other tapes I have discussed, there are no "Oriental" devices. And although Sum Yung Mahn and all the men of color are inevitably fucked (without reciprocating), there is mutual sexual engagement between the white and nonwhite characters.

In this tape Sum Yung Mahn is Brad, a film student making a movie for his class. Brad is the narrator, and the film begins with a self-reflexive "head and shoulders" shot of Sum Yung Mahn explaining the scenario. The film we are watching supposedly represents Brad's point of view. But here again the tape is not targeted to black, Asian, or Latino men; though Brad introduces all of these men as his friends, no two men of color ever meet on screen. Men of color are not invited to participate in the internationalism that is being sold, except through identification with white characters. This tape illustrates how an agenda of integration becomes problematic if it frames the issue solely in terms of black–white, Asian–white mixing: it perpetuates a system of white-centeredness.

The gay Asian viewer is not constructed as sexual subject in any of this work—not on the screen, not as a viewer. I may find Sum Yung Mahn attractive, I may desire his body, but I am always aware that he is not meant for me. I may lust after Eric Stryker and imagine myself as the Asian who is having sex with him, but the role the Asian plays in the scene with him is demeaning. It is not that there is anything wrong with the image of servitude per se, but rather that it is one of the few fantasy scenarios in which we figure, and we are always in the role of servant.

Are there then no pleasures for an Asian viewer? The answer to this question is extremely complex. There is first of all no essential Asian viewer. The race of the person viewing says nothing about how race figures in his or her own desires. Uniracial white representations in porn may not in themselves present a problem in addressing many gay Asian men's desires. But the issue is not simply that porn may deny pleasures to some gay Asian men. We also need to examine what role the pleasure of porn plays in securing a consensus about race and desirability that ultimately works to our disadvantage.

Though the sequences I have focused on in the preceding examples are those in which the discourses about Asian sexuality are most clearly articulated, they do not define the totality of depiction in these tapes. Much of the time the actors merely reproduce or attempt to reproduce the conventions of pornography. The fact that, with the exception of Sum Yung Mahn, they rarely succeed—because of their body type, because Midwestern-cowboy-porn dialect with Vietnamese intonation is just a bit incongruous, because they groan or gyrate just a bit too much— more than anything brings home the relative rigidity of the genre's codes. There is little seamlessness here. There are times, however, when the actors appear neither as simulated whites nor as symbolic others. There are several moments in *International Skin*, for example, in which the focus shifts from the genitals to hands caressing a body; these moments feel to me more "genuine." I do not mean this in the sense of an essential Asian sexuality, but rather a moment is captured in which the actor stops pretending. He does not stop acting, but he stops pretending to be a white porn star. I find myself focusing on moments like these, in which the racist ideology of the text seems to be temporarily suspended or rather eclipsed by the erotic power of the moment.

In "Pornography and the Doubleness of Sex for Women," Joanna Russ writes

> Sex is ecstatic, autonomous and lovely for women. Sex is violent, dangerous and unpleasant for women. I don't mean a dichotomy (i.e., two kinds of women or even two kinds of sex) but rather a continuum in which no one's experience is wholly positive or negative.[23]

Gay Asian men are men and therefore not normally victims of the rape, incest, or other sexual harassment

to which Russ is referring. However, there is a kind of doubleness, of ambivalence, in the way that Asian men experience contemporary North American gay communities. The "ghetto," the mainstream gay movement, can be a place of freedom and sexual identity. But it is also a site of racial, cultural, *and* sexual alienation sometimes more pronounced than that in straight society. For me sex is a source of pleasure, but also a site of humiliation and pain. Released from the social constraints against expressing overt racism in public, the intimacy of sex can provide my (non-Asian) partner an opening for letting me know my place—sometimes literally, as when after we come, he turns over and asks where I come from.[24] Most gay Asian men I know have similar experiences.

This is just one reality that differentiates the experiences and therefore the political priorities of gay Asians and, I think, other gay men of color from those of white men. For one thing we cannot afford to take a libertarian approach. Porn can be an active agent in representing *and* reproducing a sex–race status quo. We cannot attain a healthy alliance without coming to terms with these differences.

The barriers that impede pornography from providing representations of Asian men that are erotic and politically palatable (as opposed to correct) are similar to those that inhibit the Asian documentary, the Asian feature, the Asian experimental film and videotape. We are seen as too peripheral, not commercially viable—not the general audience. *Looking for Langston* (1988),[25] which is the first film I have seen that affirms rather than appropriates the sexuality of black gay men, was produced under exceptional economic circumstances that freed it from the constraints of the marketplace.[26] Should we call for an independent gay Asian pornography? Perhaps I am, in a utopian sort of way, though I feel that the problems in North America's porn conventions are manifold and go beyond the question of race. There is such a limited vision of what constitutes the erotic.

In Canada, the major debate about race and representation has shifted from an emphasis on the image to a discussion of appropriation and control of production and distribution—who gets to produce the work. But as we have seen in the case of *Asian Knights*, the race of the producer is no automatic guarantee of "consciousness" about these issues or of a different product. Much depends on who is constructed as the audience for the work. In any case, it is not surprising that under capitalism, finding my penis may ultimately be a matter of dollars and cents.

Acknowledgments

I would like to thank Tim McCaskell and Helen Lee for their ongoing criticism and comments, as well as Jeff Nunokawa and Douglas Crimp for their invaluable suggestions in converting the original spoken presentation into a written text. Finally, I would like to extend my gratitude to Bad Object-Choices for inviting me to participate in "How Do I Look?"

Notes

1. J. Philippe Rushton and Anthony F. Bogaert, University of Western Ontario, "Race versus Social Class Difference in Sexual Behaviour: A Follow-up Test of the r/K Dimension," *Journal of Research in Personality* 22 (1988), 259.

2. See Eric Williams, *Capitalism and Slavery* (New York: Capricorn, 1966).

3. Feminists of color have long pointed out that racism is phrased differently for men and women. Nevertheless, since it is usually heterosexual (and often middle-class) males whose voices are validated by the power structure, it is their interests that are taken up as "representing" the communities. See Barbara Smith, "Toward a Black Feminist Criticism," in *All the Women Are White, All the Blacks Are Men, But Some of Us Are Brave: Black Women's Studies* (Old Westbury, NY: The Feminist Press, 1982), 162.

4. The mainstream "leadership" within Asian communities often colludes with the myth of the model minority and the reassuring desexualization of Asian people.

5. In Britain, however, more race–sex stereotypes of South Asians exist. Led by artists such as Pratibha Parmar, Sunil Gupta, and Hanif Kureishi, there is also a growing and already significant body of work by South Asians themselves which takes up questions of sexuality.

6. Renee Tajima, "Lotus Blossoms Don't Bleed: Images of Asian Women," *Anthologies of Asian American Film and Video* (New York: A distribution project of Third World Newsreel, 1984), 28.

7. Ibid., 29.

8. See Stephen Gong, "Zen Warrior of the Celluloid (Silent) Years: The Art of Sessue Hayakawa," *Bridge* 8, no. 2 (Winter 1982–3), 37–41.

9. Frantz Fanon, *Black Skin White Masks* (London: Paladin, 1970), 120. For a reconsideration of this statement in the light of contemporary black gay issues, see Kobena Mercer, "Imaging the Black Man's Sex," in *Photography/ Politics: Two*, ed. Pat Holland, Jo Spence, and Simon Watney (London: Comedia/Methuen, 1987); reprinted in *Male Order: Unwrapping Masculinity*, ed. Rowena Chapman and Jonathan Rutherford (London: Lawrence and Wishart, 1988), 141.

10. I do not think that this could happen in today's Toronto, which now has the second largest Chinese community on the continent. Perhaps it would not have happened in San Francisco. But I still believe that there is an onus on gay Asians and other gay people of color to prove our homosexuality.

11. The term *minority* is misleading. Racism is not a matter of numbers but of power. This is especially clear in situations where people of color constitute actual majorities, as in most former European colonies. At the same time, I feel that none of the current terms are really satisfactory and that too much time spent on the politics of "naming" can in the end be diversionary.

12. To organize effectively with lesbian and gay Asians, we must reject self-righteous condemnation of "closetedness" and see coming out more as a process or a goal, rather than as a prerequisite for participation in the movement.

13. Racism is available to be used by anyone. The conclusion that—because racism = power + prejudice—only white people can be racist is Eurocentric and simply wrong. Individuals have varying degrees and different sources of power, depending on the given moment in a shifting context. This does not contradict the fact that, in contemporary North American society, racism is generally organized around white supremacy.

14. From simple observation, I feel safe in saying that most gay Asian men in North America hold white men as their idealized sexual partners. However, I am not trying to construct an argument for determinism, and there are a number of outstanding problems that are not easily answered by current analyses of power. What of the experience of Asians who are attracted to men of color, including other Asians? What about white men who prefer Asians sexually? How and to what extent is desire articulated in terms of race as opposed to body type or other attributes? To what extent is sexual attraction exclusive and/or changeable, and can it be consciously programmed? These questions are all politically loaded, as they parallel and impact the debates between essentialists and social constructionists on the nature of homosexuality itself. They are also emotionally charged, in that sexual choice involving race has been a basis for moral judgment.

15. See Richard Dyer, *Heavenly Bodies: Film Stars and Society*

(New York: St. Martin's Press, 1986). In his chapter on Marilyn Monroe, Dyer writes extensively on the relationship between blondness, whiteness, and desirability.

16. Print porn is somewhat more racially integrated, as are the new safe sex tapes—by the Gay Men's Health Crisis, for example—produced in a political and pedagogical rather than a commercial context.

17. Richard Dyer, "Coming to Terms," *Jump Cut*, no. 30 (March 1985), 28.

18. Tom Waugh, "Men's Pornography, Gay vs. Straight," *Jump Cut*, no. 30 (March 1985), 31.

19. *International Wavelength News* 2, no. 1 (January 1991).

20. Tom Waugh, "Men's Pornography, Gay vs. Straight," 33.

21. It seems to me that the undressing here is organized around the pleasure of the white man in being served. This is in contrast to the undressing scenes in, say, James Bond films, in which the narrative is organized around undressing as an act of revealing the woman's body, an indicator of sexual conquest.

22. Interestingly, the gay video porn from Japan and Thailand that I have seen has none of this Oriental coding. Asianness is not taken up as a sign but is taken for granted as a setting for the narrative.

23. Joanna Russ, "Pornography and the Doubleness of Sex for Women," *Jump Cut*, no. 32 (April 1986), 39.

24. Though this is a common enough question in our postcolonial, urban environments, when asked of Asians it often reveals two agendas: first, the assumption that all Asians are newly arrived immigrants and, second, a fascination with difference and sameness. Although we (Asians) all supposedly look alike, there are specific characteristics and stereotypes associated with each particular ethnic group. The inability to tell us apart underlies the inscrutability attributed to Asians. This "inscrutability" took on sadly ridiculous proportions when during World War II the Chinese were issued badges so that white Canadians could distinguish them from "the enemy."

25. Isaac Julien (director), *Looking for Langston* (United Kingdom: Sankofa Film and Video, 1988).

26. For more on the origins of the black film and video workshops in Britain, see Jim Pines, "The Cultural Context of Black British Cinema," in *Blackframes: Critical Perspectives on Black Independent Cinema*, ed. Mybe B. Cham and Claire Andrade-Watkins (Cambridge, Mass.: MIT Press, 1988), 26.

27.
QUEER EYE FOR THE STRAIGHT GUISE
Camp, Postfeminism, and the Fab Five's Makeovers of Masculinity
Steven Cohan

The big hit on American cable television in the summer of 2003 was the Bravo series *Queer Eye for the Straight Guy*, airing on Tuesday evenings. Every week five gay men, collectively referred to as the "Fab Five," take on a domestically and sartorially challenged straight man. He serves as their "trade" but not in the sense of the term suggested by the double entendre of the title; rather, they do a complete makeover of the straight guy. Each member of the queer team represents what is taken as a gay-identified specialty: Carson Kressley is in charge of fashion, Kyan Douglas grooming, Thom Filicia decorating, Ted Allen cooking, and Jai Rodriguez something vaguely called "culture" but more accurately a hybrid of dating or hosting etiquette and leisure entertainment skills. Typically, each episode focuses the straight guy's makeover around a particular "mission," with the Fab Five's renovation directed toward his achieving a personal or professional goal so that he can attain "confidence" and "grow up," as is frequently said on the show. Regardless of the particulars, the Fab Five's primary objective is to teach the straight guy how to satisfy the emotional and domestic needs of a present or potential female partner.

Queer Eye adheres to the makeover show format insofar as it defines a confident, mature masculinity through consumption and then normalizes it through a heterosexual couple, leaving the queer guys out of the loop except as spectators. Just as important, though, while decidedly aimed at restoring the straight guy's cultural capital in a postfeminist marketplace, *Queer Eye* also makes a concerted effort through camp

to visualize queerness in its contiguous relation to straightness. How one weighs these concerns, I am going to argue, determines what one can find in the Fab Five's makeovers of the straight guys.[1] My discussion of the first season of *Queer Eye* will thus aim to situate its legibility as a queer show in light of this collection and the conference that inspired it. I have in mind (and am, to be candid, intentionally resisting) how some formulations of postfeminism have so readily absorbed the impact of queer theory but left out the queerness. Witness how, in addressing the woman now seemingly liberated by feminism, consumer culture and the mass media have transformed the visible gay male into what Baz Dreisinger aptly describes as "the trendy accessory for straight women," namely, the "postfeminist" female's best friend and confidante, and the inspiration for her ideal consort, that hip, het "metrosexual."[2] While recognizing the extent to which *Queer Eye* encourages a highly comforting view of homosexuality as a useful accessory of postfeminist femininity, I want to examine how the series simultaneously enables a queer viewer to see past that agenda.

Good Fairies to the Rescue?

Queer Eye for the Straight Guy was Bravo's effort to exploit the popularity of makeover shows, twisting the format a bit with its five gay experts. Moreover, Bravo paired it with another gay version of a reality TV genre, the dating show *Boy Meets Boy*, to create a two-hour bloc of "alternative" programming on Tuesday nights.

The intent was to establish a niche identity, thereby overcoming the blandness of this NBC-owned cable network, and possibly to find a signature show. Having gay or gay-coded hosts on a cable reality series was not new; nor did *Queer Eye* make any pretense of reinventing the makeover format. All the same, in the absence of a big, tabloid, TV event in the summer of 2003, *Queer Eye* immediately received a great deal of media coverage because, unlike *Boy Meets Boy*, it featured five gay men perfectly comfortable with their homosexuality and openly identified itself as a series respectful of queer tastes and attitudes.

Exploiting the buzz that resulted from so much attention, NBC subsequently reran episodes several times in its powerhouse Thursday night lineup during the summer months (a significant spot for advertising the opening of new movies each week), and the series' success prompted an appearance of the Fab Five on the network's *Tonight Show* in August to do a makeover of the host, Jay Leno. They performed the same job for preselected audience members on Oprah Winfrey's afternoon talk show in early autumn. In the fall as well, the Comedy Central satire *South Park* parodied *Queer Eye*, indicating how quickly this new series had entered popular culture awareness. Aside from the expected gay demographic, the series quickly attracted a strong female following, prompting a Yahoo! discussion group dedicated to this important segment of the viewing audience, "A Girl's View of *Queer Eye*." Yet the series also drew a cadre of straight men. One fan site, "Straight Eye for the Queer Shows" (now apparently defunct), featured four openly heterosexual men who rotated responsibility for writing detailed, tongue-in-cheek recaps of each week's episode. This is not to suggest that the male segment of the series' audience took its makeover lessons lightly. A December 2003 survey conducted by Jericho Communications revealed that whenever a new episode aired on Tuesday evenings it encouraged more males to go shopping with a buddy the day afterward than at any other time during the week.[3]

The currency of *Queer Eye* throughout its first season occurred at the same time that same-sex marriage became a controversial, publicly debated issue.[4] Two Canadian provinces legalized such unions in the summer of 2003, making it possible for gay and lesbian couples to travel there from the United States

and marry, and in November of that year the Massachusetts Supreme Court upheld same-sex marriages, prompting local civil resistance to the federal Defense of Marriage Act in states on the East and West Coasts. This timeliness certainly contributed, if indirectly, to the attention *Queer Eye* and its five hosts received in the months following the premiere. In its year-end chronicle of events, the American Film Institute (AFI) listed *Queer Eye* as one of the two major cultural developments of 2003 (the other was the issue of film piracy). The AFI singled out *Queer Eye* because it brought "gay culture to the national fore by spoofing and celebrating stereotypes, and unlike other reality shows, it did so in a winning and genuine manner that developed a bond between the gay and straight man."[5] The AFI was not alone in applauding the series' liberal viewpoint. Oprah Winfrey expressed much the same sentiment, often tearfully, several times during the Fab Five's appearance on her show.

Alongside that liberal approval, *Queer Eye* received its fair share of negative criticism for perpetuating, not debunking, gender-sexual stereotypes. News stories on the suddenly hot new show balanced criticism and praise in their accounts of the response from gay viewers.[6] Skimming several gay-oriented discussion boards during the months following the series premiere, I found that the strongest charge against the Fab Five was directed at their "unmasculine" appearance and mannerisms, epitomized by their flamboyant personification of effeminate stereotypes, with Carson and Jai targeted in particular.

Inevitably, a comparison was made with the more attractive gay men to be found on Bravo's other new series, *Boy Meets Boy*. Its hook was that the gay bachelor did not know his dating pool included straight men. While this premise appeared to belie the distinction between gay and straight on the basis of appearance, *Boy Meets Boy* reinscribed the axiom that the most attractive gay men are those who can successfully pass as straight, and the series only proved that, when it comes to dating, gay men can be just as banal and superficial as their straight counterparts. But *Boy Meets Boy* capitalized on the thinking that motivates the many gay personal ads seeking straight-acting men, and it exploited the fantasy, a staple of gay erotica, that straight men are seducible. What stood out in the contrasting remarks about *Queer Eye*'s circulation of gay stereotypes was the discomfort felt by hostile viewers precisely because the Fab Five were not gym junkies; they did not conform to the "Abercrombie & Fitch" ethos inspiring (not to say inciting desire in) gay men of their generation, which, as Michael Joseph Gross observes, is to look like everyone else, to be "regular guys—[but] with better-than-average bodies."[7] In short, these viewers preferred the buff, twenty-something, heterosexual-looking guys on *Boy Meets Boy.* While the criticism declared that *Queer Eye* reconfirmed straight prejudices about nelly gay men, it could be reduced to the simpler question: why can't these five queers act and look more like straight guys?

When watching that first season of *Queer Eye,* my own answer at the time was: if they did, we wouldn't be able to tell the difference. True, *Queer Eye* defines the queerness of the Fab Five through their expertise as consumers, not through their sexual orientation. As Anna McCarthy points out, "The Fab Five are totally sexless. They may tease their subjects, but there is no chance that they will get to sleep with them."[8] Their queer eye is for the most part not focused through a gay gaze—it's not *that* kind of queer eye for a straight guy—but is meant to illuminate for heterosexual men what their girlfriends, wives, or mothers already know, namely, the value of "products," perhaps the most repeatedly used term on the show, as the cornerstone of heterosexual self-confidence and maturity. The five hosts function for each episode not as protagonists but in the capacity that narratology calls helper figures, serving the needs of a domesticated heteronormality; this subordinate role in the narrative of each episode enables a makeover to be focused through a decidedly straight eye for the queer guy, which is why the five hosts may encourage what is actually "the fantasy that [the series'] straight viewers gain entry into an otherwise inaccessible, unfamiliar gay culture."[9] With their homosexuality serving mainly as consumer culture's equivalent of professional counseling for the straight couple, and gay culture itself reduced to shopping, the Fab Five do end up seeming all too reminiscent of the three drag queens in *To Wong Foo, Thanks for Everything! Julie Newmar* (1995): the asexual good fairies who bring a hip Manhattanite's taste for style, flair, color, and cleanliness into a bland and dingy straight world and quickly depart as soon as they have spread their gay cheer.

As for its depiction of straights, *Queer Eye* follows the example of all the self-help relationship books that binarize the difference between men and women, depicting the genders as "different species entirely" and consequently promoting the expectation that heterosexual romance "is not a walk in the park but an arduous expedition."[10] I think it is safe to assume that the appeal of the series for many women lies in its mission of softening masculinity's rough edges for successful male-female cohabitation. Registering what Sasha Torres observes is "the incapacity of the heterosexual families that spawned the straight guys to sustain even a minimal quality of life," *Queer Eye* depicts not only the domestic rehabilitation but also the class elevation of straight men for the benefit of their women."[11] Like other makeover shows, the series teaches its viewers that this dual mission is most easily performed through one's appearance, and the urgency of such instruction is expressed every time the Fab Five obsess over men needing to shave in "the right way" and to remove all that gristly body hair, whether it's the straight guy's back hair, ear hair, or unibrow. As Torres notes, the show's preoccupation with shaving crystallizes, through the Fab Five's intervention, both the necessity of male-male tutelage in perpetuating the protocols of civil masculinity and the heterosexual family's failure to perform this crucial function for its unruly sons, much to the dismay of their future girlfriends and wives.

With successful straight coupling requiring endless negotiation between alien creatures polarized in their libidinal, emotional, and domestic needs, *Queer Eye* brings in the Fab Five to mediate heterosexual difference; their visible queerness then functions to speak for women in an unthreatening male voice. As a result, the series brings out the contradiction constructing the postfeminist female viewer being addressed from this vantage point. Straight masculinity is identified as problematic more than oppressive, and it can be remedied through a male's consumption of the same kind of products that enhance in order to regulate femininity. However, even though the makeovers serve the interests of women, *Queer Eye* concentrates on "the pleasures of companionship" between straight guys and their gay cohorts, relegating women to "a shadow presence on the show."[12] A female's main function is to nod approval at what the queer guys have achieved for her in her absence, which involves their pedagogical bonding with the straight guy as well as his makeover.

The cultural ideal of masculinity aimed for here—though it is a standard the straight guys on the series at best only approximate to provide the link between the makeovers and the advertising and product placement—is what the media has termed the metrosexual, the youngish, upscale, heterosexual male who spends so much time on his appearance (and so much money on hairstyling, fashionable clothing, and skin products) that he is readable as "gay" and too liberal to mind the mistake—but hands off, please! On the Fab Five's return visit (21 November 2003) several months after their makeover of the *Tonight Show*, Carson Kressley defined this suddenly ubiquitous yet sexually ambiguous figure for Jay Leno as the straight guy who moisturizes but doesn't have sex with other men. More accurately, the fashion guru quipped, he's "a moistrosexual."

A recent invention of marketing and the urban press, the metrosexual male gives every impression of revising how straight masculinity has traditionally been defined in opposition to feminine activities such as shopping, grooming, and cooking, as Martin Roberts points out elsewhere in this volume [*Interrogating Postfeminism: Gender and the Politics of Popular Culture*].[13] Such a refiguration of masculinity has a longer history, though, deriving from an earlier representation of what was termed the New Man in advertising, TV, and films of the 1980s, itself an outgrowth of the kind of marketing aimed directly at male consuming, which *Playboy* magazine perfected in the 1950s.[14] Somewhat like the metrosexual, the New Man of the 1980s was depicted as being "tough but tender, masculine but sensitive—he can cry, cuddle babies and best of all buy cosmetics."[15] This newly styled image of a straight masculinity geared toward consuming was perhaps first signaled by *American Gigolo* (1980), the neo-noir film starring Richard Gere that put the clothing designer Georgio Armani on the map, and it was featured in advertising campaigns for products such as Levi's 501 jeans and Grey Flannel cologne. By the end of the decade, when the Liz Claiborne company introduced its own brand of men's cologne, the marketing was specifically aimed at the New Man, "who attends Rob Reiner romances and tipples kir royales [and] might also want to take

an introspective and vulnerable approach to the way he smells."[16]

According to Suzanne Moore, the 1980s New Man drew on the visual iconography of soft-core gay pornography, drawing attention to the male body "as a pleasurable object [but] on condition that his pleasure can be contained within a narcissistic/auto-erotic discourse."[17] Just as important, this image addressed women by offering "the possibility of an *active female gaze*."[18] Moore attributes this kind of radical shift in depicting the masculine, which blurs the distinction between the active male voyeur and the passive female exhibitionist, to popular culture's awareness of the "renegotiations over masculinity brought about by radical political discourses," feminism, and the gay and lesbian rights movement in particular.[19] Because of the homoeroticism informing the visual representation of the New Man, however, the heterosexuality of this image of masculinity was never fully secure. Hence paying attention to how one smelled could signal vulnerability as well as introspection, just as it still connoted suspicion about—and feminized-as narcissistic—the type of man who was *too* concerned with how he looked.

The 1980s New Man, in short, could always turn out to be a closet case. By contrast, as the newer term suggests, the metrosexual willingly displays his toned but moisturized body as a means of performing his masculinity through his ability to consume, using his exhibitionism to assert his identity as an urban, middle-class male. While this newest incarnation of a male attuned to the same consumerist desires as his domestic partner is presumed to be heterosexual, he is still poised between assumptions about what makes a man readable as "straight" and what makes him readable as "queer," which is why he is more "metro" than "hetero." Appropriating the tropes formerly used to identify the gay male consumer, the metrosexual reimagines masculinity from a postfeminist perspective, but the price remains this new man's sexual ambiguity—the very anxiety that *Boy Meets Boy* appeared to celebrate but actually fostered by keeping its gay bachelor in the dark about the sexual orientation of the men he was scrutinizing, flirting with, and sharing his feelings with in one-on-one encounters. For single straight women, even if the metrosexual moisturizes but doesn't swing with the other team, his sexual ambiguity renews the motive for the much-quoted worry that all the best men are either already married or gay—for if they aren't gay they certainly look like they are, so how is a girl to tell?

This is where the Fab Five come in: to clarify who is and who isn't. *Queer Eye for the Straight Guy* outwardly deploys their queerness to facilitate the mating of a metrosexual wannabe with his postfeminist partner, but these makeovers of the sleeping woolly beast for his date with Princess Charming are primarily structured around the opposition of "queer" and "straight," not "masculine" and "feminine." The series' humor and its potential edginess reside in this opposition. The Fab Five's queer eye slyly acknowledges the regulation and deregulation of domestic and urban spaces through that dualism, which places gay men outside straight culture yet makes them central to its successful operation. At issue is the spatial differentiation pointed out by the series' title. *Queer Eye for the Straight Guy* does something akin to what Joshua Gamson argues about daytime talk shows, which perform "an ambivalence about just who is doing what and how in public—and, more fundamentally, just to whom public space belongs." "It's not so much *the gayness* that is bothersome," Gamson concludes, "it's the *publicness*."[20] *Queer Eye* does not represent that disturbance through violent confrontations in the manner of Jerry Springer or Ricki Lake. Rather, in order to stage the queer eye—straight guy encounter as a momentary deregulation of boundaries, *Queer Eye* foregrounds the public visibility of queerness in its adjacency to straightness through *camp*, although the Fab Five do not always maintain this viewpoint coherently or consistently in each episode.

Camping with the Fab Five

Historically speaking, in the pre-Stonewall era of the closet (a crucial space for *Queer Eye* as it turns out), camp was a strategy of cultural differentiation for queers, one highly responsive to the imperative of passing—a "queer eye for the straight *guise*"—even more than it was a "sensibility" and "style" or a category of "taste," to refer to Susan Sontag's and Andrew Ross's early commentaries on camp.[21] As I have written elsewhere, "In response to that era's oppression and censorship of homosexuality, camp allowed for

the ironic, self-reflective style of gay men passing as straight, who kept a 'straight face' so as not to let outsiders in on the joke, while simultaneously winking at the initiated in shared acknowledgment of it. *Camp* can be defined as the ensemble of strategies used to enact a queer recognition of the incongruities arising from the cultural regulation of gender and sexuality."[22] Despite its later appropriation by the mainstream during the 1960s and 1970s, which began to efface its history and politics, camp still works by exaggerating the homologous boundaries of the visible/straight/natural and invisible/queer/unnatural in order to locate one side of the polarity in more direct tension with the other. This is why, as Esther Newton observes, "Camp is not a thing. Most broadly it signifies a *relationship between* things, people, and activities or qualities, and homosexuality."[23]

Today camp may seem politically incorrect because of its association with the oppressive politics of the closet, but its significance for gay culture, while reinflected according to the times, has not diminished. Camp still enables a queer perspective to be discerned through its *effect* (the ironic inflection of a witty putdown or pun, a coded allusion for those in the know, the exaggeration of artifice and theatricality) and, more profoundly, in its *affect* (the queer pleasure in perceiving, if not causing, the disruption of gender-sexual categories whether in representations of heterosexual normality, the values that reiterate it, or the commodities that derive from and reinscribe it). Although first feminism and then postfeminism have provocatively taken camp as a ground for theorizing the artifice of gender construction and regulation, and to serve as a strategy for reading against: oppressive representations of women, I want to insist on what is still, to my mind, the intractable *queerness* of camp. It may illuminate the subordination of women alongside that of gay men, but because of its queer bias it is not reducible to either feminist political aims or postfeminist awareness of the interaction between feminine identities, gender performativity, and consumption.[24]

On *Queer Eye*, from Carson's double entendres to Jai's exaggeration of a drag queen in mufti to Ted's understated, straight-faced irony, the Fab Five engage in camp at the level of both effect (what they do and say to make viewers laugh at the straight people) and affect (how that laughter then yields pleasure in watching the makeovers, though a pleasure that exceeds the series' ideological purpose of recuperating heterosexual coupledom). Their camp enables them to be readily perceivable as "gay," in contrast to the straight men they remake for straight women, but it also allows them to cast a queer eye on their job of serving heterosexuality as its asexual helpers.

Rather effortlessly, yet somewhat violently, the team moves in and out of the regulatory boundaries that uphold the distinction, in private and public, between queer and straight spaces. Each episode begins with the Fab Five speeding across Manhattan in their sport-utility vehicle as they briefly describe their mission of the day. The opening credits then identify each member of the team individually according to his expertise; pictures them in a group as if they were the Mod Squad, the A-Team, and Charlie's Angels combined; and locates them at the imaginary intersection of Gay and Straight Streets. Following the credits, the first segment records them arriving at their destination like a gay brigade of terrorists or kidnappers invading the presumed sanctity of the straight guy's home and disrupting its heterosexual space. With pseudo-militaristic fervor, the five charge inside and register their offense at what they find there: disarray, dysfunctionality, and dirt. In this first segment, edited in a fast-paced montage that does not follow temporal chronology, they appropriate items from the kitchen, bathroom, or bedroom closet in order to mock the straight guy's ad hoc domesticity, indifference to sanitation, ineptitude with clothing, and, whenever the opportunity arises—for instance, if they find porn or condoms or even his underwear—his sexual prowess. The humiliated straight guy stands by watching helplessly, often laughing but rarely offering resistance to this demeaning ridicule except to avoid physical contact, while the five queer men proceed to trash the place literally as well as verbally, even going so far as to toss his furniture or clothing out a window or over a balcony.

The next set of sequences leads the straight guy through the physical makeover, which amounts to a takeover. He passively puts himself in Carson's hands for a shopping spree and in Kyan's for grooming at a salon or spa; usually there is a third outing with one of the others for furniture or cuisine. The ostensible point of these sequences is his instruction—on what

clothes suit his body, what areas of his face, hair, or body need immediate attention, and how to select furniture or food. Visually and verbally, the camp humor in these sequences depends on the extent to which the team can expose how this consuming disturbs their subject's comfortable occupation of public space as a heterosexual male. These are indeed "outings." Not only is the straight guy undertaking an activity of specialized consuming presumed to be a gay man's preoccupation with his appearance for the appreciative gaze of another man, but this straight guy is doing it in public with an openly gay guy, so the act of consuming places the two together in a hybrid space that confounds a straight-queer dichotomy. Anyone who observes the straight guy in an upscale clothing store with Carson is not going to presume that these are two straight buddies—the pair identified by the Jericho Communications survey—picking up a new pair of jeans or polo shirt to replace a worn one. Flamboyantly rushing through the store with his straight guy in tow, Carson announces his queer presence at every turn by means of his camp manner. The straight guy, meanwhile, submits to a scrutinizing queer eye that is superior to his when Carson appraises his appearance; using a quick wit as well as a keen sense of style to exploit his discomfort and objectify him, Carson dresses down the straight guy while dressing him up.

Similarly, when Kyan supervises the straight guy's subjection to exfoliating, tweezing, plucking, and waxing—the work that goes into "femininity"—he also exposes him to the gaze of a queer eye. Although it does not occur in each episode, here the crossing of boundaries can most disturbingly question how *queer* and *straight* are still defined according to spatial regulation. This is most vividly apparent in episode 108, "Law and Disorder" (first shown on Bravo on 19 August 2003), which recounts the makeover of John Verdi, an Italian American cop living on Staten Island. A bald, pudgy, pasty, white man with gross toenails, John is taken to the Completely Bare spa for a spray-on tan. All he can mutter throughout is how embarrassed he is, not so much for appearing practically naked on national television as for doing so side-by-side with a gay guy. "See how he has a farmer's tan," Kyan remarks to the female attendant while pointing it out on John's chest and verifying that the process can contour and slendorize the body through the way the color is blended. John, in the meantime, has his eyes shut tight. "Dude," Kyan comments, "I have to say this is the most embarrassing thing ever done to help out a straight guy." But John seems more flummoxed: "Dude, this is so embarrassing, to be standing next to a gay guy in skivvies and . . . disposable skivvies, I might add."

Kyan: Well, you're no Prince Charming either, Big Boy.

John: I'm not—I'm not even looking at you. I don't want to look that way.

Kyan: Are you serious?

John: Dude, it's like . . . uh . . . you don't understand.

Kyan: What's gay about this situation?

John: Are you kidding me right now?

Kyan: I mean, over here it's gay. But (*pointing to John's space in the tanning booth*) what's gay about that?

John: Cause I'm in skivvies next to a gay—you don't understand.

But Kyan *does* understand. A short time later, he pressures the straight guy again, wondering to the attendant, "Can you make his penis look bigger?" "Guy," John asks defensively, "why are you looking at my penis?" Kyan laughs, and John begs, "Come on, please." Although Kyan demurs, his joke taken, the camera then focuses on crotch and butt shots of John as the tanning process is completed.

This segment questions what makes one space gay and another straight, and does so at the straight guy's expense, triggering his homophobic panic at being in such intimate proximity to a gay male body—the seminude Kyan, the member of the group whom fans and the media consider the "hottest." His gayness is for the moment defined in explicitly sexual terms as a queer eye not for products but for the straight guy's penis. This definition is then overlaid with the erotic display of Kyan's body for a gay and female viewer, as well as the camp deflation of John's endowment, which encourages one to infer that perhaps it is already looking a little "bigger." Joking about penis anxiety is an obvious sign of the discomfort that arises when heterosexual identity comes into contact with homosexual desire, harking back to the embarrassment, insecurity, curiosity, and/or excitement that

characterizes all those group showers straight boys have had to take after high school gym classes. However, the John Verdi episode is more complex than this for it also brings out how this straight guy's "Guido Mumbo" masculinity, as Jai calls it later in the hour, is not only a performance of heterosexual codes for the benefit of the queer guys but is also, shall we say, blended, contoured, and slenderized by homosexual codings as the condition of his being made over in order to be more compatible with his female partner.

As happens in each episode, following the physical makeover John Verdi returns home with his new queer buddies in order to see what Thom has accomplished in his absence ("You don't feel like you live in some gay guy's apartment?"), to perform a fashion show of the clothing Carson has selected for him ("Hip hop with a little more class," but remember to zhuzh up the sleeves), to learn from Kyan how to establish a grooming regimen (proper use of products, which happen to vary each week, for "long-term skin care"), and to receive final instructions on preparing and serving food for the evening from Ted (in this case, a torte or quiche, though Ted reassures John that this torte is "a manly quiche, a quiche with balls"—even though it is made with eggs). Then the Fab Five depart for an apartment in Manhattan where, in the final segment, cocktails in hand and getting visibly looped, they observe how successfully the straight guy follows their tutelage on closed-circuit television.

Once again this episode reveals how camp identifies a distinctly queer eye for the show. John's mission has been to rekindle his romance with his live-in girlfriend, Ayana, a "hot" African American model who is tired of mothering him. As soon as she enters, John abruptly readjusts his masculine persona: "Isn't this re-mahk-able?" he asks, further showing his excitement about the makeover of his body and their home by jumping up and down and talking baby talk, all the while appreciating how her "boobages" look in her new outfit, which was also selected by Carson. In the meantime, much as if they were watching *Sex and the City*, the Fab Five gather in front of the TV for some camp camaraderie. "He's bouncing around like a little girl, isn't he?" Kyan asks in disbelief. "He's acting gayer than I do," Carson agrees. "He was all tough guy around us, and now he's . . ." Ted cannot find the words, so he makes a flaming gesture. "He totally hopped out of the bedroom," Thom adds. Throughout this segment, the Fab Five note every potential disaster or faux pas, as well as every sign of slippage, between queer and straight in John's demeanor, as when he describes the dessert he has prepared as "divine." "Divine? He used the word *divine*," Ted exclaims, to which Carson replies, "He *is* gay." John confesses to Ayana how for a while he has been lacking confidence but now he has "a spark in his pants" again, and Thom mutters, "Don't look at me—I didn't put it there." "There's a lot of power in a pedicure and a spray-on tan," Kyan concludes, restoring the consumer orientation of the makeover. Mission complete, the Five toast their success in rescuing another straight guy from drabness.

Queer Eye may deserve the critiques it has received for its endorsement of class hierarchies based on consuming, but that does not mean the overt ideological agenda of the series warrants outright dismissal of the additional cultural work it performs as a queer show. The series remakes straight masculinity according to bourgeois norms, but it does so through the mediation of queerness, which foregrounds the instability of both masculinity and straightness. For all their disavowals, most of the straight guys appear to realize the fragility of their heteromasculinity at some point in the hour. For instance, while shopping, John Verdi tells Carson that he'd do anything for his female partner, "even start with five gay guys and get made over." His problem, however, is that he doesn't know "what sexy is." All he knows is that he wants it and the queer guys know how to gain access to it, so he submits to their tutelage.

John's confession makes explicit the gender instability on which the series' camp outlook spins. Straight masculinity is just another cultural product and a confused one at that. As John's makeover illustrates, the series just as explicitly recognizes how a so-called normative masculinity is a performance, frequently multiple in its signifying effects; that it achieves an impression of stability by maintaining the perceived boundaries strictly differentiating between and culturally locating hetero- and homosexual male identities; and that it occurs in a consumer-oriented society that, needing to exploit the male market, overlaps these two identities (as in the metrosexual advertising image), thereby requiring the performance in the first place. The series' understanding of how straightness

is organized according to its disavowed proximity to queerness is best epitomized in the opening segment, which depicts the Fab Five's invasion of a heterosexual domicile, during which they ridicule the straight guy's veneer of manliness, exposing his dirty underwear literally and figuratively, and in the closing one, which records the Fab Five's withdrawal into their own camp camaraderie, where they laugh once more at the spectacle of a straight guy's performance of his newly acquired, upscale masculinity. This framing vantage point enables *Queer Eye for the Straight Guy* to pass, in effect, as "safe" entertainment and yet display an edgier outlook, as the John Verdi episode well illustrates. The series can be read as straight or nonstraight, as noncamp or camp, depending on which eye you look with.

The central joke driving the series, it bears repeating, is that men with no sexual interest of their own in women have to be brought in from outside a clearly delineated heterosexual space in order to teach a straight guy "what sexy is," which enables heartfelt appreciation by heterosexual men and women alike of this needed queer intervention. This joke defines what the queer eye can see in the makeover because it also highlights what the straight eye fails to see. Thus, the remarks posted by females on the "Girl's Eye View of Queer Eye" Web site, right after the John Verdi episode aired, confined themselves to appreciating how "adorable" the Fab Five looked or behaved at certain points and how striking John appeared in his new clothes, making him such an attractive date. A more interesting response appeared in the recap of this episode on the "Straight Eye for the Queer Shows" fan site. The writer, "Larry," goes into great detail; he describes all the bristly interactions between the cop and the Fab Five from their entrance through each stage of the makeover, including the trip to Completely Bare (although the point seems to be what NBC edited out when it reran this episode), and he quotes much of their dialogue. However, except for noting that the gay men dwell on the size of Ayana's breasts (their response to John's appreciation of her "boob-ages"), "Larry" ignores the final segment, in which the team watches the results of the makeover. Instead, as if the Fab Five's viewpoint were transparent, this straight fan disregards their camp commentary and only describes what they see—John and Ayana's night out.

Expressing his appreciation of John's efforts to please Ayana, "Larry" concludes:

> Now a number of people have complained how John gets such a hot chick. In his defense, he's tall, pretty fit, and strong (though he's gained some weight) and a cop. He's apparently good at the kissing (full alignment with light tongue tizzle) and it seems like he had a good sized package while being spray tanned. Many women out there want a guy who can take care of them and really love them and this guy can do it. Any man willing to stretch himself to keep his relationship fresh, is a good catch, and most women should be so lucky.[25]

The difference between queer and straight viewpoints depends on the extent to which, as "Larry" typifies here, a viewer disregards the Fab Five's camp mediation and identifies primarily with the woman as the motivating force behind the straight guy's makeover—he's doing it solely for her, and she then serves as his private audience when he shows off the results of his makeover. However, in fulfilling that role for this type of viewer, Ayana is also participating in the performance, which the Fab Five simultaneously watch on their closed-circuit TV. Because they filter the straight couple through their camp spectatorship, it is difficult to extract a bona fide feminine viewpoint from the closure, however much "Larry" tries to do so. The couple themselves are rarely if ever shown recognizing any camp element in their performance of heterosexuality, even when they acknowledge the performative dimension of the makeover and its subsequent test run as the straight guy shows off what he has learned for his partner's inspection and approval.

Yet, by casting his closing response to this episode through an awareness of Ayana's needs and not the Fab Five's camp, "Larry" can display the post-feminist male sensibility that, one has to assume, allows him to take pleasure in the series and coauthor the "straight guy" Web site. No doubt influenced by all those self-help relationship books, which are supposedly written in the wake of feminism but present an option other than feminism when it comes to women's relations with men, "Larry" writes as a male seemingly liberated from sexist attitudes and, what is more, since he did notice John's "package," as a male not subject to insecurity about the stability of his own heteromasculinity. To sustain this viewpoint, he has to ignore both the Fab Five's camp eye and the subordinate role of women in the makeover. For her part, Ayana knows very well her limited contribution to the makeover process; on departing the premises so that the Fab Five can take charge of John's makeover, she loudly announces, "The vagina is leaving the nest." "Larry's" summary does indicate why a woman's presence, at least in the closure of each episode, is still a crucial element in the series' success. She facilitates the more sanguine, straight male response to the Fab Five's queer intervention in heterosexuality, which Larry typifies when he in effect rewrites the John Verdi episode to concentrate solely on the couple through Ayana's point of view.

A Straight Eye for Those Queer Guys

That a female figure cannot easily be removed from the series' formula stands out all the more when we look at the guest appearances of the Fab Five on the Oprah Winfrey and Jay Leno shows. Not surprisingly, given their target audience, each guest spot retains the series' premise but not its structure, more noticeably marginalizing the five gay men as outsiders for a predominantly straight female and male audience, respectively. The difference between the two spots is quite revealing. Winfrey's singling out of the female motivation for the makeovers considerably tames the Fab Five's impact, negating any jarring collision of straight and gay spaces, whereas a female's absence from the Leno makeover brings out more clearly the disturbance that the series itself manages more insightfully through camp.

On the Winfrey show (first shown in syndication on 22 September 2003), the queer makeovers of the various straight guys selected for a much-needed rescue, at least according to Oprah and the men's wives, cause members of the female audience to cry, with everyone who had a stake or hand in the renovations gathered together onstage for a big group hug at the end of the hour. One exemplary moment occurs in the final segment, when a formerly shaggy middle-aged man named Roland returns to display his new appearance, supervised by Kyan. Previously Roland had not shaved his beard or cut his hair in over twenty years, during which time his wife and two daughters had never seen what lay behind all the hair. Not only does the family break down in tears at the revelation that a well-groomed Roland is as handsome as "a movie star," but Oprah herself is open-mouthed when gazing at his dramatically different look. While Kyan, as befitting his role as product endorser, reflects that "shaving is all about preparation and products," Roland himself confesses, "I feel like I'm alive again." He grabs Oprah in a tight hug and begins to weep, and she gets caught up in the emotions too. "Let's all just have a cry," she sobs, inviting the predominantly female audience in the studio and at home to participate in the emotional outburst that confirms feminine gratitude for the queer intervention on behalf of what Oprah has earlier called "frustrated wives" who are unable to assist their "helpless husbands." The way the show is shot encourages such empathetic participation throughout the hour, and it does not involve the visual or verbal mediation of the Fab Five, despite the many times Oprah laughs heartily at Carson's camp barbs. The desperate wives who have "turned in" their husbands, as Oprah puts it, sit in the front rows as audience members, whereas the husbands stand uncomfortably onstage like wanted men; repeated close-ups of the wives' disgruntled then delighted faces equate their reactions with those of the audience members at large, fostering identification with this point of view by the home viewer as well.

By contrast, no tears are shed when Jay Leno receives his makeover. To publicize it, the Fab Five show up the night before the big reveal, appearing after Kevin Costner, who is promoting his new western, *Open Range* (2003), which was broadcast on NBC on 14 August 2003. As soon as the Fab Five make their entrance, Leno begins to bait Costner, implying that the star's heteromasculinity, not Leno's own, is in doubt because of its proximity to queerness. After describing the *Queer Eye* slogan, "Five gay men out to make over the world—one straight guy at a time," Leno turns to Costner, warning, "and you're next, buddy." Leno goes on to joke that Costner intentionally lowered his voice when greeting the Fab Five, to tease Costner about getting his buttocks pierced, to propose that the Fab Five should plan Costner's upcoming wedding, and to suggest that, possibly because he had already spent too much time on the open range when making his movie, Costner is now re-thinking the whole marriage thing. Although at moments Costner does

seem uncomfortable, especially when the Fab Five first descend on him en masse, at other times he gets into the spirit of things (asking Jai, for instance, what he means by "working a room"), but Leno repeatedly attributes discomfort to him. Additionally, Leno turns every comment made by his guests into a joke about straight masculinity that actually endorses it as the impeachable norm—just in case anyone is wondering. For instance, when Thom explains that the worst offense he finds in straight domiciles is bad lighting, typically supplied by a single torchiere halogen lamp, Leno again makes a joke at Costner's expense: "Straight guys like that porno lighting," Leno explains. "See, Kevin knows what I'm talking about." When Ted comments on straight guys' insecurity about ordering fine wines at restaurants, Leno similarly reasons, "it comes from going to strip shows."[26]

Without a straight male ally onto whom he can deflect his anxiety, the following night Leno resorts to homophobic jokes about the makeover process, playing up the gayness of the Fab Five in contrast to his own resistant straightness (broadcast on NBC on 15 August 2003). Distancing himself from the makeover even while going through it, Leno repeats his worry that the process effeminizes him by forcing him to think about fashion and skin conditioning. Not deterred, the Fab Five keep their banter going, chiding Leno for his appearance and his show's decor. They anticipate his stale straight-guy jokes, beating him to the punch line or turning the jokes awry, and four members of the team have an opportunity, with their customary chat and drinks, to view the remodeled set's disclosure and Ted's gourmet spot with Leno on a TV monitor from behind the scenes.

Somewhat like the tanning booth segment with John Verdi but with less good-natured candor, what seems disturbing to Leno, because it motivates so many of his jokes during the makeover, is how intimate contact with these gay guys makes his body vulnerable to anal penetration. Indeed, the makeover edition of the *Tonight Show* begins by explicitly identifying this fear and making it central to the whole enterprise of renovating Leno. On this night, the program forsakes its usual opening credits and begins instead with an imitation of the Fab Five's own series opening. As the team discusses its new mission, making over a famous talk show host, Kyan remarks that Leno is "a spa virgin" and Jai rejoins, "You're going to pop his spa cherry." Whether improvised or scripted, this exchange predetermines how the audience will subsequently view both Leno's discomfort during the shopping and spa montages and his many attempts to go for the easy, homophobic laughs. "I feel like the new guy on his first day in prison," Leno announces as the Fab Five inspect him, a sentiment also included in the teaser for the makeover shown the night before. Kyan's discovery of "a pubic hair" growing out of Leno's ear is just the proverbial tip of the iceberg. Carson insists on doing a "booty check" when Leno tries on pants. Displaying for a whining Leno a broad pinstripe suit (the one he will wear on the show), Carson compares the pattern to racing stripes, which Leno confirms he likes but does not want up his ass. During his hairstyling, Leno complains, "These guys are putting, like, KY Jelly in my hair."

On the two *Tonight Show* appearances by the Fab Five, women are excluded from all phases of the encounter. Without a woman to motivate the makeover and safeguard the straight guy's heterosexuality, the Fab Five's difference as gay men is more homosexualized and shown to be more potentially tempting to a straight guy, though not to Leno of course. On a shopping spree to buy new furniture for the show's set, Jai does a Christina Aguilera impersonation and Thom remarks to the young salesman, "It's kinda scary when he does that. He's so good acting like a woman." Sitting on the floor, the salesman replies, "The scary thing is, it doesn't bother me," so Jai mimes, "call me," drawing a big laugh from the studio audience. While this brief encounter seems daring for the *Tonight Show*, even as it reiterates the stereotype that gay men are at heart women (both are reasons for the laughter), it actually goes far beyond that (the reason I laughed). From the return of looks, we are encouraged to see the straight-looking salesman responding to Jai with homosexual interest, and, what is more, this not so straight guy is neither attracted to nor put off by Jai's effeminacy—rather, it just doesn't bother him. The Winfrey show, on the other hand, places the makeover's value for the straight guys' wives always in the foreground, which keeps queer and straight men at a much safer distance from each other while also sentimentalizing the beneficial results of their interaction, little of which is shown to viewers. The Fab Five

serve as the wives' domesticating surrogates; unable to do the work of civilizing their mates themselves, for whatever reason, these wives, like the women on the series, have to rely on the kindness of queer strangers to clean up the mess.

In contrast to the Fab Five's appearances on the Winfrey and Leno shows, their own camp spectatorship of the straight guy's makeover in the closing segment of each *Queer Eye* episode parodies the hegemony of the straight guy and his mate in order to reverse the inside-outside dichotomy that marginalizes the queer. Even more than their expertise as specialists in fashion, grooming, cooking, decor, and "culture," their camp is the sign that these five men are the true insiders—the savvy cultural observers—as far as the series is concerned. When an episode can develop its edgy camp outlook, as in the John Verdi example, *Queer Eye* skillfully engages both queer and postfeminist viewpoints but also takes care not to make them identical. The series' camp target, after all, is straight masculinity, not femininity; while the Fab Five mockingly introduce straight guys to the domesticating regimes of grooming and housework long associated with femininity, the Fab Five never challenge the validity of such protocols, instead offering women the compensation of laughing at the ineptitude and insecurity of straight men when it comes to performing the social rituals that they have had to master in order to attract the guys in the first place. This camp perspective enables queerness to be visible amid straightness, just as it distinguishes the queer eye from a postfeminist one even though both arc acutely aware of the construction of masculinity and femininity alike through consumption.

As telling of the culture industry's absorption of difference, though, *Queer Eye* has been unable to sustain its camp perspective week after week with any degree of rigor or consistency. The rigid formula of the makeover structure, the budgetary restriction to Manhattan and its outlying boroughs and suburbs, the sameness of the straight guys willing to expose themselves, the necessity for seemingly endless product endorsements on the series, and the Fab Five's own gleeful emersion in popular culture as the latest media darlings all work against the camp humor that made *Queer Eye* seem more queer than one could have expected when it first aired. The Fab Five have gone on to do a music video, star in commercials, and write self-help books; their celebrity keeps their queerness visible and in circulation but homogenizes it as a product—the gay accessory—for lifestyle consumption. As success begets repetition on television, it also breeds boredom, and even camp gets dull and predictable when prepackaged as a commodity in its own right.

Notes

1. In a substantive analysis of *Queer Eye* that appeared after I wrote this essay, Beth Berila and Devika Dibya Choudhuri examine the multiple ways in which, by re-inscribing a white, middle-class bias through effacement or minimalization of racial, sexual, and class hierarchical differences, the series "contains gayness by reducing it to a commodity that services heteronormality" ("Metrosexuality the Middle Class "Way," para. 4). I do not disagree with their careful and lengthy critique, which shares but develops much more fully the concerns of critics noted below; however, I think it is important to place alongside that kind of critique consideration of how the Fab Five's performance of the show's ideological agenda can at times also allow some viewers to see its transparency and laugh at it. Thus, while Berila and Choudhuri note that *Queer Eye* "troubles heteronormality on one level while reinscribing it through the commodification of gayness on the other" (para. 8), I am arguing that the series does not always manage this strategy so easily or readily and specifically that its cultural impact during its first season had much to do with the way episodes were not necessarily reducible to a single, recuperative, and heteronormative viewpoint in the makeover narratives.
2. Dreisinger, "The Queen in Shining Armor," 3.
3. "Survey Finds 'Queer Eye' Affects Shopping," Zapit.com, 4 December 2003.
4. Gallagher, "*Queer Eye* for the Heterosexual Couple," 224.
5. "Piracy, 'Queer' on AFI Timeline," *Hollywood Reporter*, 16 December 2003.
6. During the summer of 2003, a Web search turned up articles reporting on both the positive and negative responses to the series and not only in the dailies of large urban areas. See, for example, Potts, "'Queer Eye' Makes over View of Homosexuals"; and Moon, "'Queer Eye' Opens Window to Gay Life."
7. Gross, "The Queen Is Dead," 64.
8. McCarthy, "Crab People from the Center of the Earth," 99.
9. Gallagher, "*Queer Eye* for the Heterosexual Couple."
10. Dreisinger, "The Queen in Shining Armor," 4.
11. Torres, "Why Can't Johnny Shave?" 96.
12. Gallagher, "*Queer Eye* for the Heterosexual Couple," 223.
13. See Roberts, "The Fashion Police," in this volume [*Interrogating Postfeminism*]. Toby Miller chronicles the 1990s marketing invention of the metrosexual figure in "A Metrosexual Eye on *Queer Guy*."
14. See Cohan, *Masked Men*.
15. Moore, "Here's Looking at You, Kid!" 45.
16. Rothenberg, "Claiborne's Approach to Today's Man."
17. Moore, "Here's Looking at You, Kid!" 55.
18. Ibid., 45.
19. Ibid., 48.
20. Gamson, *Freaks Talk Back*, 201, 203.
21. Sontag, "Notes on Camp"; Ross, "Uses of Camp."
22. Cohan, *Incongruous Entertainment*, 1. The book's introduction elaborates more fully the historical understanding of camp that I am summarizing here (see pp. 1–19). For further discussion of the mainstream appropriation of camp, see pages 208–10.
23. Newton, *Mother Camp*, 105.
24. My point is that, while recognizing the affinities of camp and feminism, I do not want to erase the queer location of camp, which is crucial to understanding how it operates in practice, beginning with its ironic stance toward the regulation of heteronormality. To be sure, camp—in large part when it is solely equated with drag queens and their adoration of female stars—has a history of being read for its hostility to feminism. Camp was repudiated for its apparent misogyny in parodying "women's oppression," reflecting the tension between the feminist and gay rights movements of the 1970s, as Michael Bronski notes in *Culture Clash: The Making of Gay-Sensibility* (205). Camp still bears this dubious status for many feminists. Yet, while certain instances of camp may be misogynistic, camp as a cultural strategy has another history of being quite valuable to feminism and of serving its transition into postfeminism. Although her source in camp is at best implicit, rendered through the extended example of drag, Judith Butler, in *Gender Trouble: Feminism and the Subversion of Identity*, has offered what is perhaps the most influential theorization of gender as a performance of identity through the convergence of camp and feminism. it is worth noting, however, that, even though *Gender Trouble* has become a landmark text for both queer theory and postfeminism, in her new preface to the 1999 edition Butler locates the agenda of her book in feminism, not queer theory, nor does she identify her project as a postfeminist one (rather, she cites its genealogy in poststructuralist French theory). For a different sort of example of how camp has been usefully linked with feminism as a cultural strategy taken up by women, see Robertson,

Guilty Pleasures, though here, too, note the author's need to call what she is analyzing feminist camp in order to point out her paralleling of women's camp strategies and gay men's. From a different perspective, in *Female Masculinity*, Judith Halberstam examines the possibilities of a recent phenomenon, lesbian camp. According to her, masculinity stills tends to rely on tropes that efface its performativity, which resists the predication of camp "on exposing and exploiting the theatricality of gender," so she proposes, as an alternative to "the camp humor of femininity," a new term, *king-drag*, to designate "[lesbian] drag humor associated with masculinity" (237–38). While the enhanced theatricality of femininity has always been an easy target for camp humor and display—hence the long-standing but also somewhat limiting reduction of camp to drag—I think that camp can be sharply attuned to the performative dimensions of masculinity, as *Queer Eye for the Straight Guy* illustrates. But see also my chapter on Gene Kelly's camp masculinity in *Incongruous Entertainment* (149–99).

25. "Queer Eye #108—Law and Disorder: Special Picnic Unit," Posted by "Larry," www.straighteye.com, downloaded 21 March 2004.

26. During the Fab Five's return visit to the *Tonight Show* in November 2003, Leno baited the comedian Colin Quinn in the same way, causing the irritated guest to exclaim, "Jay, I thought it was going to be *me* and *you* against *them*!

References

Berila, Beth, and Devika Dibya Choudhuri. "Metrosexuality the Middle Class Way: Exploring Race, Class and Gender in *Queer Eye for the Straight Guy*." *Genders OnLine Journal* 42 (2005), http://www.genders.org/g42/g42_berila_choudhuri.html.

Bronski, Michael. *Culture Clash: The Making of Gay Sensibility.* Boston: South End Press, 1984.

Butler, Judith. *Gender Trouble: Feminism and the Subversion of Identity.* New York: Routledge, 1999.

Cohan, Steven. *Incongruous Entertainment: Camp, Cultural Value, and the MGM Musical.* Durham: Duke University Press, 2005.

———. *Masked Men: Masculinity and the Movies in the Fifties.* Bloomington: Indiana University Press, 1997.

Dreisinger, Baz. "The Queen in Shining Armor: Safe Eroticism and the Gay Friend." *Journal of Popular Film and Television* 28:1 (spring 2000): 2–11.

Gallagher, Mark. "*Queer Eye* for the Straight (... *Media Studies* 4:2 (2004): 223–26.

Gamson, Joshua. *Freaks Talk Back: Tabloid ... Sexual Nonconformity.* Chicago: Universi... Press, 1998.

Gross, Michael Joseph. "The Queen Is De... *Monthly*, August 2000.

Halberstam, Judith. *Female Masculinity.* Dur... University Press, 1998.

McCarthy, Anna. "Crab People from the Cent... Earth." *GLQ* 11:1 (2005): 99.

Miller, Toby. "A Metrosexual Eye on *Queer Guy*." (... (2005) 112–17.

Moon, Troy. "'Queer Eye' Opens Window to Gay Li... Wins over Straight Crowd, but Not Everyone Se... to Eye." *Pensacola News-Journal*, 14 August 2003.

Moore, Suzanne. "Here's Looking at You, Kid!" In *The ... Gaze: Women as Viewers of Popular Culture*, ed. Lor... Gammon and Margaret Marshment. London: Won... Press, 1988.

Newton, Esther. *Mother Camp: Female Impersonators in A... ica.* Chicago: University of Chicago Press, 1979.

"Piracy, 'Queer' on AFI Timeline," *Hollywood Reporter*, ... December 2003.

Potts, Leanne. "'Queer Eye' Makes over View of Homosex... uals." *Albuquerque Journal*, 12 August 2003.

"Queer Eye #108—Law and Disorder: Special Picnic Unit," Posted by "Larry," www.straighteye.com, downloaded 21 March 2004.

Roberts, Martin. "The Fashion Police: Governing the Self in *What Not to Wear*." In *Interrogating Postfeminism: Gender and the Politics of Popular Culture*, ed. Yvonne Tasker and Diane Negra. Durham: Duke University Press, 2007.

Robertson, Pamela. *Guilty Pleasures: Feminist Camp from Mae West to Madonna.* Durham: Duke University Press, 1996.

Ross, Andrew. "Uses of Camp," In *Camp Grounds: Style and Homosexuality*, ed. David Bergman. Amherst: University of Massachusetts Press, [1988] 1993.

Rothenberg, Randall. "Claiborne's Approach to Today's Men." *New York Times*, 18 August 1989.

Sontag, Susan. "Notes on Camp." In *Camp: Queer Aesthetics and the Performing Subject*, ed. Fabio Cleto. Ann Arbor: University of Michigan Press, [1964] 1999.

"Surveys Finds 'Queer Eye' Affects Shopping," Zapzit.com, 4 December 2003.

Torres, Sasha. "Why Can't Johnny Shave?" *GLQ* 11:1 (2005) 96.

28.
'SLAVES WITH WHITE COLLARS"

Persistent Performances of Masculinity in Crisis
Karen Lee Ashcraft and Lisa A. Flores

The whole generation is womanized; the masculine tone is passing out of the world; it's a feminine, a nervous, hysterical, chattering, canting age,
an age of hollow phrases and false delicacy and
exaggerated solicitudes and coddled sensibilities,
which, if we don't soon look out, will usher in the
reign of mediocrity, of the feeblest and flattest and
the most pretentious that has ever been.

(Basil Ransom, *The Bostonians*, 1886 (qtd. in
Rotundo 252))

I swear it's not a world of men [. . .] It is a world
of clockwatchers, bureaucrats, office holders. It's
a fucked-up world. No adventure in it [. . .] We're
the members of a dying breed.

(Ricky, *Glengarry, Glen Ross*, 1992)

From sitcoms to social movements, commercial
campaigns to scholarship, we are witnessing the
growth of interest in men as men. Increasingly, U.S.
representations of manhood converge on the claim
that masculinity is in the midst of crisis. The rise of
men's movements like the Promise Keepers and
mythopoetic men, not to mention popular television
programs like *The Man Show*, suggest the broad resonance of this crisis narrative and the perceived need
for curative forms of manliness. Though scholars have
begun to examine the alleged crisis (e.g., Horrocks;
Robinson), few have attended to the particular role
of work, and those who have tend to stress working-
class frailties (e.g., Faludi; Fine, Weis, Addelston, and
Maruszsa).

In this essay, we spotlight the performance of
a subjectivity that has drawn little direct discussion. Specifically, we trace an emerging discourse
that offers identity politics to white/collar[1] men. To
focus our analysis of this freshly politicized subjectivity, we explore two illustrative yet distinct film performances: *Fight Club* and *In the Company of Men*. The
discourse that weaves across these texts mourns the
imminent collapse of the corporate man, over-civilized and emasculated by allied obligations to work
and women. To rebuild this haggard creature, the films
(re)turn to what we call a "civilized/primitive" masculinity, embodied by the hardened white man who finds
healing in wounds. This resilient figure obscures the
race and class hierarchy on which it rests by explicitly
appealing to gender division, if not outright misogyny. The current discourse of dominant men in crisis bears conspicuous resemblance to other historical discourses, such as a similar narrative of threatened masculinity in play one century ago. Ultimately,
we argue that this pattern reveals chronic conflicts
embedded in the ongoing performance of white/
collar masculinity and so, potential vulnerabilities in
patriarchal capitalism.

Organizing Masculinity

Research on masculinity has become a truly inter-
disciplinary venture, including feminist analyses that
span rhetorical, historical, psychoanalytic, and sociological perspectives. Below, we clarify our interest in
the meeting of dominant masculinities and labor

identities. We begin by establishing our conception of masculinity and, more specifically, the role of discourse and performance in the social construction of gender. We then narrow our focus to professional masculinity, drawing upon relevant historical and contemporary discourses of gender, labor, and identity to theorize enduring dilemmas that appear to haunt white/collar performances. Our theoretical frame integrates insights gleaned from three principal literatures: masculinity and film studies, feminist and critical organization research, and historical accounts of masculinity rhetoric.

Studying and Defining Men and Masculinity

Scholarly interest in masculinity continues its dramatic rise. A recent proliferation of monographs, anthologies, and journals confirms the development of a diverse body of work that interrogates gender identities and explores how masculine forms relate to patriarchal systems.[2] This research has generated pivotal insights that inform our work. For example, masculinity may be conceptually detached from actual male bodies (Cheng "Men") and broadly defined as "the set of images, values, interests, and activities held important to a successful achievement of male adulthood" (Jeffords *Remasculinization* xii). Masculinity is not a stable or unified phenomenon; its meanings shift over time and in relation to culture, context, and person (Spitzack "Production"). Multiple narratives of manhood abound at once, and the subjectivities and practices they enable engender differential, consequential performances of power and resistance (Corey; Mechling and Mechling; Nakayama "Significance"). More specifically, theories of intersectionality push us to recognize that gender identity is inevitably raced and classed (C. Crenshaw; K. Crenshaw; Dace; Orbe). Thus, talk of "men" and "the masculine"–however generalized–always refers to a type of masculinity (Dines; Eng; Wiegman).

Most masculinity studies coalesce around a concern shared with feminist scholarship: the need to mark masculinity and men as gendered subjects. In particular, scholars challenge the invisibility of dominant masculinities, since all forms of manhood do not enjoy similar privilege. Hence, the term "hegemonic masculinity" has come to capture the socially con-

structed, institutionalized yet shifting form of masculinist identity that systematically dominates femininities and alternative masculinities (Connell "Big Picture" and *Gender*; Donaldson). Ironically, studies of hegemonic masculinity run the risk of re-centering the subject they seek to dismantle: white, heterosexual, middle-class men (Robinson).[3] Not oblivious to such danger, many masculinity scholars assume the risk to shatter illusions of homogenous, indelibly privileged male selves (e.g., Eng; Mumby; Spitzack "Theorizing"). In a similar vein, we stress how popular performances of masculinity offer identity politics to middle-class, heterosexual, white men. Accordingly, we do not directly study men *per se* but rather discourses of dominant masculinity.

Masculinity as Discourse and Performance: Filmic Fragments

By "discourse," we refer to temporarily fixed (i.e., predictable but not determined), coherent (though also conflicted), abstract, and dispersed social narratives about people, objects, and events. Multiple discourses (e.g., of masculinity and race) circulate and intersect at once, although some enjoy greater institutional support, and so, "look" and "feel" more persuasive than others (Hall "Signification" and "The Work"). Discourses generate possible conditions in that they enable ways of seeing, being, and doing (Laclau and Mouffe). In dramaturgical terms, they supply social actors with roles and scripts, with rough guides to public and mundane performances of identity and social relations. Discourses–of gender, for example–come to life and assume concrete form as we perform and thus, affirm or revise the possibilities they offer. In this sense, accomplishing gender necessarily entails performance, whether improvised in the mundane moments of everyday life or memorialized on screen for countless witnesses (Butler; West and Zimmerman).

Appearing in various mediated forms, discourses are dynamic and partial. While we may select various texts (e.g., popular films or literature, interview data) for analysis, we do not presume that any one contains nor completely represents a discourse; rather, apparently discrete texts can be understood as fragments of larger narratives (McGee). Attention to complementary *and* contradictory strands enables a contextual analysis, for texts do not exist in cultural vacuums but become promiscuous players in larger social structures. Although various public texts comprise cultural discourses, we stress popular culture, and specifically, film. Our discursive approach to film highlights vocabularies and ideologies of masculinity, necessarily excluding empirical claims about male behaviors or psyches. This is not to say that we see no connection between filmic and other performances of gender, such as those found in mundane interaction. Rather, we take interest in film performance as it shapes the social imagination, extending invitations to "new" performances of subjectivity in everyday life. In short, we treat film as a meta-performance wherein actors recognized as such articulate gendered possibilities for social actors. We are especially concerned with how film performances both highlight and obscure intersections of masculinity with other facets of identity. This focus reflects our aim to understand how "representational intersectionality" operates in popular performances (K. Crenshaw). In other words, we explore how "symbolic images applied to different race, class, and gender groups interact in maintaining systems of domination and subordination" (Collins 33). When not qualified in political terms, masculinity discourse tends to summon a homogenous, static image that is white, middle-class, and heterosexual (Mandziuk).

Guiding our venture is a considerable body of work on gender and film.[4] In particular, some feminist film scholars criticize a tendency to take masculinity as given, thereby perpetuating the notion that it is a fixed entity occupying the space of privilege (e.g., Cohan and Hark; Wiegman). In an effort to rupture its silence and normativity, these authors investigate performances of masculinity in film, targeting race, class, and sexuality as central poles around which masculinities converge and diverge (e.g., Beavers; Dyer *White*; Jeffords *Hard*; Tasker "Fists"). Not surprisingly, this work extends the larger interest in hegemonic masculinity, demonstrating the flexibility with which it co-opts discourses of race, class, and sexuality without deposing its white, heterosexual, and middle-class footing.[5]

To complicate masculinity, some film scholars have turned to the male body, observing contrasting

bodily depictions and their relationship to dominant and subordinated identities.[6] This work has uncovered the centrality of hard bodies to hegemonic masculinity (e.g., Jeffords *Hard*; Tasker *Spectacular*, and S. Willis). Additionally, it indicates visual pleasures available through voyeuristic attention to the male body and heterosexual anxieties aroused by male-on-male gazing.[7]

Masculinities That Work

The masculinity and film literature yields crucial insights, but a key question remains understudied: How do forms of labor facilitate distinctive masculine performances? Certainly, film scholars acknowledge the importance of work to masculinity. Yet they tend to stress a limited range of working (class) subjects, as evident in their extensive attention to action films featuring soldiers and police officers. While Jeffords provides a convincing chronicle of the reign of hard-body masculinity in the 1980s, she does not address connections with professional identity (*Hard*). Similarly, Robinson's provocative account of white male crisis rhetoric concentrates elsewhere, though the book's cover figures a white businessman, briefcase and cell phone in tow. Such cursory attention to labor, much less the professions, is striking, particularly given professed scholarly interest in the meeting of masculinities and class. Moreover, work has anchored U.S. white, middle-class manhood since the early 19th century (Rotundo; Trujillo).

Organizational scholars are poised to provide the most nuanced treatment of masculinity and work. Though they have begun to do so, the majority of gendered organization research addresses the professional dilemmas of white, middle-class women.[8] This work guides us to the import of two historical formations: the discourse of separate spheres (i.e., public and private) and the discourse of gender difference (i.e., masculine and feminine as complementary opposites).[9] Still today, these notions intersect in a manner so familiar as to barely necessitate review. The public realm is commonly seen as the legitimate site of production and politics, the more "natural" turf of men/masculinity. Divorced from "real" labor, the private sphere is linked to intimacy, sexuality, reproduction, emotion, and domestic concerns, deemed the expertise of women/femininity (Martin; Mills and Chiaramonte). Feminist scholars compellingly contend that the discourses of public-private and gender difference come together to naturalize workplace control and exclusion of femininities (Acker).

While these accounts enhance our understanding of some women's subordination, they also neglect a different consequence of the same discursive union. Namely, some men are expected to travel competently across spheres, although the masculine is aligned with only one. As the spheres are thought to entail opposing demands and habits, white masculine subjectivity bears a sort of schizophrenia or double bind. Consequently, many men may struggle to negotiate selves that work in public and private. Recent scholarship indicates another layer of the paradox: expectations for civilized *and* primitive male selves in public *and* private arenas (Bordo; Robinson; Rotundo). At least in the U.S., the civilized-primitive dualism evokes slippery evolutionary images of man-savage-animal, tinged with racial hierarchy (Bederman). Though diluted, such racist meanings hang on the tips of our tongues, and the dualism still serves as a powerful way to (racially) mark approaches to violence and sexuality (e.g., primitive release, civilized restraint) (Orbe; Sloop). Moreover, the dualism remains one of the primary ways we distinguish types of work (e.g., manual or mental labor), suggesting that constructions of class are also deeply raced.

Forms of public labor have long been coded in terms of how they blend masculinity with the primitive-civilized. For example, organizational scholars have begun to explore how blue-collar labor produces a primitive masculinity replete with images of raw physicality–hard, hands-on work performed by dirty, sweaty bodies (e.g., Collinson; Gibson and Papa; P. Willis). Accordingly, working-class subjects enjoy (suffer?) closer ties to primal, near-bestial savagery and sexuality (Gherardi). Such coding will likely shape the way in which masculinity dilemmas manifest themselves. For example, primitive blue-collar masculinity can dominate the "soft" private and even "soften" (i.e., feminize, make impotent) its white-collar superiors. Simultaneously, it is prone to charges of being uncivilized, which depict working-class men as dumb, juvenile, or overgrown brutes.

Since white-collar labor leans toward the civilized pole, we might expect scholars to find mirror-image vulnerabilities. To the contrary, the burgeoning literature on managerial masculinity implies that corporate life furnishes a persistent, resilient home for white male dominance, despite dramatic changes in capitalism and the organization of work.[10] Like film theorists, then, organization scholars tend to presume intact the uniform, enduring, and seamless reign of businessmen. In addition, they have scarcely begun to address race (Ashcraft and Allen; Nkomo). We seek to redress these oversights by problematizing the performance of white/collar masculinity.

Professional Masculinity: Voices of Crisis from the Turn of the Centuries

As we hinted above, white/collar masculinity is susceptible to feminization, given its reputed lack of physicality and bureaucratic sterility, suppression of the body, self-imposed discipline, and obligatory ingratiation. Perhaps tellingly, professional discourses summon the primitive and civilized at once. Consider this dizzying array of business imagery: the corporate jungle, the rational actor, unbridled competition and aggression, self-discipline and impulse-control, intellectual (i.e., "clean") labor, dog-eat-dog world. We argue that white/collar masculinity straddles both primitive and civilized poles; to overstress one is to risk failure at the other and, therefore, to render masculinity, professionalism, or whiteness suspect. In this sense, a chronic anxiety plagues professional identity, as it is no simple feat to perform hard and soft, primitive and civilized at once, especially given their varying depiction as unequal opposites. For help in this thorny endeavor, white/collar masculinity depends on affiliation with other gender, race, and class discourses. For instance, it can appeal to images of dark savagery or working-class men as powerfully primal *and* subordinate (i.e., professional minds dominate primitive bodies). At times, it can affiliate with white women, who become a taming force that nurtures the advancement of civilization. Upon inspection, each alliance sparks its own vulnerabilities. For example, if civilization is emphasized and associated with whiteness, white women can stake a claim to equality; if an essential male primitive is stressed, men of color and diverse class can do so. How can professional masculinity draw on these discourses without undermining itself? How can white/collar masculinity retain its race, class, and gender dominance all at once? How are these tensions discursively and performatively managed? Or perhaps first, how *were* they managed?

From Civilized Restraint to Primitive Passions: Turning the Last Century

This is not the first time that public representations of dominant masculinity in crisis have circulated in the U.S. For example, a similar surge of crisis discourse surfaced around the turn of the last century. That wave is worth reviewing not only due to arresting parallels, but because "our lives a century later are still bound by this reshaping of manhood" (Rotundo 222). Attention to historical context can expose the political economies that give rise to particular gendered discourses—or, put with different emphasis, the political and material circumstances that such discourses struggle to manage.

Rotundo identifies a change in hegemonic masculinity between the 18th and 19th centuries: from a communal manhood based on moral community obligations to a self-made manhood proven by individual work achievement. In the late 19th century, the notion of masculinity in crisis swept the country. The principal fear was that men, especially white professionals, were overcivilized to the point of impending extinction. Two key changes in capitalist labor arrangements lay at the core of the crisis narrative: (a) the increasingly bureaucratic nature of work minimized opportunities for entrepreneurial achievement, trading independence for subordination to other men; and (b) women began to infringe on the public sphere (Bederman; Rotundo). Among other ways, the crisis narrative materialized in a medical discourse of "neurasthenia," a nervous disorder thought to result from overcivilization and, specifically, too much mentally stimulating work. The U.S. saw an outbreak of male neurasthenia diagnoses between 1880 and 1910, and those deemed at greatest risk "were middle- and upper-class businessmen and professionals whose highly evolved bodies had been physically weakened by advances in civilization" (Bederman 87). Widespread worry about

the alleged disease flagged a puzzling paradox: "Only white male bodies had the capacity to be truly civilized. Yet, at the same time, civilization destroyed white male bodies. How could powerful, civilized manhood be saved?" (Bederman 88).

In response to the crisis narrative, public discourse of the time embraced "natural" male passions long disciplined out of white men. As Bordo summarizes, "fantasies of recovering an unspoiled, primitive masculinity began to emerge, and with them, a 'flood of animal metaphors' poured forth to animate a new conception of masculinity. White men drew on the images and ideology of the savage Other to help them articulate this emerging construction of 'passionate manhood'" (249). In the new subjectivity, "savages and animals fade together," as "middle-class men [. . .] were drawn to both groups for the same qualities" (Rotundo 229). What became of white civilized professionalism amid this turn to the primitive? Bederman argues that, rather than discursive division or death, it allied with the primitive, joining contradictory notions of manhood with "'civilization's larger narrative of millennial advancement toward a higher race and perfect manhood" (218). But white/collar man's anxiety would persist, for his was a conflicted and contestable right to the primitive.

Modern Man's Neurasthenia? Contemporary Cries of Crisis

Recently, abundant public and scholarly discourse has converged on another so-called masculinity crisis (Faludi; Horrocks; Robinson). Those who trace it to work stress the fragility of working-class identities, weakened by economic and social conditions (e.g., Fine et al.). We tease out a strand of discourse that has garnered less attention. Specifically, we argue that public performances of white/collar masculinity in crisis are gaining momentum and bear startling resemblance to themes from the last turn of the century. Consider the rash of recent films that portray mounting tension between professional men and work: *Falling Down* (1989); *Glengarry, Glen Ross* (1992); *Disclosure* (1994); *Wolf* (1994); *In the Company of Men* (1997); *Office Space* (1999); *American Beauty* (1999); *Fight Club* (1999); *The Big Kahuna* (2000); and *Boiler Room* (2000)—to name a few. In contrast to the usual films featuring men at work, this trend suggests that corporations amount to an increasingly inadequate stage that stifles and emasculates the performance of white/collar masculinity. Evidence suggests some similarities to the early 20th century, even a familiar yearning for the primitive. Bordo details how "today, with many men feeling that women–particularly feminists–have been pushing them around for a couple of decades, the idea of a return to manhood 'in the raw' has a fresh, contemporary appeal" (251).

Across most current scholarship, then, the hegemony of white/collar masculinity appears relatively smooth, even when marked. Despite growing testament to the ambiguities of masculinity, we continue to neglect how even the most dominant forms require relentless maintenance. This gap becomes pressing in an age of patriarchal and managerial capitalism, for which the professional subject is a central character (Deetz and Mumby). The dearth of attention to white/collar dilemmas also contributes to the continued invisibility of multiple intersections in masculinity. Accordingly, we highlight how professional masculinity depends upon discourses of race, class, sexuality, and labor.

Healing Wounds: Violence and the Civilized/Primitive

To interrogate white/collar masculinity, we selected two films that shoulder its tensions and manage them in seemingly contradictory ways: *In the Company of Men*, a critically acclaimed independent film, and *Fight Club*, a Hollywood blockbuster based on the best-selling novel of the same name. Two questions organize our analysis: How do the films stage the masculinity crisis, and what performances bring comfort and resolution?

The Wounds of the White/Collar Man

As soon as we meet them, the men of both films inform us that something has gone wrong. Women and work are at varying degrees of fault, and the situation is dire. Below, we trace how the films convey the professional man's breaking point, and we identify common themes of crisis.

In the Company of Men

This film follows the lives of two corporate men on a six-week assignment at a non-specific company in Anytown, USA. In the opening scenes, we meet the two central characters, clad in standard business attire and waiting in an airport courtesy lounge. Howard– a glaringly insecure, sulky man recently promoted to manage the project–marvels that he has just been slapped by a woman from whom he simply asked the time. Chad Piercewell, an attractive and swaggering figure, is Howard's old college friend and new underling. For Chad, the slap epitomizes the sorry state of businessmen's lives. In the airport, on the plane, and in a restaurant at their destination, the two men proceed to mourn the "doom" they face "as a race–men like us, guys who care a smidgen about the workplace, their women." They trade tales of abandonment and rejection by the women in their lives, interspersed with cautionary words about vile colleagues and maddening corporate politics. Howard observes that "everything– work, these women–feel like they're getting out of balance, don't they?" Chad concurs, "Yeah, they really do, Howard [. . .] We ought to do something about it." Soon after, Chad professes the urgency of the situation: "Circle the date on this one, big guy. If we keep playing along with this pick-up-the-check, can't-a-girl-change-her mind crap–we can't even tell a joke in the workplace–there's gonna be hell to pay down the line, no doubt about it. We need to put our foot down pronto." Despite Howard's formal rank, Chad immediately surfaces as the alpha male. He almost single-handedly articulates the crisis and aggressively solicits Howard's help in addressing it. Howard meekly assents, interjecting the occasional "I hear ya."

It is thus in the first few minutes of the film that work and women are linked together as the cause of professional men's impending downfall. In brief, women expect men's sensitivity in romantic and work relationships, as well as their financial support. Yet women offer nothing but ingratitude and abuse in return. Men give and give, while women bite the hand that feeds them. What's more, corporations have become a sterilized den of thieves, thanks in part to women's invasion and a merciless corporate elite. Women control us; corporations consume us; and if this continues, the common businessman will soon be extinct. The situation demands immediate action. And–make no mistake–that action is a noble struggle to reclaim something lost, to restore a rightful order.

Fight Club

This film begins at its end. The two main characters, a nameless narrator and Tyler Durden, are engaged in a conversation laden with tense expectancy. Immediately, the intimacy between the two is apparent, as are the profound differences that divide them. The narrator sits small and tentative, curiously un/dressed in his boxer shorts. Tyler stands in a pose that exudes militaristic power; and in his sleeveless tight shirt and low-slung camouflage pants, he vibrates with a sexual intensity enhanced by his hardened body and muscled arms.

In flashback style, the narrator takes us back to a time when he was a numbed shell of a man. Corporate servitude engulfs him. He is locked in a sterile, white/collar world where mere imitations of life abound: "Everything's a copy of a copy of a copy." Bureaucratic objectification and meaningless existence emerge in techno-jargon, as he dully asks his boss: "You want me to deprioritize my current reports until you advise of a status upgrade?" Corporate control threatens complete takeover; even scientific dreams of space exploration can only produce "the IBM stellarsphere, the Microsoft Galaxy, Planet Starbucks." Service to the company enables a second crippling factor: an obsession with material perfection as defined by corporate gods. This all-encompassing materialism sucks men into illusions of identity. Wondering what "kind of dining set defines me as a person," the narrator seeks to create the perfect home, an absolute replica of a catalog image. Consumed by consumption, young businessmen are, in Tyler's words, "by-products of a lifestyle obsession" who occupy ornamental bodies and spaces (Bordo; Faludi).

Part of a "generation raised by women," Tyler and the narrator suffer from the absence of men in their lives. They are children of divorce–of fathers who abandoned them to "franchise" new lives and families. They are victims of fathers' false promises about careers, marriage, and social responsibility. Even God, the ultimate father, is absent and uncaring. A sense of utter disposability and despondency floods their expe-

rience. Nobody's heroes, they enjoy no great moment in history, for the noble wars of the past belong to other men. As Tyler later proclaims, "Our great war is a spiritual war [. . .] Our great depression is our lives." These young men are not simply denied access to the masculine; they are invaded by femininity on all sides. Early in the film, the narrator frames his tale around women: "I realized that all of this [. . .] had something to do with a girl named Marla Singer." Beyond the physical presence of women, the feminine threatens to overtake. We witness the narrator battle his insomniac stupor with feminized tools, including "Martha Stewart" materialism, sleeping pills, meditation, and therapeutic retreats to his "inner cave." Weak and impotent, he finds temporary relief in a new addiction, support groups. During his first attendance–to a testicular cancer group called "Remaining men together"–he meets Bob, a one-time body-building champion now literally castrated. Nestled between Bob's "bitch tits," the narrator finds release through sobbing, temporarily curing his insomnia. The threat of the feminine emerges further in the form of Marla, another "tourist" on the therapy circuit. Her presence at the support groups disrupts the narrator's relief, plunging him back into insomnia and desperation.

In short, *Fight Club* codes the corporate world and all its trappings–bureaucratic sedation, materialism, isolation, deception, and the crushing presence of things feminine–as a force that kills men. Tyler captures this subordination when he asks, "Now, why do guys like you and I know what a duvet is? Is this essential to our survival in the hunter-gatherer sense of the word?" As Tyler explains, young men have become "slaves with white collars," stuck in "jobs we hate, so we can buy shit we don't need." They must mobilize and fight to regain control, if not life.

Producing the Wounded Corporate Figure

Despite different takes on whether corporations are conducive to masculinity, the white/collar men of both films are united by their search for more dignified, satisfying identities, if not outright revenge. They share a keen sense that work and women are not as they once were. Jobs are more competitive; corporate environments are increasingly cruel and hygienic; and the possibility of a secure future looms ever distant and unsatisfying. Women bear the blame for many of these changes, and their intrusions and orders have become unbearable. Specifically, women have feminized and disabled men with conflicting demands for emotional, financial, and political support and sensitive, over-civilized behavior. To make matters worse, "woman" is the ultimate source of men's corporate bondage; it is largely because of her that men subject themselves to the whims and abuses of an elusive, all-powerful, corporate elite. It is no longer tolerable that her insidious presence grows with her confusing list of demands. In theoretical terms, she is unraveling an ambivalent web of dominance, duty, and resentment that has long sutured relations between white, middle-class masculinity and femininity (Lyman; Rotundo). Or, as film critic Hershenson puts it, "the old roles continue to crumble" and "you're pretty much on your own, buddy" (par. 3).

Given this discourse of wounded businessmen, it is not surprising that the central characters of each film define their quest as resistance to an oppression that, as one film critic noted, is "worth rising up against" (Smith par. 2). They do not experience the crisis in their lives as a disruption of male privilege that might facilitate more inclusive social relations. On the contrary, they perceive it as injustice and violence—a thing expected but denied, a promise wrongly snatched away (Hearn "Organization"; Linstead). In this way, men's collective corporate dominance becomes eclipsed by the individual man's personal experience of powerlessness (Hamada; Horrocks).

As to what must be done, the characters concur on a few points. First, any "new manhood" premised on men's exploration and development of the traditionally feminine is grossly insufficient. They fear their status as drained, cloned, impotent "yes men" who perform meaningless work at others' bidding. They mourn the passing of an age when work was a world of adventurous, virile men. As one critic of *Fight Club* remarked, "Nice is over and hard is where it's at" (Watson par. 2). Second, they believe their load is too heavy, and something must give. Chad takes a first step to freedom when he lets go of caring: "You know why I'm still chipper? Big grin on my face, Howie? . . . Because I realized something [. . .] I do not give a shit, not about anybody." Meanwhile, Tyler liberates the narrator from the promise of corporate success, the

throes of materialism, and all debilitating fears, goading him to hit bottom: "It's only after we've lost everything that we're free to do anything." Both films imply that if one rejects the rules of the current game, he becomes free to write, play, and win his own game. However, this requires a radical switch from a passive to an active approach to life. Chad announces, "Life is for the taking, is it not?"

At the end of the day, a man who continues to obey the rules will be an impotent, feminized bureaucrat who has sold his soul to borrow the power of others. It is in imaginative, daring manipulation of the rules or bold, outright rebellion that a real man can be made. Next, we trace two disparate paths toward healing the wounded white/collar man. While *In the Company of Men* depicts a professional jungle ruled by the sadistic warrior, *Fight Club* nurtures a corps of masochistic soldiers who burn that jungle to the ground.

Business as Sadistic Sport

In the Company of Men As Chad and Howard sip scotch and commiserate over their crisis, Chad devises a "refreshing" and "very therapeutic" scheme to "fuck somebody up for good" and "restore a little dignity to our lives":

> Say we were to find some gal [. . .] just vulnerable as hell [. . .] disfigured in some way [. . .] just some woman who is pretty sure that life—and I mean a full, healthy sexual life, romance, stuff like that—is just lost to her forever. Anyhow, we take a girl of that type [. . .] and we both hit her. You know, small talk, a dinner date, flowers [. . .] see an ice show, something like that. And we just do it, you know, you and me, upping the ante all the time. And suddenly she's got two men; she's calling her mom; she's wearing makeup again. And on we play and on and on. Then one day, out goes the rug and us pulling it hard. And Jill? She just comes tumbling after [. . .] Trust me, she'll be reaching for the sleeping pills within a week, and we will laugh about this 'til we are very old men.

Though initially hesitant, Howard consents by the end of the evening like a kid caving to peer pressure. Soon after, Chad meets Christine, a young deaf woman employed in the company's typing pool. Given her evident vulnerabilities, Chad concludes that she's a perfect target and takes her out. Goaded by Chad, Howard agrees to court her as well. The rest of the film follows Chad and Howard's pursuit of two shared and parallel projects: they work, date Christine, and swap stories about both. Before long, it becomes clear that the twin projects are proceeding differently. Howard develops what he sees as genuine feelings for Christine, while Christine falls for Chad. Even worse, Howard's first management assignment unravels; he and Chad discuss faulty reports and other mishaps that perturb the guys at the home office. Ultimately, Christine rejects Howard, proclaiming her love for Chad, and Howard is demoted from his management position. Chad callously discards a devastated Christine, returning home to a promotion and his live-in girlfriend. Despite his cruel cons in business and romance, Chad's world only improves. Despite Howard's tireless efforts to be "the good guy" (at least in his eyes), his world collapses. The film concludes with a smug and smirking Chad, enjoying his lover's services, juxtaposed against a pathetically collapsing Howard, whose strident screams—"Listen to me . . . Listen, listen, listen!"–fall on Christine's deaf ears.

What can we learn about healing white/collar masculinity from such a disturbing tale? We begin by elucidating the film's depiction of dominant and subordinate, potent and impotent, masculinities. Chad's character reveals that performing victory over and at the expense of opponents is the core passion and proof of manliness. Any man is entitled to compete, but only those with "big, brass ones" can win. Climbing the corporate hierarchy is the only game that counts, and all other contests are mere training for the ultimate competition among men. So how does a man win the all-important sport of business, thereby earning and flaunting his superior balls?

From the striking contrast between Chad and Howard, we learn that a potent man carefully and constantly hones specific aptitudes. Chief among these is a fundamental suspicion of everyone. Throughout, Chad cautions Howard to expect betrayal–to "watch your back," "cover your ass," to "be careful" of this "bunch of vultures" hovering to "feed on my insides"– citing various company men to build his case for an ever-vigilant, always-defensive ethos. Chad's paranoia

does not discriminate; he warns that one should be especially wary of the company of women, who are all made of "meat and gristle and hatred just simmering." Women lie in wait to ambush men, and they'll "kick you straight in the teeth" just "when you start to feel sorry" for them.

A basic distrust and disgust for humanity calls for a second key aptitude: ruthless, unflinching, impenitent violence toward others. To sustain his startling ability to "not give a shit," Chad objectifies the targets of his violence. When presented with personalizing details about someone, Chad routinely dismisses or ignores the information. For example, when a co-worker cagily observes that Christine is a "nice girl [. . .] types like 95 a minute [. . .] she's kind of pretty," Chad rises to leave and retorts, "Anyway, see you later," in the shrill, dolphin-like tone with which he imitates Christine's voice. Chad paints all people as useless caricatures, pure enemies to be decimated, disposable things. Frequently, he whets and validates his paranoia, rehearsing the dehumanization of possible targets. In one scene, for instance, with co-workers, he reviews colleagues depicted in a company newsletter: "I hate this guy. Oh, I hate that guy too. He's a little bastard [. . .] Oh, I hate that dude right there [. . .] one of those from Pittsburgh. Oh, he sucks dick [. . .] Oh man, I despise that dude. Sales rep from Indiana [. . .] Now, he's a new breed of fuck, like a special strain of fucker. Oh, I hate that little prissy cocksucker." Importantly, a wary and violent stance is more than a necessary survival strategy for the corporate winner; it is his primary source of pleasure. Chad's newsletter review is far more than an angry, vicious outburst. It is playful, cunning, and hilarious; and he joyously savors the moment. Likewise, with a twisted smile, Chad eagerly asks his various victims "So how does it feel?" and relishes their palpable shock and pain. In this sense, the vigilant violence practiced by the corporate victor is profoundly sadistic.

Thus far, the corporation is characterized as a specific sort of jungle; it's a kill-or-be-killed, every-man-for-himself world in which only the strongest survive. Accordingly, a successful businessman sees himself as perpetually wounded and all others as the possible cause. For white masculinity, "the threat of castration is everywhere present and everywhere hidden" (Holmlund 153). For this reason, the corporate jungle entails guerilla warfare, which real men enjoy. Success under these conditions requires a third aptitude: relentless self-interest, often cloaked as partnership. That is, a man must be politically savvy enough to know when his interests can be served by temporary alliance with others. Such coalitions require a form of hypocrisy: the effective performance of feelings one does not allow himself to actually experience. Chad brilliantly executes this feat with Christine and Howard, who respectively mistake him for a sincere lover and friend. Chad further displays his charlatan skills in the newsletter scene described above. When his amused and admiring co-workers ask if he likes a colleague who just left the room (and with whom he had just exchanged pleasant conversation), he casually responds, "Him? You kiddin' me? I hate that prick." Throughout the film, Chad's capacity for persuasive kindness followed by swift malice goes unrivaled. As he observes to his girlfriend at the end of the film, "When I get working, I can sound like practically anyone." Conversely, one of Howard's key frailties becomes his inability to discern performance from authenticity. With both Chad and Christine, he confuses instrumental alliance with meaningful relationship and, worse yet, falls prey to his own feeble performances.

Victory amid corporate guerilla warfare requires an additional aptitude for constant and stringent control of self and others. In Chad's words, "Never lose control [. . .] that is the total key to the universe." As indicated above, a man of suspicion and sadism keeps a tight reign on the emotions he feels, much less publicly displays. He also disciplines his body such that, ironically, it appears to require no control. For example, Chad limits himself to more refined forms of violence: clever verbal attacks, never physical brawls. He wears the corporate uniform with comfort and confidence, head and shoulders erect, body rarely prone. In striking contrast, Howard's body appears in endless disarray. We watch him eat, defecate, and vomit; and these bodily functions seem exceptionally awkward and time-consuming, akin to a "leaking" feminized body (Trethewey). Moreover, we see and hear that Howard stoops to physical scraps with women, which create a visual effect more akin to a "catfight" than domestic violence. And while assertive Chad grabs every opportunity to seize an upper

hand, bumbling Howard tends to babble on toward embarrassment.

Finally, a man who would win the corporate game never retreats to the petty comforts found in the company of boys. In the film, corporate losers are synonymous with boys. Two characters vividly occupy this position and expose the perils of a boy's world. The most prominent is Howard, tellingly referred to as "Howie" by Chad. We listen to Howie vie for freedom from his mother and ex-fiancé; we then watch him brace for similar bondage when he recycles an old engagement ring and shops for china with Christine in mind. The second character is a Black intern, who appears in a brief and poignant scene discussed later. For now, it is sufficient to note that Chad assails the intern group as a "bunch of juvenile fuckers" who mistake work for "summer camp" and "still want their mommies wiping their bottoms every time they go potty." Hence, a boy's world is suspect because it is subject to domineering women and because its members are too infantile and negligent to comprehend the rules that distinguish life in the company of men.

In sum, a man who is susceptible to human trust and care, whose conscience impedes violent pleasures, who cannot uphold the masquerade, and who lacks control of himself and others is a despicable figure–a corporate loser, a soft boy. Howie embodies this pitifully impotent creature. By the film's conclusion, he loses more than his managerial voice and metaphorical balls to a virile corporate warrior; he is literally rendered silent by a gullible, feminine "handicap" who dared to claim the right to choose among suitors. Whereas *In the Company of Men* marks the corporate world as the space in which real masculinity can emerge, the players of *Fight Club* treat corporations as the very site that tames, emasculates, and so, must be destroyed.

Masochism: To Wage War Against the Corporation—Fight Club

Over beers at a local dive, Tyler reframes the recent explosion of the narrator's condo and possessions. The loss is opportunity, not tragedy: "I say never be complete [. . .] I say let's evolve." Devoid of the material goods he so desperately sought, the narrator should see the demolition as freedom. Intrigued but skeptical, he wavers, unable to let go of his perfectly dissatisfying life.

Emerging from the bar, Tyler invites the narrator to hit him. With that first hesitant punch, they launch "Fight Club," an underground club "for men only" in which pairs of men brawl to the cheers of on-lookers, gladiator-style. Its exponential national growth attests to its resonance, and men everywhere are drawn to it as a site that exposes and celebrates men's wounds. Eventually, Fight Club evolves into war, and Project Mayhem—a militaristic venture in which Tyler and his all-male corps fight the corporate enemy—is born. Meanwhile, we witness the narrator's increasing attraction to Tyler and his jealousy over Tyler's relationships with others, including Marla. We also see the narrator's growth, from slumping to swaggering, as well as his moral struggle with Tyler's boyish and reckless approach to life. The film climaxes when we learn, with the narrator, that he and Tyler are literally the same person. In his desperate attempt to escape his sedated life, the narrator created a persona embodying all he is not. With this split personality, the narrator and Tyler manifest the classic double bind of masculinity (Bordo; Robinson; Rotundo). As the film ends, the narrator attempts to heal himself, ironically by killing Tyler and turning to Marla.

The narrator and Tyler's youthful approach to healing includes various escapades into mischief and malice. Defining manhood as boyish rebellion, the film promotes a visceral manliness in which men strip their corporate attire and (re)turn to a primitive age filled with physical contests. Adventure replaces work, and pranks expose social niceties. The antithesis of masculinity is the man afraid to fight, controlled by social demands rather than raw instinct. Such men are mindless robots.

An initial step toward men's "evolution" entails rejection of materialism and conspicuous consumption. If, as Tyler believes, "the things you own end up owning you," then a simplistic life devoid of "things" enables growth. Violent and complete separation is necessary, and Tyler models a life free from senseless spending. Suddenly homeless, the narrator moves in with Tyler. Living in a dilapidated house, filled with bare, stained mattresses and rust-red water, Tyler and the narrator cut themselves off from the mate-

rial world. This lifestyle frees them from the hold of image-based masculinity promoted by the likes of Gucci and Calvin Klein. Tyler helps the narrator as well as the men of Fight Club and Project Mayhem see that "You are not your job, you're not how much money you have in the bank, you're not the car you drive, you're not the contents of your wallet, you're not your–*fucking–khakis.*"

Evolution requires this brutal honesty to expose and reject the lies of fathers. Ultimately, men must uncover social myths and fabrications about masculinity. Tyler forces men to hear the truth: "We've all been raised on television to believe that one day we'd all be millionaires and movie gods and rock stars, but we won't. And we're slowly learning that fact, and we're very, very pissed off." Reveling in their anger at this betrayal, the men of Fight Club and Project Mayhem join Tyler in sharing these difficult lessons. Tyler's chant–"You are not special; you are not a unique or beautiful snowflake"–becomes a lesson shared among the soldiers of Project Mayhem. Only upon learning these truths can men sever the ties that enslave them and unleash their stifled selves. A primary arena for such enlightenment is Fight Club.

Prior to joining Fight Club, members are living lies, performing a fraudulent masculinity akin to femininity. This emasculating masquerade emerges in the narrator's early addiction to therapy groups, where he finds life by mimicking disability and impending death. A phony pretending to be wounded, the narrator craves the pain he witnesses in others. Tyler provides the cure in Fight Club. In brutal, bloody fights, the narrator learns to feel and wear pain with pride. Unlike the "bitch tits" that prove Bob's pain, the bruises, scars, and blood the narrator sports stand as virile wounds. A far cry from the zombie-like plod that plagued his early life, he is soon strutting down the street, parading ugly bruises and utter disregard for social decorum, openly scoffing at colleagues obsessed with corporate efficiency and whether they can "get the icon in cornflower blue." In stark contrast to stuffed-shirt corporate conformity, the narrator becomes deliberately disheveled, shirt untucked and tie askew. Rather than acquiescing, the narrator flaunts disrespect, finally bullying his boss. He reflects on his own behavior, "I used to be such a nice guy."

Fight Club adds more than fleeting bruises and scars; it engenders a ritualistic and masochistic fascination with pain (Robinson). Violence is a stimulating addiction. The narrator and Tyler bask in its glow, pushing the body to its ultimate limits. We witness Tyler pour lye onto the narrator's hand and hold him still until he can relish the exquisite pain. We watch Tyler viciously beaten, begging for more with orgasmic overtures: "That's right Lou, get it out [. . .] ooh yeeaah [. . .] oooh Loouu." Why this masochism? Burned and beaten, the narrator learns the limits of his body and uncovers new strength. Even as he hits bottom, he is not defeated, evincing a warrior-like mentality in which he refuses to die. Parallels to Schwarzenegger's and Stallone's hard-body, action-adventure masculinity, in which wounds are redemptive, are compelling (Jeffords *Hard*). As Savran maintains, white masculinity has developed a pain fixation, "torturing himself to prove his masculinity" (par. 4).

Importantly, Fight Club and Project Mayhem enable the creation of male bonds and intimacies, advancing evolution by recentering men in men's lives. Joy emerges among the men as they roll around, punching, beating, touching each other. As victims, they forge bonds in their shared identity. Victor and defeated embrace, anticipating their next encounter. These ties that bind prepare men to engage battle and defeat the corporate enemy. And Project Mayhem provides the site. A sort of boot-camp, Project Mayhem spawns an army of soldiers—young men with shaved heads and black uniforms who destroy corporate art and coffee franchises, who start fires in corporate buildings, who infiltrate local businesses. That war must be declared and corporations defeated is more than metaphor. Project Mayhem becomes a tightly organized, minutely planned operation (ironically, bureaucratic in structure). It allows neither weakness nor vulnerability; it accepts neither tears nor regret over casualties; it admits no diversions to its ultimate goal—destruction of the corporate enemy and liberation of its subjects. Men and masculinity will not be under siege.

Haunting the narrator throughout much of this war is the (feminine) fear of uncontrolled excessive masculinity. While the lure of the hard body is desirable and the moral quest to regain it important, the rebellious mentality of Tyler is often frightening and intense. Ultimately, the narrator knows that the wild boy must be contained, and thus the film concludes with the narrator's recognition of and gratitude for the lessons learned. With this realization, he destroys Tyler.

For Chad, Tyler, and his narrator apprentice, sadistic or masochistic violence awakens a businessman's taste for virility and pleasure. Next, we consider how these complementary tales of hegemonic masculinity—one that dominates, one that resists the corporation—respond to the contemporary discourse of crisis.

Across the Films: Traces and Implications of the "New" Professional

Modern Neurasthenia: Managing Masculine Double Binds

The films do not simply cure modern neurasthenia tensions; rather, they relish a perpetual sense of anxiety and unrest. First, neither film articulates the reconciliation of men's public and private selves. *In the Company of Men* marks the private as indulgent excess—a source of softening or weakening that disables a man's paranoid violence. For instance, Howard is ultimately ruined by myriad vulnerabilities to private virtues (e.g., morality, love), regulating figures, (e.g., mothers, fiancés), and bodily leaks. Trifling with the private stunts his capacity for sadism and renders him an incompetent manager—of his work, his ties to women, and even his own body. He caves and confesses the plot against Christine when he smells defeat and, ostensibly, when he begins to care for her. It is no coincidence that these sensations develop simultaneously. In a Chad-like logic, Howard is foolish enough to seek solace and healing in private relationships, or at least in their public markers. Thus, in the face of corporate loss and an increasingly shaky friendship with Chad, he is frantic to possess romance and prove some semblance of virility. Chad designed the game with this in mind, for he enticed Howard with assurances that "no matter what happens after [. . .] jumped over for promotions, wife runs off with some biochemist [. . .] we would always have this thing to fall back on. Could always say, 'Yeah fine. But they never got me like we got her.'" In this light, even if Howard could win Christine, it would prove a hollow victory. For in the company of real men, the private realm we know is dead, resurrected in the image and service of the corporate jungle.

Fight Club offers another way to maneuver. Neurasthenic from corporate over-civilization and engulfed by the private to the point of symbolic castration, the narrator literally develops a split personality to reconcile the competing demands of masculinity. His discovery of the primal pleasures of fight helps him to overcome his fears and to see, accept, even cherish his wounds. By forging male intimacy through violent contact and a shared goal or moral quest, Fight Club and Project Mayhem offer men—especially young ones who live in the shadow of great heroes and memories—the opportunity to play at war and learn its manly lessons. Emerging from this military space, which has historically lent men a public/private means to foster hard bodies, the narrator can engage the private and reach out to Marla with fewer fears of future emasculation.

In brief, whereas Chad scorns the world of women, saving a mask to perform within it, *Fight Club's* narrator destroys Chad's corporate jungle and returns to the private a stronger man. Yet both films remain leery of the private as a safe space for masculinity. Both reify the need for hard bodies and public balls as a kind of armor against the private. And, though in opposite ways, both mark the resilient male body as a public figure and corporate product.

Second, neither film consistently embraces nor rejects the primitive and civilized. Indeed, the characters approach this masculine dialectic as a constant juggling act. On the one hand, both films ironically imply that men must rediscover the primitive to rescue civilization. Concurrently, these primitive habits must be curbed by civilized norms. Rationality, restraint, and strategic duplicity package the primitive in civilized form *In the Company of Men;* in *Fight Club*, vague notions of morality, honor, and human connection serve as civilizing tools. We contend that, despite manifold differences, both films construct a civilized/primitive subjectivity that allows professional men to hold conflicting selves together in temporary, partial, adaptable, and strategic performances, however loose their grip might be. For example, Chad alternately performs calculated control with apparent sensitivity (e.g., courting Christine, befriending Howard) and raw aggression-derived genitalia: "Listen, you got a pair the kind that men are carrying around, you practically wear 'em on your sleeve. That's what business

is all about—who's sporting the nastiest sac of venom and who is willing to use it." For Chad, "the idea that real manliness (and sexuality vitality and zest for life) is to be found outside man-made culture is merged with the idea of the workplace as the man-made jungle where a man might realize himself, if he's the right sort of animal" (Bordo 253). In a different civilized/primitive performance, Tyler embodies a primal physicality, rationalized by his social consciousness; later, his primitive club assumes militaristic, near-bureaucratic form. Determined to erase external controls of men, Tyler ironically assumes the role of corporate father, ruling over a rule-governed and hierarchical entity. Eventually, the narrator internalizes Tyler's lessons in primal pain but slays his primitive excess in the name of ethics. In sharp contrast to the other characters, Howard remains the archetypal neurasthenic, a transparent impostor who confuses strategic performance with an "authentic" self. As he succumbs to, or becomes, the performance, he cannot adjust to changing primitive/civilized demands and, consequently, gets consumed by both.

In sum, the films cast the primitive/civilized as a masculine dialectical tension with many possible and creative performances. Central to managing this dialectic is the elusive quest for an ideal blend of control and excess. At various times, Chad, Tyler, and the narrator portray a keen sense of the shifting faces the two may take, the fine line between them, and the dangers wrought by too much of either. As a result, the characters develop adoration *and* loathing for control and excess—a flexible stance that allows them to invoke one to tame the other and, thereby, to manage shifting accountabilities to the primitive/civilized.

Ultimately, we argue that neither film moves to heal the battered white/collar man. While *Fight Club* incessantly pushes him to reopen his wounds and celebrate them as spectacle, *In the Company of Men* harbors the ubiquitous threat of bruises to fuel the fire of violence directed outward. Put simply, the wounds don't need to be healed; they *are* a healing force, creating an already broken and thus unbreakable professional body. Hence, the display of wounds becomes indefinitely central to the performance of professional masculinity, which finds stimulation in the notion that it too is injured (Jeffords *Hard*; Savran). In this sense, civilized/primitive subjectivity stakes a claim to identity politics for white/collar men (Robinson). Below, we consider how this professional character plays with other politicized subjects.

Gender, Race, Sexuality, Class, and the Civilized/Primitive

For Men Only, but Which Ones?

While some (e.g., white) masculinities and femininities lay claim to diverse dimensions of the civilized (e.g., scientific rationality, private virtues), the films insist that only men can access the primitive. The primitive emerges as a suppressed male essence, which is presumably available to all men. Significantly, across the films, only white men get to teach the primitive, and their primary pupils are other white men. However, two strikingly parallel scenes depict pupils of color. In the first, Chad chastises a young Black intern–one of the "juvenile fuckers" at "summer camp" alluded to earlier. The pretense of their meeting is that Chad is graciously showing the intern the ropes, "rolling out the opportunity" for him to "hang with the money people." When the intern shrugs off Chad's initial advice, Chad demands gratefulness from his student: "You know, I could've held back on this [. . .] let you figure out life all on your little lonesome. But I think I would've been doing you a disservice [. . .] cherish this." Chad stresses his confusion over whether the intern's name is "Keith" or "Keif" and sniggers at Keif's pronunciation of "axe": "Let me give you a professional tip. The word is *ask*." With his arm around Keif, Chad informs him that he needs "the big brass ones" to climb the corporate ladder: "Let's see 'em then, these clankers of yours." When Keif hesitates and mumbles a disbelieving protest, Chad removes all doubt of his command: "Show–Me–Your–Balls!" After Keif complies, Chad asks him to fetch a cup of coffee on his way out: "Black's fine."

Like Chad, Tyler excels in his role as teacher, even with the most difficult lessons. Viewers watch as Tyler, embarking on a "human sacrifice," drags an Asian/ American clerk out of the convenience store where he works, pushes him to his knees, and holds a gun to his head. Perusing the clerk's wallet, Tyler announces, "Raymond, you are going to die [. . .] There's going to be nothing left of your face." Tyler discovers Raymond's school ID and asks, "what'd you study,

Raymond?" Violently shaking, Raymond stutters, "st-st-st-stuff," at which Tyler hits Raymond with the gun, demanding "I asked you, what'd you study?" Unsatisfied with the answer, Tyler continues, "Why? [. . .] What'd you want to be, Raymond K. Hessel?" As the clerk continues to sob, Tyler cocks the gun and repeats, "The question–Raymond, was–What–Did–You–Want–To Be?" Finally, Tyler releases Raymond, warning that he will return to see that Raymond is pursuing his goals. Mockingly, as Raymond runs off, Tyler taunts, "Run, Forrest, Run." Questioned by the narrator as to the point, Tyler proclaims assuredly that Raymond's life will now have meaning.

In both powerful scenes, the tone of white men's teaching takes a dramatic turn that reveals the ways in which civilized/primitive masculinity entails racialized performance. With their primary and most serious (white) pupils, the teachers devote extensive time and adopts a tone of relative equality and intimacy. Tyler acts as a buddy mentor who guides his chief trainee through the primitive; Chad too engages Howard as a chummy peer and a possible player, despite his agenda to the contrary. With men of color, the tone is contrastingly brief, distant, condescending, and violent; and the relation shifts from mentor-apprentice to (abusive) father-boy or tyrant-minion. These peons apparently necessitate a harsher hand and deserve to be put in their place. As such, both films invite audiences to gaze upon these racially marked and crumbling bodies. We watch Keif nervously undo his pants; we witness Raymond shaking and sobbing. While both films provide space to morally question these violent moments, they simultaneously fix or mark racial difference as visibly and immediately other (S. Willis).[11] Moreover, both scenes underscore the inability of these pupils to rightfully claim civilized/primitive subjectivity. Keif could have it all if only he would stop "screwing around," start using his head, and speak professionally (i.e., get civilized, where civilized equals white). Raymond could find a new life if he would stop blubbering like a sissy and grab his future by the horns (i.e., get primitive in pursuit of career achievements– a whitened primitive, not to mention an ironic message for a work-suspicious film). The films' reliance on familiar racial imagery here (e.g., Black man as dumb primal brute, Asian man as over-cultured and effeminate) needs little elaboration (e.g., Dines; Eng).

The notion of white men as teachers of the primitive is telling, for it rejects the conventional discourse of the primitive as the domain of dark savage rapists (Bederman). We suggest that white masculinity can now appropriate the teaching role precisely because the emerging ideal embraces a *civilized*/primitive masculinity. This flexibility in itself marks whiteness, for dark masculinities are granted access only to savage primal modes or feminized civil ones (Dines; Eng). It is also notable that the mentors of both films grant white pupils more serious and sustained attention. These insights come together in Chad's depiction of the masculinity crisis: "OK, well we're doomed then, seriously, as a race." Chad characterizes white/collar men as an advanced civilization, entitled to "put our foot down" and damned unless they do. In this light, going primitive becomes a means of (white) race preservation. Handily, the primitive no longer threatens to taint the white man with dark savage excess, because the sophisticated white primitive retains a firm foothold in–and, actually, aims to serve and protect–civilization (Bederman).

In the Company of Men self-consciously exposes raced and classed restrictions as to which men can pull off the performance of civilized/primitive subjectivity. In addition to the Chad-Keif scene, we hear Howard denounce his working-class heritage as a quaintly impotent "Norman Rockwell" life. *Fight Club* appears less self-conscious about its class and racial limitations. With its more visually diverse membership, *Fight Club* extends a civilized/primitive brotherhood to men of all ages, races, and classes. Indeed, a Black man enjoys pummeling the narrator in one scene (though the narrator is in the midst of explaining that Fight Club is not about winning or losing). And oddly, while Fight Club develops in response to professional neurasthenia, its members are increasingly working class. By mid-film, for example, Tyler pronounces the significance of his army of men as he threatens to castrate a police commissioner: "Look, the people you are after are the people you depend on. We cook your meals; we haul your trash; we connect your calls; we drive your ambulances. We guard you while you sleep." The centrality of anti-materialism to Fight Club also reaches out to men of diverse class. At the same time, it erases racial wounds, subordinating all other injuries to those inflicted by a faceless corporate capitalism. Strategically here, through

the creation of all-male clubs with trans-racial memberships, the discourse co-opts contemporary ideological debates, particularly racial ones, to its own ends (Hanke; S. Willis). Men of color are invited to act, but only in those secondary roles approved by white directors. A similar effect is produced by the film's age appeals. Although men of various ages initially flock to Fight Club, most of the key players that emerge are young, lean, white boy-men. And besides the MTV-feel of the film, the main source of identification between the narrator and Marla is a kind of "Gen X" despondency: drifting young adults discarded by divorced parents, disillusioned by American dreams, skeptical of traditional work ethics, and so forth. This youthful emphasis further serves to conceal the white, middle-class character of this generational narrative.

The Feminine, Effeminate, and Manly Desire

The masculine identities and bonds that surface in the films are opposed to and explicitly deny the feminine. Women and things feminized appear soft, weak, hypersensitive, overcivilized, frazzled, psychobabbling, indecisive, disabled, unduly restrained yet too excessive–dripping with private (non-) sensibilities. Paradoxically, women and the feminine are also decidedly threatening, for they pose seductive entrapment. Worse yet, they rule the private realm but then refuse to be contained there. Their strides in the company of men exacerbate men's neurasthenic anxieties. It is this final and most recent violation that seems to spawn the intensified loathing and vigorous misogyny at work in these films. Simply put, femininities are menacing because they are intruding, exposing, captivating, captive-making, and necessary all at once (Horrocks). Donning the primitive helps a man stand strong amid the feminine, in part because it restores his control of it. The evolution of the relationship between Marla and the narrator nicely illustrates the point. Initially, Marla calls the shots, assertively defending her therapy group turf. Yet as Fight Club grows, she becomes increasingly neurotic and dependent. By the film's end, the relation of control has flipped: Marla feels ruined by the newly alive and virile narrator, who then rescues her and, by implication, earns her affection.

The enhanced misogyny that suffuses both films is also colored with race hierarchy. While all men may join the war, invitations are neither equal nor sufficient to disrupt racial superiority (Wiegman). As hinted earlier, Tyler's first "human sacrifice" victim becomes the symbolic equivalent of a whimpering woman, whereas Chad dismisses Keif as an ignorant boy. As such, the Asian/American clerk is a far cry from the male primitive, while the Black intern is little but primal. These scenes surface more than the import of historically racialized access to the civilized and primitive. Namely, masculinities of color are also evaluated according to their degree of closeness to things feminine. And femininities are all the more odious when expressed in a male body. After all, the obese, castrated Bob is the only Project Mayhem soldier to die in battle.

As the latter point implies, the racist and misogynist civilized/primitive is also homophobic, as revealed by Chad's choice of profanities (e.g. "prissy cocksucker") in the newsletter review scene. And while *Fight Club* flirts with the homosocial, it concludes with compulsory heterosexuality (Wittig). Yet, in seeming contradiction, the civilized/primitive can engender homoeroticism. For example, the male bonds built in *Fight Club* are joined by homosocial desire (Roper; Sedgwick). Tyler's beautifully virile physicality brings this hunger to *Fight Club*. His flamboyant apparel, ranging from vibrant vintage to hipster to camouflage to a pastel coffee-cup bathrobe, marks him as spectacle. In scene after scene, the camera hovers lovingly over his sculpted, tanned, near-naked form, as it struts around the house or writhes around on a filthy floor, interlocked with various men. That men patently adore Tyler's body is made permissible in interesting ways. First, the narrator's relationship with Tyler is fraught with the symbolism of heterosexual courtship and marriage. On their first evening together, Tyler directs the narrator to "cut the foreplay" and ask if he can spend the night. The conclusion of their first physical brawl is laden with sexual imagery: With glazed, satisfied expressions, the two share a cigarette and a beer, musing, "We should do this again sometime." After the men move in together, the narrator's cynical references to "playing Ozzie and Harriet" depict the two as a less-than-ideal married couple. We watch the narrator gaze at Tyler in the bathtub; we observe his possessive and admiring smirks when he watches

Tyler fight. Later, the narrator interprets Tyler's budding interest in a young, lithe, beautiful, blonde Fight Club member—referred to as "Angel Face"—as a sort of extramarital affair. Like a spurned lover, the narrator nips the affair in the bud by destroying Angel's face in a fight, proclaiming an "inflamed sense of rejection." Meanwhile, the potential for romantic relations between Tyler and the narrator is denied by Tyler's "sportfucking" of Marla, coupled with the narrator's own muted attraction to Marla. Here, we are assured that the homoerotic is not the homosexual, while the heterosexuality of both men gets affirmed. The narrator is hardly the only man in the film who gazes on Tyler with yearning awe; but Fight Club soon adopts the frame of war, which construes such desire as hero worship and the intense physical intimacy of bonds forged in battle. But only the white male body appears worthy of worship. Although all members arrive with an "ass made of cookie dough" and come away "carved out of wood," Tyler's stylishly primal and brutally militaristic body remains special throughout, supporting Jeffords claim that hard body masculinity was never meant to include anyone but white men (*Hard*).

In the Company of Men also toys with the homoerotic in a less frequent and visible but more explicitly racialized way. Arguably, Chad's interest in Keif's balls reflects his curiosity about the mythic genitalia of Black men (hooks *Outlaw*). Chad bluntly deflects any such reading by avowing, "I'm not a homo, Keith," and recasting the scenario as an evaluation of whether Keif is "man enough" for management. This frame negates Chad's possible desire and diffuses the threat of primitive Black bodies and sexuality, affirming the superiority of Chad's civilized/primitive masculinity in the name of corporate prowess. Taken together, the human sacrifice and Keif scenes emasculate the bodies of men of color and enforce the entitled strength and beauty of the white male body. This is not surprising, for discourses of the dangers of Black male bodies (Dines; Orbe), of the lewd nature of Latino bodies (Berg), and of the feminized Asian/American male bodies (Nakayama "Show/down") encumber the formation of a civilized/primitive body of color.

In sum, the characters of both films use intensified—and, usually, misogynistic and homophobic—gender division to seduce a civilized/primitive brotherhood composed of all races and classes. However, it seems that the "unfortunate" inability of all but white men to adapt to both sides of this malleable self will preclude them from potent performance. Through such powerful discursive tactics, professional masculinity can once again manage to morph yet retain its gender, race, and class dominance all at once.

Conclusion

Thus far, we have traced two parallel yet divergent threads of a contemporary discourse of white/collar men in crisis. Like the crisis narrative a century ago, these fragments are all about manhood threatened by feminizing forces. But this time around, corporations are figured as *the* emasculating force, sterilized by women's civilization. This novel motif suggests the need to attend to the ways in which work enables and constrains the performance of hegemonic masculinity.

White men have long been construed as public characters. In the 19th century, the stage shifted from community to work, where it has largely remained until now. The crisis narrative that ensued eventually rescued business by crafting it as a jungle of men, fertile ground for potent masculinity (Bederman; Rotundo). Today, amid serious public clamor for quality of work life and fashionably derisive caricatures like Dilbert, corporate ground seems ever more barren. In short, contemporary discourse casts suspicion on the white collar, as well as the notion that a man is defined by his professional achievements and material possessions. In the discourse chronicled here, white/collar masculinity alternately appears as socially destructive, as hinted by *In the Company of Men's* satirical tone, or as personally dissatisfying, as in *Fight Club*. As noted earlier, these films are part of a recent surge of works that explore the failings of white/collar masculinity. Arguably, many of these films—such as *American Beauty* (1999), *Office Space* (1999), and *Wolf* (1994)—also take up with the neurasthenic tensions analyzed here and depict disabling contradictions between corporate life and a potent masculine self. Ours may well be a time when hegemonic masculinity flirts with a new public home.

In this sense, the critique embedded in the rise of such films is penetrating, pushing men to seek other options. For example, both films analyzed here open space for criticizing hegemonic masculinity, especially *In the Company of Men*, whose tongue-in-cheek caricature is captured by Chad "Piercewell." While *Fight Club* does not extend the same invitation, the narrator and occasionally Tyler perform discomfort with moral excess. And in the final moments of both films, we are left with empty images: Howard screaming at the deaf Christine, Chad gloating in the sexual adulation of his lover, radical Tyler destroyed by the narrator, and a dazed and confused narrator. We submit that these spaces constitute a window of opportunity through which to re-vision dominant masculinity. Whereas corporations have long supplied an institutional anchor for white, middle-class masculinity, they now ironically become the force that strips this weary subject of his manhood. In this way, the characters' perceptions of personal powerlessness–however whiny, victimizing, or otherwise perilous–facilitates the sort of resistance that could undermine patriarchal, managerial capitalism, which depends on white/collar men to devote themselves to a game they will likely lose (Donaldson). If the present discourse continues to gain steam, we suspect that the nature of corporate commitment will have to change or white, middle-class masculinity may drift toward another public base.

Lest we sound too optimistic, we acknowledge at least two discursive hitches to sustainable resistance. First, the essay reveals the tremendous historical weight and contemporary pressure of the neurasthenic paradox, which demands that white/collar men (among others) simultaneously perform accountability to conflicting expectations for civilized and primitive selves in public and private arenas. Alternation between soft, sensitive and hard, violent masculinities constitutes one cultural means of managing this dilemma. Indeed, violence has become a familiar balm for embattled professional men (Hearn "Organization"; Linstead). We maintain that feminist and other calls for masculinity transformation must take seriously the difficulty of navigating this tension.

A second catch follows our analysis of the political relations at work in the film. Specifically, even if white, middle-class masculinity begins to dislodge from corporations, there is no reason to believe it will lose hold of its race, class, sexuality, and gender dominance. Consider, for example, what we learn about possibilities from the film tales. In general, we are offered four potential subject positions: (a) the debilitated neurasthenic (i.e., Howie, early narrator); (b) the eternally suspicious and sadistic corporate fighter (i.e., Chad); (c) the wild, masochistic boy rebel, playfully and maliciously violent (i.e., Tyler); and (d) the morally conflicted young man who killed him, only to (re)join with a woman (i.e., "evolved" narrator). Option one is immediately undermined, and the others are never embraced. To different degrees, these faulty performances of masculinity concede the inevitability of the hegemonic masculinities they seek to disrupt. Certainly, *In the Company of Men* is less at fault in this regard, yet even it depends on the audience to supply a critique frame and to connect its more and less subtle dots between gender, race, homophobia, and classism. That not everyone can or will do so becomes evident in some public reactions to the film. One viewer, frustrated by a recent romantic break-up, noted, "I actually walked out of the movie with a smile" (Kohn par. 5). Another critic observed that Chad is "so charming that he's irresistible, but what a poisonous man–just the type who often makes it in business" (Hershenson par. 9).

Alone, these twin caveats leave us with a final caution: Hegemonic masculinity remains an elastic, "historically mobile relation" (Connell *Masculinities* 77). Temporarily itinerant, perhaps. In search of a more supportive stage. But definitely not daunted.

Notes

1. Throughout the essay, our use of "white/collar" is meant to mark the masculinity's race and class profile, without subordinating one to another.

2. In addition to journals such as *Men and Masculinities and Journal of Men's Studies*, see for instance, Brittan; Brod and Kaufman; Hearn and Morgan; Kimmel and Messner; Segal; Seidler *Rediscovering* and *Unreasonable*; and Stecopoulos and Uebel.

3. This concern is shared among scholars of whiteness, for whom the parallel fear of reinscribing white dominance exists in tension with the desire to render it visible (e.g., Flores and Moon; Projansky and Ono).

4. See, for instance, Byars; De Lauretis *Alice* and *Technologies*; Mulvey "Afterthoughts" and "Visual"; Penley; Powrie; and van Zoonen.

5. See, for instance, Bird; hooks *Reel*; Jeffords *Hard*; Tasker "Dumb" and *Spectacular*; and S. Willis.

6. See Bordo; Dyer *White*; Kirkham and Thumim *You Tarzan*; Ray; and Tasker "Fists."

7. Such arguments are explored in Cohan; Dyer "Rock"; Fuchs; Neale; and Stukator.

8. For discussions of masculinity and work, see Alvesson; Cheng *Masculinities*; Collinson and Hearn "Naming", *Men*, and "Men"; and Mumby. Studies of women and work include Ashcraft "Empowering" and "Managing"; Buzzanell; Konek and Kitch; Marshall; Pringle; Rosener; and Trethewey.

9. For an extended account of the rise of these formations and their implications for masculinity, see Rotundo.

10. See, for instance, Burris; Hearn *Men* and "Deconstructing"; Kerfoot and Knights; Kilduff and Mehra.

11. As we later clarify, *In the Company of Men* marks race more self-consciously and purposefully than *Fight Club*, where it appears incidental.

Works Cited

Acker, Joan. "Hierarchies, Jobs, Bodies: A Theory of Gendered Organizations." *Gender and Society* 4 (1990): 139–58.

Alvesson, Mats. "Gender Relations and Identity at Work: A Case Study of Masculinities and Femininities in an Advertising Agency." *Human Relations* 51 (1998): 969–1005.

American Beauty. Dir. Sam Mendes. Universal Studios, 1999.

Ashcraft, Karen Lee. "Empowering 'Professional' Relationships: Organizational Communication Meets Feminist Practice." *Management Communication Quarterly* 13 (2000): 347–92.

——. "Managing Maternity Leave: A Qualitative Analysis of Temporary Executive Succession." *Administrative Science Quarterly* 44 (1999): 40–80.

Ashcraft, Karen Lee, and Brenda J. Allen. "The Racial Foundation of Organizational Communication." *Communication Theory*, 13 (2003): 5–38.

Beavers, Herman. "'The Cool Pose': Intersectionality, Masculinity, and Quiescence in the Comedy and Films of Richard Pryor and Eddie Murphy." Stecopoulos and Uebel 253–85.

Bederman, Gail. (1995). *Manliness and Civilization: A Cultural History of Gender and Race in the United States, 1880–1917*. Chicago: U of Chicago P, 1995.

Berg, Charles Ramirez. "Stereotyping of Films in General and of the Hispanic in Particular." *Latin Looks: Images of Latinas and Latinos in the U.S. Media*. Ed. Clara E. Rodriguez. Boulder: Westview, 1997, 104–20.

The Big Kahuna. Dir. John Swanbeck. Universal Studios, 2000.

Bird, Sharon R. "Welcome to the Men's Club: Homosociality

and the Maintenance of Hegemonic Masculinity." *Gender and Society* 10 (1996): 120–32.

Boiler Room. Dir. Ben Younger. New Line Studios, 2000.

Bordo, Susan. *The Male Body: A New Look at Men in Public and in Private*. New York: Farrar, Straus, and Giroux, 1999.

Brittan, Arthur. *Masculinity and Power*. New York: Basil Blackwell, 1989.

Brod, Harry, and Michael Kaufman, eds. *Theorizing Masculinities*. Thousand Oaks: Sage, 1994.

Burris, Beverly H. "Technocracy, Patriarchy, and Management." Collinson and Hearn 61–77.

Butler, Judith. *Gender Trouble: Feminism and the Subversion of Identity*. New York: Routledge, 1990.

Buzzanell, Patrice M. "Reframing the Glass Ceiling as a Socially Constructed Process. Implications for Understanding and Change." *Communication Monographs* 62 (1995): 327–54.

Byars, Jackie. "Gazes/Voices/Power: Expanding Psychoanalysis for Feminist Film and Television." *Female Spectators: Looking at Film and Television*. Ed. E. Deidre Pribram. New York: Verso, 1988. 110–31.

Cheng, Cliff, ed. *Masculinities in Organizations*. Thousand Oaks, CA: Sage, 1996.

——. "Men and Masculinities are not Necessarily Synonymous: Thoughts on Organizational Behavior and Occupational Sociology." Cheng xi–xx.

Cohan, Steven. "Masquerading as the American Male in the Fifties: *Picnic*, William Holden and the Spectacle of Masculinity in Hollywood Film." *Camera Obscura* 25/26 (1991): 43–72.

Cohan, Steven and Ina Rae Hark, eds. *Screening the Male: Exploring Masculinities in Hollywood Cinema*. New York: Routledge, 1993.

Collins, Patricia Hill. "Toward a New Vision: Race, Class, and Gender as Categories of Analysis and Connection." *Race, Sex and Class* 1 (1993): 25–45.

Collinson, David L. "'Engineering Humour': Masculinity, Joking, and Conflict in Shop-floor Relations." *Organization Studies* 9 (1988): 181–99.

Collinson, David L. and Jeff Hearn, eds. *Men as Managers, Managers as Men*. Thousand Oaks, CA: Sage, 1996.

——. "'Men' at 'Work': Multiple Masculinities/Multiple Workplaces." *Understanding Masculinities: Social Relations and Cultural Arenas*. Ed. In Máirtín Mac an Ghaill. Buckingham, UK: Open UP. 61–76.

——. "Naming Men as Men: Implications for Work, Organization and Management." *Gender Work, and Organization* 1 (1994): 2–22.

Connell, R. W. "The Big Picture: Masculinities in Recent World History." *Theory and Society* 22 (1993): 597–623.

——. *Gender and Power*. Palo Alto, CA: Stanford UP, 1987.

——. *Masculinities*. Berkeley: U of California P, 1995.

Corey, Frederick C. "Masculine Drag." *Critical Studies in Media Communication* 17 (2000): 108–10.

Crenshaw, Carrie. "Women in the Gulf War: Toward an Intersectional Feminist Rhetorical Criticism." *Howard Journal of Communications* 8 (1997): 219–35.

Crenshaw, Kimberlé. "Mapping the Margins: Intersectionality, Identity Politics, and Violence Against Women of Color." *Stanford Law Review* 43 (1991): 1241–99.

Dace, Karen L. "'Had Judas Been a Black Man . . .': Politics, Race, and Gender in African America." *Judgment Calls: Rhetoric, Politics, and Indeterminacy*. Ed. John M. Sloop and James P. McDaniel. Boulder: Westview, 1998. 163–81.

De Lauretis, Teresa. *Alice Doesn't: Feminism, Semiotics, Cinema*. Bloomington: Indiana UP, 1984.

De Lauretis, Teresa. *Technologies of Gender: Essays on Theory, Film, and Fiction*. Bloomington: Indiana UP, 1987.

Deetz, Stan, and Dennis Mumby. "Power, Discourse, and the Workplace: Reclaiming the Critical Tradition." *Communication Yearbook* 13 (1990): 18–47.

Dines, Gail. "*King Kong* and the White Woman: Hustler Magazine and the Demonization of Black Masculinity." *Violence Against Women* 4.3 (1998). 24 Aug. 2000 <http://ehostvgw3.epnet.com/ehost1.asp>.

Disclosure. Dir. Barry Levinson. Warner Brothers, 1994.

Donaldson, Mike. "What is Hegemonic Masculinity?" *Theory and Society* 22 (1993): 643–58.

Dyer, Richard. "Rock–The Last Guy You'd Have Figured?" *You Tarzan: Masculinity, Movies and Men*. Ed. Pat Kirkham and Janet Thumim. New York: St. Martin's Press, 1993. 27–34.

——. *White*. New York: Routledge, 1997.

Eng, David L. *Racial Castration: Managing Masculinity in Asian America*. Durham: Duke UP, 2001.

Falling Down. Dir. Joel Schumacher. Warner Brothers, 1993.

Faludi, Susan. *Stiffed: The Betrayal of the American Man*. New York: William Morrow, 1999.

Fight Club. Dir. David Fincher. Twentieth Century Fox, 1999.

Fine, Michelle, Lois Weis, Judi Addelston, and Julia Marusza. "(In)secure Times: Constructing White Working-class Masculinities in the Late 20th Century. *Gender and Society* 11 (1997): 568.

Flores, Lisa A., and Dreama G. Moon. "Rethinking race, revealing dilemmas: Imagining a new racial subject in *Race Traitor*." *Western Journal of Communication* 66 (2002): 181–207.

Fuchs, Cynthia J. "The Buddy Politic." Cohan and Hark 194–210.

Gherardi, Silvia. *Gender, Symbolism, and Organizational Cultures*. Newbury Park, CA: Sage, 1995.

Glengarry, Glen Ross. Dir. James Foley. Artisan Entertainment, 1992.

Gibson, Melissa K., and Michael J. Papa. "The Mud, the

Blood, and the Beer Guys: Organizational Osmosis in Blue-collar Work Groups." *Journal of Applied Communication Research* 28 (2000): 66–86.

Hall, Stuart. "Signification, Representation, Ideology: Althusser and the Poststructuralist Debates." *Critical Studies in Mass Communication* 2 (1985): 91–114.

——. "The Work of Representation. *Representation: Cultural Representations and Signifying Practices*. Ed. Stuart Hall. London: Sage/Open UP, 1997. 13–64.

Hamada, Tomako. "Unwrapping Euro-American Masculinity in a Japanese Multinational Corporation." Cheng 160–76.

Hanke, Robert. "Hegemonic Masculinity in *thirtysomething.*" *Critical Studies in Mass Communication* 7 (1990): 231–48.

Hearn, Jeff. "Deconstructing the Dominant: Making the One(s) the Other(s). *Organization* 3 (1996): 611–26.

——. *Men in the Public Eye: The Construction and Deconstruction of Public Men and Public Patriarchies*. New York: Routledge, 1992.

——. "The Organization of Violence: Men, Gender Relations, Organizations, and Violences." *Human Relations* 47 (1994): 731–54.

Hearn, Jeff and David Morgan, eds. *Men, Masculinities and Social Theory*. London: Unwin Hyman, 1990.

Hershenson, Karen. "In the Company of Men." *The News—Times*. 15 Sep. 1997. 6 Sep. 2000 <http://www.news-times.com/archive97/sep1597/mvd.htm>.

Holmlund, Chris. "Visible Difference and Flex Appeal: The Body, Sex, Sexuality, and Race in the 'Pumping Iron' Films." *Out of Bounds: Sports, Media, and the Politics of Identity*. Ed. Aaron Baker and Todd Boyd. Bloomington: Indiana UP, 1997. 145–60.

hooks, bell. *Outlaw Culture: Resisting Representations*. New York: Routledge, 1994.

——. *Reel to Real: Race, Sex and Class at the Movies*. New York: Routledge, 1996.

Horrocks, Roger. *Masculinity in Crisis*. New York: St. Martin's Press, 1994.

In the Company of Men. Dir. Neil LaBute. Tristar, 1997.

Jeffords, Susan. *Hard Bodies: Hollywood Masculinity in the Reagan Era*. New Brunswick: Rutgers UP, 1994.

——. *The Remasculinization of America: Gender and the Vietnam War*. Bloomington: Indiana UP, 1989.

Kerfoot, Deborah, and David Knights. "Management, Masculinity and Manipulation: From Paternalism to Corporate Strategy in Financial Services in Britain. *Journal of Management Studies* 30 (1993): 659–77.

Kilduff, Martin, and Ajay Mehra. "Hegemonic Masculinity Among the Elite: Power, Identity, and Homophily in Social Networks." Cheng 115–29.

Kimmel, Michael, and Michael Messner, eds. *Men's Lives*, 2nd ed. Boston: Allyn & Bacon, 1995.

Kirkham, Pat, and Janet Thumim, eds. *Me Jane: Masculinity,*

Movies and Women. New York: St. Martin's Press, 1995.

——. *You Tarzan: Masculinity, Movies and Men*. New York: St. Martin's Press, 1993.

Kohn, Dan. "In the Company of Men." 12 Sep. 1997. 6 Sep. 2000 <http://xent.ics.uci.edu/FoRKo-archive/sept97/0080.html>.

Konek, Carol Wolfe, and Sally L. Kitch, eds. *Women and Careers: Issues and Challenges*. Thousand Oaks: Sage, 1994.

Laclau, Ernesto, and Chantal Mouffe. *Hegemony and Socialist Strategy: Towards a Radical Democratic Politics*. London: Verso, 1985.

Linstead, Stephen. "Abjection and Organization: Men, Violence, and Management." *Human Relations* 50 (1997): 1115–45.

Lyman, Peter. "The Fraternal Bond as a Joking Relationship: A Case Study of the Role of Sexist Jokes in Male Group Bonding." Kimmel and Messner 86–96.

Mandziuk, Roseann M. "Necessary Vigilance: Feminist Critiques of Masculinity." *Critical Studies in Media Communication* 17 (2000): 105–8.

Marshall, Judi. "Viewing Organizational Communication From a Feminist Perspective: A Critique and Some Offerings." *Communication Yearbook* 16 (1993): 122–43.

Martin, Joanne. "Deconstructing Organizational Taboos: The Suppression of Gender Conflict in Organizations." *Organization Science* 1 (1990): 339–59.

McGee, Michael Calvin. "Text, Context, and the Fragmentation of Contemporary Culture." *Western Journal of Communication* 54 (1990): 274–89.

Mechling, Elizabeth W., and Jay Mechling. "The Jung and the Restless: The Mythopoetic Men's Movement." *Southern Communication Journal* 59 (1994): 97–111.

Mills, Albert, and Peter Chiaramonte. "Organization as Gendered Communication Act." *Canadian Journal of Communication* 16 (1991): 381–98.

Mulvey, Laura. "Afterthoughts on 'Visual Pleasure and Narrative Cinema.'" *Feminism and Film Theory*. Ed. Constance Penley. New York: Routledge, 1988. 69–79.

——. "Visual Pleasure and Narrative Cinema." *Screen* 16 (1975): 6–18.

Mumby, Dennis K. "Organizing Men: Power, Discourse, and the Social Construction of Masculinity(s) in the Workplace." *Communication Theory* 8 (1998): 164–83.

Nakayama, Thomas K. "Show/down Time: 'Race,' Gender, Sexuality, and Popular Culture." *Critical Studies in Mass Communication* 11 (1994): 162–79.

——. "The Significance of 'Race' and Masculinities." *Critical Studies in Media Communication* 17 (2000): 111–13.

Neale, Steve. "Masculinity as Spectacle: Reflections on Men and Masculinity in Mainstream Cinema." Prologue. Cohan and Hark 9–20

Nkomo, Stella M. "The Emperor Has No Clothes:

Rewriting 'Race in Organizations.'" *Academy of Management Review* 17 (1992): 487–513.

Office Space. Dir. Mike Judge. Twentieth Century Fox, 1999.

Orbe, Mark P. "Constructions of Reality on MTV's 'The Real World': An Analysis of the Restrictive Coding of Black Masculinity." *Southern Communication Journal* 64 (1998): 32–47.

Penley, Constance, ed. *Feminism and Film Theory.* New York: Routledge, 1988.

Powrie, Phil. *French Cinema in the 1980s: Nostalgia and the Crisis of Masculinity.* Oxford: Clarendon, 1997.

Pringle, Rosemary. "Bureaucracy, Rationality, and Sexuality: The Case of Secretaries." *The Sexuality of Organization.* Ed. Jeff Hearn, Deborah Sheppard, Peta Tancred-Sheriff, and Gibson Burell. Newbury Park, CA: Sage, 1989. 158–77.

Projansky, Sarah, and Kent A. Ono. "Strategic Whiteness as Cinematic Racial Politics." *Whiteness: The Communication of Social Identity.* Ed. Thomas K. Nakayama and Judith N. Martin. Thousand Oaks, CA: Sage, 1999. 149–74.

Ray, Sid. "Hunks, History, and Homophobia: Masculinity Politics in *Braveheart* and *Edward II.*" *Film and History* 29 (1999): 22–31.

Robinson, Sally. *Marked Men: White Masculinity in Crisis.* New York: Columbia UP, 2000.

Roper, Michael. "'Seduction and Succession': Circuits of Homosocial Desire in Management." Collinson and Hearn 210–26.

Rosener, Judy B. "Ways Women Lead." *Harvard Business Review* 6 (1990): 119–25.

Rotundo, E. Anthony. *American Manhood: Transformations in Masculinity From the Revolution to the Modern Era.* New York: Basic Books, 1993.

Savran, David. "The Sadomasochist in the Closet: White Masculinity and the Culture of Victimization." *Differences: A Journal of Feminist Cultural Studies* 8 (1996). 13 Jun. 2001 <www.softlineweb.com/softlineweb/bin/KaStasGw.exe>.

Sedgwick, Eve K. *Between Men: English Literature and Male Homosocial Desire.* New York: Columbia UP, 1985.

Segal, Lynne. *Slow Motion: Changing Masculinities, Changing Men.* New Brunswick: Rutgers UP, 1990.

Seidler, Victor J. *Rediscovering Masculinity: Reason, Language and Sexuality.* New York: Routledge, 1989.

——. *Unreasonable Men: Masculinity and Social Theory.* New York: Routledge, 1994.

Sloop, John M. "Mike Tyson and the Perils of Discursive Constraints: Boxing, Race, and the Assumption of

Guilt." *Out of Bounds: Sports, Media, and the Politics of Identity.* Ed. Aaron Baker and Todd Boyd. Bloomington: Indiana UP, 1997. 102–22.

Smith, Christopher. "'Fight Club' Worth Catching in Video Version." *Bangor Daily News.* 27 April 2000. 6 Sep. 2000 <http://proquest.umi.com/pqdweb>.

Spitzack, Carole. "The Production of Masculinity in Interpersonal Communication." *Communication Theory* 8 (1998): 143–64.

——. "Theorizing Masculinity Across the Field: An Intradisciplinary Conversation." *Communication Theory* 8 (1998): 141–43.

Stecopoulos, Harry, and Michael Uebel, eds. *Race and the Subject of Masculinities.* Durham: Duke UP, 1997.

Stukator, Angela. "'Soft Males,' 'Flying Boys,' and 'White Knights': New Masculinity in *The Fisher King.*" *Literature Film Quarterly* 25 (1997): 214–21.

Tasker, Yvonne. "Dumb Movies for Dumb People: Masculinity, the Body, and the Voice in Contemporary Action Cinema." Cohan and Hark 230–44.

——. "Fists of Fury: Discourses of Race and Masculinity in the Martial Arts Cinema." Stecoupoulos and Uebel 315–36.

——. *Spectacular Bodies: Gender, Genre and the Action Cinema.* New York: Routledge, 1993.

Trethewey, Angela. "Disciplined Bodies: Women's Embodied Identities at Work." *Organization Studies* 20 (1999): 423–50.

Trujillo, Nick. "Hegemonic Masculinity on the Mound: Media Representations of Nolan Ryan and American Sports Culture." *Critical Studies in Mass Communication* 8 (1991): 290–308.

Van Zoonen, Liesbet. *Feminist Media Studies.* Thousand Oaks, CA: Sage, 1994.

Watson, Shane. "Give Us Manly Men with Stubby Fingers!: Shane Watson on the Macho Revival." *The Guardian.* 26 May 2000. 6 Sep. 2000 <http://www.proquest.umi/pqdweb>.

West, Candace, and Don H. Zimmerman. "Doing Gender." *Gender and Society,* 1 (1987): 125–51.

Wiegman, Robyn. "Feminism, 'The Boyz,' and Other Matters Regarding the Male." Cohan and Hark 173–93.

Willis, Paul. *Learning to Labor: How Working Class Kids Get Working Class Jobs.* New York: Columbia UP, 1977.

Willis, Sharon. *High Contrast: Race and Gender in Contemporary Hollywood Film.* Durham: Duke UP, 1997.

Wittig, Monique. *The Straight Mind and Other Essays.* Boston: Beacon, 1992.

Wolf. Dir. Mike Nichols. Columbia, 1994.

29.
A BODY OF TEXT

Revisiting Textual Performances of Gender and Sexuality on the Internet
Niels van Doorn, Sally Wyatt, and Liesbet van Zoonen

Introduction

Over the past decade, research on internet culture has displayed an increased interest in the concept of embodiment, particularly in relation to the performance of (gender) identities (Bell 2001). Whereas early debates about gender identity and CMC (computer-mediated communication) focused on either the liberating potential of a textual, disembodied space (Bruckman 1992, 1993; Danet 1996; Reid 1993, 1994), or the discursive reiteration of traditional gender norms (Herring [1993] 1996, 1995, 1996; Herring, Johnson & Dibenedetto 1995; Jaffe, Lee, Huang & Oshagan 1995; Savicki, Kelley & Lingenfelter 1996), more recent studies have directed their attention towards the embodied everyday experiences of internet users (for an overview, see Van Doorn & Van Zoonen 2008). The most recent incitement of this academic interest has been the proliferation of the "Web 2.0," with its emphasis on user-generated content and social networking. Websites such as MySpace, FaceBook, and YouTube (to name the most popular ones) have turned the sharing of personal narratives and the construction of communities into a multi-billion dollar industry. However, this "revolution" in digital culture could not have taken place without the social software that has shaped the infrastructure of today's web. These technologies have gradually transformed online culture into a visual experience, making it possible for users to include images, webcams and video material on their weblogs or MySpace profiles. These developments have transported the ordinary "real" lives of millions of internet users onto the web, foregrounding their physically situated existence. At the same time, the internet itself has become evermore integrated into people's daily practices, making it less a separate sphere than an extension of everyday life.

While research on these phenomena is certainly indispensable for our understanding of contemporary culture in relation to new media, and more specifically the relation between gender and internet use, we feel that a general focus on the internet's graphical spaces tends to ignore the fact that text-based interaction still constitutes a large part of online social life. Second Life might have attracted a lot of buzz, but many text-based formats for social interaction have remained popular, such as public chat rooms (i.e. Yahoo Chat) or private forms of online communication (MSN Instant Messenger, Gmail). This study revisits the textual element of online interaction by looking at an "old favorite" of CMC research: IRC (internet relay chat), one of the internet's first social spaces. We examine how bodies, which have become increasingly visible in contemporary internet culture, play a role in the text-based environment of IRC, and analyze how this shapes the discursive performances of gender and sexuality. Are conventional notions of embodiment reinstated in a social space without visually represented bodies, or does this textual setting attract people who are interested in escaping the omnipresence of the corporeal in mainstream (web) culture? How does the exhibition of everyday life in relation to gender take shape on IRC?

In order to answer these questions, we first reassess the work of Rodino (1997) and O'Brien (1996, 1999), two authors whose perspectives have been important in shaping the understanding of gender performance in relation to text-based communication. Based on this discussion we specify the research questions in more detail.

Gender and Embodiment Online

In her article on the performance of gender on IRC, Rodino (1997) claims that studies providing evidence for or against women's inequality online inevitably support the reification of men and women as two distinct groups. She states:

> Research that considers the relationship between gender and power in language necessarily confronts binary gender, because looking at this relationship means looking at "men" and "women". The binary is always already constructed when one considers women's oppression in CMC, because women's oppression has been described in relation to male domination.
>
> (Michelle Rodino 1997)

The fact that the position of women is continually described in relation to the position of men has reified the binary gender system, which functions as a normative mechanism that categorizes individuals as either male or female and subsequently decides which identities are both culturally legible and legitimate. In Rodino's view, studies that examine gender identity and CMC would be fortified by incorporating a "performative" view of gender. She uses Butler's conception of performativity as the discursive constitution of regulatory notions and their effects, whereby the repeated citation of gendered norms effectively creates a subject who appears to precede the process of gendering (Butler 1993). However, Rodino infuses Butler's interpretation of performativity with Goffman's notion of interactional gender performance, in which subjects are granted a more pronounced sense of agency. In Goffman's view, people are actively "doing" gender, rather than being mainly an effect of its regulatory regime (Brickell 2005).

Although the notion of embodiment is implicitly present in Rodino's critique, it is never clearly brought forward. While stressing that the performance of gender is not linked to a "biological sex," her main criticism of theorists like Reid (1993) is that they too easily neglect the role of the body. This still leaves the relation between bodies and CMC uncomfortably underdetermined. A more elaborate discussion of the corporeal and its status in relation to online interactions is provided by authors such as Sundén (2003) and O'Brien (1999). For Jodi O'Brien the significance of the body is deeply rooted in modern epistemology:

> The political authenticity of the modern self is grounded in the assumption that personhood is located in the physical body, which, in turn, is located in a state of nature as a single, classifiable object . . . The female/male dichotomy is the main line of classification, not only of bodies, but, by extension of the logic of a single, embodied self, the central distinction of "self". Based on what are generally taken to be naturally occurring distinctions in physical sex attributes, it is assumed that gender is the most natural, immutable aspect of "self."
>
> (1999, p. 78)

Achieving a convincing gender performance in practice requires "interactional acknowledgement" (O'Brien 1999). This means that people rely on others to have knowledge about the "gender script" through which they are performing their identity, since this is the only way in which their interactions can be meaningful.

It is the reliance on what O'Brien calls "classification schemes" that causes people to make continual references to their bodies as connected to their "self," even though these bodies are not physically present in the realm where communication is taking place. In this sense, "sexed" bodies provide people with a common point of reference, a kind of "physical truth" that structures and classifies the textual communication and gives it meaning (Nakamura 2002). Conventional gender norms are thus transported online through the classification schemes people rely on both off- and online. As the amount of visual material on the internet is ever growing, this physical truth gets more and more pervasive, reaffirming the binary gender-body connection in online discourse.

Like Rodino, O'Brien believes that it is not the internet itself that facilitates a possible shift in the way people perform gender and perceive its relation to the body, as if the internet is some kind of "thing." Instead, this shift could be initiated by the coming together of individuals who have already had experiences with "gender bending" in their everyday lives. O'Brien uses the example of the "queer": "those for whom the conventional connections between desire/ body/mind/self do not fit" (O'Brien 1996, p. 63). She continues:

> The "alternative" experiences that are enacted in "alternative" or queer spaces are based on realities of the flesh: real, embodied experiences and/or fantasies cultivated through exposure to multisensory stimuli. The online relations that reflect these altered forms are generally enacted in spaces where there is a mutual suspension of the belief that "reality" is connected with one's gendered body.
>
> (Jodi O'Brien 1996, pp. 64–65)

However, the conclusion that a "critical mass of queer bodies online" will consequently provide a challenge to the traditional view of gender and the sexed body might turn out to be premature. Jodi O'Brien concludes:

> Although access to "alternative" gender communities has increased through online communication, for real change to occur there will need to be considerable interaction between those who carry altered gender expectations and those who maintain traditional representations of both fact/ fiction and male/female.
>
> (1996, p. 66)

The work by Rodino and O'Brien evokes the following research questions:

1. Which discursive practices of embodiment exist on IRC and how do they articulate gender?
2. How does the performance of gender and

embodiment on IRC differ between "straight" and "non-straight" participants and is there interaction between them?

Method

Our study focuses on IRC: a form of text-based, synchronous CMC. It is one of the larger chat services on the internet, which can be accessed via an IRC client that can be downloaded from its website (www.mirc. com). Once this client is installed, it is possible to log on to one of the IRC servers and select a "channel," which is the IRC equivalent of a chat room. Conversations that take place in the public part of the channel are visible to everyone who is logged on, but there is also the option of engaging in private conversations through PM (personal messaging). Before engaging in conversation, participants are asked to select a nickname that matches their "virtual self" (MIRC n.d.). They then have access to thousands of channels featuring a plethora of topics and interests. While some of these channels are quite permanent, others come and go. Since IRC is a purely text-based form of CMC, it forms a suitable site for the investigation of the performance of gender and sexuality in a realm where bodies are neither physically nor visually present.

Participants' interactions on two different IRC channels were observed and "logged"[1] on a daily basis over a five-week period (January 5–February 9, 2005). During this period, the average amount of time that was spent logged on to both channels accumulated to approximately five hours per day. The two IRC channels under investigation are #Cyberbar, a channel that hosts predominantly "straight" male/female gender performances, and #Queer, a channel mostly visited by participants who articulate "gay male" gender identities. These two channels were selected for comparison in order to investigate the notion that avowedly queer online spaces might provide for alternative performances of gender identity and sexualized embodiment, thus offering a potential challenge to traditional "straight" gender roles (O'Brien 1996).

Taking into account both ethical and practical considerations, we decided to ask for the participants' consent after data collection was complete (Mann & Stewart 2000). The reason for not seeking consent prior to data collection is because that by doing so we would have introduced ourselves as researchers, thus possibly influencing the outcomes of the interactions we wanted to observe. The intention was to "lurk" (observe while entering no text) in the two selected channels so that we could examine the public conversations without being part of them. If participants had been aware of the presence of researchers, we believe that they would not have conversed as freely as they did without this awareness.

It turned out to be a rather difficult task to obtain consent from all participants. This was mainly due to the considerable turnover in the channels: some of the participants were no longer present in the channels when we returned to gain their consent. Also, many of the participants who were still active in #Cyberbar and #Queer did not seem very interested in our research. We tried to gain consent on three separate occasions, by posting an explanation of our research and an accompanying request for consent on both channels. While some participants gave their consent, a larger number never replied to our request. No participants explicitly refused to provide us with their consent. As there were no refusals, and since all of the observed conversations took place in publicly accessible channels, we decided to use the data. In order to ensure some level of privacy for the participants, the names of the two IRC channels have been altered. However,

we have continued to use the participants' nicknames, as these constitute an important part of our analysis and nicknames themselves function as pseudonyms for participants' real names.

After multiple preliminary observations, in which the complete data set was read and assessed, usable data was selected. We considered data to be "usable" when it contained interactions that somehow referred to gender, sexuality and/or embodiment. For example, in the left column of Table 29.1, three participants in #Cyberbar discuss hair growth on their bodies and ways of grooming it. The right column illustrates how we analyzed and interpreted this conversation.

Of course our interpretation in the right-hand column of Table 29.1 is only one possible reading of the text. Empirical data, like the excerpt presented above, never yield single, straightforward meanings, and "it is only through the interpretative framework of the researcher that understandings of the 'empirical' come about" (Ang 1996, p. 46). While we recognize the importance of our own interpretative framework, we have tried to read the conversations in a way that does justice to the particular situations in which they came about. This means we have opted for an interpretation that takes into account the context of an interaction, which structures and delimits the possible meanings of the text under investigation. In practice, this

Table 29.1 Discussing body hair in #Cyberbar

<SpawnX> i got stubble <SpawnX> ive been to lazy to shave <LushPuppy> where? <SpawnX> and my face <niceguy420> i dont even have that <LushPuppy> ah <SpawnX> and ya there to pete <niceguy420> when i start to get stubble on my head <LushPuppy> hey I didn't say anything? <niceguy420> i take my mach 3 turbo and shve <SpawnX> but last time i cut my balls with the electric clippers <LushPuppy> could have been on the top of your head? <SpawnX> man they bleed	SpawnX reveals to the other participants that he has been too lazy to shave and thus has "got stubble". LushPuppy questions the location of this "stubble," while iceguy420 claims he doesn't "even have that" because he always shaves his head with his razor. Then SpawnX discloses that he recently cut his "balls," which caused them to bleed. In this conversation, a version of masculinity is discursively constructed by referring to a bodily practice (shaving) in relation to one's "real" male body: the discussion of hair and testicles articulates the physical foundation of their "manhood." While the shaving of one's testicles does not fit the traditional norm of masculinity, the foregrounding of these primary markers of the "male sex" conjures up an image of the male body that fits into the conventions of a binary gender system.

demanded that we interpret the specific utterances of the participants in relation to the larger discussions of which they are a part. In turn, we could only make sense of these larger discussions through the interpretation of the specific utterances that together create meaning. All three authors applied this "hermeneutic circle" in their interpretations of the data to enable a shared understanding of the texts. We are aware that different, more intricate or radical readings might be possible, especially if the researcher adopts a framework based on poststructuralist or queer theory, but we doubt whether many of the participants who read/ write these conversations share similar academic frameworks. Instead of purposefully reading against the grain, we feel it is more interesting to locate the "dominant" meaning that was shared by the participants engaged in particular interactions.

After selecting the usable data, they were transferred from the log files into Word documents. These documents, a total of 267 pages, were then filed chronologically. An interpretative discourse analysis was conducted on this data.[2] The first part of the analysis introduces some of the socio-cultural issues within the discursive environment of the two channels: the articulation of physically located bodies; the use of nicknames; the occurrence of "cross-over"; and the matter of homogeneity in #Queer. The second part demonstrates how these issues relate to the use of certain "interpretative repertoires" within the discourse of #Cyberbar and #Queer (Wetherell & Potter 1988, 1990).

Results: Socio-Cultural Issues in #Cyberbar and #Queer

The Articulation of Physically Located Bodies

Our analysis shows that participants often refer to the physical location of their "real life" selves as they introduce themselves to others in the channel. In turn, these participants expected others to also disclose this sort of information during these introductory conversations. In almost all instances these expectations were met, as it turned out that the physical location of a "real body" features as a common point of reference in many interactions that took place in the channels. In addition, the notion of a geographical location

gives rise to the discursive invocation of other aspects of the "real" body behind the screen, as the following excerpts show:

> <badwolf> hello
> <koainy> hi
> <badwolf> where are u right now?
> <koainy> in front of the computer
> <koainy> why?
> <badwolf> i mean location country city
> <badwolf> just asking
> <koainy> malaysia
> <koainy> and u?
> <badwolf> romania
> <koainy> ok
> <koainy> very far away
> <badwolf> what are u boy girl?
> <koainy> frm the nick, u guess!
> <badwolf> i am not a good quesser
> <koainy> f (#Cyberbar, January 5)

> <adritelles> I am from Brazil
> <CyberDawg^> Brazil
> <adritelles> yes
> <adritelles> Where are you from?
> <CyberDawg^> Texas
> <adritelles> boy or girl?
> <CyberDawg^> boy
> <adritelles> Kimo? How old are you?
> <LadyRaven> 72, adritelles
> <CyberDawg^> I'm 37
> <adritelles> I'm 35 (#Cyberbar, January 18–19)

As can be gathered from these examples, the disclosure of one's physical location quickly leads to questions about one's sex and, in the latter case, age. These inquiries that revolve around the "a/s/l" (age, sex, and location) of physical bodies can be seen as an example of how participants use "classification schemes" (O'Brien 1999) to reduce the uncertainty in their online interactions, using the physical location of "real life" bodies as a common point of reference.

The excerpts above pointed to the discursive invocation of "real," physical bodies. However, participants were also exchanging links to webcams and trading photographs to surpass IRC's textual realm and provide visual proof of their "real life" embodied selves. Whether it was being used as a way for regulars to keep up with each other's altered looks, or to gain attention from possible love/lust interests, the various visual representations of the participants' physical bodies proved to be a vital point of reference during many textual interactions in both channels. The following excerpt, in which some regulars in #Queer discuss the use of pictures in relation to disclosing corporeal features, serves as a good example:

<Buck> he is at work right now
<Healer1> making porn
<Buck> lol nah he is too shy for that
<Healer1> no one is too shy
<Buck> he wont even let me take a pic to show u guys:
<Buck> :\
<Buck> oh he aint shy in bed lol [laugh out loud]
<InHawaii> good for him.
<Healer1> LOL Buck smart boy
<veryh0t> that bad?
<Healer1> can I have the first pic
<Buck> sure .. actually i HAVE a pic but its not scanned. my sister took it for me
<Buck> i need to go to a copy shop 2morrow
<Healer1> a naked one buck
<Buck> nah i know he wont go for that
<veryh0t> candid camera
<Buck> he got pissed off a month ago when i pointed the cam at him for serverguy (#Queer, January 12–13)

As this excerpt shows, the practice of referring to pictures and webcams as a way to reveal someone's "real self" (in this case Buck's offline partner) is incorporated into the textual interactions, which demonstrates how the participants are accustomed to the visual technologies available to them. The assumption, here, is that you can only be who you say you are to the extent that you can visually back it up, making corporeal proof a requirement for "interactional acknowledgement" (O'Brien 1999). Thus, in some instances, text-based communication and visual technologies are integrated in the performance of embodied gender and sexuality on IRC.

The Use of Nicknames

Nicknames play a crucial part in performing an identity in both channels, as they can be used to display information that contributes to the performance of one's age, sex, location, and body type (amongst others). The next excerpt serves as a good example:

<AzureCat> <== Not a gal despite the name
<SpawnX> well there might be some here
<SpawnX> lol
<kat-kat> hi!!
<AzureCat> Guess I should have picked a more manly name
<_HyPNOS_> <== hemaphrodite
<AzureCat> Like DEATHCAT
*kat-kat has left #Cyberbar
<AzureCat> or something
<AzureCat> lol
<SpawnX> lol
<SpawnX> bad
<_HyPNOS_> AzureCat no..real manly name is AnotherBeerBitch
<AzureCat> Yeah (#Cyberbar, January 11–12)

Apparently, AzureCat notices the gender ambiguity surrounding his nickname, so he feels it necessary to explicitly articulate his alleged gender: "not a gal," but a guy. He goes on to suggest a "more manly" nickname, namely DEATHCAT. This conjures up a rather morbid imagery of masculinity as destructive power over life, which is apparently found to be so over-the-top that it evokes laughter ("lol") in the channel. Meanwhile, HyPNOS seems to suggest (s)he is a hermaphrodite, but when this statement appears to be ignored (s)he returns with another suggestion for a "real manly" nickname: "AnotherBeerBitch." This strategy produces the idea of nicknames that are masculine as opposed to feminine. A nickname seems to be considered more masculine when it addresses the opposite sex in a derogatory way, thereby establishing the male dominance of the participant who uses it. At the same time, any suggestion of identification outside of the male-female dichotomy is ignored. Thus, it appears that the nicknames in this example are subjected to the logic of a binary gender system that only allows for either a male or female subject position.

"Cross-Over"

Recalling O'Brien's notion about the need for "considerable interaction between those who carry altered gender expectations and those who maintain traditional representations of both fact/fiction and male/female" (1996, p. 66), we looked at the occurrence of "cross-over": the interaction between "straight" and "non-straight" participants in both channels. First, our analysis shows that #Queer is predominantly populated by participants who construct a gay male identity, while #Cyberbar mostly features participants who perform heterosexual male and female identities. Second, although the amount of participants "crossing-over" is marginal, its most prominent manifestation takes place in the form of "gay bashing." In the online version of "gay bashing," self-proclaimed "straight" people enter #Queer (and most likely other channels) in order to display their disdain for the "abject" and to subsequently articulate their heterosexual identity through these negative expressions. Some examples of homophobia in #Queer include:

> <Realist-01> This channel is profane!! The only purpose for sex is reproduction! Homosexuality is without purpose and therefore must be eliminated! (#Queer, January 8/9)

> <Negative0> Heh, fags:>
> <fade> :(
> * fade is scared
> <Negative0> O_o
> <fade> aha heres a chick
> <fade> or no
> <Negative0> Where ?
> <fade> its some guy pretending to be one
> <fade> :(
> <fade> i wanna lovebang a girl
> <DecK19> well done
> <fade> with big GREAT titties!
> <fade> mmmmmm tits
> <Negative0> And sweet ass
> <Negative0> Pussy:>
> <Greeklove> is this a gay channel?i wonder
> <fade> oh yeah
> <fade> PUSSEH (#Queer, January 8–9)

Homogeneity in #Queer

Finally, it is important to return to a notion that emerged in the discussion about interaction between "straight" and "non-straight" participants. It has already been mentioned that #Queer is predominantly populated by participants who perform a gay male identity, which means that only a small segment of queer identity is articulated in this channel.[3] While lesbian, transvestite, and transsexual identities have been prominent within queer culture and theory, they are rarely performed in #Queer. As far as they do occur in this channel, the regulars treat them as outsiders who must have mistakenly entered "their domain." The following examples serve as illustrations:

> <xdressed> anyone wanna cyber with hot punk crossdress bitch?
> <xdressed> whats a good channel to go on?
> <VoyAger4u> xdressed, what kind of fun do you want?
> <xdressed> any to be honest
> <VoyAger4u> hehe
> <VoyAger4u> then just try some
> <VoyAger4u> see what suits you the most
> <xdressed> mmmmm can't find any shemale rooms or crossdresser rooms
> <VoyAger4u> how do you search?
> <xdressed> search buttton
> <VoyAger4u> okie (#Queer, January 8–9)

> <veryh0t> guys in drag please dont message me
> <Alecxx> does this happne to you a lot veryh0t?
> <veryh0t> does what happen to me a lot alexcc??
> <Alecxx> guys in drag hitting on you
> <veryh0t> i wouldnt know, it was a warning (#Queer, January 18–19)

In the first excerpt, "xdressed" enters #Queer looking for other cross-dressers, but to no avail. (S)he is politely asked to try somewhere else. This excerpt shows that although there are requests for transvestite or transsexual interactions, they are redirected to some space other than #Queer. The fact remains that most of the participants in #Queer are performing homosexual male identities and are not interested in interactions with participants who articulate an alternative gender. This kind of "gay male normativity" can even lead to apprehensive behavior, as demonstrated by "veryh0t" in the second excerpt.

Interpretative Repertoires: The Perseverance of the Body

As discussed above, the body plays an instrumental role within the discursive interactions in both channels. Whether it is through the articulation of physically located bodies, the adoption of gendered nicknames, the violent practice of gay bashing, or the reinforcement of a "gay male norm," the notion of embodiment constitutes a red thread throughout the channels' discourse. Accordingly, when focusing on the construction of specific "interpretative repertoires" in the participants' discursive exchanges, our analysis resulted in the identification of three such repertoires that involved an invocation of embodiment: the "real life body" repertoire; the "phallic" repertoire; and the "physical motion" repertoire.[4]

The "Real Life Body" Repertoire

One of the ways in which embodiment comes into play is through the invocation of "real life" bodies. During numerous conversations, the participants articulate a body behind the screen to "add weight" to the identities they are trying to construct.

The conversation in the first excerpt focuses on the modification of the "real body" behind the screen and the discursive signifying practices that give this modification meaning. The conversation starts when niceguy420 is asked whether he had his ear pierced:

> <TheLuvBunnys> bro u got yer ear pierced?
> <niceguy420> now i do
> <niceguy420> i got both pierced
> <TheLuvBunnys> ackkkkkkk
> <TheLuvBunnys> but u aint gay lol
> <niceguy420> i know
> <TripleNut> Always the left.
> <TripleNut> Always.
> <TripleNut> Right is gay.
> <TheLuvBunnys> yup

> <niceguy420> my friend has em both pierced
> <TripleNut> So never the right.
> <TripleNut> Never.
> <TheLuvBunnys> me whacks TripleNut
> <niceguy420> and he gets more women than i used to
> <TheLuvBunnys> roflmao
> <TheLuvBunnys> now wait a minute
> <TheLuvBunnys> how the hell ya gonna get more wimmin with 2 ears pierced pfft lol
> <niceguy420> cause
> <niceguy420> in washinton state
> <niceguy420> gays wear tight pants and see through net shirts
> <TheLuvBunnys> ewww
> <TripleNut> Yuck (#Cyberbar, February 6–7)

After niceguy420 reveals he has both ears pierced, TheLuvBunnys react with shock and need affirmation of his heterosexual identity. TripleNut then emphasizes that the piercing should "always" be in the left ear, since the "right is gay." He subsequently repeats that it thus should never be on the right side, suggesting a fear of and/or an animosity towards gay people. In an attempt to reaffirm the masculine heterosexual intention behind getting both of his ears pierced, niceguy420 states that his friend has both of his ears pierced as well and "gets more women" than he used to. TheLuvBunnys are seemingly amused by this statement, as can be gathered from the abbreviation "roflmao" (rolling on the floor laughing my ass off). In answer to TheLuvBunnys question about "how the hell" he is going to get more women with two ears pierced, niceguy420 explains that where he comes from "gays wear tight pants and see through net shirts." This is received with disgusted outcries such as "ewww" and "yuck."

This example clearly shows how a supposed modification of the "real body" behind the screen can function as a discursive signifier, the symbolic value of which leads certain participants to discursively establish a schism between the "normal" (in this case the heterosexual) and the abnormal, or abject (in this case the homosexual).

In the next excerpt, a different version of the previously explained abbreviation "roflmao" proves to be the catalyst in a conversation about buttocks:

<pdavid> i need to get blasted
<BIAsT3d> lmfao . . . not today!;)
<pdavid> ojk whats the f does the f mean in there
<VoyAger4u> f = friends
<VoyAger4u> f = fabulous
<BIAsT3d> *grin*
<VoyAger4u> f = feminine gay
<BIAsT3d> yeah . . . fabulous . . .;-) for my wonderful ass
<BIAsT3d> lol
* VoyAger4u pings BlAsT3d in one of his fabulous buttocks:-) and marks it 'approved by VoyAger4u':-)
<Crazednut> lol
<BIAsT3d> Woot!!
<BIAsT3d> ;)
<pdavid> heard mine is a ten
<VoyAger4u> woot indeed:-)
<pdavid> never really see much of it
<VoyAger4u> show me, pdavid:-) (#Queer, February 3–4)

As stated above, "lmao" means "laughing my ass off." But the addition of an "f" by BIAsT3d causes some confusion in the channel. After some guesses about the possible meaning of the "f," BIAsT3d jokingly affirms VoyAger4u's conjecture by stating that it indeed stands for "fabulous," in reference to his "wonderful ass." VoyAger4u then simulates "pinging" (a virtual pinching) BIAsT3d's "fabulous buttocks" and marks it "approved by VoyAger4u." Not wanting to be left out, pdavid mentions that his behind is valued at a "ten," to which VoyAger4u mischievously asks for some visual proof. In this excerpt, the references to the participants' real life buttocks function as a way of expressing their desire for "real" physical male bodies, and to consecutively perform their identity as gay men. Whereas the discussion in the previous example explicitly positioned male bodies in a heterosexual matrix, it here becomes an object of both pride and homosexual lust, which challenges the traditional conceptions of masculine identity. However, while these participants discursively deviate from the norm (i.e. traditional male heterosexuality), the male-female gender binary remains intact.

The "Phallic" Repertoire

A certain amount of the discourse in both channels focused on the "male" genitals, in particular on the penis. Based on this outcome, a "phallic" repertoire could be identified, which is closely related to the "real life body" repertoire. The main difference between the two is that the "phallic" repertoire focuses solely on this particular body part and its symbolic power as gendered signifier.

In the first excerpt, two participants are engaged in a mock fight in which they try to outdo each other in more ways than one:

* Amoot beats off Kipper with a pair of chopsticks
<Kipper> my stick is bigger than your stick;P
<Amoot> i've got two sticks:p
<blade_uk> now now
<Kipper> hehheh
<Amoot> twice the fun
<blade_uk> lets not go there
* Amoot giggles
<Amoot> and one question
<Kipper> hockey stick you dirty minded git blade_uk;)
<blade_uk> me
<Amoot> yeah, my 5ft pole
<Amoot> hmm how long is the hockey stick?
<blade_uk> you wish
<Amootsgirl> lol
<Kipper> mine is 5.5 foot
<Amoot> darn, you do have a bigger stick than me
<Amoot> mines only 5ft even
<Amootsgirl> lol as tall as me babe im 5 ft even lol
<Amoot> yup, you've seen my big stick between my legs babe
<Amoot> i sent ya photos remember? (#Cyberbar, January 12–13)

What first appears to be an innocent chopstick fight rapidly becomes a tongue-in-cheek competition about who has the biggest "hockey stick." This showdown can be read as a scene of macho bravado, where self-proclaimed male participants brag about the size of their "real life" penises (represented here through the "hockey stick" image). Even if there was any doubt concerning the subject matter, Amoot bluntly puts an end to this when he refers to the "big stick" between "his" legs. What this example illustrates, then, is how participants use metaphors to refer to the size of their "real life" male genitals, discursively constructing a masculine dominance that is derived from the symbolic power of the "phallus." This also explains the use of the "hockey stick" metaphor: since the participants' physical genitals stand in stark contrast to the mythical power of the symbolic "phallus," they are discursively substituted by a much larger piece of "equipment" with a phallic shape.

Just like in #Cyberbar, the conversations in #Queer focused on the male genitals of the participants, but in this channel the use of a traditional "phallic" metaphor is replaced by a homo-erotic discourse that evokes sexual desire rather than authority and admiration. The following excerpt shows some participants engaged in a fairly raunchy conversation about making a cast of their penis:

> <Buck> me and the new hubby were at a motel when we were dating and they had xxx movies and commercials.. one of them was the kit to make a replica of ur own dick
> <Healer1> Hey buck you can bid on one on ebay LOL
> <Buck> lol probably
> <Healer1> they have the two inch and 24 inch sizes left
> <Buck> 2 inches would only piss me off
> * Luiggi18 has joined #Queer
> <Healer1> it wouldnt even tickle me
> <InHawaii> I'd love to make a replieca of some of my friends, life size, and have them sitting around the place.
> <Buck> hehe
> <Healer1> or you sitting around the place on them LOL
> <veryh0t> thats sick
> <veryh0t> thats even better
> <InHawaii> LOL
> <Buck> ur nasty (keep talking)
> <InHawaii> that could be fun too. (#Queer, January 12–13)

As discussed above, the conversation in this example focuses on producing a replica of a "real life" penis as an object of homosexual desire, rather than the masculine power signified by the phallus in heteronormative discourse. This can be understood as follows: participants who perform a masculine gender identity in #Cyberbar have to make use of the symbolic power of the phallus to construct their identity as a dominant male *in opposition to* the participants who articulate female identities, whose identification with the symbolic phallus is denied in heteronormative discourse. In addition, the relationship between these participants who construct masculine identities is one of competition, since this performance requires them to position themselves as authoritarian and victorious. In contrast, the majority of the participants in #Queer are performing gay male identities, in which the phallus is not only the source of symbolic power, but also a physical object to be sexually desired. As this latter position is traditionally reserved for heterosexual women, this "queered" discourse breaks with traditional gender roles in relation to their presupposed heterosexuality. In addition, these performances "stretch" the traditional conception of masculinity by inserting it into a homo-erotic discourse.

The "Physical Motion" Repertoire

The "physical motion" repertoire, like the previous two repertoires, also functions to foreground the body in an otherwise disembodied realm. But whereas in the previous two repertoires the "real" physical body (or the symbolic power derived therefrom) is invoked, it is the suggestion of physical motion in a virtual space (i.e. the IRC channel) that forms the discursive center of this repertoire.

In the most revealing example, we come across Aragorn, a participant who has previously articulated a masculine identity. "He" has just received the head of a Barbie doll from SpawnX, and is now flirting with LadyRaven:

> * Aragorn^ tongues LadyRaven
> <niceguy420> woa
> <LadyRaven> lol
> <niceguy420> grab a room would ya

<Pluckster> lol niceguy
<SpawnX> took long enough to quit with the head
<LadyRaven> where's Kalasin when I need her >
:D
<niceguy420> unless i get to join in
<niceguy420> j/k
<Pluckster> lol
* Aragorn^ gives LadyRaven head. THE head. the
barbie head
<Aragorn^> lol
<LadyRaven> LOL
<niceguy420> aragon gave LR head (#Cyberbar,
January 5)

Aragorn's suggestion of physical intimacy with Lady-Raven evokes amused "outrage" from the other regulars in the channel, as illustrated by niceguy420's comment "grab a room would ya." Aragorn then takes it a step further by simulating giving LadyRaven "head," suggesting the performance of oral sex. He immediately revokes his act by stating he meant the Barbie head, but his intentions are obvious to the rest of the room. Following the participants' interpretation of this scene, it makes most sense to read this interaction as an attempt by a participant to express his masculine heterosexuality by making sexual insinuations to a participant who performs a feminine identity. These insinuations are discursively enacted by simulating the physical act of oral sex, in order to add credibility to his advances and, in turn, his online gender identity.

Discussion and Conclusion

The most important conclusion of this study is that the interactions in both #Cyberbar and #Queer contain various discursive performances of embodiment that, in general, have reinforced the norms of a binary gender system through the reiteration of a "natural" connection between gender and sexed bodies. However, while the male-female dichotomy remains unchallenged in both channels, a number of participants in #Queer articulated alternative interpretations of masculinity, which did destabilize traditional heteronormative standards concerning "male behavior."

O'Brien's suggestion that the establishment of online queer spaces could transgress conventional performances of gender and embodiment seems

thereby only partly corroborated. Yet as discussed above, #Queer proved to almost exclusively host participants who performed a gay male identity, instead of representing a larger variety of queer performances.[5] The majority of the participants in #Queer presented themselves as "male" and closely related this identification to a physical body. While homosexuality certainly poses a challenge to the heteronormative matrix that forms the foundation of our binary gender system (through its reinforcement of a desire for the "opposite" sex), the object of desire in #Queer was still the traditional male body, providing little reason to seek out alternatives beyond the male-female dichotomy. Even though the participants in #Queer did expand conventional notions of masculinity, they simultaneously created their own "gay male norm" that did not allow for performances which transgressed its boundaries.

This supports O'Brien's view that the "alternative experiences" enacted in online environments are based on "real life" experiences. People who have not experienced what it is like to continuously "live" an alternative gender on a day-to-day basis can hardly be expected to perform an online identity that challenges something as pervasive as our binary gender system. In this way, we also concur with O'Brien's stance that it is not the internet itself that facilitates a discursive space capable of reconceptualizing gender. The internet, or in this case IRC, is indeed not an autonomous "thing," but is made up of people who bring their everyday experiences to a realm where their actions together constitute a shared, temporal reality. It is important to keep in mind, then, that this "reality" consists of discourses that originate from an embodied understanding of how our world works and who/what/how we can be to make our lives as livable as possible. In Lisa Nakamura's words:

> In order to think rigorously, humanely, and imaginatively about virtuality and the "posthuman," it is absolutely necessary to ground critique in the lived realities of the human, in all the particularities and specificity. The nuanced realities of virtuality—racial, gendered, othered—live in the body, and though science is producing and encouraging different readings and revisions of the body, it is premature to throw it away just yet, particularly

since so much postcolonial, political and feminist critique stems from it.

(2002, p. 7)

Contemporary technoculture contains a paradox: on the one hand it cherishes a fetish for the transcendence of the material, striving for and depending on an increasingly faster and more efficient exchange of information in the most compressed, least space-consuming way possible. In this sense, we are still chasing the cyberpunk dreams that are now often considered hyperbolic and naïve. We still want to think and talk beyond our corporeal capabilities. Yet on the other hand another fetish is cherished, up to the point that it tends to become an obsession. The massive surge of people engaged in blogging, social networking, photo sharing, and vodcasting has exhibited an intense fascination with the mundane, everyday experiences of people exposing their embodied selves to those willing to watch. This preoccupation with real life/live body images on the computer screen firmly reassures us that the material body is still present, albeit in a technologically mediated way.

Within this paradoxical technoculture, textual internet communication occupies a peculiar position. In a sense it still contains the aspiration to "leave the body behind," but at the same time it is continually haunted by the "specter of embodiment" that enforces its law and governs our discourse. In the context of gender, this specter continues to enforce a discourse that links gender to a dichotomously sexed body, whether visible or not.

Acknowledgements

We are grateful for the financial support of the Netherlands Organisation of Scientific Research (NWO), grant number: NWO-MES 014–43–701, entitled "Gender bending on the Internet." We are also grateful to all of the members of the Internet PhD club within ASCoR for their many and helpful comments on an earlier draft.

Notes

1. "Logging" is the act of storing all of the data from an IRC channel into a "log file."

2. Obviously, this analysis focused solely on the public part of the two channels.

3. This is something that was discovered after a large part of the data had already been analyzed. It then became apparent that #Queer largely consisted of participants who performed a gay male gender identity.

4. A "Pop-Cultural" repertoire was also identified but since it had no relation to the notion of embodiment we decided not to discuss it here. For a complete discussion of all four repertoires, see van Doorn (2005).

5. If #Queer had indeed hosted a broader array of queer performances, it is very plausible that the results would have been different and that alternative repertoires might have been identified.

References

Ang, Ien (1996) *Living Room Wars: Rethinking Media Audiences for a Postmodern World*, Routledge, London.

Bell, David (2001) *An Introduction to Cybercultures*, Routledge, New York.

Brickell, Chris (2005) 'Masculinities, performativity, and subversion: a sociological reappraisal', *Men and Masculinities*, vol. 8, no. 1, pp. 24–43.

Bruckman, Amy (1992) *Identity Workshop. Emergent Social and Psychological Phenomena in Text-Based Virtual Reality*, [Online] Available at: http://www.cc.gatech.edu/fac/Amy.Bruckman/papers/index.html#IW (March, 2005).

Bruckman, Amy (1993) 'Gender swapping on the internet', *Proceedings of INET93*, The Internet Society, Reston, VA, [Online] Available at: http://www.cc.gatech.edu/~asb/papers/gender-swapping.txt.~asb/papers/gender-swapping.txt (January, 2005).

Butler, Judith (1993) *Bodies that Matter: On the Discursive Limits of Sex*, Routledge, London and New York.

Danet, Brenda (1996) *Text as Mask: Gender and Identity on the Internet*, [Online] Available at: http://atar.mscc.huji.ac.il/~msdanet/mask.html (January, 2005).

Herring, Susan C. [1993] (1996) 'Gender and democracy in computer-mediated communication', *Electronic Journal of Communication*, vol. 3, no. 2, repressed in *Computerization and Controversy*, 2nd edn, ed. Rob Kling, Academic Press, New York.

Herring, Susan C. (1995) 'Men's language on the internet', Tromso University Working Papers on Language and Linguistics, Nordlyd.

Herring, Susan C. (1996) 'Posting a different voice: gender and ethics in computer mediated communication', in *Philosophical Perspectives on Computer Mediated Communication*, ed. Charles Ess, SUNY Press, Albany, pp. 115–145.

Herring, Susan C., Johnson, D. & Dibenedetto, T. (1995) 'This discussion is going too far! Male resistance to female participation on the internet', in *Gender Articulated: Language and the Socially Constructed Self*, eds Mary Buchholtz & Kira Hall, Routledge, New York, pp. 67–96.

Jaffe, J. Michael, Lee, Y., Huang, L. & Oshagan, H. (1995) 'Gender, pseudonyms and CMC: masking identities and baring souls', paper presented at the 45th annual conference of the International Communication Association, Albuquerque, NM, [Online] Available at: http://members.iworld.net/yesunny/genderps.html (January, 2005).

Mann, Chris & Stewart, Fiona (2000) *Internet Communication and Qualitative Research*, Sage, London.

MIRC (website) (n.d.) Available at: http://www.mirc.com/irc.html (December, 2004).

Nakamura, Lisa (2002) *Cybertypes. Race, Ethnicity, and Identity on the Internet*, Routledge, New York.

O'Brien, Jodi (1996) 'Changing the subject', *Women & Performance: A Journal of Feminist Theory*, vol. 17, no. 9, pp. 55–67.

O'Brien, Jodi (1999) 'Writing in the body: gender (re)production in online interaction', in *Communities in Cyberspace*, eds Marc A. Smith & Peter Kollock, Routledge, London, pp. 76–104.

Reid, Elisabeth (1993) 'Electronic chat: social issues in internet relay chat', *Media Information Australia*, vol. 67, pp. 62–70.

Reid, Elisabeth (1994) *Cultural Formations in Text-Based Virtual Realities*, [Online] Available at: http://www.ludd.luth.se/mud/aber/articles/cult-form.thesis.html (January, 2005).

Rodino, Michelle (1997) 'Breaking out of binaries: reconceptualizing gender and its relation to language in computer mediated communication', *Journal of Computer-Mediated Communication*, vol. 3, no. 3, [Online] Available at: http://www.ascusc.org/jcmc/vol3/issue3/rodino.html (January, 2005).

Savicki, V., Kelley, M. & Lingenfelter, D. (1996) 'Gender language style and group composition in internet discussion groups', *Journal of Computer-Mediated Communication*, vol. 2, no. 3, [Online] Available at: http://ascusc.org/jcmc/vol2/issue3/savicki.html (January, 2005).

Sundén, Jenny (2003) *Material Virtualities: Approaching Online Textual Embodiment*, Peter Lang Publishing, New York.

Van Doorn, Niels (2005) *A Body of Text: Gender and Sexuality in Synchronous Computer-Mediated Communication*, unpublished MA thesis, University of Amsterdam.

Van Doorn, Niels & Van Zoonen, Liesbet (2008) 'Theorizing gender and the internet: past, present, and future', in *The Handbook of Internet Politics*, eds Andrew Chadwick & Philip Howard, Routledge, New York, pp. 261–274.

Wetherell, Margaret & Potter, Jonathan (1988) 'Rhetoric and ideology. Discourse analysis and the identification of interpretative repertoires', in *Analyzing Everyday Explanation. A Casebook of Methods*, ed. Charles Antaki, Sage, London, pp. 168–183.

Wetherell, Margaret & Potter, Jonathan (1990) 'Discourse: noun, verb or social practice?', *Philosophical Psychology*, vol. 3, no. 2/3, pp. 205–219.

PART IV

TEXTS: GENRE, MODE, AND OTHER NARRATIVE STRATEGIES

Introduction

Analyses of gender, genre, and other narrative strategies compose Part IV of this collection. Since critical media studies has as its primary focus fictional, entertainment texts and owes much of its academic heritage to literature and drama studies, questions of narrative are commonly privileged in such scholarship. Building from foundational analyses of gendered media representation that exposed patriarchal patterns of storytelling, such as Laura Mulvey's "Visual Pleasure and Narrative Cinema,"[1] the studies included here explore how gender is produced and negotiated via different narrative practices, including genre, movement, and character. Genre plays an important role in the majority of these chapters, although it is differently construed depending on the medium in question (e.g., film, television, music).[2]

The objects of study and methodological approaches in narrative-based feminist and queer media studies have been diverse. In order to study gendered storytelling practices in cinema, early feminist film scholars adopted the psychoanalytic approach made popular in feminist literary studies in the 1970s and 1980s.[3] Although originally focused on discerning patriarchal narrative strategies in mainstream media, such studies commonly led to explorations of female-centered texts, such as women's films, soap operas, and fashion magazines, as well as searches for agential, feminist characters.[4] Once manhood and masculinity became specific objects of study for media scholars, male-centered texts, such as action/adventure films, came under greater scrutiny. Although narrative genres have long been understood as gender-specific, many media texts produced today, particularly within film and television, are hybridized generically in order to appeal to both male and female audience members. Studies of narrative and genre in contemporary feminist and queer media scholarship have veered from this subfield's early psychoanalytic path in order to consider other factors impacting storytelling practices, such as performance, commerce, medium specificity, sociohistorical context, and text–reader relations. Indeed, given the common understanding among media scholars today that textual meaning is produced by consumers, it is not surprising that many chapters in this part explore narrative strategies and reception practices simultaneously.

The chapter that opens Part IV is Teresa de Lauretis's "Oedipus Interruptus."[5] As with Mulvey, De Lauretis adopts a psychoanalytic approach and is concerned here with the difficulty of female spectators' identification and pleasure in cinema, yet she looks to narrative to theorize this dilemma. De Lauretis starts from the common psychoanalytic notion that narrative is Oedipal—that is, story movement operates in relation to male desire, following the male protagonist through his journey to mature adulthood as the female character operates as the point of narrative closure. De Lauretis argues that to find pleasure in narrative films female spectators identify both with the images they see on the screen (including women) and with the movement of the narrative (although it is male-driven), thus resolving one of the contradictions in Mulvey's theory. In turn, she advocates feminists' different filmmaking strategies via their creation of texts that disrupt the traditional Oedipal narrative schema by calling attention to a cultural practice that has historically limited female desire.

Michael Schiavi's "A 'Girlboy's' Own Story" explores the storytelling strategies of *Ma Vie en Rose*, a film whose pre-pubescent, cross-dressing lead character rejects the heteronormative and patriarchal strictures of Oedipal narrative analyzed by De Lauretis. A seemingly untellable story, *Ma Vie en Rose*, Schiavi argues, bravely represents the identity explorations of a child who subverts all gender and sexual categories (is he gay? is he genderqueer? is he a she?) and thus reveals the progressive potential of both narrative and gender today, two structures traditionally limited by fears of deviance, particularly as embodied by effeminate boys.

Moving the discussion of narrative toward media modes that are female-centered, Christine Gledhill's "Speculations on the Relationship between Soap Opera and Melodrama" approaches her project not via case study but via history and theory. Gledhill begins by noting the common scholarly subsumption of soap opera under melodrama and argues for a teasing out of the two in order to better understand their relation and differences. Examining the development of each genre, Gledhill discusses both male and female participation in early melodramatic culture, yet the increasing gendering of that mode as feminine during the late nineteenth century. Meanwhile, she notes that soap opera developed from women's domestic fiction, which sets it apart from melodrama in terms of formal strategies, narrative structure, and presentation of personal relationships. Nevertheless, Gledhill finds that the prominence of the family and a serial structure in soap opera open the genre to melodramatic devices, even though those are differently utilized based on cultural context.

Also focusing on the mode of melodrama, Linda Williams's "Film Bodies: Gender, Genre, and Excess" adds two other sensational film genres to her objects of study: horror and pornography. Pushing reception analyses toward studies of real consumers, Williams focuses on elements of excess, perversion, and fantasy in each of these "body genres" in order to better understand viewers' embodied responses to their violent, emotional, and sexual sensationalism. As a feminist, Williams is concerned also with how gender operates in each of these genres, particularly women's masochistic construction, as well as the processes of gendered spectatorship. Yet Williams's theory also allows for shifts in such genres' representation and viewership, noting that all display great fluidity with regard to gender in their explorations of sexual identity, power, and pleasure.

Sarah Banet-Weiser and Laura Portwood-Stacer's "'I Just Want to Be Me Again!'" similarly concerns the body, yet their study is a comparative analysis of shows within a particular genre of television. Focusing on the Miss American Pageant and makeover shows, like *The Swan* (FOX 2004) and *Extreme Makeover* (ABC 2002–2007), they explore the intersecting themes of beauty, femininity, agency, commercialism, and citizenship. Through a discursive analysis of such texts' constructions of women's beauty, Banet-Weiser and Portwood-Stacer comment on the difference between pageants' seemingly outdated concern with inner beauty and social empowerment and makeover series' focus on self-actualization via superficial, physical transformation. They link this latter approach to postfeminism, a contradictory commercial discourse that advocates individual improvement and agency through consumption and avoids critical reflection on power, oppression, and structural inequality.[6]

Taking up yet another sensational body genre, Yvonne Tasker's "Fists of Fury" explores the martial arts film. In this work, Tasker moves the study of gender in the action genre beyond its typical masculine framing by considering its intersections with race and ethnicity in the martial arts performers and cinemas of Hollywood and Hong Kong. Through her study, Tasker reveals the dominant place of the male body in martial arts films, a body that is often featured as hard, resilient, and triumphant, yet one that is also impacted by the different contexts productive of its representation, not the least of which is nationality.

Susan Douglas's "Letting the Boys Be Boys" concerns the variations of gender in the genre of male-hosted talk radio. Centering on the gender performances of Howard Stern, Rush Limbaugh, and Don Imus, Douglas argues that such hosts created a variety of gender performances in response to the popularization of feminism in the late twentieth century. While some of these white, male hosts demonstrated their racial and gender bigotry daily, others showed characteristics long associated with women, such as being overly emotional. As much as Douglas sees progressive potential in the gender hybrid of the male hysteric as performed by hosts like Limbaugh, she nevertheless concludes that such gender performances can be seen as part of a larger conservative movement in the 1980s and 1990s whose objective was saving the United States from the "soft" values of feminists and Democrats.

Martha Nochimson's "'Waddaya Lookin' At?'" examines a similarly masculinized cultural structure: the gangster genre. Focusing on *The Sopranos* (HBO 1999–2007), Nochimson brackets the gangster narrative from other types of crime stories in order to explore how HBO's hit series reveals the complex emotional subtext of what is ostensibly a melodramatic submode, albeit one that is muscular and violent rather than feminine and weepy. Indeed, as Nochimson argues, *The Sopranos* foregrounds its melodramatic heritage via its lead character's domestic relations, psychotherapy sessions, and conflicting impulses of duty and desire, innocence and immorality.

Henry Jenkins's "Never Trust a Snake" also explores the melodramatic mode, yet this time from within the world of sports and manhood. Building upon earlier work by Roland Barthes and taking the World Wrestling Federation (WWF) televised shows as his object of study, Jenkins theorizes professional wrestling as masculine melodrama. He is particularly concerned with the structure and reception of WWF broadcasts, and explores pro wrestling's cathartic effect on its primarily male, working-class audience. Arguing that such texts are both progressive and reactionary, Jenkins demonstrates their homophobic, jingoistic, racist, and misogynist tendencies, while also appreciating their ability to provide a legitimated space for male bonding and emotional release, as well as class resistance.

Robert Walser's "Forging Masculinity" is one of the first studies of gender in a rock music genre.[7] Focusing on heavy metal, Walser is specifically concerned with the constructions and negotiations of masculine power present in this musical scene. He explores heavy metal's gender work with regard to not only its lyrical and sonic styles, but also the visual representation of bands and, like Jenkins, the reception practices of their mostly white, working-class audience members. Although Walser is keen to understand how male metal fans negotiate the various representations of masculinity and misogyny circulating within this genre, he also notes an increase in romance as a lyrical theme since the 1980s and spends time analyzing female fans' reception practices as well as the androgynous performances of male "hair bands."

Diane Railton's "The Gendered Carnival of Pop" explores gender in the genre of pop music, a form traditionally derided by academics and music critics for its perceived superficiality, spectacularity, anti-intellectualism, and commercialism, not to mention its young female fans. Utilizing theories of the carnivalesque, Railton argues that pop is liberatory, providing girls—performers and consumers alike—with an opportunity to experience the bodily pleasures of music without sanction and to engage with a cultural form that places them center stage. Pop, in other words, challenges cultural and social hierarchies. Interestingly, despite its transgressions, it is a style taken seriously by the music industry as it struggles to cash in on popular trends. Nevertheless, within a bourgeois, patriarchal culture that continues to privilege ostensibly "serious" musical styles, such as rock, pop remains disparaged, the genre girls are meant to leave behind them as they grow up. Pop's potential remains constrained by its association with a particular generational identity as well as gender identities.

Notes

1. Laura Mulvey's article is reprinted in Part I of this reader.
2. For some media scholars, genres are used to categorize texts based on their common formal and narrative strategies. For others, genres have a ritual function, helping audiences to explore and negotiate particular social problems. Today, many media scholars adopt the perspective outlined by Jason Mittell, understanding genres as cultural categories that are collectively produced by media producers, critics, and audiences. See "A Cultural Approach to Television Genre Theory," *Cinema Journal* 40.3 (2001) 3–24.
3. For example, see Tania Modleski, *Loving with a Vengeance: Mass-Produced Fantasies for Women* (Hamden, CT: Archon Books, 1982).
4. For example, see Christine Gledhill, ed., *Home Is Where the Heart Is: Studies in Melodrama and the Woman's Film* (London: British Film Institute, 1987).
5. De Lauretis expands considerably on this argument in *Alice Doesn't: Feminism, Semiotics, Cinema* (Bloomington: Indiana University Press, 1984).
6. For another analysis of postfeminist media culture, see Rosalind Gill's chapter reprinted in Part I of this reader.
7. Walser takes this analysis much further in *Running with the Devil: Power, Gender, and Madness in Heavy Metal Music* (Hanover, NH: University Press of New England, 1993).

30.
OEDIPUS INTERRUPTUS
Teresa de Lauretis

My title is polemical and intentionally misleading. For in the context of a discussion about narrative and the avant-garde, whose historical and theoretical antipathy have long been established, or at least presumed, in film studies, the pun of "Oedipus Interruptus" is likely to be read more or less as follows: avant-garde cinema interrupts the pleasure of the text, that "passion of meaning" which, Roland Barthes observed, is "an Oedipal pleasure (to denude, to know, to learn the origin and the end), if it is true that every narrative (every unveiling of the truth) is a staging of the (absent, hidden, or hypostatized) father."[1] The avant-garde, therefore, is anti-Oedipal. Yet this is but the first, the easiest, and most obvious, of the implications intended by the pun, and one which it is my purpose to debate.

Within Barthes' Oedipal metaphor, the other kind of text, the text of *jouissance*, disrupts narrative pleasure by withholding from the reader or the writer not simply the possibility of coming to meaning and closure but also the consequently—one might say— the male seed which is necessary for reproduction. Barthes, most probably, had just this in mind: one aim of the writerly, or creative, activity is to stop the reproduction of society as we know it. And women want that too, or so we feminists believe. However, if we pursue that metaphor in its often asserted relevance to the avant-garde as a politically radical practice of cinema, we come to this paradox: by denying narrative and instead affirming a kind of material *jouissance* of the apparatus, or by analyzing the operations of cinema as Marx analyzed the operations of capital,

avant-garde cinema would withhold from the spectator (or the filmmaker) the seed necessary to social reproduction; that is to say, it would withhold the possibility of control of, or even access to, the means of production. I am speaking, obviously, of the production of imaging, not babies; but that's the point of the metaphor.

What I am leading up to suggesting, in short, is that Barthes' preference for the texts of *jouissance* modernist or postmodernist, and his concern to undermine the father may be admirable and praiseworthy in themselves, but are not altogether pertinent to a feminist theory of narrative and representation; nor are they immediately applicable to the political-textual practices of feminism. Women do have a stake in (re)production for, unlike Barthes' reader-writer or the "speaking subjects" of whom Kristeva speaks, they belong to a social category whose control of the means of production is severely restricted. I will then propose that, from where a woman stands—or lies, or looks, or works—to interrupt Oedipus can be quite a different thing.

Barthes' view of the pleasure of the text, at once erotic and epistemological, develops from his earlier hunch (during his semiological period) of an intimate connection between language, narrative, and the Oedipus. In the famous "Introduction to the Structural Analysis of Narratives" (1966), he first pointed out what has since become a basic semiotic postulate— that "narrative is international, transhistorical, transcultural: it is simply there, like life itself."[2] Then, after a lengthy and detailed analysis of narrative instances and the logic of their paradigmatic and integrative relations, he ended his essay with a curious statement: "it may be significant that it is at the same moment (around the age of three) that the little human 'invents' at once sentence, narrative, and the Oedipus."[3] Pleasure and meaning move along this triple track, and the tracking is from the point of view of Oedipus, so to speak; its movement is that of masculine desire. Thus, as the myth of Oedipus is paradigmatic of all narrative, it seems to follow quite logically that any anti-narrative textual practice will produce an anti-Oedipus. But equally, I again suggest, anti-Oedipus is *not* a useful feminist conceit.

When Claire Johnston first noted, back in 1974, that "women's cinema must embody the working through of desire," what she had in mind was narrative cinema or, as she put it, "the entertainment film."[4] Very much out of a similar concern, in a recent essay on sexual identity and melodrama, Laura Mulvey addresses the question of the female spectator's pleasure and the positionalities of identification available to her in narrative cinema, which are "triggered by the logic of narrative grammar."[5] It is indeed time to reexamine the nature of narrative structure and the working of narrativity intra- and inter-textually in light of questions, like desire and identification, that have been preempted in semiotic studies or, in film theory, displaced by other interests (such as the long debate on the psychoanalytic definition of the subject). For feminist criticism, in particular, the reexamination of narrative theories amounts to a rereading of certain sacred texts—filmic or written, fictional or theoretical, like the Barthes texts just cited—in line with the passionate urging of a different question, a different practice, and a different desire.

The necessity for such theoretical return to narrative can be argued for both pragmatically, in view of the increasing presence of narrative in independent filmmaking and what is actually called "new narrative cinema," and ideologically; for insofar as narrative pervades commercial cinema and television, any avant-garde or critical practices of cinema cannot hold a stance of non-intervention, especially considering their institutional and pedagogic component in American universities. But I would like to make the case for narrative in a more drastic manner. I will state it first in the form of a proposition: there

is no image outside of narrative, and no filmic image outside of history, which is also to say the history of cinema including avant-garde and mainstream, classical and contemporary cinema.

Now, however, I must backtrack a little and offer some support for such a drastic proposition. Two notions have become accepted within film theory. One is the notion of cinema as both a social technology and a signifying or semiotic practice. The other is the notion of the subject as historically constituted in practices; that is, the subject is constituted not just *by* symbolic systems (such as cinema or language) but *in* the practices of signification and meaning production that take place through those systems, of which cinema is one among others.

If the film-theoretical notion of cinema as a semiotic practice is to have any value at all, the problem of making a film cannot be solely one of enunciation, of expressive modalities, of struggle with the material; it cannot be a problem of art as construed in traditional aesthetics. It must be as well a problem of address, of who is making (or writing or saying) what, when and for whom. And so both filmmakers and spectators must be understood as historical subjects and, more specifically, as gendered subjects. In fact, one might wish to consider the question of address as perhaps the most important parameter by which to characterize the practice of independent avant-garde cinema. While all cinema, by the fact of its being a social technology, is involved in certain relations of production and circulation, the qualitative distance between commercial and independent cinema can be located initially in the sphere of reception—the relationship with audiences. If spectators are construed not as consumers but as subjects engaged in the viewing process, personally and subjectively involved in the relations of meaning and imaging that the film inscribes or sustains, cinematic representation appears to be a kind of mapping of social vision into subjectivity. For not only semantic and social values, but affect and fantasy as well, are bound to images in the film. This then allows us to redefine the sphere of production in a broader sense than merely the funding or the making of a film as object, product, or commodity for given sectors of a consumer market; that sphere extends to the production of a social imagination, of forms of subjectivity that are individually shaped but unequivocally social.

Secondly, however, if the notion that the subject is historically constituted in practices (in the world and in cinema, too) is to be taken seriously, what we think happens in film viewing must be related or relatable to what happens elsewhere. Processes of spectatorship must be understood more complexly than is implied, for example, by the currently popular notion that female spectators identify with the image because, as women, they are constructed in narcissistic nearness to the body (of the mother). I have begun to argue elsewhere that narrativity, as a hegemonic cultural mode, overdetermines identification as well as the spectator's other relations to the film, and thus affects our reading and our very seeing of the images; so that all images are implicated with narrativity whether they appear in a narrative, non-narrative, or anti-narrative film.[6] The overwhelming diffuseness of the narrative form in all cultural discourses renders identification itself, to some extent, narrativized.

Film spectators enter the movie theater as either men or women, which is not to say that they are simply male or female, but rather that each person goes to the movies with a semiotic history, personal and social, a series of previous identifications, by which she or he has been somehow engendered. And because she and he are historical subjects, continuously engaged in a multiplicity of signifying practices which, like narrative and cinema, rest on and perpetuate the founding distinction of culture—sexual difference—the film's images for them are not neutral objects of a pure perception, but already "significant images," as Pasolini observed; already significant by virtue of their relation to the viewer's subjectivity, coded with a certain potential for identification, placed in a certain position with respect to desire. They already bear, even as the film begins, what Mulvey has called a certain "place of the look."[7]

This is the reason for reexamining narrative theories, for asking again Barthes' question: in what ways does narrative work to engender the subject in the movement of its discourse, as it defines positions of meaning, identification and desire? But if we leave the point of view of Oedipus, and instead ask the question from the place of the historical woman spectator, we may prefer to put it like this: in which ways does narrative (in or through cinema) solicit the female subject's identification in the narrative movement?

Does it offer any pleasure beside that of a purely passive, narcissistic or masochistic, position (which is, I think, an impossible place for identification, a non-subject effect)? What manner of seduction operates in cinema to procure the complicity of women in a desire whose terms are those of the Oedipus?

I said that a theoretical return to narrative requires or instigates a rereading of the sacred texts. One could, for instance, reread Propp's work on the historical roots of folic narratives, especially his fascinating essay on Oedipus, written in 1944, against Lotman's recent theory of plot typology.[8] (One could read these works of Propp's, that is, if one reads Russian—or Italian, the only Western language in which they have been translated, to my knowledge.) Or one might read the 1980 special issue of *Critical Inquiry* on the presence of the narrative form in genres as diverse as myth and anthropological description, literature and film, or historical narration and the case history; and reading the 1980 volume, compare it with the 1966 issue of *Communications* on the structural analysis of narrative, which Barthes introduced as quoted earlier. What one would then discover, as I have, is that most of the recent studies, while they fashionably scorn structuralism as reductivist or ahistorical, in fact exude a very traditional, integrative view of narrativity. In their attempt to distance themselves from structuralism by emphasizing process and transformation over structure and code, they de-historicize and *a fortiori* de-gender the subject, and ironically end up universalizing the "narrative process" as such.

While some argue convincingly, Lotman for example, that "narrative is a powerful means of making sense of life," since it derives from myth the social function of establishing distinctions, of classifying phenomena and regulating events into anomalies and norms, they seem to be unaware of the fully mythical terms in which their own discourse is cast.[9] Narrative, according to Lotman, endlessly reconstructs the world as a two-character drama in which, the human being, the mythical subject, creates and recreates himself out of a purely symbolic other, indifferently seen as the earth, the grave, the womb or woman. Female is what is not susceptible to transformation, to life or death; she (it) is the obstacle to be overcome, the boundary to be crossed, an element of plot-space, a topos, a resistance, matrix and matter. In short, this

"Oedipal drama"—as Stephen Heath has aptly called the classical narrative film—has the movement of a passage, an actively experienced transformation of the human being into . . . man. This is the "sexual difference" on which are based not only narrative as the production of Oedipus, but equally and concurrently Lotman's and other theories of narrative.

And this is why the work of people like Propp and Freud must be seriously reconsidered—Propp's because of its emphasis on the interdependence of material social relations and cultural productions, which Lotman all but disregards; Freud's because of its emphasis on the inscription of those relations into the sphere of subjectivity. But rather than reread Propp and Freud here, I prefer to turn to another sacred text, particularly relevant in this context, Mulvey's "Visual Pleasure and Narrative Cinema." Not the least reason for my choice is that in her most recent essay, probably not by chance, she too has seen fit to reread Propp and Freud. Probably, like me, she found no answers in either Lotman or Barthes.

I will start from a marvelous sentence, in the *Screen* essay, which sets out practically all the specifications of the cinematic apparatus, its terms, components, and operations:

> . . . cinematic codes create a gaze, a world, and an object, thereby producing an illusion cut to the measure of desire.[10]

It is an amazingly concise and precise description of cinema, not only as a social technology, machine, institution or apparatus to produce images and meanings; but also as a semiotic practice, a working of the codes to engage the subject's desire in the very processes of vision, looking and seeing, it is, or could be, a perfectly good description of cinema *tout court*. But, in the context of the essay, the description only refers to dominant or Hollywood cinema. Within the discursive framework that opposes mainstream to avant-garde cinema, "illusion" is associated with the former and charged with negative connotations: naive reflection-theory realism, bourgeois idealism, sexism and other ideological mystifications. Hence, in this Brechtian-Godardian program, a radical film practice can only constitute itself against the specifications of that cinema, in counterpoint to it, and must set out

to destroy the "satisfaction, pleasure and privilege" it affords. The alternative, as has been pointed out, is brutal, especially for women to whom pleasure and satisfaction, in the cinema and elsewhere, are not easily available. And indeed the program has not been rigorously followed by feminist filmmakers, including Mulvey herself.

I do not mean this as a *post factum* criticism of an ideological analysis that has promoted the politicization of film practice and sustained an intensely productive phase of feminist work with film. On the contrary, the point is to assess its historical significance and to locate the usefulness of its lesson in the very limits it has posed and allowed to be tested. For one, that notion of political avant-garde, which today retains its critical force only to the extent that we are willing to historicize it, and to give it up as the paragon or absolute model of any radical cinema. Thus I would like to re-propose that description of cinema and to start again from there:

> . . . cinematic codes create a gaze, a world, and an object, thereby producing an illusion cut to the measure of desire.

Narrative and visual pleasure (Freud's *Schaulust* or scopophilia) constitute the frame of reference of cinema for, like Alberti's window, they incorporate the standard unit of measurement and judgment; the knowledge and the meaning of the sensible world (for Alberti) and of the social imaginary (for us) are given to the spectator as vision, a vision which is "cut to the measure of desire."[11] If the inheritance of renaissance perspective that comes to cinema with the camera and, by engaging the scopic drive, maps desire into representation, is a function of social memory, so is narrativity, which brings to cinema the capacity for organizing meaning it has had since the time of the classical myths, the capacity to reproduce distinctions and so provide the standard of judgment by which the things of the world become visible in cinema. That standard, of course, is man, the mythical subject; for the "visible things" of cinema, the object and the modalities of vision, pleasure and meaning, have been defined on the basis of perceptual and conceptual schemata provided by patriarchal ideologies and social formations. In the frame of reference of men's cinema and theoretical discourses, man is the measure of desire, quite as the phallus is its signifier and the standard of visibility in psychoanalysis.

The project of feminist cinema, therefore, is not so much "to make visible the invisible," as the saying goes, or to destroy vision altogether, as it is to construct another (object of) vision and the conditions of visibility for a different social subject. Valuable as the work of the avant-garde has been and still is as a radical analysis of what Mulvey calls "the monolithic accumulation of traditional film conventions," its usefulness for an avant-garde cinema of women would be assessed in relation to the feminist project. That is, as I see it, to articulate the relations of the female subject to representation, meaning and vision, and in so doing to set out the terms of another measure of desire, the conditions of presence of another social subject. The problem is how to reconstruct vision from the contradictory—but not impossible—place of female desire, how to represent her double identification in the process of "looking at her looking," and so to perform the contradictions of women in language, in imaging, in the social.[12]

When Mulvey turns to the questions of sexual identity and spectator identification in the *Framework* article, she states:

In *Visual Pleasure* my argument was axed around a desire to identify a pleasure that was specific to cinema, that is the eroticism and cultural conventions surrounding the look. Now, on the contrary, I would rather emphasise the way that popular cinema inherited traditions of story telling that are common to other forms of folk and mass culture, with attendant fascinations other than those of the look.[13]

She says, "on the contrary," and that puzzles me. She seems to make a distinction between the fascinations of the look and the others—the fascinations of narrative, of storytelling. But isn't the (system of the) look precisely what joins image and story into a narrative image, and by interlocking the visual and the narrative registers, maps the narrative movement with places and positionalities for spectator identification? The essay's title, "Afterthoughts on 'Visual Pleasure and Narrative Cinema' inspired by 'Duel in the Sun'," all but reiterates that join. So I would say that what this essay explores is not another, distinct question, but the other side of the same question Mulvey had addressed in the *Screen* essay, and I here reformulate thus: what manner of seduction operates in cinema to solicit the complicity of women spectators in a desire whose terms are those of the Oedipus?

Mulvey, rereading Freud and Propp, ventures the idea of a narrative identification with the masculine position. Female spectators, she argues, have access to the film's fantasy of action "through the metaphor of masculinity": the character of Pearl (Jennifer Jones), by dramatizing the oscillation of female desire between "passive" femininity and "regressive masculinity," encapsulates the position of the female spectator "as she temporarily accepts 'masculinization' in memory of her 'active' phase." However, Mulvey concludes, Pearl's story illustrates that masculine identification for the female spectator is always "at cross purposes with itself, restless in its transvestite clothes."[14] This is a crucial point, which I have also discussed and elaborated at greater length in *Alice Doesn't*. Although, my discussion there develops in rather different ways, I fully share Mulvey's concern to displace the active-passive and gaze-image dichotomies in the theorization of spectatorship, and to rethink the possibilities of *narrative* identification as a subject-effect in female spectators, an effect that is persistently denied by the prevailing notion of woman's narcissistic over-identification with the image.[15] Here I can only state my argument in brief.

Cinematic narrative, Stephen Heath has argued convincingly, is governed by an Oedipal logic; it is a process of restoration that depends ultimately on the image of woman, generalized into what he calls the *narrative* image, a function of exchange within the terms of the film's contract.[16] The female position, produced as the end result of narrativization, is a figure of narrative closure, the "narrative image" in which the film "comes together." Narrativization, thus, is the process by which the flow of images is articulated into a meaningful view, a "welding together" of space and spectator, a coherence of spectator and vision.

What moves in film, finally, is the spectator, immobile in front of the screen. Film is the regulation of that movement, the individual as subject held in a shifting and placing of desire, energy, contradiction. ... The spectator is *moved*, and *related* as subject in the process and images of that movement.[17]

But if the movement or "passage" of the spectator-subject through the film is modulated on the movement of the film, its "placing" of desire (and indeed precisely because of this), we must not overlook the fact that the movement of the film, as the movement of narrative, is possessed of a direction and an orientation—better still, in Freud's good word, a teleology.[18]

Film narrative, too, if Lotman's typology be credited, is a process by which the text-images distributed across the film (be they images of people, objects, or of movement itself) are finally regrouped in the two zones of sexual difference, from which they take their culturally preconstructed meaning: mythical subject and obstacle, maleness and femaleness. Therefore, if it is granted that spectators enter the movie theater as either men or women, in the sense I discussed earlier, then it seems evident to me that the kinds of identification available to women spectators, and the nature of the process whereby female subjectivity is engaged in narrative cinema, demand a separate and specific analysis.

I would propose that female spectators can be "related as subject" in the film's images and movement only insofar as they are engaged by a two-fold process of identification, sustaining two distinct sets of identifying relations.

The first set is well known in film theory: the masculine, active, identification with the gaze (the looks of the camera and of the male characters) and the passive, feminine identification with the image (body, landscape, view). The second set, which has received much less attention, is implicit in the first as its effect and specification, for it is produced by the apparatus which is the very condition of vision (that is to say, the condition under which what is visible acquires meaning). It consists of the double identification with the figure of narrative movement, the mythical subject, and with the figure of narrative closure, the narrative image.

Were it not for the possibility of this second, figural identification, the female spectator would be stranded between two incommensurable entities, the gaze and the image. Identification, that is, would be either impossible, split beyond any act of suture, or entirely masculine. The figural (narrative) identification, on the contrary, is double; both figures can and in fact must be identified with at once, for they are inherent in narrativity itself. It is this narrative identification that assures "the hold of the image," the anchoring of the subject in the flow of the film's movement; rather than, as Christian Metz proposes, the primary identification with the all-perceiving subject of the gaze.[19]

Thus I would provisionally answer Mulvey's question (and mine) by saying that *this* is the operation by which narrative and cinema procure the spectators' consent and seduce women into femininity: by a double identification, a surplus of pleasure produced by the spectators themselves for cinema and for society's profit.

When a film within the standard frame of reference accidentally or unwisely puts in play the terms of a double female desire (for the Father and for the Mother)—for instance *Vertigo* (1958), or *Rebecca* (1940), as Tania Modleski shows—it usually displays that desire as impossible or duplicitous, finally contradictory; and then proceeds to resolve the contradiction much in the same way as myths or the mythologists do—by the massive destruction or the territorialization of women.[20] However, there are also films being made from other standards, working to construct that other measure of desire.

What I see now possible for women's cinema is to answer the plea for "a new language of desire" expressed by Mulvey, Johnston and others in the early Seventies; and I see it possibly even bypassing the stoic, brutal prescription of self-discipline that seemed inevitable at the time. But if the project of feminist cinema—to enact the contradiction of female desire in the terms of narrative, to perform it in the figures of movement and closure, image and gaze—now seems more possible, and indeed actual to a certain extent, this is largely due to the work produced in response to that self-discipline and the knowledge generated from the practice of feminism and film.[21]

What does my title mean, after all this? What could *oedipus interruptus* do for us? I am not advocating the replacement or the appropriation of Oedipus by women; nor am I darkly intimating his emasculation. For, on the contrary, access to the means of production is as important as ever. I am simply proposing that an interruption, a dis-alignment of the triple track by which meaning and pleasure and narrative are constructed from his point of view, is necessary for women's work and pleasure in cinema and in the world. The really avant-garde work in cinema and in feminism today is not anti-narrative or anti-Oedipal. Quite the opposite, it is narrative and Oedipal with a vengeance, since it seeks to stress the duplicity of that scenario and the specific contradiction of the female subject in it—the contradiction whereby historical women must work with and against Oedipus.

Notes

1. Roland Barthes, *The Pleasure of the Text*, tr. Richard Miller (New York: Hill and Wang, 1975), p. 10.
2. Roland Barthes, *Image-Music-Text*, tr. Stephen Heath (New York: Hill and Wang, 1977), p. 79.
3. *Ibid.*, p. 124,
4. Claire Johnston, ed., *Notes on Women's Cinema* (London: SEFT, 1974), p. 31.
5. Laura Mulvey, "Afterthoughts on 'Visual Pleasure and Narrative Cinema' Inspired by 'Duel in the Sun' (King Vidor, 1946)," *Framework*, No. 15/16/17 (1981), p. 13.
6. Teresa de Lauretis, "Snow and the Oedipal Stage," *Screen*, 22, No. 3 (1981), 24–39.
7. Laura Mulvey, "Visual Pleasure and Narrative Cinema," *Screen*, 16, No. 3 (1975), 17.
8. Vladimir Ja. Propp, "Edip *v* svete fol'klora," first published in *Serija filologiceskich nauk*, 9, No. 72 (1944), 138–75; Italian tr. in Clara Strada Janovič; ed., *Edipo alla luce del folclore* (Torino: Einaudi, 1975), pp. 85–137.
9. Jurij M. Lotman, "The Origin of Plot in the Light of Typology," tr. Julian Graffy, *Poetics Today*, 1, No. 1–2 (Autumn 1979), 161–84; originally published in 1973. See also the essays by Victor Turner, Roy Schafer and Seymour Chatman in *Critical Inquiry*, 7, No. 1 (Autumn 1980).
10. Mulvey, "Visual Pleasure and Narrative Cinema," p. 17.
11. I am indebted to Joel Snyder, "Picturing Vision," in W. J. T. Mitchell, ed., *The Language of Images* (Chicago and London: the Univ. of Chicago Press, 1980), pp. 219–46 for a thought-provoking rereading of Alberti's theory of perspective.
12. A more thorough discussion of these questions may be found in Teresa de Lauretis, *Alice Doesn't: Feminism, Semiotics, Cinema* (Bloomington: Indiana Univ. Press, 1984).
13. Mulvey, "Afterthoughts . . .," p. 13.
14. *Ibid.*, p. 15.
15. For example, see Mary Ann Doane, "Film and the Masquerade: Theorising the Female Spectator," *Screen*, 23, No, 3–4 (1982), 74–87.
16. Stephen Heath, *Questions of Cinema* (Bloomington: Indiana Univ. Press, 1981), p. 121: "Narrative contains a film's multiple articulations as a single articulation, its images as a single image (the 'narrative image', which is a film's presence, how it can be talked about, what it can be sold and bought on, itself represented as—in the production stills displayed outside a cinema, for example)."
17. *Ibid.*, pp. 53 and 62.
18. Cf. Freud's famous account of the female Oedipus complex, or the little girl's journey to womanhood: "it is our impression that more constraint has been applied to the libido when it is pressed into the service of the feminine function, and that—to speak teleologically—Nature takes less careful account of its [that function's] demands than in the case of masculinity. And the reason for this may lie—thinking once again teleologically—in the fact that the accomplishment of the aim of biology has been made to some extent independent of women's consent." ("Femininity," in *The Standard Edition of the Complete Psychological Works of Sigmund Freud*, ed. James Strachey [London; Hogarth Press, 1955], Vol. XXII, p. 114.)
19. Christian Metz, *The Imaginary Signifier*, tr. Ben Brewster et al. (Bloomington: Indiana Univ. Press, 1981).
20. Tania Modleski, "Never To Be Thirty-Six Years Old: *Rebecca* as Female Oedipal Drama," *Wide Angle*, 5, No. 1 (1982), 34–41.
21. See E. Ann Kaplan, *Women and Film: Both Sides of the Camera* (London and New York: Methuen, 1983).

31.
A "GIRLBOY'S" OWN STORY

Non-Masculine Narrativity in Ma Vie en Rose

Michael R. Schiavi

I. Anti-Narrative "Girlboys"

Alain Berliner's film *Ma Vie en Rose* [*My Life in Pink*] (1997) puts at center screen an aggressively narrative-resistant protagonist: an effeminate, cross-dressing, boy-loving, girl identified, pre-pubescent male. Seven-year-old Ludovic Fabre (Georges Du Fresne) lives a life that defies plotting.[1] Deflecting the social engagement required of basic storytelling, Ludo's most salient traits court narrative elimination rather than inclusion. His habitual cross-dressing, for example, registers to uncertain snickers and then nearly vanishes behind parental rage and medical intervention. Such markers of effeminacy as his choice of toys, cherished long hair, and emulation of hyper-feminine heroines only inspire tableaux of censorship and peer abuse; they seem never to chart the tale of a boy's evolving sensibility. Ludo's love of Jérôme (Julien Rivière), the boy next door and also the son of his father's boss, prompts professions of disbelief, dismissal—and even a full swoon—but it certainly enjoys no narrative space in which to develop its own plotline. Several years shy of sexual maturity, Ludo is presumed by all adult onlookers to be reparably diverted from the path of normative development. If a "girlboy" (Ludo's own term) has any story to tell, it would seem to be that of compulsory integration within recognizable narrative passages of heterosexual love and family.

Literary and film theory, psychological studies, (auto)biographical writing, and film typically elide gay and/or effeminate boys from narrative radar. When portrayed at all, these boys are self-censoring to the point of anti-narrativity, or they become unwitting antagonists in brief, violent warfare that ends either in their defeat or in their expulsion from the *mise-en-scène*. Neither scenario allows for a detailed unpacking of young non-masculine lives. Of necessity, therefore, Ludo's story employs tropes of silence, warfare, and expulsion, yet it also posits sustaining narrative structures little seen in tales of non-masculine childhood.[2] Berliner bases Ludo's characterological tenability on the boy's foregrounded spectatorship: his committed watching and remobilization of "feminine" performance detach even his parents from the prescribed gender rituals that comprise traditional narrative. Seduced into participation within "girlboy" fantasies, Pierre and Hanna belatedly recognize their son's subjective independence beyond correctional discourse. The deliberately hazy—indeed, archly unresolved—end of Berliner's film leaves a viewer with ample opportunity to speculate on the potential narrative flights of "girlboys" who have traditionally found very few unblocked avenues to public representation.

Feminist theorists of prose and cinema have long noted the thwarting of non-heterosexual and non-masculine subjects within Western narrative. Julie Abraham, for instance, details ways in which

> [t]he heterosexual plot constructs heterosexuality . . . as the norm . . . by providing a basis for narratives into which the heterosexuality of subjects can disappear. When it is not the focus, heterosexuality remains the precondition for whatever is being addressed, whether that is the intricacies of

particular relationships, adolescent angst, or adult ambition. (Abraham 1996, 3)

Without heterosexuality as their bedrock, Abraham implies, conventional narrative treatments of interpersonal relations, self-determination, and labor have no stable ground upon which to build. Non-heterosexual characters must, therefore, speak themselves into existence against the tacit "heterosexual plot" engulfing them. But what of characters who are psychologically or intellectually unprepared to declare any sexual affiliation? In Ken Corbett's cogent observation, "[h]omosexual boyhood as a conceptual category does not exist. . . . There has been virtually no effort to speak of the boyhood experience of homosexuals other than to characterize their youth as a disordered and/or non-conforming realm from which it is hoped they will break free . . ." (1999, 108). Corbett is critiquing the cultural mandate that presumes children to be asexual or, at most specific, latently heterosexual. Boys whose behavior, however broadly, connotes or portends homosexuality have no story until puberty allows them both an active sexuality and a reasonably informed subject position from which to claim their orientation along with whatever traumas and triumphs it occasions.

By these specifications, Ludo's story is untellable. His affect clashes mightily against social narratives that deem tacit heterosexuality—even in children—a functional prerequisite. Yet while no character witnessing Ludo's tastes or activities presumes him to be currently heterosexual, and although Ludo proclaims his love for Jérôme openly, at seven he is not seen as making a definitive statement about his sexuality. This ambiguity constitutes his narrative entrée. Early in the film, trying to explain away Ludo's wish to look "pretty" in drag, Hanna shares her *Marie Claire* certainty that "until the age of 7, we all search for our identity." Too young to declare credibly that he is either homosexual or transsexual, Ludo is presumed innately heterosexual by default[3]—and thus cannot initially rise even to the basic narrative level of conflict.

Film theorist Teresa de Lauretis defines "the movement of narrative discourse" as that force which "specifies and even produces the masculine position as that of the mythical subject and the feminine position as mythical obstacle or, simply, the space in which movement occurs" (1984, 143). Following De Lauretis's theory, the non-masculine subject, be it female or non-masculine male, exists only to the extent it opposes a masculine character position. Unable to act, compelled to react only, it produces with the masculine subject a kind of gendered, sadomasochistic agon that, Laura Mulvey argues in her seminal essay "Visual Pleasure and Narrative Cinema," informs the very essence of cinematic storytelling: "Sadism demands a story, depends on making something happen, forcing a change in another person, a battle of will and strength, victory/defeat . . ." (1975, 29).

In Ludo's narrative, the sadistic antagonist is less a masculine subject than a masculinist discourse that exists precisely to annihilate non-masculine boys. To be sure, adult and child sadists, who shear Ludo's hair and threaten his safety, crowd the story, but they don't quite determine the film's narrative thrust: Ludo is too young and too passive to engage in full-scale "battle." The sadism propelling *Ma Vie en Rose* is less literal than taxonomic, the brutal process by which, Pat Califia notes, "differently-gendered" subjects are divested of the voice that makes them subjects: "To be differently gendered is to live within a discourse where other people are always investigating you, describing you, and speaking for you; and putting as much distance as possible between the expert speaker and the deviant and therefore deficient subject" (1997, 2). The "expert's" words take on particular force when categorizing a boy whose behavior rivets the notice of everyone around him but who, paradoxically, cannot speak for himself. As David Plummer remarks, these children end up viciously spoken for rather than speaking: "[b]oys who don't observe boundaries [of gender codes] run a risk of becoming defined by their 'transgressions' . . ." (1999, 219). An individual "defined by [his] 'transgressions'" has little narrative existence outside the "normalizing gaze" that, Michel Foucault posits, exists "to qualify, to classify, and to punish" deviant subjects passing before its omnipresent stare (1977, 184). How compelling a story can any screenwriter create around the ritual sighting, punishment, or even well-intentioned "reform" of a resolutely deviant boy?

In writing *Ma Vie en Rose*, Berliner and screenwriter Chris Vander Stappen, whom Berliner describes as a lesbian living as a man, deliberately flirted with narrative impossibility. Rather than draw on Vander Stappen's own tomboy experience, the pair wished, in Berliner's account, "to dramatize the stronger taboo of a boy acting like a girl [rather] than vice-versa. A woman wearing trousers is not shocking anymore. But a little boy wearing a dress is" (Sherman 1998, N9). Tomboy Chris, the only child beside Jérôme who ever solicits Ludo's company, passes for a boy until her mother (Marine Jolivet) calls out the full name of "Christine." Comfortably androgynous, Chris can wear whatever she wants—as when she steals the "Three Musketeers" costume that Ludo dons for her birthday party—and play slingshot games to her heart's content without fear of children's snickers or adult hysteria. Swimming in Chris's outsized princess dress, Ludo faces a wholly different reception.

In numerous films, adult male transvestism serves as both a source of surefire mainstream amusement and a semiotic smokescreen. In such movies as *La Cage aux Folles* (Molinaro, 1978), *Adventures of Priscilla, Queen of the Desert* (Elliott, 1994), *To Wong Foo, Thanks for Everything, Julie Newmar* (Kidron, 1995), *Flawless* (Schumacher, 1999), *Never Again* (Schaeffer, 2002), and *Connie and Carla* (Rambeck 2004) colorful transvestism diverts attention from homosexuality that may be stated, but remains unpracticed, by protagonists. The silver screen is evidently too small to accommodate both size 14 pumps *and* gay romance. Gay-male romantic relationships have figured centrally in recent cinema—consider *Alive and Kicking* (Meckler, 1997), *Billy's Hollywood Screen Kiss* (O'Haver, 1998), *I Think I Do* (Sloan, 1998), *Trick* (Fall, 1999), *The Broken Hearts Club* (Berlanti, 2000)—and even amorous gay teenagers have received multiplex due in such films as *Beautiful Thing* (MacDonald, 1996) and *Edge of Seventeen* (Moreton, 1998). However, none of these films stacks its narrative deck with the wild cards of transvestite or child protagonists, two groups who, receiving little discursive credibility, would not strengthen the tenuous reception afforded gay relationships in popular representation. There is, therefore, no narrative precedent for a tiny drag queen who blithely insists that he will marry the unfazed boy next door.[4] Not only does Ludo sexualize clothing that, draped over a filmed male body, typically connotes asexuality; not only does he sexualize an undeveloped body that would not yet communicate, to a Western observer, in any carnal register; but he also receives enthusiastic reciprocation from his male object of desire. Cinema has never before seen the likes of Ludovic.[5]

Nor has gay film scholarship. The work of pioneering historians Parker Tyler, Vito Russo, Boze Hadleigh, Raymond Murray, David Ehrenstein, and William J. Mann[6] has been invaluable for demonstrating the symbiotic rise of cinema and homophobic language, and for illuminating the closets in which gay artists navigated the homophobia of an industry that vilified but deeply depended on their sensibilities. Building on this historical criticism, Steven Cohan, Ellis Hanson, Alexander Doty, Brett Farmer, Matthew Tinkcom, and Richard Dyer[7] have theorized gay lensings and receptions of the adult male body, thereby mapping valences of gay auteurship/spectatorship and widening the fields of gender and cinema studies. Yet Ludo and *Ma Vie en Rose* fall outside the parameters of gay representation proffered by these writers. As the film is the product of an avowedly straight-male director and lesbian screen writer, Ludo does not come to audiences from closeted circumlocution. Nor does he, at seven, evoke the deliberate homoerotics of filming and watching that have occupied much recent gay scholarship. Not an object of camp, not a sexualized object of the gaze, not a witting contributor to identity politics, Ludo fits no better on the page than he does on the screen.[8]

When first declaring oneself "gay," a speaker releases accumulated, generally fraught self-knowledge in a revelation of certain social consequence. Ludo is too young to have any such sense of personal disclosure and effect; in fact, far from determining through conscious declaration his own rhetorical status, he learns of it from reactions to his ingenuous expression. Ludo's relationship to his sexuality, therefore, does not constitute recognizable coming-out narrative. As Chantal Nadeau argues, the film "is not about coming out; on the contrary, it ambiguously plays with the question of coming *in* as a queer child" (2000, 138). Nadeau's phrase "coming *in*" is felicitous for its implication of the interiority and silence that generally contain youthful homosexual self-awareness, speech acts, and narrative possibility.

The literature on gay youth testifies to children's early, necessarily silent, sense of their own difference from peers and family. From his wide professional contact with young gay subjects, psychologist Ritch C. Savin-Williams states that "the vast majority of the . . . youths [he] interviewed . . . attributed to themselves an early sense that in some fundamental way they differed from other boys . . . [that they detected in themselves] how a boy should *not* act, think, and feel" (1998, 23, 27). Comparably, Robert E. Owens, Jr. has found that "[s]eventy percent or more of lesbian, gay, and bisexual adolescents and adults report feeling different at an early age, often as early as four or five . . . . Many sexual-minority youths state that before they even knew what the difference was they were convinced of its importance" (1998, 16). Gay boys' sense of self is thus often formed in opposition to, rather than identification with, other boys; any story they might tell or have told about them must generically be a tale of deviance—beginning with the tropes of difference-naming and enforced atonement. Ludo evinces awareness of his difference early in the film. When Hanna gently informs him that at seven he is "too old for [transvestite] dress-up," he grins and happily agrees to wash off his lipstick. Soon after, during Show and Tell, doll-toting Ludo faces classmates' laughter and registers bewilderment when his teacher (Anne Coesens) suggests that Ludo only wishes to "be like Ben," the "Ken" doll of his pair. Imitating Pam is Ludo's favorite pastime, but he quickly sees the impossibility of sharing his hobby when an authority figure dismisses Ludo's identification with Pam before he can speak it. His mere display of dolls in the classroom makes him the target of peer hostility. In no place can Ludo name his tastes, much less act on them.

The reaction of Ludo's peers to his effeminate behavior is typical among children and tends to obliterate young, non-masculine expression and storytelling. Psychologist William Pollack avers that boys who display "feminine" traits "are usually greeted not with empathy but with ridicule, with taunts and threats that shame them for their failure to act and feel in stereotypically 'masculine' ways" (1998, 24). In their shame, psychologists suggest, non-masculine boys typically lapse into silence, withholding substantial pain and self-doubt. Savin-Williams comments that his subjects' "most common responses" to the "almost universal harassment they received from their peers" were "to ignore, withdraw, or cry" (1998, 32, 30)—none of which repeated reactions can generate

narrative. In large measure, the boys' silence is a survival technique, one initiated on the fraught understanding that they "cannot let . . . feelings show [or] flinch for fear of ending up humiliated, seriously injured, or dead" (Pollack 2000, 107). Appropriately, psychoanalyst Domenico Di Ceglie posits "breaking the cycle of secrecy" as one of his ten "primary therapeutic aims" for children of atypical gender affect on the theory that this secrecy promotes the devastating equation of a boy's natural expression with shame, crippling child and family alike (1998, 187).

As dramatized in *Ma Vie en Rose*, non-masculine boyhood first manifests narratively through tropes of apocalyptic family crisis. Homophobia, in Plummer's analysis, has imbued "homosexuality with symbolic significance as the antithesis of . . . family and individual continuity" (1999, 27). To the extent that a non-masculine boy connotes homosexuality and thus dangerous foreignness within the family,[9] the family's own stories become restricted to certain narrative structures: chaos, battle, halting resolution. How can the family maintain historical or narrative "continuity" until the foreign element is either "corrected," expelled, or accepted? Savin-Williams, though arguing that 21st-century parents are more accepting than their predecessors of gay children, excoriates current "popular literature [for] promot[ing] the view that no task is . . . riskier for family relationships than the disclosure of same-sex desires by children to family members," even as he notes in his counseling sessions an ultimately "positive response" from mothers to gay children (2001, 24, 23). These responses, however, are hardly guaranteed.

More typical may be psychologist Kenneth J. Zucker and psychiatrist Susan J. Bradley's definitely worded postulate that ". . . most parents, not surprisingly, prefer that their children do not develop a homosexual orientation . . ." Zucker and Bradley seek to "block" homosexuality (or transsexualism) in young patients on the contention that "a homosexual lifestyle in a basically unaccepting culture simply creates unnecessary social difficulties" (1995, 269). Zucker and Bradley sugarcoat their pathologizing of non-masculine children with the consolation that if a boy's homosexuality is arrested in time, he will be able to participate in social structures that might otherwise reject him and cut off his life-story before it properly begins. This notion of homosexuality as an acquired social affront, rather than as a genetic predisposition, casts the gay or proto-gay child as a willful destroyer of family image and narrative. Describing his own coming-out, teenager Simeon Maraspini articulates in the film *Gay Youth* the legendary stakes implicit in a gay child's self-disclosure: "With being gay, everything that I wanted to be, everything that my parents wanted me to be, just was shot. It was . . . all over because the foundation was destroyed, the heterosexual family was destroyed, and I didn't think I had anything to look forward to" (1992). What can be the next step in a story whose primal presumptions of procreation, continuity, and normativity have been arrested? On what terms can any of the players move forward?

With family so predominant an element in the narrative of most small children, the story of an effeminate boy must detail first not the subject's own self-awareness, but the reactions he receives. Particularly in the story of a child Ludo's age, family reaction inevitably supplants first-person narrative. Indeed, behaviors typical of Ludo's extreme youth elicit family outrage far more than a teenager's coming out, which, as a single speech act, literally vanishes on utterance and thus may be contained within family walls. Psychotherapist Peter Wilson argues that whatever the individual distinctions among small children with "gender identity problems," they share the "strength of their assertions and beliefs about themselves" (1998, 2); comparably, Zucker and Bradley have found that for many of their young patients, "cross-dressing has an obligatory quality (e.g., insistence on cross-dressing outside the home) and is not restricted to play situations" (1995, 15). Ludo's deviation manifests less in verbal declaration than in insistent wardrobe and behavioral "affectations" inspiring punitive measures that, initially, steal from Ludo the film's narrative focus.

Even when scolded, children of Ludo's age and sensibilities may not be able to change behaviors that the most sympathetic parents find trying. Lisen Stromberg, for example, adores her three-year-old "janegirl" (her own riff on "tomboy"), but, following countless caustic comments from family and neighbors, she allows that "sometimes even [she is] a little embarrassed by [her] son's behavior." She writes wearily of the near "family feud" her toddler inadvertently caused on announcing his intention to be a ballet dancer, and wonders realistically how she will "protect him from the inevitable taunting that will occur as he ages" (1999, 57). Unlike a self-naming teenager, a younger child such as Ludo presents both mortifying present and uncertain, frightening future. The family's efforts to contain their embarrassment necessarily usurp the child's subjectivity and story. For a believable telling of Ludo's narrative, Berliner and Vander Stappen must begin with the parents who, given their way, would rewrite their son completely.

II. Situating Ludo within "Girlboy" Narrative

Berliner and Vander Stappen assign Ludo's effeminate affect dizzyingly high stakes on his initial appearance. Brief expository set-up informs us that the Fabres have moved to Mennecy at the wish of Pierre 's boss and new neighbor, Albert (Daniel Hanssens). In this candy-colored suburb, public vigilance and gender conformity rule. An early overhead tracking shot maps the entire neighborhood on interlocking streets that erase personal space; yet the viewer quickly realizes that Pierre and Hanna should have no trouble with communal scrutiny. The story opens with crosscut tableaux of Pierre and Hanna performing with their neighbors—Albert and Lisette (Laurence Bibot), Thierry (Jean-François Gallotte) and Monique (Caroline Baehr)—an almost identical gender ballet as everyone prepares for the Fabres' neighborhood barbecue.

Judith Butler famously asserts that ". . . gender identity might be reconceived as a personal/cultural history of received meanings subject to a set of imitative practices which refer laterally to other imitations and which, jointly, construct the illusion of a primary and interior gendered self " (1999, 176). The "imitative" nature of those gender identities bespeaks an implicit conformity that Pierre, Hanna, and their adult neighbors seem to have mastered without consultation these characters, the film suggests, are male and female to the degree that they match their peers' performances of masculinity and femininity. In the opening montage, all three wives are assisted or watched by their husbands as they zip themselves into dresses and Jungian script, and their children are clearly being prepared to follow gendered suit: Albert enforces masculine dress code by insisting that Jérôme don a bowtie, however constraining, for the Fabres' party, and Sophie (Morgane Bruna), Thierry and Monique's daughter, is preparing to play feminine archetype Snow White, to her parents'—and Ludo's—fascination.

Ludo emerges into this setting an incipient gender disaster, a *sui generis* deviant without mentor or peers. Before we see him in full, Yves Cape's camera atomizes the child at his toilette as disparate effeminate parts: a Cinderella-slippered foot, a pair of painted lips, an adorned earlobe, and perfectly arched fingers that suggest less a seven-year-old boy than Norma Desmond. Soon to be the object of perpetual observation, he emerges theatrically through patio curtains to the applause of spectators thinking him his older sister Zoé (Cristina Barget), whose fairy princess costume he has ceremonially appropriated for his introduction to the new neighbors. A shocked Pierre, having already categorized his sons Tom (Gregory Diallo) and Jean (Erik Cazals De Fabel) "the brainy one" and "the naughty one," attempts to denominate Ludo a boyish "joker," but the Pandoran narratives of effeminacy and homosexuality have already been uncovered. Tiny Ludo instantly connotes alarm to neighbors who talk pointedly of alarm systems. Mentioned by Thierry and approved by Albert, these systems remain unseen and unheard, but they are on constant alert for intrusion. Foucault's characterization of historic police presence captures the stealthy vigilance surrounding the Fabres: "this power had to be given the instrument of permanent, exhaustive, omnipresent surveillance, capable of making all visible, as long as it could itself remain invisible. It had to be like a faceless gaze that transformed the whole social body into a field of perception: thousands of eyes everywhere . . ." (1977, 214). When Pierre, scrambling for community trust, invites his neighbors to "look in anytime," they instantly and incessantly oblige him.

With Pierre's job hanging on the continued favor of Albert, who verbally equates sexual deviation with Divine disfavor, Ludo's transvestism precipitates a family crisis that, in keeping with the coming-out narratives Savin-Williams cites, threatens to pirate Ludo's own coming-of-age narrative. His behavior will eventually fray his parents' marriage, test his older brothers' loyalty to him and to each other, and force the family to abandon their idyllic neighborhood when Pierre loses his job. Even though Pierre and Hanna do not echo Albert's pseudo-religious bigotry or Thierry's careless contempt for "bent" boys, they immediately recognize the material threat that Ludo represents to their lives. Ludo's "wedding" to Jérôme may not destroy Hanna's love for her son, but his subsequent appearance in backward button-fly briefs convinces her that a gender nightmare is brewing under her roof. Before a third of the film has elapsed, Ludo becomes less a character proper than an object of masculine remediation and psychiatric evaluation.

Pollack delineates the frequency with which boys "feel forced to become extremely watchful, carefully monitoring how other boys act and expending huge amounts of time and energy desperately trying to fit in and pass muster" (2000, 21). Ludo is no exception, and his narrative is quickly skewed by scenarios of macho self-reconstruction. Temporarily believing in his anatomical boyhood, he kicks an array of dolls under his bed and submits to two haircuts designed to make him "neat and trim" like his father and brothers. Goaded by Albert to remove Ludo from Hanna's maternal (hence effeminizing) influence, Pierre enrolls his son in soccer lessons that present Ludo at his most awkward. In opposition to the studied grace Ludo displays at his toilette, he emerges on the soccer field a collection of parts on the verge of masculine breakdown. Cinematographer Cape features in close-up a pair of fragile, fluttery legs; a mop of abundant hair flopping from under a too-large baseball cap; a sweaty, confused little face squinting at Papa's shouted directions in between painful falls to the derriere.

Eager to please his parents, Ludo doggedly appends masculine semiotics onto his delicate frame. Staging his own Lacanian sketch, Ludo stares at himself in a full-length mirror, dubiously cups his genitals, and tries to recreate the gunman's pose ("Bang! Bang!") that he has seen in other children's play.[10] As visible in his flaccid face and posture, Ludo has not convinced even himself of his masculinity, yet he abruptly tries to impose his performance, along with an aggressive kiss, on a female peer who only stops giggling long enough to shove him down, barking, "I don't kiss girls!" Ludo's cultivation of John Wayne, like his visit to the soccer field, literally lands him on his behind and sends him skipping back to Jérôme and Pam.[11]

Following Ludo's masculine failure, *Ma Vie en Rose* could very well metastasize into the underplotted, doomed battle between inexplicable child, horrified parents, and intrepid medical intervention. When Hanna admits to Ludo's therapist (Marie Bunel) that she and Pierre had hoped their fourth child would be a girl, the screenplay offers viewers a classic psychoanalytic tease: did Pierre and Hanna "cause" Ludo to identify as female? The therapist implies as much and directs the Fabres not to "expect miracles" in her treatment of Ludo, who is briefly positioned as victim in the narrative. Therapy ends, however, when Ludo refuses to speak further with the therapist, and *Rose* ceases to be the story of etiology and correction. The blame reverts to Ludo himself.

In her study of aberrant children in film, Kathy Merlock Jackson holds that "[c]hildren who act like monsters are not fully guilty; further exploration reveals that their behavior is not really their fault"; she later substantiates the tendency of film "parents [to] worry about a child's physical normality but never his or her moral sense" (1986, 137, 141). Jackson implies that narrative cannot accommodate brusque parental expulsion of a deviant child. Parents must unearth the root of the unwanted behavior, thereby advancing the tale via the child's recuperation within social structures. When Ludo himself thwarts this plotline, the Fabres depart from Jackson's narrative rubric: they stop attempting to restore Ludo to "physical normality" on the presumption that his "moral sense" is indeed warped. When Pierre loses his job, Hanna informs Ludo that it is his fault, that "everything" the family has suffered—economic ruin along with exile from Mennecy—is his fault. This is not momentary rage; Hanna repeats her blame of Ludo after the family has moved to their smaller, cramped house in Clermont-Ferrand, telling the boy that he "really mess[es] up [the family's] lives," and finally, beating him severely, bellows at her small son to give the family "a fucking break" when she finds him once again in drag.

By this point, the Fabres have spent themselves scrutinizing Ludo for any sign, however fleeting, of presumed normalcy. Having invested considerable time and money in trying to make Ludo heterosexual and masculine, Hanna simply gives up. Coldly informing her son that he is "bent," she saddles him with a

hated crew cut and addresses him with unremitting chilled rage almost to the closing credits. In marked opposition to Hanna, however, critics seem to take Ludo at his earnest word as a little boy who thinks himself a heterosexual girl and dresses and loves accordingly. Brian D. Johnson, for instance, applauds Berliner and Georges Du Fresne for "play[ing] it straight, portraying the confused child with matter-of-fact charm that speaks volumes" (1998, 70). If Ludo seems "confused," he is so not about himself, but only in response to the furor surrounding his determination to select wardrobe and boyfriend much as he sees his older sister do. When Ludo wails to Granny Elisabeth that his parents "say I refuse to change and only bring them trouble," he voices bewilderment and sincerity in equal measure. To his mind, he needn't "change" anything about himself, a conviction validated by Stanley Kaufmann's assertion that the boy's behavior "is not perversity . . . it is Ludovic" (1998, 25).

Berliner has indicated audiences' comparable tendency to colonize Ludo according to their own sexual and/or political agenda. Though he insists that "[n]obody knows how Ludo is going to end up," Berliner also wryly notes that "transsexuals see Ludo as a transsexual, gays say that he is gay, and straights say that he is 'just going through a phase'" (Thomas 1997, 12). Ludo, however, remains his own uncategorizable self, which makes for significant narrative problems and generic crisis. Nadeau characterizes *Rose* as the "hybrid of a fairy tale and a freak show" (2000, 137); yet the former invokes narrative structures in which no non-heterosexual, non-masculine small boy has ever played even a supporting, much less leading, role, and the latter implies shocking spectacle devoid of plot. At no time do Vander Stappen and Berliner objectify Ludo as freakish, and while the term "fairy tale" may apply in cruel pun, Ludo is in far greater control than Cinderella or Snow White of what his audience sees and how his story unfolds. Additionally, Pam—of whom more shortly—disallows fairy-tale narrative simply by being a princess possessed of a prince whom she herself magically summons. Her world contains neither the supernatural villainy nor divine intervention of classic fairy tales, and the uninterrupted through-line of her romantic pursuits is what Ludo most covets. By flatly refusing to acknowledge the dragons and witches of censuring family and community, Ludo divests his tale of fairy-tale trapping and generic categorization altogether.

What plot structure accommodates a child who obeys no sexual, gender, or generic boundary? Were *Rose* a horror film, the abnormal child could turn killer (*Halloween* [Carpenter, 1978]),die at the finale for his sins (*The Bad Seed* [LeRoy, 1956]), be freed from a demon (*The Exorcist* [Friedkin, 1973]), or ultimately emerge as Satan proper and inspire several sequels (*The Omen* [Donner, 1976]). Ludo, however, inhabits not a horror film but a domestic family drama in which no murder committed by or against the young protagonist would fit. And yet Ludo's tale, defiantly titled with first-person possessive adjective, does not defer so easily to the more conventional family narrative surrounding it. A *nouveau* deviant, Ludo keeps silent control of his own tale by refusing to relinquish interpretive sway over it. Ludo's therapist, who is more sympathetic to Ludo than the screenplay initially leads us to believe, tells him that "there may be things [his] parents will never understand," and that he "may have to wait until [he is] older to say them out loud." Her kindly advice implies that Ludo knows himself best, but it also leaves the film's protagonist with very little to say or do. How, then, do Berliner and Vander Stappen manage to hang their entire film on a comparatively mute protagonist who seems thwarted at every narrative turn?

III. A "Girlboy's" Own Narrative Terms

Midway through the film, low on patience and impromptu remedies, Hanna declares to Pierre, "We have no idea what goes on in [Ludovic's] mind." By keeping Ludo inscrutable, Berliner and Vander Stappen make possible the shaping of his story. Ironically, the less his resistance, the wider his narrative options. For instance, the abuse that Ludo faces from peers—an inevitable, potentially murderous motif in the story of any non-masculine boy—seems not to faze him. Faced by laughing children during Show and Tell or while in drag at Sophie's party, Ludovic registers only mild surprise that his peers do not cherish his toys and clothes as much as he does. Even when the laughter turns ugly, Ludo remains unruffled: a classmate's cruel pantomime of him prods Ludo not toward abashed self-monitoring but toward even more elaborate, dis-

missive application of imaginary make-up. Only when other boys threaten him physically in a locker room does Ludo cry out briefly.

At first glance, Ludo seems preternaturally precocious in his ability to squelch the pain he must feel. It gradually becomes clear, however, that he is less staunch before, than impervious to, the homophobia and effeminaphobia surrounding him. A miniature Walter Mitty, Ludo maintains firm interpretive control over the tropes that would colonize his story. Critic Leonard Maltin identifies as one of *Rose*'s chief virtues that "[a]ll points of view are well served" (2002, 891), but ultimately it is Ludo's worldview that informs the film's narrative and aesthetic structures. Competing discourses fall before his considerable appreciation and reconstruction of feminine performance. So powerful are both, in fact, that they ultimately seduce Hanna and Pierre into the only resolution possible for the film: full family acceptance of Ludo, whose final appearance in Christine's princess costume, echoing his entrance in Zoé's gown, neatly brackets the film with the insistent visibility of pre-pubescent queer sensibility.

Berliner paints his suburban *mise-en-scène* as an *Edward Scissorhands* (Burton, 1990) backlot, replete with hot pinks, reds, yellows, and greens. As in the earlier film, *Rose*'s make-believe kingdom evokes the question of what may happen to a deviant who treads unbidden this bizarrely cheery landscape. Yet in a community so wary of deviance, Berliner's dollhouse colors also speak an ironic queer shorthand established and filmed long before Ludo's birth.[12] Despite the community's exclusion of Ludo, its aesthetics belong to a little boy who reminds adults of the subversiveness skipping just beyond their alarm systems' jurisdiction. Before panning the neighborhood's color scheme, Berliner starts the film within the scope of Ludo's spectatorship. For the technically remarkable credit sequence filmed within Pam's dollhouse, cinematographer Cape sweeps over the electric burgundy of Pam's ornate headboard; the brilliant violet of her lamp; the candy-box red of her heart-shaped mirror, dressing table, and Victorian sofa (nicely offsetting pink iron and heart-shaped pink windows). Her vivid house is complemented by yards of plastic daisies, each more geometrically perfect and purely white than anything found in nature. Cape blurs this survey to a pink haze before abruptly cutting to Thierry and Monique's pink-walled bedroom—via a shot banked off the mirror hanging over their bed.

Berliner's opening juxtaposition captures the dueling sensibilities that inform his film's principal conflict. Soon after the Fabres's barbecue, we see Ludo watching *Le Monde de Pam* [*Pam's World*] on television and realize that Pam's house—hence Ludo's aesthetic—has determined our first glimpse of his world. An avatar of postmodern femininity with blond extensions, deeply exposed cleavage, and pastel dreamhouse, Pam provides Ludo with a magical escape from the masculine expectation hampering his every move. Adopting her sinuous choreography, which suggests the union of Madonna's "Vogue" video (1990) and the incantatory repertoire of Agnes Moorehead in *Bewitched* (1964–72), Ludo literally dances away from taunts and the vexing body that has yet to turn female for him. In Pam's hyperfeminine milieu, to be extremely "girlish" is to be rewarded with one's own television show, magical powers, and a handsome, marriage-proposing boyfriend whom one can conjure at will.[13] Yet when Ludo appropriates Pam's over-the-top femininity by arranging florally a bright red napkin in a drinking glass, Monique labels him "a real little housewife"—a gratuitous crack that Elisabeth derides as "not too subtle"—and remarks in his presence that a television program about transsexuals once "made [her] cry."

In her idealized *monde*, Pam need never fear seeming over-the-top; she has no neighbors to deride the chromatic extremity of her home, her scanty orange velvet dress, or her flagrantly stagy movements. Though Ludo's neighborhood appears to have been pelted by Pam's brush, its residents dread any public recreation of her flamboyant colors and self-presentation. In the privacy of the opening montage, Pierre and Hanna allude to their active sexuality, while Thierry and Monique begin to act theirs out beneath the deliberately placed mirror in which we first glimpse them. At the barbecue, however, Monique, knowing that her crowd shuns any behavior or color that draws attention to itself, worriedly asks the Fabres whether everyone must "mind [their] P's & Q's." Thierry has already called his new neighbors "flashy" for throwing a party before they've unpacked; Pierre seems to have anticipated this criticism when he asks Hanna to

change her red dress before the party. Even Elisabeth, who arrives at the party in a bright yellow convertible, finds the Fabres' florid pink "Welcome" sign "a bit too much" for the neighborhood.

Though Elisabeth, who dresses wildly and earns her son-in-law's scorn for "pretend[ing] to be young," is in many ways "the sustaining life force of any budding queer boy's lonely hours" (Stuart 1997, 52), she also recognizes the spectacular limitations of the socially unsanctioned body. As she tries to teach Ludo, this body—whether elderly or cross-dressed, raucous or effeminate—requires certain tailoring for social and narrative efficacy. Like her grandson, Elisabeth would emulate a "slim and smooth" young doll (in the music box given to her by a married admirer), but she realizes that to try to do so at her age would make her look "ridiculous." Like Ludo's therapist, Elisabeth advises her transvestite grandson that "we all have to face reality" and confine fantasy selves within private fantasy moments. Neither woman intends to change Ludo; they simply wish to keep his appearance and utterance uninflected until he can present himself publicly without inviting the phobic "next steps" that could put a permanent end to his story. In the private fantasies that Elisabeth prescribes, Ludo need participate in no plotting at all, as when he imagines himself waking one morning a satin-draped girl in Pam's pink and purple bedroom. Lasting only 30 seconds, his vision unfolds very simply; Ludo has already learned that to imagine any "sequel" for his fantasies invariably means trouble.

From what we see of her life, Pam also lives outside plotting. Of only a few minutes' duration, her show seems to involve no more than a survey of her colorful landscape, Ben's proposal, and her swoony acceptance. A figure of children's television, Pam presents only the glamour of femininity and the excitement of courtship itself; there is no call for her to dramatize the heterosexuality or actual marital life that would elude Ludo. She instills in Ludo a taste for triumphant—if transient—tableaux that become for him both escape hatch as well as force of narrative control. Ludo's development of various scenarios, both imagined and literal, come to comprise a great deal of *Rose*'s screen time as they dramatically elevate the war between self and society that drives the film's main plot. His invented narratives chiefly detail his transformation into a girl and marriage to Jérôme. Like Pam's scenarios, they end abruptly before competing plotlines can invalidate his self-image. Through his fantasies, Ludo grows adept at brands of audience seduction that require no plotting, only momentary attention. And Ludo is never at a loss for onlookers' attention.

When he mounts Pam-like vignettes for his own audience, they react with total captivation. At the film's start, when he steps through patio-cum-theater curtains to join his parents' barbecue, Ludo realizes that observers can't take their eyes off him. At first wholly convincing as a girl, he receives enthusiastic applause; when revealed as a boy, he only silences the crowd into polite stares. No serious consequence ensues. Playing at Jérôme's house, Ludo stages a wedding with his willing friend by appropriating the boy's dead sister's clothes and converting her intact bedroom into a chapel. Unaware of the girl's fate, Ludo treats her room and possessions as his well-appointed back-stage workshop. Naming a stuffed bear "vicar," he populates the stage, assigns himself and Jérôme the roles of Pam and Ben, and even provides voiceover ("We walk down the aisle. I look gorgeous.") as he and his beloved approach the altar. Lisette, unseen by the boys and rapt by their proceedings, seems to pre-empt the climactic kiss in a faint that demonstrates to Ludo his sway over spectators: what surer sign of a performer's ability to overpower an audience?

The parental scoldings following this episode do not dissolve Ludo's determination to marry Jérôme for the much larger audience attending his school's *Snow White* pageant. Mournfully cast against type as a bearded dwarf, Ludo locks Sophie, the female lead, in a bathroom and takes her supine place onstage beneath Snow White's translucent veil. It's not enough that he has previously "married" Prince Charming in a private ceremony; Ludo now wants the public kiss that will wake him from the curse of boyhood into a feminine symbol revered throughout Western culture. The plan backfires when Jérôme, informed by his parents that association with Ludo means flirtation with hellfire, balks at a homosexual kiss, and when Ludo, unveiled, sits up to face an audience that would expel him from school and remove him permanently from their stage. Yet even this critical reception does not discourage Ludo, who requests—and secures—permission to wear a skirt to Snow White's birthday

party ("We're letting him enact his fantasy [in order] to banalize [and banish] it," an exhausted Pierre explains to doubting neighbors).

To be sure, Ludo's scenarios are doomed to derail, as they can only mimic, not effect, the anatomical change and social reintegration he desires. Following the joyful fantasia of attaining sudden girlhood, enlisting Pam to tie up meddlesome mothers, and choreographing a wedding attended by beaming parents and grandmother, Ludo fails to imagine anything of a female's daily life. He has no particular interest in what happens after a bride has won both her groom and her parents' approval. The click of haircutting scissors and the pounding of a For Sale stake in front of his house interrupt Ludo's visions of the perfect girlish bob and of rooftop twirling, before adoring masses, in bridal regalia with Jérôme. Like his real-life dramas, these dreams offer neither gratifying permanence nor a rising story action, but they do signal Ludo's ability to deploy imagination in maintenance of his much contested self-image.

However failed Ludo's scenarios, they teach him that popular narratives—e.g., those of marriage, gender codes, fame—can be manipulated to private ends. Armed with this knowledge, Ludo learns to apply popular and scientific discourse to his interpretive advantage. Dissatisfied by impatient parental declarations that he is male and will be for life, he undertakes to prove his claim to girlhood via sweet recourse to an essentialism that rivals his parents'. With the aid of Zoé's biology text, Ludo learns about "XX" and "XY" chromosomes and hypothesizes, as Berliner films in much fanciful detail, that God assigned him a double-X but—Divine fumble!—accidentally dropped one "X" into a trashcan rather than down the Fabre chimney. Hence Ludo's development as a "girlboy" who waits patiently for God to restore his missing "X." While his parents insistently (and noisily) hew to the argument that Ludo is a boy simply because he is, Ludo seeks to complicate the matter by "proving" his female status: he can urinate while seated, and he has stomach cramps that feel suspiciously like the complaint that makes Zoé, in the proud maternal blessing on which Ludo eavesdrops, a "real little lady." Naturally, Pierre and Hanna are less than convinced by Ludo's explications of the evidence, but Jérôme, who informs Ludo that the ability to urinate from a seated position does not necessarily a girl make, does not discount the possibility of Ludo's eventual girlhood. Jérôme may not accept the term "girlboy," but he doesn't wholly dismiss the possibility of marrying Ludo—contingent only upon "what kind of girl" Ludo finally becomes.

Ludo and Jérôme's belief in his fantasies keeps Ludo alive and prevents his story from shutting down altogether. If Ludo accepted his parents' insistence on gender-prescribed behavior and clothes, if he allowed his therapist to convince him he is male, if he believed Albert and Lisette's conviction that he is evil, then his narrative could not continue. He would have no choice but to change (which he expressly tells Elisabeth he does not want to do) or to destroy himself, a fate he escapes only by generic necessity.[14] When Ludo climbs into a freezer unit, attempting to halt permanently the body that has brought him and his family such trouble, the audience of *Ma Vie en Rose* finds itself in an almost unbearable spectatorial position. We've already seen the child ridiculed, bullied, beaten, expelled from school, and moved far from Elisabeth, the one sympathetic constant in his life. How much more abuse can the story—or the tiny body at center screen—endure? Charles Dickens earned the preeminent reputation in Victorian letters by chronicling the plight of despised boys, but Oliver Twist, Pip, David Copperfield, and *Bleak House*'s Jo do not have the added burden of reviled gender affect to seal off rescue at every turn. The destruction of a tremendously sympathetic child hero would be excruciating to watch, but it is nigh impossible to imagine any other fate for Ludo or from his family.

Domenico Di Ceglie posits as "an important therapeutic aim" the enabling of "a child/adolescent [of atypical gender identity] to tolerate uncertainty in the area of gender identity development" (1998, 194). It is also a vital narrative aim. Without some embrace of an unspecified sexual future, the story of a gay or transsexual child cannot reach the nominal resolution expected of family narrative. *Ma Vie en Rose*'s considerable tension abruptly dissipates before the credit crawl when, minutes after beating Ludo about the head and shoulders for appearing in drag, Hanna murmurs to her son, "Whatever happens, you'll always be our child. . . . I've tended to forget it lately." Even Pierre, throughout the film no champion of his fey son, tells Ludo to "[d]o whatever feels best"

when the child offers to remove the lacy blue frock that inspired Hanna's rage. The film's finale follows the gowned Ludo back to Chris's birthday party in his new neighborhood, where he happily romps amid a new group of children who, unlike his previous peers, seem wholly unflustered by the junior drag queen in their midst. Cape pulls away from the cavorting children to feature a blue sky—the perfect match for Ludo's dress—across which floats the winking figure of Pam, wafting pixie dust over the throng. Credits.

Understandably, critics have found this coda unsatisfactory. After all, the other children have forced Ludo into Christine's dress, which he is, at the film's close, wearing in the rarefied context of a costume party. How would the children and adults of Clermont react the following Monday morning if Ludo sailed into school so attired? This question remains unanswered, prompting critics, of whom Joe Holleman is a fair representative, to fault *Ma Vie en Rose* for ending too "neatly—and somewhat unrealistically" (1998, E3). Eleanor Ringel argues that the "film's denouement seems less earned than targeted at . . . an American audience" eager to see unambiguous narrative resolution for its protagonist (1998, 11). While Berliner does not seem to have intended Americans as his principal audience, the director has gratefully noted that "Americans and Anglo-Saxons in general . . . seem to get from the film what I'd hoped they'd get from it—they understand what we were aiming at way more than the French do" (Nesselson 1998). Mainstream Hollywood narrative, particularly family narrative, does not endorse lasting divisiveness: in a country where *Forrest Gump* (Zemeckis, 1994) makes a suitable foster parent, and where only death can sever *American Beauty*'s (Mendes, 1999) Lester Burnham (Kevin Spacey) from the wife (Annette Bening) he has long detested, little Ludo's ultimate drift from the family hearth would be anathema. At whatever cost of narrative credibility, Ludo must reintegrate within the Fabre milieu in order to secure the kind of U.S. attention that wins Golden Globes (for Best Foreign Film of 1997) and greases worldwide distribution. Still—for those wedded to verisimilitude—the question remains: just how *do* Hanna, Pierre, and a crowd of anonymous children suddenly accept the figure who has grated so violently against spectatorship throughout the film?

How does Ludo suddenly claim territory within a set of social boundaries that could never previously accommodate him?

The answer seems to lie in Pam—or, more specifically, in Ludo's consumption, redeployment, and dissemination of her image. We never see the adults in Ludo's life watching Pam's show with him, yet each of them, through the power of his spectatorship, becomes transfixed by her moves. Elisabeth, who watches her grandson's choreography poised as if to rebuke its effeminate movements, suddenly plays along with Ludo, imitating with him Pam's cross-armed, index-fingers-aloft, torso-twisting variations. Pierre, recently fired and witness to the roadside kiss that Hanna, vengefully seeking to drive her neighbors mad, plants on Albert before Lisette, takes comfort in Pam's repertoire. The camera traces Pierre from feet up as he twirls in the syncopated circle Ludo has modeled, and he uses prop cups to blow Pam's pixie-dust kiss to an imaginary audience. Finishing the routine, Pierre puts down his cups and grins sheepishly, as if embarrassed to be caught performing a routine for which he would certainly attack his youngest son.

Hanna is not shown emulating Pam's motions, but like her mother, husband, and Jérôme, she seems to believe implicitly in the transformative powers of Ludo's scopophilia. When Ludo attempts to escape Hanna's beating of him, Berliner shifts into a surreal sequence that finds Hanna scaling a *Monde de Pam* billboard, hallucinating that Ludo has gotten a ladder, climbed into the artwork, and disappeared with his idol. That Ludo is too small to carry even a step-ladder does not seem to occur to Hanna, who, trying to "pursue" Ludo into the picture, "falls" through Pam's shockingly green landscape and awakens on her own sofa, surrounded by concerned friends and family, including Ludo. Finding herself back in familiar surroundings does not convince Hanna of her vision's unreality; she asks Ludo whether he "really [wanted] to go away with that doll?" This is the same woman who earlier forced on her seven-year-old child the decision of whether to stay with his immediate family or to live with his grandmother. It seems that Hanna has divorced herself sufficiently from Ludo to believe that his overwhelming identification with Pam could take him on escapes that realistic storytelling could never realize. Hanna's acceptance

of Ludo, much like Pierre's, reflects the sudden, serene credibility she assigns her son's ability to recreate himself and his world through performance and narrative.

Conclusion

Ma Vie en Rose has much to teach us about how we read—and instruct our students to read—stories about boys. By all normative narrative rights, Ludovic Fabre has no story of his own to tell. Injecting both homosexuality and transsexualism into a self-monitoring suburb, Ludo's story seems to fit very restricted plot structures: absurdist comedy or social warfare to the point of expulsion or death. Add to this mix a grade school protagonist and the narrative options narrow further still: the notion of sexualizing a prepubescent child before a camera invokes horrible images of pedophilia and exploitation,[15] and the notion of naming a homosexual or transsexual child seems almost to baffle language—how can a child be a "sexual" anything before adolescence? At its most sophisticated, it would seem that Ludo's story traces the family stalemate of parents and siblings vs. distraught child declaring outlaw status well before anyone might expect such affiliation. Yet Ludo shows not even the expected reaction of lamenting his sexual or gender orientation; he asserts himself with complete candor after being informed of his deviance. His cannot, therefore, be a story of internal battle against nature, nor can we see him vacillating between his own viewpoint and that of his parents, nor, given his age, can we see him striking out on his own and creating a free, unquestioned life.

That Berliner and Vander Stappen manage to create a thoroughly compelling story around these daunting limitations demonstrates the breadth of narrative paths—to say nothing of life paths—open to boys who do not follow mainstream gender or sexual expectations. The power of Ludo's theatrical sense and the inventiveness with which he respins canonical genders and tales demonstrate that even a small child can carve narrative space for himself where none has previously existed. Ludovic Fabre points us toward a wealth of boys' stories that have yet to find their way to page, stage, or screen.

Notes

The research and writing of this article were supported by a research grant from the New York Institute of Technology chapter of the American Association of University Professors. My thanks to Alain Berliner, Scott Stoddart, John Fitzgerald, Kathy Williams and an anonymous reader at *College Literature* for their invaluable assistance with this article.

1. The story of *Ma Vie en Rose* is easily summarized for those unfamiliar with the film. Pierre and Hanna Fabre (Jean-Philippe Écoffey and Michèle Laroque) have just moved with their four children, of whom Ludovic is the youngest, to the middle-class suburb of Mennecy, approximately 40 km from Paris. The warm welcome the family receives quickly chills as Ludo's transvestism and determination to marry Jérôme, his young neighbor, disrupt school, community, and finally the Fabre household itself. The unflappable Ludo disregards all escalating prohibitions against dresses and homosocial relationships. He clings to unconventional Granny Elisabeth (Hélène Vincent), Hanna's flamboyant, pot-smoking mother, and Pam (Delphine Cadet), the televised Barbie knockoff Ludo adores and emulates. Yet the solace offered by Elisabeth and Pam cannot spare Ludo from Jérôme's abrupt rejection of him, nor can it stem his bewilderment when he finds himself expelled from school. When Ludo's unwavering transsexual convictions pre-empt his "corrective" therapy and get his father fired, the child finds himself temporarily bundled off to the home of his sympathetic grandmother. The Fabres's economic misfortune soon exiles them to remote Clermont-Ferrand, where Ludo, rejoining the family, discovers that even Hanna has turned against him. Only his eleventh-hour friendship with tomboy Christine (Raphaelle Santini) and his imaginative flights with Pam seem to provide Ludo the simultaneous social connection and escape that he needs. At the film's conclusion, we are left to wonder about the future of Ludo's family and community relations. Pierre and Hanna have reached a beaten truce with their determined "girlboy," but will the truce last as neighbors continue to discover this small boy in chiffon, poised for his next Prince Charming?

2. Two outstanding children's books have attempted to incorporate effeminate children—or ducklings—within mainstream. Tomie dePaola's *Oliver Button Is a Sissy* (1979) and Harvey Fierstein's *The Sissy Duckling* (2002) both feature young effeminate protagonists at first reviled, but later embraced, by friends and family for their uniqueness. Remarkable as they are, these books are written for very young children and do not grapple extensively with the devastating discourses that circumscribe "sissy" boys' lives. Fed up with his bullying father, for example, Fierstein's Elmer simply runs away and sets up his own housekeeping, an option unknown to his real-life human counterparts. Both *Oliver Button* and *Sissy Duckling* teach an indispensable lesson of tolerance, but they cannot be considered fully evolved "girl-boy" narratives of material and psychological consequence.

3. This essay's denotations of Ludo as "gay," "transvestite," "transsexual," or "effeminate" refer exclusively to *how Ludo appears* within the film's normative *mise-en-scène*. An anatomical male in love with another male, thinking himself innately female, enamored of "feminine" trappings and activities, Ludo registers to spectators on and offscreen through various identities that he himself cannot yet articulate. My purpose is not to specify the "truth" of Ludo's identities but to isolate his particular affect within larger narratives that label him, for corrective purposes, an abject boy.

4. It is important to note that other prepubescent male film characters have confessed their love to male friends: *This Boy's Life* (Caton-Jones, 1993) and *Billy Elliot* (Daldry, 2000) both find avowedly heterosexual boys responding sympathetically but without interest to amorous pals. This is not a dynamic unique to lensings of English-language boyhood. In *Les roseaux sauvages* (Téchiné, 1994), teen-aged François (Gaël Morel) takes as his object of affection heterosexual Serge (Stéphane Rideau), a boy who may indulge in some random wrestling with his friend but then advises him, as far as romance and concomitant narrative go, to "forget it." Conversely, *Ma Vie en Rose* finds Jérôme complicit in Ludo's affection to the point of pursuing and kissing him back, but their romantic play, countenanced by no adult character, receives very little narrative attention—a tradition evident in earlier prose and film treatments of boyhood homosexuality.

   Arnie Kantrowitz's memoir, *Under the Rainbow: Growing Up Gay* (1977), Paul Monette's autobiography *Becoming a Man: Half a Life Story* (1992) and Henry Jaglom's film *Last Summer in the Hamptons* (1995) all acknowledge the existence of active boyhood homosexuality, but only as the catalyst for silent family embarrassment and resentment. Interrupted mid-fellatio with a friend, 12-year-old Kantrowitz found himself branded a family "disgrace" until his mother's frantically consulted physician declared him "normal" and just "experimenting" (1977, 35). Lingering maternal suspicions were not voiced again for years, thereby banishing the topic of homosexuality from family lore. When nearly caught in sexual play with a male friend, nine-year-old Monette dismissed the incident as "nothing" to his mother, beginning a decades-long silence in which "[h]er closet was as airless as mine" (1992, 28, 30). *Last Summer*'s Jake (Jon Robin Baitz) remembers being discovered at age eleven *en flagrante* with a male playmate by his powerful director-father (Andre Gregory), whose sole curt comment—"Don't do it again. If his [actor-] father finds out, he'll never work with me again"—sets off the embittered stalemate that characterizes their relationship into Jake's adulthood. In none of these memories does a gay boyhood experience lead to further dialogue or substantive repercussion beyond silent impasse. As in *Ma Vie en Rose,* Kantrowitz, Monette, and Jake's boyhood sexual experiences do not figure in larger plotting.

5. Ludo's closest filmed American counterpart might be Bruno Battaglia, the 8-year-old protagonist of *The Dress Code* (MacLaine, 1999). Like Ludo, Bruno (Alex D. Linz), who favors glam-drag à la Diana Ross or Dolly Parton, shuns boys' attire whenever possible. Unlike Ludo, however, there is no suggestion that Bruno might be gay—in fact, a classmate's taunting question on this subject prompts the only retaliatory action Bruno takes against children who berate and beat him throughout the film. Moreover, whereas Ludo wears girls' outfits in order to look "pretty," Bruno refers to his beloved dresses as "holy vestments," i.e., garb of the angels whose power he would appropriate. At no point does David Ciminello's screenplay ascribe to Bruno any particular effeminacy or desire to be female. Ludo in drag is, therefore, a far more destabilizing signifier than Bruno.

6. See, for example: Tyler (1972), Russo (1987), Hadleigh (1993), Murray (1996), Ehrenstein (1998), and Mann (2001).

7. See, for example: Cohan and Hart (1993), Hanson (1999), Doty (2000), Farmer (2000), Tinkcom (2002), and Dyer (2003).

8. Eve Kosofsky Sedgwick attributes the "eclipse of the effeminate boy from adult gay discourse" to the "marginal or stigmatized position which even adult men who are effeminate have often been relegated in the [gay-rights] movement," and to the need to effect "relative deemphasis of the links between gay adults and gender-nonconforming children" (1993, 158, 157). Sedgwick references here the gay dislike of effeminacy that runs riot through personal ads seeking, with no awareness of their sad irony, "straight-acting" partners: if "straight"-coded masculinity is only an "act," what happens when the performer tires and reverts to his "natural," decidedly *not* sexy effeminacy? She also alludes to panicky post-Stonewall efforts to separate inevitably conflated effeminacy, weakness, and male homosexuality—"rescue" efforts that personals of 30 years later perpetuate quite undaunted. To the extent, then, that gay films and gay film scholarship are informed by contemporaneous gay discourse, the

absence of non-masculine boys from both media can only seem culturally consistent.

9. On its U.S. release, the Motion Picture Association of America (MPAA) assigned *Ma Vie en Rose* an "R" rating for "brief strong language." This "restricted" categorization is baffling in that the film displays only momentary violence, and the script's profanity extends to one single use of the word "fuck," a term that appeared, often repeatedly, in earlier American films (e.g., *All the President's Men* [Pakula, 1976], *Mommie Dearest* [Perry, 1981], *Tootsie* [Pollack, 1982], *Terms of Endearment* [Brooks, 1983]) assigned a "PG" rating. By demanding that children under 17 see *Ma Vie en Rose* with a parent or adult guardian, the MPAA endorses the notion that gender and sexual difference are both antithetical to family viewing and must be rigidly monitored by parents to ensure "damage control." (For a passionate argument against *Rose*'s MPAA rating, see Phil Weinstein's Website, www.WhyIsMaVieEnRose RatedR.com.) Moreover, marketed in the U.S. principally as an "arthouse" or "gay" product, *Rose* received relatively limited distribution. In New York City, for example, the film played only at Greenwich Village's Quad Cinema and the Upper West Side's Lincoln Plaza Cinemas; both are Manhattan arthouses that do not bring films to mainstream audiences, much less to children. But in Europe, *Ma Vie en Rose* was permitted a much wider audience—albeit with certain caveats. In the U.K., Finland, and France, for instance, the film was only restricted to children under 12. Berliner notes, however, that French "exhibitors had to put a note at the windows of the box office, saying that 'this movie could hurt the sensibilities of teenagers because of its purpose.' " With understandable anger, the director assails the "ambivalent" French distribution that straitjacketed his film as " 'an arthouse movie that could make a success' " (2003). Neither mainstream nor arthouse per se, *Ma Vie en Rose* did not quite find its European niche.

10. Interestingly, John Colapinto isolates an "angular, gunslinger's stride" as the very factor that gave away the true male gender of "Brenda"/David Reimer, a young boy whose botched circumcision prompted his castration and unwitting tenure as a girl. The innate boyishness of the "gunslinger's" walk that "Brenda" could not hide beneath frilly dresses is the same affect that Ludo cannot muster in his game emulation of masculinity (2000, 146).

11. It seems no coincidence that John Wayne also turns up in both *La Cage aux Folles* and its American remake, *The Birdcage* (Nichols, 1996), as the masculine archetype to which Albin/Albert (Michel Serrault and Nathan Lane, respectively), like Ludo, cannot begin to aspire.

12. Of his first visit to Fire Island in 1971, Arnie Kantrowitz

relates that he felt "as if [he] were living in a pop-up picture book, a town over 90 percent gay, filled with dollhouses trimmed to the eaves in charming gingerbread, pastel paints . . . gardens profuse with black-eyed Susans, tiger lilies, sunflowers, daisies, petunias, and no-nonsense pansies" (1977, 193). A certain segment of post-Stonewall gay American society clearly relished the dollhouse aesthetic that dominates *Ma Vie en Rose*, much as it does the earlier films *The Detective* (Douglas, 1968), *The Gay Deceivers* (Kessler, 1969), *Norman, Is That You?* (Schlatter, 1976), *The Ritz* (Lester, 1976), and *Torch Song Trilogy* (Bogart, 1988).

13. To be sure, some critics have taken exception to the portrayal of Ludo's model. Eleanor Ringel, for instance, argues that "Ludo's guileless fantasies about a Belgian [*sic*] Barbie Doll named Pam are spooky in the way they suggest the pressure on 7-year-old girls to grow up to be domestic-goddess sex kittens" (1998, 11). Ringel, however, misses the point that Ludo is a small *boy* whose emulation of Pam reveals considerable courage, to say nothing of a rupture in the gender economy that limits children of both sexes to certain stultifying roles.

14. The theme of suicidal youth has enjoyed decided vogue in popular cinema of the past 35 years. Teenage characters have attempted to kill themselves in such dramas as *Up the Down Staircase* (Mulligan, 1967) and *Ordinary People* (Redford, 1980), as well as in the comedies *Beetlejuice* (Burton, 1988) and *Heathers* (Lehmann, 1989). Successful teen suicides have been featured in such films as *Romeo and Juliet* (Zeffirelli, 1968; Luhrmann, 1996), *One Flew Over the Cuckoo's Nest* (Forman, 1975), and *The Virgin Suicides* (Coppola, 2000); successful teen suicides prompted by guilt over male homosexuality comprise central plot threads in *Ode to Billy Joe* (Baer, 1976) and *Six Degrees of Separation* (Schepisi, 1993). *Blue Car* (Moncrieff, 2003) features a suicidal child (the heroine's younger sister), but her death comes early in the narrative and does not become a story unto itself. None of these films, in short, offers a suicidal protagonist younger than 15. The ghastly notion of a prepubescent protagonist's suicide has not yet reached popular cinema—which may be, in part, why Hanna just happens to look in the garage freezer and save her son from suffocation.

15. Significantly, *Ma Vie en Rose* was released in Belgium and France some six months after the capture of Marc Dutroux, a Belgian pedophile who abducted six girls, four of whom he murdered. In Andrew Osborn's analysis, "no other single event, bar[ring] the Second World War . . . has had such a traumatic and damaging effect to the country's self-image." Such was the Belgian outrage, in fact, that in October 1996, roughly 300,000 protestors—"the largest public march of its kind"—assembled in Brussels to express their shock and grief (2002). The protest kicked off the so-called "white year," during which, Jean-Marie Chauvier notes, Belgians, who previously had been "renowned for their timid protests or just turning their backs on [outrage] . . . had suddenly decided to speak out" (1997). According to Osborn, however, righteous indignation against pedophiles blossomed into "harassment of homosexuals [including Deputy Prime Minister Elio Di Rupo] and other 'deviants.' . . ." How ironic that in this witch-hunting context, Belgians managed to keep *Ma Vie en Rose* in proper perspective as the story of a child discovering, without exploitation of the child or the topic itself, his sexuality. The film's Belgian classification as acceptable for all audiences emerges in even greater relief alongside its U.S. "R" rating. At what point does representation of childhood become too "adult" for children to see?

Works Cited

Abraham, Julie. 1996. *Are Girls Necessary? Lesbian Writing and Modern Histories*. New York: Routledge.

Berliner, Alain. 2003. E-mail to author, 14 May.

Butler, Judith. 1999. *Gender Trouble: Feminism and the Subversion of Identity*. 2nd. ed. New York: Routledge.

Califia, Pat. 1997. *Sex Changes: The Politics of Transgenderism*. San Francisco: Cleis Press.

Chauvier, Jean-Marie. 1997. "The 'White' Year Turns to Grey." Trans. Karen Wilkin. *Mondediplo.com* (October). Date of access: 4 May 2003.

Cohan, Steven, and Ina Rae Hart, eds. 1993. *Screening the Male: Exploring Masculinities in Hollywood Cinema*. London: Routledge.

Colapinto, John. 2000. *As Nature Made Him: The Boy Who Was Raised as a Girl*. New York: HarperCollins.

Corbett, Ken. 1999. "Homosexual Boyhood: Notes on Girlyboys." In *Sissies and Tomboys: Gender Nonconformity and Homosexual Childhood*, ed. M. Rottnek. New York: New York University Press.

De Lauretis, Teresa. 1984. *Alice Doesn't: Feminism, Semiotics, Cinema*. Bloomington: Indiana University Press.

DePaola, Tomie. 1979. *Oliver Button Is a Sissy*. New York: Harcourt Brace Jovanovich.

Di Ceglie, Domenico, with David Freedman, eds. 1998. *A Stranger in My Own Body: Atypical Gender Identity Development and Mental Health*. London: Karnac Books.

Doty, Alexander. 2000. *Flaming Classics: Queering the Film Canon*. New York: Routledge.

Dyer, Richard, with Julianne Pidduck. 2003. *Now You See It: Studies on Lesbian and Gay Film¸* 2nd ed. New York: Routledge.

Ehrenstein, David. 1998. *Open Secret: Gay Hollywood, 1928–1998*. New York: William Morrow & Co.

Farmer, Brett. 2000. *Spectacular Passions: Cinema, Fantasy, and Gay Male Spectatorship*. Durham, NC: Duke University Press.

Fierstein, Harvey. 2002. *The Sissy Duckling*. New York: Simon and Schuster.

Foucault, Michel. 1995. *Discipline and Punish: The Birth of the Prison*. Trans. Alan Sheridan. 1977. Reprint. New York: Vintage.

Gay Youth. 1992. Produced, directed, and written by Pam Walton. 40 min. Filmmakers Library. Videocassette.

Hadleigh, Boze. 1993. *The Lavender Screen: The Gay and Lesbian Films: Their Stars, Makers, Characters, and Critics*. Secaucus, NJ: Carol Publishing Group.

Hanson, Ellis. ed. 1999. *Out Takes: Essays on Queer Theory and Film*. Durham, NC: Duke University Press.

Holleman, Joe. 1998. "French Take on Problem Is Done With Style." *St. Louis Post-Dispatch*, 27 February, E3.

Jackson, Kathy Merlock. 1986. *Images of Children in American Film: A Sociocultural Analysis*. Metuchen: Scarecrow Press.

Johnson, Brian D. 1998. Review of *Ma Vie en Rose*. *Maclean's*, 23 February, 70.

Kantrowitz, Arnie. 1977. *Under the Rainbow: Growing Up Gay*. New York: William Morrow.

Kaufmann, Stanley. 1998. Tough Guys and Others. Review of *Ma Vie en Rose*. *New Republic*, 26 January, 25.

Ma Vie en Rose. 1997. Directed by Alain Berliner. 88 min. Sony Pictures Classics and Haut Et Court.

Maltin, Leonard. 2002. *2003 Movie & Video Guide*. New York: Signet.

Mann, William J. 2001. *Behind the Screen: How Gays and Lesbians Shaped Hollywood, 1910–1969*. New York: Viking.

Monette, Paul. 1992. *Becoming a Man: Half a Life Story*. New York: Harcourt Brace Jovanovich.

Mulvey, Laura. 1992. "Visual Pleasure and Narrative Cinema." In *The Sexual Subject: A Screen Reader in Sexuality/Screen*. 1975. Reprint. London: Routledge.

Murray, Raymond. 1996. *Images in the Dark: An Encyclopedia of Gay and Lesbian Film and Video*, 2nd ed. Philadelphia: TLA Video.

Nadeau, Chantal. 2000. "Life with Pinky Dots." *GLQ: A Journal of Lesbian and Gay Studies* 6:1: 137–44.

Nesselson, Lisa. 1998. "Alain Berliner." *Variety Online*, 14 January. www.variety.com. Date of access: 4 May 2003.

Osborn, Andrew. 2002. "Belgium Still Haunted by Pedophile Scandal." Guardian unlimited 26 January. www.guardian.co.uk/elsewhere/journalist/story/0,7792,639371. oo.html. Date of access: 4 May 2003.

Owens, Robert E., Jr. 1998. *Queer Kids: The Challenges and Promises for Lesbian, Gay, and Bisexual Youth*. New York: Haworth Press.

Plummer, David. 1999. *One of the Boys: Masculinity, Homophobia, and Modern Manhood*. New York: Haworth Press.

Pollock, William. 1998. *Real Boys: Rescuing Our Sons from the Myths of Boyhood*. New York: Random House.

Pollock, William, and Todd Shuster. 2000. *Real Boys' Voices*. New York: Random House.

Ringel, Eleanor. "A Boy Who's Pretty in Pink." Review of *Ma Vie en Rose*. *The Atlanta Journal-Constitution*, 27 February, 11.

Russo, Vito. 1987. *The Celluloid Closet: Homosexuality in the Movies*. 2nd ed. New York: Harper & Row.

Savin-Williams, Ritch C. 1998. "*. . . And Then I Became Gay*": *Young Men's Stories*. New York: Routledge.

———. 2001. *Mom, Dad, I'm Gay. How Families Negotiate Coming Out*. Washington, DC: American Psychiatric Association.

Sedgwick, Eve Kosofsky. 1993. "How to Bring Your Kids Up Gay: The War on Effeminate Boys." In *Tendencies*. Durham: Duke University Press.

Sherman, Betsy. 1998. "A Rosy Ending for Belgian Director: *Ma Vie en Rose*, Winner of Golden Globe, Will Compete for Oscar." *Boston Globe*, 1 February, N9.

Stromberg, Lisen. 1999. "The Boy in the Blue Tutu: My Son Loves Dresses. You Got a Problem with That?" *Mothering* 93 (March/April): 57.

Stuart, Jan. 1997. Review of *Ma Vie en Rose*. *Advocate*, 23 December, 51–52.

Thomas, Kevin. 1997. "The Blooming of *Rose*: For Director Alain Berliner, the Response to His First Feature Film Has Been Amazingly Positive." *Los Angeles Times*, 25 December, 12.

Tinkcom, Matthew. 2002. *Working Like a Homosexual: Camp, Capital, Cinema*. Durham: Duke University Press.

Tyler, Parker. 1972. *Screening the Sexes: Homosexuality in the Movies*. New York: Holt, Rinehart, and Winston.

Wilson, Peter. 1998. "Development and Mental Health: The Issue of Difference in Atypical Gender Identity Development." In *A Stranger in My Own Body*, ed. D. Di Ceglie, with D. Freedman. London: Karnac Books.

Zucker, Kenneth J., and Susan J. Bradley. 1995. *Gender Identity Disorder and Psychological Problems in Children and Adolescents*. New York: The Guilford Press.

32.
SPECULATIONS ON THE RELATIONSHIP BETWEEN SOAP OPERA AND MELODRAMA

Christine Gledhill

This paper explores the relationship between melodrama and an increasingly popular area of Television Studies—soap opera. A cursory glance at recent literature on soap opera suggests a certain ambiguity about this relationship. Most frequently an identity between soap opera and melodrama is assumed, but the opposite may be the case—as when soap opera is discussed in the context of realism.

For example, Robert Allen's scholarly study, *Speaking of Soap Opera* (1985), makes no reference to melodrama. "Homey drama of the type that appeals to 'just folks'" is offered as a typical broadcaster's conception of 30s Radio soap opera.[1] In the 50s, Allen suggests, televised soap opera turned for visual style to the transparency and seamlessness of "classic Hollywood," dictated according to film theory by the demands of realism—a far cry from the "problem of style and articulation" which Thomas Elsaesser (1987) names as the hallmark of melodrama.[2]

Similarly, the writers of the BFI monograph on the British soap opera *Coronation Street* (1981) trace the aesthetic sources of the serial not to melodrama but, rather, to a tradition of British social realism. Marion Jordan, for instance, pointing to the compatibility between the conventions of social realism and the serial form used by soap opera, argues that "soap opera realism" represents a specific televisual mode.[3]

Tania Modleski (1982), on the other hand, in her seminal essay "The Search for Tomorrow in Today's Soap Opera," deploys the contrary term, "soap opera melodrama," implicitly endorsing identification between the forms, while recording soap opera's for-mal and ideological divergence from *film* melodrama, a difference she explains in gender terms.[4] And Ien Ang, in *Watching Dallas* (1985), points to early British soap operas as non-melodramatic examples of the genre, while arguing that the soap opera format, especially in American primetime examples such as *Dallas*, is particularly hospitable to the "melodramatic imagination." At the same time she introduces the new category of "emotional realism" which she argues lies at the heart of contemporary soap opera.[5]

What is the explanation for these apparently discrepant accounts of soap opera's aesthetic allegiances? This paper makes the plea that before continuing to talk about "television melodrama" and subsuming soap opera into its embrace, we step back to take stock of our terms. It therefore looks at some recent work on melodrama and soap opera in order to reflect on what knowledge we have in the hope of starting a process of clarification that will further debate.

My provisional conclusions are that soap opera's beginnings as an advertising vehicle directed at women meant that it drew on women's cultural forms themselves operating within frameworks of domestic realism and romance. However, as soap opera became established as an independent aesthetic form, certain thematic and formal features made it prone to melodramatization. This becomes increasingly marked as soap opera is drawn from its ghetto as "women's" programming into the mainstream, where its particular, once historically specific, resources begin to serve needs in "male" culture and a wider popular imagination. The degree of melodramatization, however, varies according to the particular soap opera in question and national cultural characteristics it draws on.

To arrive at this view, however, I look at the historical formation of both melodrama and soap opera in order to deduce the imaginative resources which grew out of historically contingent moments of cultural innovation.

Methodological Preliminaries

Soap opera is a twentieth-century form, whose sources and general formal and institutional characteristics are relatively accessible to investigation. Melodrama, on the other hand, arose in the early nineteenth century in a wide range of institutional sites, aesthetic forms, and national cultures. This has given rise to considerable discrepancy in historical accounts of nineteenth-century melodrama and, applied to twentieth-century popular culture, either vague generalization or an overly narrow use of the term.

Aesthetic history teaches that cultural categories are not fixed and that the boundaries between categories shift under pressure of social change. Analyzing the fluidity of cultural processes, however, requires some conception of stability in order to locate the continuity that enables us to identify transformation and change. Rather than enumerating sets of conventions or stylistic traits which serve only to construct static genres, the notion of a cultural "project" enables us to grasp both an aesthetic identity and a dynamic process. For instance, the history of realism displays an epistemological and aesthetic project—to represent the real world—the terms and conventions of which change as the social construction of reality, the philosophy of knowledge and means of representation change. In this perspective, realism as cultural practice and aesthetic theory constitutes an arena of debate in which the construction of reality itself is contested.

I want to suggest that melodrama represents a related "project," one which intersects with and complicates the project of realism in contemporary popular culture. Unlike realism, however, melodrama is only just becoming visible critically speaking. Recent examination of the historical institutional, aesthetic, and ideological conditions of melodrama's formation identifies a set of structures and devices, of aesthetic pleasures and ideological processes, from which can be derived the melodramatic project, an orientation to the world that distinguishes it from realism at the same time as making its relationship to that mode clearer. In this century, however, the aesthetic and cultural functions of melodrama have been obscured by the values of contemporary criticism. Until very recently, melodrama had been abandoned as a nineteenth-century phenomenon—displaced in modern consciousness by the superior values of realism or modernism and retained merely as a derogatory term to berate the products of mass culture for a backwardness excusable only in women and children.

Soap opera shares this denigrated cultural space with melodrama and this, arguably, is a large factor in the equation of the two forms. For example, Peter Brooks, writer of *The Melodramatic Imagination* (1976) which is fast becoming a major influence in film studies, begins his attempt to reclaim melodrama for academic consideration with the casual remark that contemporary usage of the term "most often refers to a cheap and banal melodrama—to soap opera."[6] Peter Brooks uses soap opera to carry the brunt of devaluation while he seeks to represent nineteenth-century melodrama to twentieth-century sensibilities as worthy of attention.

It is clear, then, that historizing cultural forms is not simply a question of aesthetic and ideological affiliations and difference, but also of shifting cultural valuations. Popular critical categories and values determine how a product is circulated, what slots it appears in, how it is treated by reviewers, and how perceived and enjoyed by audiences. However, the repression of melodramatic aesthetic values—or their mis-recognition—through the pre-eminence of realism as a touchstone of cultural worth, does not mean that melodrama ceases to function in the twentieth century, simply that there exists a level of cultural expression not articulated in, or displaced from the center of critical categories and values. As Ien Ang suggests in her interesting analysis of the ambiguity with which *Dallas* watchers explain their responses to the serial, pleasures in popular culture often co-exist with an ironic disparagement of those pleasures. We know very well that we are not supposed to find melodrama and soap opera satisfying; but, frequently even, we find pleasurable on one level what on another is objectionable to us.

Critical Categories and Gender

The source of the shared devaluation of melodrama and soap opera is not far to find in any standard review of either product. The proclivity of female audiences for domestic melodrama and soap opera links the two in the presumption that they constitute "women's forms"—a gendered categorization supported by the central place these genres accord socially mandated feminine concerns: family, domestic life, personal relationships, and "feelings" which frequently run to tears.

According to Robert Allen, the term *soap opera* was generated in the trade press of the late 30s to position culturally what broadcasters knew as the "daytime dramatic serial." The term stuck and has since passed into common usage, expressing an ironic putdown of a humble form for the emotional demands it makes on behalf of trivial subjects.[7] The new form was also popularly known as the "washboard weeper," in part because women were said to listen while at their housework. The woman's film, which emerged from the major film studios at roughly the same time and for the same commercial reasons, accrued similar tags such as "4-handkerchief pictures," "woman's weepie," "sudsers," "tear-jerkers."[8] While the term *soap opera* starts with the material fact of soap manufacturing sponsorship (Proctor and Gamble, Colgate-Palmolive, Lever Brothers), its watery connotations give scope to pejorative evaluation of the feelings evoked by the form, particularly tears. Soap produces suds, froth, foam, lather—terms of insubstantiality emphasized in the ironic juxtaposition of soap to "opera"—the elite form of high culture, given over to the grandiose expression of elevated feelings of important people and always to be treated with solemn seriousness. The tears produced by the woman's film or soap opera, on the other hand, are considered unjustified by their trivial domestic or personal content and explainable only in terms of a "feminized" sensibility. Robert Allen suggests that class denigration hides behind devaluation by gender.[9] Significantly, "grand opera," the preserve of the establishment, is the one remaining cultural space where melodrama can still be respectably

indulged. No one, however, tries to suggest that opera is a woman's form.

Melodrama similarly makes apparently unjustified demands on our emotional responses—a view pinpointed by Thomas Elsaesser's essay title, "Tales of Sound and Fury" or Peter Brooks's "large but unsubstantiable claims on meaning."[10] So the term *melodramatic* in twentieth-century usage comes to refer to emotions demanded for insignificant situations. Since soap opera is known to have been devised to reach female audiences and to deploy subject matter designated "feminine," namely family and personal relationships and a focus on emotion, it is assumed that such concerns are "melodramatic" and in a circular process that melodrama is somehow a "woman's" cultural form. Description and evaluation are in complete harmony, and a critical trap is laid for unwary "progressive" cultural analysts. The term *melodramatic* comes to signify the oppression of women in the home (as, for example in Michele Mattelart's (1985) "From Soap to Serial"[11]), or more generally a kind of feminizing oppression dished out by mass culture. The result is that we neither grasp what melodrama means in general, nor what goes on in the cultural sphere designated "woman's." A counter tendency in feminist recuperation of melodrama and soap opera as women's forms worthy of critical respect reinforces this conflation.[12] The gender specification of melodrama, however, is a twentieth-century phenomenon. Thomas Elsaesser, Peter Brooks, and others have argued that the nineteenth century conceived its world in melodramatic categories.[13] In other words melodrama, as well as producing a specific theatrical genre, with highly codified plot structures, character types, staging and performance conventions, also gave rise to an imaginative mode which informed not only artistic production across the media, but intellectual, social, and political thought as well. Twentieth-century gender specification has obscured melodrama's existence as a central imaginative and epistemological mode, and its role in the institutional and aesthetic foundation of popular culture.

In the nineteenth century, men and women, the middle and working classes, participated in a theatrical, fictional, and intellectual melodramatic culture—albeit in different cultural or institutional sites. However, in the latter half of the nineteenth century a division took place which separated audiences by class, gender, and aesthetic category. The middle-class intellectual elite, men, realism, tragedy, and modernism are categorized on one side of the divide. The working-class, women and children, melodrama and, latterly, soap opera on the other. However, the ascription of melodrama to all things feminine and only things feminine marks a huge contraction in the reach of the term.

But we are here talking of critical categories and values, not about what actually gets produced, for, as I have argued elsewhere, melodrama survived its critical relegation to mesh with realism as a founding mode of mainstream film and television culture, and not just as a woman's genre.[14]

The Melodramatic Project

According to Peter Brooks, the melodramatic mode organizes an imaginative world constructed on the principle of terminal conflict between polarized moral forces that run through the social fabric and are expressed in personal and familial terms extending beyond the biological family into all areas of social life. Peter Brooks argues that melodrama arises in response to the process of secularization attendant on capitalism's rise to dominance in the western world. Economic imperatives displaced religion—the sacred order represented in the hierarchy of God, Church, and State—which until then had supplied meaning to individual lives and justification for prevailing socio-political arrangements. Melodrama emerges to fill this gap, seeking, in a circular movement, to prove (by making visible) the presence of ethical forces at work in everyday life, and thereby to endow the behavior of ordinary persons with dramatic and ethical consequence. Ideologically speaking, melodrama forges what Peter Brooks calls the "moral occult," which replaces religion as a form of "social glue," giving individual lives an overriding moral significance not supplied by economic structures alone.[15]

Melodrama and Realism

The nineteenth century is more frequently characterized by its codification of realism, notoriously in the "classic realist novel." This is not the paradox it may seem, for the melodramatic mode is committed to making a particular kind of sense of everyday life and on one level is bound not only by contemporary realities but also by the prevailing conventions of realism. Nicholas Vardac (1949) has charted in detail what he calls a "romantic-realist" sensibility, in which the more improbable the fictional strategies to which melodrama resorts in the interest of its sense-making, the more literally its fictions must be "realized" in faithful surface detail.[16] Moreover, nineteenth-century melodrama was highly sensitive to the topical issues of the day and frequently took as subject matter "real life" problems and events. The difference lies in melodrama's use of verisimilitude and in its approach to explanation and resolution of the real world's problems.[17]

Personalization, the mechanism through which melodrama forges a moral order for the secular world, derives from the same ideological sources as the individualism of the realist novel. However, whereas realism can produce individualized characters who at the same time are types representing social forces and whose interrelations describe the movements of social and political change—thereby moving from the individual outwards to society—melodrama works in reverse, understanding the social and political only as they touch on the moral identities and relationships of individuals.

Melodrama's aesthetic problem, according to Peter Brooks, is to demonstrate, to make real, social and ethical forces at work at that point in personal life where politics touch on the psychic. But realism is constrained by the boundaries of the empirically knowable and permissible. Melodrama, on the other hand, while never denying those boundaries, demands that the real world match up to the imagination. Melodramatic aesthetics have survived because they offer to bridge this contradictory pressure, taking, in Peter Brooks's terms, authentic documents from the "real world" and pushing them towards the symbolic activity of metaphor.[18]

Thus verbal discourse is subordinated to an expressive language of visible and musical signs which reach for metaphor. The human body provides a rich vocabulary of gesture, facial expression, and attitude. Episodic narrative action, disregarding logical cause and effect, brings about juxtapositions and confrontations which isolate moments of climactic declaration.

Schematic plot devices such as the discovery of hidden relationships, fatal coincidences, missed meetings and lost chances, engineer encounters and contacts necessary to the moral drama, while bearing metaphoric witness to powerful underlying forces at work in individual lives. Music carries climactic moments, giving an emblematic quality to the resounding cliches that arise from confrontation, recognition, declarations of identity. Melodrama's personae, bearing the brunt of emotional trauma, become personalized metaphors for particular states of being and moral identity, at the same time playing roles—villain, victimized heroine, and absent hero—designed to make the wheels of the drama turn.

In melodrama what people feel and do, how they relate to each other, is of utmost consequence—the source of meaning, the justification for human action. Personalization in this respect is not simply a realist technique for individualizing the social world. Nor does it simply, as is often said, "displace" social and political issues into personal or familial terms in order to achieve a bourgeois fantasy resolution. Personalization is melodrama's primary strength. The webs of economic, political, and social power in which melodrama's characters get caught up are represented not as abstract forces but in terms of desires which express conflicting ethical and political identities and which erupt in the actions and transactions of daily life.

Melodrama and the Family

Personalization, however, does not *per se* make melodrama "family drama." Rather, melodrama uses familial relations in order to access the desires, ethical identities, and ideological conflicts which provide its rationale. Familial desires and hatreds can be enacted in all sorts of social forms, and are not tied to the biological family, for as Freud teaches, psychic drives and familial relationships are intimately linked in western society. As an imaginative mode, nineteenth-century melodrama produced many genres including nautical and military melodrama, cape and sword melodrama, frontier melodrama, alongside the domestic variant. It is only negative twentieth-century gender specification that has prevented acknowledgement of the melodramatic base of so-called "male" cinematic genres such as the western or gangster film.

My concern here, then, is to distinguish between the melodramatic as an imaginative mode that can inform any genre whether "male" or "female," and those instances of cultural production that seek to address female audiences by drawing on women's cultural forms which may be informed variously by realism, melodrama, romance, comedy, and so on. In other words melodrama is not to be identified by a subject matter—emotion and family—alone. Not all expression of emotion or domestic crisis constitutes melodramatic expression and not all melodramatic expression speaks to and from female concerns.

Women's Culture, the Mass Media and Soap Opera

Unlike melodrama, soap opera *was* devised as a woman's form. It therefore raises the question of how gender specification intervenes in a popular cultural field marked out by the interrelated but distinct projects of melodrama and realism. The sponsored continuous serial on U.S. 30s radio was developed as a vehicle for advertising and fictionalized product pitches directed at women in the home. According to Robert Allen, it was devised as a more effective alternative to the radio/magazine/advice column format initially used for this purpose because of the power of serial fiction to capture audiences for the advertising message—which could be given direct from sponsor to audience, or be embedded in the fiction. Given the purpose of the serials to promote domestic consumption, plots concerned female characters and their roles in the family. On somewhat similar lines, the woman's film was developed in the 30s by Hollywood's major film studios as a means of bring a large female audience (who market research suggested constituted the principal film-goers) both into the cinemas and into reach of manufacturers whose need to showcase a wide range of domestic consumer goods led to lucrative deals around "product tie-ins."[19]

If the motive for the production of mass media forms aimed at a female market lay in the need of advertisers to attract women as consumers, the problem remained how to address this audience. In the 30s, the radio and film industries turned to previous formats through which women's cultural concerns have circulated—material often produced by women or out of traditions associated with female writing: novelettes, short stories, serial fiction, romances, letter pages, advice columns, fashion pages, etc. According to Frank Hummert, who with his wife, Anne, was a major pioneer of soap opera on American radio, the idea of using the serial format came from women's magazines.[20] Perhaps the most celebrated instance of transmutation between cultural forms is offered by Olive Higgins Prouty's *Stella Dallas* which was first serialized in *The American* between 1922–3, appeared as a novel in 1923, a play in 1924, a silent film in 1925, the much debated woman's film of 1937, and finally provided the source for a Hummert radio soap opera that ran seventeen years, from 1938–55.

The term *women's culture* requires caution. Clearly it cannot be used to suggest some pure feminine space where women speak freely to each other outside patriarchal constraints. Rather it refers to a place on the margins of a dominant culture where the social and psychic consequences of women's different positioning in society is acknowledged and allowed a degree of expression. I am here using "culture" in its widest sense to refer to how women live their daily lives in the home, in the workplace in women's jobs, or in competition with men, to the social forms through which women interact with each other—mother and toddler groups, townswomen's guilds, women's campaign groups, health groups, etc.—as well as to the gender specific forms of cultural expression women use amongst others.

Soap Opera and Domestic Fiction

Both Tania Modleski and Robert Allen place American soap opera in a cultural tradition that begins with the nineteenth-century American genre of domestic fiction written by and for women. This tradition has also been argued by Ann Kaplan (1987) and Maria LaPlace (1987) as a major source of the woman's film.[21] What is interesting about this "female" genre is how it relates to the cultural conditions within which it emerged and particularly to melodrama and realism.

A major factor in the twentieth-century ghettoization of melodrama as a female genre is the space it gave to female characters. For central to the moral world of Victorian melodrama was the symbolic role of woman as persecuted innocence and representative

of virtue. The heroine is the occasion of the climactic conflict between hero and villain; her perseverance through social and psychic threats, loyalty to and efforts on behalf of an often imperceptive or incompetent hero and steadfast resistance to the villain make everything come out all right in the end.

The centrality of this symbol to patriarchal society raises questions for women's culture. How have women related to their own metaphoric image? What have they done with it? For in that melodrama uses the female figure as a central symbol for its world—as maternal icon or sexual predator—women's culture has been formed in an overdetermined relationship to it. Nineteenth-century women's fiction was forced to reinterpret or challenge this image in order to reclaim "woman" as representative not of generalized psychic need, but of a specific social group, women. The work of Nina Baym (1978) suggests ways in which the domestic novel sought to detach itself from its melodramatic surroundings, both ideologically and aesthetically. In particular this fiction departed from scenarios based on woman as victim—succumbing to male seduction, rape, and abandonment. Against the patriarchal fantasy locked into these motifs, domestic fiction produces a "heroine's text" in which the woman overcomes adversity in the context of a world constructed in realist domestic detail. The domestic novel offers the inverse of the melodramatic process. Rather than metaphorizing the real world to produce symbolic enactments expressing the demands of the patriarchal imagination, women's fiction, through a process of "transvaluation" treats domestic ideology "realistically" as a realizable social program for human betterment. Self-sacrifice and perseverance are translated ideologically as practical ways of dealing with a world that offers women very little and has a habit of disappointing expectation. Domestic feminism illuminates the heroine's search for herself, enabling her to realize her superior moral strength which in turn gives her a social goal. The utopias these novels construct involve less the magical reversals of melodrama's happy ends, than realizable social programs in which the superior values of the domestic sphere are extended to embrace society as a whole and bring about male reformation.[22]

The domestic novel was not the only response made by women writers to the ideologies that circulated with nineteenth-century melodramatic cosmology. Its authors can be distinguished from writers who worked within rather than against the melodramatic tradition. There were those who exploited the pathos of melodrama's victimized heroines and of mother-child bondings and separations—the woman standing in for an underclass to whom social justice is due—as a means of focusing on the intolerable or "tragic" aspects of women's lives. And others who developed the reverse fantasy, the transgressive power of the villainess.[23] However, the domestic novel, particularly in its American variant, was hugely successful.

The demarcation of "domestic realism" as a category worthy of critical attention not only detaches familial and personal relations from the negative connotations of melodrama, it also engages with given understandings of what can be embraced by the "classic realist novel." For women's fiction displays a shift of emphasis in the treatment of family and personal relationships that contests both melodramatic and realist values. These novels take family and personal relationships at face value rather than as mechanisms for melodrama or social representation. Interpersonal or familial conflicts provide a means of exploring the dynamics of human interaction and the female situation. Particularly significant is the role of dialogue in articulating a subjective dimension reached by melodrama only through a series of highly metaphoric expressive codes. In domestic fiction conversation takes the place of action and there is consequently less need for plotting that bounces the drama from one high point to another. This has led, as Sally Mitchell (1977) points out, to the denigration of women's fiction for its apparent formlessness and lack of interest in the progress of events.[24]

According to feminist literary historians such as Nina Baym, the radical aspirations of the American domestic novel died in the late decades of the nineteenth century. Serious women writers branched out into forms and genres that until then had belonged to men. The targeting of the home as a source of domestic consumption by manufacturers and advertisers coincided with a retraction of domestic feminism from wider social application and its incorporation into the dominant view of home as respite from industrial society. However, Robert Allen argues the importance of the genre in establishing a huge popular female readership which didn't disappear with the

genre that established it but supported "women's culture" as a central, if derided, branch of mass production. Not only did a tamer form of women's novelette maintain domesticity as a source of fiction, but women's magazines and newspaper pages spoke in different ways—short stories, serials, poems, recipes, fashion and beauty columns, advice pages, etc.—to the contradictory ideological and social situation of women in the personal and domestic sphere.

Although separated from the woman's film and soap opera by a distance of forty or fifty years, domestic fiction, through the heritage it passed on to women's magazine and "novelette" writing, provided a cultural resource to both genres in their need to fictionalize the sphere of domestic consumption. Not only did such fiction provide subject matter, it provided, as Maria LaPlace argues, an ideology, the Victorian aspects of which—namely the value of sacrifice, self-control, perseverance, duty—were again highly functional in the Depression-ridden 30s, offering a way of coping with life "realistically" and with a degree of dignity and self-respect.[25] Finally, the emphasis on dialogue in women's fiction clearly served both the needs of a radio format addressed to women and the development of the woman's film, the emergence of which with the coming of synchronized sound to the movies was, Andrea Walsh (1984) suggests, no accident.[26]

However, the woman's film, in so far as it is constituted as the single fiction and therefore bounded within the time limits of the feature, demands a compression that invites melodramatic enactment. The film industry was not slow to tag such films as melodrama. There existed already a developed cinematic melodramatic tradition in silent cinema, at the same time as cinema sought prestige as a realist medium. The critical contraction (discussed above) of the term *melodrama* to family and love relationships led to the designation of the woman's film as melodrama and there is evidence that male directors, script-writers, and composers tended to impose a melodramatic framework on novelistic sources more inclined towards domestic realism.[27]

Soap Opera as Serial Form

If the woman's film fell prey to the covertly melodramatic assumptions of its producers, soap opera is arguably situated more ambiguously between modes and forms.

The initially accidental but ultimately defining feature of soap opera which emerged only with the passage of time is its endless seriality. Serial fiction, of course, had a vigorous nineteenth-century life, when its episodic format conformed quite happily to melodramatic requirements, notably in the work of Eugene Sue, George Reynolds, and Charles Dickens. As written fiction, such serialization developed a type of episodic narrative action which according to Nicholas Vardac was central both to the melodramatic stage and to the development of film fiction.[28] However, while serialization led to convoluted, action-filled plotting, such fictions were goal oriented and eventually, their intertangled threads knotted, they did come to an end. Perhaps their television equivalents are the Brazilian telenovelas—said to function highly melodramatically—which also achieve closure after a hundred or so episodes.

Continuous serialization, however, can work against melodrama. In the first place, the experience of seriality through the fixed schedule of radio or television is very different from more flexible encounters with magazine or serialized novel parts which can be consumed at chosen times, and is consequently dependent on the "cliffhanger" to retain its readership. Arguments for the diegetic realism of the continuous radio or TV serial are based on the way it runs parallel to and is integrated into the listener's or viewer's everyday life through its habit-forming regularity. Christine Geraghty (1981) has enumerated a range of formal entailments on this aspect of seriality—for example what she calls "unchronicled growth" whereby we assume that in between episodes time passes for the characters in line with our time, the incorporation of seasonal celebrations or major public events, the sense of a future not yet written, and the recall to a past we share with the characters, which may embrace major changes in their and our lives—births, marriages, deaths, changes in social attitudes, and so on.[29] Finally, the serial world is extended beyond the fiction through a series of secondary texts which elaborate on it as if it were a part of the real world: newspaper speculation or revelation of what is about to happen, articles on the actors, and so on.

Here must be remembered the initial promise of the soap opera to produce measurable social effects—a rise in consumption off the supermarket shelves, which would convince advertisers to buy airtime. The purpose of seriality was to address women as they went about their daily lives in the home, enabling the fiction to offer parallel, "true to life" situations which could "realistically" speaking be improved by the purchase of certain products.

Soap Opera and Women's Culture

Recent feminist analysis of soap opera suggests that the conjunction of seriality with the need to invent a new women's cultural form continued the process begun by women's fiction of negotiating the metaphoric image of woman deployed by melodrama.[30] At a structural level, for example, endless seriality may be antagonistic to melodrama. Whereas melodrama, in order to produce its symbols and moral lessons—in particular its deus-ex-machina resolutions—is dependent on the freeze-frame of tableau and narrative closure, soap opera must continually destroy equilibrium and frame in order for the show to go on. As Tania Modleski and others have pointed out, the endlessness of soap opera means that its resolutions can only be temporary.

Melodrama, nevertheless, contains within itself the seeds of such serial destruction, which its particular strategies seek to contain. According to Peter Brooks, melodrama differs from tragedy because it can no longer draw on an overriding order to which individual lives can be securely reconciled.[31] Therefore its resolutions must be continually re-won. Moreover, within melodrama itself, as Louis James (1981) points out, the dynamic of the tableau resides in the contrary tensions caught up in the freeze frame which will serve to break the picture up in a return to action.[32]

In the context of soap opera where the focus is women's lives, the contrary tension within any moment of stasis resides close to the surface in the manifest contradictions surrounding female roles in patriarchy and emerges in currents that run counter to dominant ideology—around divorce, marital fidelity, sisterhood, and so on. Thus Tania Modleski talks of the *impossibility* of resolution in narratives which take women's lives as their subject matter.[33] In particular the happy end that is sealed in marriage must be disrupted in order for the serial to keep rolling. A wedding merely constitutes, as Terry Lovell (1981) has remarked, an interruption to the real business of life—the vicissitudes and problems of personal relationships.[34] The centrality to soap opera of female characters who cannot be fixed in marriage, then, may lead to figures that slip out of the symbolic placements designed by melodrama.

Equally important as seriality in defining soap opera is the dominance of dialogue over action. Initially a necessary entailment of radio fiction, talk, as we have seen, is a major element of women's fictional forms. So that when soap opera left radio for television, the exigencies of the by now well established format, reinforced by low production values, meant that as visual fiction soap opera consisted mainly of talking heads.

Like the endlessness of soap opera's seriality, the centrality of "talk" cuts across the purposes of melodrama. In soap opera, events can hardly be said to be enacted. They are announced over the telephone, or through letters or gossip retailing what has been overseen or overheard. Narrative is pieced together by the audience from the fragments of conversation through which these announcements are discussed, argued about, and generally chewed over. Such exchanges use colloquial, conversational forms of speech and follow everyday patterns of reasoning. They represent different characters' attempts to understand within the limits of their character type and prevailing common-sense what is happening or ought to happen in a given situation. They offer an arena for learning, for bringing things out into the open, talking problems over and working them through. Robert LaGuardia notes how the repetitive nature of the daily soap opera tends to "slow" the pace of modern living down in order to permit this kind of reflective process.[35]

Soap opera constructs a feminine world of personal conversation, into which male characters are integrated. In this respect, soap opera, in its construction of male characters, frequently offers female audiences the pleasurable effect of "estrangement," particularly in recent times when the repertoire of male figures entering soap opera and participating in its personal conversations has expanded.

The social diversity of soap opera characters is devised to provide a balanced range of types for the particular milieu. Difference is essential to keep the conversation going. Considerable negotiation takes place between differing points of view—particularly between dominant conservative views and alternative, provocative notions introduced by young or marginal types. In this way personal conversation becomes social conversation. In this context events are important for the extra charge they give to the narrative and incentive to the audience to keep watching. But their major function is to give the characters something to keep talking about.

Soap Opera and Melodrama

How then does soap opera relate to melodrama? Given the contracted reach of the latter term in twentieth-century criticism, soap opera appears to share a subject matter with melodrama, namely the home, family, and heterosexual relations. But the connection with domestic fiction discussed above suggests that soap opera also shares its different approach to family and personal relationships. I have already suggested that such fictions take family and personal relationships at face value rather than as mechanisms for melodramatic enactment, that dialogue similarly displaces the expressive codes of melodrama, and finally that endless seriality cuts across the formal demands of the melodramatic worldview.

This shift can now be further elaborated. Thomas Elsaesser argues that the flamboyant *mise en scene*, theatrical performance, spectacular actions, and grandiose delivery of banal sentiments which carry the over-arching ethical, social, and political conflicts of melodrama are predicated on inadequate, inarticulate characters who submit to the repressed ideological contradictions of their society. But while similar narrative situations may occur in melodramas, domestic novels, and soap operas, writers drawing on women's culture have access to a set of female discursive forms which are highly articulate—conversation, the confessional heart-to-heart, gossip—and exist precisely to work through the psychic and social contradictions which melodrama must externalize through non-verbal means. Moreover, as Laura Mulvey suggests of woman-oriented melodrama, such contradictions, far from being unconscious, are part of the acknowledged experience of female audiences.[36] Thus in domestic fiction and soap opera, narrative events are relatively incidental and *mise en scene* relatively unimportant, since it is precisely the intervening social webbing of events through personal talk that constitutes their sphere of action. Far from representing an internalized "excess" of emotion in place of extraverted action, as Jon Stratton (1987) suggests, talk in soap opera *is* action—a feminine type of extraversion—while action in the more conventional (male) sense represents unexpressed emotion.[37]

Recent feminist writing has stressed further homologies between the structural features of soap opera and women's cultural and social forms. Tania Modleski, for example, suggests that seriality applied to domestic and familial content reproduces aesthetic patterns—multiple points of identification, fragmented and interrupted story lines, the play on endless expectation, the impossibility of closure—which conform closely to how women actually experience life. Charlotte Brunsdon (1982) has argued that soap opera developed the serial format both to suit the conditions of female listening or viewing in the home and to exploit the special kind of reading competence that the contradictory multiplicity of women's social roles foster—i.e., constant interruptability, distraction, and automated attentiveness to personal and social nuances, which the fragmented, conversational mode of soap opera's narration mirrors.[38]

In this context, it is interesting to consider the functioning of mechanisms deployed by the continuous serial which *are* shared with the melodramatic repertoire: the fatal coincidence or missed opportunity, the reappearance of a long lost relative or unknown figure from the past, or mysteries about parentage and legitimacy. Such mechanisms are almost inevitable if narrative is to be endlessly generated in a world constrained by the limits of domestic relations, and where endless seriality means the virtual impossibility of letting a story line rest in a desired or ideologically acceptable conclusion with the consequent need to engineer disruptions and reversals to the status quo. Clearly such mechanisms can be and often are developed for their melodramatic frisson. However, within soap opera's intense preoccupation with the lived experience of women's lives these

mechanisms may be drawn in a different direction. Rather than engineering symbolic confrontations, soap opera's sudden reversals or coincidences may render life's habit of disappointing expectation or of throwing up undesirable complications—much in the tradition of the domestic novel which seeks stoically to face life's problems rather than to make grandiose gestures or seek magical solutions.

One further feature of soap opera needs addressing in considering soap opera's designation as melodrama, namely its incorporation of romance. This can be traced back to the beginning of soap opera. For insofar as the sponsored soap opera sought to address the everyday life of women in order to affect their behavior as consumers, it had also to address female desire. In American radio soap operas of the 30s—especially those devised by the Hummerts whose work Robert LaGuardia opposes to the domestic realism of Irna Phillips—familial relationships shared airtime with romantic relationships, as they did in the more diffused context of women's magazine culture from which the Hummerts drew inspiration.[39] This aspect of soap opera has attracted wide condemnation as escapist fantasy, particularly as the serials of the 30s were constructed within a strict Victorian morality which appeared to mean a virtual absence of sexual fulfillment.

Popular critical wisdom barely distinguishes romance from melodrama in that both appear to pursue wishfulfilling rather than realistic resolutions. However, feminist analysts such as Janice Radway (1984), Alison Light (1984), and Maria LaPlace (1987) have begun to reconsider the role of romance in women's culture, alongside melodrama and soap opera.[40] Their work suggests ways of reading women's romance as re-figuring patriarchal sexuality in order to make space, albeit within boundaries marked out by negation, for fantasies within which a different mode of sexual reality can be hinted at. The reading of the frequent sacrificial conclusions of women's fictions as masochism too easily assumes that coital coupling is the desired end of female fantasy. Just as domestic realism reworks the familial ideology of melodrama, so it can be suggested that romance fiction rearranges the components of dominant fantasies of heterosexuality in order to disclose alternative fantasies of strong, enduring, often single women, of female bonding, and of heterosexual relations characterized by equality and mutuality rather than by scenarios of dominance and submission. To read the romantic relations of soap opera in this way is to enter once more a contestation of the way the "real" is constructed through culture.

Cultural Forms and National Cultures

To this point I have discussed soap opera as a somewhat abstract, singular model, assuming its production as a form directed at women. While this holds true of American radio soap opera of the thirties and its transference to daytime television in the 50s, it is not necessarily true of its later development, nor of its adoption in different national cultures. According to Peter Buckman (1984), it was to a large degree the commercial origins of American soap opera, with their appeal to the fantasies of mass (and female) audiences, that made the BBC, under the leadership of Lord Reith, reject the form as "encouraging mindless listening."[41] This did not, however, prevent British audiences from becoming familiar with American soap opera when in their millions they tuned into Radio Luxemburg and the Hummert serials which it bought in.

According to Buckman, it was propaganda rather than commercial requirements which during the war prompted the BBC to initiate its first continuous serial, designed to convince the home front and allies that "Britain can take it." Peter Buckman's account of this and post-war serials such as *Mrs. Dale's Diary* and *The Archers* highlights the BBC's refusal of the soap opera category and determination to distance its serial fiction from the presumed romantic, wishfulfilling escapism of the American type. Realism was to distinguish the British serial from its American counterpart, to ward off the taint of romance and melodrama that characterized the products of a commercial mass and feminized culture. But the American serials, as Robert LaGuardia points out, also claimed to be "true to life" and "realistic."[42] That the BBC was in fact appealing to a particular national cultural formation in its claim to realism is supported by the commercial company, Granada's, similar refusal to locate its first long running serial, *Coronation Street*, in the soap opera category. Marion Jordan's analysis of this serial finds a

perfect fit between its formal and thematic characteristics and those of British social realism.[43]

At issue in the comparison of American and British soap operas is the different way melodrama and realism inform their respective cultures, and the gender implications of this difference. In fact rarely do these early British soap operas set out to construct a specifically female ambience. In preference they choose social communities: the hospital in *Emergency Ward 10*, a magazine office in *Compact*, a football club in *United*, or the problem of new towns in *The Newcomers*. In those that center more explicitly on the family, such as *Mrs. Dale's Diary, The Archers*, or *The Groves*, British realist treatment of the family and the individual women within it frequently lead outwards to the community and social issues. *The Archers*, for example, has always been used to convey a large amount of general information about farming.

Such national comparison is a subject for another project; but important to note here is the complication of national specificities by the international circulation of television fiction, through which the practices of, in particular, American popular culture, provide resources to others. As Robert LaGuardia suggests, from the seventies on, soap opera, with its extraordinary successes and excesses, its integration into the imaginary lives of millions of people, its widening transnational audiences and growing cultural and academic respectability, creates news headlines—and no television company of whatever cultural persuasion can afford to be without one.[44]

Soap Opera Realism: Soap Opera Melodrama

The international circulation of soap opera suggests that to pursue the contradictory formation of soap opera requires consideration not only of the cultural space into which it emerged, but, once established, of its implications as a resource to other areas of cultural production. Just as the "melodramatic" spiraled off from the specific theatrical genre in which it crystallized to become a very much more wide-ranging resource that has survived into the twentieth-century, I would argue that the same is true for soap opera; as a form that passed from radio to television programming for women and laterally into a wider cultural sphere, it has generated a far more extensive potential than its early progenitors ever envisaged. Crucial to this potential is the intersection in soap opera of domestic realism and melodrama as they bear on gender representation.

If realism is, as Peter Brooks suggests, constrained by limits set by what social, cultural, psychic and ideological convention recognizes or permits, it must at the same time continually re-establish its claims to show the world as it is by breaking with convention. As new social forces exert pressure on the limits of representation, demanding recognition, the realist work must in the end, however much resistance there is in its system, attempt to show what has not been represented before in order to justify its claims.

Melodrama is also driven to break with the limits of representation: not, however, in order to renew verisimilitude, but rather to render the world as humanly significant, to deal with the real as it touches psychic nerves or activates the moral imagination. Hence melodrama functions both referentially and metaphorically, bearing witness to the underlying desires and impulses which fuel social processes. In this respect melodrama feeds off the ideological conflicts that accompany social change. Thus realism in pioneering new fields of representation offers melodrama the material for renewed symbolic enactment, in reverse process, melodrama's capacity to cut short the logical processes of realism to arrive at overdetermined confrontations can make covertly available as melodrama what realism avoids or represses as too threatening. This interdependence seems to me particularly pertinent to the way soap opera has responded to changes in gender roles and ideologies since the 50s.

Soap Opera and Gender

I have argued that while melodrama uses familial relations as a mechanism that achieves the personalization of social and ideological conflict, soap opera in drawing on the traditions of the domestic novel, takes the family as its subject matter. However, by the 50s, as David Rodowick (1987) has pointed out, the set of familial relations that nineteenth-century melodrama could rely on as ethical touchstones became highly problematic.[45] The family no longer offers relations that unquestioningly produce loyalty, devotion, duty,

or betrayal. While still expressing deeply-seated psychic desires, the family has itself become a problem for society. The symbolic weight it has brought with it from its nineteenth-century melodramatic inheritance has proved too much for its ill-founded and fragile structure, as is evidenced in the 50s Hollywood family melodrama. Critical to this shift are the ideological conflicts which surfaced in the late 50s and early 60s around the role of women. Soap opera, which gives pre-eminent place to female characters and family subjects, is prone to melodramatic enactment on behalf of society as a whole. At the same time in the USA, soap opera made the successful shift from radio to daytime television. While low production values maintained the pre-eminence of dialogue and the talking head, the visual dimension of television fiction increased the possibility of melodramatic values—particularly in the role of the glance, gesture, and body movement as major channels of communication when verbal exchanges fail to express or conceal underlying facts and feelings. Higher production values in later soap operas intensify their potential for melodramatic expression.

If this potentiality for the melodramatic lay dormant while 50s family melodrama in the cinema carried the brunt of the growing pressure on gender roles, the late 70s and 80s saw a renewed search in popular fictional forms for enacting heterosexual and family crisis. In cinema, attempts were made to revive the family melodrama and woman's film. But soap opera appears to have provided the most fertile format for these renewed negotiations—arguably because melodrama and realism, women's and men's culture, intersect in soap opera in a particularly productive way. In primetime serials such as *Dallas* and *Dynasty*, which supported high production values, the potential offered by soap opera for melodramatizing the family comes into tension with the project of soap opera as women's cultural form. For example, in a particular phase of *Dallas*, the melodramatic construction of Pamela and Sue Ellen as contrary types and rivals began to give way under pressure of a plot that took them to Hong Kong on a rescue mission during which the absence of the immediate family allowed space for a certain comradeship and exchange of sisterly views about life, men, and relationships far more reminiscent of the soap opera aimed at women.[46]

Soap Opera and Men's Culture

The recent change in the status and production values of soap opera with its shift from daytime to primetime television suggest to me a recognition of a potentially new dimension of male culture. As a women's form, soap opera pioneered in the margins of popular cultural production a space for representing a particular kind of aesthetic experience—namely, personal life—which, if devalued in the immediate post-war years of economic reconstruction, becomes an invaluable cultural resource in the late 70s when international economic and political crises throw the gender roles and patriarchal values underlying capitalist production into question. The question "how to live"—in other words the question of personal meaning and justification—becomes acute when warfare, law-enforcement, politics, multinational business (the arenas of masculine endeavor and achievement) spell corruption, torture, terrorism, and annihilation, and the women's movement makes the cultural validation of machismo no longer an easy option. In the first instance we can observe the spread of soap opera structures into male preserves such as the crime series—*Hill Street Blues*—and the entry in their own right of a widening range of male characters into soap operas. But for male characters to enact male dramas inside soap opera or for soap opera structures to operate inside a "male" genre, a break is required with conventions of gender representation—which dictate taciturnity and invincibility as marks of masculinity and construe talk about personal feelings as "feminizing." Melodrama provides the means for devising and structuring situations which build to crisis points such that taboos around masculinity and feeling can be broken. Melodrama enables male genres to draw on the resources of soap opera, so that for example, we can find out about exchanges of male intimacy in the washroom; it legitimates the stronger, expressive roles played by men in contemporary primetime soap operas from *Dallas* to *East Enders*.[47]

Conversely, if women's domestic realism opens up areas for melodramatic enactment not visible to mainstream forms, melodrama's taboo-breaking capacity can open socially proscribed areas to the problem-raising of soap opera, particularly those areas in which women have a vested and not always conformist interest—for example abortion, separation, illegitimacy, career building, and so on. In many instances, soap opera will resort to melodramatic formulation when the nearly unthinkable is offered as a plot complication. However, once melodrama has put the problem on the agenda, soap opera's diagnostic technique of conversation will frequently dissipate the melodramatic charge as characters chew over in their various different social and personal contexts the emotional, moral, and social implications and consequences of the event. For example, in an episode of the Australian soap opera, *Neighbours*, when the fact is about to be made known to Rosemary that it is her mother's brief affair with Rosemary's fiancé which lies behind her broken engagement, the style shifts into a melodramatic orchestration of parallel lines of action, significant glances, one liners, and haunting music on the sound-track. For a brief episode, the world of *Neighbours* is held in the balance while incestuous implications and matricidal feelings reverberate as Rosemary swears she will never speak to her mother again. Several discussions between interested parties, a few interventions and a couple of episodes later, mother and daughter talk their way back to the feminine commonsense of personal relations and daily business can take its course.

Here melodrama's schematic plotting, which serves to construct improbable inter-personal conjunctures, permits emotional enactments within fantasies disallowed by social or cultural convention, which can then be worked over according to the processes of women's fictional forms as if they are real. Arguably the emotional realism which Ien Ang discerns in the melodrama of *Dallas* is carried in such verbal dissections of events by involved characters.[48]

Provisional Conclusions

In conclusion, soap opera has evolved from the intersection of a number of institutional, ideological, and aesthetic processes. For the broadcaster and advertisers, the motivation to produce soap opera lay in the need to reach a female audience in the home. Economic and ideological conditions dictated the subject matter—home, family, relationships—while the social and aesthetic traditions of women's culture provided formal influence. Women's writing had developed in uneasy relations with melodrama, which lays powerful claim to the image of woman as a symbol for the whole culture, and which women's fictional forms had to negotiate in order to open up the drama of women's lives. Advertisers' needs to produce material effects in the patterns of women's consumption, the influence of the realist mode of domestic fiction, and the need of the serial form to produce a fictional world to parallel its listeners' lives all tended to lead soap opera towards a low budget, conventional realism.

Seriality contributes a solidity to this enterprise, producing a format in which a few central families are involved in a wider community—dominated by women— the multiplicity of whose relationships and life stories provides continuous occasion for storytelling and a three dimensional reality to a tale that runs in parallel to its listeners' lives. At the same time the continuousness of the serial produces problems in the need for endless self-generation. The combination of the family and seriality produces conditions in which devices employed by melodrama are almost inevitable: the return from the past, reversals of fortune, painful confrontations, and the interpolation of topical social, economic, or political reference into personal, family dramas. Structural tactics such as these hold the potentiality for the overdetermination of events and conflicts towards the metaphorical that characterizes melodrama. But cultural context and audience address determine the degree to which these devices are exploited melodramatically.

However, the soap opera format, at first despised for its address to devalued female concerns, demonstrates an extraordinary power to hold audiences. And ideological tensions around the organization of gender in both economic and personal life which rise to the surface in the 70s and 80s discover in the soap opera formal and subject matter an ideal site for melodramatic enactments that now begin to draw "men's culture" and "women's culture" together into an arena of contest and negotiation.

Notes

This paper was originally presented to the third International Television Studies Conference held in London during July 1988. I am more than glad that the revised version can appear in this issue of QRFV [*Quarterly Review of Film and Video* 14.1–2] devoted to the memory of Beverle Houston.

QRFV provided the occasion of my first encounter with Beverle when she drove me to complete a piece on feminist criticism that I had wanted to give up on. Later I met Beverle in Los Angeles and behind the generation of the present piece lie animated discussions with her on *Stella Dallas* as melodrama and women's culture. The only time that I could return her hospitality was during her visit to London for the first ITSC. When I came to give this paper at the third Conference, I sorely missed her energizing and encouraging presence. I am glad therefore of this opportunity to acknowledge my debt of gratitude for these brief but vital moments of contact with her.

1. Robert Allen, *Speaking of Soap Opera* (Chapel Hill: University of North Carolina Press, 1985), p. 11.
2. Thomas Elsaesser, "Tales of Sound and Fury: Observations on the Family Melodrama" in Christine Gledhill (ed.), *Home Is Where the Heart Is* (London: BFI, 1987), p. 50.
3. Marion Jordan, "Realism and Convention" in Richard Dyer, et al. (eds.), *Coronation Street*, Television Monograph 13 (London: BFI, 1981), p. 28.
4. Tania Modleski, "The Search for Tomorrow in Today's Soap Operas" in *Loving With a Vengeance* (Hamden, Connecticut: The Shoe String Press, 1982), p. 93.
5. Ien Ang, *Watching Dallas: Soap Opera and the Melodramatic Imagination* (London: Methuen, 1985), p. 87.
6. Peter Brooks, *The Melodramatic Imagination: Balzac, Henry James, Melodrama and the Mode of Excess* (New Haven: Yale University Press, 1976), p. 12.
7. Robert Allen, *Speaking of Soap Opera*, op. cit., p. 9. Significantly the similar term "horse opera" for the western has had nothing like the same currency.
8. See Jeanine Basinger, "When Women Wept," *American Film*, vol. 12 no. 10, September 1977.
9. Robert Allen, *Speaking of Soap Opera*, op. cit.
10. Peter Brooks, *The Melodramatic Imagination*, op. cit., p. 199.
11. Michele Mattelart, "From Soap to Serial," in *Women, Media and Crisis* (London: Comedia, 1985).
12. Jon Stratton, "Watching the Detectives: Television Melodrama and its Genres" in *Australasian Drama Studies*, no. 10, April 1987 discusses this conflation in a very interesting analysis of the relations between melodrama, seriality, soap opera, and gender which both overlaps with and diverges from the arguments I make here.
13. For example, Wylie Sypher, "Aesthetic of Revolution: The Marxist Melodrama" in Robert W. Corrigan (ed.), *Tragedy: Vision and Form* (New York: New York University Press, 1965).
14. See "The Melodramatic Field: An Investigation" in Gledhill (ed.), *Home Is Where the Heart Is*, op. cit.
15. Peter Brooks, *The Melodramatic Imagination*, op. cit., p. 20.

16. Nicholas Vardac, *Stage to Screen: Theatrical Origins of Early Film: David Garrick to D. W. Griffith* (Cambridge: Harvard University Press, 1949).

17. See David Mayer, "*The Ticket-of-Leave Man* in Context," *Essays in Theatre*, vol. 6 no. 1, November 1987.

18. Peter Brooks, *The Melodramatic Imagination*, op. cit., p. 9.

19. See Leo Handel, *Hollywood Looks at its Audience* (1950), and Charles Eckert, "The Carol Lombard in Macy's Window" (1976), both quoted in Maria LaPlace, "Producing and Consuming the Woman's Film: Discursive Struggle in *Now, Voyager*," in Gledhill (ed.), *Home Is Where the Heart Is*, op cit.

20. Frank Hummert, quoted in Peter Buckman, *All for Love: A Study in Soap Opera* (London: Secker and Warburg, 1984), p. 9.

21. E. Ann Kaplan, "Mothering, Feminism and Representation: The Maternal Melodrama and the Woman's Film 1910–40" and Maria LaPlace, "Producing and Consuming the Woman's Film: Discursive Struggle in *Now, Voyager*," both in Gledhill (ed.), op. cit.

22. See Nina Baym, *Woman's Fiction: A Guide to Novels by and about Women in America, 1820–1870* (Ithaca: Cornell University Press, 1978), p. 36.

23. See Elaine Showalter, "Desperate Remedies: Sensation Novels of the 1860s," *The Victorian Newsletter*, no. 49, Spring 1976.

24. Sally Mitchell, "Sentiment and Suffering," *Victorian Studies*, vol. 21 no. 1, 1977.

25. Maria LaPlace, "Producing and Consuming the Woman's Film: Discursive Struggle in *Now, Voyager*," in Gledhill (ed.), op. cit.

26. Andrea Walsh, *Women's Film and Female Experience* (New York: Praeger, 1984).

27. Jeanne Alien, for example, quotes Edmund Golding's treatment of Olive Higgins Prouty's novel, *Now, Voyager* in which he recommends "tightening the narrative line and making Charlotte and Jerry bolder and more resilient characters. He believed that the thread to develop was the basic premise of melodrama: 'the grim opposition to the heroine's and the audience's deep desires.'" Jeanne Allen, "Introduction" to *Now, Voyager* (Madison, Wisconsin: University of Wisconsin Press, 1984), p. 19.

Olive Higgins Prouty herself records her struggles against the demand for "cliffhangers" in the seven part serialization which was her first means of publishing *Stella Dallas*, declaring, "There are two things I want to avoid in my writing—sentimentality and melodrama." Not surprisingly she also resisted her (male) publisher's suggestion for an alternative title, *Greater Love Hath No Woman*. She had little time for the film versions and less still for the soap opera, which was fabricated by the Hummerts without her permission. See Olive Higgins

Prouty, *Pencil Shavings* (Cambridge, Massachusetts: Riverside Press, 1961), pp. 152–174 and Robert LaGuardia, *Soap World* (New York: Arbor House, 1983), pp. 16–17.

28. Nicholas Vardac, *Stage to Screen*, op. cit.

29. Christine Geraghty "The Continuous Serial—a Definition" in Dyer, *Coronation Street*, op. cit.

30. For example, Tania Modleski, "The Search for Tomorrow in Today's Soap Operas" in *Loving With a Vengeance*, op. cit. and Charlotte Brunsdon, "Crossroads: Notes on Soap Opera," *Screen*, vol. 22 no. 4, 1982.

31. Peter Brooks, *The Melodramatic Imagination*, op. cit.

32. Louis James, "Is Jerrold's Black-Eyed Susan More Important than Wordsworth's Lucy?" in David Bradby, et al., *Performance and Politics in Popular Drama* (Cambridge: Cambridge University Press, 1981).

33. Tania Modleski, "The Search for Tomorrow in Today's Soap Operas" in *Loving With a Vengeance*, op. cit. See also, Jane Feuer, "Melodrama, Serial Form and Television," in *Screen*, vol. 25 no. 1, January-February 1984.

34. Terry Lovell, "Ideology and *Coronation Street*" in Dyer, et al., *Coronation Street*, op. cit.

35. Robert LaGuardia, *Soap World*, op. cit., p. 4.

36. Laura Mulvey, "Notes on Sirk and Melodrama," in Gledhill (ed.), op. cit.

37. Jon Stratton, "Watching the Detectives: Television Melodrama and its Genres," op. cit. Soap operas are often compared to gossip. Christine Geraghty discusses the structural function of gossip for soap opera in "The Continuous Serial—a Definition," in Dyer, *Coronation Street*, op. cit. But the centrality of "talk" to women's fictional forms is also seen as a pejorative gender characteristic, trying the patience of at least one British television reviewer who complained of the "relentless drip of . . . domestic dialogue" in Andrea Newman's thirteen part serial, *Mackenzie* (Richard Last in *The Daily Telegraph*, 5.4.80).

38. See Tania Modleski, "The Search for Tomorrow in Today's Soap Operas" in *Loving With a Vengeance*, op. cit. and Charlotte Brunsdon, "*Crossroads*: Notes on Soap Opera," op. cit.

39. Robert LaGuardia, *Soap World*, op. cit.

40. See Janice Radway, *Reading the Romance: Women, Patriarchy, and Popular Culture* (Chapel Hill: University of Carolina Press, 1984); Alison Light, "'Returning to Manderley'—Romance Fiction, Female Sexuality and Class," *Feminist Review*, no. 16, April 1984; Maria LaPlace, "Producing and Consuming the Woman's Film: Discursive Struggle in *Now, Voyager*," in Gledhill (ed.), op. cit.

41. Peter Buckman, *All For Love: A Study in Soap Opera*, op. cit., p. 5.

42. Robert LaGuardia, *Soap World*, op. cit., pp. 12–18.

43. Marion Jordan, "Realism and Convention" in Dyer, et al. (eds.), *Coronation Street*, op. cit.

44. Robert LaGuardia, *Soap World*, op. cit., p. 40.

45. David Rodowick, "Madness, Authority and Ideology: The Domestic Melodrama of the 1950s," in Gledhill (ed.), op. cit.

46. Jackie Byars analyzes these episodes as feminine discourse in "Reading Feminine Discourse: Prime-Time Television in the US," *Communications*, Slimmer 1986.

47. Charlotte Brunsdon discusses the recent intermeshing of women's and male genres in "Women Watching Television," *Medie Kultur*, no. 4, November 1986.

48. Ien Ang, *Watching Dallas: Soap Opera and the Melodramatic Imagination*, op. cit., p. 87.

33.
FILM BODIES

Gender, Genre, and Excess

Linda Williams

When my seven-year-old son and I go to the movies we often select from among categories of films that promise to be sensational, to give our bodies an actual physical jolt. He calls these movies "gross." My son and I agree that the fun of "gross" movies is in their display of sensations that are on the edge of respectable. Where we disagree—and where we as a culture often disagree, along lines of gender, age, or sexual orientation—is in which movies are over the edge, too "gross." To my son the good "gross" movies are those with scary monsters like Freddy Krueger (of the *Nightmare on Elm Street* series) who rip apart teenagers, especially teenage girls. These movies both fascinate and scare him; he is actually more interested in talking about than seeing them.

A second category, one that I like and my son doesn't, are sad movies that make you cry. These are gross in their focus on unseemly emotions that may remind him too acutely of his own powerlessness as a child. A third category, of both intense interest and disgust to my son (he makes the puke sign when speaking of it), he can only describe euphemistically as "the 'K' word." K is for kissing. To a seven-year-old boy it is kissing precisely which is obscene.

There is no accounting for taste, especially in the realm of the "gross." As a culture we most often invoke the term to designate excesses we wish to exclude; to say, for example, which of the Robert Mapplethorpe photos we draw the line at, but not to say what form and structure and function operate within the representations deemed excessive. Because so much attention goes to determining where to draw the line, discussions of the gross are often a highly confused hodgepodge of different categories of excess. For example, pornography is today more often deemed excessive for its violence than for its sex, while horror films are excessive in their displacement of sex onto violence. In contrast, melodramas are deemed excessive for their gender- and sex-linked pathos, for their naked displays of emotion; Ann Douglas once referred to the genre of romance fiction as "soft-core emotional porn for women" (Douglas, 1980).

Alone or in combination, heavy doses of sex, violence, and emotion are dismissed by one faction or another as having no logic or reason for existence beyond their power to excite. Gratuitous sex, gratuitous violence and terror, gratuitous emotion are frequent epithets hurled at the phenomenon of the "sensational" in pornography, horror, and melodrama. This essay explores the notion that there may be some value in thinking about the form, function, and system of seemingly gratuitous excesses in these three genres. For if, as it seems, sex, violence, and emotion are fundamental elements of the sensational effects of these three types of films, the designation "gratuitous" is itself gratuitous. My hope, therefore, is that by thinking comparatively about all three "gross" and sensational film body genres we might be able to get beyond the mere fact of sensation to explore its system and structure as well as its effect on the bodies of spectators.

Body Genres

The repetitive formulas and spectacles of film genres are often defined by their differences from the classical realist style of narrative cinema. These classical films have been characterized as efficient action-centered, goal-oriented linear narratives driven by the desire of a single protagonist, involving one or two lines of action, and leading to definitive closure. In their influential study of the Classical Hollywood Cinema, Bordwell, Thompson, and Staiger call this the Classical Hollywood style (1985).

As Rick Altman has noted in a recent article (1989), both genre study and the study of the somewhat more nebulous category of melodrama has long been hampered by assumptions about the classical nature of the dominant narrative to which melodrama and some individual genres have been opposed. Altman argues that Bordwell, Thompson, and Staiger, who locate the Classical Hollywood Style in the linear, progressive form of the Hollywood narrative, cannot accommodate "melodramatic" attributes like spectacle, episodic presentation, or dependence on coincidence except as limited exceptions or "play" within the dominant linear causality of the classical (Altman, 1988, 346).

Altman writes: "Unmotivated events, rhythmic montage, highlighted parallelism, overlong spectacles—these are the excesses in the classical narrative system that alert us to the existence of a competing logic, a second voice." (345–6) Altman, whose own work on the movie musical has necessarily relied upon analyses of seemingly "excessive" spectacles and parallel constructions, thus makes a strong case for the need to recognize the possibility that excess may itself be organized as a system (347). Yet analyses of systems of excess have been much slower to emerge in the genres whose non-linear spectacles have centered more directly upon the gross display of the human body. Pornography and horror films are two such systems of excess. Pornography is the lowest in cultural esteem, gross-out horror is next to lowest.

Melodrama, however, refers to a much broader category of films and a much larger system of excess. It would not be unreasonable, in fact, to consider all three of these genres under the extended rubric of melodrama, considered as a filmic mode of stylistic and/or emotional excess that stands in contrast to more "dominant" modes of realistic, goal-oriented narrative. In this extended sense melodrama can encompass a broad range of films marked by "lapses" in realism, by "excesses" of spectacle and displays of primal, even infantile emotions, and by narratives that seem circular and repetitive. Much of the interest of melodrama to film scholars over the last fifteen years originates in the sense that the form exceeds the normative system of much narrative cinema. I shall limit my focus here, however, to a more narrow sense of melodrama, leaving the broader category of the sensational to encompass the three genres I wish to consider. Thus, partly for purposes of contrast with pornography, the melodrama I will consider here will consist of the form that has most interested feminist critics—that of "the woman's film" or "weepie." These are films addressed to women in their traditional status under patriarchy—as wives, mothers, abandoned lovers, or in their traditional status as bodily hysteria or excess, as in the frequent case of the woman "afflicted" with a deadly or debilitating disease.[1]

What are the pertinent features of bodily excess shared by these three "gross" genres? First, there is the spectacle of a body caught in the grip of intense sensation or emotion. Carol Clover, speaking primarily of horror films and pornography, has called films which privilege the sensational "body" genres (Clover, 189). I am expanding Clover's notion of low body genres to include the sensation of overwhelming pathos in the "weepie." The body spectacle is featured most sensationally in pornography's portrayal of orgasm, in horror's portrayal of violence and terror, and in melodrama's portrayal of weeping. I propose that an investigation of the visual and narrative pleasures found in the portrayal of these three types of excess could be important to a new direction in genre criticism that would take as its point of departure—rather than as an unexamined assumption—questions of gender construction, and gender address in relation to basic sexual fantasies.

Another pertinent feature shared by these body genres is the focus on what could probably best be called a form of ecstasy. While the classical meaning of the original Greek word is insanity and bewilderment, more contemporary meanings suggest components of direct or indirect sexual excitement and rapture, a rapture which informs even the pathos of melodrama.

Visually, each of these ecstatic excesses could be said to share a quality of uncontrollable convulsion or spasm—of the body "beside itself" with sexual pleasure, fear and terror, or overpowering sadness. Aurally, excess is marked by recourse not to the coded articulations of language but to inarticulate cries of pleasure in porn, screams of fear in horror, sobs of anguish in melodrama.

Looking at, and listening to, these bodily ecstasies, we can also notice something else that these genres seem to share: though quite differently gendered with respect to their targeted audiences, with pornography aimed, presumably, at active men and melodramatic weepies aimed, presumably, at passive women, and with contemporary gross-out horror aimed at adolescents careening wildly between the two masculine and feminine poles, in each of these genres the bodies of women figured on the screen have functioned traditionally as the primary *embodiments* of pleasure, fear, and pain.

In other words, even when the pleasure of viewing has traditionally been constructed for masculine spectators, as is the case in most traditional heterosexual pornography, it is the female body in the grips of an out-of-control ecstasy that has offered the most sensational sight. So the bodies of women have tended to function, ever since the eighteenth-century origins of these genres in the Marquis de Sade, Gothic fiction, and the novels of Richardson, as both the *moved* and the *moving*. It is thus through what Foucault has called the sexual saturation of the female body that audiences of all sorts have received some of their most powerful sensations (Foucault, 104).

There are, of course, other film genres which both portray and affect the sensational body—e.g., thrillers, musicals, comedies. I suggest, however, that the film genres that have had especially low cultural status—which have seemed to exist as excesses to the system of even the popular genres—are not simply those which sensationally display bodies on the screen and register effects in the bodies of spectators. Rather, what may especially mark these body genres as low is the perception that the body of the spectator is caught up in an almost involuntary mimicry of the emotion or sensation of the body on the screen along with the fact that the body displayed is female. Physical clown comedy is another "body" genre concerned with all manner of gross activities and body functions—eating shoes, slipping on banana peels. Nonetheless, it

has not been deemed gratuitously excessive, probably because the reaction of the audience does not mimic the sensations experienced by the central clown. Indeed, it is almost a rule that the audience's physical reaction of laughter does not coincide with the often dead-pan reactions of the clown.

In the body genres I am isolating here, however, it seems to be the case that the success of these genres is often measured by the degree to which the audience sensation mimics what is seen on the screen. Whether this mimicry is exact, e.g., whether the spectator at the porn film actually orgasms, whether the spectator at the horror film actual shudders in fear, whether the spectator of the melodrama actually dissolves in tears, the success of these genres seems a self-evident matter of measuring bodily response. Examples of such measurement can be readily observed: in the "peter meter" capsule reviews in *Hustler* magazine, which measure the power of a porn film in degrees of erection of little cartoon penises; in horror films which measure success in terms of screams, fainting, and heart attacks in the audience (horror producer William Castle specialized in this kind of thing with such films as *The Tingler*, 1959); and in the longstanding tradition of women's films measuring their success in terms of one-, two-, or three-handkerchief movies.

What seems to bracket these particular genres from others is an apparent lack of proper esthetic distance, a sense of over-involvement in sensation and emotion. We feel manipulated by these texts—an impression that the very colloquialisms of "tear jerker" and "fear jerker" express—and to which we could add pornography's even cruder sense as texts to which some people might be inclined to "jerk off." The rhetoric of violence of the jerk suggests the extent to which viewers feel too directly, too viscerally manipulated by the text in specifically gendered ways. Mary Ann Doane, for example, writing about the most genteel of these jerkers—the maternal melodrama—equates the violence of this emotion to a kind of "textual rape" of the targeted female viewer, who is "feminized through pathos" (Doane, 1987, 95).

Feminist critics of pornography often evoke similar figures of sexual/textual violence when describing the operation of this genre. Robin Morgan's slogan "pornography is the theory, and rape is the practice" is well known (Morgan, 139). Implicit in this slogan is the notion that women are the objectified victims of pornographic representations, that the image of the sexually ecstatic woman so important to the genre is a celebration of female victimization and a prelude to female victimization in real life.

Less well known, but related, is the observation of the critic of horror films, James Twitchell, who notices that the Latin *horrere* means to bristle. He describes the way the nape hair stands on end during moments of shivering excitement. The aptly named Twitchell thus describes a kind of erection of the hair founded in the conflict between reactions of "fight and flight" (Twitchell, 10). While male victims in horror films may shudder and scream as well, it has long been a dictum of the genre that women make the best victims. "Torture the women!" was the famous advice given by Alfred Hitchcock.[2]

In the classic horror film the terror of the female victim shares the spectacle along with the monster. Fay Wray and the mechanized monster that made her scream in *King Kong* is a familiar example of the classic form. Janet Leigh in the shower in *Psycho* is a familiar example of a transition to a more sexually explicit form of the tortured and terrorized woman. And her daughter, Jamie Lee Curtis in *Halloween*, can serve as the more contemporary version of the terrorized woman victim. In both of these later films the spectacle of the monster seems to take second billing to the increasingly numerous victims slashed by the sexually disturbed but entirely human monsters.

In the woman's film a well-known classic is the long-suffering mother of the two early versions of *Stella Dallas* who sacrifices herself for her daughter's upward mobility. Contemporary film goers could recently see Bette Midler going through the same sacrifice and loss in the film *Stella*. Debra Winger in *Terms of Endearment* is another familiar example of this maternal pathos.

With the above genre stereotypes in mind we should now ask about the status of bodily excess in each of these genres. Is it simply the unseemly, "gratuitous" presence of the sexually ecstatic woman, the tortured woman, the weeping woman—and the accompanying presence of the sexual fluids, the blood and the tears that flow from her body and which are presumably mimicked by spectators—that mark the excess of each type of film? How shall we think

of these bodily displays in relation to one another, as a system of excess in the popular film? And finally, how excessive are they really?

The psychoanalytic system of analysis that has been so influential in film study in general and in feminist film theory and criticism has been remarkably ambivalent about the status of excess in its major tools of analysis. The categories of fetishism, voyeurism, sadism, and masochism frequently invoked to describe the pleasures of film spectatorship are by definition perversions. Perversions are usually defined as sexual excesses, specifically as excesses which are deflected away from "proper" end goals onto substitute goals or objects—fetishes instead of genitals, looking instead of touching, etc.—which seem excessive or gratuitous. Yet the perverse pleasures of film viewing are hardly gratuitous. They have been considered so basic that they have often been presented as norms. What is a film, after all, without voyeurism? Yet, at the same time, feminist critics have asked, what is the position of women within this pleasure geared to a presumably sadistic "male gaze"? (Mulvey, 1976) To what extent is she its victim? Are the orgasmic woman of pornography and the tortured woman of horror merely in the service of the sadistic male gaze? And is the weeping woman of melodrama appealing to the abnormal perversions of masochism in female viewers?

These questions point to the ambiguity of the terms of perversion used to describe the normal pleasures of film viewing. Without attempting to go into any of the complexities of this discussion here—a discussion which must ultimately relate to the status of the term perversion in theories of sexuality themselves—let me simply suggest the value of not invoking the perversions as terms of condemnation. As even the most cursory reading of Freud shows, sexuality is by definition perverse. The "aims" and "objects" of sexual desire are often obscure and inherently substitutive. Unless we are willing to see reproduction as the common goal of the sexual drive, we have to admit, as Jonathan Dollimore has put it, that we are all perverts. Dollimore's goal of retrieving the "concept of perversion as a category of cultural analysis"—as a structure intrinsic to all sexuality rather than extrinsic to it—is crucial to any attempt to understand cultural forms—such as our three body genres—in which fantasy predominates.[3]

Structures of Perversion in the "Female Body Genres"

Each of the three body genres I have isolated hinges on the spectacle of a "sexually saturated" female body, and each offers what many feminist critics would agree to be spectacles of feminine victimization. But this victimization is very different in each type of film and cannot be accounted for simply by pointing to the sadistic power and pleasure of masculine subject positions punishing or dominating feminine objects.

Many feminists have pointed to the victimization of the woman performers of pornography who must actually do the acts depicted in the film, as well as to the victimization of characters within the films (Dworkin, 1979; MacKinnon, 1987). Pornography, in this view, is fundamentally sadistic. In women's weepies, on the other hand, feminists have pointed to the spectacles of intense suffering and loss as masochistic.

In horror films, while feminists have often pointed to the women victims who suffer simulated torture and mutilation as victims of sadism (Williams, 1983), more recent feminist work has suggested that the horror film may present an interesting, and perhaps instructive, case of oscillation between masochistic and sadistic poles. This more recent argument, advanced by Carol J. Clover, has suggested that pleasure, for a masculine-identified viewer, oscillates between identifying with the initial passive powerlessness of the abject and terrorized girl-victim of horror and her later, active empowerment (Clover, 1987).

This argument holds that when the girl-victim of a film like *Halloween* finally grabs the phallic knife, or ax, or chain saw to turn the tables on the monster-killer, that viewer identification shifts from an "abject terror gendered feminine" to an active power with bisexual components. A gender-confused monster is foiled, often symbolically castrated by an "androgynous" "final girl" (Clover, 206–209). In slasher films, identification with victimization is a roller-coaster ride of sadomasochistic thrills.

We could thus initially schematize the perverse pleasures of these genres in the following way: pornography's appeal to its presumed male viewers would be characterized as sadistic, horror films' appeal to the emerging sexual identities of its (frequently adolescent) spectators would be sadomasochistic and

women's films appeal to presumed female viewers would be masochistic.

The masochistic component of viewing pleasure for women has been the most problematic term of perversion for feminist critics. It is interesting, for example, that most of our important studies of masochism—whether by Deleuze (1971), Silverman (1980; 1988) or Studlar (1985)—have all focused on the exoticism of masculine masochism rather than the familiarity of female masochism. Masochistic pleasure for women has paradoxically seemed either too normal—too much the normal yet intolerable condition of women—or too perverse to be taken seriously as pleasure.

There is thus a real need to be clearer than we have been about what is in masochism for women—how power and pleasure operate in fantasies of domination which appeal to women. There is an equal need to be clearer than we have about what is in sadism for men. Here the initial opposition between these two most gendered genres—women's weepies and male heterosexual pornography—needs to be complicated. I have argued elsewhere, for example, that pornography has too simplistically been allied with a purely sadistic fantasy structure. Indeed, those troubling films and videos which deploy instruments of torture on the bodies of women have been allied so completely with masculine viewing pleasures that we have not paid enough attention to their appeal to women except to condemn such appeal as false consciousness (Williams, 1989, 184–228).

One important complication of the initial schema I have outlined would thus be to take a lesson from Clover's more bisexual model of viewer identification in horror film and stress the sadomasochistic component of each of these body genres through their various appropriations of melodramatic fantasies that are, in fact, basic to each. All of these genres could, for example, be said to offer highly melodramatic enactments of sexually charged, if not sexually explicit, relations. The sub-genre of sadomasochistic pornography, with its suspension of pleasure over the course of prolonged sessions of dramatic suffering, offers a particularly intense, almost parodic, enactment of the classic melodramatic scenario of the passive and innocent female victim suffering at the hands of a leering villain. We can also see in horror films of tortured women a similar melodramatization of the innocent victim. An important difference, of course, lies in the component of the victim's overt sexual pleasure in the scenario of domination.

But even in the most extreme displays of feminine masochistic suffering, there is always a component of either power or pleasure for the woman victim. In slasher horror films we have seen how identification seems to oscillate between powerlessness and power. In sadomasochistic pornography and in melodramatic woman's weepies, feminine subject positions appear to be constructed which achieve a modicum of power and pleasure within the given limits of patriarchal constraints on women. It is worth noting as well that *non*-sadomasochistic pornography has historically been one of the few types of popular film that has not punished women for actively pursuing their sexual pleasure.

In the subgenre of sadomasochistic pornography, however, the female masochist in the scenario must be devious in her pursuit of pleasure. She plays the part of passive sufferer in order to obtain pleasure. Under a patriarchal double standard that has rigorously separated the sexually passive "good" girl from the sexually active "bad" girl, masochistic role-playing offers a way out of this dichotomy by combining the good girl with the bad: the passive "good girl" can prove to her witnesses (the super-ego who is her torturer) that she does not will the pleasure that she receives. Yet the sexually active "bad" girl enjoys this pleasure and has knowingly arranged to endure the pain that earns it. The cultural law which decides that some girls are good and others are bad is not defeated but within its terms pleasure has been negotiated and "paid for" with a pain that conditions it. The "bad" girl is punished, but in return she receives pleasure.[4]

In contrast, the sadomasochistic teen horror films kill off the sexually active "bad" girls, allowing only the non-sexual "good" girls to survive. But these good girls become, as if in compensation, remarkably active, to the point of appropriating phallic power to themselves. It is as if this phallic power is granted so long as it is rigorously separated from phallic or any other sort of pleasure. For these pleasures spell sure death in this genre.

In the melodramatic woman's film we might think to encounter a purer form of masochism on the part

of female viewers. Yet even here the female viewer does not seem to be invited to identify wholly with the sacrificing good woman, but rather with a variety of different subject positions, including those which empathically look on at her own suffering. While I would not argue that there is a very strong sadistic component to these films, I do argue that there is a strong mixture of passivity and activity, and a bisexual oscillation between the poles of each, in even this genre.

For example, the woman viewer of a maternal melodrama such as *Terms of Endearment* or *Steel Magnolias* does not simply identify with the suffering and dying heroines of each. She may equally identify with the powerful matriarchs, the surviving mothers who preside over the deaths of their daughters, experiencing the exhilaration and triumph of survival. The point is simply that identification is neither fixed nor entirely passive.

While there are certainly masculine and feminine, active and passive, poles to the left and right of the chart on which we might position these three genres (see below), the subject positions that appear to be constructed by each of the genres are not as gender-linked and as gender-fixed as has often been supposed. This is especially true today as hard-core pornography is gaining appeal with women viewers. Perhaps the most recent proof in this genre of the breakdown of rigid dichotomies of masculine and feminine, active and passive is the creation of an alternative, oscillating category of address to viewers. Although heterosexual hard core once addressed itself exclusively to heterosexual men, it has now begun to address itself to heterosexual couples and women as well; and in addition to homosexual hard core, which has addressed itself to gay and (to a lesser extent) lesbian viewers, there is now a new category of video called bisexual. In these videos men do it with women, women do it with women, men do it with men and then all do it with one another, in the process breaking down a fundamental taboo against male-to-male sex.[5]

A related interpenetration of once more separate categories of masculine and feminine is what has come to be known in some quarters as the "male weepie." These are mainstream melodramas engaged in the activation of the previously repressed emotions of men and in breaking the taboos against male-to-male hugs and embraces. The father-son embrace that concludes *Ordinary People* (1980) is exemplary. More recently, paternal weepies have begun to compete with the maternal—as in the conventional *Dad* (1989) or the less conventional, wild paternal displays of *Twin Peaks*.

The point is certainly not to admire the "sexual freedom" of this new fluidity and oscillation—the new femininity of men who hug and the new masculinity of women who leer—as if it represented any ultimate defeat of phallic power. Rather, the more useful lesson might be to see what this new fluidity and oscillation permits in the construction of feminine viewing pleasures once thought not to exist at all. (It is instructive, for example, that in the new bisexual pornography women characters are shown verbally articulating their visual pleasure as they watch men perform sex with men.)

The deployment of sex, violence, and emotion would thus seem to have very precise functions in these body genres. Like all popular genres, they address persistent problems in our culture, in our sexualities, in our very identities. The deployment of sex, violence, and emotion is thus in no way gratuitous and in no way strictly limited to each of these genres; it is instead a cultural form of problem solving. As I have argued in *Hard Core*, pornographic films now tend to present sex as a problem, to which the performance of more, different, or better sex is posed as the solution (Williams, 1989). In horror a violence related to sexual difference is the problem, more violence related to sexual difference is also the solution. In women's films the pathos of loss is the problem, repetitions and variations of this loss are the generic solution.

Table 33.1 An Anatomy of Film Bodies

Genre:	Pornography	Horror	Melodrama
Bodily excess	sex	violence	emotion
Ecstasy:	ecstatic sex	ecstatic violence	ecstatic woe
—shown by	orgasm	shudder	sob
	ejaculation	blood	tears
Presumed audience:	men	adolescent boys	girls, women
	(active)	(active/passive)	(passive)
Perversion:	sadism	sadomasochism	masochism
Originary fantasy:	seduction	castration	origin
Temporality of fantasy:	on time!	too early!	too late!
Genre cycles: "classic"	stag films	"classic" horror:	"classic" women's films:
	(20's–40's):	*Dracula*	maternal melodrama:
	The Casting Couch	*Frankenstein*	*Stella Dallas*
		Dr. Jekyll/Mr. Hyde	*Mildred Pierce*
		King Kong	romance:
			Back Street
			Letter from an
			Unknown Woman
contemporary	feature-length	post-*Psycho*:	male and female
	hard core porn:	*Texas Chainsaw*	"weepies":
	Deep Throat, etc.	*Massacre*	*Steel Magnolias*
	The Punishment of Anne	*Halloween*	*Stella*
	Femme Productions	*Dressed to Kill*	*Dad*
	Bi-sexual	*Videodrome*	
	Tri-sexual		

Structures of Fantasy

All of these problems are linked to gender identity and might be usefully explored as genres of gender fantasy. It is appropriate to ask, then, not only about the structures of perversion, but also about the structures of fantasy in each of these genres. In doing so, we need to be clear about the nature of fantasy itself. For fantasies are not, as is sometimes thought, wish-fulfilling linear narratives of mastery and control leading to closure and the attainment of desire. They are marked, rather, by the prolongation of desire, and by the lack of fixed position with respect to the objects and events fantasized.

In their classic essay "Fantasy and the Origins of Sexuality," Jean Laplanche and J. B. Pontalis (1968) argue that fantasy is not so much a narrative that enacts the quest for an object of desire as it is a setting for desire, a place where conscious and unconscious, self and other, part and whole meet. Fantasy is the place where "desubjectified" subjectivities oscillate between self and other occupying no fixed place in the scenario (16).

In the three body genres discussed here, this fantasy component has probably been better understood in horror film, a genre often understood as belonging to the "fantastic." However, it has been less well understood in pornography and women's film melodrama. Because these genres display fewer fantastic special effects and because they rely on certain conventions of realism—the activation of social problems in melodrama, the representation of real sexual acts in pornography—they seem less obviously fantastic. Yet the usual criticisms that these forms are improbable, that they lack psychological complexity and narrative closure, and that they are repetitious, become moot as evaluation if such features are intrinsic to their engagement with fantasy.

There is a link, in other words, between the appeal of these forms and their ability to address, if never *really* to "solve," basic problems related to sexual identity. Here, I would like to forge a connection between Laplanche and Pontalis's structural understanding of fantasies as myths of origins which try to cover the discrepancy between two moments in time and the distinctive temporal structure of these particular genres. Laplanche and Pontalis argue that fantasies which are myths of origins address the insoluble problem of the discrepancy between an irrecoverable original experience presumed to have actually taken place—as in the case, for example, of the historical primal scene—and the uncertainty of its hallucinatory revival. The discrepancy exists, in other words, between the actual existence of the lost object and the sign which evokes both this existence and its absence.

Laplanche and Pontalis maintain that the most basic fantasies are located at the juncture of an irrecoverable real event that took place somewhere in the past and a totally imaginary event that never took place. The "event" whose temporal and spatial existence can never be fixed is thus ultimately, according to Laplanche and Pontalis, that of "the origin of the subject"—an origin which psychoanalysts tell us cannot be separated from the discovery of sexual difference (11).

It is this contradictory temporal structure of being situated somewhere between the "too early" and the "too late" of the knowledge of difference that generates desire that is most characteristic of fantasy. Freud introduced the concept of "original fantasy" to explain the mythic function of fantasies which seem to offer repetitions of and "solutions" to major enigmas confronting the child (Freud, 1915). These enigmas are located in three areas: the enigma of the origin of sexual desire, an enigma that is "solved," so to speak, by the fantasy of seduction; the enigma of sexual difference, "solved" by the fantasy of castration; and finally the enigma of the origin of self, "solved" by the fantasy of family romance or return to origins (Laplanche and Pontalis, 1968, 11).

Each of the three body genres I have been describing could be seen to correspond in important ways to one of these original fantasies: pornography, for example, is the genre that has seemed to endlessly repeat the fantasies of primal seduction, of meeting the other, seducing or being seduced by the other in an ideal "pornotopia" where, as Steven Marcus has noted, it is always bedtime (Marcus, 269). Horror is the genre that seems to endlessly repeat the trauma of castration as if to "explain," by repetitious mastery, the originary problem of sexual difference. And melodramatic weepie is the genre that seems to endlessly repeat our melancholic sense of the loss of origins—impossibly hoping to return to an earlier state which is perhaps most fundamentally represented by the body of the mother.

Of course each of these genres has a history and does not simply "endlessly repeat." The fantasies activated by these genres are repetitious, but not fixed and eternal. If traced back to origins each could probably be shown to have emerged with the formation of the bourgeois subject and the intensifying importance to this subject of specified sexualities. But the importance of repetition in each genre should not blind us to the very different temporal structure of repetition in each fantasy. It could be, in fact, that these different temporal structures constitute the different utopian component of problem-solving in each form. Thus the typical (non-sadomasochistic) pornographic fantasies of seduction operate to "solve" the problem of the origin of desire. Attempting to answer the insoluble question of whether desire is imposed from without through the seduction of the parent or whether it originates within the self, pornography answers this question by typically positing a fantasy of desire coming from within the subject *and* from without. Non-sadomasochistic pornography attempts to posit the utopian fantasy of perfect temporal coincidence: a subject and object (or seducer and seduced) who meet one another "on time!" and "now!" in shared moments of mutual pleasure that it is the special challenge of the genre to portray.

In contrast to pornography, the fantasy of recent teen horror corresponds to a temporal structure which raises the anxiety of not being ready, the problem, in effect, of "too early!" Some of the most violent and terrifying moments of the horror film genre occur in moments when the female victim meets the psycho-killer-monster unexpectedly, before she is ready. The female victims who are not ready for the attack die. This surprise encounter, too early, often takes place at a moment of sexual anticipation when the female victim thinks she is about to meet her boyfriend or lover. The monster's violent attack on the female victims vividly enacts a symbolic castration which often functions as a kind of punishment for an ill-timed exhibition of sexual desire. These victims are taken by surprise in the violent attacks which are then deeply felt by spectators (especially the adolescent male spectators drawn to the slasher subgenre) as linked to the knowledge of sexual difference. Again the key to the fantasy is timing—the way the knowledge of sexual difference too suddenly overtakes both char-acters and viewers, offering a knowledge for which we are never prepared.

Finally, in contrast to pornography's meeting "on time!" and horror's unexpected meeting "too early!," we can identify melodrama's pathos of the "too late!" In these fantasies the quest to return to and discover the origin of the self is manifest in the form of the child's fantasy of possessing ideal parents in the Freudian family romance, in the parental fantasy of possessing the child in maternal or paternal melo-drama, and even in the lovers' fantasy of possessing one another in romantic weepies. In these fantasies the quest for connection is always tinged with the melancholy of loss. Origins are already lost, the encounters always take place too late, on death beds or over coffins. (Neale, 1988).

Italian critic Franco Moretti has argued, for example, that literature that makes us cry operates via a special manipulation of temporality: what triggers our crying is not just the sadness or suffering of the character in the story but a very precise moment when characters in the story catch up with and realize what the audience already knows. We cry, Moretti argues, not just because the characters do, but at the precise moment when desire is finally recognized as futile. The release of tension produces tears—which become a kind of homage to a happiness that is kissed goodbye. Pathos is thus a surrender to reality but it is a surrender that pays homage to the ideal that tried to wage war on it (Moretti, 1983, 179). Moretti thus stresses a subversive, utopian component in what has often been considered a form of passive powerlessness. The fantasy of the meeting with the other that is always too late can thus be seen as based upon the utopian desire that it not be too late to remerge with the other who was once part of the self.

Obviously there is a great deal of work to be done to understand the form and function of these three body genres in relation to one another and in relation to the fundamental appeal as "original fantasies." Obviously also the most difficult work of understanding this relation between gender, genre, fantasy, and structures of perversion will come in the attempt to relate original fantasies to historical context and specific generic history. However, there is one thing that already seems clear: these "gross" body genres which may seem so violent and inimical to women cannot be dismissed as evidence of a monolithic and unchanging misogyny, as either pure sadism for male viewers or masochism for females. Their very existence and popularity hinges upon rapid changes taking place in relations between the "sexes" and by rapidly changing notions of gender—of what it means to be a man or a woman. To dismiss them as bad excess whether of explicit sex, violence, or emotion, or as bad perversions, whether of masochism or sadism, is not to address their function as cultural problem-solving. Genres thrive, after all, on the persistence of the problems they address; but genres thrive also in their ability to recast the nature of these problems.

Finally, as I hope this most recent example of the melodrama of tears suggests, we may be wrong in our assumption that the bodies of spectators simply reproduce the sensations exhibited by bodies on the screen. Even those masochistic pleasures associated with the powerlessness of the "too late!" are not absolutely abject. Even tear jerkers do not operate to force a simple mimicry of the sensation exhibited on the screen. Powerful as the sensations of the jerk might be, we may only be beginning to understand how they are deployed in generic and gendered cultural forms.

Notes

I owe thanks to Rhona Berenstein, Leo Braudy, Ernest Callenbach, Paul Fitzgerald, Jane Gaines, Mandy Harris, Brian Henderson, Marsha Kinder, Eric Rentschler, and Pauline Yu for generous advice on drafts of this essay.

1. For an excellent summary of many of the issues involved with both film melodrama and the "women's film," see Christine Gledhill's introduction to the anthology *Home Is Where the Heart Is: Studies in Melodrama and the Woman's Film* (Gledhill, 1987). For a more general inquiry into the theatrical origins of melodrama, see Peter Brooks's (1976) *The Melodramatic Imagination*. And for an extended theoretical inquiry and analysis of a body of melodramatic women's films, see Mary Ann Doane (1987), *The Desire to Desire*.
2. Carol J. Clover (1987) discusses the meanings of this famous quote in her essay, "Her Body/Himself: Gender in the Slasher Film."
3. Dollimore (1990, 13). Dollimore's project, along with Teresa de Lauretis's more detailed examination of the term perversion in Freudian psychoanalysis (in progress) will be central to any more detailed attempts to understand the perverse pleasures of these gross body genres.
4. I discuss these issues at length in a chapter on sadomasochistic pornography in my book *Hard Core* (1989).
5. Titles of these relatively new (post 1986) hard-core videos include: *Bisexual Fantasies; Bi-Mistake; Karen's Bi-Line; Bi-Dacious; Bi-Night; Bi and Beyond; The Ultimate Fantasy; Bi and Beyond II; Bi and Beyond III: Hermaphrodites.*

Works Cited

Altman, Rick. 1989. "Dickens, Griffith, and Film Theory Today." *South Atlantic Quarterly* 88:321–359.

Bordwell, David, Janet Staiger and Kristin Thompson. 1985. *The Classical Hollywood Cinema: Film Style and Mode of Production to 1960.* New York: Columbia University Press.

Clover, Carol J. 1987. "Her Body, Himself: Gender in the Slasher Film." *Representations* 20 (Fall): 187–228.

Deleuze, Gilles. 1971. *Masochism: An Interpretation of Coldness and Cruelty.* Translated by Jean McNeil. New York: Braziller.

Doane, Mary Ann. 1987. *The Desire to Desire: The Woman's Film of the 1940's.* Bloomington: Indiana University Press.

Doane, Mary Ann, Patricia Mellencamp, and Linda Williams, eds. 1983. *Re-vision: Essays in Feminist Film Criticism.* American Film Institute Monograph Series, vol. 3. Frederick, MD: University Publications of America.

Dollimore, Jonathan. 1990. "The Cultural Politics of Perversion: Augustine, Shakespeare, Freud, Foucault." *Genders* 8.

Douglas, Ann. 1980. "Soft-Porn Culture." *The New Republic*, 30 August 1980.

Dworkin, Andrea. 1979. *Pornography: Men Possessing Women.* New York: Perigee Books.

Foucault, Michel. 1978. *The History of Sexuality, Vol. 1: An Introduction.* Translated by Robert Hurley. New York: Pantheon Books.

Freud, Sigmund. 1915. "Instincts and their Vicissitudes." Vol. 14 of the *Standard Edition of The Complete Psychological Works of Sigmund Freud.* London: Hogarth. 14.

Laplanche, Jean, J. B. Pontalis. 1968. "Fantasy and the Origins of Sexuality." *The International Journal of Psycho-Analysis.* 49:1–18.

MacKinnon. 1987. *Feminism Unmodified: Discourses on Life and Law.* Cambridge, MA: Harvard University Press.

Marcus, Steven, 1964/74. *The Other Victorians: A Study of Sexuality and Pornography in Mid-Nineteenth Century England.* New York: New American Library.

Morgan, Robin, 1980. "Theory and Practice: Pornography and Rape." In *Take Back the Night: Women on Pornography*, edited by Laura Lederer. New York: Morrow.

Moretti, Franco. 1983. "Kindergarten." In *Signs Taken for Wonders*. London: Verso.

Mulvey, Laura. 1975. "Visual Pleasure and Narrative Cinema." *Screen* 16, no. 3: 6–18.

Neale, Steve. 1986. "Melodrama and Tears." *Screen* 27 (Nov.–Dec): 6–22.

Silverman, Kaja. 1980. "Masochism and Subjectivity." *Framework* 12:2–9.

———. 1988. "Masochism and Male Subjectivity." *Camera Obscura* 17: 31–66.

Studlar, Gaylyn. 1985. *In the Realm of Pleasure: Von Sternberg, Dietrich and the Masochistic Aesthetic*. Urbana: University of Illinois Press.

Twitchell, James. 1985. *Dreadful Pleasures: An Anatomy of Modern Horror*. New York: Oxford.

Williams, Linda. 1983. "When the Woman Looks." In *Re-Vision: Essays in Feminist Film Criticism*. See Doane (1983).

———. 1989. *Hard Core: Power, Pleasure and the "Frenzy of the Visible."* Berkeley: University of California Press.

34.
"I JUST WANT TO BE ME AGAIN!"

Beauty Pageants, Reality Television and Post-feminism
Sarah Banet-Weiser and Laura Portwood-Stacer

A Miss America has to have this image of being this wholesome, holier-than-thou, up-on-a-pedestal woman. In this day and age of reality TV, when people want the nitty gritty and the foibles, that's diametrically opposed. You really need to get to real women letting their hair down.

(Paula Shugart, president, Miss Universe Organization, cited in Godleski, 2005)

After the 2004 Miss America televised pageant attracted a record-low 9.8 million people, the US television network ABC dropped the event as a ratings loser (Godleski, 2005). The fate of the pageant was unknown for a while, but recently the Miss America Organization has signed a multi-year broadcast deal with cable country music network CMT (de Moraes, 2005). The move to CMT indicates a clear shift in genre for the pageant, and airing the programme on a narrowly defined niche cable channel certainly challenges the pageant's historical claim of 'universal' femininity. Indeed, in this post-network era, where hundreds of cable channels attract smaller and smaller audiences, it is no surprise that Miss America had difficulty finding their audience on a broadcast network such as ABC. Beauty pageants and country music have both been more popular in Southern states of the US, and thus CMT may turn out to be Miss America's niche. As media analyst Larry Gerbrandt (2005) comments, 'Miss America is sort of a heartland kind of event . . . It's Mom, Dad, the flag and apple pie. That's their demographic'.

Before the move to CMT, however, there was talk about remaking the pageant in the style of a reality television show, where viewers would watch the pageant unfold over a number of weeks, investing in individual contestants in a *Survivor*-type manner, until the fateful night when one of them wins. Indeed, in an effort to connect more closely with an audience that tunes in regularly to reality programmes such as *Survivor, American Idol, The Swan* and *Extreme Makeover*, the Miss America pageant in recent years has adjusted its script to contain more reality-style gimmicks, such as *Who Wants to be a Millionaire*-style questions during the on-stage interview portion of the event (where the host asks 'Is that your final answer?'), or new rules that allow the previous contestants who did not make the top ten to come back for a second chance at the crown (Godleski, 2005; Peterson, 2005).

During this historical moment, however, Miss America didn't just find reality television useful—reality television discovered the theme of Miss America as a driving narrative in the form of a new genre, the cosmetic surgery makeover show. At the same time that Miss America was losing its television audience, the cosmetic surgery makeover show made its debut on network television, and became an immediate hit. These shows offer personal narratives of individuals (both women and men) as they undergo extensive cosmetic surgery as a way to 'make over' their lives; the surgical procedures are positioned as effective means through which one can achieve a more general life transformation. Reality makeover shows clearly and uncritically legitimate the increasing normalization of the cultural practice of cosmetic surgery in US culture, and transparently conflate personal fulfilment and individual achievement with the attainment of a physically ideal body.

Televised performances of gender have shifted focus, then, from the intensely scripted, out-of-touch Miss America to reality makeover shows that normalize cosmetic surgery as a means to become the 'ideal' woman. What does this genre redefinition mean in terms of gender representation and performance? It is clear—at least as measured by television ratings—that the Miss America pageant is widely understood as irrelevant and old-fashioned, and that shows such as *Extreme Makeover* and *The Swan* seem to resonate more with their audience, but does this indicate anything deeper than the popularity of faddish television? In this essay, we are interested in the shift in popular appeal from more traditional performances of beauty such as the beauty pageant to the surgically enhanced performances of beauty that form the logic of contemporary reality makeover shows. While there has been a great deal of scholarship produced over the past decade about the appeal of reality television, what interests us is not so much the change in television genre, but rather the definition of femininity that is produced through this genre. Specifically, how do the cultural conditions of the current media environment provide an opportunity to construct a particular version of femininity that resonates with contemporary ideologies of personal transformation, celebration of the body, and female empowerment? These contemporary ideologies comprise a commercially driven 'post-feminism', and it is within this context that reality makeover shows are both created and legitimated.

Thus, a related concern in this essay is the on-going relationship between dominant norms of femininity and particular versions of mainstream feminism. Certainly, the Miss America pageant has been engaged in a relationship with feminism since its inception in 1921, and feminist critiques of pageants have questioned (among other things) the relationship between pageant-defined femininity and claims of national representation, exposing the implicit premise that the 'ideal' American female citizen is defined in terms of white, heterosexual or subordinate femininity. The 1968 feminist protest of the Miss America pageant perhaps best exemplified the ways that the meanings of this particular spectacle have been understood,

challenged, and struggled over in terms of its relationship to feminism (Echols, 1989; Dow, 2003). Yet, along with beauty pageants and other dominant rituals of hegemonic femininity, feminism itself has undergone a 'makeover' in the late 20th and early 21st centuries.[1] Post-feminism has become a dominant form of mainstream feminism in the United States, where a media creation and legitimation of post-feminist 'power', combined with the increasing cultural recognition of adolescent girls and women as both powerful citizens and consumers, offers what at times looks like a radical gesture in terms of disrupting dominant gender relations (Findlen, 1995; Baumgardner and Richards, 1999). However, this consumer post-feminism is often individualized and constructed as personal choice or individual equality, and thus is figured quite differently from a historical feminist emphasis on social change and liberation. This is the feminism of reality makeover shows such as *The Swan* and *Extreme Makeover*, where a 'celebration' of the body, the pleasure of transformation, and individual empowerment function as a justification for a renewed objectification of female bodies. In the following sections, we examine how the Miss America pageant and reality makeover shows each work to construct a particular version of the liberal feminine self in connection with discourses of feminism.

Miss America and National Representation

In 1960, the televised broadcast of the Miss America pageant attracted 85 million viewers—an almost unheard-of number in today's competitive television context (Huus, 2005). In 2003, the ratings for the pageant, which is one of television's longest running franchises, fell to only 10.3 million viewers (Huus, 2005), prompting the network ABC to consider how to change the pageant to suit a more contemporary television audience. The Miss America pageant clearly had a kind of identity crisis, in which the spectacle not only failed to attract a television audience, but also seemed to fail in its construction of ideal femininity itself. Since its beginning in 1921, the Miss America pageant was largely understood as an important civic ritual in the United States, a vital source of knowledge for many young women about the disciplinary practices of femininity (Banet-Weiser, 1999). Perhaps most importantly, the pageant resonated with its audience and with American women—the Miss America crown has been held up to be attainable by 'ordinary' women; this crown, like commercial success, like the American dream, is there for those who try. The Miss America pageant was expert at navigating between the individual and the ideal—it claimed to be all-inclusive and to depict a national community. The Miss America contestant's body, through her disciplined physique, her commitment to virtue, and her testimony to stability, represented a well-managed collective American body. In this way, the beauty pageant helps to transform American culture's anxiety about its stability as a coherent nation into a spectacular re-enactment and overcoming of that very anxiety. In other words, the Miss America pageant contestants perform the abstract character of liberal personhood—white and middle class—within a particular national imaginary. As Susan Bordo (2003), Sandra Lee Bartky (1988), and many others have pointed out, theories of power and agency that understand gendered and raced bodies as effects and enactments *of* power rather than passive sites *for* power are required to generate a more complex understanding of productions of femininity—as both represented by media events and also through self-representation. A theory of power—such as one provided by feminist readings of Foucault—calls for a reconfiguring of gendered bodies on a political, social, and cultural landscape that assists in analysing the complicated and contradictory ways these bodies are disciplined and regulated (Bartky, 1988). Beauty pageants such as the Miss America pageant are not simply sites for the objectified feminine body, but are rather places in which this feminine body is articulated within the terms of liberal ideology—as an individual with choices and freedoms. Importantly, the television context of the Miss America pageant allows for this kind of liberal production, encouraging audiences to focus relentlessly on the visual character of women's bodies, as testimony for the collapse of identity with representation.

As Sarah Banet-Weiser (1999), Maxine Craig (2002), and others have argued, the Miss America pageant has historically prided itself on its commitment to liberal ideology, especially the theme of equal opportunity. Through a visual focus on female bodies and particular visions of individualism, pageants attempt to resolve contradictions within liberal ideology—contradictions about the exclusivity of who can access wealth, employment, housing, and so forth—by relying on classic liberal stories about individual achievement and pluralist tolerance. By making invisible the social technologies that produce difference, these liberal stories result in the retrenchment of a national identity defined by white middle-class norms. It is the active commitment to making these technologies *invisible* that connects media events such as the Miss America pageant to a conventional notion of liberal politics; the pageant is committed to maintaining the illusion of the liberal subject in the US, one defined by personal freedoms and public protections. Beauty pageants can be thus situated as a particular cultural form that accommodates a liberal feminist rhetoric, which relies on particular fantasies of agency, voice and citizenship as crucial components of identity construction for most American women. The pageant, in other words, offers a sensationalized venue for constructing liberal identity that both draws from and resists a mainstream feminist agenda. Beauty pageant contestants are particular kinds of theorizing agents: contestants perform liberal narratives about women's rights, individual achievement, pluralism, self-determination, and voluntarism in a similar way and on similar grounds as liberal feminists who have articulated these very same narratives.

Liberal ideology clearly remains a political force in contemporary US society, but the Miss America pageant, and its own version of liberal femininity, does not seem to be able to connect with an audience any longer. What has happened? Have the contours of liberal ideology shifted so that the version performed by Miss America contestants is no longer relevant? Certainly, the association between Miss America and the nation has been characterized by pitfalls, contradictions, and unevenness in every given historical moment. The relationship between gender and nation has, in the US, always been a crucial one to maintain, and that maintenance requires a glossing over of contradiction and conflict. What occurs on the stage of a national beauty pageant is the enactment of a particular kind of national dilemma, one that must continuously attempt to resolve tensions that characterize dominant practices of femininity within an increasingly diversified society—even as the pageant simultaneously celebrates and reinvents precisely these categories of experience.

One of the problems, then, that the Miss America pageant has been facing in the last five years concerns this process of reinvention—the pageant cannot seem to create and sustain an ideal definition of femininity for the contemporary US. This is not because in 1960 there was a more coherent ideal definition of femininity for the nation, but instead simply because the relationship between contemporary Miss America contestants and feminine national identity is situated within a different media environment. These factors include the obvious, such as a racially diverse population that is plainly not reflected in the make-up of Miss America contestants, but also the more subtle, such as a post-network television environment, where hundreds of niche cable channels belie the illusion of a universal television audience (and thus the illusion of a universal liberal citizen such as Miss America), and a postmodern media audience that is savvy about both its own self-identity and its media choices. These factors—a diverse and savvy media audience and a multitude of channel choices on cable television—have forced the Miss America Organization to consider particular kinds of changes to the pageant, so that the event would seem more 'relevant' to a contemporary audience.

Not surprisingly, these changes came in the form of reality television, where tropes and themes that had proven successful (read: attracted audiences and thus ratings) for shows such as *Survivor* and *American Idol* were incorporated into the pageant to liven up the show and make it more contemporary and in touch with its audience (Huus, 2005). As Art McMaster, the CEO of the Miss America Organization, claimed about the past year's show, 'It dragged too much . . . We decided to cut it down to get a faster-paced, hipper type of show this year' (Huus, 2005). The pageant attempted to be more spontaneous, in an era that celebrated and rewarded the unscripted television show. And, while the objectification of women's bodies as entertainment never seems to go out of style, the particular ways that the Miss America pageant objectified contestants came across as *too* sincere, not enough tongue-in-cheek, not cynical or hip enough. Even those loyal to the pageant seemed to agree; past CEO Leonard Horn has stated that the pageant

needed a 'radical update', claiming that 'By the time [the contestants] reach the national level they no longer look like fresh girls or 21-year-olds . . . They look like 40-year-old Stepford Wives . . . If they are going to relate to the women in [the] audience, they have to look and act like their peers' (Huus, 2005). In the current post-feminist context, when media audiences are routinely tuning in to reality television that offers edgier, more personal, and more spontaneous gender performances, Miss America could not find an audience niche.

Cosmetic Surgery and Post-feminism

The politics of feminism are quite obviously different for different generations, and post-feminists are produced in a very different cultural and political context than, say, second wave feminists. This generational divide situates the specific politics of post-feminism as a politics of contradiction and tension: the dynamics between the ideological claims of this cultural phenomenon—girls are strong and independent—and the commercial merchandising of these claims—where identity characteristics such as strength and independence function as effective marketing strategies—demonstrate a profound ambivalence about these feminist politics in general. Reality television contributes to this ideology through its relentless focus on individual pleasure and choice, and through the explicit suggestion that accessing choices and individual pleasures is enabled by consumerism (through cosmetic surgery, new clothes, new houses, cars, etc.). In other words, post-feminism boldly claims that women possess active political agency and subjectivity, yet the primary place in which this agency is recognized and legitimated is within individual consumption habits as well as within general consumer culture. The contradiction lies within this dynamic, where it is in fact true that media representations of women are more 'positive' in the contemporary climate, but it is equally true that these positive representations are part of aggressive new market strategies rather than indications of social and political changes within dominant gender relations in the US.

Angela McRobbie (2004), writing about post-feminism, argues that contemporary commercial popular culture uses sexist imagery in an ironic way to deflect feminist critiques of this kind of imagery, so that the exploitation of one's body and sexuality is positioned as a matter of personal and individual choice and disconnected from feminist theories of power. As she points out,

> If we turn attention to some of the participatory dynamics in leisure and everyday life which see young women endorse (or refuse to condemn) the ironic normalization of pornography, where they indicate their approval of and desire to be pinup girls for the centerfolds of the soft porn lad mags, where it is not at all unusual to pass young women in the street who are wearing T-shirts bearing phrases such as Porn Queen or Pay to Touch across the breasts, and where (in the United Kingdom, at least) young women quite happily attend lap dancing clubs (perhaps as a test of their sophistication and cool), we are witness to a hyperculture of commercial sexuality, one aspect of which is the repudiation of a feminism invoked only to be summarily dismissed.
>
> (McRobbie, 2004: 8)

The Miss America pageant, despite its lukewarm attempts to appeal to a media-savvy post-feminist audience, remains irrevocably connected to a particular Puritan ideal of sex and sexuality; one simply cannot imagine a Miss Oklahoma answering interview questions wearing a t-shirt emblazoned with 'Porn Star' across the breasts. This, perhaps, is why the pageant has seen its final days on network television, and why reality television programmes such as *The Swan* and *Extreme Makeover* gain more popularity with contemporary audiences. Both pageants and makeover shows purport to endorse individual choice and personal freedoms; it is what one is encouraged to *do* with those choices and freedoms that differentiates the two genres—and ultimately it is this difference that comes to define contemporary notions of femininity and citizenship.

The increasing normalization of cosmetic surgery in the US is one expression of post-feminism. Cosmetic surgery, through its legitimation of a particular idealized feminine beauty, is perhaps the ultimate expression of an individual transformation and a kind of empowerment. Indeed, it is precisely because of this celebration of a 'beautiful' body that many feminists have taken issue with the practice of cosmetic surgery. The increasing normalization of cosmetic surgery and the resulting idealized feminine body have forced feminist attention to this issue, in much the same way as feminists have examined and critiqued the cultural practices and performances of femininity exhibited on the beauty pageant stage. Feminist philosophers such as Susan Bordo (2003) and Kathryn Pauly Morgan (1991) have written persuasively about how decisions by women to undergo cosmetic surgery are often masked as expressions of female agency. On the contrary, Bordo and Morgan argue, the practice of cosmetic surgery *should* enable feminist questions about whether and how women are agents of their own oppression, how this kind of surgery is a clear demonstration of masculinist power, or the ways in which cosmetic surgery functions as a significant example of what Sandra Lee Bartky (1988: 65) called a 'disciplinary practice of femininity'. Bartky uses Foucault's notion of the 'docile body' as a way to explain disciplinary practices of femininity such as wearing make up, weight loss, and bodily comportment. The docile body—a body willing to be disciplined as a process of normalization—is clearly present in the individuals featured on reality makeover shows, as they willingly and emotionally surrender their bodies to cosmetic surgeons ready to coax the 'authentic' beautiful self out of the 'old' body. These shows are premised on the notion that in order to lead a rewarding, fulfilling psychological and personal life, the cost is nothing less than a perfect, medically enhanced body: firm breasts and buttocks, no cellulite, white sparkling teeth, beautiful healthy hair. Indeed, it is difficult for feminists *not* to theorize the cultural practice of cosmetic surgery—and especially its televisual expression—as anything short of objectifying and alienating.

However, as with the beauty pageant, there have also been significant challenges to a feminist theorizing of cosmetic surgery as simply a 'paradox of choice', where women who choose to undergo radical surgeries are understood as victims of false consciousness who are duped into conforming to cultural norms (Morgan, 1991: 35). For example, in her discussion of the surgical alteration of racialized features among Asian-American women, Eugenia Kaw (2002) insists that cosmetic surgery involves a complex process of negotiating between cultural identity and hegemonic norms of whiteness in US society. Kaw asks us to consider cosmetic surgery as less about beauty than about attaining some minimum level of social acceptability that can then serve as a base from which to practise the more 'normal' regimen of feminine beauty within contemporary US society. Kathy Davis (1995) similarly discusses cosmetic surgery as a practice that is not simply about female oppression, complicating the notion that women are striving for perfect beauty by her assertion that women more often elect cosmetic surgery in order to attain a feeling of *normalcy*, not perfection.

We also see a need for complicating the feminist theorizing of cosmetic surgery, but from a slightly different perspective. The cosmetic surgery makeover television genre is enabled in the present context in part because of the normalization of post-feminism. The earlier feminist critique of beauty pageants such as the Miss America pageant positioned itself in stark opposition to the spectacle. While there are certainly feminists who challenge the normalization of cosmetic surgery, it is precisely *a kind of feminism*—post-feminism—that also legitimates the practice, especially in the form of the television makeover show. In other words, while several scholars have argued that a traditional feminist approach to beauty pageants that understands pageant contestants as victims of false consciousness is both over-determined and over-simplified, in order to theorize the ways in which dominant norms of femininity are produced in a spectacle such as Miss America it is necessary to recognize power as a constitutive force in the cultural production of feminine bodies. However, a post-feminist critique often neglects a careful consideration of power relations in contemporary performances of gender. Indeed, as McRobbie (forthcoming) argues, when mainstream feminism became a kind of commodity in the early 1990s (one of the 'flashpoints' of post-feminism), young feminists rightly embraced this move as important and significant. Yet, a superficial focus on the post-feminist slogan 'girl power' allowed for a deflection away from some of the ways in which mainstream feminism became connected with dominant forms of power and subjugation. Calling specifically for a re-engagement with theories of power, McRobbie points out that

[w]ithout serious engagement with Freud, or with the work of Foucault, or indeed Deleuze, the dynamics of pain within pleasure, the uncertainty and ambivalence of pleasure, the whole pink and frilly world of affect and emotion within which the girl herself is permitted to 'become,' the intensity of focus on body and its surfaces, and of course the heteronormative assumptions underpinning these endless rituals of sexual differentiation, which are conditions of youthful female subjecthood, have been quite absent from much of this recent dialogue.

(McRobbie, forthcoming)

One of the things that troubles McRobbie about contemporary post-feminist theories of gender is this refusal to engage theories of power with gender construction. Even the most over-simplified feminist account of pageants as an alienating, oppressive site for false consciousness engages theories of power—a Marxist theory of power, an Althusserian rendering of ideology, or a Foucauldian application of the disciplined feminine body. However, within post-feminism, theories of power are absent, replaced by a celebratory notion that women 'own' their power. Thus, there is an erasure of earlier efforts of feminism to engage in collective struggle about issues of female subjection practised on women's bodies; rather, the cosmetic surgeries practised on female bodies become a kind of evidence for a post-feminist transformed self.

The Reality Makeover Show in the Post-feminist Context

In post-feminist fashion, then, the reality makeover show is precisely about making *visible* the technologies used to construct self. In this way, the makeover show is committed to a kind of newly entrenched liberal politics, dedicated more to 'lifestyle politics' than to traditional assertions of citizen rights and liberties. McRobbie (forthcoming) points this out in her discussion of the ways in which current theories of the liberal self 'take feminism into account, perhaps politely referencing some key texts of feminist scholarship; but otherwise they have moved on'. This 'moving on' is signalled by 'the emergence of a different kind of popular political formation, a shift away from emancipatory politics (of which feminism is one example) toward life politics . . .' (McRobbie, 2004: 10). In this scenario, the makeover show functions as a kind of 'life politics' and is positioned as much more contemporary—and more 'connected' with contemporary women—than the traditional beauty pageant. In other words, the liberal subjects that are produced through the beauty pageant and the makeover show connect with different theories of who and what the liberal subject should be. In makeover shows, using a reframed rhetoric of individual choice, technological transformation, and celebration of the body, the individual women featured claim to be freeing themselves of their earlier lives. In fact, what is happening is a more intense policing of the body, a body that is ever more docile as it is literally reshaped according to a set of dominant norms.

A dominant feminist critique of beauty pageants is that events such as Miss America claim to present the ideal representatives of the citizenry, marginalizing the types of bodies that are not displayed (Banet-Weiser, 1999). Reality show subjects are also chosen for their 'representativeness', but in their case, they represent the perceived flaws and shortcomings experienced by audience members. Although they may begin with more diverse bodies than the pageant ever did, makeover shows continue to reinforce a certain dominant beauty ideal when they literally cut away physical features that deviate from this ideal. The racism, sexism, and classism of beauty ideals that have been the traditional target of critiques of 'representative' femininity exist unproblematically in the current cultural context, because the post-feminist assumption is that these issues no longer have to be challenged—they've already been addressed through historical struggles. There are no narratives in these programmes to explain the pressures to conform to a particular (white, middle-class, heterosexual) norm of femininity, so individuals merely see their non-attainment of beauty norms as personal obstacles to be overcome. Within the context of post-feminism and its consequent emphasis on individual transformation and consumer citizenship, then, this process of 'overcoming' is more important—and more indicative of a dominant norm of femininity—than the final product.

The ideologies of post-feminism, then, found a niche in reality television, when in 2002 cosmetic surgery and makeovers became a novel theme for new reality television programmes. Although women have been receiving surface-level makeovers on television since the inception of the medium (e.g. *Queen for a Day*), the popularity of these cosmetic surgery shows is a phenomenon unique to this particular historical moment, as is their particular vision of feminine identity. ABC's *Extreme Makeover* features women and men undergoing cosmetic surgery procedures as part of an 'extreme makeover' of all areas of their lives—job satisfaction, personal fulfilment, higher self-esteem. Despite the rhetoric of 'overall' transformation, however, the programme is clearly about the medically explicit cosmetic surgeries. After the success of *Extreme Makeover*, cosmetic surgery makeover shows were clearly established as a successful sub-genre of reality television. In March of 2004, the reality programme *I Want a Famous Face* premiered on MTV. This programme featured individuals who wished to alter their faces to resemble movie stars such as Brad Pitt and Jennifer Lopez. As Leigh Turner (2005) succinctly puts it: '*I Want a Famous Face* takes fantasies about beauty and stardom and inscribes them on flesh. Call it cosmetic surgery karaoke'. Later in 2004, Fox network debuted *The Swan*, a combination of reality makeover show and beauty pageant. In this programme, there are sixteen contestants who undergo cosmetic surgery in hopes of winning a beauty pageant held at the end of the series. The contestants are apparently chosen because of their 'ugly duckling' status, and a variety of cosmetic surgeries, ranging from liposuction to laser eye surgery to breast augmentation, are offered as a means for contestants to emerge as victorious, beautiful 'swans'. As Turner (2005) describes, all of these shows attempt to call attention to the ways in which they function as vehicles, not simply for physical beauty, but also for psychological growth and personal transformation. As Turner (2005) puts it,

> The new bodies do not just have bigger breasts, more pronounced cheekbones, and whiter teeth. Rather, the programs suggest that individuals undergoing multiple cosmetic surgery procedures become livelier, more outgoing, and psychologically content individuals. Personal growth or spiritual development used to be connected to taking a pilgrimage to Thailand, watching Oprah, or

training for marathon runs. Now, apparently, you need buttock implants or breast augmentation to let your authentic self emerge.

The theme of authenticity is, of course, key to reality television.[2] The reality television genre of makeover shows demystifies the ideal female body by showing *how* it is produced, in excruciating detail (details which were, although perhaps assumed, nonetheless hidden behind the scenes with beauty pageants). Savvy viewers do recognize that editing and casting ensure that the subjects of reality television perform very clearly defined roles. However, there is no question that form and content of reality television work to hide the constructed nature of the programme and thus present the subjects of the programme as eminently authentic and genuine. Indeed, part of what makes reality television so effective is its presentation of the depicted events as *actually taking place*. A scripted drama can teach viewers how to fall in line with social norms, but there is no guarantee that the strategies advocated will result in success. Even beauty pageants are ambiguous on this score, because viewers are not privy to the processes by which contestants achieved their perfect bodies. But televised depictions of plastic surgery seem to leave nothing out. These presentations perform their realism by doing work on actual bodies. The physical evidence of transformation, along with what appear to be the unadulterated expressions of pain by the subjects, provide unequivocal proof that change has taken place, and leave no room for doubt that the procedures depicted have resulted in a beautiful body. This mode of presentation not only naturalizes a faith in the positive effects of plastic surgery, but also affirms a contemporary post-feminist ideology about individual transformation and the pleasure that eventually comes from constructing the perfect feminine body.

Of course, witnessing this kind of feminine production has been supported by television for years, where an at-home audience could vicariously identify with Miss America, and admire her accomplishments and overcoming of adversity (which may be vaguely alluded to), while remaining oblivious to her actual process of becoming ideal. Witnessing the process itself has historically not been important for television—it was the visual presentation of the *result* that

provided 'evidence' of a female liberal subjectivity. In an era of unscripted television, however, the process has become the product. Reality television promises to give viewers a glimpse at 'real' life, complete with flaws and everyday problems.[3] Of course, the 'reality' aspect of reality television is a particular kind of reality: unscripted television programmes are not 'realist' in the documentary sense, but rather are a mixture of realism and spectacular entertainment. The subjects of reality programmes are 'real'; that is, they are presumably representative of the television audience, particularly insofar as they are not actors portraying a scripted role. And the action of the show—the transformation—is seen as 'real' because it is at least partially confirmed by physical changes that occur before the viewers' eyes. Indeed, at the most basic level, the 'reality' genre is different from other types of programming that may technically fit the generic conventions of reality television (e.g. the live, unscripted beauty pageant) because it carries 'the open and explicit sale of television programming as a representation of reality' (Friedman, 2002: 7). This claim to realism has significance in the normalization of gender identity, especially in those programmes dedicated to the transformation of gender identity. Because makeover programmes depict 'real' people undergoing cosmetic surgery, the narrative of these shows normalizes undergoing cosmetic surgery and other extremes to change and 'improve' one's appearance.

The Swan and *Extreme Makeover*

The Swan's self-stated goal is to 'take ordinary women and radically transform them into beauty queens'.[4] The opening to each episode introduces the 'team of experts', including plastic surgeons, a dentist, therapist, physical fitness expert, and a 'life coach'. The beginning words of the show feature each 'expert' offering a pithy sentence about what *The Swan* intends: 'We help women transform their lives . . . We rebuild and enhance their bodies . . . Help them overcome life-long obstacles . . . and drive them to reach beyond themselves'. In both *The Swan* and *Extreme Makeover*, there is a focus on the corporeal, where flabby stomachs are grabbed and measured, large bodies are exaggerated and intentionally made to look unattractive (e.g. *The Swan* features a 'before' picture of each subject wearing grey, dingy underwear that resembles a kind of prison garb), and a general visual privileging of excessive flesh. This initial focus makes the finished product more spectacular, as the subject views herself in an enormous mirror as part of a ritual that is called the 'reveal'.

The Swan and *Extreme Makeover* construct their transformation narratives using very specific strategies and themes that resonate within a post-feminist context of neo-liberalism, individual agency and celebration of technology. For instance, both programmes are structured by an implicit (and sometimes explicit) class discourse. Plastic surgery shows often select as their subjects a 'certain class' of woman, which translates frequently into working-class women. The selection of working-class subjects contributes to the seemingly inexhaustible ideology of the American dream, where those of a lower socio-economic class can succeed at becoming middle-class subjects, and the media audience participates in this transformation by tuning in to watch (Palmer, 2004). *The Swan* normalizes the use of services such as cosmetic surgery, 'life coaches', and therapists (services which are presumably only available to those with disposable income). At the end of the show, the subjects are taken to 'The Swan Mansion', which is the realm of the experts and the site for the reveal of the finished product (the pre-surgery subject apparently never sullies the environment with her pre-surgery 'ugliness'). Although the subjects of reality television may actually represent a more diverse range of identities than previously seen in the medium, the outcome of these subjects' transformations is usually a mainstreaming, a construction of a new, improved self who conforms even more readily to dominant norms. Moreover, as Laurie Ouellette (2004: 232) has argued, reality television programmes

> do not subvert elusive democratic ideals, then, as much as they *construct* templates for citizenship that complement the privatization of public life, the collapse of the welfare state, and most important, the discourse of individual choice and personal responsibility.

Another factor in this template for citizenship involves overcoming of personal and psychological obstacles. The personal history of each subject chosen to participate in *The Swan* is part of the narrative theme. In one episode of the show, a woman, 'Jennifer', needs a surgical and physical makeover to cover the scars she received during a house fire when she was a child. However, of great significance (apparently) is the fact that her mother left her in the house to burn in the fire, thus her physical scars are compounded by the emotional ones of abandonment. Within this psychological context, her scars are surgically removed (or altered), she loses weight, has multiple cosmetic and dental surgeries, and then is 'revealed' to both herself and the audience at the end of the episode, so that the audience can take part in her individual, physical, and moral transformation.

The process of becoming a 'swan' is dramatized and technologized using simple and culturally recognizable pseudo-scientific visual techniques. Before the makeover begins, the woman's body is graphically displayed in a boxed-in grid, complete with cross-hairs, digital sound effects, and an inexplicable running set of numbers in the bottom left-hand corner (one can't help but be reminded of the Arnold Schwarzenegger film, *Total Recall*). Off to one side, there is a listing of the various procedures that will be conducted during the makeover, including liposuction, dental veneers, tummy tucks, and breast augmentation. The visual trope of the technologized body as displayed in *The Swan* is emblematic of post-feminist culture, where surgical 'choices' about idealized femininity are cast in the same wide commercial net as watching MTV, wearing t-shirts that say 'Girls Rule!', and watching the quintessential teenage US television network, the WB (Bordo, 2003).

The visual display of the plastic, technologized body that is created in *The Swan* privileges a more general cultural narrative about the plasticity of the self (Bordo, 2003). Indeed, after the technology involved in the makeover is displayed, the programme focuses in on whatever emotional trauma the subject has endured, blatantly 'resolving' the psychological obstacles along with the technological solutions. So, to help Jennifer confront the emotional scars from her traumatic house fire, *The Swan* insists that she undergo weekly therapy and life coaching—but more importantly, her scars will be healed through multiple surgeries, a 1200 calorie-a-day diet and 2 hours daily in the gym.

In another *Swan* example, a woman ('Kimberly') is yearning for a self-transformation because, again, she endured a traumatic childhood as an orphan without a stable home environment. *The Swan*—and more obliquely, the practices involved in becoming the ideal feminine figure—can help Kimberly with this trauma, again through an alteration of the physical body. As Kimberly says in this episode, 'It is painful to wake up and know you have a beautiful figure underneath a bunch of flab. I just want to be me again!' While the connection between her tragic childhood and being slightly overweight by contemporary standards is left unclear, it is a connection that is unproblematically—indeed, necessarily—made throughout the programme. The logic of a programme such as *The Swan* unequivocally revolves around transformation—and like so many other themes within post-feminism, the transformation is one of becoming more like 'yourself'.

The transformations depicted on *Extreme Makeover* are similarly articulated as a process of 'becoming' oneself. In one episode, 'Elisa' is seeking a transformation in order to overcome her poor self-image that dates back to her childhood. The narrative clearly positions her as the classic liberal subject who has overcome many obstacles (though these are never specified) in order to become the successful woman she is today. However, as Elisa states, 'The one thing I haven't overcome is my image'. Time after time in this episode, Elisa's 'image' is privileged as the site of the most important transformation, the one that will 'seal the deal' of her self-actualization. In one particularly explicit expression of this, the narrator says 'Elisa's nose [has been] reshaped, along with her poor self-image'. Here, self-image is unproblematically bound to the corporeal, with no acknowledgement that self-image might be much more dependent upon cultural pressures and psychological issues than actual physical appearance.

Becoming a Better "You"

Although both the beauty pageant and the surgical makeover show are about subjects' endeavours to attain a cultural ideal of feminine attractiveness, the makeover show is much more overt in acknowledging the importance of *physical* transformation. Within

beauty pageants such as the Miss America pageant, there is an implicit articulation of physical perfection with 'inner beauty'. In surgical makeover programming, there is nothing implicit or subtle about this articulation. Over and over again, the women undergoing surgery to improve their appearance state that they want to be beautiful as a *means* to the various ends of being more successful in their relationships, effective in their careers, respected in their communities, or prized for their femininity. As one subject's husband commented on *The Swan*, 'I'm anxious to see how *The Swan* empowers her'. The underlying assumption made by these women, and thus by these programmes, is that appearance *is* one's character and capacity for achievement in all aspects of life. Indeed, according to Gareth Palmer (2004: 184), '[makeover] television is possible because it is now widely agreed and understood that "appearance is everything"'. Within the contemporary media environment, the meanings inscribed on the bodily surface come to be increasingly central to individual identity. This focus on individual subjectivity is characteristic of post-feminism's celebration of media visibility and the pleasure of consumption practices, as well as indicative of post-feminism's shift away from questions of power and domination (McRobbie, forthcoming). Gender performance is, within this context, one more pleasurable commodity, one more way to celebrate the individual body. Reality makeover shows exploit this feature of post-feminism by offering the pleasure of transforming the self. Within these shows, the submission of one's body to a group of cosmetic surgeons to be reworked and redefined is never positioned as an issue about gender inequity or unattainable femininity—indeed, shows such as *The Swan* and *Extreme Makeover* provide 'evidence' that *any* body is possible, if one simply has the desire.

This normalization of flawless femininity is obviously problematic for feminists, and the problem is compounded by a liberal logic that celebrates disciplinary practices of femininity as 'free' choice and individual pleasure. This kind of rhetoric, celebrated and maintained within a post-feminist cultural context, makes it difficult to generate a discourse that is about struggle or structural inequality. Indeed, the feminist critiques of unreal standards of appearance come to seem, as McRobbie (2004) points out, cranky and reactionary (and certainly old-fashioned) within this contemporary context. Rather, the historical feminist insistence that disciplinary femininity is a symptom and effect of gender oppression is re-shifted in this context as a denial of women's agency and the pleasures that can be won through physical attractiveness.

Given both the economic and cultural normalization of cosmetic surgery in the United States over the past decade, it is no real surprise that the reality makeover genre would prove so successful a venture. However, personal transformation through surgery is especially consistent with the context of post-feminism and contemporary commodity culture, because these programmes sensationalize individual improvement through consumption. All makeover programmes are about becoming a better 'you' by making better purchases and adopting better lifestyle habits (remember the plea of one *Swan* contestant: 'I just want to be me again!'). Cosmetic surgery shows not only capitalize on this ideology, but are products of this ideological climate where the consumption of medical procedures rather than (or in addition to) a new haircut or a new pair of jeans is normalized.

While both the Miss America pageant and reality makeover shows offer their viewers performances of femininity, these performances need to be understood as emerging from the cultural and political conditions in which they are produced. This difference in presentation of the subjects of beauty pageants and makeover programmes respectively speaks to the changing role of media in the normalization of performances of femininity, as well as to the affiliation many young women have with post-feminist politics. Before its downturn, the Miss America pageant presented female citizens who embodied a liberal discourse of opportunity and empowerment. Pageant contestants symbolized personal achievement, which for American women is supposed to be defined by the moral discipline that results in feminine beauty and wholesome values. In contrast, the femininity that is normalized by reality makeover programmes has less to do with the ideals of traditional American citizenship and more to do with an individual celebration of the self within the sphere of consumer culture—a consumer citizenship. This celebration is the post-feminist version of 'empowerment'; it is a logic that implies that

loving one's own (surgically enhanced) female body is as much a promotion of (post-) feminist values as staging a political protest with one's revolutionary sisters was in 1968. Within this media context, a woman's right to citizenship is passé and hardly worth talking about; post-feminism now seems to be about a woman's right to sculpt her body to approximate more closely a constructed ideal.

And so it is that reality makeover shows present us with a newly defined liberal feminine subject. The women of these programmes are as invested in cultural norms of femininity as any Miss America contestant ever was. But the untempered enthusiasm with which makeover subjects embark upon a project of self-actualization almost wholly within the consumer market differentiates and marks the new genre as part of a post-feminist media culture. Building upon the traditional liberal trope of the disciplined self in search of fulfilment against all odds, the new feminine subject transcends even the limitations of her own body to participate in a discourse that encourages her to '"imagine the possibilities" and close [her] eyes to limits and consequences' (McRobbie, forthcoming). The message of reality makeover programming is that nothing, and certainly not your own body, should stand between you and what you want to become.

Notes

1. Clearly, this does not assume that all feminism could be considered 'post-feminism'. Rather, the version of liberal feminism that became part of mainstream television in the 1980s and 1990s—from, as Bonnie Dow (1996) points out, *Designing Women* to *Murphy Brown*—has actually shifted and become more 'post-feminist'. The television heroines of the post-feminist era range from *Ally McBeal* to *Buffy (the Vampire Slayer)* to the women on *Sex and the City.*

2. Television theorist Mark Andrejevic (2003) refers to Walter Benjamin's prediction that the apparatus of mechanical production would demystify the product, because the presence of the apparatus challenges the magic of production, and makes it clear that objects are produced. The technique of reproduction detaches the reproduced object from the domain of tradition, substituting copies for a unique existence. Benjamin's subject was, of course, art, and his primary argument was that the means of production—mechanical reproducibility—disrupts the aura or the authenticity of a product. Applying this concept

to reality television, Andrejevic argues that aura has now been displaced onto the apparatus itself.

3. Economically, this shift in programming has certainly favoured the industry. Reality television is partially the result of the dual trends of corporate media consolidation since the Telecommunications Act of 1996 and increasing globalization of media markets. With these trends there is a consequent reluctance on the part of networks and media conglomerates to make large investments in media content. Reality television's reduced need for acting, writing, directing, and producing talent fits the bill. As Mark Andrejevic (2003) has pointed out, everyday people are willing to do 'the work of being watched' and developers of television content have been only too happy to exploit this willingness. With a compelling concept, ratings hits can be cobbled together requiring a minimum of overhead costs, resulting in a maximization of profits for media corporations.

4. All examples and text from *The Swan* and *Extreme Makeover* are from episodes airing on Fox and ABC, respectively, in the fall of 2004.

References

Andrejevic, M. (2003) *Reality TV: The Work of Being Watched.* Lanham, MD: Rowman & Littlefield.

Banet-Weiser, S. (1999) *The Most Beautiful Girl in the World: Beauty Pageants and National Identity.* Berkeley: University of California Press.

Bartky, S. L. (1988) 'Foucault, Femininity, and the Modernization of Patriarchal Power', pp. 63–82 in I. Diamond and L. Quinby (eds) *Feminism and Foucault: Reflections on Resistance.* Boston: Northeastern University Press.

Baumgardner, J. and A. Richards (1999) *ManifestA: Young Women, Feminism, and the Future.* New York: Farrar, Straus and Giroux.

Bordo, S. (2003) *Unbearable Weight: Feminism, Western Culture, and the Body.* Berkeley: University of California Press.

Craig, M. L. (2002) *Ain't I a Beauty Queen? Black Women, Beauty, and the Politics of Race.* Oxford: Oxford University Press.

Davis, K. (1995) *Reshaping the Female Body: The Dilemma of Cosmetic Surgery.* New York: Routledge.

Dow, B. J. (1996) *Prime-Time Feminism: Television, Media Culture, and the Women's Movement since 1970.* Philadelphia: University of Pennsylvania Press.

Dow, B. J. (2003) 'Feminism, Miss America, and Media Mythology', *Rhetoric and Public Affairs* 6(1): 127–49.

Echols, A. (1989) *Daring To Be Bad: Radical Feminism in America, 1967–1975.* Minneapolis: University of Minnesota Press.

Findlen, B., ed. (1995) *Listen Up: Voices from the Next Feminist Generation.* New York: Seal Press.

Friedman, J., ed. (2002) *Reality Squared: Televisual Discourse on the Real.* New Brunswick, NJ: Rutgers University Press.

Gerbrandt, L. (2005) 'Miss America Pageant Goin' Country' [online], The Boston Channel. URL: http://www.the-bostonchannel.com (accessed June 2005).

Godleski, M. (2005) 'Reality TV Makes it Tough for Miss America' [online], Associated Press. URL: http://www.usatoday.com (accessed 13 October 2005).

Huus, K. (2005) 'Miss America Seeks Relevance and Ratings: Pageant Telecast Slashes Talent, Takes a Page from Reality Programs' [online], MSNBC. URL: http://www.msnbc.com (accessed 6 July 2005).

Kaw, E. (2002) 'Medicalization of Racial Features: Asian-American Women and Cosmetic Surgery', pp. 167–83 in R. Weitz (ed.) *The Politics of Women's Bodies: Sexuality, Appearance, and Behavior.* Oxford: Oxford University Press.

McRobbie, A. (2004) 'Notes on Postfeminism and Popular Culture: Bridget Jones and the New Gender Regime', pp. 3–14 in A. Harris (ed.) *All About the Girl: Culture, Power, and Identity.* New York: Routledge.

McRobbie, A. (forthcoming) 'Consumer Citizenship?', in *Post-Feminist Disorders? Gender, Culture and Social Change.* London: Sage.

Moraes, L. de (2005) 'Miss America Pageant Two-steps over to CMT' [online], *Washington Post.* URL: www.washingtonpost.com (accessed 13 October 2005).

Morgan, K. P. (1991) 'Women and the Knife: Cosmetic Surgery and the Colonization of Women's Bodies', *Hypatia* 6(3): 25–53.

Ouellette, L. (2004) '"Take Responsibility for Yourself": Judge Judy and the Neoliberal Citizen', pp. 231–50 in S. Murray and L. Ouellette (eds) *Reality TV: Remaking Television Culture.* New York: New York University Press.

Palmer, G. (2004) '"The New You": Class and Transformation in Lifestyle Television', pp. 173–90 in S. Holmes and D. Jermyn (eds) *Understanding Reality Television.* London: Routledge.

Peterson, I. (2005) 'Miss America a Reality Show? Surely, no Bugs' [online], *New York Times News Service.* URL: http://www.signonsandiego.com (accessed 13 October 2005).

Turner, L. (2005) 'Television on the Cutting Edge: Cosmetic Surgery Goes Prime-Time' [online], American Medical Association. URL: http://www.ama.org (accessed 3 October 2005).

35.
FISTS OF FURY

Discourses of Race and Masculinity in the Martial Arts Cinema

Yvonne Tasker

It was undeniably the figure of Bruce Lee who popularized martial arts movies with Western audiences of the 1970s, even before his untimely death made him the stuff of legend. As well as being the first Chinese actor to become a major star in the West, Lee played a significant role in the redefinition of both the Hong Kong and the American action cinema. The martial arts cinema, itself part of the broader action traditions of a popular cinema that is defined by physicality and spectacle, encompasses a vast range of forms and subgenres. Chinese and American martial arts films, from both the 1970s and the present day, offer a fertile ground for an investigation of the play of sexualized racial discourses within the popular cinema.[1] In the pages that follow the operation of these discourses are discussed primarily in relation to the dominating figure of Bruce Lee, but also with reference to the work of recent Western martial arts stars, and the kung fu comedy associated with Jackie Chan. If these traditions have received little sustained critical attention, perhaps this is because critics tend to dismiss the products of the popular cinema as mindless, objecting to the visceral pleasures of physicality that are on offer. This lack of attention, however, will come as no surprise when we consider the marginal audiences with which the films are popular in the West, as well as the relative invisibility of Asian film culture.[2]

The typical action narrative operates around an axis of power and power-lessness, which is complexly articulated through the discourses of race, class, and sexuality that constitute the body of the hero. Themes of activity and passivity are central to all these discourses, as well as to the construction of the action hero. While the hero is, by definition, an active figure, he is also frequently rendered passive, subject to a range of restraints and oppressive forces. The hero is also defined in part by his suffering, which both lends him a certain tragic status, and demonstrates his remarkable ability to endure. The trajectory of tragic suffering is at its most extreme when enacted through the figure of the white male hero of recent Western action movies. While the black protagonists of these films, who usually act as partners to the white hero, are often damaged in some way. this seems to render them symbolically safe. By way of contrast, these same Western movies seem to need obsessively to cut up and punish the body of the white male hero, a body that they, not coincidentally, also offer up as sexual spectacle. In *Cyborg* (1989) the hero, played by Jean-Claude Van Damme, is described as a "walking wound." This phrase comes close to encapsulating the role of the white male hero in the contemporary action movie. He is both massively damaged and yet still functioning. It also indicates the potential purchase of a psychoanalytic discourse in understanding the complex ways in which figures of power and powerlessness are written over the body of a hero who is represented as both invincible and castrated.

"Race," Masculinity, and the Action Tradition

In the action cinemas of both Hong Kong and America, the body of the hero or heroine is their ultimate, and often their only, weapon. A point of distinction between the two traditions lies in the way the Chinese hero often fights for and as part of a community, while within the American tradition the hero has become an increasingly isolated figure.[3] Both, however, tend to find themselves confronting a political system that is almost entirely corrupt, a villain who is the complete personification of evil. In Hong Kong films the use of the colonial past as a setting provides a specific populist point of reference. While some films are set in an unspecified or mythological past, the invocation of Japanese, Russian, or British forces allows for a more historically and culturally located narrative threat.[4] While Western films often tend toward the articulation of narratives centered on class conflict within a context of supposed racial harmony—the interracial male buddies—Hong Kong films are more likely to enact conflict in terms of the figures of colonial oppression, in which the enemy represents a threat from outside. The context of the anticolonial narrative is crucial for thinking about the racial discourses of masculine identity that are worked through in the Hong Kong martial arts cinema. As is evidenced most clearly in Bruce Lee's internationally successful films, the martial arts film of the 1970s deployed a discourse of macho Chinese nationalism that proved popular with a range of audiences. While the assertion of a powerful Chinese hero has an obvious appeal for Asian audiences, both in Asia and America, martial arts films were also hugely popular with black and white working-class audiences in the United States and in Europe during the 1970s. Such popularity can obviously be understood in terms of the production of fantasies of physical empowerment. These fantasies respond to the *constitution of the body through limits.*[5]

The redefinition of the swordplay film into the martial arts format familiar from the 1970s involved the increasing centrality of the fight, and hence the body, as a set piece. The action shifted to settings such as the martial arts school or the tournament, providing a showcase for the skills of the various performers.[6] A typical scenario consists of the fighting schools, in which the hero or heroine, who may be single or plural, fights to defend the honor of their school and the particular style of fighting associated with it against the incursion of a corrupt school, often associated with the Japanese.[7] In *The Chinese Boxer* a rogue Chinese who has been thrown out of the town some

years before returns, bringing with him three Japanese karate experts who defeat the good school and take over the town. Only Wang Yu's character survives to take on and defeat these corrupt forces. In the film's final sequence, Wang Yu triumphs over the karate experts despite the machinations of their treacherous Chinese go-between, who has hidden himself under the snow. Within the anticolonial narrative of revenge, the collaborator is an ambiguous enemy. The figure of the traitorous intermediary, who in *The Chinese Boxer* is also a rapist, is interestingly written through sexual imagery in Bruce Lee's *Way of the Dragon* (U.S.: *Return of the Dragon*). A gender dysfunction of some kind comes to define the threat represented by this figure.

Way of the Dragon is set in contemporary Rome, a re-location that does not significantly alter the basic formulation of a Chinese community, here the owners and workers of a restaurant, under threat from an archetypal white capitalist with an army of hired thugs. The European location does allow for an explicit address to issues of Westernization, largely expressed through discourses of sexuality. The treacherous Chinese go-between is styled as a camp gay man who, dressed in outrageously bright Western clothes, minces about the restaurant cooing over Bruce Lee's muscles. Interestingly, he is one of the first characters in the film to realize what Bruce Lee's body is *for*, commenting on its hardness. As in his other movies, Lee's character holds back from fighting for some time and the film teases the audience as to when Lee will "reveal" himself, a double moment in which he both reveals his body, removing his jacket, and his "hidden" strength. The go-between functions not only as a passive figure against which the tough masculinity of Lee's character can be defined, but is also figured here in terms of a specifically (homo)sexual threat associated with Europe. The sexual naiveté of Lee's character, Tang Lung, is indicated through his encounter with a European prostitute who takes him back to her apartment. He happily works out in front of a mirror but is horrified when she appears before him naked, running away in panic. Lee's absorption in his own image here is played off against those characters who have sexual designs on his body.

Set in Shanghai's international settlement. *Fist of Fury* (U.S.: *The Chinese Connection*) portrays the struggles of a Chinese school who are powerless against the political power of the Japanese school. A famous image from the film has Bruce Lee as Chen destroying a park sign saying "No Dogs and Chinese." This moment specifically enacts a fantasy that involves the refusal of physical limits. The film militantly champions a muscular Chinese national identity, despite the strictures of the law and against the insults of the Japanese. The go-between in this film acts as a translator for the Japanese—mediating between both language and culture. Disrupting a memorial service for their teacher, the go-between brings the Chinese a challenge, contemptuously referring to them as the "Sick Man of Asia." A close-up shows Chen's fist tightening, with the accompanying soundtrack amplifying and intensifying this physical expression of anger. Finally eschewing his promised restraint, Chen goes to the Japanese, defeating them all and declaring "we are not sick men." This assertion of nationalism is very clearly inscribed through the revelation of Lee's body—as he ritualistically removes his jacket—so that discourses of masculinity and nationhood are complexly bound up together in his star image. It is Lee's body that marks the assertion of a masculine national identity.

The American action cinema is more visibly concerned than other Hollywood forms with discourses of racial difference and masculinity. In a genre defined so much by physicality, black and Asian performers have had more opportunities to take on major roles. The spaces offered by such roles inevitably reinscribe stereotypical definitions of the physical, often further positioning black and Asian characters within a fantasized marginal space of criminality or deviance. Yet the martial arts film is also a genre in which racially overdetermined bodies, spaces for the projection of a range of fantasies, come into intimate physical contact. To this extent, racial difference functions partly within the films as a term that can deflect anxieties around their implicit homoeroticism. A violent physical confrontation, usually between men, forms the climax of the martial arts movie, which can be seen in terms of the staging or the performance of competing masculinities. In the memorable final fight from *Way of the Dragon*, Bruce Lee takes on karate champion Chuck Norris against the setting of Rome's Coliseum, a location that indicates the grandeur or at least the proportions of the occasion. The film offers compet-

ing masculinities and male bodies as a way of speaking about colonial conflict. Ritual images of limbering up, or extended training sequences, as well as the fights themselves, offer the male body as a sexualized spectacle, a spectacle that is inevitably overlaid with the complex meanings of the racially defined body.

The language and images through which the figure of the hero is articulated pose questions of gendered identity in terms of visual and verbal metaphors of hardness and softness. The hero's masculine identity is constructed as hardness. Using a range of methods to fight their opponents, the hero must avoid letting any stray kick or punch through his/her defense, so that the body functions as a sort of armor.[8] In *The Chinese Boxer* Wang Yu must make his hands *like iron*. The film's training sequences detail his disciplined struggle to become invincible, with images of him hardening his hands by placing them in a vat of heated iron filings, running and jumping with iron rods attached to his legs. These images provide a clear, since amplified, instance of the process by which a gendered identity is constituted through the necessary act of imagining, as well as resisting, bodily boundaries. We identify with a masculine identity that is constituted before our eyes, enacted through these narrative images of physical hardening. Judith Butler takes up this point when she suggests that "the body is not a 'being,' but a variable boundary, a surface whose permeability is politically regulated." Butler sees the body as "a signifying practice within a cultural field of gender hierarchy and compulsory heterosexuality," but the purchase of her analysis can also be extended in order to think about the racial constitution of the body (*Gender Trouble* 139). The symbolic centrality of a rhetoric of hardness in the martial arts films finds its parallel in those visual metaphors that express a fear of penetration, or of the softness that would allow it. As we'll see in the case of Bruce Lee, these fears are in part routed through the history of representation in which Chinese men and women have been constituted by the West as "soft."

A metaphoric language of gender that is intimately entwined with issues of place and status, is in operation in the fight film generally. For Western movies of recent years, a fear of softness is more directly connected to the deployment of a sexual, usually homoerotic, imagery of bodily penetration. The terrain of the action

cinema is haunted by questions of masculine identity, that are in turn bound up with complex configurations of power and authority. As I've already implied, these ideological figures must be considered not only as they operate textually, but in terms of the audiences' relationship of identification to the figure of the hero. At the most obvious level, the figure of the graceful and ultimately triumphant martial arts hero offers a more perfect figure of identification for both male and female audiences, and in this sense our relationship to the image is one of primary narcissism.[9] The hero performs astounding physical feats with which we can identify—a process in which identity is *constituted through an identification* with the performance of the body. The notorious soundtrack of grunts that accompanies martial arts films forms part of the sensuous assertion of a physicality that transgresses limits. Our relationship as an audience to the adventures portrayed is also mediated through an identification with the Oedipal figure of the hero who struggles, who rebels against, but is subject to, the strictures of the social world.

Martial arts films combine sets of images that define the body in terms of aggression and sensuousness. It is no accident though that, given a particular understanding of masculinity, Western censors have read the films as primarily having to do with aggression. The sensuousness of movement is effaced, leaving only the violence of the body, a violence that is then projected onto a pathologized marginal audience. Yet if we reinstate the eroticized aspects of the graceful movement played out in these films, it also becomes apparent that the martial arts film has evolved as a cinematic form that allows men to look at men. In this the films legitimate a taboo look. More than this, they allow an identification with a male figure who other men will look at and who will enjoy being the object of that admiring gaze. In understanding this, the juxtaposition of martial arts and dance is a useful one. In Western culture, dance is constructed in opposition to fighting. It is also linked to the feminine, and often explicitly to images of male homosexuality. It is important to note though that this does not mean the *feminization* of the male dancer, a formulation that operates within a simple gender binary. Rather, dance offers the possibility of occupying a feminine position that involves, as with the martial arts film, an explicit location of the male body on display.

While Freud's theorized relationship between primary narcissism and homosexual desire (love of the self and the same) has proved problematic, I want to invoke this relationship here as one possible way of talking about the "regressive" pleasures of the fight films. To some extent psychoanalysis functions to provide a framework within which terms such as "regressive" and "childish" do not carry the pejorative connotations that they do in everyday speech. Clearly regressive or childish pleasures are in operation through our identification with the hero as a more complete figure who triumphs over adversity. This fantasy of empowerment emerges from and speaks to those who, like children, find themselves in a position of powerlessness. In particular, an identification with the physical aspects of the hero's triumph is crucial—offering a very different set of pleasures to an intellectual identification. The regression at stake in the films can be seen as a resistance to (becoming) the father, a resistance that is radically different but nonetheless present in both the Chinese comedy films and the more earnest, or anxious, products associated with Bruce Lee and with more recent white stars. This resistance relates to the hero's location within a fantasy of omnipotence that is to some extent "outside" the institutions that represent power.

In the revenge narratives around which many martial arts films are structured, the fight has an immense importance. The "shift of the narrative discourse to violence," suggests Chiao Hsiung-Ping, "allows such a particularly intense and coherent statement of conflicts that the fight scenes become the real force carrying the narrative flow" ("Bruce Lee" 35). This understanding is echoed by Stuart Kaminsky who finds a Western point of reference for the films in the Hollywood musical, which has dance as its physical center, expressed in the set-piece musical number (see Kaminsky). Chiao Hsiung-Ping also links the figure of dance to images of physicality and the success of the martial arts films rather more effectively through an image from another hit film of the 1970s, *Saturday Night Fever*. We see the near-naked hero, Tony Manero (John Travolta) alone in his bedroom. On the wall are images of Sylvester Stallone (as Rocky) and Bruce Lee. All three men are figures who have achieved or seek to achieve success through their physicality—dance, boxing, kung fu—escaping the marginal spaces in which they find themselves through their achievements. The bodies of these working-class, marginalized men, which are their only resource, are turned through these forms into a spectacular site of pleasure rather than labor. Such images offer a physical constitution of identity that attempts to escape the policing to which the body is subject. The emphasis on physicality, then, allows the audience to identify with the construction of an oppositional identity sited on the body. This is pleasurable partly because the body is constituted through oppressive physical limitations.

Whilst Chiao's analysis was written retrospectively, critics at the time were not slow to posit links between the Western success of the martial arts films and a "ghetto myth" through which dispossessed groups might identify with the hero's struggle to overcome. B. P. Flanigan's speculation on the success of the films is representative, asserting how it is "obvious" that "people who represent the most oppressed segment of a society would obtain great satisfaction, indeed enjoyment, in watching an antagonist be literally destroyed by the kung fu hero" (10). These equations—between audience and hero—are often rather schematic. The reference to the success of martial arts films with a black urban audience in the United States seems to represent an end point. The lack of further critical work suggests perhaps that the *process of accounting* is all, a process not unlike those regulatory processes of classification familiar from other spheres. An "obvious" explanation can ultimately operate to confirm the marginalized audience in their marginal place, since explaining the appeal of the films somehow exhausts them. Is this because the films, like their audiences, are assumed to be "simple"? By contrast, Chiao's analysis begins to unravel the complex articulation of race, class, and sexuality that is elaborated in the differing Chinese and American reception of these films, as well as within the revenge narratives of the films themselves.

While I am wary of generalization in relation to an area so often characterized precisely as "simple," I wish to risk one at this stage. This is to suggest that while both Hong Kong and American martial arts films are staging fantasies, the primary focus in each tradition is different. Within the Hong Kong cinema the films can be seen as primarily working through fantasies of empowerment that emphasize social relations.

By contrast, the Americanized version of the martial arts format has increasingly become used as a space within which to stage homoerotic fantasies, primarily working through issues and anxieties around white male sexuality. Now it is nonetheless the case that both traditions employ a gendered rhetoric through which they articulate their narratives of revenge and struggle.[10]

Bruce Lee and the Remasculinization of the Chinese Body

"Remasculinization" may be a problematic notion within discourses about race and sexuality, potentially implying a return to a mythical gender stability, yet it nonetheless provides a way of situating a discussion of the central figure of Bruce Lee.[11] The significance of Lee's Western success lies partly in his articulation of a tough masculinity within nationalistic films that can be read against a history of "feminizing" Western representations of Chinese men. The significance of this shift becomes even more apparent when we consider the one Western vehicle in which Lee starred. *Enter the Dragon*, a film that gives him an asexual persona and that seeks to rewrite his image into that of a representative of colonial authority. Before moving on to a discussion of Lee's films in this context, I want to make a brief digression into literature. In her novel of Chinese-American womanhood, *The Woman Warrior*, Maxine Hong Kingston writes fantasies of omnipotence precisely in terms of shifting gendered identities. Thus her narrator tells us "[W]hen we Chinese girls listened to the adults talking-story, we learned that we failed if we grew up to be but wives or slaves. We could be heroines, swordswomen." She speculates on whether women "were once so dangerous that they had to have their feet bound" (*Woman Warrior* 25). The polarized terms, of bondage and of the swordswoman's raging freedom, are initially assigned a sex and a gender—female/feminine and male/masculine—from which the text seeks to break free. Kingston uses another opposition—that between China and America—in order to partly deconstruct this gendered binary. Her various narrators are, for much of the text, caught between the two. Kingston's writing invokes a variety of cross-cultural perspectives within an American context, in which China is read, through Orientalist discourses, as a mystical/ feminine space.

Kingston's second book, *China Men*. opens with a short fragment, "On, discovery," which describes Tang Ao's journey to America, the "land of women." He is captured by women who remove his armor and slowly, painfully "feminize" him. He is made up, his ears are pierced and his feet bound until, when he is serving food at court, we are told that his "hips swayed and his shoulders swivelled because of his shaped feet." He has become a beautiful and painful spectacle: "'She's pretty, don't you agree?' the diners said, smacking their lips at his dainty feet as he bent to put dishes before them" (*China Men* 10). In this fragment and in the different narratives that follow, King-Kok Cheung sees both the book and its hostile critical reception from Asian critics as revealing "not only the similarities between Chinese men's and Chinese women's suffering but also the correlation between these men's umbrage at racism and their misogynist behaviour" (240). In this she points to the impossibility of tackling questions of gender "in the Chinese American cultural terrain without delving into the historically enforced 'feminization' of Chinese American men, without confronting the dialectics of racial stereotypes and nationalist reactions or, above all, without wrestling with die-hard notions of masculinity and femininity in both Asian and Western cultures" (234). This perception is crucial in enabling King-Kok Cheung to both critique and contextualize the attempts by male literary editors to reproduce and update a heroic masculine tradition of Asian literature. In a footnote Cheung also refers to Bruce Lee, pointing to his significance in representations of Chinese masculinity but also to his rather inhuman characterization in *Enter the Dragon*, the American film that is taken up below.

When Bruce Lee died in 1973 he was given two funerals. Chiao Hsiung-Ping writes of the thirty thousand people who attended his Hong Kong funeral, suggesting though that the event "*was only symbolic*" since the real thing "was held in Seattle, and Steve McQueen and James Coburn were among the pallbearers" ("Bruce Lee" 31; emphasis added). What was this double ceremony symbolic of? Perhaps it indicates something of the way in which Lee was positioned, and positioned himself, as a star in both Asia and America. Bruce Lee was, and remains, the only

Chinese star to achieve an international visibility that included the West. He was also a very *visible* star in that his films tended to emphasize his physicality in a way that some have characterized as narcissistic. Given that the role of the movie actor is defined by display, the designation "narcissistic" tends to be invoked only when critics feel such display is inappropriate or unsettling. In this sense it is significant that Lee's assertion of a strong, muscular Chinese hero should be so often dubbed unsettling by contemporary Western critics. Within his films Lee's lithe muscularity is played off in spectacular film battles against huge, white, muscular opponents: Chuck Norris in *Way of the Dragon*, Robert Baker in *Fist of Fury*. I've already noted the way in which Lee's films build up to the moment when he will fight, keeping him clothed up to that point as a form of disguise. Assuming a variety of disguises in *Fist of Fury*, Lee/Chen uses his *invisibility* as a Chinese man to spy on the Japanese school. The play of disguise and revelation is also a play, once more, on an accumulated history of images of softness and hardness, passivity and masculinity.

The hardness of Lee's body and of his star image emerges from a history of softness, a history of images in which both Chinese men and women had been represented as passive and compliant. In an early film appearance as a heavy in *Marlowe* (1968), James Garner suggests that Lee's character is gay, thus leading him to lose his temper and leap to his death. Garner's jibe picks up on the extent to which the display of Lee's body and physical grace was to be emphasized in his persona. The display of the male body in action is felt to be unsettling here, making too explicit as it does the homoeroticism implicit in these man-to-man showdowns. Later on in his career, Lee was turned down in favor of David Carradine for the lead role in the television series *Kung Fu*. Of Carradine, Chuck Norris is reported to have said, with rather disarming honesty, that he "is about as good a martial artist as I am an actor." Lee himself pondered whether perhaps "they weren't ready for a Hopalong Wong" (qtd. in Glaessner 91). The earnestness of the Lee persona, along with the comedic sections of his films, can be situated against this cinematic context. Lee's struggle within America, which can be contrasted sharply with his success in Hong Kong, has emerged as a key element in the star image that has developed since his death. Chuck Norris conveys something of this in the following description of Lee, which is taken from Norris's indicatively entitled autobiography, *The Secret of Inner Strength:* "Bruce lived and breathed the martial arts. I still recall the night I dropped in on him at home and found him in the den watching television. He was lying on his back in front of the TV set with his young son, Brandon, sitting on his stomach. Bruce had leg weights wrapped around his ankles. He had barbells in his hands. While bouncing Brandon on his stomach, he was inhaling and exhaling, thus tightening the muscles of his abdomen. At the same time, he was doing leg-ups and arm exercises" (67). Such testimonies form part of the mythology surrounding Bruce Lee, a mythos that is constructed through images of an obsessive commitment to training and the struggle to succeed, to become a star.

Lee's image speaks of a struggle to become hard, to negate an imputed softness. Another aspect of this is Lee's reputed refusal to follow any one school of fighting, instead appropriating and adapting a range of styles. Lee is complexly positioned as a star in both, and "in-between," Asia and America. Chiao Hsiung-Ping explores this positioning "in-between" in terms of what she calls Lee's "cross-cultural savvy." Having worked in both industries, she points out, Lee was in a good position to judge what would appeal across the two. He was responsible for moves toward the use of martial artists rather than actors in Hong Kong films, as well as the reduction of rapid editing, camera tricks, the use of trampolines, and so on. Lee "knew the generic importance of the fighting scene, but . . . strove for a 'believable' kung fu. . . . Oriental fantasies were reduced and western realism was emphasized" ("Bruce Lee" 33). In cinematic terms the meaning of this opposition between fantasy and realism is clear, avoiding trick camera work and so on. At an ideological level this opposition echoes a history of racial stereotypes, a history that seeks to represent the kinds of fantasies at work in the Western imaginary as somehow "real."[12]

If a strong masculinity is central to Bruce Lee's image, then this is accompanied by anxieties that prefigure the uncertainties that surround the personae of many white male stars today. That this image of the Chinese man was perceived as problematic within Hollywood is evident in *Enter the Dragon*. The film centers on three men, heroes who are constructed through the use of racial stereotypes. Bruce Lee plays Lee, who is the center of a film that is to a large extent a showcase for his skills. Along with Lee are a white American character called Roper, played by John Saxon (a B movie actor who received equal billing with Lee), and an African American, Williams, played by Jim Kelly, who went on to play the part of "Black Belt Jones." *Enter the Dragon* does not, however, go in for the extensive interracial male bonding that typifies many action pictures of recent years. While the three heroes talk to each other at various points, they do not act together and their stories are kept discrete. There is one key moment of recognizable male bonding in the film, between Williams and Roper when they first meet. Significantly, this moment centers on their shared experiences in Vietnam. Indeed, within the narratives of many American martial arts movies, Vietnam functions as the space/time when the hero acquired his fighting skills. Perhaps because of the very centrality of a "Vietnam" constituted against an Oriental Other in American films, *Enter the Dragon* is clearly uncomfortable with its racial mix, a mix that represents Warner Bros.'s very tentative attempts to promote a Chinese star. Anecdotally, while the film is often seen by Western audiences as Lee's greatest achievement—and it is the film for which he is best known in the West, Asian audiences were suspicious of the film (Chiao, "Bruce Lee" 37; see also Glaessner 93–96).

We are introduced to Lee in the Shaolin Temple, where an English official, Braithwaite, enlists his help against the evil Han (Shek Kin) who is involved in both drugs and sexual slavery. Han holds a martial arts tournament every three years on his fortress island as a way for him to recruit talent to his organization. The struggles against colonial opponents found in *Fist of Fury* and *Way of the Dragon* are replaced by Han who, with his white cat, is very clearly derived from a James Bondian lineage. Such a tradition does not offer a particularly fruitful space for the articulation of a Chinese identity, so that Lee seems to be placed once more in the role of Kato, the sidekick he had played years before in the American television series *The Green Hornet*. After Lee has agreed to act on behalf of the British, he is given a further motivation in a flashback that tells of the death of his sister (Angela Mao Ying). Roper is a compulsive gambler whose debts have led him to fight in the upcoming tournament. Williams's motivation for attending is less clear since we see him saying his good-byes wordlessly in an all-black martial arts school. As he is traveling to the airport Williams is harassed by two white policemen. Williams knocks the men out and steals their police car, signaling an underdeveloped narrative of racial conflict within America—a narrative that is displaced through images of the Orient.

In the complex relationship between the articulation of a Chinese and a masculine identity in Lee's image, the following comments from Robert Clouse, director of *Enter the Dragon*, are indicative:

> He [Lee] had this strut. . . . they showed me his first three films at Warner Bros. and . . . I said the first thing we have to do is kick the strut out of Bruce Lee. We're going to Westernize him to some degree. They wanted an international star. I said we would put him in carefully tailored suits instead of just his Chinese suits. We'll show him both ways. He should look as though he'd be comfortable in New York or London. . . . [In *Enter the Dragon*] he comes strutting down the field toward the end of the big battle. . . . And I said . . . "You're beyond that now. A Western audience doesn't like the obvious strut. Let's play it straight there."
>
> ("Interview with Robert Clause" 43)

Caught up in fantasies of racial and sexual identity, Clouse speaks through oppositions of savagery and civilization, Western suits versus Chinese suits. Gail Ching-Liang Low heads her discussion of cultural cross-dressing with a pertinent statement from Frantz Fanon that the "colonised is elevated above his jungle status in proportion to his adoption of the mother country's cultural standards. He becomes whiter as he renounces his blackness, his jungle" (qtd. in Low 83). Such a logic structures Clouse's desire to put Lee in Western clothes in order that he be "comfortable" in the West, which is really to say that the West would be comfortable with him. Clouse's reference to "playing it straight" in this context unwittingly indicates the homoerotic imaginary that underpins the cinematic performance of Lee's body—a performance in which the body is offered as sexual spectacle, as a site of pleasure rather than subjection.

This same logic is also expressed through Clouse's (failed) intention to *kick the strut* out of Lee. This phrase signals something of the fear and mistrust that develops around Bruce Lee's star status in the West, fears bound up with the tough nationalistic male identity that is championed in his Hong Kong films. I don't want to suggest that Lee was completely controlled by this discourse, since the parts of *Enter the Dragon* that he directed, and his own performance in particular, do emerge (complete with strut) as to some extent separate from the messy compromise that is the film's attempt to cater to a range of audiences. The confusion of the film is expressly clear in its mobilization of sexualized discourses of race. The three fighters are, in appropriately Bondian-decadent style, offered the choice of a harem of women. Roper selects the white woman who seems to be in charge, while Williams selects four Asian women. Predictably enough, Lee's character absents himself, selecting a woman he knows to be a spy who has been placed on the island.

It is Kelly as Williams who must bear the burden of the film's discourse about race. It is no surprise then that the stereotype of the black stud is invoked or that Williams does not survive to the end of the movie. It is he who also voices the film's social commentary, pointing regretfully to the ghettos of the city. Amidst the general success of Hong Kong action pictures in the America of the 1970s, producers were not slow to notice the appeal of these films to an urban black audience. Black martial arts films, which built on the success of films like *Shaft* (1971), invoked a hypersexualized image of the black man. By contrast, one of the most enduring Western stereotypes of the East is as a site of a mystical, asexual knowledge. Richard Fung captures this, setting out a representational dichotomy in which Asian men are either an "egghead/wimp" or "the kung fu master/ninja/samurai." He is "sometimes dangerous, sometimes friendly, but almost always characterized by a desexualized Zen asceticism." Fung uses Fanon, who describes how "the Negro is eclipsed. He is turned into a penis. He is a penis," to draw a contrast with Western representations of the Asian man who "is defined by a striking absence down there" (148). In *Enter the Dragon* Chinese sexuality is erased while blackness, in the figure of Jim Kelly, becomes the overdetermined space through which the film signifies both sexuality and racial difference.

Western Stars and the Martial Arts Cinema

A commentary on the workings of the Western action cinema is useful here in contextualizing the kinds of operation at work in a film like *Enter the Dragon* or more recent Orientalist fictions, such as *Showdown in Little Tokyo*, which I discuss below. The American martial arts film, which is a subsidiary of the big-budget action picture, has very little cultural prestige attached to it. Indeed, Western martial arts stars frequently express the desire to move on from the so-called "chop-socky" action film into more conventional action movies. Jean-Claude Van Damme is no exception, and his films have gradually moved away from showcasing martial arts into more traditional heroics. In any case, the overdeveloped muscular frames of the white Western stars are geared much more toward the sort of static, posed display involved in bodybuilding than the quick-fire action seen in the Hong Kong films. Given this tendency toward static display, it is perhaps not surprising to find that the films are centrally concerned with the sexual commodification of the (usually white) male body. The body is portrayed as sexual spectacle within a narrative that offers a critique of such commodification. Though there is not space here to develop the point fully, the different status of martial arts and other American action pictures can be understood partly through the sense that the martial arts form already carries the kinds of feminized associations that the Western imaginary has long ascribed to the East. The insistent homoeroticism of films featuring stars such as Van Damme, only makes it more important to distance him from such implicit feminization. Thus, it is black characters who once again take up the burden of a pathologized (homo)sexuality in the Western films.

A.W.O.L. (1990) casts Van Damme as Lyon, a soldier who has deserted the legion to visit his dying brother in America. He works his passage stoking the boilers of a ship, a typical plot device in that it both stresses the body as a site of manual labor and allows Van Damme to remove his clothes. Such moments of display are combined with set-piece fights. On his arrival Lyon meets Joshua, a crippled but street-smart black man, who initially seeks to exploit Lyon's fighting skill, though the two soon become buddies. The theme of the commodification of the working-class male body, typical of American fight movies, is also explicitly bound into the sexual implications of that commodification here, as Lyon finds himself working for "The Lady," who runs a high-class bare-knuckle fighting operation. The controlling figure of Cynthia, "The Lady," is a deeply fearful image of the powerful woman who at first seeks to control Lyon and then, when he spurns her sexually, matches him against a vicious white fighter known as Attila, who literally tears his opponents in two. The anxiety attendant on the commodification of the white male body is mediated here through the figure of the powerful (masculine) woman. The version of black masculinity articulated in these films is also crucial to securing the symbolic position of the hero. The recurrent figure of the "damaged" black man is central, with the crippled Joshua fulfilling this role in *A.W.O.L.*, and Hawkins (who has a "dead" eye) befriending Van Damme in *Death Warrant* (1991). The physical flaws of these initially hostile but ultimately dependable men make them symbolically safe in an anxious representational world. Blackness also functions then as a space within which to deal with fears around homosexual desire.

In *Death Warrant* Van Damme plays Burke, a cop who goes undercover in a maximum-security jail. The prison narrative is a favorite of the American action cinema, allowing as it does for the free play of homoerotic images and for the repressive mobilization of stock characters, such as the sadistic white warden and guards, dependable black old-timers, and hysterical, knife-wielding Latins. Here the hero is explicitly threatened with rape, an assault that the film's editing implies, though it cannot seem to explicitly state. While Western martial arts and other action movies thrive on interracial same-sex friendships, homosexuality or any notion of gay desire remains almost exclusively expressed in terms of threat and violence. The fight then provides the perfect space for male physical intimacy—since that intimacy is accompanied by a compensatory brutal violence. Serving to highlight the sexual significance of the "castrated" black man in these fictions is another level of blackness conjured up by *Death Warrant* in the figure of Priest. He inhabits a mysterious realm beneath the prison: "The lower you go the funkier it gets in this place," Burke's cell mate tells him cheerfully, adding that he should "cover his ass" and "I mean that literally—it's not a figure of speech." We are told that even the guards won't come here—it is a space then that is both sexual and totally other. Here we find Priest, surrounded by his "ladies," male/female inmates who function as profoundly unstable and hauntingly present figures in the film—images of the subterranean depths that lie beneath the sexual relations as relations of power that structure the prison world. The film both acknowledges and plays to the existence of gay desire, in its images and its narrative, while finally projecting this desire onto a space of pathologized black masculinity, in which sexuality is part of a more general excess.

An earlier Van Damme movie, *Kickboxer* (1989), not only teams the hero with a "damaged" black man—Taylor, a cynical veteran scarred by his experiences in Vietnam—but also employs stereotypical images of the East. Thai kickboxing champion Tong Po embodies the Orient as sexual threat, alongside the figures of the mythic sage and the virginal maiden. The structure of this film is a familiar one in the West. A young white man persuades an ancient "Oriental" man to teach him the skills of a secret martial art. At the same time, he typically meets an "innocent" girl and falls in love. Although he seems to face impossible odds, he ultimately wins out in the final moments of the film. Now this is to some extent a familiar narrative of the Hong Kong cinema in the 1970s. The hero is initially beaten, learns a secret technique that makes him invincible, and, after extended torturous training, is ultimately triumphant—this is roughly the plot of *The Chinese Boxer*. But the version of this narrative that places the white hero at the center represents a significant rewriting.

To think about this further I'll refer briefly to an American cop movie, *Showdown in Little Tokyo* (1991). Starring Dolph Lundgren and Brandon Lee, this is a rare film in its casting of a Chinese actor in a major heroic role. The film seeks to capitalize on an action-comedy tradition by casting Lee as a thoroughly Westernized Japanese-American, who to some extent undercuts the strong-silent performance of costar Dolph Lundgren.[13] In a perverse colonial logic, Aryan beefcake Lundgren plays a cop brought up in Japan who styles himself as a samurai warrior. His knowledge of Japanese tradition, language, and culture is played off against Lee's Westernized persona. The film's fantasy of cultural cross-dressing operates both to negate the homoeroticism implicit in the buddy rela-

tionship and to produce a complex fantasy of white mastery through the appropriation and penetration of the other's culture. Speaking of fantasies of cultural cross-dressing in nineteenth-century imperialist literature, Gail Ching-Liang Low points out that since "the Orient becomes, through western imagination, a site of excess sexuality and deviant behaviour that must be penetrated and controlled," then the "violation of a subject-culture may also be read as a sexualised text" (95).[14] *In Showdown in Little Tokyo* this fantasy might be directly interpreted in terms of the racist articulation of American fears around Japanization. That these fears are bound up with masculine identity is perhaps most apparent in the "comic" moment when Lee's character compliments Lundgren's on the size of his penis. Recalling Richard Fung's comments on Western myths of Asian sexuality as asexuality, it is clear that Lundgren's superwhite, muscular body functions as a fetish within the film. The body is clearly constituted by "race," and yet it also refuses the limits of that constitution. The freedom to shift, transgress, and adopt racial identities in this way is, of course, as Ching-Liang Low points out, available to different groups differently (98).[15]

Jackie Chan: Masculinity and Kung Fu Comedy

Jackie Chan's combination of action with slapstick comedy is quite distinct from the earnest and anxious suffering of the white stars, and from the dominating figure of Bruce Lee. His films are much more at ease with the hectic heroics of their male protagonists, heroics that are at once offered as spectacle and comically undercut. Comic interludes and punch lines punctuate even relatively tense narratives such as the *Police Story* films. I'd like to make some brief comments on Jackie Chan's films here as a way of talking about a very different kind of Hong Kong film-making to that associated with Bruce Lee. The films use a variety of physical set pieces—both comic and violent—drawing on a theatrical tradition that is committed to a different kind of spectacle than the more static bodily display at work in many American films. This is most apparent in the orchestration of group fights of amazing complexity, as in the bar room brawl and the final showdown of *Project A*. The more restrained playground battle in *Police Story* 2 pitches

Chan against a group of thugs, but even here, when the hero fights alone, the camera work is carefully choreographed around the scene, rather than the individual hero, as spectacle.

Of course, many of the films I've already discussed include comic moments, though I've not focused on this aspect of the action tradition. What distinguishes the quick-fire timing and slapstick comedy for which Chan has become famous is the infiltration of comedy into the fight scenes themselves, fights that as we've seen, form the center of the martial arts movie. In Chan's films, fights are played both seriously and for laughs, as when opponents come to blows and then back off shaking their fists or rubbing their heads in pain. Such moments admit both the possibility of pain and the vulnerability of the body. There is an indicative moment in *Wheels on Meals* when costars Chan and Yuen Biao are involved in a street fight. They look at each other, agree that their opponents are too tough and simply run away. Chan, while at times a very graceful fighter, also plays on the way in which both the body and technology lets its owner down. Thus he often seems to win his fights more by good luck and determination than skill. In the middle of a tense fight at the end of *Wheels on Meals*, Chan frees himself from a hold by tickling his opponent. Similarly, most of the people in a Jackie Chan film are *at some point* a fighter—characters are not written as professional fighters and they are not necessarily students or teachers in a martial arts school. Pauline Yeung, the romantic lead in *Dragons Forever*, who spends most of her time being rescued or wooed, suddenly, and quite inexplicably, produces a short set-piece display of fighting skill, knocking out a bad guy in the films final showdown.

In Chan's movies it is more often the case that women are either explicitly cast as, or ultimately revealed to be, girlish. They increasingly seem to represent a troublesome presence, both an annoying and a fascinating distraction from adventures and from the concerns of male friendship. Heterosexual romance is an important term for the definition of an adult masculine identity in the films, but is also the cause of myriad problems, as in the two *Police Story* films. The chorus of three women who keep getting in Chan's way in *Operation Condor: Armour of God 2* (1991) represents an extreme articulation of women-as-femininity-as-chaos.

An inordinate amount of screen time is given over to the comic demonstration of female incompetence, by contrast to Western movies that are much more likely to exclude women altogether. The original *Armour of God* was reviewed and marketed in the West as Chan's attempt to cash in on the success of the *Indiana Jones* films. While these successful films do provide a reference point, there is more than a little naiveté in the assumption that Hong Kong always follows in the wake of Hollywood, especially given Hong Kong's long tradition of producing epic adventure films. So while some critics suggested the film was Westernized, they didn't in turn acknowledge the ways in which *The Armour of God* redefines and undercuts those Hollywood traditions that it does draw on. Indeed, Chan emerges from a changed industrial context in Hong Kong, and the figure of the adventurer is rewritten within its existing traditions. Chan plays Jackie, the "Asian Hawk," an ex–pop star turned adventurer who tracks down ancient artifacts for sale to the highest bidder. The film allows Chan to explore a Europe that is constructed as an alien and exotic territory. The hero is pitted against a fabulously bizarre sect of evil monks who are ensconced in a mountain retreat. A rather camp waiter tells them that the monks come down once a month to fetch supplies and women, establishing both the opponents and the terrain as sexually decadent. The terms of Orientalist fantasies are turned around on themselves, as Europe becomes the site of an exotic adventure for the Chinese heroes and heroine.

The film turns on the relationship between Jackie and his best friend Alan. Though Alan is to some extent a clownish character, this is set up differently to the physical comedy constructed around Chan. Though we see him early on performing in a spectacular stage show before a huge Hong Kong crowd, he lacks masculine competence within the film's terms. He is something of a fashion plate, modeling a series of stylish clothes throughout the film. Given this characterization it is not surprising that Alan is useless in a fight, pointing out hysterically that he doesn't believe in violence while holding onto Jackie for protection, getting them into trouble and needing to be rescued. If the fight bears the narrative discourse of the martial arts film, then a hero who cannot fight is an oddity. Within the film's discourse about masculinity Alan is clearly situated within a feminine position that is played for laughs. The comedy format allows for an articulation of masculinity that is to some extent fluid, not expressed exclusively in terms of a muscular hardness. Ultimately, though, *The Armour of God* falls back on blackness as a space of sexualized deviance. In one of the film's final sequences, when Jackie is attempting to steal the armor, four black furies are turned on him. These fighting women are kitted out in black corsets and stilettos. Both comic and fetishistic, these women represent the displacement of an exaggerated sexuality onto blackness. This image echoes the opening of the film, located in a fantasized Africa, in which Jackie fools a black tribe by talking gibberish. He escapes, stealing the sword that is part of the "armour of god," using a variety of gadgets and stunts. The structures at work here are replicated in the recent sequel. *Operation Condor* (1991), which again begins with Jackie fooling a black African tribe. This time he only narrowly escapes from the threat of marriage. The "Asian Hawk" achieves his heroic identity at the expense of an Africa constructed as primitive and easily fooled.

Unlike Bruce Lee, the struggle for American success is not foregrounded in Jackie Chan's star image, though he also made a rather disastrous American movie with Robert Clouse at one point in his career.[16] "Bruce had that hard tight look whenever he wanted it," observes Clouse, the man who we recall wanted to "kick the strut" out of Lee. Clouse goes on to remark that he "thought Jackie Chan had it but he was soft" ("Interview with Robert Clouse" 9). Chan's "softness" does not consist in a lack of muscularity or an inability to fight, but more in a refusal either to take the male body too seriously or to play the part of Oriental other. Chan's persona is built on the cheerful admission of vulnerability at work in his films—most obviously in the inclusion at the end of the movies of outtakes featuring stunts gone wrong. And while he frequently gets beaten up in his films, he is nonetheless in control. As Chan put it: "In Hong-Kong, I can control everything. In Hollywood I'm just a Chinese actor who speaks bad English" (Rayns 84).

Discourses of race and masculinity are elaborated in vastly different ways in the various martial arts films discussed in this essay. I have sought to comment on some of the many contrasting traditions and

subgenres, and to argue that the construction of racial and gendered identities in the genre is not as simple or as easily characterized as it may seem. Though many films work to reinscribe sexual and racial stereotypes, our readings also need to be situated within a historical and a cinematic context. The discussion of the very distinct star images and films of Bruce Lee, Jean-Claude Van Damme, and Jackie Chan emphasizes the radically different ways that the ideas, images, and themes associated with the martial arts genre can be inflected. Indeed, though I have used the term "genre" here, it is probably evident from the range of films discussed that there is no clearly definable set of rules that can encapsulate the martial arts film across either the output of decades or the different industries of Hollywood and Hong Kong.

I have sought to argue, though, that there are certain themes recurring across different films—power and powerlessness, physical limitations and their transgression, narratives of revenge, and so on—that have a clear resonance for the discussion of the construction of masculine identities in the cinema. A central focus for this discussion has been the role of the body in the genre, with the suggestion that we can see the constitution of gendered identities in the cinema as operating through the act of imagining and resisting bodily boundaries. The discussion of various films and stars offered here can only further emphasize the extent to which ideas and images of masculine power—defined through such figures as the "hard" male body, the ability to bear suffering, and ultimately to triumph—are intertwined with discourses of race, class, sexuality, and nationality.

Notes

Thanks to Val Hill, Leon Hunt, and Gwion Jones for their ideas and comments.

1. While the primary focus of this essay is male martial arts stars, Hong Kong cinema has a long tradition of female fighters. Western martial artist Cynthia Rothrock went to Hong Kong to make films such as *Above the Law* (with Yuen Biao), while in Hollywood producers seem more likely to cast her as a "girlfriend."

2. Popular Asian cinema has an extensive circulation in the West through forms such as video. The point I'm making here is that these forms are marginal in comparison to the more widely available and more widely discussed Hollywood material. There are complex links between

the popular cinemas of Hong Kong, Taiwan, Japan, and Bombay. These traditions are often ignored by Western criticism, though attention has been paid to more prestigious Asian films. For an excellent industrial survey see Lent.

3. This tendency is most evident in the frequent use of the figure of the Vietnam veteran, portrayed as a slightly unbalanced man who has lost his comrades in battle and been betrayed by his government.

4. I do not know of any Hong Kong action films that deal explicitly with the colonial present, though British figures are very visible, if marginal, in films—for example, the *Police Story* and *Project A* films. Chiao Hsiung-Ping describes *Project A: II* (1987) as "given over to addressing the contradictory situation whereby Hong Kong now fears the 1997 return to the mainland and would rather remain colonised" ("Distinct Taiwanese" 160).

5. In The *Wretched of the Earth* Frantz Fanon writes that "The native is a being hemmed in; apartheid is simply one form of the division into compartments of the colonial world. The first thing which the native learns is to stay in his place and not go beyond certain limits" (40). Fanon also emphasizes that the experience of the world through such oppressive limits generates fantasies of physical empowerment. See also Robins and Cohen, especially *Knuckle Sandwich: Growing Up in the Working-Class City* 94–103, in which they discuss the appeal of the martial arts; and see Walkerdine, for a discussion of class in relation to narratives of fighting. A key reference point for my argument here is Butler's *Gender Trouble*. Butler uses Foucault to discuss the constitution of the body through signs.

6. See Glaessner 54.

7. Glaessner outlines the function of the antagonist school in these films as "a straightforward stand-in for the institutions involved in Japanese imperialism or for their less overt infiltration into Chinese life" (36).

8. The most useful reference point for a consideration of this play of qualities is in the work of anthropologist Mary Douglas, such as *Natural Symbols* and *Purity and Danger*. Theweleit takes up the image of the body as armor in relation to militarist culture in *Male Fantasies*. Theweleit, however, tends toward a pathologization of the ways in which identity is constructed through the establishment of bodily limits.

9. I'm referring here to Freud's essay "On Narcissism" (1914), in which narcissism is situated as part of human development rather than a property of a perverse few.

10. Male buddy relationships are crucial to the Hong Kong action film and have become more explicitly eroticized in some recent films such as *The Killer* (1989). See Chiao, "The Distinct Taiwanese" 163, for what she describes as a "macho/gay feel" to some recent Hong Kong films.

The distinction I'm seeking to draw here, though, is around the extent to which recent Western films quite obsessively center on relationships between men.

11. Jeffords interestingly uses the term "remasculinization" in the context of recent representations around Vietnam. See her *The Remasculinization of America*.

12. Though he doesn't discuss China in an extensive way, Said's *Orientalism* is a crucial point of reference here. Bhabha's writings on colonial discourse develop these points within a psychoanalytic framework. See his "Of Mimicry and Man: The Ambivalence of Colonial Discourse" and "Sly Civility."

13. Jackie Chan was also called on to play a Japanese character in the *Cannonball Run* films, part of an early attempt to break into Western markets. Brandon Lee seems aware that his father's name has given him an access to the American industry denied to other Chinese actors. The publicity machine seems determined to push this line, dubbing him "Son of the Dragon." See, for example, "Interview with Brandon Lee." Since this essay was originally written, Brandon Lee died in unusual circumstances and we have seen the much hyped release of his last film, finished with the help of computer technology. The turn to be taken by media mythology around his death remains to be seen.

14. Bhabha's writings (see note 12) are relevant here in terms of the processes of failed identification at work in the complex fantasies of mastery that structure colonial discourse.

15. Mercer offers an interesting discussion of Michael Jackson's changing image in this context in his "The Boy Who Fell to Earth" 34–35.

16. The film was *The Big Brawl* (1980), which Clouse directed. This is not to suggest that Chan is somehow a more "subversive" figure than Lee. Rather that the two emerged from very different historical moments.

References

Bhabha, Homi K. "Of Mimicry and Man: The Ambivalence of Colonial Discourse," *October* 28 (Spring 1984): 125–33.

———. "Sly Civility." *October* 34 (1985): 71–80.

Butler, Judith. *Gender Trouble: Feminism and the Subversion of Identity*. New York: Routledge. 1990.

Cheung, King-kok. "The Woman Warrior versus the Chinaman Pacific: Must a Chinese American Critic Choose between Feminism and Heroism?" *Conflicts in Feminism*. Eds. Marianne Hirsch and Evelyn Fox Keller. New York: Routledge, 1990. 234–51.

Chiao Hsiung-Ping. "Bruce Lee: His Influence on the Evolution of the Kung Fu Genre." *Journal of Popular Film and Television* 9.1 (1981) 30–42.

———. "The District Taiwanese and Hong Kong Cinemas." *Perspectives on Chinese Cinema*. Ed. Chris Berry. London: BFI, 1991. 155–65.

Douglas, Mary. *Natural Symbols*. Harmondsworth: Penguin, 1973.

Fanon, Frantz. *The Wretched of the Earth*. 1961. Trans. Constance Farrington. Harmondsworth: Penguin, 1967.

Flanigan, B. P. "Kung Fu Crazy, or The Invasion of the 'Chop Suey Easterns.'" *Cineaste* 15.3 (1974).

Freud, Sigmund. "On Narcissism." *The Standard Edition of the Complete Psychological Works of Sigmund Freud*. Ed. James Strachey. 24 vols. London: Hogorth, 1953–1974. 14: 69–102.

Fung, Richard. "Looking for My Penis: The Eroticized Asian in Gay Video Porn." *How Do I Look?: Queer Film and Video*. Ed. Bad Object-Choices. Seattle: Bay, 1991. 145–60.

Glaessner, Verina. *Kung Fu: Cinema of Vengeance*. London: Lorrimar, 1974.

Jeffords, Susan. *Hard Bodies: Hollywood Masculinity in the Reagan Era*. New Brunswick, N.J.: Rutgers UP, 1994.

Kaminsky, Stuart M. "Kung Fu Film as Ghetto Myth." *Journal of Popular Film* 3 (1974): 129–38.

Kingston, Maxine Hong. *China Men*. London: Picador, 1981.

———. *The Woman Warrior*. London: Picador, 1977.

Low, Gail Ching-Liang. "White Skin/Black Masks: The Pleasures and Politics of Imperialism." *New Formations* 9 (Winter 1989): 83–103.

Mercer, Kobena. "The Boy Who Fell to Earth." *Marxism Today* (July 1988).

Rayns, Tony. "Entretien avec Jacky Chan." *Cahiers du cinema* (Sept. 1984).

Robins, David, and Philip Cohen. *Knuckle Sandwich: Growing Up in the Working-Class City*. Harmondsworth: Penguin, 1978.

Theweleit, Klaus. *Male Fantasies*. Trans. Erica Carter, Chris Turner, and Stephen Conway. 2 vols. 1977, 1978. Minneapolis: U of Minnesota P. 1987, 1989.

Walkerdine, Valerie. "Video Replay: Families, Films, and Fantasy." *Formations of Fantasy*. Eds. Victor Burgin, James Donald, and Cora Kaplan. London: Methuen, 1986. 167–89.

36.
LETTING THE BOYS BE BOYS

Talk Radio, Male Hysteria, and Political Discourse in the 1980s

Susan J. Douglas

"Listening to [Howard] Stern," wrote *Boston Globe* columnist Mike Barnicle in 1994, "is the electronic equivalent of loitering in the men's room of a bus terminal."[1] Apparently, despite such slurs, this was a place a lot of listeners wanted to go. Why was this, for some, such an appealing destination in the 1980s and '90s? Howard Stern, Don Imus, and Rush Limbaugh, as well as other local talk jocks, revitalized radio beginning in the mid-1980s, soaring to the top of the ratings during morning drive time or, with Limbaugh, taking a time slot thought hopeless and turning it into a gold mine. Most of the commentary about talk radio, whether journalistic or scholarly, has focused on two things: its rudeness (the threat it posed to civility) and its unrepresentative amplification of right-wing politics (the threat it posed to democracy).

But what is obvious, and yet much less frequently discussed, is talk radio's central role in efforts to restore masculine prerogatives to where they were before the women's movement. After all, over 80% of the hosts, and a majority of the listeners, particularly to political talk radio, are male.[2] Talk radio is as much—maybe even more—about gender politics at the end of the century than it is about party politics. There were different masculinities enacted on radio, from Howard Stern to Rush Limbaugh, but they were all about challenging and overthrowing, if possible, that most revolutionary of social movements, feminism. They were also about challenging buttoned-down, upper-middle-class, corporate versions of masculinity that excluded many men from access to power. The "men's movement" of the 1980s found its outlet—and that was talk radio. In

this essay I'd like to provide a brief overview of the rise of talk radio and consider how the recuperation of certain types of masculinities played a central role in the genre's success and in the ongoing American debate about what is and is not our "national identity." And I'd like to suggest that a new gender hybrid, the male hysteric, emerged on talk radio as a deft if sometimes desperate fusion of the desire to thwart feminism with the reality of having to live with and accommodate to it.

Talk radio began to make national headlines in the mid-1980s, when Howard Stern gained increasing notoriety and earned the moniker "shock jock," and Alan Berg, an especially combative talk show host in Denver, was murdered—presumably, it was thought, by one of his infuriated listeners. More headlines came in 1989, when a coalition of approximately thirty talk show hosts coordinated a major attack on a proposed 51% congressional pay increase that then Speaker of the House Jim Wright planned to push through without a floor vote.[3]

The number of radio stations with all talk or a combined news and talk format quadrupled in ten years, from approximately 200 in the early 1980s to more than 850 in 1994.[4] As music programmers and listeners evacuated the AM dial in favor of FM in the 1970s, previously thriving, profitable stations were faced with a crisis. Some tried the all-news format while others clung to music, but by 1980 the talk format—whether the host was a sexologist dispensing advice or a political consultant fielding calls—was proving to be a solution to AM's abandonment. Talk radio didn't require stereo or FM fidelity, and it was unpredictable, incendiary and participatory. By the mid-1990s talk radio was one of the most popular formats on the air, second only to country music.[5] Talk radio—and its particular version of radio populism—had arrived.

Like some of the most successful popular culture—one thinks of P.T. Barnum's early "museums," or *National Geographic*, or *60 Minutes*—talk radio entertained and educated, fused learning with fun, allowed people to be titillated and informed, and encouraged them to be good citizens and unruly rebels, all at the same time.

Station managers also discovered that talk show audiences were extremely loyal—once they listened and liked what they heard, many got hooked. In fact, stations discovered that some advertisers were willing to pay twice as much to reach the talk radio audience because of what was called its "foreground" aspects—people didn't use it for background noise, like they sometimes did with a music format.

Satellite technology, first used in radio broadcasting by NPR in 1978, also allowed some stations to maximize profits by distributing their shows nationally. In comparison to the old method of relaying shows from one station to another using telephone lines, satellite technology provided a much cheaper and technically superior method of transmitting a local broadcast nationally. With satellites, managers could chose what they wanted to broadcast and when from a variety of options, and all for less money than land lines. While stations downlinked one event or program to air, they could also record another program to air at a later time. Satellite technology would come to be Larry King's, Rush Limbaugh's, and Howard Stern's best friend.

Another invention that especially fueled the popularity of call-in talk radio, and shifted the demographics of the audience, was the cell phone. Virtually unheard of as a car accessory in the mid-1980s, the sales of cell phones exploded between 1989 and 1992. During that period the number of subscribers to cell phone services increased by 215%; by 1993 there were twelve million cellular phones in use, with ten thousand new subscribers signing up each day; by 1995 there were thirty-three million subscribers.[6] And one of the things they did, as they drove to and from work or in between meetings, was call in to radio talk shows.

By 1984 *Time* was able to feature a major story on the talk show format, titled "Audiences Love to Hate Them." There was a new dynamic here, one that had been developing since at least the late 1960s, in which certain radio shows sought to rile up their audiences, following the notion that fury equals—and begets—attention, and thus profits. Unlike TV in the 1950s and early 1960s, which sought to avoid controversy so as not to alienate its audiences, talk radio pursued controversy and, again in total contradiction to the earlier years, used this as a selling point to advertisers looking for loyal, large, engaged audiences. In other words, controversy and marketability were joined, so that talk radio developed a "financial dependence on sensation."[7] By 1995, one general manager of a talk radio station was able to give the following explanation for why conservative hosts dominated the air: Liberals "are genetically engineered to not offend anybody. People who go on the air afraid of offending are not inherently entertaining."[8]

Talk radio spoke to a profound sense of public exclusion from and increasing disgust with the mainstream media in general and TV news in particular. It became an electronic surrogate for the public sphere, where people imagined their grandparents—even their parents, for that matter—might have gathered with others to chat, however briefly, about the state of the town, the country, the world.

Talk radio tapped into the sense of loss of public life, the isolation that came from overwork and the privatization of American life, and the huge gap people felt between themselves and those who run the country. Talk radio was also a reaction against changes in the network news and the newsmagazines in the 1980s when news staffs were cut, stories became shorter, the sound bites allowed even presidential candidates shrank to about nine seconds, and in-depth reporting was eclipsed by celebrity journalism. Talk radio represented a new, sometimes brashly assertive way of constructing a sense of special group identity within the homogenizing onslaught of mainstream media fare.[9] Remember too that by the 1980s, much of FM, once so vibrant and experimental, had been sliced up into predictable, homogenized formats that offered little surprise and no interaction.[10]

The talk on political talk radio, as well as the talk about talk radio, was, from the start, decidedly macho and loud. The imaginary audience, the one most hosts seemed to speak to, was male. And what these hosts and their audiences did was assert that talking over the phone, talking about your feelings and experiences, talking in often emotional registers was no longer the province of women. These guys were going to take America's traditional assumptions of associating talk, or "chatter," with women and throw that stereotype out the window.[11] In fact, despite the plethora of talk show shrinks and sexologists, by the 1980s it was the male culture of political talk radio that had become noteworthy. Some hosts were promoted simply and proudly with the moniker "radio's bad boy."

Characterizing most talk show hosts' abrasive style as "a verbal adjunct to street fighting," *Time* acknowledged that their success stemmed, in part, from the fact that "the decade's mood has become more aggressive."[12] Talk radio hosts helped build imagined communities that made quite clear who was included and who was excluded. The guy nobody wanted was the new male pariah of the 1980s, the wimp.[13] No yes-men, mama's boys here, beaten-down types who obeyed too eagerly, who had responded too sympathetically to the civil rights or the women's movement. Hosts insulted and yelled at listeners like abusive fathers, and tough callers knew how to take it. In fact, talk radio proved to be a decidedly white male preserve in a decade when it became much more permissible to lash out at women, minorities, gays, lesbians, and the poor—the very people who had challenged the authority and privileges of men, of white people, of the rich and powerful, and of heterosexuals, in the 1960s and 1970s. Now it was payback time.

As Susan Jeffords, Yvonne Tasker, and Michael Kimmel, among others, have noted, the late 1970s was a period of greatly heightened anxiety about manhood in America.[14] Indeed, one could argue that this was a true moment of crisis for masculinity. Feminists had made gender politics front-page news, and they had demonstrated how patriarchy undermined and threatened core American values, particularly democracy and equality of opportunity for all. At the same time a panic, it seems, about the legitimacy of America's patriarchal power structure took hold as the country watched one president resign in disgrace, another continually tripping, stumbling, and hitting people in the head with out-of-control golf balls, and

a third stand by helplessly as Americans were held hostage by a "third-rate" military power. All of the presidents of the 1970s had lost control, and control and mastery are central to most conceptions of true manhood. And manhood is central to conceptions of American national identity. A new term—the "Vietnam syndrome"—characterized American reluctance to engage in military action, as if this were an ailment or disease. Flaccid men had made for a flaccid foreign policy, according to Richard Nixon and other conservative critics.

Ronald Reagan, through his rhetoric, policies, and appearance, sought to change all that. Screw feminist politics and getting in touch with your feminine side, said the Reagan presidency. All that had done was to make the country vulnerable, flaccid, and weak. It was time to reassert male supremacy. As if in response, Hollywood in the 1980s pumped out high-action, bloated-budget beef-cake movies in which Sylvester Stallone, Arnold Schwarzenegger, Bruce Willis, and others used their tough, muscled bodies to remasculinize America's self-image, which played all too well into Reagan's efforts to pump a great deal of testosterone into American foreign policy, the fight against crime, and the "war on drugs."[15]

But Reagan and these "hard-body" movies had hardly resolved the issue. The 1988 presidential campaign was all about manhood, with George Bush and his handlers working round the clock to jettison his "wimp" image, and Michael Dukakis getting pilloried in the press for looking like a little boy instead of a real man as he rode around in a tank wearing an oversized helmet. Wall Street insiders revealed that men with power were referred to as "big swinging dicks." The fear that American men weren't "real men" anymore, and a determination on the part of many men to abandon certain traditional masculine behaviors and roles, coexisted with an insistence that some men were never going to respond to the women's movement, period.

There were also genuine anxieties about and frustration with what came to be called "political correctness." For women and people of color, sexism and racism had assumed both overt and subtle forms. Many men thought they were being genial when they kept telling a woman she looked nice or persisted in calling her "honey"—why were these women so sensitive all of a sudden? And just when white people thought that *black* was perfectly acceptable, they learned they should use the term *African-American*—not *Afro-American*—or *people of color*. Diversity training and sexual harassment workshops became de rigueur in many workplaces. So many white men came to feel that they were walking on eggshells, that they didn't know what was right and wrong to say anymore, that they wanted a place where they could exhale. Talk radio gave them that refuge. As one talk show host put it, "[T]oday, you have to hyphenate everything. People have no sense of humor. Talk radio allows people to break away from that. As a host I can be like grandpa—you know, 'there goes grandpa again'—I can say anything."[16]

On talk radio, the trend was the same as in many mainstream films—to take over public discourse, purge it of conciliatory, bland, or feminine tendencies, and reclaim it for men. But not men such as Peter Jennings, Dan Rather, or Tom Brokaw, well-groomed, decorous, polite types who told us the news without any passion and who, by their very demeanor, embodied goody-two-shoes men with money and influence who had probably, in their youth, been president of the student council or captain of the debating team.

No, the masculinity on talk radio was different, over the years, fusing some working-class politics and sensibilities with the language and attitude of the locker room. There were clear exceptions to this—the suave, urbane Michael Jackson in Los Angeles, and Larry King, who by 1984 was reaching 3.5 million listeners nationally with his interview show. But Don Imus, Bob Grant, Howard Stern, and their many imitators would become famous for their verbal dueling and for assuming the persona of a horny, insubordinate twelve-year-old boy. At first, growing out of the bitterness of political and economic alienation of the late 1970s and 1980s, some talk radio—especially the version offered by Stern and Imus—was a rebellion against civilization itself, against bourgeois codes of decorum that have sought, especially, to silence and tame the iconoclastic, delinquent, and defiant impulses in which adolescent boys especially seem to revel and delight. Here the transgressions of the unreconstructed class troublemaker were packaged up and sold to an audience of eager buyers. But Imus and Stern were not just mindlessly celebrating pubescent anarchy for its own sake, although certainly at

times it seemed that way. They, and Limbaugh, spoke to many men on the wrong end of power relations, men excluded from the upper levels of America's social hierarchies where restraint, rationality, good taste, good manners, and deference marked who was allowed in. They insisted there was a place—an important place—for disobedience, hedonism, disrespect, bad taste, and emotionalism.

In *Talk Radio and the American Dream*, the only book on those early years of the format, Murray Levin describes talk radio as "the province of proletariat discontent, the only mass medium easily available to the underclass."[17] Focusing on two political talk shows in New England between 1977 and 1982, including the highly successful *Jerry Williams Show*, Levin found that callers felt themselves to be quite marginalized from media versions of the political mainstream, deeply distrustful of political and business institutions, and profoundly anxious about the collapse of community and civility.

Levin cites pollster Daniel Yankelovich, who documented various manifestations of Americans' escalating mistrust of a range of national institutions. "Trust in government," he reported in the late 1970s, "declined dramatically from almost 80% in the late 1950s to about 33% in 1976. Confidence in business fell from approximately a 70% level in the late '60s to about 15% today." The press, the military, and elite professionals such as doctors and lawyers all suffered a similar sharp drop in trust, according to the polls. More to the point, noted Yankelovich, "[a] two-thirds majority felt that what they think 'really doesn't count.'"[18]

It was lower-middle-class and working-class men especially. Levin reports, who eagerly sought an outlet, a platform, for what they thought. And call-in talk radio shows, beginning in the late 1970s, provided access to such a podium, while also keeping the caller invisible and preserving his or her anonymity. While television news and talk shows such as *Inside Washington* and *This Week with David Brinkley* favored as commentators, experts, and guests those who were well spoken, well educated, influential, or famous, the radio version invited those with poor grammar, polyester clothes, bad haircuts, and only a high school education to hold forth on national and local affairs. Levin argued that the absence of those stiff protocols that delimited and restrained a commentator's performance on television was key to talk radio's spontaneity and informality, which in turn were key to the format's appeal.[19] We should also note that talk radio didn't require codified, elite ways of speaking. Those not savvy in official-speak were welcome, even urged to call in, at least, in the early days. Of course, such callers also helped to make the host appear more knowledgeable, more in command, more deserving of controlling the mike.

Levin taped seven hundred hours of talk radio and found among callers a discourse "preoccupied with emasculation." The proper order of things now seemed inverted, upside down, so that crime, blacks, rich corporations, women, and inept bureaucracies all had the upper hand.[20] The Iranian hostage crisis—and Jimmy Carter's failed efforts to overcome it—further exacerbated a sense that America had become weak, could be bullied, and was being compromised by soft-spoken New Age guys. As with the linguistic slapstick of 1930s radio comedy, the "verbal martial arts," as Levin puts it, assumed center stage here too. Talk radio was a linguistic battleground, and few callers had the skills, or position of authority, to deflect the verbal salvos and put-downs of the host. Yet they kept coming back for more.

It was the participatory ethos of talk radio, its suggestion that it would reverse years of the ongoing consolidation and centralization of power—especially in Washington—that was central to its appeal. The great irony is that his very kind of talk radio, with its new macho populism, was the product of government deregulation, merger mania, and corporate consolidation during the 1980s and beyond. Populism and participation were the public faces of radio; they masked increased economic concentration and heightened barriers to entry for all but the very rich in the industry itself. But then again, that was the Reagan administration's great genius—selling the increased concentration of wealth as a move back toward democracy.

Mark Fowler's FCC championed the deregulation of radio in the 1980s, allowing companies to own greater numbers of stations, and eliminating restrictions on how long a company had to hang onto a station before turning around and reselling it for a higher price. The other significant deregulatory move in the 1980s was the abandonment of the Fairness Doctrine, which the FCC announced in 1987 it would no longer enforce.[21] In practice the doctrine was meant to do two things: mandate that stations were required to cover controversial issues of public importance, and provide differing points of view about such issues.

Abandonment of the Fairness Doctrine means, in part, that a radio station can air Rush Limbaugh followed by G. Gordon Liddy and is not required then to air a liberal talk show or to bring on anyone who might challenge or correct these guys; assertions. It was this powerful constellation of forces in the 1980s—satellite technology, deregulation, and a sense among many Americans, and especially many men, that they were not being addressed or listened to by the mainstream media—that propelled the new genre, talk radio, into a national phenomenon and a national political force. By 1992 the talk radio format claimed 875 stations nationally, up from 2.38 in 1987.

The 1989 fax attacks on the proposed congressional pay raises alerted those out of the talk radio loop that something was afoot, but it was the 1992 presidential campaign and the torpedoing of Zoë Baird's nomination for attorney general that made talk radio, and Rush Limbaugh in particular, national, frontpage news. Ross Perot launched his presidential campaign on talk radio and TV, and Bill Clinton, eager to circumvent the mainstream press after reporters put him on the spot for his alleged affair with Gennifer Flowers, sought out radio and TV talk show hosts. Some listeners, already alienated by the network news, were turning increasingly to talk radio and political talk TV to get more thorough discussion of the issues. And in 1992 they were not to be disappointed. One study showed that television talk shows often featured three times as much substantive coverage of the issues themselves than did the network news.[22] Poll respondents said they felt they learned things about the candidates from talk radio during the 1992 campaign that they didn't learn elsewhere.

Limbaugh became the poster boy for all of political talk radio. He boasted that in 1994 alone there were 4,635 stories written about him.[23] Although his political influence was no doubt exaggerated, he raised fears that a conservative, activist minority was circumventing representative government, undermining the role of objectivity in the press, and imposing the will of an unrepresentative minority on public policy. While acknowledging that talk radio was "a needed jolt to sclerotic Washington," *Newsweek* also cautioned that "it raises the specter of government by feverish plebiscite—an entertaining, manipulable and trivializing process that could eat away at the essence of representative democracy."[24] As *Time* put it in 1989, "the current radio activism . . . has elements of a *Meet John Doe* nightmare."[25] In part, of course, this was a potential nightmare for *Time* itself, and for newspapers and the networks news, all of whom were experiencing a decline in their audiences. Talk radio was a new, sexy competitor—for people's attention, for political influence, and for advertising dollars. And media coverage of talk radio, which more often than not was alarmist and negative, reflected these anxieties. In the aftermath of the Zoe Baird debacle, *Newsweek* did a cover story titled "The Power of Talk." The blaring headlines were superimposed over a huge, open, angry, yelling mouth that took up the entire cover.[26]

Much of the debate about the possible pernicious influences of talk radio stemmed from this very real threat that the new genre posed to its more established rivals. But the debate also reflected pronounced concerns about a decline of "civility" and the collapse of "civil discourse." These are debates about the public sphere, about how to reconstruct one, and about just *whose* public sphere it's going to be anyway, the educated bourgeoisie's or the rabble rousers'.

What was being threatened, especially from the academic and journalistic point of view, were middle-class, elite notions about the public sphere and citizenship, as well as established notions about journalism, commentary, experts, and who gets to be a source. These were hardly frivolous concerns, given that G. Gordon Liddy advocated the killing of federal agents, Ken Hamblin referred to James Brady as "that cripple," J. Paul Emerson of KSFO announced that he "hated the Japs," and Bob Grant called African Americans "sub-humanoids, savages."[27] Nor were journalists, who were compelled to fact-check everything, sanguine about many of these hosts offering their own, often misinformed opinion as fact, or about allowing callers to start a panic about cellular phones causing cancer.

But many in the talk show business felt that the more outrageous types—Liddy, Stern, and Grant—were singled out to stand for all talk show hosts in a way that was alarmist about the entire genre. "There is much more diversity than the stereotypes suggest," insisted industry analyst Jim Casale, adding that "we've been demonized."[28] Talk show host Mark Williams also felt that the attention given to talk radio was "all out of proportion to its influence."[29] This was part of the ongoing battle in America over control of public discourse, a battle that has always been based on class, gender, and racial antagonisms. Talk show hosts were not just storming the media citadel; they were thumbing their noses at bourgeois conventions about political debate, public dialogue, and who deserves access to the soapbox.

No discussion of talk radio can proceed without considering the meteoric rise of Howard Stern and his archrival Don Imus, both of whom worked for Infinity Broadcasting and each of whom claimed five million listeners by the mid-1990s.[30] Stern's revisionist and, in the end, cowardly movie *Private Parts* sought to whitewash the depth of his racist, sexist, and vulgar remarks throughout his tenure on the air—his voiceover in the film kept claiming, "Everything I do is misunderstood"—but it was these very transgressions that made him a millionaire. So did his celebration of locker room masculinity, bullying yet self-deprecating, working-class yet college-educated, quintessentially adolescent yet adult. The Stern of *Private Parts* was a mensch, like Woody Allen before Soon-Yi, who bemoaned the fact that he was "hung like a three-year-old," threw up after he was forced to fire someone, and only wanted to be loved by the public; his main targets were pigheaded and autocratic broadcasting executives. The Stern on the air, however, was something else.

He was perfect for the Reagan years. The Reagan administration, with its attacks on affirmative action, "welfare queens," "bleeding heart" liberal politics, and abortion, and its celebration of greed, often used coded terms and laden symbols to give Americans permission to be selfish, sexist, racist, uncharitable. There was nothing coded about Stern, with the possible exception of his flowing-over-the-shoulders hair. Buoyed up by this political climate, he took the gloves off and articulated in explicit terms what this new backlash politics was all about. His deejay persona as a shock jock emerged on WWDC-FM in Washington, DC, in 1981, and tripled the station s morning drive-time audience. He then went to WNBC-AM in New

York and got fired three years into the job, presumably because of routines such as "Bestiality Dial-a-Date." Infinity's WXRK, known as K-Rock, quickly hired him for the morning slot, and his show soon zoomed to number one (beating out Imus, also on in New York at the same time).

In 1990 he signed a five-year contract, with Infinity reportedly worth $10 million, and by 1992 he was heard in ten cities around the country.[31] He was the first local deejay to have a national drive-time audience, thanks to the marvels of satellite technology. His core audience was white, often working-class men ages eighteen to thirty-four,[32] but he also attracted others, including women, and many listeners had a love-hate relationship with him. His draw was that each day you never knew which taboos he would violate next, what scandal he might commit.

How far would he go today? Would it be farther than yesterday? Stern was a linguistic stripper, teasing his audience that maybe today, maybe tomorrow, he would really take it all off, although it was often hard to imagine what boundaries there were left to violate. He was also often very funny—not, to my mind, when he was humiliating women, people with disabilities, and blacks, although clearly others found this hilarious, but when he took on celebrities he thought were arrogant, hypocritical, or both. People with real distaste for many of Stern's routines adored his skewering of Kathie Lee Gifford, Bryant Gumbel, and Tom Hanks's bathetic acceptance speech when he won the Oscar for *Philadelphia*. Stern's populism emerged especially when he ridiculed the self-importance and mediocrity of a celebrity culture that the rest of the media profited from, promoted, and took all too seriously. With celebrity journalism spreading like anthrax and the Hollywood publicity juggernauts ramming through all the media, Stern just said no. This was the antithesis of the TV talk show host who had to suck up to celebrities who were pushing their latest "projects." Stern gleefully flattened these hierarchies and exposed them as arbitrary, ridiculous, and often utterly without justification.

Stern's on-air persona was that of the class troublemaker—and often the bully—in seventh grade, the guy who made fart noises during study hall and tried to snap girls' bra straps in the cafeteria. He was obsessed with sex and was also relentlessly self-absorbed. One of the adjectives most frequently used to describe him was *pubescent*. This is telling in more than the obvious way. Because Stern assumed different identities at different times—one minute the insecure, almost feminized boy, the next minute the mouthy, arrogant stud—he enacted those swings between masculine and feminine, confident and abject, that young men really experienced. While it's true that his commentary seemed aimed at twelve-year-old boys, this characterization also lets him off the hook. For the persona was also that of a grown man, and a deeply cynical one at that, who hated liberal politics and who insisted that unreconstructed white men get back on top. He was antigovernment and anti-immigrant, and said the L.A. police were right to beat Rodney King.[33] He combined adolescent humor about toilets, breasts, penises, passing gas, and jerking off with politically reactionary jokes that harked back to minstrel shows and burlesque. He was especially determined to defy the new, liberal sensibilities about race, gender, physical disabilities, and sexual preference that had emerged from the social movements of the 1960s and '70s. He was also determined to expose the hypocrisy of a culture that is often prudish and pornographic at exactly the same time.

This was a volatile and, it seems, deliberately incoherent combination of libertarian, liberal, and conservative sensibilities. He was pro-choice and, in what came to be one of his most oft-cited quips, suggested that any woman who voted for George Bush might as well mail her vagina to the White House. His defiance of all codes of decorum, his insistence that sex was something you talked about in the open, and that nothing and no one were sacred made him very hip, very 1980s. Yet in his on-air comments to female and African-American guests he alluded longingly back to the 1950s, when Jim Crow was still the law of the land and the objectification of women was both commonplace and celebrated. He told the Pointer sisters that he wished he could be their "Massa Howard." "The closest I came to making love to a black woman," he announced, "was masturbating to a picture of Aunt Jemima." On newscaster Connie Chung: "For an Oriental woman, she has big breasts."[34]

In other words, Stern embodied the edict "Question authority" and challenged convention, tradition, and bourgeois morality every chance he got. Yet the framework within which this occurred could not have been more utterly conventional, more conformist to deep-seated American attitudes and prejudices about men, women, people of color, and the order of things circa 1952. So Stern's listeners could be, vicariously, iconoclasts and traditionalists at the same time, totally hip yet stick-in-the-mud.

Stern was a brilliant Peter Pan. He created a space where men didn't have to overcome their socialization as boys—they didn't have to grow up and leave never-never land and go back to that stuffy old. Victorian nursery, at least not until the show was over. Moms and middle-class mores said that you had to learn how to be a gentleman, be polite to girls and deferential to superiors, learn how to make a living and become a responsible and civilized young man. Not on Stern's show you didn't.

The bridge person between Stern and Limbaugh was Don Imus, the real pioneer of the format. As early as 1971, when he was a deejay on WNBC in New York, Imus was offering irreverent, insulting humor in between Top 40 hits.[35] He became enormously successful, and *Life* magazine labeled him "the most outrageous disc jockey anywhere." But his alcoholism seriously hampered his work, and he was fired in 1977. He subsequently returned to WNBC but then became addicted to cocaine. It was not until 1988, after Imus had gone through a rehab program and got a new show on his old WNBC-AM station, now owned by Infinity and redubbed WFAN, that he began to be, again, a major figure in talk radio. Within three years *Imus in the Morning* was the third-ranked program among men between twenty and fifty-four, but he had more male listeners making over $100,000 than any other morning talk show.[36]

Imus has not escaped the adjective *juvenile*, and Dinitia Smith, writing for *New York* magazine, likened listening to *Imus in the Morning* to "being stuck in a classroom with a bunch of prepubescent boys while the teacher is out of the room. Imus lets the educated male who grew up in the sixties and was taught not to judge women simply by the size of their breasts to be, for one glorious moment of his day, an unreconstructed chauvinist pig."[37] Like Stern, nothing is sacred, and Imus's show was replete with the de rigueur breast and penis jokes, attacks on homosexuals and African Americans, and tasteless characterizations of women, especially

famous ones such as Madonna, who was referred to as a "two-legged yeast infection," and Monica Lewinsky, "the fat slut."[38] He is simultaneously infantile and autocratic, as one of his favorite things to do is ban somebody "for life" from appearing on the show.

But the difference between Imus and Stern was that Imus was more explicitly political. "Imus," notes media critic Howard Kurtz, "meshed eighth-grade locker-room jokes with fairly serious talk from pundits and politicians."[39] He featured commentary by Jeff Greenfield and Anna Quindlen, read and deconstructed items from the day's newspapers, and invited politicians on the show. He made national headlines when Bill Clinton, whom Imus had been trashing throughout the spring of 1992 as a "hick" and a "bubba," appeared on his show and charmed listeners—and, temporarily, Imus himself—by holding his own against Imus and quipping that "Bubba is just southern for 'mensch.'"[40] Imus expressed grudging admiration, and when Clinton won the New York State primary, some credited Imus's endorsement as helping push Clinton over the top. His stock as star maker went up. By the late 1990s Imus also was syndicated on over a hundred stations in cities around the country and could also be seen on MSNBC, reaching over ten million listeners.

In focus groups, Imus fans say they especially like his parodying of public figures, bringing them down from their pedestals and stripping them of their aura. As one man put it, "[H]e's not afraid to poke fun at people and poke hard," even with prominent political guests or media stars. This fan added, quite tellingly, that Imus in the morning "gets me going real good." He liked that Imus got his juices flowing first thing, that he knew, with every show, he would be jolted out of a politically and intellectually dulled state and made to think and laugh at the same time. Fans like this are sick of spin and news management, weary of the deferential constraints that bond journalists and politicians together in their staged minuets, and eager for a deflation of decorum and pretense. They want hierarchies flattened, and Imus gives this to them. They can't say whatever they feel like at work; Imus can. Most TV morning show hosts, and certainly late night talk show hosts, have to please and flatter their guests. Not Imus. The guest must entertain and inform *him* or be subject to his withering dismissals, and now that he has taken to plugging books that he likes, single-handedly creating best-sellers, guests with books to sell are only too eager to please. For many of his listeners, Imus turns the tables on money, power, and entitlement, where polite people in prestigious and influential jobs have to "suck up," as Imus puts it, to a man who breaks all the rule of bourgeois, upper-middle-class decorum.

Stern's and Imus's success as "shock jocks" raised alarm that now radio was cultivating the worst in its white male listeners by encouraging them to repudiate the achievements, however partial, won by women, people of color, gays and lesbians, and the disabled. But when the press itself, and much of the white male power structure in Washington, felt threatened by talk radio, this became a major story. And the man who made political talk radio a national concern, rightly or wrongly, was Rush Limbaugh. By the early 1990s all sorts of power was attributed to him, and he himself boasted that he was "the most dangerous man in America." When former congressman Vin Weber introduced Rush Limbaugh to freshmen Republicans in 1994, celebrating their takeover of Congress, he said, "Rush Limbaugh is really as responsible for what has happened as any individual in America."

Limbaugh was, to the early 1990s, what Father Coughlin was to the early 1930s: a radio orator who made many people feel that he gave voice to what they really felt but hadn't yet put into words. One fan especially liked Limbaugh because he "articulates things in a way they haven't been articulated before." Limbaugh "fills in the blanks." When conservatives hear Limbaugh, according to this listener, they say to themselves "Why can't I say it like that?" and "Yes, that's the way I feel."[41] While only somewhere between 6 and 9% percent of the population listens to him on a daily basis, this still amounted to, by 1992, the largest, audience in political talk radio, estimated at somewhere between twelve million and twenty million listeners. In 1992 Limbaugh was heard on 529 stations; three years later 660 stations aired his show. He earned $1.7 million a year.[42] And he had gone national only in 1988.

Limbaugh did the unprecedented: he gathered a large audience in the early afternoon, a slot thought to be dead compared to morning and evening drive time. And he succeeded in having a New York-based show go national. Some restaurants and bars opened "Rush rooms" so that his fans, who called themselves "dittoheads," could gather and listen together while having lunch.[43] Most of his listeners were white, and many had a higher income than the general population. Nearly 80% of those who listened often to Limbaugh expressed Republican sentiments; two-thirds identified themselves as conservative. They often expressed significantly greater interest in politics and public affairs than nonlisteners. For example, a whopping 90% of those who reported listening often to Limbaugh said they voted in the off-year elections of 1994. His listeners are more likely to talk about politics and to engage in political activities.[44] So even though Limbaugh may be preaching to the choir, the fact that this is an activist choir that can be mobilized to fax, write letters to Congress, and jam the White House switchboard gave him and his listeners considerable clout.

By 1990 Limbaugh had become a critically important opinion leader for many, who didn't necessarily have their positions changed by Limbaugh but who learned how to think about particular issues after listening to him.[45] His brilliance was in bringing humor and irreverence to what had been a pretty laced-up, overly serious form, conservative commentary. He was particularly skillful in his use of metaphors and had a talent for distilling issues down to their most simple elements. He delighted in conjuring up vivid mental images of environmentalists as wacko tree-huggers and feminists as combat-boot-wearing, goose-stepping "feminazis." He zoomed right into signifiers of class privilege. Academics, for example, were the "arts-and-croissant, wine-and-Brie crowd." He nicknamed the anchor of *CBS Nightly News* "Dan Blather." Clinton was "the Schlickmeister."

Another of Limbaugh's brilliant strokes was that his show provided an on-air political Elderhostel for those long out of the classroom who wanted and needed guidance in a media-saturated, spin-governed world. He labeled his show the "Institute for Advanced Conservative Studies" and addressed his listeners as if he sensed that they missed the act of being educated, of being privy to knowledge that others don't have. Limbaugh has been denounced for being a demagogue, but his real persona is that of pedagogue. He brought his listeners into a spectral lecture hall and helped them see themselves as part of a literate community where everyday people, and not just elites, must have knowledge, because knowledge is power. This wasn't a one-shot class; this was an ongoing seminar in which you didn't just learn isolated infobits but acquired a broader framework that constituted a worldview.

While, increasingly, the network news and the newsmagazines addressed their audiences as consumers, Limbaugh addressed his as citizens. Limbaugh read to his audience from the *New York Times* and the *Washington Post*, quoted from the network news, and juxtaposed these excerpts with hot-off-the-press faxes that he received from "inside" conservative sources who allegedly had the "real" truth. Limbaugh fans emphasize that his show "provides information you can't get anyplace else" and that he increases people's "political savvy."

Limbaugh was also deft at flattering his audience. He encouraged listeners to see themselves as competent media critics who could detect media bias, sensationalism, and superficiality. But at the same time they still needed a teacher. As he said in 1996, "I believe that the most effective way to persuade people is . . . to speak to them in a way that makes them think that they reached certain conclusions on their own."[46] Yet his caller screening practices gave preference to sycophants who offered very high teacher evaluations on the air. As Limbaugh told Howard Kurtz, "The purpose of a call is to make me look good."[47] Savvy callers knew it was important to play the courtier, and those who did usually didn't get dissed by Limbaugh. These flattering remarks, laid lovingly before Rush's feet, seemed to serve as "sacrificial offerings to win acceptance and entry" into the "discursive kingdom" presided over by the great professor.[48]

Of course, Limbaugh was a conservative activist, and it was his politics and their effect on national discourse—and national elections—that have received the most attention. But let's remember that his listeners were primarily male, with one study claiming that his core, diehard audience was as much as three-quarters male.[49] Another study reported that nearly one-third of all men listened to Limbaugh at least sometimes, compared to only 13% of all women. It wasn't necessarily true that women hated Limbaugh—although clearly many did—but they just didn't tune in.[50]

What did Limbaugh offer these men, in addition to an on-air Elderhostel and forum for conservative views? Limbaugh was a gender activist, an ideological soldier in the war to reassert patriarchy, to reclaim things as they "ought to be." He himself lamented the state of masculinity in the 1990s: "On the one hand, we want men who are sensitive and crying, like Alan Aldas, and then, after so much of that, women finally get tired of wimps and say, 'We want real men again!' O.K., so now we gotta change, we've got to go back to tough guys, we're not gonna take any shit. And our memories tell us, we go back to high school, look at who the girls went for—the assholes! The mean, dirty, greasy sons of bitches."[51] The ads on the show, for hair loss products, memory enhancers, and health care organizations that seek to prevent heart attacks, impart a worried subtext about emasculation that can, and must, be reversed.

But Limbaugh was more than a throwback. He personified a new kind of 1990s man, the antithesis of the allegedly New Age, sensitive, feminized kind of guy. Real men didn't eat quiche; they had a point of view and voiced it. Yet, interestingly, Limbaugh deftly *did* blend "feminine" traits into his persona, because he gave men permission to get passionate about politics. Here was a man who was emotionally unchecked—at times hysterical—yet simultaneously reasonable, combative, and avowedly anti-feminist.

To put it bluntly, Limbaugh was a male hysteric. So were other male talk show hosts. This was not the persona of the organization man who keeps his lip zipped, goes along with institutional idiocy because his boss says to, and keeps his own reactions in check. This is not some Dilbert forced to seethe in silence in his cubicle. No, this man got outraged, his naturally deep voice shooting up an octave as he denounced something he thought didn't make a lick of sense. Limbaugh, and many of his fellow hosts, attacked post-Vietnam, media, and corporate versions of masculinity; they attacked what Christopher Lasch had labeled in the late 1970s the narcissistic personality, the bureaucratic operator desperately dependent on the approval of others who learns how to wear a variety of amiable masks to get by.

There was no equivocation here, no "on one hand, on the other hand," no genial, get-along stance. Here real men had a point of view. Through their phone calls and faxes, their radio activism, they could still "ride to the rescue, and be saviors," as host

Mark Harrison put it.[52] They also had passion. Rush lost it on the air—not totally, not in a way that was out of control—but he was a man who became easily exasperated and said so. It was this delicately calibrated balance between letting go and holding on that staked out the male hysteric as not just a reasonable but enviable persona, a man more authentic, more in touch with the connection between his feelings and his ideas than circumscribed TV reporters or political spin doctors. Feminist-bashing is essential to Limbaugh—he frequently gives "feminist updates" on the movement's alleged idiocies. If masculinity has to be recuperated on a regular basis, especially for a guy who is a male hysteric, then it is crucial to combine feminist bashing with your own more emotionally varied (dare I say more "feminine") performances.

On talk radio in the 1980s and '90s, masculinity was constructed as a hybrid, a fusion of traditionally "male" and "female" trails. Boys were supposed to be boys, meaning white, heterosexual boys—horny, outspoken, brash, impolite, rude, combative—who regarded women as sex objects, people of color as inferiors, and disabled people as jokes. But whether these jocks had long flowing hair or got overly emotional on the air, they were also gender poachers, recuperating masculinity at the end of the century by infusing it with the need to chat, the need to confess insecurities, the need to be hysterical and overwrought about politics, the need to make the personal political. Masculinity had become too fake, too bland, too corporate, too manufactured, too much of a processed masquerade, they suggested—let the testosterone flow, and male authenticity will follow.

This discourse about masculinity was—and is—embedded in a deeply conservative political discourse about the nation's need for discipline, responsibility, strength, and "tough love." Liberal models for achieving social justice were wrong, these guys suggested, because they were coded as feminine: too nurturing, too compassionate, too weak. Since masculinity has, from the beginning, been a central component of America's identity as a nation, this particular fusion of gender and politics on talk radio was hardly inconsequential. Talk radio's attacks on Clinton as being, in part, too pussy-whipped and too soft, indecisive, and feminized played an important role in pushing Clinton further to the right and marginalizing feminist politics

in the 1980s and '90s. But under talk radio's working-Joe, regular-guy populism also lurked class antagonisms about which class of men deserved access to the mike. It was men who were facile with words, who were skilled at using words as weapons, whose linguistic one-upmanship got proved day in and day out who got to be the leaders. In other words, gender politics, in which all us guys are in it together against "them," loudly and brilliantly disguised the class politics that truly divided the men from the boys.

So it's not just that Stern, Limbaugh, and their ilk were and are vulgar loudmouths who coarsen public discourse. They and talk radio were major players in the ongoing national struggle about what America is and should be, which gender codes it should embody as a nation, and what the connection between gender politics and national politics should be. While it is essential that we keep taking Limbaugh on for his anti-feminist attacks, I hope you will feel free to use the term "male hysteric" when referring to Rush. Because as much as he deplores feminism, his politics and his carefully crafted gender-poaching persona would be nowhere without the second wave. It is this hybridization of gender, and what that means for national and international politics, that I hope will remain a central area of inquiry for American studies.

Notes

1. Mike Barnicle, "Allow Stern to Be Stupid," *Boston Globe*, 13 Jan. 1994: 25.
2. Kurtz, *Hot Air* 259.
3. Wayne Munson, *All Talk*, 93.
4. "Talk Show Democracy," CQ Researcher, 29 Apr. 1994: 375.
5. Howard Kurtz, *Hot Air: All Talk, All the Time* (New York: Times Books, 1996), 257.
6. *Statistical Abstracts of the United States: 1996* (Washington: U.S. Bureau of the Census, 1996), 565.
7. Munson 42.
8. Richard Corliss, "Look Who's Talking," 24.
9. Chaney 100.
10. Michael Harrison, interview, 20 June 1997.
11. Munson 114.
12. "Audiences Love to Hate Them," *Time*, 9 July 1984: 80–81.
13. Michael Kimmel, *Manhood in America* (New York: Free, 1996), 294.
14. Kimmel, *Manhood in America*; Susan Jeffords, *Hard*

Bodies: Masculinity in the Reagan Era (New Brunswick: Rutgers UP 1993)

15. See Jeffords, *Hard Bodies*.
16. Mark Williams, interview, 20 June 1997.
17. Murray Levin, *Talk Radio and the American Dream* (New York: Lexington, 1987) xiii.
18. Cited in Levin, 4–5.
19. Levin 16.
20. Levin 27, 147.
21. For a detailed discussion see Patricia Aufderheide, "After the Fairness Doctrine: Controversial Broadcast Programming and the Public Interest," *Journal of Communication* 40, (1990): 47–72.
22. "Talk Show Democracy," *CQ Researcher*, 29 Apr. 1994: 364.
23. Margaret Carlson, "My Dinner with Rush," *Time* 23 Jan. 1995: 26.
24. Howard Fineman, "The Power of Talk," *Newsweek* 8 Feb. 1993: 25.
25. Richard Zoglin, "Bugle Boys of the Airwaves," *Time* 15 May 1989: 88.
26. "The Power of Talk Radio," *Newsweek* 8 Feb. 1993.
27. Corliss, "Look Who's Talking," 22–24.
28. Interview, Jim Casale, 21 June 1997.
29. Interview, Mark Williams, 20 June 1997.
30. Richard Turner, "An Ear for the CBS Eye," 59.
31. Jeanie Kasindorf, "Bad Mouth," *New York Magazine*, 23 Nov. 1992: 43.
32. Kurtz, *Hot Air* 274.
33. Kurtz, *Hot Air* 274.
34. Cited in Kasindorf, "Bad Mouth,"; Richard Zoglin, "Shock Jock," *Time*, 30 Nov. 1992, 72–73; Kurtz, 275.
35. Biographical material on Imus from Dinitia Smith, "Morning Mouth," *New York Magazine*, 24 June 1991: 28–35; and Kurtz, *Hoi Air* 278–83.
36. Dinitia Smith, "Morning Mouth," 30.
37. Dinitia Smith, "Morning Mouth," 30.
38. Smith, "Morning Mouth," 31; Ken Auletta, "The Don," *The New Yorker*, 25 May 1998: 59.
39. Kurtz, *Hot Air.* 283.
40. "Sacred and Profane," *The New Yorker*, 21 Dec. 1992: 47.
41. Marsh Center Focus Groups, 28 Jan. 1997.
42. Peter J. Boyer, "Bull Rush," *Vanity Fair*, May 1992, 205.
43. Boyer, 206.
44. Knight and Barker, 10–11.
45. Knight and Barker, 12, 14, 15–16.
46. Cited in Knight and Barker, 3.
47. Kurtz, *Hot Air.*
48. Paddy Scannell, 129.
49. Knight and Barker, 10.
50. Knight and Barker, 10.
51. Cited in Boyer, "Bull Rush," 208.
52. Interview, Mark Harrison, 20 June 1997.

Bibliography

"Audiences Love to Hate Them," *Time*, 9 July 1984: 80–81.
Aufderheide, Patricia. "After the Fairness Doctrine: Controversial Broadcast Programming and the Public Interest," *Journal of Communication* 40 (1990): 47–72.
Auletta, Ken. "The Don," *The New Yorker* 25 May 25, 1998: 59.
Barnicle, Mike. "Allow Stern to be Stupid," *Boston Globe* 13 Jan. 1994: 25.
Boyer, Peter J. "Bull Rush," *Vanity Fair*, May 1992: 159.
Carlson, Margaret. "My Dinner with Rush," *Time* 23 Jan. 1995: 26.
Chaney, David C. *The Cultural Turn: Scene-Setting Essays on Contemporary Cultural Theory.* New York: Routledge, 1994.
Corliss, Richard. "Look Who's Talking," *Time* 23 Jan. 1995: 24.
Fineman, Howard. "The Power of Talk," *Newsweek* 8 Feb. 1993: 25.
Jeffords, Susan. *Hard Bodies: Masculinity in the Reagan Era.* New Brunswick, NJ: Rutgers University Press, 1993.
Kasindorf, Jeanie. "Bad Mouth," *New York Magazine* 23 Nov. 1992: 43.
Kimmel, Michael. *Manhood in America*, New York: Free, 1996.
Knight, Kathleen, and David Barker. "'Talk Radio Turns the Tide'?: The Limbaugh Effect: 1993–1995," unpub. ms., 1996.
Kurtz, Howard. *Hot Air: All Talk, All the Time.* New York: Times Books, 1996.
Levin, Murray. *Talk Radio and the American Dream.* New York: Lexington Books, 1987.
Munson, Wayne. *All Talk: The Talkshow in Media Culture.* Philadelphia: Temple UP, 1993.
"Sacred and Profane," *The New Yorker* 21 Dec. 1992: 47.
Scannell, Paddy. *Radio, Television and Modern Life.* Cambridge, MA: Blackwell, 1996.
Smith, Dinitia. "Morning Mouth," *New York Magazine* 24 June 1991: 28–35.
Statistical Abstracts of the United States: 1996. Washington: U.S. Bureau of the Census, 1996.
"Talk Show Democracy," *CQ Researcher* 29 Apr. 1994: 375.
Turner, Richard. "An Ear for the CBS Eye," *Newsweek* 16 Dec. 1996: 58–59.
Zoghn, Richard. "Bugle Boys of the Airwaves," *Time* 15 May 1989: 88.
———. "Shock Jock," *Time* 30 Nov. 1992: 72–73.

37.
WADDAYA LOOKIN' AT?

Re-reading the Gangster Genre Through The Sopranos

Martha P. Nochimson

The beast in me is caged by frail and fragile
    bands,
Restless by day and by night rants and rages at
    the stars
God help the beast in me.

           (Nick Lowe, "The Beast in Me")

Perceived as hypermasculine fare, the gangster picture is generally understood to be popular because of its explosive virility and its close connection to reality. Yet despite these entrenched truisms, hindsight and the progeny that have been spawned by the early masterpieces of the genre suggest that the situation is more complex. An extended narrative of the world of fin-de-siècle New Jersey mob boss Tony Soprano (James Gandolfini), "The Sopranos" reveals the media gangster as the core of a highly emotional mode of storytelling in which the pleasures of action and violence exist to speak not only about macho aggressiveness "ripped from today's headlines," but also about vulnerabilities that the display disguises and about troubling cultural conditions. "The Sopranos," David Chase's HBO series, is clearly an elegiac, self-conscious, tragicomic meditation on America's lost innocence, but less obviously it is also about the otherness of body and family to American corporate culture, and, above all, it is about the undying connections human beings have to one another despite a social system that maintains its hold through a divide-and-conquer strategy. In this, "The Sopranos" may seem to be an inversion of generic traditions, but, in fact, it grows from elements in this species

of media representation that have been simmering since its inception.

In order to explore "The Sopranos" as the unmasking of the heretofore thickly disguised emotional subtext of gangster stories, I will invoke a very precise, exclusive rather than inclusive definition of this category of entertainment. In so doing, I take a distinctly different approach from that of both casual public discourse and almost all serious scholarly discussion to date, which has conflated the gangster narrative with many other kinds of crime stories as part of one amorphous genre.

This discussion of the gangster project will read it as a subgenre of the media crime story set apart by three essential characteristics. First, in the gangster film the protagonists with whom we empathize reverse our usual patterns of identification by engaging us and our feelings with career criminals, often to the exclusion of empathy with law-abiding citizens. This can happen in other sub-genres of crime entertainment, but not within a dense social context, which is the second essential trait of the gangster project. The gangster subgenre is epic in nature, highly social, and generally paints a panoramic picture of society and its values—all in all a departure from the usual emphasis in Hollywood on the purely personal and individualistic. Gangland protagonists are embedded in a well-articulated hierarchy of colleagues whose relationships may be turbulent but remain crucial to their well-being. For this reason, the final essential characteristic of the gangster subgenre is its unusually even matching of the opposing claims of the personal and the social, unusual in that Hollywood almost always weights the scale for the personal. Some major examples of this discrete subgenre are *Little Caesar* (1930), *Public Enemy* (1931), *Scar-face* (1932), *White Heat* (1949), The "Godfather" trilogy (1972/74/90), *Prizzi's Honor* (1985), and *Goodfellas* (1994).

These defining characteristics leave for other discussions about other issues a wide range of other crime entertainment stories, including those in which ordinary people uncharacteristically commit a crime—Walter Neff in *Double Indemnity* (1944); Frank Chambers in *The Postman Always Rings Twice* (1946); Marion Crane in *Psycho* (1960)—and those that focus on lone wolves or outlaw couples with scarcely a shred of social connection—*Bonnie and Clyde* (1967); *Badlands* (1973). They also rule out films and television shows in which the gangsters are the antagonists and the police, reporters, detectives, or intended victims of the crime organization are the protagonists—*Deadline-U.SA.* (1952); the "Dirty Harry" series (1971/76/88); *Dick Tracy* (1990). Movies about lone bandits, crime couples on the run, and intrepid lawmen are informed more by romanticism than by epic, and are generally studies in individualism—both of the policeman and the criminal. They either mark crime as an individual pathology or the individual as a persecuted being. They promote a complicated means for the audience to form an ephemeral, symbiotic relationship with voluptuous, perhaps masturbatory, lonely transgressive pleasures bearing on the disconnect between the group and the self.

In contrast, one equally transgressive subgenre permits a unique audience catharsis that speaks of the violence that erupts specifically because we are and need to be connected to other people. The catharsis is unique because its nuanced depiction of human connections, particularly with family, allows a forbidden look at "sacred" ties, which, despite the saccharine pronouncements of radical right-wing politics and much popular domestic drama, not only tempt but also trouble us. In the gangster drama, as in our lives, a strong desire for filiation complicates autonomy and the drive to succeed in a competitive economic system.

The media gangster's dilemma strikes a chord in the law-abiding public, resonating against the secret knowledge of the ordinary moviegoer that in a competitive capitalist society the emotional claims of the family are in crucial ways "other" to materialist success. Thus it is no accident that crime families in the gangster subgenre are noticeably foreign, immigrant. Their foreignness serves as a vehicle for portrayal of the ancient, pre-American call of family ties, while modern success is conveyed by the clean-cut Americans on the police force and in the FBI, who, not un-coincidentally, are almost always presented without reference to their families or to any connections that are not official. At varying levels of consciousness, the gangster film draws the audience into a radical alliance with an inversion of the usual definitions of "like" and "other," making American audiences adhere to the foreign.

"I'm Not So Tough"

The audience's surprising compact with the foreign element of blood and family connection in the gangster story makes possible a number of alternative perspectives, one of the most important being identification with a masculinity that is at once intensely virile *and* other to the standard self-contained masculine image. The gangster protagonist is in the most profound way a family man who gives the audience a means of obliquely exploring family life, free from the stigma attached to emotions and "women's entertainment" (often erroneously identified as the whole of melodrama). What is ordinarily identified as family melodrama is feminized and openly emotional, while the domestic melodrama of the gangster subgenre is muscularized, displacing emotion onto the tumult associated with violence.

"The Sopranos," as the inheritor of a long line of texts which disguise familial tensions, brings this displacement to the surface. When Tony Soprano's mother Livia (Nancy Marchand) conspires with his uncle Corrado "Junior" Soprano (Dominic Chianese) to have him killed, they are operating (albeit confusedly) within the imperatives of a gangland struggle for rule of the Northern New Jersey mob. But each is also trenchantly expressing garden-variety familial anger: Livia a familiar generational rage, because Tony has put her in a nursing home, and Junior a familiar fury about rank in families, because the leadership of the mob has been given to his nephew instead of to him. What also distinguishes the gangster melodrama from the domestic melodrama is how directly and intensely emotions are expressed in the domestic melodrama, while here the emotions of the situation are displaced onto the violent crime story. In "The Sopranos," Junior and Livia give each other permission to rid themselves of Tony with such minimalism that the audience is not sure what has transpired between them until the plans to kill Tony are put into action. The violence in the scenes in which an attempt is made on Tony's life expresses their rage with such displacement that they are not even present. Certainly this is standard operating procedure for gangster films. But that is the point: it is representative of the tradition of emotional displacement in this genre. The aggressor is invisible as the rage is expressed, as opposed to domestic melodrama, which unabashedly shows the venting of anger. Displacement protects the virility of the genre and gives the (male) viewers access to emotional situations they need not see in directly emotional terms.

The thinly disguised familial drama in "The Sopranos" is not a new wrinkle; the drama is just more visible. In *Public Enemy*, when Tommy Powers (James Cagney) collapses in the rain murmuring, "I'm not so tough," the low emotion/high violence scene, as with the scene of Tony's near assassination, utilizes an action sequence to raise the issue of family conflicts. Tommy's collapse is the result of a gangland shootout, but its import is dramatized in relationship to his mother, as it sets the scene for her impending discovery of his final appearance as a mummified corpse, horrifically evocative of a swaddled infant. On one level, then, Tommy's crime agon is a shoot-'em-and-die blood circus. But any gangster entertainment that is purely that is doomed to oblivion.

The abiding importance of *Public Enemy* is its early use of the gangster milieu as a metaphor for the complex tensions between individuation and family. It is an early example of the self-image of a culture awash in pious pronouncements about the value of both individualism and family which allows no way to integrate the blood ties of family with the isolating drive necessary to individuals bound for success. Comparison with *Public Enemy* and other classic gangster films is encouraged by "The Sopranos," which contains numerous allusions to *Scarface*, the "Godfather" trilogy, and *Public Enemy*. In the second episode

of the third season, Tony watches *Public Enemy* the day his mother dies, with specific emphasis on scenes between Tommy Powers and his mother. Indeed, after her funeral, Tony watches the "I'm not so tough" scene and the scenes with Tommy's mother that the collapse sets up. The series is fully aware that Tony Soprano's thwarted attempts at meshing family and individuation is part of a long tradition. What is new in current gangster entertainment is that blunt, reflexive awareness of the genre's dark secret. "The Sopranos" deals openly in representations that were suppressed in the earlier classics. The cat is out of the bag from the very first episode. In the first image of the series, gang boss Tony Soprano is in dialogue with familial confusions, specifically the maternal influence: he is sitting in the office of a female psychiatrist, completely framed by the legs of a female nude sculpture (recalling his origins in the birth canal and the power of the mother). His curious gaze upward at the nude sculpture is a radical reversal of the conventionally possessive male gaze.

Tony begins the series already having discovered that he's "not so tough," collapsing as he periodically does from panic attacks, a debilitating condition whose cause, we later discover, is his extremely troubled connection with his mother and father. Tommy Powers never got a chance to process that thought, but like all other great media gangsters, he was suffused with ambivalence about mothers, sisters, and wives in the context of a similar confusion about brothers and father figures, and about the sexual and territorial implications of that ambiguity. "The Sopranos" offers Tony the opportunity for therapy and with a woman doctor, thereby making almost explicit its displaced investigation of the American family.

Linda Williams' seminal essay "Melodrama Revised" explores the melodramatic infrastructure of Hollywood entertainment and suggests a way to pierce the layers of historical misperception of the gangster subgenre. Williams' theory lays the groundwork for my proposal that the gangster project is not a genre but a subgenre of a subgenre (crime entertainment) of melodrama. In her essay she explores a structuring tension between (realistic) action and (certain intensities of) melodrama as the inner dynamic of most Hollywood entertainment, giving us a vocabulary for speaking of the perennial (if veiled) importance of emotion, family, and women in the gangster classics.

Williams theorizes that the Hollywood action genres are really all varieties of melodramas played out within a variety of discrete action conventions that each stage a narrative of misprized innocence: "If emotional and moral registers are sounded, if a work invites us to feel sympathy for the virtues of beset victims, if the narrative trajectory is ultimately more concerned with a retrieval and staging of innocence than with the psychological causes of motives and action, then the operative mode is melodrama."[1]

Surprisingly, an extended discussion of the Hollywood gangster—Cagney, Robinson, Muni, Pacino— reveals that his drama *is* the staging of his innocence and his victimhood, though not in the tropes associated with domestic melodrama. The gangster's behavior is related to a social setting (and beginning with *White Heat*, a psychological circumstance) that has coerced a capable, forceful man into extortion and murder. Misprized innocence, relative to the gangster, is more complex than it is in domestic melodrama, since, clearly, the gangster *is* guilty at the most literal level. But though the screen gangster is depicted as not only legally culpable but also essentially corrupt by nature in all other categories of crime entertainment (with the possible exception of the lone outlaw category), in the true gangster film there shine through the Hollywood mobster's villainous deeds the remnants of what his initial innocence might have been like.

There is a longing in the gangster subgenre for its protagonist's lost purity, staged on the level of the physical, for the Hollywood gangster typically has an "innocent," spontaneous relationship to his body and physicality in general.[2] Almost all the action is written onto the bodies of the gangsters in a subgenre that places great emphasis on physical touch in general, on drinking, and sometimes on food. The infamous grapefruit-in-the-face scene in *Public Enemy* is as much a deeply embedded evocation of loss for Tommy as it is an abuse of Kitty. Tommy assaults Kitty because she is concerned about his welfare; apparently he needs to summon up considerable energy to deny that kind of filiation with anyone but his mother. In "The Sopranos" an overt consciousness of the relevance of food and touch to this genre is everywhere; but this is not a simple awareness: kisses and shared meals are both powerful and ambiguous signs, perhaps of connection, perhaps of betrayal and rejection.

Tony Soprano's rich physicality is a particularly important part of his characterization, a primary vehicle for our experience of his intricately marbled guilt and innocence. We know that he has a history behind him that pushes him involuntarily into mob life, and we also share his pleasure in the body of the world, in both its perverse and its sweet aspects, which makes a powerful suggestion to the audience that Tony, given other historical circumstances, could have been a very different person. Moreover, this physicality contrasts favorably with the unsatisfying, sterile aphysicality of the law-abiding citizens, which makes us feel that Tony had (or perhaps has) the potential to be much better than they are. Tony touches and is touched, a source of his immense appeal.

Despite his potbelly and balding head, James Gandolfini has become an unexpected sex symbol because of his frank involvement with the sensual body. He has made touch an integral part of Tony's management technique: embracing, kissing, shaking, and smacking the men whom he leads. Tony's relationship to food is unashamedly enthusiastic: not only is much business conducted by him over meals, but he appealingly expresses affection with food in a way that also expresses his power, as in a good-night ritual with his son when he sprays whipped cream from a can into his own mouth as a bedtime treat and then sprays some into his son's. The paternal and even maternal warmth that he displays is the positive side of his gangster tendency to understand the world in purely physical terms. The emphasis on Tony's body is also a seminal mode of representing his problematic allure. While he lives a life shockingly contained by physical orientation in which murder is just another form of saying "that's the way it is," the warmth of his engagement in the touchable world points up a lack—a physical coldness—in the characters who occupy a variety of moral and ethical positions. With this troubling irony, Chase permits sophisticated viewers a new insight into a fundamental aspect of what has always been the enigmatic attractiveness of gangsters. Certainly Tommy Powers is much more physically alive than his wooden, good, older brother Michael. We find the same contrast in many of Tony's predecessors.[3]

Tony Soprano's guilt of murder—and more—is complicated by the fact that he was born (did not choose) to rule the Northern New Jersey mob and by his utterly spontaneous, child-like joy in physicality. The series follows in the footsteps of not only the great gang classics but also many important classics of American literature which represent the moral double bind. "The Sopranos" is as complex as Herman Melville's *Billy Budd* in exploring the issues of innocence and crime; in contrast, the moralist critics of gangster film and television have shown themselves to be simplistic. Reductive criticism of the great media gangster classics has a venerable history, from the Production Code to Marge Roukema, though today's self-appointed censors fall short of the standards of yesteryear's. The critics of "The Sopranos" mainly raise their voices in horror at the violence and ethnic representation of Italian Americans, yet they fail to note critiques of so-called good citizens of all types that the old Production Code Administration would have been eager to condemn.[4]

"The Sopranos" portrays a broad spectrum of characters who are building lives as career criminals, and does so with explicit ethnic markings. This would have disturbed the PCA, but—and this might have been even more irritating to the old in-house censor—the series also depicts the sniveling hypocrisy of mainstream middle-class Caucasian professionals (clergy, teachers, lawyers, therapists, politicians, doctors), who are supposed to be guardians of the public sphere, but who are cowardly and morally derelict in varying ways. However, "The Sopranos" is not using the mob simply to make good citizens more thoughtful about their own compromised actions in the lawless climate of contemporary America. Rather, the series is trying for a much more profound interrogation of our blind spots relative to the pleasure we take in the infantile innocence of the gangster.

"Cunnilingus and Psychiatry Brought Us to This"

At the end of the first season, Tony Soprano tells wife Carmela, in the aftermath of the failed contract on his life, "Cunnilingus and psychiatry brought us to this"—a twenty-first-century translation of "I'm not so tough." The "this" of this statement is the nub of the

significance of this television series for the gangster tradition. For Tony, "this" expresses his exasperation with the strains modern life has placed on the gangster's macho code. However, for the viewer, "this" is the possibility inherent in modern life for a new understanding of the ambiguous charm of the gangster. Tony's mob issues are actually pretty standard, but they become new in "The Sopranos," which insightfully reconfigures the delicate balance between right, might, and delight that has historically made the gangster sub-genre such a seething cauldron of unresolved drives. The series works episode by episode, season by season to establish a complex point of view that inevitably requires us to acknowledge, despite its power over us, the insufficiency of Tony's charm in the face of murder and other forms of social devastation.

Central to the series' revolutionary take on the appeal of the immediacy of the gangster is its revelation of a dark secret about family through a juxtaposition between the roles of Carmela and Dr. Melfi in Tony's life. Instead of comparing an innocent family with a guilty career, the series juxtaposes Tony's criminal activities with a family held together by his wife Carmela's unacknowledged, self-destructive attachment to the excitement and allure of Tony's violence, to which she is blinded by a reductive attitude toward religion that serves as a powerful form of denial rather than as a mode of fighting against evil. Only Melfi's psychiatry, with its ethical roots deeply anchored in a conscious connection with the beneficial aspects of the subconscious, can offer any hope of dealing with the attractions of the innocence (and power) of gangster spontaneity. In this, "The Sopranos" represents an impressive advance over both the rigid code of ethics and morals in the 1930s gangster film and the post-Code relativity instigated by Francis Ford Coppola, neither of which dealt honestly with its material.

The untenably simplistic nature of the Code rendered the "good people" one-dimensional and unintentionally made the gangsters seem more exciting and desirable. In post-studio Hollywood, post-Godfather gangster narratives tended to follow Coppola's simplistic lead in relativizing values, which ultimately disappeared into the maelstrom of Michael Corleone's id and ego, seemingly lost forever in the glamour of gang potency. In contrast, the old Hollywood definition of "good" people is severely challenged and the romanticizing of the gangster in the "Godfather" series is commented on in "The Sopranos," particularly in the second-season episode "Commeditori," when Tony and "the guys" go to Italy expecting the operatic glamour of Coppola's films, only to be disappointed by the putrefaction and emptiness under the pretty surfaces. The continuous thrust of "The Sopranos" is an examination of the way Americans (even gangsters themselves) are bedazzled by the same impulsive human desire that mesmerized Coppola. Chase deliberates the need to use our human capacity to mediate desire so as to allow for important longer-range needs and interests.

Tony's interlude with a family of wild ducks in the first episode, his pure delight in nature's gift to him, is the series' introduction of the problem of Tony's seductive "innocence." The ducks come to him literally out of the blue, bringing their natural bodies and their unsullied family behavior smack into the middle of his contradiction-ridden home and business life when they land in his backyard pool. The positioning of the ducks creates the maximum of complexity about Tony, coming as it does after a main title sequence that contains a mass of aggressively virile resonances: Tony Soprano returning home to New Jersey from New York, a huge cigar in his mouth, driving through a maze of evocations of masculine power in America—bridges, highways, electric wires, and industrial sites. The sequence is shot through the driver's POV, further emphasizing Tony's dominance as he negotiates the twists and turns. Aurally, the montage is scored by a guttural rendition of "Woke Up this Morning," a song with the refrain "Got yourself a gun."

These images immediately collide with Tony's position of subjective, child-like confusion in the psychiatrist's office and his discomfort as he meets Dr. Melfi for the first time. As he speaks with her, we see him suppressing the information about his violent operations and frolicking in his pool, like a delighted child, with a mother duck and her ducklings, clad only in an open robe and his boxer shorts. The entrance of the ducks into the analysis puts a strain on the already powerful imbalances of Tony's characterization.

These dissonances and contrasting fragments are bracketed by the linearity of Tony's conversation with Melfi. Unexpectedly, it is a curative rather than a repressive linearity that makes its first dent in Tony's macho defenses as he fulminates about the weakness involved in going to a psychiatrist. Melfi keeps him focused, finally thwarting his evasions as she insistently repeats the question, "Are you depressed?" He finally stops spinning his cover stories and answers reluctantly, "Yeah, since the ducks left." What to make of a protagonist who thrives on brutality and grieves for departed ducks? Ultimately, a great deal. For Tony's infantile obsession with the ducks is a distillation of his confusion about immediacy—a confusion shared by everyone in the show but his therapist—which he is able to sentimentalize and compartmentalize so that his worship of his own visceral responses blocks him from experiencing a mature sting of conscience about his life of crime.

Tony's retreat into Melfi's inner sanctum suggests that he can gain the needed insight, and this marks an enormous change in the life of the media gangster. Unlike Tommy Powers, Tony Soprano does not have to have his body destroyed in order to cut through his defenses. Unlike Henry Hill in *Goodfellas*, the gangster project Chase considers "the Bible" for his creation, Tony is not forever lost in the false glamour of the gangster life, in comparison with which ordinary life is a second-rate business that makes "schnooks" of all of us.[5] Tony has begun a quest that will slowly and with great pain, sorrow, and difficulty lead to other possibilities than the unthinking release of chaotic energy and false glamour that have locked previous gangsters into a doomed cycle of savagery. Not for one second does "The Sopranos" deny the moment-to-moment pleasure of the infantilized life that the American media gangster leads. But neither does the series fall into the moral confusion of the "Godfather" trilogy and its descendants, which are so enchanted by spontaneous pleasure that they have barely a shred of defense against the infantile, violent sprees of its protagonists. In a flash of insight, "The Sopranos" takes heed of that oddly seductive innocence in all its thrilling excitement and chilling myopia.

The characteristic myopia of Tony and his colleagues threads the series, continually provoking ambivalence about the gangster's spontaneity, one of the most revealing episodes being "Boca," the ninth of the first season. The episode weaves two stories, one about Uncle Junior's taste for cunnilingus and one about the sexual abuse of one of Meadow's (Tony's daughter) friends by Don Hauser, the coach of the girls' soccer team at Verbum Dei, Meadow's high school. "Boca," which means "mouth" in Italian, is also the nickname for Boca Raton, the upscale resort town in Florida to which Junior takes his main squeeze, Roberta "Bobbi" Sanfillipo, for some rest, recreation, and cunnilingus. The juxtaposition of Junior's time-out from the male world of the mob and the abuse story sets up a set of contrasts that suggest the problematic nature, not of Junior's particular and perfectly innocent sexual desire, but of its proscription by a male subculture that, ironically, enthusiastically endorses a wide variety of other instinctual drives that are dangerous and destructive. When Tony learns of Junior's sexual preferences, Junior has to terminate his relationship with Bobbi, and the reflection cast by the Hauser story pairs these events to imply that all aspects of the lives of the gangsters are occasions for male self-indulgence as long as they fit within the conventional macho image.

The soccer-coach thread begins as Tony and the other suburban gangster fathers and their satellites are beside themselves with joy at their daughters' triumph on the playing field. However, the thrill of victory foregrounds their male sense of dominance: they do not take their daughters out to celebrate; they take the coach for a drink at Bada Bing!, the topless bar where the Sopranos gang hangs out. Their infectious euphoria turns slightly unpalatable when it generates an equally spontaneous anger at the news that Hauser has negotiated a new and better contract and is leaving the school. Impulsive forms of intimidation to get him to stay escalate when the final shoe drops and it becomes clear that Hauser has sexually abused one of the girls on the team. Tony and his soldiers decide to kill him. This complicates audience relationships with the characters. The "good fellas" are suddenly not amusing, but frightening. Yet at the same time there is a nagging admiration for the gangsters: Who is not outraged by child molestation? Except that, cleverly, Chase makes us confront the problem of dealing with such rage spontaneously.

Tony is the fulcrum of this episode because only he, by virtue of the combination of his gangster power and his analysis with Melfi, can begin to mediate the huge energies in play. He finds himself unable to

blithely indulge his instincts, to enjoy without reservation either the damage to Junior's reputation because of his pleasure in giving Bobbi pleasure or the plan to avenge the young girl by killing Hauser. The newly emerging Tony is no longer completely proof against doubt. He aborts the contract on Hauser primarily because Melfi asks him why he has to control everything after he heaps contempt on the solutions posed by what he sees as the ineffective legal and psychiatric communities: "Who's gonna stop him? You?" In the context established by the episode, it becomes clear to the audience and to Tony himself that he is motivated by some dubious needs of his own for control and domination in seeking to kill Hauser, and the enthusiastic endorsement of those needs by Tony's soldiers contrasts suspiciously with their proscription of Junior's sexuality. The physical spontaneity of cunnilingus is too openly emotional, too tender for the soldiers, sounding yet a further note of warning about the limitations of the lure of gangster immediacy. The warnings become ever more insistent, and awareness for both characters and audience grows as the series continues.

For Tony, there is a modicum of new insight because of Melfi's interventions. For the audience, though there is a certain attractiveness to Tony's take-charge position, since we know the problematic relationship between legal justice and sex offenders, there is also a certain horror inherent in his propensity toward murder. When he finally cancels the hit, Tony feels neither liberated nor evolved, but rather radically out of control, and to commemorate the loss that ethical behavior inspires in him, he floods his system with alcohol and Prozac, babbling that he hasn't hurt anyone. Like Tony, the audience is and continues to be in a conflicted position in which it is difficult to reject either Melfi's moral stance with its long-range implications or the short-term immediacy of Tony's practical approach toward survival. Yet at the end of "Boca," Tony is at a tantalizingly different place from any gangster in the history of the subgenre, just because of psychiatry and cunnilingus.

This conflict is actively refracted in every transaction and relationship in the series, but particularly in the juxtaposition of Tony's wife and his therapist, by means of which the series makes its main contribution to the gangster project by breaking with both small-minded PCA moralism and the relativist "God-father" phenomenon. Having profited from Coppola's infusion of a new vocabulary and a more overt portrayal of family and gangster vocation into the subgenre, Chase takes on the task of restoring values to mass-culture fiction about gangsters, but with an unprecedented complexity, and a new twist for the genre. The problematic nature of the joy associated with Tony's spontaneous virility is most uniquely confronted in the juxtaposition of Carmela's problematic, self-serving form of Catholicism and the painful integrity of Jennifer Melfi's commitment to our human relationship to the subconscious.

The old gangster tradition, in deference to the extremely conservative Catholicism of the men who governed the Production Code Administration, would ritually haul out a highly idealized, cardboard impersonation of a priest to pass harsh judgement on the infectious excitement of the gangster mayhem. Ironically, this worked nicely to liberate audiences from their ordinary limits by permitting them to enjoy the gangster while taking in the obligatory pieties at the same time. The "Godfather" series exploded this disguise not only by implicating the Church as a financial dependent of the Corleones, but also by cross-cutting between Michael's role in the baptism of his nephew and his "family's" role in the killing of the principal members of the rival mobs. As Michael is being asked, "Do you renounce Satan?" his will is being carried out by numerous assassins, a chilling evocation of the Church as the house of Satan in this world. With the Church unmasked as a fraud, and with no other source of values in *The Godfather*, the vitality of the gangster assumes an uncontested sovereignty in the film. In contrast, David Chase also envisions a corrupt Church financially beholden to the mob, but "The Sopranos," by placing Tony between Carmela and Dr. Melfi, raises to the surface from the depths of the gangster tradition the possibilities of human allegiance to ethics by taking heed of the energy of the subconscious.

The subconscious, along with the Catholic Church, has always played a role, albeit a shadowy one, in the gangster subgenre, but never before as a potential source of values. It has always lurked as the negative source from which gangsters draw nervous energy and the reason they are subject to fits. After

World War II, the psychology of criminal behavior became more explicit, as in *White Heat*, which linked Cody Jarrett's (James Cagney) migraine headaches to his incestuous relationship with his mother, and ostensibly both to his propensity for violence. After *The Godfather*, interestingly, abnormal psychology was relegated to the lesser gangsters, Vito and Michael Corleone becoming the templates for the gangster as hero in a totally degenerate society. But the TV series casts a cold eye on Tony's belief that he is of the latter type, and suggests his lack of connection to subconscious energies.

The juxtaposition of Carmela and Dr. Melfi highlights the melodrama of Tony's choices, not a sexual choice—the cliché of sexual competition between women is present only if it is imposed by a clichéd reading of the series—but a choice of values: Carmela's travesty of morality that actually enables Tony to continue in a life of crime, or Melfi's honest confrontation of the subconscious that might aid him in coping with the infantile charms of criminal mayhem. That Carmela is married to the mob works on more than one level. She is, in many ways, an allegory for the confusion in the general American public about deviance. A devoted mother, with a sincere concern for other people and community as she understands it, she is nevertheless unaware that she is sexually excited by transgressive behavior, and especially by violence. Endlessly tinkering with her Catholicism to calm her conscience, her piety is explicitly revealed, in part, as self-deception by her sexuality. She becomes aroused with Tony only in response to his criminal behavior. When he brings home a stolen fur coat, she expresses her appreciation by initiating sex: fascinatingly, she is the partner on top. In an even more chilling sequence, utterly unprecedented in gangster lore, Carmela initiates unusually warm and tender sex when Tony, in an episode entitled "From Where to Eternity," returns from murdering a 23-year-old boy. This is not a deed that Tony has explicitly mentioned to her, but the sequences before and after indicate that she knows the basics of his intent, a situation that patently horrifies and arouses her. It is noteworthy that her physical approach to Tony is linked to the infantilization that the worship of immediacy spawns; she caresses his face and body as a mother might caress a baby. In fact, Tony's relationship to his home stresses the infantile; he spends a disproportionate amount of time in his bed, like a baby in his crib (as Henry Bronchtein, the director of the episode, has noted).[6] Tony's home is not built in opposition to his gang life, but on a disguised attraction to the "bad boy" energy of the criminal.

The audience too would like to stay in its crib, fiercely fighting against what Chase reveals about Tony through the polarities inherent in Carmela and Melfi. Chat rooms buzz with audience desire to get lost in erotic fantasies about Tony with both women. But the series relentlessly chips away at those fantasies, revealing some hard home truths about sexual attraction/repulsion concerning Tony. Chase links Carmela's morality to an infantilized relationship with the Church through her psychosexual liaison with the parish priest, Father Philip Intintola. (It says much about this character that his name—if you say it quickly, which they all do—sounds like "Rin-Tin-Tin.") Father Phil spends cozy evenings with Carmela in front of the Home Entertainment Center. He even spends the night once, ostensibly for practical reasons, while Tony is away, and they have a close brush with sex. But, as Carmela realizes and tells Father Phil, he has made a life work of arousing needy women, and enjoying the whiff of sexuality without following through. Would that Carmela could turn her formidable insights on herself. Even in the third season, when she can no longer endure her own complicity with the poisoned wellsprings of her affluence, she escapes into rhapsodies about the innocence of the Baby Jesus in paintings in the Metropolitan Museum of Art—her version of Tony's fixation on the ducks. And when she consults a psychologist, who bluntly refuses to let her pay him with what he calls Tony's blood money and tells her that her only productive recourse is to leave her husband, Carmela decides that this Jewish doctor "can't understand" the Catholic attitude toward marriage. Chase contextualizes this attitude in a less than flattering light when Carmela accepts the counsel of a priest (not Father Intintola), who insists that she honor the sacrament of marriage by taking from the marriage only that which isn't tainted by Tony's criminal activities—a stunning exercise in sophistry that continues to lock Carmela into her painful dynamic with Tony and results in no more than a renunciation of some flashy jewelry.

Chase also frustrates the fantasies that the audience wants to cultivate about Dr. Melfi. Although there is some subtextual sexual interest aroused in Jennifer Melfi by Tony Soprano, she, in contrast to Carmela, is prepared to deal with and fight it. Paying what must be one of the highest compliments ever accorded psychiatry on television, Chase suggests that beyond the clichés that associate permissiveness with therapeutic treatment—clichés Tony periodically hurls in Melfi's face—there exists a core in the psychiatric process that fosters an honesty about the attractions of the gangster way of life that may be our only hope, even if it cannot promise a complete solution to the problem.

From the moment Tony Soprano first enters Dr. Melfi's office, he continually attempts to ensnare her in the exercise of raw power that passes for sexuality and even love among the women with whom he deals. (It passes for love between Tony and the men too.) Often his displays toward her take an "adorable" child-like form of impetuousness, impulsiveness, spontaneity, and socially immature gestures—putting his feet up on her coffee table and flapping them back and forth, for example. But Tony's attempts to create a crib away from home for himself are not successful. Melfi will not give in to any of his gangster erotics—sudden attempts to kiss her, attempts to extend the protection of his power to her—or to his belief that violence can change the truth. His declaration of love in the first season is met with her calm analytical approach to transference. When he learns that she needs repairs on her car, he "steals" it and takes it to his own mechanic, thinking this will be a romantic surprise. But Melfi confounds him by insisting that he will receive credit on her bill for the cost. She does let him get her and her date a table at a crowded restaurant to prevent a scene, but when he threatens her with extreme physical violence at her analytical suggestion that his mother is behind the attempt on his life, she leaves him to deal with the doubts she has encouraged, doubts that cannot just be pounded into submission.

When Tony's violent way of life reaches into Melfi's life, forcing her to go into hiding, she terminates her association with him on what she assures him is a permanent basis. There seems to be no temporizing on her part, as there is on Carmela's, until in the middle of the second season, plagued by dreams about abandoning him, she decides to resume his therapy despite the urgent pleas of her therapist ex-husband, Richard La Penna (Richard Romanus), and her control psychiatrist, Eliot Kupferberg (Peter Bogdanovich), to stay away from a person they deem a dangerous sociopath. Their doubts stand unanswered in the second season: Is Melfi in the process of giving in to her own adolescent longings about Tony?

In the third-season episode "Employee of the Month," we must come to the conclusion that Melfi has important, mature, professional—not personal and infantile—reasons for continuing to treat Tony. The show, primarily about the rape of Dr. Melfi by Jesus Rossi (employee of the month at the local fast-food restaurant that she patronizes), quashes the innocence of spontaneity within the violent context. While Carmela has permitted violence to be hidden and eroticized, the violence in Melfi's life is too available in all its ugliness to evoke anything but horror. Rossi's attack on Melfi is a motiveless hatred unleashed on her in a spur-of-the-moment urge, the worst aspect of spontaneity unmasked. Even for the audience, which (given the evidence of the chat rooms) was charmed by Tony and Carmela's post-murder bedroom scene, this is an act impossible to romanticize. Melfi's demeanor is utterly business-like as she descends a metal staircase in a cinderblock stairwell, a surrounding devoid of any sensual ambience, when Rossi assaults her. Her response is an unambiguous struggle to escape him. For the audience, trained by decades of gangster lore, sentimentalization is displaced onto its yearning for this terrible moment to foster in Melfi a desire to turn toward Tony as her protector and avenger.

A selective interpretation of the episode can suggest that this is a desire encouraged by the show. The police have casually released Rossi because of procedural snafus, and there is no one but Tony who can give Melfi the immediate gratification of vengeance. Melfi feels the same childish impulses to avail herself of that solace: she finds herself yelling at Dr. Kupferberg with the same rage that Tony yelled at her when she suggested that Hauser be turned over to the police instead of dispatched by efficient mob execution, "That employee of the month cock-sucker is back on the street, and who's gonna stop him, you?" But a more comprehensive understanding of events reveals that the show raises this desire in order to reject it. Despite her rage, Melfi's use of Tony to avenge her is restricted to the world of the imagination—the proper use for a gangster fantasy. It is important that Chase does not construct her as being above the desire to throw herself on Tony's mercy, for it reflects the audience's divided position. Indeed, Melfi is overtaken by a spasm of fear during a therapy session with Tony, which upsets him to the point that he intrudes on the distance between analyst and patient by walking over to comfort her. The moment is filled with unspoken feelings and ideas as Tony searches Melfi's bruised face for some clue to this unprecedented outburst, and Melfi wrestles silently with a decision that has hovered over this episode. "What? Do you want to say something?" asks Tony, genuinely concerned, expressing the tenderness that is embedded in his rich access to physical immediacy. The camera lingers on Melfi's now impassive swollen and bruised face. "No," she says, and the episode cuts abruptly, with finality, to black. Tony's momentarily naïve openness cannot be accepted because of its place in a much larger constellation of unacceptable behavior.

In raising our fantasies that Tony will be Melfi's hero, and then dramatizing her ethical rejection of that childish romanticism about gangsters, "The Sopranos" as a postmillennial gangster entertainment stakes out the highest ground yet claimed by any production in this subgenre, if complexity is a measure of ethical value. It refuses to make things easy for us. On an emotional level, all people in this series are equal. Tony has many a genuine and profound emotional response. Even the most brutal and heedless of the gangsters might have one now and again. Yet if the human common denominator of intense feeling is a basis for occasional empathy and identity with characters, that empathy does not become a substitute for ethics in this series. A true melodrama, "The Sopranos" stages the innocence of its protagonist: Tony has a certain purity of heart. But that innocence is more troubling than in previous gangster melodramas.

"The Sopranos" proclaims, and loudly, that if the innocence of bodily immediacy is attractive, still that is not enough. Tony's disregard for ethics and law cannot be condoned because of his spontaneous, generous charm. Carmela represents that untenable attitude of the mass audience excited by the lies unspoken, while Melfi will not lose herself in them, although at times—to quote Sam Spade—everything in her wants to. This is no valentine, as Mario Puzo's novel is to Vito Corleone.[7] Nor is it an arch wink at the joke the gangster world has played on straitlaced America, as in Richard Condon's "Prizzi" series.[8] David Chase and his creative community are inviting us to be very adult in our consideration of the crime culture and very sophisticated about its role as a metaphor for the tangled desires of our daily lives.[9] We might even say that with "The Sopranos," mass culture comes of age as entertainment provides a truly popular examination of important popular realities. Would a public that could learn the lesson Tony offers continue voting for presidential candidates on the basis of a perceived warmth and spontaneity that annihilates known facts about the insufficiency of their administrative records and/or unacceptable ideological commitments?

Notes

1. Linda Williams, "Melodrama Revised," in *Refiguring American Film Genres: Theory and History*, ed. Nick Browne (Berkeley, CA: University of California Press, 1998), 42.

2. In the gangster subgenre, the spontaneous body of the gangster protagonist is always rendered appealing; in other genres of crime entertainment, where the gangster is an antagonist, that spontaneity is generally rendered repulsive; indeed, it is often inscribed as a nauseating violation of cleanliness, proportion, and order. It is no accident that James Cagney, a dancer, was so effective in gangster films: the attractions of his lithe, feline, grace set him apart from the wooden, if morally correct, bodies of the good men and the slothful, obdurate bodies of lesser gangsters.

3. In non-gangster crime entertainment, the coolness of the policeman's body is often one of his central attractions; the heat of the gangster's body being associated with putrefaction and fetidity. Clint Eastwood's Dirty Harry is a prime example. Humphrey Bogart's physical coolness is also the center of his character when he fights crime, a hallmark that made him in many ways a more memorable lawman than he was a criminal. But in the gangster subgenre, the physical coolness of the lawmen is asexual, antiseptic rather than enticing. In "The Sopranos," the police and the FBI are much in evidence, and, for the most part, are of unquestionable integrity. Accordingly, they are clean-cut, if somewhat indistinguishable from each other. Their cool detachment from their job, in which there is no personal body, works similarly against audience empathy with their plans to get evidence on Tony, even if we know that it is the right thing to do.

4. Marge Roukema, a conservative Republican Congresswoman who admits to never having seen the show, is representative of a myopia about the show's ethical complexity.

5. An unrepentant Henry Hill, in the witness protection program at the end of *Goodfellas*, mourns the loss of "the good life": "We were treated like movie stars with muscle. We had it all just for the asking. . . . We ran everything. We paid off cops, we paid off judges. . . . Everything was for the taking. And now it's all over. And that's the hardest part. . . . I have to wait around like everyone else. . . . I'm an average nobody, get to live the rest of my life like a schnook." The film gives us no reason to second-guess Henry; it implies the existence of nothing that is as worthwhile in life as having "everything for the taking."

6. Henry J. Bronchtein, Commentary, "From Where to Eternity," Disc 3, *The Sopranos, The Complete Second Season*, DVD, HBO Home Video, 2001.

7. Mario Puzo, *The Godfather* (Greenwich, CT: Fawcett, 1969). Puzo's novel depends on a fantasy medieval, personal hierarchy, in which Vito rises to the top because his supremely warm, generous instincts and mental acuteness enable him to manage the affairs of human beings while the abstract legal system flounders. It is a profoundly relativistic book that idealizes men who "know how to use violence," the tone of which is perfectly translated to the screen by Francis Ford Coppola.

8. Richard Condon's "Prizzi" trilogy is an elaborate joke about the United States, proposing the gangster as the quintessential American: a person with absolutely portable ethics and identity, rooted in nothing but the exigencies required for success. The trenchant irony of the tale speaks of the blindness of American society from a perspective outside of American relativism that locates the trilogy as an ethical statement. *Prizzi's Honor* (New York: Coward, McCann & Geoghegan, 1982); *Prizzi's Family* (New York: Putnam, 1986); *Prizzi's Glory* (New York: Dutton, 1988).

9. Although the "Sopranos" online chat rooms give no evidence of a broad spectrum of sophisticated viewers, they also give no indication that the fears of the

would-be censors are justified. The enthusiastic participants do not express negative attitudes about ethnic groups, nor do they seem to lose respect for cultural institutions; in fact quite the reverse. By and large, the audience is intrigued by questions of loyalty to family and among "soldiers," although they are also swept up by sexual interest in the obvious objects of desire: Tony, Dr. Melfi, and Carmela.

38.
"NEVER TRUST A SNAKE"

WWF Wrestling as Masculine Melodrama

Henry Jenkins

See, your problem is that you're looking at this as a *wrestling* battle—two guys getting into the ring together to see who's the better athlete. But it goes so much deeper than that. Yes, wrestling's involved. Yes, we're going to pound each other's flesh, slam each other's bodies and hurt each other really bad. But there's more at stake than just wrestling, my man. There's a morality play. Randy Savage thinks he represents the light of righteousness. But, you know, it takes an awful lot of light to illuminate a dark kingdom.

(Jake "the Snake" Roberts)[1]

There are people who think that wrestling is an ignoble sport. Wrestling is not a sport, it is a spectacle, and it is no more ignoble to attend a wrestled performance of Suffering than a performance of the sorrows of Arnolphe or Andromaque.

(Roland Barthes)[2]

Like World Wrestling Federation superstar Jake "the Snake" Roberts, Roland Barthes saw wrestling as a "morality play," a curious hybrid of sports and theater. For Barthes, wrestling was at once a "spectacle of excess," evoking the pleasure of grandiloquent gestures and violent contact, and a lower form of tragedy, where issues of morality, ethics, and politics were staged. Wrestling enthusiasts have no interest in seeing a fair fight but rather hope for a satisfying restaging of the ageless struggle between the "perfect bastard" and the suffering hero.[3] What wrestling offers its spectators, Barthes tells us, is a story of treachery

and revenge, "the intolerable spectacle of powerlessness" and the exhilaration of the hero's victorious return from near-collapse. Wrestling, like conventional melodrama, externalizes emotion, mapping it onto the combatants' bodies and transforming their physical competition into a search for a moral order. Restraint or subtlety has little place in such a world. Everything that matters must be displayed, publicly, unambiguously, and unmercilessly.

Barthes's account focuses entirely upon the one-on-one match as an isolated event within which each gesture must be instantly legible apart from any larger context of expectations and associations: "One must always understand everything on the spot."[4] Barthes could not have predicted how this focus upon the discrete event or the isolated gesture would be transformed through the narrative mechanisms of television. On television, where wrestling comes with a cast of continuing characters, no single match is self-enclosed; rather, personal conflicts unfold across a number of fights, interviews, and enacted encounters. Television wrestling offers its viewers complexly plotted, ongoing narratives of professional ambition, personal suffering, friendship and alliance, betrayal and reversal of fortune. Matches still offer their share of acrobatic spectacle, snake handling, fire eating, and colorful costumes. They are, as such, immediately accessible to the casual viewer, yet they reward the informed spectator for whom each body slam and double-arm suplex bears specific narrative consequences. A demand for closure is satisfied at the level of individual events, but those matches are always contained within a larger narrative trajectory which is itself fluid and open.

The WWF broadcast provides us with multiple sources of identification, multiple protagonists locked in their own moral struggles against the forces of evil. The proliferation of champion titles—the WWF World Champion belt, the Million Dollar belt, the Tag Team champion belt, the Intercontinental champion belt—allows for multiple lines of narrative development, each centering around its own cluster of affiliations and antagonisms. The resolution of one title competition at a major event does little to stabilize the program universe, since there are always more belts to be won and lost, and in any case, each match can always be followed by a rematch which reopens old issues. Outcomes may be inconclusive because of count-outs or disqualifications, requiring future rematches. Accidents may result in surprising shifts in moral and paradigmatic alignment. Good guys betray their comrades and form uneasy alliances with the forces of evil; rule-breakers undergo redemption after suffering crushing defeats.

The economic rationale for this constant "buildup" and deferral of narrative interests is obvious. The World Wrestling Federation (WWF) knows how to use its five weekly television series and its glossy monthly magazine to ensure subscription to its four annual pay-per-view events and occasional pay-per-view specials.[5] Enigmas are raised during the free broadcasts which will be resolved only for a paying audience. Much of the weekly broadcast consists of interviews with the wrestlers about their forthcoming bouts, staged scenes providing background on their antagonisms, and in-the-ring encounters between WWF stars and sparring partners which provide a backdrop for speculations about forthcoming plot developments. Read cynically, the broadcast consists purely of commercial exploitation. Yet this promotion also has important aesthetic consequences, heightening the melodramatic dimensions of the staged fights and transforming televised wrestling into a form of serial fiction for men.

Recent scholarship has focused on serial fiction as a particularly feminine form.[6] Television wrestling runs counter to such a sharply drawn distinction: its characteristic subject matter (the homosocial relations between men, the professional sphere rather

than the domestic sphere, the focus on physical means to resolve conflicts) draws on generic traditions which critics have identified as characteristically masculine; its mode of presentation (its seriality, its focus on multiple characters and their relationship, its refusal of closure, its appeal to viewer speculation and gossip) suggests genres often labeled feminine. These contradictions may reflect wrestling's uneasy status as masculine melodrama. Critics often restrict their discussion of melodrama to the domestic melodrama, a form particularly associated with feminine interests and targeted at female audiences.[7] Such a definition ignores the influence of melodrama on a broader range of genres, including some, such as the western or the social-problem drama, which focus on a masculine sphere of public action. Our inability to talk meaningfully about masculine melodrama stems from contemporary cultural taboos against masculine emotion. Men within our culture tend to avoid self-examination and to hide from sentiment, expressing disdain for the melodramatic. After all, we are told, "real men don't cry." Yet masculine avoidance of the public display of emotion does not mean that men lack feelings or that they do not need some outlet for expressing them. Patriarchy consequently constructs alternative means of releasing and managing masculine emotion while preserving the myth of the stoic male. A first step toward reconsidering the place of male affective experience may be to account for the persistence of melodramatic conventions within those forms of entertainment that "real men" do embrace— horror films, westerns, country songs, tabloid newspapers, television wrestling, and the like. By looking more closely at these forms of sanctioned emotional release for men, we may be able to locate some of the central contradictions within our contemporary constructions of masculinity.

This chapter will thus consider WWF wrestling as a melodramatic form addressed to a working-class male audience. In focusing on this particular audience here, I do not mean to suggest that this is the only audience interested in such programming. The WWF's multi-focused narrative creates space for multiple audience segments—children, young and older women, gays, etc.—who take their own pleasures in its narrative. Nor does my focus on the melodramatic imply that televised wrestling is not readable in terms of other generic traditions, such as the carnivalesque dimension John Fiske locates.[8] My subtitle, "WWF Wrestling as Masculine Melodrama," signals my focus on one of a number of possible readings of the program. As Peter J. Rabinowitz has suggested, "Reading is always 'reading as,'" and our decision about a generic frame shapes subsequent aspects of our interpretations.[9] This essay, thus, reads wrestling *as* masculine melodrama, placing particular emphasis upon its relationship to a masculine audience and a melodramatic tradition. Such a focus invites an inquiry into the complex interplay of affect, masculinity, and class, issues which surface in both the formal and the thematic features of televised wrestling, in its characteristic narrative structure(s), its audience address, its treatment of male bonding, and its appeal to populist imagery.

Playing with Our Feelings

Norbert Elias and Eric Dunning's pathbreaking study *The Quest for Excitement: Sport and Leisure in the Civilizing Process* invites us to reconsider the affective dimensions of athletic competition. According to their account, modern civilization demands restraint on instinctive and affective experience, a process of repression and sublimation which they call the "civilizing process." Elias has spent much of his intellectual life tracing the gradual process by which Western civilization has intensified its demands for bodily and emotional control, rejecting the emotional volatility and bodily abandon that characterized Europe during the Middle Ages:

> Social survival and success in these [contemporary] societies depend . . . on a reliable armour, not too strong and not too weak, of individual self-restraint. In such societies, there is only a comparatively limited scope for the show of strong feelings, of strong antipathies towards and dislike of other people, let alone of hot anger, wild hatred or the urge to hit someone over the head.[10]

Such feelings do not disappear, but they are contained by social expectations:

> To see grown-up men and women shaken by tears and abandon themselves to their bitter sorrow

in public . . . or beat each other savagely under the impact of their violent excitement [experiences more common during die Middle Ages] has ceased to be regarded as normal. It is usually a matter of embarrassment for the onlooker and often a matter of shame or regret for those who have allowed themselves to be carried away by their excitement.[11]

What is at stake here is not the intensity of feeling but our discomfort about its spectacular display. Emotion may be strongly felt, but it must be rendered invisible, private, personal; emotion must not be allowed to have a decisive impact upon social interactions. Emotional openness is read as a sign of vulnerability, while emotional restraint is the marker of social integration. Leaders are to master emotions rather than to be mastered by them. Yet, as Elias writes, "We do not stop feeling. We only prevent or delay our acting in accordance with it."[12] Elias traces the process by which this emotional control has moved from being outwardly imposed by rules of conduct to an internalized and largely unconscious aspect of our personalities. The totality of this restraint exacts its own social costs, creating psychic tensions which somehow must be redirected and released within socially approved limitations.

Sports, he argues, constitute one of many institutions which society creates for the production and expression of affective excitement.[13] Sports must somehow reconcile two contradictory functions— "the pleasurable de-controlling of human feelings, the full evocation of an enjoyable excitement on the one hand and on the other the maintenance of a set of checks to keep the pleasantly de-controlled emotions under control."[14] These two functions are never fully resolved, resulting in occasional hooliganism as excitement outstrips social control. Yet the conventionality of sports and the removal of the real-world consequences of physical combat (in short, sport's status as adult play) facilitate a controlled and sanctioned release from ordinary affective restraints. The ability to resolve conflicts through a prespecified moment of arbitrary closure delimits the spectator's emotional experience. Perhaps most important, sports offer a shared emotional experience, one which reasserts the desirability of belonging to a community.

Elias and Dunning are sensitive to the class implications of this argument: the "civilizing process" began at the center of "court society" with the aristocracy and spread outward to merchants wishing access to the realms of social and economic power and to the servants who must become unintrusive participants in their masters' lives. Elias and Dunning argue that these class distinctions still surface in the very different forms of emotional display tolerated at the legitimate theater (which provides an emotional outlet for bourgeois spectators) and the sports arena (which provides a space for working-class excitement): the theater audience is to "be moved without moving," to restrain emotional display until the conclusion, when it may be indicated through their applause; while for the sports audience, "motion and emotion are intimately linked," and emotional display is immediate and uncensored.[15] These same distinctions separate upper-class sports (tennis, polo, golf) which allow minimal emotional expression from lower-class sports (boxing, wrestling, soccer) which demand more overt affective display. Of course, such spectacles also allow the possibility for upper- or middle-class patrons to "slum it," to adopt working-class attitudes and sensibilities while engaging with the earthy spectacle of the wrestling match. They can play at being working-class (with working-class norms experienced as a remasculinization of yuppie minds and bodies), can imagine themselves as down to earth, with the people, safe in the knowledge that they can go back to the office the next morning without too much embarrassment at what is a ritualized release of repressed emotions.

Oddly absent from their account is any acknowledgment of the gender-specificity of the rules governing emotional display. Social conventions have traditionally restricted the public expression of sorrow or affection by men and of anger or laughter by women. Men stereotypically learn to translate their softer feelings into physical aggressiveness, while women convert their rage into the shedding of tears. Such a culture provides gender-specific spaces for emotional release which are consistent with dominant constructions of masculinity and femininity—melodrama (and its various manifestations in soap opera or romance) for women, sports for men. Elias and Dunning's emphasis upon the affective dimensions of sports allows us to more accurately (albeit schematically) map the

similarities and differences between sports and melodrama. Melodrama links female affect to domesticity, sentimentality, and vulnerability, while sports links male affect to physical prowess, competition, and mastery. Melodrama explores the concerns of the private sphere, sports those of the public. Melodrama announces its fictional status, while sports claims for itself the status of reality. Melodrama allows for the shedding of tears, while sports solicits shouts, cheers, and boos. Crying, a characteristically feminine form of emotional display, embodies internalized emotion; tears are quiet and passive. Shouting, the preferred outlet for male affect, embodies externalized emotion; it is aggressive and noisy. Women cry from a position of emotional (and often social) vulnerability; men shout from a position of physical and social strength (however illusory).

WWF wrestling, as a form which bridges the gap between sport and melodrama, allows for the spectacle of male physical prowess (a display which is greeted by shouts and boos) but also for the exploration of the emotional and moral life of its combatants. WWF wrestling focuses on both the public and the private, links nonfictional forms with fictional content, and embeds the competitive dimensions of sports within a larger narrative framework which emphasizes the personal consequences of that competition. The "sports entertainment" of WWF wrestling adopts the narrative and thematic structures implicit within traditional sports and heightens them to ensure the maximum emotional impact. At the same time, WWF wrestling adopts the personal, social, and moral conflicts that characterized nineteenth-century theatrical melodrama and enacts them in terms of physical combat between male athletes. In doing so, it foregrounds aspects of masculine mythology which have a particular significance for its predominantly working-class male audience—the experience of vulnerability, the possibilities of male trust and intimacy, and the populist myth of the national community.

Remaking Sports

Elias and Dunning offer a vivid description of the dramaturgy of the ideal soccer match: "a prolonged battle on the football field between teams which are well matched in skill and strength. . . . a game which sways to and fro, in which the teams are so evenly matched that first one, then the other scores." The emotional consequences of the close and heated action are viscerally felt by the spectators. Each subsequent play intensifies their response, "until the tension reaches a point where it can just be borne and contained without getting out of hand." A decisive climax rewards this active engagement with "the happiness of triumph and jubilation."[16] The writers emphasize many traits which football shares with melodrama—the clear opposition between characters, the sharp alignment of audience identification, abrupt shifts in fortune, and an emotionally satisfying resolution. Yet there is an important difference. While melodrama guarantees emotional release through its conformity to tried and true generic structures, actual athletic competition, unlike staged wrestling, is unrehearsed and unscripted. Matches such as the ones Elias and Dunning describe are relatively rare, since so much is left to chance. Where the actual competition lacks narrative interest, that gap must be filled by sports commentary which evokes and intensifies the audience's investment. However, as Barthes notes, wrestling is not a sport but rather a form of popular theater, and as such, the events are staged to ensure maximum emotional impact, structured around a consistent reversal of fortunes and a satisfying climax. There is something at stake in every match—something more than who possesses the title belts.

As a consequence, wrestling heightens the emotional experience offered by traditional sports and directs it toward a specific vision of the social and moral order. Peter Brooks argues that melodrama provides a postsacred society with a means of mapping its basic moral and ethical beliefs, of making the world morally legible.[17] Similarly, wrestling, Barthes argues, takes as its central problematic the restoration of moral order, the creation of a just society from a world where the powerful rule. Within the World Wrestling Federation, this battle for a higher justice is staged through the contest for the title belts. Like traditional melodrama, wrestling operates within a dualistic universe: each participant is either a good guy or a villain, a "fan favorite" or a "rule-breaker." Good guys rarely fight good guys, bad guys rarely fight bad guys. Championship is sometimes unjustly granted to rule-breakers but ultimately belongs to the virtuous.

WWF wrestling offers its viewers a story of justice perverted and restored, innocence misrecognized and recognized, strength used and abused.

Might Makes Right

Within traditional sports, competition is impersonal, the product of prescribed rules which assign competitors on the basis of their standings or on some prespecified form of rotation. Rivalries do, of course, arise within this system and are the stuff of the daily sports page, but many games do not carry this added affective significance. Within the WWF, however, all competition depends upon intense rivalry. Each fight requires the creation of a social and moral opposition and often stems from a personal grievance. Irwin R. Schyster (IRS) falsely accuses the Big Boss Man's mother of tax evasion and threatens to throw her in jail. Sid Justice betrays Hulk Hogan's friendship, turning his back on his tag team partner in the middle of a major match and allowing him to be beaten to a pulp by his opponents, Ric Flair and the Undertaker. Fisticuffs break out between Bret Hart and his brother, "Rocket," during a special "Family Feud" match which awakens long-simmering sibling rivalries. Such offenses require retribution within a world which sees trial by combat as the preferred means of resolving all disputes. Someone has to "pay" for these outrages, and the exacting of payment will occur in the squared ring.

The core myth of WWF wrestling is a fascistic one: ultimately, might makes right; moral authority is linked directly to the possession of physical strength, while evil operates through stealth or craftiness (mental rather than physical sources of power). The appeal of such a myth to a working-class audience should be obvious. In the realm of their everyday experience, strength often gets subordinated into alienated labor. Powerful bodies become the means of their economic exploitation rather than a resource for bettering their lot. In WWF wrestling, physical strength reemerges as a tool for personal empowerment, a means of striking back against personal and moral injustices. Valerie Walkerdine argues that the *Rocky* films, which display a similar appeal, offer "fantasies of omnipotence, heroism and salvation . . . a counterpoint to the experience of oppression and powerlessness."[18] Images of fighting, Walkerdine argues, embody "a class-specific and gendered use of the body," which ennobles the physical skills possessed by the working-class spectator: "Physical violence is presented as the only way open to those whose lot is manual and not intellectual labor. . . . The fantasy of the fighter is the fantasy of a working-class male omnipotence over the forces of humiliating oppression which mutilate and break the body in manual labor."[19]

A central concern within wrestling, then, is how physical strength can ensure triumph over one's abusers, how one can rise from defeat and regain dignity through hand-to-hand combat. Bad guys cheat to win. They manipulate the system and step outside the rules. They use deception, misdirection, subterfuge, and trickery. Rarely do they win fairly. They smuggle weapons into the ring to attack their opponents while their managers distract the referees. They unwrap the turnbuckle pads and slam their foes' heads into metal posts. They adopt choke holds to suffocate them or zap them with cattle prods. Million Dollar Man purposefully focuses his force upon Roddy Piper's wounded knee, doing everything he can to injure him permanently. Such atrocities require rematches to ensure justice; the underdog heroes return next month and, through sheer determination and willpower, battle their antagonists into submission.

Such plots allow for the serialization of the WWF narrative, forestalling its resolution, intensifying its emotional impact. Yet at the same time, the individual match must be made narratively satisfying on its own terms, and so, in practice, such injustices do not stand. Even though the match is over and its official outcome determined, the hero shoves the referee aside and, with renewed energy, bests his opponent in a fair (if nonbinding) fight. Whatever the outcome, most fights end with the protagonist standing proudly in the center of the ring, while his badly beaten antagonist retreats shamefully to his dressing room, justice triumphs both in the long run and in the short run. For the casual viewer, it is the immediate presentation of triumphant innocence that matters, that satisfactorily resolves the drama. Yet for the WWF fan, what matters is the ultimate pursuit of justice as it unfolds through the complexly intertwined stories of the many different wrestlers.

Body Doubles

Melodramatic wrestling allows working-class men to confront their own feelings of vulnerability, their own frustrations at a world which promises them patriarchal authority but which is experienced through relations of economic subordination. Gender identities are most rigidly policed in working-class male culture, since unable to act *as* men, they are forced to act *like* men, with a failure to assume the proper role the source of added humiliation. WWF wrestling offers a utopian alternative to this situation, allowing a movement from victimization toward mastery. Such a scenario requires both the creation and the constant rearticulation of moral distinctions. Morality is defined, first and foremost, through personal antagonisms. As Christine Gledhill has written of traditional melodrama, "Innocence and villainy construct each other: while the villain is necessary to the production and revelation of innocence, innocence defines the boundaries of the forbidden which the villain breaks."[20] In the most aesthetically pleasing and emotionally gripping matches, these personal antagonisms reflect much deeper mythological oppositions—the struggles between rich and poor, white and black, urban and rural, America and the world. Each character stands for something, draws symbolic meaning by borrowing stereotypes already in broader circulation. An important role played by color commentary is to inscribe and reinscribe the basic mythic oppositions at play within a given match. Here, the moral dualism of masculine melodrama finds its voice through the exchanges between two announcers, one (Mean Jean Okerlund) articulating the protagonist's virtues, the other (Bobby "the Brain" Heenan) justifying the rule-breaker's transgressions.

Wrestlers are often cast as doppelgängers, similar yet morally opposite figures. Consider, for example, how *WWF Magazine* characterizes a contest between the evil Mountie and the heroic Big Boss Man: "In conflict are Big Boss Man's and the Mountie's personal philosophies: the enforcement of the law vs. taking the law into one's own hands, the nightstick vs. the cattle prod, weakening a foe with the spike slam vs. disabling him with the nerve-crushing carotid control technique."[21] The Canadian Mountie stands on one page, dressed in his bright red uniform, clutching his cattle prod and snarling. The former Georgia prison guard, Big Boss Man, stands on the other, dressed in his pale blue uniform, clutching an open pair of handcuffs, with a look of quiet earnestness. At this moment the two opponents seem to be made for each other, as if no other possible contest could bear so much meaning, though the Big Boss Man and the Mountie will pair off against other challengers in the next major event.

The most successful wrestlers are those who provoke immediate emotional commitments (either positive or negative) and are open to constant rearticulation, who can be fit into a number of different conflicts and retain semiotic value. Hulk Hogan may stand as the defender of freedom in his feud with Sgt. Slaughter, as innocence betrayed by an ambitious friend in his contest against Sid Justice, and as an aging athlete confronting and overcoming the threat of death in his battle with the Undertaker. Big Boss Man may defend the interests of the economically depressed against the Repo Man, make the streets safe from the Nasty Boys, and assert honest law enforcement in the face of the Mountie's bad example.

The introduction of new characters requires their careful integration into the WWF's moral universe before their first match can be fought. We need to know where they will stand in relation to the other protagonists and antagonists. The arrival of Tatanka. on the WWF roster was preceded by a series of segments showing the Native American hero visiting the tribal elders, undergoing rites of initiation, explaining the meaning of his haircut, makeup, costume, and war shout. His ridicule by the fashion-minded Rick "the Model" Martel introduced his first antagonism and ensured the viewer's recognition of his essential goodness.

Much of the weekly broadcasts centers on the manufacturing of these moral distinctions and the creation of these basic antagonisms. A classic example might be the breakup of the Rockers. A series of accidents and minor disagreements sparked a public showdown on Brutus "the Barber" Beefcake's Barber Shop, a special program segment. Shawn Michaels appeared at the interview, dressed in black leather and wearing sunglasses (already adopting iconography signaling his shift toward the dark side). After a pretense of reconciliation and a series of clips reviewing their past together, Michaels shoved his partner, Marty Jannetty,

through the barber-shop window, amid Brutus's impotent protests.[22] The decision to feature the two team members as independent combatants required the creation of moral difference, while the disintegration of their partnership fit perfectly within the program's familiar doppelgänger structure. *WWF Magazine* portrayed the events in terms of the biblical story of Cain and Abel, as the rivalry of two "brothers":

> [The Rockers] were as close as brothers. They did everything together, in and out of the ring. But Michaels grew jealous of Jannetty and became impatient to succeed. While Jannetty was content to bide his time, work to steadily improve with the knowledge that championships don't come easily in the WWF, Michaels decided he wanted it all now—and all for himself.[23]

If an earlier profile had questioned whether the two had "separate identities," this reporter has no trouble making moral distinctions between the patient Jannetty and the impatient Michaels, the self-sacrificing Jannetty and the self-centered Michaels. Subsequent broadcasts would link Michaels professionally and romantically wirh Sensational Sherri, a woman whose seductive charms have been the downfall of many WWF champs. As a manager, Sherri is noted for her habit of smuggling foreign objects to ringside in her purse and interfering in the matches to ensure her man's victory. Sherri, who had previously been romantically involved with Million Dollar Man Ted Dibiase, announced that she would use her "Teddy Bear's" money to back Michael's solo career, linking his betrayal of his partner to her own greedy and adulterous impulses. All of these plot twists differentiate Jannetty and Michaels, aligning spectator identification with the morally superior partner. Michaels's paramount moral failing is his all-consuming ambition, his desire to dominate rather than work alongside his long-time partner.

The Rockers' story points to the contradictory status of personal advancement within the WWF narrative: these stories hinge upon fantasies of upward mobility, yet ambition is just as often regarded in negative terms, as ultimately corrupting. Such a view of ambition reflects the experience of people who have worked hard all of their lives without much advancement and therefore remain profoundly suspicious of those on top. Wrestling speaks to those who recognize that upward mobility often has little to do with personal merit and a lot to do with a willingness to stomp on those who get in your way. Virtue, in the WWF moral universe, is often defined by a willingness to temper ambition through personal loyalties, through affiliation with others, while vice comes from putting self-interest ahead of everything else. This distrust of self-gain was vividly illustrated during a bout between Rowdy Roddy Piper and Bret "the Hitman" Hart at the 1992 Wrestlemania. This competition uncharacteristically centered on two good guys. As a result, most viewers suspected that one fighter would ultimately be driven to base conduct by personal desire for the Intercontinental Championship belt. Such speculations were encouraged by ambiguous signs from the combatants during "buildup" interviews and exploited during the match through a number of gestures which indicate moral indecision: Rowdy stood ready to club Hart with an illegal foreign object; the camera cut repeatedly to close-ups of his face as he struggled with his conscience before casting the object aside and continuing a fair fight. In the end, however, the two long-time friends embraced each other as Piper congratulated Hart on a more or less fairly won fight. The program situated this bout as a sharp contrast to the feud between Hulk Hogan and Sid Justice, the major attraction at this pay-per-view event. Their budding friendship had been totally destroyed by Justice's overriding desire to dominate the WWF: "I'm gonna crack the head of somebody big in the WWF. . . . No longer is this Farmboy from Arkansas gonna take a back seat to anybody."[24] Rowdy and Hart value their friendship over their ambition; Justice lets nothing stand in the way of his quest for power.

WWF wrestlers are not rounded characters; the spectacle has little room for the novelistic, and here the form may push the melodramatic imagination to its logical extremes. WWF wrestlers experience no internal conflicts which might blur their moral distinctiveness. Rather, they often display the "undividedness" that Robert Heilman sees as a defining aspect of nineteenth-century melodramatic characters:

> [The melodramatic character displays] oneness of feeling as competitor, crusader, aggressor; as defender, counterattacker, fighter for survival;

he may be assertive or compelled, questing or resistant, obsessed or desperate; he may triumph or lose, be victor or victim, exert pressure or be pressed. Always he is undivided, unperplexed by alternatives, untorn by divergent impulses; all of his strength or weakness faces in one direction.[25]

The WWF athletes sketch their moral failings in broad profile: The Mountie pounds on his chest and roars, "I am the Mountie," convinced that no one can contest his superiority, yet as soon as the match gets rough, he slides under the ropes and tries to hide behind his scrawny manager. The Million Dollar Man shoves hundred-dollar bills into the mouths of his defeated opponents, while Sherri paints her face with gilded dollar signs to mark her possession by the highest bidder. Ravishing Rick Rude wears pictures of his opponents on his arse, relishing in his own vulgarity. Virtue similarly displays itself without fear of misrecognition. Hacksaw Jim Duggan clutches an American flag in one hand and a two-by-four in the other.

The need for a constant recombination of a fixed number of characters requires occasional shifts in moral allegiances (as occurred with the breakup of the Rockers). Characters may undergo redemption or seduction, but these shifts typically occur quickly and without much ambiguity. There is rarely any lingering doubt or moral fence-straddling. Such characters are good one week and evil the next. Jake "the Snake" Roberts, a long-time hero—albeit one who enjoys his distance from the other protagonists—uncharacteristically offered to help the Ultimate Warrior prepare for his fight against the Undertaker. Their grim preparations unfolded over several weeks, with Jake forcing the Warrior to undergo progressively more twisted rituals—locking him into a coffin, burying him alive—until finally Jake shoved him into a room full of venomous snakes. Bitten by Jake's cobra, Lucifer, the Ultimate Warrior staggered toward his friend, who simply brushed him aside. As the camera pulled back to show the Undertaker standing side by side with Jake, the turncoat laughed, "Never trust a snake." From that moment forward, Jake was portrayed as totally evil, Barthes's perfect bastard. Jake attacks Macho man Randy Savage's bride, Elizabeth, on their wedding day and terrorizes the couple every chance he gets.

The program provides no motivation for such outrages, though commentary both in the broadcasts and in the pages of the wrestling magazines constantly invites such speculation: "What makes Jake hate Savage and his bride so fiercely? Why does he get his jollies—as he admits—from tormenting her?" What Peter Brooks said about the villains of traditional melodrama holds equally well here: "Evil in the world of melodrama does not need justification; it exists, simply. . . . And the less it is adequately motivated, the more this evil appears simply volitional, the product of pure will."[26] Jake is evil because he is a snake; it's in his character and nothing can change him, even though in this case, less than a year ago, Jake was as essentially good as he is now totally demented. We know Jake is evil and without redemption, because he tells us so, over and over:

I'm not really sure I have any soul at all. . . . Once I get involved in something—no matter how demented, no matter how treacherous, no matter how far off the mark it is from normal standards—I never back down. I just keep on going, deeper and deeper into the blackness, far past the point where any sensible person would venture. You see, a person with a conscience—a person with a soul—would be frightened by the sordid world I frequent. But Jake the Snake isn't scared at all. To tell you the truth, I can't get enough of it.[27]

Jake recognizes and acknowledges his villainy; he names it publicly and unrepentantly.

Peter Brooks sees such a process of "self-nomination" as an essential feature of the melodramatic imagination: "Nothing is spared because nothing is left unsaid; the characters stand on stage and utter the unspeakable, give voice to their deepest feelings, dramatize through their heightened and polarized words and gestures the whole lesson of their relationship."[28] The soliloquy, that stock device of the traditional melodrama, is alive and well in WWF wrestling. Wrestlers look directly into the audience and shove their fists toward the camera; they proclaim their personal credos and describe their sufferings. Tag team partners repeat their dedication to each other and their plans to dominate their challengers. Villains profess their evil intentions and vow to perform various forms of mayhem upon their opponents. Their rhetoric is excessively metaphoric, transforming every fight into a life-and-death struggle. Much as nineteenth-century theatrical melodrama used denotative music to define the characters' moral stances, the wrestlers' entry into the arena is preceded by theme songs which encapsulate their personalities. Hulk's song describes him as "a real American hero" who "fights for the rights of every man." The Million Dollar Man's jingle proclaims his compelling interest in "money, money, money," while Jake's song repeats "trust me, trust me, trust me."

This public declaration ensures the constant moral legibility of the WWF narrative and thereby maximizes the audience's own emotional response. Spectators come to the arena or turn on the program to express intense emotion—to cheer the hero, to boo and jeer the villain—without moral ambiguity or emotional complexity. (Wrestling fans sometimes choose to root for the villains, taking pleasure in their self-conscious inversion of the WWF's moral universe, yet even this perverse pleasure requires moral legibility.) Operating within a world of absolutes, WWF wrestlers wear their hearts on their sleeves (or, in Ravishing Rick Rude's case, on the seat of their pants) and project their emotions from every inch of their bodies. Much as in classic melodrama, external actions reveal internal states; moral disagreements demand physical expressions. As Brooks writes, "Emotions are given a full acting-out, a full representation before our eyes. . . . Nothing is *under*stated, all is *over*stated."[29] The Million Dollar Man cowers, covering his face and retreating, crawling on hands and knees backward across the ring. Sherri shouts at the top of her ample lungs and pounds the floor with her high-heel shoe. Rowdy Roddy Piper gets his dander up and charges into the ring. With a burst of furious energy, he swings madly at his opponents, forcing them to scatter right and left. Roddy spits in the Million Dollar Man's eyes, flings his sweaty shirt in his face, or grabs Sherri, rips off her dress, throws her over his knee, and spanks her. Such characters embody the shameful spectacle of emotional display, acting as focal points for the audience's own expression of otherwise repressed affect.

Invincible Victims

Fans eagerly anticipate these excessive gestures as the most appropriate means of conveying the characters' moral attitudes. Through a process of simplification, the wrestler's body has been reduced to a series of iconic surfaces and stock attitudes. We know not only how the performer is apt to respond to a given situation but what bodily means will be adopted to express that response. Wrestlers perform less with their eyes and hands than with their arms and legs and with their deep, resounding voices. Earthquake's bass rumble and Roddy's fiery outbursts, Ric Flair's vicious laughter and Macho Man's red-faced indignation are "too much" for the small screen, yet they articulate feelings that are too intense to be contained.

This process of simplification and exaggeration transforms the wrestlers into cartoonish figures who may slam each other's heads into iron steps, throw each other onto wooden floors, smash each other with steel chairs, land with their full weight on the other's prone stomach, and emerge without a scratch, ready to fight again. Moral conflict will continue unabated; no defeat can be final within a world where the characters are omnipotent. If traditional melodrama foregrounded long-suffering women's endurance of whatever injustices the world might throw against them, WWF wrestling centers around male victims who ultimately refuse to accept any more abuse and fight back against the aggressors.

Such a scenario allows men to acknowledge their own vulnerability, safe in the knowledge that their masculine potency will ultimately be restored and that they will be strong enough to overcome the forces which subordinate them. Hulk Hogan has perfected the image of the martyred hero who somehow captures victory from the closing jaws of defeat. Badly beaten in a fight, Hulk lies in a crumpled heap. The referee lifts his limp arms up, once, twice, ready to call the fight, when the crowd begins to clap and stomp. The mighty hero rises slowly, painfully to his feet, rejuvenated by the crowd's response. Blood streams through his blond hair and drips across his face, but he whips it aside with a broad swing of his mighty arms. Hulk turns to face his now-terrified assailant.

"Seeing Is Believing"

Such broad theatricality cuts against wrestling's tradition of pseudorealism; the programs' formats mimic the structures and visual style of nonfiction television, of sports coverage, news broadcasts, and talk shows.

The fiction is, of course, that all of this fighting is authentic, spontaneous, unscripted. The WWF narrative preserves that illusion at all costs. There is no stepping outside the fiction, no acknowledgment of the production process or the act of authorship. When the performers are featured in *WWF Magazine*, they are profiled in character. Story segments are told in the form of late-breaking news reports or framed as interviews. The commentators are taken by surprise, interrupted by seemingly unplanned occurrences. During one broadcast, Jake the Snake captured Macho Man, dragging him into the ring. Jake tied him to the ropes and menaced him with a cobra which sprang and bit him on the forearm. The camera was jostled from side to side by people racing to Macho's assistance and panned abruptly trying to follow his hysterical wife as she ran in horror to ringside. A reaction shot shows a child in the audience reduced to tears by this brutal spectacle. Yet, at the same time, the camera refused to show us an image "too shocking" for broadcast. Macho Man's arm and the snake's gaping mouth were censored, blocked by white bars, not unlike the blue dot that covered the witness's face at the William Kennedy Smith rape trial that same week. (A few weeks later, the "uncensored" footage was at last shown, during a prime-time broadcast, so that viewers could see "what really happened.") The plot lines are thus told through public moments where a camera could plausibly be present, though such moments allow us insight into the characters' private motivations.

As Ric Flair often asserted during his brief stay in the WWF, "Pictures don't lie; seeing is believing," and yet it is precisely seeing and not believing that is a central pleasure in watching television wrestling. What audiences see is completely "unbelievable," as ring commentators frequently proclaim—unbelievable because these human bodies are unnaturally proportioned and monstrously large, because these figures who leap through the air seem to defy all natural laws, and, most important, because these characters participate within the corny and timeworn plots of the nineteenth-century melodrama. The pleasure comes in seeing what cannot be believed, yet is constantly asserted to us as undeniably true. Fans elbow each other in the ribs, "Look how fake," taking great pride in their ability to see through a deception that was never intended to convince.

Such campy self-acknowledgment may be part of what makes male spectators' affective engagement with this melodramatic form safe and acceptable within a traditionally masculine culture which otherwise backs away from overt emotional display. Whenever the emotions become too intense, there is always a way of pulling back, laughing at what might otherwise provoke tears. WWF wrestling, at another level, provokes authentic pain and rage, particularly when it embraces populist myths of economic exploitation and class solidarity, feeds a hunger for homosocial bonding, or speaks to Utopian fantasies of empowerment. The gap between the campy and the earnest reception of wrestling may reflect the double role which Elias and Dunning ascribe to traditional sports: the need to allow for the de-controlling of powerful affects while at the same time regulating their expression and ensuring their ultimate containment. The melodramatic aspects are what trigger emotional release, while the campy aspects contain it within safe bounds. The plots of wrestling cut close to the bone, inciting racial and class antagonisms that rarely surface this overtly elsewhere in popular culture, while comic exaggeration ensures that such images can never fully be taken seriously.

Romance in the Ring

WWF's plots center on the classic materials of melodrama: "false accusation. . . . innocence beleaguered, virtue triumphant, eternal fidelity, mysterious identity, lovers reconciled, fraudulent revealed, threats survived, enemies foiled."[30] The ongoing romance of Macho and Elizabeth, bears all of the classic traces of the sentimental novel. The virginal Miss Elizabeth, who almost always dresses in lacy white, stands as the embodiment of womanly virtues. WWF fans were fascinated by her struggle to civilize her impassioned and often uncontrollable Macho Man, withstanding constant bouts of unreasoning jealousy, tempering his dirty tactics. As a profile of Miss Elizabeth explained, "She embodies the spirit of a grass-roots American wife. She cares for her man. She provides him with comfort in the midst of chaos. She provides him with a sense of unity when his world seems to be disintegrating. Elizabeth calmly handles these difficult situations with grace and tact."[31] WWF fans watched the course

of their romance for years, as Macho rejected her, taking up with the sensuous and anything-but-virtuous Sherri, but he was reunited with Elizabeth following a devastating defeat in a career-ending match against the Ultimate Warrior. They followed her efforts to rebuild her Macho Man's self-confidence, his fumbling attempts to propose to her, and their spectacular pay-per-view wedding. They watched as the beloved coupled were attacked during their wedding party by Jake and the Undertaker, as Macho begged the WWF management to reinstate him so that he could avenge himself and his wife against this outrage, and as he finally returned to the ring and defeated the heartless Snake during a specially scheduled event. No sooner was this conflict resolved than Ric Flair produced incriminating photographs which he claimed show that Elizabeth was his former lover. In a locker-room interview, Ric and Mr. Perfect smirkingly revealed the photographs as evidence that Elizabeth is "damaged goods," while the fumbling announcer struggled to protect Elizabeth's previously unquestioned virtue. Once again, this domestic crisis motivated a forthcoming bout, creating narrative interest as the all but inarticulate Macho defended his wife with his muscles.

The Macho Man-Elizabeth romance is unusual in its heavy focus on domestic relations, though not unique: Sherri's romantic entanglements with the Million Dollar Man and Shawn Michaels offer a similar (albeit morally opposite) narrative, while the complex family drama of the Hart family (whose patriarch, Stew, was a long-time wrestler and whose four sons have all enjoyed WWF careers) has motivated images of both fraternal solidarity and sibling rivalry. More often, however, the masculine melodrama of WWF wrestling centers on the relationships between men, occupying a homosocial space which has little room for female intrusions. There are, after all, only two women in the WWF universe—the domestic angel, Elizabeth, and the scheming whore, Sherri. A more typical story involved Virgil, the black bodyguard of the Million Dollar Man, who, after years of being subjected to his boss's humiliating whims, decided to strike back, to challenge his one-time master to a fight for possession of his "Million Dollar Belt." Virgil was befriended by the feisty Scotsman Rowdy Roddy Piper, who taught him to stand tall and broad. The two men fought side by side to ensure the black man's dignity.

The antagonism between Virgil and the Million Dollar Man provoked class warfare, while the friendship between Virgil and Roddy marked the uneasy courtship between men.

Here and elsewhere, WWF wrestling operates along the gap that separates our cultural ideal of male autonomy and the reality of alienation, themes that emerge most vividly within tag team competition. The fighter, that omnipotent muscle machine, steps alone, with complete confidence, into the ring, ready to do battle with his opponent. As the fight progresses, he is beaten down, unable to manage without assistance. Struggling to the ropes, he must admit that he needs another man. His partner reaches out to him while he crawls along the floor, inching toward that embrace. The image of the two hands, barely touching, and the two men, working together to overcome their problems, seems rich with what Eve Sedgwick calls "male homosocial desire."[32] That such a fantasy is played out involving men whose physical appearance exaggerates all of the secondary masculine characteristics frees male spectators from social taboos which prohibit the open exploration of male intimacy. In their own brutish language, the men express what it is like to need (and desire?) another man. Consider, for example, how *WWF Magazine* characterizes the growing friendship between Jake the Snake and Andre the Giant:

> At a glance, Andre gives the impression of granite—unshakable, immutable and omnipotent. Inside, there is a different Andre. His massive size and power belie the fact that his spirit is as fragile as anyone's. And that spirit was more bruised than was his body. Like Andre, Jake projects a sense of detachment from the world of the average guy. Like Andre, Jake has an inner self that is more vulnerable than his outer shell.[33]

The story describes their first tentative overtures, their attempts to overcome old animosities, and their growing dependency on each other for physical and emotional support. As Jake explains:

> Andre was afraid of serpents. I was afraid of people—not of confronting people, but of getting close to them. We began to talk. Slow talk. Noth-

ing talk. Getting to know one another. The talk got deeper. . . . I never asked for help from anybody. I never will. But Andre decided to help me; I won't turn him down. I guess we help one another. You might call it a meeting of the minds.[34]

Jake's language carefully, hesitantly negotiates between male ideals of individual autonomy ("I never asked for help") and an end to the isolation and loneliness such independence creates. Will Jake find this ideal friendship with a man who was once his bitter enemy, or does he simply lay himself open to new injuries? These images of powerful men whose hulking bodies mask hidden pains speak to longings which the entire structure of patriarchy desperately denies.

Such a narrative explores the links that bind and the barriers that separate men. Yet, at the same time, its recurring images of betrayed friendship and violated trust rationalize the refusal to let down barriers. Texas Tornado describes his relationship to his former tag team partner: "I know the Warrior as well as any man in the World Wrestling Federation. . . . Of course, in wrestling, you never get too close with anybody because one day you might be facing him on the other side of the ring. Still, Warrior and I have traveled and trained together. We've shared things."[35] Wrestling operates within a carefully policed zone, a squared ring, that allows for the representation of intense homosocial desire but also erects strong barriers against too much risk and intimacy. The wrestlers "share things," but they are not allowed to get "too close."

Consider what happened when the Beverley Brothers met the Bushwhackers at a live WWF event at the Boston Gardens. The two brothers, clad in lavender tights, hugged each other before the match, and their down-under opponents, in their big boots and work clothes, turned upon them in a flash, "queer baiting" and then "gay bashing" the Beverley Brothers. I sat there with fear and loathing as I heard thousands of men, women, and children shouting, "Faggot, faggot, faggot," I was perplexed at how such a representation could push so far and spark such an intense response. The chanting continued for five, ten minutes, as the Bushwhackers stomped their feet and waved their khaki caps with glee, determined to drive their "effeminate" opponents from the ring. The Beverley Brothers protested, pouted, and finally submitted, unable to stand firm against their tormentors. What may have necessitated this homophobic spectacle was the need of both performers and spectators to control potential readings of the Bushwhackers' own physically intimate relationship. The Bushwhackers, Butch and Luke, are constantly defined as polymorphously perverse and indiscriminately oral, licking the faces of innocent spectators or engaging in mutual face-wetting as a symbolic gesture of their mutual commitment. By defining the Beverley "Sisters" as "faggots," as outside of acceptable masculinity, the Bushwhackers created a space where homosocial desire could be more freely expressed without danger of its calling into question their gender identity or sexual preference. This moment seems emblematic of the way wrestling more generally operates—creating a realm of male action which is primarily an excuse for the display of masculine emotion (and even for homoerotic contact) while ensuring that nothing which occurs there can raise any questions about the participant's "manhood."[36]

Populist Pleasures

One key way that wrestling contains this homoerotic potential is through the displacement of issues of homosocial bonding onto a broader political and economic terrain. If, as feminism has historically claimed, the personal is the political, traditional masculinity has often acknowledged its personal vulnerabilities only through evoking more abstract political categories. Populist politics, no less than sports, has been a space of male emotional expression, where personal pains and sufferings can be openly acknowledged only through allegorical rhetoric and passionate oratory. Melodramatic wrestling's focus on the professional rather than the personal sphere facilitates this shift from the friendship ties between individual males to the political ties between all working men. The erotics of male homosocial desire is sublimated into a hunger for the populist community, while images of economic exploitation are often charged with a male dread of penetration and submission.

Although rarely described in these terms, populism offers a melodramatic vision of political and economic relationships. Bruce Palmer argues that populism is characterized by its focus on a tangible reality of immediate experience rather than political abstraction, its emphasis on personal rather than impersonal causation, and its appeal to sentimentality rather than rationality (all traits commonly associated with the melodramatic). As he summarizes the basic axioms of the southern populist movement, "what is most real and most important in the world was that which was most tangible, that which could be seen and touched. . . . People made things move and if some people were moved more than movers, it was because others, more powerful, moved them."[37] American populism sees virtue as originating through physical labor, as a trait possessed by those who are closest to the moment of production (and therefore embodied through manual strength), while moral transgression, particularly greed and ruthlessness, reflects alienation from the production process (often embodied as physical frailty and sniveling cowardice). Populism understands politics through the social relations between individuals rather than between groups, though individuals are understood in larger allegorical categories—the simple farmer vs. the slick Wall Street lawyer, the factory worker vs. the scheming boss, the small businessman vs. the Washington bureaucrat, the American voter vs. the party bosses. Social changes come, within this model, through personal redemption rather than systemic change. A populist utopia would be a community within which individuals recognized their common interests and respected their mutual responsibilities. As Palmer explains, "The only decent society was one in which each person looked out for every other one, a society in which *all* people enjoyed equal rights and the benefits of their labor."[38] Such a movement made common cause between workers and farmers (and in its most progressive forms, between whites and blacks) in their mutual struggle for survival against the forces of capitalist expansion and technological change.

If populism draws on melodramatic rhetoric, populism has also provided the core myths by which the masculine melodrama has historically operated. French melodrama might concern itself with the struggles of the aristocracy and the bourgeois; American faith in a classless society translated these same conventions into narratives about scheming bankers and virtuous yeomen, stock figures within the populist vision. American melodrama, David Grimsted tells us, imagines a democratic universe which rewards a commitment to fraternity and hard work and demonizes appeals to privilege.[39] Michael Denning argues that the sentimental fiction provided by turn-of-the-century dime novels similarly interpreted the economic relations between labor and capital within essentially melodramatic terms.[40] While such visions of American democracy were not automatically populist and often lent themselves to middle-class social reform, melodrama was always available as a vehicle for populist allegory, especially within masculine forms which displace melodrama's characteristic interest in the domestic into the public sphere.

In that sense, melodramatic wrestling fits squarely within the larger tradition of masculine melodrama and populist politics. What is striking about the mythology of WWF wrestling is how explicitly its central conflicts evoke class antagonisms. Its villains offer vivid images of capitalist greed and conspicuous consumption. The Million Dollar Man wears a gold belt studded with diamonds and waves a huge wad of hundred-dollar bills. Magazine photographs and program segments show him driving expensive cars, eating in high-class restaurants, living in a penthouse apartment, or vacationing in his summer house at Palm Beach. What he can't grab with brute force, he buys: "Everybody has a price." In one notorious episode, he bribed Andre the Giant to turn over to him the sacred WWF championship belt; another time, he plotted a hostile takeover of the WWF. Similarly, Ric Flair brags constantly about his wealth and influence: "I'll pull up [to the match] in my stretch limousine with a bottle of Dom Perignon in one hand and a fine-looking woman holding my other. The only thing I'll be worried about is if the champagne stays cold enough."[41] Mean Gene Okerlund interviews him on his yacht, *Gypsy*, as he chuckles over his sexual humiliation of the Macho Man and brags about his wild parties. The Model enjoys a jet-setting lifestyle, displays the "finest in clothing," and tries to market his new line of male perfumes, "the scent of the 90s, Arrogance." Irwin R. Schyster constantly threatens to audit his opponents, while Repo Man promises to foreclose on their possessions: "What's mine is mine. What's yours is mine too! . . . I've got no mercy at all for cheats. Tough luck

if you've lost your job. If you can't make the payment, I'll get your car. Walk to look for work, Sucker."[42]

The patriotic laborer (Hacksaw Jim Duggan), the virtuous farm boy (Hillbilly Jim), the small-town boy made good (Big Boss Man), the Horatio Alger character (Virgil, Rowdy Roddy Piper, Tito Santana) are stock figures within this morality play, much as they have been basic tropes in populist discourse for more than a century. WWF heroes hail from humble origins and can therefore act as appropriate champions within fantasies of economic empowerment and social justice. A profile introducing Sid Justice to *WWF Magazine* readers stressed his rural origins: "Sid Justice comes from the land. . . . Born and raised on a farm in Arkansas, imbued with the hardworking values of people who rise before dawn to till the earth and milk the cows. . . . A lifestyle that is the backbone of this country."[43] Justice developed his muscles tossing bales of hay onto his grandfather's truck, and his integrity reflects the simplicity of an agrarian upbringing: "Don't confuse simplicity with stupidity. A man who learned to make the land produce its fruits has smarts." Sid Justice understands the meaning of personal commitments and the value of simple virtues in a way that would be alien to "people who get their dinner out of a cellophane package from a super market."

Pride in where one comes from extends as well to a recognition of racial or ethnic identities. Tito Santana returns to Mexico to rediscover his roots and takes lessons from a famous bullfighter, changing his name to El Matador. Tatanka emerges as the "leader of the New Indian Nation," demonstrating his pride in his "Native American heritage." He explains, "the tribes of all nations are embodied in me."[44] The creation of tag teams and other alliances cuts across traditional antagonisms to bring together diverse groups behind a common cause. Tag team partners Texas Tornado and El Matador, the Anglo and the Mexicano, join forces in their shared struggle against economic injustice and brute power. "Rule-breakers" are often linked to racial prejudice. The "Brain" releases a steady stream of racial slurs and epithets; the Million Dollar Man visits the "neighborhoods" to make fun of the ramshackle shack where El Matador was raised or to ridicule the crime-ridden streets where Virgil spent his youth. What WWF wrestling enacts, then, are both contemporary class antagonisms (the working man against the Million Dollar Man, the boy from the barrio against the repo man, the farmer against the IRS) and the possibilities of a class solidarity that cuts across racial boundaries, a common community of the oppressed and the marginal.

The rule-breaker's willingness to jeer at honest values and humble ancestry, to hit the proletarian protagonists with economic threats and to shove their own ill-gotten goods in their faces, intensifies the emotions surrounding their confrontations. These men are fighting for all of our dignity against these forces which keep us down, which profit from others' suffering and prosper in times of increased hardship. Big Boss Man defends his mother against false allegations leveled against her by the IRS: "My Mama never had a job in her life. All she did was take care of her children and raise food on the farm down in Georgia."[45] Virgil strikes back not only against the man who forced him to wipe the perspiration from his brow and pick the dirt from between his toes, but also against the conditions of economic subordination which made him dependent on that monster.

Coming to Blows

Such evil must be isolated from the populist community; its origins must be identified and condemned because it represents a threat to mutual survival. This attempt to name and isolate corruption emerges in a particularly vivid fashion when Sgt. Slaughter discusses the Nasty Boys' delinquency:

> The Nasty Boys are un-American trash. You know, their hometown of Allentown is a very patriotic town. Its people have worked in the steel mills for years. Their hard work is evident in every skyscraper and building from coast to coast. Allentown's people have worked in the coal mines for years. Their hard work has kept America warm in the dead of winter. But the Nasty Boys don't come from the same Allentown I know. . . . They spit on hard-working Americans. They spit on Patriotic people. And they spit on the symbol of this great land, Old Glory herself.[46]

Slaughter's rhetoric is classic populism, linking virtue and patriotism with labor, treating evil as a threat originating outside of the community which much be contained and vanished.

This process of defining the great American community involves defining outsiders as well as insiders, and it is not simply the rich and the powerful who are excluded. There is a strong strand of nativism in the WWF's populist vision. When we move from national to international politics, the basic moral opposition shifts from the powerless against the powerful to America and its allies (the United Kingdom, Australia and New Zealand, Canada) against its enemies (especially the Arabs and the Communists, often the Japanese). The central match at the 1993 Survivor Series, for example, pitted the "All-Americans" against the "Foreign Fanatics" (a mix that involved not only predictable villains such as Japan's massive Yokozuma but also less predictable ones, such as Finland's Ludwig and the Montrealers). The appeal to racial stereotyping, which had its progressive dimensions in the creation of champions for various oppressed minorities, resurfaces here in a profound xenophobia. Arab wrestlers are ruthless, Asian wrestlers are fiendishly inscrutable or massive and immovable. While America is defined through its acceptance of diversity, foreign cultures are defined through their sameness, their conformity to a common image. This is true for sympathetic foreigners, such as the Bushwhackers, as it is for less sympathetic foreigners, such as Col. Mustafa and Gen. Adnan. At this level, Hulk's longtime possession of the WWF title becomes an issue of national sovereignty, with threats coming from outside not only the populist community but the American nation-state as well; "Foreign Fanatics" are trying to take what belongs always in American hands, and they must be taught that they can't mess with Uncle Sam.

American's foreign relations can be mapped through the changing alliances within the WWF: Nikolia Volkov, one of the two Bolsheviks, retired from view when the Cold War seemed on the verge of resolution but reemerged as a spokesman for the new Eastern Europe, redefined as a citizen of Lithuania. The WWF restaged the Gulf War through a series of "Body-bag" bouts between Hulk Hogan and Sgt. Slaughter. Slaughter, a former Marine drill sergeant, was brainwashed by Iraqi operatives Col. Mustafa and Gen. Adnan. Under their sinister tutelage, he seized the WWF championship belt through brutal means and vowed to turn the entire federation and its followers into "POWs." In a series of staged incidents, Slaughter burned an American flag and ridiculed basic national institutions. The turncoat leatherneck smugly pounded his chest while his turbaned sidekick babbled incessantly in something resembling Arabic. Hulk Hogan, the all-American hero, vowed that his muscles were more powerful than patriot missiles and that he could reclaim the belt in the name of God, family, and country. He dedicated his strength to protect the "Little Hulkamaniacs" whose mothers and fathers were serving in the Gulf. The blond-haired, blue-eyed Hulkster looked directly into the camera, flexing his pythons and biceps, and roared, "What ya gonna do, Sarge Slaughter, when the Red, White and Blue runs wild on you?" Hulk and Hacksaw Jim Duggan incited the crowd to chant "USA" and to jeer at the Iraqi national anthem. Here, the working-class heroes emerge as flag-waving patriots, fighting against "unAmericanism" at home and tyranny abroad.

Yet, however jingoistic this enactment became, WWF's melodramatic conventions exercised a counterpressure, bridging the gap between otherwise sharply delimited ideological categories. Humiliated by a crushing defeat, Slaughter pulled back from his foreign allies and began a pilgrimage to various national monuments, pleading with the audience, "I want my country back." Ultimately, in a moment of reconciliation with Hacksaw Jim Duggan, the audience was asked to forgive him for his transgressions and to accept him back into the community. Sarge kneeled and kissed an American flag, Hacksaw embraced him, and the two men walked away together, arm in arm. That moment when one tired and physically wounded man accepted the embrace and assistance of another tired and psychically wounded man contained tremendous emotional intensity. Here, male homosocial desire and populist rhetoric work together to rein in the nationalistic logic of the Gulf War narrative, to create a time and space where male vulnerability and mutual need may be publicly expressed. Here, the personal concerns which had been displaced onto populist politics reassert their powerful demands upon the male combatants and spectators to ensure an emotional resolution to a story which in the real world refused satisfying closure. The story of a soul-less turncoat

and a ruthless tyrant evolved into the story of a fallen man's search for redemption and reunion, an autonomous male's hunger for companionship, and an invincible victim's quest for higher justice.

Such a moment can be described only as melodramatic, but what it offers is a peculiarly masculine form of melodrama. If traditional melodrama centers upon the moral struggle between the powerful and the vulnerable, masculine melodrama confronts the painful paradox that working-class men are powerful by virtue of their gender and vulnerable by virtue of their economic status. If traditional melodrama involves a play with affect, masculine melodrama confronts the barriers which traditional masculinity erects around the overt expression of emotion. If traditional melodrama centers on the personal consequences of social change, masculine melodrama must confront traditional masculinity's tendency to displace personal needs and desires onto the public sphere. The populist imagery of melodramatic wrestling can be understood as one way of negotiating within these competing expectations, separating economic vulnerability from any permanent threat to male potency, translating emotional expression into rage against political injustice, turning tears into shouts, and displacing homosocial desire onto the larger social community. Populism may be what makes this powerful mixture of the masculine and the melodramatic popularly accessible and what allows wrestling to become such a powerful release of repressed male emotion.

Laura Kipnis's thoughtful essay "Reading *Hustler*" cautions us against reading popular culture (or working-class ideology) in black-and-white, either-or terms, imposing upon it our own political fantasies: "There is no guarantee that counter-hegemonic or even specifically anti-bourgeois cultural forms are necessarily also going to be progressive."[47] Kipnis finds that *Hustler* "powerfully articulates class resentments" but does so in terms which are "often only incoherent and banal when it means to be alarming and confrontational." Kipnis does not deny the profound "anti-liberalism, anti-feminism, anti-communism and anti-progressivism" which characterizes the magazine's contents; she does not attempt to rescue Larry Flynt for progressive politics. She does, however, see *Hustler* as speaking to an authentic discontent with middle-class values and lifestyles, as a voice that challenges entrenched authority. Kipnis's essay is controversial because it neither condemns nor romanticizes *Hustler* and because its writer struggles in print with her own conflicted feelings about pornography.

WWF wrestling poses this same problematic mixture of the antihegemonic and the reactionary. It is a fascist spectacle of male power, depicting a world where might makes right and moral authority is exercised by brute force. It engages in the worst sort of jingoistic nationalism. It evokes racial and ethnic stereotypes that demean groups even when they are intended to provide positive role models. It provokes homophobic disgust and patriarchal outrage against any and all incursions beyond heterosexual male dominance. But, as Jake the Snake reminds us, "it goes much deeper than that. . . . There's more at stake than just wrestling, man." WWF wrestling is also a form of masculine melodrama which, like its nineteenth-century precedents, lends its voice to the voiceless and champions the powerless. Wrestling allows a sanctioned space of male emotional release and offers utopian visions of the possibility of trust and intimacy within male friendship. It celebrates and encourages working-class resistance to economic injustice and political abuse. It recognizes and values the diversity of American society and imagines a world where mutual cooperation can exist between the races. In short, wrestling embodies the fundamental contradictions of the American populist tradition. The politics of WWF wrestling is punch-drunk and rambunctious, yet it builds upon authentic anger and frustrations which we cannot ignore if we want to understand the state of contemporary American culture. Wrestling makes you want to shout, and perhaps we have had too much silence.

Notes

1. "WWF Interview: A Talk with Jake 'the Snake' Roberts," *WWF Magazine*, February 1992, p. 17.
2. Roland Barthes, "The World of Wrestling," in Susan Sontag, ed., *A Barthes Reader* (New York: Hill and Wang, 1982), p. 23.
3. Ibid., p. 25.
4. Ibid., p. 29.
5. For useful background on the historical development of television wrestling, as well as for an alternative reading of its narrative structures, see Michael R. Ball, *Professional Wrestling as Ritual Drama in American Popular Culture* (Lewiston: Edwin Mellen Press, 1990). For a performance-centered account of WWF Wrestling, see Sharon Mazer, "The Doggie Doggie World of Professional Wrestling," *The Drama Review*, Winter 1990, pp. 96–122.
6. John Fiske, *Television Culture* (London: Methuen, 1987); Tania Modleski, *Loving with a Vengeance: Mass Produced Fantasies for Women* (London: Methuen, 1982); Jane Feuer, "Melodrama, Serial Form and Television Today," *Screen* 25 (1984): 4–16.
7. Gledhill, pp. 12–13. David Thorburn similarly finds melodramatic conventions underlying much of prime-time television programming. See Thorburn, "Television Melodrama," in Horace Newcomb, ed., *Television: The Critical Eye*, 4th ed. (New York: Oxford University Press, 1987), p. 7.
8. John Fiske, *Understanding Popular Culture* (Boston: Unwin Hyman, 1989), chapter 4.
9. Peter J. Rabinowitz, "The Turn of the Glass Key: Popular Fiction as Reading Strategy," *Critical Inquiry* 12, no. 2 (1985): 421.
10. Norbert Elias and Eric Dunning, *The Quest for Excitement: Sport and Leisure in the Civilizing Process* (New York: Basil Blackwell, 1986), p. 41.
11. Ibid., pp. 64–65.
12. Ibid., p. 111.
13. Ibid., p. 49.
14. Ibid.
15. Ibid., p. 50.
16. Ibid., pp. 86–87.
17. Peter Brooks, *The Melodramatic Imagination: Balzac, Henry James, Melodrama and the Mode of Excess* (New Haven: Yale University Press, 1976).
18. Valerie Walkerdine, "Video Replay: Families, Films and Fantasy," in Victor Burgin, James Donald, and Cora Kaplan, eds., *Formations of Fantasy* (London: Methuen, 1986), pp. 172–74.
19. Ibid., p. 173.
20. Christine Gledhill, "The Melodramatic Field: An Investigation," in Christine Gledhill, ed., *Home Is Where the Heart Is: Studies in Melodrama and the Woman's Film* (London: BFI, 1987), p. 21.
21. Keith Elliot Greenberg, "One Step Too Far: Boss Man and Mountie Clash over Meaning of Justice," *WWF Magazine*, May 1991, p. 40.
22. Brutus was injured in a motorcycle accident several years ago and had his skull reconstructed; he is no longer able to fight but has come to represent the voice of aged wisdom within the WWF universe. Brutus constantly articulates the values of fairness and loyalty in the face of their abuse by the rule-breaking characters, pushing for reconciliations that might resolve old feuds, and watching as these disputes erupt and destroy his barber shop.

23. "The Mark of Cain: Shawn Michaels Betrays His Tag Team Brother," *WWF Magazine*, March 1992, p. 41.

24. "WWF Superstars Talk about Wrestlemania," *WWF Magazine*, March 1992, p. 18.

25. Robert Bechtold Heilman, *The Iceman, the Arsonist and the Troubled Agent: Tragedy and Melodrama on the Modern Stage* (Seattle: University of Washington Press, 1973), p. 53.

26. Brooks, p. 34.

27. "WWF Interview: A Talk with Jake 'the Snake' Roberts," p. 17.

28. Brooks, p. 4.

29. Ibid., p. 41.

30. Robert Bechtold Heilman, *Tragedy and Melodrama: Versions of Experience* (Seattle: University of Washington Press, 1968), p. 76.

31. "Elizabeth Balancing Family with Business," *WWF Wrestling Spotlight*, March 1992.

32. Eve Kosofsky Sedgwick, *Between Men: English Literature and Male Homosocial Desire* (New York: Columbia University Press, 1985).

33. "Meeting of the Minds: Jake and Andre—Psychological Interplay," *WWF Magazine*, August 1991, p. 52.

34. Ibid.

35. Keith Elliot Greenberg, "The Darkness Is in Me Forever . . .," *WWF Magazine*, August 1991, p. 47.

36. This incident could also be read as a response to a series of rumors and tabloid stories centering on the sexuality of WWF athletes. The Ultimate Warrior was "outed" by one tabloid newspaper, while charges of sexual harassment surfaced on an episode of the Phil Donahue show. Complicating an easy reading of this incident is the strong popularity of wrestling within the gay male community and the existence of gay fanzines publishing sexual fantasies involving wrestlers.

37. Bruce Palmer, *"Man over Money": The Southern Populist Critique of American Capitalism* (Chapel Hill: University of North Carolina Press, 1980), p. 3.

38. Ibid., p. 5.

39. David Grimsted, *Melodrama Unveiled: American Thought and Culture, 1800–1850* (Chicago: University of Chicago Press, 1968).

40. Michael Denning, *Mechanic Accents: Dime Novels and Working-Class Culture in America* (London: Verso, 1987), p. 80.

41. "WWF Superstars Talk about Wrestlemania," p. 18.

42. "Personality Profile: Repo Man," *WWF Magazine*, February 1992, p. 11.

43. "Salt of the Earth: Sid Justice Comes from the Land," *WWF Magazine*, November 1991, pp. 47–48.

44. "Tatanka: Leader of the New Indian Nation," *WWF Magazine*, April 1992, p. 55.

45. "A Talk with Big Boss Man," *WWF Magazine*, November 1991, p. 18.

46. "American Pride: Sarge and Duggan Protect Old Glory from the Nastys," *WWF Magazine*, March 1992, p. 52.

47. Laura Kipnis, "Reading *Hustler*," in Lawrence Grossberg, Cary Nelson, and Paula Treichler, eds., *Cultural Studies* (New York: Routledge, Chapman and Hall, 1992), p. 388.

39.
FORGING MASCULINITY
Heavy-Metal Sounds and Images of Gender
Robert Walser

The spectacle is not a collection of images, but a social relation among people, mediated by images.

(Guy Debord)[1]

Orpheus, the god-like musician of Greek mythology, was a natural figure for opera plots, which must reconcile heroics and song; his legendary rhetorical powers made him the most popular subject of early seventeenth-century dramatic music, with settings by Monteverdi, Peri, Caccini and many other composers. But his story contains a built-in contradiction: Orpheus must sing in such a way as to demonstrate his rhetorical mastery of the world, yet such elaborate vocal display threatens to undermine Orpheus' masculine self-control. Flamboyant display of his emotions is required as evidence of his manipulative powers, but such excess makes him into an object of display himself, and suggests a disturbing similarity to the disdained emotional outbursts of women. Western constructions of masculinity often include conflicting imperatives regarding assertive, spectacular display and rigid self-control. Spectacles are problematic in the context of a patriarchal order that is invested in the stability of signs and which seeks to maintain women in the position of object of the male gaze.[2]

Today's heavy-metal musicians must negotiate the same contradiction. Like the story of Orpheus, heavy metal often stages fantasies of masculine virtuosity and control. Musically, heavy metal often depends upon a dialectic of controlling power and transcendent freedom. Metal songs usually include impressive technical and rhetorical feats on the electric guitar, counterposed with an experience of power and control that is built up through vocal extremes, guitar power chords, distortion and sheer volume of bass and drums. Visually, metal musicians typically appear as swaggering males, leaping and strutting about the stage, clad in spandex, scarves, leather and other visually noisy clothing, punctuating their performances with phallic thrusts of guitars and microphone stands. The performers may use hyper-masculinity or androgyny as visual enactments of spectacular transgression. Like opera, heavy metal draws upon many sources of power: mythology, violence, madness, the iconography of horror. But none of these surpasses gender in its potential to inspire anxiety and to ameliorate it.

Heavy metal is, inevitably, a discourse shaped by patriarchy. Circulating in the contexts of Western capitalist and patriarchal societies, for much of its history metal has been appreciated and supported primarily by a teenage, male audience. But it is crucial to specify not only age and gender, but the corresponding political position of this constituency: it is a group generally lacking in social, physical and economic power, but one besieged by cultural messages promoting such forms of power, insisting on them as the vital attributes of an obligatory masculinity. As John Fiske concluded from his study of 'masculine' TV shows such as *The A-Team*, 'our society denies most males adequate means of exercising the power upon which their masculinity apparently depends. Masculinity is thus socially and psychologically insecure; and its insecurity produces the need for its constant reachievement. . . .'[3] I would emphasize in Fiske's analysis the words 'apparently' and 'socially', for I see sex roles as contradictory, mutable social constructions, rather than as normative formations somehow grounded in biology or an ahistorical psychology. Moreover, it is not only masculinity that is insecure; none of the components of identity are stable or natural. Heavy metal, like all other culture, offers occasions for doing 'identity work': among other things, for 'accomplishing gender'.[4] That is, notions of gender circulate in the texts, sounds, images and practices of heavy metal; and fans experience confirmation and alteration of their gendered identities through their involvement with it.

For Fiske, the contradictions built into male sex roles and the insecurity that men feel as a result help explain the episodic and generic aspects of male culture. Television shows such as *The A-Team* are structured as repeated enactments of paradigmatic narratives and representations because their function is to address anxieties that can never be resolved. Fiske's ideas are easily transferable to music and music video, where repetition and genre are also crucial phenomena. The purpose of a genre is to organize the reproduction of a particular ideology, and the generic cohesion of heavy metal until the mid-1980s depended upon the desire of young white male performers and fans to hear and believe in certain stories about the nature of masculinity. But metal's negotiations of the anxieties of gender and power are never conclusive; that is why, as Fiske says, these imaginary resolutions of real anxieties must be re-enacted over and over again. That such representations can never be definitive or totally satisfying also means that they are always open to negotiation and transformation. But social circumstances may change such that particular forms of culture are no longer relevant: metal fans tend mostly to be young because much of metal deals with experiences of powerlessness that may be, to some extent, overcome. As they get older, fans may acquire some amount of economic power, or they may beget children who replace them at the bottom of the familial and social ladders, whose physical power and mobility is far less than theirs and who thus assuage some of their culturally-produced anxieties.[5]

Such a theoretical perspective cannot be a comprehensive one for the study of gender in heavy metal, though, for there are many female metal fans, for whom such explanations are inadequate. Indeed, since around 1987, concert audiences for metal shows have been roughly gender-balanced. But metal is overwhelmingly concerned with presenting images and confronting anxieties which have been traditionally understood as peculiar to men, through musical means which have been conventionally coded as masculine. Since the language and traditions of heavy metal have been developed by and are still dominated by men, my discussion of gender in metal will initially be an investigation of masculinity; I will return later to issues of the reception of these male spectacles by female fans.

Heavy metal, for two decades, has offered a variety of compensatory experiences and opportunities for bearing or resolving the contradictions of masculinity as they have been constructed by societies which are aligned by patriarchy, capitalism and mass-mediation. Thus one of the most important items on the heavy-metal agenda has long been to deal with what patriarchy perennially perceives as the 'threat' of women. I will be framing my discussion of heavy-metal songs and videos in terms of a loose list of strategies concerning gender and power: misogyny, exscription, androgyny and romance. Heavy-metal musicians and fans have developed tactics for modelling male power and control within the context of a patriarchal culture, and metal's enactions of masculinity include varieties of misogyny as well as 'exscription' of the feminine—that is, total denial of gender anxieties through the articulation of fantastic worlds without women—supported by male, sometimes homoerotic, bonding. But heavy metal also participates in rock's tradition of rebellion, and some metal achieves much of its transgressiveness through androgynous spectacle. Until recently, one of these three strategies—misogyny, exscription, androgyny—tended to dominate each heavy-metal band's 'aesthetic'. A fourth approach, increasingly important in recent years, 'softens' metal with songs about romance; this kind of music has drawn legions of female fans to metal since the mid-1980s.

In spite of the fact that this categorization of metal might look like a menu for sexual abuse, I intend neither to denounce utterly, nor to try to rescue wholesale, heavy metal's politics of gender. To do only the former would be to ignore the politics of critique, particularly the fact that criticism of popular culture never takes place apart from implicit comparisons with more prestigious culture. Like racism, sexism is sustained and naturalized across class lines. Writers who expose racism and sexism in popular culture must take care that their critique does not collude with those who want to identify such barbarisms with an economic and cultural underclass which can thus be more self-righteously condemned and oppressed. Critics of popular music must take care to acknowledge the politics of their work: while it is imperative to be critical, to avoid bland enthusiasm or dispassionate positivism, analyses of popular culture must also be empathetically drawn if they are to register accurately the contradictions and subtleties of popular practices. Otherwise they too easily serve as mandates for elitist condemnation and oppression. It is beyond dispute that some of the images and ideologies of heavy metal are violent and irresponsible. But of course the violence and irresponsibility of much so-called 'high' culture, and of the economic elite that underwrites its existence, is also demonstrable. The politics of prestige work to position 'high' culture beyond scrutiny, and 'low' culture beneath it. But in either case the effect is to forestall critique by mythologizing constructions that are in fact never natural, no matter how powerfully they work to constitute subjectivity. It is less important simply to denounce or defend cultural representations of gender than to critique them in the context of an explanation of how they work, what social tensions they address, where they come from, and why they are credible to particular audiences.

Gender constructions in heavy-metal music and videos are significant not only because they reproduce and inflect patriarchal assumptions and ideologies, but more importantly because popular music may teach us more than any other cultural form about the conflicts, conversations and bids for legitimacy and prestige that comprise cultural activity. Heavy metal is, as much as anything else, an arena of gender, where spectacular gladiators compete to register and affect ideas of masculinity, sexuality and gender relations. The stakes are as high in metal as anywhere, and they are more explicitly acknowledged there, both in visual and musical tropes and in the verbal and written

debates of fans. By taking the trouble to distinguish carefully among the varieties of representation within heavy metal, we can gain a better understanding of larger interrelationships of gender and power.[6]

Behind the Screen: Listening to Gender

In her pathbreaking study of music video, *Rocking Around the Clock*, E. Ann Kaplan makes two main points about metal videos: that their violence and rebelliousness place them in the 'nihilistic' category of her typology of videos, and that their reputation for blatant sexism is well deserved.[7] Neither of these might seem particularly bold assertions; but taken together, I think, they are contradictory. Sexism is in fact a major ideological constituent of much heavy metal, but sexism is never nihilistic: the intensity and variety of modes of sexist discourse must be understood as indices of the urgency and influence of patriarchal ideals. To call such discourse nihilist is to obscure its real ideological functions.

Kaplan's readings of videos as texts embedded in the contexts of MTV and consumer culture are sometimes acute and illuminating. But two serious methodological shortcomings flaw her comments on heavy metal. First, beyond her observation that metal audiences are made up of 'young males' (not entirely true even when her book was written, and certainly not now), Kaplan's comments appear to be uninformed by any ethnographic or personal contact with the heavy-metal musicians and fans whose texts and lives she presumes to explain. While Kaplan's conclusions are based on her analysis of MTV as a spectacular reinforcement of universal decentredness and passivity, the interviews and questionnaires I have received from heavy-metal fans point to a wide range of activities connected to their involvement with the music. *Headbangers' Ball*, the weekly three-hour MTV programme devoted to heavy metal, is quite popular with the fans I surveyed, but it is hardly the most important aspect of their involvement with metal. Concerts, records, radio, fan magazines and quite often playing an instrument figure as primary components of metal fans' lives. A significant number of fans (especially male) watch MTV seldom or never, and for many (especially female) the glossy photographs of rampant musicians to be found in the copious fan literature are more important sources of visual plea-sure than videos. This is not to argue that metal vid-eos are unimportant, but rather to say that they do not operate in a social vacuum: their analysis must be inflected by knowledge of the lives and cultural invest-ments of the viewers.

Second, certainly the most serious shortcoming of Kaplan's book is the almost total absence of analy-sis pertaining to the *music* of music video. Kaplan's few comments addressing musical details of heavy-metal songs are hardly helpful: she characterizes heavy metal as 'loud and unmelodious', filled with 'relatively meaningless screaming sounds'.[8] Though musical discourses are invisible, they are nonetheless susceptible to analysis, and musical analysis is cru-cial for music video analysis because aural texts are indisputably primary: they exist prior to videos and independently of them, and fans' comments make it clear that it is the music of music video that carries the primary affective charge. That is, it is the music that is mostly responsible for invoking the libidinal and corporeal investment that intensify belief, action, com-mitment and experience. The challenge of analysing music videos is that of interpreting and accounting for *both* musical and visual discourses, simultaneous but differently articulated and assuming a variety of relations.

If the cinema, as Laura Mulvey asserts, 'has struc-tures of fascination strong enough to allow temporary loss of ego while simultaneously reinforcing the ego', the same was surely true of music long before cinema was invented.[9] Musical constructions, in metal or else-where, are powerful in part because they are made to seem so natural and unconstructed. We experience music's rhetorical pull apart from language, seem-ingly apart from all social referents, in what is usu-ally thought a pure, personal, subjective way. Yet that impression of naturalness depends on our responding unselfconsciously to complex discursive systems that have developed as historically and socially specific practices. It is not only lyrics or visual imagery, but the music itself that constructs gendered experiences.[10] The musicians I will discuss have used musical codes to articulate visions of the world that are filled with the pleasures of energy, freedom, power and a sense of community. Discursively, specific details of rhythm, pitch and timbre *signify*—some of them through the

conventions of heavy metal proper, some as part of a complex, mutable tradition of musical semiotics that stretches back centuries. Such signification always occurs in social contexts structured through political categories such as gender, class and race; and musical meanings are thus inseparable from these fundamen-tal constituents of social reality.

Only with its complex sonic texts and ethno-graphic contexts disregarded, as in analyses such as Kaplan's, can heavy metal be casually characterized as both sexist and nihilistic, or as a monolithic, ado-lescent deviance. For 'heavy metal' is a genre label which includes a substantial and growing female audience, a number of distinctive and sophisticated musical discourses, and many different 'solutions' to complex problems of gender relations. As I discuss several heavy-metal songs and their videos, I hope to delineate their musical and ideological strategies more precisely than is accomplished by such vague but pervasive terms of dismissal. As I work through the various gender strategies I have identified in heavy metal, I will be arguing on the one hand that music videos cannot reasonably be analysed without the musical component of such texts being examined; and on the other hand, that it is crucial for the cultural critic to develop an understanding of the interests and activities of the communities who find meaning in their encounters with these texts.

No Girls Allowed: Exscription in Heavy Metal

The most distinctive feature of heavy-metal videos is that they typically present the spectacle of live per-formance; bands are shown on stage, performing in sync with the song. Other kinds of pop music videos also frequently feature 'live' synced performances, but pop songs are less often 'performed' on a stage than mimed in front of fantastic or arty backgrounds, or in unlikely locations; often only vocals are synced, as only the singer is visible. In the typical metal video, however, actual concert footage is often used, and when it is not, sets, backdrops and musicians' postur-ings usually imitate the spectacle of an arena concert. Bands as different in their styles and constituencies as Guns N' Roses, Poison and Metallica all rely on scenes of 'live' performance for most of their videos. Heavy metal has long had the most loyal touring support of any popular musical genre, and the arena concert experience of collectivity and participation remain the ideal which many videos seek to evoke.

Besides the videos of metal singles to be seen on programmes like MTV's *Headbangers' Ball*, full-length heavy-metal concerts are popular rentals at video stores. Since a favourite performer might come through town once a year at best, and since many younger fans are not allowed by their parents to attend concerts, heavy-metal videos make more widely available the singular events which are most highly valued by fans. The video in a concert setting, with or without fans, presents the performers in all their glory, as larger-than-life figures whose presence is validated by feelings of community and power, and evoked by venue and music.

Many such performance videos offer for the pleasure of young males a fantasy not unlike that constructed by *The A-Team*, as John Fiske describes it: a world of action, excess, transgression, but little real violence; one in which men are the only actors, and in which male bonding among the members of a 'hero-team' is the only important social relationship. As Barbara Ehrenreich has pointed out, for young men maturing in a patriarchal world where men dominate the 'real' world while women raise kids, growing up means growing away from women.[11] Fiske's analysis of the television show stresses the value of male bonding for creating close social ties while excluding the threat of the feminine: 'Feminine intimacy centers on the relationship itself and produces a dependence on the other that threatens masculine independence. . . . Male bonding, on the other hand, allows an interpersonal dependency that is goal-centered, not relationship-centered, and thus serves masculine performance instead of threatening it.'[12] Even in many non-performance metal videos, where narratives and images are placed not on a stage but elsewhere, the point is the same: to represent and reproduce spectacles that depend for their appeal on the exscription of women.

Even exceptions to the metal concert video format emphasize the performative. In Judas Priest's 'Heading out to the highway', a song from 1981 that was still popular as a video in 1988 and 1989, performance is not literally represented. The band's two guitar players drag race on an empty highway in the middle of nowhere, flagged on by the singer, whose macho

stances, gestures and singing are the only elements of the real performance retained in the fantastic setting. The song and the images are about freedom and adventure, and we don't even need the initial 'Hit 'em, boys' to know that we're talking about a specifically male kind of freedom. There are no women to be seen in this video, and what is there to be seen—the cars, the road, the leather, the poses—have long been coded as symbols of male freedom, linked as signs of aggressiveness and refusal to be bound by limits.

The performance enacts this in musical terms as well. The vocals and guitars constantly anticipate the downbeats, punching in ahead of the beat defined by the bass and drums throughout the song. Halford's rough, powerful voice finds support in harmony vocals that sound as menacing as a gang's chant. He sustains triumphant high notes at the end of each chorus, in a display of power that has counterparts in the guitar's solo section and the bass pedal under the verse. Not only his voice, but the singer's writhing and posing provide a spectacle of male potency for a male audience, including both the band on screen and the presumed male viewer of the video.[13]

But images of masculine display are available to be construed in a variety of ways. Gay heavy-metal fans sometimes celebrate forthrightly the homoeroticism that is latent in such displays of exclusive masculine bonding. This can be seen, for example, in the activities of the Gay Metal Society, a social club of over 100 members, based in Chicago. In addition to sponsoring and organizing parties and nights out on the town for its members, GMS publishes a monthly newsletter, which contains commentary on the history, criticism and discography of heavy metal. The GMS *Headbanger* also functions as a forum for debate of issues involving sexuality and music. Gay fans celebrate metal musicians whom they believe are gay, such as Judas Priest's Rob Halford, and confirm and contest each other's 'negotiated' readings of popular texts. They may see metal videos as erotic fantasies, while straight fans resist the homoerotic implications and insist on identification with the power and freedom depicted.[14] Of course, straight fans must negotiate their readings, too. Some of Accept's lyrics are explicitly homosexual if studied closely; despite this, the band is quite popular among heterosexual, often homophobic, men. As with classical music, heterosexual and even homophobic audiences can negotiate their reception and find the constructions of gay composers powerfully meaningful.

Male bonding itself becomes crucial to the reception of metal that depends on masculine display, for it helps produce and sustain consensus about meaning. Exscripting texts do occasionally refer to sexuality, but typically as just another arena for enactments of male power. Mutual erotic pleasure rarely appears in the lyrics of heavy metal, just as it is seldom discussed by men in any other context. Metal shields men from the danger of pleasure—loss of control—but also enables display, sometimes evoking images of armoured, metallized male bodies that resemble the Freikorps fantasies analysed by Klaus Theweleit.[15] The historical context and social location of these fantasies marks them as very different from heavy metal, but the writings and drawings of the German soldiers Theweleit studied evince a similar exscription of women, and a concomitant hardening and metallic sheathing of the male body as a defence against culturally-produced gender anxieties. Such images from heavy-metal lyrics and album cover art could be cited by the hundreds, in a tradition that goes back to one of the founding texts of heavy metal, Black Sabbath's *Paranoid* (1970), which included the song 'Iron man'.[16]

The seductive women who sometimes intrude into otherwise exscripting videos signify in several ways. First, these shots function just as they do in advertising: to trigger desire and credit it to the appeal of the main image. But the sexual excitement also serves as a reminder of why exscription is necessary: the greater the seductiveness of the female image, the greater its threat to masculine control. Moreover, the presence of women as sex objects stabilizes the potentially troubling homoeroticism suggested by the male display. I will have more to say about the anxieties produced by homoerotic display in my discussion of androgyny below. There are, however, many videos which attempt to manage gender anxieties more overtly, through direct representations of women.

The Kiss of Death: Misogyny and the Male Victim

Blatant abuse of women is uncommon in metal videos. There are unequivocal exceptions, such as the brutal

stage shows of W.A.S.P., or the forthrightly misogynistic lyrics in some of the music of Guns N' Roses and Mötley Crüe. But despite heavy metal's notorious reputation among outsiders, few heavy-metal videos have ever approached the degree of narcissistic misogyny routinely displayed by, for example, pop star Michael Jackson (e.g., his videos for 'Dirty Diana', or 'The way you make me feel'), if the exscripting music of Judas Priest or AC/DC conflates power and eroticism, making pleasure contingent upon dominance, many of heavy metal's critics have similarly confused the issue. Tipper Gore, for example, makes it clear that she considers rape and masturbation equal threats to 'morality'. And William Graebner has offered an analysis of 'the erotic and destructive' in rock music that too often fails to distinguish between the two themes.[17] But articulations of gender relations in contemporary patriarchy are complex, and if constructions of sexuality in popular music are to be understood, their relationship to structures of power and dominance must be delineated, not crudely presumed.

Like heavy metal, sexually explicit films have an undeserved reputation for physical violence, according to a recent historical study of hard-core pornographic films. Building on the observation that sex is more shocking than violence in the United States, Joseph W. Slade explains the rampant violence in 'legit' films as a result of prohibitions of dealing with eroticism. Violence is often used as a metaphor for passion, Slade maintains, in discourses where explicit depiction of sexual activity is banned. In X-rated films, on the other hand, where representation of sex is not only permissible but primary, power relations are articulated through sexual relations rather than violence. The central purpose of pornography, Slade summarizes, has been 'to assuage male anxieties about the sexuality of females'.[18] Male authority is characteristically made secure through porn because that authority is represented as being founded in love: women are seen to submit themselves voluntarily and gladly, and force is unnecessary.

While non-violent fantasies of dominance might be, for some, no less repugnant than blatant misogyny, it is important to recognize that they are different. As is typical of hegemonic constructions, overt force is not only unnecessary in pornography, but it would be disruptive of a representation that depends on presenting itself as natural and uncoerced. Heavy metal too relies much less on physical violence against women than on a number of more hegemonic representations. Because metal has developed discourses of male victimization, exscription and androgyny, its power to reproduce or adapt patriarchy is often contingent on the absence of overt violence. Although some of these discourses embody challenges to or transformations of hegemonic ideology, some reproduce rather directly the hegemonic strategies of control and repression of women that pervade Western culture.

For example, there is the strategy of confronting the 'threat' head-on: one of the more successful representations of women in metal is the *femme fatale*. Such images are quite popular, from Mötley Crüe's 'Looks that kill' to Whitesnake's 'Still of the night', but the metal band Dokken could be said to have specialized in such constructions, embedded in narratives of male victimization. Many of their best-known songs enact the same basic story of the male entrapped, betrayed or destroyed by the female: 'Heaven sent', 'Prisoner (chained by love)', 'Just got lucky', Into the fire' and 'Kiss of death'.[19] Dokken's success with this formula was enabled by two of the band's particular assets: singer Don Dokken's voice and face are clean and soulful, the perfect complement to his tragic, self-pitying lyrics; and guitarist George Lynch is a powerful rhetorician whose solos and fills demonstrate a perhaps unmatched command of the semiotics of frantic but futile struggle.

Dokken's 'Heaven sent' (1987) is reminiscent of nineteenth-century operatic constructions such as Salome and Carmen in the way it locates women at a nexus of pleasure and dread.[20] Dokken sings of a woman who is simultaneously angel and witch, temptress and terror. A slim young woman in the video appears inexplicably, metamorphosed from a much heavier and older woman. She never speaks, but walks alone through the night, sometimes in black mini-skirt and leather, sometimes in a flowing white gown, holding a candelabra; she is followed by a rushing, tipping camera until she mysteriously dissolves. Jump-cuts and shifts in point of view fragment the video, but the decentring and transformations are precisely the point: the boys in the band, first seen playing chess in a bar (in an unlikely portrait of innocence), wind up doing their onstage posturing in a graveyard, to the

tune of their own victimization. Of course, the woman in the video never actually does anything threatening; it is enough that she exists. Women are presented as essentially mysterious and dangerous; they harm simply by being, for their attractiveness threatens to disrupt both male self-control and the collective strength of male bonding.

Musically, 'Heaven sent' constructs this victimization through images of constraint and struggle. The song opens with the repetition of a pair of open fifths, a whole step apart. But the fifths are not the usual power chords—they lack sufficient sustain and distortion. Instead, they sound haunting and ominous, and their syncopation and sparseness give them an anticipatory air, in contrast to the rhythmic control and driving energy of the rest of the song (and of most other metal songs). Once the song gets under way, the rhythm is inexorable and precise, in that articulation of power and control that is one of the primary musical characteristics of heavy metal. In tension with the rhythmic stability, though, are the sudden and unexpected harmonic shifts that articulate 'Heaven sent' formally. Like the jump-cuts in the video, these key changes are initially disorienting; but since the song stays in its gloomy Aeolian/Dorian mode throughout, each new section is affectively felt as the same scene, however distant harmonically—just as the various manifestations of less 'woman' in the video are linked by an aura of mystery and dread.

The guitar solo, often the site of a virtuosic transcendence of a metal song's constructions of power and control, is in 'Heaven sent' a veritable catalogue of the musical semiotics of doom. As with 'ground bass' patterns in seventeenth-century opera, the harmonic pattern uses cyclicism to suggest fatefulness; as in certain of Bach's keyboard pieces, the virtuoso responds to the threat of breakdown with irrational, frenzied chromatic patterns.[21] The guitar solo is an articulation of frantic terror, made all the more effective by its technical impressiveness and its imitations of vocal sounds such as screams and moans. After the solo, the song's chorus intensifies these images through elusion: seven measures long instead of the normal, balanced eight, the pattern cycles fatalistically, without rest or resolution.

Visual images, narrative and the music itself combine in this video to represent women as threats to male control and even male survival. The mysterious-ness of women confirms them as a dangerous Other, and their allure is an index of the threat.[22] Female fans, who now make up half the audience of heavy metal (though only a very small fraction of metal musicians are women), are invited to identify with the powerful position that is thus constructed for them; it is a famil-iar one, since women are encouraged by a variety of cultural means to think of appearance as their natu-ral route to empowerment. Men, on the other hand, are reassured by such representations that patriarchal control is justified and necessary. Such constructions are by no means to be found only in heavy metal, of course; not only do they belong to a long and esteemed tradition of Western cultural history, but their success in the 1980s has been widespread in a political con-text marked by reactionary governmental policies and a significant backlash against feminism. It is crucial to recognize that heavy metal itself, then, is not the aberrant 'Other' that many conservative critics would have it be. The sexual politics of heavy metal are a conflicted mixture of confirmation and, as we will see, contradiction of dominant myths about gender.

Living on a Prayer: Romance

Heavy metal changed a great deal in the last half of the 1980s, and one particular album of 1986 is a good register of the shift, as well as a major factor in precip-itating it. With *Slippery When Wet*, one of the biggest-selling hard-rock albums of all time (over 13 million copies), Bon Jovi managed to combine the power and freedom offered by metal with the constructed 'authenticity' of rock and, most important, the roman-tic sincerity of a long tradition of pop. Though Bon Jovi offered typical experiences of the heavy-metal dialectic of absolute control and transcendent free-dom in a performative context of male bonding, lead singer Jon Bon Jovi also projected a kind of sincerity and romantic vulnerability that had enormous appeal for female fans. It is this discursive fusion that enabled the band's Top 40 success, and which helped spark the unprecedented entry of much heavy metal and metal-influenced music into the Top 40 of the late 1980s.

Bon Jovi was certainly not the first to achieve this fusion; bands like Van Halen, Boston, Journey, For-eigner, Loverboy and others were engaged in similar

projects some time before. But Bon Jovi's music was a phenomenal success, and it helped transform what had long been a mostly male subcultural genre into a much more popular style with a gender-balanced audience. The fusion was developed and managed very deliberately: once a standard leather/chains/eye-liner heavy-metal band, with lots of tragic, macho songs about running, shooting and falling down, the band sought to capture a wider audience for *Slippery When Wet*. The most obvious change was in the lyrics: abandoning heavy-metal gloom, doom and creepy mysticism, they began cultivating a positive, upbeat outlook, where the only mystical element was bour-geois love. Writing songs about romantic love and per-sonal relationships, they tempered their heavy-metal sound and image and pitched their product to appeal as well as to a new female market.

There is still a lot of metal in Bon Jovi's music, although the question of his inclusion in the genre is vigorously contested among various factions of metal fans. Features of heavy metal are evident in the tim-bres and phrasing of both instruments and vocals, the emphasis on sustain, intensity and power, the fascina-tion with the dark side of the daylit respectable world. But by not wearing makeup anymore, and by wearing jeans, not leather or spandex, Bon Jovi abandoned much of heavy metal's fantastic dimension in favour of signs of rock 'authenticity'. Moreover, from pop music the band got its constructed sincerity, just the right degree of prettiness, and a conscious appeal to a female audience. The sustained and intense sounds of heavy metal are channelled behind the romantic sincerity of pop, while smooth, sometimes poignant synthesizer sounds mediate the raw crunch of dis-torted guitars.

The biggest hit song from *Slippery When Wet* was 'Livin' on a prayer', which invites us to sympathize and identify with Tommy and Gina, a young cou-ple who are good-hearted but down on their luck. Tommy, now out of work, is a union man, working-class, tough—but also tender, caring and musical. He used to make music, that is, until he had to hock his guitar; Tommy's loss of his capacity to make music is a sign of the couple's desperate circumstances. The lyrics of the song fall into three groups, each with a different sort of text and musical affect: the verses of the song tell the story of Tommy and Gina's troubles;

the pre-choruses are resolutions not to give up, the pair's exhortations to each other about the power of love; and the choruses are Tommy's affirmation that such hope and faith in love is justified, that love really can transcend material problems.[23]

The source of the song's main pleasures is its musical construction of romantic transcendence. As with most pop songs, the transcendent moment is the place in the chorus where the title hook is presented, where the affective charge is highest: it is there, if ever, that we are convinced that Tommy and Gina *will* make it, that love *must* triumph over adverse social conditions, that bourgeois myths *can* survive even the despair of joblessness. Such affirmative stories have led to critical dismissal of Bon Jovi as fatuous rock 'perfect for the Reagan era'.[24] But such disparagements typically ignore gender as a site of political formation, and critical sneering does little to help us understand the tensions that are mediated by such a vastly popular song.

There are at least three ways of understanding how this sense of transcendence is constructed musically. First, and simplest, it is at this moment that the piece moves out of its minor key and into its relative major. Such a key change accomplishes a tremendous affective change, moving from what is conventionally perceived as the negativity or oppression of the minor key to the release and affirmation of the major. Experientially, we escape the murk that has contained us since the beginning of the song. Second, this moment in the chorus offers an escape from the C–D–E pattern that has been the only chord progression the song has used until this point, and which thus has seemed natural and inevitable, however cheerless.[25] 'Livin' on a prayer' breaks out of its gloomy treadmill at this point of transcendence, moving from C to D to *G*, not E. By breaking free of its oppressive minor tonality, and by doing so through a brand-new progression, the song leaps into an exciting new tonal area and constructs a transcended context for Tommy and Gina, and for the song's audience. To clinch it, a background group of voices joins in here to support Tommy's tough solo voice; the rest of the social world seems to join in this affirmation.

Finally, this new progression C–D–G has discursive significance. This pattern has been one of the most important formulas for establishing resolution and closure in Western music from Monteverdi to the 'Monster mash'; it is not, however, a common progression in heavy metal. The C–D–E progression upon which most of 'Livin' on a prayer' is built, on the other hand, is strongly associated with metal. Thus when 'Livin' on a prayer' reaches its moment of transcendence, the shift in affect is marked by the use of a different harmonic discourse. The transcendence is in part an escape from heavy metal itself, with all its evocation of gloominess, paranoia and rebellion. 'Livin' on a prayer' breaks away from the musical discourse of heavy metal at the point where it offers its bottom line: transcendence through romantic love. To offer such a payoff, it *must* break away from metal.

The success of the song depends on the contrast of and tension between two affective states: the Aeolian grunge of the beginning, which sets up the story of Tommy and Gina's hardship; and the transcendent change to G major in the chorus, which symbolically and phenomenologically resolves it. For most of the song, the grunge frames and contains the chorus. It seems more realistic, since it returns as though inevitable whenever Bon Jovi's fervent vocalizing stops. The utopian promise is thus made contingent on the singer's efforts. Only at the end of the song, where the chorus endlessly repeats through the fade-out, does it seem that the transcendence might be maintained—and then only if the singer never ceases. At the same time that the magical power of romantic love, transcending material conditions, is being touted as the solution to what are in fact social problems, the Horatio Alger solution of hard individual work is also suggested, in the end the utopian moment wins out, keeping the realistic grunge at bay and even suggesting that the transcendent fantasy is more real. But all of this is possible only because Bon Jovi has created these realities: a bleak, resonant social landscape, the power of romantic love to offer transcendence, and a tough but sensitive male to make it work. The patriarchal premises of Bon Jovi's fusion are clear.

Towards the end of the song the transcendent moment is kept fresh through a key change, up a half step. Not only does the pitch rise, creating an overall affective elevation, but it also forces Bon Jovi's voice higher, charging it with even more effortful sincerity and, since he meets the challenge successfully, utopian promise. Moreover, the key change is made to coincide with a dropped beat so the music jumps for-ward suddenly, unexpectedly, onto this new, higher harmonic plateau. In the concert footage used in the video of 'Livin' on a prayer', Jon Bon Jovi sails out over the audience on a wire at precisely this moment, tripling the transcendent effect.

The rest of the video seems, to have little to do with the song as I have analysed it. It consists mostly of grainy black-and-white footage of Jon and the band backstage and in rehearsal, without any visual connection to the romantic narrative of the song. Nei-ther is it a typical performance video like the ones I discussed above, since more camera time is devoted to backstage and rehearsal scenes than to actual or even faked (synced) performance. Yet the video is closely connected to the music; the biggest visual gesture is the sudden switch to colour film and a live concert audience, which occurs two-thirds of the way through the song, precisely at the climactic moment of transcendence indicated by the song's chorus. The video marginalizes the literal narrative of the lyrics, in accordance with the way that typical heavy-metal videos cater to fans' enjoyment of live concerts. The transcendence constructed by the music, originally mapped onto the story of Tommy and Gina, has now become the transcendence available through Bon Jovi: the music, the concert and even the grainy black-and-white footage that purports to let the fan in on the behind-the-scenes lives of the musicians. What was framed by the lyrics as a moment of transcendence for a romantic, heterosexual couple, made possible by the male narrator, is now a celebration of the band members as objects of desire, and of the concert as an experience of collective pleasure. The 'Livin' on a prayer' video is less a romantic story than a spectacle of masculine posturing, and the musically-constructed transcendence of the song is linked to patriarchy through both narrative and visual pleasure.

It has been argued that the cinema has only recently begun to present the masculine as spectacle, in something like the way that women have been so presented. This is in contrast to theorizations of ear-lier cinematographic practice, where women were typically presented as erotic objects of the male gaze, but representations of men functioned as embodi-ments of a powerful, ideal ego.[26] Such a develop-ment is of great interest, because the contradictions

historically coded into representations of gender result in an almost androgynous glamour being attached to male objects of desire. Bon Jovi's image has been carefully managed so as to simultaneously maintain two different kinds of appeal to male and female fans. For example, the release order of singles from *Slippery When Wet* was carefully balanced between romantic and tougher songs, in order to sustain inter-est in the band from both genders.[27] But we will see more serious problems of managing desire in the face of gender blurring in a sub-genre of heavy metal dis-tinguished by blatant visual androgyny.

Nothing but a Good Time? Androgyny as a Political Party

Androgyny in heavy metal is the adoption by male performers of the elements of appearance that have been associated with women's function as objects of the male gaze—the visual styles that connote, as Laura Mulvey put it, 'to-be-looked-at-ness'.[28] The members of bands like Poison or Mötley Crüe wear garish make-up, jewellery and stereotypically sexy clothes including fishnet stockings and scarves, and sport long, elaborate, 'feminine' hairstyles. Though they are normally included within the genre of heavy metal, such 'glam' bands are considered by most fans to be less 'heavy' than the mainstream. This is due less to musical differences than to their visual style, which is more flamboyant and androgynous than heavier metal.[29]

Androgyny has a long history in music; I have already mentioned problems of gender and represen-tation in Baroque opera. (And one could also mention the seventeenth-century castrati—perhaps the most dedicated androgynes in history.) Recent examples of male androgyny outside of heavy metal range from Liberace to Little Richard to Lou Reed, not to mention the androgynous glamour of many country-and-western stars.[30] Some of this history has faded through supercession: some thought the Beatles' hair, for example, threateningly androgynous in 1964. But in glam metal, androgyny has found popular success to a degree unique in the rock era. And it's a particular sort of androgyny; unlike the 1970s' great androgyne, David Bowie, heavy metal lacks ironic distance. It is this absence of irony more than anything else that leads rock critics to scorn glam metal, for the ridiculous seriousness of metal's gender constructions is at odds with the patriarchal premisses undergirding the ideologies and institutions of rock.

Poison is a good example of a successful glam-metal band: one that boasts millions of fans and no critical approval. 'Nothin' but a good time', from Poison's multi-platinum album *Open Up and Say . . . Ahh!* (1988), is shot almost entirely as a performance video, one that presents the band as though actually performing the song we hear. It includes, however, two framing scenes, which I will describe and discuss briefly before focusing on Poison's androgyny. The opening scene shows us a young man, with a metal fan's long hair, washing dishes in the back of a restaurant. He is swamped with work, surrounded by dirty plates and hot steam, and he is alone except for a small radio, which is playing a song by Kiss, the founders of spectacular metal. Next we meet his boss, loud and rude, who has stomped back to apply a verbal whip; he threatens and insults the dishwasher, flipping off the radio as he leaves. Disgusted and exhausted, the kid sullenly turns the radio back on as soon as the boss leaves. Then he kicks open a nearby door, as though to grab a bit of air before returning to the grind. When the door opens, we are instantly plunged into a Poison performance, taking place just outside. 'Nothin' but a good time' begins with that door-opening kick, and while it lasts, the framing narrative is suspended; we don't see the dishes, the washer or the boss until the song is over. Afterwards, we are returned to the same scene as at the beginning. Having heard the music, the boss storms back into the frame to lash again at the kid; he suddenly notices, however (at the same time that we notice it), that all the dishes, miraculously, are clean. Confounded, he sputters and withdraws, as the dishwasher relaxes and smiles.

The framing scenes of this video call to mind cultural critics' debates about class and resistance in popular culture. The issue is whether or not popular narratives such as that presented by this song and video contain any oppositional potential or critical perspective, whether they offer viewers anything more than an experience of rebellion that is ultimately illusory and inconsequential. We must be wary of simply dismissing such 'unreal' resolutions of real social antagonisms; as Fredric Jameson has argued, although mass culture has conservative functions, though it commonly arouses utopian hopes but perpetuates their containment within hegemonic social forms, the very representation of social fantasies is risky, and maintenance of dominant ideologies is never complete.[31] However, the overt political lesson of the video's framing narrative may be far less important than the implications of the band's visual and musical styles for notions of authenticity and gender. 'Nothin' but a good time' can serve as an example of those subcultural challenges to hegemony which, as Dick Hebdige has argued, are not issued directly, but rather are 'expressed obliquely, in style'.[32]

In the 'Nothin' but a good time' video, the song itself is framed as a fantastic experience. Reality is the world of the frame, the world of work, steam, sweat and abuse; as in *The Wizard of Oz*, the real world is shot in muted colour so as to enable the fantasy to seem more real. When the dishwasher kicks open the door, Poison explodes in colour and musical sound, and the real world, the one which supposedly includes the fantasy, vanishes; the fantasy takes over as a more real reality. Even the dishwasher himself disappears for the duration of the song, in a kind of dissolution of the ego in the flux of musical pleasure. This fantasy is credited with magical agency as well: at the end of the song, we are returned to grey reality to find the dishes done, the impossible task fulfilled. The boss's torrent of abuse is plugged; something has been put over on him, though he can't say what or how.

When combined with the song's lyrics, the video's message seems fairly simple self-promotion: the good time being sung about is something that can be accessed through Poison's music, no matter what the 'real' conditions. As with many TV advertisements, Poison's fantasy is represented as more real than mundane reality, and the fantasy is to be enjoyed through involvement with a commercial product. Such an appeal, though, must evoke our desires for community and for greater freedom and intensity of experience than are commonly available in the real world. Poison, like Pepsi, uses narrative and image to arouse these longings and then present us with a particular kind of consumption as the means of satisfying them.

But it would be a mistake to exaggerate the importance of the narrative framing of the song; however obvious the 'political' message of the framing narrative may seem, it may be far less important than the gender politics of the song and its performance. Debates over the liberatory possibilities of mass culture all too often proceed in terms that neglect the gendered character of all social experience. Yet popular music's politics are most effective in the realm of gender and sexuality, where pleasure, dance, the body, romance, power and subjectivity all meet with an affective charge. The significance of the musical section of the video may be overlooked because it seems to be simply a representation of a live performance, whereas the frame is more arbitrary, and thus presumably more meaningful. But it is the band's performance that is privileged visually, through colour, free movement and spectacle—and through the transgressive energies of male display and flamboyance. Most tellingly, it is the performance rather than the framing narrative that benefits from the affective invigoration of the music. If the framing scenes address labour relations, they do so in a rather flat, pedantic way. It is the video of the song itself that deals with the issues of greatest importance to metal fans: the power, freedom, transcendence and transgression that are articulated through fantastic, androgynous display. The young man we meet in the frame finds his release from drudgery in Poison's spectacular androgyny.

Significantly, the video's 'live' performance of 'Nothin' but a good time' is neither live nor a real performance, but a constructed fantasy itself. The musicians undergo impossibly frequent and sudden changes of costume, without narrative explanation, through the invisible, extra-diegetic powers of editing. Along with similar metamorphoses of the guitar player's instrument, which is a different model and colour each time we see it, these unreal transformations contribute to the fantastic aura of the performance by offering an experience of freedom and plenitude. Moreover, there is no audience; the band 'performs' in an abstract space, a contextless setting for pure spectacle. Such a location can serve as a 'free space' for Poison's play of real and unreal, authenticity and desire, and the ambiguous subversiveness of androgyny, supported by the energy of the music.

The lyrics of the song are fairly simple: they combine a lament about overwork with a celebration of partying. The music is similarly straightforward, built around a vigorous rock beat and standard power chords on the scale degrees I, ♭VII and IV. The musical mode is mixolydian, quite commonly used in pop-oriented hard rock or metal, as it combines the positive effect of the major third with the 'hard' semiotic value of the minor seventh.[33] 'Nothin' but a good time' derives much of its celebratory energy from the repeated suspension of the fourth-scale degree over this major third, and the conventional move to ♭VII adds to the song's rebellious or aggressive tone. The visual narrative and the musically-coded meanings are roughly parallel; the lyrics are supported by music that is energetic, rebellious and flamboyant.

But in 'Nothin' but a good time' we can also detect the association of androgynous visual styles with a particular set of musical characteristics. The song features compelling rhythmic patterns, it contains the requisite guitar solo, it utilizes the distorted timbres one would expect in the electric guitar and vocals of a metal song; in short, the song meets generic criteria in every way. It is, of course, successful music, deploying discursive potentials with skill and effectiveness. However, one would be hard pressed to find it very distinctive in any way; this is not especially innovative or imaginative music. Androgynous metal usually includes less emphasis on complexity and virtuosity than other styles of metal, and many arguments among fans are provoked by the collision of visual spectacle and transgression with metal's dominant aesthetic (masculine) valorization of sonic power, freedom and originality.

This alignment of androgynous spectacle with a musical discourse relatively lacking in sonic figurations of masculinity is crucial, for it signals the extent to which a linkage of 'feminine' semiotic instability with monolithic, phallic power is deemed impossible. To be sure, if the music of glam metal were separated from its visual context, it would still sound like hard rock. Compared to other kinds of popular music, glam rock is replete with constructions of masculine power. But within the context of heavy metal, glam metal's relative lack of virtuosity, complexity and originality are aural contributors to androgyny. Fans link visual signs of androgyny with an abdication of metal's usual virtuosic prowess. 'It seems like if you have the makeup you're thought of as less than a musician', complains Poison's guitarist C. C. Deville, 'It seems because of the image we can't get past that hurdle. Now we try to stay away from the glam thing. When we first came out we were a little extreme.'[34]

Indeed, I was quite surprised when I attended a Poison concert and discovered that their drummer, Rikki Rockett, was actually an excellent musician whose featured solo was marked by sophisticated polyrhythms and rhetorical intelligence. I was surprised by this because his playing on Poison's recordings had always been extremely simple, however accurate and appropriate. But Poison's simplicity is constructed, like that of much American popular music throughout its history. From Stephen Foster to Madonna (not to mention Aaron Copland), many musicians have used great skill to craft musical texts that communicate great simplicity. The musical construction of simplicity plays an important part in many kinds of ideological representations, from the depiction of pastoral refuges from modernity to constructions of race and gender. Poison succeeded in a genre dominated by virtuosity because their musical simplicity complemented their androgynous visual style and helped them forge a constituency. As Deville's comment indicates, the band now yearns to be respected musically as well, and though they have yet to make much progress towards this goal, they have drastically reduced the amount of make-up they wear, in pursuit of it.

'Real Men Don't Wear Make-up'

In the case of bands such as Poison, we might understand androgyny as yet another tactic for dealing with the anxieties of masculinity. Androgynous musicians and fans appropriate the visual signs of feminine identity in order to claim the powers of spectacularity for themselves. But while it is certainly important to understand heavy metal androgyny as patriarchal, metal takes part in a rock'n'roll tradition of Oedipal rebellion as well: the musical and visual codes of heavy metal may function to relieve anxieties about male power, but they are incompatible with the styles previous generations of men developed for doing the same thing. Teenage boys and young men chafe under patriarchal control even as women do, and boys often develop innovative ways of expressing control over women as simultaneous proof of their achievement of manhood and their rebellion against dominant

men. This internal tension is never entirely manageable or predictable, and heavy metal transgresses against patriarchal control in ways that sometimes undermine, sometimes affirm, its tenets.

Musicians themselves may notice how the ambiguities of androgyny provoke compensatory strategies. Aerosmith's hit song and video 'Dude looks like a lady' (1987) confronts the gender anxieties aroused by androgyny, airing the problem with a tone of mock hysteria. And singer David Lee Roth self-reflexively connects his enthusiasm for bodybuilding and martial arts training to his 'feminized' image on stage: 'A lot of what I do can be construed as feminine. My face, or the way I dance, or the way I dress myself for stage . . . . But to prove it to myself, to establish this [his masculinity], I had to build myself physically. I had to learn to fight'.[35]

Roth's private regimen allows him to go on being androgynous in public. His personal anxieties about masculinity are shaped by conventional patriarchy, yet the attraction of androgynous transgression is also strong. Among the most leering of rock's lyricists, Roth seems neither personally nor artistically to have resisted sexist objectification of women, as is attested by his notorious paternity insurance policy, or the video for his swaggering remake of the Beach Boys' 'California girls'. Yet Roth has also publicly criticized the sexism of a society that discourages women from becoming professional musicians:

> What if a little girl picked up a guitar and said 'I wanna be a rock star'. Nine times out of ten her parents would never allow her to do it. We don't have so many lead guitar women, not because women don't have the ability to play the instrument, but because they're kept locked up, taught to be something else. I don't appreciate that.[36]

Roth's ideal of personal freedom is in conflict with the limitations of conventional gender definitions, though he doesn't grapple with the problem of how patriarchal power relations might be further strengthened by transgressions that rely on objectified representations of women.

In the journalism of heavy metal, the most heated debates are over 'authenticity', which often implicitly revolves around issues of gender and sexuality. Fans frequently write to the letters columns of metal magazines to denounce or defend glam-metal bands. Attackers label such musicians 'poseurs', implying either that the band is all image with no musical substance, or that they find androgyny fundamentally offensive, a perversion. As one female fan complained in a letter to a fan magazine, 'real men don't wear makeup'.[37] On the other side, defenders of glam metal are quick to respond, though they rarely defend androgyny *per se:*

> This is to Kim of Cathedral City . . . who said that real men don't wear makeup. I have just one question: Do you actually listen to the music, or just spend hours staring at album covers? True, Metallica and Slayer kick f?!kin' ass and Megadeth rules—but Poison, Mötley Crüe and Hanoi Rocks f?!kin' jam too.[38]

Unwilling to discuss gender constructions directly, or lacking cultural precedents for doing so, fans usually defend the musical abilities of the band's members or argue for the intensity of experience provided by the group. But they may also respect the courage that is required of those who disrupt the symbolic order through androgyny, those who claim social space by having 'the guts to be glam'.[39]

Male fans of 'harder' styles of heavy metal are often frantic in their denunciations of androgyny, seeing in it a subversion of male heterosexual privilege and linking it to the threat of homosexuality. On the cover of an album by MX Machine (*Manic Panic*, 1988), a picture of a grimacing boy with his fist in the air is accompanied by a sticker proclaiming 'No Glam Fags! All Metal! No Makeup!' Both homosexuality and symbolic crossing of gender boundaries threaten patriarchal control, and they are thus conflated in the service of a rhetoric which strives to maintain difference and power. Musicians who wear make-up often compensate in private for their transgressions with homophobic banter, insulting each other in order to call masculinity into question and provide an opportunity for collective affirmation of heterosexuality,[40] An interview with Charlie Benante, drummer in the thrash-metal band Anthrax, confirms that even instruments themselves are conventionally gender-coded, and that the use of a feminine-coded instrument in the context of heavy metal evokes the spectre of homosexuality. When an interviewer asked, 'Would you ever consider using keyboards as a major part of the song?' Benante replied, 'That is gay. The only band that ever used keyboards that was good was UFO. This is a guitar band. . . . '[41]

However, since many glam-metal performers appeal in particular to young women, an analysis of heavy metal that understands it only as a reproduction of male hegemony runs the risk of duplicating the exscription it describes. Heavy-metal androgyny presents, from the point of view of women, a fusion of the signs specific to current notions of femininity with musically- and theatrically-produced power and freedom that are conventionally male. Colourful make-up; elaborate, ostentatious clothes; hair that is unhandily long and laboriously styled—these are the excessive signs of one gender's role as spectacle. But on stage in a metal show, these signs are invested with the power and glory normally reserved to patriarchy. As usual, women are offered male subject positions as a condition of their participation in empowerment; but the men with which they are to identify have been transformed by their appropriations of women's signs, in their bid for greater transgression and spectacularity, the men on stage elevate important components of many women's sense of gendered identity, fusing cultural representations of male power and female erotic surface. At the symbolic level, prestige—male presence, gesture, musical power—is conferred upon 'female' signs which, because they mark gender difference and are used to attract and manipulate, adolescent men pretend are trivial but take very seriously.

Feminist scholars have long been concerned with investigating the gendered aspects of the relationship of symbolic and political orders, and the longstanding linkage of women with ephemeral spectacle is highly relevant to metal videos. Kaja Silverman has pointed out that the instability of female fashion has historically marked women as unstable, while male sartorial conservatism represents the stable and timeless alignment of men with the symbolic and social orders.[42] Heavy-metal androgyny challenges this 'natural' alignment, drawing on the power of musical and visual pleasures. It is true that there is no inherent link between subversive textual practices and subversive politics, but the relationships I have delineated among the lyrics, music, images, fans, musicians and ideologies of heavy metal, particularly with respect to gender, are intended to make the case for a conventional link.[43] Glam metal has prompted a great deal of thought and discussion about gender by demonstrating, even celebrating, the mutability of gender, by revealing the potential instability of the semiotic or symbolic realms that support current gender configurations. In some ways, heavy metal reflects the impact of what Jane Flax has called the greatest achievement of feminist theory, the problematization of gender.[44]

Metal replicates the dominant sexism of contemporary society, but it also allows a kind of free space to be opened up by and for certain women, performers and fans alike. Female fans identify with a kind of power that is usually understood in our culture as male—because physical power, dominance, rebellion and flirting with the dark side of life are all culturally designated as male prerogatives. Yet women are able to access this power because it is channelled through a medium—music—that is intangible and difficult to police. Female performers of heavy metal can become enabled to produce and control very powerful sounds, if they meet other genre requirements and acquiesce in the physical display that is so sexist and widespread in society generally, but which may in fact seem less so in metal, where men similarly display themselves.[45] Thus when metal guitarist and singer Lita Ford brags 'I wear my balls on my chest', she combines her seemingly inevitable status as an object of sexual spectacle with her metallic stature as an object embodying the spectacle of power.[46]

Women's reception of these spectacles is complex, and female performers of heavy metal may be advancing provocative arguments about the nature and limits of female claims to power. I have observed and interviewed female fans who dress, act and interpret just like male fans, for example, particularly at concerts of bands like Metallica—bands which avoid references to gender in their lyrics, dealing instead with experiences of alienation, fear and empowerment that may cut across gender lines. Elements of rock music that had been coded as masculine, such as heavy beats, are negotiable, in so far as female fans are willing to step outside of traditional constrictions of gender identity.[47] It may well be, then, that the participation of female metal fans reflects the influence that feminism has had in naturalizing, to a great extent, the

empowerment of women. Even in the 1970s, fewer women would have been comfortable identifying with power, when power was more rigidly coded as male. The choice was between being powerful and being a woman, a dichotomy which has since eroded somewhat.

But female fans also maintain their own distinctive modes of engagement with heavy metal, including practices which are often too quickly dismissed as degrading adoration. Sue Wise has argued that the young women who screamed and swooned over Elvis were not so much worshipping him, as so many male rock critics have assumed, as *using* him. Instead of a subject who caused his helpless fans to go into frenzies, Elvis was for many women an object, by means of which they explored their own desires and formed friendships.[48] Similarly, many female heavy-mental fans take great pleasure in collecting, owning and looking at pictures of male heavy-metal musicians. Predictably, male fans tend to be scornful of the pin-up magazines and their devotees.[49] But the enthusiasm of young women for glam styles of heavy metal is not simply an example of masochistic submission to male idols. Such spectacle also infuses with power the signs of women's hegemonically constructed gender identity, offers visual pleasures seldom available to women, and provides them with opportunities to form their own subsets of the fan community.

The channelling of so much masculine prestige through feminine forms thus represents a risky sexual politics, one that is open to several interpretations. Heavy metal's androgyny can be very disturbing, not only because the conventional signs of female passivity and objectification are made dynamic, assertive, transgressive, but also because hegemonic gender boundaries are blurred and the 'natural' exclusiveness of heterosexual male power comes into question.[50] For all its rhetoric of male supremacy—phallic imagery, macho posturing, the musical semiotics of male power—metal's rebellion and fantastic play offer its fans, both male and female, opportunities to make common cause against certain kinds of oppression, even as the same texts may enable each gender to resolve particular anxieties in very different ways. The level of discussion of gender among heavy-metal fans is impressive, in statements that reflect their awareness of the mutability of gender roles and other cultural constructions. Practically every issue of the fan magazine *RIP* in 1989 contained letters from fans protesting sexism, racism and even homophobia.[51] Glam metal fostered greater perception of the conventionality of gender roles, and thus helped lead to greater participation in metal by women, and to debates over gender stereotypes, masculinity, behaviour and access to power.

Androgyny offers male performers (and vicariously, male fans) the chance to play with colour, movement, flamboyance and artifice, which can be a tremendous relief from the rigidity expected of them as men. Philip Gordon argues that singer Dee Snider 'grew his hair and wore women's clothes and make-up, not merely to assert a difference between himself and his parents (as if any sign of difference would be equally effective), but as a carefully constructed style signifying attractiveness, energy and opposition to authoritative restrictions on particular pleasures.'[52]

Critics have not generally understood glam metal in this way. E. Ann Kaplan denies any significance to heavy metal's gender politics: 'Unlike the genuine Bakhtinian carnival, the protest remains superficial: mere play with oppositional signifiers rather than a protest that emerges from a powerful class and community base.'[53] But Kaplan can make such a statement only because she made no efforts to discover anything about the 'class and community base' of heavy metal. There is nothing superficial about such play; fans and musicians do their most important 'identity work' when they participate in the formations of gender and power that constitute heavy metal. Metal is a fantastic genre, but it is one in which real social needs and desires are addressed and temporarily resolved in unreal ways. These unreal solutions are attractive and effective precisely because they seem to step outside the normal social categories that construct the conflicts in the first place.

Like many other social groups, metal musicians and fans play off different possibilities available to them from mainstream culture, at the same time that they draw upon the facts of a social situation that is not mainstream. Androgynous metal's bricolage of male power and female spectacle, and its play of real and unreal, are complex responses to crucial social contradictions which its fans have inherited. Heavy metal's fantastic representations clash with the visions of many other social groups in the cultural competition to define social reality, and like the tensions to which they are a response, metal's fantasies are themselves richly conflicted. If male heavy-metal fans and musicians sometimes assert masculinity by co-opting femininity, what they achieve is not necessarily the same kind of masculinity that they sought, as the conflicting demands of masculinity and rebellion are mediated through new models, and the free play of androgynous fantasy shakes up the underlying categories that structure social experience.

However, androgyny is by no means a purely utopian sign. Capitalism, after all, feeds on novelty as a spur to consumption, and mass culture may colonize existing tensions and ambiguities for consumer purposes rather than to prefigure new realities. As Fred Pfeil points out, mass audiences are increasingly offered 'scandalously ambivalent pleasure', and the same 'de-Oedipalization' of American middle-class life that makes androgyny possible, attractive and thrilling can also block further development towards new collective social forms, beyond fragmentation.[54] Moreover, postmodern cultural 'decentring' can serve capitalism by playing to sensual gratification in ways that deflect people from making the connections that might enable critique.

But postmodern disruptions also open up new possibilities and enable new connections and formulations to be made by delegitimating conceptual obstacles; androgynous metal's defamiliarization of social categories that are still thought normative by many must be given its due. Poison's music and images reflect a concern with shifting boundaries of gender and reality that cannot simply be disregarded as nothing but inauthentic or commodified fantasies. For such fantasies are exercises in semiotic power, offering challenges at both the level of what representations are made and who gets to make them. Dismissing fantasy and escapism 'avoids the vital questions of *what* is escaped from, *why* escape is necessary, and *what* is escaped to.'[55]

Simon Frith and Angela McRobbie ended their early theorization of rock and sexuality with what they saw as a 'nagging' question: 'Can rock be non-sexist?'[56] The obvious answer would seem to be 'no', for there is no way to step outside the history of a discourse, and Frith and McRobbie's question begs for a kind of music that is recognizably—that is, discursively—rock, but which does not participate in the sexism that rock has articulated. Rock can never be gender-neutral, because rock music is only intelligible in its historical and discursive contexts. Rock can, however, be anti-sexist; instead of dreaming of a kind of music that might be both 'rock' and 'nonsexist', we can spot many extant examples of rock music that use the powerful codings of gender available in order to engage with, challenge, disrupt or transform not only rock's representations of gender, but also the beliefs and material practices with which those representations engage. The point of criticism should not be to decide whether rock music is oppositional or co-optive, with respect to gender, class or any other social category, but rather to analyse how it arbitrates tensions between opposition and co-optation at particular historical moments.[57]

I have ranged widely within heavy metal in this paper, turning to a number of very different bands, and to various visual and musical strategies for dealing with the contradictions inherent in the gender roles in the 1980s. The range of examples is necessary, I think, in order to demonstrate that heavy metal as a genre includes a great variety of gender constructions, contradictory negotiations with dominant ideologies of gender that are invisible if one is persuaded by metal's critics that the whole enterprise is a monolithic symptom of adolescent maladjustment. In fact, it is those most responsible for the very conditions with which metal musicians and fans struggle—the contradictory demands of subordination and socialization, of 'masculine' aggressiveness and communal harmony, the possibilities of transcendent pleasure and street pain—who insist on reading this music as impoverished and debased 'entertainment'.

Heavy metal, like virtually all cultural practices, is continually in a flux, driven by its own constitutive contradictions. Patriarchy and capitalism form the crucible, but human experience can never be wholly contained within such a vessel: there are aspects of social life that escape the organization of one or the other; there are also aspects organized in contradictory ways by the pair. Culture cannot transcend its material context, but culture very often transcends hegemonic definitions of its context: heavy metal perpetuates some of the worst images and ideals of

patriarchy at the same time that it stands as an example of the kinds of imaginative transformations and rebuttals people produce from within such oppressive systems. Masculinity is forged whenever it is hammered out anew through the negotiations of men and women with the contradictory positions available to them in such contexts. It is also forged because masculinity is passed like a bad cheque, as a promise that is never kept. Masculinity will always be forged because it is a social construction, not a set of abstract qualities but something defined through the actions and power relations of men and women—because, with or without make-up, there are no 'real men'.[58]

Notes

1. Guy Debord (1983) *Society of the Spectacle*, Detroit: Black & Red, §4.
2. See Susan McClary (1991) 'Constructions of gender in Monteverdi's dramatic music', in *Feminine Endings: Music, Gender, Sexuality*, Minneapolis: University of Minnesota Press, pp. 35–52.
3. John Fiske (1987) *Television Culture*, New York: Methuen, p. 202. See also Fiske (1987) 'British cultural studies and television', in *Channels of Discourse*, Robert C. Allen, (ed.) Chapel Hill: University of North Carolina Press, pp. 254–89.
4. See Arthur Brittan (1989) *Masculinity and Power*, New York: Basil Blackwell, especially pp. 36–41.
5. Deena Weinstein (1991) believes that heavy metal 'celebrates the very qualities that boys must sacrifice in order to become adult members of society'; see her *Heavy Metal: A Cultural Sociology*, New York: Lexington Books, p. 105. I argue the opposite of this: that the same patriarchal ideals are largely held in common by 'boys' and 'adult members of society'.
6. Heavy metal engages with many other social formations and historical tensions than those subsumable under 'gender'. For more comprehensive musical and social analysis of heavy metal, see my forthcoming book, *Running with the Devil: Power, Gender, and Madness in Heavy Metal Music*, Hanover, New England: Wesleyan University Press, 1993.
7. E. Ann Kaplan (1987) *Rocking Around the Clock: Music Television, Postmodernism, and Consumer Culture*, New York: Methuen.
8. Kaplan, *Rocking Around the Clock*, p. 107.
9. Laura Mulvey (1985) 'Visual pleasure and narrative cinema', in *Movies and Methods*, vol. 2, Bill Nichols (ed.), Berkeley: University of California Press, p. 308.
10. For a full discussion of this point, see Susan McClary,

'Introduction: a material girl in Bluebeard's castle', in *Feminine Endings*, pp. 3–34.

11. See Barbara Ehrenreich (1990) *The Worst Years of Our Lives*, New York: Pantheon, pp. 251–7. It is crucial to recognize that exscription is not subcultural deviance but a mainstream ideological convention. Daniel Patrick Moynihan once proposed that the 'character defects' of young black men be solved by removing them to a 'world without women' in the military. Adolph Reed Jr and Julian Bond (1991) 'Equality: why we can't wait', *The Nation*, 9 December, p. 733.

12. Fiske, 'British cultural studies', p. 263. Fiske properly discusses the links between such a concept of masculinity and its context of patriarchal capitalism.

13. Of course, some women also find such images attractive, as I will discuss below. But the point is that 'the social definition of men as holders of power is translated not only into mental body images and fantasies, but into muscle tensions, posture, the feel and texture of the body' (not to mention the music). R. W. Connell (1987) *Gender and Power: Society, the Person, and Sexual Politics*, Cambridge, MA: Polity Press, p. 85.

14. When I first started studying metal, a friend and I discovered we were reading a Judas Priest concert film in these two very different ways. Occasionally, the 'threat' (for straight men) of homoeroticism is addressed directly, as by metal star Ted Nugent, who remarking during a concert, 'I like my boys in the band, as long as they don't fucking touch me.' On the theory of 'negotiated' readings of popular texts, see Horace M. Newcomb (1984) 'On the dialogic aspects of mass communication', *Critical Studies in Mass Communication*, 1, pp. 34–50.

15. Klaus Theweleit (1989) *Male Fantasies*, vol. 2, Minneapolis: University of Minnesota Press.

16. For example, many Judas Priest songs, such as 'Hard as iron' and 'Heavy metal', from *Ram It Down*, and the album cover art from *Ram It Down*, *Screaming For Vengeance* and *Defenders of the Faith*.

17. Tipper Gore (1987) *Raising PG Kids in an X-rated Society*, Nashville: Abingdon Press, pp. 17–18. William Graebner (1988) 'The erotic and destructive in 1980s rock music: a theoretical and historical analysis', *Tracking: Popular Music Studies*, 1 (2), 8–20.

18. Joseph W. Slade (1984) 'Violence in the pornographic film: a historical survey', *Journal of Communication*, 34 (3), 153. See also Linda Williams (1989) *Hard Core: Power, Pleasure, and the 'Frenzy of the Visible'*, Berkeley: University of California Press.

19. All from the album *Back for the Attack* (1987); further examples of this type of song can also be found on earlier Dokken albums, such as *Tooth and Nail* (1984). 'Looks that kill' is from Mötley Crüe's *Shout at the Devil* (1983); 'Still of the night' is on Whitesnake's *Whitesnake* (1987).

20. On this reading of the presentation of women in nineteenth-century opera, see Catherine Clément (1988) *Opera, or the Undoing of Women*, Minneapolis: University of Minnesota Press.

21. See, for example, the E Minor Partita; or see Susan McClary's (1987) analysis of the Brandenburg Concerto No. 5: 'The blasphemy of talking politics during Bach year', in *Music and Society: The Politics of Composition, Performance, and Reception*, Richard Leppert and Susan McClary (eds), Cambridge: Cambridge University Press, pp. 13–62. As I have argued elsewhere, such comparisons are neither arbitrary nor coincidental: album liner credits, published interviews with musicians and the musical analyses in guitarists' trade journals all make explicit the relation of Baroque musical discourse to that of heavy metal, a relationship resulting from the continuing circulation of classical music in contemporary culture, and metal guitarists' conscious and meticulous study. See Robert Walser (1992) 'Eruptions: heavy metal appropriations of classical virtuosity', *Popular Music* 11 (3), 263–308.

22. In a stunning projection of violence onto the victim, the lyrics of 'Midnight maniac', by Krokus *(The Blitz*, 1984), warn of a female sex maniac creeping about at night, breaking in and killing; the singer evokes the terror of the presumably male victim.

23. I have written elsewhere about the musical organization of this song; see Robert Walser (1989) 'Bon Jovi's alloy: discursive fusion in Top 40 pop music', *OneTwoThreeFour*, 7, 7–19.

24. Rob Tannenbaum (1989) 'Bon voyage', *Rolling Stone*, 9 February, pp. 52–8, 132–3.

25. This distinctive harmonic progression is more fully discussed in Chapters Two and Three of *Running with the Devil*.

26. See Steven Neale (1983) 'Masculinity as spectacle: reflections on men and mainstream cinema', *Screen*, November–December, 24 (6), 2–16; and Laura Mulvey, 'Visual pleasure and narrative cinema'.

27. Susan Orleans (1987) 'The kids are all right', *Rolling Stone*, 21 May, pp. 34–8, 108–11.

28. Mulvey, 'Visual pleasure and narrative cinema', p. 309.

29. See the album cover photos in Poison's *Open Up and Say . . . Ahh!* and the even more androgynous look on their first album. *Look What the Cat Dragged In*. See Mötley Crüe's photos on the albums *Shout at the Devil*, *Theatre of Pain* and *Girls, Girls, Girls*. Such images fill the pages of metal fan magazines like *Hit Parader*, *Metal Mania*, *Faces*, *Metal Edge* and *RIP*.

30. See Steven Simels (1985) *Gender Chameleons: Androgyny in Rock'n'Roll*, New York: Timbre Books. In 1987 the same costume designer was employed by both Liberace and the metal band W.A.S.P.; see Anne M. Raso (1987) 'Video: behind the reel', *Rock Scene*, July, p. 68.

31. Fredric Jameson (1979) 'Reification and utopia in mass culture', *Social Text*, I (1), 130–48.

32. Dick Hebdige (1979) *Subcultures: The Meaning of Style*, New York: Methuen, p. 17.

33. For explanations of the affective character of the various musical modes and their self-conscious deployment by heavy-metal musicians, see *Running with the Devil*, especially Chapters Two and Three.

34. John Stix (1989) 'Ready or not', *Guitar for the Practicing Musician*, March, p. 56.

35. Roberta Smoodin (1986) 'Crazy like David Lee Roth', *Playgirl*, August, p. 43.

36. Dave Marsh (ed.) (1985) *The First Rock & Roll Confidential Report*, New York: Pantheon, p. 165.

37. Kim of Cathedral City (1989) *RIP*, February, p. 6.

38. Ray R., Winter Springs, Florida (1989) *RIP*, May, p. 6.

39. Interview with Scott, 30 June 1989, St Paul, Minnesota.

40. Besides observing this behaviour among members of various bands, I discussed it openly with musicians during two interviews. Such behaviour is equally widespread among orchestral musicians; indeed, it occurs whenever men transgress against hegemonic norms of masculinity by acting expressive, sensitive or spectacular.

41. George Sulmers (1987) 'Anthrax: metal's most diseased band', *The Best of Metal Mania* #2, p. 24.

42. Kaja Silverman (1986) 'Fragments of a fashionable discourse', in *Studies in Entertainment*, Tania Modleski (ed.), Bloomington: Indiana University Press, pp. 139–52.

43. For a critical view of this position, see Rita Felski (1989) *Beyond Feminist Aesthetics; Feminist Literature and Social Change*, Cambridge, MA: Harvard University Press. Felski's criticism of avant-garde strategies of textual disruption as political action rests on her perception of a conflation of gender and class: avant-garde art is as elitist as anything it might challenge. It is worth noting that the same problem hardly exists with heavy metal.

44. See Jane Flax (1990) 'Postmodernism and gender relations in feminist theory', in Linda J. Nicholson (ed.), *Feminism/Postmodernism*, New York: Routledge, Chapman & Hall, pp. 39–62.

45. Pat Benatar discusses the difficulty of creating her own hard-rock image: 'I never considered the character [I play] to be a sex symbol. I just was looking for extreme strength and self-assuredness. ... I listened to a lot of male-dominated groups like the Stones and Led Zeppelin. There weren't a lot of women around to emulate, no one female figure, so I took a shot in the dark and tried to figure out a way to do this without looking stupid and victimized.' Joe Smith (1988) *Off the Record*, New York: Warner Books, pp. 406–7.

46. Laurel Fishman (1988) 'Lita Ford', *Metal*, May, pp. 36–8. One fan told me that she was contemptuous of Ford and other female metal musicians because they are 'stupid sex objects', but also that she saw some of the male musicians the same way. Interview with Rita, 30 June 1989.

47. For writings which focus on female reception of heavy metal and hard rock, see Daniel J. Hadley, (1991) '"Girls on Top": women and heavy metal', unpublished paper, Department of Communications, Concordia University, Montreal; and Lisa A. Lewis (1990) *Gender Politics and MTV: Voicing the Difference*, Philadelphia: Temple University Press, especially pp. 149–71. Both Hadley and Lewis discuss the fanzine *Bitch*, wherein female heavy-metal fans debated the meanings of their own involvement with metal.

48. Sue Wise (1990) 'Sexing Elvis', in Simon Frith and Andrew Goodwin (eds), *On Record: Rock, Pop, and the Written Word*, New York: Pantheon, pp. 390–8.

49. This was debated at length during an interview with Lisa, Tammy and Larry, 30 June 1989.

50. From her cross-cultural study of androgyny, Wendy Doniger O'Flaherty asserts that the androgyne expresses 'conflict between one sex's need for and fear of the other, ... primarily the male's need for and fear of the female'. She concludes: 'Dangling before us the sweet promise of equality and balance, symbiosis and mutuality, the androgyne, under closer analysis, often furnishes bitter testimony to conflict and aggression, tension and disequilibrium. . . .' Wendy Doniger O'Flaherty (1980) *Women, Androgynes, and other Mythical Beasts*, Chicago: University of Chicago Press, pp. 331, 334.

51. See, for example, the letter from 'Hard rockin' and homosexual, Boston, Massachusetts' (1989) *RIP*, August, p. 5; and a letter decrying sexism in metal by a female musician in *RIP*, May, 1989, p. 5.

52. Philip Gordon (1989) 'Review of Tipper Gore's *Raising PG Kids in an X-rated Society* and *Dee Snider's Teenage Survival Guide*', *Popular Music*, 8 (I), January, p. 122.

53. Kaplan, *Rocking Around the Clock*, p. 72.

54. Fred Pfeil (1988) 'Postmodernism as a "structure of feeling"', in *Marxism and the Interpretation of Culture*, Cary Nelson and Lawrence Grossberg (eds), Urbana: University of Illinois Press, pp. 381–403.

55. Fiske, *Television Culture*, p. 317. Moreover, such explorations are not unique to capitalist societies, nor are they reducible to epiphenomena of commerciality. From his study of the music of the Venda people of South Africa, ethnomusicologist John Blacking learned that fantastic music is not an escape from reality; it is a creative exploration of reality, and of other possibilities. John Blacking (1973) *How Musical is Man?*, Seattle: University of Washington Press, p. 28.

56. Simon Frith and Angela McRobbie (1978/9) 'Rock and sexuality', *Screen Education*, 29.

57. See George Lipsitz (1990) *Time Passages: Collective Memory and American Popular Culture*, Minneapolis: University of Minnesota Press, p. 102.

58. I would like to thank Susan McClary, George Lipsitz, Wendy Kozol, Carolyn Krasnow, Andrew Goodwin and Diane Shoos for their helpful comments on earlier drafts of this paper, and Metal Mark, Gary Thomas, Nancy Armstrong and many heavy-metal fans for illuminating conversations. For a fuller discussion of heavy-metal music and politics, see *Running with the Devil*.

40.
THE GENDERED CARNIVAL OF POP
Diane Railton

One of the ironies of popular music studies is that the music that is the most popular, in terms of contemporary chart success, is rarely discussed by academics writing in the field. In this article I want to suggest that this is because some forms of 'mainstream' chart pop music, and the discourse of the magazines that promote this type of music, pose a threat to the certainties of both gender and genre that underpin 'serious' popular music. The music I am concerned with here is that provided by 'boy bands' like Boyzone, Westlife or Five, and 'girl groups' like The Spice Girls, Atomic Kitten or Precious, as well as mixed-sex groups such as Steps, SClub7 and Hear'Say, and singers such as Britney Spears and Billie—music that is the mainstay of magazines such as the UK publications *Smash Hits, Top of the Pops* and *Live and Kicking.* I shall argue that this music, and the way of enjoying music promoted by the magazines that support it, can best be understood in terms of a carnivalesque disruption that challenges all stable ideas about what makes music good, and what popular music should be about. Furthermore, I shall argue that, just as this music is perhaps the only form of popular music to have a predominantly female audience, the threat that it poses is the threat of the feminine, and of female encroachment into what is still predominantly a male, and masculine, world.

To this end, I will argue that the development of particular types of popular music as a focus for academic study and serious enjoyment can be likened to the development of bourgeois society in the eighteenth and nineteenth centuries. 'Pop' music, of the type I have described above, can be seen as the carni-valesque 'low other' that was a source of both horror and fascination to the emerging bourgeoisie (Stallybrass and White 1986, p. 202). I will begin by outlining my reasons for suggesting a resemblance between the establishment of 'serious' popular music genres and the development of bourgeois hegemony, before going on to explore the carnivalesque nature of 'pop' and the response of 'serious' popular music to this.

The concept of 'the bourgeois public sphere' is a useful starting point for discussion. The term derives from the work of Jürgen Habermas and describes a particular site of social intercourse that developed in the late seventeenth and eighteenth centuries and facilitated bourgeois hegemony in both politics and the arts. The coffee houses and spas that proliferated at this time were places of informed, critical discussion between the emerging bourgeoisie and sympathetic members of the aristocracy. They provided the impetus for the development of newspapers and journals, through which critical debate could be disseminated to a wider audience. They helped to construct the notion of a reasoned and informed public whose opinion was worthy of consideration. Through the institutions of the public sphere, informed public discussion, rather than royal decree or courtly practice, became the basis on which matters of taste and of politics could be decided. The public sphere could do this because it was independent of both church and state: it was not part of the institutions of high culture. The bourgeois public sphere constituted a challenge to the position of the court as the arbiter of taste and holder of political power (Habermas 1995).

Stallybrass and White describe the response of the emergent bourgeois society to 'low' culture as a mixture of revulsion and fascination—simultaneously a rejection of and a desire for the bodily in culture. They argue that the public sphere developed not only in opposition to aristocratic, high culture but also to the low culture of the circus, the carnival, and so on. It was as much about distancing bourgeois taste from plebeian taste, and sophisticated bourgeois cultural practices from the coarseness of the lower classes at play, as it was about challenging courtly privilege. It was about demonstrating distinctions by displaying civility and manners (Stallybrass and White 1986, p. 191). The importance of the public sphere is that it was neither high nor low. It avoided both the excesses of aristocratic dilettantism and the degradation of low revelry. The bourgeoisie was only able to obtain the successes it did against the aristocracy by defining itself in contradistinction to the 'low'. Yet members of the bourgeoisie always maintained a fascination with that which they were distancing themselves from. The circus, the carnival, the bodily, and sexual performance were constant sources of both dread and allure.

It almost goes without saying that the bourgeois public sphere was both male and masculine in its constitution. It was based on what are traditionally considered masculine values (reason, objectivity, the mind), and eschewed the traditionally feminine (emotion, the home, the body). As early as 1674, women were criticising the institution of the coffee house for excluding them (Habermas 1995, fn. 8). It was a realm from which women were excluded by both their position in society and their femininity. The public sphere was defined by masculinity—by values that since the time of the Ancient Greeks had been seen as the province of men (Lloyd 1984).

At this point, I want to argue that parallels can be drawn in a number of ways between rock music culture as it developed in the late 1960s and early 1970s, and the bourgeois public sphere. Just as the bourgeois public sphere was a starting point that facilitated the hegemony of bourgeois ideals and political power, rock culture served as the starting point for the hegemony within popular music discourse of particular ways of understanding and appreciating music. As Laing suggests:

> For more than two decades, popular music studies and the higher journalism of record and concert reviewing have been dominated by an all-embracing discursive pattern that has coiled itself around a single four letter word: rock.
>
> (Laing 1997, p. 116)

In the first instance, it must be stressed that the inherent masculinity of the bourgeois public sphere was mirrored by the masculinity of rock culture. Feminist writers of the time, like their counterparts of the seventeenth century, condemned the exclusionary masculinity of rock culture. Writers such as Mary Meade and Susie Hiwatt criticised the way that rock culture was masculine in terms of band membership and production, its lyrical content, and its political agenda. Women were marginalised by being denied a mind and reduced to their bodies:

> Seldom [in song lyrics] does one come across a mature, intelligent woman, or for that matter, a woman who is capable enough to hold a job.
>
> (Meade 1972, p. 175)

They were sexualised and deemed incapable of handling the intellectual sophistication of the music:

> Frank Zappa laid it out when he said that men come to hear the music and chicks come for sex thrills.
>
> (Hiwatt 1971, p. 145)

If they tried to make music, they were treated as figures of fun:

> The very idea of a woman's rock band is looked upon as weird (. . .) a freak show good for a few giggles.
>
> (Meade 1972, p. 176)

In a world of sex and drugs and rock 'n' roll, women's role was to provide the sex. Just as the bourgeois public sphere functioned by excluding the feminine, rock culture as it developed in the 1960s and 1970s, despite its claims to revolutionary politics, worked in much the same way. It can, of course, be argued that music cultures have changed significantly since the early

1970s. However, as I will argue later in this paper, rock hegemony remains strong.

Secondly, just as the public sphere developed in distinction from the court, basing political practice on discussion rather than decree, rock music developed as distinct from Western art music. Its influences were the blues and jazz of African-American culture, the spirituality of Eastern religions, the culture of Native Americans. Its instruments were far removed from the orchestras of Western art music. Its musicians could rarely read music but learned their craft through imitating the blues guitarists of the past, and by solitary practice rather than through the formal institutionalised training associated with classical music. Musicians were proud of their self-taught status: classical training could stunt originality and creativity. Rock culture was a way of making 'serious' music that was free from the institutional and stylistic demands of art music.

This did not mean that it was understood by those who made it and those who enjoyed it as 'not art', however. Frith and Horne (1987) have documented the influence of the Art School on the development of British rock culture. Many of the influential musicians of this period, and their 1970s punk counterparts, were introduced, through their experience of Art School, to the avant-garde and the bohemian. In Frith and Horne's words: 'artistic self-consciousness started to feed into all aspects of pop' (p. 92). As pop became rock, eschewing art music practice most certainly did not mean eschewing *art*.

Moreover, like the bourgeois public sphere, rock culture was supported by sympathetic members of the art elite, whether this was Andy Warhol using rock music as part of his challenge within the field of high art (Cagle 1995), or musicologist Wilfred Mellers bringing the methods of high art criticism to bear on the music of the Beatles (Mellers 1973). So, although rock culture was not high culture, it *was* linked to the avant garde/bohemian internal critique of the high. As such, it was part of a tradition that, as Frith and Horne note, was distinctly anti-family. Frith and Horne (1987) argue that this does not mean that it was anti-woman (p. 90). I would argue, however, that it *was* anti-feminine. Most notable in the work of bohemian writers, but also apparent in the work of many rock musicians, were the assumptions that the private sphere of the home and domestic life was antithetical to masculine creativity, and that female sexuality was a temptation that could lure men from a properly masculine life (Cassady 1990).

It is important to note that the art sensibility of rock music culture meant that, like the emerging bourgeois culture of two centuries earlier, rock was at pains to distinguish itself from 'low culture'; in this case, the mass-produced, commercial popular music that was the youth music of the early 1960s. Rock distanced itself from the 'low' in a way that can be seen as very similar to the methods common within the bourgeois public sphere: by masculinising itself, and by introducing a particular way of enjoying music that eschewed the feminine, emotional and physical response of early 1960s pop fans in favour of cool, laid-back and thoughtful appreciation of the music. Where the public sphere had developed as a place of civility and manners, disinterested discussion and public debate, rock culture developed as a site of political and cultural discussion and debate that contrasted strongly to the simple, physical enjoyment of 'pop'. Although rock music was very different from Western art music, it *was* art.

This is not to say that rock culture of the late 1960s and early 1970s was not physical music. Many writers have argued strongly that rock was sexual in both form and content. This was, however, the time of the 'sexual revolution' and the counterculture. Sexual behaviour could be intellectualised as a political or artistic act. Rock, therefore, was music for people with a mind as well as a body—people who politicised bodily pleasure.

'Pop' music of the late 1950s and early 1960s, by contrast, was seen by those who criticised it, and by many of those who made it, as mindless music appealing to the bodies of those who enjoyed it, not to their minds. It was music of adolescent sexuality, of youthful energy, and *only* that. An evening at the disco was even compared to working out at a gym (Blum 1966). Music was judged on whether it had a catchy tune, whether it had popular appeal, whether you could dance to it. Even television programmes such as *Juke Box Jury* did not ask if a record was good but rather if it would sell, if it would be popular. This was not music for intellectual contemplation, for discussion of value and worth.

Can any pop music be considered in terms of quality and judged musically superior to any other, as one judges symphonies or concert arias?

(*The Times*, 16 July 1966).

The advent of rock music changed all this. It changed it by introducing a mind to the music as well as a body. The lyrics to songs became less and less the love songs or novelty songs of the earlier era. Eric Burdon, lead singer of The Animals, summed it up well when he suggested that:

Eventually I would like to reach the stage where I didn't have to write about love and kisses and all that stuff. I wish I could write about really ultimate things. That's where I think all of us want to go really. All the groups seem to be heading towards a kind of pop music that deals with ultimate things.

(Burdon cited in Marks 1968, no page numbers)

Music was to have meaning. It had to deal with issues more serious than young love. It was to be about 'ultimate things'. Burdon's language suggests strongly that this shift was gendered. The music he is distancing himself from—the music of 'love and kisses'—clearly connotes the feminine sphere. Moreover, his use of the phrases 'all of us' and 'all the groups' refers directly to the, predominantly male, makers of rock music and culture.

This was not the only way music changed at this time, however. Stress was placed on the skill and virtuosity of musicians. Bands wrote and performed their own music, no longer relying on professional songwriters. Even the drugs of choice that influenced the music were changing their focus from the body to the mind—from the physical high of speed to the 'mind-expanding' psychedelics. 'Rock' was not just a form of music but a culture, a politics, a lifestyle, based on informed discussion, critical awareness and political challenge. As the bourgeois public sphere before it, rock music culture was distinct from the high, supported by sympathetic members of the elite, and defined in contradistinction to the low. And the low from which it distinguished itself was inextricably linked to the feminine.

Thirdly, as with the bourgeois public sphere, rock culture created its own spaces and its own infrastruc-

ture for the production and discussion of rock music. It developed its own sites of discourse in clubs and universities. Women were not physically excluded from the sites of rock music as they had largely been from the coffee houses of the eighteenth century. As early feminist writers point out, however, they were excluded from the intellectual involvement in those spaces. They were there to be the physical, and only the physical.[1] Rock, too, developed its own magazines and newspapers through which informed discussion of culture and politics could be spread to a wider audience. In the discourses that emerged from the sites of rock culture, rock was neither part of the staid institutions of Western art music nor was it part of the mindless, mass music that had preceded it.

The clubs and festivals that were the sites of rock music performance in the late 1960s and early 1970s were not the youth clubs, theatres and coffee bars of the late 1950s and early 1960s. They were distinct, separate, new. Television music changed. In the UK, where there had been *Juke Box Jury* there was now *The Old Grey Whistle Test*. The paternalistic and somewhat condescending presenter now became the knowledgeable member of rock culture. David Jacobs had given way to Bob Harris. The content of the programmes was different too. The emphasis shifted from what might be a 'hit', or what would be popular, to performance by little known, obscure bands that did not aim for chart success. Magazines changed, and new ones were produced. *Valentine*, with its love stories based on the hits of the day, gave way to U.S. publications *Rolling Stone* and *Crawdaddy*, with their political and philosophical dimension. The news-oriented UK magazines, *New Musical Express (NME)* and *Melody Maker* began to change their style. The new music magazines were for discussion, opinion and critique. They were not so much about 'news', or 'stars', as forums for debate about what music was, and what music meant. Writers such as Meltzer could get their philosophy papers published as rock criticism (Meltzer 1992, p. 86). It was no longer enough for popular music to have a good beat. To be good it needed to be something that could be talked about. It had to have meaning—political or artistic. It had to have a tradition, a history, a philosophy behind it. It had to be about 'ultimate things'. It had to be very obviously not feminine.

In the fourth instance, just as the bourgeois, public sphere became the springboard for bourgeois political power and eventually bourgeois hegemony, the rock, public sphere led to a hegemonic way of enjoying music that other genres followed. Very few genres that have emerged since the early 1970s have adopted the complete 'rock' model where music was given artistic, political *and* philosophical status. However, with the exception of mainstream pop, all genres have adopted some of these criteria for judging music, for deciding what makes a band or a record good. Punk, for example, rejected 'rock' virtuosity but insisted on the political significance of the music whether it was as 'dole queue rock' or anarcho/situationist disruption. Disco had no credibility as a genre until it could be seen as linked to gay identity politics and discussed in terms of camp or body politics (Dyer 1992A).

This is something that persists in both academic and popular discussions of popular music. Regev refers to the 'rockization' of different musical forms, where genres such as folk took on rock musical patterns to produce new sub-genres (Regev 1994, p. 97). It is not only in musical form, however, that this 'musical colonialism' (Ibid., p. 97) exists. Despite claims that rock is dead (Frith 1988) or at least seriously ill (Grossberg 1994), the high art sensibilities and abhorrence of commercialism unmediated by artistic value persist across a range of musical genres. Dance music,[2] seemingly the most bodily of musical forms, has become an art form, played as part of installations in art galleries and discussed in terms of its complexity and intelligence:

> [Drum and Bass] It's an *intelligent* music made for a *discerning* audience.
> (Tod Terry, cited in *The Observer*, 11 April 1999, emphasis mine)

Other contemporary genres maintain this position. Alec Empire can list philosopher Giles Deleuze among his heroes in *NME* (5 August 2000), while Sizzla can discuss the politics of repatriation (*NME*, 2 September 2000), and Chuck Dee can declare that what is wrong with hip hop is that it has become 'hip pop' (*Touch*, November 1996). From the hardcore politics and music of straightedge to the complex artistry of trance, popular music, if it is to be treated seriously,

must have an underlying philosophy, it must be something that can be discussed and debated in terms of politics, lifestyle, art. It must have a mind; the bodily in the music must be available for intellectualisation. This is a move that is intrinsically gendered: the feminine body must be under the control of the masculine mind.

Finally, just as the culture that developed from the bourgeois public sphere maintained a horrified fascination with the 'low', so the genres that have developed out of rock culture constantly relate to the 'pop' low in terms of a sexualised fascination and revulsion. Magazines such as *NME* and *Melody Maker* regularly feature reviews of 'pop' bands that one would imagine to fall outside of their remit. They invariably discuss, and condemn, them in highly sexualised terms that often link a liking for 'pop' music to hormonal changes in adolescent girls. For example, at a Peter Andre concert, there is an 'efflorescence of underage oestrogen' as the fans are driven by 'gusset-moistening lust' (*NME* 31 May 1997). In a recent television programme about 'teen idols', Desmond Morris claimed that, after a Beatles' concert, the menstrual cycles of young women fans would become synchronised (*Top 10 Teen Idols*, Channel 4, 3 February 2001). If young women like commercial pop music they must do so for purely physical reasons; the mind can play no part.

A similar pattern can be seen on the letters pages of music magazines where readers' criticisms are spelled out in what is often crudely sexualised, and sexist, terms. This is particularly true when the bands in question are women:

> Can no one see that the Spice Girls are a bunch of talentless slappers.
> (*NME*, 11 January 1997)

> [The Spice Girls] They're clearly just a collection of 'need to get famous any way I can' tarts.
> (*NME*, 11 January 1997).

> [Destiny's Child] All you have to do is dress like a prostitute, wear wet make up and an expression that says 'give it to me'.
> (*NME*, 17 February 2001)

The criticisms, 'slappers', 'tarts', etc., almost invariably relate to commercialised sex. This is not restricted to any particular genre. If you are a woman at the 'pop' end of the genre you will be insulted in sexualised terms. So, for example, Lil' Kim is described as a 'corporate whore' in *Hip Hop Connection* (September 2000). As Lees has argued, such terms are frequently used as a way of controlling the behaviour, sexual and otherwise, of young women (Lees 1993). In the case of women involved in commercial pop music, however, this terminology is particularly pertinent. To be a woman, in rock hegemony, is to be sexual. To be sexual and produce music that is purely commercial easily transforms into prostitution and commercial sex.

If women pop singers are not directly sexualised by the serious music press, they are discussed in unflattering terms in relation to their physical appearance, as the following readers' comments illustrate. Daphne and Celeste, for instance, are 'ugly':

> How can anyone as ugly as those two fucking fat c-s possibly judge anyone on how they look?
>
> (*NME*, 10 June 2000)

> What are those ugly mutant monkeys talking about?
>
> (*Melody Maker*, 31 May 2000)

The three women of the group Hear'Say are 'scary', described as:

> Scarier than the picture of Kylie smiling at the NME Carling Awards where it looks like the top half of her face has been botoxed rock solid.
>
> (*NME*, 10 March 2001)

The writer manages, thereby, to insult the appearance of four women in one letter. And Hilary from JJ72 provokes the following comment:

> Judging from last week's cover shot she was an extra in Jim Henson's 80s' Muppet Fest The Dark Crystal.
>
> (*NME*, 3 February 2001)

Rather than simply being ignored or marginalised, as one might expect from 'serious' music magazines, women who make successful 'pop' music are a source of fascination, and their music and performance are likened to prostitution, while their bodies are described

as grotesque. They are the feminine, 'low' other by which rock (or other generic) music is defined.

I want, at this point, to suggest that this is because of the carnivalesque nature of commercial pop music. Carnival, in early modern times, was a time of legitimate illegitimacy. For a day, or a week, the traditional order could be overturned. It was a time when the world was turned upside down and this was depicted in many drawings and other representations of the time. Cities were shown floating in the sky, men dressed as women and women dressed as men. Races were run where the winner was the one who came last. Tableaux were enacted where the 'fool', or an animal, was a scholar or a cleric, or where the peasant was a lord. Subjects that were otherwise forbidden could now be brought to the fore. It was a time of crude humour. Sex and the body were central, status was undermined, and no one was safe from the rotten egg or the sexual advance. Linked, in many countries, to Lent, it was a time of feasting rather than fasting. Pigs were depicted running around ready roasted with a knife stuck in their back. It was party time and stood in direct contrast both to the restrictions of Lent and to the deprivations of everyday life (Burke 1978). Even the highly commercialised carnival of today, in Rio de Janeiro, for example, pays tribute to this as spectacle replaces the everyday, and norms of gender and sexuality are transgressed.

Pop and carnival are interlinked in many ways. In the first instance, pop is music of the body, and not only the sexual body. It is physical in its performance, in its representation, in the response it provokes and in its self-conscious 'mindlessness'. Of course, all music involves physical activity, whether in front of an audience or in a recording studio. The groups I am talking about here, however, often do not make the *music* in the sense of the instrumental part of the song: they are primarily singers and dancers, and rarely play instruments. In live performance, their bodies are exposed to view rather than protected by instruments. Instrumentation is provided by backing tapes. They move about. They are dancers. They cannot maintain a stationary position. They perspire. Their bodies become sweaty. They become breathless. The performance is defined by its physicality.

Similarly, the visual representations in the 'pop' music press are both more frequent and more revealing than in their 'genre' music counterparts. Whereas publications such as *Melody Maker, NME, Q* or *Select* often publish pictures of artists, these are often only of the head, or of the head and upper body covered by an instrument. By contrast, pictures of both men and women that appear in *Smash Hits, TOTP* or *Live and Kicking* are often full-figure, standing or lying with legs splayed. Clothes may be pulled aside to reveal a bodily adornment such as a navel ring or a tattoo (e.g. *Smash Hits*, 6 September 2000, p. 3); trousers may be lowered (e.g. *TV Hits*, March 2000, p. 28); or chests may be bared (e.g. *Smash Hits*, 28 June 2000).

Furthermore, pictures in 'genre' music magazines are rarely simply about display. They are almost invariably linked to a more intellectual pursuit: they accompany interviews, reviews, or 'news' items. In 'pop' magazines this is not necessarily the case. Pictures may accompany articles but they do not have to. There is invariably a 'photo section' with few, if any, of those featured being mentioned elsewhere in the magazine. Pictures in pop magazines stand alone: they are there to be looked at, not to illustrate more serious commentary.

It is not only the performers that are involved in the physicality of pop, however. A constant image of fans of this type of music is of a girl or young woman, screaming, out of control, totally absorbed in the bodily experience. And the image that is reproduced time and time again is not usually of *one* girl but of a heaving, screaming 'mass' of femininity (Garratt 1990; Ehrenreich, Hess and Jacobs 1992). 'Pop' music of this type is about losing control; surrendering the rational mind to the body and the emotions. It is here that we can get some clue as to the (horrified) fascination in which such music is held by the 'serious' music press. From time to time it is argued in the music press and elsewhere that popular music *should* be about *jouissance*, and that rock criticism, both popular and academic, serves to render it mere *plaisir* (Reynolds 1990): the excitement of the music is lost in the intellectualisation of it. However, in the young women screaming and swooning at the sight of their favourite pop star, we get the epitome of the *jouissance* of 'pop'. We see what music appreciation could be like if we eschewed the mind. Yet, because of the art sensibilities that are an intrinsic part of rock hegemony, it is only by distancing music from this sort of bodily response that it can be taken seriously.

It is not only in its emphasis on the body, however, that pop music can be seen as carnivalesque. Pop music, as it is discussed in magazines like *Smash Hits*, is about the humorous undermining of established hierarchies. It simultaneously constructs a 'star' system and undermines the very system it constructs. This undermining is done in a variety of ways. In the first instance, stars featured in magazines such as *Smash Hits* are rarely afforded the dignity of their full name. For the most part they are identified by the group to which they belong. Articles and photographs refer simply to Darren Savage Garden, Lee 911, Shane Westlife, Paul 7, and so on (*Smash Hits*, 15 November 2000). This serves to take away their individual identity, and make them simply part of a collectivity rather than a person, or an artist, in their own right. And art demands an artist. It makes it difficult, therefore, to take them seriously. Others are renamed by the magazines. It was in teenage music magazines, for example, that the Spice Girls first became Ginger, Sporty, Scary, Posh and Baby. It is in *Smash Hits* that Christina Aguilera becomes Christina AquaLibra (*Smash Hits*, 9 August 2000) and Mariah Carey becomes Scary Mary or Mazza (*Smash Hits*, 17 November 1999).

Moreover, the irreverent names are accompanied by irreverent questions. *Smash Hits* asks the sort of questions that you will not find in the more serious magazines. 'Embarrassing moments' are a common theme, where stars talk about when they first learned about the 'birds and the bees' (*TV Hits*, November 2000), or how their trousers fell down in public (*TV Hits*, March 2000). Alternatively they may be asked about the mundane, everyday, bodily aspects of their lives: 'How much is a loaf of bread?' (*TOTP*, December 1996); 'How long does it take you to change a nappy?' (*TOTP*, January 1997), and so on. They may be given quizzes to see if, as with Mark Owen, they are 'still in touch with the real world' (*TOTP*, December 1996), or, as with 'Darren Savage Garden', if they are really as their name suggests: 'How savage is Darren?' (*Smash Hits*, 4 October 2000). So, people may be famous, successful and popular, but they cannot escape from the mundane and the everyday. They are not allowed to 'get above themselves', or to put on airs. There is even a regular feature in *Smash Hits* called 'Yowser look at those trousers', where stars are mocked for fashion gaffes and readers are encouraged to write in with examples of famous people in embarrassing outfits (see, for example, *Smash Hits*, 15 November 2000, p. 7, where 'AJ Backstreet' is shown wearing 'hideous trousers').

Moreover, this humorous undermining of status is not restricted to 'pop' stars. Eminem, discussed in *NME* as 'the greatest all-American pop anti-hero since Kurt Cobain' (*NME*, 12 August 2000), is 'a birrova naughty boy' in *Smash Hits* (9 August 2000). His unquestioned status as an 'artist' is further undermined by his being criticised for his 'strong language' and questioned about his responsibility to impressionable fans (*TOTP*, October 2000).

It is not only stars who are undermined, however. The whole system of categorising music falls by the wayside when we look at these magazines. Almost any genre of music can be featured as long as it is from the commercially successful part of the genre. Oasis or the Verve are welcome, as are Mary J. Blige, Sisqo and Lil' Kim. What is more, they are not segregated into discrete categories such as *NME*'s 'On the Decks' dance music section. Genre boundaries have no place for the girls and young women who make up the bulk of the readership for these magazines. In a recent *Smash Hits* poll (1996), for example, the Spice Girls came second in the 'soul music' category. It seems unlikely that they would have been considered in this category anywhere else. It could, of course, simply be that the voters did not understand the categorisation, or did not know what the genre 'soul' meant. I prefer, however, to think that they simply refused to be bounded by established categories. If someone is the best, they are the best in every category: boundaries cease to have meaning. This approach is mirrored in the magazines themselves, where pop, indie, soul, hip hop, even nu-metal bands are featured.

The carnivalesque therefore appears in pop magazines and pop music through the way in which they are concerned primarily with the physical, eschewing the mind. It appears through the humour and lack of respect that undermine existing hierarchies of stardom and of genre. Most of all, however, it appears in the way these magazines and performers 'turn the world upside down'. They turn the world upside down by placing the needs and desires of young women to the fore in a society that is still geared to the needs and desires of adult men.

The main role of the 'pop star' is to entertain. Dyer has argued that:

> Entertainment offers us the image of 'something better' to escape into, or something that we want deeply that our day-to-day lives don't provide. Alternatives, hopes, wishes—these are the stuff of Utopia, the sense that things could be better, that something other than what is can be imagined and may be realised.
>
> (Dyer 1992B, p. 18)

If they are to be successful, entertainers must meet the needs, the dreams and the fantasies of a better life that entertainment gives us. This means that pop stars, with a target audience of girls and young women, must put girls and young women centre stage, must focus on *their* needs rather than on the needs of the performer or of musical credibility. They must understand what is missing from the day-to-day lives of young women and provide it in fantasy form.

We must remember, however, that carnival was a time of legitimate illegitimacy. The world could only be turned on its head at specific times of the year. The challenge of carnival was controlled by the temporal limits that were placed on it. It could not pose a real threat to the social order. In fact the freedom of carnival could be seen as a way of maintaining social order by giving people a safety valve that helped them cope with the pressures of day-to-day hard work and deprivation.

A similar role can be seen for the carnivalesque of 'pop'. It, too, is temporally bounded, seen only as a fitting taste for *very* young women. The pleasures of 'pop' are something that we must learn to grow out of. After all, as everyone knows:

> When you reach 12 years old, you should begin to grow out of pop pap music.
>
> (Jerry Pounds, *NME*, 14 January 1996)

It is not simply the music that women are expected to grow out of, however. As Cheryl Cline puts it:

> For an adult woman to admit, in mixed company, to a crush on a rock star is to overstep the bounds

of proper [adult] feminine behaviour (. . .). To as much as mention Bruce Springsteen's biceps is to leave yourself open to charges of immaturity, bad taste, political incorrectness and general mush-mindedness.

(Cline 1992, p. 70)

It is not only the music that must be left behind, but the physical, the sexual, in the music. The feminine in music must be abandoned as women grow up. It is only permissible for girls and young women.

Pop music provides a brief taste of freedom for young women—a time when they are placed at centre stage, when the world is turned upside down. It is a time when they can let themselves go, enjoy the bodily pleasures of music and experience the *jouissance* of pop. It is the commercial nature of pop music that means that those who produce the music must take young women's pleasures seriously, and must give them what they want. As the target audience, for both the music itself and the magazines that support it, young women's needs and desires are of prime importance. This is something, however, that does not last: they must put it behind them as they grow up. The carnivalesque of pop can provide no real challenge to the masculine world of popular music until it becomes acceptable not to grow out of 'pop pap music', but to carry its pleasures with us into adult life.

Notes

1. Elizabeth Wilson suggests that the ambition of the female bohemian 'was not to be a "Great Artist but to be a Great Artist's Mistress"' (Wilson 1982, cited in Frith and Horne 1987, p. 92).
2. Straw notes, too, that dance music culture associates the commercial with the feminine (Straw 1995), a point also made by Thornton (1995).

References

Blum, L. H. 1966. 'The discotheque and the phenomenon of alone-togetherness: a study of the young person's response to the Frug and comparable current dances', *Adolescence*, 1/3, pp. 351–66

Burke, P. 1978. *Popular Culture in Early Modern Europe* (London)

Cagle, V. M. 1995. *Reconstructing Pop/Subculture: Art Rock and Andy Warhol* (London)

Cassady, C. 1990. *Off the Road: 20 Years with Cassady, Kerouac and Ginsberg* (London)

Cline, C. 1992. 'Essays from Bitch: the women's rock newsletter with bite', in *The Adoring Audience: Fan Culture and Popular Media*, ed. L. A. Lewis (London)

Dyer, R. 1992A. 'In defence of disco', in R. Dyer, *Only Entertainment* (London)

1992B. 'Entertainment and Utopia', in R. Dyer, *Only Entertainment* (London)

Ehrenreich, B., Hess, E., and Jacobs, G. 1992. 'Beatlemania: a sexually defiant consumer culture?' in *The Adoring Audience: Fan Culture and Popular Media*, ed. L. A. Lewis (London)

Frith, S. 1988. *Music for Pleasure* (Oxford)

Frith, S., and Horne, H. 1987. *Art into Pop* (London)

Garratt, S. 1990. 'Teenage dreams', in *On Record: Rock, Pop and the Written Word*, ed. S. Frith and A. Goodwin (London)

Grossberg, L. 1994. 'Is anybody listening? Does anybody care? On talking about "the state of rock"', in *Microphone Fiends: Youth Music and Youth Culture*, ed. A. Ross and T. Rose (London)

Habermas, J. 1995. 'Institutions of the public sphere', in *Approaches to Media: A Reader*, ed. O. Boyd-Barret and C. Newbold (London)

Hip Hop Connection. September 2000 (London)

Hiwatt, S. 1971. 'Cock rock', in *Twenty-Minute Fandangos and Forever Changes: A Rock Bazaar*, ed. J. Eisen (New York), pp. 141–7

Laing, D. 1997. 'Rock anxieties and new musical networks', in *Back to Reality? Social Experience and Cultural Studies*, ed. A. McRobbie (Manchester)

Lees, S. 1993. *Sugar and Spice: Sexuality and Adolescent Girls* (London)

Lloyd, G. 1984. *The Man of Reason: 'Male' and 'Female' in Western Philosophy* (London)

Marks, J. 1968. *Rock and Other Four Letter Words: Music of the Electric Generation* (London)

Meade, M. 1972. 'The degradation of women', in *The Sounds of Social Change*, ed. S. Denisoff and R. Peterson (Chicago), pp. 173–8

Mellers, W. 1973. *Twilight of the Gods: The Music of the Beatles* (New York)

Melody Maker. 31 May 2000 (London)

Meltzer, R. 1992. 'The aesthetics of rock', in *The Penguin Book of Rock and Roll Writing*, ed. C. Heylon (London)

New Musical Express. 14 December 1996, 11 January 1997, 31 May 1997, 10 June 2000, 5 August 2000, 12 August 2000, 2 September 2000, 3 February 2001, 17 February 2001, 10 March 2001 (London)

The Observer. 11 April 1999 (London)

Regev, M. 1994. 'Producing artistic value: the case of rock music', *Sociological Quarterly*, 35/1, pp. 85–102

Reynolds, S. 1990. *Blissed Out: The Raptures of Rock* (London)

Smash Hits. *17* November 1999, 28 June 2000, 9 August 2000, 6 September 2000, 4 October 2000, 15 November 2000 (London)

Stallybrass, P., and White, A. 1986. *The Politics and Poetics of Transgression* (London)

Straw, W. 1995. 'The booth, the floor and the wall: dance music and the fear of falling', in *Popular Music: Style and Identity*, ed. W. Straw (Montreal), pp. 249–54

The Times. 16 July 1966 (London)

Thornton, S. 1995. *Club Cultures: Music, Media and Subcultural Capital* (Cambridge)

Top of the Pops Magazine. December 1996, January 1997, October 2000 (London)

Touch. November 1996 (London)

TV Hits. March 2000, November 2000 (London)

Wilson, E. 1982. *Mirror Writing* (London)

PART V

CONSUMPTION: SPECTATORS, FANS, USERS, AND GAMERS

Introduction

The chapters in Part V concern the study of gender and media consumption. As with other forms of gender-based media analysis, the objects of study, theoretical perspectives, and methodological approaches to gender and media consumption have shifted over time.[1] As discussed in Part II, most early scholarship on gender and media was focused on representation. Yet media reception was never far from such concerns. In fact, much of the feminist media research of the 1970s demonstrates scholars' strong interest in audiences' interpretations and uses of texts. For example, Gaye Tuchman was concerned with how the negative portrayal and "symbolic annihilation" of women in mass media might affect the socialization of girls.[2] Adopting a psychoanalytic approach, Laura Mulvey's study of the male gaze explored the gendered psychological dynamics of narrative cinema that place all viewers in the position of the male spectator.[3]

While Mulvey's article has drawn criticism for its inability to theorize active female viewers and queer spectators, since the expansion of cultural studies in the 1980s, hers and other theories of film reception have been critiqued also for their constructions of an abstract, ahistorical spectator with little connection to the lived experiences of the real people who watch movies. This criticism posed a significant problem within feminist film studies, which at that point still privileged analyses of the gaze informed by Freudian and Lacanian psychoanalytic theory. Influenced by ethnographic work in both cultural studies and the then-new field of television studies, Annette Kuhn's "Women's Genres," published in 1984, contains one of the first arguments for more feminist studies of real film audiences. Importantly, the audience research Kuhn and others helped to inspire was not in the empirical tradition associated with effects-based communication studies. Instead, media scholars interested in audiences have focused on consumers as active producers of textual meanings rather than passive dupes of the culture industries. Feminist scholars, such as Janice Radway, were at the forefront of this shift from reception analyses to audience studies.[4]

Unfortunately, research on real film audiences is still minimal in comparison to that on television viewers, magazine readers, music fans, and gamers.[5] Nevertheless, several important studies have encouraged film scholars to explore instances of filmgoers' active negotiations of the gendered messages offered by media culture. Although much feminist inquiry into film audiences has focused on white women, bell hooks's "The Oppositional Gaze" helped to bridge feminist and critical race theory by arguing that gendered viewing practices are also intersected by racial identity. Resisting the psychoanalytic schema of feminist film theory while insisting on the materialist arguments of critical race theory and cultural studies, hooks avers that, in a white supremacist culture, black people develop a resistant, oppositional gaze. It is this practice that allows black people to find pleasure in hegemonic constructs and negative imagery. Taking black women's independent cinema as her secondary object of study, hooks also explores how the oppositional gaze can be powerfully redirected into the creation of films whose nonhegemonic narrative and representational strategies speak more directly about and to members of socially disenfranchised groups.

Part of a larger book-length project that reconfigures film spectatorship via queer theory,[6] Alexander Doty's "There's Something Queer Here" also discusses an oppositional gaze, yet this time such deviance is sexual rather than racial. By arguing that queerness is central to, rather than subtextual within, mass media texts, Doty problematizes the assumed dominance of heteronormativity in media texts and reception practices. Helping to introduce "queer" as a verb (as in "queering a text"), Doty's work encourages scholars to consider the many ways in which consumers, particularly those in the LGBTQI community, reconfigure media narratives in order to find pleasure. In particular, he explores cross-gender spectatorial identifications and the homosexualizing of same-sex friendships.

As television scholars became interested in studying real media audiences in the 1980s, some feminist researchers began to focus on the gendered aspects of TV reception. One of the few studies of that period to take technology into consideration, Ann Gray's "Behind Closed Doors" revealed the gendered aspects of home entertainment equipment, particularly videocassette recorders, the precursor to today's digital videodisc players. As Gray's work demonstrates, men's and women's different uses of such technology are related to domestic labor, authority relationships, and structures of power within the private sphere.

Will Straw's "Sizing Up Record Collections" also moves audience studies toward material culture, this time by examining record collecting, a practice historically dominated by men. With a particular focus on the gendered aspects of connoisseurship and consumption, Straw explores competing forms of masculinity within record collectors' culture, such as hipness and nerdishness, as well as the relationship of those forms to media representations of such collectors.

One of the most productive branches within audience studies today focuses on media fandom and fan communities.[7] A precursor to her book-length study of women film fans of the mid twentieth century,[8] Jackie Stacey's "Feminine Fascinations" takes up Kuhn's decade-earlier challenge to study real female filmgoers. Nevertheless, Stacey does not abandon the heretofore dominant psychoanalytic approach to reception, but rather merges it with ethnographic methods in order to explore the various ways in which female fans' same-sex identifications with stars are psychologically processed and differently embodied.

Although his work has more ties to reception studies than audience studies, Brett Farmer continues this critical conversation of star–fan relations in "The Fabulous Sublimity of Gay Diva Worship." Through his use of Eve Kosofsky Sedgwick's theory of reparative cultural practices,[9] Farmer complicates the notion that gay men's adoration of musical divas is merely escapist. Using his own experiences and scenes from films like *Philadelphia* (1993) as his evidence, Farmer avers that the cross-gender practices of diva worship allow queer men to find self-affirmation and transcendence in an otherwise hostile, homophobic society.

The most recently emergent sub-area of scholarship on media consumption concerns the users of digital media technologies, specifically the World Wide Web and video games. Building on the considerable research of fan "prosumers" (media consumers who also make media and other cultural artifacts related to their objects of fandom) inspired by Henry Jenkins's *Textual Poachers*,[10] Sharon Cumberland's "Private Uses of Cyberspace" concerns the construction of the Internet as a liminal, private/public space by women writers of fan fiction. In particular, she focuses on the Web's facilitation of women's expression of erotic desire within public space, a historically taboo practice, as well as the Web's support of women's community and cultural production. Hence, Cumberland participates in discussions similar to those of feminist scholars whose research concerns girls' and women's zines.[11]

The other primary area of scholarship on digital media consumers concerns video game users or "gamers." Since research to date on gamers has largely avoided gender analysis, the final two chapters in this part are representative of a very small pool of scholarship available at the time of this reader's inception. The first, "Women and Games" by Pam Royse, Joon Lee, Undrahbuyan Baasanjav, Mark Hopson, and Mia Consalvo, examines adult women's reasons for playing games, their levels of game play, and their genre preferences in order to explore variances in gendered video game use. Questioning how games and gender are mutually constituting, the researchers discovered three different types of game play among women in their sample, which in turn suggests the users' differing gender performances and thus relations to gender norms. Such research challenges stereotypes of women gamers and expands our understanding of gendered gaming practices.

Esther MacCallum-Stewart's "Real Boys Carry Girly Epics," the second chapter on video game users, explores the gender game play of *World of Warcraft*, a massively multiplayer online role-playing game.

She is especially interested in male *World of Warcraft* gamers who use female avatars while playing video games. Comfortable in the gender crossing this game and others facilitate, this particular group of gamers, MacCallum-Stewart argues, is helping to reconfigure the traditional gender dynamics of video game culture. Indeed, such gender crossings have become naturalized within the gaming community and have impacted avatar design. Nevertheless, some gamers' heterosexualizing of their cross-gender game play reveals an uneasiness that this practice may be indicative of homosexuality or transgenderism, and thus suggests the ongoing need for gamers to negotiate traditional real-world norms when engaged in virtual play.

Notes

1. For an overview of this field, see Janet Staiger, *Media Reception Studies* (New York: New York University Press, 2005).
2. Gaye Tuchman's essay on symbolic annihilation is reprinted in Part I of this reader.
3. Laura Mulvey's article on the male gaze is reprinted in Part I of this reader.
4. See Janice Radway, *Reading the Romance: Women, Patriarchy, and Popular Literature* (Chapel Hill: University of North Carolina Press, 1984).
5. To date, most film audience research is historical in nature.
6. Alexander Doty, *Making Things Perfectly Queer: Interpreting Mass Culture* (Minneapolis: University of Minnesota Press, 1993).
7. For an overview of this field, see Matt Hills, *Fan Cultures* (New York: Routledge, 2002).
8. Jackie Stacey, *Star-Gazing: Hollywood Cinema and Female Spectatorship* (New York: Routledge, 1994).
9. Eve Kosofsky Sedgwick, "Paranoid Reading and Reparative Reading; or, You're So Paranoid, You Probably Think This Introduction Is about You," *Novel Gazing: Queer Readings in Fiction*, ed. Eve Kosofsky Sedgwick (Durham, NC: Duke University Press, 1997) 1–37.
10. Henry Jenkins, *Textual Poachers: Television Fans and Participatory Culture* (New York: Routledge, 1992).
11. For example, see Kristen Schilt's chapter in Part II.

41.
WOMEN'S GENRES

Melodrama, Soap Opera, and Theory

Annette Kuhn

I

Television soap opera and film melodrama, popular narrative forms aimed at female audiences, are currently attracting a good deal of critical and theoretical attention. Not surprisingly, most of the work on these 'gynocentric' genres is informed by various strands of feminist thought on visual representation. Less obviously, perhaps, such work has also prompted a series of questions which relate to representation and cultural production in a more wide-ranging and thoroughgoing manner than a specifically feminist interest might suggest. Not only are film melodrama (and more particularly its subtype the 'woman's picture') and soap opera directed at female audiences, they are also actually enjoyed by millions of women. What is it that sets these genres apart from representations which possess a less gender-specific mass appeal?

One of the defining generic features of the woman's picture as a textual system is its construction of narratives motivated by female desire and processes of spectator identification governed by female point-of-view. Soap opera constructs woman-centred narratives and identifications, too, but it differs textually from its cinematic counterpart in certain other respects: not only do soaps never end, but their beginnings are soon lost sight of. And whereas in the woman's picture the narrative process is characteristically governed by the enigma-retardation-resolution structure which marks the classic narrative, soap opera narratives propose

competing and intertwining plot lines introduced as the serial progresses. Each plot . . . develops at a different pace, thus preventing any clear resolution of conflict. The completion of one story generally leads into others, and ongoing plots often incorporate parts of semi-resolved conflicts.[1]

Recent work on soap opera and melodrama has drawn on existing theories, methods and perspectives in the study of film and television, including the structural analysis of narratives, textual semiotics and psychoanalysis, audience research, and the political economy of cultural institutions. At the same time, though, some of this work has exposed the limitations of existing approaches, and in consequence been forced if not actually to abandon them, at least to challenge their characteristic problematics. Indeed, it may be contended that the most significant developments in film and TV theory in general are currently taking place precisely within such areas of feminist concern as critical work on soap opera and melodrama.

In examining some of this work, I shall begin by looking at three areas in which particularly pertinent questions are being directed at theories of representation and cultural production. These are, firstly, the problem of gendered spectatorship; secondly, questions concerning the universalism as against the historical specificity of conceptualisations of gendered spectatorship; and thirdly, the relationship between film and television texts and their social, historical and institutional contexts. Each of these concerns articulates in particular ways with what seems to me the central issue here—the question of the audience, or audiences, for certain types of cinematic and televisual representation.

II

Film theory's appropriation to its own project of Freudian and post-Freudian psychoanalysis places the question of the relationship between text and spectator firmly on the agenda. Given the preoccupation of psychoanalysis with sexuality and gender, a move from conceptualising the spectator as a homogeneous and androgynous effect of textual operations[2] to regarding her or him as a gendered subject constituted in representation seems in retrospect inevitable. At the same time, the interests of feminist film theory and film theory in general converge at this point in a shared concern with sexual difference. Psychoanalytic accounts of the formation of gendered subjectivity raise the question, if only indirectly, of representation and feminine subjectivity. This in turn permits the spectator to be considered as a gendered subject position, masculine or feminine: and theoretical work on soap opera and the woman's picture may take this as a starting point for its inquiry into spectator-text relations. Do these 'gynocentric' forms address, or construct, a female or a feminine spectator? If so, how?

On the question of film melodrama, Laura Mulvey, commenting on King Vidor's *Duel in the Sun*[3], argues that when, as in this film, a woman is at the centre of the narrative, the question of female desire structures the hermeneutic: 'what does *she* want?' This, says Mulvey, does not guarantee the constitution of the spectator as feminine so much as it implies a contradictory, and in the final instance impossible, 'phantasy of masculinisation' for the female spectator. This is in line with the author's earlier suggestion that cinema spectatorship involves masculine identification for spectators of either gender[4]. If cinema does thus construct a masculine subject, there can be no unproblematic feminine subject position for any spectator. Pam Cook, on the" other hand, writing about a group of melodramas produced during the 1940s at the Gainsborough Studios, evinces greater optimism about the possibility of a feminine subject of classic cinema. She does acknowledge, though, that in a patriarchal society female desire and female point-of-view are highly contradictory, even if they have the potential to subvert culturally dominant modes of spectator-text relation. The characteristic 'excess' of the woman's melodrama, for example, is explained by Cook in terms of the genre's tendency to '[pose] problems for itself which it can scarcely contain.'[5]

Writers on TV soap opera tend to take views on gender and spectatorship rather different from those advanced by film theorists. Tania Modleski, for example, argues with regard to soaps that their characteristic narrative patterns, their foregrounding of 'female' skills in dealing with personal and domestic crises, and the capacity of their programme formats and scheduling to key into the rhythms of women's work in the home, all address a female spectator. Furthermore, she goes as far as to argue that the textual processes of soaps are in some respects similar to those of certain 'feminine' texts which speak to a decentred subject, and so are 'not altogether at odds with . . . feminist aesthetics'.[6] Modleski's view is that soaps not only address female spectators, but in so doing construct feminine subject positions which transcend patriarchal modes of subjectivity.

Different though their respective approaches and conclusions might be, however, Mulvey, Cook and Modleski are all interested in the problem of gendered spectatorship. The fact, too, that this common concern is informed by a shared interest in assessing the progressive or transformative potential of soaps and melodramas is significant in light of the broad appeal of both genres to the mass audiences of women at which they are aimed.

But what precisely does it mean to say that certain representations are aimed at a female audience? However well theorised they may be, existing conceptualisations of gendered spectatorship are unable to deal with this question. This is because spectator and audience are distinct concepts which cannot—as they frequently are—be reduced to one another. Although I shall be considering some of its consequences more fully below (in part III), it is important to note a further problem for film and television theory, posed in this case by the distinction between spectator and audience. Critical work on the woman's picture and on soap opera has necessarily, and most productively, emphasised the question of gendered spectatorship. In doing this, film theory in particular has taken on board a conceptualisation of the spectator derived from psychoanalytic accounts of the formation of human subjectivity.

Such accounts, however, have been widely criticised for their universalism. Beyond, perhaps, associating certain variants of the Oedipus complex with family forms characteristic of a patriarchal society and offering a theory of the construction of gender, psychoanalysis seems to offer little scope for theorising subjectivity in its cultural or historical specificity. Although in relation to the specific issues of spectatorship and representation there may, as I shall argue, be a way around this apparent impasse, virtually all film and TV theory—its feminist variants included—is marked by the dualism of universalism and specificity.

Nowhere is this more evident than in the gulf between textual analysis and contextual inquiry. Each is done according to different rules and procedures, distinct methods of investigation and theoretical perspectives. In bringing to the fore the question of spectator-text relations, theories deriving from psychoanalysis may claim—to the extent that the spectatorial apparatus is held to be coterminous with the cinematic or televisual institution—to address the relationship between text and context. But as soon as any attempt is made to combine textual analysis with analysis of the concrete social, historical and institutional conditions of production and reception of texts, it becomes clear that the context of the spectator/subject of psychoanalytic theory is rather different from the context of production and reception constructed by conjunctural analyses of cultural institutions.

The disparity between these two 'contexts' structures Pam Cook's article on the Gainsborough melodrama, which sets out to combine an analysis of the characteristic textual operations and modes of address of a genre with an examination of the historical conditions of a particular expression of it. Gainsborough melodrama, says Cook, emerges from a complex of determinants, including certain features of the British film industry of the 1940s, the nature of the female cinema audience in the post World War II period, and the textual characteristics of the woman's picture itself.[7] While Cook is correct in pointing to the various levels of determination at work in this instance,

her lengthy preliminary discussion of spectator-text relations and the woman's picture rather outbalances her subsequent investigation of the social and industrial contexts of the Gainsborough melodrama. The fact, too, that analysis of the woman's picture in terms of its interpellation of a female/feminine spectator is simply placed alongside a conjunctural analysis tends to vitiate any attempt to reconcile the two approaches, and so to deal with the broader issue of universalism as against historical specificity. But although the initial problem remains, Cook's article constitutes an important intervention in the debate because, in tackling the text-context split head-on, it necessarily exposes a key weakness of current film theory.

In work on television soap opera as opposed to film melodrama, the dualism of text and context manifests itself rather differently, if only because—unlike film theory—theoretical work on television has tended to emphasise the determining character of the contextual level, particularly the structure and organisation of television institutions. Since this has often been at the expense of attention to the operation of TV texts, television theory may perhaps be regarded as innovative in the extent to which it attempts to deal specifically with texts as well as contexts. Some feminist critical work has in fact already begun to address the question of TV as text, though always with characteristic emphasis on the issue of gendered spectatorship. This emphasis constitutes a common concern of work on both TV soaps and the woman's picture, but a point of contact between text and context in either medium emerges only when the concept of social audience is considered in distinction from that of spectator.

III

Each term—spectator and social audience—presupposes a different set of relations to representations and to the contexts in which they are received. Looking at spectators and at audiences demands different methodologies and theoretical frameworks, distinct discourses which construct distinct subjectivities and social relations. The *spectator*, for example, is a subject constituted in signification, interpellated by the film or TV text. This does not necessarily mean that the spectator is merely an effect of the text, however, because modes of subjectivity which also operate outside spectator-text relations in film or TV are activated in the relationship between spectators and texts.

This model of the spectator/subject is useful in correcting more deterministic communication models which might, say, pose the spectator not as actively constructing meaning but simply as a receiver and decoder of preconstituted 'messages'. In emphasising spectatorship as a set of psychic relations and focusing on the relationship between spectator and text, however, such a model does disregard the broader social implications of filmgoing or televiewing. It is the social act of going to the cinema, for instance, that makes the individual cinemagoer part of an audience. Viewing television may involve social relations rather different from filmgoing, but in its own ways TV does depend on individual viewers being part of an audience, even if its members are never in one place at the same time. A group of people seated in a single auditorium looking at a film, or scattered across thousands of homes watching the same television programme, is a *social audience*. The concept of social audience, as against that of spectator, emphasises the status of cinema and television as social and economic institutions.

Constructed by discursive practices both of cinema and TV and of social science, the social audience is a group of people who buy tickets at the box office, or who switch on their TV sets; people who can be surveyed, counted and categorised according to age, sex and socio-economic status.[8] The cost of a cinema ticket or TV licence fee, or a readiness to tolerate commercial breaks, earns audiences the right to look at films and TV programmes, and so to be spectators. Social audiences become spectators in the moment they engage in the processes and pleasures of meaning-making attendant on watching a film or TV programme. The anticipated pleasure of spectatorship is perhaps a necessary condition of existence of audiences. In taking part in the social act of consuming representations, a group of spectators becomes a social audience.

The consumer of representations as audience member and spectator is involved in a particular kind of psychic and social relationship: at this point, a conceptualisation of the cinematic or televisual apparatus as a regime of pleasure intersects with sociological and economic understandings of film and TV as institutions. Because each term describes a distinct set of relationships, though, it is important not to conflate social audience with spectators. At the same time, since each is necessary to the other, it is equally important to remain aware of the points of continuity between the two sets of relations.

These conceptualisations of spectator and social audience have particular implications when it comes to a consideration of popular 'gynocentric' forms such as soap opera and melodrama. Most obviously, perhaps, these centre on the issue of gender, which prompts again the question: what does 'aimed at a female audience' mean? What exactly is being signalled in this reference to a gendered audience? Are women to be understood as a subgroup of the social audience, distinguishable through discourses which construct *a priori* gender categories? Or does the reference to a female audience allude rather to gendered spectatorship, to sexual difference constructed in relations between spectators and texts? Most likely, it condenses the two meanings; but an examination of the distinction between them may nevertheless be illuminating in relation to the broader theoretical issues of texts, contexts, social audiences and spectators.

The notion of a female social audience, certainly as it is constructed in the discursive practices through which it is investigated, presupposes a group of individuals already formed as female. For the sociologist interested in such matters as gender and lifestyles, certain people bring a pre-existent femaleness to their viewing or film and TV. For the business executive interested in selling commodities, TV programmes and films are marketed to individuals already constructed as female. Both, however, are interested in the same kind of woman. On one level, then, soap operas and women's melodramas address themselves to a social audience of women. But they may at the same time be regarded as speaking to a female, or a feminine, spectator. If soaps and melodramas inscribe femininity in their address, women—as well as being already formed *for* such representations—are in a sense also formed *by* them.

In making this point, however, I intend no reduction of femaleness to femininity: on the contrary, I would hold to a distinction between femaleness as social gender and femininity as subject position. For example, it is possible for a female spectator to be addressed, as it were, 'in the masculine', and the converse is presumably also true. Nevertheless, in a culturally pervasive operation of ideology, femininity is routinely identified with femaleness and masculinity with maleness. Thus, for example, an address 'in the feminine' may be regarded in ideological terms as privileging, if not necessitating, a socially constructed female gender identity.

The constitutive character of both the woman's picture and the soap opera has in fact been noted by a number of feminist commentators. Tania Modleski, for instance, suggests that the characteristic narrative structures and textual operations of soap operas both address the viewer as an 'ideal mother'—ever-understanding, ever-tolerant of the weaknesses and foibles of others—and also posit states of expectation and passivity as pleasurable:

> the narrative, by placing ever more complex obstacles between desire and fulfilment, makes anticipation of an end an end in itself.[9]

In our culture, tolerance and passivity are regarded as feminine attributes, and consequently as qualities proper in women but not in men.

Charlotte Brunsdon extends Modleski's line of argument to the extra-textual level: in constructing its viewers as competent within the ideological and moral frameworks of marriage and family life, soap opera, she implies, addresses both a feminine spectator and female audience.[10] Pointing to the centrality of intuition and emotion in the construction of the woman's point-of-view, Pam Cook regards the construction of a feminine spectator as a highly problematic and contradictory process: so that in the film melodrama's construction of female point-of-view, the validity of femininity as a subject position is necessarily laid open to question.[11]

This divergence on the question of gendered spectatorship within feminist theory is significant. Does it perhaps indicate fundamental differences between film and television in the spectator-text relations privileged by each? Do soaps and melodramas really construct different relations of gendered spectatorship, with melodrama constructing contradictory identifi-

cations in ways that soap opera does not? Or do these different positions on spectatorship rather signal an unevenness of theoretical development—or, to put it less teleologically, reflect the different intellectual histories and epistemological groundings of film theory and television theory?

Any differences in the spectator-text relations proposed respectively by soap opera and by film melodrama must be contingent to some extent on more general disparities in address between television and cinema. Thus film spectatorship, it may be argued, involves the pleasures evoked by looking in a more pristine way than does watching television. Whereas in classic cinema the concentration and involvement proposed by structures of the look, identification and point-of-view tend to be paramount, television spectatorship is more likely to be characterised by distraction and diversion.[12] This would suggest that each medium constructs sexual difference through spectatorship in rather different ways: cinema through the look and spectacle, and television—perhaps less evidently—through a capacity to insert its flow, its characteristic modes of address, and the textual operations of different kinds of programmes into the rhythms and routines of domestic activities and sexual divisions of labour in the household at various times of day.

It would be a mistake, however, simply to equate current thinking on spectator-text relations in each medium. This is not only because theoretical work on spectatorship as it is defined here is newer and perhaps not so developed for television as it has been for cinema, but also because conceptualisations of spectatorship in film theory and TV theory emerge from quite distinct perspectives. When feminist writers on soap opera and on film melodrama discuss spectatorship, therefore, they are usually talking about different things. This has partly to do with the different intellectual histories and methodological groundings of theoretical work on film and on television. Whereas most TV theory has until fairly recently existed under the sociological rubric of media studies, film theory has on the whole been based in the criticism-oriented tradition of literary studies. In consequence, while the one tends to privilege contexts over texts, the other usually privileges texts over contexts.

However, some recent critical work on soap opera, notably work produced within a cultural studies context, does attempt a *rapprochement* of text and context. Charlotte Brunsdon, writing about the British soap opera *Crossroads*, draws a distinction between subject positions proposed by texts and a 'social subject' who may or may not take up these positions.[13] In considering the interplay of 'social reader and social text', Brunsdon attempts to come to terms with problems posed by the universalism of the psychoanalytic model of the spectator/subject as against the descriptiveness and limited analytical scope of studies of specific instances and conjunctures. In taking up the instance of soap opera, then, one of Brunsdon's broader objectives is to resolve the dualism of text and context.

'Successful' spectatorship of a soap like *Crossroads*, it is argued, demands a certain cultural capital: familiarity with the plots and characters of a particular serial as well as with soap opera as a genre. It also demands wider cultural competence, especially in the codes of conduct of personal and family life. For Brunsdon, then, the spectator addressed by soap opera is constructed within culture rather than by representation. This, however, would indicate that such a spectator, a 'social subject', might—rather than being a subject in process of gender positioning—belong after all to a social audience already divided by gender.

The 'social subject' of this cultural model produces meaning by decoding messages or communications, an activity which is always socially situated.[14] Thus although such a model may move some way towards reconciling text and context, the balance of Brunsdon's argument remains weighted in favour of context: spectator-text relations are apparently regarded virtually as an effect of socio-cultural contexts. Is there a way in which spectator/subjects of film and television texts can be thought in a historically specific manner, or indeed a way for the social audience to be rescued from social/historical determinism?

Although none of the feminist criticism of soap opera and melodrama reviewed here has come up with any solution to these problems, it all attempts, in some degree and with greater or lesser success, to engage with them. Brunsdon's essay possibly comes closest to an answer, paradoxically because its very failure to resolve the dualism which ordains that spectators are constructed by texts while audiences have

their place in contexts begins to hint at a way around the problem. Although the hybrid 'social subject' may turn out to be more a social audience member than a spectator, this concept does suggest that a move into theories of discourse could prove to be productive.

Both spectators and social audience may accordingly be regarded as discursive constructs. Representations, contexts, audiences and spectators would then be seen as a series of interconnected social discourses, certain discourses possessing greater constitutive authority at specific moments than others. Such a model permits relative autonomy for the operations of texts, readings and contexts, and also allows for contradictions, oppositional readings and varying degrees of discursive authority. Since the state of a discursive formation is not constant, it can be apprehended only by means of inquiry into specific instances or conjunctures. In attempting to deal with the text-context split and to address the relationship between spectators and social audiences, therefore, theories of representation may have to come to terms with discursive formations of the social, cultural and textual.

IV

One of the impulses generating feminist critical and theoretical work on soap opera and the woman's picture is a desire to examine genres which are popular, and popular in particular with women. The assumption is usually that such popularity has to do mainly with the social audience: TV soaps attract large numbers of viewers, many of them women, and in its heyday the woman's picture also drew in a mass female audience. But when the nature of this appeal is sought in the texts themselves or in relations between spectators and texts, the argument becomes rather more complex. In what specific ways do soaps and melodramas address or construct female/feminine spectators?

To some extent, they offer the spectator a position of mastery: this is certainly true as regards the hermeneutic of the melodrama's classic narrative, though perhaps less obviously so in relation to the soap's infinite process of narrativity. At the same time, they also place the spectator in a masochistic position of either—in the case of the woman's picture—identifying with a female character's renunciation or, as in soap opera, forever anticipating an endlessly held-off resolution. Culturally speaking, this combination of mastery and masochism in the reading competence constructed by soaps and melodramas suggests an interplay of masculine and feminine subject positions. Culturally dominant codes inscribe the masculine, while the feminine bespeaks a 'return of the repressed' in the form of codes which may well transgress culturally dominant subject positions, though only at the expense of proposing a position of subjection for the spectator.

At the same time, it is sometimes argued on behalf of both soap opera and film melodrama that in a society whose representations of itself are governed by the masculine, these genres at least raise the possibility of female desire and female point-of-view. Pam Cook advances such a view in relation to the woman's picture, for example.[15] But how is the oppositional potential of this to be assessed? Tania Modleski suggests that soap opera is 'in the vanguard not just of TV art but of all popular narrative art'.[16] But such a statement begs the question: under what circumstances can popular narrative art itself be regarded as transgressive? Because texts do not operate in isolation from contexts, any answer to these questions must take into account the ways in which popular narratives are read, the conditions under which they are produced and consumed, and the ends to which they are appropriated. As most feminist writing on soap opera and the woman's melodrama implies, there is ample space in the articulation of these various instances for contradiction and for struggles over meaning.

The popularity of television soap opera and film melodrama with women raises the question of how it is that sizeable audiences of women relate to these representations and the institutional practices of which they form part. It provokes, too, a consideration of the continuity between women's interpellation as spectators and their status as a social audience. In turn, the distinction between social audience and spectator/subject, and attempts to explore the relationship between the two, are part of a broader theoretical endeavour: to deal in tandem with texts and contexts. The distinction between social audience and spectator

must also inform debates and practices around cultural production, in which questions of context and reception are always paramount. For anyone interested in feminist cultural politics, such considerations will necessarily inform any assessment of the place and the political usefulness of popular genres aimed at, and consumed by, mass audiences of women.

Notes

1. Muriel G Cantor and Suzanne Pingree, *The Soap Opera*, Beverley Hills, Sage Publications, 1983, p 22. Here 'soap opera' refers to daytime (US) or early evening (UK) serials . . . not prime-time serials like *Dallas* and *Dynasty*.

2. See Jean-Louis Baudry, 'Ideological Effects of the Basic Cinematographic Apparatus', *Film Quarterly* vol 28 no 2 (1974–5), pp 39–47; Christian Metz, 'The Imaginary Signifier', *Screen* Summer 1975, vol 16 no 2, pp 14–76.

3. Laura Mulvey, 'Afterthoughts on "Visual Pleasure and Narrative Cinema"', *Framework* nos 15/16/17 (1981), pp 12–15.

4. Laura Mulvey, 'Visual Pleasure and Narrative Cinema', *Screen* Autumn 1975, vol 16 no 3, pp 6–18.

5. Pam Cook, 'Melodrama and the Women's Picture', in Sue Aspinall and Robert Murphy (eds), *Gainsborough Melodrama*, London, B F I 1983, p 17.

6. Tania Modleski, *Loving With a Vengeance: Mass Produced Fantasies for Women*, Hamden Connecticut, The Shoe String Press, 1982, p 105. See also Tania Modleski, 'The Search for Tomorrow in Today's Soap Operas', *Film Quarterly* vol 33 no 1 (1979), pp 12–21.

7. Cook, op cit.

8. Methods and findings of social science research on the social audience for American daytime soap operas are discussed in Cantor and Pingree, op cit, Chapter 7.

9. Modleski, *Loving With a Vengeance*, op cit, p 88.

10. Charlotte Brunsdon, 'Crossroads: Notes on Soap Opera', *Screen*, vol 22 no 4 (1981), pp 32–37.

11. Cook, op cit, p 19.

12. John Ellis, *Visible Fictions*, London, Routledge and Kegan Paul, 1982.

13. Brunsdon, op cit. p 32.

14. A similar model is also adopted by Dorothy Hobson in *Crossroads: the Drama of a Soap Opera*, London, Methuen, 1982.

15. Cook, op cit. E Ann Kaplan takes a contrary position in 'Theories of Melodrama: a Feminist Perspective', *Women and Performance: a Journal of Feminist Theory* vol 1 no 1 (1983), pp 40–48.

16. Modleski, *Loving with a Vengeance*, op cit, p 87.

42.
THE OPPOSITIONAL GAZE

Black Female Spectators

bell hooks

When thinking about black female spectators, I remember being punished as a child for staring, for those hard intense direct looks children would give grown-ups, looks that were seen as confrontational, as gestures of resistance, challenges to authority. The 'gaze' has always been political in my life. Imagine the terror felt by the child who has come to understand through repeated punishments that one's gaze can be dangerous. The child who has learned so well to look the other way when necessary. Yet, when punished, the child is told by parents, 'Look at me when I talk to you.' Only, the child is afraid to look. Afraid to look, but fascinated by the gaze. There is power in looking.

Amazed the first time I read in history classes that white slave-owners (men, women, and children) punished enslaved black people for looking, I wondered how this traumatic relationship to the gaze had informed black parenting and black spectatorship. The politics of slavery, of racialized power relations, were such that the slaves were denied their right to gaze. Connecting this strategy of domination to that used by grown folks in southern black rural communities where I grew up, I was pained to think that there was no absolute difference between whites who had oppressed black people and ourselves. Years later, reading Michel Foucault, I thought again about these connections, about the ways power as domination reproduces itself in different locations employing similar apparatuses, strategies, and mechanisms of control. Since I knew as a child that the dominating power adults exercised over me and over my gaze

was never so absolute that I did not dare to look, to sneak a peep, to stare dangerously, I knew that the slaves had looked. That all attempts to repress our/black peoples' right to gaze had produced in us an overwhelming longing to look, a rebellious desire, an oppositional gaze. By courageously looking, we defiantly declared: 'Not only will I stare. I want my look to change reality.' Even in the worse circumstances of domination, the ability to manipulate one's gaze in the face of structures of domination that would contain it, opens up the possibility of agency. In much of his work, Michel Foucault insists on describing domination in terms of 'relations of power' as part of an effort to challenge the assumption that 'power is a system of domination which controls everything and which leaves no room for freedom.' Emphatically stating that in all relations of power 'there is necessarily the possibility of resistance,' he invites the critical thinker to search those margins, gaps, and locations on and through the body where agency can be found.

Stuart Hall calls for recognition of our agency as black spectators in his essay 'Cultural Identity and Cinematic Representation.' Speaking against the construction of white representations of blackness as totalizing, Hall says of white presence: 'The error is not to conceptualize this "presence" in terms of power, but to locate that power as wholly external to us—as extrinsic force, whose influence can be thrown off like the serpent sheds its skin. What Franz Fanon reminds us, in *Black Skin, White Masks*, is how power is inside as well as outside:

. . . the movements, the attitudes, the glances of the Other fixed me there, in the sense in which a chemical solution is fixed by a dye. I was indignant; I demanded an explanation. Nothing happened. I burst apart. Now the fragments have been put together again by another self. This 'look,' from— so to speak—the place of the Other, fixes us, not only in its violence, hostility and aggression, but in the ambivalence of its desire.

Spaces of agency exist for black people, wherein we can both interrogate the gaze of the Other but also look back, and at one another, naming what we see. The 'gaze' has been and is a site of resistance for colonized black people globally. Subordinates in relations of power learn experientially that there is a critical gaze, one that 'looks' to document, one that is oppositional. In resistance struggle, the power of the dominated to assert agency by claiming and cultivating 'awareness' politicizes 'looking' relations—one learns to look a certain way in order to resist.

When most black people in the United States first had the opportunity to look at film and television, they did so fully aware that mass media was a system of knowledge and power reproducing and maintaining white supremacy. To stare at the television, or mainstream movies, to engage its images, was to engage its negation of black representation. It was the oppositional black gaze that responded to these looking relations by developing independent black cinema. Black viewers of mainstream cinema and television could chart the progress of political movements for racial equality *via* the construction of images, and did so. Within my family's southern black working-class home, located in a racially segregated neighborhood, watching television was one way to develop critical spectatorship. Unless you went to work in the white world, across the tracks, you learned to look at white people by staring at them on the screen. Black looks, as they were constituted in the context of social movements for racial uplift, were interrogating gazes. We laughed at television shows like *Our Gang* and *Amos 'n' Andy*, at these white representations of blackness, but we also looked at them critically. Before racial integration, black viewers of movies and television experienced visual pleasure in a context where looking was also about contestation and confrontation.

Writing about black looking relations in 'Black British Cinema: Spectatorship and Identity Formation in Territories,' Manthia Diawara identifies the power of the spectator: 'Every narration places the spectator in a position of agency; and race, class and sexual relations influence the way in which this subjecthood is filled by the spectator.' Of particular concern for him are moments of 'rupture' when the spectator resists 'complete identification with the film's discourse.' These ruptures define the relation between black spectators and dominant cinema prior to racial integration. Then, one's enjoyment of a film wherein representations of blackness were stereotypically degrading and dehumanizing co-existed with a critical practice that restored presence where it was negated. Critical discussion of the film while it was in progress or at its conclusion maintained the distance between spectator and the image. Black films were also subject to critical interrogation. Since they came into being in part as a response to the failure of white-dominated cinema to represent blackness in a manner that did not reinforce white supremacy, they too were critiqued to see if images were seen as complicit with dominant cinematic practices.

Critical, interrogating black looks were mainly concerned with issues of race and racism, the way racial domination of blacks by whites overdetermined representation. They were rarely concerned with gender. As spectators, black men could repudiate the reproduction of racism in cinema and television, the negation of black presence, even as they could feel as though they were rebelling against white supremacy by daring to look, by engaging phallocentric politics of spectatorship. Given the real life public circumstances wherein black men were murdered/lynched for looking at white womanhood, where the black male gaze was always subject to control and/or punishment by the powerful white Other, the private realm of television screens or dark theaters could unleash the repressed gaze. There they could 'look' at white womanhood without a structure of domination overseeing the gaze, interpreting, and punishing. That white supremacist structure that had murdered Emmet Till after interpreting his look as violation, as 'rape' of white womanhood, could not control black male responses to screen images. In their role as spectators, black men could enter an imaginative space of phallocentric power that mediated racial negation. This gendered relation to looking made the experience of the black male spectator radically different from that of the black female spectator. Major early black male independent filmmakers represented black women in their films as objects of male gaze. Whether looking through the camera or as spectators watching films, whether mainstream cinema or 'race' movies such as those made by Oscar Micheaux, the black male gaze had a different scope from that of the black female.

Black women have written little about black female spectatorship, about our moviegoing practices. A growing body of film theory and criticism by black women has only begun to emerge. The prolonged silence of black women as spectators and critics was a response to absence, to cinematic negation. In 'The Technology of Gender,' Teresa de Lauretis, drawing on the work of Monique Wittig, calls attention to 'the power of discourses to "do violence" to people, a violence which is material and physical, although produced by abstract and scientific discourses as well as the discourses of the mass media.' With the possible exception of early race movies, black female spectators have had to develop looking relations within a cinematic context that constructs our presence as absence, that denies the 'body' of the black female so as to perpetuate white supremacy and with it a phallocentric spectatorship where the woman to be looked at and desired is 'white.' (Recent movies do not conform to this paradigm but I am turning to the past with the intent to chart the development of black female spectatorship.)

Talking with black women of all ages and classes, in different areas of the United States, about their filmic looking relations, I hear again and again ambivalent responses to cinema. Only a few of the black women I talked with remembered the pleasure of race movies, and even those who did, felt that pleasure interrupted and usurped by Hollywood. Most of the black women I talked with were adamant that they never went to movies expecting to see compelling representations of black femaleness. They were all acutely aware of cinematic racism—its violent erasure of black womanhood. In Anne Friedberg's essay 'A Denial of Difference: Theories of Cinematic Identification' she stresses that 'Identification can only be made through

recognition, and all recognition is itself an implicit confirmation of the ideology of the status quo.' Even when representations of black women were present in film, our bodies and being were there to serve—to enhance and maintain white womanhood as object of the phallocentric gaze.

Commenting on Hollywood's characterization of black women in *Girls on Film*, Julie Burchill describes this absent presence:

> Black women have been mothers without children (Mammies—who can ever forget the sickening spectacle of Hattie MacDaniels waiting on the simpering Vivien Leigh hand and foot and enquiring like a ninny, 'What's ma lamb gonna wear?') . . . Lena Horne, the first black performer signed to a long term contract with a major (MGM), looked gutless but was actually quite spirited. She seethed when Tallulah Bankhead complimented her on the paleness of her skin and the non-Negroidness of her features.

When black women actresses like Lena Horne appeared in mainstream cinema most white viewers were not aware that they were looking at black females unless the film was specifically coded as being about blacks. Burchill is one of the few white women film critics who has dared to examine the intersection of race and gender in relation to the construction of the category 'woman' in film as object of the phallocentric gaze. With characteristic wit she asserts: 'What does it say about racial purity that the best blondes have all been brunettes (Harlow, Monroe, Bardot)? I think it says that we are not as white as we think.' Burchill could easily have said 'we are not as white as we want to be,' for clearly the obsession to have white women film stars be ultra-white was a cinematic practice that sought to maintain a distance, a separation between that image and the black female Other; it was a way to perpetuate white supremacy. Politics of race and gender were inscribed into mainstream cinematic narrative from *Birth of a Nation* on. As a seminal work, this film identified what the place and function of white womanhood would be in cinema. There was clearly no place for black women.

Remembering my past in relation to screen images of black womanhood, I wrote a short essay, 'Do you

remember Sapphire?' which explored both the negation of black female representation in cinema and
television and our rejection of these images. Identifying the character of 'Sapphire' from *Amos 'n' Andy* as
that screen representation of black femaleness I first
saw in childhood, I wrote:

> She was even then backdrop, foil. She was bitch—
> nag. She was there to soften images of black men,
> to make them seem vulnerable, easygoing, funny,
> and unthreatening to a white audience. She was
> there as man in drag, as castrating bitch, as some-
> one to be lied to, someone to be tricked, someone
> the white and black audience could hate. Scape-
> goated on all sides. *She was not us.* We laughed
> with the black men, with the white people. We
> laughed at this black woman who was not us. And
> we did not even long to be there on the screen.
> How could we long to be there when our image,
> visually constructed, was so ugly. We did not long
> to be there. We did not long for her. We did not
> want our construction to be this hated black female
> thing—foil, backdrop. Her black female image was
> not the body of desire. There was nothing to see.
> She was not us.

Grown black women had a different response to Sapphire; they identified with her frustrations and her
woes. They resented the way she was mocked. They
resented the way these screen images could assault
black womanhood, could name us bitches, nags. And
in opposition they claimed Sapphire as their own, as
the symbol of that angry part of themselves white folks
and black men could not even begin to understand.

Conventional representations of black women
have done violence to the image. Responding to this
assault, many black women spectators shut out the
image, looked the other way, accorded cinema no
importance in their lives. Then there were those spectators whose gaze was that of desire and complicity.
Assuming a posture of subordination, they submitted
to cinema's capacity to seduce and betray. They were
cinematically 'gaslighted.' Every black woman I spoke
with who was/is an ardent moviegoer, a lover of the
Hollywood film, testified that to experience fully the
pleasure of that cinema they had to close down critique, analysis; they had to forget racism. And mostly
they did not think about sexism. What was the nature
then of this adoring black female gaze—this look that
could bring pleasure in the midst of negation? In her
first novel, *The Bluest Eye*, Toni Morrison constructs
a portrait of the black female spectator; her gaze is
the masochistic look of victimization. Describing
her looking relations, Miss Pauline Breedlove, a poor
working woman, maid in the house of a prosperous
white family, asserts:

> The onliest time I be happy seem like was when I
> was in the picture show. Every time I got, I went,
> I'd go early, before the show started. They's cut
> off the lights, and everything be black. Then the
> screen would light up, and I's move right on in
> them picture. White men taking such good care
> of they women, and they all dressed up in big
> clean houses with the bath tubs right in the same
> room with the toilet. Them pictures gave me a lot
> of pleasure.

To experience pleasure, Miss Pauline sitting in the
dark must imagine herself transformed, turned into
the white woman portrayed on the screen. After
watching movies, feeling the pleasure, she says, 'But it
made coming home hard.'

We come home to ourselves. Not all black women
spectators submitted to that spectacle of regression
through identification. Most of the women I talked
with felt that they consciously resisted identification
with films—that this tension made moviegoing less
than pleasurable; at times it caused pain. As one black
woman put, 'I could always get pleasure from movies
as long as I did not look too deep.' For black female
spectators who have 'looked too deep' the encounter
with the screen hurt. That some of us chose to stop
looking was a gesture of resistance, turning away was
one way to protest, to reject negation. My pleasure in
the screen ended abruptly when I and my sisters first
watched *Imitation of Life*. Writing about this experience in the 'Sapphire' piece, I addressed the movie
directly, confessing:

> I had until now forgotten you, that screen image
> seen in adolescence, those images that made me
> stop looking. It was there in *Imitation of Life*, that
> comfortable mammy image. There was something

familiar about this hard-working black woman who loved her daughter so much, loved her in a way that hurt. Indeed, as young southern black girls watching this film, Peola's another reminded us of the hardworking, churchgoing, Big Mamas we knew and loved. Consequently, it was not this image that captured our gaze; we were fascinated by Peola.

Addressing her, I wrote:

> You were different. There was something scary in his image of young sexual sensual black beauty betrayed—that daughter who did not want to be confined by blackness, that 'tragic mulatto' who did not want to be negated. 'Just let me escape this image forever,' she could have said. I will always remember that image. I remembered how we cried for her, for our unrealized desiring selves. She was tragic because there was no place in the cinema for her, no loving pictures. She too was absent image. It was better then, that we were absent, for when we were there it was humiliating, strange, sad. We cried all night for you, for the cinema that had no place for you. And like you, we stopped thinking it would one day be different.

When I returned to films as a young woman, after a long period of silence, I had developed an oppositional gaze. Not only would I not be hurt by the absence of black female presence, or the insertion of violating representation, I interrogated the work, cultivated a way to look past race and gender for aspects of content, form, language. Foreign films and US independent cinema were the primary locations of my filmic looking relations, even though I also watched Hollywood films.

From 'jump,' black female spectators have gone to films with awareness of the way in which race and racism determined the visual construction of gender. Whether it was *Birth of a Nation* or Shirley Temple shows, we knew that white womanhood was the racialized sexual difference occupying the place of stardom in mainstream narrative film. We assumed white women knew it too. Reading Laura Mulvey's provocative essay, 'Visual Pleasure and Narrative Cinema,' from a standpoint that acknowledges race, one sees clearly why black women spectators not duped by mainstream cinema would develop an oppositional gaze. Placing ourselves outside that pleasure in looking, Mulvey argues, was determined by a 'split between active/male and passive/female.' Black female spectators actively chose not to identify with the film's imaginary subject because such identification was disenabling.

Looking at films with an oppositional gaze, black women were able to critically assess the cinema's construction of white womanhood as object of phallocentric gaze and choose not to identify with either the victim or the perpetrator. Black female spectators, who refused to identify with white womanhood, who would not take on the phallocentric gaze of desire and possession, created a critical space where the binary opposition Mulvey posits of 'woman as image, man as bearer of the look' was continually deconstructed. As critical spectators, black women looked from a location that disrupted, one akin to that described by Annette Kuhn in *The Power of The Image*:

> ... the acts of analysis, of deconstruction and of reading 'against the grain' offer an additional pleasure—the pleasure of resistance, of saying 'no': not to 'unsophisticated' enjoyment, by ourselves and others, of culturally dominant images, but to the structures of power which ask us to consume them uncritically and in highly circumscribed ways.

Mainstream feminist film criticism in no way acknowledges black female spectatorship. It does not even consider the possibility that women can construct an oppositional gaze via an understanding and awareness of the politics of race and racism. Feminist film theory rooted in an ahistorical psychoanalytic framework that privileges sexual difference actively suppresses recognition of race, reenacting and mirroring the erasure of black womanhood that occurs in films, silencing any discussion of racial difference—of racialized sexual difference. Despite feminist critical interventions aimed at deconstructing the category 'woman' which highlight the significance of race, many feminist film critics continue to structure their discourse as though it speaks about 'women' when in actuality it speaks only about white women. It seems ironic that the cover of the recent anthology *Feminism and Film Theory* edited by Constance Penley has a graphic that is a reproduction of the photo of white actresses Rosalind Russell and Dorothy Arzner on the 1936 set of the film *Craig's Wife* yet there is no acknowledgment in any essay in this collection that the woman 'subject' under discussion is always white. Even though there are photos of black women from films reproduced in the text, there is no acknowledgment of racial difference.

It would be too simplistic to interpret this failure of insight solely as a gesture of racism. Importantly, it also speaks to the problem of structuring feminist film theory around a totalizing narrative of woman as object whose image functions solely to reaffirm and reinscribe patriarchy. Mary Ann Doane addresses this issue in the essay 'Remembering Women: Psychical and Historical Construction in Film Theory':

> This attachment to the figure of a degeneralizible Woman as the product of the apparatus indicates why, for many, feminist film theory seems to have reached an impasse, a certain blockage in its theorization . . . in focusing upon the task of delineating in great detail the attributes of woman as effect of the apparatus, feminist film theory participates in the abstraction of women.

The concept 'Woman' effaces the difference between women in specific socio-historical contexts, between women defined precisely as historical subjects rather than as *a* psychic subject (or non-subject). Though Doane does not focus on race, her comments speak directly to the problem of its erasure. For it is only as one imagines 'woman' in the abstract, when woman becomes fiction or fantasy, can race not be seen as significant. Are we really to imagine that feminist theorists writing only about images of white women, who subsume this specific historical subject under the totalizing category 'woman,' do not 'see' the whiteness of the image? It may very well be that they engage in a process of denial that eliminates the necessity of revisioning conventional ways of thinking about psychoanalysis as a paradigm of analysis and the need to rethink a body of feminist film theory that is firmly rooted in a denial of the reality that sex/sexuality may not be the primary and/or exclusive signifier

of difference. Doane's essay appears in a very recent anthology, *Psychoanalysis and Cinema* edited by E. Ann Kaplan, where, once again, none of the theory presented acknowledges or discusses racial difference, with the exception of one essay, 'Not Speaking with Language, Speaking with No Language,' which problematizes notions of orientalism in its examination of Leslie Thornton's film *Adynata*. Yet in most of the essays, the theories espoused are rendered problematic if one includes race as a category of analysis.

Constructing feminist film theory along these lines enables the production of a discursive practice that need never theorize any aspect of black female representation or spectatorship. Yet the existence of black women within white supremacist culture problematizes, and makes complex, the overall issue of female identity, representation, and spectatorship. If, as Friedberg suggests, 'identification is a process which commands the subject to be displaced by an other; it is a procedure which breeches the separation between self and other, and, in this way, replicates the very structure of patriarchy.' If identification 'demands sameness, necessitates similarity, disallows difference'—must we then surmise that many feminist film critics who are 'over-identified' with the mainstream cinematic apparatus produce theories that replicate its totalizing agenda? Why is it that feminist film criticism, which has most claimed the terrain of woman's identity, representation, and subjectivity as its field of analysis, remains aggressively silent on the subject of blackness and specifically representations of black womanhood? Just as mainstream cinema has historically forced aware black female spectators not to look, much feminist film criticism disallows the possibility of a theoretical dialogue that might include black women's voices. It is difficult to talk when you feel no one is listening, when you feel as though a special jargon or narrative has been created that only the chosen can understand. No wonder then that black women have for the most part confined our critical commentary on film to conversations. And it must be reiterated that this gesture is a strategy that protects us from the violence perpetuated and advocated by discourses of mass media. A new focus on issues of race and representation in the field of film theory could critically intervene on the historical repression reproduced in some arenas of contemporary critical practice, making a discursive space for discussion of black female spectatorship possible.

When I asked a black woman in her twenties, an obsessive moviegoer, why she thought we had not written about black female spectatorship, she commented: 'We are afraid to talk about ourselves as spectators because we have been so abused by "the gaze".' An aspect of that abuse was the imposition of the assumption that black female looking relations were not important enough to theorize. Film theory as a critical 'turf' in the United States has been and continues to be influenced by and reflective of white racial domination. Since feminist film criticism was initially rooted in a women's liberation movement informed by racist practices, it did not open up the discursive terrain and make it more inclusive. Recently, even those white film theorists who include an analysis of race show no interest in black female spectatorship. In her introduction to the collection of essays *Visual and Other Pleasures*, Laura Mulvey describes her initial romantic absorption in Hollywood cinema, stating:

> Although this great, previously unquestioned and unanalyzed love was put in crisis by the impact of feminism on my thought in the early 1970s, it also had an enormous influence on the development of my critical work and ideas and the debate within film culture with which I became preoccupied over the next fifteen years or so. Watched through eyes that were affected by the changing climate of consciousness, the movies lost their magic.

Watching movies from a feminist perspective, Mulvey arrived at that location of disaffection that is the starting point for many black women approaching cinema within the lived harsh reality of racism. Yet her account of being a part of a film culture whose roots rest on a founding relationship of adoration and love indicates how difficult it would have been to enter that world from 'jump' as a critical spectator whose gaze had been formed in opposition.

Given the context of class exploitation, and racist and sexist domination, it has only been through resistance, struggle, reading, and looking 'against the grain,' that black women have been able to value our process of looking enough to publicly name it. Centrally, those black female spectators who attest to the oppositionality of their gaze deconstruct theories of female spectatorship that have relied heavily on the assumption that, as Doane suggests in her essay, 'Woman's Stake: Filming the Female Body,' 'woman can only mimic man's relation to language, that is assume a position defined by the penis-phallus as the supreme arbiter of lack.' Identifying with neither the phallocentric gaze nor the construction of white womanhood as lack, critical black female spectators construct a theory of looking relations where cinematic visual delight is the pleasure of interrogation. Every black woman spectator I talked to, with rare exception, spoke of being 'on guard' at the movies. Talking about the way being a critical spectator of Hollywood films influenced her, black woman filmmaker Julie Dash exclaims, 'I make films because I was such a spectator!' Looking at Hollywood cinema from a distance, from that critical politicized standpoint that did not want to be seduced by narratives reproducing her negation, Dash watched mainstream movies over and over again for the pleasure of deconstructing them. And of course there is that added delight if one happens, in the process of interrogation, to come across a narrative that invites the black female spectator to engage the text with no threat of violation [. . .]

Talking with black female spectators, looking at written discussions either in fiction or academic essays about black women, I noted the connection made between the realm of representation in mass media and the capacity of black women to construct ourselves as subjects in daily life. The extent to which black women feel devalued, objectified, dehumanized in this society determines the scope and texture of their looking relations. Those black women whose identities were constructed in resistance, by practices that oppose the dominant order, were most inclined to develop an oppositional gaze. Now that there is a growing interest in films produced by black women and those films have become more accessible to viewers, it is possible to talk about black female spectatorship in relation to that work. So far, most discussions of black spectatorship that I have come across focus on men. In 'Black Spectatorship: Problems of Identification and Resistance' Manthia Diawara suggests that 'the components of "difference" ' among elements of sex, gender, and sexuality give rise to different readings of the same material, adding that these conditions produce a 'resisting' spectator. He focuses his critical discussion on black masculinity.

The recent publication of the anthology *The Female Gaze: Women as Viewers of Popular Culture* excited me, especially as it included an essay, 'Black Looks,' by Jacqui Roach and Petal Felix that attempts to address black female spectatorship. The essay posed provocative questions that were not answered: Is there a black female gaze? How do black women relate to the gender politics of representation? Concluding, the authors assert that black females have 'our own reality, our own history, our own gaze—one which sees the world rather differently from "anyone else." ' Yet, they do not name/describe this experience of seeing 'rather differently.' The absence of definition and explanation suggests they are assuming an essentialist stance wherein it is presumed that black women, as victims of race and gender oppression, have an inherently different field of vision. Many black women do not 'see differently' precisely because their perceptions of reality are so profoundly colonized, shaped by dominant ways of knowing. As Trinh T. Minh-ha points out in 'Outside In, Inside Out': 'Subjectivity does not merely consist of talking about oneself . . . be this talking indulgent or critical.'

Critical black female spectatorship emerges as a site of resistance only when individual black women actively resist the imposition of dominant ways of knowing and looking. While every black woman I talked to was aware of racism, that awareness did not automatically correspond with politicization, the development of an oppositional gaze. When it did, individual black women consciously named the process. Manthia Diawara's 'resisting spectatorship' is a term that does not adequately describe the terrain of black female spectatorship. We do more than resist. We create alternative texts that are not solely reactions. As critical spectators, black women participate in a broad range of looking relations, contest, resist, revision, interrogate, and invent on multiple levels. Certainly when I watch the work of black women filmmakers Camille Billops, Kathleen Collins, Julie Dash, Ayoka Chenzira, Zeinabu Davis, I do not need to 'resist' the images even as I still choose to watch their work with a critical eye.

Black female critical thinkers concerned with creating space for the construction of radical black female subjectivity, and the way cultural production informs this possibility, fully acknowledge the importance of mass media, film in particular, as a powerful site for critical intervention. Certainly Julie Dash's film *Illusions* identifies the terrain of Hollywood cinema as a space of knowledge production that has enormous power. Yet, she also creates a filmic narrative wherein the black female protagonist subversively claims that space. Inverting the 'real-life' power structure, she offers the black female spectator representations that challenge stereotypical notions that place us outside the realm of filmic discursive practices. Within the film she uses the strategy of Hollywood suspense films to undermine those cinematic practices that deny black women a place in this structure. Problematizing the question of 'racial' identity by depicting passing, suddenly it is the white male's capacity to gaze, define, and know that is called into question.

When Mary Ann Doane describes in 'Woman's Stake: Filming the Female Body' the way in which feminist filmmaking practice can elaborate 'a special syntax for a different articulation of the female body,' she names a critical process that 'undoes the structure of the classical narrative through an insistence upon its repressions.' An eloquent description, this precisely names Dash's strategy in *Illusions*, even though the film is not unproblematic and works within certain conventions that are not successfully challenged. For example, the film does not indicate whether the character Mignon will make Hollywood films that subvert and transform the genre or whether she will simply assimilate and perpetuate the norm. Still, subversively, *Illusions* problematizes the issue of race and spectatorship. White people in the film are unable to 'see' that race informs their looking relations. Though she is passing to gain access to the machinery of cultural production represented by film, Mignon continually asserts her ties to black community. The bond between her and the young black woman singer Esther Jeeter is affirmed by caring gestures of affirmation, often expressed by eye-to-eye contact, the direct unmediated gaze of recognition. Ironically, it is the desiring objectifying sexualized white male gaze that threatens to penetrate her 'secrets' and disrupt her process. Metaphorically, Dash suggests the power of black women to make films will be threatened and undermined by that white male gaze that seeks to reinscribe the black female body in a narrative of voy-euristic pleasure where the only relevant opposition is male/female, and the only location for the female is as a victim. These tensions are not resolved by the narrative. It is not at all evident that Mignon will triumph over the white supremacist capitalist imperialist dominating 'gaze.'

Throughout *Illusions*, Mignon's power is affirmed by her contact with the younger black woman whom she nurtures and protects. It is this process of mirrored recognition that enables both black women to define their reality, apart from the reality imposed upon them by structures of domination. The shared gaze of the two women reinforces their solidarity. As the younger subject, Esther represents a potential audience for films that Mignon might produce, films wherein black females will be the narrative focus. Julie Dash's recent feature-length film *Daughters of the Dust* dares to place black females at the center of its narrative. This focus caused critics (especially white males) to critique the film negatively or to express many reservations. Clearly, the impact of racism and sexism so over-determine spectatorship—not only what we look at but who we identify with—that viewers who are not black females find it hard to empathize with the central characters in the movie. They are adrift without a white presence in the film.

Another representation of black females nurturing one another *via* recognition of their common struggle for subjectivity is depicted in Sankofa's collective work *Passion of Remembrance*. In the film, two black women friends, Louise and Maggie, are from the onset of the narrative struggling with the issue of subjectivity, of their place in progressive black liberation movements that have been sexist. They challenge old norms and want to replace them with new understandings of the complexity of black identity, and the need for liberation struggles that address that complexity. Dressing to go to a party, Louise and Maggie claim the 'gaze.' Looking at one another, staring in mirrors, they appear completely focused on their encounter with black femaleness. How they see themselves is most important, not how they will be stared at by others. Dancing to the tune 'Let's get Loose,' they display their bodies not for a voyeuristic colonizing gaze but for that look of recognition that affirms their subjectivity—that constitutes them as spectators. Mutually empowered

they eagerly leave the privatized domain to confront the public. Disrupting conventional racist and sexist stereotypical representations of black female bodies, these scenes invite the audience to look differently. They act to critically intervene and transform conventional filmic practices, changing notions of spectatorship. *Illusions*, *Daughters of the Dust*, and *A Passion of Remembrance* employ a deconstructive filmic practice to undermine existing grand cinematic narratives even as they retheorize subjectivity in the realm of the visual. Without providing 'realistic' positive representations that emerge only as a response to the totalizing nature of existing narratives, they offer points of radical departure. Opening up a space for the assertion of a critical black female spectatorship, they do not simply offer diverse representations, they imagine new transgressive possibilities for the formulation of identity.

In this sense they make explicit a critical practice that provides us with different ways to think about black female subjectivity and black female spectatorship. Cinematically, they provide new points of recognition, embodying Stuart Hall's vision of a critical practice that acknowledges that identity is constituted 'not outside but within representation,' and invites us to see film 'not as a second-order mirror held up to reflect what already exists, but as that form of representation which is able to constitute us as new kinds of subjects, and thereby enable us to discover who we are.' It is this critical practice that enables production of feminist film theory that theorizes black female spectatorship. Looking and looking back, black women involve ourselves in a process whereby we see our history as counter-memory, using it as a way to know the present and invent the future.

References

Burchill, Julie, *Girls on Film* (New York: Pantheon, 1986).

Diawara Manthia, 'Black Spectatorship: Problems of Identification and Resistance'. *Screen*, Vol. 29, No. 4 (1988).

Diawara, Manthia, 'Black British Cinema: Spectatorship and Identity Formation in Territories'. *Public Culture*, Vol. 1, No. 3 (Summer 1989).

Doane, Mary Ann, 'Woman's Stake: Filming the Female Body'. In *Feminism and Film Theory*, edited by Constance Penley (New York: Routledge, 1988).

Doane, Mary Ann, 'Remembering Women: Psychical and Historical Constructions in Film Theory'. In *Psychoanalysis and Cinema*, edited by E. Ann Kaplan (London: Routledge, 1990).

Fanon, Franz, *Black Skin, White Masks* (New York: *Monthly Review*, 1967).

Friedberg, Anne, 'A Denial of Difference: Theories of Cinematic Identification'. In *Psychoanalysis and Cinema*, edited by E. Ann Kaplan (London: Routledge, 1990).

Gamman, Lorraine and Marshment, Margaret (eds), *The Female Gaze: Women as Viewers of Popular Culture* (London: The Women's Press, 1988).

Hall, Stuart, 'Cultural Identity and Diaspora'. In *Identity: Community, Culture, Difference*, edited by Jonathan Rutherford (London: Lawrence & Wishart, 1990).

hooks, bell, 'Do You Remember Sapphire?'. In hooks, *Talking Back: Thinking Feminism, Thinking Black* (Boston: South End Press, 1989).

Kuhn, Annette, *The Power of the Image: Essays on Representation and Sexuality* (New York: Routledge, 1985).

Minh-ha, Trinh T., 'Outside In, Inside Out'. In *Questions of Third Cinema*, edited by Jim Pines (London: British Film Institute, 1989).

Morrison, Toni, *The Bluest Eye* (New York: Holt, Rinehart and Winston, 1970).

Mulvey, Laura, 'Visual Pleasure and Narrative Cinema'. *Screen* Autumn 1975, Vol. 16, No. 3, pp. 6–18.

Mulvey, Laura, *Visual and Other Pleasures* (Bloomington: University of Indiana Press, 1989).

43.
THERE'S SOMETHING QUEER HERE
Alexander Doty

There's Something Queer Here

But standing before the work of art requires you to act too. The tension you bring to the work of art is an action.

Jean Genet[1]

I'm gonna take you to queer bars
I'm gonna drive you in queer cars
You're gonna meet all of my queer friends
Our queer, queer fun it never ends.

"The Queer Song,"
Gretchen Phillips, Two Nice Girls[2]

The most slippery and elusive terrain for mass culture studies continues to be negotiated within audience and reception theory. Perhaps this is because within cultural studies, "audience" is now always already acknowledged to be fragmented, polymorphous, contradictory, and "nomadic," whether in the form of individual or group subjects. Given this, it seems an almost impossible task to conduct reception studies that capture the complexity of those moments in which audiences meet mass culture texts. As Janice Radway puts it:

No wonder we find it so difficult to theorize the dispersed, anonymous, unpredictable nature of the use of mass-produced, mass-mediated cultural forms. If the receivers of such forms are never assembled fixedly on a site or even in an easily identifiable space, if they are frequently not uniformly or even attentively disposed to systems of cultural production or to the messages they issue, how can we theorize, not to mention examine, the ever-shifting kaleidoscope of cultural circulation and consumption?[3]

In confronting this complexity, Radway suggests that mass culture studies begin to analyze reception more ethnographically by focusing upon the dense patterns and practices "of daily life and the way in which the media are integrated and implicated within it," rather than starting with already established audience categories.[4] Clearly the danger of making essentializing statements about both audiences and their reception practices lurks behind any uncritical use of categories such as "women," "teenagers," "lesbians," "housewives," "blue-collar workers," "blacks," or "gay men." Further, conducting reception studies on the basis of conventional audience categories can also lead to critical blindness about how certain reception strategies are shared by otherwise disparate individuals and groups.

I would like to propose "queerness" as a mass culture reception practice that is shared by all sorts of people in varying degrees of consistency and intensity.[5] Before proceeding, however, I will need to discuss—even defend—my use of "queer" in such phrases as "queer positions," "queer readers," "queer readings," and "queer discourses." In working through my thoughts on gay and lesbian cultural history, I found that while I used "gay" to describe particulars of men's culture, and "lesbian" to describe particulars of women's culture, I was hard-pressed to find a term to describe a cultural common ground between lesbians and gays as well as other nonstraights—a term representing unity as well as suggesting diversity. For certain historical and political reasons, "queer" suggested itself as such a term. As Adele Morrison said in an OUT/LOOK interview: "Queer is not an 'instead of,' it's an 'inclusive of.' I'd never want to lose the terms that specifically identify me."[6]

Currently, the word "gay" doesn't consistently have the same gender-unifying quality it may once have possessed. And since I'm interested in discussing aspects of cultural identification as well as of sexual desire, "homosexual" will not do either. I agree with those who do not find the word "homosexual" an appropriate synonym for both "gay" and "lesbian," as these latter terms are constructions that concern more than who you sleep with—although the objects of sexual desires are certainly central to expressions of lesbian and gay cultural identities. I also wanted to find a term with some ambiguity, a term that would describe a wide range of impulses and cultural expressions, including space for describing and expressing bisexual, transsexual, and straight queerness. While we acknowledge that homosexuals as well as heterosexuals can operate or mediate from within straight cultural spaces and positions—after all, most of us grew up learning the rules of straight culture—we have paid less attention to the proposition that basically heterocentrist texts can contain queer elements, and basically heterosexual, straight-identifying people can experience queer moments. And these people should be encouraged to examine and express these moments *as* queer, not as moments of "homosexual panic," or temporary confusion, or as unfortunate, shameful, or sinful lapses in judgment or taste to be ignored, repressed, condemned, or somehow explained away within and by straight cultural politics—or even within and by gay or lesbian discourses.

My uses of the terms "queer readings," "queer discourses," and "queer positions," then, are attempts to account for the existence and expression of a wide range of positions within culture that are "queer" or non-, anti-, or contra-straight.[7] I am using the term "queer" to mark a flexible space for the expression of all aspects of non- (anti-, contra-) straight cultural production and reception.[8] As such, this cultural "queer

space" recognizes the possibility that various and fluctuating queer positions might be occupied whenever *anyone* produces or responds to culture. In this sense, the use of the term "queer" to discuss reception takes up the standard binary opposition of "queer" and "nonqueer" (or "straight") while questioning its viability, at least in cultural studies, because, as noted earlier, the queer often operates within the nonqueer, as the nonqueer does within the queer (whether in reception, texts, or producers). The queer readings of mass culture I am concerned with in this essay will be those readings articulating positions *within* queer discourses. That is, these readings seem to be expressions of queer perspectives on mass culture from the inside, rather than descriptions of how "they" (gays and/or lesbians, usually) respond to, use, or are depicted in mass culture.

When a colleague heard I had begun using the word "queer" in my cultural studies work, she asked if I did so in order to "nostalgically" recapture and reassert the "romance" of the culturally marginal in the face of trends within straight capitalist societies to co-opt or contain aspects of queer cultures. I had, in fact, intended something quite different. By using "queer," I want to recapture and reassert a militant sense of difference that views the erotically "marginal" as both (in bell hooks's words) a consciously chosen "site of resistance" and a "location of radical openness and possibility."[9] And I want to suggest that within cultural production and reception, queer erotics are already part of culture's erotic center, both as a necessary construct by which to define the heterosexual and the straight (as "not queer"), and as a position that can be and is occupied in various ways by otherwise heterosexual and straight-identifying people.

But in another sense recapturing and reasserting a certain nostalgia and romance is part of my project here. For through playfully occupying various queer positions in relation to the fantasy/dream elements involved in cultural production and reception, we (whether straight-, gay-, lesbian-, or bi-identifying) are offered spaces to express a range of erotic desire frequently linked in Western cultures to nostalgic and romantic adult conceptions of childhood. Unfortunately, these moments of erotic complexity are usually explained away as part of the "regressive" work of mass media, whereby we are tricked into certain "unacceptable" and "immature" responses as passive subjects. But when cultural texts encourage straight-identified audience members to express a less-censored range of queer desire and pleasure than is possible in daily life, this "regression" has positive gender- and sexuality-destabilizing effects.[10]

I am aware of the current political controversy surrounding the word "queer." Some gays, lesbians, and bisexuals have expressed their inability to also identify with "queerness," as they feel the term has too long and too painful a history as a weapon of oppression and self-hate. These nonqueer lesbians, gays, and bisexuals find the attempts of radical forces in gay and lesbian communities (such as Queer Nation) to recover and positively redefine the term "queer" successful only within these communities—and unevenly successful at that. Preferring current or freshly created terms, non-queer-identifying lesbians, gays, and bisexuals often feel that any positive effects resulting from reappropriating "queer" are more theoretical than real.

But the history of gay and lesbian cultures and politics has shown that there are many times and places where the theoretical can have real social impact. Enough lesbians, gays, bisexuals, and other queers taking and making enough of these moments can create a more consistent awareness within the general public of queer cultural and political spaces, as these theory-in-the-flesh moments are concerned with making what has been for the most part publicly invisible and silent visible and vocal. In terms of mass culture reception, there are frequent theory-in-the-flesh opportunities in the course of everyday life. For example, how many times do we get the chance to inform people about our particular queer perspectives on film, television, literature, or music during conversations (or to engage someone else's perhaps unacknowledged queer perspective)? And how often, even if we are openly lesbian, gay, or bisexual, have we kept silent, or edited our conversations, deciding that our queer opinions are really only interesting to other queers, or that these opinions would make people uncomfortable—even while we think family, friends, and strangers should, of course, feel free to articulate various heterosexual or straight opinions in detail at any time?

Of course, queer positions aren't the only ones from which queers read and produce mass culture.

As with nonqueers, factors such as class, ethnicity, gender, occupation, education, and religious, national, and regional allegiances influence our identity construction, and therefore are important to the positions we take as cultural producers and reader-consumers. These other cultural factors can exert influences difficult to separate from the development of our identities as queers, and as a result, difficult to discuss apart from our engagement in culture as queers. For example, most people find it next to impossible to articulate their sexual identities (queer or non-queer) without some reference to gender. Generally, lesbian- and gay-specific forms of queer identities involve some degree of same-gender identification and desire or a cross-gender identification linked to same-gender desire. The understanding of what "gender" is in these cases can range from accepting conventional straight forms, which naturalize "feminine" and "masculine" by conflating them with essentializing, biology-based conceptions of "woman" and "man"; to imitating the outward forms and behaviors of one gender or the other while not fully subscribing to the straight ideological imperatives that define that gender; to combining or ignoring traditional gender codes in order to reflect attitudes that have little or nothing to do with straight ideas about femininity/women or masculinity/men. These last two positions are the places where queerly reconfigured gender identities begin to be worked out.[11]

"Begin to be," because most radically, as Sue-Ellen Case points out, "queer theory, unlike lesbian theory or gay male theory, is not gender specific."[12] Believing that "both gay and lesbian theory reinscribe sexual difference, to some extent, in their gender-specific constructions," Case calls for a queer theory that "works not at the site of gender, but at the site of ontology."[13] But while a nongendered notion of queerness makes sense, articulating this queer theory fully apart from gendered straight feminist, gay, and lesbian theorizing becomes difficult within languages and cultures that make gender and gender difference so crucial to their discursive practices. Through her discussions of vampire myths, Case works hard to establish a discourse that avoids gendered terms, yet she finds it necessary to resort to them every so often in order to suggest the queerness of certain things: placing "she" in quotation marks at one point, or discussing R. W. Fassbinder's film character Petra von Kant as "a truly queer creature who flickers somewhere between haute couture butch lesbian and male drag queen."[14]

Since I'm working with a conception of queerness that includes gay- and lesbian-specific positions as well as Case's nonlesbian and nongay queerness, gender definitions and uses here remain important to examining the ways in which queerness influences mass culture production and reception. For example, gay men who identify with some conception of "the feminine"[15] through processes that could stem from conscious personal choice, or from internalizing longstanding straight imperatives that encourage gay men to think of themselves as "not men" (and therefore, by implication or by direct attribution, as being like "women"), or from some degree of negotiation between these two processes, are at the center of the gay culture cults built around the imposing, spectacular women stars of opera (Maria Callas, Joan Sutherland, Beverly Sills, Renata Scotto, Teresa Stratas, Leontyne Price), theater (Lynn Fontanne, Katharine Cornell, Gertrude Lawrence, Maggie Smith, Angela Lansbury, Ethel Merman, Tallulah Bankhead), film (Bette Davis, Joan Crawford, Judy Garland, Marlene Dietrich, Vivien Leigh, Bette Midler, Glenda Jackson), popular music (Midler, Garland, Eartha Kitt, Edith Piaf, Barbra Streisand, Billie Holiday, Donna Summer, Diana Ross, Debbie Harry, Madonna), and television (Carol Burnett, the casts of *Designing Women* and *The Golden Girls*, Candice Bergen in *Murphy Brown*, Mary Tyler Moore and the supporting cast of women on *The Mary Tyler Moore Show*).[16] For the past two decades in the gay popular press, book chapters and articles on the connections between gay men and women stars have been a commonplace, but only occasionally do these works go beyond the monolithic audience label "gay men" to suggest the potential for discussing reception in a manner attuned to more specific definitions of sexual identity, such as those constructed to some degree within the dynamics of gender and sexuality.[17]

Given this situation, one strand of queer mass culture reception studies might be more precisely focused upon these networks of women performers who were, and are, meaningful at different times and places and for different reasons to feminine-identified gay men. One of the most extended analytic pieces

on feminine gay men's reception of women stars is the "Homosexuals' Girls" chapter of Julie Burchill's *Girls on Film*. But Burchill is clearly writing critically *about* a particular queer reception position; she is not queerly positioned herself. Indeed, Burchill's analysis of how "queens" respond to women stars seems written to conform to very narrow-minded ideas about audience and reception. For Burchill, all "feminine homosexual" men's investment in women stars is rooted in envy, jealousy, misogyny, and cruelty—and she concludes this even as she relates a comment by one of her gay friends: "You may have a flaming faggot's taste in movies, kid, but your perspective is pure Puritan."[18]

Clearly we need more popular and academic mass culture work that carefully considers feminine gay and other gendered queer reception practices, as well as those of even less-analyzed queer readership positions formed around the nexus of race and sexuality, or class and sexuality, or ethnicity and sexuality, or some combination of gender/race/class/ethnicity and sexuality.[19] These studies would offer valuable evidence of precisely how and where specific complex constructions of queerness can and do reveal themselves in the uses of mass culture, as well as revealing how and where that mass culture comes to influence and reinforce the process of queer identity formation.

One of the earliest attempts at such a study of queers and mass culture was a series of interviews with nine lesbians conducted by Judy Whitaker in 1981 for *Jump Cut*, "Hollywood Transformed." These interviews touched upon a number of issues surrounding lesbian identity, including gender identification. Although careful to label these interviews "biographical sketches, not sociological or psychological studies," Whitaker does make some comments suggesting the potential for such studies:

> Of the nine women who were interviewed, at least six said they identified at some time with male characters. Often the explanation is that men had the interesting active roles. Does this mean that these lesbians want to be like men? That would be a specious conclusion. None of the women who identified with male characters were "in love" with the characters' girl friends. All of the interviewees

were "in love" at some time with actresses, but they did not identify with or want to be the male suitors of those actresses. While the context of the discussion is film, what these women are really talking about is their lives. . . . Transformation and positive self-image are dominant themes in what they have to say. Hollywood is transcended.[20]

After reading these interviews, there might be some question about how fully the straight ideologies Hollywood narratives encourage are "transcended" by these lesbian readers' uses of mainstream films, for as two of the interviewees remark, "We're so starved, we go see anything because something is better than nothing," and "It's a compromise. It's a given degree of alienation."[21] This sense of queer readings of mass culture as involving a measure of "compromise" and "alienation" contributes to the complexity of queer articulations of mass culture reception. For the pathos of feeling like a mass culture hanger-on is often related to the processes by which queers (and straights who find themselves queerly positioned) internalize straight culture's homophobic and heterocentrist attitudes and later reproduce them in their own queer responses to film and other mass culture forms.

Even so, traditional narrative films such as *Sylvia Scarlett, Gentlemen Prefer Blondes, Trapeze, To Live and Die in L.A., Internal Affairs*, and *Thelma and Louise*, which are ostensibly addressed to straight audiences, often have greater potential for encouraging a wider range of queer responses than such clearly lesbian- and gay-addressed films as *Scorpio Rising, Home Movies, Women I Love*, and *Loads*.[22] The intense tensions and pleasures generated by the woman-woman and man-man aspects within the narratives of the former group of films create a space of sexual instability that already queerly positioned viewers can connect with in various ways, and within which straights might be likely to recognize and express their queer impulses. For example, gays might find a form of queer pleasure in the alternately tender and boisterous rapport between Lorelei/Marilyn Monroe and Dorothy/Jane Russell in *Gentlemen Prefer Blondes*, or in the exhilarating woman-bonding of the title characters in *Thelma and Louise*. Or lesbians and straights could queerly respond to the erotic elements in the relationships between the major male characters in *Trapeze, To*

Live and Die in L.A., or *Internal Affairs*. And any viewer might feel a sexually ambiguous attraction—is it gay, lesbian, bisexual, or straight?—to the image of Katharine Hepburn dressed as a young man in *Sylvia Scarlett.*

Of course, these queer positions and readings can become modified or can change over time, as people, cultures, and politics change. In my own case, as a white gay male who internalized dominant culture's definitions of myself as "like a woman" in a traditional 1950s and 1960s understanding of who "a woman" and what "femininity" was supposed to be, my pleasure in *Gentlemen Prefer Blondes* initially worked itself out through a classic gay process of identifying, alternately, with Monroe and Russell; thereby experiencing vicarious if temporary empowerment through their use of sexual allure to attract men—including the entire American Olympic team. Reassessing the feminine aspects of my gay sexual identity sometime in the 1970s (after Stonewall and my coming out), I returned to the film and discovered my response was now less rooted in the fantasy of being Monroe or Russell and gaining sexual access to men, than in the pleasure of Russell being the "gentleman" who preferred blonde Monroe, who looked out for her best interests, who protected her against men, and who enjoyed performing with her. This queer pleasure in a lesbian text has been abetted by extratextual information I have read, or was told, about Russell's solicitous and supportive offscreen behavior toward Monroe while making the film.[23] But along with these elements of queer reading that developed from the interaction of my feminine gay identity, my knowledge of extratextual behind-the-scenes gossip, and the text itself, I also take a great deal of direct gay erotic pleasure in the "Is There Anyone Here for Love?" number, enjoying its blatantly homo-historic and erotic ancient Greek Olympics mise-en-scène (including Russell's large column earrings), while admiring Russell's panache and good humor as she sings, strides, and strokes her way through a sea of half-naked male dancer-athletes. I no longer feel the need to mediate my sexual desires through her.

In 1985, Al La Valley suggested that this type of movement—from negotiating gay sexual desire through strong women stars to directly expressing desire for male images on screen—was becoming increasingly evident in gay culture, although certain forms of identification with women through gay connections with "the feminine" continue:

> One might have expected Stonewall to make star cults outmoded among gays. In a sense it did: The natural-man discourse, with its strong political and social vision and its sense of a fulfilled and open self, has supplanted both the aesthetic and campy discourses. . . . A delirious absorption in the stars is now something associated with pre-Stonewall gays or drag queens, yet neither gay openness nor the new machismo has completely abolished the cults. New figures are added regularly: Diana Ross, Donna Summer, Jennifer Holliday from the world of music, for example. There's a newer, more open gay following for male stars: Richard Gere, Christopher Reeve [and, to update, Mel Gibson], even teen hunks like Matt Dillon [Christopher Atkins, Johnny Depp, Jason Priestley, and Luke Perry].[24]

One could also add performers such as Bette Midler, Patti LaBelle, and Madonna to La Valley's list of women performers. While ambivalent about her motives ("Is she the Queen of Queers. . . . Or is she just milking us for shock value?"), Michael Musto's *Outweek* article "Immaculate Connection" suggests that Madonna is queer culture's post-Stonewall Judy Garland:

> By now, we finally seem willing to release Judy Garland from her afterlife responsibility of being our quintessential icon. And in the land of the living, career stagnation has robbed Diana [Ross], Liza [Minnelli], and Barbra [Streisand] of their chances, while Donna [Summer] thumped the bible on our heads in a way that made it bounce back into her face. That leaves Madonna as Queer Queen, and she merits the title as someone who isn't afraid to offend straight America if it does the rest of us some good.[25]

Musto finds Madonna "unlike past icons" as she's "not a vulnerable toy"; this indicates to him the need to reexamine gay culture's enthusiasms for women stars with greater attention to how shifting historic (and perhaps generational) contexts alter the meanings and uses of these stars for particular groups of gay men.[26]

Examining how and where these gay cults of women stars work in relation to what La Valley saw in the mid-1980s as the "newer, more openly gay following for male stars" would also make for fascinating cultural history. Certainly there have been "homosexual" followings for male personalities in mass culture since the late nineteenth century, with performers and actors—Sandow the muscleman, Edwin Booth—vying with gay enthusiasms for opera divas and actresses such as Jenny Lind and Lillian Russell. Along these lines, one could queerly combine star studies with genre studies in order to analyze the gay appreciation of women musical performers, and the musical's "feminine" or "effeminized" aesthetic, camp, and emotive genre characteristics (spectacularized decor and costuming, intricate choreography, and singing about romantic yearning and fulfillment), with reference to the more hidden cultural history of gay erotics centered around men in musicals.[27]

In film, this erotic history would perhaps begin with Ramon Navarro (himself gay) stripped down to sing "Pagan Love Song" in *The Pagan*. Beyond this, a gay beefcake musical history would include Gene Kelly (whose ass was always on display in carefully tailored pants); numbers like "Is There Anyone Here for Love?" (*Gentlemen Prefer Blondes*) and "Y.M.C.A." (*Can't Stop the Music*) that feature men in gym shorts, swimsuits (Esther Williams musicals are especially spectacular in this regard), military (especially sailor) uniforms, and pseudo-native or pseudo-classical (Greek and Roman) outfits; films such as *Athena* (bodybuilders), *Seven Brides for Seven Brothers* (Western Levis, flannel, and leather men), *West Side Story* (Hispanic and Anglo t-shirted and blue-jeaned delinquents, including a butch girl); Elvis Presley films (and those of other "teen girl" pop and rock music idols—Frank Sinatra, Ricky Nelson, Fabian, Cliff Richard, the Beatles, and so on); and the films of John Travolta (*Saturday Night Fever, Grease, Staying Alive*), Patrick Swayze (*Dirty Dancing*), and Mikhail Baryshnikov, who in *The Turning Point* and *White Nights* provided the impetus for many gays to be more vocal about their "lowbrow" sexual pleasure in supposedly high-cultural male bodies. If television, music video, and concert performers and texts were added to this hardly exhaustive list, it would include David Bowie, Morrissey, David Cassidy, Tom Jones, and Marky Mark, among many others, and videos such as *Cherish, Express Yourself,* and *Justify My Love* (all performed by Madonna), *Being Boring* (The Pet Shop Boys), *Love Will Never Do Without You* (Janet Jackson), *Just Tell Me That You Want Me* (Kim Wilde), and *Rico Suave* (Gerardo), along with a number of heavy-metal videos featuring long-haired lead singers in a variety of skintight and artfully opened or ripped clothes.[28]

I can't leave this discussion of gay erotics and musicals without a few more words about Gene Kelly's "male trio" musicals, such as *On the Town, Take Me Out to the Ball Game,* and *It's Always Fair Weather.*[29] Clad in sailor uniforms, baseball uniforms, and Army uniforms, the male trios in these films are composed of two conventionally sexy men (Kelly and Frank Sinatra in the first two films, Kelly and Dan Dailey in the last) and a comic, less attractive "buffer" (Jules Munshin in the first two, Michael Kidd in the last) who is meant to diffuse the sexual energy generated between the two male leads when they sing and dance together. Other Kelly films—*Singin' in the Rain, An American in Paris,* and *Anchors Aweigh*—resort to the more conventional heterosexual(izing) narrative device of using a woman to mediate and diffuse male-male erotics.[30] But whether in the form of a third man or an ingenue, these devices fail to fully heterosexualize the relationship between Kelly and his male costars. In *Singin' in the Rain,* for example, I can't help but read Donald O'Connor maniacally unleashing his physical energy to entertain Kelly during the "Make 'Em Laugh" number as anything but a case of overwrought, displaced gay desire.[31]

Kelly himself jokingly refers to the queer erotics of his image and his many buddy musicals in *That's Entertainment!,* when he reveals the answer to the often-asked question, "Who was your favorite dancing partner . . . Cyd Charisse, Leslie Caron, Rita Hayworth, Vera-Ellen?," by showing a clip of the dance he did with Fred Astaire ("The Babbit and the Bromide") in *Ziegfeld Follies.* "It's the only time we danced together," Kelly remarks over the clip, "but I'd change my name to Ginger if we could do it again." As it turned out, Kelly and Astaire did "do it again" in *That's Entertainment 2,* and their reunion as a dancing couple became the focus of much of the film's publicity campaign, as had been the case when Astaire reunited with Ginger Rogers in *The Barkleys of Broadway.*[32]

While there has been at the very least a general, if often clichéd, cultural connection made between gays and musicals, lesbian work within the genre has been less acknowledged. However, the evidence of lesbian viewing practices—in articles such as "Hollywood Transformed," in videos such as *Dry Kisses Only* (1990, Jane Cottis and Kaucyila Brooke) and *Grapefruit* (1989, Cecilia Dougherty), and in informal discussions (mention *Calamity Jane* to a group of thirty- to forty-something American lesbians)—suggests that lesbian viewers have always negotiated their own culturally specific readings and pleasures within the genre.[33] Although it never uses the word "lesbian," Lucie Arbuthnot and Gail Seneca's 1982 article "Pre-text and Text in *Gentlemen Prefer Blondes*" is perhaps the best-known lesbian-positioned piece on the musical. While couched in homosocial rhetoric, this analysis of the authors' pleasures in the film focuses upon Lorelei/Monroe's and Dorothy/Russell's connection to each other through looks, touch, and words ("lovey," "honey," "sister," "dear"). Noting that a "typical characteristic of [the] movie musical genre is that there are two leads, a man and a woman, who sing and dance together, and eventually become romantically involved," Seneca and Arbuthnot recognize that in *Gentlemen Prefer Blondes* "it is Monroe and Russell who sing—and even harmonize, adding another layer to the metaphor—and dance as a team."[34] Since the men in the film are "never given a musical role," the authors conclude "the pretext of heterosexual romance is so thin that it scarcely threatens the text of female friendship."[35]

One note hints at a possible butch-femme reading of the Russell/Monroe relationship, centered upon Russell's forthright stride and stance: "The Russell character also adopts a 'masculine' stride and stance. More often, Monroe plays the 'lady' to Russell's manly moves. For example, Russell opens doors for Monroe; Monroe sinks into Russell's strong frame, allowing Russell to hold her protectively."[36] Released in 1953, during the height of traditional butch-femme role-playing in American urban lesbian culture, *Gentlemen Prefer Blondes* could well have been read and enjoyed by lesbians at the time with reference to this particular social-psychological paradigm for understanding and expressing their sexual identity.[37] The film continues to be read along these lines by some lesbians as well as by other queerly positioned viewers. Overall, Seneca and Arbuthnot's analysis of *Gentlemen Prefer Blondes* qualifies as a lesbian reading, as it discusses the film and the musical genre so as to "re-vision . . . connections with women" by focusing upon the pleasures of and between women on the screen and women in the audience, rather than on "the ways in which the film affords pleasure, or denies pleasure, to men."[38]

Working with the various suggestive comments in this article and considering actual and potential lesbian readings of other musicals can lead to a consideration of other pairs and trios of song-and-dance women performers (often related as sisters in the narratives), certain strong solo women film and video musical stars (Eleanor Powell, Esther Williams, Carmen Miranda, Lena Horne, Eartha Kitt, Doris Day, Julie Andrews, Tina Turner, Madonna), and musical numbers performed by groups of women, with little or no participation by men.[39] Of particular interest in this latter category are those often-reviled Busby Berkeley musical spectacles, which appear in a different light if one considers lesbians (and other queers) as spectators, rather than straight men. I'm thinking here especially of numbers like "The Lady in the Tutti-Frutti Hat" in *The Gang's All Here*, where Carmen Miranda triggers an all-woman group masturbation fantasia involving banana dildos and foot fetishism; "Dames" in *Dames*, where women sleep, bathe, dress, and seek employment together—some pause to acknowledge the camera as bearer of the voyeuristic (straight) male gaze, only to prohibit this gaze by using powder puffs, atomizer sprays, and other objects to cover the lens; "The Polka-Dot Ballet" in *The Gang's All Here*, where androgynized women in tights rhythmically move neon hoops and large dots in unison, then melt into a vivid, hallucinogenically colored vaginal opening initially inhabited by Alice Faye's head surrounded by shiny cloth; "Spin a Little Web of Dreams" in *Fashions of 1934*, where a seamstress falls asleep and "spins a little web of dreams" about a group of seminude women amid giant undulating ostrich-feather fans who, at one point, create a tableau called "Venus with Her Galley Slaves"; and parts of many other numbers (the two women sharing an upper berth on the Niagara Limited who cynically comment upon marriage in *42nd Street*'s "Shuffle Off to Buffalo," for example).[40]

Since this discussion of queer positions and queer readings seems to have worked itself out so far largely as a discussion of musical stars and the musical genre, I might add here that of the articles and books written about film musicals only the revised edition of June Feuer's *Hollywood Musicals* goes beyond a passing remark in considering the ways in which this genre has been the product of gay film workers, or how the ways in which musicals are viewed and later talked about have been influenced by gay and lesbian reception practices.[41] From most accounts of the musical, it is a genre whose celebration of heterosexual romance must always be read straight. The same seems to be the case with those other film genres typically linked to gays, lesbians, and bisexuals: the horror/fantasy film and the melodrama. While there has been a rich history of queers producing and reading these genres, surprisingly little has been done to formally express this cultural history. There has been more queer work done in and on the horror film: vampire pieces by Richard Dyer, Bonnie Zimmerman, and Sue-Ellen Case; Bruna Fionda, Polly Gladwin, Isiling Mack-Nataf's lesbian vampire film *The Mark of Lilith* (1986); Amy Goldstein's vampire musical film *Because the Dawn* (1988); a sequence in *Dry Kisses Only* that provides a lesbian take on vampire films; an article by Martin F. Norden on sexuality in *The Bride of Frankenstein*; and some pieces on *The Rocky Horror Picture Show* (although most are not written from a queer position), to cite a few examples.[42]

But there is still much left unexamined beyond the level of conversation. Carl Dreyer's lesbophobic "classic" *Vampyr* could use a thorough queer reading, as could Tod Browning's *Dracula*—which opens with a coach ride through Transylvania in the company of a superstitious Christian straight couple, a suit-and-tie lesbian couple, and a feminine gay man, who will quickly become the bisexual Count Dracula's vampirized servant. Subsequent events in the film include a straight woman who becomes a child molester known as "The Woman in White" after the count vampirizes her. It is also amazing that gay horror director James Whale has yet to receive full-scale queer auteurist consideration for films such as *Frankenstein* (the idea of men making the "perfect" man), *The Bride of Frankenstein* (gay Dr. Praetorius; queer Henry Frankenstein; the erotics between the blind man, the monster, and Jesus on the cross; the overall campy atmosphere), *The Old Dark House* (a gay and lesbian brother and sister; a 103-year-old man in the attic who is actually a woman), and *The Invisible Man* (effete, mad genius Claude Rains spurns his fiancée, becomes invisible, tries to find a male partner in crime, and becomes *visible* only after he is killed by the police).[43] Beyond queer readings of specific films and directors, it would also be important to consider how the central conventions of horror and melodrama actually encourage queer positioning as they exploit the spectacle of heterosexual romance, straight domesticity, and traditional gender roles gone awry. In a sense, then, *everyone's* pleasure in these genres is "perverse," is queer, as much of it takes place within the space of the contra-heterosexual and the contra-straight.

Just how much everyone's pleasures in mass culture are part of this contra-straight, rather than strictly antistraight, space—just how *queer* our responses to cultural texts are so much of the time—is what I'd finally like this chapter to suggest. Queer positions, queer readings, and queer pleasures are part of a reception space that stands simultaneously beside and within that created by heterosexual and straight positions. These positions, readings, and pleasures also suggest that what happens in cultural reception goes beyond the traditional opposition of homo and hetero, as queer reception is often a place beyond the audience's conscious "real-life" definition of their sexual identities and cultural positions—often, but not always, beyond such sexual identities and identity politics, that is. For in all my enthusiasm for breaking down rigid concepts of sexuality through the example of mass culture reception, I don't want to suggest that there is a queer utopia that unproblematically and apolitically unites straights and queers (or even all queers) in some mass culture reception area in the sky. Queer reception doesn't stand outside personal and cultural histories; it is part of the articulation of these histories. This is why, politically, queer reception (and production) practices can include everything from the reactionary to the radical to the indeterminate, as with the audience for (as well as the producers of) "queercore" publications, who individually and collectively often seem to combine reactionary and radical attitudes.

What queer reception often does, however, is

stand outside the relatively clear-cut and essentializing categories of sexual identity under which most people function. You might identify yourself as a lesbian or a straight woman yet queerly experience the gay erotics of male buddy films such as *Red River* and *Butch Cassidy and the Sundance Kid*; or maybe as a gay man your cultlike devotion to *Laverne and Shirley, Kate and Allie*, or *The Golden Girls* has less to do with straight-defined cross-gender identification than with your queer enjoyment in how these series are crucially concerned with articulating the loving relationships between women.[44] Queer readings aren't "alternative" readings, wishful or willful misreadings, or "reading too much into things" readings. They result from the recognition and articulation of the complex range of queerness that has been in popular culture texts and their audiences all along.

Notes

1. Jean Genet, *Gay Sunshine Interviews*, ed. Winston Leyland (San Francisco: Gay Sunshine Press, 1978), 73.
2. Gretchen Phillips, "The Queer Song," performed by Two Nice Girls, *Chloe Likes Olivia* (Rough Trade Records, 1991). Lyrics quoted by permission.
3. Janice Radway, "Reception Study: Ethnography and the Problems of Dispersed Audiences and Nomadic Subjects," *Cultural Studies* 2, no. 3 (October 1988): 361.
4. Ibid., 366.
5. Stuart Hall's article "Encoding/Decoding" informs much of my general approach to queer cultural readings of mass culture. This important essay is in *Culture, Media, Language*, ed. Stuart Hall, Andrew Lowe, and Paul Willis (Birmingham: Center for Contemporary Cultural Studies, 1980), 128–38.
6. Adele Morrison as quoted in "Queer," Steve Cosson, *OUT/LOOK* 11 (Winter 1991): 21.
7. Although the ideas that comprise "straightness" and "heterosexuality" are actually flexible and changeable over time and across cultures, these concepts have been—and still are—generally understood within Western public discourses as rather clearly defined around rigid gender roles, exclusive opposite sex desires, and such social and ideological institutions as patriarchy, marriage, "legitimate" child-bearing and -rearing, and the nuclear, patrilineal family. And all of this has been/is placed in binary opposition to "homosexuality" or "queerness." However, if we consider the notion of "queerness" in relation to the terms of the still commonly evoked utopian binary of sexuality (with its implicit dynamics of heterosexual

gender stability versus homosexual [cross-]gender insta-bility), it becomes clear that queerness, not straightness, describes an enormous space of cultural production and reception. For it is *deviance* from the demands of strict straight/heterosexual paradigms (however they are defined in a given time and place) that most often defines and describes our sexualized and/or gendered pleasures and positions in relation to movies, television, videos, and popular music. Indeed, many so-called straight mass cul-ture texts encourage "deviant" erotic and/or gendered responses and pleasures in straight viewers.

8. These thoughts about queer spaces in mass culture are most immediately indebted to Robin Wood's "Respon-sibilities of a Gay Film Critic," *Movies and Methods II*, ed. Bill Nichols (Berkeley: University of California Press, 1985), 649–60, and Marilyn R. Farwell's "Heterosexual Plots and Lesbian Subtexts: Toward a Theory of Les-bian Narrative Space," *Lesbian Texts and Contexts: Radi-cal Revisions*, ed. Karla Jay and Joanne Glasgow (New York: New York University Press, 1990), 91–103. Con-cerned with the politics of film critics/theorists (Wood) and the creation of uniquely lesbian narrative spaces for characters in literature (Farwell), these articles lucidly combine academic theory with gay- and lesbian-spe-cific cultural concerns to suggest how and where being gay or lesbian makes a difference in cultural production and reception.

9. bell hooks, "Choosing the Margins as a Space of Radical Openness," *Yearning: Race, Gender, and Cultural Politics* (Boston: South End Press, 1990), 153.

10. While I use the term "regression" here in relation to queerness and mass culture, I don't want to invoke conventional psychoanalytic and popular ideas about queerness as a permanently infantilized stage past which heterosexuals somehow progress.

11. In "On Becoming a Lesbian Reader," *Sweet Dreams: Sexuality, Gender and Popular Fiction*, ed. Susannah Rad-stone (London: Lawrence and Wishart, 1988), Alison Hennegan offers many incisive examples of the com-plex workings of gender in the construction of queer identities and cultural reading practices, as well as indi-cating the reciprocity between sexual identity formation and reading cultural texts. Speaking of her adolescence, Hennegan states: "That I turned to ancient Greece need come as no surprise. If there's one thing every-one knows about the Greeks it's that they were all That Way. . . . That women's own voices were virtually silent, bar a few precious scraps of lyric poetry and the occa-sional verbatim transcript from a court hearing, did not then worry me. What I was looking for were strong and passionate emotions which bound human beings to members of their own sex rather than to the other. That the bonds depicted existed primarily between men didn't

matter. In part this was because I spent at least half my adolescence 'being male' inside my own head: 'gender identity confusion' in today's terminology, or 'male iden-tified,' but neither phrase is right or adequate. I never for one moment thought I was a man nor wished to be. But somehow I had to find a way of thinking of myself which included the possibility of desiring women. And those who desire women are men" (p. 170).

12. Sue-Ellen Case, "Tracking the Vampire," *differences* 3, no. 2 (Summer 1991): 2.

13. Ibid., 3.

14. Ibid., 8, 12.

15. Some gay men will prefer the terms "effeminate" or "woman-identified" where I use "feminine" in this section, and throughout the text. I find the former term still too closely connected to straight uses that simultane-ously trivialize and trash women and gay men, while the latter term might appear to place gay men in the position of essentializing theoretical transsexuals. Where I use "effeminate" in this book [*Making Things Perfectly Queer*], it should be understood as describing culturally dictated heterosexist ideas about gays and gender (which queers might also employ).

16. Although most of these performers have an interna-tional gay following, this list is rather Anglo-Ameri-can. To begin to expand it, one would add names like Zarah Leander (Germany), Isa Miranda (Italy), Dolores del Rio, Maria Felix, Sara Montiel (Latin America and Spain), and Josephine Baker (France). As is the case in the United States and Great Britain, while some national and regional queer cultural work has been done regard-ing (feminine) gays and women stars, much more needs to be done. Television series cited in this section: *Design-ing Women* (1986–present, CBS), *The Golden Girls* (1985–92, NBC), *Murphy Brown* (1989–present, CBS), *The Mary Tyler Moore Show* (1970–77, CBS).

17. Among the work on women stars that concerns femi-nine gay reception (with the "feminine" aspects usu-ally implied) are: Parker Tyler, "Mother Superior of the Faggots and Some Rival Queens," *Screening the Sexes: Homosexuality in the Movies* (Garden City, N.Y.: Anchor Books, 1973), 1–15 [on Mae West]; Quentin Crisp, "Star-dom and Stars," *How to Go to the Movies* (New York: St. Martin's Press, 1989), 11–30; Gregg Howe, "On Iden-tifying with Judy Garland" and "A Dozen Women We Adore," *Gay Life*, ed. Eric E. Rofes (New York: Double-day, 1986), 178–86; Seymour Kleinberg, "Finer Clay: The World Eroticized," *Alienated Affections: Being Gay in America* (New York: St. Martin's, 1980), 38–69; Michael Bronski, "Hollywood Homo-sense," *Culture Clash: The Making of Gay Sensibility* (Boston: South End Press, 1984), 134–43; Jack Smith, "The Perfect Filmic Appo-siteness of Maria Montez," *Film Culture* 27 (1962–1963):

28–32. I might also include critic John Simon's *Private Screenings* (New York: Macmillan, 1967) on this list, for its Wildean bitchy-witty critiques of stars such as Elizabeth Taylor, Barbra Streisand, Anna Karina, and Monica Vitti, which are embedded in film reviews. Simon may be a self-declared straight, but his style and sensibility, in this collection at least, are pure scathing urban queen—which works itself out here, unfortunately, to include a heavy dose of misogyny.

18. Julie Burchill, *Girls on Film* (New York: Pantheon Books, 1986), 109.

19. More work is being done in these areas all the time. Some of the more recent essays include: Richard Fung, "Looking for My Penis: The Eroticized Asian in Gay Video Porn," *How Do I Look? Queer Film and Video*, ed. Bad Object-Choices (Seattle: Bay Press, 1991), 145–60; Kobena Mercer, "Skin Head Sex Thing: Racial Differences and the Homoerotic," ibid., 169–210; Mark A. Reid, "The Photography of Rotimi Fani-Kayode," *Wide Angle* 14, no. 2 (April 1992): 38–51; Essex Hemphill, "*In Living Color:* Toms, Coons, Mammies, Faggots and Bucks," *Outweek* 78 (December 26, 1990): 32–40; Marlon Riggs, "Black Macho Revisited: Reflections on a Snap! Queen," *The Independent* 14, no. 3 (April 1991): 32–34; Manthia Diawara, "The Absent One: The Avant-Garde and the Black Imaginary in *Looking for Langston*," *Wide Angle* 13, nos. 3/4 (July-October 1991): 96–109; Anthony Thomas, "The House the Kids Built: The Gay Imprint on American Dance Music," OUT/LOOK 2, no. 1 (Summer 1989): 24–33; Jackie Goldsby, "What It Means to Be Colored Me," OUT/LOOK 3, no. 1 (Summer 1990): 8–17; Kobena Mercer and Isaac Julien, "Race, Sexual Politics and Black Masculinity: A Dossier," *Unwrapping Masculinity*, ed. Rowena Chapman and Jonathan Rutherford (London: Lawrence and Wishart, 1988), 97–164.

20. Judy Whitaker, "Hollywood Transformed," *Jump Cut* 24/25 (1981): 33. Gail Sausser's "Movie and T.V. Heart-Throbs" chapter of *Lesbian Etiquette* (Trumansburg, N.Y.: Crossing Press, 1986) offers another expression of lesbian reception practices, their connection to gender identity, and the evolution of both through time: "I loved romantic movies when I was a teenager. I unconsciously identified with all the heroes who got the girl. Since I came out, however, my identifications have changed. Now I yell, 'No, no, not him!' at the heroine and root for her female roommate. What a difference a decade (or two) makes" (p. 57).

21. Whitaker, "Hollywood," 34.

22. Films mentioned in this section: *Sylvia Scarlett* (1936, RKO, George Cukor), *Gentlemen Prefer Blondes* (1953, Twentieth Century-Fox, Howard Hawks), *Trapeze* (1956, United Artists, Carol Reed), *To Live and Die in L.A.* (1985, New Century, William Friedkin), *Internal Affairs* (1990,

Paramount, Mike Figgis), *Thelma and Louise* (1991, MGM, Ridley Scott), *Scorpio Rising* (1962–63, Kenneth Anger), *Home Movies* (1972, Jan Oxenberg), *Women I Love* (1976, Barbara Hammer), *Loads* (1980, Curt McDowell).

When I say certain mainstream films elicit a "wider range of queer responses" than films made by, for, or about lesbians, gays, and bisexuals, I am not commenting upon the politics of these films or their reception, only about the multiplicity of queer responses. And while the lesbian and gay films listed here are much more direct and explicit about the sex in them being homo, the sexual politics of these films are not necessarily more progressive or radical than that of the mainstream films.

23. The strength of the Monroe-Lorelei/Russell-Dorothy pairing on and off screen was publicly acknowledged shortly after the film's release when, as a team, the two stars went through the ceremony of putting prints of their hands and feet in the forecourt of Grauman's Chinese Theatre in Hollywood.

24. Al La Valley, "The Great Escape," *American Film* 10, no. 6 (April 1985): 71.

25. Michael Musto, "Immaculate Connection," *Outweek* 90 (March 20, 1991): 35–36.

26. Ibid., 36.

27. In the revised edition of *The Hollywood Musical* (London: BFI/Macmillan, 1993), Jane Feuer has added a brief section focusing on MGM's Freed Unit and Judy Garland that suggests ways of developing gay readings of musicals with reference to both production and queer cultural contexts. Mentioned in Feuer's discussions, Richard Dyer's chapter "Judy Garland and Gay Men," in *Heavenly Bodies: Film Stars and Society* (New York: St. Martin's Press, 1986), 141–94, is an exemplary analysis of how and why queers and queer cultures read and, in certain ways, help to create star personas.

28. Films mentioned in this section: *The Pagan* (1929, MGM, W. S. Van Dyke), *Athena* (1954, MGM, Richard Thorpe), *Seven Brides for Seven Brothers* (1954, MGM, Stanley Donen), *West Side Story* (1961, United Artists, Robert Wise and Jerome Robbins), *Saturday Night Fever* (1977, Paramount, John Badham), *Grease* (1980, Paramount, Randall Kleiser), *Staying Alive* (1984, Paramount, Sylvester Stallone), *Dirty Dancing* (1987, Vestron, Emile Ardolino), *The Turning Point* (1977, Twentieth Century-Fox, Herbert Ross), *White Nights* (1987, Paramount, Taylor Hackford).

29. Films cited: *On the Town* (1950, MGM, Gene Kelly and Stanley Donen), *Take Me Out to the Ball Game* (1949, MGM, Busby Berkeley), *It's Always Fair Weather* (1955, MGM, Gene Kelly and Stanley Donen). For a more extended discussion of Gene Kelly and the "buddy"

musical, see Steven Cohan's chapter, "Les Boys," in *Masked Men: American Masculinity and the Movies in the Fifties* (Indianapolis and Bloomington: Indiana University Press, 1997).

30. Films cited: *Singin' in the Rain* (1952, MGM, Gene Kelly and Stanley Donen), *An American in Paris* (1951, MGM, Vincente Minnelli), *Anchors Aweigh* (1945, MGM, George Sidney).

31. In *The Celluloid Closet: Homosexuality in the Movies*, rev. ed. (New York: Harper and Row, 1987), Vito Russo uncovers material on *Singin' in the Rain*'s production history that reveals that the erotics between Kelly and O'Connor were referred to in the original script: "One line of dialogue in Betty Comden and Adolph Green's screenplay for *Singin' in the Rain* (1952) was penciled out by the censors because it gave 'a hint of sexual perversion' between Donald O'Connor and Gene Kelly. When O'Connor gets the idea of dubbing the voice of Debbie Reynolds for the high-pitched, tinny voice of Jean Hagen in a proposed musical, *The Dancing Cavalier*, he illustrates his idea for Kelly by standing in front of Reynolds and mouthing the words to "Good Morning" while she sings behind him. When the song is over, O'Connor turns to Kelly and asks 'Well? Convincing?' Kelly, not yet catching on, takes it as a joke and replies, 'Enchanting! What are you doing later?' The joke was eliminated" (pp. 98–99).

32. Films cited: *That's Entertainment!* (1974, MGM, Jack Haley, Jr.), *Ziegfeld Follies* (1946, MGM, Vincente Minnelli), *That's Entertainment 2* (1976, MGM, Gene Kelly), *The Barkleys of Broadway* (1949, MGM, Charles Walters).

33. Film cited: *Calamity Jane* (1953, Warners, David Butler). Some lesbians also take what they would describe as a gay pleasure in musicals, and perform readings of individual films and of the genre in terms they identify as being influenced by their understanding of the ways gay men appreciate musicals. These kinds of gay approaches might take the form of specific star cult enthusiasms (for Judy Garland, Barbra Streisand, or Bette Midler, for example) that individual lesbian readers feel aren't important in lesbian culture, or of an appreciation for certain aesthetic or critical approaches (camp, for example) which seem unpopular, inoperative, or not "politically correct" in the lesbian culture(s) within which the individual reader places herself.

34. Lucie Arbuthnot and Gail Seneca, "Pre-text and Text in *Gentlemen Prefer Blondes*," *Film Reader* 5 (1982): 20. This essay is reprinted in *Issues in Feminist Film Criticism*, ed. Patricia Erens (Bloomington and Indianapolis: Indiana University Press, 1990), 112–25.

35. Arbuthnot and Seneca, "Pre-text and Text," 21.

36. Ibid., 23.

37. Alix Stanton's "Blondes, Brunettes, Butches and Femmes" (unpublished seminar paper, Cornell University, 1991) offers a more extended consideration of butch-femme roles and cultures in relation to readings of *Gentlemen Prefer Blondes* (and *How to Marry a Millionaire* [1953, Twentieth Century-Fox, Jean Negulesco]).

38. Arbuthnot and Seneca, "Pre-text and Text," 21. For another approach to the lesbian aspects of this film, see Maureen Turim's "Gentlemen Consume Blondes," in *Issues in Feminist Film Criticism*, ed. Erens, 101–11; originally in *Wide Angle* 1, no. 1 (1979), also reprinted in *Movies and Methods, Volume II*, ed. Bill Nichols (Berkeley and Los Angeles: University of California Press, 1985): 369–78. As part of an addendum to the original article, Turim considers lesbianism and *Gentlemen Prefer Blondes* in light of certain feminist film theories about straight male spectatorship. Turim sees the main characters as male constructed "pseudo-lesbians," and the film's use of them as being related to "how lesbianism has served in male-oriented pornography to increase visual stimulation and to ultimately give twice as much power to the eye, which can penetrate even the liaisons which would appear to deny male entry" (pp. 110–11).

39. While not a lesbian-specific reading, Shari Roberts's "You Are My Lucky Star: Eleanor Powell's Brief Dance with Fame" (from an unpublished Ph.D. dissertation, "Seeing Stars: Female WWII Hollywood Musical Stars," University of Chicago, 1993) is suggestive of how and where such a reading might begin, with its discussion of Powell's (autoerotic) strength as a solo performer and its threatening qualities: "If . . . Powell represents a recognition of women as independent, working women, her films also reflect society's related fear of this 'new' woman, and potential gender confusion. . . . This anxiety is demonstrated with homophobic and cross-dressing jokes in the Powell films" (p. 7).

40. Films mentioned in this section: *The Gang's All Here* (1943, Twentieth Century-Fox, Busby Berkeley), *Dames* (1934, Warners, Ray Enright), *Fashions of 1934* (1934, Warners, William Dieterle), *42nd Street* (1933, Warners, Lloyd Bacon).

41. Feuer's "Gay Readings of Musicals" section in *Hollywood Musicals* (cited in note 27) concentrates on gay male production and reception of musicals.

42. Articles mentioned in this section: Richard Dyer, "Children of the Night: Vampirism as Homosexuality, Homosexuality as Vampirism," *Sweet Dreams: Sexuality, Gender and Popular Fiction*, ed. Susannah Radstone (London: Lawrence and Wishart, 1988), 47–72; Bonnie Zimmerman, "*Daughters of Darkness*: Lesbian Vampires," *Jump Cut* 24/25 (1981): 23–24; Sue-Ellen Case, 'Tracking the Vampire," *differences* 3, no. 2 (Summer 1991): 1–20; Martin F. Norden, "Sexual References in James Whale's *Bride of Frankenstein*," *Eros in the Mind's Eye: Sexuality*

and the Fantastic in Art and Film, ed. Donald Palumbo (New York: Greenwood Press, 1986), 141–50; Elizabeth Reba Weise, "Bisexuality, *The Rocky Horror Picture Show*, and Me," *Bi Any Other Name: Bisexual People Speak Out*, ed. Loraine Hutchins and Lani Kaahumanu (Boston: Alysou, 1991), 134–39.

43. Films mentioned in this section: *Vampyr* (1931, Gloria Film, Carl Theodore Dryer), *Dracula* (1931, Universal, Tod Browning), *Frankenstein* (1931, Universal, James Whale), *The Bride of Frankenstein* (1935, Universal, James Whale), *The Old Dark House* (1932, Universal, James Whale), *The*

Invisible Man (1933, Universal, James Whale). In light of the discussion of musicals in this essay, it is interesting to recall here that Whale's biggest success apart from his horror films was directing Universal's 1936 version of *Show Boat*.

44. Films and television series mentioned in this section: *Red River* (1948, United Artists, Howard Hawks), *Butch Cassidy and the Sundance Kid* (1969, Twentieth Century-Fox, George Roy Hill), *Laverne and Shirley* (1976–83, ABC), *Kate and Allie* (1984–90, CBS), *The Golden Girls* (1985–92, NBC).

44.
BEHIND CLOSED DOORS
Video Recorders in the Home

Ann Gray

The video cassette recorder is arguably the major innovation in home entertainment in Britain since television. When we address questions of how women watch television and video we inevitably raise a complex set of issues which relate to women and their everyday lives. In talking to women about home video cassette recorders (VCR) and television use, I have identified some of the determining factors surrounding these activities which take place within the domestic environment.[1] With the development of VCRs and other products such as home computers and cable services, the 1980s is seeing an ever-increasing trend towards home-centred leisure and entertainment. New technology in the home has to be understood within a context of structures of power and authority relationships between household members, with gender emerging as one of the most significant differentiations. This far from neutral environment influences the ways in which women use popular texts in general and television and video in particular, and the pleasures and meanings which these have for them.

The Video Revolution

Although it is a relatively recent phenomenon, home video arrived as long ago as 1972 with Philips VCR and Sony U-matic. But it wasn't until Sony Betamax and VHS (video home system), both of which use 19 mm tape, brought the cost down significantly, that the stage was set for a consumer boom. In 1983 15 per cent of households in the United Kingdom had access to a VCR, by 1986 the figure had reached 40 per cent.

An important factor in the British VCR experience is that the distribution of recorders operates through the already existing television rental networks, thereby making it possible to rent a VCR on a monthly basis, without the necessity for large capital investment. This results in video recorders being made available to a much wider range of socio-economic groups than might at first be imagined. We are not, in the British case, considering a 'luxury' item which graces the affluent household, rather, a widely available home entertainment facility which has rapidly become an accepted and essential part of everyday life, cutting across economic and class boundaries.

The development and marketing of entertainment consumer hardware can often outpace the provision of 'software' or 'content'. Raymond Williams points out that when domestic radio receivers were first marketed there was very little to receive in terms of programming content, 'It is not only that the supply of broadcasting facilities preceded the demand; it is that the means of communication preceded their content' (Williams, 1974: 25).

There are two major uses for VCRs: time-shift, which involves recording off-broadcast television in order to view at a different time, and the playing of pre-recorded tapes.[2] These can be purchased, though the majority are hired through video rental 'libraries'. Although off-air recording is an attractive proposition, it has become obvious to a few entrepreneurs that there is a large potential market for the hiring of pre-recorded tape. In Britain during the early 1980s one feature of almost every high street was a new phenomenon known as the 'video library'. These were often hastily converted small shops offering tapes, mainly of movies, for hire. In these early days, in order to finance their purchase of new material, the libraries demanded a membership fee, often as high as £40, as well as a nightly fee for the hiring of tapes. Nowadays it is possible to join a video library free of charge, with a nightly rental fee of £1.00–1.50 per tape. There are now upwards of 6,500 movies[3] available for hire on video tape and at a rough estimate four million tapes are hired a week. Indeed, 97 per cent of film watching is now done outside the cinema, mainly on broadcast television, but the hiring of films accounts for a significant proportion of this viewership (Howkins, 1983).

The video library industry—and I use this term to describe the distributors and retailers of pre-recorded tapes for purchase or hire—has experienced major change. Many of the smaller retail outlets have gone by the board, forced out by the larger and well-established distributors who moved in once the market had been tested. The industry has established its own quasi-professional organizations in order to protect itself against 'video piracy' and to professionalize and improve its image, which has not been good. The 'moral panic' which resulted in the Video Recordings Bill of 1984, providing for every film on hire to be censored for home viewing, had a devastating effect on the public image of the video libraries. This was fuelled enthusiastically by the popular press (Petley, 1984; Kuhn, 1984*a*; Barker, 1984). On 1 September 1982 the *Sun* carried the headline 'Fury over video nasties' and referred to the video distributors and retailers as 'the merchants of menace' who were threatening the well-being of our children. This kind of response to a new development in mass cultural production is similar to those precipitated by the novel in the nineteenth century, cinema in the 1920s, and television in the 1950s. The moral reformers were then, as now, fearful for the effects of these new mass-produced cultural forms on those 'weaker' members of society—women, children, and the 'lower orders' in general—whom they sought to protect.

Video and Family Life

Although there are many aspects of the video phenomenon which are worthy of study, my research initially

focuses on the potential choice which the VCR offers for viewing within the domestic and family context. The major reason for this is that, until recently, attention to the context of viewing seems to have been largely neglected in media and cultural studies.[4] The relationship between the viewer and television, the reader and text, is often a relationship which has to be negotiated, struggled for, won or lost, in the dynamic and often chaotic processes of family life. As video recorders offer, above all, extended choice of content and time management for viewing within the home, research into its use has to be focused within that very context. The context of 'the family' is, for my purposes, conceived of as a site of constant social negotiation within a highly routinized framework of material dependency and normative constraint,[5] and all these elements enter into the negotiations which surround viewing decisions. This family setting, with its power relationships and authority structures across gender, is an extremely important factor in thinking more generally of 'leisure' and, specifically, home-based leisure. The home has increasingly become the site for entertainment, and we can see VCRs as yet one more commodity which reduces the necessity for household members to seek entertainment outside the home, a situation reinforced by the present economic climate in Britain:

> JS: Well, we can't really afford to go out to the pictures, not any more. If we all go and have ice-creams, you're talking about eight or nine pounds. It's a lot of money.

What is especially important for women is that the domestic sphere is increasingly becoming defined as their only leisure space. Many married women are in paid work outside the home, but women are still largely responsible for the domestic labour in the home. Childcare, food provision, laundry, shopping, and cleaning the living space, are ultimately women's responsibility even if their male partners help. While men in paid employment come home to a non-work environment, women who either work in the home all day or go out to paid employment still have to work at home in the evenings and at weekends:

> AS: Him? Oh, he sits on his backside all night, from coming in from work to going to bed.

Indeed, many women do not consider themselves as having any leisure at all (Deem, 1984). And many certainly would not allow themselves the luxury of sitting down to watch television until the children are fed and put to bed and the household chores have been completed:

> JK: I'd feel guilty, I'd feel I was cheating. It's my job and if I'm sat, I'm not doing my job.

This is a context which, at the most basic and practical level, positions women in relation to the whole area of leisure, but particularly in relation to television and video viewing:

> AS: Like, if he comes in and he's rented a video, straight after tea he wants to put it on. I say 'well let me finish the washing-up first'. I mean, I just wouldn't enjoy it if I knew it was all to do.

Video as Technology

Women and men have differential access to technology in general and to domestic technology in particular. The relations between domestic technology and gender are relatively unexplored,[6] though there is more work on gender and technology in the workplace, where, as Jan Zimmerman notes, new technology is entering existing and traditional sets of relations. Old values in this way become encoded in new technologies (Zimmerman, 1981; Cockburn, 1983, 1985). It is interesting to note that American researchers discovered that in the early 1970s the full-time housewife was spending as much time on housework as her grandmother had done fifty years earlier. Domestic technology may be labour-saving, replacing the drudgery of household work, but it is time-consuming in that each piece of equipment requires work if it is to fulfil its advertised potential. Rothschild argues that far from liberating women from housework, new technology, embedded as it is in ideological assumptions about the sexual division of labour, has further entrenched women in the home and in the role of housewife (Rothschild, 1983).

When a new piece of technology is purchased or rented, it is often already inscribed with gender expectations. The gender specificity of pieces of domestic technology is deeply implanted in the 'commonsense' of households, operating almost at an unconscious level. As such it is difficult for the researcher to unearth. One strategy I have employed which throws the gender of domestic technology into high relief is to ask the women to imagine pieces of equipment as coloured either pink or blue.[7] This produces almost uniformly pink irons and blue electric drills, with many interesting mixtures along the spectrum. The washing machine, for example, is most usually pink on the outside, but the motor is almost always blue. VCRs and, indeed, all home entertainment technology would seem to be a potentially lilac area, but my research has shown that we must break down the VCR into its different modes in our colour-coding. The 'record', 'rewind', and 'play' modes are usually lilac, but the timer switch is nearly always blue, with women having to depend on their male partners or their children to set the timer for them. The blueness of the timer is exceeded only by the deep indigo of the remote control switch which in all cases is held by the man:

> SW: Oh, yes, that's definitely blue in our house. He flicks from channel to channel, I never know what I'm watching—it drives me mad.

It does appear that the male of the household is generally assumed to have knowledge of this kind of technology when it enters the household, or at least he will quickly gain the knowledge. And certain knowledges can, of course, be withheld and used to maintain authority and control:

> AS: Well, at first he was the only one who knew how to record things, but then me and my young son sat down one day and worked it out. That meant we didn't have to keep asking him to record something for us.

Although women routinely operate extremely sophisticated pieces of domestic technology, often requiring, in the first instance, the study and application of a manual of instructions, they often feel alienated from operating the VCR. The reasons for this are manifold and have been brought about by positioning within the family, the education system, and the institutional-ized sexism with regard to the division of appropriate activities and knowledges in terms of gender. Or there may be, as I discovered, 'calculated ignorance':

> CH: If I learnt how to do the video it would become my job just like everything else.

If women do not feel confident or easy in approaching and operating the recorders, let alone in setting the timer for advance recording, they are at an immediate and real disadvantage in terms of exercising the apparent choices which the VCR offers. This, combined with constraints in the hiring of video tapes, either financial or simply normative, means that for women the idea of increased freedom and choice of viewing may well be spurious.

Genre and Gender

If women are 'positioned' within the context of con-sumption, it seems that they are also positioned, or even structured in absence, by the video industry itself in terms of the kind of audience it seems to be addressing. To enter a video library is to be visually bombarded by 'covers' depicting scenes of horror, action adventure, war, westerns, and 'soft' pornogra-phy, traditionally considered to be 'male' genres.[8] Is it therefore mainly men who are hiring video tapes, and if so, what do women feel about the kinds of tapes they are watching at home? Do women ever hire tapes themselves, or do they feel alienated from both the outlets and what they have to offer? In other words, what are the circumstances surrounding the use of video libraries and what is the sexual divi-sion of labour associated with the hiring and view-ing of tapes? I have already made reference to the so-called 'male' genres which imply that certain kinds of films address themselves to and are enjoyed by a male audience and the same, of course, could be said for 'female' genres. But why do certain kinds of texts or genres appeal to women and not to men and vice versa and how should we conceive of the audience for these texts made up of women and men?

The 'gendered audience' has a theoretical history which, as Annette Kuhn usefully points out, has devel-oped within two different perspectives, one emerging from media studies and the other from film theory (Kuhn, 1984*b*). This has resulted in two quite different notions of the gendered audience. The sociological emphasis of media studies has tended to conceive of a 'social audience', that is, an audience made up of already constituted male and female persons who bring (among other things) maleness or femaleness to a text, and who decode the text within that particular frame of reference. Film theory on the other hand, has conceived of a 'psychological audience', a collec-tion of individual spectators who do not read the text, but rather the text 'reads' them. In other words, the film offers a masculine or feminine subject position and the spectator occupies that position. Of course, this is not automatic and there is nothing to prevent, for example, a female spectator taking up a masculine subject position. However, the construction of mas-culinity and femininity across the institutions within society is so powerfully aligned to the social catego-ries 'male' and 'female' that the two usually coincide apparently seamlessly. But, as Kuhn points out, what is suggested by these two perspectives is a distinction between femaleness as a social gender and femininity as a subject position. The problem here is that neither of these two perspectives is sufficient in themselves to gain a full understanding of what happens when men and women watch films. In the former case, con-text is emphasized over text and in the latter text over context. The spectator-text relationships suggested by the psychoanalytic models used in film theory tend to disregard those important factors of social context involved in film and TV watching. Also, they find it dif-ficult to allow for the subject constituted outside the text, across other discourses, such as class, race, age, and general social environment. The social audience approach, conversely, sees the response to texts as a socially predetermined one, and in this way does not allow for consideration of how the texts themselves work on the viewers/readers.

There have been some attempts to link text with context by examining the particular features of 'women's genres'. Soap operas, for example, have been looked at in terms of their distinctive narrative pattern, which is open-ended and continuous; their concern with so-called 'female' skills; their scheduling on television which fits into the rhythm of women's work at home, all of which can be seen as specifically addressing a social audience of women (Brunsdon, 1981; Modleski, 1982). However, this would still seem to stress context over text and in this area the film theory perspective has certainly been limited by its implicit assumption of an intense and concentrated relationship between spectator and text in a darkened cinema. For television this relationship is more likely to be characterized by distinction and diversion. As Kuhn points out:

> This would suggest that each medium constructs sexual difference through spectatorship in rather different ways: cinema through the look and spectacle, and TV—perhaps less evidently—through a capacity to insert its flow, its characteristic modes of address and the textual operations of different kinds of programmes into the rhythms and routines of domestic activities and sexual divisions of labour in the household at various times of day.
>
> (Kuhn, 1984*b*:25)

This distinction is important and useful, but when thinking about the use of VCRs the two media are viewed in the same context. Movies have long been a part of television's nightly 'flow' as well as part of daytime viewing. But in video recording movies off television for watching at a later date, and in hiring movies, we have a discrete 'event' which disrupts the flow of television and its insertive scheduling:

> AC: Oh yes, we all sit down and watch—'we've got a video, let's sit down'—TV's different, that's just on.

Concepts of the psychological audience and the social audience are not sufficient in themselves to explore the whole complexity of text, subject, and context and the ways in which they intersect. But both are necessary, representing as they do different instances within the process of consumption of popular texts. While the psychological model posits an unacceptably homogeneous and 'universal' audience, it does allow us to consider the importance of how texts work, not only in terms of subject positioning and interpellation, but also in terms of pleasure and desire. The social model demands that the audience is heterogeneous and requires us to explore those other

differences and contexts which, to a greater or lesser extent, determine the ways in which women and men read those texts. It seems clear that the problem of the relationship between text and gendered audience cannot be resolved at the theoretical level, but rather must be kept in play and, if possible, problematized throughout the research enterprise.

Viewing Contexts

It would seem that women do have certain preconceptions about what constitutes a 'film for men' as against a 'film for women', and furthermore, a typology of viewing contexts is beginning to emerge, along with appropriate associated texts (see Table 44.1).

I wish to focus mainly on Context (Female alone), but before I do it is worth mentioning the difference between the negotiations around Contexts (Male

Table 44.1 Typology of viewing context[9]

Context	Film	TV
1 Family together	*Superman* Walt Disney *Jaws* Comedy	Children's TV Quiz shows Comedy *EastEnders*
2 Male and female partners together	*An Officer and a Gentleman* *Kramer v. Kramer* The Rockys Any Clint Eastwood	*Auf Wiedersehen, Pet* *Minder* Shows *Coronation Street* *EastEnders*
3 Male alone	War Action adventure* Horror* Adults*	Sport News Documentaries
4 Female alone	*Who Will Love My Children?* *Evergreen* Romance	*Coronation Street* *Crossroads* *Dallas* *Dynasty* *A Woman of Substance* *Princess Daisy*

* These are the category headings used by many video libraries.

alone) and (Female alone). For the latter to exist, the male partner must normally be out of the house, either at work or at leisure, whereas Context (Male alone) would be likely to exist when both male and female were in the house together. The women simply wouldn't watch:

BA: If he's watching something I'm not enjoying, I'll either knit or read.

JS: Well, I can read when the telly's on if it's something I don't like.

DS: I usually go to bed with a book, or sometimes I'll watch the portable in the kitchen, but it's damned uncomfortable in there.

CH: Well, when he's in, Father has priority over what's on. Yes, he does, but I can go in the other room if I don't want to watch it.

Women Only

For women who are at home all day, either with very small children or children of school age, and whose husbands are out at work, there are obvious opportunities for them to view alone. However, most of the women I have talked to are constrained by guilt, often referring to daytime viewing as some kind of drug:

SW: No, I've got too many things to do during the daytime, I couldn't do it to myself, I'd be a total addict.

JK: Well, I watch *Falcon Crest*—it's a treat, when I've done my work, then I sit down and it's my treat. But I'm not one to get videos during the day because I think you can get really addicted, then everything else suffers.

The second woman quoted indicates what is a fairly common strategy—that of using daytime television programmes to establish some time for herself as a reward to which completion of household tasks will lead. This assuages the guilt to a certain extent and the pleasure afforded by this particular viewing context seems to go far beyond the pleasures of the text itself. What it represents is a breathing space when the busy mother can resist the demands of her children and domestic labour for a brief period of time. One

of the most popular daytime programmes cited was *Sons & Daughters*, an Australian imported soap opera, transmitted three afternoons a week in the Yorkshire region. Most of the women preferred to watch this alone, some taking the telephone off the hook to ensure uninterrupted concentration, but they would watch it with a friend if they happened to be in each other's houses at the time. Janice Radway in her study of women and romantic fiction talks with regret of the isolated context within which popular romances are consumed by women (Radway, 1984).The next viewing context I wish to discuss reveals a more optimistic state of affairs for women.

This context is again female only, but is one in which several women get together to watch a video which they have hired jointly. This would normally happen during the day when their children are at school. Far from being instrumental in isolating women, it would seem that there is a tendency to communal use of hired videos, mainly on economic grounds, but also on the grounds that the women can watch what they want together without the guilt or the distraction of children:

BS: There are three of us, and we hire two or three films a week and watch them together, usually at Joyce's house when the kids are at school. We can choose what we want then.

JK: Yes, if there's something we want to see we wait 'til the kids have gone back to school so's we can sit and watch it without them coming in saying 'can 1 have . . . can I have . . .' it makes it difficult.

The idea of viewing together during the day for this particular network of women living on the same street came when one of them found herself continually returning the video tapes which her husband had hired the night before. She discovered that there were films which she would like to watch but which her husband never hired. A good relationship was established with the woman who worked in the video library who would look out for good films:

BS: She comes into the shop where I work and I go 'have any new videos come out?' She tells me. She knows what we like.

One favoured form for this viewing network is that of the long family saga, often running to two or three tapes:

JK: We like something in two or three parts; something with a really good story to it so's you can get involved.

BS: Mm . . . the other week we had a Clint Eastwood and Burt Reynolds film because she [MD] likes Clint Eastwood but we talked all the way through that, didn't we?

When the group views sagas which extend over two or three tapes there is obvious pleasure in anticipating both the outcome of the narrative and the viewing of the following tape. A considerable amount of discussion and speculation ensues and a day for the next viewing is fixed:

MD: We like to spread them out—every other day, it helps to break the week up. Sometimes we have them on an evening, if our husbands are away or out. We'll have a bottle of wine then, then we don't even have to get up to make a cup of tea.

These women are also devotees of the American soap operas and operate a 'failsafe' network of video recording for each other, refusing to discuss each episode until they have all seen it. These popular texts form an important part of their friendship and association in their everyday lives and give a focus to an almost separate female culture which they can share together within the constraints of their positions as wives and mothers. Furthermore, they are able to take up the feminine subject positions offered by these texts comfortably and pleasurably. In contrast, the films which their husbands hire for viewing Context (Male and female partners together) mainly offer a masculine subject position which the women seem to take up through their male partners, who in turn give their approval to such texts.

The major impetus for a viewing group like this is that films which women enjoy watching are rarely, if ever, hired by their male partners for viewing together because they consider such films to be 'trivial' and 'silly' and women are laughed at for enjoying them:

BA: I sit there with tears running down my face and he comes in and says 'you daft thing.'

This derision also applies to soap operas, and is reproduced in male children:

JK: Oh, my son thinks I'm stupid because I won't miss *Dallas*—perhaps I am.

It is the most powerful member within the household who defines this hierarchy of 'serious' and 'silly', 'important' and 'trivial'. This leaves women and their pleasures in films downgraded, objects and subjects of fun and derision, having to consume them almost in secret. But the kinds of films and television soap operas which women enjoy watching alone deal with things of importance to them, highlighting so-called 'female' concerns—care of children, concern for members of one's own family, consideration for one's own sexual partner, selflessness in character—all of which are the skills of competence, the thought and caring which husbands and children expect of women and assume as a matter of natural course.[10] This is a deeply contradictory position for women, lying between the realities of their day-to-day lives and the pleasures and gratifications that they seek to find in texts that their partners, and very often their children, look upon as so much rubbish:

JS: I think a lot of story-lines in soap operas are very weak and I think a man needs something to keep his interest more than a woman. That makes a man sound more intelligent, but that's not what I mean. It's got to be something worth watching before he'll sit down and actually watch it, but I'd watch anything. I think he thinks it's unmanly to watch them.

SW: All the soap operas are rubbish for men, fantasy for women.

AG: *Do you think men need fantasy?*

SW: They need fantasy in a different way, detectives and wars, that's their fantasy world, and science fiction, a tough, strong world. Not sloppy, who's fallen in love with who, who's shot JR—it's rubbish. Men know it's rubbish, that's the difference.

Here are two women talking about a genre they love in relation to their male partners, giving us a sense of the 'power of definition' within the partnerships, but also the ways in which the women themselves think of their own pleasures.

Conclusion

Theories of the gendered audience as they have been developed are useful, but when women and men watch movies and television they become that hybrid, the *social spectator* (Kuhn, ibid.) and, in understanding the subject-text-context relationship, the social and the psychological have to be kept in play to a proportionately greater or lesser degree. This allows us to consider how texts and contexts (both the specific and the wider social context) combine together in producing the gendered reading subject. Charlotte Brunsdon, writing on *Crossroads*, has attempted to resolve this dualism and suggests that, 'The relation of the audience to the text will not be determined solely by that text, but also by positionalities in relation to a whole range of other discourses—discourses of motherhood, romance and sexuality for example' (Brunsdon, 1981: 32). This enables us to think of the subject in the social context occupying different positions in relation to different discourses which change across time. As particular discourses become central issues, they will affect the ways in which the social subject occupies, or resists, the subject position constructed by a text.

The viewing and reading of texts takes place, for the majority of people, within the domestic context. However, this is a context which is not singular and unchanging, but plural and open to different permutations, dependent upon the negotiations between members of the household and the particular texts involved. The VCR offers the potential for extended choice of viewing in terms of text and context. But in order to explore how this potential is being used the particular conditions of its consumption must be addressed. The viewing contexts and their associated texts which I have outlined here have emerged from my discussions with women who occupy different social positions and there are remarkable similarities in the ways in which all the women have spoken about their domestic viewing practices. However, it is simply not sufficient to have identified these similarities,

and my analysis of the interview 'texts' continues in an attempt to make visible the important differences between the women's accounts of these practices. These differences must be seen in relation to their particular social positioning and the various specific discourses which they inhabit. The interview material I have gathered demands a framework of analysis which uses theories and concepts developed within different disciplines and will, I am sure, test their relative strengths and weaknesses in revealing the complexity of how women relate to television and video in their everyday lives.

Acknowledgement

I am grateful to Andrew Tudor for his thorough reading of an early draft of this article, and indebted to the women who gave me much more than their time.

Notes

1. This research was initially funded by the Economic and Social Research Council and has taken the form of long, open-ended discussions with women whose age, social position, employment, and family circumstances differ (race is a variable which has not been introduced). Part of my strategy has been to encourage open discussion and allow the women themselves to introduce topics which are of importance to them. By keeping the discussions open they can take pleasure in having the opportunity to explore and express their own ideas and feelings on these matters. For discussions on feminist research methods see Roberts (ed.), 1981; Stanley and Wise, 1983, Bell and Roberts, 1984.

2. VCRs can also be used in conjunction with a video camera to produce home video tapes.

3. 'Movies' in this context include films made specially for video distribution, films made for TV, both British and American, as well as 'feature' films which are produced primarily for the cinema.

4. There are notable exceptions (Hobson, 1981 and 1982, Morley, 1986; Collett, 1986).

5. I am grateful to Elizabeth Shove and Andrew Tudor for this working definition.

6. However a recent publication by W. Faulkner and E. Arnold (eds.), *Smothered by Invention: Technology in Women's Lives* (Pluto Press, 1985), does address issues of domestic technology and gender.

7. These were ideas discussed at a seminar given by Cynthia Cockburn at York University, June 1985. See also Cockburn, 1985.

8. It is interesting to note that video tapes *are* now being distributed which *are* specifically aimed at a female audience; IPC and Videospace combined magazine and video to market their *Woman's Own Selection*, along with their more recent label *Images of Love*, while Polygram Video are offering a label, *Women's Choice*. However, in the North of England certainly, these have a very limited distribution.

9. These are the names which the women themselves gave to the different texts and genres.

10. Charlotte Brunsdon has made this point in relation to *Crossroads*, but we can see that it can apply to other 'women's genres' (Brunsdon, 1981).

References

Barker, M. (1984) (ed.), *The Video Nasties* (London: Pluto Press).

Bell, C., and Roberts, H. (1984) (eds.), *Social Researching* (London: Routledge & Kegan Paul).

Brunsdon, C. (1981), '*Crossroads*: Notes on a Soap Opera', *Screen*, 22/4: 32–7.

Cockburn, C. (1983), *Brothers* (London: Pluto Press).

—— (1985), *Machinery of Dominance* (London: Pluto Press).

Collett, P. (1986), 'Watching the TV Audience', paper presented to International Television Studies conference 1986.

Deem, R. (1984), 'Paid Work, Leisure and Non-Employment: Shifting Boundaries and Gender Differences', paper presented to British Sociological Association conference 1984.

Faulkner, W., and Arnold, E. (1985) (eds.), *Smothered by Invention* (London: Pluto Press).

Hobson, D. (1981), 'Housewives and the Mass Media', in S. Hall *et al.* (eds.), *Culture, Media, Language* (London: Hutchinson).

—— (1982), '*Crossroads*': The Drama of a Soap Opera (London: Methuen).

Howkins, J. (1983), 'Mr Baker: A Challenge', *Sight & Sound* (autumn), 227–9.

Kuhn, A. (1984*a*), 'Reply to Julian Petley', *Screen*, 25/3 (May/June), 116–17.

—— (1984*b*), 'Women's Genres', *Screen*, 25/1 (Jan./Feb.), 18–28.

Modleski, T. (1982), *Loving With a Vengeance* (Hamden, Conn.: Shoe String Press).

Morley, D. (1986), *Family Television: Cultural Power and Domestic Leisure* (London: Comedia).

Petley, J. (1984), 'A Nasty Story', *Screen*, 25/2 (Mar./Apr.), 68–74.

Radway, J. A. (1984), *Reading the Romance* (Chapel Hill: Univ. of North Carolina Press).

Roberts, H. (1981) (ed.), *Doing Feminist Research* (London: Routledge & Kegan Paul).

Rothschild, J. (1983), *Machina ex Dea* (New York: Pergamon Press).

Stanley, L., and Wise, S. (1983), *Breaking Out* (London: Routledge & Kegan Paul).

Williams, R. (1974), *Television Technology and Cultural Form* (London: Fontana).

Zimmerman, J. (1981), 'Technology and the Future of Women: Haven't we Met Somewhere Before?', *Women's Studies International Quarterly*, 4/3: 355.

45.
SIZING UP RECORD COLLECTIONS
Gender and Connoisseurship in Rock Music Culture
Will Straw

For example, suppose we required a dense texture of classical allusion in all works that we called excellent. Then, the restriction of a formal classical education to men would have the effect of restricting authorship of excellent literature to men. Women would not have written excellent literature because social conditions hindered them. The reason, though gender-connected, would not be gender per se.

(Baym, 1985: 64–5)

I wish Riot Grrrl had inspired girls to be more curious about the great female musicians of yesteryear. Boys bond around discussing used records and obscure bands. With girls it's like every generation has to exhaust itself reinventing the wheel. So we end up with bands that are good but less original than they think they are.

(Vincentelli, 1994: 24)

You don't have to be a German genius to figure out that any pop combo is only as good as their record collection . . .

(Moore, 1993)

Introduction

When I had almost finished writing this article, I was interviewed by the director of *Vinyl*, a documentary film-in-progress whose subject is record collecting. By the time shooting of the film is completed, its director told me, he will have interviewed almost 100 record collectors. Only five of these, he admitted, were women. He had tried (he claimed, convincingly) to find more female collectors, following up on every lead and making certain that his search was well publicised, but had met with no success. (In response to my own concern that my collection might not be spectacular enough, the director reassured me that some interview subjects had collections of only a few hundred records.) With the director of this film, as with everyone who has discussed the subject with me, there was easy and intuitive acceptance of the idea that record collecting, within Anglo-American cultures at least, is among the more predictably male-dominated of music-related practices.

The challenge, however, is to determine what might be said next. When people are pressed to account for the gendered, masculinist character of record collecting, the certainty that it is so gives way to hesitant and often contradictory explanations as to why. As I shall argue, this uncertainty is rooted in competing images of the collection as cultural monument and private haven. Record collections are seen as both public displays of power/knowledge and private refuges from the sexual or social world; as either structures of control or the by-products of irrational and fetishistic obsession; as material evidence of the homosocial information-mongering which is one underpinning of male power and compensatory undertakings by those unable to wield that power. Indeed, the confusion underlying these characterisations is such that, were one presented with statistical evidence that the typical record collector was female, one could easily invoke a set of stereotypically feminine attributes to explain why this was the case. One might note, for example, that collecting is about the elaboration of a domestic context for consumer goods; that, within collecting, the values of consumption come to assume priority over those of production; and that, in the collection, an immediate, affective relationship to the object takes precedence over collective, spectacular forms of cultural involvement (for a discussion which explores some of these claims, see Belk and Wallendorf, 1994).

Taxonomies of Male Identity

At the very least, we may say of record collecting, as of most practices of connoisseurship and systematic consumption, that it stands in an uncertain relationship to masculinity. As part of the material culture of music, records themselves participate in the gendering of cultural habits at a number of levels. From one perspective, records are merely the physical residues of processes of commodity turnover and stylistic change, and, as such, are part of the ongoing, unofficial relocation of objects from the public, commercial realm into the domestic environment. In this, they contribute to the differentiation of domestic spaces, and it is as an effect of the male collector's salvaging of popular cultural artefacts from the world outside that many of the distinctive or stereotypically resonant aspects of men's domestic space take shape. (The slovenly bachelor, his apartment collapsing into disorder amidst the chaos of clutter, is one such stereotype; the apartment which is little more than a compulsively ordered archive is another.) It is often in his relationship to his collections that a male's ideas about domestic stability or the organisation of a domestic environment find their fullest or most easily decipherable elaboration. (Writing of the 1950s, Keir Keightley (1966) has discussed the role of hi-fi equipment in nourishing a masculine ideal of the listening room as refuge from the noise and interruptions which come with married or family life.)

Were record collections merely graveyards for exhausted commodities, however, their connection to what Medovoi has called the 'masculinist politics' which surround so much popular music might not be apparent (Medovoi, 1984). As accumulations of material artefacts, record collections are carriers of the information whose arrangement and interpretation is part of the broader discourse about popular music. In a circular process, record collections, like sports statistics, provide the raw materials around which the rituals of homosocial interaction take shape. Just as ongoing conversation between men shapes the composition and extension of each man's collection, so each man finds, in the similarity of his points of reference to those of his peers, confirmation of a shared universe of critical judgement.

In the psychological literature on collecting, it is sometimes noted that males and females tend to accumulate objects with equal intensity. If men's accumulations of objects tend, more frequently, to be considered 'collections', one explanation is that this simply signals the higher prestige which has accrued, historically, to the sorts of objects amassed by men. Baekeland has suggested that this argument is not sufficient, and that, in fact, male practices of accumulation take shape in an ongoing relationship between the personal space of the collection and public, discursive systems of ordering or value. These public systems are no less arbitrary, of course, in their choice of objects or criteria of value, but they tie each male's collection to an ongoing, collective enterprise of cultural archaeology. Baekeland cautions that:

> we should not forget that many women privately amass personal possessions far in excess of any practical need, without any thought of public exhibition other than adornment: we rarely think of accumulations of dress, shoes, perfumes, china and the like as collections. They consist of relatively intimate and transient objects intended directly to enhance their owners' self-images, to be used until they are worn out or broken, and then to be discarded. Men's collections, however, be they of stamps, cars, guns or art, tend to have clear-cut thematic emphases and standard, external reference points in public or private collections. Thus, women's collections tend to be personal and ahistorical, men's impersonal and historical, just as, traditionally, women have tended to have a relatively greater emotional investment in people than in ideas and men to some extent the reverse.

> (Baekeland, 1994: 207)

This opposition of 'people' to 'ideas', however, misses the extent to which it is an ideal of systematicity itself which typically grounds the masculinist inclination to collect. Images of the stamp collector as armchair traveller or the phonecard collector as folklorist miss, in their emphasis on the object itself, the degree to which any corpus which may be differentiated in consensual ways will become the focus of collective collecting. Indeed, the most satisfying (albeit under-theorised) explanation of the masculine collector's urge is that it lays a template of symbolic differentiation over a potentially infinite range of object domains. (In this, railroad systems offer the most perfect image of the collector's object, both in the flat, geometric structure of such systems themselves, and in the fact that all there is to be collected, ultimately, are the numbers through which trains are differentiated.)

This vision of collecting leaves unanswered the reasons as to why it might be so. One explanation is that collecting works to displace the affective or corporeal aspects of particular practices (sports, music-listening) onto series and historical genealogies, in what might be seen as a fetishistic act of disavowal. Another might tie the compulsion to contextualise to a broader male preoccupation with the subject's place within symbolic configurations of identity, a preoccupation whose links to Oedipal anxiety should be apparent. 'What motivates the purchase', Baudrillard writes of the collector, 'is the pure imperative of association' (1994: 23). These are both, it must be acknowledged, pop-psychoanalytic accounts of collecting and the compulsion to contextualise, and each is convincing only to the extent that it sheds light on the social dimensions of collecting – its role in structuring and excusing relations between men.

Wearing Knowledges

Several years ago, film studies scholars noted that skills and knowledge have a problematic place within dominant representations of an ideal masculinity, and that there is ongoing anxiety over whether the most valorised forms of masculine mastery are social or asocial. (See, for a summary and development, Neale, 1983.) Forms of expertise acquired through deliberate labour of a bookish or archival variety are typically so dependent upon bureaucratised institutions

of knowledge that they are poor supports for ideals of masculinity as transcendent strength. In Neale's words, this subservience to the terms of a symbolic order will 'threaten any image of the self as totally enclosed, self-sufficient, omnipotent' (Neale, 1983: 7). A disavowal of the social, discursive origin of such knowledges is necessary if skill is to be seen to be instinctual, the sign of 'power, omnipotence, mastery and control' (1983: 5).

The variable relations between knowledge and mastery help to generate the range of masculine identity formations which circulate within popular culture and nourish our everyday classifications. In any discussion of this range, we would do well to recall Eve Kosofsky Sedgwick's insight that positions in what she calls the 'male homosocial spectrum' have long been marked by the variable susceptibility of each to accusations of homosexuality (Sedgwick, 1990: 185). Within the peer cultures of adolescent males – groups which typically show a high involvement in popular music – the contours of public postures will be shaped to significant degrees by the possibility of such accusations. Positions in this spectrum are individuated through the ways in which the possession of knowledges is signalled in self-presentation, in 'the most automatic gesture or the apparently most insignificant techniques of the body – ways of walking or blowing one's nose, ways of eating or talking' (Bourdieu, 1984: 466). Males police themselves, not only in terms of the looseness or control which mark bodily gesture, but in the ways they 'wear' and release the knowledges they have cultivated. While the dandy, for example, manifests a mastery of the most social of codes, the sense that his persona is frivolous or depthless, reducible to the surface on which this mastery is displayed, is the frequent basis of his denigration. Inversely, the nerd is noted for a mastery of knowledges whose common trait is that they are of little use in navigating the terrains of social intercourse. (Indeed, nerdish dispositions are marked by their ability to turn virtually any domain of expertise into a series of numbers on a checklist.) Both the dandy and the nerd are characterised by a relationship to knowledge which is semiotically rich and easy material for parody. For the dandy, this is the result of a labour which transforms cultivated knowledges into the basis of an ongoing public performance. For the nerd, knowledge (or, more precisely, the distraction which is its by-product) stands as the easily diagnosed cause of performative social failure, blatantly indexed in the nerd's chaotic and unmonitored self-presentation.

We might add to this taxonomy (if only as the marker of an extreme position) the figure of the brute, the male persona characterised by a pure and uncultivated instinctuality. The brute shares with the nerd an obliviousness to the rules of social comportment, and, as with the dandy, there is a sense of explicitness, of little depth beyond the immediately visible. What the brute most famously suggests, however, is a strength and mastery independent of knowledges which originate and find value within the social and the symbolic. In Western popular culture of the postwar period, for the most part, the brute has not been a principal source of heroic or appealing imageries of the male. (As Sharon Willis (1993/4) has noted, with respect to the films of Quentin Tarantino, even the racist positing of certain African-American cultural figures as purely instinctual has seemed to require the interpretive gaze of a cultivated white man who is able to recontextualise such figures within popular cultural traditions.)

In popular music, ostensibly dependent upon the expression of raw, erotic energy, we might expect the figure of the brute to be prominent, but this has been the case only in isolated instances. Throughout most of the recent history of that music, the privileged masculine stances have been those which move between the immediacy of unfettered expression and the acknowledgement that a tradition or genealogy is being reworked or updated. (The postures of recent Britpop stars, marked by both libidinous laddishness and knowing references to Burt Bacharach or Ray Davies, are almost perfect examples of this ambiguity.) Indeed, an image of instinctual strength which is not informed by an awareness of progenitors or not anchored in the solidity of a canon and tradition risks appearing naive (as has often been the case with Heavy Metal performers). It is from the raw material of instinctuality, nevertheless, that the most appealing images of a cool, hip masculinity within popular musical culture have been formed (e.g. Chris Isaac or Damon Albarn). Hipness almost always requires a knowledge which is more or less cultivated, but must repress any evidence that this knowledge is easily acquired in the mastery of lists or bookish sources. In this respect, as Andrew Ross suggests, hipness is one point in an economy which threatens to flounder on the opposed alternatives of being over- or under-informed (Ross, 1990: 83). What counts, however, is not simply the degree of knowledge but the amount of restraint with which it is deployed or guarded. The jazz musician quizzed at length about his influences by the eager fan will almost always insist that music is a question of an elusive 'feel,' even when, like Kirk Douglas in the film *Young Man With a Horn*, he carries his record collection with him from town to town. Similarly, it has long been common in the hipper circles of science fiction fandom to belittle as nerdish those who see that fandom as a cultural space in which to discuss science fiction. To actually introduce science fiction into conversation – to take the pretext for fannish intercourse as its ongoing focus – is to risk being denounced as 'sercon' (*serious* and *conservative*), someone unable to sustain effortless and generalised sociality. A familiarity with the symbolic universe of science fiction is a long-term necessity for a subcultural career within fandom, but this familiarity must be signalled in ways which do not show the marks of contrived effort.

Hipness and nerdishness both begin with the mastery of a symbolic field; what the latter lacks is a controlled economy of revelation, a sense of when and how things are to be spoken of. Hipness maintains boundaries to entry by requiring that the possession of knowledge be made to seem less significant than the tactical sense of how and when it is made public. Cultivation of a corpus (of works, of facts) assumes the air of instinctuality only when it is transformed into a set of gestures enacted across time. The stances of hip require that knowledge and judgement be incorporated into bodily self-presentation, where they settle into the postures of an elusive and enigmatic instinctuality and may therefore be suggested even when they are not made blatantly manifest.

It is within social constructions of hipness that values we might call masculinist and strategies whose effect is to reproduce social stratification interweave in interesting ways. The male club disc jockey who refrains from discussing labels and producers with a fan avoids the dissipation of his power within meshes of trivial knowledge and is thus part of a line of descent that includes the silent but effective hero of western films. However, he is also, by insisting on the instinctual and uncultivated nature of his choices, limiting access to the set of practices which are his own ticket to social mobility. If the worlds of club disc jockeys or rock criticism seem characterised by shared knowledges which exclude the would-be entrant, this functions not only to preserve the homosocial character of such worlds, but to block females from the social and economic advancement which they may offer.

In general terms, it might be said that most forms of collecting are devalorised within male peer groups. They are viewed as the sign of a retreat from those realms in which patriarchal power is most obviously deployed and enjoyed. At worst, collections are taken as evidence that blocked or thwarted sexual impulses have been sublimated into lifeless series of facts or objects. At best, the distraction which characterises the collector is seen as causing an obliviousness to the implicit rules of public presentation which govern dress, gesture and bodily comportment. Collecting is an important constituent of those male character formations, such as nerdism, which, while offering an alternative to a blatantly patriarchal masculinity, are rarely embraced as subversive challenges to it.

Record collecting, nevertheless, is almost never irredeemably nerdish. While canonical forms of nerdishness take shape around domains of knowledge (such as computer science) which may only in special circumstances emerge as heroic or eroticised, there are lines of flight which easily connect record collecting to a variety of stances which are more easily recuperable. These stances include hipness which, as discussed above, may draw sustenance from those skills which the cultivation of a collection may provide. Other such stances include the connoisseurship which furnishes historical depth to musical practice itself, and through which canons and terms of judgement take shape. Record collecting also converges with those anti-consumerist ethics which tie the collector's investment in the obscure to the bohemian's refusal of the blatantly commercial. Finally, with growing frequency, images of the collector circulate which cast him as adventurous hunter, seeking out examples of the forgotten or the illicit.

Acquisition and Obsession

In three recent novels, men whose lives and relationships to women are in crisis take refuge within intense (even obsessive) relationships to works of popular culture. In the most well-known of the three, Nick Hornby's *High Fidelity*, the protagonist's successful passage into middle age is marked by his renouncing the secure refuge of his record shop and the system of values and homosocial relations which has taken form around it (Hornby, 1995). In Tim Lucas's novel *Throat Sprockets*, the protagonist is driven obsessively to see, over and over again, a low-budget porn film (itself entitled *Throat Sprockets*) and to seek out its makers (Lucas, 1994). In *Glimpses*, by Lewis Shiner, a troubled man on the verge of middle age imagines that he travels back in time to participate in the final completion of such legendary unfinished albums as the Beach Boys' *Smile* and Jimi Hendrix's *Church of the New Rising Sun* (Shiner, 1995).

At the conclusion of *High Fidelity*, the male protagonist learns that he is now able to visit middle-aged professionals with horribly middle-brow record collections (Peter Gabriel, Simply Red) and still finds reasons to value their friendship. He comes, as well, by novel's end, to organise club nights on which cover bands and disc jockeys play oldies for an ageing audience hopelessly out of touch with contemporary music. Both these transformations are meant to signal a (belated) coming of age, and the signs of this new maturity are a declining interest in policing other's tastes and the withering of the main character's commitment to anti-commercial, connoisseurist musical tastes. As it moves towards its conclusion, the novel becomes increasingly ironic. Changes described to us (in the protagonist's own voice) as logical adaptations to changing material or romantic circumstances are clearly, from our vantage-point as readers, an ageing male's strategies for survival in a cultural realm in which his place is no longer certain.

That these changes are both conservative (a capitulation to mass, uninformed taste) and liberating (a release from structures of judgement which limit social and sexual opportunity) takes us to the heart of the male record collector's increasingly problematic political status. On the one hand, as Eric Weisbard suggests, the record collector's obscurantist interest in the marginal may be seen to be fully continuous with rock culture's myths of oppositionality (Weisbard, 1994b: 19). To collect the obscure is to refuse the mainstream, and, therefore, to participate in an ongoing fashion in what Lawrence Grossberg has called rock culture's processes of 'excorporation', 'operating at and reproducing the boundary between youth culture and the dominant culture' (Grossberg, 1984: 231). This sense of rock music culture as marked by a permanent division has always given the investment in the obscure and the margin a heroic edge, and made of it the very foundation of rock politics.

What *High Fidelity* suggests, however, is that the only real choice is between entry into an world of adult sexuality and responsibility and remaining within the immature, homosocial world of the record store where obscurantist tastes continue to appear political. Elsewhere, Eric Weisbard notes that the wave of female alternative rockers who emerged in the early 1990s offered 'the first version of punk we've had in ages that doesn't require owning a big record collection' (1994a: 24). One effect of new movements in rock music (initiated by women and queers), he suggests, is to reveal a 'consumption-based ethic of oppositionality' as not much more than the only readily accessible political stance for the white rock musician or fan (Weisbard, 1994b: 19). Elsewhere, writing of moves to render dance music 'militant', I suggested that when the militant credibility of a cultural group can no longer be grounded in a sense of itself as political agency, it will be installed as a set of constraints or expulsions set in place against the lure of vulgarity (Straw, 1995: 252). For some time, now, the status of collecting has been caught within the dilemma discussed here and thematised within *High Fidelity*. To collect is to valorise the obscure, and yet such valorisation increasingly stands revealed as dependent on the homosocial world of young men, a world in which boundaries between the acceptably collectable and the vulgar or commercial are strengthened and perpetuated as the only available and heroic basis for political claims.

Tim Lucas's novel *Throat Sprockets* is not about records, but in its emphasis on a degraded, obscure work of popular culture which becomes the focus of an intensely private obsession, it leads us to consider the libidinal dynamic of boy-dominated trash fandoms. These fan formations have been a persistent part of Anglo-American popular musical culture for some two decades, fixing their attention on the marginal spaces of garage psychedelia, surf music and, more recently, what has come to be called Space Age Bachelor Pad Music or loungecore. At one level, the impulses behind these fandoms are directed at activities of documentation and vernacular scholarship, producing ongoing series of compilation albums, discographies and fanzine reconstructions of performer careers and historical moments. At the same time, however, the dispositions of trash fandoms depart from those of an indie rock obscurantism in that, while both privilege a notion of the culturally marginal, the former often ties this to an idea of the illicit. In the spaces of trash culture, the implicit claim runs, one finds the purest glimpses of a sexual energy or a transgressive anti-conventionalism.

In their privileging of illicit, even abject texts (such as strip-club music) trash fandoms run the risk, as Bryan Bruce has noted, of an amorality which valorises transgression irrespective of its content or purpose (Bruce, 1990). Indeed, in the current easy listening revival, the most prominent dynamics are those which diverge from the more respectable and populist anti-rockism which was one of this revival's original impulses. In place of that impulse, one finds an ongoing move to rehabilitate ever more scandalous musical currents, from the soundtracks to German porn films through baroque orchestral versions of late Beatles songs. Here, as in trash fandoms more generally, collecting is refigured as anthropology, an expedition into the natural wilderness of discarded styles and eccentric musical deformations. Indeed, within the easy listening revival, the civilised sound of tinkling Martini glasses is counterbalanced by the image of intrepid explorers marching from one thrift store to another. As the editors of *Incredibly Strange Music II* note, admittedly with some irony:

> In search of amazing endangered records as well as insights as to their genesis, we interviewed not just original musical innovators (who once experienced fame), but trail blazing collectors who, without benefit of discography or reference guide, went out into backwater flea markets and thrift stores to search through that which society has discarded. Experiencing the thrill and adventure of the hunt,

they made their selections and then listened for hours to ferret out exceptional recordings.

(Juno and Vale, 1993: 3)

This evocative account may be seen as part of a broader history of moves which cast the spaces of popular music consumption as primitive and adventurous. Michael S. Kimmel has written about those transformations in American popular fiction which, after the turn of the century, presented the city as 'wilderness' or 'jungle' and the male inhabitant of such settings as manly adventurer (Kimmel, 1994). In the 1950s, a prominent television genre joined private investigators and the world of the jazz club (for example, *77 Sunset Strip*), turning urbanised spaces of musical consumption into natural spaces of danger or illicit promise. Trash fandoms themselves perpetuate the sense that particular moments or spaces of popular culture (the mid-1960s, for example) will remain chaotic or unpacified, forever yielding up hitherto unimagined and possibly scandalous artefacts for the adventurer/collector. In this they depart from those fan/collector formations (such as those centring on jazz) which seek explicitly to bring order to a corpus and history of formidable scope.

In Lewis Shiner's *Glimpses*, the narrator's personal collection functions in a minor way as refuge, of the sort seen in *High Fidelity*, but the novel's more central concern is the canon, the virtual collection of unfinished albums by such masters as the Beach Boys, the Doors, Jimi Hendrix and the Beatles. Here, the narrator seeks release, not in the comfort of domestic accumulation, nor in the lure of the illicitly obscure text, but in a reassuring experience of rock history as a series of recognisable and, finally, completed monuments. Indeed, the central concern here is not simply the composition of this canon, but the sense that rock music is principally about that canon, about completing the unfinished history of the 1960s.

The gendering of musical consumption has, as one of its most sharply-drawn axes, the relationship of record collection to canon. Elizabeth Vincentelli's claim (quoted at the beginning of this article), that new female bands are not sufficiently aware of their predecessors, signals the problematic relationship, within rock music's history, between the idea of cyclical rupture and the critical investment in the idea of

a stable canon. Histories of punk which foreground its origins in socio-cultural conditions (working-class anger or art world interventionism) on either side of the Atlantic have steadily lost ground to arguments which assert the continuity of a dissident tradition beginning in the USA and running through the New York Dolls and the Ramones. In part, such arguments are about empirically verifiable patterns of imitation and communication, but they centre, as well, on the manner in which punk was to be heard.

One way to hear punk, of course, was as the centre of new relationships between the cultural spaces of art, fashion and music, and to pursue these threads of dissemination and influence outwards to their respective destinations. As a means of building a context for punk, this road was highly likely to encounter female figures or feminist practices, and offer a diminished view of the importance of specifically musical ancestors. The other way meant being sent back to investigate a whole series of progenitors of punk, buying Velvet Underground or New York Dolls' albums and building a collection which embodied the transformed rock canon inaugurated in the late 1970s. This was the road mapped out, in the late 1970s, in such publications as *New York Rocker*. In a debate long posed as one between those who held to a theory of spontaneous working class uprising and others who held to the idea of a steady, imperceptible weaving of trans-Atlantic influences, the latter position would always seem more historiographically comfortable. Over time, nonetheless, the debate over the sources of punk has become a debate about influences (British pub rock versus downtown New York punk) rather than the status of specifically musical influences, each side offering its canon of forebears to be added to a representative record collection.

Conclusion

Just as I began writing this article, I was interviewed by the maker of a National Film Board of Canada documentary on 'nerds'. (I was chosen, the director assured me, as an 'expert' and not as a case study.) The film was inspired, in part, by the sentiment that the nerds of youth are the Bill Gates of adulthood, and that, in the interests of long-term economic stability, the social pressures exercised upon the young should nourish nerdish sentiments rather than work to repress them. From a perspective which locates the most harmful forms of masculinist power in blatant displays of physical or technical prowess, the nerd may well seem an enlightened frog awaiting the kiss which will turn him into a cool and suave prince of the post-industrial economy.

And yet, it might be argued, the nerdish homosociality of those who collect popular music artefacts is as fundamental to the masculinism of popular music as the general valorisation of technical prowess and performative intensity more typically seen to be at its core. Eric Weisbard has noted, in connection with the rise of alternative rock after 1991, that '[r]ock stars no longer make a pageant of their power, as modesty and constant allusions to unknown underground bands become required decorum' (Weisbard, 1994b: 17). At one level, this suggests a historical change, as semiotic competence in reading the state of the musical field comes to assume greater importance, within musical culture, than the public display of technical mastery. At a more conspiratorial level, this account might be taken as describing the successful adaptation of rock music's masculinist impulses to an era of sampling or niche market obscurantism. Interviews with contemporary female rock musicians frequently describe how, having learned to play guitars and play them loud, women find that the lines of exclusion are now elsewhere. They emerge when the music is over, and the boys in the band go back to discussing their record collections.

Acknowledgement

As always, I owe an enormous debt to Keir Keightley, for incisive ideas, ongoing and productive debate and tips as to sources. Conversations with David Galbraith and Graciela Martinez-Zalce, as we drove from one record store to another during their visits to Montreal, helped me develop many of the ideas here. The ongoing research out of which this article grows has been financed in part by grants from the Fonds pour la Formation de Chercheurs et l'Aide à la Recherche (Quebec) and the Social Sciences and Humanities Research Council of Canada. Small portions of this article have appeared in Straw (1995).

References

Baekeland, Frederick (1994) 'Psychological Aspects of Art Collecting', in Susan M. Pearce (ed.) *Interpreting Objects and Collections*, London: Routledge, pp. 205–19.

Baudrillard, Jean (1994) 'The System of Collecting', in John Elsner and Roger Cardinal (eds) The *Cultures of Collecting*, Cambridge, MA: Harvard University Press, pp. 7–24.

Baym, Nina (1985) 'Melodramas of Beset Manhood: How Theories of American Fiction Exclude Women Authors', in Elaine Showalter (ed.) *The New Feminist Criticism: Essays on Women, Literature, Theory*, New York: Pantheon Books.

Belk, Russell W. and Wallendorf, Melanie (1994) 'Of Mice and Men: Gender Identity in Collecting', in Susan M. Pearce (ed.) *Interpreting Objects and Collections*, London: Routledge, pp. 240–53.

Bourdieu, Pierre (1984) *Distinction: A Social Critique of Judgement*, trans. Richard Nice, Cambridge, MA: Harvard University Press.

Bruce, Bryan (1990) 'Right Wing Chic: Adam Parfrey and R. Kern Fingered!!' *CineAction* 19/20 (May): 3–10.

Grossberg, Lawrence (1984) 'Another Boring Day in Paradise: Rock and Roll and the Empowerment of Everyday Life', *Popular Music* 4: 225–58.

Hornby, Nick (1995) *High Fidelity*, New York: Riverhead Books.

Juno, Andrea and Vale, V. (1993) 'Introduction', *Incredibly Strange Music* (San Francisco: Re/Search Publications) 1: 2–5.

Keightley, Keir (1996) '"Turn it Down!" She Shrieked: Gender, Domestic Space, and High Fidelity, 1948–1959', *Popular Music* 15(2): 1–28.

Kimmel, Michael S. (1994) 'Consuming Manhood: The Feminization of American Culture and the Recreation of the Male Body, 1832–1920', *Michigan Quarterly Review* 33(1) (Winter): 7–36.

Lucas, Tim (1994) *Throat Sprockets*, New York: Delta.

Medovoi, Leerom (1992) 'Mapping the Rebel Image: Postmodernism and the Masculinist Politics of Rock in the U.S.A.', *Cultural Critique* 20 (Winter): 153–88.

Moore. Rob (1993) Liner notes to the CD album *Here's to the Lovers*, by the group Love Jones, Toronto: BMG Music.

Neale, Steve (1983) 'Masculinity as Spectacle', *Screen* 24(6) (November–December): 2–16.

Ross, Andrew (1990) *No Respect: Intellectuals and Popular Culture*, London: Routledge.

Sedgwick, Eve Kosofsky (1990) *Epistemology of the Closet*, Berkeley and Los Angeles: University of California Press.

Shiner, Lewis (1995) *Glimpses*, New York: Avon Books.

Straw, Will (1995) 'The Booth, the Floor and the Wall: Dance

Music and the Fear of Falling', in Will Straw, Stacey Johnson, Rebecca Sullivan and Paul Friedlander (eds) *Popular Music-Style and Identity*, Montreal: The Centre for Research on Canadian Cultural Industries and Institutions/International Association for the Study of Popular Music, pp. 249–54.

Vincentelli, Elisabeth (1994) Letter excerpted in 'Year of the Woman' Music Supplement, *Village Voice* 8 (1 March): 24.

Weisbard, Eric (1994a) Letter excerpted in 'Year of the Woman' Music Supplement, *Village Voice* 8 (1 March): 24.

Weisbard, Eric (1994b) 'Over & Out: Indie Rock Values in the Age of Alternative Million Sellers', *The Village Voice Rock & Roll Quarterly* (Summer): 15–19.

Willis, Sharon (1993/94) 'The Fathers Watch the Boy's Room', *Camera Obscura* 32 (September–January): 42–73.

46.
FEMININE FASCINATIONS
Forms of Identification in Star–Audience Relations
Jackie Stacey

The Lost Audience

Throughout this book—as throughout most film studies—the audience has been conspicuous by its absence. In talking of manipulation . . . consumption . . . ideological work . . . subversion . . . identification . . . reading . . . placing . . . and elsewhere, a concept of audience is clearly crucial, and yet in every case I have had to gesture towards this gap in our knowledge, and then proceed as if this were *merely* a gap. But how to conceptualise the audience—and the empirical adequacy of one's conceptualisations—is fundamental to every assumption one can make about how stars and films work.[1]

My mother obtained a job at the State cinema when I was ten. For me that meant a ticket to Paradise, and regularly I worshipped at the shrine of the gods and goddesses. I couldn't wait for the moment to come when the velvet curtains would sweep apart, the lights dim, and a shared intimacy would settle on the hushed audience.

(D. H.)

The first quotation is taken from the conclusion of Richard Dyer's study on stars, the second is written by a film fan remembering the pleasures offered by Hollywood stars in the 1940s and 1950s. Since the publication of *Stars* in 1982 there has been little work to fill the gap referred to in Dyer's conclusion. It is particularly important for feminists to challenge the absence of audiences from film studies, since it has reproduced an assumed passivity on the part of women in the cinema audience. Wanting to find out about female audiences and their relationship to stars, I advertised in two of the leading women's weekly magazines for readers to write to me about their favourite Hollywood star of the forties and the fifties. These decades interested me since much feminist work on Hollywood has looked at the films of this period, which was, as well, a time of changing definitions of femininity in Hollywood and in society generally.

The enthusiastic response of over 300 letters, including some from Canada, the United States and Australia, testifies to the continuing significance of Hollywood stars in women's lives and imaginations. Many letters were several pages long and offered detailed recollections of particular favourite stars, as well as of the cinema generally during this period. Respondents included photos, scrapbooks and original newspaper cuttings about their favourite stars, as well as detailing their appeal in their own words. The letters covered a broad range of topics including how much the cinema, and stars in particular, meant in women's lives; the role of the cinema in wartime Britain; why women stopped being fans of stars; and the particular pleasures of the cinema experience in the context of the 1940s and 1950s. This chapter looks firstly at the reasons for the continued absence of the audience from film studies and then offers some preliminary findings from research in progress into aspects of the relationship between female Hollywood stars and women in the audience.

Within film studies generally, the study of stars has remained predominantly textual. Although Dyer's work challenges some of the existing boundaries of film studies, by linking textual models of semiotic and narrative analysis to a sociological approach to stars, very few studies have succeeded in developing this project in relation to questions about cinema audiences. Analyses of stars have continued to focus on the production of particular significations within the film text, or within other aspects of the cinema industry such as publicity, rather than on how audiences might read them within particular cultural and historical contexts.[2]

There is surprisingly little feminist work on Hollywood stars, and even less on their audiences. Attention to genre (especially melodrama, the woman's film and film noir), to narratives (especially those reproducing the oedipal drama) and to forms of looking (especially voyeurism and fetishism) have tended to dominate the feminist agendas of the 1980s. It is especially puzzling that stars have remained a relatively undeveloped aspect of Hollywood cinema within feminist work since female stars might seem an obvious focus for the analysis of the construction of idealised femininities within patriarchal culture. In the work which has emerged, feminist film theorists have also tended to reproduce a textual analysis of stars. Despite their very different theoretical positions, the two key perspectives within feminist film theory, namely the 'images of women'[3] approach and the 'woman as image'[4] approach, have also shared a common reliance on textual analysis, ignoring the role of the audience in the cinema.

Molly Haskell, for example, discusses the female stars in Hollywood cinema in terms of stereotypes which limit and control definitions of femininity in a male dominated culture. She contrasts, for example, the 'treacherous woman', associated with stars such as Rita Hayworth in *Gilda* and *The Lady from Shanghai* with the 'superfemale', such as Bette Davis in *Jezebel*, who, 'while exceedingly "feminine" and flirtatious, is too ambitious and intelligent for the docile role society has decreed she play', and with the 'superwoman' who 'instead of exploiting her femininity, adopts male characteristics in order to enjoy male prerogatives, or simply to survive'.[5] This latter female type is exemplified by stars such as Katharine Hepburn and Joan Crawford and is different again from the 'sweet and innocent' type, associated with June Allyson, Olivia de Havilland and Judy Garland: 'For every

hard-boiled dame there was a soft-boiled sweetheart . . .'.[6] Although Haskell's analysis refers outside the film texts to feminine stereotypes in society generally, and to a patriarchal culture in whose interest they are perpetuated, Haskell's discussion of the stars themselves is restricted to the characters portrayed and their narrative treatment in the films.

The other approach to stars within feminist film criticism has been the investigation of female stars as objects of the 'male' gaze. Laura Mulvey, for example, analyses Sternberg's use of Dietrich as the 'ultimate fetish' in her well-known essay 'Visual Pleasure and Narrative Cinema':

> The beauty of the woman as object and the screen space coalesce; she is no longer the bearer of guilt but a perfect product, whose body, stylised and fragmented by close-ups, is the content of the film and the direct recipient of the spectator's look.[7]

This fetishism of the female star within Hollywood cinema is one form of scopophilia (or pleasure in looking) offered to the spectator, the other is the voyeuristic pleasure in the objectification of the female star on the screen. To illustrate this latter process, Mulvey discusses the heroines of Hitchcock's films who are constructed as passive objects of the sadistic controlling voyeurism of the male protagonist, and, by extension, the spectator: 'The power to subject another person to the will sadistically or to the gaze voyeuristically is turned onto the woman as object of both.'[8]

Little attention, then, has been paid to female stars in Hollywood by feminist film theorists outside the ways in which the stars function within the film text.[9] There are, however, a few exceptions which have tried to bring together textual analysis either with ethnographic investigation or with a historical contextualisation of audiences. Helen Taylor's recent book *Scarlett's Women*, for example, analyses audiences' readings of Vivien Leigh in *Gone with the Wind*.[10] Jane Gaines has examined the different definitions of femininity constructed in 1940s fan magazines through which female stars could be read.[11] Angela Partington, whilst maintaining the focus on genre, offers a convincing analysis of the place of female stars in the production of an 'excess' of femininity in melodrama in the 1950s, which can only be understood in relation to other representations and consumer practices, not solely in terms of its own textual operations.[12] Finally, in *Heavenly Bodies*, Richard Dyer offers a reading of Judy Garland's star image through discourses of gay male subculture. Based on responses to an advert, Richard Dyer's analysis demonstrates the importance of meanings produced outside the film text to the readings audiences make of Hollywood stars. Indeed there could not be better evidence to illustrate the argument against textual determinism, since the readings made by these fans are so clearly based not just outside the film text, or even the cinema, but outside mainstream culture itself, and within a subculture which reverses and parodies dominant meanings.[13]

Investigating Audiences

Whilst these studies show that work on audiences is developing,[14] there remain several difficulties in this emerging area of work. One of the particular difficulties with analysing audiences from past decades is that they are not easily accessible. What then are the possible sources for their investigation?[15] First, box-office statistics can give us an indication of which films, and perhaps which stars, were popular and when. Film magazines such as *Cinematograph Weekly*, or *Picturegoer*, ran popularity polls on stars, and these may also indicate in more detail which stars were favoured, when, and for how long. Other surveys done at the time may indicate who went to which films and why, such as the work at the Mass Observation Archive at Sussex University,[16] or the market research produced for commercial reasons, or the sociological research on the 'effects' of films on audiences. Sometimes this information is broken down according to class and gender divisions, which enables conclusions to be drawn about which genres were popular among specific audiences, for example.[17] However, this information, whilst it may give a broad indication of likes or dislikes, offers little insight into the more qualitative dimensions of those preferences.

A richer source of information which offers more details on preferences and audiences' tastes has been what audiences wrote about stars at the time. Letters pages in film magazines contain examples of audience opinion about stars, as well as about other issues. Magazines' and newspapers' letters pages typically include complaints, criticism, appreciation and likes and dislikes letters. They are generally responding to an article or feature on a particular star, film or director, or to controversial questions set up by the editor. The most popular magazine of this kind in the 1940s and 1950s, *Picturegoer*, for example, regularly featured provocative pieces such as 'Charm not Curves' by Vincent Keene, which questioned what constituted desirable femininity.[18] The letters pages in the weeks following were full of differing and wide ranging answers to this question. Letters from readers could be a useful indicator of audiences' preferences and responses to stars, bearing in mind that the topics raised in the letters are shaped by the magazine as a whole and its own editorial criteria. The mode of the magazine thus produces very particular generic conventions through which the readers' letters are channelled.

In addition, the editorial decisions about which letters get published clearly determine what kinds of opinions we can have access to now.[19] Thus letters pages in weekly magazines are interesting in terms of studying the magazine and its role in framing Hollywood in Britain, but less useful in terms of offering detailed sources on audiences.

Fan clubs offer another source of information about audiences in the 1940s and 1950s, but these are often difficult to trace, and much of the fan mail written at this time has been lost or destroyed. The fan clubs which responded to my letters of enquiry said they no longer possessed such old fan mail from Britain.

The final possibility for investigating audiences of the 1940s and 1950s is to analyse people's memories and recollections of the cinema at that time. Yet, as is true of all the sources discussed so far, the rules of enquiry frame the kind of information elicited. Answers to an advertisement asking for recollections of favourite stars inevitably produce a particular set of representations, which are clearly framed by a specific cultural context. First, in my own case, the research concerns women's *memories* of Hollywood stars. The kinds of selections respondents make when remembering what Hollywood stars meant in their lives are therefore mediated in a particular way. Which stars are remembered and how they are remembered must additionally be influenced by the cultural constructions of those stars since that time. For example, audiences may remember stars differently depending on whether the stars are still alive, and if not, how they died (e.g. Marilyn Monroe); whether they still have a fan club (e.g. Deanna Durbin); whether the star continued to have a successful career (e.g. Katharine Hepburn and Bette Davis); whether their films have been shown frequently on television and indeed whether the stars went on to have a television career (e.g. Barbara Stanwyck).

In addition to these factors, memory introduces a particular kind of selection process. What gets remembered and what gets forgotten may depend not only on the star's career since the time period specified, but also upon the identity of the cinema spectator. Having asked women to write about female stars, the kinds of representations offered will be informed by issues such as self-image and self-perception, particularly in relation to gender identity. The different constructions of femininity within Hollywood, such as the power and rebelliousness of Bette Davis or the sexual attractiveness of Marilyn Monroe, or the clean-livingness of Deanna Durbin may have particular appeal in retrospect, and may have come to mean something over the years which it did not in the 1940s and 1950s.[20]

It is this final approach to historical audiences that I am using in this chapter. In particular I want to explore one of the recurring themes of the letters which were sent to me by women in response to my advertisement: the processes of identification at stake in the exchange between female stars and the female spectator. I have chosen to focus on this aspect of the relationship between stars and spectators not only because of its recurrence as a theme in the letters, but also because of its theoretical centrality within feminist criticisms of Hollywood cinema.

A Question of Identification

The term 'identification' has been central to many debates within psychoanalytic theory and film studies. Within psychoanalytic theory, 'identification' has been seen as the key mechanism for the production of identities. Freud analysed the unconscious mechanisms through which the self is constituted in relation to external objects. In her paper 'Identification and the

Star: A Refusal of Difference', Anne Friedberg quotes Freud on identification:

> First, identification is the original form of emotional tie with an object; secondly, in a regressive way it becomes a substitute for a libidinal object-tie, as it were by means of introjection of the object into the ego; and thirdly, it may arise with any new perception of a common quality shared with some other person who is not an object of sexual instinct. The more important this common quality is, the more successful may this partial identification become, and it may thus represent the beginning of a new tie.[21]

The role of vision in identification has always been part of the Freudian formulation (the emphasis on the moment of the sight of sexual difference, for example) but the 'specular role of identification' has taken centre stage in Lacan's theories of the mirror phase, through which subjects are 'constituted through a specular misrecognition of an *other*'.[22]

These models of identification employed within psychoanalysis to explore the developments of unconscious identities have been seen by some film theorists, such as Christian Metz,[23] as analogous to the cinematic experience of spectatorship. As Friedberg outlines:

> Primary identification as Metz describes it (as distinct from Freud's 'original and emotional tie') means a spectator who identifies with both camera and projector, and like the child positioned in front of the mirror, constructs an imaginary notion of wholeness, of a unified body. . . . Secondary identification is with an actor, character or star . . . any body becomes an opportunity for an identificatory investment, a possible suit for the substitution/misrecognition of self.[24]

Psychoanalytic film theorists have thus developed a complex analysis of cinematic identification, based on an analogy between the construction of individual identities in infancy in relation to others, and the process of watching a film on a screen. Whilst this may be an appealing analogy, especially given the centrality of the specular in later psychoanalytic accounts of the development of identity, the question remains as to the validity of such a straightforward transposition: how similar are these processes, and what is being left out of the account of spectatorship by focusing so exclusively on its psychic dimensions? Such a framework offers limited purchase on understanding cinematic identification, with no evidence other than a conceptual analogy of the processes occurring in individual psyches.

In film studies more generally, the term 'identification' has been widely used to suggest a broader set of processes. Drawing on literary analysis, identification has often been used rather loosely to mean sympathising or engaging with a character. It has also been used in relation to the idea of 'point of view', watching and following the film from a character's point of view. This involves not only *visual* point of view, constructed by type of shot, editing sequences and so on, but also *narrative* point of view, produced through the sharing of knowledge, sympathy or moral values with the protagonist. Identification has thus been used as a kind of common-sense term within film and literary studies, referring to a very diverse set of processes, and has yet to be adequately theorised in a manner which provides a satisfactory alternative to the more reductive psychoanalytic models.

Interestingly, feminist writing on the subject of identification in relation to gender identities has developed in two opposing directions. On the one hand, the psychoanalytically informed film criticism following Laura Mulvey's original attack on the visual pleasure of narrative cinema is still marked by a suspicion of any kind of feminine role model, heroine or image of identification. Mulvey's films (such as *Amy!*, 1980), as well as her influential theoretical work, have advocated a rejection of the conventions of popular representations, not simply for the images of femininity constructed, but also for the processes of identification offered to the cinema spectator. 'Identification' itself has been seen as a cultural process complicit with the reproduction of dominant culture by reinforcing patriarchal forms of identity. Anne Friedberg sums up what feminists have seen as the problematic functions of identification thus:

Identification can only be made through recognition, and all recognition is itself an implicit confirmation of an existing form. The institutional sanction of stars as ego ideals also operates to establish normative figures. Identification enforces a collapse of the subject onto the normative demand for sameness, which, under patriarchy, is always male.[25]

On the other hand, some feminist cultural theorists have attempted to rescue the process of identification from such criticism, and have instead drawn attention to the empowerment through certain forms of identification within the consumption of popular culture. Valerie Walkerdine, for example, offers an analysis of the way the different members of a working-class family read *Rocky II*, which demonstrates the shifting significance of the metaphor of fighting in Rocky's character.[26] Gender differences produce different and conflicting identifications in Walkerdine and the family members; nevertheless identification is reclaimed in Walkerdine's analysis as potentially producing rebellious feelings and a desire to fight the dominant system, as well as being a necessary aspect of cultural consumption.

These two perspectives, then, represent opposite positions on processes of identification in the visual media: the first criticises identification of any kind for reproducing sameness, fixity and the confirmation of existing identities, whilst the second reclaims it as potentially empowering and expressive of resistance. They coincide, however, in taking psychoanalytic accounts of identification as central to their understanding of spectatorship.

Whilst there are detailed psychoanalytic accounts of the psychic processes of identification,[27] however, there has been less investigation of the broader cultural and social dimensions of identification in the cinema. Therefore instead of applying psychoanalytic theory to a film text to investigate identification in the cinema, I shall take the audiences' representations of this process and its meanings as my starting point. This is not to argue that audiences are the source of 'the true meanings' of films or of stars; clearly audiences' recollections are themselves a highly mediated set of cultural representations, as I have discussed above. Instead, the purpose of this investigation is to look at the production of the meaning of stars in the terms of how audiences construct them.

Particularly striking in the letters I received was the diversity of processes represented which could loosely be termed identification. To the extent that identification involves various processes which negotiate the boundaries between self and other,[28] these processes take on a particular significance in the context of popular cinema where women in the audience are offered idealised images of femininity in many different forms. Some of these quite clearly relate back to the psychic processes described by psychoanalysis, and others move into the domain of cultural consumption more generally.

There is a problem finding a term to refer to the women in the audience whose letters are used in this analysis. The term 'female spectator', used so widely within feminist film theory, has been a confusing one; it has been used to refer both to the textual positions constructed by the film, and, often implicitly, to the female members of the cinema audience.[29] At best it is acknowledged that the two processes may, to some extent, be separate, but generally an implicit textual determinism defines assumptions about spectatorship.[30] In addition, the singularity of the reference of the term spectator implies a unified viewing experience, and its usage carries with it a very passive model of how audiences watch films.

I am using 'spectator' here in a rather different way to refer to members of the cinema audience. However, there is a further problem using the term to discuss practices which take place beyond the cinema, since spectator, in this broader sense, refers to a person still in the cinema. This is itself symptomatic of the limited interest in what spectatorship might mean outside or beyond the cinema experience. Spectatorship, when considered as an aspect of cultural consumption, should no longer be seen simply as an extension of a film text replicating infantile misrecognition, nor as an isolated viewing process, but rather as part of a more general cultural construction of identities.

The analysis of the letters which follows is divided into two sections. The first addresses processes of identification which involve fantasies about the relationship between the identity of the star and the identity of the spectator. On the whole these forms of identification relate to the cinematic context. The second section examines forms of identification which involve practice as well as fantasy, in that spectators actually transform some aspect of their identity as a result of their relationship to their favourite star. These practices extend beyond the cinema itself and thus spectatorship is considered in relation to the construction of feminine identities more generally.

Cinematic identificatory fantasies
Devotion and worship

> I wanted to write and tell you of my devotion to my favourite star Doris Day. I thought she was fantastic, and joined her fan club, collected all the photos and info I could. I saw *Calamity Jane* 45 times in a fortnight and still watch all her films avidly. My sisters all thought I was mad going silly on a woman, but I just thought she was wonderful, they were mad about Elvis, but my devotion was to Doris Day.
>
> (V. M.)

Some letters do not even mention the self, but simply offer evidence of devotion to a female star. However, this is unusual; most letters I received framed their comments on stars in relation to their own identities. In this first group, many of the letters speak of the pleasure produced by some kind of difference from the star, the distance produced by this difference providing a source of fascination. Stars are frequently written about as out of reach, and belonging to a different world or plane of existence:

> Film stars . . . seemed very special people, glamorous, handsome and way above us ordinary mortals.
>
> (J. T.)

> I'll never forget the first time I saw her, it was in *My Gal Sal* in 1942, and her name was Rita Hayworth. I couldn't take my eyes off her, she was the most perfect woman I had ever seen. The old cliché 'screen goddess' was used about many stars, but those are truly the only words that define that divine creature. . . . I was stunned and amazed that any human being could be that lovely.
>
> (V. H.)

Stars were fabulous creatures to be worshipped from afar, every film of one's favourite gobbled up as soon as it came out.

(P. K.)

These statements represent the star as something different and unattainable. Religious signifiers here indicate the special status and meaning of the stars, as well as suggesting the intensity of the devotion felt by the spectator. They also reinforce the 'otherness' of the stars who are not considered part of the mortal world of the spectator. The last example, however, does introduce the star into the mortal world by a metaphor of ingestion reminiscent of the act of communion. Worship of stars as goddesses involves a denial of self found in some forms of religious devotion. The spectator is only present in these quotes as a worshipper, or through their adoration of the star. There is no reference to the identity of the spectator or suggestion of closing the gap between star and fan by becoming more like a star; these are simply declarations of appreciation from afar. The boundaries between self and ideal are quite fixed and stable in these examples, and the emphasis is very strongly on the ideal rather than the spectator. Even in the last statement, where the self is implicit in that the star is to be gobbled up, the star none the less remains the subject of the sentence.

The Desire to Become

In other examples, the relationship between star and audience is also articulated through the recognition of an immutable difference between star and spectator: 'Bette Davis was the epitome of what we would like to be, but knew we never could!' (N. T.). Yet here the desire to move across that difference and become more like the star is expressed, even if this is accompanied by the impossibility of its fulfilment.[31] The distance between the spectator and her ideal seems to produce a kind of longing which offers fantasies of transformed identities.

These desires to become more like the stars occur on several levels. Many of them are predictably articulated in relation to appearance:

I finally kept with Joan Crawford—every typist's dream of how they'd like to look.

(M. R.)

And of course her [Betty Grable's] clothes—how could a young girl not want to look like that?

(S. W.)

Although I wished to look like a different star each week depending what film I saw, I think my favourite was Rita Hayworth, I always imagined, if I could look like her I could toss my red hair into the wind . . . and meet the man of my dreams . . .

(R. A.)

Clearly, stars serve a normative function to the extent that they are often read as role models, contributing to the construction of the ideals of feminine attractiveness circulating in culture at any one time. The age difference between the star and the younger fans is central here: stars provide ideals of femininity for adolescent women in the audience, preoccupied with attaining adult femininity. Part of this kind of identification involves recognising desirable qualities in the ideal and wanting to move towards it:

Doris Day . . . seemed to epitomise the kind of person who, with luck, I as a child could aspire to be.

(B. C.)

I loved to watch Deanna Durbin. I used to put myself in her place. She lived in a typical girl's dream.

(J. G.)

These examples demonstrate not simply the desire to overcome the gap between spectator and star, but a fantasy of possible movement between the two identities, from the spectator to the star.

Pleasure in Feminine Power

However, the difference between the female star and the female spectator is a source of fascination not only with ideals of physical beauty, but also with the stars' personalities and behaviour, which are often admired or envied by spectators. These identifications demonstrate the contradictory pleasures offered by Hollywood stars, on the one hand reproducing normative models of feminine glamour, whilst on the other hand offering women fantasies of resistance. For example, some female stars represented images of power and confidence. These were frequent favourites because they offered spectators fantasies of power outside their own experience.

> We liked stars who were most different to ourselves and Katharine Hepburn, with her self-assured romps through any situation was one of them. We were youngsters at the time, and were anything but self confident, and totally lacking in sophistication, so, naturally, Bette Davis took the other pedestal. She who could be a real 'bitch', without turning a hair, and quelled her leading men with a raised eyebrow and sneer at the corners of her mouth . . .
>
> (N. T.)

> Bette Davis . . . was great, I loved how she walked across the room in her films, she seemed to have a lot of confidence and she had a look of her own, as I think a lot of female stars had at that time . . .
>
> (E. M)

Powerful female stars often play characters in punishing patriarchal narratives, where the woman is either killed off, or married, or both, but these spectators do not seem to select this aspect of their films to write about. Instead, the qualities of confidence and power are remembered as offering pleasure to female spectators in something they lack and desire.

Identification and Escapism

This movement from spectator to star is part of the pleasure of escapism articulated in many of the letters. Instead of the difference between the spectator and the star being recognised and maintained, the difference provides the possibility for the spectator to leave her world temporarily and become part of the star's world:[32]

> It made no difference to me if the film was ushered in by a spangled globe, the Liberty Lady or that roaring lion, I was no longer in my seat but right up there fleeing for my life from chasing gangsters, skimming effortlessly over silver ice, or singing high and sweet like a lark.
>
> (D. H.)

I was only a girl, but I could be transported from the austerity and gloom of that time to that other world on the silver screen.

> (J. T.)

> Joan Crawford—could evoke such pathos, and suffer such martyrdom . . . making you live each part.
>
> (M. B.)

In these examples, the movement from self to other is more fluid than in the previous categories, and this fluidity provides the well-known pleasure of the cinema: 'losing oneself' in the film. Here, in contrast to the distinction between self and ideal maintained in the processes of spectatorship discussed above, the spectator's identity merges with the star in the film, or the character she is portraying.

In this first section I have discussed processes of spectatorship which involve negotiating the difference between the star and the spectator in various ways: beginning with the denial of self, in favour of praising the screen goddesses, and moving on to the desire to become like the star, but realising the impossibility of such desires, and ending with the pleasure in overcoming the difference and merging with the ideal on the screen.

Extra-cinematic Identificatory Practices

Now I want to move on to discuss representations which concern what I shall call 'identificatory practices' of spectatorship. These nearly all relate to forms of identification which take place outside the cinematic context. These practices also involve the audience engaging in some kind of practice of transformation of the self to become more like the star they admire, or to involve others in the recognition of their similarity with the star.

Pretending

> . . . there was a massive open-cast coal site just at the tip of our estate—there were 9 of us girls— and we would go to the site after school, and play on the mounds of soil removed from the site. The mounds were known to us as 'Beverley Hills' and we all had lots of fun there. Each of us had our own spot where the soil was made

into a round—and that was our mansion. We played there for hours—visiting one mansion after another and each being our own favourite film star. . .

(M. W.)

I really loved the pictures, they were my life, I used to pretend I was related to Betty Grable because my name was Betty, and I used to get quite upset when the other children didn't believe me.

(B. C.)

Pretending to be particular film stars involves an imaginary practice, but one where the spectator involved knows that it is a game. This is rather different from the processes of escapism in the cinema discussed above whereby the spectator feels completely absorbed in the star's world and which thus involves a temporary collapsing of the self into the star identity. The first example given above is also different in that it involves a physical as well as an imaginary transformation. Furthermore pretending does not simply involve the privatised imagination of the individual spectator, as in the process of escapism, but also involves the participation of other spectators in the collective fantasy games. This kind of representation of the relationship between star and fan is based more on similarity than difference, since the fan takes on the identity of the star in a temporary game of make-believe, and the difference between them is made invisible, despite the recognition of the whole process as one of pretending.

Resembling

Bette Davis—her eyes were fabulous and the way she walked arrogantly . . . I have dark eyes, in those days I had very large dark eyebrows . . . and my Dad used to say . . . 'Don't you roll those Bette Davis eyes at me young lady. . . .' Now Doris Day, that's a different thing—we share the same birthday . . .

(P. O.)

There are numerous points of recognition of similarities between the spectator and the star. These are not based on pretending to be something one is not, but rather selecting something which establishes a link between the star and the self based on a pre-existing part of the spectator's identity which bears a resemblance to the star. This does not necessarily involve

any kind of transformation, but rather a highlighting of star qualities in the individual spectator. The significance of particular features, such as 'Bette Davis eyes', seems to exceed physical likeness, to suggest a certain kind of femininity, in this case a rebellious one which represented a challenge to the father's authority.

Imitating

Unlike the above process of recognising a resemblance to a star, many spectators wrote about practices which involved transforming themselves to be more like the star. This is different from the fantasy of becoming the star whilst viewing a film, or even expressing the desire to become more like the star generally, since it involves an actual imitation of a star or of her particular characteristics in a particular film. In other words this identificatory practice involves a form of pretending or play-acting, and yet it is also different from pretending, since pretending is represented as a process involving the whole star persona, whereas imitation is used here to indicate a partial taking-on of part of a star's identity.

Several letters gave examples of imitating singing and dancing of favourite stars after the film performance:

We used to go home and do concerts based on the songs and dances we had seen in the films, and one of my friends had an auntie who was a mine of information on the words of songs from films . . .

(B. F.)

The films we saw made us sing and sometimes act our way home on the bus . . .

(J. T.)

My favourite female star was Betty Grable. The songs she sang in the film, I would try to remember, I would sing and dance all the way home . . .

(P. G.)

The imitation of stars was not limited to singing and dancing, but was clearly a pleasure in terms of replicating gestures, speech and star personalities: 'I had my favourites of course. . . . One week I would tigerishly pace about like Joan Crawford, another week I tried speaking in the staccato tones of Bette Davis and puffing a cigarette at the same time'

(D. H.).

Copying

Although imitation and copying are very closely linked as practices, I want to use them here differently to distinguish between audiences *imitating* behaviour and activities, and copying appearances. As the attempted replication of appearance, then, *copying* relates back to the desire to look like stars discussed above. However it is not simply expressed as an unfulfillable desire or pleasurable fantasy, as in the earlier examples, it is also a practice which transforms the spectators' physical appearance.

Copying is the most common form of identificatory practice outside the cinema. Perhaps this is not surprising given the centrality of physical appearance to femininity in general in this culture, and to female Hollywood stars in particular. The 'visual pleasure' offered by the glamour and sexual appeal of Hollywood stars has been thoroughly criticised by feminists elsewhere.[33] Here I am interested in how women audiences related to these ideals of femininity as presented by Hollywood stars on the screen, and particularly in how identification extends beyond individualised fantasies into practices aimed at the transformation of identity.

> I was a very keen fan of Bette Davis and can remember seeing her in *Dark Victory*. . . . That film had such an impact on me. I can remember coming home and looking in the mirror fanatically trying to comb my hair so that I could look like her. I idolised her . . . thought she was a wonderful actress.
>
> (V. C.)

This process involves an intersection of self and other, subject and object. The impact of the film on the spectator was to produce a desire to resemble physically the ideal. In front of a reflection of herself, the spectator attempts to close the gap between her image and her ideal image, by trying to produce a new image, more like her ideal. In this instance, her hair is the focus of this desired transformation. Indeed hairstyle is one

of the most frequently recurring aspects of the star's appearance which the spectators try to copy:

> My friends and I would try and copy the hair styles of the stars, sometimes we got it right, and other times we just gave up, as we hadn't the looks of the stars or the money to dress the way they did.
>
> (E. M.)

> Now Doris Day. . . . I was told many times around that I looked like her, so I had my hair cut in a D.A. style. Jane Wyman was a favourite at one stage and I had hair cut like hers, it was called a tulip. . . . Now Marilyn Monroe was younger and by this time I had changed my image, my hair was almost white blonde and longer and I copied her hairstyle, as people said I looked like her.
>
> (P. O.)

These forms of copying involve some kind of self-transformation to produce an appearance more similar to Hollywood stars. Some spectators clearly have a stronger feeling of their success than others; the first example includes a sense of defeat whilst the last seems to be able to achieve several desired likenesses, especially bearing in mind this respondent is the one who had 'Bette Davis eyes'. The difference then between the star and the spectator is transformable into similarity through the typical work of femininity: the production of oneself simultaneously as subject and object in accordance with cultural ideals of femininity.

Copying and Consumption

Copying the hairstyles of famous film stars can be seen as a form of cultural production and consumption. It involves the production of a new self-image through the pleasure taken in a star image. In this last section I want to consider an extension of the identificatory practice of copying where it intersects with the consumption of cultural products in addition to the star image. The construction of women as cinema spectators overlaps here with their construction as consumers.

To some extent copying the hairstyles of the stars overlaps with this. However I have separated hairstyles from other aspects of this process, since changing hairstyles does not necessarily involve the actual purchasing of other products to transform the identity of the spectator, although it may do. The purchasing of items such as clothing and cosmetics in relation to particular stars brings into particularly sharp focus the relationship between the cinema industries and other forms of capitalist industry. Stars are consumable feminine images which female spectators then reproduce through other forms of consumption.

> and I bought clothes like hers [Doris Day] . . . dresses, soft wool, no sleeves, but short jackets, boxy type little hats, half hats we used to call them and low heeled court shoes to match your outfit, kitten heels they were called . . . as people said I looked like her [Marilyn Monroe] I even bought a suit after seeing her in *Niagara*.
>
> (P. O.)

> It was fun trying to copy one's favourite stars with their clothes, hats and even make-up, especially the eyebrows. Hats were very much in vogue at that time and shops used to sell models similar to the styles the stars were wearing. I was very much into hats myself and tried in my way (on a low budget) to copy some of them.
> Naturally I bought a Deanna Durbin model hat and a Rita Hayworth one.
>
> (V. C.)

> I'd like to name Deanna Durbin as one of my favourite stars. Her beautiful singing voice, natural personality and sparkling eyes made her films so enjoyable, and one always knew she would wear boleros; in one film she wore six different ones. I still like wearing boleros—so you can tell what a lasting effect the clothes we saw on the screen made on us.
> (J. D. Member of the Deanna Durbin Society)

Stars are thus identified with particular commodities which are part of the reproduction of feminine identities. The female spectators in these examples produce particular images of femininity which remind them of their favourite stars. In so doing they produce a new feminine identity, one which combines an aspect of the star with their own appearance. This is different from imitation, which is more of a temporary reproduction of a particular kind of behaviour which resembles the star. It transforms the spectators' previous appearance, and in doing so offers the spectator the pleasure of close association with her ideal.

> As teenagers and young girls we did not have the vast variety of clothing and choices of make-up that is available today, so hairstyles and make-up were studied with great interest and copied . . . I seem to remember buying a small booklet by Max Factor with pictures of the stars, M.G.M. mostly, with all the details of their make-up and how to apply it. . .
>
> (E. H.)

> Their make-up was faultless and their fashion of the forties platform shoes, half hats with rows of curls showing at the back under the hat. . . . We used to call the shoes 'Carmen Miranda' shoes . . . I felt like a film star using Lux Toilet soap, advertised as the stars' soap.
>
> (V. B.)

Through the use of cosmetic products, then, as well as through the purchasing and use of clothing, spectators take on a part of the stars identity and make it part of their own. The self and the ideal combine to produce another feminine identity, closer to the ideal. This is the direct opposite of the process of identification I began with in the first section, in which the spectator's own identity remained relatively marginal to the description of the pleasure taken in female Hollywood stars. In this final process, the star becomes more marginal and is only relevant in so far as the star identity relates to the spectator's own identity. As has been noted by other commentators, these latter practices demonstrate the importance of understanding Hollywood stars and their audiences in relation to other cultural industries of the 1940s and 1950s.[34]

Concluding Comments

Having outlined some of the different forms of identification in audience-star relationships represented in these letters, it is now important to reconsider some of the earlier models of identification and spectatorship in the light of this research. First, the diversity of processes of identification, including forms of desire, evident in these letters is striking. The idea of a singular process of identification, so often assumed in psychoanalytic film theory, seems unsatisfactory in the light of the range of processes discussed above. In addition, the use of the term 'female spectatorship' to refer to a single positioning by a film text seems equally inappropriate in the light of the diversity of readings of stars by different women in the cinema audiences in the 1940s and 1950s.

As well as categorising the many different kinds of identification in the relationships between audiences and stars, I have also drawn attention to the broad distinction between two different forms of identification: identificatory fantasies (pp. 149–52) and identificatory practices (pp. 153–7). This is not to suggest that the practices do not also involve fantasies, nor that fantasies cannot also be considered as practices. But rather, it is important to extend our understanding of cinematic identification, previously analysed solely at the level of fantasy, to include the practices documented by these spectators, in order to understand the different forms of overlap between stars' and audiences' identities.

Another significant distinction is that between cinematic identification, which refers to the viewing experience, and extra-cinematic identification, referring to the use of stars' identities in a different cultural time and space. So far, film studies has, not surprisingly, been concerned with the former. However, the importance of these extra-cinematic forms of identification to the women who wrote to me came across very forcefully in their letters. Not only was this one of the most written-about aspects of the relationship between stars and audiences, but the pleasure and force of feeling with which they recalled the details of the significance of stars in this context was also striking.

All the above forms of identification relate to a final distinction which I have used to frame the sequence of the quotations: identification based on difference and identification based on similarity. The early categories of identification concern processes where the differences between the star and the spectator produce the sources of pleasure and fascination.

The representations of these processes tended to emphasise the presence of the star and de-emphasise the identity of the spectator. The later categories concern processes where the similarity, or at least the possibility of closing the gap produced by the differences between stars and spectators, is the source of pleasure expressed. In these examples the reproduction of the spectators' identities tended to be the focus of the commentary. Thus identifications do not merely involve processes of recognition based on similarity, but also involve the productive recognition of differences between femininities.

Indeed the processes of identification articulated most strongly in terms of difference seem to be those relating more directly to the cinematic context where the image of the star is still present on the screen. The processes, and practices, which involve reproducing similarity seem to be those extra-cinematic identifications which take place more in the spectator's more familiar domestic context, where the star's identity is selectively reworked and incorporated into the spectator's new identity. Even in these cases, identification does not simply involve the passive reproduction of existing femininities, but rather an active engagement and production of changing identities.

The assumption behind much of the psychoanalytic work discussed earlier is that identification fixes identities: 'identification can only be made through recognition, and all recognition is itself an implicit confirmation of existing form'.[35] Many of the examples I have discussed contradict this assumption and demonstrate not only the diversity of existing forms, but also that recognition involves the production of desired identities, rather than simply the confirmation of existing ones. Many forms of identification involve processes of transformation and the production of new identities, combining the spectator's existing identity with her desired identity and her reading of the star's identity.

This research also challenges the assumption that identification is necessarily problematic because it offers the spectator the illusory pleasure of unified subjectivity. The identifications represented in these letters speak as much about partial recognitions and fragmented replications as they do about the misrecognition of a unified subjectivity in an ego ideal on the screen. Thus, cultural consumption does not necessarily fix identities, destroy differences and confirm sameness. If we take audiences as a starting point for understanding the consumption of stars, the active and productive elements of the star-audience relationships begin to emerge.

In challenging previous models of passive female spectatorship, and demonstrating the diversity and complexity of identifications between stars and women in the audience, however, I am not suggesting feminists look at cultural consumption uncritically. Taking audiences as a starting point can present problems for a feminist analysis: how can we remain critical of the dominant meanings of gender produced by Hollywood, whilst at the same time taking seriously the pleasures female spectators articulate about their favourite stars? Perhaps this problem is itself a reason for the reluctance by feminists to analyse female audiences and their relationship to dominant idealised feminine images, such as Hollywood stars.

In asking women to write to me about the appeal of Hollywood stars, it was inevitable I would receive an enthusiastic response. The discrepancy between the passion with which women spectators wrote about their Hollywood favourites and feminist criticisms of the patriarchal constructions of femininity in Hollywood produces a familiar dilemma for feminists working in many areas of cultural analysis. Simply to use what women wrote to me to illustrate the subordinating operations of patriarchal capitalism seems to me to be overwhelmingly patronising, as well as rather pessimistic. But simply to embrace the enthusiastic spirit of the pleasures they describe would be equally problematic, and would reproduce an uncritical populism which leaves behind crucial feminist insights. It therefore remains a challenge to feminists analysing Hollywood cinema to produce critical accounts of dominant cultural representations whilst at the same time developing theories of female cultural consumption as an active and productive process.

Acknowledgments

I would very much like to thank Richard Dyer, Sarah Franklin, Anne Gray, Hilary Hinds, Richard Johnson and Celia Lury for their helpful comments on earlier drafts of this paper, and their encouragement and support for this research project. I would also like to thank Christine Gledhill for her interest, enthusiasm and patience.

Notes

1. Richard Dyer, *Stars* (London, BFI Publishing, 1979).
2. A notable exception to this is Leo Handel's *Hollywood Looks at its Audience* (Urbana, University of Illinois Press, 1950). Handel's findings are developed further in Andrew Tudor, *Image and Influence: Studies in the Sociology of Film* (London, Allen & Unwin, 1974), chapter 4.
3. Typical of the 'images of women' approach are Molly Haskell, *From Reverence to Rape: The Treatment of Women in the Movies* (Harmondsworth, Penguin, 1974); Marjorie Rosen, *Popcorn Venus* (New York, Coward, McCann and Geoghegan, 1973); and Brandon French, *On The Verge Of Revolt: Women in American Films of the Fifties* (New York, Frederick Ungar Publishing Co., 1978).
4. Typical of the 'woman as image' approach are Laura Mulvey, *Visual and Other Pleasures* (London, Macmillan, 1989); and Constance Penley, ed., *Feminism and Film Theory* (New York, Routledge, and London, BFI Publishing, 1988).
5. Molly Haskell, *From Reverence to Rape,* 214.
6. Ibid., 194.
7. Laura Mulvey, *Visual,* 22.
8. Ibid., 23.
9. Robyn Archer and Diana Simmonds, *A Star Is Torn* (London, Virago, 1986).
10. Helen Taylor, *Scarlett's Women: 'Gone With the Wind' and its Female Fans* (London, Virago, 1989).
11. Jane Gaines, 'War, women and lipstick: fan mags in the forties', in *Heresies,* 18 (1986), 42–7.
12. Angela Partington. 'Melodrama's gendered audience', in Sarah Franklin, Celia Lury and Jackie Stacey, eds, *Off Centre: Feminism and Cultural Studies* (London, Unwin Hyman, 2006).
13. Richard Dyer, *Heavenly Bodies: Film Stars and Society* (London, BFI/Macmillan, 1986), chapter 3.
14. See Bruce A. Austin, *Immediate Seating: A Look at Movie Audiences* (Belmont, California, Wadsworth Publishing Co., 1989).
15. For discussions of historical audiences see Janet Staiger, 'The handmaiden of villainy: methods and problems for studying the historical reception of a film', *Wide Angle,* 8, 1 (1986); Philip Corrigan, 'Film entertainment as ideology and pleasure: towards a history of audiences', in James Curran and Vincent Porter, eds, *British Cinema History* (London, Weidenfeld & Nicolson, 1983); and Sue Harper, 'Popular taste and methodological problems: British historical films in the 1930s', paper given at *Popular European Cinema* conference, University of Warwick, September 1989.
16. See Jeffrey Richards and Dorothy Sheridan, eds, *Mass-Observation at the Movies* (London and New York, Routledge & Kegan Paul, 1987).

17. See Janet Thumim, 'Super special long-run propositions: revenue, culture and popularity in "Cinematograph Weekly"'s annual review', paper at *Popular European Cinema* conference, University of Warwick, September 1989.

18. Vincent Keene, 'Charm not curves', *Picturegoer*, 14 October 1950. Letters responding directly to this article appeared in *Picturegoer,* 9 December 1950.

19. I am grateful to Jane Gaines for pointing out to me that the authenticity of the letters published on film magazine letters' pages remains in question. However the Mass-Observation Archive at Sussex University holds all the original letters written to *Picturegoer* in the year 1940, which would provide a more reliable source for the historical analysis of cinema-goers.

20. See Popular Memory Group, 'On popular memory', in Bill Schwarz *et al.,* eds, *Making Histories: Studies in History, Writing and Theory* (London, Hutchinson, 1982).

21. S. Freud, *Group Psychology and the Analysis of the Ego,* 1921, chapter 7, quoted in Anne Friedberg, 'Identification and the Star: a refusal of difference', in Christine Gledhill, ed., *Star Signs* (London, BFI Publishing, 1982).

22. Ibid., 49.

23. Christian Metz, 'Le Signifiant imaginaire', *Communications,* 23 (1975); tr. Celia Britton, Anwyl Williams, Ben Brewster, Alfred Guzetti, *Psychoanalysis and Cinema: The Imaginary Signifier* (London, Macmillan, 1983).

24. Anne Friedberg, 'Identification and the Star', p. 50.

25. Ibid., 53.

26. Valerie Walkerdine, 'Video replay: families, films and fantasies', in Victor Burgin, James Donald and Cora Kaplan, eds, *Formations of Fantasy* (London, Methuen, 1986).

27. For example, see Jacqueline Rose, *Sexuality in the Field of Vision* (London, Verso, 1986), Mary Anne Doane, *The Desire to Desire: The Woman's Film of the 1940s* (Bloomington and Indianapolis, Indiana University Press, 1987), and Teresa de Lauretis, *Alice Doesn't: Feminism, Semiotics, Cinema* (London, Macmillan, 1984).

28. For a typology of audience–star relations, see Andrew Tudor, *Image and Influence,* 80.

29. See Tania Modleski, 'Introduction: Hitchcock, feminism and the patriarchal unconscious', in *The Woman Who Knew Too Much: Hitchcock and Feminist Theory* (London, Methuen, 1988).

30. This problem is addressed by Annette Kuhn, 'Women's genres', in *Screen,* 25, 1 (1984), 18–28.

31. For a discussion of the representation of desire between women produced by their differences, see Jackie Stacey, 'Desperately seeking difference', in *Screen,* 28, 1 (1987), 48–61.

32. For a discussion of the pleasurable feelings escapism offers to the cinema audience, see Richard Dyer, 'Entertainment and Utopia', *Movie,* 24 (Spring 1977), 2–13.

33. See Laura Mulvey, *Visual,* and E. Ann Kaplan, *Women and Film: Both Sides of the Camera* (London, Methuen, 1983).

34. See Partington, 'Melodrama's gendered audience'.

35. Friedberg, 'Identification and the Star', 53.

47.
THE FABULOUS SUBLIMITY OF GAY DIVA WORSHIP

Brett Farmer

At the beginning of his collection of essays in queer studies, Jeffrey Escoffier makes the at once portentous and banal assertion that "the moment of acknowledging to oneself homosexual desires and feelings . . . and then licensing oneself to act . . . is *the* central drama of the homosexual self." That "moment of self-classification," he explains, "is an emergency—sublime, horrible, wonderful—in the life of anyone who must confront it."[1] In the theater of my own biography, I am unsure how or when I first played out this epiphanic drama of queer self-acknowledgment, but I can vividly recall the first time someone else enacted it for me. In elementary school, at the age of ten, a fellow pupil cornered me in the school playground and announced with calculated precocity to anyone who cared to listen that I was, as he put it, "a homo." Unlike some of my congregated peers whose chorus of "what's a homo?" provoked a dizzying exchange of infantile misinformation, I was only too well aware of the term's meaning and, shocked that my queerness should not only be revealed but be so transparently legible that even a boorish bully might detect it, I slid away in fearful embarrassment. What proved most unsettling to me, however, was that my nascent homosexuality should have been evidenced in this playground spectacle of queer exposure not on the basis of same-sex desire but on the basis rather of passionate devotion to a woman.

Earlier that day, our schoolteacher had directed us to write and then read aloud to the class a composition titled "My Hero." Where most of my classmates wrote predictable tributes to normative role models of

the time like Neil Armstrong, Greg Chappell, Muhammad Ali, and even Jesus Christ, I penned an effusive homage to what I described in the essay as that "radiant star of stage and screen, Miss Julie Andrews." It was this profession of ardent admiration for a female film star that led directly to my schoolyard outing. As my accuser put it when explicating the deductive rationale behind his sexual detection, "Only a homo would love Julie Andrews!" Even at age ten, the paradoxical (il)logic of this formulation was so glaring as to all but slap me hard across the face—an action transposed from the metaphoric to the literal by my playground adversary who, not content to let "the homo" escape too readily or lightly, pursued me across the schoolyard and pushed me face-first into the asphalt. How could my declaration of desire for a female star—which in strictly definitional terms should have seemed, if anything, eminently heterosexual—be taken so assuredly as a marker of homosexuality? Why and how could my loving Julie Andrews provoke such an explosive manifestation of juvenile homophobia? The answers to these questions were already known, if only intuitively and, thus, only partially, to the ten-year-old me. Like many other elements of my childhood, my love for Julie Andrews formed part of what I was fast recognizing was an ever-expanding and ever-consolidating category of bad object-choices: a diverse array of cultural and social cathexes variously abjected, proscribed, or deemed otherwise inconsonant with dominant modes of sexual selfhood. Redefined as an indexical symptom of sexual dissonance, my devotion to Andrews suddenly became a catalytic signifier of shame, a palpable marker of my failure to achieve heteronormality and, thus, another attachment to cache away in the cavernous closet of protogay childhood.

That this scenario will sound instantly familiar to many is evidence of the extent to which a politics of shame is routinely mobilized—most potently, though by no means exclusively, in childhood—to stigmatize and thus discipline queer subjectivities. Much of the breathtaking success with which mainstream culture is able to install and mandate a heteronormative economy depends directly on its ability to foster a correlative economy of queer shame through which to disgrace and thus delegitimate all that falls outside the narrow purview of straight sexualities. Not that such processes of juridical stigmatization are necessarily successful. *Shameful* and *shameless* are, after all, but a suffix apart, and a good deal of the productivity of queer cultures—as of queer lives—resides precisely in the extraordinary capacity they obtain for not only clinging stubbornly and defiantly to the outlawed objects of their desire but also investing these objects with a near-inexhaustible source of vitalizing energy. The scene of my schoolyard shaming may have effected a public occlusion of my love for Julie Andrews, but it in no way quelled or attenuated that love. Indeed, transformed into a sign of my developing homosexuality, my attachment to Andrews became more than ever an integral component of my subjectivity and an indefatigable resource for survival in the face of what I perceived to be an unaccommodating social world.

Eve Kosofsky Sedgwick dubs these survivalist dynamics of queer culture "reparative" in the sense given the term by object-relations theory as an affirmative impulse to repair or make good the losses of subjective constitution. Unlike the competing paranoid positionality, which in object-relations theory is understood to fracture the world into colliding part-objects and is marked by "hatred, envy, and anxiety," the reparative dynamic is marked by love and seeks to reassemble or repair the subject's world into "something like a whole" that is "available both to be identified with and to offer one nourishment and comfort in turn."[2] For Sedgwick, this idea of a reparative impulse speaks powerfully to the inventive and obstinate ways in which queer subjects negotiate spaces of self-affirmation in the face of a hostile environment, or, as she evocatively puts it, the ways in which queer "selves and communities succeed in extracting sustenance from . . . a culture whose avowed desire has often been not to sustain them" (35). As a paradigmatic example of and governing trope for this reparative tradition of queer survivalism, Sedgwick offers, significantly for my purposes, the image of the protoqueer child or adolescent ardently (over)attached to a cultural text or object, passionately investing that text or object with almost talismanic properties to repair or make good a damaged *socius*. "Such a child," she writes, "is reading for important news about herself, [even] without knowing what form that news will take; with only the patchiest familiarity with its codes; without, even, more than hungrily hypothesizing to what questions this news may proffer an answer" (2–3).

This characterization of a reparatively positioned proto-queer reader resonates profoundly with my own fiercely loving attachments to Julie Andrews. Much of the energy of these attachments—certainly in childhood and, perhaps less urgently but no less decisively, in adulthood—springs directly from the reparative performances to which this particular star has been cast in the playhouse of my own imaginary. To wit: a cherished ritual from childhood. In the days when I was growing up, the days before VCRs and cable television, my Andrews fandom was of necessity organized less around her films than around her recordings. While I had of course seen her films, and these were vital, generative sites for my fan passions, the primary focus for those passions—where they were practiced, indulged, nurtured—was her vocal recordings. On long, listless afternoons, returned home from school, I would rush to the living room, position myself squarely in front of the family hi-fi and blissfully listen my way through my expansive collection of Julie Andrews LPs. My favorite, without doubt, was the soundtrack recording for *The Sound of Music*, which I would play and replay for hours. I can still recall the palpable sense of breathless anticipation when, unsheathed from its cover and reverently placed on the turntable, the disc would crackle to life. A whispering breath of wind, an echo of birdsong, a rapid swell of violins, and Julie's inimitable voice would break forth in fortissimo triumph, leaping through the speakers and enveloping the room with melodic abundance. To augment the sense of excitement, I would, while listening, gaze intently at the record cover with its celebrated image of Julie leaping in midflight like a preternatural oread, skirt billowing up with carefree delight, arms swinging open in joyous welcome, effortlessly holding aloft a guitar case and a traveling bag, twin symbols of musical expressivity and liberating escape. Projecting myself into the scene, I would twirl with Julie in imaginary freedom, riding the crest of her crystalline voice in rapturous transport from the suburban mundanities of family, school, and straightness. Invested with the attentive love and astonishing creativity of juvenile fandom, Andrews provided not just the promissory vision of a life different from and infinitely freer than the one I knew, but the phantasmatic means through which to achieve and sustain this process of transcendence. If I adored Julie Andrews as a child, it was because that adoration functioned as a process through which to resist and transfigure the oppressive banalities of the heteronormative everyday.

Though unaware of it at the time, my childhood mobilization of a female star as a vehicle of and for quotidian transcendence has a long and rich pedigree in queer cultures, especially male homosexual cultures. From the enthusiasms of the nineteenth-century dandies for operatic *prime donne* and the fervent gay cult followings in the mid-twentieth century of Hollywood stars such as Judy Garland and Bette Davis, to contemporary queer celebrations of pop goddesses like Madonna, Cher, Kylie Minogue, and Jennifer Lopez, female star adoration or, as it is more commonly known in queer contexts, "diva worship" has been a vital staple of gay male cultural production, where it has sustained a spectacularly diverse array of insistently queer pleasures.[3] While loath to generalize its heterogeneous functions and values, I submit that much of the enduring vitality of diva worship in gay male cultures resides in the commodious scope it affords for reparative cultural labor. Most critical discussions of gay diva worship posit in some fashion that gay men engage divas as imaginary figures of therapeutic escapism. "At the very heart of gay diva worship," opines Daniel Harris, is "the almost universal homosexual experience of ostracism and insecurity" and the desire to "elevate [one]self above [one's] antagonistic surroundings."[4] Wayne Koestenbaum similarly claims that "gay culture has perfected the art of mimicking a diva—of pretending, inside, to

be divine—to help the stigmatized self imagine it is received, believed, and adored."[5] Tuned to the chord of reparative amelioration, diva worship emerges here as a practice of resistant queer utopianism, or what might be more suggestively termed *queer sublimity*: the transcendence of a limiting heteronormative materiality and the sublime reconstruction, at least in fantasy, of a more capacious, kinder, queerer world.

Significantly, the category of the sublime has fundamental and enduring associations with queerness. One could even go so far as to suggest that queerness *is* the sublime within a different nomenclature and critical idiom. In its traditional Romantic form, the sublime nominates the delirious feeling of metaphysical ecstasy that is evoked by certain unlimited, immense, or incomprehensible phenomena: "a quality of overwhelming power which, in a flash of intensity could ravish the soul with a sudden transport of thought or feeling."[6] Conventionally associated with the awesome power of nature, the sublime is frequently cast in this classic tradition as a mode of religious transcendence, an apprehension of the divine through an encounter with that which exceeds the limits of everyday experience and cognition. In contemporary critical theory, the concept of the sublime has been inevitably revised and updated. Congruent with the increased secularization of the modern age, it has lost much of its overt religious significance, and the range of objects potentially evocative of sublimity has broadened to include not just natural but artistic, architectural, and even—following David E. Nye's influential claims—technological, electrical, and consumerist phenomena.[7] Yet the dynamic structure of the sublime as a radical discontinuity in sensory experience through which the quotidian is ruptured and transposed remains essentially the same. Jean François Lyotard, for example, defines the contemporary, or what he terms postmodern, sublime as "that which . . . puts forward the unpresentable in presentation itself" and, by so doing, enables "new presentations" of identity and thought.[8]

It is in this context that sublimity assumes its queer correspondences, for like queerness it is effectively a project of categorical rupture, a breaching of conventional subjective boundaries that encounters and imagines the obscene or excluded otherness of discursive normativity. Etymologically derived from the Latin *sub-limen*, meaning to move up or through a threshold, the sublime enacts a constitutive process of border crossing, a breaching and renegotiation of the definitional divisions that order hegemonic taxonomies, or what Michael Warner memorably terms "regimes of the normal."[9] Frequently allied to notions of sexual dissidence and transgression, even within its conventional form—Warren Stevenson, for example, argues that a discourse of psychic androgyny, "a transcendence of self and sex," is integral to the Romantic sublime—the border crossings of sublimity obtain immediate and wide-ranging queer import.[10]

Without doubt, it is the enormous potential of diva worship for the transgression and disorganization of various categorical boundaries that marks much of its transcendent sublime effect. The categorical binarism of sexual difference, of male/female, is the most obvious casualty of gay diva worship—grounded as it is in a sustained male identificatory cathexis of the feminine—but it is merely one of many. Other cherished cultural distinctions, including those of generation, race, ethnicity, class, and nationality, are equally disrupted in practices of diva worship, as are the even more vital ontological binarisms of self/other, subject/object, image/reality, and identification/desire. Indeed, the categorical crisscrossings of gay diva worship are so multiple and insistent as to destabilize that which they would seem ostensibly to articulate: the distinction homosexual/heterosexual. While many commentators assert that gay men's interest in divas is essentially platonic, functioning in the register of what Stephen Maddison terms "heterosocial bonding," the overwhelming intensity of affect and obsessive passion at the heart of diva worship problematize any simple attempt to void it entirely of heteroeroticism.[11] Diva worship may be a central forum for the production of identitarian discourses of gayness, but its constitutive predication upon a hetero-oriented desire introduces a fundamental excess into those discourses that undercuts any notion of an essential, stable male homosexuality. It is a process of radical discursive rupture that importantly if paradoxically invests gay diva worship with its wide-ranging scope for sublime transcendence and utopian queer reconstruction.

To anchor gay diva worship to the transcendent operations of sublimity in this way risks courting arguments, popularized in some recent gay commentaries, that it has become an increasingly outdated practice because it is invested in social and affective conditions that no longer prevail. In his summarily titled *The Rise and Fall of Gay Culture*, Daniel Harris claims that diva worship has declined in contemporary gay culture to the point of virtual obsolescence because the oppressive social and political environments of disenfranchisement and alienation that once made it a vital practice of utopian escapism for gay men have ceded to a new liberal era of acceptance and assimilation. It is a heroic narrative of Darwinian supersession that Harris pegs quite specifically to the historical watershed of Stonewall as symbolic index of gay liberation. "Before Stonewall," he writes, gay men turned to divas as "a therapeutic corrective" with which "to counteract their own sense of powerlessness as a vilified minority" and "triumph . . . over the daily indignities of being gay," but the increasing social tolerance of the post-Stonewall era and the development of more open, assertive gay male identities and cultures have attenuated the oppressive conditions that traditionally inspired and governed diva worship, making the latter ever more irrelevant to the needs of contemporary queer life.[12] "For gay men under the age of 40," he writes, the diva "has become the symbolic icon of an oppressed early stage in gay culture," "the politically repugnant fantasy of the self-loathing pansy whose dependence on the escapism of cinema [or opera, theater, music, etc.] must be ritually purged from his system."[13]

There can be little argument that the advent of gay liberation has had wide-ranging, radical impacts on queer identities and cultures, and I do not doubt that practices of diva worship have changed as a result, but it would be wrong, or at the very least unhelpful, to consign gay diva worship to the historical dustbin of pre-Stonewall obsolescence. Not only does it disregard the presence of diva worship in contemporary queer cultural productions—in which, contrary to Harris's sweeping claims, female stars continue to function as significant, highly visible foci of investment and are often openly styled and marketed as such[14]—it also enforces a reductive reading of gay cultures that ignores—indeed does not even allow for—historical persistences and continuities. Though hardly the first to do so, Harris works with an artificially rigid, homogenizing division of queer history into mutually exclusive, self-contained categories of pre- and post-Stonewall, in which the former is freighted with all the negative signs of queer experience—oppression, marginalization, shame: in short, the tropology of the closet—and the latter emerges as its sunny, rainbow flag-waving antithesis. Within such a representational schema, diva worship, in its traditional capacity as practice of transcendent queer utopianism, can be understood only as an outmoded anachronism with no place in, let alone relevance for, the liberated cultural economies of post-Stonewall gay pride. Again, I would not want to diminish the important social and political advances that have been realized in the wake of gay liberation, but just as pre-Stonewall homosexual cultures were hardly absolute wells of loneliness devoid of any sense of empowerment, self-worth, and joy, contemporary post-Stonewall gay cultures are certainly not quit of those painful experiences of exclusion and oppression that continue to be structural features of queer selfhood in a hetero-normative world.[15] Further, as I hope my discussion will by this stage at least have signaled, gay diva worship may take much of its initial affective drive from the emotional vicissitudes of queer pathos, but its operative value, that which assures and sustains its continued vitality as a productive practice of queer cultural life, is precisely the transcendence of those oppressive deformations, the social exclusions and impossibilities, that occasion queer pathos in the first place. It is in essence an exercise in queer empowerment, a restorative amendment in which the aberrant excesses and life-affirming energies of divadom are harnessed to variable projects of queer authorization and becoming: something that remains pressingly relevant, even indispensable.[16]

The transcendent dynamics evoked by what I am calling the queer sublimity of diva reception form a standard, if variably articulated, element of many textual representations of gay diva worship. A particularly celebrated example, and one that offers a crystalline illustration of the sorts of issues outlined here, is the "Mamma morta" sequence—or what Roy Grundmann and Peter Sacks dub the "infamous opera scene"—in Jonathan Demme's earnest 1993 social message film, *Philadelphia* (US).[17] A hybrid deathbed melodrama cum social realist film cum courtroom

drama, *Philadelphia* is widely considered a historical landmark as the first mainstream Hollywood film to deal centrally and openly with the AIDS crisis. Andy Beckett (Tom Hanks) is a gay PWA who has been fired from his position at a high-profile Philadelphia law firm after his HIV status is discovered. Facing discrimination at every turn, Andy decides to file a lawsuit for unfair dismissal against his former employers and enlists the professional help of a straight attorney, Joe Miller (Denzel Washington). True to his name, Joe functions in *Philadelphia* as the textual embodiment of mainstream normativity, the everyman through which the film articulates and peddles its liberal message of tolerance. Indeed more than one critic has claimed that, despite its ostensible focus on the plight of gay Andy, *Philadelphia* is effectively the story of straight Joe, who is at once the agent of narrative action and the lodestone of audience identification. Initially reluctant to take Andy on as a client, Joe is progressively forced in the film to confront and reassess his own prejudiced views of both gay men and PWAs, thus as Dennis Allen notes, "playing out, on the level of the individual, the larger abstract narrative of social acceptance" that is foundational to the film's generic and ideological profile.[18]

Situated halfway through the film's 120-minute running time and thus literally at its heart, the "Mamma morta" sequence is vital to *Philadelphia*'s diegetic and rhetorical economies. Joe is in Andy's apartment to finish details before the start of court proceedings the following day. Having just spent the evening with Andy and his partner at "a gay party," Joe is evidently unsettled and, in an effort to regain some measure of experiential equilibrium, is keen to get back to the familiar stability of work. Sitting across the table from Andy, he repeatedly attempts to focus attention on the pending court case but is consistently foiled as Andy steers the conversation into ever more abstract, metaphysical directions before finally launching into an ecstatic reverie inspired by Maria Callas's performance of "La mamma morta," an aria from Umberto Giordano's *Andrea Chénier*, which is playing in the background as diegetic music through the apartment's stereo system. Rising from his chair, Andy turns up the volume and, to Joe's obvious consternation, becomes transported by the music, surrendering himself entirely to the rapturous lure of Callas's voice, waltzing across the floor in a burnished red glow, tears streaming down his face.

In his review of the film, Andrew Sullivan calls *Philadelphia* "a work of translation" because its function is, as he sees it, to translate between divergent cultural registers: most notably, between homosexual and heterosexual as the film strives to reframe and interpret gay experiences and dynamics for the straight audiences that are its intended addressees.[19] This is why *Philadelphia* is so "unsettling," he suggests, and why it seems to fail on so many critical fronts because it must speak with translation's in-between voice. Certainly the "Mamma morta" sequence enshrines an obvious logic of translation: quite literally, as Andy interprets the Italian lyrics of the Callas aria into English, but also more abstractly, as he seeks to paraphrase and explain to Joe both his operatic and, by metonymic index, his sexual desires. In fact, the scene assumes something of a pedagogic structure with Andy an impassioned if histrionic teacher to Joe's curious if reluctant pupil. It is a structure that has raised the ire of several commentators. John Simon of the *National Review*, for example, lambastes the scene as "tasteless, patronizing and offensive" because it implies that "homosexuals . . . have something wonderful to impart to the rest of us ignorant slobs."[20] At the other end of the spectrum, gay critics Roy Grundmann and Peter Sacks attack the scene for what they see as its "misappropriation of gay culture" in the service of an "ethnographic perspective" that objectifies Andy as a sort of gay "noble savage" displayed for the instruction or simple entertainment of a straight spectatorship.[21] More recently, Charles I. Nero mounts a revealing critique of what he terms the trope of "operatic tutelage" in *Philadelphia*, as well as a number of other films of the mid-nineties, for its investment in a sexist and racist structure of Eurocentric male homosociality.[22] As he reads it, Andy's "gift" of opera to Joe functions ostensibly as a symbolic contract—a male traffic in opera divas—whereby a culturally superior white man uses the recorded voice of the female soprano to enlighten and forge friendship with a socially subordinate man of color.

I would not want to discount the legitimacy and insight of these critiques, but there is another—and to my mind more interesting—process of translation at work in the scene than the nominally liberal,

educative, homosocial one between Andy and Joe, and that is the translation that takes place between Andy and the diva. Pace a reading like Nero's, for example, which apprehends the voice of the diva as a subsidiary vehicle of exchange within the primary medium of male bonding, I would suggest that Andy's relationship to the diva is a crucial medium of exchange in its own right. In many ways, the latter relationship is the focus of the sequence—certainly its primary source of semiotic power—and it is one that quickly moves to marginalize if not displace all other relational networks. Entering deeper into his reverie, Andy increasingly diminishes his external engagement with Joe and his surroundings—turning away, closing his eyes—while correspondingly expanding and intensifying his engagement with the vocal presence of the diva. It is a movement that is signaled quite openly at the level of speech by a marked grammatical transition from an initial structure of standard interpersonal dialogue and second-person narration ("This is Maddalena. Do you hear the heartache in her voice? . . . Can you feel it, Joe?") to a much more fluid syntax where Andy assumes and speaks in the first-person subjective of, variously, Callas, the diegetic subject of the aria, Maddalena, and even Maddalena's dead mother: a syntactic slide of mobile identifications that culminates in a final audacious embodiment of divinity itself. "I am divine, I am oblivion," Andy cries through the ventriloquial agency of the diva's voice before finally reaching for and, in frenetic mime, nailing the piercing high note that marks both the aria's and the sequence's emotional crescendo. Descending from the climax, his body quivering in metaphoric glissando, Andy weeps the closing doublet of the aria, "I am love, I am love," a deep sob swallowing the last word, so that all that comes out is an open-ended "I am . . ." A more forceful articulation of the sublime effects of gay diva worship could scarcely be imagined. His ferociously loving engagement with the diva produces for Andy not just an overwhelming transport of feeling, but also a delirious transcendence of embodied identity itself. Moving blithely across the multiple positions of the diva's fluid performativity, Andy enacts what Dennis Allen terms an "osmosis of the self," a rupturing of the boundaries that frame and constitute identity and a radical dispersal of the self across the differential field of alterity.[23]

It is a movement of structural rupture and dissolution that is equally and openly replicated in the sequence at the level of textual form, with the carefully composed two-shots, measured continuity editing, and general classical realism that mark the opening scenes of the sequence ceding to a high expressionist aesthetic of canted angles, colored gels, and chiaroscuro lighting. The overall effect is an intensely melodramatic articulation of the transcendent sublimity of diva worship where the passionate encounter between the diva and her gay male devotee is signaled as and through a rapturous breakdown of conventional systems of textuality, meaning, and representation. As this aesthetic excess might indicate, the operations of melodrama are crucial to the sequence's staging of the disorganizational impulses of queer diva worship. Indeed, the sequence is so heavily invested in a melodramatic formal economy—featuring many of its generic elements, from overwrought emotionalism and histrionic mise-en-scène to a pathos-filled scenario focused on moral injustice and suffering—that it effectively functions as what Lea Jacobs terms a "situation," a high moment of spectacular arrest that serves to crystallize the melodramatic text's foundational emotional dilemmas.[24] Literalized in the Delsartean tableaux of classical stage melodramas, the convention of the situation—which Jacobs posits as a core element of the mode—continues in film melodrama as a localized instance of affective crescendo where action is arrested and the protagonists' and narrative's desires are expressed in essential form. Though Jacobs doesn't make the claim, the situation might be taken to enshrine the psychoanalytic logic of "acting out" that has been claimed by a long line of critics as foundational to the melodramatic imagination. As Peter Brooks writes in a seminal argument: "Melodrama handles its feelings and ideas virtually as plastic identities, visual and tactile models held out for all to see and to handle. Emotions are given a full acting-out, a full representation before our eyes. We come to expect and to await the moment at which characters will name the wellsprings of their being. . . . They proffer to one another, and to us, a clear figuration of their souls, they name without embarrassment eternal verities."[25] That this acting out should occur in *Philadelphia* through the excessive affect of an operatic aria doubles its impact and significance.

In a recent meditation on the close affinities between melodrama and opera, Brooks argues for the operatic aria as the correspondent of the melodramatic situation—or in his broadly analogous term, "set piece"—for both operate through a shared dynamic of spectacular hystericization.[26] Like the hysteric who articulates repressed desire through the body, melodrama and opera, especially in the privileged moments of situation and aria, speak their "unspeakable" meanings through a weighted somaticism. Where the hysterical somaticization of melodrama has traditionally been focused on the physical body—"distorting it and arresting it in postures and gestures that speak symbolically of powerful affects" (122)—opera extends its hysterical ambit to the realm of vocality: "The hystericized voice of the operatic aria . . . become[s], in the manner of the melodramatic body, symptomatic of an extreme situation, an emotional impasse . . . [and] works it through in an internal dialogue of passion and measure, that of song" (126). With its combined accent on the visual spectacle of Hanks's bravura performance, which works through a veritable canonical repertoire of hysterical gestures—what might be described through Didi Huberman's striking turn-of-phrase as "the postures of delirium": "attacks, cries, *attitudes passionelles*, crucifixion, ecstasy"[27]—and the aural spectacle of Callas's histrionic bel canto vocals, *Philadelphia* conjoins both modes of hysterical spectacularization—body and voice—to its melodramatic economy of acting out. The result is a scenarization that is almost overwhelming in its hysterical intensity: the body and the voice are both gripped by affective representation, yoked inexorably to the demands of psychic and cultural conversion to the point where they cease to perform their traditional semiotic functions, becoming instead overdetermined texts of densely symbolic meanings.

Typically, of course, the hystericized body of melodrama and the hystericized voice of opera are female. The profane collocation in *Philadelphia* of a male body and a female voice as coupled subjects of hysterical acting out complicates these normative gendered codings, even as it depends on them to produce its perverse effects, thereby intensifying the text's capacity for both disruptive hystericization and sublimity. Much of the fascination of the sequence—its lure of uncanny, dare we say queer, captivation—stems precisely from its willful staging of transgendered, transsexual mutability: its multiple movements across various representational registers traditionally understood as gender and sexual exclusive. These movements are arguably central to hysteria as a condition, which, as Claire Kahane details, has been profitably understood in feminist psychoanalytic theories as a resistant questioning of sexual difference and identity: "Am I a man? Am I a woman? How is sexual identity assumed? How represented?"[28] They are also arguably central to the functions of diva worship, as evidenced by the constitutive indexing of hysteria, qua disruptive sexual lability, in discourses of gay diva fandom. The gay diva devotee (the opera queen or any of his multiple "sisters"—the show queen, Hollywood queen, disco queen) is routinely envisioned as male hysteric: excessive, irrational, feminized. While the reading formations of gay diva worship habitually focus on moments and figures of hysterical eruption: the "mad scenes" of opera; the "eleven o'clock" showstoppers of musical theater; the scenery-chewing *grande damerie* of the woman's film; the vocal gymnastics of the dance-floor diva. These moments of hysterical excess, of extreme passions and outrageousness, so integral to cultural definitions—and receptions, good and bad—of the diva, constitute powerful points of transcendence where the constraints of sexual, social, and textual normativity are refused and space is opened, however partially, for alternative visions and structures of meaning.[29]

This capacity for transcendent reimagining fuels and frames the hysterical energies of diva worship in *Philadelphia*, in which the inflated extravagance of Callas's aria furnishes Andy with a means through which to exceed the juridical binds of normative disciplinarity and stage a resistant performance of queer self-expression. Forbidden by the homophobic discourses of mainstream culture and cinematic textuality to speak his queer desire directly, or at the very least forbidden by those discourses to give adequate value to his desire, Andy "acts out" through the hysterical authority of the diva. It is not a displacement or substitution of his queer desire. As Brooks reminds us, acting out, for Freud, constitutes a reproduction, and not just an imitation, of affect, a "reproduction that abolishes the distance between mental ideation and physical action."[30] Andy's delirious performance

of diva-oriented desire, like performance of gay diva worship more generally, thus signals not some second-order index of queerness but, to rephrase an earlier quote from Brooks, its "full acting-out, [its] full representation before our eyes."

The imaging of gay diva worship as excessive, disruptive sublimity constructed in *Philadelphia* clearly admits competing evaluations. In his essay "Homosexuality and Narrative," Dennis Allen is highly critical of the "Mamma morta" sequence for instating what he claims is a homophobic representation of homosexuality as "an indeterminate locus of shifting identifications."[31] Drawing from Lee Edelman's concept of "homographesis," which he defines as "the heterosexual fantasy of the inevitable visibility of homosexuality," Allen contends that the sequence works entirely to ensure heterosexual privilege "by projecting unstable, incoherent or multiple identity onto the homosexual so that the heterosexual can stand, in contrast, as internally coherent" (625). There can be little argument that this sort of depreciatory counterpoint is an operative element in the "Mamma morta" sequence and its visualization of homosexual difference through the sublime spectacle of diva worship. Indeed it is revealing, and more than a little ironic, that the litany of homophobic myths recited by Joe at the start of the sequence as the popularly held representational face of "homosexuality"—placed by Denzel Washington's emphatic performance in demonstrative scare quotes lest these misinformed views be somehow confused with the enlightened liberalism of the film's own enunciative regime—provides the very tropological script enacted in the ensuing floorshow where, wandering around like a demented oracle in the grips of spiritual possession, Andy furnishes visible and quite literal confirmation that "queers are funny, queers are weird" and, in acoustic terms at least, "queers dress up like their mothers." As irascible playwright and AIDS activist Larry Kramer quips in a polemic summarily titled "Why I Hate *Philadelphia*," "even I'd be afraid of someone who—out of the blue—behaved like this."[32]

Fear is, however, a standard—some would even claim definitionally requisite—response to sublimity, in which the rupture of categorical divisions and the consequent encounter with otherness that mark the sublime experience fill the observer with an awe and wonder so extreme as to be potentially terrifying. It is a response that importantly need not be disabling; it may in fact prove empowering, even liberatory. As the sensorial registration of transfixing awe, the "terror of ecstasy," as Burke famously described the emotional impact of sublimity, is arguably a prime affective mechanism through which the sublime provokes its transcendent (re)visions. To admit therefore that the awful sublimity of diva worship may be explicitly yoked in *Philadelphia* to a project of visibilizing homosexual difference as abject and terrifying does not cancel nor deplete the broad range of competing significances to which this formation, once articulated, gives rise. Following an earlier cue, the inscription of homosexuality in the field of the visible is always and inevitably the site of what Lee Edelman claims is "a double operation: one serving the ideological purposes of a conservative social order intent on codifying identities in its labor of disciplinary inscription, and the other resistant to that categorization, intent on *de*scribing the identities that order has so oppressively *in*scribed."[33]

Certainly the fearsome spectacle of diva worship unfurled in *Philadelphia* functions on many levels to upset and complicate the sort of banal disciplinary operations of sexual classification to which many critics seem driven—obsessively and perhaps symptomatically—to reduce it. Far from enacting an untroubled inscription of normalizing sexual binarisms, the "Mamma morta" sequence arguably stages the scene for their delirious breakdown. Consider, for instance, the simple—or, as it happens, not so simple—question of erotic relationality in Andy's literally obscene performance. That the performance obtains a profoundly erotic gravitas is undoubtable. The interdependent registers of dramaturgy, narrative thematics, and cinematographic style conspire to give it the decided look and feel of a slightly arty sex scene, complete with appropriately scarlet camera gels, tumescent accelerative montage, and heaving postcoital breathlessness. At the same time, the increasingly frozen gawp of wide-eyed shock on Joe's face in the reaction shots leaves little doubt that he—and we—are witnessing an act of monumental gross indecency. But just what precise form that indecency takes and how it can be read and made sense of is another matter altogether. Neither evidently nor coherently heterosexual or homosexual; solipsistic or intersubjective;

unitary, dyadic, or triangular: the erotic relations in the sequence are simply so variable and shifting and contain so many permutations between and across the multiple players and positions in the scene as to defy basic interpretability let alone classificatory regulation. Perhaps, then, the truly terrifying aspect of the sublime spectacle of gay diva worship as envisioned in *Philadelphia*, what sends the otherwise stouthearted Joe running anxiously from the apartment, is not its display of a homosexuality demonized as the other of a stable heterosexual norm but its display rather of a (homo)sexuality run amok, one that refuses to remain within the categorical divisions that regulate the scripts and legibilities of hegemonic sexuality and that thus problematizes the possibility of any stable term of erotic reference: hetero or homo.[34]

As suggested, it is this structural predilection to categorical transgression and rupture, portrayed so evocatively in *Philadelphia*, that furnishes gay subcultural practices of diva reception with much of their dazzling capacity for sublime effect. The erotic and discursive indeterminacies at the heart of diva worship offer a rich and ready-made framework for the transcendence of heteronormative boundaries and the cathexis of those conditions of alterity that Lyotard claims as the signs of true sublimity: "heterogeneity, . . . optimal dissensus and radical openness."[35] It would be wrong, however, to assume this emphasis on rupture and dissolution as the ultimate logic of gay diva worship or of the affective economies of queer sublimity within which it operates. A central condition of the sublime—and I would contend that this holds especially true of the sublime dynamics operative in gay diva worship—is that it moves simultaneously and paradoxically toward both subjective fracture *and* subjective restoration. In his canonical philosophical treatise on the subject, Immanuel Kant describes the sublime experience as a movement through self-erasing awe to a heightened awareness of subjective reason. This developmental reading of the sublime is explicated further by Thomas Weiskel, who posits a tripartite process of sublimity from an initial stage of habitual complacency through an intermediate stage of momentary rupture and subjective indeterminacy to a final "reactive" stage of rebalance and transcendent bliss.[36] While I am uncomfortable with its rather static temporal linearity—surely any sublimity worth its rapturous salt holds stages two and three, inde-terminacy and masterful transcendence, in constant, irresolvable tension—this account nevertheless high-lights the central movement of the sublime toward both a disintegration and a reintegration of self, or to put it another way, toward both subjective incoher-ency and (transformed) subjective meaning.

Gay diva worship's blatant disorganization, if not dissolution, of orthodox subjective boundaries undoubtedly instates a rapturous jouissance in which the coherency of self is shattered, but through that process it also enables the production of new modes of subjectivity that are receptive of queer possibilities precisely because of their antinormative incoherency. Queerness is after all a supreme paradigm of identifi-catory transformation, an opening out from the limit-ing scripts of subjective normativity to other forms of sexual and social selfhood. José Muñoz has sugges-tively deployed the term *disidentification* to describe the "nonlinear and nonnormative modes of identifi-cation with which queers predicate their self-fashion-ing."[37] He argues that, unlike majoritarian subjects who access with relative ease dominant fictions of coher-ent, masterful identity, queers and other minoritarian subjects must "activate their own senses of self" by engaging "multiple and sometimes conflicting sites of identification" and "interfac[ing] with different subcul-tural fields" (5). It is a complex and fraught process of (dis)identificatory production that ensures queer identity is always in a condition of constant becoming and hybridized difference, always "a point of depar-ture, a process, a building" (200). Gay diva worship, I submit, is a vital cultural forum for the enactment of just such processes of queer becoming.[38] Through the perverse practices, the aberrant cathexes and desires, of diva worship, gay cultures have fashioned a unique and insistently affirmative cultural space within which to produce and experience shifting and multiple forms of queer subjecthood.[39]

To return one last time to *Philadelphia*, if, as I have detailed, Andy's rapturous engagement of the diva stages a hysterical breakdown of normative discourses of identity, it equally and simultaneously stages a restorative production of renewed subjective mean-ing and queer empowerment. His passionate encoun-ter with Callas propels Andy to a delirious transport that breaches the categorical borders—male/female,

hetero/homo, self/other, identification/desire—that bound and give orthodox form to subjectivity and its cultural locations, provoking him, quite literally, to fall apart; but at the same time, and as part of the same process, it clears the way for a virtuoso performance of subjective authorization. It is an ambivalent process of transcendent rupture and counterassertive renewal that can be neatly traced through the film's allegorical correspondence of diva worship to something about which I have till now kept strategically silent but that is so crucial as to be all-pervasive: a thematics of death. *Philadelphia* is after all a deathbed melodrama, and by the point of the "Mamma morta" scene, Andy is evidently in the terminal stages of AIDS, a fact given visual underscoring through the simulated cadaver-ousness of Hanks's cosmeticized face and the intrave-nous drip that hangs off him throughout the sequence like a ghostly paramour in a *danse macabre*. Should these visual cues go unheeded, the script spells it out, with Andy commenting to Joe in solemn resignation at the outset of the sequence, "There's a possibility I won't be around to see the end of this trial." Sig-nificantly, it is this recognition of impending death that initiates Andy's diva-fueled delirium: no sooner does he make the comment than the background music suddenly, and conveniently, amplifies before segueing into Callas's, and Andy's, big number. It hardly needs mention that the choice of aria here is richly pointed. As made plain by its title, "La mamma morta" ("The Dead Mother") is a song all about death. In its original context in *Andrea Chénier*, Umberto Giordano's opera about a pair of doomed aristocratic lovers during the French Revolution's Reign of Terror, the aria is sung as a plea for clemency by the female protagonist, Maddalena. In a bid to save the life of Andrea, her imprisoned lover, Maddalena entreats the sympathies of Gérard, the revolutionary who had Andrea jailed on trumped-up charges of treason because he secretly desires Maddalena, by narrating her tragic tale of bereavement. To the rich strains of Giordano's high romantic melody, she relates how her mother was killed while protecting her from mobs that burned her family home to the ground, and how afterward her life, and that of those she loved, plunged into an inexorable downward spiral. Though the finer points of the opera's admittedly circuitous narrative don't quite make the translation to screen in *Philadelphia*, the film is careful to explicate the fundamental scenario of death and loss, with Andy setting the scene through general synopsis and select quotations from the libretto. "Look, the place that cradled me is burning," he sings in echo of Maddalena's lament. That the voice expressing this tale of tragic demise is none other than that of Maria Callas augments the significances. Not only is Callas "the operatic diva most closely (if only tacitly) associated with gay fandom," as Wayne Koestenbaum notes, but her troubled life and premature death have inexorably anchored her star image to a semiotics of fatality, securing her legend as what Sam Abel terms "the goddess of opera's gay cult of death."[40] As such, Andy's identificatory assumption of Callas and the multiple positionalities signaled through her performance of "La mamma morta" assimilates him, unavoidably and emphatically, to a discourse of death.

On one level, the thematic parallels between Andy and death serve a fairly straightforward process of narrative foreshadowing, prefiguring a fatal closure that the film has already set up and that the genre of the deathbed melodrama has effectively prescribed. However, in the immediate context of the sequence and its articulation of queer desire through the sublime spectacle of diva worship, they assume a slightly more symbolic cast. As the extinction of human life, the end of known existence, death is a—if not *the*—primordial categorical limit, that which marks the bounds of lived identity and the interface with absolute alterity. This is why death evokes such enduring fascination for most, and enduring fear for many. It is also why death serves as such a powerful source of sublimity. As Jahan Ramazani notes, although they "often refer to it by other names . . . : castration, physical destruction, semiotic collapse, defeat by a precursor, and annihilation of the ego," theories of the sublime are traditionally obsessed with death and "from the eighteenth century on, they increasingly pair the sublime with death, as death seems to become ever more solitary, final, and secular."[41] Taking a cue from Burke, who famously claimed the sublime to be occasioned by "ideas of pain, and above all death," Ramazani posits death as the supreme inspirator of sublimity, arguing that the sublime is, at heart, "a staged confrontation with death" (110). Certainly much of the sublime energy at play in the "Mamma morta" sequence may be seen

to spring directly from its presentation of an encounter with death. Drawn to confront mortality face on, both at the narrative level of his lived situation and the phantasmatic level of his diva identification, Andy cathects the most radical form of dissolution imaginable, the final extinction of selfhood, and experiences the full force of emotional intensity thus engendered. Through the doubled conduit of Callas/Maddalena, he not only imagines but acts out his own annihilation: "I am oblivion," "I bring sorrow to those that love me," he cries in imitation of the diva's song. Importantly, however, neither the diva's song nor Andy's reiterative performance of it stops here. Circling dazedly around the floor, eyes closed in ecstatic meditation on some imagined internal focus, Andy underlines through his fractured commentary an all-important shift in the tenor and import of the aria. "In come the strings and it changes everything," he murmurs, "The music fills with a hope." It is a shift equally underlined through formal mise-en-scène, with the lighting of the scene dropping suddenly into dramatic chiaroscuro and the color tone balance turning noticeably red. What follows is an extended passage by Andy of direct citation from the aria that is worth quoting here at length:

> It was during this sorrow that love came to me,
> A voice filled with harmony,
> It said, "Live still, I am life,
> Heaven is in your eyes.
> Is everything around you just the blood and the mud?
> I am divine, I am oblivion.
> I am the god that comes down from the heavens,
> And makes of the earth a heaven.
> I am love, I am love!"

In a fascinating study on the intersections between opera and shifting cultural discourses of death, Linda and Michael Hutcheon argue for opera as the closest modern equivalent to the medieval *contemplatio mortis*, a form of *ars moriendi*, or "the art of dying," that "dramatized and 'performed' imaginatively the experience of dying."[42] As they detail, the principal aim of the *contemplatio mortis* was to give meaning and positive value to the concept and experience of death through a process of meditation and narrativization that enabled the subject to prepare, spiritually and emotionally, for death, but also, through the fact of "awakening" from the contemplation and returning to worldly activity, "to appreciate life more fully by contrast" (25). In a culture such as ours that obsessively denies death and fosters a generalized social phantasm of technomedical-driven immortality, the idea of a positive valorization of death can seem flatly counterintuitive, but forms of *contemplatio mortis* continue, it is suggested, in a range of arts, most notably in opera, where death is a veritable thematic stock in trade and where the distinctive combination of emotive music and drama with highly stylized presentation offers the perfect environment for the sort of ritualized "working through" of death described via the practice of *contemplatio mortis*.

Whether or not this reading constitutes a legitimate account of opera as a generalized cultural practice I cannot say, but it certainly provides a resonant take on "La mamma morta" and Andy's intense reception of it. His staged confrontation with death via the heightened affective economy of a Callas aria seems quite openly to offer Andy a potent form of "ritual bereavement" and "working through," where he "imaginatively experienc[es] the emotions associated with dying" in order to "find not only consolation but also meaning in death and, indeed, in life" (185). The latter point is vital and helps link this reading to the overarching argument about sublimity and the move toward transcendent meaning and renewed subjective value. The central effect of the *contemplatio mortis*, as of the broader formations of sublimity it arguably indexes, is not a melancholic embrace of self-annihilation, a total triumph of the death drive, but rather a positive processing of death, a direct engagement and transcendence of it as categorical limit, that, as paradoxical as it may seem, affirms and gives renewed value to life through its emotive and experiential structure of momentary death and reawakening, of dissolution and resolution, self-shattering and transcendent bliss. Like Callas/Maddalena—indeed, *as* Callas/Maddalena—Andy passes through the terrifying boundary of death and accedes to an enlarged vision and an ecstatic counterassertion of life, a reparative revisioning that "makes of [his] earth a heaven" imbued with love.

To conclude in this way is not to give death the final word, as it were, on gay diva worship, and it certainly is not to continue the deformational stereotype of the opera queen—or queer diva fan, more generally—as tragi-pathetic figure of moribund self-loathing. There is nothing remotely pathetic or tragic in Andy's sublime adoration of Callas; indeed, it is the very means through which he transcends the tragic and reinvests his life with value. Through the queer sublimity of diva devotion, Andy is able to confront and move beyond the ultimate abjection of death to a triumphal affirmation of empowered and expanded selfhood. As such the "Mamma morta" sequence signals a sort of extreme narrativization of the logic of reparative survivalism that I have suggested subtends and works through formations of diva worship in gay male cultures. In a passage that, with happy pertinence to *Philadelphia*, comments on the gay reception of Maria Callas but that as readily speaks to the practice of gay diva worship at large, Wayne Koestenbaum writes: "Callas was a refuge, where a forbidden sexuality, a forbidden alienation from masculinity, could spread its wings. Listening to Callas, I acquire spaciousness. If consciousness, as determined by gender and sexuality, has certain limits, a voice like Callas's has the power to turn the mind's closed room into an immensity: she bestows the illusion that the view continues endlessly on the other side of the mirror, and that wherever you expected to find limits, instead you find continuations."[43]

In many respects, it makes perfect sense that gay male cultures should have mobilized and privileged the figure of the diva for such processes of sublime queer transcendence and expanded self-creation. Born out of nineteenth-century traditions of operatic spectacle and melodramatic theatricality and bred throughout the twentieth century in the auratic grandiloquence of mediatized glamour, the diva is nothing if not a consummate figure of self-authorization, a magisterial image of triumphant identificatory production. Blazing her way across the cultural landscape in defiant disregard of orthodox conventions of social discipline and patriarchal injunctions against feminine potency, the diva offers a lesson to all who care to attend in the resistant production of aberrant subjectivity. Put simply, the diva is a figure that is "fabulous" in both senses of the term, as "marvelous and astonishing" but also "fable-like, fictitious, and invented" and, in her fabulousness, the diva extends to her devotees untold possibilities for the production of equally fabulous modes of empowered selfhood. Therein lies perhaps the primary source of the diva's enduring appeal for queer cultures and her inexhaustible productivity as a sublime site of reparative gay labor.

Notes

1. Jeffrey Escoffier, *American Homo: Community and Perversity* (Berkeley: University of California Press, 1998), 1.

2. Eve Kosofsky Sedgwick, "Paranoid Reading and Reparative Reading; or, You're So Paranoid, You Probably Think This Introduction Is about You," in *Novel Gazing: Queer Readings in Fiction*, ed. Eve Kosofsky Sedgwick (Durham, NC: Duke University Press, 1997), 8.

3. Originally coined in the nineteenth century as an aggrandizing honorific for principal operatic sopranos, the term *diva*, from the Latin for goddess, has been consistently broadened in use and meaning in gay cultures to refer to an expansive range of female performers across genres and strata of popular culture whose spectacular, strong personae and performative extravagance inspire various forms of queer popularization and devotion.

4. Daniel Harris, *The Rise and Fall of Gay Culture* (New York: Hyperion, 1997), 10.

5. Wayne Koestenbaum, *The Queen's Throat: Opera, Homosexuality, and the Mystery of Desire* (New York: Poseidon, 1993), 133.

6. D. B. Morris, *The Religious Sublime: Christian Poetry and Critical Tradition* (Lexington: University of Kentucky Press, 1972), 1.

7. David E. Nye, *American Technological Sublime* (Cambridge, MA: MIT Press, 1994).

8. Jean-François Lyotard, *Lessons on the Analytic of the Sublime: Kant's Critique of Judgment, Sections 23–29*, trans. Elizabeth Rottenberg (Stanford, CA: Stanford University Press, 1994).

9. Michael Warner, "Introduction," in *Fear of a Queer Planet: Queer Politics and Social Theory*, ed. Michael Warner (Minneapolis: University of Minnesota Press, 1993), xxvi.

10. Warren Stevenson, *Romanticism and the Androgynous Sublime* (Cranbury, NJ: Associated University Presses, 1996), 10.

11. Stephen Maddison, *Fags, Hags, and Queer Sisters: Gender Dissent and Heterosocial Bonds in Gay Culture* (New York: St. Martin's, 2000).

12. Harris, *The Rise and Fall of Gay Culture*, 13. It is an argument that has been made by others. In a recent op-ed piece, online journalist Damien Cave asserts, "with the new millennium upon us, diva worship is dying in the gay community. With extended life spans for HIV sufferers becoming reality, a booming economy and the increasing ease of assimilation, divas are no longer needed as a unifying force against oppression and discrimination in the gay community" ("The Descent of the Divas," *Salon.com*, 10 January 2000, salon.com/people/feature/2000/01/10/divas).

13. Harris, *The Rise and Fall of Gay Culture*, 22.

14. Indeed, the effective pith of Harris's argument seems less that contemporary gay cultures have abandoned diva worship than that they don't worship the same divas as earlier generations. "Many homosexuals under the age of 30 have never even seen a film starring Joan Crawford," he laments, "let alone relished the magnificent biographical ironies of *A Star Is Born* or seen Bette Davis's hair fall out in *Mrs. Skeffington* or Rita Hayworth dance in *Gilda*" (32). Possibly true, but many of them will have thrilled to Madonna, Jennifer Lopez, and Janet Jackson in concert; danced with wild abandon at an all-night rave to Kylie Minogue, Christina Aguilera, and Gwen Stefani; wept to the heartfelt ballads of Tori Amos and Celine Dion; delighted at the resistant femininities of Christina Ricci, Margaret Cho, *Absolutely Fabulous* (1992–96, 2001, 2003), and *Sex and the City* (1998–2004); or reveled in any of the other queer cult figures and texts that form the basis for contemporary practices of diva worship among many young gay and queer men. Harris just needs to get out more.

15. In a typically insightful essay, David Halperin suggests that, for all its benefits and gains, gay liberation has equally produced its own constraints, one of the more problematic being what he terms the refusal of "the life of queer affect and feeling." He writes: "The problem, it turns out, is that instead of ending up in triumphant possession of a gay pride and freedom we can wholeheartedly call our own, we have constructed a gay identity that actively represses both the pathos and the pleasure of those residual queer affects that we prefer to think we have liberated ourselves from and that we claim have simply vanished from our consciousness" (David Halperin, "Homosexuality's Closet," *Michigan Quarterly Review* 41 [2002]: 24). See also Heather Love, "Spoiled Identity: Stephen Gordon's Loneliness and the Difficulties of Queer History," *GLQ* 7 (2001): 487–519.

16. A further argument might be made that the unapologetic queerness of diva worship—its relentless perversity, about which I have more to say later—offers a thrilling alternative, if not corrective, to the antiseptic, normalizing neoliberalism of assimilationist gay culture, giving it renewed significance and appeal.

17. Roy Grundmann and Peter Sacks, "*Philadelphia*," *Cineaste*, Summer 1993, 53.

18. Dennis W. Allen, "Homosexuality and Narrative," *Modern Fiction Studies* 41 (1995): 623.

19. Andrew Sullivan, "Wouldn't Normally Do," *New Republic*, 21 February 1994, 42.

20. John Simon, "*Philadelphia*," *National Review*, 7 February 1994, 68.

21. Grundmann and Sacks, "*Philadelphia*," 53.

22. Charles I. Nero, "Diva Traffic and Male Bonding in Film: Teaching Opera, Learning Gender, Race, and Nation," *Camera Obscura*, no. 56 (2004): 48.

23. Allen, "Homosexuality and Narrative," 625.

24. Lea Jacobs, "The Woman's Picture and the Poetics of Melodrama," *Camera Obscura*, no. 31 (1993): 121–47.

25. Peter Brooks, *The Melodramatic Imagination: Balzac, Henry James, Melodrama, and the Mode of Excess* (New Haven, CT: Yale University Press, 1976, rev. ed. 1995), 41.

26. Peter Brooks, "Body and Voice in Melodrama and Opera," in *Siren Songs: Representations of Gender and Sexuality in Opera*, ed. Mary Ann Smart (Princeton, NJ: Princeton University Press, 2000).

27. Didi Huberman, *Invention of Hysteria: Charcot and the Photographic Iconography of the Salpêtrière*, trans. Alisa Hartz (Cambridge, MA: MIT Press, 2003), xi.

28. Claire Kahane, "Introduction: Part Two," in *In Dora's Case: Freud, Hysteria, Feminism*, ed. Charles Bernheimer and Claire Kahane (New York: Columbia University Press, 1985), 22.

29. While *Philadelphia*, and perforce my analysis, focuses primarily around the operatic diva, the diversity of cultural figures and genres feted in gay diva worship should affirm that the operatic prima donna is hardly unique as agent of queer transcendence. The Hollywood, Broadway, pop, disco, or television diva can and does work in similar fashion. That the operatic diva is still routinely privileged in popular representations—if not always popular practices—of queer diva worship is due to a raft of interacting factors, not the least of which is the enduringly persistent cultural associations of opera, and in particular the operatic soprano, with sublimity and sacralization. See Felicia Miller Frank, *The Mechanical Song: Women, Voice, and the Artificial in Nineteenth-Century French Narrative* (Stanford, CA: Stanford University Press, 1995).

30. Brooks, "Body and Voice in Melodrama and Opera," 123.

31. Allen, "Homosexuality and Narrative," 624–25.

32. Larry Kramer, "Why I Hate *Philadelphia*," Films about AIDS, newton.uor.edu/AIDS/Kramer.htm (accessed 27 November 2004).

33. Lee Edelman, *Homographesis: Essays in Gay Literary and Cultural Theory* (New York: Routledge, 1994), 10, emphasis original.

34. Undoubtedly it is the unbridled sexual and semiotic excess, the patent perversity of the sequence, that endows it with queer fascination and that allows it to break, however momentarily, from the textual straitjacket of earnest social realism and anodyne bourgeois liberalism that constrains much of the rest of *Philadelphia*. As self-confessed opera queen and diva devotee Sam Abel dryly notes, "It is, unfortunately, the only truly electric scene in the entire film" (*Opera in the Flesh: Sexuality in Operatic Performance* [Boulder, CO: Westview, 1996], 203n10).

35. Lyotard quoted in Hans Bertens, *The Idea of the Postmodern: A History* (London: Routledge, 1995), 133.

36. Thomas Weiskel, *The Romantic Sublime: Studies in the Structure and Psychology of Transcendence* (Baltimore: Johns Hopkins University Press, 1976), 23–24.

37. José Esteban Muñoz, *Disidentifications: Queers of Color and the Performance of Politics* (Minneapolis: University of Minnesota Press, 1999), 33.

38. Although he focuses his readings primarily around contemporary practices of performance art, especially those produced by queers of color, Muñoz actually nominates diva worship as a classic practice of queer disidentification. In a brief discussion of Wayne Koestenbaum's personalized account of gay male opera culture, Muñoz argues that "Koestenbaum's disidentification with the opera diva . . . fuels his identity-making machinery." He writes, "A diva's strategies of self-creation and self-defense, through the criss-crossed circuitry of cross-identification, do the work of enacting self for the gay male opera queen" (30).

39. That the forms of queer selfhood enabled by diva worship are indeed shifting and multiple is a point worth underscoring. Diva worship may be an insistently visible and enduring practice of modern metropolitan queer cultures, but its operations and effects are far from singular. In particular, the modes of queer self-actualization and becoming facilitated by diva worship shift, often radically, from one context to the next, animated by the manifold contingencies of time and place.

40. Koestenbaum, *The Queen's Throat*, 133; Abel, *Opera in the Flesh*, 56.

41. Jahan Ramazani, *Yeats and the Poetry of Death: Elegy, Self-Elegy, and the Sublime* (New Haven, CT: Yale University Press, 1990), 109.

42. Linda Hutcheon and Michael Hutcheon, *Opera: The Art of Dying* (Cambridge, MA: Harvard University Press, 2004), 11.

43. Koestenbaum, *The Queen's Throat*, 153.

48.
PRIVATE USES OF CYBERSPACE
Women, Desire, and Fan Culture
Sharon Cumberland

The writing of an erotic story is a public articulation of desire . . . what begins as a private act, a woman, a computer, becomes a community of women and computers. To place a story on the internet mirrors and amplifies the act of writing it in the first place.

(helen)

The subject of this essay is fiction writing on the Internet, specifically, the erotica written by women in the context of fan culture. Fan fiction is a genre of noncommercial writing that features an original plot using characters and settings from commercially produced film and television. Such fiction has been a social and literary phenomenon since fans started writing their own *Star Trek* episodes in the 1960s, though some would argue that fan fiction can be traced back to early literary parodies and sequels such as Lydgate's *Siege of Thebes* (a continuation of *The Canterbury Tales*) or the many "metanovels" that have been written as sequels to such works as Austen's *Pride and Prejudice*, Conan-Doyle's *Sherlock Holmes*, or Stowe's *Uncle Tom's Cabin*.[1] While a great deal of critical attention has been given recently to fan cultures and fan arts in all media, my particular focus is on the proliferation of fan fiction on the Internet and the communities that have encouraged fans to become writers as well as readers.[2] In this essay I examine the way in which women are using the paradox of cyberspace—personal privacy in a public forum—to explore feelings and ideas that were considered risky or inappropriate for women in the past. I will suggest that the protection and freedom of cyberspace is enabling these writers to defy many of the social taboos that have inhibited self-exploration and self-expression before the emergence of the Internet.

Problems of Internet Research

But how do I prove to other fen [plural of "fan"] that I'm real, if I only interact with fandom virtually? How does anyone?

(Kass)

Any discussion based upon Internet phenomena must begin with a disclaimer (confession might be a better word) concerning the limitations of "cyberfacts" and, by extension, the limitations of any claim a scholar makes based upon them.[3] The virtues of cyberspace are access and anonymity, which I call the "paradox of cyberspace" because of the incongruity of hidden identities seeking and finding exposure to the public. Cybercitizens can express thoughts and ideas in a public forum while concealing identifying markers that in the past might have caused their voices to be dismissed or diminished: race, gender, age, appearance, and economic status, to name the most obvious general categories. These virtues are two-sided coins, however, each with a corresponding "vice" or problem for scholars.

Untold millions have access to cyberspace, and the number of people going online increases every day. Google.com, the dominant search engine on the World Wide Web, documents 1.4 billion unique pages, of which 71.2% were less than one year old in

December, 2000. Furthermore, cyberspace is equally weighted. While certain "homesteads" are very large, such as GeoCities (5.5 million pages) and America Online (1.7 million pages), one homepage or threaded discussion is as valid as any other. There is no capital city in cyberspace, and no Great Chain of Cyberbeing. Without a central point from which a hierarchy can be constructed, even a modest commitment of resources will enable the humble to stake a claim in cyberspace beside the mighty. The corresponding "vice," however, is that quantification of Internet phenomena is nearly impossible because the number of participants is so vast. For instance, the volume of fan fiction on the Internet makes it impossible for me to verify some basic facts for this essay, such as how many fan communities there are on the Internet, how many fan fiction writers are posting stories on the Internet, and how many of these writers are women, (not to mention how many are heterosexual, lesbians, married, single, mothers, etc). As with any large media group, one can use sampling methods to estimate general numbers, and then use ethnographic methods to create a sense of individual characteristics. But like Neilson ratings for television and telephone polling for elections, the results are highly stylized constructions for which no verification exists.

The other virtue of cyberspace is anonymity, which permits self expression without retaliation, both for the historically oppressed and for those with unpopular or unconventional ideas, as well as for those who wish to experiment with their identities. The corresponding "vice" is that you don't know who you're talking to and can not verify claims of identity short of meeting informants face to face. For instance, I have interviewed many writers of fan fiction for this essay, and I believe that they are women because they say they are. But though I have no reason to doubt them, I also have no way to authenticate their identities unless I attend fan fiction conferences to meet them in person. Until new conventions or new technologies emerge to address this issue, a certain amount of unscholarly faith in the good will of cybercitizens is required for studying the Internet. As Kass observes, "[U]ntil we meet in RL [real life]—or if we never meet in RL—we have to take each others' identities on faith".[4] This essay makes a reasonable (i.e. highly personal) investment in the good will of the writers I quote.

Women in Disguise

> Anonymity isn't important, but there's just too much crap in the world around the issues of homosexuality for me to waste my time trying to explain to people why I write what I write if I don't have to. It's primarily a pragmatic approach for me.
>
> (elynross)

In her article entitled "Drag Net: From Glen to Glenda and Back Again . . . Is it Possible?," Sherry Turkle examines the benefits of concealing one's biological gender while participating in multi-user discussion groups (MUDs). Since male and female gender identity must be constructed in real life anyway, she argues, reconstructing identity in a MUD by changing gender enables both men and women to escape the expectations of their biological sex and to gain insight into the opposite sex. While the authors of internet fan fiction do not, as a general rule, conceal their genders, the majority of them—especially those writing erotica—conceal their real life identities with pseudonyms, as does "clynross," a prolific writer of the erotic genre called "slash."

Pseudonyms, avatars, and "handles" allow writers to avoid the real world "crap" that many of the women who write fan erotica would face if their work was published under their legal names, or in the print media. The ability to conceal identity on the Internet grants the woman author a level of liberation, like those in Turkle's MUD culture, that goes beyond first amendment rights. For while authors who publish in print media are free to write uncensored erotica, social mores inhibit most women writers from doing so. By writing on the internet under pseudonyms, women can go directly to their readers without risking their reputations with editors, publishers, or—as Henry Jenkins describes in *Textual Poachers*—anti-erotica fans. In pre-internet times the only way to buy fan erotica was to attend conferences and buy fan zines sold by the authors themselves. This made the authors vulnerable to being "outed" (publicly humiliated) by those who wished to discourage the use of their celebrity heroes in sexually explicit stories.

This ability to go directly to the reader on the Internet is the second part of the cyberspace equation. In the past, the desire or need for privacy would have either limited the author's access to an audience or would have placed the author at risk of discovery. In cyberspace, however, the audience for anonymous fan erotica is very large, since people can access and read it in the privacy of their homes (Google.com reports that the number one search term on the World Wide Web is "sex"). Though it is impossible to know precisely how large the readership for adult fan fiction may be, a conservative approach would be to assume that the readership is at least as large as the "writership" because, as we shall see below, fan fiction writers are part of an actively supportive community that encourages writing as much as reading.

Bearing in mind the impossibility of actually quantifying the phenomenon, I turned to Yahoo's WebRing program on the Internet to determine the scope of the fan erotica "writership" and their productions. WebRing allows any interested person with a home page about a special topic to become a "ringmaster" by inviting others on the internet who have relevant sites to join in their ring. As the WebRing advertisements claim, there are "84 affinity groups (in the ringworld directory), 66,000 rings on any conceivable topic, and 1.5 million member sites." The press release goes on to say that "The WebRing system can support an unlimited number of separate and distinct Rings across the Internet." This allows the visitor to move through the indirection of cyberspace in what feels like a circular pattern, either by jumping from site to site in a designated order or skipping along the ring randomly. Though Web rings are not comprehensive (there is no guarantee that all *Star Trek* home pages are on *Star Trek* Web rings, for instance) using web rings to select samples of fan populations offers some sense of the extent of the fan community devoted to erotic fan fiction on the Internet.

Though I could only explore a fraction of the choices offered on the Adult Fan Fiction webring because of the extremely large size of the field, at the time of this writing there were 145 separate rings listed in the ringworld sub-directory. A more comprehensive category, "alternative fan fiction," includes lesbian and gay fan fiction and all permutations of S&M and bondage. In this division there were 601 webrings, with over fifteen thousand individual sites. By selecting one percent of these sites and averaging the number of stories on each—more than a dozen stories per homepage—a rough estimate suggests that there are over 180 thousand fan-authored erotic

stories on the "alternative fan fiction" list.[5] If there is even one non-writing reader for every writer in the alternative fan fiction webring, then the readership for this genre alone is thirty thousand.

Although there is no way to prove the widely held impression that the majority of these writers are women, some fan writers themselves identify their communities as predominantly female, as does delle, a writer in the *La Femme Nikita* universe who says that their authors "are, to the best of my knowledge, 99.9% female." Different fandoms will have different gender proportions, of course, but if fan writers reflect the general population of cybercitizens, then at least half of fan fiction writers are female . . . a very conservative estimate given early claims that as many as ninety percent of fan writers were women. While few researchers accept that claim across all fan communities today—if for no other reason than that more and more male writers are contributing to fandoms on the Web (assuming, of course, that they are not gender experimenters)—fan culture, especially fan erotic culture, still has the earmarks of a woman's community: interest in topics such as the status of women in society, women's ability to express desire, the blurring of stereotyped gender lines (powerful women; nurturing men), as well as enthusiastic discussion and support groups for new writers. Regardless of numbers, however, there is no doubt that women benefit from the ability to explore their erotic fantasies on the Internet, and to share them with enthusiastic and supportive "sister" writers.

Fanfic Communities

Is this noble? Is this arrogance? To hope that my writing can give someone the desire to push on? Ease them out of their pains for a while? Make them giggle?

(James Walkswithwind)

Ethnographic studies conducted over the past ten years have documented fan communities and their creative productions, as well as the migration of these communities to the Internet.[6] "A remarkable aspect of the development of online fandoms and fan fiction ("fanfic") communities is the culture of inclusion that embraces anyone (including men) who joins in, both as readers and writers. I have written elsewhere about the powerful sense of sisterhood that develops among women who work together to build websites for their collaborative writing focused on iconic celebrity figures.[7] Much larger communities have formed around fandoms devoted to television and film, such as *Xena: Warrior Princess, The X-Files, Buffy the Vampire Slayer, The Sentinel, The Professionals, Highlander, Hercules, Babylon 6*, and all iterations of *Star Wars* and *Star Trek*, to name only a few of the hundreds listed on general fan Web sites. As James Walkswithwind suggests in the quotation above, motivations for fanfic writing are non-commercial, and focus on imaginative identification not only with the appropriated protagonists from popular culture, but with the community of fanfic readers. Within general fandoms, the writers of fanfic—their sites, symposia, support sites, and ree sites (recommendations of favorite stories or expert writers)—make an elite subculture.

Though the term "elite" seems to contradict the concept of inclusiveness and equality found on the Internet, talent among fanfic authors is cultivated, appreciated, and awarded status in the community since these writers have the ability to extend the sagas of favorite characters and to invest them with the sexuality and interior lives that are only implied in the commercial productions. In an article that compares fanfic writing to the Northwest Indian gift-giving tradition of the potlatch, fan author Rachel Sabotini describes the basis for "creation of status within the fan community" as the giving of gifts: "The gifts—art, songvids, and fan fiction—all require some level of artistry to master and are thus highly prized". Fanfic communities have many methods of encouraging writers to hone their skills for their own sakes and for the sake of the community.

An excellent example is *Lunacy's Fan Fiction Reviews*, a rich online support system for the communities devoted to *Xena Warrior Princess* and *Star Trek: Voyager*. On her large and detailed site, Lunacy offers resources for both readers and writers, casing the way for readers to gain the expertise required to attempt fan writing. For the neophyte there is a glossary of several hundred terms used in fanfic culture, including definitions for various genres (slash, het, alt, gen, Mary Sue . . .), common abbreviations (TPTB: The Powers That be; UST: Unresolved Sexual Tension . . .), terms specific to particular fandoms (*X-Phile*, n. Also *phile*: an X-Files fan; *PGP*, adj. Acronym for Post Gauda Prime:

stories set after the *Blake's 7* series finale, which took place on Gauda Prime . . .), and terms specific to the writing of fanfic (*beta*, v. to edit a fanfic story; *canon*, n.: refers to facts established by the original fiction . . .). On a separate page of Lunacy's site are definitions of sub genres in the *Xena* and *Voyager* universes, such as "Uber-Xena," "Warlord/Slave," and "Hurt/Comfort," with detailed descriptions of their histories, nuances, and variations. Lunacy includes links to essays that describe the art of fanfic writing, recruiting and working with a "beta reader" (volunteer story editor), and official Web sites, as well as to the original series and plot summary sites (for learning the "canon" and tracking studio activity).

One of the most impressive offerings for *Xena* and *Voyager* fanfic writers is Lunacy's Experts Directory, which contains twenty-four topic headings under which volunteers can list their areas of expertise for fanfic writers to consult. From "Animals" to "Weapons," there are over a hundred experts willing to advise on languages, ancient coins, black-smithing, medicine and herbs, karate, musical instruments, and myriad other areas that will make the futuristic universe of *Star Trek* or the ancient universe of *Xena* seem more authentic. Finally, Lunacy offers hundreds of reviews of *Xena* and *Voyager* fanfic, organized by genre, author, and special topics. On her "Highest Recommendation" page she leads the reader to the most polished exemplars of each genre, giving both the apprentice writer and the fan reader the means of enjoying and studying the best in the field. Sites like Lunacy's offer a profound service to the fan community that enables the fanfic culture to exist by educating and encouraging the newest readers, the most experienced writers, and fans at all stages on the continuum between. Their efforts enable authors like Walkswithwind to write as an act of both community and personal creativity; to "give someone the desire to push on," or, to quote an earlier passage in his essay, to let them "read something erotic that makes them smile, laugh, cry, turn to someone and say 'let's get naked.' "

E-Genres: Emotional, Erotic, Electronic

I don't read or write fanfic to get more of the show. I read fanfic to get what was missing in the show.

(Lorelei Jones)

"Getting naked" is the central act of the e-genres of fanfic, in which "e" stands not only for "electronic" but for "erotic" and "emotional." It is that which is "missing" in almost all of the commercial film and television stories that inspire fanfic writers. Lorelei Jones continues:

> I read for a favorite character who didn't get enough screen time. I read for overt declarations of love or physical intimacy. I read for realistic consequences to actions, a sense of continuity, deeper exploration of a theme barely touched on in the show, I read for the things I wish had been in the show but weren't.

Reading and writing erotica on the Internet is not simply a matter of exploring the forbidden, but of exploring the fully human. Popular culture productions in America tend to valorize violence and a type of clever, shallow relationship in which the protagonists "meet cute" and short-circuit their intimacy with snappy dialogue. Yet the commercial characters in film or a television series who must perform these abbreviated versions of their potential humanity—Spock and Kirk, Xena and Gabrielle, Han Solo and Princess Leia, for example—all have the capacity for love, physical intimacy, and emotional depth, since without this potential they would not attract even the 18–25 year old male who is target of most popular culture productions. Given the demographic that runs Hollywood, however, intimacy and complexity must be implied rather than allowed to interfere with the physical action that sells tickets and advertising.

Thus, a great deal of fan fiction is the product of longing by women for stories that bear some semblance to the realities of the human struggle for understanding, affection, and communication—all the things that studios believe would be slow and boring if developed on the screen. And sex, while not boring, needs to be slow—or approached slowly in the context of character-driven relationships—in order to have the emotional content that women find satisfying. Clearly the Internet's unique combination of personal privacy and access to a sympathetic public has enabled a huge subculture of adult fan fiction to thrive, in which the abbreviated characters of popular culture can be "fleshed out" by fan writers. "Getting naked" is

both an emotional and an erotic act, in which the soul of a character as well as the body is exposed.

Though there are many permutations of e-genres emerging on the Internet, the three major forms are "het" or heterosexual fiction, "alt." or lesbian fiction, and "slash" or homoerotic fiction. Women who write for adult audiences are experimenting with and challenging the conventional gender definitions imposed upon them in real life by imagining themselves into characters experiencing a full range of erotic engagement. In cyberspace, where a woman can avoid criticism of (or even identification with) her own writing, fanfic writers are able to explore areas of curiosity and concern that could not be explored in print media. In real world print environments, women writers would have to pass through editorial hierarchies or expose themselves to the expectations of gender appropriateness. When asked if they would have written erotica if they had not found fanfic on the Internet and sympathetic readers, most of the fanfic writers I interviewed answered in the same vein as Killashandra: "I *do* think I would have written regardless, but whether I would have written pure erotica? I doubt it. Not without the community of other women out there reading it and responding to it."

Het: Female ≠ Fanatic

> Knowing that I am not alone in my appreciation of Antonio Banderas as an actor gives my "obsession" with him approval and validates it.
>
> (Deena Glass)

Because heterosexual erotica is the most conventional and (apparently) least transgressive of the e-genres, it is the most likely to conjure up the classic stereotype of female fans as desperate women who are "fanatics" for an iconic celebrity male. The image of a female whose love endangers a male hero is a basic trope (Adam/Eve; Odysseus/Calypso; Launcelot/Guinevere, etc.) that constructs the female as a renegade who is untrustworthy unless controlled by a powerful male. Yet the modern image of an anonymous female fan swooning over a celebrity male is the invention of the romantic age. Women fainting at Chopin concerts and Byron chased through the streets of London, foreshadow hysterical Elvis and Beatles fans—always young females, always screaming and crying, overwhelmed by unrequited and unrequitable lust. This image of the anonymous female fan represents a threat to male authority. She functions outside the domestic sphere (and cannot be kept at home); she expresses open desire for a man who is not her mate (implying by her behavior that she would give him sexual favors if only he would accept them); and she is hysterical in public (out of patriarchal control). The female fan is, in effect, the woman who makes the private public, who makes sexuality, which was confined to the domestic sphere, a matter of public display. She humiliates the men who are charged with controlling her.

That, at least, is the patriarchal subtext handed down through ages of male-authored literature (with some notable exceptions, including Chaucer's *Wife of Bath's Tale*). Yet the erotic genre called "het" (predominantly woman-authored fanfic which engages male and female protagonists in erotic relationships) seems to come from a parallel universe in which men have as much capacity for emotional attachment and meaningful communication as do women. The image of women as rogue characters, whose unbridled lust for men endangers hearth and home (as in *Fatal Attraction*), is replaced with passionate yet rational relations between the sexes. As a fan of the Spanish actor Antonio Banderas, I have followed the het fiction written in Web communities devoted to him since 1994. Fan writers use his many film characters as protagonists for sequels and expansions of such films as *The 13th Warrior* and, at the time of this writing, the erotic thriller *Original Sin*. Yet in every case I have found the het erotica written about the Banderas iconic hero to be as much focused on complexity and communication as on sex. Other fandoms devoted to het treatments of characters like the *X-Files*' Fox Mulder make no apology for their open lust for their erotic hero, with sites devoted to the actor who portrays Mulder bearing such titles as the David Duchovny Estrogen Brigade, and DROOL (David's Revelry of Obsessed Lusters). Without the patriarchal presence that converts het lust into home-wrecking, desire into danger, or fans into fanatics, women writing and reading het erotica on the Internet are free to share and enjoy their common fantasy of sexy, communicative, non-oppressive males. And, as Deena Glass observes, the company of other women in the Banderas fanfic community legitimizes and validates her "obsession."

Alt.: The f/f Alternative

As is the case with m/m slash, the majority of writers seem to be female but the difference, at least with XWP/Xena Warrior Princess/fanfic, is that many of the female writers are lesbian or bisexual—though certainly not all. We have many fantastic het AND male writers.

(Maribel Piloto)

Erotic fanfic that pairs female protagonists, such as *Xena Warrior Princess*'s Xena with the bard Gabrielle, or *Star Trek: Voyager*'s Captain Janeway with Borg shipmate Seven of Nine, is referred to as "alternative fiction" or "alt.," sometimes expressed as f/f, meaning female to female. The presence of a slash, in the fanfic world, has always indicated homoerotic sex scenes—a venerable convention dating from the Kirk/Spock *Star Trek* erotica of the 1970s zine culture. (Even though "slash" is a general term for homoerotic fiction, it is sometimes used, however, as a general indication of sex in fanfic, with m=male and f=female: m/m, f/f, m/m/f, f/f/m, m/f . . .).

Fanfic writers in the alt. community present the sexual passion between female protagonists as natural and inevitable, rather than as transgressive relative to a heterosexual worldview. While both Xena and Captain Janeway could be interpreted within their settings as "masculine" women who hold positions of power and authority traditionally occupied by men, gender struggles are not a thematic strain in either canon. Janeway does not have bitter and disobedient men around her who disrespect her authority, nor does Xena struggle to assert herself in a male-dominated world. Furthermore, their partners in the alt. iterations—Seven of Nine and Gabrielle—are not playing particularly "female" roles relative to their partners. Seven of Nine is a Borg-enhanced human whose detachment is reminiscent of the Vulcan Mr. Spock and the android Data in previous *Star Trek* series, while Gabrielle is as athletic and energetic as her warrior counterpart. Male characters in each series occupy the full spectrum of masculinity, from drag queens, to mild dependency on women, to equal partners with women, and chest-thumping he-men. Female characters follow the same full range of gender types, giving the genders equal sway by acknowledging that there are many ways to be both male and female. Because of the basic sympathy of the original series characters to lesbian (or feminist) issues, the re-conceptualized alt. universe is highly plausible.

For example, fan writer G. L. Dartt has accomplished the notable feat of adding two complete seasons to *Star Trek: Voyager* by writing 50 stories in her own alt. universe. Called the "Just Between" series, or the "JB universe," the episodes conform to the canonical behavior of characters and, in general terms, to the events in the television series. The difference, however, is in the richness of Janeway's interior life, as she struggles over the inappropriateness of falling in love with a female subordinate (whereas the Janeway of the TV series remains aloof from emotional attachments). The first two episodes, "Just Between Us," and "Just Between Them," are classic "First Time" stories in which the reader shares in the emotional tension of both protagonists as they come to terms with their love for each other, go through the first awkward stages of private and public encounters, and find the balance between their personal and professional lives. The love story between Janeway and Seven of Nine is told in the context of other characters familiar to *Voyager* fans, and against a full program of events and plot developments, so that the *Voyager* setting is not a mere backdrop for a love story or a PWP (Plot What Plot?) sex story. Dartt not only constructs a tense story line concerning an alien culture that may (or may not) be as hospitable as it seems, but also manages to address contemporary issues of concern to the lesbian community without allowing ideological intrusiveness.

For instance, in "Just Between Them," Janeway and Seven of Nine are dancing at a formal event hosted by aliens whose world they are visiting. As they dance, they discuss the difficulty of not being able to touch each other in public whenever they feel moved to do so. Janeway asks Seven, "Does it really bother you that you can't touch me unless we're alone?" Her partner answers that it does, but that she understands how it would make others feel if they have private moments in their professional settings: ". . . were I to touch you in the way that I like to touch you, it would make others uncomfortable as well . . . and that is not good for the functionality of the ship." The conversation addresses several layers of problems that the protagonists face: the distinction between a captain and her subordinate, the distinction between public and private behavior, the need to maintain the good will of the crew, and the ability to read each other's signals. But outside the universe of *Voyager*, which takes place three hundred years into the future in a time when, presumably, no prejudice exists against homosexual expression, the episode carries a contemporary subtext concerning the plight of homosexual couples. In early twenty-first century America, neither gay nor lesbian couples have the freedom of displaying affection in public to the same degree that heterosexuals enjoy. The discussion between Janeway and Seven transposes the essential dilemma facing contemporary lesbians into the present and offers the reader some advice and comfort on a difficult aspect of life.

Convincingly written alt. fiction performs another service to its readership by modeling for the heterosexual community lesbian relationships that are successful and natural as well as passionate. Without being two-dimensional moralists (they are, after all, writing erotica) the authors of the alt. fanfic I have read, which I selected from Lunacy's Highest Recommended page, demonstrate that lesbian relationships are as normal—even ordinary—in their arguments, disappointments, and passions as heterosexual relationships. And as Maribel Piloto notes, not all readers and writers in the alt. community are lesbian and bisexual. Het fans of alt. provide the world with one more group of people who do not demonize alternative lifestyles.

Slash: Queen (King?) of E-genres

> Slash fiction, devoted to same gender couplings, produces consumers of nearly exclusively one gender. This is a sexual community, an explicit community, in which desire is looked upon as normal and a fixation with sex is rewarded, with readership, with feedback. This, for many women, is a community that is significantly lacking in life off the Internet.
>
> (helen)

Of all the erotic genres of fan fiction on the Internet, "slash" is the most evolved, analyzed and, if sheer volume is an indication, the most popular. There are hundreds of slash pages devoted to fandoms of all kinds, as well as chat rooms, discussion groups and symposia devoted to analyzing the genre. There is an annual conference for writers and readers of slash, in addition to slash discussion groups in the major fan conferences world wide.[8] And while the history and evolution of slash is well documented and will not be repeated here, it presents the most complex analytical issues of all the erotic genres, since, as helen points out, "in a slash story, there is no place for a woman—thus, the writer is nowhere and everywhere. She must be both the aggressor and the recipient of romantic overtures." This point—the whereabouts of a woman author in the m/m world of slash—is the subject of much discussion in the slash community.[9]

The debate follows two major themes through fan discussions. The first theme is preoccupied with whether or not a protagonist is gay if he is portrayed as having sex with another male protagonist, and whether this constitutes a departure from canon. This discussion, set in motion by Joanna Russ in 1985, implies that the author is straight identified, since she is worried that a favorite character may be diminished by being labeled gay.[10] In a culture that persists in seeing gayness as "effeminate," as Shomeret observes in "Is Methos a Woman?," the heterosexual female reader or writer will have difficulty imaging sex with a favorite character if he is feminized, since she herself wants to be his opposite. Put another way, how can she have sex with him if he's playing the female role?

The second, related, discussion theme is whether or not the female author is projecting herself into the story as a man or a woman, which is to ask, obliquely, whether or not the author is experiencing androgyny, a transgendered (phallic) experience, or an out of body experience when writing or reading slash. The Internet has changed the terms of this discussion a great deal, since women slash fans are no longer confined to the objectivity of the printed word, but can enter into the spirit of interactivity, subjectivity, and experimentation that the Internet has encouraged. Sherry Turkle has written extensively on the subject of online identities, as observed earlier, and there is no reason to suppose that experimentation with gender is less prevalent in slash culture than it is in the MUD culture she identifies, though its implementation is somewhat different. In the privacy of the home, writing under a pseudonym and with the encouragement of a community that will never "out" you to your friends and

family, gender experimentation has lost its undercurrent of seediness and danger. Slash writers and readers are no longer constructed as "perverts" or "pornographers" as Russ used the terms in 1985.

Two examples of slash fiction from the *Highlander* fandom will demonstrate the range of possibilities for slash writers and readers for projecting or experimenting with their sexual projections onto protagonists. D/M stories involve Duncan MacLeod, an immortal born in Scotland 400 years ago, and Methos, the oldest living immortal, born five thousand years ago. In the *Highlander* universe, potential immortals only achieve immortality if they suffer untimely death (after which they inexplicably wake up again). They can be killed innumerable times and return to life, as long as they are not decapitated. Since Methos suffered his "first death" in his early thirties, be remains that age forever, in spite of his five thousand years. Duncan, killed in his mid-thirties, is likewise vital and—need it be said?—handsome and sexy for eternity. Methos is slender, birdlike, winsome, and one for whom discretion is the better part of valor. Duncan is brawny, powerful, aggressive, one for whom valor involves every martial art known to man. For the slash writer, this is a match made in heaven.

The physical stature of each protagonist suggests that the answer to Shomert's question is yes, Methos is a woman, and Duncan is the man, or, to use language from the gay porn world, Methos is the bottom, Duncan the top. "Interlunation" by Bone follows this general pattern of small = feminine, large = masculine, but constructs Methos as a "pushy bottom," one who makes passive aggressive demands on his top so that it is clear to the reader who is in charge of the emotional encounter. Unlike gay porn, however, Bone delays sexual interaction between the protagonists until the character's situation and relationship has been fully developed. So much of the development has happened in the commercial aspect of the fan universe (which is why readers are required to "do their homework" by mastering the series canon before reading) that sex is delayed only enough for anticipation. Although Bone calls her story "less than a real plot, but more than a PWP," the sex scenes that comprise most of the action occur simultaneously with both men's thoughts, memories, and emotions as they discover that sex is a form of forgiveness and renewal. Thus the reader or writer who is "everywhere and nowhere" may move from top to bottom with her favorite character, but is always rewarded with the rich interior lives that distinguish slash from porn.

The second *Highlander* story draws its pleasures from inverting the D/M relationship and making Methos a slaveholder and Duncan the slave. *The Seduction of the Desert Prince* is an illustrated novel of twenty-three chapters by a writer's collective called The Krell. Set in an alternative universe (meaning, in slash culture, a setting other than that provided by the creators of the television series) it takes place in a non-specific past and is set in the romantic, imaginary desert first presented in *The Sheik*. Though there are extended sex scenes, they are few in number and embedded in a plausible and suspenseful plot. Duncan and Methos are canonical in that they conform to the essence of their personalities and obey the laws of the *Highlander* universe. But the reader and writers have the pleasure of seeing the brawny Duncan chained like Samson at Methos's feet, forced to serve his sexual pleasures with initial reluctance, growing enthusiasm, and then—as their emotional needs take precedence—as an equal and a free man.

In e-mail exchanges with the authors of this novel, one member of The Krell told me that she wrote what she wanted to read since erotica in bookstores is focused on sex and not relationships: "I write erotic stories because I like to explore the themes of emotional intimacy, and I write fan fiction because it lets me do that with characters that already interest me." This is a perfect summation of slash fiction—erotica that occurs only in the context of emotional relationships, involving familiar and favorite characters. Whether the reader or writer sees herself as experimenting with male identity and sexuality, as a disembodied power to whom powerful males are subject, as a woman masked in a male body, or as some other variation of gender mixing, the most satisfying slash seems to integrate the best of both worlds—emotional complexity with the simple pleasure of great sex.

Conclusion: Original Borrowings, Communal Pleasures

We're in the business of stealing ideas. That's what we do. We take cultural offering's and we manipu-

late them, involve ourselves in them, shape them to our taste. Besides which. Shakespeare wasn't exactly Original Story Gay, either.

(Justine)

Women are using the paradox of cyberspace—personal privacy in a public forum—to explore feelings and ideas that were considered risky or inappropriate for women in the past. The protection and freedom of cyberspace is enabling these writers to defy many of the social taboos that have inhibited self-exploration and self-expression before the emergence of the Internet. At the same time, the inclusiveness of fanfic communities has encouraged more and more women (and some men) to participate actively by writing their own stories. Fan writers have found the resources—such as Lunacy's Experts Directory—to support their inventions, beta readers to critique them, audiences to read them, and symposia to debate their meaning and worth. Our notions of the relationship between sexuality and privacy are challenged by the fact that many—perhaps the majority—of these women would not have written erotica in the absence of a community of appreciative female readers. The Internet fanfic world provides these authors with safe, anonymous and, paradoxically, public places to meet with like-minded women in order to experiment with ideas of sexuality and gender identity.

The sum of this activity is community—a place where the cultural offerings of a detached and commercialized world are manipulated and "shaped to our taste." Women are using erotica not only to explore their inner lives, but also to expand their outer connections with the world. Fanfic Web sites have, in effect, become women's clubs, where erotica can be safely explored without damage to the reputation, the career, or the domestic life.

Notes

1. See !Super Cat, *A (Very) Brief History of Fanfic* [Online] (Rebecca Lucy Busker, 1999 [cited August 10 2001]); available from <http://www.trickster.org/symposium/symp5.htm>.
2. For an introduction to fan culture and fan media, see Henry Jenkins, *Textual Poachers: Television Fans and Participatory Culture. Studies in Culture and Communication* (London: Routledge, 1992); Camille Bacon-Smith,

Enterprising Women: Television Fandom and the Creation of Popular Myth, ed. Dan Rose and Paul Stoller, Series in Contemporary Ethnography (Philadelphia: University of Pennsylvania Press, 1992); Chery Harris and Alison Alexander, eds., *Theorizing Fandom: Fans, Subculture and Identity*, Hampton Press Communication Series: Communication Alternatives (Cresskill, NJ: Hampton Press, 1998); and Henry Jenkins, "Quentin Tarantino's *Star Wars?*: Digital Cinema, Media Convergence, and Participatory Culture," in this volume. [*Rethinking Media Change: The Aesthetics of Transition,* eds. David Thorburn and Henry Jenkins (Cambridge, MA: MIT Press, 2003)]

3. The instability of Internet sources is a well-documented problem that I will not address here. For a discussion of online documentation issues, see Janice R. and Todd W. Taylor Walker, *The Columbia Guide to Online Style* (New York: Columbia University Press, 1998) and Joseph Gibaldi, *MLA Style Manual and Guide to Scholarly Publishing*, 2nd ed. (New York: Modern Language Association of America, 1998).

4. Some would argue that search engines, such as Google and Yahoo, constitute hierarchical powers because they control the terms that allow cybercitizens to find one another. As media companies converge (the dystopian argument goes) barriers to entry will constrict competition in cyberspace. This argument is focused on the commercialization of cyberspace and may not have the same implications for non-commercial enterprise such as fan fiction. Programs such as WebRing provide non-commercial web communities with ways of finding one another apart from search engines. See Robert McChesney, "So Much for the Magic of Technology and the Free Market: The World Wide Web and the Corporate Media System," in *The World Wide Web and Contemporary Cultural Theory,* ed. Andrew and Thomas Swiss Herman (New York: Routledge, 2000).

5. See Rebecca Lucy Busker, *Cereta's Fanfic Symposium* [Online] (1999–2001 [cited June 5 2001]); available from http://www.trickster.org/symposium/. Many fan fiction writers are the most insightful critics of their own work and cultures. I am grateful to Cynthia Jenkins for introducing me to this symposium and many other rich sources of fan criticism and analysis.

6. For another approach to estimating the scope of fan fiction on the Internet see Mary Ellen Curtin, *The Fan Fiction Universe: Some Statistical Comparisons* [Online] (1999: 2000 [cited]; available from <http://www.eclipse.net/~inecurtin/au>. Curtin's conservative estimate of general fan fiction stories on the Internet, based upon counting archived stories in the largest fandoms, is over half a million (in 2000).

7. See the citations listed in note 1 as well as Nancy K. Baym, *Tune In, Log On: Soaps, Fandom, and Online Community* (Thousand Oaks, CA: Sage, 2000); Julian Dibbell, *My Tiny Life: Crime and Passion in a Virtual World* (New York: Henry Holt, 1998); Harris and Alexander, eds., *Theorizing Fandom,* Marc A. Smith and Peter Kollock, eds., *Communities in Cyberspace* (New York and London: Routledge, 1999); and Sherry Turkle, *Life on the Screen: Identity in the Age of the Internet* (New York: Touchstone, 1997).

8. Two fan conferences devoted entirely to slash are ZebraCon, which had its sixteenth biannual meeting in October 2002, and Escapade, which had its thirteenth annual meeting in February 2003. Both conferences protect slash writers and media artists from moral and legal objections by limiting attendance to their own membership.

9. While the chapter on slash in *Textual Poachers* covers both history and ideological issues, a more recent article gives an update on the status of the genre. See Shoshanna Green, Cynthia Jenkins, and Henry Jenkins, "Normal Interest in Men Bonking: Selections from The *Terra Nostra Underground* and *Strange Bedfellows*" in *Theorizing Fandom: Fans, Subculture and Identity,* ed. Cheryl Harris and Alison Alexander, Hampton Press Communication Series (Cresskill, NJ: Hampton Press, 1998). For fan discussions see especially helen, *nt* [Online] (2001 [cited August 13, 2001); available from <http://www.waxjism.net/helen/domnatrix.htm> and Busker, *FanFic Symposium* [cited].

10. See "Pornography By Women For Women, With Love" in Joanna Russ, *Magic Mommas, Trembling Sisters, Puritans and Perverts: Feminist Essays* (Trumansburg, NY: Crossing, 1985).

Bibliography

Austin, Shelley. *Web Ring Press Release* [Online]. Yahoo.com, 1999 [cited October 8, 1999]. Available from <http://nav.webring.org/egi-bin/navegi?ring=adulfic;list>.

Bacon-Smith, Camile. *Enterprising Women: Television Fandom and the Creation of Popular Myth.* Philadelphia: University of Pennsylvania Press, 1992.

Baym, Nancy K. *Tune in, Log On: Soaps, Fandom, and Online Community.* Thousand Oaks, CA: Sage, 2000.

Bone. *Interlunation* [Online]. 2000 [cited June 18, 2001]. Available from <http://business/mho.net/houseofslash/bslash.htm>.

Boutin, Paul. "1.6 Billion Served: The Web According to Google." *Wired* (December 2000): 118–119.

Busker, Rebecca Lucy. *Cereta's Fanfic Symposium* [Online]. 1999, 2001 [cited June 5, 2001]. Available from <http://www.trickster.org/symposium/>.

Cat, !Super. *A (Very) Brief History of Fanfic* [Online]. Rebecca Lucy Busker, 1999 [cited August 10, 2001]. Available from <http://www.trickster.org/symposium/symp5. htm>.

Clerc, Susan. "Estrogen Brigades and 'Big Tits' Threads: Media Fandom Online and Off." In *Wired Women: Gender and New Realities in Cyberspace*, ed. Lynn Cherny and Elizabeth Reba Weise. Seattle: Seal Press, 1996.

Cumberland, Sharon. "The Five Wives of Ibn Fadlan: Women's Collaborative Fiction on Antonio Banderas Websites." In *Reload: Rethinking Women + Cyberculture*, ed. Austin Booth and Mary Flanagan. Cambridge, MA: MIT Press, 2001.

Curtin, Mary Ellen. *The Fan Fiction Universe: Some Statistical Comparisons* [Online], 1999, 2000, available from <http://www.eclipse.net/~mecurtin/au>.

Dartt, G. L. *Just Between Them* [Online]. 2001 [cited August 13, 2001]. Available from <http://www.northco.net/ ~janeway/JBSeries/Seson l/jb02them.htm>.

delle. *The Overuse of H/C, or, Why Do We Torture Our Characters (and, Perhaps, Our Readers?)* [Online]. Rebecca Lucy Busker, 2000 [cited June 5, 2001]. Available from <http://www.trickster.org/symposium/symp50.htm>.

Dibbell, Julian. *My Tiny Life: Crime and Passion in a Virtual World*. New York: Henry Holt, 1998.

Gibaldi, Joseph. *M.L.A. Style Manual and Guide to Scholarly Publishing*, 2nd ed., New York: Modern Language Association of America, 1998.

Glass, Deena. Electronic mail, 1999.

Green, Shoshanna, Cynthia Jenkins, and Henry Jenkins. "Normal Interest in Men Bonking: Selections from the *Terra Nostra Underground* and *Strange Bedfellows*." In *Theorizing Fandom: Fans, Subculture and Identity*, edited by Cheryl Harris and Alison Alexander. Cresskill, NJ: Hampton Press, 1998.

Harris, Cheryl, and Alison Alexander, eds. *Theorizing Fandom: Fans, Subculture and Identity*. Cresskill, NJ: Hampton Press, 1998.

helen, *nt* [Online]. 2001 [cited August 13, 2001]. Available from <http://www.waxjism. net/helen/dominatrix. htm>.

Jenkins, Henry. "*Quentin Tarantino's Star Wars?*: Digital Cinema, Media Convergence, and Participatory Culture," in this volume [*Rethinking Media Change*]. See also <http://web.mit.edu/21fms/www/faculty/henry3/starwars. html>

———. *Textual Poachers: Television Fans and Participatory Culture*. New York and London: Routledge, 1992.

Jones, Lorelei. *Reasons for Fanfic and Impact on Characterization* [Online]. Rebecca Lucy Busker, 2000 [cited June 5, 2001, 2001]. Available from <http://www.trickster.org/ symposium/symp67.htm>.

Justine, *And Now Back to Our Show: A Rant by Justine* [Internet]. Rebecca Lucy Busker, 1999 [cited October 4, 1999]. Available from <http://trickster.org/radiofree/ justine/Rant 1.html>.

Kass. *Becoming Real or, the Invisible Fan* [Online]. Rebecca Lucy Busker, 2000 [cited June 5, 2001]. Available from <http://www.trickster.org/symposium/symp65. htm>.

Killashandra. Electronic mail, October 4, 1999.

McChesney, Robert. "So Much for the Magic of Technology and the Free Market: The World Wide Web and the Corporate Media System." In *The World Wide Web and Contemporary Cultural Theory*. ed. Andrew Herman and Thomas Swiss, 5 36. New York: Routledge, 2000.

Piloto, Maribel, Electronic mail, September 6, 2000.

———. *Lunacy's Fan Fiction Reviews* [Online]. 2001 [cited August 13 2001]. Available from <http://www.geocities. com/Area51/Shire/6930>.

Russ, Joanna, *Magic Mommas, Trembling Sisters, Puritans and Perverts: Feminist Essays*. Trumansburg, NY: Crossing, 1985.

Sabotini, Rachel. *The Fannish Potlatch: Creation of Status within the Fan Community* [Online]. Rebecca Lucy Busker, 1999 [cited June 5, 2001]. Available from <http://www. trickster.org/symposium/symp41.htm>.

Shomeret. *Is Methas a Woman?* [Online]. Rebecca Lucy Busker, 1999 [cited] June 5, 2001]. Available from <http://www.trickster.org/symposium/symp19.htm>.

Smith, Marc A., and Peter Kollock, eds. *Communities in Cyberspace*. New York and London: Routledge, 1999.

Turkle, Sherry, *Life on the Screen: Identity in the Age of the Internet*. New York: Touchstone, 1997.

Walker, Janice R., and Todd W. Taylor, *The Columbia Guide to Online Style*. New York: Columbia University Press, 1998.

Walkswithwind, James, *Musings* [Online]. Rebecca Lucy Busker, 2000 [cited June 5, 2001]. Available from <http://www.trickster.org/symposium/symp46.htm>.

49.
WOMEN AND GAMES
Technologies of the Gendered Self

Pam Royse, Joon Lee, Undrahbuyan Baasanjav, Mark Hopson, and Mia Consalvo

Introduction

The gaming industry and most popular media have begun to recognize that women play digital games. The rise in 'casual games', coupled with sales of diverse game titles such as *Dance Dance Revolution* and Sony's *Eyetoy* indicate that women and girls are a growing part of the gaming audience. Yet this diverse group is still misunderstood and too often conflated as having a single perspective or experience. This article explores more deeply why some adult women play and how they choose to integrate gaming technologies into their daily lives or reject them.

Past research concerning females and video games has fallen into two general areas: assessing the gender representations found in games (Beasley and Standley, 2002; Heintz-Knowles and Henderson, 2002; Kinder, 1991; Okorafor and Davenport, 2001; Provenzo, 1991); and surveying or interviewing female gamers (as contrasted with male gamers) regarding their level of play, particular interests and thoughts regarding games and gaming culture (Cassell and Jenkins, 1998; Cunningham, 2000; Ivory and Wilkerson, 2002; Media Analysis Laboratory, 1998; Schott and Horrell, 2000; Yates and Littleton, 2001). This growing body of work has produced valuable knowledge about users as well as content but it has often been conflated, when in reality the research studies and results do not always (or should not always) fit together easily, or even belong together.

In particular, there are two issues of concern. First, when researching female gamers, mention is often made of images of females in games. Although some research reports do make an explicit link between respondent concerns and the importance of these images, other reports seem to mix them together without justification, or through suggestions that the images must be having 'effects' on game players. Second, research on female gamers initially focused on girls and has now broadened to encompass adult women players, but the interests, preferences and play habits of girls and women are usually combined without any discussion of how such conflations might be problematic. To illustrate how unusual the practice of such combinations is, consider television audience research and how rarely women and girls are examined as part of the same sample group.

This article seeks to make a more careful examination of women gamers by bracketing the discussion of female representations in games (unless explicitly discussing the comments of female gamers about such images) and focusing exclusively on research done on adult women gamers. This article also approaches the subjects of women and gaming from a feminist, critical-cultural point of view, seeing gender and technology as mutually shaping. Thus, following the work of Yates and Littleton, we view 'computer gaming as something that is constructed out of a set of practices that computer gamers engage in' (2001: 106), and further, that through these constructions gamers also negotiate and create gendered identities.

To do so, this article brings in the work of gender and technology theorists such as Balsamo (1996) and Haraway (1991), but also draws on and expands the work of Foucault (1988), in particular his conceptualization of technologies or techniques of the self. Thus it views computer games and gaming as a set of practices or technologies that multiple individuals use in different and at times contradictory ways to construct a gendered self that is culturally, socially and historically specific.

Past Research: Women and Games

Research examining the play habits, interests and preferences of women includes the work of Consalvo and Treat (2002), Ivory and Wilkerson (2002), Kerr (2003), Schott and Horrell (2000), Taylor (2003) and Yates and Littleton (2001). All of these reports indicate that women do play games and while on average the amount of that play is less than for men of a similar age, women vary considerably as a group in playing time, favorite genres and particular interests or reasons for gaming.

In the most basic study of gendered play patterns, Ivory and Wilkerson (2002) surveyed 150 college students (half men and half women). They found that while only four women had 'never' played a video game, 77 percent of males said that they played video games at least once a week, while only 46 percent of women did so.

Similarly, Consalvo and Treat (2002) found that 75 percent of men and 51 percent of women reported playing games currently and that 'power' users (those playing for more than 20 hours a month) were disproportionately male—42 percent of men reported such power levels of playing, while only 15.6 percent of women did the same. The authors also found differences in favorite genres for men and women. From a list of eight types of genres, men's top three genres were sports, action/adventure and simulation. Women chose puzzle-solving, platform and sports genres. Yet, when considering what elements of game play were most important, men and women scored equally the ability to succeed in playing a game as the most important element. Overall then, while women and men had different play frequencies and favorite genres, they did not differ much in the elements of gameplay that were most important.

Similarly, Yates and Littleton (2001) conducted a participant observation ethnographic study of adult computer gamers aged 20–35, finding that women had a wide variety of gaming interests that were not necessarily tied to gendered expectations. Further, some women resented 'gender appeals' in game literature, arguing that such games were offensive to them and not at all a draw for playing. They found that

> women [were] selecting and negotiating subject positions—drawn from their own life worlds—that allow[ed] them to engage with games software through the employment of specific cultural competencies. The women, however, clearly articulated some of the problems faced in negotiating and countering the male-gendered preferred readings within the games.
>
> (2001: 113)

Yates and Littleton argue that the more fruitful approach to studying women who play games is not to look for reified 'women' that play 'games' (or do not), but instead to determine how various players construct the act of gaming and how that process plays into (or challenges) their own particular sense of self, including their own specific gendered identity. By doing so, it is possible to reach a better understanding of the real differences between women who prefer more 'male-oriented' games, as well as those who would prefer a more 'feminine' flavor to their games (whatever this might mean).

Kerr problematizes gendered identities in games 'with a masculine and heterosexual player in mind' (2003: 284). Conducting semi-structured interviews, Kerr found that women contested and appropriated gaming technology for their own means. Consequently, the construction of particular characters and identities reveals that gender and technology is a dynamic practice for women who play video games. Although the participants expressed concerns about the gendered nature of game culture and game content, their perceptions varied in terms of the extent to which this gendering informed views of themselves as women.

As indicated, the digital gaming culture has largely negated the empowerment of women. However, Taylor's (2003) interviews with women gamers reveals that gender-neutral games also equated to virtual spaces where competition is based solely on skill. Within the virtual world one can assume any identity—resulting in a freedom of movement and advancement not always afforded to women. Nonetheless, Taylor's research foregrounds virtual bodies and virtual space as significant to present and potential audiences. The author calls for producers and consumers to meet the challenge of understanding how digital games inform notions of gender in general, and the sociology of the body in particular.

In a similar vein, Schott and Horrell (2000) conducted open-ended interviews with both girls and women and found a range of interests and play frequencies. Again, gender and technology helped to construct each other, as 'for adult gamers, it appeared that gaming slots into the existing nexus of domestic power' (2000: 49). Thus, many adult women gamers felt that their male partners had more time available for game play, as they did not feel as obligated to engage in housework or domestic chores—tasks which women felt took precedence over leisure activities.

Gender and Technology: Relevant Theory

Many if not most, feminist theorists of gender and technology would argue that these two concepts are socially constructed in specific historical, political and cultural contexts. Further, these two concepts are theoretically intertwined, informing each other in important ways.

One classic example of such mutual shaping is Rakow's (1992) social history of the telephone and her explanation of how it became gendered (as a female medium for socializing) in a specific way and led to particular ways of defining what is (and is not) 'women's work' in relation to family and group communication. Here, gender helps to define a technological medium and a technology is (re)configured gender-wise, to the feminine.

More recent work addresses how technologies that promise greater choice can often end up reifying traditionally gendered body norms. Theorists such as Anne Balsamo (1996) have argued that computer technologies have been employed in the service of redefining appropriately gendered bodies, through such mechanisms as cosmetic surgery. These technologies themselves are bound up in discourses concerning gendered identities of users as well as producers or inventors. Balsamo builds on and expands the (classic) work of Haraway (1991), who argues that women must embrace technology and grapple with its contra-

dictory and potentially dangerous meanings if we are to have a hand in its future development and implementation.

More recently, Liesbet van Zoonen echoed and reinforced these findings, arguing that 'both technology and gender are multidimensional processes that are articulated in complex and contradictory ways which escape straightforward gender definitions' (2002: 6). Further, she makes the pertinent point that 'the decisive moment in the circuit of culture is in the moment of consumption, when technologies are domesticated in everyday lives' (2002: 16). That concern underscores the desire in this article to focus on the consumption (or use) of games, to determine whether and how they may morph from their production culture of a mainly masculine domain to something more complex in gender terms (for more information on the gendered production of games, see Davies, 2002).

Although feminist theorists such as Rakow, Balsamo and van Zoonen have produced critical insights into how gender and technology can mutually shape each other and do so in ways that resist as well as comply with existing (gendered) power hierarchies, their models tend to see the gendered use of technologies in ways that do not account for differences in use—other than in a dualistic use/non-use conceptualization. For example, Balsamo's excellent critique of the rise of digital imaging in cosmetic surgery demonstrates how women's choices reinscribe traditional ideas about female beauty. Yet the analysis is limited to either engaging or not engaging in cosmetic surgery. Similarly Rakow's inquiry into telephone use mainly focuses on the differences between men and women and does not examine deeply how various women might use the telephone in different frequencies. Although such critiques of differential use are usually related to identity factors such as ethnicity or class, it is also important to look at the level of use of a technology and determine how women who are invested in differential use patterns or practices may come to understand a technology differently and therefore have different attitudes about it, and how they also may see the technology as 'gendered' differently.

Perhaps such concerns can be addressed usefully by integrating Foucault's 'technologies of the self' into the feminist model of 'technologies of gender'. Doing so allows for greater understanding of how individual women, or groups of women, may experience video game play and help us to understand how different women come to have very different patterns of use and attitudes concerning games and game culture.

In his later work, Foucault came to see the limitations of his system of all-pervasive power, which led to docile bodies and did not account for any types of resistance to that generalized system—particularly for women (as feminists would point out; see McNay, 1992). Foucault's later theorizing moved to a consideration of the self and how individuals—shaped in specific cultural contexts—could come to choose actions and behaviors knowingly from a range of options, perhaps even choosing actions that would produce sanctions, but doing so willingly. He termed the range of alternatives 'technologies of the self'.

Such a conceptualization can be applied to the study of digital game use by women, and in so doing can help to clarify some of the contradictions found in women's use and interests in games and gaming. Different researchers have identified women with different play frequencies, styles and interests. These differential uses make it impossible for researchers to make ready conclusions about how digital games may operate as 'technologies of gender', for they seem to operate in different ways for different women. Some women, for example, readily play the more 'masculine' first-person shooter (FPS) games and relish the opportunity to 'blow away' other competitors—especially males. Yet, other women play occasionally or sporadically and prefer more 'gender neutral' games such as *The Sims*. A blanket term such as 'technologies of gender' cannot be applied easily here—which is the 'correct' use of the technology in relation to women (or men)?

A better alternative is offered by the combination 'technologies of the gendered self'. This model solves two problems: it allows researchers a way in which to understand differential play patterns and interests among women (and men), and gives us a more useful theoretical tool for understanding how women negotiate particular technologies and how their various work of negotiation can produce different results and different interpretations of the consumption of technology as a gendered practice.

To that end, this study has examined women's experiences of games and gaming from their per-

spectives, as they seek to integrate (or reject) gaming technology into their lives, in various ways. It examines how games and gaming function as technologies that help them to define their gendered selves. This can be through integration, negotiation or rejection. This investigation looks at women with different levels of play, as well as different interests in genres and individual games. These differences (and their consequences) offer a better picture of both how women define themselves in terms of gaming, and how gaming culture responds. The research questions are as follows.

RQ1: Why do female gamers play digital games?

RQ2: What are female gamers' perceptions of themselves and their gaming experiences? How do these perceptions influence their decisions to play and purchase digital games?

RQ3: How can women's gaming perceptions be understood from the perspective of power dynamics of technologies of the gendered self?

RQ4: Do electronic games influence women's self-identity or self-image, or perception of women in general?

Method

The integration of female gamers into gaming culture is best understood in its 'most complex whole' (Geertz, 1973: 299). As recommended by Geertz, this study strived to create a 'thick description' of how women blend, negotiate and negate digital gaming and gender. This study grew from a graduate methods class which conducted individual in-depth interviews, as well as focus groups with a diverse group of participants in terms of the level of expertise in gaming—from non-players to expert players—and geographic and demographic diversification.

One group of researchers conducted three focus groups to understand the collective processes of interpretations of gaming culture by female gamers and non-gamers among students in the local area. The guided discussions focused on how women described their electronic gaming experiences and how they constructed their own perspectives about gaming culture. Twenty female students from a Midwestern public university were recruited for three separate focus groups: power users, moderate users and non-users. These groups were assembled, based on the number of hours that the participants spent playing digital games and on the level of expertise as determined by the participants in pre-focus group questionnaires. Operationally, non-gamers did not play any games, moderate gamers spent approximately one to three hours a week playing, while power gamers ranged from three to more then 10 hours weekly. The demographic characteristics of the participants for the focus groups reflected the population of the local university town: mostly Caucasian with a few Asians, ages ranging from 18–37 and with annual incomes below $25,000.

The second group of researchers conducted in-depth interviews. In-depth interviews provide a more personal and individualized account compared to focus groups. By asking questions and probing different answers, the researchers captured women's experiences, views, perceptions and the meaning that they give to computer games. In this project, 15 in-depth interviews were conducted using the following interview techniques: face-to-face (FTF); computer-mediated communication (CMC); and telephone. The CMC interviews enhanced the comprehensiveness of this study by allowing the research team to investigate participants who were savvier in regard to online or digital gaming but geographically located as far away as Europe. The participants for the project can be characterized best as evocative. The researchers selected this group to 'provide a flavor' (Mason, 2002: 126) of the different perspectives of female gamers with varying commitments to playing. The demographic characteristics of the informants were similar to those of the focus group interviews, but with a wider age range, from 18–52. The ethnicity and socio-economic status of these participants were not gathered at the time of the original research.

All the interviews and focus groups were conducted in January and February of 2003 and were transcribed by multiple researchers. All the names used in this article are pseudonyms. Although there are many advantages to the interview method, the method relies heavily upon the responses of subjects and does not allow researchers to observe actual behavior of playing digital games. Nonetheless, we believe that the collaborative approach and the use of different qualitative methods have produced data that is rich and reliable.

Findings

While we wish to avoid the suggestion that female gamers can be easily categorized or that their preferences can be predicted, it was revealing that the data cleaved along lines corresponding to the level of play in which the women engaged. Furthermore, these women expressed variations in their definitions of gendered self. Specifically, it was found that gaming technology and gender were most well integrated for power gamers, whereas for moderate gamers, gaming technology and gender is more carefully negotiated, creating an uneasy truce. By comparison, non-gamers asserted themselves—by their very rejection of gaming technology—in ways that might be considered more traditionally feminine. The following discusses the integration, negotiation and rejection of gaming as it is manifested in the women's choice of genre and characters, their attitudes toward the representations of women in game texts and their exercise of control in integrating, negotiating or rejecting gaming technology.

Integration of Gaming: Gender and Technology Fusion

> There are many computer games that portray women as a sex object, but I don't care. You might think I am a little unusual . . . The games with extreme violence and sexuality are not allowed for those under age to play, so I don't think it matters.
> (Roselyn, a power-gamer from Korea)

Power gamers place high importance on gaming and engage in it frequently; it is not surprising, then, that these gamers appear more comfortable with gaming technology and game themes and that gaming is better integrated into their lives. The degree of integration is demonstrated not only by the frequency with which they play, but also by their facility with the technology and their revelations that they enjoy multiple genres. The power gamers that were interviewed tended to distinguish between the various pleasures that gaming provides and astutely recognized that different genres promote different pleasures. The women were technologically adept, and consequently reported that they actively choose specific genres to fulfill their desires for particular pleasures, such as sociability, intellectual stimulation and competitive challenge. For example, Kara said:

> I play RPGs [role-playing games] to relax and enjoy, because they tell thrilling stories like interactive storybooks. I play fighting games when I feel the 'urge' or when someone challenges me. I play strategy games to work out my logic.

One particular pleasure which power gamers emphasized is the challenge that certain games provide; these women take pleasure from mastering the skills required by the game and from competing with other players. Several of the participants cited their preferences for online, multiplayer FPS games and they spoke in detail about the pleasures of this particular genre. Kylie, who studies digital game design in the UK, said: '*Counter-Strike* is a hard game to master. If you become very good, you earn the respect of everyone.' *Counter-Strike* requires considerable time and effort to play and requires social and technical skills in order to connect successfully with people on the internet. For the women who play this game, pleasure also stems from their accomplishments in successful competition. Chris, who has played digital games since the second grade, finds *Counter-Strike* to be 'an exhilarating competitive exercise', which she compares to 'scoring a goal in hockey or soccer'. Despite the fact that typically, FPS games are played by males and have violent content, several of the participants indicated that they consciously choose this genre for its unabashed aggressiveness. Ivy, who has played FPS games for seven years, said:

> Sometimes, if I blew up a guy and he would type 'Bitch' . . . Well, that just makes me smile and go after him more.

Competition provides an arena in which power gamers are able to define and extend their definitions of self and gender. As Taylor (2003) has observed, one of the most salient pleasures for women gamers is the opportunity to engage in game combat, a space which permits them to challenge gender norms by exploring and testing their aggressive potentiality Indeed, several of the power gamers interviewed take tremendous

pleasure in challenging gender norms through their choice of genre. Ivy, for example, said: 'I liked running around with a rocket launcher and shooting people I didn't know.' At the same time, however, Ivy adamantly asserted her femininity, which she marked by such feminine signs as long fingernails, which she referred to at several points in the interview. Ivy refuses to cut her nails and thus we are presented with a paradox of sorts—the gamer who embodies 'femininity', while performing 'masculinity'. For power gamers, digital games are not a problematic technology. Even as they themselves admit to the hypersexualization of some female images in games and the sexism of some male players, they have defined games successfully for themselves as being about pleasure, mastery and control. Technology here is not a problem but an integral part of life.

This paradox crops up in regard to power gamers in a second area. Power gamers also perform their definitions of gender via the representations of the game characters that they employ. Power gamers are certainly not oblivious to the hypersexualized representation of female avatars and they do realize that such representations pander to male fantasies. However, such representations do not necessarily limit the pleasure of this study's participants. On the contrary, such characters appear to enhance pleasure for a number of these women. Several of the power gamers indicated that they purposefully choose and create characters that are feminine and sexy as well as strong. In an online interview, Kara expressed her appreciation for sexualized female characters:

> When I create a character in an RPG, I like to make them as sexy as possible. Haha! I love a sexy and strong female character. A character who is sexy and strong and can still kick a guy's butt 10 ways to Sunday!

Some additional insight was provided by Chris, another power gamer who writes and reviews games and characters for several women's gaming websites:

> It's not like women want to play ugly characters. They just want to be attractive on their own terms.

Those terms appear to combine [feminine] sexy attributes with [masculine] characteristics like 'strength' and 'intelligence'.

The salient factor for the power gamer in this regard appears to involve choice and control. Having a choice of characters, as well as control over their representations, appeared to maximize these women's sense of agency and pleasure. Chris expressed it this way:

> It's not that I don't want to play a sexual character—it's fantasy role-playing after all and I have fantasies, too. It's that I want it to be my own fantasy, not his.

To the extent that games can provide women with a choice of characters, combined with control of their representation, games function as technologies for explorations of the gendered self, producing paradoxical enactments that challenge cultural norms. Furthermore, when power gamers voiced their concerns about gender bias in games, they cited the weaker power levels of stock female characters; this observation signals their desire for more choice and control within the context of game play. The following exchange occurred in the power gamers' focus group and illustrates how their concerns are tied to their desire for control:

Erin: I wish there were more characters, where they actually did stuff instead of, like, they help the little princesses.

Linda: Oh, princesses, that's the worst.

Lauren: Oh, I hate that one. Just like, 'Oh, save me Morion'. I just wish there [were] more words, like you could actually be the person controlling all this stuff.

A little while later, Lauren commented about the Growling Chicken, a stock character in the second *Lord of the Rings* game:

> The second *Lord of the Rings* has a Growling Chicken, which is nice, but she is a lot weaker than the guys. Like her power level is lower and she just can't do as much and she dies faster and it's kinda weird. Just like, she can't do as much as some of the guys can. I wish it wasn't that way, but that's the way they program it . . . She is in the book; I read about her. She is a strong character. I mean, she's still fighting everything, but she is not powerful. She is just very weak and kind of de-de-de . . . can't fight this now, and then she is dead.

The desire for control of a character's representa-tion is linked to the pleasure sought from the gaming experience. Female characters might also promote player identification and enhance women's pleasure in this regard.[1] As Kara reported: 'I use my characters to reflect the way I wish I had the courage to be.' It is clear that for Kara, control of the character's representation increases her pleasure and enjoyment. It is significant then, that in role-playing games where she is able to create her own characters, she chooses a combination of (feminine) sexuality and (masculine) strength. For power gamers, technology encourages them to enact new definitions of the gendered self. One might say that they just want to look sexy while they're 'kicking butt'.

Negotiation of Gaming: Gender and Technology in an Uneasy Truce

> I like games where you can control the world. And I just started playing *Civilization,* where you get to control the whole world. I think that's fun and the one that I recently acquired was *The Sims.* You cannot play a short game of *The Sims.* Just controlling them where it's a controlled environment, where in your [real world] environment you cannot control everything. But you can control everything that happens on the screen. It's like an escape, you get to just control it and not worry about other stuff you cannot control in your life.
>
> (Jenn, a participant in the moderate gamers' group)

For moderate gamers, as Jenn's comments illustrate, control is once again a salient factor related to the particular pleasures of the gaming experience. However, as Jenn's comments suggest, the nature of control is radically different for this group of women. Whereas control for power gamers relates to the characters that they use to explore new definitions of gender and self, for moderate gamers, control is largely environmental. For a number of the moderate gamers in this study, games provide the pleasure of an ultimately controllable environment. For others in this group, gaming offers an escape or distraction from everyday life, a vehicle used to escape momentarily the gendered role of life's caretaker; here, distraction can be seen as a means of self-control, a way to cope with the demands of women's daily lives.

Commensurate with these particular pleasures and uses, it is not surprising that the moderate gamers expressed preferences for some RPGs, puzzles, cards and problem-solving games. While a few of these women enjoyed competitive games, the moderate gamers as a group tended to reject violent genres such as the FPS games. Kristin's response was typical of this group of women: 'I don't like shooting, zombies, blood here and blood there . . . it's not my type of game.' In addition to choosing genres that are less violent, the moderate gamers veered toward games that provide more opportunities to win. Winning for these women does not necessarily mean defeating an opponent; rather, winning can mean beating the game by predicting and making the right moves in order to solve a puzzle or problem. This type of gratification is the reason that Karen, a 52-year-old housewife, prefers to play *Free Cell*. As she explains, 'If you make the right moves, it is never a non-winnable game.' By playing games like *Free Cell,* Karen is able to control even the very experience of gaming in order to ensure that it provides the particular pleasure that she seeks.

Because control is configured differently for moderate gamers than for power gamers, we need to tease the data in order to understand how gaming functions as a technology of gendered self for this group of women. One set of data provides at least two clues to this end. The first we have briefly mentioned already: moderate gamers seek control and/or distraction from their real-life pressures. The second clue concerns the ways in which moderate gamers tended to draw a line between the genres that women play and those that men play. Thus, while these women emphasized control and distraction as their pleasures, they negotiate gaming in ways that tend to reinscribe traditional gender divisions. For example, many moderate gamers assign fantasy games and violent genres to men. Amy, a moderate gamer, said:

> Most of the men I know play PlayStations, or Xbox, or Nintendo and they are more into it. They get into a drama, even if it is a shoot 'em up drama. If I'm gonna go to a virtual world, I'm going to go for distraction from my life, but not to replace it.

According to Amy, women play games for distraction. She perceives that men become more fully immersed in the virtual game world—they enter more easily into the fantasy and drama and tend to devote more time to games. This line between reality and fantasy helps to explain other remarks made by moderate gamers such as Kerry who said: 'I am kind of annoyed by people who talk about video games like real life.' The distinction between women and men and reality and fantasy carried over to a focus group discussion about the representations of women in games:

> I think that most video games are geared towards younger males. They just don't think that there's an audience, like, female. They're geared more towards the man . . . Anytime you have a female fighter, she's got like huge breasts and a flat stomach and long legs and it's always [an] exact outfit you'll never see in real life. It's all, like, glorified.
>
> (Danni)

A little while later, Rachel noted that *The Sims* game that she prefers permits players to choose more realistic characters:

> In *The Sims* you can choose your body. They do have, like, slender, big-boob woman and . . . the arousing man [who is] rippled out. But they also have, like, the overweight woman-in-her-thirties character.

When asked by the moderator whether they could identify with game characters, or whether some character representations might be empowering for women, the moderate gamers again asserted a difference between the real world and the game world:

> For me it's just a video. It's not like . . . I mean like women in magazines and stuff. Yeah, that's the difference, coz those are like real people. But it's just a video game.
>
> (Lauren)

In doubting that such representations might be empowering for women and in denying any identification with the game's characters, moderate gamers provide a clue about how they define gender and self. Inasmuch as self and gender remain tethered to the moderate gamers' realities, their habits of negotiating game technology seem to reinscribe a game technology or gender division for these women. So even as they admit to playing games and having fun doing so, the culture of gaming overall is largely seen as a male domain. Here, the technology of gaming must be negotiated, as for this group it is still largely gendered masculine, even as more women play games themselves.

With one foot firmly in the 'real world' at all times, it should not be surprising then that moderate gamers talk a lot about the pleasures of control and distraction. In some respects, 'control' would seem to signal an intense involvement with the games, almost diametrically opposed to distraction. However, it can be argued that for the women in this study, control and distraction are two sides of the same coin. In their discussion, control and distraction bracket real life, providing two approaches for coping with its stressors. To demonstrate this, the moderate gamers' 'control' discourse will be vetted further.

For some of the women who expressed pleasure in being able to exercise control over an environment or situation, computer games appear to be useful as a rehearsal for the challenges of life. Eva, for example, faced a daunting cultural adjustment when she came to the USA 10 years ago. When we specifically asked her to compare the difficulties of her real life and the challenges that she finds in computer games, she replied:

> I think it's almost the same thing . . . Because I tried the game [that] I can do . . . [In] real life I can do the same thing. I think, almost the same. Whatever I put my effort, I can do in real life and the game.

Eva shares a characteristic with several other gamers who played in order to control an environment—a need to think through problems. Eva prefers war (strategy) games:

> [B]ecause [I] have to think what I have to do . . . how can I move . . . how can I improve my characters . . . how I can win. I have to think.

Many of the moderate gamers indicated that they enjoyed the mental challenge that games provide. Lily spoke about this pleasure as she reflected on her 'role' in the mystery games that she plays:

> You're like, the conscience, you know. You're pretty much in control of his mind. And you get his mind and . . . all the clues that he knows about to figure it out. And then you have to tell *him* . . .

It puts you up on a pedestal, even over the main character.

We read Lily's comment as further evidence of both gender division and the line that moderate gamers impose between reality and the gameworld. Lily's description of her 'role' as the male character's conscience suggests that she sees herself as positioned outside the game world. It seems likely, then, that the pleasure she derives from this game also works to construct or reinforce her sense of gendered self. By describing her pleasure in the terms of being placed on a pedestal above the main (male) character, we might even read her particular construction of gendered self to be one of superiority. For Lily, the self is constructed as exceedingly competent but nonetheless embedded in the gender conventions of reality.

Although some moderate gamers seek their pleasure in games that help them to think through problems, others among this group play in order to stop thinking about the worries of their daily lives. Michelle, who plays for distraction in order to relieve stress and to stop thinking about her problems and commitments, compared computer games to rock climbing:

> You give all your attention to something, so it is like the rest of the world just, you know, falls away, because you are focusing . . . so intensely . . . on this one thing. I heard when people talk about . . . rock climbing. That is, people like rock climbing so much, because . . . the only thing they have to think about is the place to put their hand. They don't think about the next mortgage payment, a girlfriend, or whatever; they are, like, just completely taken out by the next motion they have to make.

The moderate gamer uses games in order to cope with her everyday life. For some women, games provide a way to think through and solve various problems and situations; for others, computer games provide a temporary respite from the worries that plague their minds. The desire for control and the desire for distraction are two sides of the same coin, pleasures that bracket the moderate gamer's position. These indicate that the moderate gamer is situated at an intersection where the virtual gameworld intersects with their reality The moderate gamer negotiates gaming technologies in order to help cope with the routines of their daily life, yet they are not quite fully immersed in the gaming world. This particular negotiation of gaming technology enables 'care of the self' (Foucault, 1988). Nonetheless, this self appears to be gendered within the conventions of traditional social norms.

Rejection of Gaming: Gender Triumphs over Technology of Gaming

> You know, girls, I'm in my mid-20s. The girls I hang out with, they're just way more into going out with friends and doing things, like in their different clubs and organizations. And they have full-time jobs, or they have part-time jobs while they're going to school . . . Everything they do is more interaction-based. There's not time to be doing something with the computer or with a TV.
>
> (Michelle, a participant in the non-gamers' group)

The non-gamers had critical, negative perceptions of gaming. They rejected gaming as a waste of time and were quite vocal about asserting other priorities. In the focus groups, non-gamers expressed the strongest opinions about a perceived 'gaming culture'. They were concerned about the sexualized and violent content of games, but acknowledged that this is a problem with other media products as well. Non-gamers also speculated that players become addicted to computer games. These women viewed gaming as an asocial and solitary activity and believed most gamers to be interpersonally inept. By their implied and expressed comparisons to players, non-gamers define themselves in ways that might be considered more traditionally female: completely grounded in reality, interpersonally competent and with their priorities set on things that really matter.

For non-gamers, the rejection of gaming was expressed as control over time and the assertion of other priorities. The amount of time required to play was discussed at some length in the non-gamers' focus group. Several of the participants stated that the length of time required to play was 'ridiculous'. Speaking about *Final Fantasy,* a role-playing game with which she had some familiarity Lindsay observed that 'it takes you like 20 hours until you reach the end'. When asked what type of games she might consider playing, Michelle again asserted that time was a primary consideration; if she did decide to play, she would look for games with 'an endpoint' which do not continue 'on for years' and that can be completed 'within a certain amount of time'.

Time appears to be significant in these women's rejection of games because it is a practical obstacle to their participation and because their leisure time is determined largely by family and work responsibilities:

> Women usually have more things to do. I mean, lets face it, they're out there working. Not only do [women] work outside of the home, but then they come in and have to make dinner, do the laundry, get the kids ready for school the next day . . . They don't have any time for games much less for themselves, to do things they wanna do.
>
> (Kathy)

While Kathy's comments demonstrate the practical consequences of limited leisure time, they also suggest that the non-gamer's time is configured in relation to their established gender roles and responsibilities.

According to the non-gamers, their rejection of gaming is not simply a matter of daily responsibilities limiting their available leisure time. While several of the women indicated that they might play games if they could be completed within a short period of time, by and large the non-gamers echoed Michelle, whose comments open this section, in asserting that they choose other priorities.

The choices that non-gamers make appear to align with traditional female expectations, and include interpersonal activities which are 'interaction based'. This particular choice is centered in the way that non-gamers define themselves and is positioned in opposition to their perceptions of players. Non-gamers viewed gaming as a 'solitary' activity which attracts individuals who lack interpersonal skills. For example, Jill observed that players become so absorbed in games that they 'ignore everyone around them'. Similarly, Michelle perceives her own brother and sister, who are both avid gamers, as 'very introverted':

> They are very good at like computer language and decoding this and doing that in the role-playing game, [but] if you take them out to a social event they are not sure how to act with other physical human beings. But put them behind a keyboard and they can talk to people outside of the country, but they can't deal with one-on-one behaviors.

By comparison, then, non-gamers imply their own interpersonal competence. Ironically, despite non-gamers' interpersonal competence, their self-definitions construct a gendered, split-sphere arrangement that is quite long established. It is possible to read how separate spheres conflict with traditionally-gendered interpersonal objectives in Amber's comments:

> If they are my age, which is just under 30, then I'm thinking of the guys in the long, black trench coats who are playing the role-playing games online. Where it's a strangely solitary event, but it's still a group event in a very solitary way. This is why I think that I am still single. Because I think that all the eligible men my age are somewhere in a room playing video games.

We might conclude that non-gamers are playing another game by real-world rules. In addition, non-gamers were more concerned about the sexualized representations of women in computer gamers, but recognized that other media contribute to these stereotypes, creating an intertextual effect:

> I've noticed . . . that some of the qualities of some of these women, that I've seen in some of these video games or ads, seem to be extremely desirable by men, such as their sluttiness. Uh, and it's just, it's been relationship breakers before and . . . I don't know where it comes from. I don't know if that's from TV, magazines or it's from these games.
>
> (Amber)

Amber and some of the other non-gamers worry that these stereotypes create expectations on the part of men, which spill over into the real world:

> I think that men . . . It's kind of the virgin–whore dichotomy, in that they'd like to date a nice girl, but really, they'd really like her to act like this . . . Or do those things in the bedroom that I see on TV. Especially the Japanamation kind of look and those girls seem really domineering, but yet are also coy and shy, but yet very strong sexual overtones.
>
> (Amber)

A few lines later, this is followed by Kathy:

> I'm reminded of all the pornography literature that stated, well, they have found it doesn't make . . . men want to go out and rape women. But when they ask them specific questions about, you know, why women are here, what is their purpose in life, what do you look for in women? They found that the very heavy pornography users were more likely to have really, really shitty opinions about women. Excuse my language. But it's true, the way they perceive women is not what women really are.

In Kathy's comments, especially, one can hear a paradox. While non-gamers seem to define themselves in ways that align with traditional ideas of femininity, she insists that she is an interpersonally competent agent who exercises active choice in how she determines priorities and controls her time. She also appears to feel the real effects of sexism most acutely.

Gaming as a Gendered, Technological Practice: Re-integrating Theory

'Technologies of the gendered self' refers to the dynamic relationship between women, gender and technological use. This concept helps us to understand how women negotiate game play, gender expectations and roles in relation to technology use. It acknowledges that practices are often multiple and conflicting and seeks to expand rather than conflate ambiguities and differences. In this way this concept should be useful in understanding a wider range of technological uses and how gender relates, as it more broadly takes account of active users and multiple uses of technologies.

The results of this research demonstrate that this concept is useful in understanding how female gamers integrate different levels of gaming technologies with their perceptions of gender and self. Additionally, by allowing for variations in the degree of technological integration, the concept allows an exploration of how different gender constructions are implicated in the way that gamers negotiate the tensions of gaming and reality. As part of that negotiation, in fact, gamers create different boundaries for their game-playing activities, with some seeing gaming as squarely separate from 'real life' or reality and others acknowledging that the two overlap and co-constitute each other.

Power gamers who have integrated gaming technologies into their everyday lives construct a gendered self that might be described as more fluid and androgynous, in that it is comprised of a palette of chosen traits and interests; this contrasts with a gendered female self that embodies 'traditional' norms reflective of a masculine/feminine binary. The integration of gaming technology empowers women with a confidence that prevails in the challenge and competition that they encounter in games. Even 'conventional' signs of femininity, such as long nails and sexualized representations, were viewed by many of these women as pleasurable and emancipating, rather than as subjugating them in male–female power dynamics.

By comparison, the gendered self of moderate gamers is situated in a liminal space between 'real life' and gaming. Although moderate gamers enjoy playing and can be quite good at it, they have not fully integrated gaming technologies with their gendered identity. While power gamers perform a more fluid and androgynous gender in gaming, moderate gamers' self-constructions do not demonstrate this degree of fusion but rather they suggest an uneasy alliance between identity and activity. For them, gaming functions as a coping mechanism, a vehicle of escape from reality, and games provide an opportunity to control an environment on their own terms. For them, gaming is a sphere apart from 'reality'. Moderate gamers perceive gaming as a predominantly male activity and situate themselves as more closely aligned with 'the real world' than the fantasy worlds of particular games. Subsequently in thus making the distinction and then negotiating reality and gaming, moderate gamers construct a gendered self that appears to be positioned in an uneasy truce between two worlds.

In contrast, non-gamers, who rejected gaming and its culture as totally masculine, positioned themselves as successfully living in the 'real world'. Here again, gameworlds are separate from the 'real' world, as articulated by this group. In this study, these women frequently rejected gaming because it takes too much time, a commodity they perceive as already limited and better spent on 'social' activities—interests and pursuits that are often generalized as more traditionally feminine. The non-gamers studied had less understanding of gaming technologies and tended to depict players as interpersonally inept and 'addicted' to gaming. Unlike power and moderate gamers, the non-gamers did not appear to appreciate the emancipative potential of games, neither did they discern the possibility of negotiating a 'truce' between gaming and reality, or even less likely, see how the two might merge in any way.

Finally, we want to acknowledge that in outlining this conceptualization of 'technologies of the gendered self', this study has relied on three somewhat artificial categories in order to describe female gamers and non-gamers. These categories, and the levels of technological integration that they represent, need not be viewed as a rigid matrix for understanding gender and gaming. With further research, the model can be expanded, modified and refined to represent better the complexities and power dynamics that operate at the intersection of gender and games.

Conclusion

This study began by asking how individual differences in the consumption of computer games intersect with gender and how it is that games and gender mutually constitute each other. To examine this question, its efforts were focused on adult women, seeking to understand the gaming experience from their perspectives, with particular attention to differences in level of play, as well as their genre preferences. Based on the participants' responses, three levels of game consumption were identified. For power gamers, those participants who reported the highest levels of consumption, technology and gender appear to be most highly integrated. These women play more frequently and tended to play multiple genres, deriving different pleasures from different types of games, including the mastery of game-based skills and competition. These women seemed most likely and willing to exploit gaming technology in order to explore different enactments of a gendered self.

By comparison, moderate gamers play games in order to cope with their lives. These women reported that they take pleasure in controlling the gaming environment, or alternately, that games provide a necessary distraction from the pressures of their daily lives. Moderate gamers enjoy games, but negotiate technology in a way that reinscribes the gender divisions that we traditionally associate with the lived world.

The non-gamers who participated in the study expressed strong criticisms about game-playing and gaming culture. For these women, games are a waste of time—a limited commodity better spent on other activities. Their decisions not to play define a self that might be viewed as more traditionally feminine, but which these women insist is interpersonally competent and grounded in the things that matter.

The findings here support the work of other feminist scholars who have previously argued that gender and technology have a reciprocal relationship. This study has tried especially to respond to van Zoonen's (2002) arguments concerning the complexity of technology and gender by accounting for differences in game consumption. By examining three levels of consumption, it has developed a more nuanced understanding of the ways in which gender and technology are articulated. In addition, it has proposed a concept, 'technologies of the gendered self', which offers flexibility and moves us closer to a better understanding of how technology and gender intersect in individuals' resistance or compliance to existing gender hierarchies.

Acknowledgements

The authors would like to acknowledge the work of Emmanuel Adugu in the planning and conceptualization of this article. Further, we thank the members of the Qualitative Research Methods class, who contributed data to this project.

Note

1. In this article we do not explore in depth the relationship between identification of players and their avatars, although we do subscribe to Gee's (2003) belief that such relationships are complex in their construction. This limitation is due in part to our lack of specific questioning of women regarding their identification with avatars (or not)—we mainly talked about game-play and representation. In reflecting on the evidence, however, we can see that power gamers are more likely to identify fully with their avatars (viewing themselves as controlling the character, the character in the virtual world and their hopes and plans for the character), while moderate gamers are more conflicted. In using Gee's taxonomy of levels of identification, we could argue that moderate gamers cannot construct a projective identity. That is, they can view themselves as controlling avatars in different games, but do not make a complete interface between 'the real-world person and the virtual character' (2003: 56). For moderate gamers, the avatar (virtual identity) and their own identity (real world) are not meshed, but remain distinct.

References

Balsamo, A. (1996) *Technologies of the Gendered Body: Reading Cyborg Women.* Durham, NC: Duke University Press.

Beasley, B. and T. C. Standley (2002) 'Shirts vs. Skins: Clothing as an Indicator of Gender Role Stereotyping in Video Games', *Mass Communication and Society* 5(3): 279–93.

Cassell, J. and H. Jenkins (1998) *From Barbie to Mortal Kombat: Gender and Computer Games.* Cambridge, MA: MIT Press.

Consalvo, M. and R. Treat (2002) 'Exploring Gameplay: A Survey of Game Players' Preferences', unpublished manuscript.

Cunningham, H. (2000) '*Mortal Kombat* and Computer Game Girls', in J. Caldwell (ed.) *Electronic Media and Technoculture*, pp. 213–26. New Brunswick, NJ: Rutgers University Press.

Davies, J. (2002) 'Male Dominance of Video Game Production and Consumption: Understanding the Social and Cultural Processes', URL (consulted 30 June 2004): http://www.gamasutra.com/education/theses/20020708/davies_01.shtml

Foucault, M. (1988) 'Technologies of the Self: A Seminar with Michel Foucault', in L. H. Martin, H. Gutman and H. Hutton (eds) *Technologies of the Gendered Self: A Seminar with Michel Foucault*, pp. 16–49. Amherst, MA: University of Massachusetts Press.

Gee, J. (2003) *What Video Games Have to Teach Us about Learning and Literacy.* New York: Palgrave.

Geertz, C. (1973) 'Thick Description: Toward an Interpretive Theory of Culture', in *The Interpretation of Cultures*, pp. 298–320. New York: Harper.

Haraway, D. (1991) *Simians, Cyborgs and Women.* New York: Routledge.

Heintz-Knowles, K. and J. Henderson (2002) 'Gender, Violence and Victimization in Top-selling Video Games', paper presented at the Annual Meeting of the Association for Education in Journalism and Mass Communication, Miami Beach, FL, August.

Ivory, J. and H. Wilkerson (2002) 'Video Games Are from Mars, Not Venus: Gender, Electronic Game Play and Attitudes toward the Medium', paper presented at the Annual Meeting of the Association for Education in Journalism and Mass Communication, Miami Beach, FL, August.

Kerr, A. (2003) 'Women Just Want to Have Fun: A Study of Adult Female Players of Digital Games', in M. Copier and J. Raessens (eds) *Level Up: Digital Games Research Conference*, pp. 270–85. Utrecht: University of Utrecht.

Kinder, M. (1991) *Playing with Power in Movies, Television and Video Games: From Muppet Babies to Teenage Mutant Ninja Turtles*. Berkeley, CA: University of California Press.

Mason, J. (2002) *Qualitative Researching* (2nd edn). London: Sage.

McNay L. (1992) *Foucault and Feminism*. Boston, MA: Northeastern University Press.

Media Analysis Laboratory (1998) 'Video Game Culture: Leisure and Play Preferences of B.C. Teens', *Media Awareness Network*, URL (consulted 30 June 2004): http://www.media-awareness.ca/

Okorafor, N. and L. Davenport (2001) 'Virtual Women: Replacing the Real', paper presented at the Annual Conference of the Association for Education in Journalism and Mass Communication, Washington, DC, August.

Provenzo, E. (1991) *Video Kids: Making Sense of Nintendo*. Cambridge, MA: Harvard University Press.

Rakow, L. (1992) *Gender on the Line: Women, the Telephone and Community Life*. Urbana, IL: University of Illinois Press.

Schott, G. and K. Horrell (2000) 'Girl Gamers and Their Relationship with the Gaming Culture', *Convergence* 6(4): 36–53.

Taylor, T. L. (2003) 'Multiple Pleasures: Women and Online Gaming', *Convergence* 9(1): 21–46.

Van Zoonen, L. (2002) 'Gendering the Internet: Claims, Controversies and Cultures', *European Journal of Communication* 17(1): 5–23.

Yates, S. and K. Littleton (2001) 'Understanding Computer Game Cultures: A Situated Approach', in E. Green and A. Adam (eds) *Virtual Gender: Technology, Consumption and Identity*, pp. 103–23. London: Routledge.

50.
REAL BOYS CARRY GIRLY EPICS

Normalising Gender Bending in Online Games

Esther MacCallum-Stewart

> The fact that many games are designed for a teenage male market probably goes some way to explaining the predominance of stereotypical and sometimes demeaning representations of women, That does not mean, however, that all players 'read' or use the signifiers of gender and appearance in the same way.
>
> (King and Kryzwinska, 2006, pp. 183–4)

This paper was initially intended to be about the roles women like to take when playing games. How do they socialise? What roles do they prefer and how do they imagine them in terms of role-play? It quickly became apparent however, that a more pressing issue was at stake, prompted largely by the responses to questions asked amongst players of both genders. Why do men like playing women so much, and how do they understand this role?

The intense speculation around Lara Croft as a site of gendered tension in games has skewed a more pressing factor for the players of games,—namely that players of all genders are accustomed to approaching female avatars as one option amongst many, and that they often chose these for ludic, rather than gendered reasons. This act has normalised the adoption of female avatars by male players to the extent that they feel more comfortable with assuming them as gameplay devices. In beat 'em up games, the female characters have evolved so that they often possess the more technical, difficult moves to reproduce, meaning that they are often regarded both as challenging to play and as a marker of proficiency. Furthermore,

the social context in which beat 'em up players engage with each other and the game often means that they are in direct contact—in the same room or arcade, for example. There is thus nothing to mask the players 'real' appearance from each other. Thus, man playing woman has become a normal practise, and not one that is seen as either aberrant or subversive.

Lara Croft altered this perception. In *Tomb Raider* and its sequels, the player exists in isolation to others. Speculation over the role of the male as female, over the site of Lara's own body, and over the relative consideration given to the cross-gendered performance is therefore related to directly. Whilst many have expressed unease about Lara's appearance and her relationship with the player, Helen Kennedy suggests that the experience is a deliberate act of transgendering:

> One potential way of exploring this transgendering is to consider the fusion of player and game character as a kind of queer embodiment, the merger of the flesh of the (male) player with Lara's elaborated feminine body of pure information. This new queer identity potentially subverts stable distinctions between identification and desire and also by extension the secure and heavily defended polarities of masculine and feminine subjectivity.
>
> (Kennedy, 2002)

However, whilst Lara was alone with the player, she was not alone in a rapidly developing game world, where a multiplicity of female characters was emerging. Alongside Lara, other game genres were already making active use of female avatars for various purposes. Whilst these did often conform to derogative images of women, they were increasingly used for different purposes—by female players to express self, and by all players in order to play in a completist manner. Additionally, the introduction of figures such as Elaine Marley (*The Secret of Monkey Island*, 1990) allowed feminine expression which did not necessary always conform to passive ideals of the damsel in distress.

More recently, the MMORPG (Massively Multiplayer Online Roleplaying Game) has become one of the most popular forms of gaming. Within this construction, players can usually adopt either a male or female avatar without there being a statistical difference between genders (these differences are instead enacted through more traditional Dungeons and Dragons—style differentiations of class and race). The choice of male or female avatar again becomes a site for examination, with studies noting that there is a predominance of male characters who choose female avatars—Nick Yee estimates that over 80% of male players cross gender during play (Yee, 2007). Most often, this is attributed by researchers as 'more concerned with mastery and control of a body coded as female within a safe and unthreatening context' (Kennedy, 2002). However, although there is a great deal of weight to this argument, the viability of computer avatar within an established historical games context, where players already have established responses towards avatar selection, is not considered.

In a series of interviews and observations recorded within the MMORPG *World of Warcraft* by the author, considerable resistance to the idea of cross-gendered experimentation was encountered. Users described, candidly, the many reasons for choosing to play either gender. This paper argues that the relative freedom with which these players express their arguments is in part derived from their familiarity with adopting avatars of both genders throughout their gaming lives. By the time of MMORPGs, the adoption of a female form was such a naturalised action that many players now choose to move across gender for aesthetic pleasure, rather than from a need to experience a new form of being. Players are so used to this action that

they do not see it as deviant. Rather, they celebrate it as a fan activity unique to them.

Early Games, Special Moves and Spinning Bird Kicks

> Computer games as we know them were invented by young men around the time of the invention of graphical displays. They were enjoyed by young men, and young men soon made a very profitable business of them, dovetailing to a certain extent with the existing pinball business. Arcade computer games were sold into male-gendered spaces, and when home computer consoles were invented, they were sold through male-oriented consumer electronics channels to more young men. The whole industry consolidated very quickly around a young male demographic—all the way from the gameplay design to the arcade environment to the retail world.
>
> (Laurel, 1998)

As Brenda Laurel suggests, there were few early female characters simply because the target demographic of games did not anticipate them as users. Significant previous work in Games Studies, not least through the discussions presented in *From Barbie to Mortal Kombat* (Cassell et al. 1998), trace both the beginnings of gender studies concerning games, as well as the early patterns of female involvement in games' play, design and participation. It is however worth noting, that the presence of women in games has in some cases been overlooked. The blue valkyrie from *Gauntlet* (1985) may have been a blur of pixels and thus hardly female in form, but she was still a formidable gameplay choice, the heroine sidekicks of Lucas Arts point and click adventures are feisty as well as fully clothed and Samus Aran is of course, famously revealed as female at the end of *Metroid* (1986).

Streetfighter II (1986) is however a landmark in gaming. Although not the first beat 'em up, it reconfigured the genre in new ways, with manga-style animations enabling cartoonish movement; bright, lively scenery; strong characterisation and a revolutionary new style of 'special moves' which differentiated each character not simply by speed, strength or health, and demanded that the player activate a series of complicated yet intentionally organic manipulations of buttons and joystick in order to complete each action successfully.

In *Streetfighter II* the player had to choose between eight central characters (later, the four boss characters were also available to play through unlocking Easter Egg secrets). One of these was Chun Li, a Chinese detective for Interpol on the hunt for her missing father. Chun Li was strikingly dressed in a blue qipao (a long tunic with split sides allowing the legs more freedom), which showed most of her rather chunky thighs, her hair in 'ox horn' buns with ribbons. Chun Li's special moves included the *Hyakuretsukyaku*, the Hundred Rending Leg (more commonly know as the Lightening Kick), which enabled her to kick her opponent in an animated 'blur' of feet, a smaller but faster version of the *hadoken* fireball thrown by counterparts Ryu and Ken, the Spinning Bird Kick, in which she leapt onto her hands and span across the screen, repeatedly hitting her opponent in the head with her upside-down kicks, and an ability that allowed her to bounce herself off walls (in this case, the 'wall' being the players screen—so one might perhaps ironically refer to this as bouncing off the Fourth Wall), then stomp on the opposing player's head. Overall, Chun Li was the fastest of the characters in the game and the one whose moves were also the easiest overall to execute, although they had less relative power than most of her male counterparts, making her a formidable opponent. These abilities, rather than her femininity, led her to quickly become a favourite amongst the hardcore arcade gamers that David Surman identifies in his analysis of the series, as well as amongst tournament and casual players in arcades and later, on consoles (Surman, 2007a).

The *Streetfighter* series prides itself on the tactile identification with its audiences—the first arcade console was predicted on how hard a player hit the buttons, for example, a legacy that was continued in the 'light, medium, hard' buttons that replaced this formation in its second iteration, and the special moves that a player must perform mirror joystick movement with the animated resultant action (Surman, 2007a, p. 211). The game deliberately presented characters that were fast, slow, long reaching, more powerful, more agile or able to carry out more devastating moves. Difference in fighting style was therefore an essential part of the game. Chun Li therefore became one of these

differences—she was the fast, nimble character who sacrificed power for speed. These elements clearly gave her an advantage and meant that frequently she was chosen for statistical gain, not for gender preference.

Chun Li's obvious advantages to a novice player were coupled with her engagement with the audience. She is easier to play by a novice than her male counterparts, allowing a far greater degree of luck in winning if her player button bashes and swivels the joystick wildly to execute a special move. However, her avatar is also altogether more playful. After winning a bout, the hardened Interpol warrior again breaks the fourth wall, facing outwards towards the player and leaping up and down in a triumphant dance, or giving a 'victory' sign with her fingers and loudly proclaiming 'Ya Ta!' ('I did it'). This admission of fallibility (she might not have 'done it'), as well as the glee of Chun Li's avatar as she celebrates her victory in such an obviously childish manner is far more satisfying than male counterparts such as Ryu, who never says anything, instead folding his arms and letting the wind blow through his hair, or E. Honda the wrestler, who merely grunts a taciturn acknowledgement of his win.

The tradition of Chun Li as fast, endearing and also skilful had a lasting affect on the beat 'em up genre. From the *Streetfighter* series onwards, the option to play at least one female character was usually present in beat 'em ups. Clear descendants from Chun Li can be seen in many of these figures; Mileena and Kitana (*Mortal Kombat*, 1992), Pai Chan (*Virtua Fighter*, 1993), Jung Chan and Ling Xiaoyu (*Tekken*, 1994) and Kasumi and Lei Fang (*Dead or Alive*, 1996) all wear the qipao, for example. Jill Valentine and Claire Redfern of the *Resident Evil* series (1997, 1998) also exemplify the ways in which a female protagonist with slightly different skills from a male counterpart can be used to alter gameplay of the same scenario.

It also possible that Chun Li validated the pleasure of allowing the player to admire self as avatar. In *Streetfighter II Turbo* on the SNES (1991), an Easter Egg allowed Chun Li to appear in a different coloured qipao; and from *Super Streetfighter II: the New Challengers* (1993) onwards, characters had multiple colours available and this developed throughout games until by the time of *Dead or Alive*, the aesthetic appearance of each woman was not only of paramount importance, but completing the game on various levels of difficulty, attaining certain scores or finishing with a particular character many times allowed multiple costumes, appearances and sometimes even hair colour and style changes. Even at this stage however, these women were firmly encoded within a male gaze—*Dead or Alive* had a notorious setting which allowed a player to change the extent to which each avatars' breasts bounced during combat, for example, and the subsequent release of games such as *Dead or Alive Xtreme Beach Volleyball* (2003) confirmed the link between attractive women and impressive costumes.

At this point there are several important things to note. Firstly, the assumption that female avatars generally appeared in skimpy, revealing costumes does hold true, but equally, many of these alternative appearances emphasised intricate costumes and graphical patterns that displayed the prowess of the designers. The ability to uncover [sic] alternative costumes also activated the ever-popular gameplay facet of collecting; once the game was finished, it was not 'complete' until the whole array of alternatives was assembled. Thus the pleasure of viewing female avatars was accompanied by a gameplay aesthetic that encouraged users to keep playing for different gains.

Secondly, beat 'em ups were primarily social games—although players could play on their own (and presumably try to collect all the costumes available), the real pleasure was in playing them against real opponents. Thus the player who chose a woman did not exist in an imaginary limbo to their opponent; usually they were sitting or standing right next to them, presenting the player with both the physical and imagined identity of their opposition at once, and normalising the virtual/real difference.

Thirdly, although female avatars clearly did pander to the male gaze, their statistical benefits against other players meant that they were often popular choices. Nina Williams from *Tekken*, for example, was often considered the most technically precise character, and the emphasis throughout on the game on long, very detailed special moves for women avatars meant that often the female characters were difficult to master, but very powerful once this was achieved. The female avatar was slowly becoming the avatar of choice; not because of appearance, but because of ludic gain.

Along Came Lara

A great deal has been written about Lara Croft—so much so that a casual observer into Games Studies might at first think that she constitutes the only female avatar in the history of games, and certainly the only one of feminist note. This is regrettable. Firstly, much of the early theory surrounding Lara prioritises her as a single female character from the emerging genre of the FPS, suggesting that previously, the choice to become a female character was limited. Secondly, detrimental readings of her physical appearance often overrule the pleasure of Lara herself, emphasising her bionic breasts rather than her dry wisecracks, and her curved appearance rather than her prowess as a gymnast and warrior.

It is thus useful to remember that Lara Croft did not exist in a vacuum; she was instead born into a world where female avatars already took an active part in gameplay lives. In 1996, when *Tomb Raider* was first introduced, the role of female characters in games was already well established, and as described above, it was often one of choice.

Lara is undeniably a figure of male desire. From her various incarnations as filmic idol, digital treasure hunter and front page pin-up, the sexuality of Lara cannot be denied . . . except perhaps by the role of the Tomb Raider franchise in promoting a fizzy drink. In 1999, Eidos and the Lucozade sports drink launched the 'Gone a bit Lara' campaign, following on from a series of animated advertisements starring Lara herself. In this, young women dressed as Lara Croft and presumably also under the influence of Lucozade hide on buses, are chased by dogs and ambush strange men in gorilla masks (http://www.youtube.com/watch?v=DADWwvfI33k). At the close of the advertisement, two women in an Accident and Emergency ward nod in recognition to each other, immediately cutting into a final shot of many 'Laras' running desperately across a road.

In the 'Gone a Bit Lara' campaign, the implication is that many women, having played and enjoyed the game, were now trying to live out, or were perhaps subsumed by their fantasies in the real world. The advertisement Laras are desperate, frantic, alarming, but the emphasis is on their normality—they bear a passing resemblance to Lara in that they all have dark, plaited hair and wear Lara's trademark combat shorts, green vest and thigh holsters, but otherwise they are surprisingly 'everyday' in appearance. They are most emphatically not Angelina Jolie, the actress chosen to play Lara Croft in the film version of the game. The implication was that anyone, *especially* women, could go 'a bit Lara', presumably from playing too much *Tomb Raider* and drinking too much Lucozade.

It is this latter point that is crucial. Lara Croft may be demeaning, unrealistic, a site of horrific sexual deviance, a site of playful experimentation, bionic, sadistic and troublesome, but she was also a heroine to women as well as to men. For a generation of players accustomed to trudging around with the grunting protagonist of the *Doom* games and newer 'heroes' such as Duke Nukem (who gives cash to dancing girls during the game with the injunction 'Shake it, baby'), Lara was not only a welcome relief, but also a fantastic opportunity.

Tanya Krzywinska describes Lara Croft as 'a combination of both object and wilful subject' (King and Krzywinska, 2006, p. 181). It is undeniable that her appearance (highly sexualised) and her actions (highly aggressive) are problematic, but they are problematic because they throw into contrast an issue that was already of concern—the adoption of a foreign body within a gaming sphere as a virtual representation of self.

MMORPG: Many Men Online Role Playing Girls

> Through role-playing it is possible to test out new frontiers and new roles. As a player of games, I have the leisure and luxury to explore what it is like to be something totally other. 'What are you', you ask, and I don't answer with my real gender, nationality or age. I am an orc, a shaman, in Kalimdor . . . I still know very well who I am, but I am also something else, something other—and online, playing a role-playing game, I set some of that other free.
>
> (Mortensen, 2007, p. 305)

The research concerning the question of men who play women has been fraught with difficulty. Many critics argue that in some form that men primarily

cross gender in order to experiment as part of natural sexual development, to 'play' with gender ideas, or for reasons to do with the gaze, which are offset by traditional Freudian anxieties (Carr, 2002, Kennedy, 2002). The media frequently portray cross-gendered play to demonstrate the 'otherness' of players, and to some extent to encourage paranoia about players' identity online. Programmes such as *Wonderland—Virtual Adultery and Cyberspace Love* (aired 30th January, BBC 1) emphasise the potential titillation factor of gendered online identity, encouraging sexual prejudices that suggest cross-gendered play is aberrant or deviant in form, and that it is predominantly sexual in nature. Gender switching therefore is seen as a site of tension, and these positions have largely informed gendered readings of male–female positioning within games.

There are also other elements that support the problematic depiction of gendered play in game worlds. Players often support the notion that many men choose female avatars because, as one parody on You Tube states 'you all know this is as close as I'm gonna get to an actual girlfriend' (IceflowStudios, 2007). Finally, as David Surman has noted, what players say about their female avatars and why they play them, and what they actually believe to be true, can be two separate things, with the latter a subject that they may feel embarrassment about, and predicated on their own social preconceptions and inhibitions (Surman, 2007b).

This research was therefore performed in a climate where players have been in some ways socially conditioned to believe that they are a minority. When asking them about their gender switching, however, the results were surprising. Informal questioning was carried out across a broad spectrum of *World of Warcraft* (Blizzard, 2004–present) players—by asking a specific guild, by recording abstract comments or actions made by players, and by observing comments made on the forums that any player with an account can access. *World of Warcraft* (*WoW*) was chosen because of its popularity—to date it is the largest online game in the world, with over ten million accounts. *WoW* has a reputation for attracting a broad spectrum of players, and for being responsible for introducing many new people to the world of gaming.

In *World of Warcraft*, all avatars (or 'toons') are the same body shape, weight and height, dependent on race and sex. They are differentiated by their clothes (gained usually by questing), and various customisable aspects chosen when the player selects an avatar, including hair colour and style, jewellery, horn size or shape, and facial features. A female human joke typifies this; 'Me and my girlfriends exchange clothes all the time; we're all the same size!' indeed, they are *exactly* the same size. This is an unusual option—changing shape is allowed in games such as *Lord of the Rings, Online* (where players can choose female hobbits with fat tummies or big bottoms, or choose male figures without the usual quotient of musculature) (2007–present), *Oblivion, the Elder Scrolls* (2006–present), and *City of Heroes* (2004–present). However, it is useful in this context as the set body form means that the female/male shape is uniform from the onset, and thus also regarded as a given by players. This is also interesting, as the specifics detailed above that initially drew players towards female avatars—the difference that female players offer, are *not* present within these games—instead of females being faster, having more detailed moves and so on, these statistical differences are determined by race (dwarf, undead, troll, gnome . . .) and class (mage, warrior, shaman, hunter . . .).

The ability to costume and display one's avatar is a core part of online gaming. The equipment that players wear is gained through questing and adventuring together, often in large groups or very difficult gameplay circumstances. High-level equipment tends to be ornate and distinctive (Eynalir, 2007, provides a visual record of this), thus clothing also denotes status. Very often, the form of the female displays this to better effect—ironically, it is the curves and protuberances of the female form that emphasise areas such as chest, stomach and head in a far more obvious way than the thickset appearance of the male form. Morie et al. suggest that:

> Perhaps the conflation of the 'masculine' space of the computer, combined with the notion of 'gear' (armor and weapons) actually regenders costume play in more masculine direction[s]. What this suggests is that while costume play on computers may be creating more female-friendly play opportunities, conversely, it may also be opening up more avenues of dress-up for men.
>
> (Morie, 2007)

In addition to normal costuming, various festivals, special events and quests during the year provide players with costumes or objects that are entirely cosmetic—Santa Klaus outfits, Festival robes, free pets that vary from year to year (and thus are an indication of how long a player has been active), and so on, all of which encourage the idea of the avatar as something to be admired. This is borne out in the way that players most commonly justify their choice of an avatar of alternative sex. Players argue consistently that they choose women avatars because they like to look at them, specifically because the long term nature of play in MMORPGs means that if they are going to have to look at the same avatar repeatedly they want it to be an attractive one. This is as true of women players who choose to play men, as it is of men who choose to play women.

Many players specifically use this action to reaffirm normative ideas about all forms of gender identity. Heterosexual males specifically stated they were appreciating the female form whilst playing it, thus setting themselves in a sexual dichotomy in regards to their adopted avatar. Women who played women also broadly agreed with these ideas; in particular arguing that some avatars gained more attention than others. Several argued that alongside an attractive avatar, they enjoyed the ability to play a 'strong' female who is also good looking, therefore highlighting positive female attributes as well as looks (this was a particularly common argument on the web forums by female players). Although Nick Yee estimates that only 1 in 100 women play male characters (Yee, 2007), the ones spoken to during this study who chose male avatars argued that they found them 'cute' or more overtly 'sexy', or in one were compared to the player's real life dog as a less sentient, but still loveable figure. All of the women directly questioned who played male avatars expressed ideas of sexual empowerment through what they considered a subversive activity, either through being hidden (in a majority of men), or through their exposure of male ideals. One of the women who played a male described incidents in which she would tease other male players by using her avatar to emote light-hearted actions targeted at their avatar such as /flirt, /kiss and /hug, regarding this as an act of empowerment, 'getting her own back', and playing with sexual norms (woman as male, woman interacting as homosexual male) from which surrounding players 'in the know' took amused enjoyment and interpreted specifically as teasing. Players on the WoW forums predominantly cite visual aesthetic (not liking the way certain avatars looked or moved) (WoW Forums 2007a-d), as well as playing male characters in order to avoid unwanted attention. (WoW Forums, 2007b): At the same time, the description of the male avatars as 'cute' seems to suggest that women players also chose more sexually passive representations of the male figure. No players identified themselves as gay, and it is fair to say that preconceptions and bigotry on this matter are an extremely distasteful part of play, even though the use of sexually offensive language is forbidden in the EULA (End Users License Agreement) and subject to a ban. Overall however, avatars were deliberately and consciously objectified by players, who often used this definition to reaffirm their own sexual potency in order to negate claims of deviance or atypical responses about their adoption of differently gendered avatars.

Players are absolutely unrepentant about the fact that they find the female avatars more attractive. This is a subject of almost continual debate, on the forums, in guild channels, and even in roleplay activities. Interestingly, this is also related to definitions of maturity. Players, by and large, feel that the skinnier, or overtly sexualised female characters are the domains of younger, more sexually immature players. Conversely, players who like curves also style themselves as older and more mature. (Whether this has any actual relationship to a player's real age is not clear). Furthermore, players justify their adoption of the attractive females by arguing against the aesthetic of the male forms. They find these appearances off-putting and 'unrealistic', an interesting commentary on a body which is as objectified as the females; most of the males have traditional fantasy style bulging muscles and shoulders bigger than their heads. Interestingly, it appears that the hyper aggressive forms of the males are seen as intimidating; one player described his glee at being able to play a skinny wizard in *Lord of the Rings Online*, suggesting that both wizards ought to be skinny, and that a more normative body shape made him feel more at ease with the form (Parsler 2007). It is ironic perhaps, that male players recognise the objectification of their own bodies, and

do not like it, whilst still responding to the over-exaggerated female form as an object of desire.

The argument that appearance adds to the overall aesthetic of the game is in fact a valid one, regardless of whether it inspires the activation of female objectification. As Geoff King and Tanya Kryzwinska argue; 'the fact that the player's sense of being-in-the-game-world is mediated is made explicit in third-person games because the player-character can be *seen*, as an entity entirely separate from the player. The character is designed to-be-looked-at, as well as to-be-played-with (King and Krzywinska, 2005: 100). In this respect, the act of transgendering is therefore crucial to the spectacle of play, as well as clearly existing 'apart' from the player:

Perhaps one of the most interesting aspects of gendered objectification is that players also regard swapping gender as interchangeable with race or other signifiers of difference:

> . . . something that I like about women chars is that they allow me to play something that I am not and . . . if I am going to be a half rotten walking copse . . . what's so strange about wanting to switch gender?
>
> (Azeroth Elders, L)

> . . . I would never roll a human male or female because 1) I am already human (vaguely) so whats the point of playing a fantasy game and being something I am already?
>
> (Azeroth Elders, L)

This suggests that the normalisation of adopting a cross gendered avatar is simply seen as one of many selections, none of which have bearing on a players' actual real life orientation. In the case of the second respondent, male and female roles are seen as equivalent, and not as interesting as being something new. The fact that choosing a gender is seen as equivalent to choosing a race or a character class is in fact heartening—defined as normative choice rather than subversive activity, and thus implying that sexual difference is accepted as a familiar act of gameplay.

One of the reasons for this identification with the avatar as an aesthetic or a character, rather than as a 'person', is the response to role-playing within the game. Some players very strongly identify with their characters as role-played identities; characters that they create and that have backstories exterior to gameplay. This is not usually sexual in nature (another common misconception associated with the term elsewhere), and players are very aware of their identities as constructed beings that they then act out:

> I'm a guy playing a female character because that's just what it is for me. A character which I control . . . She's just a character I developed over some years, just like a writer would design the people in his novel or whatever.
>
> (Azeroth Elders, Ja)

> Me, I have rolled a female char for the challenge of Roleplay, see if I can 'fit' into the role of a female, being a male myself. . . . I mean, I know about everything about being a guy, I wanted to see if I had sufficient knowledge of the feminine world to play a girl.
>
> (Azeroth Elders, A)

An alternative to this presents itself through players who simply regard their avatar as a tool. If male and female both have the same function, then why not choose either? It is important to note, as we have done elsewhere, that MMORPGs do not have to be played as 'roleplaying' games, certainly if one defines roleplay as the conscious adoption of a created identity. (MacCallum-Stewart and Parsler, 2008). MMORPGs, despite their moniker, have a relationship with role-playing games which take the statistical elements of tabletop and live action roleplay games rather than the imaginative ones (Eyles, 2007), and many players regard their actions within them within this context. The gender of an avatar is therefore irrelevant, since 'roleplay' itself is a minority occupation, and gameplay where the realisation of self as a characterised entity is not really possible supersedes this action (Parsler and MacCallum-Stewart, 2008).

Players are aware that the avatars they interact with, especially if they are female, are unlikely to be the same gender as their online counterparts. This is however often taken to extremes, with players making the assumption that virtually all players are male. A lack of concrete evidence about the relative percentage of female players, as well as consistent depiction by the media of the gamer as male, white and middle class also supports this assumption. From personal experience, it is common for female avatars to be asked if they are 'really' women in real life by other players, and often to be disbelieved particularly if one's play is of a high standard, should the answer be an affirmative.

Perhaps one of the reasons for this is that players feel that women avatars are given more help, given more social leeway, and are allowed to make gameplay mistakes with fewer consequences, another common subject for the WoW Forums (WoW Forums, 2006, 2007a). Most female players counter this by arguing that not expecting or requiring gifts, and refusing them if they do appear to be given on the basis of gender, particularly in order to make this behaviour stop, is more common. 'Real' female players therefore do not like this perception and frequently resist it.

Overall, a clear pattern emerges—players are continuously seeking to normalise the playing of avatars of the opposite gender, but at the same time they genuinely see it as a standard practise. Male players who adopt female avatars are not seen as usual or freakish within what can be an extremely male orientated environment. Players are certainly not laughed at or shunned for gender-bending; in fact it is seen as perfectly normal behaviour within the context of the game:

The idea that games are the domain of geeks with few social skills is so institutionalised, that like fan cultures, players often support these ideas as a form of self-defence. The gamer as a solitary and sexually inexperienced figure is also part of this construction. Surrounded by a bevy of pixelated beauties, this mythology then reconstructs the salivating fan as redirecting desires inwards towards unrealistic 'fake' avatars. This type of behaviour is seen by Henry Jenkins as typical of fan cultures, where groups take the accusations levelled against them and support them in both an ironic and a self-conscious form. The textual poachers idea argues that fans will appropriate images of themselves and celebrate them, often reinforcing ideas that may not necessary hold true (Jenkins, 1992). In fact, although the percentage of male/female players is unknown, it is acknowledged that many more players are female than gaming communities might often claim. However, because most players will appear to others simply in the form of the avatar, and not, for example, be subjected to direct questioning about their gender, or not have their real gender 'discovered' through forums, additional technologies such as the Teamspeak or Ventrillo voice programs, or through meeting in person to the majority of other players at large, the stigma that most players are young, insensitive and male still predominates.

Unease does remain. Players affirm that their behaviour is not deviant by continually having the same conversations about why they choose an alternative gender; one of the responses to such a question on the WoW forums asking for stories about cross gendering players was 'This topic again? Is it that time of the week already? Good lord . . .' (Clearsky, WoW Forums, 2007e). The answers too, seem to have become largely stock-in-trade; men like the female avatars, women want to avoid undue, gendered attention and be regarded as gaming equals. These reaffirmations serve not only to normalise cross-gendering, but also to render it safe, heterosexual and emancipating rather then associated with homosexual desire or transgendered desires.

Conclusion

In his preface to *Undertones of War*, Edmund Blunden defiantly asked his reader, 'Why should I not write it?' (Blunden, 1933) challenging the conspiracy of silence that had hitherto surrounded the conditions of the First World War, but which nevertheless, virtually every combatant was aware of. This striking 'Undertone', which had survived for nearly fifteen years after the war ended before it found a voice in the war poets and writers, bears incredible similarity to the player, whose attitude when adopting a cross gender avatar is very much 'Why should I not play it?' Naturalised by years of play in which swapping gender was a statistical, technical or mandatory choice, players are also drawn to the female body by cultural conditioning which invites them to admire and appreciate the female form far more than the male.

Like many fan communities before them, these players have embraced their oddities and now celebrate them as part of their uniqueness. Cross gendered play is one of these things—little understood from an exterior perspective, which often seeks to pillory the playful adaptation from male to female and vice versa. Unlike other worlds, game worlds are immersive spaces where a player is their own agent; free to take their own actions, but crucially enmeshed between the avatar they play on the screen, and their own identity. This causes an irresolvable tension, but it is a tension that players fully embrace during play. Their responses to their transgendered counterparts are playful, self-aware, unselfconscious, deviant, and played for as many different reasons as there are people themselves. However, these players come from a standpoint in which the actions they take are normalised—although increasing amounts of women play games and online games, the assumption that a player may be male irrespective of what avatar stands on the screen predominates.

More than any other media, the videogame allows players to revel in their own embodiment as alternative beings. This may involve the conscious adoption of objectified bodies within each game world, but these are bodies that that player also recognises they cannot 'own' in a physical sense, and that do not belong to them as corporeal figures. The videogame body can however come to represent the player for considerable amounts of time; in online games, one's avatar becomes a persistent, representation of self; one that often remains immutable once it has been chosen.

In a world of heroes, in fantasy and science fiction settings, players see adoption of the hyper-real body as a clear signifier of heroic qualities. This may indeed include disenfranchising representations of both sexes—willowy women and bulging brutes, but it is interesting to see how extreme the tendency to choose the female form has become. The Conan-style hero now appears to be associated with qualities of oafishness, aggression and bravado that also make the more passive yet simultaneously feisty qualities of a heroine more desirable. An over-abundance of muscles seems to have the opposite effect to an excess of curves, with older players repeatedly and specifically stating that they find this type of avatar visually unattractive and difficult to identify with. At the same time, there are still points of tension—'ugly' avatars are still defined primarily through pejorative sexual terms by players, and the statistics for avatar choice support the fact that more sexualised body forms are more popular than those deemed to be either less attractive or simply sexually absent (Rollie, 2007). This does not obscure the fact however, that choice, even if it is regarded through sexual 'norms' still passes freely across gender, with aesthetic pleasure overriding the potentate sexual anxiety of playing the opposite sex.

For all these complicated issues, however, it is still 'play'. Thus it offers a dynamic forum for exploring identity issues where mistakes are not terminal and new ideas can always be tried. It encourages serious study into the issues as well as allowing casual exploration.

(Antunes, 1999)

References

Antunes, Sandy (1999) 'Leaping into Cross-Gender Role-Play' [online]. Available from: <http://www.mud.co.uk/richard/ifan195.htm> [Accessed 1 February 2008].

Azeroth Elders Forums (2007) 'Who do you like to play and why?' [online]. Available from: <http://ae.guildhome.nl/> [Accessed 1 February 2008].

Blunden, Edmund (1933) *Undertones of War*. London: Penguin Books.

Carr, Diane (2002) 'Playing with Lara'. In Screenplay: Cinema/Videogames/Interfaces. London: Wallflower Press, pp. 171–80.

Cassell, Justine & Jenkins, Henry (1998) *From Barbie to Mortal Kombat: Gender and Computer Games*. Massachusetts: The MIT Press.

Clearsky (2007) 'To Males Playing Female Chars' [online]. Available from: <http://forums.worldofwarcraft.com/thread.html?topicId=1778011663&sid=1&p ageNo=1> [Accessed 1 February 2008].

Eyles, Mark (2007) 'Ambient Role Playing Games: Towards a Grammar of Endlessness', presented at Women in Games, Newport.

Eynalir 'WoW Tier 7 Gear' [online]. Available from: http://www.youtube.com/watch?v=Zo9HDU-5TtY&feature=related> [Accessed 1 February 2008].

IceFlowStudios 'WoW Commercial Parody #3' [online]. Available from: <http://www.youtube.com/watch?v=tPKAUQA1TZc&feature=related> [Accessed 1 February 2008].

Kennedy, Helen (2002) 'Lara Croft, Feminist Icon or Cyber Bimbo: The Limits of Textual Analysis. *Game Studies*, 2 (2), 2002. Available from: <http://www.gamestudies.org/0202/kennedy/>

King, G & Krzywinska T. (2006) *Tomb Raiders and Space Invaders: Forms and Meanings of Videogames*. London: IB Tauris.

Laurel, Brenda. 'Keynote address given at CHI 98 conference April 1998' [online]. Available from: <http://www.tauzero.com/Brenda_Laurel/Recent_Talks/Technological_Humani sm.html> [Accessed 1 February 2008].

Ludica, Fron, Janine, Fullerton, Tracy, Morie, Jacquelyn Ford, and Pearce, Celia, 'Playing Dress-Up: Costumes, Roleplay and Imagination'. Women in Games 19th–21st April 2007, University of Wales, Newport.

Mortensen, Torill. (2007) 'Me, the Other' in eds. Harrigan, Pat and Wardrip-Fruin, Noah. *Second Person, Roleplaying and Story in Games and Playable Media*. Massachusetts: The MIT Press.

Parsler, Justin. Conversation online, May 2007. Reproduced with permission.

'Rollie' 'Adding Gender Graphs', at Warcraft Realms, [online]. Available from: <http://www.warcraftrealms.com/forum/viewtopic.php?t=2996> (see also WoW Census at http://www.warcraftrealms.com/census.php) [Accessed 14 February 2008].

Surman, David (2007a) 'Pleasure, Spectacle and Reward in *Streetfighter II*' in Atkins, B & Kryzwinska, T, eds. *Videogame, Player, Text*. Manchester: Manchester University Press: 2007a. pp. 204–21.

Surman, David (2007b). conversation at the Women in Games Conference, Newport. (reproduced with permission).

WoW Forums [Accessed 1 February 2008]:

    (2007a) 'Female Toon Stories' [online]. Available from: <http://forums.worldofwarcraft.com/thread.html?topicId=2856015211>

    (2007b) 'To all guys that pick girl toons!' [online]. Available from: <http://forums.worldofwarcraft.com/thread.html?topicId=2518906045>

    (2007c) 'Are there any women that play male toons?' [online]. Available from: <http://forums.worldofwarcraft.com/thread.html?topicId=36653742>

    (2007d) 'Poll your favourite female Wow Toon' [online]. Available from: <http://forums.wow-europe.com/thread.html;jsessionid=04BE8B9B442470EF10BDCD85094CA31 8.app03_01?topicId=2405318027>

    (2007e) 'to males playing female chars' [online]. Available from: <http://forums.worldofwarcraft.com/thread.html? topicId=1778011663>

Yee, Nick (2007) 'WoW Gender Bending' [online]. Available from: <http://www.nickyee.com/daedalus/archives/001369.php> [Accessed 5 February 2007].

PERMISSIONS

(Organized by Appearance in Reader)

The editor gratefully acknowledges permission to reproduce the following essays:

Part I – Foundations

Van Zoonen, Liesbet. "Feminist Perspectives on the Media." *Mass Media and Society*. Ed. James Curran and Michael Gurevitch. New York: Edward Arnold, 1991. 33–54.

Tuchman, Gaye. "The Symbolic Annihilation of Women by the Mass Media." *Hearth and Home: Images of Women in the Mass Media*. Eds. Gaye Tuchman, Arlene Kaplan Daniels, and James Benét. New York: Oxford University Press, 1978. 3–45.

Mulvey, Laura. "Visual Pleasure and Narrative Cinema." *Screen* 16.3 (1975) 6–18.

D'Acci, Julie. "Defining Women: The Case of *Cagney and Lacey*." *Private Screenings: Television and the Female Consumer*. Eds. Lynn Spigel and Denise Mann. Minneapolis: University of Minnesota Press, 1992. 169–200.

Shohat, Ella. "Gender and the Culture of Empire: Toward a Feminist Ethnography of the Cinema." *Quarterly Review of Film & Video* 13.1–3 (1991) 45–84.

Crenshaw, Kimberlé Williams. "Beyond Racism and Misogyny: Black Feminism and 2 Live Crew." *Words that Wound: Critical Race Theory, Assaultive Speech, and the First Amendment*. Eds. Mari J. Matsuda, Charles R. Lawrence III, Richard Delgado, Kimberlé Williams Crenshaw. Boulder: Westview Press, 1993. 110–132.

Butler, Judith. "Imitation and Gender Insubordination." *Inside/Out: Lesbian Theories, Gay Theories*. Ed. Diana Fuss. New York: Routledge, 1991. 13–31.

Gill, Rosalind. "Postfeminist Media Culture: Elements of a Sensibility." *European Journal of Cultural Studies*, 10.2 (2007) 147–166.

Part II – Production

Bielby, Denise D. and William T. Bielby. "Women and Men in Film: Gender Inequality among Writers in a Culture Industry." *Gender & Society* 10.3 (1996) 248–270.

Citron, Michelle. "Women's Film Production: Going Mainstream." *Female Spectators: Looking at Film and Television*. Ed. E. Deidre Pribram. New York: Verso, 1990. 45–63.

Meehan, Eileen R. "Gendering the Commodity Audience: Critical Media Research, Feminism, and Political Economy." *Sex and Money: Feminism and Political Economy in the Media*. Eds. Eileen R. Meehan and Ellen Riordan. Minneapolis: University of Minnesota Press, 2002. 209–222.

Brookey, Robert Alan and Robert Westerfelhaus. "Hiding Homoeroticism in Plain View: The *Fight Club* DVD as Digital Closet." *Critical Studies in Media Communication* 19.1 (2002) 21–43.

Levine, Elana. "Fractured Fairy Tales and Fragmented Markets: Disney's *Weddings of a Lifetime* and the Cultural Politics of Media Conglomeration." *Television and New Media* 6.1 (2005) 71–88.

Shade, Leslie Regan. "Gender and the Commodification of Community: Women.com and gURL.com." *Community in the Digital Age: Philosophy and Practice*. Eds. Darin Barney and Andrew Feenberg. Lanham, MD: Rowman & Littlefield, 2004. 143–160.

Schilt, Kristen. "'I'll Resist With Every Inch and Every Breath': Girls and Zine Making as a Form of Resistance." *Youth & Society* 35.1 (2003) 71–97.

Kelley, Robin D. G. "Looking to Get Paid: How Some Black Youth Put Culture to Work." *Yo' Mama's Disfunktional!: Fighting the Culture Wars in Urban America*. Boston: Beacon, 1997. 43–77.

Bayton, Mavis. "Women and the Electric Guitar." *Sexing the Groove: Popular Music and Gender*. Ed. Sheila Whiteley. New York: Routledge, 1997. 37–49.

Part III – Texts: Representation

Mooney, Annabelle. "Boys Will Be Boys: Men's Magazines and the Normalisation of Pornography." *Feminist Media Studies* 8:3 (2008) 247–265.

Carrillo Rowe, Aimee and Samantha Lindsey. "Reckoning Loyalties: White Femininity as 'Crisis.'" *Feminist Media Studies* 3.2 (2003) 173–191.

Molina Guzmán, Isabel and Angharad N. Valdivia. "Brain, Brow, and Booty: Latina Iconicity in U.S. Popular Culture." *Communication Review* 7 (2004) 205–221.

Sellen, Eliza. "Missy 'Misdemeanor' Elliott: Rapping on the Frontiers of Female Identity." *Journal of International Women's Studies* 6.3 (2005) 50–63.

Ciasullo, Ann M. "Making Her (In)visible: Cultural Representations of Lesbianism and the Lesbian Body in the 1990s." *Feminist Studies* 27.3 (2001) 577–608.

Sgroi, Renee M. "*Joe Millionaire* and Women's Positions: A Question of Class." *Feminist Media Studies* 6.3 (2006) 281–294.

Cooper, Brenda. "*Boys Don't Cry* and Female Masculinity: Reclaiming a Life and Dismantling the Politics of Normative Heterosexuality." *Critical Studies in Media Communication* 19.1 (2002) 44–63.

Messner, Michael A., Michele Dunbar, and Darnell Hunt. "The Televised Sports Manhood Formula." *Journal of Sport and Social Issues* 24.4 (2000) 380–394.

Fung, Richard. "Looking for My Penis: The Eroticized Asian in Gay Video Porn." *How Do I Look?: Queer Film and Video*. Eds. Bad Object-Choices. Seattle: Bay Press, 1991. 145–160.

Cohan, Steven. "Queer Eye for the Straight Guise: Camp, Postfeminism, and the Fab Five's Makeovers of Masculinity." *Interrogating Postfeminism: Gender and the Politics of Popular Culture*. Eds. Yvonne Tasker and Diane Negra. Durham: Duke University Press, 2007. 176–200.

Ashcraft, Karen Lee and Lisa A. Flores. "'Slaves with White Collars': Persistent Performances of Masculinity in Crisis." *Text and Performance Quarterly* 23.1 (2003) 1–29.

Van Doorn, Niels, Sally Wyatt, and Liesbet van Zoonen. "A Body of Text: Revisiting Textual Performances of Gender and Sexuality on the Internet." *Feminist Media Studies* 8.4 (2008) 357–374.

Part IV – Texts: Narrative

De Lauretis, Teresa. "Oedipus Interruptus." *Wide Angle* 7.1 (1985) 34–40.

Schiavi, Michael R. "A 'Girlboy's' Own Story: Non-Masculine Narrativity in *Ma Vie en Rose*." *College Literature* 31.3 (2004) 1–26.

Gledhill, Christine. "Speculations on the Relationship between Soap Opera and Melodrama." *Quarterly Review of Film and Video* 14.1–2 (1992) 103–124.

Williams, Linda. "Film Bodies: Gender, Genre, and Excess." *Film Quarterly* 44.4 (1991) 2–13.

Banet-Weiser, Sarah and Laura Portwood-Stacer. "I Just Want to Be Me Again!": Beauty Pageants, Reality Television and Post-feminism." *Feminist Theory* 7. 2 (2006) 255–272.

Tasker, Yvonne. "Fists of Fury: Discourses of Race and Masculinity in the Martial Arts Cinema." *Race and the Subject of Masculinities*. Eds. Harry Stecopoulos and Michael Uebel. Durham: Duke University Press, 1997. 315–336.

Douglas, Susan. "Letting the Boys Be Boys: Talk Radio, Male Hysteria, and Political Discourse in the 1980s." *Radio Reader: Essays in the Cultural History of Radio*. Ed. Michele Hilmes. New York: Routledge, 2002. 485–503.

Nochimson, Martha P. "Waddaya Lookin' At? Re-reading the Gangster Genre Through *The Sopranos*." *Film Quarterly* 56.2 (2003) 2–13.

Jenkins, Henry. "Never Trust a Snake: WWF Wrestling as Masculine Melodrama." *Out of Bounds: Sports, Media and the Politics of Identity*. Eds. Aaron Baker and Todd Boyd. Bloomington: Indiana University Press, 1992. 48–80.

Walser, Robert. "Forging Masculinity: Heavy-Metal Sounds and Images of Gender." *Sound and Vision: The Music Video Reader*. Eds. Simon Frith, Andrew Goodwin, and Lawrence Grossberg. London: Routledge, 1993. 153–181.

Railton, Diane. "The Gendered Carnival of Pop." *Popular Music* 20.3 (2001) 321–331.

Part V – Consumption

Kuhn, Annette. "Women's Genres: Melodrama, Soap Opera, and Theory." *Screen* 25.1 (1984) 18–28.

hooks, bell. "The Oppositional Gaze: Black Female Spectators." *Black Looks: Race and Representation*. Boston: South End, 1992. 115–131.

Doty, Alexander. "There's Something Queer Here." *Making Things Perfectly Queer: Interpreting Mass Culture*. Minneapolis: University of Minnesota Press, 1993. 1–16.

Gray, Ann. "Behind Closed Doors: Video Recorders in the Home." *Boxed In: Women and Television*. Eds. Helen Baehr and Gillian Dyer. London: Pandora Press, 1987. 38–54.

Straw, Will. "Sizing Up Record Collections: Gender and Connoisseurship in Rock Music Culture." *Sexing the Groove: Popular Music and Gender*. Ed. Sheila Whiteley. New York: Routledge, 1997. 3–15.

Stacey, Jackie. "Feminine Fascinations: Forms of Identification in Star–Audience Relations." *Stardom: Industry of Desire*. Ed. Christine Gledhill. New York: Routledge, 1991. 141–166.

Farmer, Brett. "The Fabulous Sublimity of Gay Diva Worship." *Camera Obscura* 59 (2005) 165–194.

Cumberland, Sharon. "Private Uses of Cyberspace: Women, Desire, and Fan Culture." *Rethinking Media Change: The Aesthetics of Transition*. Ed. David Thorburn and Henry Jenkins. Cambridge: MIT Press, 2003. 262–279.

Royse, Pam, Joon Lee, Undrahbuyan Baasanjav, Mark Hopson, and Mia Consalvo. "Women and Games: Technologies of the Gendered Self." *New Media & Society* 9.4 (2007) 555–576.

MacCallum-Stewart, Esther. "Real Boys Carry Girly Epics: Normalising Gender Bending in Online Games." *Eludamos: Journal for Computer Game Culture* 2.1 (2008) 27–40.

INDEX